Ford's The Modern Theologians

The Great Theologians

A comprehensive series devoted to highlighting the major theologians of different periods. Each theologian is presented by a world-renowned scholar.

Published

Ford's The Modern Theologians

An Introduction to Christian Theology since 1918

Fourth Edition

Edited by

Rachel Muers and Ashley Cocksworth

WILEY Blackwell

Registered Offices
John Wiley & Sons, Inc., 111 River Street, Hoboken, NJ 07030, USA
John Wiley & Sons Ltd, The Atrium, Southern Gate, Chichester, West Sussex, PO19 8SQ, UK

For details of our global editorial offices, customer services, and more information about Wiley products visit us at www.wiley.com.

Wiley also publishes its books in a variety of electronic formats and by print-on-demand. Some content that appears in standard print versions of this book may not be available in other formats.

Library of Congress Cataloging-in-Publication Data
Names: Muers, Rachel, editor. | Cocksworth, Ashley, editor. | John Wiley &
    Sons, publisher.
Title: Ford's The modern theologians : an introduction to christian
    theology since 1918 / edited by Rachel Muers, Ashley Cocksworth.
Other titles: Great theologians.
Description: Fourth edition. | Hoboken, NJ : Wiley-Blackwell, 2024. |
    Series: The great theologians | Includes index.
Identifiers: LCCN 2023050166 (print) | LCCN 2023050167 (ebook) | ISBN
    9781119746744 (paperback) | ISBN 9781119746768 (adobe pdf) | ISBN
    9781119746782 (epub)
Subjects: LCSH: Theology, Doctrinal–History–20th century. | Theology,
    Doctrinal–History–21st century. | Theologians–History–20th century.
Classification: LCC BT28 .F665 2024 (print) | LCC BT28 (ebook) | DDC
    230.09/04–dc23/eng/20231206
LC record available at https://lccn.loc.gov/2023050166
LC ebook record available at https://lccn.loc.gov/2023050167

Cover Design: Wiley
Cover Image: Courtesy of Magnus Aronson/Ikon

Set in 10/12pt Galliard by Straive, Pondicherry, India
Printed and bound by CPI Group (UK) Ltd, Croydon, CR0 4YY

C9781119746744_140224

Contents

Notes on Contributors

Susan Abraham is Professor of Theology and Postcolonial Cultures, Pacific School of Religion, Berkeley, CA

Nicholas Adams is Professor of Philosophical Theology, University of Birmingham, UK

Sammy Alfaro is Professor of Theology, Grand Canyon University, Phoenix, AZ

Rachel Sophia Baard is Assistant Professor of Theology and Ethics at Union Presbyterian Seminary in Richmond, VA

Brian Bantum is Neil F. and Ila A. Fisher Professor of Theology, Garrett-Evangelical Theological Seminary, Evanston, IL

Lilian Calles Barger is an independent historian based in New Mexico

Michael Barnes is Emeritus Professor of Interreligious Relations, University of Roehampton, and Research Associate, School of Advanced Study, University of London, UK

Jeremy S. Begbie is Thomas A. Langford Distinguished Research Professor of Theology at Duke Divinity School, Durham, NC

Elias Kifon Bongmba is Harry and Hazel Chavanne Chair in Christian Theology, Rice University, Houston, TX

Luke Bretherton is Robert E. Cushman Distinguished Professor of Moral and Political Theology, Duke Divinity School, Durham, NC

Stephen Burns is Professor of Liturgical and Practical Theology at Pilgrim Theological College, University of Divinity, Melbourne

Patrick S. Cheng is Visiting Professor of Anglican Studies, Union Theological Seminary, New York, NY

Alexander Chow is Senior Lecturer in Theology and World Christianity, University of Edinburgh, UK

Sung Wook Chung is Professor of Christian Theology, Denver Seminary, Littleton, CO

Ashley Cocksworth is Reader in Theology and Practice, University of Roehampton, UK

Ernst M. Conradie is Senior Professor, Department of Religion and Theology, University of the Western Cape, South Africa

Katie Cross is Christ's College Lecturer in Practical Theology, University of Aberdeen, UK

Jenny Daggers is Honorary Fellow in the Department of Theology, Philosophy and Religious Studies, Liverpool Hope University, UK

Celia Deane-Drummond is Director of the Laudato Si' Research Institute and Senior Research Fellow in Theology at Campion Hall, University of Oxford, UK, and Visiting Professor in Theology, Durham University, UK

David F. Ford is Emeritus Regius Professor of Divinity, University of Cambridge, UK

Ben Fulford is Senior Lecturer in Systematic Theology, University of Chester, UK

Joseph D. Galgalo is Assistant Bishop of All Saints Cathedral Diocese, Nairobi and the Provincial Secretary of the Anglican Church of Kenya and former Vice-Chancellor of St Paul's University, Limuru

Brandon Gallaher is Associate Professor of Systematic Theology, University of Exeter, UK

K. Healan Gaston is Lecturer in American Religious History and Ethics, Harvard Divinity School, Cambridge, MA

Kevin Hart is Edwin B. Kyle Professor of Christian Studies, University of Virginia, Charlottesville, VA

Karen Kilby is Bede Professor of Catholic Theology, Durham University, UK

Paul Ladouceur is Adjunct Professor at the Orthodox School of Theology at Trinity College, University of Toronto, and Professeur associé, Faculté de théologie et de sciences religieuses, Université Laval, Canada

Jenny Leith is Lecturer in Christian Ethics, Westcott House, Cambridge, UK

Julius Lipner is Emeritus Professor of Hinduism and the Comparative Study of Religion, University of Cambridge, UK

Clive Marsh is Principal of the Queen's Foundation for Ecumenical Theological Education, Birmingham, UK

Joshua Mauldin is Associate Director of the Center of Theological Inquiry, Princeton, NJ

Mark McInroy is Founding Co-Director of the Claritas Initiative on Beauty, Goodness, and Truth and Associate Professor of Theology at the University of St Thomas, St Paul, MN

Eleanor McLaughlin is Lecturer in Theology, Ripon College Cuddesdon, Oxford, UK

Jolyon Mitchell is Principal of St John's College and Professor in the Department of Theology and Religion, Durham University, UK

Esther Mombo is Lecturer in the Faculty of Theology, St Paul's University, Limuru, Kenya

Rachel Muers is Professor of Divinity, University of Edinburgh, UK

Paul D. Murray is Professor of Systematic Theology in the Department of Theology and Religion, Durham University, UK

Karen O'Donnell is Academic Dean and Lecturer in Worship and Community, Westcott House, Cambridge, UK

Odair Pedroso Mateus was until 2022 the Director of the Commission on Faith and Order, World Council of Churches

Andrew Prevot is the Joseph and Winifred Amaturo Chair in Catholic Studies and Professor of Theology and Religious Studies at Georgetown University, Washington, DC

Joshua Ralston is Reader in Christian-Muslim Relations, University of Edinburgh, UK

Randi Rashkover is Nathan and Sofia Gumenick Professor of Judaic Studies and Professor of Religious Studies, William & Mary, Williamsburg, VA

Chloë Reddaway is McDonald Agape Research Fellow in Theology and the Visual Arts and Deputy Director, Centre for Arts and the Sacred, King's College London, UK

Anthony G. Reddie is Professor of Black Theology at the University of Oxford, UK. He is also Director of the Oxford Centre for Religion and Culture at Regent's Park College, University of Oxford, and an Extraordinary Professor of Theological Ethics, University of South Africa

Hanna Reichel is Associate Professor of Reformed Theology, Princeton Theological Seminary, Princeton, NJ

Ulrich Schmiedel is Senior Lecturer in Theology, Politics and Ethics, University of Edinburgh, UK

Devin Singh is Associate Professor of Religion, Dartmouth College, Hanover, NH

Susannah Ticciati is Professor of Christian Doctrine, King's College London, UK

David Tombs is Howard Paterson Professor of Theology and Public Issues, University of Otago

O. Ernesto Valiente is Associate Professor of Systematic Theology, Boston College School of Theology and Ministry, Brighton, MA

Felix Wilfred is Emeritus Professor of Philosophy and Religious Thought, State University of Madras, India

David Wilkinson is Professor in the Department of Theology and Religion, Durham University, UK

Sung Bihn Yim is Professor of Christianity and Culture, Presbyterian University and Theological Seminary, Seoul

Philip G. Ziegler is Professor of Christian Dogmatics, University of Aberdeen, UK

Acknowledgments

With its fourth edition, *The Modern Theologians* – now *Ford's The Modern Theologians* – has moved to a new stage with a new editorial team. David F. Ford, who shaped, developed, and carried through the groundbreaking and field-shaping project that was *The Modern Theologians* in its first three editions (1989, 1997, 2005), has remained involved as a consulting editor. We are deeply grateful to David, not only for making *The Modern Theologians* a vital part of the theological landscape but also for his unfailing support and encouragement as the fourth edition took shape. It is a tribute to David's vision, and its enduring significance, that succeeding academic generations have been able to take *The Modern Theologians* forward.

Much of the distinctive value of *The Modern Theologians* lies in the breadth and depth of scholarship that its authors bring. Every author in this volume contributes a unique and essential voice – and every author has also had to fit this work around a unique set of commitments and challenges. We thank all the authors for their time, dedication, and enthusiasm. With any project on this scale, and even without the challenges of the COVID-19 pandemic, there are bound to be unforeseen problems. We extend particular gratitude to those authors who joined the project at a late stage, or who took on additional and unexpected work to enable us to complete the volume.

Behind the editors named on the cover stand many others, without whose work the book would never have reached the press. We are grateful to Declan Kelly for his thorough, well-informed, and highly professional work as our specialist editorial assistant. We thank the team at Wiley-Blackwell for all their efforts and for their exemplary patience with the shifting timescales involved in a complex project. In particular, Juliet Booker was involved with the development of this fourth edition at the crucial early stages and we gratefully acknowledge her input. We thank the anonymous readers who offered us both challenge and encouragement during our planning process.

We are indebted to our wider communities of colleagues and friends for numerous forms of support throughout the project. We thank our families for living with *The Modern Theologians* as well as with their own modern theologians. Ash is especially grateful to Hannah, and to Lucy and Maisie who were both born during the production of this book. Rachel is especially grateful to Gavin – who probably thought that he would never have to hear about "TMT" again after the third edition – and to Matthew and Peter.

As we have worked on this volume, correspondents have frequently told us about their fond memories of *The Modern Theologians* and about its significance for their formation. We have seen how much *The Modern Theologians* matters to current and former students of theology, around the world, at many levels, and in many contexts. While this has made us all the more aware of the scale of the responsibility we have taken on, it has also reminded us of the strength and vitality of the intergenerational community of theologians. We hope that readers of this new edition will be inspired to join that community.

List of Modern Theologians

Introduction

Rachel Muers and Ashley Cocksworth

In the epilogue to the second edition of *The Modern Theologians*, published in 1996, David Ford referred to the "global upsurge" of diverse theological voices in the twentieth century and proposed that this diversity should be read as "testimony to the polyphonic abundance of God." Three decades later, this new edition captures some of the multiple voices of Christian theology, in a diverse and intensely interconnected world – and again invites readers to find a testimony to "polyphonic abundance" in this multiplicity. Our introduction seeks to draw out connections and resonances between the theologies presented here, and to point to the common enterprise in which they are engaged.

Why "Modern" Theologians?

In titling this book "The Modern Theologians," we foreground modernity as the determining context for Christian theology since 1918 – and theology in this era has indeed been shaped by ongoing debates about the legacy of modernity. To quote the introduction to an earlier edition of this volume:

> Theologians have been members of societies, churches, and academic institutions through this innovative, traumatic period, and their theology has inevitably been influenced by it. That is how, in a minimal sense, their theology is modern: by taking account of such developments, even if sometimes in order to dismiss, criticize, resist, or try to reverse them.[1]

Modernity, of course, has its origins long before the period discussed in this book – perhaps with the Renaissance, with the Enlightenment, with industrialization, with the beginning of Western European colonial movements, with scientific and political revolutions, or with one of the many other large-scale transformations of social conditions and contexts since the late 1400s.[2] This list of possible points of origin already indicates that we should be cautious about taking "modernity" as the sole frame for theology since

Ford's The Modern Theologians: An Introduction to Christian Theology since 1918, Fourth Edition.
Edited by Rachel Muers and Ashley Cocksworth.
© 2024 John Wiley & Sons Ltd. Published 2024 by John Wiley & Sons Ltd.

1918. Modernity generally refers to social and intellectual developments originating from Europe, and its global impact and implications are bound up with European power and influence.

Thus, although all the theologians considered in this volume *are* affected by modernity, it is still the case that allowing a narrow concept of modernity to set the agenda for theology risks allowing that agenda to be dominated by European elite perspectives. We can say that all these theologians are engaging to differing extents with the challenges of modernity – but we should be careful about telling too simple a story of what those challenges are; we may need, in Christian theology as elsewhere, to think in terms of multiple modernities.[3] More than this, recognizing modernity's complexity also enables us to take a fresh look at the history of modern theology – rereading twentieth-century classics (such as, in this volume, Karl Barth or the Niebuhrs) in relation to a new set of questions.

Engaging Modernity Theologically

What features of "modernity" remain significant for understanding Christian theology since 1918? Among the key intellectual moves characteristic of modernity that appear across this volume in many different ways are the turn to the subject, the turn to history, and the turn to suspicion.

First, modernity – from the Renaissance onwards – is often associated with a new focus on the human subject as knower and agent. Theologically, this modern turn is associated with questions about knowledge of God in relation to knowledge more generally, and about the practical and moral import of Christian faith in relation to morality more generally – and is represented, at least in theologies influenced by Western European modernity, by the long and ongoing history of theological responses to Kant. When we look at the broader picture of Christian theology since 1918, however, we also see an extended and many-faceted theological interrogation of the very idea of *the* human subject. What does it mean to speak of, and as, humanity in relation to God when humanity is irreducibly plural? Who has been included in, and who excluded from, the normative vision of humanity, and how can Christian theology name and challenge the exclusions? How does the figure of Jesus Christ confront and transform the various understandings of humanity – implicit or explicit, theoretical or practical – that operate in modernity? Thus, for example, theologies of liberation (for example, the chapters on Gustavo Gutiérrez and on Latin America), theologies engaging directly with human embodiment (for example, the chapter on queer theology), and theologies considering humanity's place among other creatures (for example, the chapter on the environmental crisis) all deepen and complexify the modern turn to the human subject.

Furthermore, the essays in this volume show Christian theology engaging with multiple ways of knowing. There are obvious reasons – going back much further than the modern era – to see Christian theology as having particularly close connections with philosophy (see Chapter 29). However, knowledge in modernity is most obviously dominated, not by philosophy but by the sciences – and theologians have responded critically and constructively both to scientific paradigms of knowledge and to the ever-changing understandings of the world that emerge from scientific research (see Chapters 38 and 39). Meanwhile, theology's inextricable links to the life and practice of Christian communities opens up engagement with ways of knowing that were sometimes neglected in the modern academy – for example, knowledge connected with spirituality, liturgy, and practice in general (Chapters 28, 31, and 32). Theological engagements with the arts and with culture, besides pointing to still more ways of knowing to which theology can attend, are of particular interest in modernity because they often raise questions about the boundary between the religious and the secular – as well as about what kinds of intellectual production can count as theology. As Chapters 33–37 demonstrate in different ways, the arts and culture often enable engagement with theological issues – with or without the explicit recognition of theological frameworks or concepts.

The very naming of "modernity" points to the emergence of historical consciousness and the foregrounding of questions of continuity, change, and the relationship to the past. Christian theology, by its nature, cannot escape questions of meaning in history – as Ford puts it, "Christianity ... cannot do without the authority of the past in some form."[4] This also means that Christian theology is of necessity a hermeneutical enterprise. Since the emergence of modern biblical criticism, engagement with biblical scholarship has been one of the contexts in which Christian theology has wrestled with questions of meaning in history (see Chapter 30) – and, as with the other academic disciplines with which theology engages, it is important to recognize that biblical scholarship as a practice of engagement itself is self-critical and ever changing.

To recognize theologies as shaped by distinctive contexts – as this volume does, by locating individual theologians in geographical regions, in translocal movements and in ecclesial contexts – is already to locate oneself in the modern turn to history. Beyond this, key strands of Christian theology since 1918 have been decisively shaped by new engagements with history and tradition, both methodologically and substantively. The Second Vatican Council (see Chapter 18), with its emphases on both *aggiornamento* ("bringing up to date") and *ressourcement* (recovery of living tradition), represents a clear turning point in the middle of the period covered by this volume, opening up new approaches to history and historicity in Roman Catholic theology. Another crucial turning point for modern theologies of history – as well as modern theology more generally – occurred just before the period of this volume, at the origins of Pentecostalism. The Pentecostal emphasis on the present activity of the Holy Spirit, bringing about a new thing in history, provokes new questions about how to interpret and respond to *this* historical moment – and how to relate present experience of the Spirit to scripture and tradition (see Chapter 19). More broadly, however, all of theology's ecclesial contexts invite theologians to engage with specific strands of Christian history (see, for example, Chapter 22 on Anglican theology and Chapter 21 on evangelical theology).

Saying that Christian theology raises questions of meaning in history and involves hermeneutical work, however, also points to Christian theology's encounter in modernity with the hermeneutics of suspicion. Notoriously, in the work of the nineteenth- and early twentieth-century "masters of suspicion," Christian theology is read in ways that call into question, or claim to debunk, its claims to knowledge.[5] Relatedly but differently, from both within and outside the Christian community, Christian theology is read in ways that interrogate its character as ideology and its implication in structures of power, including oppressive or unjust power. In many of the contexts and movements covered in this book, particularly from the second half of the twentieth century onwards, this movement of suspicion and critique is incorporated into theology's self-understanding as something that must be reckoned with. Theologians are less likely, toward the end of this volume's time period, to think they have to reject or accept a "suspicious" reading *tout court* – and more likely to recognize the suspicious reading, particularly where it comes as ideology critique, as a contribution to theology's perennial task of anti-idolatry. Having said that, it is again important to recognize contextual differences – much theology is done in contexts where Christianity is *not* allied with power (see, for example, Chapter 17 on Chinese theology).

One further, contested, aspect of "modernity" needs to be acknowledged. Modernity is frequently associated with *secularization* – with the marginalization of Christianity in the public square and the associated marginalization of theology in the academy and other spaces of public reason. In the North and the West, it makes sense to tell the story of modern theology, at least in part, as a story of engagement with the challenges of universalizing secular rationality – a rationality that itself emerges from a Christian cultural and intellectual heritage. Chapters in this volume on North American (5) and Western European (10) theology tell parts of that story. However, the picture looks very different in contexts where Christianity has not historically been culturally dominant, or where modernization has not been associated with the retreat of religion from the public realm – as is shown, for example, in the chapters on African theology. Indeed, even in supposedly "secular" post-Enlightenment contexts, it has become impossible in the twenty-first century to ignore the public and political role of religion. Even in countries not affected by the much-studied "resurgence of religion" in the early twenty-first century, that same period saw a *turn* to religion in the academy and a wider public recognition of the political and social significance of religion.[6]

A Proposal for Reading Contemporary Theology: Five Dynamics

Introductions to earlier editions of this book picked up Hans Frei's typology of Christian theology's engagements with universalizing secular rationality, in its relation to Christian particularity.[7] Frei's typology, developed in the late twentieth century, already demonstrates the variety of different ways in which theology can be both modern and Christian – different ways of performing the relationship between the Christian community's traditioned claims, on the one hand, and the questions and intellectual approaches arising in a modern context, on the other. For Frei and for many of the theologians discussed in this volume, the institutional context where this relationship was worked through was the modern university, and one of the key background questions for Christian theology since 1918 is that of theology's place among the academic disciplines.

To engage fully with the diversity of Christian theology since 1918, however, we must recognize that the modern university is only one of the many institutional contexts for disciplined intellectual work on Christian faith in relation to contemporary thought – and thus that theology has a wider set of questions to answer than just "how is what you are doing a respectable academic enterprise?" Broader questions arise as to what theologians think they are doing. For example: What makes a particular theological debate worth having? What genres or forms are best for theology? What is the mission or the vocation of a theologian in a particular context? Questions like this invite a switch of focus, from purportedly universal criteria according to which theology can be judged, to more pragmatic and contexualized judgments about how and why theologians are engaging with specific tasks. Indeed, in shaping this volume, we have sought authors from a range of different contexts, with different theological experiences and vocations, to offer their judgments about aspects of modern theology.

One way to approach questions about "what theologians are doing," in a way that enables cross-contextual comparisons, is to identify common *dynamics* that may be found across theologies with different main foci, institutional locations, or genres. In this section, we discuss a set of five dynamics of theology, loosely drawn from the story of Jacob at the Jabbok ford (Gen 32:24–41): wrestling with the given, asking the name, following the community, demanding a blessing, and crossing the border.[8]

Wrestling with the given

Wrestling with the given refers to engagement with the complex specifics of Christian scripture and traditions, taking "traditions" in the broadest possible sense. Givenness – beginning "in the middle of things," relying on testimony, recognizing the indissoluble connection between theology and hermeneutics – is easy to identify in many strands of twentieth and early-twenty-first-century theology. It appears, for example, in the turn to *ressourcement* in post-Second Vatican Council theology (Chapter 18), or in contemporary evangelical theology's revisiting of classic debates (Chapter 21), as much as in the rereading of scripture and in the givens of practice. Beyond this, however, readers might consider what the crucial "given" might be in *each* theological project. Where, for this theologian or this group of theologians, is God encountered, and on what specific given material should our reasoning about God do its work? Consider, for example, the central importance of African women's religious experience in the theologies discussed in Chapter 2, or of specific formative histories of racial oppression in James Cone's work

(Chapter 6). Moreover, a wide range of philosophical and other scholarly methods borrowed and put to work in theology may facilitate "wrestling with the given" – as demonstrated, for example, in the discussions of the social sciences, of philosophy and of the arts in this volume.

Asking the name

Our second dynamic, asking the name, refers to that point in the story of Jacob's wrestling when he puts a wider question about what is going on. As part of its work with the given, theology puts questions that might be put in comparable or analogous situations and that thereby relate *just this* given to a wider context. In the classic "modern" framing of theology's task, this move of putting wider questions might be understood as a move, through philosophy, to relate theology to a supposedly universal secular horizon. Within this volume, however, we see a more diverse range of questions that relate theology's particular "given" to its wider horizon. To give two contrasting examples, postcolonial theologies (Chapter 25) relate theology to a theoretical horizon that is decidedly *not* claiming to be universal or secular; and pastoral and practical theologies relate to a "horizon" of multiple theories concerning human flourishing (Chapter 24).

Following the community

Following the community points to a core issue for contemporary theological work, helpfully framed by Ada María Isasi-Díaz in terms of a theologian's "communities of accountability."[9] It is important to note in this regard that a community of accountability as Isasi-Díaz understands it is not simply the community to whom this has to make intellectual sense; it is also the community whose lives set the theological agenda. Everyone speaks from somewhere, but a distinctive dynamic is set up where a theologian *thematizes* and locates a community of accountability – be that community geographical, confessional, based on gender or race or some other aspect of identity, or specified in some other way. One of the questions that is worth asking in many of the chapters of this volume – perhaps especially of the geographically-focused chapters in the first section – is whether and to what extent the theologians who are grouped under a specific heading explicitly regard themselves as answerable to, or responding to, the community designated in that way. For example, in any of the geographically-focused chapters we find many theologians who are explicitly developing their work in response to the specific concerns of a particular nation or region – but also strands of theology that, whatever their geographical location, look to the concerns of one or another international audience.

Demanding a blessing

Demanding a blessing points to theological engagement with the needs, concerns, and desires emerging in a particular time and place. We would argue that it is important to distinguish this from the idea of communities of accountability, especially given the global and cross-contextual nature of many of the most urgent concerns of contemporary theology. It is important to ask not only "who you are doing this theology with and for?" but "why you are doing it?" We might consider, for example, the wealth of theological work emerging from reflection on the many dimensions of the environmental crisis – from multiple geographical and confessional locations and with the wider global horizon that the subject matter necessitates (Chapter 49); or those theologies that engage from all sides with the formations and deformations of human worlds in the conditions of late capitalism (Chapter 46); or the flourishing, in our period, of science-engaged theology, engaging with the needs and the open questions of a science-dominated and science-anxious age. Theology hears, voices, and responds to "cries," the existentially affecting demands for response that are not even fully formed questions[10] – and as many of our chapters make clear, it is important to remember that Christianity and Christian theology are quite often a background cause of the problem.

Crossing the border

The final dynamic of twenty-first century theology to which we draw attention here is crossing the border. It is now very common to describe theology as inherently interdisciplinary – and sometimes to experience anxiety about that interdisciplinarity, asking whether the subject is at risk of dissolving into its disparate constituent parts. This volume suggests that theology's border crossings – between theory and practices of engagement, disciplines, between religious traditions, between geographical and ecclesial contexts – are a strength rather than a weakness; every section of the book bears witness to different informed and informing encounters between Christian theology and its neighbors. Indeed, in practice and in history, Christian theology has been formed in dialogue, not only asserting a preformed identity over against an other but rather discovering and shaping an identity through the negotiation of difference. Thus, for example, Christian theology in the twentieth and early twenty-first centuries has been transformed on many levels by a deep rethinking of Christianity's relations to Judaism (Chapter 41), and chapters in this volume on Islam, Buddhism, and Hinduism suggest the potential for comparable transformations (Chapters 42–44); moreover, as Jenny Daggers suggests (Chapter 45), all of these exercises in "theology between faiths" need to be read in the context of rethinking the imperialist impulses that relegated all kinds of "others" to the margins of Christian self-understanding.

Putting "The Modern Theologians" Together

The fourth edition of *The Modern Theologians* is in an important sense beginning in the middle of things. Successive editions have seen significant shifts in content and organization. This edition could fruitfully be read in dialogue with previous editions; it is a fascinating exercise in itself to see how different authors over the course of the series have approached the same named theologian and found new things to say.

One of the most noticeable shifts for this fourth edition is the decision not to begin with a list of named individual theologians (from Western Europe and North America). Extended engagement with a range of individual thinkers has been a hallmark of this volume since its inception; we study the *modern theologians*, not (just) modern theology. Although this is no longer the principal way in which chapters are organized, it is no accident that named theologians are still a feature across the volume. Thinking about theologians, not just theology, allows us to do justice to the systematic character of Christian theology – each theologian engages in a distinctive way with the whole picture. It also allows us to indicate how confessional belonging, geographical context, historical time period, political commitments, positioning in terms of gender and race, and other dimensions of identity and belonging contribute to, but do not determine, a theologian's distinctive work. Most important, perhaps, it thus enables us to recognize that good theology is a creative enterprise.

The risk with a focus on individuals, and even with the selection of more than one named theologian within most of the thematic chapters, is that it can reinforce the – rather modern – myth of the individual creative genius standing alone, and downplay the extent to which theology is a shared and relational endeavor. Still, bringing theologians together into various groupings, as this volume has tended to do, carries its own risks. It might be taken to represent a "postmodern condition" of theology, fragmented into its various factions that operate according to different norms and speak in mutually unintelligible terms. Such factionalism is indeed a risk for Christian theology as it enters the twenty-first century, especially as wider discursive environments are affected by polarization and extremism (as acknowledged, for example, by Ulrich Schmiedel in Chapter 48).

Our hope, however, is that this volume also indicates modern Christian theology's resistance to polarization. The various chapters show both the internal debates within, and the multiple connections between, "groupings" of theologians; and the central concerns of Christian theology, often summed up as doctrinal loci, recur across contexts and groupings. Indeed, it may be more helpful to read the groupings of theologians in this volume, not as markers of theological identity but rather as conversations or "publics" – along the lines of David Tracy's influential characterization of theology as addressed to "three publics," the academy, the churches, and society. Christian theology as a whole, and each individual theologian, relates to academic norms, from the lofty (and theologically weighted) imperative to seek truth and test everything, to the messy everyday politics of academic institutions. Likewise, all Christian theology relates to ecclesial, confessional, and interconfessional norms, whether or not it is subject to ecclesial authorization or carries ecclesial authority. Beyond this, all Christian theology, just by being published and read in some context, relates to some wider public spaces and debates, each with its own norms and concerns. This plurality of publics, inherent in the theological task, makes theology hard to confine to any of the boxes into which its readers or authors might try to fit it. This volume includes chapters organized along lines set mainly by the academy (such as the interdisciplinary conversations in Part 4), by the churches (especially in Part 2), and by wider society – but a study of the richness of any of the individual chapters shows that a theologian's significance or influence cannot be confined to just one "public." Moreover, and importantly, as can be seen already in the reception of many of the modern theologians featured in this volume, theological work is read and used far beyond its original publics or audiences. Theologians may identify and prioritize specific publics or "communities of accountability," but the reading, reception, and use of their work take it beyond their original audiences or intentions.

This volume has, inevitably, gaps and omissions. Some geographical regions are not specifically represented or are underrepresented in the volume as a whole – so, for example, there is very little here from Oceania and very little from the Middle East, and Eastern Europe is treated only under the heading of Orthodox theology (Chapter 23). Orthodoxy as a whole, it could plausibly be argued, is underrepresented, in an age when more and more of the earlier obstacles to dialogue between Eastern and Western churches are being removed (see, for example, Chapter 20 on ecumenical theology). The selection of individual theologians for chapter-length studies is still biased toward European and North American men, partly because of the need to select thinkers whose work has already – at the time of writing – had broad and lasting influence. The decision to reduce the number of chapters devoted to individual theologians made the selection for this part of the book even more difficult, and several theologians treated at length in previous editions now appear only within broader thematic chapters. Partly in response to the concern about factionalism described here, we have chosen not to focus many chapters on theological "schools" – but this might in turn mean that we have missed opportunities to highlight significant areas of shared intellectual endeavor. Future editions of this work will undoubtedly continue the dialogue, seeing further shifts and course corrections, responding to changes in the theological communities both "behind" and "in front of" the text – the theologians it describes and the theologians who read it.

In 2022, the World Council of Churches invited its various member churches and associated bodies to commit themselves to a "pilgrimage of justice, reconciliation, and unity." The timing of the invitation, in turn invites reflection on whether this captures something of the character and task of Christian theology in the early twenty-first century, as it takes up and engages with the many theologies discussed in this volume. The image is of intentional "journeying together" in which the journey itself, not only the destination, carries theological and ecclesial significance as a faithful response to God. It suggests a shared context for the journey – an interconnected and globalized world facing immense collective challenges, such as those discussed in the final section of this volume.

It also suggests a deep shared understanding of the journey, grounded in the specificity of Christian faith – the justice, reconciliation, and unity given and revealed in Christ – but also opening up space for encounter and relationship beyond the Christian community. Crucially, it does not require the movement of this diverse group through time and space to be understood as merely instrumental, a way of getting as quickly as possible to the right place or the right answer – but nor does it condemn participants to wandering aimlessly around. The process has direction, and possibly even makes progress – there are chapters of this volume that do display progress in Christian theology, including in the very respects highlighted by the World Council of Churches (justice, reconciliation, unity). However, the direction and intermediate goals are worked out *in via*, in relation to the concrete possibilities that emerge in particular historical situations. Evaluation of the journey so far, that is, of past theology's achievements and agenda – such as authors were asked to include in chapters for this volume – are themselves always conducted *in via*, rather than from a perspective outside or beyond the ongoing historical activity of theology. We invite readers from all contexts and perspectives to engage in such evaluations.

Notes

1 David F. Ford, "Introduction," in *The Modern Theologians: An Introduction to Christian Theology since 1918*, 3rd ed. (Malden, MA: Blackwell, 2005), 1.

2 See also Rachel Muers and Mike Higton, *Modern Theology: A Critical Introduction* (London: Routledge, 2012).

3 See Shmuel N. Eisenstadt, ed., *Multiple Modernities* (London: Routledge, 2002).

4 Ford, "Introduction," 6.

5 On the "masters of suspicion," see Paul Ricoeur, *Freud and Philosophy: An Essay on Interpretation* (New Haven, CT: Yale University Press, 1970).

6 See on the "resurgence of religion" Scott Thomas, *The Global Resurgence of Religion and the Transformation of International Relations: The Struggle for the Soul of the Twenty-First Century* (London: Palgrave Macmillan, 2005).

7 Hans Frei, *Types of Christian Theology* (New Haven, CT: Yale University Press, 1994). See Ford, "Introduction," 2–3.

8 For a fuller development of this idea, see Rachel Muers, "Encounters at the Jabbok Crossing: Five Dynamics of Christian Theology for the 21st Century," in Ben Fulford and Drew Collins, eds., *Hans Frei and the Future of Christian Theology* (Eugene, OR: Cascade Books, 2024).

9 Ada Maria Isasi-Diaz and Eduardo Mendieta, eds., *Decolonizing Epistemologies: Latina/o Theology and Philosophy* (New York: Fordham University Press, 2011). Monica Coleman raises the important question of *choice* in relation to one's communities of accountability, proposing that the womanist theologian does not automatically need see herself as accountable to "the historic Black church." Monica A. Coleman, "Introduction," in Monica A. Coleman, ed., *Ain't I A Womanist Too? Third-Wave Womanist Religious Thought* (Minneapolis, MN: Fortress Press, 2013), 1–31.

10 See David F. Ford, *Christian Wisdom: Desiring God and Learning in Love* (Cambridge: Cambridge University Press, 2007), 14–45.

The Modern Theologians in Their Contexts

Geographical Contexts

African Theology

Elias Kifon Bongmba

Introduction

In this chapter I discuss selected themes articulated by African theologians from the period of late colonialism to the decolonial period.[1] African theology as critical discourse and practice, which has evolved from the colonial to the postcolonial period, has inspired liberation, adaptation, reconstruction, gender equality, cultural and human dignity, and economic and social justice, and promoted the will to be church and community on African terms without diminishing critical collaboration and global partnerships. The theological mission that blossomed in late colonialism deepened its liberation priorities and later turned to address the postcolonial despoliation.[2] European incursion and colonial practice had shaped theological imagination during the long deadly night of colonialism. Strands of theological thought articulated during the revolutionary and liberation struggle for independence developed as African theology moved out of its decolonial position into the postcolonial period and addressed the malaise of the continent.[3] Theologians reviewed and rejected aspects of missionary and colonial theology and praxis and responded with a theology of critical reaffirmation, drawing resources from African intellectual, spiritual, social, and cultural systems to critique and circumscribe dominant colonial motifs about African religiosity and to open new ways of reasoning about the Christian tradition in Africa.

Survey

First, African theology has grown from multidisciplinary research and the dialectical encounter with doctrinal, biblical, cultural and philosophical perspectives. African theologians in late colonialism developed scholarship that prioritized African Christianity, rather than building theological systems as was the predominant practice in universities and seminaries. This multidisciplinary work on African Christianity did not ignore doctrinal theology. Articulations of doctrinal theology can be found, for example, in the work

Ford's The Modern Theologians: An Introduction to Christian Theology since 1918, Fourth Edition.
Edited by Rachel Muers and Ashley Cocksworth.

of J. B. Danquah, John Mbiti, E. Bolaji Idowu, Charles Nyamiti, Bénézet Bujo, Kwesi Dickson, and Kwame Bediako.[4] In addition to his book, *Concepts of God in Africa,* Mbiti's *New Testament Eschatology in an African Background* set the gold standard for a critical dogmatic and cultural theological analysis.[5] Kwesi Dickson, in *Theology in Africa*, offered a religio-cultural reading of Africa and the implications of that theology across the continent as it was evident in the project of indigenization.[6] Fabien Eboussi-Boulaga and Jean-Marc Ela conceived their work as a critique of the colonial project and the postcolony.[7] Theologians expanded their study of specific doctrinal themes with an interdisciplinary approach, under the rubrics of "adaptation and incarnation."[8]

Positions on modern African theology

First, one of the early debates in African theology focused on the extent to which one could embrace Western philosophical thought in African theology. The hesitation by many theologians stemmed from the fact that Western philosophy had established a canon and a tradition of inquiry that did not embrace some parts of the world. Despite these debates, one must always remember that there is a rich history of philosophical theology in Africa, manifested in the work of Fabien Eboussi Boulaga, Bénézet Bujo, Nimi Wariboko, John W. de Gruchy, Charles Villa-Vicencio, and James R. Cochrane, to name only a few.

Second, African theology involves dialogue with the traditions of systematic theology. The leading theologian here has been Charles Nyamiti, whose approach to theology represents an impressive blending of the systematic theological tradition and an invitation to the theology of inculturation. Nyamiti calls for the grounding of theology in African culture as a way of making the church an African church. Nyamiti's rigorous theological analysis covers major aspects and themes of Christian doctrine; several studies have been done on Nyamiti, a generative thinker and renaissance scholar whose work in music and composition is also well known.

In the twenty-first century many African theologians have published on specific doctrinal themes, especially on ecclesiology as they have sought to define the nature of the ecclesial community in the African context. Some of the most creative work has been done on African-initiated churches – such as Marthinus L. Daneel's work on Christian independency in Zimbabwe.[9] David Ngong has started to work on doctrinal themes, and Diane B. Stinton and James Kombo have produced studies on the doctrine of Christology and the doctrine of God.[10] Other related scholarship on doctrine include Esther Acolatse's work on spiritual powers. Making a case for "biblical realism" and grounding her investigation in the theology of Kwesi Dickson and Karl Barth, Acolatse invites the church, especially in the North, to recognize the presence of the Spirit and calls for a recognition of spiritual powers present in the ecclesial community today.[11] Stan Chu Ilo's studies on the ecclesial community focus on the themes of salt and light.[12]

Third, African theology is a cultural and religious project. By engaging with African worldviews, African theologians have argued that biblical revelation should be understood in the light of African religiosity.[13] Thus, for example, the landmark 1956 publication *Des Prêtres Noirs s'Interrogent (Black Priests Reflect)*, by thirteen young Francophone African priests, grounded African theology in local religious roots and Christian history.[14] Placide Temple's groundbreaking book *Bantu Philosophy* invited an African philosophical response that promoted theological thinking, and Alexis Kagame invited readers to discover categories of being in Rwanda.[15] W. T. Harris and Harry Sawyerr discussed belief in a Supreme Being among the Mande people offering a theological engagement from an African perspective.[16]

Priorities of theological imagination and praxis

Pioneers of African theology envisioned a theological engagement that would speak to African realities. Bolaji Idowu and John Mbiti, both of whom earned doctorates in theology in England, grounded the study of African Christian themes in the religious worldview of Africans. Thus Aylward Shorter called for the adaptation of theology, emphasizing the staying power of African cultures and religions, making the case that theological themes had to be understood and expressed with a view of African cultures, a process that was called the adaptation of theological ideas to reflect the African worldview.[17] This called for an interdisciplinary approach to theology; one example was the new understanding of ecclesiology as part of the rigorous study of African church history, which received a ringing endorsement in Bengt Sundkler's magisterial study, *Bantu Prophets in South Africa*.[18] Writing during the same period, Kwesi Dickson stressed the importance of African culture to religion and the development of theology for the African church.[19] Bénézet Bujo grounded his theology in the African social context, calling on theologians to take the cultures of Africa seriously in their theological reflection.[20] Jean-Marc Ela's telling title *My Faith as an African* offered a theological reflection grounded in the Cameroonian context.[21] Fabein Ebbousi Boulaga criticized missionary denigration of African culture, which demanded Africans detach themselves from their pre-Christian world.[22] Joseph Healey and Donald Sybertz have promoted a theology of inculturation grounded in African proverbs.[23] Agbonkhianmeghe E. Orobator in his brilliant book *Theology Brewed in an African Pot* alludes to the appropriateness of using local terms and ideas to express theology and religious ideas by reminding readers of Chinua Achebe's account of a missionary's proclamation of his religion when he arrived in Igbo land. The missionary referred to the son of God, and the main character Okonkwo, in criticism of an earlier proclamation, reminded the missionary that he had said that there was only one God but now he was saying that God has a son, which means that he must have a wife. Rather than explain his earlier proclamation, the missionary proceeded to complicate it by talking of the Holy Trinity. "At the end of it, Okonkwo was fully convinced that the man was mad. He shrugged his shoulders and went away to tap his afternoon palm wine."[24] The story illustrates the notion that theology is first a local before it becomes a global product. Drawing illustrations from local Nigerian ideas about God, he highlights a broad and extended dialogue on political and social disruption that took place with the coming of a new God, proclaimed by Christian missionaries.[25] In the dialogue between the missionary and the locals, who knew and worshipped God, they found it perplexing that this God had no name but given the global reach of the idea of the divine, God also had many names. The messenger of God seemed to Okonkwo to be a mad preacher (someone who might have been mentally disturbed because he also talked about three persons in one God). This account by Orobator is illustrative of the importance of a contextual approach to theology, which has also been described as a theology of inculturation because local ideas are used to express the teachings of the Christian faith.

African theologians have expanded theological analysis beyond biblical and doctrinal issues to engage in a broad critical conversation and a rigorous scrutiny of public and political life and practice.[26] The broadening of political theology in Africa in the late twentieth century started as an anticolonial project and has moved into a postcolonial project. Theological thinking in its early phase criticized the colonial racial project that marked Africa for domination and subjugation, and early African theological imagination called for justice as part of a long struggle for freedom in colonial Africa. By the 1960s when African states gained independence, the quest for freedom intensified, especially in the Southern Africa region where coloniality and racial domination endured much longer. Theologians in the region resisted White domination by rejecting racism and its most vicious manifestation in the doctrine of apartheid and calling for independence and freedom for all people in the region. Building on themes of liberation and Black liberation theology, African theologians also introduced philosophies that were grounded in Black consciousness to resist racial discrimination and apartheid. In doing so, theologians drew resources from religion, the arts, humanities, and social sciences. What emerged and thrived in the Southern African region – where White hegemony in the name of Christian civilization put together a project of separate development that privileged Whites and pauperized Blacks – was a theology of liberation.[27]

Emerging themes in public theology

After the end of apartheid, political theology in that region took an important turn to the theology of reconstruction. Charles Villa-Vicencio sketched the idea of reconstruction, and the full-blown argument was presented by Jesse N. K. Mugambi at the Rockwell Lectures at Rice University in Houston, Texas, and later expanded and published as *From Liberation to Reconstruction*.[28] Political theology expanded into the era of Afropessimism, that period during which the economic fortunes of Africa were declining due to corruption, local strife, and the global economic imbalance that called for massive intervention from the World Bank and the International Monetary Fund (through the most debated Structural Adjustment Program). While the literature on Afro-pessimism painted a dark picture, Paul Gifford's influential historical studies – notably *Christianity in Africa: Its Public Role* – offered theologians a new starting point for interdisciplinary critiques of the political practice in Africa by exposing the debilitating impact of "big man" politics that brought many African states to the brinks of financial collapse.[29] A number of theological monographs, including my *The Dialectics of Transformation in Africa*, spelled out the malaise of the state and called for a practice of love.

In addition to documenting the challenges of the continent, other theological studies mapped out the possibilities of a democratic renewal. In the landmark work *Christianity and Democracy*, John de Gruchy tracked the recent history of theological and political activism to the political revolutions of 1989 in Europe, arguing that they served as a catalyst of the democratic change around the world. De Gruchy criticized the Western liberal democratic tradition for silence on questions of justice and for emphasizing the battle between capitalism and communism. He called for a just world order driven by a democratic practice grounded on the biblical prophetic traditions, the teachings of Jesus Christ, and an appreciation of the communal life of the early Christian church. Such a theology should always also be an ethical orientation, and de Gruchy argued that the African philosophical and ethical ideal *ubuntu* and "its contemporary reaffirmation is essential for the renewal of democracy in Africa and more universally."[30] Theologians have since welcomed Mahmood Mamdani's *Citizen and Subject* and Achille Mbembe's *On the Postcolony*; both books, without ignoring centuries of European underdevelopment of Africa, prosecuted the case against misrule in Africa, a devastation Mbembe has recently described as necropolitics.[31] In an earlier theological study, James R. Cochrane called for the restoration of human dignity that had been and was being crushed by political malpractice in the postcolony.[32]

Political and public theology in Africa will have to wrestle with conflicts. Christian Cardinal Tumi published two books detailing his struggle with the regimes of President Ahidjo and President Paul Biya, in which Tumi demonstrated that the Cameroon state lacked democratic practice.[33] The recent civil strife in Cameroon has generated early theological reflection,[34] a hastily put together article as if scholars are in competition for the position of the first theologian to publish in the self-declared country of Ambazonia. In the process, rather than stick with marshaling his own arguments the author uncritically castigates Cameroon theologians and philosophers, whom he blames for not supporting Ambazonian independence. Although liberation remains a compelling motif, the theology in this article ignores or simply abandons the path of critical dialogue that could resolve some of the tensions in the country. The civil war that is raging in Ethiopia today is another demonstration that ethnic differences still loom large and tends to overshadow the quest for a political consensus. In a study that was published before the start of the present war in Ethiopia, Theodros Teklu and his colleagues have decried the politics of hatred, offering critical analysis of the ethnic diversity and the legal responsibilities that come with it.[35] The compelling text explores unity and diversity to emphasize the spirit of togetherness, calling for a balanced view of the self and the other, with authors stressing the eddies of neighbor, the individual as a self-asserting being in a perichoretic relationship that in the Christian tradition should be seen as a *paraclesis* or supplication for political theology. They also draw from the biblical image of foot washing to underscore the need for humility and emphasize the moral responsibility of embracing others from different ethnic groups.

Recently Emmanuel Katongole has redefined the terms of political theology using specific language that describes the despoliation of Africa as a sacrifice. He has also developed a theology that he aptly calls "born from lament" and both texts explore the political catastrophe in Africa that has led to the deaths of millions, the majority of them occurring in the calculated and executed genocide of Rwanda. In both texts, Katongole advances a theology of hope manifested in the political praxis of Thomas Sankara and Maggie Barankitse who worked to establish a house of hope for victims of the Rwandan genocide.[36]

Theology in Africa has focused on women's rights and women's voices. Mercy Amba Oduyoye's personal journey as well as her intellectual interaction with Brigalia Bam and other scholars, notably Letty Russell, prepared Oduyoye to start the Circle of Concerned African Women Theologians in 1989 to challenge gender discrimination in Africa and invite scholars, especially African women, to engage in theological projects that would humanize the ecclesial community and its praxis. Oduyoye and members of the Circle resolved to write and live theology that would speak to and reject male domination of women, resist patriarchy, restore gender equity, realign ecofeminism, and reinstate the project of justice as a human engagement. The work of the Circle has radically disrupted male-dominated theology and centered and prioritized women's issues. One of the foundational texts of the Circle, *The Will to Arise*, summoned African women to stand up, speak, and claim the will to be, thus launching a critical multidisciplinary theological engagement that questioned and rejected patriarchy and called for justice.[37] Members of the Circle started a quiet revolution that would reverse the biased interpretation of sacred texts and Christian history and called on African women to defend rights for all persons. A new generation of women scholars has emerged, engaged in critical and culturally informed study of theology, church history, and a feminist reading of the Bible to promote gender equality. African women theologians have rejected female genital cutting, all forms of violence against women, and the economic and political marginalization of women. Their multidisciplinary studies have brought to the table a new textual analysis that prioritized women's issues as a way of challenging prevailing paradigms.

As part of this fight for gender equity in all areas of life, Musa Dube has adopted a strategy of reading the Bible that involves retelling of biblical stories to invite reader to see injustice and gender discrimination.[38] These readings were encouraged during the HIV/AIDS pandemic, which in Africa carried a woman's face because of sexual violence against women, the subjugation of women on grounds of culture or religion, and the promotion of false sexual mythologies. The members of the Circle have published research exposing injustices and calling for action to promote justice and equality.

African theology is an ongoing ethical project. Theologians have employed interdisciplinary tools to understand and call for an ethical approach to social living that promotes communal responsibilities in light of the face of the Other – the "least of these my brethren."[39] African theologians have embraced otherness, grounding it in the philosophy of ubuntu, which means "humanity" or "humaneness." The concept embodies the best of human values – love, support, and respect for one another in the political community. In southern Africa, the term has earned a greater currency with the expression "*umuntu ngumuntu ngabantu*," meaning "a person is a person through persons." Bénézet Bujo has argued that ubuntu demonstrates that personhood is not defined strictly by *cogito* but also by *relatio* (relationship) and *cognatio* (kinship).[40] Augustine Shutte has argued that ubuntu reflects a genuine interaction of life forces with the self and others.[41]

The debates on ethics and theology in Africa continue to call for a thoughtful balance between communalism and individuality.[42] The idea of ubuntu prioritizes the other person, regardless of their origin, gender, class, religion, sexual orientation, or politics. What stands out in this proposition is the view that the individual as an entity cannot and should not be submerged into the community and lose his or her freedom to make decisions as an individual. The priority of the other does not displace the community. At best, it suggests that a strong and well-balanced view of individuals strengthens the community. Ubuntu opens the door for a theological and ethical praxis that balances individuality and community. It is important to note that in the larger political community it would take other mechanisms of governance to actualize a functional ethical community. Thus, for example, Villa-Vicencio has addressed politics and human rights in the work of nation building.[43] Central to his argument is the notion that the rule of law offers possibilities to reconstruct human rights. Villa-Vicencio argues that first-generation rights such as the Universal Declaration of Human Rights offer individual rights, liberties, freedom of expression, movement, and association. Villa-Vicencio employs legal philosophy to promote social values that contribute reconstruction. He invites theologians to engage in the study of ethics from an interdisciplinary perspective, arguing that to do so, theologians ought to promote second-generation rights, as they take their stand with the poor. This affirms what liberation theologians called a preferential option for the poor.[44]

Interdisciplinarity: Theology and ethics

In an earlier work on theology and ethics, I argued that one could approach allegations of witchcraft through a theological and philosophical analysis using the philosophy of Emmanuel Levinas's philosophy and ethics of the other.[45] Although I did not seek to dismiss or affirm the idea of witchcraft, I framed the debate in terms of the effect of the discourse and alleged practice of witchcraft on the Other as it had been framed in the ethical thought of Levinas. Central to my discussion of witchcraft was the view that one could frame and define witchcraft discourses as intersubjective engagements because what generally happens is that someone is accused of having witchcraft and uses it to hurt other people. Although these practices allegedly take place in the spiritual realm, the ethical import of the discourses point to the notion of intersubjectivity, and the transactions of these intersubjective engagements have also been described by Levinas as a face-to-face relationship. He has offered a compelling argument for restructuring ethics as face-to-face engagements where the other's face stands as an injunction against violence.[46] Although the idea of the practice of witchcraft might not always reflect a physical face-to-face relationship as Levinas grounds his argument, the connection between two people where one reportedly has spiritual or occult powers that can be and are allegedly deployed to hurt the other represents a totalizing attitude that, if true, dominates another person who according to Levinas not only should be inviolable but is absolutely Other and should not be violated.

Paulinus Ikechukwu Odozor's magisterial study, *Morality Truly Christian, Truly African,* breaks new ground in theological ethics. Odozor argues that humanity is created in the image of God to live in community as men and women who must oppose inauthentic living. Inauthentic living here refers to all ideas and practices that violate the dignity of others and create disharmony in society. Odozor argues that humans are called to build solidarity and use it to end the dehumanization of others and create conditions for human thriving.[47] Odozor affirms the notion of basic freedom, and argues that an African communitarian emphasis does not undermine individuality and the human being has value because of the redemptive work of Jesus.[48] Nimi Wariboko, a leading theological ethicist, has broken new paths by grounding this ethical discourse and praxis in an interdisciplinary approach that draws materials from theological, intercultural, philosophical, and political analysis. He also builds on his Kalabari life ethic and norms that motivate people to live lives worthy of remembrance.[49] Wariboko's scholarship on ethics and theology has opened new paths of inquiry for philosophical theology in Africa.

Theology and public health

African theologians have taken up the question of health and well-being as a major theological issue. There are several reasons why this question has particular salience in Africa. Medicines and miracles both feature in sacred texts; Africans face medical challenges in the face of which miracles do not always work, and medicines are in short supply. A particular focus of theological work on health and well-being, as mentioned previously, has been HIV/AIDS. Theologian Lado Tonlieu Ludovic has argued that solving the AIDS pandemic by promoting only individual responsibility is not working well. Faith communities in many African communities emphasized abstinence mainly. The growing number of sexual transmissions was evidence that people were not practicing abstinence or that abstinence alone was not sufficient to stem the tide of the infections. It was therefore necessary to talk openly about condoms, which unfortunately in many contexts had been fetishized by faith leaders as the epitome of loose sexuality.[50] The failure to promote a rigorous gender equity means that many women are at risk of infections with the HIV/AIDS because structural inequities and weak economies have exacerbated the sexual vulnerabilities of many women and male sex workers. There is still a need for a robust theological engagement that will address the social, economic, cultural, and political conditions that have long been identified by the Joint United Nations Program to Combat HIV/AIDS and the World Health Organization.

Evelyn Namakula Mayangja has argued that fighting AIDS has been hampered by a deficit of political leadership and that the task for the church is to work for effective liberation of the people in the spirit of *Gaudium et Spes,* the Pastoral Constitution of the Church, one of the documents of the Second Vatican Council.[51] *Gaudium et Spes* invites faith leaders to criticize bad political policies. Mayanja argues that in doing so, African theologians have carried out research on health and healing especially during the HIV/AIDS pandemic and called for the practice of justice in health care in a postcolonial world where economic disparities had grown and most of the people lived below the poverty level and could not afford basic health care. Improving healthcare systems in Africa requires a sustained medical, political, theological, and cultural approach that invites all stakeholders to think and act together. For example, during the high noon of the battle to contain HIV/AIDS, South African theologians launched the African Religious Health Assets Program (ARHAP). James R. Cochrane and Steve de Gruchy and other scholars from the University of Memphis in Tennessee highlighted the tangible and intangible assets that faith communities have that could and should be deployed in fighting the disease and creating conditions for promoting well-being.[52]

Theology and inculturation

In his magisterial study *Inculturation and Healing,* Stuart C. Bate has argued that inculturation was the key to what he called "theological judgment." A new view of inculturation that reflects relevant theological judgment should be brought to bear on crucial things like health. African theology could and must pay attention to local cultural ideas and practices because culture involve local ideas and understanding of illness, healing, and well-being. But, more important, local ideas ought to be brought into the discourses about health in order to humanize each other to strengthen individuals and communities to face the many challenges posed by the precarity of health.[53] A Christian theology of health and healing will always walk the intercultural path to arrive at a holistic approach to health and healing.

Theology and the environment

African theology is also a discourse on the environmental crisis. Theologians have recognized that with an estimated 25 percent of the surface area of Africa being desert, and the forests and wetlands disappearing, Africa faces a growing ecological crisis. In this context, Christian theologians are raising new questions about how to understand the affirmation that the earth and all its fullness belong to the Lord. That affirmation is also an invitation for the inhabitants of the earth to assume responsibility in managing and preserving the earth. M. L. Daneel initiated the African Earthkeeping project to awaken churches in Southern Africa to the reality of climate change and take steps to protect the environment.[54] Susan Rakoczy has argued that women have adopted ecofeminism as a compelling motif for ecological justice; the environmental crisis affects women the most because in many communities women are the breadwinners.[55] Rakoczy argues that it is time to recognize that in the debates about the environment and climate change, women in Africa "know from daily experience that patriarchy/kyriarchy and the domination of nature results in poverty ... Their daily household responsibilities are made much more difficult."[56]

Rakoczy rejects dualisms that associate women with nature and argues that an ecofeminist perspective rejects these dualisms, which very often are grounded in domineering male categories. She reviews women's and feminist responses and initiatives, especially in the global South, and offers a holistic theological vision grounded in intercommunion and in an ecofeminist understanding of the Spirit who gives life, heals the earth, and empowers and enables responsible stewardship. She also calls for African theologians to raise questions about the human (and animal) habitat, water, and food sustainability. Rakoczy's focus on gender is apropos because the most well-known environmentalist on the continent was Wangari Maathai of Kenya who championed the planting of trees and was recognised with the Nobel Peace Prize. Other theologians have noted that food security remains a serious concern and calls for more theological analysis and training at local level.[57] In the context of the South African drought of 2016, Ernst Conradie called on theologians to address the moral and spiritual roots of the crisis.[58]

It is safe to think that most African communities have some kind of perspective on the connection between ecology and spirituality. Nisbert Taisekwa Taringa, in an ethical study of the environment in Africa grounded in the social antienvironmental world of the Shona and Christian worldviews, has called on faith communities to see the complementarity of those worldviews in order to promote ecospirituality and ecojustice and live a life of stewardship to the environment.[59] One hopes that faith leaders will continue to promote a spirituality that recognizes the precarity of the situation, especially in Africa, and in doing so, motivate members of the faith community to take proactive stands to slow down desertification and climate change.

New Theoretical Debates on Interdisciplinary Sources

One debate, which has nearly died down now and has left a fruitful path for theology in Africa today, has to do with sources of theology in Africa. The debate here is not only about the traditional sources of theology such as the Bible, oral tradition, existing theological literature, or even the idea of "revelation." Rather, the concern is with theory, concepts, and language in the postcolonial context. For nearly half a century of modern theological practice in Africa, scholars have raised concerns about the practice of grounding theological analysis on theories articulated in western and northern countries, whereas theoretical developments in the global South have been ignored. Therefore, we are not only dealing with the issue of the bibliography a theologian employs in their research, one's interlocutors, but also raising questions about how we go about conceptualizing theological categories that would invite critical dialogue in and out of Africa. The challenge here goes beyond ideas and the construction of theories itself but involves language because the theology that has been practiced in Africa has privileged colonial languages, especially English, French, Portuguese, Spanish, and ironically, rarely Arabic, which is read and spoken in a large part of Africa. The concerns here are genuine and call for critical thought because we have also come to a point where many African languages are now used in public education across the continent. It is safe to suggest that in the near future, one can expect a new theological vocabulary that will reflect African categories and use African languages as a means of communication. Many of the major African languages (Hausa, Yoruba,

Igbo, Isizulu, Swahili, Lingala, Amharic, Doaula, Ewondo, Bakweri, Fulfude) offer opportunities for theological writing that will popularize theology in Africa.[60]

Nimi Wariboko has regrounded African philosophical theology with a new rigor and without apologies and focused on, for lack of a better expression, what Paul Ricoeur described as *la chose du texte,* or even *le monde du texte,* roughly translated *the* matter of the text or the world of the text. Wariboko pursues *le monde du text* and brings new understanding and appreciation of Pentecostal thought and praxis.[61] It is this spirit that has led Wariboko to engage a spectacular array of philosophers like Hegel, Heidegger, Alain Badiou, Georges Battaille, and Michel Foucault and theologian Paul Tillich. Wariboko has put behind apologies for using a broad philosophical background in African theology, and the result is a philosophical theological journey that examines themes like ethics, excellence, and studies of money to articulate a theology grounded in the Spirit of God for the life of the ecclesial community and the wider world. Wariboko's work puts an end to the debates about which philosopher or which philosophical texts and tradition one can use in African theology. I am convinced that his scholarship marks a new dawn for constructive African theology because theologians can carry out a debate on questions that concern Africa and use all the relevant theological tools to make their case as Wariboko has done with continental philosophy.

Second, critical theological discourse will involve an ongoing debate on contested moral questions. Research on gender remains a pivotal theological category because despite the many accomplishments of the Circle of Concerned African Women Theologians, gender discrimination remains a reality for many African women. So much has been accomplished with African women theologians publishing highly acclaimed studies, but we have not achieved liberation on the gender front. Hotly contested questions like a woman's right to choose to terminate a pregnancy through abortion, questions about the legitimacy of same-sex relations, and the dissolution of marriage through divorce invite a rigorous theological reasoning that will deploy all the tools available to the theologian. Those tools include not only past theological analysis, but as has been done for most of postcolonial history, the social, cultural, and political history of the continent.

In these debates, theologians will have to come to terms with legal questions and this can be done by drawing on a number of tools that include a careful study of the constitutions of different African countries, the Charter of the African Union and regional groupings on the continent, as well as international conventions to which African countries are signatories such as the Universal Declaration of Human Rights. The pluralistic nature of African communities means that theological resources should be used in critical dialogue with the legal infrastructure of each country. Those legal documents are all part of the interdisciplinary resources that the theologian can draw upon to study and understand the full extent of human freedom and the importance of understanding human freedom in light of gender questions. Moreover, it would be a mistake to assume that the quest to restore the rights and dignity of African women and girls has nothing to learn from African resources. This is a topic that calls for additional theological research, but there is no doubt that, although many of the myths and traditional knowledge of Africa may be tainted with male bias, it is also the case that a careful reading of the mythological corpus of Africa will offer rich narratives on which to reconstruct an egalitarian approach to gender relations. This would invite research that in addition to well-known historic queen mothers would probe into the daily lives of women to recover and embrace the ethics with which African women lived, organized their lives, and managed their families and communities. This is a critical study that must be undertaken to offer local accounts that could fill the void when an effective depatriarchalizing research on theology, biblical studies, ethics, and ecclesial life has been undertaken. Here African theologians must build on the research done by members of the Circle of Concerned African Women Theologians as they seek to learn from the movement that was shaped by *Hearing and Knowing* and *The Will to Arise.*[62]

Third, it is time to rethink the legacy of Christian proclamation in Africa. Many African Christians see moral questions as straightforward because from their perspective, the Bible offers clear directives on how one could live his or her life; but merely citing a biblical text is not enough to settle some of the complicated issues people face today. Returning to Odozor's magisterial work on morality, he argues that "the teachings of Jesus' rule in debates on abortion, same-sex relations, sex work, divorce and remarriage" ought to be the standards that members of the ecclesial community should use to adjudicate these debates on sexuality. He argues that the Igbo culture offers perspectives on sexual morality, and the term *Aru* refers to what the Igbos consider abominations. He also argues that the idea of *Aru* as an abomination also includes sexual relations between relatives. He is concerned that the current debates of sexuality and the libertarian posture of some proposals were preceded by the promotion of contraceptives and what has followed has revolutionized our thinking on sexuality, marriage, and family.[63] It is fair to say that Odozor brings in an important concept from the Igbo culture that reflects the overwhelming reaction we have seen and heard from many African theologians and church leaders who have teamed up with brutal dictators in some cases because they oppose any discussion of sexual freedoms. The debate in my view ought to be approached with interest in freedoms, which allows persons to make their own decisions about their bodies, who and when to love, and how to experience sexuality. In a pluralistic society, it is important to remember that the church and other faith communities are just part of the many voices that speak on ethical issues that cannot be legislated as long as these actions pose no danger to the actors or other members of the community.

The debates on sexuality are more complex and require a careful understanding of human freedom and dignity. One must agree with Odozor that many people who oppose nontraditional sexual behavior are often subjected to prejudice and often described as "closed minded, homophobic, non-inclusive, and intolerant."[64] Nonetheless, as contentious as these questions are, African theologians will serve the faith community best if they continue to engage in study and critical dialogue that prioritizes the freedom of the individual to make decisions about his or her body. Odozor adds his voice to African theologians and ethicists who have argued that an African moral theology ought to emerge from the African church and be carried out in critical dialogue with the rest of the faith community. An important example of such a theology can be found in *Reconciliation, Justice, and Peace*, which presents essays on the Second African Synod.[65] I have to agree that he invites African theologians to embrace some of the best ideas of the ecclesial and theological traditions that have emerged from the Synod of Africa. However, it must also be stated that the teachings of the church should employ the language of persuasion and help members of the ecclesial community feel free to engage in the kind of critical dialogue that prioritizes their God-given freedoms.

Although we live in a globalized world and ideas are going to spread and people are going to imitate what they find interesting in other cultures, it is unfortunate that often when people exercise their freedoms, church leaders lament that these are imposed or borrowed from the West. Although others may see this as standing up to the West because of the brutal colonial history, one wonders if a reactionary perspective tends to leave some aspects of the argument unexplored, and central to this is the expression of individual freedoms of Africans, who must not be thought of as robots who absorb everything from the West. For example, in the texts of the synod to which Odozor refers, the bishops lamented the fact that foreign views of gender and sex were being imposed upon Africa. This view calls for further scrutiny; it is time to recognize that a conversation that attributes everything one suspects might be wrong with African social norms to Western liberalism does two things. First, it acquiesces, unfortunately in my view, to the notion that Africans cannot think for themselves because the West does all the thinking. Second, although the arguments are made in contested moral discourses, these positions that reject *tout court* everything suspected of having a foreign provenance might hinder a full exploration of issues that do not necessarily divide us but require critical assessment and appropriation if necessary or a full rebuttal after a critical appraisal.

In theology, one must respect what Valentine Mudimbe has described as the African *prise de parole*, which he linked to African scholars, several of them theologians, who were part of a critical intellectual praxis that inaugurated modern and postcolonial African theology. The many pioneers of African theology did not want to imitate some Western thinkers by idealizing and isolating African cultures. I do not think that they also wanted to deny Africans from participating in a rigorous debate on some of the questions about natural desires with which all human societies wrestle. I think that future theological research could at best focus on the idea of human difference, understand as fully as they can the inevitability of difference as a prelude to the exercise of human freedom as they engage in conversation on disputed questions. I think that an approach that recognizes but does not demonize difference will help future theologians to reject positions that assume *prima facie* that all controversial issues in Africa are imposed from outside. One important angle from which to raise new questions will be to understand the broad scope of human dignity. James R. Cochrane's *Circles of Dignity* could offer some ideas about how to do theology in a manner that builds and respects human dignity.[66]

The fourth area of debate and future consideration is for theologians to expand and enhance ethical discourse and practice in a digital society that has contracted the world into a virtual global village. Although one can only speculate on future theological and ethical dilemmas that would invite critical dialogue, future debates in Africa will certainly involve continuing to embrace the philosophy of ubuntu, a crucial, viable and vibrant ethical concept for thinking about personal and communal life. Ubuntu must now be expanded in new directions, without losing the balance between personal and communal ethics. For now, one can only affirm that the theology of ubuntu remains viable because it reflects a generally accepted ethos of social life that will continue the praxis of the ecclesial community. Future discussions of theological ethics could take insights from Kwame Gyekye's rejection of absolute communitarianism in ethics and adopt what he calls moderate communitarianism that balances individuality and community in African life and ethics.[67]

Fifth, African theologians will be called upon increasingly to take a stand on African religions, the Indigenous religions Africans practiced before the coming of colonial Christianity. One of the most important legacies that modern social anthropology has given to Africa is the research on African religions, so much so that on the eve of independence the debates on the status of Indigenous African religions was already regarded as settled – many African theologians published studies of Indigenous religions.[68] Some modern Christian groups in Africa, especially Pentecostals, demonize African traditional religions, and African theologians cannot afford to sit on the fence. Studies of African religions should be conducted on their own terms and not merely as a preparation for the gospel and are necessary so that the younger generation growing up in Africa will learn more about Indigenous religions. What is challenging for this generation is that all they hear from pastors and church leaders is the denunciation of those Indigenous religions as devilish practices. As African theologians engage in these conversations, it would be good to reread the earlier theologians to appreciate their convictions that African religions are equal to other religions.

Sixth, there is important work to be done in African liturgical theology. Questions of liturgy in traditional theological education are often consigned to practical theology as if liturgy stands outside the dogmatic traditions of the church. African theologians have demonstrated the connection between theology and liturgy in many compelling ways. Elochuckwu Eugene Uzukwu, a theological mentor to many in Africa, has combined theology and liturgy in his persuasive study, *Worship as Body Language,* calling African churches to reimagine worship.[69] Uzukwu's biblically and culturally grounded study examines how gestures and myths shaped the cultus that linked humanity and divinity. He examines African gestures, music, and dance as practices that establish regularity in divine–human contact and demonstrate the depth of life. Therefore, they hold the key to understanding worship because they carry symbolic codes.[70]

The innovation in Uzukwu's studies is in his mapping of inculturation in the history of Christianity as local symbols and rituals were used to shape worship. They demonstrate the fact that the cultus was shaped by local thought and praxis. However, the colonial imagination and praxis-imposed limitations on African worship that would only be opened up by the declarations of the Second Vatican Council, adopting preparatory documents promoted by Joseph Malula, who served on the Commission on Liturgy. According to Uzukwu, these were changes the church had to make because the church of the future lay and still lies outside Europe and the Americas and worship in those places, involved the practice of inculturation to ground the church and its cultus in its *Sitz im Leben*. The localization involves more than carrying worship in local languages because it involves searching for local concepts that would enable worshipers to internalize the Christian message in their own language and idioms. This will be possible if theologians and clergy take traditional religious ideas and structures seriously.

Conclusion

I have discussed selected topics in African theology, which is an interdisciplinary, ecclesial, and for now, a postcolonial practice that has not only offered a critical alternative to missionary and colonial theology but promoted the inculturation of the faith community and its teachings. I have highlighted ideas from some of the pioneers and theologians, demonstrating that they grounded their theological reflection in Christian history and African realities, philosophy, and ethics. African theology today is an interdisciplinary engagement that probes doctrinal themes, sociocultural investigations, politics, the economy, the nature of the ecclesial community, and its mission of liberation and fights for human dignity. African theology was inaugurated to engage the Bible, ecclesial history, and the social and communal lives of the faithful in Africa; the many seeking to understand their faith so that they can connect the idea of eternal life with lived reality, human dignity, and care for our habitat. African theology takes seriously the fact that all of creation represents the fullness of the Lord, humans are stewards, and theology is only one of the many disciplines that challenge and cheer the ecclesial community to live a life of stewardship. Theologians carry out this stewardship best when they think beyond the faith community and embrace the practical realities of their political communities. The theme of postcoloniality has reminded theologians that domination and despoliation are equal opportunity employers and African theology must address the inequities and injustice now perpetrated by Africans. In this respect, African theologians have offered a critique of society and invited their leaders to reconstruct their societies and their institutions to serve as centers of justice and reconciliation, which must be part of the repair work that must be done to heal the wounds of brutalization. Such attempts to bring healing must include gender justice, the promotion of equality, and the respect of the dignity of all persons, especially on contested issues as sexuality. I am convinced that doing this will reframe theology as a value-driven enterprise that involves the ecclesial, social, cultural, political, and economic sectors of society. For this reason, ethics will remain an important component of theology because irrespective of what one believes, a theological position that demonizes, disparages, and destroys the conditions of well-being for those we disagree with betrays the gospel. The bright future that invites creative, critical, and constructive theological practices will offer theologians a new platform to operate from if they prioritize those whom Jesus described as "the least of these my brethren."

Notes

1 I am grateful to Professor Rachel Muers for reading several drafts of this chapter and giving me critical feedback that helped in revising the paper.

2 Elias K. Bongmba, *The Dialectics of Transformation in Africa* (New York: Palgrave Macmillan, 2006).

3 Robert S. Heaney, *Post-Colonial Theology: Finding God and Each Other amidst the Hate* (Eugene, OR: Cascade, 2019).

4 John Mbiti, *Concepts of God in Africa* (London: SPCK, 1971); E. Bolaji Idowu, *Towards an Indigenous Church* (London: Oxford University Press, 1965); Kwame Bediako, *Jesus and the Gospel in Africa: History and*

Experience (Maryknoll, NY: Orbis, 2000); Bénézet Bujo, *African Theology in its Social Context* (Maryknoll, NY: Orbis, 1992); J. B. Danquah, *The Akan Doctrine of God: A Fragment of Gold Coast Ethic and Religion* (London: Routledge, 2014).

5 John Mbiti, *New Eschatology in an African Background: A Study of the Encounter between New Testament Theology and African Traditional Concepts* (London: Oxford University Press, 1971).

6 Kwesi Dickson, *Theology in Africa* (London: Darton, Longman & Todd, 1984).

7 Fabien Eboussi-Boulaga, *Christianity without Fetishes: An African Critique and Recapture of Christianity* (Maryknoll, NY: Orbis, 1984); Jean-Marc Ela, *African Cry*, trans. Robert R. Barr (Maryknoll, NY: Orbis, 1986); Jean-Marc Ela, *My Faith as an African*, trans. John Pairman Brown and Susan Perry (Maryknoll, NY: Orbis, 1988).

8 Aylward Shorter, *African Christian Theology: Adaptation of Incarnation?* (Maryknoll, NY: Orbis, 1977).

9 Marthinus L. Daneel, *Old and New in Southern Shona Independent Churches*, Vols. 1–2 (The Hague: Mouton, 1971, 1974); *Quest for Belonging: Introduction to a Study of African Independent Churches* (Gweru: Mambo Press, 1987).

10 David Ngong, *A New History of Christian Thought: From Cape to Cairo* (New York: Routledge, 2017); David Ngong, *The Holy Spirit and Salvation in African Christian Theology* (New York: Peter Lang, 2010); Diane B. Stinton, *Jesus of Africa: Voices of Contemporary African Christology* (Maryknoll, NY: Orbis, 2004); James Henry Owino Kombo, *The Doctrine of God in African Christian Thought: The Holy Trinity, Theological Hermeneutics and the African Intellectual Culture* (Leiden: Brill, 2007).

11 Esther Acolatse, *Powers, Principalities, and the Spirit: Biblical Realism in Africa and the West* (Grand Rapids, MI: Eerdmans, 2018).

12 Stan Chu Ilo, Joseph Ogbonnaya, and Alex Ojacor, eds., *The Church as Salt and Light: Path to an African Ecclesiology of Abundant Life* (Eugene, OR: Pickwick, 2011).

13 See Kwesi Dickson and Paul Ellingsworth, *Biblical Revelation and African Belief* (Maryknoll, NY: Orbis, 1969).

14 A. Abble et al., *Des Prêtres Noirs S'Interrogent* (Paris: Les Éditions du Cerf, 1956).

15 Placide Temples, *Bantu Philosophy* (Paris: Présence Africaine, 1945); Alexis Kagame, *La Philosophie Bantu-Rwandaise de l'Être* (Bruxelles: Académie royale des sciences coloniales, 1956). See also Alexis Kagame, *La Philosophie Bantu Comparée* (Paris: Présence Africaine, 1976).

16 W. T. Harris and Harry Sawyerr, *The Springs of Mende Belief and Conduct: A Discussion of the Influence of the Belief in the Supernatural among the Mende* (Freetown: Sierra Leone University Press, 1968). See also Kwesi Dickson and Paul Ellingsworth, *Biblical Revelation and African Beliefs* (Maryknoll, NY: Orbis, 1969); E. W. Fasholé-Luke, "African Christian Theologies," *Scottish Journal of Theology* 29, no. 3 (1976): 172–3; Barney Pityana and Charles Villa Vicencio, eds., *Being Church in South Africa Today* (Johannesburg: South African Council of Churches, 1995).

17 Shorter, *African Christian Theology*, 2.

18 Bengt Sundkler, *Bantu Prophets in South Africa* (London: Routledge, 1948).

19 Kwesi Dickson, *Theology in Africa* (Maryknoll: Orbis, 1984), 32. See also South African critiques of the cultural approach in Desmond Tutu, "Black Theology/African Theology: Soul Mates or Antagonists," *Journal of Religious Thought* 32, no. 2 (1987): 25–33; Allan Boesak, *A Farewell to Innocence* (Maryknoll, NY: Orbis, 1977); Manas Buthelezi, "Toward Indigenous Theology in South Africa," in *The Emergent Gospel: Theology from the Underside of History*, ed. Sergio Torres and Virginia Fabella (Maryknoll, NY: Orbis, 1978), 7ff.

20 Bénézet Bujo, *African Theology in Its Social Context*, trans. John O'Donohue (Maryknoll, NY: Orbis, 1992)

21 Ela, *My Faith as an African*, 33–4.

22 Boulaga, *Christianity without Fetishes*, 23.

23 Joseph G. Healey and Donald Sybertz, *Towards an African Narrative Theology* (Maryknoll, NY: Orbis, 1996).

24 Agbonkhianmeghe E. Orobator, *Theology Brewed in an African Pot* (Maryknoll, NY: Orbis, 2008), 26–7.

25 Orobator, *Theology Brewed in an African Pot*, 27.

26 Bongmba, *The Dialectics of Transformation in Africa*.

27 Allan Boesak, Ntumeleng Mosala, Manas Buthelezi, John W. de Gruchy, Charles Villa-Vicencio, Steve Biko, James R. Cochrane, Gerald West, Tinyiko Maluleke.

28 Charles Villa-Vicencio, *A Theology of Reconstruction: Nation-Building and Human Rights* (New York: Cambridge University Press, 1992); Charles Villa-Vicencio, *Theology and Violence: The South African Debate* (Grand Rapids, MI: Eerdmans, 1988); Jesse N. K. Mugambi, *From Liberation to Reconstruction: African Christian Theology after the Cold War* (Nairobi: East African Educational Publishers Limited, 1995); Charles Villa-Vicencio, "Religion, Revolution and Reconstruction: The Significance of the Cuban and Nicaraguan Revolutions for the Church in South Africa," *Journal of Theology for Southern Africa* 73 (1990): 48–59.

29 Paul Gifford, *African Christianity: Its Public Role* (Bloomington, IN: Indiana University Press, 1998).

30 John W. de Gruchy, *Christianity and Democracy* (Cape Town: David Philip, 1996), 191.

31 Mahmood Mamdani, *Citizen and Subject: Contemporary Africa and the Legacy of Late Colonialism* (Princeton, NJ: Princeton University Press, 2018); Achille Mbembe, *On the Postcolony* (Chicago, IL: University of Chicago Press, 2009).

32 James R. Cochrane, *Circles of Dignity* (Minneapolis, MN: Fortress Press, 2009).

33 Christian Cardinal Tumi, *The Political Regimes of Ahmadou Ahidjo, and Paul Biya, and Christian Tumi, Priest* (Douala: MACACOS, 2006); Christian Cardinal Tumi, *My Faith: A Cameroon to Be Renewed* (Douala: Editions Veritas, 2011).

34 Daniel Pratt Morris-Chapman, "An Ambazonian Theology? A Theological Approach to the Anglophone

Crisis in Cameroon," *HTS Theological Studies* 75, no. 4 (2019): 1–11. See also Elias Kifon Bongmba, "Church and State in Cameroon: The Political Theology of Christian Cardinal Tumi," *Journal of Asian and African Studies* 51, no. 3 (2016): 283–304.

35 Theodros Teklu, *Ethnic Diversity, National Unity: Moral Pedagogies of Togetherness for Ethiopians,* (Eugene, OR: Wipf and Stock, 2021).

36 Emmanuel Katongole, *The Sacrifice of Africa: A Political Theology for Africa* (Grand Rapids, MI: Eerdmans, 2010); Emmanuel Katongole, *Born from Lament: The Theology of Politics and Hope in Africa* (Grand Rapids, MI: Eerdmans, 2017).

37 Mercy Amba Oduyoye and Musimbi R. A. Kanyoro, eds., *The Will to Arise: Women, Tradition, and the Church in Africa* (Maryknoll, NY: Orbis, 1992).

38 Musa W. Dube, *Postcolonial Feminist Interpretation of the Bible* (St. Louis, MO: Chalice Press, 2000).

39 Bénézet Bujo, Paulinus Okechukwu Odozor, Samuel Waje Kunhiyop, Nimi Wariboko.

40 Bénézet Bujo, *African Theology in its Social Context,* trans. John O'Donohue (Maryknoll, NY: Orbis, 2006).

41 Augustine Shutte, *Ubuntu: An Ethic for a New South Africa* (Pietermaritzburg: Cluster Publications, 2001).

42 Elias Kifon Bongmba, *African Witchcraft and Otherness: A Philosophical and Theological Critique of Intersubjective Relations* (Albany, NY: SUNY Press, 2001).

43 Charles Villa-Vicencio, *A Theology of Reconstruction: Nation Building and Human Rights* (Cambridge: Cambridge University Press, 1993).

44 I am indebted to James R. Cochrane's discussion of Villa-Vicencio's book and his other writings on human dignity. See James R. Cochrane, "A Critical Review of Charles Villa-Vicencio's A Theology of Reconstruction," *Journal for the Study of Religion* 8, no. 1 (1995): 85–95.

45 Bongmba, *African Witchcraft and Otherness.*

46 Emmanuel Levinas, *Totality and Infinity: An Essay on Exteriority,* trans. Alphonso Lingis (Pittsburgh, PA: Duquesne University Press, 1969).

47 Paulinus Ikechukwu Odozor, *Morality Truly Christian, Truly African: Foundational, Methodological, and Theological Considerations* (Notre Dame, IN: University of Notre Dame Press, 2014), 222–3.

48 Odozor, *Morality Truly Christian, Truly African,* 228–9.

49 Nimi Wariboko, *The Depth and Destiny of Work: An African Theological Interpretation* (Trenton, NJ: Africa World Press, 2008), 139–77. See Peter Paris, "Similarities between Nimi Wariboko and Aristotle," in *The Philosophy of Nimi Wariboko: Social Ethics, Economy and Religion,* ed. Toyin Falola (Durham, NC: Carolina Academic Press, 2021), 46–52.

50 Elias Kifon Bongmba "HIV and AIDS and Stigma," in *HIV and AIDS in Africa: Christian Reflection, Public Health, Social Transformation,* ed. Jacquineau Azetsop (Maryknoll, NY: Orbis, 2016), 264–76.

51 Evelyn Namakula Mayanja, "Biblical and Dogmatic Theology on Personhood: Application to Africa's Milieu," in *The Routledge Handbook of African Theology,* ed. Elias Kifon Bongmba (New York: Routledge, 2020), 462ff.

52 Gary R. Gunderson and James R. Cochrane, *Religion and the Health of the Public: Shifting the Paradigm* (New York: Palgrave Macmillan, 2012).

53 Stuart C. Bate, *Inculturation and Healing: Coping-Healing in South African Christianity,* 2nd ed. (Pietermaritzburg: Cluster Publications, 1997). See especially chapters 8, 9, and 10.

54 Marthinus L. Daneel, *African Earthkeepers, Vol. 2: Environmental Mission and Liberation in Christian Perspective,* (Pretoria: UNISA Press, 1999).

55 Susan Rakoczy, *In Her Name: Women Doing Theology* (Pietermaritzburg: Cluster Publications, 2004), 298ff.

56 Rakoczy, *In Her Name,* 303.

57 See Dietrich Werner and Elizabeth Jeglitzka, eds., *Eco-Theology, Climate Justice and Food Security: Theological Education and Christian Leadership Development* (Geneva: Globethics, 2016), 45.

58 Ernst Conradie, "Climate Justice, Food Security and God: Some Reflections from the Perspective of Eco-Theology," in *Eco-Theology, Climate Justice and Food Security,* 109–14.

59 Conradie, "Climate Justice, Food Security and God," 88.

60 See for example, see Bernd Heine and Derek Nurse, eds., *African Languages: An Introduction* (New York: Cambridge University Press, 2000). I think that it is time for African theologians to build on the work done by Wycliffe Bible Translators, learn the orthography of their own languages, and employ them in writing theology. I am as guilty as anyone and know the challenges here because we write to audiences who do not speak our languages.

61 For a one-stop reference on the work of Wariboko, see Falola, ed., *The Philosophy of Nimi Wariboko.*

62 Mercy Amba Oduyoye, *Hearing and Knowing: Theological Reflections on Christianity in Africa* (Maryknoll, NY: Orbis, 1986); Mercy Amba Oduyoye and Musimbi R. A. Kanyoro, eds., *The Will to Arise: Women, Tradition, and the Church in Africa* (Eugene, OR: Wipf and Stock, 1992).

63 Odozor, *Morality Truly Christian, Truly African,* 265.

64 Odozor, *Morality Truly Christian, Truly African,* 265.

65 Agbonkhianmeghe E. Orobator, *Reconciliation, Justice, and Peace: The Second African Synod* (Maryknoll, NY: Orbis, 2011).

66 James R. Cochrane, *Circles of Dignity: Community Wisdom and Theological Reflection* (Minneapolis, MN: Augsburg Fortress, 1999).

67 Kwame Gyekye, *Tradition and Modernity, Philosophical Reflections on the African Experience* (New York: Oxford University Press, 1997).
68 Examples here include E. Bolaji Idowu and John Mbiti.
69 Elochukwu Eugene Uzukwu, *God, Spirit, and Human Wholeness: Approaching Faith and Culture in West African Style* (Collegeville, MN: The Liturgical Press, 1997).
70 Uzukwu, *God, Spirit, and Human Wholeness*, 10–14.

Recommended Reading

Bongmba, Elias Kifon. *The Dialectics of Transformation in Africa*. New York: Palgrave Macmillan, 2006.

Bujo, Bénézet. *African Theology in Its Cultural Context*. Maryknoll, NY: Orbis, 1999.

Cochrane, James R. *Circles of Dignity*. Minneapolis, MN: Fortress Press, 2009.

de Gruchy, John W. *Christianity and Democracy*. Cape Town: David Philip, 1996.

Dickson, Kwesi. *Theology in Africa*. London: Darton, Longman & Todd, 1984.

Eboussi Boulaga, Fabien. *Christianity without Fetishes: An African Critique and Recapture of Christianity*. Maryknoll, NY: Orbis, 1984.

Ela, Jean-Marc. *Ma foi s'Africain*. Paris: Karthala, 1982.

Falola, Toyin, ed. *The Philosophy of Nimi Wariboko: Social Ethics, Economy, and Religion*. Durham, NC: Carolina Academic Press, 2021.

Hegba Méinrad Piere. *Émancipation d'Eglise sous tutelle: Essai sur ère post-missionnaire*. Paris: Présence Africaine, 1976.

Idowu, E. Bolaji. *Olódumare: God in Yoruba Belief*. New York: Wazobia, 1994.

Kombo, James H. O. *The Doctrine of God in African Christian Thought*. Leiden: Brill, 2007.

Katangole, Emmanuel. *The Sacrifice of Africa: A Political Theology for Africa*. Grand Rapids, MI: Eerdmans, 2010.

Mbiti, John. *Concepts of God in Africa*. London: SPCK, 1969.

Mosala, Itumeleng J. *Biblical Hermeneutics and Black Theology in South Africa*. Grand Rapids, MI: Eerdmans, 1989.

Mudimbe, V. Y. *The Invention of Africa: Gnosis, Philosophy, and the Order of Knowledge*. Bloomington, IN: Indiana University Press, 1988.

Mugambi, Jesse N. K. *From Liberation to Reconstruction: African Christian Theology after the Cold War*. Nairobi: East African Educational Publishers, 1995.

Mveng, Engelbert. *L'Afrique dans l'Eglise. Paroles d'un croyant*, Paris: L'Harmattan, 1985.

Nyamiti, Charles. *The Way to Christian Theology for Africa*. Eldoret: AMECEA Gaba Publications, 1979.

Oduyoye, Mercy Amba. *Introducing African Women's Theology*. Sheffield: Sheffield Academic Press, 2001.

Orobator, Agbonkhianmeghe E. *Theology Brewed in an African Pot*. Maryknoll, NY: Orbis, 2008.

Phiri, Isabel A. *Women, Presbyterianism and Patriarchy: Religious Experience of Chew Women in Central Malawi*. Blantyre/Bonn: Christian Literature Association in Malawi/Verlag für Kultur und Wissenschaft, 1997.

Pointenen, Mari-Anna. *African Theology as Liberating Wisdom: Celebrating Life and Harmony in the Evangelical Lutheran Church in Botswana*. Leiden: Brill, 2013.

Sawyerr, Harry. *God: Ancestor or Creator? Aspects of Traditional Belief in Ghana, Nigeria and Sierra Leone*. London: Longman, 1970.

Ter Haar, G. *Spirit of Africa: The Healing Ministry of Archbishop Milingo of Zambia*. London: Hurst, 1992.

Tshibangu, Tharcisse. *Le propos d'une théologie Africaine*. Kinshasa: Presses Universitaires du Zaïre, 1974.

Uzukwu, Eugene. *A Listening Church: Autonomy and Communion in African Churches*. Maryknoll, NY: Orbis, 1996.

Vähäkangas, Mika, *In Search of Foundations for African Catholicism: Charles Nyamiti's Theological Methodology*. Leiden: Brill, 1999.

Villa-Vicencio, Charles. *A Theology of Reconstruction: Nation Building and Human Rights*. Cambridge: Cambridge University Press, 1992.

Wariboko, Nimi. *The Split God: Pentecostalism and Critical Theory*. Albany, NY: SUNY Press, 2018.

African Women's Theology

Esther Mombo

Introduction

"Circle" theology, the focus of this chapter, was developed and written by members of the Circle of Concerned African Women Theologians, an organization founded three decades ago. It was launched in Trinity College Legon, near Accra, Ghana in 1989, a year after the Ecumenical Decade of Churches in Solidarity with Women. The Circle was formed under the leadership of Mercy Amba Oduyoye as an ecumenical and interfaith body of African women theologians. This theology is motivated by two motifs. First was the gospel story of Jesus raising the twelve-year-old dead daughter of Jairus with the words, "*Talitha cumi*" which means "Little girl, get up!" (Mark 5:4). Like the dead girl, African women had been treated as dead because their story was being told by others; Oduyoye and Kanyoro wrote that "as long as men and foreign researchers remain the authorities on culture, rituals and religion, African women will continue to be spoken of as if they were dead."[1] Second was the state of theology in Africa, which Oduyoye likened to a one-winged bird that could not fly and needed a second wing "in the form of women's voices and analysis."[2]

Oduyoye was convinced that African women had to construct their own theologies, rooted in the experiences of women. Defining Circle theology, Isabel Phiri affirms that

> African women's theologies are a critical, academic study of the causes of women's oppression, particularly a struggle against societal, cultural and religious patriarchy. They are committed to the eradication of all forms of oppression against women through a critique of the social and religious dimensions both in African culture and Christianity. African women's theologies take women's experiences as its starting point, focusing on the oppressive areas of life caused by injustices such as patriarchy, colonialism, neo-colonialism, racism, capitalism, globalisation, and sexism. It sees a need to include the voices of all women, not just theologians, because it acknowledges that the majority of African women are engaging in oral theology.[3]

Ford's The Modern Theologians: An Introduction to Christian Theology since 1918, Fourth Edition.
Edited by Rachel Muers and Ashley Cocksworth.
© 2024 John Wiley & Sons Ltd. Published 2024 by John Wiley & Sons Ltd.

At its formation, the Circle embarked on a seven-year cycle of sustained analysis of religion and culture with several specific objectives in mind:

1 To encourage and empower the critical study of the practice of religion in Africa
2 To undertake research that examines both positive and negative religio-cultural factors, beliefs, and myths that affect, influence, or hamper women's development
3 To publish theological literature written by African women with a special focus on religion and culture
4 To build a communications network among theologically trained women both in academia and beyond
5 To promote a dialogic approach to religious and cultural tensions in Africa
6 To strive toward the inclusion of women's studies in religion and culture in academia and research institutions in Africa, particularly institutions of higher education including theological institutions
7 To empower African women to contribute to the cross-cultural discourse on women's issues through engagement in critical cultural hermeneutics
8 To promote ecumenism and cultural pluralism
9 To bring African women's theology to the attention of the public[4]

The initial focus was to address the dearth of theological writings by women. The absence of these writings meant that theology, culture, and biblical interpretations were shaped by men who often used the scriptures and theology to oppress, exploit, and exclude women. This absence of women in church leadership, literature, and academic writings meant they were marginalized and silenced. In bringing these exclusions to light, the Circle authors published *Groaning in Faith: African Women in the Household of God*,[5] articulating the ways in which they had been excluded, dominated, and marginalized. They chose to use their narratives as a method to produce theology that would influence academics and clergy.

Survey

The central aim of the Circle founders was to create a safe space for women to both do and write theology with a liberation motif. This aim continues to be central for the members of the Circle, because women's agency and role as subjects are often hidden or downplayed in written theology. The Circle sought to foreground African women's experiences of religion, theology, and culture in their specific social locations and to undertake research, writing, and publishing on African issues focusing on women's perspectives. A unique feature of the Circle's approach to theology is its strong communal and narrative elements. Liberation for oppressed women and others who suffer oppression because of race, religion, culture, social class, and so forth is the motif that has always guided the Circle's engagement with society. In establishing their own space as women of faith, the founding members of the Circle felt that they were at a stage where they could claim independence – they had enough experience of the church and society and were able to ask questions about their role and place in the religious and social structures.

In the Circle, theologians engage the community in realizing liberation from a triple patriarchal oppression rooted in African culture, Christian culture, and colonial heritage. This triple oppression, they argue, is experienced by African women irrespective of their religious traditions. Attempts to emancipate African women ended up creating more room for a different aspect of oppression. The first attempt to liberate African women in the Christian tradition was through the work of missionaries. Christian missionaries from Europe and the United States organized mission work among women because it was one way of liberating women from what the missionaries then saw as women's oppressions; Modupe Labode refers to missionaries' perception of women as victims of traditional practices related to food taboos, initiation, marriage, and funeral rites.[6] From the Christian missionaries' perspective, liberation for women meant giving them an education for motherhood, teaching them about child care and hygiene, nutrition, and different feeding methods. This culminated in the preparation of Christian homes, which were viewed to be important places for moral and spiritual training. The education of women became a tool for "civilization" at home and a means of communicating gender roles to women.

This lopsided form of liberation, however, gave birth to very strong women's organizations in most mainline churches, and these women's organizations form the backbone of mainline churches. Most of the women's groups in the churches provide spiritual and moral support for women. In many cases, women in these groups find a way to exercise their freedom to minister to one another. Their exploration of scriptures enables them to speak about their families and their lives.[7] These organizations, though limited in their hermeneutical critique of patriarchy, remain the source of strength for many women in these denominations. These women's groups are also a source of financial support for the churches through their fundraising activities. Despite the critical numbers and the financial support they offer in the church, they are not in the mainstream. Instead, they are on the margins of the ecumenical leadership structures, which are highly patriarchal.

On liberation, these groups did not have the tools to critique the skewed power structures. This and other situations in society laid a foundation for the liberation motif by the Circle. Fiedler observes that the founders of the Circle joined other liberation groups to articulate the issues of women's oppression.[8] Members of the Circle began searching for revolutionary models and visions for the liberation of all societies by critically evaluating religious-cultural norms and values, without excluding economics and politics. Members of the Circle began to use their experiences as women, listening to other women in the church to name the inherent oppressions. They also began to rediscover the dignity and respect of all humanity.

Content

Culture

> African culture is perceived to be the thread which strings the community beliefs and social set-up together. It is therefore a great threat to community security to be critical of culture for there are elements in these cultures which are the veins through which the solidarity of communities is nurtured. Women are custodians of cultural practices.... For generations, women have guarded cultural prescriptions strictly governed by the fear of breaking taboos ... In the guise of culture, harmful practices and traditions are perpetuated. . .. Culture silences many women in African and makes it impossible for them to experience the liberating promises of God of which the Bible speaks.[9]

As a result of insights like these, Circle theologians focused on culture and religion, and in particular an objective critique of culture. The study of culture laid a foundation for articulating the liberation of women. Although African theologians focused on liberation from socioeconomic and theological domination, searching for an enculturated theology, they did not pay particular attention to the liberation of African women in the various facets of life.

The Circle employed a critique of culture from the perspective of women – a critique that did not advocate for a complete rejection of African culture, or a blind apology for it, but instead interrogated culture in the light of both oppressive and affirming aspects. In critiquing African culture, the Circle writers applied the same balanced and selective criteria. In an objective vein, they concede that "there *are* favourable aspects of our culture which enhance the wellbeing of women," but unfortunately such aspects have been suppressed. Meanwhile, "those aspects which diminish women continue to be practised in various degrees by our societies, often making women objects of cultural preservation."[10] Moreover, culture is significant in doing circle theology because of the ways in which women have been socialized to be custodians of culture.

In the Circle volume titled *The Will to Arise*, Circle members analyzed the different situations of women in Africa and how culture is used to determine their position, interrogating both the negative and positive aspects of African culture. They also highlighted the impact of these cultural traditions on the members of specific communities. In *Groaning in Faith*, the contributors discuss what it means to be a member of a particular faith and the common challenges therein.[11] In the same light, the contributors to the volume titled *Talitha Cum: Theologies of African Women* engage in their theological reflections using the lens of culture.[12] The Circle's theology emphasizes advocating for liberation from oppressive cultural practices while affirming and reclaiming positive practices. Culture as a category for doing theology is also shown in Oduyoye's *Daughters of Anowa*. In this book Oduyoye investigates the influence of African culture on the lives of African women. According to her, African myths, folktales, and proverbs have been socialized into oppressive roles in communities, thus marginalizing life-affirming spaces, regardless of their cultural expressions.

The Bible

Due to the importance of religious texts for the shaping of adherents' worldviews, which affects the status of women within faith communities, the Circle studies and interprets religious texts within Africa's major religions. This includes a critical analysis of the hidden gender-oppressive scripts in the Bible as well as the use of the Bible in subjugating women. The Circle writers noted that the translation of the Bible into local languages led to the massive expansion of Christianity in Africa. It is also the translation of the Bible that led to the founding of some of the African-instituted churches. Adopting the hermeneutic of suspicion in interpreting scripture, the Circle writers noted that the biblical texts were read through the lenses of the missionary and colonial positions, and in a gendered way. The Circle employed other ways of reading the texts that revealed how centuries of biblical patriarchal interpretation have left the plight of African women unresolved. These methods of reading interrogate and question the underlying patriarchal tendency of attempting to explain or justify texts that appear to sanction women's oppression.

Circle theologians have chosen not to remain in models of interpretation that are not liberating. It has been creative and versatile for members of the Circle to use methods such as hermeneutics of suspicion, cultural hermeneutics, and postcolonial hermeneutics to read the Bible.[13] For the Circle members, biblical studies shifted from historical exegesis to contextual reading and pragmatic interpretation. This meant that women were no longer interested in reconstructing the original text of the Bible but in finding meaning, guidance, and empowerment in the biblical narrative for present-day life. Mercy Oduyoye admits to the complexities of the Bible as a sexist book that also holds narratives of liberation, especially of those that are on the margins of society such as

> the stories of the exodus, exile and to other biblical motifs in which "the least" are recognised and affirmed, are saved or held up as beloved of God ... These narratives have been for me the bearer of good news. Despite entrenched patriarchal and ethnocentric prepositions of the Bible, it is a book I cannot dispense with as long as I remain in the Christian community and that community means more to me than my personal hurts.[14]

Similarly, Musimbi Kanyoro asserts that

> The Bible is a message of liberation for African women, much as it is also used to deny their freedom. For women to find justice and peace through the texts of the Bible, they have to try and recover the women participants as well as their possible participation in the life of the text. Secondly, women will need to read the scriptures side by side with the study of cultures and learn to recognise the boundaries between the two. Such recognition will help women to interpret biblical passages within the proper

hermeneutical understanding of ourselves and our contexts as Christian women. Women will need to sincerely claim biblical liberation without being apologetic to the culture set-up in which the message of the biblical passage has found its audience.[15]

The major thrust of Oduyoye and Kanyoro, in the cited statements, is that it is not so much the Bible that is an instrument of oppression of women as a lopsided *interpretation* of the Bible, vested with ulterior motives. Therefore, women do not really need liberation from the Bible as such but from an oppressive *interpretation* of the Bible.

For members of the Circle, their hermeneutics is determined by the context in which they live and work. The context includes that of survival in harsh conditions of oppression, exploitation, and male dominance. Therefore, the reader-centered approach to scripture is more appropriate than the "historical-critical method," which is said to suit "white, male and middle-class academics, because they alone can afford to be 'impartial,' which literally means 'non-committed.'"[16] African women theologians audaciously began to reclaim the power to reinterpret scriptures and to assert their right to read, interpret, and listen to the scriptures through their own eyes and ears. This was in a manner that was life-affirming to them.

Writing about feminist interpretations in Africa, Teresa Okure notes that African women's distinctive approach to biblical interpretation is doing theology from women's perspective. This approach has distinctive characteristics of inclusiveness; it takes note of both men and women in interpreting scripture. It includes scholars and nonscholars, the rich and the poor; it is also inclusive of scientific, creative, and popular methods.[17] The volume titled *Other Ways of Reading*, using the communal and narrative methods of reading the Bible, is an example of how women chose to interpret the text.[18] Using narratives, reason, tradition, cultural and historical conditions, and experiences, the authors unveil the cultural baggage hidden in scriptures that emphasizes the subordination of women. The narrative methodology is closer to the African communities as it is a way of reenacting the stories of the communities. Within African communities, stories have been told to entertain and impart knowledge and the values of a certain group. Storytelling is prevalent in many African cultures; it is a method used mostly by women to reenact history, to instill moral discipline, and to pass on information. It is also a way in which human beings identify, think of, and represent themselves. This pivotal role of storytelling in African communities has therefore spurred the Circle writers also to embrace this method in their writing. "African women accept story as a source of theology and so tell their stories as well as study the experiences of other women including those outside their own continent, but especially those in Africa whose stories remain unwritten."[19] By telling their stories of pain, adversity, victory, and hope as they read and interpret the Bible, the Circle writers bring the biblical text closer to the audience's lived realities.

Reading Biblical stories in juxtaposition with African cultural folktales is a form of cultural hermeneutics that is significant for African women's liberation. This is because "all questions regarding the welfare and status of women in Africa are explained within the framework of culture."[20] This does not imply that Circle members failed to consider biblical authority or difficult portions of scriptures from their own perspective. For instance, in her writings about the text and authority, Teresa Okure makes a distinction between the timeless truths in the Bible and its cultural underpinnings when she writes:

> Rereading the Bible as a patriarchal book demands that sustained efforts be made to discern between the divine and the human elements in it. For, while the former embodies timeless truth for our salvation, the latter inculcates practices that are socio-culturally conditioned, hence inapplicable universally.[21]

In their publications, the Circle writers resorted to focus on reading the Bible using the cultural lenses. The volume by Musimbi Kanyoro titled *Introducing Feminist Cultural Hermeneutics* is significant in analyzing both the African context and reading the Bible.[22] Cultural hermeneutics is significant because it empowers unheard women and men to speak out; it also provides an opportunity for their questions and their perspectives to contribute to understanding what God has to say to us through his word.

Gender-based violence

Because gender-based violence (GBV) and sexual gender-based violence (SGBV) are endemic in most patriarchal societies, particularly in Africa, numerous Circle publications have been dedicated to raising a clarion call against GBV in our homes, churches, communities, workplaces, political forums, and so forth. The gravity and prevalence of GBV as a major theme for the Circle is captured in the statement by Denise Ackermann writing in the context of South Africa:

> I suggest that there are two pressing issues at present that should be central to women doing theology in our part of the world, the first is the endemic nature of sexual violence against women and children. A war is being waged against bodies of women and children in this country.[23]

The title of Isabel Phiri's article asks a heart-wrenching question, "'Why does God allow our husbands to hurt us?': Overcoming violence against women."[24] Both Ackermann's and Phiri's statements echo the realities all Circle members face in their different contexts, as is apparent from the bibliographical data.[25] Circle studies of GBV make the connection between culture and the reading of the texts. In the article "Saved but Not Safe," Mombo and Joziazze discuss the different forms of violence, which include cultural, physical, economic, spiritual, emotional, and psychological violence in broad terms.[26] An important aspect that is brought to light is silence around violence. This silence is rooted in the hegemony of patriarchy that is invisible in culture, the Bible, and theology. Patriarchy as a system thrives on dichotomies that are based on power. The patriarchal understanding of relationship is foundational – not only on gender-based violence but also the inability of those who are being violated to seek liberation. The ideology of patriarchy presupposes that power is about aggression, domineering and the use of force. The Circle theology has made attempts to break the ideology of patriarchy by naming it in writing and showing connections to the ways in which GBV and SGBV are connected to the ideology of patriarchy. As well as writing, Circle theologians have been engaged in lobbying and advocacy using programs such as the Tamar Campaign and observing "Thursdays in Black." Over the last thirty years, the Circle has highlighted the need for transformative pastoral engagement toward addressing GBV and SGBV not only toward women but on other members of God's family as well.

Health and healing

Circle theology has engaged with embodied liberation in different themes, centering healing and health as significant for women and society as well. Over the last thirty years, the organization has been affected by pandemics including HIV, Ebola, and COVID-19. The onslaught of the HIV epidemic prompted the Circle to devote time and resources to writing and publishing on health and healing, mainstreaming HIV in theological curricula and using it as a lens to look at society. The Circle was among the first organized groups to focus not only on researching and publishing on HIV and AIDS but also on equipping communities on how to deal with the epidemic through conducting seminars and workshops. At the third Pan-African Circle conference held in Addis Ababa, Ethiopia in 2002, the executive committee was mandated to encourage Circle members to continue researching and writing about HIV and AIDS, including stories of those living with the virus.

During the peak of the global HIV epidemic, HIV was like a magnifying glass that brought to light in a more significant way the issues the Circle members were writing about – including religion, culture, and poverty. Cultural challenges were revealed as people grappled with questions around widowhood rites and other practices. HIV brought to the fore the economic challenges in communities, particularly how they affect women's lives. It revealed the issues of discrimination and the marginalization of women. Most significantly, HIV and AIDS have presented a convenient excuse for entrenching stigma and negative stereotyping on the basis of gender or sexuality. Several publications emerged out of the Circle's engagement with HIV.[27] In these books, the Circle provided both information and responses to the challenges of HIV, with topics such as HIV/AIDS prevention, treatment, intervention, and care; SGBV, cross-generational relationships and the spread of HIV; child marriages and widowhood rites; women as caregivers in the HIV and AIDS context; persons living with disabilities and HIV/AIDS; targeting men in HIV responses; and stigma, discrimination, and the HIV epidemic. In writing about HIV, the Circle members have shown how women bear the brunt of HIV and they have also created ways of engagement that are empowering.

During the global crisis of COVID-19, Circle theologians engaged questions raised by this pandemic and how it affected those on the margins. Chisale writes about COVID-19 and women with disabilities and observes that "as the COVID-19 pandemic spreads across the globe, particularly in Africa, women and girls with disabilities become vulnerable to sexual and gender-based violence, highlighting that the home is no longer a safe space for the vulnerable."[28] COVID-19 exacerbated the challenges that society was facing such as hunger, poverty, and high unemployment. The theology of the Circle on COVID-19 includes two volumes that show the multiple vulnerabilities of women through their life experiences. *COVID-19: African Women and the Will to Survive* is a witness to women's resilience in navigating multiple challenges arising from the virus and the methods of dealing with it including lock down. *A Time Like No Other* is about women's stories on the pandemic: "The stories carry audible voices of women's pains and trauma of living in fear of violence in their homes – for themselves and for their children, fear of illness and death by the virus, and loss of loved ones. The truth is that poor women have suffered the effects of the pandemic the worst."[29]

Christology

In her *Introducing African Women's Theology*, Mercy Amba Oduyoye emphasizes that in African women's Christology there is no distinction between salvation and liberation.[30] In the same vein Susan Rakoczy concludes that "to be saved is to be free; to be free is to experience the saving work of Christ. In the holistic African view of life, Jesus is experienced as responding to the totality of life."[31] There is a strong link between salvation and liberation. Christology is a major theme in circle theology, and the works of Oduyoye, Amoah, Hinga, and Nasimiyu are among the first contributions on this topic.

In 1988, Oduyoye and Amoah wrote an article titled "The Christ for African Women."[32] In this article, they argued that

> amidst the dehumanizing experiences for women, culturally, economically, socially, regiously; Jesus Christ is the liberator and a saviour of women from all the oppressive contexts. He is the one who empowers them in the contexts of powerlessness, and he is their friend and ally in the context of alienation and pain that women may be confronted with.[33]

Christ therefore becomes the voice of the voiceless, the power of the powerless. Hinga continues with the theme of liberation in her article titled "Jesus Christ and the Liberation of Women in Africa." She emphasizes that the received theology in which Christ is presented as the primordial scapegoat is not liberating but perpetuates the oppression of women. Hinga contends that "his emulation would lead women to take on a role which they are already playing, for women, in any case, fulfil the role of victims and scapegoats in their various cultures."[34]

Nasimiyu in her article "Imaging Jesus Christ in the African Context on the Dawn of a New Millennium" emphasizes Jesus as protector and nurturer of life. She writes:

By Jesus' redemptive incarnation, the humanity of Jesus is united to every other human being, granting everyone dignity, which mandates justice for all. In following the way of Jesus we are called to care and to be committed to the suffering neighbor, to critique and call for changes of the systems which cause suffering, and to endeavor to uncover the logic that is used to keep people in oppressive situations.[35]

In African women's Christologies, the narrative method is central. Narration brings the everyday experiences, the faith experiences with Jesus Christ, the ideas, and practices of women, hence, the importance of life stories, testimonies, and songs as a channel for coming to know the meaning of Jesus, the Christ-event, according to women. Male African theologians use titles drawn from the African cultural context: for example, Jesus as ancestor. Female African theologians rarely use such images derived from culture; they view this as part of the patriarchal system, and at the same time it is not part of their experience.

Achievement and Agenda: Teaching Circle Theology

It is Mercy Oduyoye who observed that "theology was something you struggle to do – not something you receive."[36] Circle theology is a struggle for liberation by women. The theme of liberation has featured prominently in the resources used at academic institutions where African women's theology is included in the curriculum. When Helen Joziasse and I wrote the article "From the Pew to the Pulpit,"[37] we were reiterating what Circle theology has done for the past three decades. Conscious of the fact that the pulpit is a space dominated by the patriarchs, making it susceptible to being used as a platform for spreading the oppressive patriarchal aspects on women, African women theologians have been making concerted efforts to dismantle the pulpit's patriarchal power. This is intended to transform the church into an inclusive and healing space.

By teaching African women's theologies, the Circle is claiming a space for Circle theology, which Phiri defined as an expression of African women's theologies belonging to a "wider family of feminist theology and which may further be categorized as a form of liberation theology."[38] This theology is committed to listening to, reflecting on, and understanding the experiences of women and helps to penetrate areas where theology has been a product of men. As Hinga observes,

> Recognizing the practice of injustices in church and society as a sinful betrayal of the vision of Jesus ... African Christian women see their task as a prophetic one of unmasking and challenging such sinful practices and structures of injustices. Thus, they see no contradiction ... in being both feminist and Christian.[39]

Circle publications include the textbook *Introducing African Women's Theology,* in which a wide range of topics are covered, as well as the perspectives of women on religion and culture. These topics include the problem of doing inclusive theology as well as the questions emerging from the concept of eschatology.

A major focus of Circle work at the time of writing is earth, gender, and religion. The aim is to investigate the impact of climate change on African women and to interrogate the role of religion in imagining the Earth.[40] The work is structured around a range of themes, such as mother earth and the Bible, mother earth and theology, mother earth and African Indigenous religions, and postcolonial and liberation theologies. In each of these volumes the authors interrogate climate change in relation to the impact on women and provide ways of dealing with the challenge. For example, in the words of the editors, *Mother Earth, Mother Africa and Biblical Studies* unapologetically points a critical finger at anthropocentrism for the widely recognized devastation of the ecosystem. In the context of the global discussion on environmental degradation it provides a holistic examination of the mindset behind the ecological catastrophe.[41]

Conclusion

In this overview of the Circle's work in the past thirty years, I have outlined the milestones the Circle has made in writing theology from experience. The choice of writing topics, such as the doctrine of God, the Bible, anthropology, the church, mission, and spirituality, emerged from the lived realities of women in the community. The major concerns have been the ways African religion and culture shape and influences the experiences of African women. On culture, the Circle authors show how it is a two-edged sword; it provides women with their communal identity and sense of belonging, while at the same time it can be manipulated and used as a tool of domination and exclusion. The theology of African women is both a critique of dominant theologies and a contribution to theology.

Notes

1 Mercy Oduyoye and Musimbi Kanyoro, eds., *The Will to Arise: Women, Tradition, and the Church in Africa* (Maryknoll, NY: Orbis, 1992), 10.

2 Teresa M. Hinga, "African Feminist Theologies, the Global Village, and the Imperative of Solidarity across Borders: The Case of the Circle of Concerned African Women Theologians," *Journal of Feminist Studies in Religion* 18, no. 1 (2002): 79–86.

3 Isabel Phiri, "Southern Africa," in *Introduction to Third World Theologies*, ed. John Parratt (Cambridge: Cambridge University Press, 2004), 156.

4 Hinga, "African Feminist Theologies," 82.

5 Mercy A. Oduyoye and Musimbi Kanyoro, eds., *Transforming Power: Women in the Household of God. Proceedings of the Pan-African Conference of the Circle* (Pietermaritzburg: Cluster, 1997), 199.

6 Modupe Labode "From Heathen Kraal to Christian Home: Anglican Mission Education and African Christian Girls, 1850–1900," in *Women and Missions: Past and Present Anthropological and Historical Perceptions*, ed. Shirley Ardener, Fiona Bowie, and Deborah Kirkwood (Oxford: Berg, 1993), 126.

7 Isabel Phiri, *Women, Presbyterianism and Patriarchy: Religious Experience of Chewa Women in Central Malawi* (Lilongwe: CLAIM, 1997); Nyambura Njoroge, *Kiama Kia Ngo: An African Christian Feminist Ethic of Resistance and Transformation* (Accra: Legon Theological Studies, 2000); Esther Mombo, "Haramisi/jumaa: The Story of the Women's Meetings in East Africa. Yearly Meeting, 1902–1979," *Woodbrooke Journal* 5 (1999): 1–25.

8 Rachel Fiedler, *A History of the Circle of Concerned African Women Theologians 1989–2007* (Luwunga: Mzuzu Press, 2017), 9.

9 Musimbi Kanyoro, *Introducing Feminist Cultural Hermeneutics: An African Perspective* (Sheffield: Sheffield Academic Press, 2002), 14, 15.

10 Mary Getui and Grace Wamue, *Violence against Women: Reflections by Kenyan Women Theologians* (Nairobi: Acton, 1996), 5.

11 Musimbi Kanyoro and Nyambura Njoroge, *Groaning in Faith: African Women in the Household of God* (Nairobi: Acton, 1996).

12 Nyambura Njoroge and Musa W. Dube, eds. *Talitha Cum!: Theologies of African Women* (Pietermaritzburg: Cluster, 2001).

13 Musa W. Dube, *Postcolonial Feminist Interpretation of the Bible* (St. Louis, MO: Chalice Press, 2000).

14 Mercy Oduyoye, *Hearing and Knowing: Theological Reflections on Christianity in Africa* (Maryknoll, NY: Orbis, 1986), 147.

15 Mercy Oduyoye and Musimbi Kanyoro, *Talitha Qumi!: Proceedings of the Convocation of African Women Theologians, Trinity College, Legon-Accra, September 24–October 2, 1989* (Accra North: Sam-Woode, 2001), 52–3.

16 Kwok Pui-lan, "Racism and Ethocentrism in Feminist Biblical Interpretation," in *Searching the Scriptures, Vol. 1: A Feminist Introduction*, ed. Elisabeth Schüssler Fiorenza (New York: Crossroad, 1993), 103.

17 Teresa Okure, "Feminist Interpretations in Africa," in *Searching the Scriptures*, ed. Fiorenza, 77.

18 Musa W. Dube, ed., *Other Ways of Reading: African Women and the Bible* (Geneva: World Council of Churches, 2001).

19 Mercy A. Oduyoye, *Introducing African Women's Theology* (Sheffield: Sheffield Academic Press, 2001), 10.

20 Musimbi Kanyoro, *Introducing Feminist Cultural Hermeneutics* (Sheffield: Sheffield Academic Press, 2002), 18.

21 Virginia Fabella and Mercy Oduyoye, eds., *With Passion and Compassion: Third World Women Doing Theology* (Maryknoll, NY: Orbis, 1988), 56.

22 Musimbi Kanyoro, *Introducing Feminist Cultural Hermeneutics* (Sheffield: Sheffield Academic Press, 2002).

23 Denise Ackerman, "Forward from the Margins: Feminist Theologies for Life," *Journal of Theologies in Southern Africa* 99 (November 1997): 67.

24 Isabel Phiri, "'Why Does God Allow Our Husbands to Hurt Us?' Overcoming Violence against Women," *Journal of Theology for Southern Africa* 114 (November 2002): 19–30.

25 Mary Getui and Grace Wamue, eds., *Violence against Women: Reflections by Kenyan Women Theologians* (Nairobi: Acton, 1996).

26 Esther Mombo and Helen Joziasse, "Saved but Not Safe: A Parish Discussion on the Absence of Safety in the Church; A Case Study of Kabuku Parish Church," *Interkulturelle Theologie* 41, no. 4 (2015): 385–99.

27 Musa W. Dube and Rachel Angogo Kanyoro, eds., *Grant Me Justice! HIV/AIDS & Gender Reading of the Bible* (Pietermaritzburg: Cluster, 2003); Bev Haddad, Isabel Apawo Phiri, Madipoane Joyce Masenya, eds., *African Women, HIV and AIDS and Faith Communities* (Pietermaritzburg: Cluster, 2003); Elizabeth Amoah, Dorothy Akoto, and Dorcas Akintunde, eds., *Cultural Practices and HIV/AIDS: African Women's Voices* (Accra, Ghana: Sam-Woode: 2005); a volume in honor of Mercy Oduyoye as the founder of the Circle, Mercy Amba Oduyoye, Isabel Apawo Phiri, and Sarojini Nadar, eds., *Women, Religion and Health: Essays in Honour of Mercy Amba Ewudziwa Oduyoye* (Maryknoll, NY: Orbis, 2006); Teresia M. Hinga, Anne Nkirote Kubai, Philomena Mwaura, and Hazel Ayanga, eds., *Women, Religion and HIV/AIDS in Africa: Responding to Ethical and Theological Challenges* (Pietermaritzburg: Cluster, 2007); Musa W. Dube, ed., *Africa Praying: A Handbook on HIV/AIDS Sensitive Sermon Guidelines and Liturgy* (Geneva: World Council of Churches, 2006); Helene Yinda and Bernadette Mbuy Beya, eds., *Sexe, Stigma et VIH-SIDA: Les Larmes Secretes des Femmes Africaines* (Yaoundé: Sherpa, 2007); Kavira Wangahemuka Julienne, ed., *La petite fille la femme, la religion et le VIH_SIDA: les theologiennes à l'épreuve des réalités africaines* (Pietermaritzburg: Circle of Concerned African Women Theologians, 2007); Maria Victoria Pereira and Felicidade Cherinda, eds., *Tempo de Mudar; Tempo de Agir: Mulheres reflection teologicamente sobre a problematica do HIV/SIDA* (Pietermaritzburg: Circle of Concerned African Women Theologians, 2007), Nontando Hadebe and Ezra Chitando, eds., *Compassionate Circles: African Women Theologians Facing HIV* (Geneva: World Council of Churches, 2009); Ezra Chitando and Sophia Chirongoma, eds., *Redemptive Masculinities: Men, HIV, Religion and Culture* (Geneva: World Council of Churches, 2012); and Ezra Chitando and Sophie Chirongoma, *Justice Not Silence: Churches Facing Sexual and Gender Based Violence* (Stellenbosch: Sun Press, 2013).

28 Sinenhlanhla S. Chisale, "COVID-19 and Ubuntu Disruptions: Curbing the Violence against Women and Girls with Disabilities through African Women's Theology of Disability," *Journal of International Women's Studies* 24, no. 4 (2022): 1.

29 Helen A. Labeodan, Johanna Stiebert, Mark S. Aidoo, and Rose Mary Amenga-Etego, eds., *COVID-19: African Women and the Will to Survive* (Bamberg: University of Bamberg Press, 2021); Nontando Hadebe, Daniela Gennrich, Susan Rackoczy, and Nobesuthu Tom, eds., *A Time Like No Other: Covid-19 in Women's Voices* (Pietermaritzburg: Cluster, 2021), 4.

30 Oduyoye, *Introducing African Women's Theology*, 64.

31 Susan Rakoczy, *In Her Name: Women Doing Theology* (Pietermaritzburg: Cluster, 2004), 118.

32 Elisabeth Amoah and Mercy Amba Oduyoye, "The Christ for African Women," in *With Passion and Compassion: Third World Women Doing Theology*, ed. Fabella and Oduyoye, 35–46.

33 Amoah and Oduyoye, "The Christ for African Women," 44.

34 Teresa Hinga, "Jesus Christ and the Liberation of Women in Africa," in *The Will to Arise: Women, Tradition, and the Church in Africa*, ed. Mercy Amba Oduyoye and Musimbi R. A. Kanyoro (Maryknoll, NY: Orbis, 1992), 185.

35 Anne Nasimiyu Wasike, "Imaging Jesus Christ in the African Context at the Dawn of a New Millennium," in *Challenges and Prospects of the Church in Africa*, ed. Nahashon W. Ndungu and Philomena Mwaura (Nairobi: Paulines Publications Africa, 2005), 112–13.

36 Christina Landman, "Mercy Amba Ewudziwa Oduyoye: Mother of Our Stories," *Studia Historiae Ecclesiasticae* 33, no. 1 (2007): 188.

37 Esther Mombo and Helen Joziassee, "From the Pew to the Pulpit: Engendering the Pulpit through Teaching African Women's Theologies," in *Men in the Pulpit, Women in the Pew? Addressing Gender Inequality in Africa*, ed. H. Jurgens Hendriks, Elna Mouton, Len Hansen, and Elisabet Le Roux (Stellenbosch: Sun Press/ESFA, 2012), 183.

38 Phiri, "Southern Africa," 151.

39 Teresa Hinga, *African Christian Feminist: The Enduring Search for What Matters* (Maryknoll, NY: Orbis, 2017), 8.

40 Sidney K. Berman, Paul L. Leshota, Ericka S. Dunbar, Musa W. Dube, and Malebogo Kgalemang, eds., *Mother Earth, Mother Africa and Biblical Studies: Interpretation in the Context of Climate Change* (Bamberg: University of Bamberg Press, 2021); Sophia Chirongoma and Esther Mombo, eds., *Mother Earth, Postcolonial and Liberation Theologies* (New York: Lexington Press, 2021); Sophia Chirongma and Scholar Wayua Kiilu, eds., *Mother Earth, Mother Africa: World Religions and Environmental Imagination* (Stellenbosch: Sun Media Press, 2022); Sophia Chirongoma and Sue Rakoczy, eds., "Sacred Earth and African Women's Theology

African," a special issue of *Journal of Gender and Religion* 27, no. 1 (2021); Sinenhlanhla Chisale and Rozelle Robson Bosch, eds., *Mother Earth, Mother Africa and Theology* (Cape Town: AOSIS, 2021); Ezra Chitando, Esther Mombo, and Masiiwa Ragies, eds.,

That All May Live! Essays in Honour of Nyambura J. Njoroge (Bamberg: University of Bamberg Press, 2021).

41 Sidney K. Berman, Paul L. Leshota, Ericka S. Dunbar, Musa W. Dube, and Malebogo Kgalemang, "Editorial," in *Mother Earth, Mother Africa and Biblical Studies*, 17.

Recommended Reading

Amoah, Elizabeth. *Divine Empowerment of Women in Africa's Complex Realities.* Accra: Sam-Woode, 2001.

———. *Where God Reigns: Reflections on Women in God's World.* Accra: Sam-Woode. 1997.

Amoah, Elizabeth, and Pamela Martin, eds. *Heart, Mind and Tongue: A Heritage of Woven Words.* Accra: Sam-Woode, 2001.

Berman, K. S., P. L. Leshota, E. S. Dunbar, M. W. Dube, and M. Kgalemang, eds. *Mother Earth, Mother Africa and Biblical Studies: Interpretation in the Context of Climate Change.* Bamberg: University of Bamberg, Press, 2021.

Chirongoma, Sophia, and Esther Mombo, eds. *Mother Earth, Postcolonial and Liberation Theologies.* New York: Lexington Press, 2021.

Chisale, Sinenhlanhla S., and Rozelle Robson Bosch, eds. *Mother Earth, Mother Africa and Theology.* Pretoria: AOSIS, 2021.

Chitando, Ezra, Esther Mombo, and Masiiwa Ragies, eds. *That all May Live: Essays in Honor of Nyambura Njoroge.* Bamberg: University of Bamberg Press, 2021.

Claassens, L. Juliana, Christl M. Maier, and Funlola O. Olojede, eds. *Transgression and Transformation: Feminist,* *Postcolonial and Queer Biblical Interpretation as Creative Interventions.* New York: T&T Clark, 2021.

Dube, Musa W., ed. *Other Ways of Reading: African Women and the Bible.* Geneva: World Council of Churches. 2001.

———. *Postcolonial Feminist Interpretation of the Bible.* St. Louis, MO: Chalice. 2000.

Fabella, Virginia, and Mercy Amba Oduyoye, eds. *With Passion and Compassion: Third World Women Doing Theology.* Maryknoll, NY: Orbis, 1988.

Gachiri, Ephigenia W. *Female Circumcision: with Special Reference to the Agikuyu of Kenya.* Nairobi: Pauline, 2000.

Getui, Mary, and Hazel Ayanga, eds. *Conflicts in Africa: A Women's Response.* Nairobi: Faith Institute of Counselling, 2002.

Getui, Mary, and Matthew M. Theuri, eds. *Quest for Abundant Life in Africa.* Nairobi: Action Publishers, 2002.

Getui, Mary, and Grace Wamue, eds. *Violence against Women: Reflections by Kenyan Women Theologians.* Nairobi: Acton, 1996.

Hinga, T. M., A. N. Kubai, P. Mwaura, and H. Ayanga, eds. *Women, Religion and HIV/AIDS in Africa: Responding to Ethical and Theological Challenges.* Pietermaritzburg: Cluster, 2008.

Latin American Liberation Theology

Rebecca S. Chopp, Ethna Regan, and David Tombs

Introduction: Character, Origins, and Influences

Latin American liberation theology – hereafter liberation theology – emerged in the late 1960s as a prophetic reflection on God's activity and transforming grace among those who are the victims of modern history. The movement developed in the 1970s and matured further in the 1980s. Since the 1990s, liberation theology has been less influential as an organized movement within the church; nonetheless, the principles and insights offered by liberation theologians continue to be a profound and inspirational influence in many areas of theology. Although liberation theology is now weaker within the church, there has been something of a revival of interest in the academy in recent years. Liberation theology continues to promote innovative and engaged theological reflection and there is ongoing debate on how liberation theology might find new expressions in the twenty-first century.[1]

Many factors contributed to the emergence of liberation theology as a distinctive voice in Latin America. The most important catalyst was the awareness of inequality and poverty as a regional and global problem. The poor in Latin America often watched their children die from lack of adequate food, health care, and sanitation. They suffered frequent unemployment and, when they did find work, the wages were not enough to provide a decent standard of living. Liberation theology speaks of God as manifest in the poor of history. It arises out of the poor's distinctive experience of God, an experience that is dependent, as Gustavo Gutiérrez insisted, upon God's choosing to reveal God's self in the poor.[2] It seeks to guide the transformation of all human beings into new ways of being human, ways not dependent upon structures of division between rich and poor, the persons and the non-persons of history.[3]

Although democracy has made significant progress, life in Latin America is marked by economic and social inequality. The challenges that gave rise to liberation theology have not disappeared. These challenges derive from the "modern" history of Latin America, a history that, since the "discovery of the New World," has been marked by oppression and colonization.[4] Spain and Portugal settled the New World through the devastation of native cultures in order to make slaves for the conquerors and to Christianize the "heathens." Even with the emergence of many Latin American nations in the early nineteenth century, neocolonialism, a system of economic dependency and exploitation, existed between these nations and global North countries, first with Great Britain

Ford's The Modern Theologians: An Introduction to Christian Theology since 1918, Fourth Edition.
Edited by Rachel Muers and Ashley Cocksworth.
© 2024 John Wiley & Sons Ltd. Published 2024 by John Wiley & Sons Ltd.

and later with the United States. The 1950s and 1960s saw international commitments to develop dependent countries to be like rich nations such as the United States and Western Europe, but this movement only augmented dependent relations, this time through military oligarchies and multinational corporations.[5]

A major factor in the development of liberation theology was the commitment to justice and peace taken by Roman Catholicism and Protestantism in the 1950s and 1960s. Most important among these was the social teaching of the Second Vatican Council concerning human dignity and the need for structural change. Latin American bishops met in Medellín, Colombia, in 1968 to discuss the impact of the Second Vatican Council for Latin America; the papers adopted by the bishops became the founding documents of liberation theology.[6] At Medellín, the struggle for change that would guide liberation theology was invoked, a struggle against the institutionalized violence suffered by the poor as a result of an "international imperialism of money," represented by the upper classes and foreign monopolies.

A new vision of faith was articulated in the view of the poor as human subjects active in history. This vision was located in small grassroots communities where the poor could determine their own destiny and express their faith as they participated in conscientization or consciousness-raising.

Besides these historical events, three other influences must be noted: political theology, Marxism, and popular religion. Political theology arose in West Germany as a critique of modern Christianity's concern for the ahistorical authenticity of the bourgeois subject and a reformulation of Christian theology in light of events of massive suffering, such as the Holocaust. The works of political theologians such as Jürgen Moltmann and Johann Baptist Metz suggested new theological terms such as privatization, oppression, ideology, and liberation. Metz offered a new anthropology that was social and political, whereas Moltmann constructed an understanding of God in and through the reality of suffering. Both theologians spoke of Christianity as a critical witness in society.[7]

Marxism influenced liberation theology as both a theoretical tool of social analysis and a philosophy of history.[8] As a tool of social analysis, Marxism supplied a dialectical, rather than functional, analysis, which focused on the relations of power and force in a society instead of cloaking such forces in an ideology of society as an organism needing balance. As a philosophy of history, Marxism contributed, along with other philosophies, toward a view of the human subject as socially or historically constituted, history as open to change and transformation, and oppression and alienation structured through the productive relations of society. Liberation theologians, especially in the early years, critically adopted some of the language and insights from Marxism; but they did so only by transforming these insights and language into their own theological reflections.

A quite different, and more recent, influence is that of popular religion. As theologians focused increasingly on the "option for the poor" as a way of life, the importance of popular religion came to the fore. Popular religion takes seriously the cultural specificity of various Latin American peoples and requires a reflection on the particularities of Amerindians, Blacks, women, and others who may have distinctive religious practices. It examines how the ideas and rituals of Christianity settled in among native religious practices. Liberation theologians, in general, came to a growing appreciation of how the people's religions included indigenous practices, African American religions, animistic traditions, the practice of magic, and various blends of religious traditions. Finally, popular religion provides an understanding not only of survival practices among the poor but also of potential resources for transformation. Devotion to Mary, for instance, includes prayer to the popular female figures Morentia of Guadalupe, the Black Aparecida, Purisima, and the Virgin of Charity, to whom the faithful pray for survival. Theological reflection and praxis also make these manifestations of the mother of the redeemer a symbol of hope for all. As María Clara Bingemer has observed:

> What is new about this work is that it reveals a Mary no longer considered individualistically, in terms of a model of ascetic virtues to be imitated, but as a collective symbol, a type of the faithful people within which the holy Spirit of God finds fertile ground to raise up the new people, the seed of the kingdom, which will inaugurate the new creation.[9]

Survey

This chapter attempts to let to liberation theology speak in its voice. The reader who is not poor must approach this logos of the theos with an attitude of respectful care to appreciate its integrity within the ancient theological task of faith seeking understanding. Although there was important systematization of liberation theology in the 1990s, it has never been primarily academic discourse for academic debate; it is, rather, church theology in the context of basic Christian communities. These are grassroots communities in which Christians seek to form and live out their Christian witness in their historical situation. Thus, the first locus of liberation theology was the church, not the academy, and it was characterized as a reflection on and guide to praxis rather than a second-level hermeneutical reflection on the theoretical meaning of Christianity. This practical theological discourse on the reality of the poor is the first, or popular, level of three levels of liberation theology described by Leonardo and Clodovis Boff. The second level is the pastoral, meaning that engaged in by theologically trained bishops, pastors, and ministers whose primary focus is pastoral ministry. These are often a bridge between the popular level and the third level of the professional theologians.[10]

Liberation theology is a critique of the structures and institutions that create the poor, including the primary identification of modern Christianity with the rich. To do this, liberation theology engages in dialogue not only with philosophy but also with the social sciences. As a theological discourse of critique and transformation in solidarity with the poor, liberation theology offers a theological anthropology that is political, an interpretation of Christianity that may be characterized through the term "liberation," and a vision of Christianity as a praxis of love and solidarity with the oppressed.

The image of human existence (and theological anthropology is always guided by an image) in liberation theology is the poor. The bishops of Latin America meeting at Puebla in 1979 identified the faces of the poor, the subjects of liberation theology:

> The faces of young children, struck down by poverty before they are born ... the faces of indigenous peoples, and frequently that of the Afro-Americans as well, living marginalized lives in inhuman situations ... the faces of the peasants; as a special group, they live in exile almost everywhere on our continent ... the faces of marginalized and overcrowded urban dwellers, whose lack of material goods is matched by the ostentatious display of wealth by other segments of society; the faces of old people, who are growing more numerous every day, and who are frequently marginalized in a progress-oriented society that totally disregards people not engaged in production.[11]

This human reality, the reality of what it is to be the poor and despised of the earth, is understood, in liberation theology, through the term "praxis," which has three distinguishable meanings. First, praxis means that human beings are constituted through political–historical reality. Where one lives, the status of the socioeconomic class, what kind of power is available, must all be clear considerations for understanding human reality. Second, praxis means that human reality is intersubjective, that human beings are not ahistorical "I's" that express their unique essences in relation to others through language, but that all subjectivity arises out of intersubjective relations between human beings. Third, praxis as the understanding of human reality means that humans must and can intentionally create history, transforming and shaping reality for the improvement of human flourishing.

This understanding of human reality through praxis is joined by an interpretation, a reformation, of Christian symbols through the central theme of liberation. It is with the centrality of this term, and many rich readings of the Bible and Christian tradition, that liberation theology is most clearly understood as not merely a form of ethics or social witness, but as a systematic theology, a radically new interpretation and transformation of Christian faith itself. Sin, for example, in liberation theology is reflected on, not merely through individual moral acts or existential separation and despair, but primarily in terms of social structures.

Sin results in suffering, whose burden is carried, time and time again, by the poor of history. Sin is radical distortion, not of some private relation with God, but of all reality, especially of the historical-political world that God gives us to live in. Redemption, correlatively, must relate to liberation, though, of course, it cannot be merely identified with any one liberating act; if redemption has to do with the reconciliation of humanity to God and salvation from sins, then it must be related to our present historical reality. Indeed, among the many readings of Christ in liberation theology – Christ as political rebel, Christ suffering as the scourged of the earth, Christ in solidarity with the poor and oppressed – it is Christ as liberator, as one who actually effects transformation, as one who brings new ways of being human, who is central.

Within the locus of this understanding of human reality and interpretation of Christian symbols, Christianity becomes a praxis of solidarity with and for the poor, working for liberation and transformation for all. Christianity represents the witness of freedom. It does not necessarily supply a new political ordering, nor offer a new theocratic state; rather, it testifies to freedom and liberation, taking sides where God takes sides with the poor and the despised of the earth. In this way, for Christians, faith and love are not separable, indeed may not be distinguishable from justice. Christianity must neither conform itself to culture nor be a radical separatist sect. Rather, Christianity must discern God's activity amid the poor and work for radical transformation of the structures of society in order that all persons may become new human subjects.

It is best, therefore, to think of liberation theology as a new genre of theology based on a specific praxis of faith. Though liberation theology shares some common resources with other theologies, its way of organizing, its criteria for reading scriptures and traditions, its tasks, purpose, and intent, are specific to Christian praxis amid the poor.

Liberation theologians write on issues such as Christology and ecclesiology, work on how to use the resources of the social sciences, investigate the relation of popular religion to liberation theology, or interpret biblical themes and narratives.

A brief survey, by alphabetical order, of some of the major figures and their books that are available in English may indicate the range of issues and interests in liberation theology. The theologians mentioned next, like most Christians in Latin America, are mainly Roman Catholic. Liberation theology has arisen primarily in the context of the Roman Catholic Church in Latin America, though there has been a parallel movement in the Protestant churches. After this overview, we consider two Roman Catholic theologians who worked in close partnership (Ignacio Ellacuría and Jon Sobrino) and then a Protestant theologian (José Míguez Bonino) for a deeper interpretation.

Hugo Assmann has taught in his native Brazil, Germany, and Costa Rica. His *Theology for a Nomad Church* considers the practical and theoretical nature of theological method in a liberation context. Like other liberation theologians, Assmann's work draws on sociology as a major source for theological reflection and formulates the basis of theological method not through eternal absolutes but through a critical engagement with historical praxis.

Clodovis Boff, a Brazilian theologian, is also concerned with the nature and method of theological reflection. His book *Theology and Praxis: Epistemological Foundations* is a thorough treatment of the epistemological presuppositions in liberation theology. Attentive to popular religion, he has also published *Feet-on the-Ground Theology: A Brazilian Journey*, a diary of his missionary work in northwestern Brazil.

Leonardo Boff, who is brother to Clodovis, is well known for his Christology, *Jesus Christ Liberator*. This Christology is based on the situation of oppression in Latin America and stresses the priority of orthopraxis over orthodoxy and the anthropological over the ecclesiological element in Christology. In *Ecclesiogenesis: The Base Communities Reinvent the Church*, Boff offers a new vision of the church, based on the experience of basic Christian communities. His book *Church, Charism and Power: Liberation Theology and the Institutional Church* seeks not only to address the concerns of the institutional church in relation to liberation theology but also to offer a new model of the church. This new model is a pneumatic ecclesiology, recalling the primitive elements of community, cooperation, and charism in Christian life. In the 1980s, this book was subjected to opposition and criticism from the Congregation of Faith within the Vatican.

José Comblin, in *The Church and the National Security State*, examined the doctrine of national security, which holds that Latin America needs military leadership to curb internal subversion and counteract Marxism. Although the church often became captive to the state's need for security, the book also testifies to Christian fidelity to the gospel under the repression of these regimes. In his later writings, the Belgian-Brazilian Comblin engages in a critique of liberation theology, and questions the adequacy of liberation theology's response to what he suggests is the main issue of the past generation, not revolution but urbanization.

Enrique Dussel's *A History of the Church in Latin America* has made a major contribution to a reinterpretation of the history of the church in Latin America, a history that has been neglected or interpreted only through the eyes of the victors. Dussel, an Argentinian Roman Catholic layman living in Mexico, is both a philosopher and a theologian, and he has developed philosophical categories for liberation theology. He considers the critique of the conquest of the New World by Antonio de Montesinos, Bartolomé de Las Casas, and Francisco de Vitoria as the first explicit liberation philosophy and the first counter-discourse of modernity. His recent work on a philosophy of liberation combines the critique of ontology born of Levinas with the Marxist critique of capitalism, engaging also in dialogue with other Western philosophers. He stresses the interrelatedness of politics and economics, and an ethics that gives centrality to the phenomenon of alterity, in which the "other" is the poor.

Ivone Gebara is a Brazilian Catholic woman religious who is well known for her book with Maria Clara Bingemer on *Mary, Mother of God, Mother of the Poor*. Gebara has also published on women's experience of suffering and injustice in *Out of the Depths: Women's Experience of Evil and Salvation*. She has been at the forefront of work in Brazil on ecofeminism. In the 1990s she was sanctioned by the Vatican because she refused to condemn abortion. During her time of public silence, she completed a second doctorate in Leuven, Belgium.

Gustavo Gutiérrez, a liberation theologian from Peru is widely recognized as the founding figure in liberation theology and the most influential of all liberation theologians. His translated books in English, include *The Theology of Liberation, The Power of the Poor in History, We Drink from Our Own Wells*, and a lengthy study of the sixteenth-century Dominican Bartolome de las Casas, *Las Casas: In Search of the Poor of Jesus Christ*.[12] Gutiérrez's influence on theology has been so great that his work merits a chapter in his own right (see chapter 4).

José Miranda is a Mexican biblical scholar who has published on religion and Marxism. His *Marx and the Bible: A Critique of the Philosophy of Oppression* and his *Being and the Messiah* suggest a new way of reading the Bible, as well as a new biblical interpretation of topics such as sin and redemption.

Juan Luis Segundo of Uruguay is concerned with the use of scripture in theology. Segundo's *The Liberation of Theology* reinterprets the hermeneutic circle in theology, addressing how the Bible is to be interpreted in a manner that does not simply repeat past doctrines, but speaks to and transforms the present historical situation. Segundo, one of the most prolific writers on liberation theology, represents many theologians who, in the course of their careers, have "become" liberation theologians, moving from a form of theological reflection in a European style to reformulating theological reflection in the Latin American situation. In fact, Segundo's five-volume series titled *A Theology for Artisans of a New Humanity*, written as liberation theology began to emerge, can be read as transitional pieces between the older European model of theology and the concerns and impulses that lie behind liberation theology. His series titled *Jesus of Nazareth Yesterday and Today* continues the methodological work of *The Liberation of Theology* and develops a contemporary Christology. Segundo's work points to the richness and breadth of liberation theology.

Elsa Tamez, a Protestant, continues the reinterpretation of basic Christian doctrines within the context of the option for the poor in her *Amnesty of Grace: Justification by Faith from a Latin American Perspective*. Tamez reinterprets justification as displaying God's affirmation of life for all human beings and thus meaning, in contemporary reality, a humanization that stands in opposition to the condemnation of human beings through poverty, oppression, and marginalization.

Prior to the late 1980s, there was little concern for the diversity of those who constituted "the poor" of Latin America. Since then, the theological voices of women, Blacks, and Amerindians have begun to be heard in liberation theology, profoundly enriching its vision and critique. Because of the breadth of issues considered, the many different approaches used, and the reformulation of theology itself, it is important to examine specific theologians and trace the development of their particular concerns, resources, and methods. The three figures discussed here are two Basque Jesuits in El Salvador, Ignacio Ellacuría SJ and Jon Sobrino SJ, and José Míguez Bonino, a United Methodist from Argentina.

Three Liberation Theologians

Ignacio Ellacuría SJ and Jon Sobrino SJ

Ignacio Ellacuría SJ (1930–1989) was an early pioneer in liberation theology.[13] He came to El Salvador from his native Spain in 1949, as part of the Central American mission. For much of his working life he was based at the Jesuit-founded Central American University (UCA) in San Salvador. His wide-ranging writings encompassed politics and philosophy as well as theology, and he frequently commented on the social problems that beset his adopted country. In 1979 he was elected rector (or president) of the UCA and this position was an important platform for commentary on national affairs. When civil war broke out in 1981 Ellacuría was a courageous voice for political negotiation and economic reform. On 16 November 1989 he was assassinated by the Salvadoran military, along with five fellow Jesuits in the UCA residence, their housekeeper, and her teenage daughter.

Ellacuría's theology consistently emphasized attention to historical reality. This was in keeping with the words of Pope John XXIII in the Bull *Humanae salutis* at the convocation of the Second Vatican Council and further elaborated in the Pastoral Constitution on the Church in Today's World, *Gaudium et Spes*. This called on the church to attend to "the signs of the times," a reference to Matthew 16:1–3. Ellacuría took up this challenge with radical honesty in the context of El Salvador. During the years of the Second Vatican Council, Ellacuría had lived in Spain as a doctoral student and worked closely with the distinguished philosopher Xavier Zubiri (1898–1983). Zubiri's work offered a profound meditation on historical reality as the task of philosophy. Ellacuría completed his doctoral dissertation on Zubiri's "theory of reality" in 1967. When Ellacuría returned to El Salvador in 1967 the commitment to reality became the metaphysical foundation and framework for all his work. Ellacuría saw the task of a scholar, and the role of the whole university, in terms of understanding and transforming the social reality around them. Again and again in Ellacuría's work, the reader is summoned to move beyond abstract understanding and become attentive to the "reality."

Concern for reality not abstraction proved a remarkably effective tool for social and ideological critique. Ellacuría showed how concern for apprehending and facing reality could highlight the destructive consequences of grinding poverty, and reframe concerns like "poverty" from distant abstractions to pressing practical challenges for the church's attention. Likewise, abstract terms like "democracy," "justice," and "peace" could be critically interrogated to show that if they remained at an abstract level they were more likely to be part of the problem than part of the solution for the everyday issues faced by the Salvadoran poor.

Ellacuría was too busy with other commitments to write a systematic account of his theological thinking. Many of his ideas were offered initially as presentations at specific events and then reworked and written up as short articles or chapters. One of the most powerful expressions of his thinking was a paper he offered during the preparatory meetings for the third conference of Latin American Bishops at Puebla (1979). At a conference in Mexico City in 1978 he spoke on "the crucified people."[14] Applying his distinctive approach, he took a subject – the cross – which was often viewed within the church in a highly abstract and spiritualized way. His paper offered a way to go beyond abstraction to a deeper understanding of present reality. His presentation of the Salvadoran poor as "crucified people" offered insight into both the oppressive situation of the poor in the present and the violent reality of the cross in the past. El Salvador's name – which means "the Savior" – encouraged Ellacuría to take seriously this theological analogy between past and present. Following Ellacuría's murder in 1989, the concern for crucified people was taken up with renewed theological concern by Ellacuría's colleague and close friend at the UCA, Jon Sobrino.

Sobrino (born 1938) is a Basque Jesuit, like Ellacuría, and has also committed his life and work to the people of El Salvador.[15] Sobrino joined the Society of Jesus in 1957 and was sent to El Salvador the following year as part of the Central American mission. Like Ellacuría, who was eight years older than him, Sobrino spent intervals during his long training outside El Salvador in the United States and Europe. Following his permanent return to El Salvador in 1974, after finishing his doctoral study in Frankfurt, Sobrino described the impact that returning to El Salvador had upon him. He described the experience as "awakening from the sleep of inhumanity."[16] Over the next fifteen years the two of them would forge a strong friendship and working partnership.

In a presentation Sobrino gave in Mexico City in 1975, which was subsequently published as the first chapter in his book *The True Church of the Poor* (1984), Sobrino drew a contrast between what he called "European theology," by which he means the progressive European theology he had studied for his doctorate, and "Latin American theology," by which he means the liberation theology he was discovering in El Salvador. He explains:

> In summary, European theology is generally interested in explaining the truth of the faith and in clarifying its meaning when it is obscured ... The questions to which it has sought answers are these: How is it possible to believe today? What meaning can faith have today when its meaning seems to have been lost? The task has been to recover the meaning of faith.[17]

Sobrino does not deny the importance of these theological tasks, but he explains that in Latin America there are other priorities which should rightly take precedence.

> Latin American theology is interested in liberating the real world from its wretched state, because it is this objective situation that has obscured the meaning of the faith. Its task is not primarily to restore meaning to the faith in the presence of the wretched conditions of the real world. It is to transform this real world and at the same time recover the meaning of the faith. The task, therefore, is not to understand the faith differently, but to allow a new faith to spring from a new practice.[18]

When Oscar Romero was Archbishop of San Salvador (1977–1980) his outspoken comments gained him the title "Voice of the Voiceless" and provoked intense opposition from the right-wing government and military. Both Ellacuría and Sobrino acted as theological consultants for Romero whenever Romero requested their advice. Romero appreciated their theological insights and expertise, and Ellacuría and Sobrino admired the courage and leadership that Romero offered to the church. Following Romero's assassination, while he was celebrating Mass in March 1980, both Ellacuría and Sobrino spoke of the inspiration that Romero gave them in their work.

Sobrino is best known as a theologian for his work in Christology. His first book, *Christology at the Crossroads* (1976, English translation [ET] 1978), reflects his conviction that the historical Jesus should serve as the foundation for a Latin American Christology. In emphasizing the historical Jesus, Sobrino's interest is not so much on the scholarly distinction between the Jesus of history and the Christ of faith since he affirms both the historical Jesus and the Christ of faith. Rather his concern is to understand Jesus within the historical context of his time. Like Ellacuría, Sobrino is suspicious of any abstraction that turns attention from reality. Furthermore, Sobrino draws attention to structural similarities between the historical conditions of oppression in which Jesus lived and the historical experience of many in El Salvador at the time.

Following the assassination of Ellacuría, Sobrino took up Ellacuría's thoughts on "the crucified people" and explored the "signs of the times" in the light of the cross. His two-volume Christology *Jesus the*

Liberator (1991, ET 1993) and *Christ the Liberator* (1999, ET 2001) offer a sustained reflection on how the experiences of those crucified today can illuminate the cross of Jesus and vice versa. In these works, and in *The Principle of Mercy* (1992, ET 1994), Sobrino also develops Ellacuría's thoughts on how Christians are called to take victims down from the cross. The primary significance of the cross is not so much as an object for contemplation, still less a focus of pious devotion, but rather a challenge that calls for radical action and transformative change.

In the late 1980s Ellacuría and Sobrino began to collaborate on an edited collection that would serve as a comprehensive overview of liberation theology. They invited a diverse group of liberation theologians to contribute chapters on key words and concepts in liberation theology. Although this was not a systematic theology as such – the number of contributors made this impractical – it was intended to offer a more systematic presentation of liberation theology than had previously been available. Most of the chapters had been submitted before Ellacuría's death and in the following year Sobrino published them in a two-volume Spanish edition (1990) and slightly abridged single volume in English (1993).

José Míguez Bonino

José Míguez Bonino's work, in books such as *Doing Theology in a Revolutionary Situation*, *Room to Be People*, and *Toward a Christian Political Ethics*, exemplifies liberation theology's understanding of history as the arena of God's action. History has its locus neither in individual historicity nor in the worldly progressive realization of the bourgeoisie, but in the total sociopolitical-economic context in which humans live and in which God continually acts. His work illustrates that history has sociopolitical determinates based not only on sociological analysis but also on theological and scriptural warrants that God acts in history. Indeed, he suggests that scripture be understood as a narrative of God's acts in history and be analogically applied to the present situation. Though God acts in history in different ways at different times, God always acts in love to transform history into the kingdom of God.

The relation of history to the kingdom is central, according to Míguez Bonino, because in the scriptures this is how God is revealed. We do not relate kingdom to history for our own political ends, but because the God of the Bible is constantly transforming history into the kingdom. This important and tensive relationship is, unfortunately, frequently misunderstood. There is a tendency to separate the kingdom and history, a position Míguez Bonino characterizes as dualism, which denies the basic biblical thrust of God in history. There is also a tendency merely to reduce the kingdom to history, or better yet a particular time and place in history, the monist solution, which denies the mission of Christianity and threatens to destroy the nonidentity between Christianity and the world. Rather, the relation of history and the kingdom must be held to as a process of transformation, a process that might be compared to the resurrection of the body, which does not deny or negate but fulfills and perfects.[19] Míguez Bonino also relates history to the kingdom of God eschatologically; like the Pauline doctrine of works, history takes on its fullness and meaning as it anticipates the kingdom of God. History has a decidedly theological meaning, not merely philosophical or materialist. We act in history because God acts, or more precisely, God acts in history through love to bring the kingdom, and, in our obedience, we act through Christ's love to bring the kingdom.

It is this praxis of obedience that calls out for theology; praxis must continually interpret God's action in history based on biblical themes and understand the Bible in light of experiencing God's activity of history. This "hermeneutical" activity, that is, the activity of discerning, interpreting, and appropriating God's activity in history into the praxis of Christian obedience, begins by realizing its own concreteness; that is, it too is historically bound, and cannot reflect outside of the categories and conditions available in a particular historical situation. All theology is therefore situated and political: situated because it is done in a particular historical situation, and political because reflection, like all other aspects of life, grows out of the full sociopolitical reality. Yet theologians must not merely mirror the sociopolitical context; rather, they must position themselves in light of their obedience to Christian praxis, or, as Míguez Bonino says, "we are situated in reality to be sure – historically, geographically, culturally, and most of all groupwise and classwise – but we can also position ourselves differently in relation to the situation."[20] Thus theology must learn to dialogue carefully with the social sciences, in order to analyze, critique, and transform the historical situation in light of God's liberating activity.

Míguez Bonino's work demonstrates both the centrality of history in liberation theology, and the sociopolitical view of history. It is important to underscore that sociopolitical history is central to understanding not only because of sociological arguments, that is, that all knowledge is historically conditioned, but also because of scriptural arguments: history is the arena of God's action, action that is the transformation of history through love. Míguez Bonino's theology calls human beings to be responsible for history: responsible in responding to God's love, and responsible for their involvement in history. He also shows us that liberation theology has a decidedly sociopolitical cast: it advocates historical transformation, it discerns God's liberating activity, and it uses social sciences for analysis, interpretation, and appropriation.

Debate

Liberation theology embarked on a bold, new interpretation of Christian witness in Latin America and was received with a great deal of debate among theologians in the other regions. Some observers responded by rethinking the basic contours and commitments of their own theological and political positions, while others dismissed liberation theology as inadequate theological reflection or a form of politics using religion. Much of the debate was centered in three broad areas: liberation theology's equation of liberation and redemption, its turn to the political as the primary locus of human life, and its theoretical arguments in relation to ethics and social theory. For some theologians in the global North, the equation of redemption and liberation tempted a kind of temporal messianism, a heralding of the reign of God on the side of one political cause.[21] This appeared too reminiscent of totalitarian movements. It was also considered unbiblical, as it seemed to place God on the side of the poor, in opposition to the rich.[22] Of course, other formulations are varied, some advocating an existentialist theology with implications to move into political realms, while others advocated a more realist power basis, noting that even Jesus said that the poor will always be with us. These arguments also touch upon a disagreement within liberation theology over how redemption and liberation are related, and upon the debate over the status of the option for the poor. As we have already seen, Míguez Bonino criticizes some liberation theologians for monist solutions, arguing for a position that distinguishes, and Gutiérrez advocates a three-level relation between redemption and liberation. The option for the poor is, as Gutiérrez suggested, a statement about God's gratuitousness and not a romanticization of the poor. This also relates to the debate among liberation theologians about the role of popular religion – whether it is a mystification of consciousness or authentic religious praxis.

Related to this criticism is the second, that liberation theology reduced human life to the political realm.[23] For many years, Roman Catholic theologians distinguished between two realms that should be separated without interference: the political and the religious. The Second Vatican Council, with its new vision of the relationship between the church and the world, gave impetus to new theological reflection on social justice and politics. Liberation theologians held a broad understanding of the political as the basis of life. Politics is not simply concerned with the managing of the state but also with how our lives are organized and expressed and how we fulfill our subjectivity. Politics is intrinsic to the definition of the human subject, not merely a secondary expression. The gospel, then, is not political in offering a particular theory of political management, but is political in terms of its promise and demand for the fulfillment of human life. Theology, like all other forms of thought, is always political, and advocating a particular view of life implies a vision of human flourishing.

But even if one grants that in some manner redemption and liberation are related, and that politics is a necessary dimension of understanding religion, questions can still be asked about liberation theology's theoretical formulations, more specifically, the relative adequacy of its ethical and social theories. Liberation theology has been criticized for lacking an adequate social theory of the relation between human consciousness and social structures.[24] Over time, however, there were significant developments in the area of ethics, although much of the literature is not available in English. Liberation theology has its origins in ethical indignation; thus, ethics is a constitutive dimension of this theology. It has placed the concerns of the poor and oppressed at the center of ethics. Developments in the area of philosophical ethics, exemplified in the writings of Enrique Dussel and Juan Carlos Scannone, were matched by a flourishing of Christian ethics in Latin America,[25] with a liberationist perspective integral to many theologians who did not necessarily identify themselves as liberation theologians. Liberation ethics embraces the concerns of human rights, feminism, bioethics, and ecology but needs more development in areas like personal freedom and conscience. Solidarity is the key theme, a theme that forges a personalism from the perspective of the poor and oppressed, based on a communitarian vision of the human person that is broader and more inclusive than North American "communitarian" thought.

Achievement and Agenda: The Future of Liberation Theology

Any evaluation of the "achievements" of liberation theology must begin with the intent and promise of this theology to be a voice of the poor and to speak of God's presence and power among the victims of history. Concerns such as liberation theology's methodological rigor or its theoretical sophistication are important, but they are secondary to the rupturing presence of this theology. It has ruptured much of the discourse of modern theology, even as it has intensified and changed many of its concepts. Modern theology's turn to the subject tended to assume the bourgeois subject confronted with atheism, but as Gutiérrez argues, the subject of liberation theology is "the nonperson." Thus, the first accomplishment of liberation theology is to enable us to hear the voice of the poor and to allow that voice to challenge our values and beliefs, even as it highlights our participation in structures and systems that oppress others. However, liberation theology's primary commitment is not to convert the rich, but to speak from the poor and for the poor, giving voice to new understandings of God, love, sin, grace, and eschatology. This second accomplishment of new theological perspectives opens new ways of speaking about the human person, community, justice, the structures of the world in which we live, and hope for the future.

The third accomplishment concerns the methodological importance of liberation theology. Latin American liberation theologians, together with Black and feminist liberation theologians, have made a convincing case for the situatedness of all knowledge. This achievement has three dimensions: (1) the situatedness of all knowledge, (2) the inclusion of ideology critique in theology, and (3) the argument for the positionality of theology, that is, the rhetorical commitments of knowledge. Liberation theologians, in a variety of ways, include ideology critique as intrinsic to the theological task, in order to reveal distortions of knowledge, interest, and power in social systems. Some years before poststructuralist claims about the relations of knowledge, interest, and power became popular in academic circles, Latin American theologians argued that reason itself is always a product of history. Liberation theologians pursue (in a way the poststructuralists often do not) a constructive vision, a world envisioned from the new subjectivity of the poor, a new relation between human consciousness and social structures.

Despite these accomplishments, and the obvious maturation from the 1970s into the 1980s, there is general agreement that liberation theology as an ecclesial movement hit a crisis in the 1990s and has sought new direction in the twenty-first century. Supporters of the movement lament its loss of momentum and the weakening of its institutional influence. Opponents suggest that the demise of socialism rendered liberation theology passé or failed. It is erroneous to view the fall of the Berlin Wall as the destruction of the cornerstone of liberation theology. The preferential, but not exclusive, option for the poor – not Marxism – was always at the heart of liberation theology. However, this option for the poor faces different and complex challenges in the new global economy. Although most liberation theologians, with varying degrees of skepticism, recognize the positive function of the market, they are concerned about the destructive impact of neoliberalism. Neoliberalism, with its absolutist view of the market and its reductionist anthropology, sees the human person merely as an income-generating unit. Although economic conditions have improved in Latin America, the masses of the poor have been joined by the newly impoverished of the middle classes. Future economic growth cannot occur at the expense of the poor and the destruction of natural resources. Liberation theology needs to engage seriously with this new economic and political reality through critique and constructive vision, maintaining the insistence on structural transformation and participatory democracy. The diversity of voices that has emerged in liberation theology has unveiled both the complexity of the poor and the complexity of oppression. Capitalism is not the only form of oppression, but there is an interrelationship between it and racism, sexism, and other forms of oppression. It is suggested that this broadening of social analysis need not blunt the socioeconomic critique that has been integral to liberation theology. Juan Carlos Scannone describes an "axial shift" from the socioeconomic to the sociocultural perspective, a shift that does not consist in substitution, but in a deepening of perspectives.[26]

The rapid growth of Pentecostal and evangelical churches in Latin America beginning in the 1980s, especially among the urban poor, was seen as some as a practical refutation of liberation theology.[27] A Brazilian pastor of the Evangelical Association told the *New York Times* "the Catholics opted for the poor, and the poor opted for the Evangelicals."[28] The attractions of Pentecostal and evangelical churches for those who are poor and seeking meaning, certainty, and practical support in a challenging world needed to be better understood because the Pentecostal and evangelical churches are part of Latin America's long-term future.[29]

Although "Pentecostalism" and "evangelicalism" are umbrella terms, embracing movements which are marked by complexity both in terms of their own composition and their relationship to politics, their continuing growth marks a major shift in Latin America's religious landscape for the twenty-first century. Some in the business sector perceive this as the arrival of the Protestant Reformation in Latin America, an arrival whose work ethic will overcome the cultural impediments to economic development. However, Pentecostalism and Evangelicalism are often criticized for being too otherworldly, individualistic, and lacking in collective social concern.[30] There also remains a Catholic tendency to see these Protestant movements as foreign imports. The growing influence of the Religious Right in North America has been a special cause for concern. In some countries there have been close associations between conservative Protestantism and right-wing politics. Religion was mobilized in the 2022 Brazilian election contested by the conservative Jair Bolsonaro and the left-wing Luiz Inácio Lula da Silva (Lula) of the Workers' Party. Bolsonaro's wife, Michelle Bolsonaro, a committed Pentecostal Christian, actively worked to promote religious support for her husband's conservative policies within Pentecostal churches.

Whether or not one considers liberation theology to be the most significant theological movement to emerge in the late twentieth century, it must be acknowledged that during the 1970s and 1980s it had a major impact on the global theological landscape. Furthermore, the methodological principles and central insights of liberation theology from this period are likely to remain profoundly relevant for many streams in Christian theology and will continue to find new expressions. These principles include (1) attention to the struggles of the marginalized and oppressed as a privileged epistemological locus for an engaged theology; (2) a commitment to lived experience and social analysis to understand the signs of the times more deeply; and (3) recognition of the political significance of all theological work.[31] Recent new initiatives suggest that liberation theology still has much to offer those who are committed to speaking of God in solidarity with those who live on the underside of our times.[32]

Notes

1 See Thia Cooper, ed., *The Reemergence of Liberation Theologies: Models for the Twenty-First Century* (New York: Palgrave Macmillan, 2013). Suggested new directions have included calls for liberation theology to strengthen its environmental concerns, see Leonardo Boff, *Ecology and Liberation: A New Paradigm* (Maryknoll, NY: Orbis, 1995); embrace sexuality and "indecent theology," see Marcella Althaus-Reid, *Indecent Theology: Theological Perversions in Sex, Gender and Politics* (New York: Routledge, 2000); deepen its economic critique, see Ivan Petrella, *The Future of Liberation Theology: An Argument and Manifesto* (New York: Routledge, 2004).

2 Gustavo Gutiérrez, "Theology and Spirituality in a Latin American Context," *Harvard Divinity Bulletin* 14, no. 3 (1984): 458–62.

3 Though a common objection to liberation theology is that it will result in making the poor rich, simply exchanging one group of oppressors for another, liberation theologians, from their earliest works on, have advocated a transformation of social structures to rid the world of the massive disparities between the poor and the rich and have offered anthropologies of transformation stressing new ways of being human for all persons.

4 For good introductions to the history of Latin America, see George Pendle, *A History of Latin America* (New York: Penguin, 1963); Hubert Herring, *A History of Latin America from the Beginnings to the Present* (New York: Alfred A. Knopf, 1961); and Enrique D. Dussel, *A History of the Church in Latin America: Colonialism to Liberation (1492–1979)*, trans. Alan Neely (Grand Rapids, MI: Eerdmans, 1981). On the role of the church in the 1960s and 1970s, see Penny Lernoux, *The Cry of the People: The Struggle for Human Rights in Latin America – the Catholic Church in Conflict with US Policy* (New York: Doubleday, 1980).

5 See José Comblín, *The Church and the National Security State* (Maryknoll, NY: Orbis, 1979) and Robert Calvo, "The Church and the Doctrine of National Security," *Journal of Interamerican Studies and World Affairs* 21, no. 1 (1979): 69–88.

6 See Joseph Gremillion, ed., *The Gospel of Peace and Justice: Catholic Social Teaching since Pope John* (Maryknoll, NY: Orbis, 1976); Alfred Hennelly, ed., *Liberation Theology: A Documentary History* (Maryknoll, NY: Orbis, 1990).

7 Representative works by these two theologians are Jürgen Moltmann, *Theology of Hope: On the Grounds and Implications of a Christian Eschatology* (New York: Harper & Row, 1967) and *The Crucified God: The Cross of Christ as the Foundation and Criticism of Christian Theology* (New York: Harper & Row, 1973); Johann Baptist Metz, *Theology of the World* (New York: Herder & Herder, 1969) and *Faith in History and Society: Toward a Practical Fundamental Theology* (London: Burns and Oates, 1980).

8 For examples of the critical uses of Marxism in liberation theology, see José Míguez Bonino, *Christians and Marxists: The Mutual Challenge to Revolution* (Grand Rapids, MI: Eerdmans, 1976) and Juan Luis Segundo, *Faith and Ideologies* (Maryknoll, NY: Orbis, 1984).

9 María Clara Bingemer, "Women in the Future of the Theology of Liberation," in *Expanding the View: Gustavo Gutiérrez and the Future of Liberation Theology*, ed. Marc H. Ellis and Otto Maduro (Maryknoll, NY: Orbis, 1990), 185.

10 Leonardo Boff and Clodovis Boff, *Introducing Liberation Theology* (Maryknoll, NY: Orbis, 1987), 11–21.

11 John Eagleson and Philip Scharper, eds., *Pueblo and Beyond: Documentation and Commentary* (Maryknoll, NY: Orbis, 1979), paras. 32–9.

12 Gustavo Gutiérrez, *A Theology of Liberation: History, Politics and Salvation* (Maryknoll, NY: Orbis, 1973, 1988); *The Power of the Poor in History: Selected Writings* (Maryknoll, NY: Orbis, 1983); *We Drink from Our Own Wells: The Spiritual Journey of a People* (Maryknoll, NY: Orbis, 1984); *On Job: God-talk and the Suffering of the Innocent* (Maryknoll, NY: Orbis, 1987); *The Truth Shall Make You Free: Confrontations*, trans. Matthew J. O'Connell (Maryknoll, NY: Orbis, 1990); *The God of Life* (Maryknoll, NY: Orbis, 1991); *Las Casas: In Search of the Poor of Jesus Christ* (Maryknoll, NY: Orbis, 1993).

13 Ignacio Ellacuría, *Freedom Made Flesh: The Mission of Christ and His Church* (Maryknoll, NY: Orbis, 1976). On Ellacuría's life and work, see Kevin Burke, *The Ground beneath the Cross: The Theology of Ignacio Ellacuría* (Washington, DC: Georgetown University Press, 2000), and Michael E. Lee, *Ignacio Ellacuría: Essays on History, Liberation, and Salvation* (Maryknoll, NY: Orbis, 2013).

14 An English translation was published posthumously as Ignacio Ellacuría, "The Crucified People," in *Mysterium Liberationis: Fundamental Concepts of Liberation Theology*, ed. Ignacio Ellacuría and Jon Sobrino (Maryknoll, NY: Orbis, 1993), 580–603.

15 On Sobrino's life and work, see Sturla Stållset, *The Crucified and the Crucified: A Study in the Liberation Christology of Jon Sobrino* (New York: Peter Lang, 2003).

16 Jon Sobrino, *The Principle of Mercy: Taking the Crucified People from the Cross* (Maryknoll, NY: Orbis, 1994), 1–11.

17 Jon Sobrino, *The True Church and the Poor* (Maryknoll, NY: Orbis, 1984), 20.

18 Sobrino, *The True Church and the Poor*, 20.

19 José Míguez Bonino, *Doing Theology in a Revolutionary Situation* (Philadelphia, PA: Fortress Press, 1975), 136–43.

20 José Míguez Bonino, *Toward a Christian Political Ethics* (Philadelphia, PA: Fortress Press, 1983), 44.

21 See, for instance, the charge by Dennis McCann that liberation theology "politicizes" the gospel: "Practical Theology and Social Action: or What Can the 1980s Learn from the 1960s," in *Practical Theology: The Emerging Field in Theology, Church, and World*, ed. Don S. Browning (San Francisco, CA: HarperCollins, 1983), 105–25.

22 For instance, the 1984 "Instruction on Certain Aspects of the Theology of Liberation," issued by the Congregation for the Doctrine of the Faith, criticized "certain forms" of liberation theology for faulty biblical hermeneutics and uncritical use of Marxism. The 1986 "Instruction on Christian Freedom and Liberation" was less critical and, although subordinating sociopolitical liberation to personal–spiritual freedom, it did endorse many of the key theological concepts of liberation theology.

23 Schubert Ogden, for example, has criticized liberation theologians for equating redemption and emancipation in his *Faith and Freedom: Toward a Theology of Liberation* (Nashville, TN: Abingdon, 1979).

24 See, for instance, Rebecca S. Chopp, *The Praxis of Suffering: An Interpretation of Liberation and Political Theologies* (Maryknoll, NY: Orbis, 1986), 144–8.

25 See Dean Brackley and Thomas L. Schubeck, "Moral Theology in Latin America," *Theological Studies* 63 (2002): 123–60, an excellent survey of recent developments in the field.

26 Juan Carlos Scannone, "'Axial Shift' instead of 'Paradigm Shift,'" in *Liberation Theologies on Shifting Grounds: A Clash of Socio-Economic and Cultural Paradigms*, ed. Georges De Schrijver (Leuven: Peeters, 1998), 91.

27 David Martin, *Tongues of Fire: The Explosion of Protestantism in Latin America* (Oxford: Blackwell, 1990); David Stoll, *Is Latin America Turning Protestant? The Politics of Evangelical Growth* (Berkeley, CA: University of California Press, 1990); Virginia Garrard-Burnett and David Stoll, eds., *Rethinking Protestantism in Latin America* (Philadelphia, PA: Temple University Press, 1993); Cecelía Loreto Mariz, *Coping with Poverty: Pentecostals and Christian Base Communities in Brazil* (Philadelphia, PA: Temple University Press, 1994); Malcolm Löwy, *The War of the Gods: Religion and Politics in Latin America* (London: Verso, 1996); Philip Berryman, *Religion in the Megacity: Catholic and Protestant Portraits from Latin America* (Maryknoll, NY: Orbis, 1996).

28 James Brooke, "Pragmatic Protestants Win Catholic Converts in Brazil," *New York Times* (4 July 1993), pp. A1, A10.

29 John Burdick, *Looking for God in Brazil: The Progressive Catholic Church in Urban Brazil's Religious Arena* (Berkeley, CA: University of California Press, 1993).

30 Rubem Alves, who is Protestant, offers a fierce critique of this lack of concern in *Protestantism and Repression: A Brazilian Case Study* (Maryknoll, NY: Orbis, 1985).

31 See David Tombs, *Latin American Liberation Theology* (Leiden: Brill, 2002), 295.

32 For an example of a recent new initiative, see the Liberation Theology podcast launched by David Inczauskis, SJ in January 2021, https://podcasts.apple.com/us/podcast/the-liberation-theology-podcast/id1551431636 (accessed 15 September 2023).

Recommended Reading

Primary

Aquino, María Pilar. *Our Cry for Life: Feminist Theology from Latin America*. Maryknoll, NY: Orbis, 1993.

Boff, Leonardo, and Clodovis Boff. *Introducing Liberation Theology*. Maryknoll, NY: Orbis, 1987.

Dussel, Enrique, D. *A History of the Church in Latin America: Colonialism to Liberation (1492–1979)*. Grand Rapids, MI: Eerdmans, 1981.

Ellacuría, Ignacio, and Jon Sobrino, eds. *Mysterium Liberationis: Fundamental Concepts of Liberation Theology*. Maryknoll, NY: Orbis, 1993.

Gebara, Ivone, and Maria Clara Bingemer. *Mary, Mother of God, Mother of the Poor*. Maryknoll, NY: Orbis, 1989.

Gutiérrez, Gustavo. *A Theology of Liberation: History, Politics and Salvation*. Maryknoll, NY: Orbis, 1973, 1988.

Míguez Bonino, José. *Doing Theology in a Revolutionary Situation*. Philadelphia, PA: Fortress Press, 1975.

Sobrino, Jon. *Christology at the Crossroads: A Latin American Approach*. Maryknoll, NY: Orbis, 1978.

——— *The Principle of Mercy: Taking the Crucified People from the Cross*. Maryknoll, NY: Orbis, 1994.

Tamez, Elsa. *The Amnesty of Grace: Justification by Faith from a Latin American Perspective*. Translated by Sharon H. Ringe. Nashville, TN: Abingdon, 1993.

Secondary

Berryman, Phillip. *Liberation Theology*. Oak Park, IL: Meyer-Stone, 1987.

Brown, Robert McAfee. *Theology in a New Key: Responding to Liberation Themes*. Philadelphia, PA: Fortress Press, 1978.

Burke, Kevin. *The Ground Beneath the Cross: The Theology of Ignacio Ellacuría*. Washington, DC: Georgetown University Press, 2000.

Chopp, Rebecca S. *The Praxis of Suffering: An Interpretation of Liberation and Political Theologies*. Maryknoll, NY: Orbis, 1986.

De Schrijver, Georges, ed. *Liberation Theologies on Shifting Grounds: A Clash of Socio-Economic and Cultural Paradigms*. Leuven: Peeters, 1998.

Ellis, Marc H., and Otto Maduro, eds. *Expanding the View: Gustavo Gutiérrez and the Future of Liberation Theology*. Maryknoll, NY: Orbis, 1990.

Hennelly, Alfred, ed. *Liberation Theology: A Documentary History*. Maryknoll, NY: Orbis, 1990.

Lee, Michael E. *Ignacio Ellacuría: Essays on History, Liberation, and Salvation*. Maryknoll, NY: Orbis, 2013.

Lernoux, Penny. *The Cry of the People: The Struggle for Human Rights in Latin America – the Catholic Church in Conflict with US Policy*. New York: Doubleday, 1980.

Tombs, David, *Latin American Liberation Theology*. Leiden: Brill, 2002.

Gustavo Gutiérrez

O. Ernesto Valiente

Introduction

For me to do theology is to write a letter, a love letter, to God, the God of my faith, to my people, and to my church.

Any adequate treatment of Christian theology in the twentieth century would be incomplete without addressing the movement of liberation theologies. Today these theologies are practiced in different contexts with different emphases and concerns but are united by their solidarity with the oppressed and the commitment to their liberation. This preferential option for the oppressed and the impoverished, they argue, is central to the God revealed to us by Jesus Christ. Although some of these theologies developed almost concurrently, Latin American liberation theology – particularly the work of Peruvian theologian Gustavo Gutiérrez – has come to mark the onset of this movement and become emblematic of this theology's approach and purpose. Indeed, today Gutiérrez is widely recognized as the "father of liberation theology."

Following the insights of liberation theology, which gives prominence to the importance of an event's context and the community's lived experience, our point of departure in examining Gutiérrez's theology turns first toward his intellectual biography and the context of his community life. Then we turn to examine the central tenets of his theology and conclude with an assessment of his work and legacy. As we will see, three historical influences are crucial to understanding Gutiérrez's approach to and development of his theology. First is his theological formation in Europe in the 1950s; second, the pastoral ministry that put him in touch with the Latin American social reality after his return to Peru in the 1960s; and third, the impact of the Second Vatican Council on Latin American theology and the council's subsequent reception in the bishops' conference at Medellín.

Ford's The Modern Theologians: An Introduction to Christian Theology since 1918, Fourth Edition.
Edited by Rachel Muers and Ashley Cocksworth.
© 2024 John Wiley & Sons Ltd. Published 2024 by John Wiley & Sons Ltd.

Survey

Roots, influences, and formation

Gustavo Gutiérrez Merino was born on 8 June 1928, in Lima, Peru to a family of Quechua and Spanish ancestry. He grew up in a close and supportive family of modest means and attended the Marist school in Lima. His youth was marked by the sickness of osteomyelitis, an infection of the bone that often kept him bedridden for long periods. Although this illness limited Gutiérrez's capacity for movement, it offered him the opportunity to read and reflect extensively. With the support of family and friends, the future pastor and theologian overcame these adversities and began his studies toward a degree in medicine at San Marcos University in Lima in 1947. As a university student, he joined the Catholic Action movement, which stressed the active role of lay people in society. Although initially interested in the field of psychiatry, at the age of twenty-four, Gutiérrez interrupted his studies to enter the seminary where he would discern a vocation to the Catholic ordained ministry.

As was customarily done with bright and promising seminarians, Gutiérrez was sent to Europe for further studies. From 1951 to 1955, he studied toward master's degrees in philosophy and psychology in Louvain, Belgium, and then moved to Lyon, France, from 1955 to 1959 to complete a master's degree in theology. Years later, in 1985, the University of Lyons would grant Gutiérrez a doctoral degree based on his published works and in recognition of his impact on Christian theology. During his time in Lyon, the theologian was introduced to the French *Nouvelle théologie,* which sought to relate the Christian faith to the modern world by returning Catholic theology to its sources, particularly scripture and the patristic tradition. The impact of theologians like Yves Congar, Henri de Lubac, and particularly M. D. Chenu, is evident in Gutiérrez's works much as it influenced other theologians such as Maurice Blondel, Karl Rahner, Edward Schillebeeckx, and the German biblical scholar Gerhard von Rad.

In 1959, Gustavo Gutiérrez was ordained to the priesthood in Rome and returned to Peru, where his work had both a fruitful academic and a pastoral dimension. He took a teaching position in the theology department at the Pontifical Catholic University of Peru and also taught courses in the faculty of letters and the social sciences there. His new academic responsibilities and the rich intellectual environment allowed Gutiérrez to establish a dialogue between theology and contemporary social thought. Among his interlocutors were important European philosophers such as Albert Camus and Karl Marx as well as seminal Peruvian literary authors like Jose Carlos Mariategui, Cesar Vallejo, and Jose Maria Arguedas.

Always close to the social reality of his country, Gutiérrez also became an advisor to the National Union of Catholic Students. This latter position allowed him to travel around Peru, be closely attuned to the social dynamics of the nation, and generate a close relationship between his pastoral and his theological work. Like other Latin American nations, Peru had begun a process of demographic transformation, as domestic manufacturing led to an increase in the migration of unemployed and underemployed rural populations into its urban centers. This process of urbanization exposed the inequality previously hidden in the rural areas of the region and enabled Latin American scholars to challenge the economic explanations put forward by scholars from industrialized nations by offering a better understanding of the causes of poverty in the region.

This was a time of broad social and political awakening, with intellectuals, workers, peasants, and other groups in civil society all questioning the status quo. The 1959 Cuban Revolution, however ambivalent its legacy, inspired many emancipatory movements elsewhere on the continent, while the liberation of many African nations from their colonial ties made the Western world more aware of the ubiquity of oppression and raised, in the developing nations, the hope for liberation. As Gutiérrez himself described it, Latin America was undergoing "a full process of revolutionary ferment" that called for new ways of confronting "the untenable circumstances of poverty, alienation, and exploitation in which the greater part of the people of Latin America live."[1]

At the same time, the Second Vatican Council (1962–5) saw a renewed attention to the historical dimension of the church and a corresponding change in attitude toward the modern world. The council also gave prominence to the role of the laity in the church, which would provide a crucial methodological framework for the church in Latin America. Within this changing social and ecclesial context, Gutiérrez became a central participant in a Latin American church that was becoming progressively aware of its distinct identity and gifts. In Latin America, the council encouraged an atmosphere of theological creativity that fostered dialogue among theologians and anticipated the development of liberation theology. At a meeting of Latin American theologians in Petrópolis, Brazil, in 1964, Gutiérrez offered a critique of the church's existing pastoral work, described theology as a critical reflection on praxis, and argued that theology should take social reality at its point of departure for pastoral action.[2] These initial theological insights were further developed at meetings in Havana, Bogota, and Cuernavaca in 1965 and were later published with other reflections under the Spanish title "Lineas Pastorales de la Iglesia en América Latina."[3]

Around this time several meetings throughout the continent were also being held as part of the preparatory work for the Second Conference of Latin American bishops to take place in Medellín, Colombia. These meetings were crucial spaces for pastoral leaders, bishops, and theologians to discern and better articulate the theological and pastoral mission of the church. Indeed, it was at a meeting sponsored by the National Office of Social Research in Chimbote, Peru, that Gutiérrez presented for the first time the basic outline for a "theology of liberation." A month later, these reflections of Gutiérrez and the other Latin American theologians informed the 1968 conference of bishops at Medellín. Following the insights of *Gaudium et Spes* and responding to the Latin American situation, the bishops identified the reality of injustice and poverty as the crucial historical sign that required the church's immediate attention. A few years after the council, in his landmark work *A Theology of Liberation*, Gutiérrez explicitly referred to this sign as the "irruption of the poor" and articulated the central theological question that would drive his work from there on: "How is it possible to tell the poor, who are forced to live in conditions that embody a denial of love, that God loves them?"[4]

The task of theology

Gutiérrez and other Latin American theologians often stress that liberation theology is a new way of doing theology. The Peruvian theologian explains that, whereas in the early church theology was understood as wisdom or spirituality, and in the Medieval period theology began to be seen as a science or rational knowledge, today's theology insists that it also be understood as "critical reflection on Christian praxis in light of the Word."[5] With this formula, Gutiérrez is not rejecting theology as an intellectual endeavor that seeks to understand the faith, but rather is stressing that "faith means not only truths to be affirmed but also an existential stance, an attitude, a commitment to God and to human beings."[6]

Christians do not just think about their faith, but experience and live it: they contemplate, pray, and commit to following God with their actions. Critical reflection, Gutiérrez avers, comes after living; echoing Hegel, "it rises only at sundown." Thus, Gutiérrez explains: "theology is a reflection – that is, it is a second act, a turning back, a reflecting, that comes after action. Theology is not first; the commitment is first ... Theology is the understanding of the commitment."[7] This inductive approach to the theological task takes the concrete faith life of Christians as its point of departure and rejects those theological approaches that separate God's revelation from a particular historical context and daily life. In a similar vein, Gutiérrez rejects those theologies that endorse any type of historical dualism. He writes, "There are not two histories, one profane and one sacred, 'juxtaposed' or 'closely linked.' Rather there is only one human destiny."[8] God not only reveals Godself in scripture and tradition but also in history and particularly in the praxis of the church community. This praxis not only *reveals* our faith but, in a sense, *is* our faith – a particular way of engaging the world.

For Gutiérrez, the term "praxis" does not simply mean human action, nor does he use the term to contrast or even separate "theory" from "practice," as if praxis were simply the application of some theory. On the contrary, the manner in which Gutiérrez uses the term praxis implies that theory and practice – that is, doctrine and action – fruitfully influence one another. In other words, theology and praxis constitute a hermeneutical circle, with theology reflecting upon those actions already informed by faith. Moreover, in solidarity with those who struggle against poverty and injustice, liberation theology embraces the perspective of those who are poor and seeks the transformation of reality according to God's will. Hence, Gutiérrez explains that "the praxis on which liberation theology reflects is a praxis of solidarity in the interests of liberation and is inspired in the gospel."[9] This option for the perspective of the poor and their liberative praxis is central to Gutiérrez's theology and liberation theology's approach to the theological task.

Scholars have noted that part of liberation theology's methodological novelty lies in its conversation partners. Unlike traditional theology that often enlists philosophy as its dialoguing partner, by choosing to reflect on historical praxis in a situation of oppression, liberation theologians often turn to the social sciences to better understand the signs of the times by recognizing who the poor are in society and identifying the different causes of their impoverishment. This emphasis on liberative praxis also helps explains why liberation theology stresses the importance of Christian charity, the connection between spirituality and social transformation, and the importance of orthopraxis as well as orthodoxy.[10]

Content

The impoverished and the preferential option for the poor

The poor are at the center of Gutiérrez's theology. Their situation and experience inform his theological perspective and explain its soteriological structure. But "poverty" is a polyvalent term that needs to be carefully examined. Gutiérrez likes to stress that poverty in Latin America is not simply a matter of fate or misfortune but rather is the consequence of human decisions and actions. It is the result of particular social arrangements, racial and cultural prejudices, and unjust economic structures. The poor are those who have been impoverished and excluded from the benefits of society; they are those who have been rendered powerless and insignificant, and destined to die before their time. Although Gutiérrez's work stresses the economic aspects of poverty, he is mindful that poverty also encompasses other social factors, among them the oppressive conditions in which Latin American women live and the exclusion of racial and cultural minorities throughout the continent.

For Gutiérrez, the preferential option for the poor is primarily a theological category rooted in the biblical vision of God. Hence, he draws from scripture to illuminate three basic understandings of poverty present in the Bible and central to the Christian life: real poverty, spiritual poverty, and solidarity with the poor. "Real poverty" in the Bible is understood as a shocking condition against human dignity and God's will. To describe the inhuman conditions of real poverty, the prophets refer to the bent-over, the beggars, and the oppressed. The prophets condemn this poverty and its different causes: unjust taxes, unjust commerce, hoarding of the lands, and other practices that perpetuate poverty and create new poor.

"Spiritual poverty," on the other hand, is the disposition to being open and dependent upon God. Rather than a condition that is contrary to God's will, this form of poverty reflects our proper stance before the divine and does not have any social or economic characteristics attached to it. From the time of Isaiah, the frequent infidelity of Israel led the prophets to develop the notion of the faithful "tiny remnant" from which the Messiah will emerge. Those who waited for the Messiah were called "the poor." Here, to be poor means to be opposed to self-sufficiency and pride. The spiritually poor are those who trust in the Lord and this trust is a condition to approach God. Perhaps the best expression of this notion in the New Testament is in Matthew's beatitudes (Matthew 5) where to be poor is to be dependent on God.

These two distinct meanings of poverty in the Bible – as a scandalous, inhuman condition and as a stance of openness to God – shed light on what the Christian witness toward poverty should be. Although real poverty is to be rejected, our attitude toward spiritual poverty expressed as a stance of total availability and dependence upon God leads us to live a life of solidarity with the poor and a life of protest against their situation. As we will see in more detail later, the spirituality that emerges from Matt. 5:3, "Blessed are the poor in spirit," leads to the praxis depicted in Matt. 25:35–36, "for I was hungry and you gave me food, I was thirsty and you gave me something to drink, I was a stranger and you welcomed me, I was naked and you gave me clothing, I was sick and you took care of me, I was in prison and you visited me." Thus, Gutiérrez avers, "The deepest meaning of the commitment to the poor is the encounter with Christ."[11] This solidarity is a commitment lived not for the sake of poverty itself but as an imitation of Christ and on behalf of those who suffer.

In explaining the preferential option for the poor, Gutiérrez insists that there is no contradiction between preference and universality. He argues that to properly understand the divine preference, it must be considered from the context of God's universal and gratuitous love. Preference "simply points to who ought to be the first – not the only – object of our solidarity."[12] God's preference exemplifies the gratuitous character of divine love. There is no indication in scripture that God's preferential concern for the oppressed is rooted in the assumption that they are more deserving than or morally superior to their oppressor or their enemies. This same sensitivity was expressed by the Latin American bishops in Puebla: "the poor merit preferential attention, whatever may be the moral or personal situation in which they find themselves" (No. 1142). Their situation often makes their moral development more difficult than those who live in situations of stability, opportunity, and comfort. Regardless of their relative moral character, Gutiérrez insists, "God loves the poor ... simply because they are poor, because they are hungry, because they are persecuted."[13] The poor are favored because they are in greater need than the nonpoor.

In retrospect, the concept of "option" may be the most ambiguous element in the "preferential option for the poor" formula. Although the term attempts to stress the freedom and commitment of a decision, it is often misunderstood to mean that the "option" is actually optional when, in fact, what is meant is that we are all – even the impoverished themselves – called to actively "opt" for the poor. As the poor become aware of their situation and the possibility of changing it, they ought to assume the leading role in the process of liberation. The demands of this renewed agency call them to make an option for themselves and for others who are oppressed. Although this option does not dictate that the nonpoor must live a life of imitation of the poor, Gutiérrez encourages the nonpoor to make friends with the poor. As he writes, just as the preferential option for the poor "aims at the promotion of justice, [it] equally implies friendship with the poor and among the poor. Without friendship there is neither authentic solidarity nor a true sharing."[14] In the final analysis, the option for the poor is not only intrinsic to living a Christian life but also a necessary step in fulfilling the call for the Christian church to become a church of the poor – one that forgets itself in order to be at the service of God and God's favored ones.

Salvation and integral liberation

In its simplest articulation, Gustavo Gutiérrez defines salvation as "the communion of human beings with God and among themselves."[15] This elegant and concise claim conceals the deeper implications of Gutiérrez's reinterpretation of the doctrine of salvation as an integrated process of liberation. To better understand Gutiérrez's contribution, we do well to remember that he is writing from a situation of injustice and oppression and reflecting on the liberating praxis of Latin American Christian communities. As noted previously, he is also attempting to develop an understanding of salvation that can overcome the constraints of a theological context that was still deeply influenced by neoscholastic theology – a theology limited by its tendency to rarify grace and separate history into the so-called profane and sacred spheres. To this point, writing in 1971, Gutiérrez complains that "one of the deficiencies of contemporary theology is the absence of a profound and lucid reflection on the theme of salvation."[16]

Gutiérrez's understanding of salvation is rooted in a unified understanding of history and a theology of grace that conceives God's self-expression not as something rare or exceptional, but as plentiful and ever present. We live in a world infused by the presence of God. All the realities that surround us – especially human beings – are means for a possible encounter with God. It is because of this sacramental quality of the world that Gutiérrez can affirm that salvation "is something which embraces all human reality, transforms it, and leads to its fulness in Christ."[17] Our encounter with God in history is enabled by God's gratuitous love. Such an encounter is an invitation to communion to which we respond with our freedom. Within our human limitations, we are free to accept or reject God's invitation. Although a deeply personal experience, our encounter with God always takes place in a social and historical setting that reflects the accumulated – positive and negative – responses to God by those who came before us. In a world that bears the ambivalent consequences of human actions, Gutiérrez, like other liberation theologians, relies on the widely held Christian tradition that distinguishes between liberation *from* and liberation *for*. "The first," Gutiérrez tells us, "refers to freedom from sin, selfishness, injustice, need, and situations calling for deliverance. The second refers to the purpose of the first freedom – namely, love and communion; this is the final phase of liberation."[18] Hence, he insists "Liberation ... is a journey toward communion. Communion ... is a gift of Christ who sets us free in order that we may be free, free to love; it is in this communion that full freedom resides."[19]

Liberation theologians consistently speak of historical salvation as the integral liberation of the whole human person: a salvation that impinges on the different dimensions of existence and establishes the necessary conditions for communion among human beings and with God. To that end, Gutiérrez asks "What relationship is there between salvation and the historical process of human liberation?" To shed light on this question, he identifies, within this single, complex, and interconnected salvific process, three "reciprocally interpenetrating levels of meaning of the term liberation": (1) the sociopolitical level, (2) the anthropological and cultural level, and (3) liberation from sin.[20] Attempting to describe the relationship among these different dimensions of the mystery of salvation, Gutiérrez writes, "These three levels mutually affect each other, but they are not the same. One is not present without the others, but they are distinct: they are all part of a single, all-encompassing salvific process, but they are to be found at different levels."[21]

The sociopolitical level stresses the interdependent nature of the human person and how each one of us is influenced by the actions of others. At this level, liberation is interpreted not only individually but socially. Thus, it has to do with the political, economic, and social arrangements that shape human existence and help promote, in some cases, the conditions that allow for communal peace to flourish, whereas in others they promote enmity and even institutionalized violence. Hence, this social dimension of liberation exposes those conflictual situations that hinder human existence and reject God's plan for humanity. Like other liberation theologians in Latin America, Gutiérrez enlists the social sciences to attempt to grasp the complex dynamics of human society, including the socioeconomic structures and inequity of the distribution of material resources; the "powers and principalities" that benefit from the status quo; and the political structures, ideologies, and juridical processes used to justify the allocation of communal power. At the same time, the sociopolitical dimension of liberation looks at social reality from "below" by engaging those social movements and revolutionary praxis that seek to transform those socioeconomic structures and political systems that negate human dignity and the God revealed by Jesus Christ.

Gutiérrez sharply delineates between the sociopolitical and anthropological and cultural levels of meaning of liberation when he argues that "persons seek likewise an interior liberation, in an individual and intimate dimension; they seek liberation not only on a social plane but also on a psychological."[22] Liberation on this second level includes the interior flourishing of the human person and the transformation of the human heart. Here history is understood as a process of liberation that engages those forces that prevent the personal realization of the human person. In Latin America, the development of a new consciousness has led oppressed people, who often saw themselves as passive victims of fate, to become aware of their rights and duties and thus become subjects of their own destiny. These qualitatively "new" human beings with a renewed social consciousness are the ones capable of envisioning the creation of a utopian but historically viable new world: a fraternal society. "To conceive of history as a process of human liberation," affirms Gutiérrez, is to understand that "the goal is not only better living conditions, a radical change of structures, a social revolution; it is much more: the continuous creation, never-ending, of a new way to be human, a permanent cultural revolution."[23]

Gutiérrez's third level or dimension of liberation stresses a theological perspective. He notes that sin is the ultimate cause of poverty, injustice, and oppression: "a breach of friendship with God and others." Although this dimension has to do with the relationship between human beings and God, it prioritizes God's salvific activity. Only through Christ in the Holy Spirit can humanity be liberated from sin. Although human beings are called to collaborate in their process of social and personal transformation, liberation comes through God's gratuitous love. Hence, it is God's saving activity that unifies the different dimensions or levels of the liberation process. God liberates us, but this liberation is not just for liberation's sake or only for our sake. Rather, it presupposes overcoming one's sin to be open to others, to reach out to others. In Gutiérrez's words, "The fulness of liberation – a free gift from Christ – is communion with God and with other human beings."[24]

These three levels or dimensions of liberation help us understand the relationship between God's free love and human cooperation in salvation history. Throughout Gutiérrez's treatment of soteriology, there is the underlying understanding that salvation is not something separated from history, waiting in our future, or only present after death. On the contrary, he stresses that salvation begins in history. Because there is a profound unity between salvation history and human history, our commitments and our actions matter. Our collaboration with God's salvific plan has a transcendent impact even if the salvation that we witness in history is partial and temporal. Our efforts have a weight of their own as they respond to the cries of a suffering world, generate hope, and anticipate God's final salvific action for creation. And yet, Gutiérrez consistently insists that our complete liberation will come only with the fullness of God's kingdom. Although human liberation can be understood as a sign of God's kingdom in history, it is not the fullness of salvation and thus should not be conflated with God's ultimate kingdom. As Gutiérrez writes, "Without liberating historical events, there would be no growth of the kingdom. But the process of liberation will not have conquered the very roots of human oppression and exploitation without the coming of the kingdom, which is above all a gift. Moreover, we can say that the historical, political liberating event is the growth of the kingdom and is a salvific event; but it is not the coming of the kingdom, not all of salvation."[25]

A liberating spirituality

The reality that one's spirituality implicitly or explicitly influences and shapes one's theology has been duly acknowledged by some of the theological giants of the last century. To stress this very point, Gustavo Gutiérrez often quotes his old teacher, Marie-Dominique Chenu. Writing in the late 1930s, the eminent French theologian asserted that, "clearly, theological systems are nothing but the expression of spiritualities. That constitutes their interest and their greatness." He then adds, "a theology worthy of the name is a spirituality that has found the appropriate rational instrument for its religious experience."[26] Implicit in these words is one of the central insights that inform Gutiérrez's understanding of a liberating theology: spirituality is the wellspring and the backbone from which a theology of liberation flows.

For this reason, Latin American liberation theologians have insisted from the onset that the practice of liberation demands more than theological categories to guide the people's struggle for liberation. They have thus stressed the central role of spirituality in shaping Christian praxis and theology. In his first book, *A Theology of Liberation,* Gutiérrez already insisted on the need for a spirituality of liberation, noting that "we need a vital attitude, all-embracing and synthesizing, informing the totality as well as every detail of our lives; we need a spirituality."[27] Although some of the basic elements of his spirituality are already present in this book, Gutiérrez develops it in much greater depth and detail in his later book, *We Drink from Our Own Wells* (1983, 2003). The title of the book, drawn from Bernard of Clairvaux, illustrates Gutiérrez's appreciation of his peoples' faith and religiosity as the "well" from which a spirituality of liberation springs.

Gutiérrez makes sure to distinguish between authentic and inauthentic spiritualities. He rejects elitist understandings that assume spirituality is something intended for a small group of Christians – monks, priests, or religious people only. He also criticizes those spiritualties that tend to divide historical reality into sacred and profane planes of existence and assume that to live a spiritual life, Christians need to escape from their daily existence and the world to encounter God. In a similar vein, Gutiérrez distrusts those spiritualities that have a strong individualistic bent that only promotes the actualization of the individual person without attending to the communal and social dimensions. Although the development of one's interior life is indispensable to the spiritual life, spirituality cannot become something private, in which one's relationship with God is disconnected from one's daily life and relationship with others. He writes, "Life according to the Spirit is therefore not an existence at the level of the soul and in opposition to or apart from the body; it is an existence in accord with life, love, and justice (the great values of the reign of God) and against death."[28]

For Gutiérrez, spirituality is the dynamism that invites and calls Christians to live according to the Spirit. As such, it involves all the different aspects of existence and can never be reduced to just a constellation of attitudes or practices that separate us from, and make us unaccountable to, the demands of our surrounding reality. At the root of any authentic spirituality is the experience of God – that is, the encounter with God in a particular place and time. But God always acts first. "To encounter the Lord," affirms Gutiérrez, "is, first of all, to be encountered by the Lord ... In this encounter, we discover where the Lord lives and what the mission is that has been entrusted to us."[29] The Peruvian theologian reminds us how the gospels vividly describe the disciples' experiences with Jesus through the intimacy that verbs such as "see," "hear," and "touch" convey. Such an encounter is deeply marked by God's gratuitous love for us and elicits in us a task – a mission – that seeks to be a gratuitous and reciprocal expression of God's initiating love.

If the encounter with God is the starting point of any authentic Christian spirituality, this encounter also marks a new itinerary in the Trinitarian path of those who become disciples: to follow Jesus toward the Father empowered and guided by the Spirit. Gutiérrez explains that in the gospels the term "to follow" is used to describe the progression of the disciples as they strive to walk in Jesus's footsteps. "It signifies both the obedient acceptance of the Lord's call and the creativity required by the new way they are to travel."[30] Gutiérrez's spirituality evinces a dynamic Trinitarian structure that invites Christian disciples to incarnate themselves in history as the location of our encounter with Christ. Embedded in history and guided by the Spirit, Christian disciples become contemplatives in action in order to discern the signs of the times and advance Jesus's mission therein.

Based on the lived experiences of the Latin American people, Gutiérrez has identified five concrete elements or dispositions that make up his spirituality of liberation: (1) conversion as a requirement for solidarity, (2) gratuitousness as the condition for efficacy, (3) joy in the victory over suffering, (4) spiritual childhood as a condition for commitment with the poor, and (5) the formation of community out of solitude. These interconnected dispositions are the fruits of Latin American Christians who have encountered with God and committed themselves to walking in the life of the Spirit. Such Christians have learned that this new way of following Jesus involves walking closely with the poor in whom God reveals Godself (Matt. 25:31–46) as well as a historical commitment to Jesus's mission and the coming of God's kingdom.

Although conversion is the beginning of every spiritual journey, Gutiérrez explains that a disposition toward conversion should be a permanent condition that allows Christians to enter into a closer relationship with God and their fellow human beings. The conversion necessary to live in solidarity with the poor is not just a definite break from a sinful past. Rather, "it is a work of concrete, authentic love for the poor that is not possible apart from bonds of real friendship with those who suffer despoliation and injustice ... without love and affection, without ... tenderness, there can be no true gesture of solidarity."[31] Such solidarity calls for an ongoing personal openness, vulnerability, and compassion characteristic of a human friendship rooted in a love that is willing to bear and partake in the consequences of sin.

The second disposition of Gutiérrez's spirituality of liberation stresses gratuity. For Gutiérrez, God's first, free, and unmerited love permeates all of Christian life. "Gratuitousness thus marks our lives so that we are led to love gratuitously and to want to be loved gratuitously."[32] Only after we have encountered and experienced God's disinterested love can we extend the same kind of love to others. This love, however, must respond to the concrete circumstance and needs of the loved ones. It must be an efficacious love that is fruitful and practical in the service of the poor, who are favored by God and with whom we stand in solidarity.

The third disposition – joy in the victory over suffering – is the disposition that allows Christians to remain hopeful even when everything seems hopeless. It echoes St. Paul's "hope against hope" (Rom. 4:18), which is the hope of the martyrs, "those who give their lives because they believe in the God life and because they love the dispossessed."[33] Although martyrdom is never sought in itself, Latin American Christians have experienced in their flesh how their love for the poor, witnessed in a world of sin, seems to inevitably lead to the cross. Even against all odds, these Christians choose to become witnesses to Easter with their conviction that the risen Lord has already vanquished death.

The fourth disposition, spiritual childhood as a condition for commitment to the poor, speaks of embracing a stance of utter dependency upon God. Following the insights of the bishops at Medellín Gutiérrez does not understand "spiritual poverty" primarily as "detachment from material goods." Rather, he connects spiritual poverty with a disposition of spiritual childlikeness, which connects to his understanding of being poor in spirit (Matt. 5:3). Gutiérrez is mindful that "poverty is lived not for its own sake, but rather as an authentic imitation of Christ; it is a poverty which means taking on the sinful condition of man to liberate him from sin and all its consequences."[34]

The fifth dimension is the formation of a community, like the Base Christian Communities, that encourages the following of Christ. Those who are committed to being in solidarity with the poor often encounter distrust, suspicion, and many difficulties that give rise to moments of great suffering and deep loneliness. In those circumstances, Gutiérrez explains, "there is a new encounter with oneself and, above all, a new face-to-face encounter with the Lord who is testing and consoling us."[35] But even in those experiences that resemble John of the Cross's frightful night, Gutiérrez adds, Christians do not fail to realize that the deep solitude they feel elicits a hunger for the most radical unity possible: "communion in the life and joy of the resurrection."[36]

Debate, Achievement, and Agenda

More than fifty years after the publication of *A Theology of Liberation,* there is widespread consensus from theologians on the rich contribution Gutiérrez has made to contemporary Christian discourse and the life of the Latin American church. Gutiérrez and other liberation theologians build on the theological insights of the Second Vatican Council to recognize the irruption of the poor in Christian consciousness and offer a response that calls for the church's solidarity with the victims of history. This response, articulated as the preferential option for the poor, has become the hermeneutical perspective that guides the church's pastoral priorities and orients Christian praxis toward a more authentic following of Jesus Christ. As theologian Roberto Goizueta rightly notes, "Today, one cannot do Christian theology, or even think theologically, without in some way confronting the claims implicit in the preferential option for the poor. As Christianity evolves from a predominantly European religion to a religion whose adherents are predominantly found in the third world, those claims will only grow in their relevance and impact."[37]

Although the preferential option for the poor has come to be recognized as the most important contribution of the Latin American church to the universal church, contradiction and criticism have often followed many of its theological champions. Gutiérrez's theological legacy reveals two contrasting dynamics in relation to the Catholic hierarchy. On the one hand, his work has been questioned, received with suspicion, and harshly criticized by the Vatican. On the other hand, over the years, he has demonstrated remarkable resilience in the face of criticism, a willingness to enter into dialogue with those who disagree with him, and the humility to improve on his work based on the suggestion of others. The conflict generated by Gutiérrez's work garnered so much attention that many came to believe that the Peruvian theologian was sanctioned, condemned, or even excommunicated from the church. It must thus be explicitly stated that, though Gutiérrez has been investigated, he has never been formally censored or condemned by the Catholic church.

In March 1983, the Congregation for the Doctrine of the Faith (CDF) sent to the Peruvian Bishops' Conference "Ten Observations on the Theology of Gustavo Gutiérrez." The document questioned his doctrinal orthodoxy and claimed that his theology makes the Marxist understanding of class struggle "the determining principle, from which he goes to reinterpret the Christian Message."[38] In the following years, the CDF published two interrelated documents on liberation theology, *Libertatis Nuntius* in 1984 and *Libertatis Conscientia* in 1986. The first criticized the use of Marxist social analysis used by some liberation theologies, and while not naming names, accused certain liberation theologians of reducing salvation to political liberation. The 1986 document is more positive in tone and offers what the CDF considered a more authentic Christian approach to freedom and liberation.

It should be noted that the polemic against Gutiérrez's work largely reflects the vitriolic reaction of the Vatican and some Latin American government officials toward liberation theology. The mistrust of liberation theology by some members of the church – clergy and laity – arose in part because of a lack of clarity in the early writings of some theologians who enlisted Marxist elements in their theological approach. But it was also fueled by what appears to have been a smear campaign organized against this theology by some influential members of the church. At a more fundamental level, this mistrust also reflected the authoritarian and repressive context in which the church was trying to renew itself. During the Cold War, particularly on a continent governed by the "national security" ideology of the then-ubiquitous military dictatorships, the term "Marxist" inspired fear and was even seen as a just cause for persecution in some Latin American circles. Thus, some church members were apprehensive of a theology that enlisted Marxist analysis as a tool to better understand the prevailing society. Many liberation theologians, including Gutiérrez, were critical of many aspects of Marxism, but their critics questioned whether these theologians could use elements of Marxist thought without also endorsing Marxism's overall atheistic philosophical framework.[39]

Gutiérrez's immediate response to the Vatican's criticism of liberation theology was measured. In an interview with the Peruvian newspaper, *La República*, he explained that the Vatican documents were not condemning liberation theology outright and added that "all together ... these criticisms will help clarify both the scope and the limitations of this theological reflection on action."[40] Indeed, his subsequent work reflects his careful engagement with his critics. For example, in his introductory essay to the fifteenth anniversary of *A Theology of Liberation*'s English language edition, Gutiérrez notes some of the limitations in the scope of his early work and explains that, due to the particular situation in Latin America at the time, he emphasized the social and economic aspects of poverty, when attention ought also to be given to other aspects of oppression such as racial, cultural, and gender discrimination. In this updated edition of *Theology of Liberation* Gutiérrez also carefully distances himself from the "dependency theory" formulated by Latin American social scientists in the mid-1960s that was widely used by liberation theologians in the 1970s. He replaces an original chapter section headed "Christian Brotherhood and Class Struggle," in response to one of the most controversial areas of his work because of its Marxist terminology, with one titled "Faith and Social Conflict." Although Gutiérrez continues to insist that class struggle is a historical fact before which Christians cannot remain neutral, in this updated section he enlists a more expansive terminology that incorporates "class struggle" within the larger category of "social conflict."[41] Here, too, he frames the discussion on conflict and class struggle explicitly within the church's magisterium, drawing heavily on Catholic social teaching and John Paul II's encyclicals. "When I speak of taking into account social conflict, including the existence of class struggle, I am not denying that God's love embraces all without exception. Nor is anyone excluded from our love, for the gospel requires that we love even our enemies."[42] A few years later, Gutiérrez even more explicitly responded to the Vatican documents in his book, *The Truth Shall Make You Free* (1990), where he emphasizes liberation theology's independence from the social analysis it utilizes and insists that Marxism is only one among several useful currents in the social sciences.

If liberation theology and Gutiérrez's works have generated such strong opposition, it is because they show how Christian revelation unveils the connection between poverty and the ethical ambiguity of our social systems and their institutions. We can no longer speak of an objective and impartial theology before a suffering world. By entering into conversation with the poor who bear the weight of our sin and reminding us of God's preferential solidarity with them, Gutiérrez has made theology a tool for the church's conversion as well as an instrument of God's reign.

The last twenty-five years have witnessed some significant changes in the life of Gustavo Gutiérrez. In 1999, he entered the Dominican order and in 2000 was offered an academic chair at the University of Notre Dame – a position he held until moving permanently back to Lima, Peru, in 2019. His sojourn in the United States allowed him to learn from, and collaborate with, other liberation theologies, particularly Latinx, Black, and North American feminist theologies. As has been widely reported, Gutiérrez's relationship with the Vatican has also undergone a remarkable transformation, particularly after the election of Pope Francis in 2013. The change seems to have begun when the Peruvian theologian coauthored a book with the former prefect of the Doctrine of the Faith, Cardinal Gerhard Müller. Pope Francis, who has made concern for the poor central to his pontificate, invited Gutiérrez and Cardinal Müller to concelebrate Mass with him in Rome during the first year of his pontificate. Most telling, in 2018, on the occasion of Gutiérrez's ninetieth birthday, Pope Francis warmly thanked the liberation theologian for his contribution "to the church and humanity through your theological service and your preferential love for the poor and discarded of society."[43]

Notes

1 Gustavo Gutiérrez, *A Theology of Liberation: History, Politics, and Salvation*, trans. and ed. Sister Caridad Inda and John Eagleson, rev. ed. (Maryknoll, NY: Orbis, 1988), 55.

2 David Tombs, *Latin American Liberation Theology* (Leiden: Brill, 2002), 84.

3 Gustavo Gutiérrez, *Líneas Pastorales de la Iglesia en América Latina, Análisis Teológico* (Lima: Centro de Estudio y Publicaciones, 1976).

4 Gutiérrez, *A Theology of Liberation*, xxxiv.

5 Gutiérrez, *A Theology of Liberation*, 3–5.

6 Gustavo Gutiérrez, *Essential Writings*, ed. James Nickoloff (Maryknoll, NY: Orbis, 2004), 24.

7 Gutiérrez, *Essential Writings*, 24.

8 Gutiérrez, *A Theology of Liberation*, 86.

9 Gutiérrez, *A Theology of Liberation*, xxx.

10 Peter Phan, "Method in Liberation Theologies," *Theological Studies* 61 (2000): 43.

11 Gustavo Gutiérrez, "The Option for the Poor Arises from Faith in Christ," *Theological Studies* 70 (2009): 320.

12 Gustavo Gutiérrez, "Option for the Poor," in *Systematic Theology: Perspectives from Liberation Theology*, ed. Jon Sobrino (Maryknoll, NY: Orbis, 1996), 28.

13 Gustavo Gutiérrez, *The Power of the Poor in History* (Maryknoll, NY: Orbis, 1983), 95.

14 Gutiérrez, "The Option for the Poor Arises from Faith in Christ," 325.

15 Gutiérrez, *A Theology of Liberation*, 85, 86, 91

16 Gutiérrez, *A Theology of Liberation*, 83.

17 Gutiérrez, *A Theology of Liberation*, 85.

18 Gustavo Gutiérrez, *The Truth Shall Make You Free: Confrontations*, trans. Matthew J. O'Connell (Maryknoll, NY: Orbis, 1990), 67.

19 Gutiérrez, *The Truth Shall Make You Free*, 106.

20 Gutiérrez, *A Theology of Liberation*, 29.

21   Gutiérrez, *A Theology of Liberation*, 103.
22   Gutiérrez, *A Theology of Liberation*, 20.
23   Gutiérrez, *A Theology of Liberation*, 21.
24   Gutiérrez, *A Theology of Liberation*, 24.
25   Gutiérrez, *A Theology of Liberation*, 104.
26   Marie-Dominique Chenu, *Le Saulchoir: Une ecole de téologie* (Casale Monferrato: Marietti, 1982), 59.
27   Gutiérrez, *A Theology of Liberation*, 117.
28   Gustavo Gutiérrez, *We Drink from Our Own Wells: The Spiritual Journey of a People*, trans. Matthew J. O'Connell (Maryknoll, NY: Orbis, 1984), 71.
29   Gutiérrez, *We Drink from Our Own Wells*, 38.
30   Gutiérrez, *We Drink from Our Own Wells*, 40.
31   Gutiérrez, *We Drink from Our Own Wells*, 104.
32   Gutiérrez, *We Drink from Our Own Wells*, 110.
33   Gutiérrez, *We Drink from Our Own Wells*, 116.
34   Gutiérrez, *We Drink from Our Own Wells*, 172.
35   Gutiérrez, *We Drink from Our Own Wells*, 131.
36   Gutiérrez, *We Drink from Our Own Wells*, 131.
37   Roberto S. Goizueta, "Gustavo Gutiérrez," in *The Blackwell Companion to Political Theology*, ed. Peter Scott and William T. Cavanaugh (Oxford: Blackwell, 2004), 299.
38   Congregation for the Doctrine of the Faith, "Ten Observations on the Theology of Gustavo Gutiérrez," in *Liberation Theology a Documentary History*, ed. Alfred Hennelly (Maryknoll, NY: Orbis, 1997), 349.
39   O. Ernesto Valiente, "The Reception of Vatican II in Latin America," *Theological Studies* 73 (2012): 810–11.
40   Gustavo Gutiérrez, "Interview Given to '*La República*,'" in *Liberation Theology a Documentary History*, ed. Alfred Hennelly (Maryknoll, NY: Orbis, 1997), 420.
41   Gutiérrez, *A Theology of Liberation*, 156.
42   Gutiérrez, *A Theology of Liberation*, 160.
43   Vatican News, "Pope Wishes Fr. Gustavo Gutierrez on 90th Birthday," 2018, https://www.vaticannews.va/en/pope/news/2018-06/pope-francis-letter-gutierrez.html (accessed 4 September 2023).

Recommended Reading

Primary

Gutiérrez, Gustavo. *The God of Life*. Translated by Matthew J. O'Connell. Maryknoll, NY: Orbis, 1991.

———. *On Job: God-Talk and the Suffering of the Innocent*. Translated by Matthew J. O'Connell. Maryknoll, NY: Orbis, 1987.

———. *The Power of the Poor in History*. Translated by Robert R. Barr. Maryknoll, NY: Orbis, 1983.

———. *Spiritual Writings*. Edited by Daniel Groody. Maryknoll, NY: Orbis, 2011.

———. *A Theology of Liberation: History, Politics, and Salvation*. Translated and edited by Sister Caridad Inda and John Eagleson. Revised edition. Maryknoll, NY: Orbis, 1988.

———. *We Drink from Our Own Wells: The Spiritual Journey of a People*. Translated by Matthew J. O'Connell. Maryknoll, NY: Orbis, 1984.

Gutiérrez, Gustavo, and Cardinal Gerhard Ludwig Müller. *On the Side of the Poor: The Theology of Liberation*. Translated by Robert A. Krieg and James B. Nickoloff. Maryknoll, NY: Orbis, 2015.

Secondary

Bingemer, María Clara. *Latin American Theology: Roots and Branches*. Maryknoll, NY: Orbis, 2016.

Brown, Robert McAfee. *Gustavo Gutiérrez: An Introduction to Liberation Theology*. Maryknoll, NY: Orbis, 1990.

Cadorette, Curt. *From the Heart of the People: The Theology of Gustavo Gutiérrez*. Oak Park, IL: Meyer-Stone, 1988.

Castillo, Daniel. *An Ecological Theology of Liberation: Salvation and Political Ecology*. Maryknoll, NY: Orbis, 2019.

Ellis, Marc H., and Otto Maduro, eds. *The Future of Liberation Theology: Essays in Honor of Gustavo Gutiérrez*. Maryknoll, NY: Orbis, 1989.

Goizueta, Roberto S. *Caminemos con Jesús: Toward a Hispanic/Latino Theology of Accompaniment*. Maryknoll, NY: Orbis, 1995.

Sobrino, Jon, and Ignacio Ellacuría, eds. *Mysterium Liberationis: Fundamental Concepts of Liberation Theology*. Maryknoll, NY: Orbis, 1993.

Twentieth-Century Theology in North America

K. Healan Gaston

Introduction

Anglophone theology in twentieth-century North America was profoundly responsive to shifting social conditions, even as many of its practitioners sought to insulate Christianity from those conditions. In the United States, especially, the massive social dislocations associated with rapid industrialization between 1870 and 1920 set the stage for a vigorous dialogue on the church's entanglements with, and roles in, specific historical settings. Whereas the dialectical analysis employed by Karl Barth and his Western European followers pointed in the direction of transcendence, the dialectic that preoccupied many Protestant theologians in the United States concerned Christianity and its social contexts: the church and the world. Such questions also loomed large for Catholic theologians, especially because the main social divisions were often replicated within the Catholic Church itself.

For many of these figures, the most theologically salient feature of "the world" was its division into various groups – nations, classes, races, ethnicities – that stood in tension or outright conflict, vitiating traditional conceptions of love and brotherhood. What could Christianity mean in a world of bitter labor conflicts, global war, and systemic oppression that sometimes spilled over into genocide? US theologians were affected less directly than their Western European counterparts by the horrors of World War I, the Holocaust, and World War II. Thus, they tended to view those particular historical events as examples of more general patterns of social conflict that Christianity could and should address, if its relationship to the particular historical conditions of the twentieth century could be properly understood.

As the century unfolded, theologians incorporated additional resources, especially from psychology, as they addressed the relations between individuals as well as groups. After the mid-1960s, as the Cold War eased and liberation movements multiplied, many theologians enlisted Christianity directly on the side of downtrodden groups – and they increasingly came from those groups themselves. But that was merely the sharpest edge of a longer and broader shift, stretching across much of the twentieth century (and beyond), toward theologically informed conceptions of pluralism that opened doors to religious outsiders and other traditionally maligned groups.

Ford's The Modern Theologians: An Introduction to Christian Theology since 1918, Fourth Edition.
Edited by Rachel Muers and Ashley Cocksworth.

This broad pluralizing impulse overlapped with multiple waves of theological attacks, unfolding over many decades, directed at the modes of liberal Protestantism that dominated the US religious scene in the early years of the twentieth century and remained powerful into the 1960s. The irony is only apparent; although liberal Protestants are now some of the most consistent champions of diversity in the United States, that was not as true of their theological forebears in 1880, 1900, or even 1920. In the late nineteenth century, a number of liberal theologians did join some of their Western European counterparts in recognizing the existence, and even the achievements, of non-Christian "world religions." Yet these figures remained Christian triumphalists in the end, welcoming other faiths temporarily in the hope of superseding them in the long run. They had inherited an evangelical sensibility and an American exceptionalist tendency that identified the United States as the site where God's plan would soon unfold, resulting in the Christianization of the world.[1] It was the succeeding generations of theologians, starting in the 1920s, who slowly began to create genuine theological room for the existence of other faith traditions, and for human difference more broadly. And many of those figures simultaneously worked to replace the conceptual pillars of theological liberalism.

Survey and Debate

Theology in the early twentieth century exhibited several important continuities with earlier developments. Although its influence had somewhat waned, for example, the colonial-era view of the United States as a "covenant nation" with a special role in the divine narrative continued to circulate in more or less diluted forms. Meanwhile, the regime of church–state separation also strongly influenced theology in the United States, not least by sustaining a general ethos of voluntarism that had produced a welter of Protestant denominational organizations by the mid-nineteenth century. Finally, as in Western Europe, controversies around historical criticism and Darwinian evolution continued to roil the Protestant churches. The timing in the United States had been somewhat different, as most theologians had grappled with both of these tendencies simultaneously and had done so only in the 1870s and 1880s, after the upheavals of the Civil War and Reconstruction. But the rise of the fundamentalist movement in the 1920s would show the strength of the theological and cultural resistance to both of these liberalizing forces.[2]

Still, while the growth of the natural sciences and biblical analysis shaped much theological effort in the late nineteenth century, the primary context for doing theology in North America in the twentieth century was social movements and social ethics. This was true of the liberalism that had taken shape since the Civil War, and it was likewise true, if often in different ways, of the oppositional theological movements that followed.[3] Protestant liberals had managed to assimilate Darwinism rather quickly, developing a "progressive evolutionism" that saw Christian morality as the goal of a thoroughly teleological and divinely ordained process of evolutionary growth. That reconciliation with modern science allowed them to focus on the social meanings of biblical texts, which the writings of Horace Bushnell and other mid-nineteenth-century thinkers increasingly inspired them to read symbolically and metaphorically rather than literally.[4]

This is not to say that theologians abandoned thorny epistemological and metaphysical questions in the early twentieth century. Some, such as Union Theological Seminary's William Adams Brown and Colgate's William Newton Clarke, asserted the independent authority of theological tenets alongside science's empirical findings. Others hewed more closely to the boundaries created by modern science. In varying ways, the empirical theology of the Canadian-born D. C. Macintosh at Yale and the religious naturalism of Chicago-based figures such as Henry Nelson Wieman found God immanent in natural processes, which served as instruments of a divine plan. Some liberal theologians, such as Borden Parker Bowne, even managed to reconcile modern tendencies with a personal view of God by defining persons as the ultimate units of reality and God as supreme among that dense web of persons.[5]

By 1900, however, the "social question" played a central role in theological debates. In the United States, the assimilation of the higher criticism and Darwinism coincided with the start of industrialization, which soon massively exceeded prior examples in both speed and its scope. The great industrial era from roughly 1880 to 1920 set off historically unprecedented movements of human beings from diverse religious, racial, and ethnic backgrounds around the globe. The United States, with its burgeoning factories, received tens of millions of these individuals. And with government regulation virtually absent, the human cost of those factories became immediately apparent: thousands upon thousands of workers – including young children – maimed or killed by machinery; the vast waves of unemployment, poverty, and hunger accompanying catastrophic business cycles; and economic inequality on a previously unimaginable scale. Where was God in relation to such a world? Already by the 1880s, that question stood front and center for theologians of many stripes. US theological liberals increasingly viewed God as immanent in history, operating through social processes.[6]

Theological liberalism and the Social Gospel

The main question was how Christians ought to respond to the emerging industrial society. In which social tendencies could God be found? How could these be strengthened? As industrialization began, many theological liberals followed a pattern characteristic of earlier Protestant responses to capitalism, tying their eschatological hopes to the economic process itself. In this view, the outcomes of industrialization – like market exchange before it – could be shaped by the churches. Pious Christian capitalists would fuel an extensive program of charitable giving, bringing every individual into the virtuous upward spiral of personal rectitude, hard work, and just rewards.[7]

Through subsequent decades, liberals remained deeply moralistic and evangelical, aiming to spread Christian love and charity throughout the population. But by the 1880s, as the full impact of industrialization came into view, the advocates of an emerging "Social Gospel" concluded that unfettered economic competition was responsible for industrial society's deeply un-Christian features. As the human costs of industrialization became a central theological problem, many contended that moral and political constraints on business enterprise embodied God's work on earth, portending a society based on cooperation and brotherhood rather than competition. The Social Gospelers become some of the most influential advocates of "Progressivism," a regulation-friendly, conflict-averse, and often explicitly Protestant sensibility that dominated electoral politics in the United States from 1900 to 1920. In its US iterations, then, liberal Protestant theology came to be closely associated with both the Social Gospel and political Progressivism. These associations would strongly shape the reactions of future theologians.

Advocates of the Social Gospel varied in their specific economic programs. Some advocated relatively mild reform programs, whereas others ventured onto the terrain of socialism. Theologically, however, figures such as Washington Gladden, George D. Herron, Charles Sheldon, and W. D. P. Bliss shared a number of common themes. Like their Protestant forebears in the United States, they focused heavily on the need for evangelism, aiming to spread Christian morality to all individuals. They also centered their theology on the historical Jesus, viewed as not only a personal savior but also an exemplar of piety and righteousness who had lived out the tenets of the Sermon on the Mount. And as postmillennialists, they expected the kingdom of God to take shape in their lifetimes, and presumably in the United States. To these relatively familiar concepts, the Social Gospel theologians added the concepts of "social sin" and "social salvation," rejecting individualistic understandings of those key Christian terms and insisting that redemption was inseparable from collective action in – and on – the surrounding social context. At a time when the growing embrace of historical criticism and Darwinism had opened up a significant gap between Protestant theologians and ministers, on the one hand, and their congregations, on the other, the pioneering Social

Gospelers worked outside the seminaries, wrote for large audiences rather than professional theologians, and had a direct and powerful impact.[8]

After 1900, the Social Gospel found its most sophisticated and influential proponent in the theologian Walter Rauschenbusch. In the late 1880s and 1890s, leading a congregation of poor German immigrants in Manhattan's notorious Hell's Kitchen, Rauschenbusch saw firsthand the impact of industrial capitalism. At Rochester Theological Seminary after 1897, he wove together strands of pietism with liberal theology, especially the varieties he had encountered in Germany during a lengthy sabbatical leave several years earlier. Rauschenbusch agreed with Albrecht Ritschl and Adolf von Harnack that theology was inseparable from its social contexts. However, he interpreted their central concept of the kingdom of God in more politically progressive terms. Calling himself a Christian socialist, he insisted that all believers needed to champion the downtrodden in order to redeem the new industrial order. It was imperative to join forces with God, engaging in sustained social action to promote economic justice.[9]

In addition to his many lectures around the United States, Rauschenbusch outlined this theological program in the widely read book *Christianity and the Social Crisis* (1907). There, he argued that the teachings of Christ and the Hebrew prophets should be viewed in historical and social, rather than eschatological, terms. In the modern world, Christian tenets spoke directly to the prevailing social crisis and could not be interpreted in isolation from it. Rauschenbusch proceeded to articulate more clearly the social and political dimensions of his vision in *Christianizing the Social Order* (1912) and the systematic theological doctrines underlying it in *A Theology for the Social Gospel* (1917). Although the latter book has proven influential in the long run, its immediate impact was muted, as Rauschenbusch's ties to Germany and calls for American neutrality in World War I brought him under suspicion.[10]

Whereas the leading Social Gospelers championed the working class, they often said less about – and sometimes reinforced – racial and sexual discrimination. Yet the Social Gospel vision was sufficiently capacious to appeal to many Black Christian leaders, though certainly not a majority. For example, Booker T. Washington and W. E. B. Du Bois made important contributions to Black Americans' understandings of the Gospel. Similarly, although the visions of the kingdom of God that circulated among many Protestants did not necessarily make room for non-Protestants, the Social Gospel also appealed to John A. Ryan and a number of other US Catholic leaders who advocated wage increases and other economic reforms. These figures worked to apply the framework of Catholic social thought developed under Leo XIII to an industrializing, multiethnic democracy. In this sense, Ryan and his counterparts reinforced an emerging sense of theology's social embeddedness, or at least social implications. Still, although shared political goals created affinities between left-leaning Protestants and Catholics, each group still expected the other's tradition – and all other contenders – to vanish in a properly Christianized world.[11]

Between the wars

The experience of World War I was not nearly as cataclysmic and disillusioning in the United States as it was in Europe. Indeed, the optimism and progressive orientation of the Social Gospel carried straight through the 1920s, as did its focus on social ethics. Yet 1920s liberals such as Harry Emerson Fosdick and Shailer Mathews were hardly uncritical celebrants of modern tendencies. To be sure, they embraced developments in the natural sciences, and many aspects of the human sciences as well. But for liberals, as for many other Protestant theologians, the main context in the early 1920s was not the shock of the war but rather the alarming implications of the new consumerism and youth culture that followed in its wake. For theologically conservative critics of the pro-business boosterism that dominated US public culture in the 1920s, that phenomenon made a mockery of the liberals' prediction that material progress would fuel moral progress. For more liberal critics, it was a sign that religious obscurantism still ruled the roost and the modernization of religion needed to be pursued even more strenuously.[12]

Other social and cultural changes produced the same kinds of theological debates. For example, the notable loosening of personal morality – especially sexual morality – among youth on college campuses and in urban areas generated similar disagreements about the proper foundations for a Christian culture. Another cause for alarm was the new way of life taking shape in the suburbs, marked by conformity, philistinism, and a technology-obsessed imperative to "keep up with the Joneses" at all costs. The liberal Shailer Mathews was no less horrified by such apparent evidences of rapid secularization than were his theologically conservative critics. They disagreed mainly as to which kind of Christianity would most effectively confront secularization and the resulting forms of moral decline.[13]

In response to such cultural and theological challenges, Social Gospelers and other liberals sought to further hone and promote their theological orientations. Questions about social movements, social ethics, and the values of the burgeoning middle class remained central for them, even as the prospect of a regime of economic regulation seemed much farther off than it had in 1910 or even 1915. One path forward involved practical cooperation between liberals across all Protestant denominations, and perhaps even with their Catholic and Jewish counterparts. But 1920s liberalism, like its forebears, did not always point the way toward religious pluralism. Even some advocates of the interfaith movement that took shape in the 1920s did not, in the end, acknowledge the legitimacy of other faiths, let alone develop a theological basis for accepting them – although decisive moves in that direction were underway in other circles. In any case, most liberals believed the main issue was Christianity's perceived irrelevance to modern social problems, and the proper response was to orient the church even more directly toward those problems. The proximate enemy was not unfettered capitalism but rather a persistent commitment to the literal truth of the Bible that, liberals believed, was steadily souring the public on Christianity.[14]

Far from a remnant of the past, that kind of literalism was actually growing in the 1920s. A resurgent movement to throw off historical criticism and take Christians back to the text of the Bible gave rise to Protestant fundamentalism in the years around World War I. For its advocates, the developments of the 1920s further reinforced the core claim that straying too far from the Bible led to moral chaos. Fundamentalists stressed the need for a personal relationship with Christ, but many placed even greater emphasis on the literal text of the Bible. This approach, known as biblical literalism, led them to reject both the higher criticism, with its emphasis on the contingent and constructed nature of the Bible and its focus on the historical Jesus, and Darwinism, which flouted the biblical account of life on earth and the very conception of an omniscient, omnipotent God. Many other theological conservatives, including the Princeton Calvinist J. Gresham Machen, likewise blamed theological liberalism for the church's apparent inability to forestall rampant moral decline. In this context, pitched battles between "fundamentalists" and "modernists" raged across the Protestant denominations, with the modernists ultimately winning the day everywhere except the Southern Baptist Convention.[15]

By the early 1930s, theological liberals faced opposition on a second front from a group of Protestants who earned the rather misleading label "neo-orthodox" but are more accurately described as Christian realists. Indeed, these figures were far from orthodox, in that they still read the Bible metaphorically rather than literally. Yet they targeted the moralism, the optimism, and the immanentism – in short, the views of humanity and of God – characteristic of US liberal theology. Unlike the European neo-orthodoxy inspired by the work of Karl Barth, American neo-orthodoxy is best understood as a critique of theological liberalism from within the liberal fold. The criticisms of such thinkers could be scathing, as when H. Richard Niebuhr described theological liberalism as the view that "a God without wrath brought men without sin into a Kingdom without judgment through the ministrations of a Christ without a Cross." But the social and political tenor of the guiding themes and questions and the undeniable opposition to many aspects of Barth's theology made American neo-orthodoxy distinct. And whereas fundamentalists, who were often aggressively anti-intellectual, operated on or beyond the fringes of the establishment, Christian realists targeted liberals within their own academic strongholds and exhibited a much higher degree of sophistication. Indeed, these figures often arrayed the cultural and intellectual authority of Europe against homegrown versions of theological liberalism.[16]

The central figures in the development of Christian realism were the brothers Reinhold and H. Richard Niebuhr. As the children of recent German immigrants to the United States, the Niebuhr brothers had an insider perspective on the kinds of group dynamics that some liberal theologians and the new field of sociology aimed to describe. Questions about religious, racial, and class identity and the dynamics of nationalism, pluralism, and secularism quickly became central to their thought. Meanwhile, their fluency in German gave them advanced access to cutting-edge German ideas; they repeatedly brought resources from German theology and sociology into the US conversation, though their immigrant consciousness in an increasingly multiethnic and multireligious country often led them to interpret such concepts quite differently than did their European counterparts.[17]

At the same time, each of the Niebuhr brothers developed his own distinctive perspectives and methods as he worked to reorient theological liberalism.[18] Although Reinhold Niebuhr's public fame would soon eclipse that of his more academically inclined brother, it was H. Richard who made the first big contribution to scholarship. As did Reinhold in his early articles, H. Richard took up the category of "the prophetic" from German sources. That concept had gone through many permutations as it traveled through the writings of the liberal theologian Adolf von Harnack, the historical theologian Ernst Troeltsch, and the early sociologist Max Weber. Having written his dissertation on Troeltsch, H. Richard sought to apply the German theologian's historical-critical method to the distinctive features of the US case in what is now seen as the founding text of US sociology of religion: *The Social Sources of Denominationalism* (1929). There, Niebuhr skewered the denominational fragmentation of American Protestantism. Because denominational Christianity ultimately took its shape from the petty conflicts of a fractured world, he contended, it could hardly offer the ethical integration that such a world desperately needed. However, in *The Kingdom of God in America* (1937), Niebuhr shifted his focus to the spiritual forces animating even these wrongheaded efforts. He sought to recover from them a strong prophetic strain in American Christianity that could not be reduced to social or economic motives and that sought to transform the United States in light of Christian ideals rather than sacralize the nation as it currently existed.[19]

As H. Richard Niebuhr's star rose in theological circles, Reinhold Niebuhr also made a major contribution to scholarship with his 1932 book *Moral Man and Immoral Society*. Today, that important book, which took its title from a phrase by Troeltsch, is widely regarded as a founding text of Christian social ethics. It emphasized the intransigency of social conflicts and insisted that neither individual morality nor scientific rationality, whether alone or in combination, could effectively address such conflicts. The sinful expressions of self-interest that haunted all human action did not exempt forms of thought such as moral philosophy and social science, let alone their translation into particular decisions on an everyday basis. Challenging the pacifist tendency of liberal Protestantism, Niebuhr argued that Christians would need to become comfortable with using power in order to achieve something like justice, even if they could never ensure the moral purity of their goals. They would also need to recognize the ubiquity of sin – which Niebuhr equated to self-interest – in human affairs, including even the most abstract forms of reasoning. Given how widespread pacifism was in progressive circles during these years, Niebuhr's meditations on the use of force created quite a stir.[20]

The Niebuhr brothers' writings of the 1930s revealed both the starting point they shared and the divergent ways in which they built upon it. For both, liberalism was not only strategically wrong but also represented a form of idolatry that substituted human goals, values, and institutions for God. Nothing human, including even love, could stand in for God. The two tended to disagree on when and how action was nonetheless needed. Reinhold saw God's will at stake in every choice – including the choice not to act – and suggested that human beings could roughly discern the proper path by taking account of their own self-interest and seeking an approximation of genuine justice. By contrast, H. Reinhold typically advocated contemplation and watchful waiting in order to discern God's larger plan, which might not conform to human conceptions of justice, let alone love. But the brothers agreed that liberalism consistently erred by erecting false human idols and divinizing human conceptions of progress.[21]

In 1933, Reinhold Niebuhr helped bring to Union Theological Seminary another preeminent theologian who had become a key source of inspiration for both brothers: the German émigré Paul Tillich. The previous year, H. Richard Niebuhr had published an English translation of Tillich's recent book *The Religious Situation*. Now, as Tillich was pushed out by the Nazis, the admiration of the Niebuhr brothers and many others facilitated his move to the United States. His work brought new dimensions and themes to US theological discourse. In the 1930s, to take just one example, Tillich's work helped Reinhold Niebuhr identify the kind of truth that he believed Christianity offered and modern science did not: namely, mythical truth, which was symbolic and yet deeper than merely empirical knowledge. During this time, Tillich was also developing his concept of the "Protestant principle," a spiritual impulse toward self-criticism that constantly pushed against the idolatrous substitution of human institutions or values for God.[22]

The explicit and implicit debates between Tillich, Reinhold Niebuhr, H. Richard Niebuhr, and their followers and interlocutors would define much of the tenor of Protestant theology in the United States into the early 1960s. One key feature of that style of theology was its openness to dialogue with thinkers from other faith traditions, especially Judaism and Catholicism. Some liberal Protestants had engaged with their Jewish counterparts, especially from the Reform tradition, since the late nineteenth century. And World War I had brought limited forms of practical cooperation between Protestants, Catholics, and Jews. These endeavors began to bear theological fruit in the 1930s. Among Protestants, Reinhold Niebuhr's emphasis on the Hebrew prophets made him especially attentive to Judaism; he became the leading Protestant advocate of Zionism as well. Tillich, likewise, had been in dialogue with Jewish thinkers in Europe and emphasized the Jewish roots and character of prophetic criticism.

By the late 1930s, a few Catholic leaders were also testing the limits of the church's ban on interreligious dialogue, seeking out theological grounds for some kind of concerted action against shared threats to all three faith traditions. Another émigré, the lay philosopher Jacques Maritain, did important work here. Decades earlier, shortly after meeting one another in France, Maritain and his wife Raïssa had converted from Protestantism and Judaism, respectively. Becoming a leading voice of neo-Thomism, he argued in his writings of the 1930s that the natural law was both fully Christian – indeed, fully Catholic – and also a common ground on which Catholics and those of other faith traditions could converge. It thus offered the possibility of a form of democracy that was infused with Christianity and yet welcoming of other faiths as well. Maritain was particularly concerned to make room for Jews in his conceptions of the natural law and democracy.[23]

After 1940, the young Jesuit theologian John Courtney Murray sought to clarify Maritain's insights about the capacity of natural law to serve as a neutral, nontheological meeting ground between the faith traditions – and, importantly, to square that argument with official church teachings about the impermissibility of theological dialogue across confessional boundaries. Given the existential threat to all religions posed by an ascendant secularism, Murray argued, Catholics should – at least in the short run – encourage Protestants and Jews to adopt more orthodox understandings of their faiths, not seek their full conversion to the one true faith. Theological differences could be worked out once the common enemy of secularism had been defeated.[24]

Murray's position reflected a growing embrace of religious pluralism that would spread far and wide after World War II. Although many US theologians, ranging from the most liberal to the most orthodox, still rejected rival traditions outright when the war began, a growing number contended that modern conditions – either the threat of secularism or the simple demand of justice – required them to acknowledge the authenticity, and perhaps even the partial validity, of other faiths.[25]

Wartime and postwar theology

As earlier, the cataclysmic events of the World War II years were considerably more abstract for most US theologians than for Europeans. Several other issues immediately impinged on those moral catastrophes as well: the passing of global leadership from Great Britain to the United States, the Cold War and remilitarization that quickly followed, the bureaucratization of many areas of daily life, and the reappearance of suburban consumer culture on a massively expanded scale. Even attempts at theological reckoning with the Holocaust were colored by these other postwar phenomena in the United States.

In this context, Reinhold Niebuhr became the country's leading public theologian, and one of its most visible intellectuals overall. His writings of the mid-1940s and beyond built on his wartime effort to systematize his theology in *The Nature and Destiny of Man*. That two-volume work articulated a theological anthropology and sought to demonstrate that the Christian tradition best captured the two key dimensions of human nature. The first was a drive toward self-transcendence, as symbolized by the *imago Dei*. The other was an inescapable finitude, captured by the images of the Fall and original sin, that stood at the meeting point of self-interest with hubris and ultimately doomed all efforts at self-transcendence to a tragic end. Although Niebuhr devoted considerable energy to explicating Western intellectual history, he also reflected on divine grace, the meaning of the Cross, and other traditional themes. His subsequent books, especially *The Children of Light and the Children of Darkness* (1944) and *The Irony of American History* (1952), wove together Niebuhr's theological insights on sin and grace with astute historical, political, and cultural analysis, influencing readers from a wide range of religious backgrounds. These works made Reinhold Niebuhr's general theological stance synonymous – for better or for worse – with the chastened, realistic liberalism that dominated US politics from the late 1940s to the mid-1960s.[26]

At the same time, the overall tenor of public religiosity in the United States moved in a rather different direction than Niebuhr's work. The "postwar religious revival" brought overt, even extravagant religious commitments into every area of US life, from film to foreign policy. Drive-in churches and revival meetings in Madison Square Garden symbolized an intense commitment to faith itself that overlapped substantially with burgeoning anticommunism. Myriad public figures portrayed the Cold War as a battle between good and evil – and in the process, implicitly divinized the consumerist, conformist society of the postwar United States. At the same time, the dominant forms of faith also challenged theological liberalism. Conservative modes of Protestant evangelicalism flourished, as Billy Graham quickly became one of the best-known religious figures in US history. However, Graham's media presence was rivaled by that of the Catholic bishop Fulton Sheen, who hosted wildly popular programs on radio and then television that attracted millions of Protestants as well as Catholics. Popular figures such as Graham and Sheen repeatedly attacked theological liberalism but were relatively sanguine about the prevailing economic and social patterns of the 1940s and 1950s.[27]

As in the 1920s, the tendency of postwar public religiosity to buttress shallow forms of consumerism and conformity presented many theologians with a conundrum. Reinhold Niebuhr was one of many who saw serious threats to Christian faith in these postwar developments rather than celebrating them as a victory. He blasted what he considered the essential secularity of postwar US religiosity: its blasphemous elevation of human phenomena such as capitalism, affluence, and even democracy itself to putatively divine status as suitable objects of worship. In his view, and that of many other theologians, postwar religiosity replicated the essential error that had vitiated liberal theology: namely, its sacralization of merely human phenomena and its consequent inability to recognize the true nature and import of the divine. Heated debates about the authenticity of the postwar revival shaped theological work in the United States through the 1950s and the early 1960s.

H. Richard Niebuhr also shared this skepticism toward the postwar explosion of overt statements of faith. Though he was not a public figure like Reinhold, his wartime and postwar works continued to break important theological ground and inspired a host of followers in that domain, including his numerous students at Yale Divinity School. Although H. Richard remained skeptical about not only the idolatrous faiths of the Cold War era but also his brother's relentless insistence on the need for human action in the world despite the ever-present reality of sin, he did view history as a key site for divine action, and even revelation. As early as 1941, in *The Meaning of Revelation*, he argued that unlike an "external" perspective on history, as it appeared from the outside, the "internal" perspective of the participants in that history could serve as an avenue for revelation, with the contours of divine action becoming gradually visible to a faith community. In a series of postwar writings, Niebuhr analyzed competing models of the relationship between Christianity and its cultural contexts, outlined a "theocentric" approach that could temper the worship of merely human or historical phenomena as false idols, and crafted a foundation for ethics rooted in the capacity of human beings to respond in a responsible fashion to God's action in the world.[28]

Paul Tillich's writings also proved extremely influential after World War II, as he increasingly wrote in a popular as well as professional register. Whereas H. Richard Niebuhr's God acted in the world, however, Tillich's God was essentially coterminous with the world. Between 1951 and 1963, Tillich published two widely read popular works and a three-volume systematics. Engaging deeply with existentialism and figures such as Heidegger, he rejected all forms of "theological theism" identifying God as merely the most important and powerful among many discrete beings. Instead, Tillich famously defined God in ontological terms as the "infinite and inexhaustible depth and ground of all being." As such, he contended, God could not be captured in rational propositions, which inevitably partook of anthropomorphism. Yet statements about God could have a mythical or symbolic truth, and therefore a sacred quality. Tillich's *Systematic Theology* elaborated this conception of a "God above the God of theism" and spelled out a "method of correlation" that identified parallels between Christian teachings and secular philosophical insights. His approach fit well with psychological and existential emphasis of postwar thought and also resonated with the new social movements of the 1960s and beyond.[29]

Some of the same tendencies appeared in postwar Catholic thought, though they remained suppressed until the Second Vatican Council reforms of 1962–5 radically altered the Catholic Church's stance on church–state separation, interfaith dialogue, and many other issues. John Courtney Murray found himself censured in the mid-1950s for his continued efforts to articulate a theological foundation for practical forms of interfaith cooperation against the shared enemy of secularism. But just a few years later, by the time of the Second Vatican Council, he had been rehabilitated and served as a primary architect of the council's statement on religious liberty, *Dignitatis humanae*. The Catholic Church's opening to new perspectives and new possibilities also created room for a host of new theological approaches that had been stirring below the surface of official doctrine, many of these echoing themes common among Protestants of the era as well. As they had all along, but now far more openly, Catholic theologians engaged Barth, Heidegger, Whitehead, existentialism, evolutionary theory, mysticism, and many other aspects of modern thought and experience.[30]

These Protestant and Catholic theologians increasingly influenced one another in the postwar years. There were important points of connection between Reinhold Niebuhr and Murray, especially. But more broadly, nonevangelical Protestants proved increasingly receptive to Catholic views after 1945, and Catholics were able to reciprocate openly after the Second Vatican Council stressed the promise rather than the danger of dialogue between faith traditions. Among Protestants themselves, meanwhile, ecumenical impulses accelerated apace, and with them cross-denominational theological exchanges. Both Protestants and Catholics also reexamined their relations with Judaism in light of the Holocaust and the creation of the state of Israel. Indeed, the broad Jewish–Christian alliance against secularism that small circles of Protestants, Catholics, and Jews had sought in the 1930s became an ever-present reality in the postwar United States, often appearing in crudely anticommunist forms but also operating among figures such as Niebuhr who deplored the easy equation of Christianity with the American way of life.[31]

In most cases, the interreligious campaign against secularism also targeted theological liberals, who were seen as having handed over cognitive and cultural authority to secular forces and abandoned the defining features of their faith traditions. It took aim as well at the stricter reading of church–state separation enshrined by the Supreme Court of the United States in the late 1940s. A broad array of critics argued that the Court's new approach would stamp out religion entirely while establishing secularism as a kind of official state faith. The ubiquitous term "Judeo-Christian" usually reflected this ecumenical antisecularism, which often entailed equally staunch resistance to both religious liberalism and strict separationism.[32]

By contrast, postwar evangelicals continued to view interreligious dialogue and cooperation as existential dangers, with one tiny but significant exception: some evangelicals, led by Lewis Sperry Chafer, proclaimed a Christian form of Zionism that described the return of the Jews to the holy land as a crucial stage in history, though it also held that Judaism itself would later disappear. Other changes also took place, as conservatives far from the spotlight of Billy Graham's revivals developed their views and debated core principles. Chafer, who had penned a series of popular works as well as theological writings since the 1910s, produced a massive *Systematic Theology* in 1947 that codified Christian Zionism as part of a broader and highly influential framework of premillennial dispensationalism. Such frameworks would anchor fundamentalism in the decades to come, while fueling intense disagreements over the rapture, the meanings of the Book of Revelation, and other key issues. Darwinism continued to preoccupy fundamentalists and other evangelicals as well. In 1961, John C. Whitcomb and Henry M. Morris rehabilitated young earth creationism, which held that geological evidence matched the literal timeline of the Bible, by updating the "flood geology" of the 1920s Adventist George McCready Price.[33]

Evangelicals, including those who rejected dispensationalism and its offshoots, also developed new apologetic arguments against unbelievers and theological liberals. One example was Carl F. H. Henry, who urged evangelicals to abandon the anti-intellectualism of the fundamentalists and spread biblical teachings throughout the secular world, including the learned professions. He insisted that any meaningful theological argument – indeed, even rationality itself – required a foundation in revelation. Another important evangelical theologian, Cornelius Van Til, developed a "presuppositionalist" approach that identified God's being as the necessary presupposition of any form of reasoning or meaning-making. Later in the century, such approaches would serve as crucial points of rapprochement between evangelicals and critics of modern thought from a range of other traditions.[34]

Theology since the 1960s

One key development after 1970 was the rapid spread of such evangelical perspectives among US citizens and their incorporation into a politically mobilized Christian Right, rooted in a convergence between conservative Protestants and Catholics that had theological as well as practical dimensions. In fact, despite its emphasis on the unchanging, literal truth of the Bible, fundamentalism, like allied forms of evangelicalism, continued to evolve in the late twentieth century. Amid the controversy triggered by the Supreme Court's legalization of abortion in *Roe v. Wade* (1973), for example, many conservative Protestants embraced the Catholic view that life begins at conception. Myriad theological disagreements about politics, personal faith, and the Bible continued to divide those who joined forces in the new Christian Right. But on one key point they agreed: Catholicism, at least in its more conservative forms, was far less dangerous than secularism or theological liberalism.

A second and very different tendency emerged on the left, where the social movements of the 1960s and 1970s spun off schools of theology that read Christian teachings through the lens of specific forms of collective oppression. The Social Gospel orientation had persisted among some Black religious leaders, most notably Howard Thurman, through and beyond World War II. In the 1950s, Martin Luther King Jr., himself a theologian as well as activist, had taken lessons about power, resistance, and the social import of theology from not only Rauschenbusch's writings and Thurman's 1949 classic *Jesus and the Disinherited* but also Reinhold Niebuhr's insights into the intransigence of power and group identity. By the 1960s, the emphasis on theology's embeddedness in particular social contexts and the insistence that Christianity demanded action on behalf of the oppressed took new forms, with a special emphasis on the collective experiences of subnational (or supranational) groups. More than mere collections of individuals, these groups had their own paths and destinies. Whereas Latin American liberation theologians tended to focus on capitalism and class, their counterparts in the United States most often identified race and gender as the main axes of oppression that obligated Christians to seek social justice through action in the world.[35]

A key development, inaugurating a self-conscious tradition of Black theology, was the 1969 publication of James H. Cone's *Black Theology and Black Power*. Cone argued that scripture should be read with regard to the collective experience of Black Americans and for the express purpose of improving their lot. He and his successors sought to reconcile the prophetic, liberatory Christianity championed by King with Malcolm X's emphasis on the brutality of the Black experience in the United States. In so doing, they drew on not only the work of professional theologians but also centuries-long vernacular traditions of Black protest and everyday faith in the service of resistance. Christianity, in this view, found its core meaning in the divinely ordained call to free those who were oppressed.[36]

The previous year, Mary Daly's *The Church and the Second Sex* had issued a parallel call to view theology – in her case, the Catholic tradition – through the lens of women's experience and for the purposes of women's liberation. If Tillich rightly understood God as the ground of being, Daly reasoned, then God could not be enlisted on the side of powerful social groups against others who partook equally of being. Also taking up the torch of feminist theology was Rosemary Radford Ruether, another Catholic theologian who observed the developments of the era from her post at the historically Black Howard University. Ruether's *Liberation Theology* (1972) ranged across multiple social movements, asserting a Christian imperative to challenge patriarchy alongside racism, imperialism, and anti-Semitism. Feminists inspired by Daly and Ruether sought to reinterpret the meanings of Christian symbols and terminology, just as they aimed to recover the lost histories of women in the church and to reform its contemporary practices.[37]

Although Ruether forged links between social movements, other theologians emphasized the specificity of particular groups' experiences. Thus, Katie Geneva Cannon and others in the womanist movement that took shape in the late 1980s adopted the perspective of Black women and emphasized their distinctiveness vis-à-vis both Black men and White feminists. Theologies rooted in queerness, disability, and other identity categories soon emerged as well. Like Black and feminist theologies, these approaches were keyed to specific systems of social oppression and aimed at the practical goal of dismantling them. A foundational call to seek justice anchored such theologies.[38]

A third characteristic mode of theological reasoning in the late twentieth century sought productive relationships between Christian insights and secular forms of knowledge and social practice. An early and dramatic example was the "death of God" theology championed by Thomas J. J. Altizer and others in the 1960s. Although that metaphor proved capable of many readings, the movement's leaders were all known for incorporating a wide range of intellectual resources. Altizer, for example, drew heavily on the poet William Blake and the iconic continental philosophers Friedrich Nietzsche and Martin Heidegger as well as Barth and other theologians. In 1965, the liberal Baptist Harvey Cox's book *The Secular City* set off a second theological debate with the secular world at its center. Informed by Tillich's depersonalization of God and attentive to modern society's reluctance to identify a separate realm of supernatural phenomena, these "secular theologies" of the 1960s foregrounded human agency, asserted the interpenetration of the sacred and secular, and sought possibilities for transcendence in and through everyday life.[39]

In addition to modern social conditions, theologians also continued to grapple with modern knowledge in the late twentieth century. For example, their engagement with continental philosophy deepened further as structuralism, poststructuralism, and other new schools of thought proliferated in Europe. Science and nature remained a central preoccupation in some circles as well, with theologians seeking various ways of squaring Christian teachings with empirical findings. Among liberal thinkers, "process theologies" rooted in the early-twentieth-century metaphysics of Alfred North Whitehead continued to circulate in the 1960s and beyond. Some Christian realists, especially those influenced by H. Richard Niebuhr, explored new ways of understanding Christianity's capacity to both humanize and divinize the thought world of the natural sciences. The environmental movement inspired a range of theological work as well, especially after 1980. A self-identified body of ecotheology, often overlapping with ecofeminism and informed by the writings of Mary Daly, emerged among theologians such as Sallie McFague.[40]

Other theologians focused more squarely on the human sciences, especially the "interpretivist" mode of reasoning that emerged in those fields as a challenge to Anglo-American empiricism and quantification from the 1960s onward. A key figure here was Bernard Lonergan, a Canadian Catholic theologian who moved to Boston College near the end of his life. Though rooted in the thought of Thomas Aquinas, Lonergan grappled with fields seemingly distant from theology, including even economics, in his quest to comprehend the nature of human understanding. Seminal works such as *Insight: A Study of Human Understanding* (1957) and *Method in Theology* (1972) inspired many others to embed the human sciences and other forms of modern knowledge in a Christian frame.[41]

A fourth mode of post-1960s theology moved in a different direction by asserting the autonomy, and perhaps even self-sufficiency, of Christian traditions, teachings, and communities. Figures in this vein argued for Christianity's priority over secular forms of reason and experience, not its compatibility with them. Of course, fundamentalists and related groups of evangelicals and Pentecostals took up this task energetically, especially with relation to Darwinism. But versions of the impulse appeared in many other theological circles as well. Many built on Karl Barth's writings, which had informed H. Richard Niebuhr's work and steadily gained new adherents by the 1960s. Like such forebears, US theologians from a variety of faith traditions emphasized that Christianity's validity did not depend on its correspondence to any secular standard, whether it was scientific evidence, ordinary experience, or formal logic. Such theologians often asserted that realists such as Reinhold Niebuhr and Paul Tillich had pulled their punches in challenging theological liberalism, ceding the realms of cognition and rationality to secular competitors and leaving Christianity with only a symbolic, metaphorical, or poetic import.[42]

The postliberal theology (also called narrative theology) pioneered by H. Richard Niebuhr's student and colleague Hans Frei offered one way to push back against Christianity's cognitive demotion. Frei's *The Eclipse of Biblical Narrative* (1974) detailed the historical process through which the truth of biblical narratives had been reduced to their compatibility with either Enlightenment philosophies or secular reconstructions of ancient historical events. To Frei, what mattered about these biblical accounts was precisely their narrative form, which mapped onto subjective human experience and thereby helped to constitute the identities of both the believer and the Christian community. The biblical stories did their work directly, not via translation into some other mode of analysis or communication.[43]

Like many of their counterparts, however, postliberal theologians also drew on numerous interpretive resources from other fields of inquiry. Although Frei, for example, followed Barth in starting with Anselm's attempt to delineate the self-understanding of faith, he also leaned on the New Critics and other literary theorists, especially Erich Auerbach. George Lindbeck, another student of H. Richard Niebuhr and a key interlocutor of Frei's at Yale, took the later Wittgenstein as his methodological guide in *The Nature of Doctrine* (1984). However, a competing school of postliberal theology takes off from the work of the French phenomenologist Paul Ricoeur, who analyzed how narratives map onto core features of immediate human experience, including its teleological flavor and its representation of the past and the future within the present. In this view, biblical narratives are like all narratives in that they stand alone and cannot be restated in other forms. The two schools of postliberal theology thus disagree on the distinctiveness of the narratives in the Bible, even as they share a belief that the form of those narratives cannot be changed without a radical loss of meaning and impact.[44]

Subsequent interpreters have combined insights from postliberal theology and other theological traditions with the "postmodern" critique of Enlightenment thought that spread through many other disciplines in the late twentieth century. For example, the postliberal theologian Stanley Hauerwas, who has influentially argued that Christians should hew to their own principles rather than alternative standards – including that of democracy – draws on sources ranging from virtue ethics to Michel Foucault. The philosopher Alasdair MacIntyre offered an important assist in 1988 by pluralizing the concept of rationality. He contended that there were competing and equally valid conceptions of rationality, each resting on an antecedent tradition of argumentation with its own presuppositions. Thus, the modes of rationality associated with modern science and secular history could not be deemed superior to Christian traditions of reasoning. Such moves to pluralize cognition by decentering Enlightenment categories have informed a host of important theological projects. As the twentieth century ended, postmodernism even began to find adherents in evangelical circles, with Carl Raschke leading the charge to throw off the shackles of modernity and return to premodern theological traditions.[45]

The new attempt to attack secularism and liberalism by describing each as one of many alternatives – if a particularly uninspiring one – rather than simply wrong or demonic also opened up new possibilities for recognizing the validity of myriad faith traditions. Postmodernism gave a major practical and conceptual boost to the already accelerating push to accept the validity of multiple interpretations of the natural world and human experience. Not all Christians fully embraced such tolerance, let alone developed explicit theological justifications for it. And many continued to regard postmodernism as merely a sharpened version of modern relativism. But in the early twenty-first century, even the most conservative of North American Christians sought allies across confessional lines – in their cases, conservative Catholics, both Roman and Orthodox, as well as Jews and perhaps even Muslims – at least as consistently as had most liberals at the turn of the twentieth century.

Influence, Achievement, and Agenda

Much else has also changed since liberal theology took hold in North America and birthed the Social Gospel. In the late nineteenth and early twentieth centuries, theologians grappled with characteristically modern developments such as industrialization, increasing religious diversity, historicism, new scientific theories, and the advent of the social sciences. Today, we face neoliberalism and increasingly sophisticated forms of finance capitalism, accelerated movements of both goods and people, the hybridization of religion and ethnoracial identities, sharp battles over entrenched structural inequalities, populist movements and other modes of skepticism toward established institutions, transformative technologies from biotechnology to artificial intelligence, and a rapid warming of the climate that threatens all life on earth.

Still, when we look more closely at such contemporary challenges, we can only marvel at how many of them stem from analogous sources. We still grapple with the same underlying forces: economic development, social diversification, secular knowledge and its offshoots. We have not solved the past's problems, it would seem. Nor, however, have we managed to simply get over them. As in the realm of ethics, the terrain of theology is always shifting because of the deeply contextual nature of our answers to the question "Where is God in the world?" Indeed, it will – and it must – always be so. Only a God who is not in the world at all would be immune from such contextual influences. And such a God would not be, in the end, the God of Christianity.

Notes

1   On this tendency, see especially Tomoko Masuzawa, *The Invention of World Religions, or, How European Universalism Was Preserved in the Language of Pluralism* (Chicago, IL: University of Chicago Press, 2005).

2   Gary J. Dorrien, *The Making of American Liberal Theology: Imagining Progressive Religion, 1805–1900* (Louisville, KY: Westminster John Knox Press, 2001); George M. Marsden, *Fundamentalism and American Culture*, 3rd ed. (New York: Oxford University Press, 2022).

3   For helpful overviews of US religious thought from this angle, see Gary J. Dorrien, *Soul in Society: The Making and Remaking of Social Christianity* (Minneapolis, MN: Fortress Press, 1995) and Dorrien, *Social Ethics in the Making: Interpreting an American Tradition* (Malden, MA: Wiley-Blackwell, 2009).

4   Dorrien, *The Making of American Liberal Theology.*

5   Jon H. Roberts, *Darwinism and the Divine in America: Protestant Intellectuals and Organic Evolution, 1859–1900* (Madison, WI: University of Wisconsin Press, 1988); William R. Hutchison, *The Modernist Impulse in*

American Protestantism (Durham, NC: Duke University Press, 1992); E. Brooks Holifield, "North American Theology," Encyclopedia of Christianity Online, accessed June 27, 2023. https://referenceworks.bril-lonline.com/browse/encyclopedia-of-christianity.

6   Ralph E. Luker, *The Social Gospel in Black and White: American Racial Reform, 1885–1912* (Chapel Hill, NC: University of North Carolina Press, 1991); Christopher H. Evans, *The Social Gospel in American Religion: A History* (New York: New York University Press, 2017).

7   Dorrien, *The Making of American Liberal Theology.*

8   Luker, *The Social Gospel in Black and White*; Evans, *The Social Gospel in American Religion.*

9   Christopher H. Evans, *The Kingdom Is Always But Coming: A Life of Walter Rauschenbusch* (Waco, TX: Baylor University Press, 2010); William H. Brackney and David P. Gushee, eds., *In the Shadow of a Prophet: The Legacy of Walter Rauschenbusch* (Macon, GA: Mercer University Press, 2020).

10 Walter Rauschenbusch, *Christianity and the Social Crisis* (New York: Macmillan, 1907); Rauschenbusch, *Christianizing the Social Order* (New York: Macmillan, 1912), Rauschenbusch, *A Theology for the Social Gospel* (New York: Macmillan, 1917).

11 Luker, *The Social Gospel in Black and White*; Evans, *The Social Gospel in American Religion*; Gary J. Dorrien, *The New Abolition: W. E. B. Du Bois and the Black Social Gospel* (New Haven, CT: Yale University Press, 2015); Harlan Beckley, *Passion for Justice: Retrieving the Legacies of Walter Rauschenbusch, John A. Ryan, and Reinhold Niebuhr* (Louisville, KY: Westminster John Knox Press, 1992); Robert G. Kennedy et al., eds., *Religion and Public Life: The Legacy of Monsignor John A. Ryan* (Lanham, MD: University Press of America, 2001). On gender, see W. J. D. Edwards et al., eds., *Gender and the Social Gospel* (Urbana, IL: University of Illinois Press, 2003).

12 For example, Harry Emerson Fosdick, *Christianity and Progress* (New York: Association Press, 1922); Shailer Mathews, *The Faith of Modernism* (New York: Macmillan, 1924).

13 Mathews lamented not only poverty and hunger but also divorce, adultery, class warfare, communism, and other modern ills, all exacerbated by scientific natural-ism. See *The Faith of Modernism*, 5–6. On these cultural shifts, see especially Lynn Dumenil, *The Modern Temper: American Culture and Society in the 1920s* (New York: Hill and Wang, 1995).

14 Mathews, *The Faith of Modernism*, 10. On the interfaith movement, see especially William R. Hutchison, *Religious Pluralism in America: The Contentious History of a Founding Ideal* (New Haven: Yale University Press, 2003); K. Healan Gaston, *Imagining Judeo-Christian America: Religion, Secularism, and the Redefinition of Democracy* (Chicago, IL: University of Chicago Press, 2019).

15 Bradley J. Longfield, *The Presbyterian Controversy: Fundamentalists, Modernists, and Moderates* (New York: Oxford University Press, 1991); J. Michael Utzinger, *Yet Saints Their Watch Are Keeping: Fundamentalists, Modernists, and the Development of Evangelical Ecclesiology, 1887–1937* (Macon, GA: Mercer University Press, 2006).

16 K. Healan Gaston, "Neo-Orthodoxy," in *The Encyclopedia of Religion in America*, ed. Charles Lippy and Peter Williams (Washington, DC: CQ Press, 2010); Robin Lovin, *Reinhold Niebuhr and Christian Realism* (New York: Cambridge University Press, 1995; H. Richard Niebuhr, *The Kingdom of God in America* (Chicago, IL: Willett, Clark, 1937), 193.

17 The best intellectual biographies remain Jon Diefenthaler, *H. Richard Niebuhr: A Lifetime of Reflections on the Church and the World* (Macon, GA: Mercer University Press, 1986) and Richard Wightman Fox, *Reinhold Niebuhr: A Biography*, 2nd ed. (Ithaca, NY: Cornell University Press, 1996).

18 On the temperamental differences between the brothers, see especially K. Healan Gaston, "'A Bad Kind of Magic': The Niebuhr Brothers on 'Utilitarian Christianity' and Democracy's Defense," *Harvard Theological Review* 107, no. 1 (2014): 1–30.

19 H. Richard Niebuhr, *The Social Sources of Denominationalism* (New York: Holt, 1929); Niebuhr, *The Kingdom of God in America*. On US adaptations of the "prophetic" discourse, see also Gaston, *Imagining Judeo-Christian America.*

20 Reinhold Niebuhr, *Moral Man and Immoral Society: A Study in Ethics and Politics* (New York: Scribner's, 1932).

21 Gaston, "'A Bad Kind of Magic,'" 21.

22 The translated book is Paul Tillich, *The Religious Situation*, trans. H. Richard Niebuhr (New York: Holt, 1932).

23 Jacques Maritain, *True Humanism* (New York: Scribner's, 1938); Maritain, *A Christian Looks at the Jewish Question* (New York: Longmans, Green, Reader & Dyer, 1939).

24 Important early statements included John Courtney Murray, "Necessary Adjustments to Overcoming Practical Difficulties," in *Man and Modern Secularism: Essays on the Conflict of the Two Cultures* (New York: National Catholic Alumni Federation, 1940), 152–7; Murray, "Current Theology: Christian Co-operation," *Theological Studies* 3 (1942): 413–31.

25 Gaston, *Imagining Judeo-Christian America.*

26 Reinhold Niebuhr, *The Nature and Destiny of Man: A Christian Interpretation* (New York: Scribner's, 1941–1943); Niebuhr, *The Children of Light and the Children of Darkness: A Vindication of Democracy and a Critique of Its Traditional Defence* (New York: Scribner's, 1944); Niebuhr, *The Irony of American History* (New York: Scribner's, 1952).

27 Helpful overviews include Mark Silk, *Spiritual Politics: Religion and America since World War II* (New York: Simon and Schuster, 1988); Patrick Allitt, *Religion in America Since 1945: A History* (New York: Columbia University Press, 2003); Mark Hulsether, *Religion, Culture, and Politics in the Twentieth-Century United States* (New York: Columbia University Press, 2007); and Jonathan P. Herzog, *The Spiritual-Industrial Complex: America's Religious Battle against Communism in the Early Cold War* (New York: Oxford University Press, 2011).

28 H. Richard Niebuhr, *The Meaning of Revelation* (New York: Macmillan, 1941); Niebuhr, *Christ and Culture* (New York: Harper, 1951); Niebuhr, *Radical Monotheism and Western Culture* (New York: Harper, 1960); Niebuhr, *The Responsible Self: An Essay in Christian Moral Philosophy* (New York: Harper & Row, 1963).

29 Paul Tillich, *The Courage to Be* (New Haven, CT: Yale University Press, 1952); Tillich, *Dynamics of Faith* (New York: Harper, 1957); Tillich, *Systematic Theology*, Vols. 1–3 (Chicago, IL: University of Chicago Press, 1951–63). On the public reception of these postwar theologies, see especially Andrew S. Finstuen, *Original Sin and Everyday Protestants: The Theology of Reinhold Niebuhr, Billy Graham, and Paul Tillich in an Age of Anxiety* (Chapel Hill, NC: University of North Carolina Press, 2009).

30 John W. O'Malley, *What Happened at Vatican II* (Cambridge, MA: Belknap Press of Harvard University Press, 2008); Mark S. Massa, *The American Catholic Revolution: How the Sixties Changed the Church Forever* (New York: Oxford University Press, 2010).

31 Herzog, *The Spiritual-Industrial Complex*; Gaston, *Imagining Judeo-Christian America*.

32 Gaston, *Imagining Judeo-Christian America*.

33 Lewis Sperry Chafer, *Systematic Theology* (Dallas, TX: Dallas Seminary Press, 1947); John C. Whitcomb and Henry M. Morris, *The Genesis Flood* (Philadelphia, PA: Presbyterian and Reformed Publishing Company, 1961); Dorrien, *The Remaking of Evangelical Theology*; Ronald L. Numbers, *The Creationists: From Scientific Creationism to Intelligent Design* (Cambridge, MA: Harvard University Press, 2006).

34 Carl F. H. Henry, *The Uneasy Conscience of Modern Fundamentalism* (Grand Rapids, MI: Eerdmans, 1947); Cornelius Van Til, *The Defense of the Faith* (Philadelphia, PA: Presbyterian and Reformed Publishing Company, 1955).

35 Howard Thurman, *Jesus and the Disinherited* (New York: Abingdon-Cokesbury, 1949); Gary J. Dorrien, *Breaking White Supremacy: Martin Luther King Jr. and the Black Social Gospel* (New Haven, CT: Yale University Press, 2018); Lilian Calles Barger, *The World Come of Age: An Intellectual History of Liberation Theology* (New York: Oxford University Press, 2018).

36 James H. Cone, *Black Theology and Black Power* (New York: Seabury, 1969); Barger, *The World Come of Age*; Gary J. Dorrien, *A Darkly Radiant Vision: The Black Social Gospel in the Shadow of MLK* (New Haven, CT: Yale University Press, 2023).

37 Mary Daly, *The Church and the Second Sex* (New York: Harper & Row, 1968); Rosemary Radford Ruether, *Liberation Theology: Human Hope Confronts Christian History and American Power* (New York: Paulist Press, 1972); Linda Hogan, *From Women's Experience to Feminist Theology* (Sheffield: Sheffield University Press, 1995); Barger, *The World Come of Age*.

38 Katie Geneva Cannon, "The Emergence of Black Feminist Consciousness," in *Feminist Interpretation of the Bible*, ed. Letty M. Russell (Louisville, KY: Westminster John Knox Press, 1985), 30–40; Cannon, *Black Womanist Ethics* (Atlanta, GA: Scholars Press, 1988); Stephanie Y. Mitchem, *Introducing Womanist Theology* (Maryknoll, NY: Orbis, 2002); Patrick S. Cheng, *Radical Love: An Introduction to Queer Theology* (New York: Seabury, 2011); Nancy L. Eiesland, *The Disabled God: Toward a Liberatory Theology of Disability* (Nashville, TN: Abingdon Press, 1994).

39 Thomas J. J. Altizer and William Hamilton, *Radical Theology and the Death of God* (Indianapolis, IN: Bobbs-Merrill, 1966); Harvey Cox, *The Secular City: Secularization and Urbanization in Theological Perspective* (New York: Macmillan, 1965); Daniel Callahan, ed., *The Secular City Debate* (New York: Macmillan, 1966).

40 C. Robert Mesle, *Process Theology: A Basic Introduction* (St. Louis, MO: Chalice Press, 1993); Sallie McFague, *Models of God: Theology for an Ecological, Nuclear Age* (Philadelphia, PA: Fortress Press, 1987).

41 Bernard Lonergan, *Insight: A Study of Human Understanding* (New York: Philosophical Library, 1957); Lonergan, *Method in Theology* (New York: Herder & Herder, 1972).

42 A historically informed example of such a critique is Douglas Sloan, *Faith and Knowledge: Mainline Protestantism and American Higher Education* (Louisville, KY: Westminster John Knox Press, 1994).

43 Hans Frei, *The Eclipse of Biblical Narrative: A Study in Eighteenth and Nineteenth Century Hermeneutics* (New Haven, CT: Yale University Press, 1974); Frei, *The Identity of Jesus Christ: The Hermeneutical Bases of Dogmatic Theology* (Philadelphia, PA: Fortress Press, 1975).

44 George Lindbeck, *The Nature of Doctrine: Religion and Theology in a Postliberal Age* (Philadelphia, PA: Westminster, 1984); Paul Ricoeur, *Time and Narrative* (Chicago, IL: University of Chicago Press, 1984–88);

Ronald T. Michener, *Postliberal Theology: A Guide for the Perplexed* (New York: T&T Clark, 2013).

45 Stanley Hauerwas and William H. Willmon, *Resident Aliens: Life in the Christian Colony* (Nashville, TN: Abingdon Press, 1989); Alasdair MacIntyre, *Whose Justice? Which Rationality?* (Notre Dame, IN: University of Notre Dame Press, 1988); Carl A. Raschke, *The Next Reformation: Why Evangelicals Must Embrace Postmodernity* (Grand Rapids, MI: Baker Academic, 2004).

Recommended Reading

Primary

Cone, James H. *Black Theology and Black Power.* New York: Seabury, 1969.

Frei, Hans. *The Eclipse of Biblical Narrative: A Study in Eighteenth and Nineteenth Century Hermeneutics.* New Haven, CT: Yale University Press, 1974.

Lonergan, Bernard. *Method in Theology.* New York: Herder & Herder, 1972.

McFague, Sallie. *Models of God: Theology for an Ecological, Nuclear Age.* Philadelphia, PA: Fortress Press, 1987.

Murray, John Courtney. *We Hold These Truths: Catholic Reflections on the American Proposition.* New York: Sheed and Ward, 1960.

Niebuhr, H. Richard. *The Meaning of Revelation.* New York: Macmillan, 1941.

Niebuhr, Reinhold. *The Nature and Destiny of Man.* Vols. 1–2. New York: Scribner's, 1941–3.

Rauschenbusch, Walter. *Christianity and the Social Crisis.* New York: Macmillan, 1907.

Ruether, Rosemary Radford. *Liberation Theology: Human Hope Confronts Christian History and American Power.* New York: Paulist Press, 1972.

Thurman, Howard. *Jesus and the Disinherited.* New York: Abingdon-Cokesbury, 1949.

Tillich, Paul. *Systematic Theology.* Vols. 1–3. Chicago, IL: University of Chicago Press, 1951–63.

Torrey, R. A., A. C. Dixon et al., eds. *The Fundamentals: A Testimony to the Truth.* Vols. 1–4. Los Angeles, CA: Bible Institute of Los Angeles, 1917.

Secondary

Barger, Lilian Calles. *The World Come of Age: An Intellectual History of Liberation Theology.* New York: Oxford University Press, 2018.

Dorrien, Gary J. *The Making of American Liberal Theology.* Vols. 1–3. Louisville, KY: Westminster John Knox Press, 2001–6.

———. *The Remaking of Evangelical Theology.* Louisville, KY: Westminster John Knox Press, 1998.

Evans, Christopher H. *Histories of American Christianity: An Introduction.* Waco, TX: Baylor University Press, 2013.

———. *The Social Gospel in American Religion: A History.* New York: New York University Press, 2017.

Gaston, K. Healan. *Imagining Judeo-Christian America: Religion, Secularism, and the Redefinition of Democracy.* Chicago, IL: University of Chicago Press, 2019.

Hutchison, William R. *The Modernist Impulse in American Protestantism.* Durham, NC: Duke University Press, 1992.

———. *Religious Pluralism in America: The Contentious History of a Founding Ideal.* New Haven, CT: Yale University Press, 2003.

Lovin, Robin. *Reinhold Niebuhr and Christian Realism.* New York: Cambridge University Press, 1995.

Marsden, George M. *Fundamentalism and American Culture.* 3rd ed. New York: Oxford University Press, 2022.

James H. Cone

Anthony G. Reddie

Introduction

James Hal Cone (1938–2018) was the "Grand Patriarch" of Black liberation theology. Although there has been a form of Black theology in existence since the era of transatlantic chattel slavery of Africans, James H. Cone is credited with creating the modern, systematic dimension of the discipline. From the outset, Cone created an epistemological break in how Black theology should be conceived when compared with hitherto established forms of theological inquiry. In establishing Black theology as a "Theology of Liberation," Cone creates alternative ways of understanding the doctrine of God, Christology, soteriology, biblical hermeneutics, theological norms, and ecclesiology.

At the outset I described James Cone as the originator of Black theology. There are many who have asserted that the true "Father" or "Grand Patriarch" of Black theology is the Reverend Albert Cleage and not James Cone.[1] It is undoubtedly the case that Albert Cleage's first book, *Black Messiah*, predates James Cone's *Black Theology and Black Power* by a year, and so many lay claim to it being the first ever Black theology book.[2] Cleage's legacy is not to be dismissed, and his early formulation for a radically pro-Black hermeneutical approach to the Christian faith is one that can claim to be an important forerunner to the later developments in Black theology.

The critical difference between the two, aside from their respective theological abilities (Cleage was a visionary church and community leader, but it cannot honestly be said that he possessed Cone's intellectual brilliance as a scholar), lies in the trajectory that followed their initial works. Following *Black Theology and Black Power* in 1969, within a year Cone had published *A Black Theology of Liberation*, arguably the first self-articulated, systematic theological text in Black theology.

Unlike Cleage, whose scholarly work largely consisted of popular essays and sermons, James Cone was committed until the very end of his life to the singular trajectory of seeking to deepen and sharpen his intellectual commitment to a freeing notion of the gospel of Jesus Christ, namely, Black liberation theology.[3]

Ford's The Modern Theologians: An Introduction to Christian Theology since 1918, Fourth Edition.
Edited by Rachel Muers and Ashley Cocksworth.
© 2024 John Wiley & Sons Ltd. Published 2024 by John Wiley & Sons Ltd.

Although some will argue for Cleage as being the founder of Black theology, I am clear, as are most experts in the field, that James Hal Cone is the creator of the academic, systematic structuring of the discipline named Black liberation theology, Black theology for short. This chapter explores the theological significance of James Cone and the development of Black theology that emerged from his brilliantly incisive work from 1969 through to his death in 2018.

Survey and Major Themes

Doctrine of God

In his second book, *A Black Theology of Liberation*, James Cone says this about God: "The reality of God is presupposed in black theology."[4] The important thing to say about this statement is that Cone was in some ways quite orthodox or conventional in his theological outlook. Whereas "aspects" of liberal theology have questioned whether God exists, or if God is merely an extension of human consciousness with no independent life or existence beyond human thought, Cone was in no doubt that God was real. The presupposed nature of God did not lead to anti-intellectualism or to lazy or sloppy thinking. On the contrary, Cone goes on to say the following:

> Black theology is an attempt to analyze the nature of reality, asking what we can say about the nature of God in view of God's self-disclosure in biblical history and the oppressed condition of black Americans. If we take the question seriously, it becomes evident that there is no simple answer to it. To speak of God and God's participation in the liberation of the oppressed of the land is a risky venture in any society. But if the society is racist and also uses God-language as an instrument to further the cause of human humiliation, then the task of authentic theological speech is even more dangerous and difficult.[5]

There is much to unpack in this statement because, in many respects, this quotation contains many, if not all of the essential ingredients to be found in Cone's recipe for talking about God and God's nature as it applies to Black theology.

For Cone to say that God is *real* is to presuppose the existence of God as an active participant in the world and, most crucially, in human history. For Cone, the God of the Bible is also the God of history, in that actions of the former are consistent with those of the latter. As we will see, the key characteristic of God for James Cone and Black theology is that of "liberation."

A God of liberation is seen to be active in the Hebrew scriptures (often traditionally known as the "Old Testament") and the Christian New Testament. God who is the same yesterday, today, and forever can be known by the deeds this God has undertaken.[6] For Cone, God is not merely a good idea. A good idea might well inspire people but whether a good idea possesses the resources to empower and transform people to fight sacrificially for radical change is open to doubt.

The God of Black theology is not a metaphor or an organizing principle. When exploring the social context out of which Black theologians undertake their theological work, Cone is clear that all theology is done within a particular context and social reality. The depth of Black suffering and oppression means that a God who is not in the business of liberating those who are socially marginalized and oppressed is no God at all.[7] Not only is God real but this God is not disinterested or oblivious to the suffering of God's people. Once again, the biblical witness to God's saving acts is clear as to the character of God. Cone writes: "The God in Black theology is the God of and for the oppressed, the God who comes into view in their liberation. Any other approach is a denial of biblical revelation."[8]

Cone's assertion that God is real finds expression in his own faith formation as a child of one of the historically Black denominations, the African Methodist Episcopal Church. Cone's formation within this Black church tradition was one that provided him with the resources of faith that would be later supplemented by his acute theological thinking.[9] Cone held to the famous dictum of St Anselm that Christian theology was "faith seeking understanding."

A God that is real is not so much a philosophical treatise for Cone as an experiential and visceral reality. Namely, the lived experience of suffering of Black people testified to the nearness and the realness of God. In one of my early books, I outline how, for the Black working-class communities of the "Windrush Generation" of post-World War II Caribbean migrants to Britain, the realness of God and the experience of God's mercy and support, expressed in the person of Jesus and the witness of the Holy Spirit, is what kept many of them going.[10]

The fact that Cone's doctrine of God assumed God's involvement within human history did present many problems, of course. One advantage of holding to a view that God is a metaphor or simply an idea that generates action by human beings is that one cannot expect such a God to be active in terms of overturning evil that leads to human suffering. But, if one believes in a God who is actively on the side of the oppressed, then the ultimate theological challenge arises when one has to account for the existence of evil and suffering in the world.

Biblical revelation

James Cone's doctrine of God is one grounded in the Bible. In *God of the Oppressed*, Cone goes to some length in outlining the biblical evidence for the liberative characteristics of a God whose existence is deeply concerned with a people whom God has identified as God's own.[11] Cone makes it clear that the biblical God is not a disinterested bystander of human history. Rather, as he states, "The God of the Bible is involved in history, and God's revelation is inseparable from the social and political affairs of Israel."[12] As Cone narrates the activity of God throughout the Hebrew scriptures, he is not so much "proof-texting" as seeking to show the consistent quality of a God who is not indifferent to human suffering and seeks to liberate a small nation that is often at the mercy of larger, more aggressive powers.

As we will see, it is this quality of God, seeking to side with those who are oppressed and at the mercy of the exploitation of others, that provides the hermeneutical grounds for asserting that "God is Black." God's identification with Diasporan Black people, the descendants of enslaved Africans, is premised on the grounds that this God does not side with the powerful and those who are oppressive. In the Exodus narrative, when God denounces the oppressive actions of Pharoah, and through Moses, declares that Pharoah should set free the oppressed Israelites, Cone is in no doubt that this facet of God's character is the consistent relational quality that supports the Black Power movement in 1960s America and is denouncing the modern-day Pharaohs who represent White supremacy.[13]

There is no doubting the importance of the aforementioned as the key revelation in Cone's doctrine of God. I believe it is no coincidence that Cone's doctoral thesis was on Karl Barth's anthropology, as there are significant remnants of the latter's thought in Cone's developing model of Black theology. Like Barth, Cone believes that the fullest expression of God's revelation can be found in Jesus Christ. Therefore, the activity of Jesus as detailed in the gospels present us with the clearest rationale for asserting that the God of the Bible is most concerned with the liberation of those whose humanity is imperiled by oppressive forces. In *A Black Theology of Liberation*, Cone writes:

> Special revelation has always occupied the central role in Christian theology. It means that there has been a self-revelation of God in biblical history and decisively in Jesus Christ. It is this conviction that Karl Barth takes seriously by using Christology as the point of departure of his *Church Dogmatics*. God has been fully revealed in the man Jesus so that the norm of all existence is determined exclusively by him.[14]

Cone's extensive reflections on Christology demonstrate its central importance in Black theology, which although orthodox in terms of its "Trinitarian" character, is nonetheless very much a Christocentric or Christ-centered movement, in which a very human Jesus, who is in solidarity with those who are marginalized, remains its central theological motif.

The biblical basis of Cone's ideological attack on all manifestations of Whiteness, including privilege, supremacy, normativity, and benign indifference to suffering, finds its most powerful anchoring in Jesus Christ. Cone's doctrine of God is not oblivious to the usefulness of other disciplines such as sociology, anthropology, psychology, or cultural studies, and these are used to help illuminate the social context in which Christian theology is undertaken.[15]

Cone's use of Marxist analysis, for example, was to enable Black theologians to better critique and deconstruct the false neutrality of White Christianity and the ways in which this phenomenon has given the world territorial conquest, chattel slavery, colonialism, genocide, apartheid, Jim and Jane Crow, segregation, and reservations.

Christology

For Cone, the centrality of Christology and Jesus in Black theology arises from two sources. In the first instance, there is Cone's historic formation within the wider African American Black church tradition. Cone was raised in the south of the United States in a Christian household. His parents were part of the African Methodist Episcopal Church, one of the historic Black denominations founded by African Americans breaking away from the hypocrisies of White Euro-American Christianity.[16]

In this crucible of cultural and religious formation, James Cone would have been introduced to a form of Christianity that was steeped in the traditions of his ancestors, enslaved African peoples.[17] This model and mold of Christianity was founded on the recontextualization of the Christian faith from within the prism of Black experience. The roots of Black theology emerge from the existential realities of being born into a Black body in a context in which Christianity was used as a justification for enslavement when coerced by the dictates of White supremacy.[18]

In the first chapter of *Said I Wasn't Gonna Tell Nobody*, Cone outlines the ways in which the Christianity of his parents and ancestors shaped him to deal with hypocrisy in the White world of America. This formation was a dialectic of defiant resistance and accommodationist pragmatism.[19] Namely, this mode of Black Christianity sought to challenge the seemingly normative assumptions of White superiority while accepting that one had to be covert in the ways in which one sought to resist, often disguising intent and strategizing beneath a veneer of acquiescence. Central to this form of Christianity was the centrality of a contexualized understanding of Jesus who sat alongside Black people in the midst of their struggles and suffering. Howard Thurman, the famed African American mystic and in many respects, a precursor of Cone in terms of Black theological scholarship, identified Jesus as having a symbiotic relationship with those he deemed the "disinherited."[20]

As a forerunner of Cone in the Black theological tradition, Thurman constructs a hermeneutical approach to critiquing the wicked machinations of White, Euro-American Christianity by focusing initially on Jesus.[21] Thurman identifies Jesus's life and the social context in which he lived as analogous to the disenfranchisement of Black people in America, more so than having anything to do the seeming normativity of White, Euro-American Christianity. Thurman says "We begin with the simple historical fact that Jesus was a Jew."[22] He continues, "The striking similarity between the social position of Jesus in Palestine and that of the vast majority of American Negroes is obvious to anyone who tarries long over the facts."[23] Here, Thurman is outlining not only some of the essential markers that would later characterize Cone's own development of Black theology, but of equal import, he is offering a summation of what would have been the basic template of the African American Black church tradition, namely, that the "Jesus of history" identified with the suffering and struggles of Black folk, more so than he did with those with power, who claimed to be his followers while oppressing others in Jesus's name. This was the truth of Jacquelyn Grant's towering work on womanist theology in the late 1980s, when she juxtaposed the "White Women's Christ," who supported the status quo of White supremacy, with the "Black Women's Jesus" who identified with the struggles and suffering of poor, Black women.[24] The roots of Black theology emerge from a Black church tradition that had already grown accustomed to critiquing the skewed ethics and problematic practices of White Christianity.

The second source for Cone's strong adherence to Christology as the point of departure in Christian theology in general and Black theology in particular, lies in his own training in Barthian anthropology in his doctoral studies at Garrett-Evangelical theological seminary. Cone's focus on Barth for his doctoral studies resulted in him sharing with him this focus on Jesus as the starting point for engaging in constructive Christian theology. Cone states, "As Christians we know God only as he has been revealed in and through Jesus. All other talk about God can have, at most, provisional significance."[25]

The focus on Jesus also derives from the practical nature of Cone's Black theology, which echoes his own formation in the African American Black church tradition. In the midst of existential despair, when Black bodies were being crushed and literally dismembered through the cruelty of lynching, Black people sought in God an immediate form of amelioration for their suffering. There was little appetite or indeed time for abstract theological musings when faced with the reality of oppression and the threat of nonbeing, i.e. of ceasing to exist due to the imposition of powerful others.[26]

The practical, experiential nature of Black Christianity across the African Diaspora (one finds echoes of this in African, Caribbean and Latin American theologies) has often seen a focus on the visible, manifest example of Jesus's life, death, and resurrection, as the basis for a faith that is trying to make sense of seemingly insoluble senselessness.[27] Although the concept of God as a being can be construed in very vague and abstract terms, the life of Jesus, especially his identification with the poor and marginalized of Judea, offers an immediate point of focus for those whose lives are besmirched by the realities of human suffering, marginalization, and oppression.

The central point of departure in James Cone's theological understanding of Jesus lies in his identity as a colonized Jewish man in Roman occupied Judea. This is nonnegotiable for Cone. He writes:

> The historical Jesus emphasizes the social context of Christology and thereby establishes the importance of Jesus' racial identity. *Jesus was a Jew!* The particularity of Jesus' person as disclosed in his Jewishness is indispensable for Christological analysis.[28]

For Cone, the fact that Jesus was not an "Aryan" White man is hugely significant. The God of the oppressed is disclosed in Jesus's identity not only as a Jewish man, but as a colonized Jew at that.

Cone is clear when he identifies Jesus as a part of an oppressed community from the moment he was born. Cone states, "The appearance of Jesus as the Oppressed One whose existence is identified exclusively with the oppressed of the land is symbolically characterized in his birth."[29] In identifying Jesus as a Galilean Jew, Cone wants to establish the critical "otherness" of his identity in order to ensure that the domestication of Jesus as "one of us" can be seriously challenged. Cone writes, "The historical Jesus must be taken seriously if we intend to avoid making Jesus into our own images."[30]

Like Cone's doctrine of God, Jesus's Blackness is understood not solely in ethnic or cultural terms, around the aesthetics of his appearance, but more so on ontological grounds, in terms of the essence and being of God that identifies with Black suffering. The Jesus in Black theology is "One of Us."[31] Being one of us, writing as a diasporan African is central to the ways in which the Judeo-Christian God of the oppressed of the Bible seeks to be in solidarity with the demonized nature of Blackness in a world that continues to echo to the strain of White supremacy. In identifying Jesus with Black suffering, Cone is not asserting that God's identification with Black people is due to inherent merit in Black people, predicated on the notion of Black acceptability when compared with White people. Rather, Cone argues that God's identification with Black people arises from God's righteousness and thirst for justice. In other words, it is Black suffering that draws God into solidarity with Black people.

The Church

In the early iteration of Black theology, Cone charts the developing understanding of the "People of God," namely Israel, who throughout the Hebrew scriptures, we see in a covenantal relationship with God.[32] God's relationship to an oppressed group of people whom God has elected provides the platform for "God's revolutionary activity" to demonstrate God's righteousness to the world.[33] The fulfilment of this process of God acting in history culminates in the work and the person called "Jesus of Nazareth." With the coming of Jesus, the church comes into being to give practical expression to the teaching and the values shared by the activism, the message and the sacrificial death of the one in whom and from whom the church takes its identity and authority. Cone writes, "The Church, then, consists of people who have been seized by the Holy Spirit and who have determined to live as if all depends on God. It has no will of its own, only God's will; it has no duty of its own, only God's duty. Its existence is grounded in God."[34]

In this regard, it is important to note that Cone has quite a "high view" of the church. In making this remark, I do not mean to say that Cone sees the church in episcopal terms in the use of the term "high," which might constitute a way of denoting a church with a pronounced sense of hierarchy that conforms to notions of apostolic succession. Rather, in using the term "high" I mean Cone does not see the church in utilitarian terms as merely a human institution that seeks to do some good. For Cone, the church is understood as a gift of God, created in order to undertake the work of liberation to which God has given expression in the witness and supreme example of Jesus Christ. Because of the divine calling of the church, Cone expects much from it and is, therefore, scathing when it fails to live up to its high calling.

Of particular importance is how Cone differentiates between the "White church" – the church that emerges from the beliefs and social practices of people of White Euro-American heritage – and the "Black church." The latter is the opposite of the former: the Black church grows out of the struggles of African Americans to give life to the liberationist impulse of God they witnessed in their lives in the power of the Holy Spirit, through their often limited engagement with the scriptures (many enslaved Africans were forbidden to read in general and not encouraged to read the Bible) and through their identification with Jesus as "One of them." The Black church, for Cone, although not beyond criticism, nonetheless, retains the identity of the "true church" that seeks to be the authentic expression of Christian love, generosity and most crucially, aligned to Christ's liberating mission to bring freedom to those bound by systemic evil and social forms of injustice.[35]

The authenticity of the church is found not in its adherence to doctrines, dogma, and creeds but rather through the extent to which it is willing to participate in the radical work of God revealed in Jesus Christ. To the extent that the church is willing to make a difference in the world and to contradict the false teachings of White supremacy and the jaundiced and biased operations of the status quo that upholds capitalistic greed and naked self-centeredness, then the church can be heralded as being what it was created to be. Yet, as Cone demonstrates throughout his work, the failure of Christian theology to denounce White supremacy, White entitlement, and privilege is the damning indictment on the "White church."[36]

Central to the identity of the church is the clear sense that it is a countercultural agency that challenges and refutes any notion of injustice and the habitual selfishness of the world. Take for example this quotation from *A Black Theology of Liberation*.

> The Christian church is that community of persons who "got the hint," as they thus refuse to be content with human pain and suffering. To receive "the power of God unto salvation" places persons

in a state of Christian existence, making it impossible for them to sit still as their neighbors are herded off to the prison camps. The hint of the gospel moves them to say no to rulers of the world: "If our brothers and sisters have to go, it will be over our dead bodies." They are the ones who believe in the gospel of liberation, convinced that personal freedom is more important than "law and order" ... Because the church is the community that participates in Jesus Christ's liberating work in history, it can never endorse "law and order" that causes suffering.[37]

One can quickly deduce from this quotation that much of what happens on a Sunday in many parts of the world is not an authentic expression of the church according to the high expectations held of it by James Cone. For most churches, "being Church" entails the coming together to sing hymns, speak prayers, enact some form of liturgy (be it formalized and prescribed or implicit and improvised), listen to some form of address/sermon, and then have coffee/tea and informal "chit-chat" afterwards. The aforementioned often takes place as a ghettoized experience separated from the wider world and the myriad problems and challenges that exist there. Of course, not every church is like this and there many notable exceptions, but in my very limited experience, the latter are the exceptions and not the rule.

Cone's words are anathema to the millions of White evangelicals in the United States who voted twice for Donald Trump and his brand of populist White Christian nationalism. The noted African American Black theologian, Josiah Young, himself a former doctoral student of Cone's at Union Theological Seminary, has outlined the intellectual and faith gap between conservative White evangelicals who voted for Trump and the majority of Black Christians who opposed him through his presidency.[38] Charting the diametrically differing ways in which both groups saw and interpreted their Christian faith in the public square, Young writes, "Many White conservative evangelicals are the progeny of racist privilege while many Black evangelicals are the progeny of enslaved African Americans."[39]

The crucial difference between the foundational moments of "White Christianity" and "Black Christianity" provide the basic template and backdrop against which Cone makes his assessment on the authentic nature of the church.

Given the propensity of White Christians in the United States to stand back and support the lynching of African Americans, one can see the extent to which White Christianity in America might be seen as anything but Christian. Cone reflects on the fundamental different between these two modes of the faith when seen through the lens of the church. He writes:

The cross has been transformed into a harmless, non-offensive ornament that Christians wear around their necks. Rather than reminding us of the "cost of discipleship," it has become a form of "cheap grace," an easy way to salvation that doesn't force us to confront the power of Christ's message and mission. Until we can see the cross and the lynching tree together, until we can identify Christ with a "recrucified" black body hanging from a lynching tree, there can be no genuine understanding of Christian identity in America, and no deliverance from the brutal legacy of slavery and white supremacy.[40]

Debate, Achievement, and Agenda

Debate: Is God a White racist?

One of James Cone's most trenchant critics was William R. Jones who, in his masterful book *Is God a White Racist?*, critiques Cone's presumed theism.[41] Jones argues that Black theologians have "compounded the confusion of an already inscrutable mystery" by assuming uncritically classical, Western constructions of "God" for their proclamations concerning God's political allegiances.[42] Jones's challenge to Cone to evidence the nature of God's allegiance to Black people as the God of the oppressed still represents one of the continuing and seemingly insoluble problems facing many Black theologians who have followed in his footsteps, including this author.[43]

Jamall Calloway provides an excellent summary of the ongoing challenge presented by William R. Jones to James Cone's continued belief in God's divine identification with Black suffering and oppression.[44] In summary, to argue for the existence of a God who possesses the characteristics of being sovereign, with the power to act in human history, one has to account for why Black people (and other marginalized and oppressed peoples) still suffer. Either an active and real God can change things but chooses not to (hence, Jones's memorable phrase "Is God a White racist?") or that God has no intent to identify with a particular experience of humanity (i.e. is not a God of the oppressed) or, even more startling, possesses no power to intervene in human history. As Calloway demonstrates, Cone spent the best part of fifty years trying to wrestle with this theological conundrum.[45] Calloway emphasizes that the faith of the Black Christian is the only relatable response Cone can make to the criticism outlined by Jones. He states:

> Jones is an internal critic whose rational critique led him to a Black humanist perspective, a perspective that is inherently a part of Black liberation theology. Nevertheless, for Cone, suffering is defeated through an acceptance of an understanding of Biblical Christology. Jesus' death and resurrection functions as the decisive event for which Jones was searching. Cone slightly rectifies this argument in his first memoir but completely rectifies it in his second and final memoir. Cone reduces his Christological defense of suffering in *My Soul Looks Back* by focusing on the faith of the people who believe in both God and liberation.[46]

Being the consummate theologian he was, Cone was always ready to debate his critics and to understand that there was no such thing as a foolproof theological system that did not carry anomalies and blind spots. For Cone, there was no intellectual proof for the belief that God is on the side of the oppressed. At one level, for all the sophistry of arguments and conceptual thinking deployed by Cone, one finally ends up falling back on the resources of faith.

Agenda: exposing white Christianity

In his fifty-plus-year career as a public intellectual, James Cone was concerned, constantly, with the need for the church to live out the mandate to be a lived and practiced experiment in the liberationist expression of the gospel of Jesus Christ. Perhaps the most consistent and sustained critique of the failure to be the church can be found in a chapter in his 1986 book *Speaking The Truth*.[47] In chapter 4, titled "A Theological Challenge to the American Catholic Church," Cone offers a coherent critique of American Catholicism that acts as a case study for a wider assessment of White American Christianity.[48] Cone makes it clear that he could write a similar critique of White American Protestantism.[49] Writing in 1986, Cone says, "The Catholic hierarchy in the United States is exclusively controlled by whites. Many black Catholics, therefore, find it difficult to challenge structures of authority in the church without enormous limitations being placed on their ministry."[50]

Cone's critique of White Christianity is enshrined in the failures of White churches to be attentive to the concerns that were uppermost in Jesus's own ministry. Care for the poor, the marginalized and neglected *should* see all churches adopting a liberationist stance in terms of their relationship to power and vested self-interests. Most crucially, it should entail a severe critique of and action to denounce White supremacy, as the latter is a clear denial of the gospel. And yet, the absence of critique at best and downright collusion with the active and more veiled workings of Whiteness at worst, have continued to besmirch the legitimacy of the church in the global North.

In more recent reflections on Black theology in Britain, post the murder of George Floyd, I have used Jesus's encounter with Pontius Pilate in John's account of the lead up to Jesus's crucifixion, as a means of engaging White British people in the paradox of their Christological gaze. In John 18:28–40 we see Jesus in conversation with Pontius Pilate, the Roman governor of Judea. Jesus is before Pilate because he has been handed over by the Jewish authorities to be tried for crimes against the state. The fact that Jesus is here in front of Pilate is because, as the text states in verses 31 and 32, only Pilate can put him to death and to underscore the type of death Jesus would die – i.e. at the hands of an invading, imperial power. I have pointed to this encounter in order to demonstrate the salient truth of Cone's Christological point of departure. In identifying Jesus as a colonized Jewish man, his encounter with Pilate, the representative of Caesar, the Godlike power that exerts control of life and death over all colonial subjects, Cone is exposing the death-dealing hypocrisy and theological sleight-of-hand of White Christianity.

Conclusion: Cone's Achievement

Black people have done theology before James Cone, but none was like him. Black people have challenged racism, segregation, and the corruption of Christianity before James Cone, but no one outlined the desecration of the very nature of Christian theology by the sin of White supremacy, as well as he did. Cone effectively created a whole new genre of academic theology. Perhaps Cone's greatest achievement, as the most influential Black theologian of them all, is his unflinching ability to root systematic theology within context and to show the significance of particularity to the development of what one might discern as universal truths. To my mind, there is no doubting the universality of Cone's writings. As he outlines the historical, religious, cultural and political contexts against which and through which his theological vision arose, it is clear that the ideas he develops have universal application, as they relate to the very nature of Christian theology and why it matters. But Cone's way of arriving at this sense of universality is by means of his deep engagement with the contextual soil in which his Black liberation theology is earthed. James H. Cone was a brilliant visionary genius and we will not see his like again!

Notes

1 See Jawanza Eric Clark, *Indigenous Black Theology: Toward an African-Centered Theology of the African-American Religious Experience* (New York: Palgrave Macmillan, 2012) and Jawanza Eric Clark, ed., *Albert Cleage Jr. and the Black Madonna and Child* (New York: Palgrave Macmillan, 2016). See also Earle J. Fisher, "Brother Malcolm, Dr King, and Black Power – A Close and Complementary Reading," *Black Theology: An International Journal* 18, no. 3 (2020): 263–87.

2 See Albert Cleage Jr., *Black Messiah: On Black Consciousness and Black Power* (New York: Africa World Press, 2017).

3 See, for example, Albert Cleage Jr., *Black Christian Nationalism: New Directions for the Black Church* (New York: Africa World Press, 1987).

4 James H. Cone, *A Black Theology of Liberation* (Maryknoll, NY: Orbis, 1970), 55.

5 Cone, *A Black Theology of Liberation*, 55.

6 Probably the most eloquent section in which this theme is explored can be found in Cone's 1975 book *God of the Oppressed* (Maryknoll, NY: Orbis, 1975), 57–76.

7 Cone, *God of the Oppressed*, 36–56.

8 Cone, *A Black Theology of Liberation*, 61.

9 See James H. Cone, *My Soul Looks Back* (Maryknoll, NY: Orbis, 1986), 64–72.

10 See Anthony G. Reddie, *Faith, Stories and the Experience of Black Elders: Singing the Lord's Song in a Strange Land* (London: Jessica Kingsley, 2001), 37–46.

11 Cone, *God of the Oppressed*, 57–76.

12 Cone, *God of the Oppressed*, 57.

13 James H. Cone, *Black Theology and Black Power* (Maryknoll, NY: Orbis, 2009), 43–46.

14 Cone, *A Black Theology of Liberation*, 51.

15 Cone, *God of the Oppressed*, 36–40.

16 For more details on this African American Black church tradition, see Anne H. Pinn and Anthony B. Pinn, *Fortress Introduction to Black Church History*

(Minneapolis, MN: Fortress Press, 2001). See also Alton B. Pollard and Carol B. Duncan, eds., *Black Church Studies Reader* (New York: Palgrave Macmillan, 2016).

17 See Linda E. Thomas, ed., *Living Stones in the Household of God: The Legacy and Future of Black Theology* (Minneapolis, MN: Fortress Press, 2003).

18 See James H. Cone, *For My People: Black Theology and the Black Church* (Maryknoll, NY: Orbis, 1984), 99–121.

19 James H. Cone, *Said I Wasn't Gonna Tell Nobody* (Maryknoll, NY, Orbis, 2018), 1–30.

20 See Howard Thurman, *Jesus and the Disinherited* (Boston, MA: Beacon Press, 1996 [1949]).

21 Thurman, *Jesus and the Disinherited*, 11–35.

22 Thurman, *Jesus and the Disinherited*, 15.

23 Thurman, *Jesus and the Disinherited*, 34.

24 See Jacquelyn Grant, *White Women's Christ and Black Women's Jesus: Feminist Christology and Womanist Response* (Atlanta, GA: Scholars' Press, 1989).

25 Cone, *Black Theology and Black Power*, 35.

26 Cone, *Black Theology and Black Power*, 43–7.

27 See, for example, Noel L. Erskine, *Decolonising Theology: A Caribbean Perspective* (Maryknoll, NY: Orbis, 1998). See also Michelle A. Gonzalez, *Afro-Cuban Theology: Religion, Race, Culture, and Identity* (Gainesville, FL: University of Florida Press, 2009). See also Mokgethi Motlhabi, *African Theology/Black Theology in South Africa: Looking Back, Moving On* (Pretoria: UNISA Press, 2009).

28 Cone, *God of the Oppressed*, 119.

29 Cone, *God of the Oppressed*, 114.

30 Cone, *A Black Theology of Liberation*, 113.

31 See Anthony G. Reddie, *Working Against the Grain: Re-imaging Black Theology in the 21st Century* (London: Equinox, 2008), 81–90.

32 Cone, *Black Theology and Black Power*, 63–4.

33 Cone, *Black Theology and Black Power*, 64.

34 Cone, *Black Theology and Black Power*, 65.

35 Cone, *God of the Oppressed*, 138–62.

36 James H. Cone, "Theology's Great Sin: Silence in the Face of White Supremacy," *Black Theology: An International Journal* 2, no. 2 (2004): 139–52.

37 Cone, *A Black Theology of Liberation*, 129–30.

38 See Josiah Ulysses Young III, "Making America Great Again? An Essay on 'The Weightier Matters of the Law: Justice and Mercy and Faith,'" *Black Theology: An International Journal* 16, no. 1 (2018): 53–60.

39 Young, "Making America Great Again?," 54.

40 James H. Cone, *The Cross and the Lynching Tree* (Maryknoll, NY: Orbis, 2013), xiv–xv.

41 William R. Jones, *Is God a White Racist?: A Preamble to Black Theology* (New York: Beacon Press, 1973/1997).

42 Jones, *Is God a White Racist?*, ix.

43 See the chapter "What Is the Point of This? A Practical Black Theology Exploration of Suffering and Theodicy" in Reddie, *Working Against the Grain*, 172–87.

44 Jamall A. Calloway, "'To Struggle Up a Never-Ending Stair': Theodicy and the Failure It Gifts to Black Liberation Theology," *Black Theology: An International Journal* 18, no. 3 (2020): 223–45.

45 Calloway, "'To Struggle Up a Never-Ending Stair,'" 239–43.

46 Calloway, "'To Struggle Up a Never-Ending Stair,'" 239–40.

47 See James H. Cone, *Speaking the Truth: Ecumenism, Liberation and Black Theology* (Maryknoll, NY: Orbis, 1986).

48 Cone, *Speaking the Truth*, 50–60.

49 Cone, *Speaking the Truth*, 55.

50 Cone, *Speaking the Truth*, 55.

Recommended Reading

Primary

Cone, James H. *Black Theology and Black Power*. Maryknoll, NY: Orbis, 1969/2009.

———. *A Black Theology of Liberation*. Maryknoll, NY: Orbis, 1970/2010.

———. *The Cross and the Lynching Tree*. Maryknoll, NY: Orbis, 2013.

———. *For My People: Black Theology and the Black Church*. Maryknoll, NY: 1984.

———. *God of the Oppressed*. Maryknoll, NY: Orbis, 1975/1997.

———. *My Soul Looks Back*. Maryknoll, NY: Orbis, 1986.

———. *Said I Wasn't Gonna Tell Nobody*. Maryknoll, NY: Orbis, 2018.

———. *Speaking the Truth: Ecumenism, Liberation and Black Theology*. Maryknoll, NY: Orbis, 1999.

———. "Theology's Great Sin: Silence in the Face of White Supremacy." *Black Theology: An International Journal* 2, no. 2 (2004): 139–52.

Secondary

Calloway, Jamall A. "'To Struggle Up a Never-Ending Stair': Theodicy and the Failure It Gifts to Black Liberation Theology." *Black Theology: An International Journal* 18, no. 3 (2020): 223–45.

Cleage, Albert, Jr. *Black Messiah: On Black Consciousness and Black Power*. New York: Africa World Press, 2017.

Erskine, Noel L. *Decolonising Theology: A Caribbean Perspective*. Maryknoll, NY: Orbis, 1998.

Fisher, Earle J. "Brother Malcolm, Dr King, and Black Power – A Close and Complementary Reading." *Black Theology: An International Journal* 18, no. 3 (2020): 263–87.

Grant, Jacquelyn. *White Women's Christ and Black Women's Jesus: Feminist Christology and Womanist Response*. Atlanta, GA: Scholars' Press, 1989.

Gonzalez, Michelle A. *Afro-Cuban Theology: Religion, Race, Culture, and Identity* Gainesville, FL: University of Florida Press, 2009.

Jones, William R. *Is God a White Racist?: A Preamble to Black Theology*. New York: Beacon Press, 1973/1997.

Parkinson, James W. *White Theology: Outing Supremacy in Modernity*. New York: Palgrave Macmillan, 2004.

Reddie, Anthony G. *Working against the Grain: Re-imaging Black Theology in the 21st Century*. London: Equinox, 2008.

Thurman, Howard. *Jesus and the Disinherited*. Boston, MA: Beacon Press, 1996.

Rosemary Radford Ruether

Lilian Calles Barger

Introduction

Rosemary Radford Ruether was a premier Catholic feminist theologian, patristic scholar, writer, and lecturer whose compelling work is expansive in theme and reach. Approaching her work as cultural criticism through a feminist lens clarifies her relationship to other systems of thought. Her theology uncovers many forms of oppression, beginning with sexism identified as part of the theological and institutional apparatus of Christianity. Widely read and globally acclaimed over four decades, she gained influence across many fields and contexts. Beyond her earned degrees, she was the recipient of fourteen honorary degrees and multiple awards. The theologian Mary Hunt has aptly compared her erudition to that of medieval abbess Hildegard of Bingen. One cannot hope to understand all the varied expressions of feminist theology without engaging with Ruether.[1]

Born in 1936 in St. Paul, Minnesota, Ruether was the youngest of three daughters of a free-thinking, yet devoted, Roman Catholic mother who attended Mass every day, and an ecumenical Episcopal father. With her father's death when she was twelve, she describes her childhood as a series of "matricentric enclaves" beginning with her mother, sisters, and aunt at home and the all-female world of the Sisters of Providence at school. Her mother's friends, including the noted social activist Helen Marston Beardsley, exposed the young Ruether to political and social activism through the local work of the Women's International League for Peace and Freedom and the American Civil Liberties Union and tagging along in public demonstrations. Her mother introduced her to Catholic spiritual classics and a circle of Quaker friends. This woman-centered, spiritually open, and politically engaged upbringing shaped the intellectual sensibility of a young Ruether.[2]

Ruether entered Scripps College, a male-directed women-only institution, where the word "feminist" was a slur and anti-Catholic sentiment was rampant. Intending to pursue art she quickly changed her focus to the humanities. While still in college she married Herman Ruether, a political scientist, in 1957 and graduated from Scripps with a BA in philosophy in 1958. Early in her egalitarian marriage, she refused to choose between domestic life and the pursuit of learning. Continuing her scholarship, along with becoming

Ford's The Modern Theologians: An Introduction to Christian Theology since 1918, Fourth Edition.
Edited by Rachel Muers and Ashley Cocksworth.
© 2024 John Wiley & Sons Ltd. Published 2024 by John Wiley & Sons Ltd.

the mother of three children, she went on to earn an MA in ancient history and a PhD in classics and patristics in 1965 from Claremont Graduate School in California. Influential in her education was the classicist Robert Palmer, who introduced her to the work of the Homeric scholar Walter Friedrich Otto. Palmer led her to the idea that religious symbols are not literal but living metaphors. Under his influence, she gained an interest in Greek and Latin culture and authored a dissertation titled *Gregory of Nazianzus, Rhetor and Philosopher*, showing the influence of Hellenistic ideas on Christian theology. Her study of classic literature and early church history became foundational for engaging in a critical theology and meeting the intellectual and political challenges of the era.

After graduate school, instead of taking a teaching position as planned, the struggle of African Americans drew her attention. In the summer of 1965, she volunteered with Delta Ministries working for civil rights in Mississippi surveying the Head Start program in rural communities. Her time with Delta Ministries exposed her to the terror of the Ku Klux Klan, racial prejudice of White churches, and a growing Black militancy, becoming a decisive point for her future work and placing her at the forefront of a social revolution.

Ruether's experience in Mississippi, the reform initiatives of the Second Vatican Council (1962–5) calling for engagement with the modern world, the civil rights movement in the United States, the rise of the modern feminist movement, and revolutionary liberation theologies of the 1960s shaped the direction of her thought. During her studies, she visited Mexico and Guatemala to learn Spanish and began reading the emergent Latin American liberation theology challenging the standing orthodoxy. Exposed to widespread demands for church reform, she completed her first book on ecclesiology at the age of thirty-one, *The Church Against Itself: An Inquiry into the Conditions of Historical Existence for the Eschatological Community* (1967), a critical assessment of the church's unwillingness to change and confront the world as it is. The book signaled the beginning of the reform-minded critique marking her career.

After her work with Delta Ministries, she and her husband moved to Washington, DC to take teaching positions, he at the American University and she at the historically Black Howard University in the School of Religion where she taught for ten years. The country was experiencing a wave of dissent with anti-imperialist New Left and peace movements marching in the streets. Ruether joined the peace movement in protesting the Vietnam War and spending time in jail with fellow radicals. The Black Power movement gained national strength creating divisions between civil rights reformers and radicals. Howard University, showing respectable restraint toward racial issues, rejected the militancy of Black Power. As a professor at Howard, Ruether defended the early Black theology of James Cone and introduced her students to it. Broader changes were afoot. With revolutionary currents running through the hemisphere, Latin American liberation theology gained strength with the publication of Gustavo Gutiérrez's *A Theology of Liberation*. Ruether read Gutiérrez, a leading Catholic theologian, in Spanish in 1971, before he was widely known in the United States. The changing cultural landscape presented by revolutionary movements and liberation theology prepared her for articulating a theological basis for the liberation of women.

The American feminist movement ignited by the publication of Betty Friedan's *The Feminine Mystique* (1963), was in full bloom by 1970. Liberal feminist activism resulted in the founding of the National Organization for Women and the passage of the Civil Rights Act of 1964 offering employment protection to women. Many radical women viewed political solutions as insufficient. Women in the New Left found radical men protesting American imperialism and the Black Power movement terminally misogynist. A younger group of militant women were not willing to settle for legal rights and demanded a new egalitarian relationship between the sexes and an equal voice within the New Left. They were demanding cultural change, not just legal change. Radical women began to question the institutions of society – government, the family, the church, and the free-market ethos. Radicals rejecting all patriarchal monotheism abandoned churches and synagogues. Friedan had pointed out how religion resisted women's freedom. Religious women touched by the broader feminist criticism became critical of the misogyny they experienced in the churches and seminaries. Reformers, instead of leaving the churches, sought a change in religious institutions, rituals, and interpretation of scripture. Women in the churches entered a crisis of faith.

Changes in consciousness among women drove Ruether to engage with the root causes of oppression, which she identified as androcentric theology marginalizing women and the earth. She questioned how theology related to social practice aware of the intersectionality of race, class, and sex. Ruether's astute theological reflection shed light on the significant social issues of the day.

Leaving Howard University, she joined the faculty of Garrett-Evangelical Theological Seminary in 1976 as one of three women faculty members. As the Georgia Harkness Professor of Applied Theology until her retirement in 2002, she pursued a fruitful collaboration with the American historian Rosemary Skinner Keller on several book projects including the three-volume *Encyclopedia of Women and Religion in North America* (2006). Highly sought after during her tenure, she had visiting professorships at Harvard Divinity School, Princeton Theological Seminary, and Yale Divinity School, among others, and kept a busy lecturing schedule at national and international conferences and symposiums. From there she spent three years at Graduate Theological Union before formally retiring. She continued with scholarship and lecturing as a visiting Professor of Feminist Theology at the Pacific School of Religion at Claremont Graduate University till becoming professor emerita.

Survey

Ruether was a prolific writer with over forty-seven books, contributing to many anthologies and producing hundreds of essays. Her oeuvre is complex, defying simple summarization – appearing in notable journals such as the *National Catholic Reporter* (publishing more than 185 columns), *Christianity and Crisis*, *Commonweal*, and *Christian Century*. Internationally recognized, widely read, and cited in and out of Catholic circles, she had influence on far-ranging issues of church reform, the liberation of women, Christian political engagement, ecology, and US imperialism. She challenged the Catholic Church's position on marriage and divorce and male-only priesthood and questioned papal infallibility. Critical of *Humanae Vitae* (1968) issued by Pope Paul VI, she addressed birth control and abortion, against the church's reaffirmation of procreation as the central purpose of marriage.[3] As a theologian she avoided biblical exegesis that begins with an unchanging standard of truth, preferring to articulate a set of principles drawn from Christian and Western history with particular attention to political and philosophical counter-movements.

Ruether's themes are expansive, drawing sociological, political, and theological lessons from the daily headlines. Looking outward beyond the walls of the church, her critique extended to the culture at large and addressed in particular the foundational dualism of the West and its theological underpinnings. Dualism sees the world as pairs of opposites, mind/body, man/woman, good/evil. The result, she argued, is sexism, racism, ecological disaster, colonialism, and political conflict between Jews and Palestinians reinforced by a complicit patriarchal and imperial Christology.

In the anti-American and anti-imperialism mood of the 1960s, and with the rise of liberation theologies, Ruether addressed the contentious issues of oppression. Her historical-critical approach draws from her vast knowledge of antiquity, the paganism of the Near East, Gnosticism, patristics, and the Hebraic prophetic tradition to unearth a usable tradition for human liberation.[4] Applying the modern method of demythologizing the Bible, a hermeneutic separating the supernatural features in the narrative from its deeper and universal moral teaching, she rooted her theology in the particular and immanent experience of the divine. She viewed the revelatory function of the scriptures as a record of an original human experience, subject to interpretation and reinterpretation by new experience rather than as a fossilized code set by church authority. She argued that controlling the margins of what is acceptable in the experience of the divine and scriptural interpretation of patriarchal authority suppresses the liberatory power of the gospel for women and other oppressed groups. Reinterpreting Christian symbols as metaphors, she offered a greater understanding of the feminine aspects of the divine and the full humanity of women as a foundational principle. Emphasizing contemporary experience arises out of Ruether's unique amalgam of post-Christian liberal philosophy recognizing equality among persons, Marxist analysis with its focus on material conditions with women as the "first and final proletariat," and the romantic utopianism of democratic socialism that sees the complementary and necessary integration of feminine and masculine attributes in individuals and communities.[5]

Ruether's work extends beyond probing the systems of oppression, to a constructive social vision of equality and hope for human flourishing. She saw the prophetic tradition beginning in the Bible and continuing through the history of religious revolutionaries and heretics as models for Christian engagement breaking the artificial wall between private religion and secular politics. She considered the church to be a fluid movement, "a happening," not an institution.[6] *The Radical Kingdom: Western Experience of Messianic Hope* (1970) presents the "free church" of dissenters escaping the boundaries of fossilized institutional religion to join the world in its ever-changing struggles. Relocating God's transcendence to the immanence of life makes her theology of hope profoundly relevant. Ruether called for a secularization of religion, a religion engaged in the politics of its own time and place. Her collection of essays *Liberation Theology: Human Hope Confronts Christian History and American Power* (1972) applied her analysis to the political effects of classic theology in undergirding relationships of oppression in anti-Semitism, racism, sexism, ecocide, and colonialism and calls on Christian socialism for its possibilities in recovering a liberating gospel.[7]

Ruether found that her early mentors and politically active coworkers did not welcome gender analysis. Neither did her colleagues at Howard University. Her early essay on sexism, "Male Chauvinist Theology and the Anger of Women," published in *CrossCurrents* in 1971, echoed the militant language of Black Power. On the leading edge of theological thinking, Ruether connected the anger of the women's liberation movement with a revolt against a long history tying women to their bodies and nature. Patriarchal psychoanalysis, philosophy, and theology had taken a flight from nature and women. Man, in the pretense of transcending nature raised himself above women, nature, and all subjugated people. Times were changing with an "ethic of liberation" appearing as an "exorcism of demonic possession." She saw "the woman's revolution [as] the most radical revolution because it threatens the fundamental social and psychic models of domination altogether." The reactionary response she asserted was a cultural-wide patriarchal backlash making even a "modest utopia" seem impossible.[8] Within Christian theology and history, she found repeated and varied patterns of domination and explored the theme in *New Woman, New Earth: Sexist Ideologies and Human Liberation* (1975). Her knowledge of ancient Greek and Roman history allowed her to name the classical inheritance received by Christianity distorting the gospel message of Jesus.

Drawn to ecofeminism, Ruether correlated the depletion of the earth to the subjugation of women as a method of analysis. She addressed ecology in *Gaia and God: An Ecofeminist Theology of Earth Healing* (1992). Drawing from the Greek earth goddess, Gaia became a modern concept for ecofeminism seeing the earth as a holistic living organism. In leading works on women's spirituality, Mary Daly and Carol P. Christ made a strong sacred connection between women and nature. Ruether critiqued both the domination paradigm of patriarchal religion and the fascination with the mystical matriarchal past in the women's spirituality movement. For Ruether, an overdetermined woman/nature paradigm was part of the problem, not the solution. She drew from Hebrew, Hellenistic, and Christian imagery to redefine Gaia as the entire cosmic process to which we all belong. Ruether called for a "new consciousness, a new symbolic culture and spirituality" making healing of the earth possible.[9]

In *Goddesses and the Divine Feminine* (2005), Ruether offered a panoramic history of ancient religion, the Hebraic and Christian borrowings, and the issues at stake in the modern Goddess revival. For Ruether, replacing God with a Goddess is not a simple or straightforward remedy. She critiqued the modern fascination with the Goddess as a symbol of women's freedom, arguing that ancient religions that include goddesses and gods did not assure ordinary women or the lower classes had much power. Ancient goddesses fulfilled roles as mothers or consorts to more powerful male gods. On the other hand, Ruether saw elements of the ancient Goddess religion buried in Judaism and Christianity as still useful for women and called for an ecumenical spirituality recovering the divine feminine aspects buried in the Western heritage.

Probing church history, Ruether showed how the patriarchs of the church adopted many dualistic Greek-Roman ideas, placing the spirit above the material world and denigrating women's bodies as sources of evil.[10] She discussed how Tertullian saw women as a source of temptation, Thomas Aquinas categorized women with slaves, and Augustine saw physical contact with women as detrimental to a man's virtuous mind. Following theological thinking into modern times, she considered how theologians from Martin Luther to Karl Barth continued to view women as subordinate to men by God's design. She pointed out the resistance of Mothers of the church who even within these patriarchal institutions became abbesses, scholars, and leaders in charitable endeavors, often renouncing association with their sex. In this way, Ruether follows historical women through the medieval and early modern periods to find both oppression and resistance.

Content

Ruether's *Sexism and God-Talk* (1983), an iconoclastic systematic theology, offered an introduction to feminist theology. Critically and constructively, she took up all the major doctrines on God, creation, anthropology, Christology, Mariology, sin and redemption, and eschatology, reinterpreting them from a feminist perspective. Following the pattern of Jewish midrash, she offered an imaginative reinterpretation of the gospel in the introduction. Through the midrash, Ruether used the lens of women's point of view to retell the story of creation, the original sin of patriarchy displacing the Queen of Heaven, the ministry of Jesus, and the beginnings of the church's hierarchy among the male disciples, a perspective running through *Sexism and God-Talk*.

Like standard systematic theologies, Ruether gave the reader the method, sources, and norms governing the scope of her theology. With women's experience as a measuring rod for symbols, doctrinal formulas, and laws, she argued, "If a symbol does not speak authentically to experience, it becomes dead or must be altered to provide new meaning."[11] She argued all theological reasoning starts with a reflection on experience rather than the truth that stands outside us. Rejecting a mystifying "objective" theological truth, she asserted that classic theology reflects a male experience alienated from the body. She defined revelation as a "breakthrough experiences beyond ordinary" illuminating the whole of life.[12] An interpretive community gives the individual experience revelatory meaning. The danger, and what often occurs, is the hardening of the original interpretation closing off any new revelatory experience or interpretation. Falling into this trap of ossification religious tradition faces corruption and a crisis of authority where more people question its veracity.

The norm for feminist theology, Ruether proposed, is the promotion of the full humanity of women. She wrote: "Whatever denies, diminishes, or distorts the full humanity of women is, therefore, appraised as not redemptive."[13] Feminist theology makes women subjects in the interpretation of scripture and tradition. The male as the norm of humanity, Ruether argued, has resulted in a sexist understanding of the "*imago dei*/Christ" and scapegoated women for sin. By extension, it marginalizes all people considered less than fully human. More broadly, Ruether rejected the exclusivity of Christianity, affirming the particularity of other religious traditions such as Buddhism or Hinduism. By reconstructing theology through the subjectivity of women, it becomes pluralistic and serves the interest of the earth.

Ruether drew from scriptural, historical, and modern sources – none uncritically – to construct her arguments. First, the broad prophetic-liberating principle embedded in scripture offers an internal condemnation of patriarchal ideology as idolatry. The liberation principle is based on the understanding of God as defending the oppressed, the poor, proclaiming judgment on dominant systems of power, a vision of a coming new age of justice, and a critique of idolatry. Feminist theology radicalizes these principles to pull the ideological cover that has distorted biblical religion.

The second source for theological reflection is the countercultural movements in church history. Beginning with the egalitarian countercultural movement in the ministry of Jesus, as a liberating figure normative for Christianity, Ruether sought counter-voices that opposed the denial of equality in the early formation of the church. Mystics, female religious communities, and movements considered heretical, such as Gnosticism, rediscover the principle of equality standing against hierarchical structures. In the Reformation, left-wing Puritans and Anabaptist groups made an important move to recover the priesthood of all believers regardless of sex. Ruether neither categorically accepted all claims of counter-voices nor rejected all classic theological insight in confronting androcentric beliefs and practices. Complementary to Christian sources, Ruether examined ancient pagan religions, their history, and belief systems for insight into how they shaped the formation of Judaism and Christianity. Ruether's use of historical sources sheds light on Christianity as a diverse movement stretching across centuries.

The third source for Ruether's theological reasoning is modern philosophical movements rejecting dualism for a unified view of reality. Liberalism, with its defense of reason, freedom, equality of opportunity, and embrace of social progress offered useful ideas. Romanticism, with its response against rationalists and the scientific approach as alienating humanity from nature, views the underclass of society, peasants, women, and native people as more attuned to nature. Marxism, as one expression of socialism, with its critique of religion and its basis in the material conditions under which people live, offers this-world possibilities. All these modern philosophical systems stripped of their androcentric assumptions can serve women's liberation. Appropriation of these systems of thought by feminists, Ruether proposed, must include a critical stance that can synthesize the best of each; freedom and equality, valuation of nature, and consciousness of material conditions shaping human experience.

Ruether probed exclusive masculine language and symbols for God by going to the origin of the male divinity. Looking at ancient agrarian civilization she found a long-standing female deity in pagan religion as a fertility symbol. The feminine deity was not transcendent but a sustaining and abiding presence in the circle of life. By the time urban societies developed, a male god of war, technology, and culture appeared as the consort and equal of the Goddess and as a sovereign power. Over a long period and through different cultural contributions an exclusive male image replaces the Goddess which stands over man and man over woman. The woman is no longer in direct association with the deity.

In the Hebrew religion the male God becomes dominant and reduces the female image to a human partner or servant of God. But God is not male, and the masculine image is not absolute, with scripture including God's "womblike" qualities. Sophia, the Wisdom of God personified as a woman, appears as an offshoot of the ancient Wisdom Goddess. Ruether brought out the forgotten elements in Christianity that once saw the Spirit of God as feminine with the power to create. Subsuming the feminine in a masculine deity had social consequences. Divine hierarchy not only places men over women, but also masters over slaves, and kings over subjects. A patriarchal God in the heavens justified hierarchal social relations on earth.[14]

Reclaiming the feminine side of God, Ruether argued, is not sufficient if the divine sovereign is still exclusively male. Male language for God reduces the divine to an idol: "When the word Father is taken literally to mean God is male and not female, represented by males and not females then this word becomes idolatrous."[15] God is neither male nor female and all language for the divine are necessarily analogies. Ruether introduced the neologism "God/ess" to suggest the multiple sides of the divine character as creator, liberator, and source of authentic humanity. The deity as an empowering matrix, rather than as a hierarchal parent or father, goes back to the earliest notions of God/ess in human history. Instead of divinity above and beyond us, God/ess is imminently near.

Ruether found the roots of domination in the opposition of humanity to the earth found in androcentric interpretations of creation. With the male standing for transcendence and above the earth, spirit and nature are dichotomous. Women are associated with animal life and the earth is subject to man's use. The earth, woman, and evil become associated in a way that demands domination by man. Ecological feminism rejects the dichotomy of spirit and nature. All matter, Ruether argued, is an ever-changing form of energy/spirit with complex life forms dependent on simpler life forms. The redemptive task of humanity, dependent as we are on nature for our existence, is restoring the right relationship with the natural world.

Ruether examined the meaning of the *imago dei,* in male and female, as created in the image of God marred by sinful alienation. She named two classic theological interpretations of the Fall with consequences for women. Both see men and women as equal at creation but having different roles. The Catholic stream of theology sees woman's subjugation to man as punishment for her participation in the Fall. To rebel against subjugation is to rebel against God's judgment. The second, Calvinist, interpretation coming out of the Reformation, saw gender hierarchy as part of God's original social order. Although men and women are equal in all respects their social function is different as assigned by God. Ruether rejected the idea of androgyny as a solution. Androgyny implies each person has a feminine and male side. Ruether rejected the dichotomy of male and female attributes for the idea that "all humans possess a full and equivalent human nature and personhood, *as male and female.*"[16] Redeemed humanity means recovering the full human potential in each person repressed by cultural stereotypes and bifurcated social values and functions.

Feminists raised the question of whether a male savior can save women. Ruether addressed this question by rejecting apolitical historical claims about Jesus that treat his maleness as normative for humanity. As a prophetic figure, Jesus, as the embodiment of Wisdom, radicalized the idea of a conquering Messianic king as a servant-liberator of the oppressed. Jesus introduced the idea of *Abba* for God, a loving parental image. The Jesus community is a family of equals with women having direct access to God/ess offering the possibility of overturning patriarchal authority. The early Jesus movement challenged the sexual double standard, undercut the power of earthly fathers, and spread an ethos of a new family of disciples not built on tradition or ethnicity. Women taking part in the early churches, gathering in the woman's domain of the home, showed their spiritual equality in the act of prophecy. Over time Christianity surrendered women's participation and equality to pagan patriarchy.

Christianity appropriated the Jewish Messiah, an anticipatory figure, for an ultimate and final savior in Christ. The transformation of Jesus into an imperial Christ, a figure of subjugation, betrayed his liberating message. Christianity became the imperial religion of the Roman Empire and installed Christ as the transcendent male mind of God over the social order. Christ served as the justification for the will of the emperor as God's reign on earth and excluded women as representatives of a male divinity. Ruether argued for a recovery of the prophetic work and iconoclastic message of Jesus in the Synoptic Gospels and saw his maleness as having no spiritual significance.

Ruether saw sin as primarily a distortion of relationships of which sexism is the most pervasive. Sin is fundamentally social. Sin occurs, not due to any original sin passed down from Adam, but because individuals are socialized into systems of oppression and domination placing men over women. This original distorted relationship affects all forms of domination. Only by a process of turning away from sexism and replacing it with relationships based on mutuality can we have hope for social healing.[17]

A theology of woman's liberation brought Ruether to reimagine the role and function of the Virgin Mary, a major icon in church history. The Virgin Mary, she argued, is open to two divergent interpretations as a source of containment and empowerment for women. Some aspects of the Virgin Mary trace back to the virgin goddess of the Greeks, and her inferior power. In the medieval period, the cult of Mary elevated her to coredemptrix with Christ to be worshiped like the Egyptian Isis. Ruether rejected the idea of the Virgin as a spotless, submissive, and passive mother or as the idealization of womanhood as compensation for the loss of power in the world. She saw Mary as a symbol of liberated humanity, one fully human cooperating with God in the incarnation and announcing liberation for all in the *Magnificat.* [18] As an exalted figure of feminine virtues, Ruether argued, Mary is not helpful. As a figure of human cooperation with the divine, Mary is a positive symbol of liberated humanity.

Turning to eschatology, the study of last things, Ruether saw some counterinterpretations in Christian eschatological sects of the first and second centuries and the hopes of modern philosophical movements. Historical mystical, monastic, and utopian sects insisting on spiritual androgyny formed communities to usher in an egalitarian future. These sects, removing themselves from the world, Ruether argued, had no vision or answers for the present injustice.

The modern philosophical system also presented problems for reimaging society. Secularizing the Fall, liberalism sees the problem not as sin but as injustice. Redemption comes in the form of progressive social reform or revolution taking place within history. She found egalitarianism in liberal feminism, with its claim to a common human nature based on shared reason and moral conscience as a positive aspect. Arguing against liberalism, however, she saw an assumption of the male experience as normative and its faith in progress as contributing to the pillage of the earth by industrialization. Marxism sees progress as reliant on the exploitation of workers and tries, not to do away with progress, but to control its direction by bureaucratic management. Control over progress continues as a key feature. Feminists taking up Marxist critique connect the exploitation of workers with women as unpaid sources of labor and see solidarity with workers as the way to liberation. Multiple expressions of Romanticism see male and female as complementary opposites with the feminine defined as intuition, emotional sensitivity, and moral purity. In turn, reason, culture-making, and aggression defined men. Romanticism rejected the technological progress of liberalism for a return to nature, and idealization of women and native people as more intuitively in touch with the sources of life. Radical feminists, taking a cue from romanticism, have insisted on the superiority of womanly values and define liberation as separation from the toxicity of men. Ruether argued that romanticism either gives women unique social power or places them in a new golden cage by excluding them from realms of culture seen as contrary to their nature. In her view, the expectation of endless progress, or of a return to some idyllic age, marred modern philosophical and political movements.

Debate/Critique

In her long scholarly career, Ruether had the opportunity for dialogue across denominational and political lines. Her interlocutors included the leading Catholic feminist theologians Elisabeth Schüssler Fiorenza and Elizabeth A. Johnson. She had exchanges with the Protestants Letty Russell and Beverly Harrison and joined feminist theologians in their ambivalence toward the Bible itself and in recognizing the need for a feminist reading. As a lifelong ecumenist, she rattled her Protestant colleagues by not breaking with Rome. The radical Goddess spirituality movement has been a source of both positive ideas and criticism in her exchange with leaders Mary Daly, a former Catholic, and Carol P. Christ. Contrary to Daly, who rejected Christianity in *Beyond God the Father* (1973) as unredeemable and hopelessly patriarchal, Ruether argued that the rejection of Christianity, the milieu in which modern women live, would take away the available power within the tradition that challenges the patriarchal system. By using masculinist theology against itself, women gain the power to effect change. Feminists have critiqued her work for wanting it both ways, in recovering the concept of the Goddess but unwilling to give up many features of a male God. Ruether's both/and approach to theological thinking escapes dualistic thought and raises points of contention from all sides.[19] Her interlocutors have been diverse, and she found affinity with the Canadian theologian Gregory Baum, instrumental in liberalizing the church at the Second Vatican Council, and the modern Catholic mystic Thomas Merton. Acting as catalysts for each other in the 1960s, Merton and Ruether exchanged forty letters collected in *At Home in the World: The Letters of Thomas Merton and Rosemary Radford Ruether* (1995). Her singular openness to a wide breadth of ideas without offhand rejection of any makes her a true modern theologian.

As one of the earliest thinkers to recognize the significance of liberation theology, Ruether was not shy about offering a critical evaluation of the first generation of Black and Latin American liberation theology for its marginalization of women. Male liberation theologians across the hemisphere tended to see feminism as a "first-world" issue and a distraction from the struggle for political and economic liberation of colonized people. They viewed their project as a recovery and contextualization of the true biblical faith. Ruether supported Latin American, Asian, and African women who were defining a contextualized feminist theology in the Ecumenical Association of Third World Theologians. "Third-world" women were dealing with their experience of colonialism, poverty, dowry and marriage traditions, and dialogue with Indigenous religions.[20] Her early exposure to the problem of racism situated her feminist theology at the intersection of race, class, and gender and her concern for all forms of oppression made her a ready source to many. She opened the way for women to rethink the Christian faith from their own localized experiences.

Ruether continually faced intense criticism from the Roman Catholic hierarchy. She skirted charges of being a heretical and a lapsed Catholic leading a radical reform movement threatening church schism. In 1986 she expressed what she believed to be chief challenges for the Roman Catholic church's future: democratic values and human rights, its response to feminism, and its stance on sexual morality in its teaching and practice. The opposition remained unabated. In 2008 the Catholic University of San Diego invited her to teach for a year as an endowed chair in the department of theology. A controversy ensued. Ruether's years of writing had gained her many admirers, but among her opponents, her reputation was of a "radical non-Christian." Opponents charged she was ill suited to teach about Catholicism and the University of San Diego rescinded the offer. Her criticism of the church and their rejection of her theology never reached a truce.

Conservative theologians viewed Ruether's work as modernist social criticism and not legitimate theology. Critiques centered on experience, i.e. feminist consciousness, as the highest authority in the interpretation and practice of Christianity, accusations of pantheism that denies God's transcendence, and syncretism. She was charged with panentheism, blurring the lines between God and creation and conceptualizing God as a cosmic power rather than a transcendent deity. Her attention to "Gaia" appears to collapse God's transcendence into immanence. She redefined sin away from rebellion against God to patriarchal distortion of relationships, which critics saw as the fruit, not the cause, of sin. She rejected the foundational doctrines of the virgin birth of Jesus and the Trinity, placing her outside classic theology.[21]

Ruether's critics have drawn attention to the issues considered a significant break from traditional theological thinking. One example is her deemphasizing of individual salvation for redeeming social and political systems of oppression. Another is her view of scripture – it is argued that her account denies the revelatory authority of the biblical writers beyond their own time and thus offers no standard for interpretation. With no normative view, interpretation becomes purely subjective. Personal experience becomes the authority and overrides the tradition that has held the Christian community together for two thousand years. Without a standard of faith, critics charged, the faith has no boundaries and no way to name the core beliefs and practices defining Christianity. The assumption of patriarchy and women's experience as the moral standard of measurement fails in defining what is patriarchal or a norm experienced by all women. Ruether, by critiquing the past for its patriarchal sins, showed a modern rationalist judgment on the motivations and circumstances that set the boundaries of Christianity. Modern hubris, critics asserted, reads the past through the lens of assumed enlightenment or moral progress. Lost in such reading is the necessary steady rudder religious tradition offers for the confusion of modern life. In her many interactions, Ruether proved herself to be too radical for conservatives and too conservative for radicals, making her difficult to categorize.

Influence, Achievement, and Agenda

Ruether's intellectual agility, broad historical knowledge, and refusal to disavow Christianity and theological synthesis have resulted in ecumenical influence. Her work is foundational in teaching women's religious history, feminist theology and ecofeminist thought. More than a scholar and prolific writer, she has put flesh on theology, elevating Christian practice as essential. From a Catholic upbringing to an ecumenical career, she has advocated radical reform through a theological intervention. She has contributed to efforts to resolve the Jewish/Palestine conflict, brought attention to earth-friendly practices of daily life, and advocated for the mentally ill, spurred by her personal experience with her son's lifelong illness. On behalf of women, she has worked for change with the Women's Ordination Conference and served on the board of Catholics for a Free Choice. Joining other feminists in the emerging Women-Church Convergence, a network of Catholic liturgical and social justice organizations advocating for a participatory, egalitarian, and self-governing gathering of women. Not a popular organizer, she has secured her place offering the necessary theological foundation by which others can actively pursue change.

Recognizing Christian feminists could no longer wait for the church to reform itself, Ruether responded to the "linguistic deprivation and Eucharistic famine." She moved ahead of institutional change by creating liturgical practices, language, and symbols that spoke to women's life passages such as puberty, marriage, childbirth, abortion, and menopause and that celebrate the universal church as an incarnational and liberating community. In *Women-Church: Theology and Practice of Feminist Liturgical Communities* (1985) she reenvisioned the sacraments of the eucharist and baptism and offered new rituals for change in seasons, and recovery from trauma such as rape and domestic violence. She offered not a prayer book or a prescription, but a blueprint for communities to develop meaningful liturgies reflecting local experience. Always opposed to feminist separatism that devalued men and with hopes for church reform, Ruether saw Women-Church as leading in the exodus to a new land. In this way, Ruether saw Christianity as a fluid, ever-changing tradition rooted in the contemporary community.[22]

Ruether has aptly used her erudition and freedom as a Catholic laywoman to reach across multiple differences. Beginning with the hopes of church reform, Ruether led the way breaking with all patriarchal teaching and practice for a radically new Christian community. The feminist theology Ruether articulated offered a necessary critique of malestream theological anthropology, instigated interest in the history of women in Christianity, buried both in the scriptures and church memory, and recovered the feminine attributes in reimagining the divine. In her writing, teaching, and advocacy, her work raised multiple issues in which debate will last long into the future, and opened new areas for further work: the place of women in Christianity, the meaning of freedom and oppression, the means and meaning of salvation, the relationship between men, women, and the earth in the community of the God/ess, and faith's relationship with the secular world and its politics. Ruether opened the conversation to women's experiences and voices, having a profound influence on theological interpretation and method.

Notes

1   Rosemary Radford Ruether, *My Quest for Hope and Meaning: An Autobiography* (Eugene, OR: Cascade, 2013); "Rosemary Radford Ruether," in *Transforming the Faith of Our Fathers: Women Who Changed American Religion*, ed. Ann Braude (New York: Palgrave Macmillan, 2004), 73–84.

2   Ruether, *My Quest*, 1.

3   Ruether, "Humanae Vitae – Twenty-Five Years Later," *Feminist Theology* 2, no. 6 (1994): 11–14.

4   References to these sources are scattered throughout her work. The most complete exploration is *Goddesses and the Divine Feminine: A Western Religious History* (Berkeley, CA: University of California Press, 2005).

5   Rosemary Radford Ruether, "The First and Final Proletariat: Social and Women's Liberation," *Soundings: An Interdisciplinary Journal* 58, no. 3 (1975): 310–28.

6   John Greenya, "Rosemary Ruether: A Most Catholic Catholic," *The Washington Star, Sunday Magazine*, 1 June 1969.

7   Rosemary Radford Ruether, "The Reformer and the Radical in the Sixteenth Century Reformation," *Journal of Ecumenical Studies* 9, no. 2 (1972): 271–82.

8   Ruether, "Male Chauvinist Theology and the Anger of Women," *CrossCurrents* 21, no. 2 (1971): 173–85; "Women's Liberation in Historical and Theological Perspective," *Soundings* 43, no. 4 (1970): 363–73.

9   Rosemary Radford Ruether, *Gaia and God: Ecofeminist Theology of Earth Healing* (London: SCM Press, 1993), 4.

10 Rosemary Radford Ruether, *Sexism and God-Talk: Toward a Feminist Theology* (Boston, MA: Beacon Press, 1983).

11 Ruether, *Sexism and God-Talk*, 13.

12 Ruether, *Sexism and God-Talk*, 13.

13 Ruether, *Sexism and God-Talk*, 18.

14 Ruether, *Sexism and God-Talk*, 56.

15 Ruether, *Sexism and God-Talk*, 66.

16 Ruether, *Sexism and God-Talk*, 111.

17 Rosemary Radford Ruether "Social Sin," *Commonweal* 108 (30 January 1981), 46–7.

18 See Ruether, *Goddesses and the Divine Feminine,* for the most comprehensive and critical review of the cultural and religious history of the feminine divine.

19 Rosemary Radford Ruether, "A Radical-Liberal in the Streets of Washington," *Christianity and Crisis* 31, no. 12 (1971): 144–7.

20 Rosemary Radford Ruether, "Crisis in Sex and Race: Black Theology vs. Feminist Theology," *Christianity and Crisis* 34, no. 6 (1974): 67–73; "Sexism and the Theology of Liberation," *Christian Century* 90 (1973): 1224–8; "Christian Feminist Theology in Global Context" (1991). *Boardman Lectureship in Christian Ethics,* 12. http://repository.upenn.edu/boardman/12 (accessed 5 September 2023).

21 Joseph Rossell, "Rosemary Radford Ruether: 'Ecofeminism Theology' vs. 'Elite White Males,'" *Juicy Ecumenism: The Institute on Religion and Democracy's Blog* (14 June 2016) https://juicyecumenism. com/2016/06/14/rosemary-radford-ruether-ecofeminist-theology-vs-elite-white-males/ (accessed 5 September 2023).

22 Rosemary Radford Ruether, *Women-Church: Theory and Practice of Feminist Liturgical Communities* (San Francisco, CA: Harper & Row, 1985), 4.

Recommended Reading

Primary

Rosemary Radford Ruether Papers, 1954–2002, The Burke Library Union Theological Seminary, New York, NY.

Ruether, Rosemary Radford. *Gaia and God: Eco-feminist Theology of Earth Healing.* London: SCM Press, 1993.

———. *Goddesses and the Divine Feminine: A Western Religious History.* Berkeley, CA: University of California Press, 2005.

———. *Liberation Theology: Human Hope Confronts Christian History and American Power.* New York: Paulist Press, 1992.

———. *My Quest for Hope and Meaning: An Autobiography.* Eugene, OR: Cascade, 2013.

———. *New Woman, New Earth: Sexist Ideologies and Human Liberation.* New York: Seabury Press, 1975.

———. *The Radical Kingdom: The Western Experience of Messianic Hope.* New York: Paulist Press, 1970.

———. *Religion and Sexism: Images of Woman in the Jewish and Christian Traditions.* New York: Simon and Schuster, 1974.

———. *Sexism and God-Talk: Towards a Feminist Theology.* London: SCM Press, 1983.

———. *Women-Church: Theology and Practice of Feminist Liturgical Communities.* San Francisco, CA: Harper & Row, 1985.

———. *Women Healing Earth: Third World Women on Ecology, Feminism, and Religion.* Maryknoll: Orbis, 2002.

Ruether, Rosemary Radford, and Herman J. Ruether. *The Wrath of Jonah: The Crisis of Religious Nationalism in the Israeli-Palestinian Conflict.* Minneapolis, MN: Fortress Press, 2002.

Secondary

Ackermann, Denise. "Rosemary Radford Ruether: Themes from a Feminist Liberation Story." *Scriptura,* 97 (2008): 37–46.

Bouma-Prediger, Steven. *The Greening of Theology: The Ecological Models of Rosemary Radford Ruether, Joseph Sittler, and Jürgen Moltmann.* Atlanta, GA: Scholars' Press, 1995.

Christ, Carol P., and Judith Plaskow. *Womanspirit Rising: A Feminist Reader in Religion.* San Francisco, CA: Harper & Row, 1979.

Daly, Mary. *Beyond God the Father toward a Philosophy of Women's Liberation.* Boston, MA: Beacon Press, 1973.

Fiorenza, Elisabeth Schüssler. *In Memory of Her: A Feminist Theological Reconstruction of Christian Origins.* New York: Crossroad, 2002.

Hogan, Linda. *From Women's Experience to Feminist Theology.* London: Bloomsbury Academics, 2016.

Johnson, Elizabeth A. *She Who Is: The Mystery of God in Feminist Theological Discourse.* New York: Crossroad, 2002.

Jones, Serene. *Feminist Theory and Christian Theology: Cartographies of Grace.* Minneapolis, MN: Augsburg Fortress Press, 2010.

Merton, Thomas, Rosemary Radford Ruether, and Mary Tardiff. *At Home in the World: The Letters of Thomas Merton and Rosemary Radford Ruether.* Maryknoll, NY: Orbis, 1995.

Russell, Letty M. *Human Liberation in a Feminist Perspective: A Theology.* Philadelphia, PA: Westminster Press, 1977.

Paul Tillich

Rachel Sophia Baard

Introduction

Paul Johannes Tillich was born on 20 August 1886 in Starzeddel, Germany, which is now part of Poland. His birthplace in this borderland symbolizes a central theme of his life, that of living on the boundary.[1] He described his childhood formation in terms of the boundary between the authoritarian moral code of his father, Johannes Tillich, a Lutheran minister, and the zest for life he associated with his mother, Mathilde Tillich (née Dürselen), who died when he was seventeen. As an adult he would inhabit many boundaries, mixing his passionate love of nature with great enjoyment of city life, teaching both philosophy and theology, and emigrating from Germany to the United States. This theme is reflected in his theology in multiple ways, most broadly in his effort to forge a path between the cultural accommodation of nineteenth-century liberal theology and the supernaturalism of twentieth-century neo-orthodoxy.

Tillich attended the Universities of Berlin, Tübingen, and Halle, and received a PhD in philosophy from the University of Breslau in 1910, and a PhD in theology from the University of Halle in 1912, both for dissertations on the German idealist Frederick Schelling, from whom he inherited a lifelong interest in the relationship between thought and reality. During his student years, he was a member of the Wingolf Christian fraternity, which was committed to a strictly moral lifestyle. Ordained as a Lutheran minister in 1912, the young Tillich worked in the working-class neighborhood of Berlin-Moabit until 1914. On 28 September 1914, mere days before leaving for the German front to serve as an army chaplain, Tillich married Margarethe (Grethi) Wever, but the union ended in divorce in 1921. In 1924 he married Hannah Werner-Gottschow, with whom he had two children, Erdmuthe (1926) and René (1935).

His biographers, Wilhelm and Marion Pauck, suggest that his time as army chaplain in World War I was "*the* turning point in Tillich's life."[2] The Tillich who emerged from the war was not the idealistic, conservative young man who had entered it. "Hell rages around us," he wrote to his father from the trenches in June 1916.[3] Twice he suffered nervous breakdowns. As he dug graves and led funeral services, he felt haunted by death, both personally and in the sense of "the actual death of this our time."[4] But he also saw this time as his personal *kairos*, referencing a biblical term that he would later utilize in his political theology to signify "a moment of time filled with unconditioned meaning and demand," to suggest the

Ford's The Modern Theologians: An Introduction to Christian Theology since 1918, Fourth Edition.
Edited by Rachel Muers and Ashley Cocksworth.
© 2024 John Wiley & Sons Ltd. Published 2024 by John Wiley & Sons Ltd.

opening up of new possibilities amidst the dying of the old.[5] For Tillich, the concept of the theistic God had died in the trenches, necessitating a new kind of faith and theology that could speak to those for whom the old answers no longer provided meaning. This is the task to which Tillich would devote the rest of his life.

From 1919 to 1924 Tillich taught at the University of Berlin, followed by three terms at the University of Marburg, where he met Martin Heidegger, whose ideas played a significant role in his later ontology. This was followed by posts at the Dresden University of Technology from 1925 to 1929 and the University of Leipzig from 1927 to 1929. In 1929 he accepted the chair of philosophy at the University of Frankfurt, where he was closely associated with members of the Institute of Social Research such as Theodor Adorno and Max Horkheimer, who sought to blend Marxist social analysis and Freudian psychoanalysis. In October 1933, having been dismissed from his post for being critical of Nazism, and subsequently invited to join the faculty of Union Theological Seminary in New York City, Tillich set sail for the United States with his family. At the age of forty-seven, Tillich was faced with the prospect of learning English and reshaping his theology for a new context. He did so with great success, eventually becoming famous, even featuring on the cover of *Time* magazine in 1959. He taught at Union Theological Seminary until 1955, subsequently at Harvard University until 1962, and finally at the University of Chicago until his death on 22 October 1965. Haunted by the issue of finitude his entire life, he faced his own with courage, saying to his wife, "today is dying day."[6] His ashes are interred in the Paul Tillich Park in New Harmony, Indiana.

Survey

Theologian of culture

Tillich's theological approach is often contrasted with that of his contemporary, Karl Barth. For both theologians the church's uncritical support of the German war effort in World War I signaled the failure of the liberal theological tradition's attempt to mediate between faith and post-Enlightenment culture. In response, both developed alternative theological approaches that, in turn, later enabled them to resist the ideological onslaught of Nazism. But whereas Barth sought to separate theology from culture, Tillich attempted to forge a new theology of culture premised upon the dynamic interplay of the religious and cultural elements of human life. He first introduced this idea in a 1919 talk to the Kant Society in Berlin and developed it further throughout his career.[7] Tillich rejected a dualism of religion and culture, arguing, instead, that "religion is the substance of culture and culture is the form of religion."[8] He did not have in mind the traditional view of religion as adherence to a particular tradition, but defined religion as Ultimate Concern, which denotes the deeply human quest for meaning that transcends finitude. As such, religion is neither something outside the human spirit, nor its product: it is, instead, an aspect of the human spirit, not in the sense of a special function, but "the dimension of depth in all of its functions."[9] This perspective is illustrated, for example, in Tillich's theology of art, in which he emphasizes *Gehalt* (revelatory content) over form (aesthetics) and *Inhalt* (content). So, in Tillich's view an ostensibly secular painting like Picasso's *Guernica* is more profoundly religious than many religiously themed paintings, because it reveals "the human predicament in our period."[10]

In sum, in Tillich's theology of culture, "the religious and the secular are not separated realms" but are "within each other."[11] He called this "theonomy," the presence of the Unconditioned within the finite. When things become distorted, the religious and the secular separate, with religion attempting to impose its values on the culture (heteronomy), and the culture celebrating itself against the imposition of religious law (autonomy).

Tillich's theology of culture is closely related to his famous "method of correlation," in which "the religious symbol is interpreted as the adequate answer to a question, implied in man's existence."[12] This should not be misread as a "secular questions/Christian answers" schema, since such a view would operate with the same culture/religion dualism that Tillich is trying to avoid. Instead, it is better to interpret this method in terms of Tillich's lifelong concern that theology must be meaningful: as he wrote in his 1947 essay, *The Problem of Theological Method*, "there is no meaningful speaking of God except in an existential attitude."[13] So, although this approach "answers the questions asked of, and the criticisms directed against, a concrete religion," he added that "an answer is possible only if there is a common ground between the one who asks and the one who answers," and the method of correlation is the way to carry this connection through. In other words, it is not a matter of subjecting culture to a new Christian heteronomy, nor of subjecting the Christian *kerygma* (proclamation) to the questions of an autonomous culture, but of finding the natural connections that exist between the structures of human existence and the symbols found in the Christian tradition. Tillich's apologetic method stands in contrast to Karl Barth's kerygmatic approach, which sought to interpret the kerygma of the Christian church without reference to cultural forms. Tillich recognized the legitimate concern behind Barth's stance, which is that the "substance of the Christian message may be lost," but countered that dangers "are not a reason for avoiding serious demand."[14] In fact, he suggested that Barth's method, while seeking to safeguard the Christian message, carries a different risk, which is that the kerygma may be isolated and elevated from the human situation. It is to be noted that, in rejecting an understanding of revelation as "supra-natural communication of knowledge," and arguing that revelation is to be found in human experience, he was not positing the latter as a source or norm of theology. Nor was he speaking of "religious experience" in the usual sense. Revelation, he said, is "the manifestation of the ultimate ground and meaning of human existence." It is a matter of ultimate concern and grasps the whole person. Therefore, it is not experience "but revelation received in experience" that provides the content of theology.[15]

Political theologian

Tillich's disillusionment in World War I was not only theological in nature but also political, as he saw "the exploitation of the common man at the hands of powers he had always taken for granted: the landed aristocracy, the army, and the church."[16] In the 1920s in Berlin, Tillich joined the Kairos Circle, a group of intellectuals who saw the kairos moment as calling for a commitment to a philosophically and religiously deepened form of socialism. In an essay published by the Kairos Circle in 1923, Tillich introduced religious socialism as rooted in the prophetic spirit that transcends both conservative and liberal political orientations.[17] The goal of religious socialism is theonomy, here defined as the "condition in which the spiritual and social forms are filled with the importance of the Unconditional as the foundation, meaning, and reality of all forms."[18] In other words, he sought a form of socialism grounded in a prophetic call to justice that transcends ideology.

Tillich's famous idea of the "Protestant Principle," the principle that identifies idolatry and absolutism, was an expression of this emphasis on the prophetic. His focus on the critical spirit of the Hebrew prophets was somewhat unique among Protestant theologians at the time, foreshadowing the political and liberation theologies of the second half of the twentieth century. For Tillich, the prophetic was a gift inherited from Judaism, which led him to emphasize the continuing importance of Judaism, both in itself and for Christian theology. This was not a merely academic point for him, as it grew from lifelong friendships with fellow Kairos Circle member Adolf Löwe, and later on, members of the Frankfurt School such as Max Horkheimer, among many others. His association of Judaism with the prophetic principle was undoubtedly somewhat reductive, but, as Albert Friedlander remarks, "We listen to Tillich the theologian because Tillich the human being extraordinaire cast his lot with the Jewish people in dark times."[19] When the Nazi secretary of education summoned him in the fall of 1933 and offered him the prestigious chair of theology at the University of Berlin upon the condition that he retract his criticism of Nazism and deny the significance of

Judaism for Christianity, he refused.[20] The official then recommended that Tillich leave Germany for his own safety, something Tillich's friends had already urged him to do, knowing that he was prone to spontaneous outbursts of indignation at the barbarity of Nazism.

But Tillich's fate had in fact already been sealed by his demand in 1932 that violent Nazi students at the University of Frankfurt be expelled and by publications in which he denounced Nazism. In his 1932 "Ten Theses: The Church and the Third Reich," he urged Protestantism to set "the cross against the paganism of the swastika" and said that the cross was against the "holiness' of nation, race, blood, and power."[21] At the end of that year, he published his most powerful analysis of Nazi ideology, *The Socialist Decision*, a book he himself would later regard as his most significant. Unfortunately, the book was quickly banned by the new Nazi regime.

The suppression of Tillich's political writing and his emigration to the United States meant that his voice was to some extent absent from the ensuing political-theological conversation in Germany. That role was left to the Confessing Church, which was heavily influenced by Karl Barth. But Tillich's rejection of Nazism had different theological origins from that of the Confessing Church. The influence of Jewish thinkers, and his belief in the continuing importance of Judaism as bearer of the prophetic spirit, helped him to realize that the persecution of Jews was integral, and not accidental, to Nazism's blood-and-soil paganism.[22] Tillich's theology was also much more explicitly political. His religious socialism was premised on the idea that the theological struggle is not against secularism (as Barthian theology might suggest) but against the demonic forces that spring forth from the depths of religion and culture. For Tillich Nazism was not to be compromised with even in matters of the state: it was to be defeated since it was a distorted, demonic cultural-religious expression. Tillich defined the demonic as "the contradiction of unconditioned form, an eruption of the irrational ground," or, more simply, as the "perversion of the creative."[23] This is no Manichean outside force, no world of spirits, nor the idea of the satanic, but the distortion of reality itself, the possibility that is present alongside the divine within the sacramental ground of existence, which emerges to sow destruction in the absence of the prophetic spirit. In his 1926 essay, *The Demonic*, Tillich identified capitalism and nationalism as the most potent demonries of his time: as form-creating expressions of human nature, they also carry with them form-destroying strength.[24]

Nationalism and capitalism make a reappearance in *The Socialist Decision*, as expressions of two political principles derived from the human condition. Borrowing from Schelling the notion of conscious and unconscious driving forces in history, Tillich developed the idea of a political principle as something dynamic, "the power of a historical reality, grasped in concepts."[25] Human beings, he said, are creatures with an internal duality: that of existence itself (Being), and that of standing over against ourselves, i.e. being self-aware (Consciousness). In other words, as human beings we find ourselves both "thrown" into this world, dependent on it, rooted in "the powers of origin" (the *Whence* of soil, family, community, race, nation), and, on the other hand, confronted by the unconditional demand of realizing something new through ourselves (the *Whither* of future-orientation that breaks the myth of origin).[26] The former is the source of conservative and romantic politics, the latter that of liberal, democratic, and socialist politics.

From this anthropological analysis, Tillich posited two opposing (yet mutually dependent) political principles: the Romantic principle that is rooted in Being, in the myth of origin; and the Bourgeois principle, which, rooted in self-awareness and future orientation, carries with it the unconditional demand that breaks the myth of origin. This unconditional demand comes from two sources: Jewish prophetism, which, in its emphasis on the God of history, breaks through the idea of the gods of blood and soil; and Enlightenment reason, which shatters the myth of origin with its rhetoric of progress. However, echoing Marx, Tillich also recognized the challenge posed to the bourgeois principle by the class struggle. But whereas Marx, who was unable to see the importance of "powers of origin" such as religion or family, predicted a future Utopia emerging from the ashes of capitalism, Tillich, being no Utopian, recognized that bourgeois hegemony not only creates economic trouble for the working classes but also causes meaninglessness by bringing cultural traditions and loyalties to family, nation, or religion under the rule of rationality. As a result, the rebellion against the bourgeoisie would not necessarily take the form of socialism but might instead give rise to a Romantic counterreaction, either in the somewhat benign form of a conservative defense of the traditional or in the disruptive form of revolutionary romanticism.

Tillich therefore recognized that Nazism was addressing a real need, an uprising against the bourgeois political center amidst the economic crisis of the day. Franklin Sherman even suggested that Tillich had a sense of sympathy with the "little people" who sought in Nazism's authoritarianism and claims of traditional values a return to the security of "mother and father."[27] But Tillich also saw that what the Nazis really represented was the demonic alliance of the revolutionary romantics and the bourgeois elites, creating an aggressive and violent nationalism. He sought to offer an alternative to this unholy alliance: theonomous socialism, which he formulated in terms of the fulfillment of the aspirations of both the bourgeois and romantic principles, because it was premised upon an integrated anthropology that recognized that Being is fulfilled in Consciousness, that the *whither* question is the consummation of the intention of the *whence* question. He proposed, in essence, a socialism that both seeks the social transformation that the Bourgeois principle stands for, and recognizes the meaning that humans find in the "powers of origin." He wrote in the final paragraph of *The Socialist Decision*, "Socialism can be victorious only in reliance on its own principle, in which powers of origin and prophetic expectation are combined." But he cautioned that the prophetic expectation should play the most important role, for only in this is human existence fulfilled. The spirit of prophetic expectation is the only hope, he concluded, for triumphing "over the death now threatening Western civilization through the resurgence of the myth of origin."[28]

Although the political dimensions of Tillich's thought became obscured during his American years, he remained deeply concerned about political matters. Between 1942 and 1944 he delivered more than 100 radio addresses that were broadcast into Nazi Germany, in which he urged Germans to recognize and reject the evil of Nazism. These broadcasts were largely unknown to the American public, destined to be recovered only decades later, as was the case with his German political writing.[29] Tillich's later political thought focused on issues such as Zionism and nuclear armament, which reflected the political climate of the 1940s and 1950s, but of the early socialist Tillich there was little to be seen in the Cold War period. The important American political movements of the 1960s, such as the Civil Rights movement and second wave feminism, came about during the final years of Tillich's life, with the result that he did not address these issues to any significant extent, although he did express the need for people to come together to fight the forces of destruction seen in racism, urging "encounters where love and justice become creatively one."[30]

Systematic theologian

It is as an existentialist philosopher and systematic theologian that Tillich is most remembered. One of his most famous books is *The Courage to Be*, in which he addressed various forms of anxiety. First published in 1952, this book marked a shift from his earlier focus on religious socialism and his political engagement during World War II, toward addressing the US context and in particular the situation of the individual in the modern age. The book introduced his characteristic theology of culture to an American audience, as well as some key concepts in his systematic theology. It showcased Tillich's blending of existentialism and depth psychology as he developed an ontology of anxiety, which is the state "in which a being is aware of its possible nonbeing."[31] He argued that our awareness of our finitude, whether in the ontological form of fate and death, the spiritual form of doubt and meaninglessness, or the moral form of guilt and condemnation, is an inevitable part of human existence. We attempt to cope with anxiety by turning it into the fear of something specific, something that can be met with an active response, but since nonbeing is part of being, anxiety cannot be eliminated. Instead, it must be faced with courage, which is affirmation of one's being despite the threat of nonbeing. This courage comes from faith, i.e. from the state of being grasped by the power of being itself. The source of that faith, and hence of that courage, is the God above God. This is not the God of theism, the God who is a Being, but is rather Being Itself, the God who appears "when God has disappeared in the anxiety of doubt."[32] Related to this is Tillich's insistence that the Protestant doctrine of justification by grace through faith includes not only the sinner in divine grace, but also the doubter, because the Reformers' central insight was that faith is not an intellectual act to be performed but was simply the receiving of divine grace.[33] Nowhere is this more beautifully expressed than in his famous sermon, *You Are Accepted.*[34]

In his magnum opus, his *Systematic Theology*, Tillich developed these and related themes in greater detail. Consisting of three volumes and five sections, the *Systematic Theology* presents a structured discussion of Christian theology in correlation with significant aspects of human existence. Part I focuses on the question of truth, correlating reason and revelation; Part II focuses on finitude, correlating being and God; Part III focuses on our existential sense of alienation, correlating existence and the Christ; Part IV examines the ambiguities that mark our lives, correlating life and the Spirit; and Part V focuses on the question of the meaning of history, correlating history and the kingdom of God.

In the first volume of the *Systematic Theology*, after showing the essential unity of reason and revelation, Tillich presented his view that God ought not to be seen as a Being but rather as Being Itself. God is that reality which sustains being: in other words, God is the Ground of Being.[35] From this view also followed his refusal to engage in arguments for the existence of God, since that would treat God as a Being among other beings. In a sense God does not "exist" since there is no Being called God.[36] Therefore, no genuine atheism is possible for anyone who has ultimate concern.

God as Being Itself is correlated to the structure of essential being, which is constituted by three sets of polar ontological elements: individualization and participation, dynamics and form, and freedom and destiny.[37] Building on this ontological analysis, Tillich then set out to reinterpret the Fall in volume II. Utilizing existentialism (which he regarded as the "good luck of Christian theology" that "helped to rediscover the classical Christian interpretation of human existence"), Tillich translated the classical teaching that we are created good but are also sinners, by saying that humans are not existentially what we essentially are.[38] We are estranged from our true being, although this also implies that we belong essentially to that from which we are estranged.[39] In a departure from a "paradise lost" view of original sin, he said that the "dreaming innocence" of essential being is not perfection, but that being drives beyond itself toward existence, despite the manifestations of estrangement that come with it.[40] The concept "estrangement" therefore captures the innermost character of sin in classical hamartiology, which is the tragic disruption of the essential unity with God, although it does not replace the concept of sin, since the latter emphasizes personal responsibility alongside the tragic element. Under the conditions of estrangement, the basic ontological structure, that of the mutual coherence of self and world, breaks apart. This leads to the disintegration of each of the ontological polarities: freedom is distorted into arbitrariness, destiny into mechanical necessity, dynamics into formless urge for self-transcendence, form into external law, individualization into loneliness, and participation into collectivization. In short, Tillich identified some of the basic tensions in human existence and the ways in which an overreach in one direction or the other leads to disintegration of being. Estranged from the power of being, our being is constrained by finitude: we live under the domination of death and are torn apart by the anxiety of having to die.[41]

It is against this background that Tillich introduced Christ as the Bearer of New Being, as "the undistorted manifestation of essential being within and under the conditions of existence."[42] The New Being stands in contrast to both the merely potential character of essential being, and the estranged character of existential being. Christ is the "one in whom the conflict between the essential unity of God and man and man's existential estrangement is overcome."[43] Tillich's Christology also reflects his existential approach in another way: he stated that the event on which Christianity is based has two sides: "the fact which is called 'Jesus of Nazareth' and the reception of this fact by those who received him as the Christ."[44] As such, what we have of Jesus is not a photograph but an "expressionist portrait."[45]

This emphasis on the Christ having "a spatial breadth" in the community of New Being opened up Tillich's theology to an expansive theology of the Spirit, which was the focus of the third volume of the *Systematic Theology*.[46] In fact, as Langdon Gilkey remarked, "Tillich is in truth a theologian of being; but what he means by being is often misunderstood if he is not also seen as a theologian of the Spirit."[47] Using the language of "the Spiritual Presence" to denote that the Spirit is "the presence of the Divine Life within creaturely life," Tillich saw the Spirit, alongside the kingdom of God and eternal life, as symbols of unambiguous life.[48] The Spiritual Presence enables, albeit fragmentarily, the overcoming of ambiguity in morality, culture, and religion, which correspond to the three ontological polarities of individualization/participation, dynamics/form, and freedom/destiny, respectively, thus enabling (fragmentary) self-integration, self-creativity, and self-transcendence. Therefore, in the Spiritual Presence, "man's essential being appears under the conditions of existence, conquering the distortions of existence in the reality of the New Being."[49] Likewise, in the realm of culture, under the impact of the Spiritual Presence, "the law can receive a theonomous quality to the extent that the Spirit is effective," becoming the justice of the kingdom of God.[50] Finally, the Spiritual Presence enables the overcoming of the ambiguity of dynamics and form in religion. Religion is not to be desired in itself: Tillich emphasized that the church is not a religious community but the New Being in community. The paradox of the church is that it participates in both the ambiguities of life in general and the unambiguous life of the spiritual community that is the work of the Spirit of God. Hence the church needs both the Catholic substance, "the concrete embodiment of the Spiritual Presence," and the Protestant principle, which is an "expression of the conquest of religion by the Spiritual Presence and consequently an expression of the victory over the ambiguities of religion, its profanization, and its demonization."[51]

The *Systematic Theology* concludes with Tillich's reflections on history, in which he wrote that the kingdom of God and eternal life are represented by the community of the Spiritual Presence (the church) fragmentarily fulfilling life within the kairos of history. The kingdom of God and eternal life are symbols that point to the eternal conquering of all the ambiguities of existence, suggesting integration of the self, theonomy, and the elevation of the temporal to the eternal.

Debate, Achievement, and Agenda

Although Tillich enjoyed considerable respect and even fame in his lifetime and continues to inspire a younger generation of scholars, he has not been without his critics. The most devastating harm to Tillich's reputation came from Hannah Tillich's memoirs, in which she shared that their marriage, forged in the bohemian atmosphere of Weimar Berlin, had been an open one marked by infidelity on both sides.[52] Those who point out that Tillich's sexual exploits reflected his longing for his mother, or that it was the result of his rejection of bourgeois values after World War I, that he enjoyed many warm friendships with women that were not necessarily sexual, and that an assessment of his ethics should not be reduced to just this one issue, all have a point.[53] As his former student Ann Belford Ulanov wrote, "He was much more than the recent gossip about his problems with women suggests," noting that he saw women as persons and listened to them with seriousness.[54] But Tillich's legacy was undoubtedly tainted by these revelations. Tillich himself wondered, "Was my erotic life a failure, or was it a daring way of opening up new human possibilities?"[55] Perhaps it would suffice to say that in this area of his life Tillich did not manage to live successfully on the boundary, in this case the boundary of freedom and commitment in matters of sexuality.

When it comes to his theological legacy itself, although Tillich is widely recognized as one of the most significant theologians of the twentieth century, his theology has often been criticized for being too reliant on German philosophical thought, of being abstract, difficult to understand, and veering from orthodoxy to the extent that it becomes unrecognizable as Christian. One significant criticism has been that his Christology ignores the historical Jesus. There is some truth to this critique, and it reflects both his translation of the meaning of Christ into existentialist terms, and the state of historical Jesus scholarship in his time, which made of the historical Jesus a shrouded figure behind the veil of the Christ. One might imagine, though, that Tillich would have relished the focus on the Jewishness of the historical Jesus in later scholarship.

Tillich's terminology, his ontology, and his reliance on existentialist philosophy can indeed pose difficulties for those steeped in more traditional theological language. But at the same time one can often trace an indebtedness to the classical theological tradition, a "hidden orthodoxy" in Tillich's theology. One particular classical theologian who influenced Tillich was Augustine, whom he described as "the foundation of everything the West had to say."[56] Despite being critical of Augustine's "ecclesiastical-conservative mentality," he believed that the Augustinian trajectory offers the possibility of overcoming the "fateful gap between religion and culture, thus reconciling concerns which are not strange to each other but have been estranged from each other."[57] In Augustine's thought "man discovers himself when he discovers God, he discovers something that is identical with himself although it transcends him infinitely."[58] It is clear how Tillich's thinking resonated with this reading of Augustine. Echoing Augustine's prayer that "our hearts are restless until they rest in you," Tillich's correlational theology suggests a connecting point between humanity and God, a sense of human longing for and belonging to divine reality. That same (be)longing is reflected in his concept of estrangement, and was clearly premised on Augustine's hamartiology, which he interpreted as offering an existentialist perspective on the human condition.[59] Within this framework, reason and revelation are not strangers to each other, but reflect a link between the *imago dei* in all human beings and the logos that is incarnate in Jesus Christ. Although less indebted to Augustine in his doctrine of God, it is clear that his vision of God as the Ground of Being does not in fact replace the personal God with an abstract foundation to life (as it has been accused of doing), but expresses a sense of the fullness of God's Being found throughout the tradition, from the biblical tetragrammaton, to Augustine's sense of our belonging to God, to Thomas Aquinas' *Ipsum Esse Subsistens*. In short, his radical rethinking of theology for the modern age was nevertheless rooted in a deep, yet critical engagement of classical theology.

It has been said that, unlike Karl Barth, Tillich did not leave a school of thought and that his theology has a certain "planned obsolescence," because he saw the task of theology as always involved in the tensions of the day. But it would be a mistake to assume that his influence has been anything other than considerable. As Martin Marty observed, "Who has done as much in our time to build bridges between Christian faith or theology and culture, particularly the arts?"[60] Among the first generation of Tillich scholars the focus was often on his theology of culture: Langdon Gilkey, for example, used Tillich to argue that even ostensibly secular culture has a religious depth dimension, and Jewish post-Holocaust theologian Richard Rubenstein's Death of God theology was partially inspired by Tillich's rejection of traditional theism and his sense of broken theological symbols.[61] His method of correlation has been particularly influential, in part because it represents a basic hermeneutical structure that "requires fidelity to Christian sources and adequacy to human existence," and as such correlation "has characterized all of the creative theology of the modern period."[62] Some feminist theologians, for instance, have found compatibility between his method and their own (Mary Daly calling it "less inadequate" than that of other male theologians).[63] Theologian David Tracy famously folded Tillich's method into his own hermeneutical approach, emphasizing that it must consist of a mutually critical correlation that recognizes that our lived experience shapes the theology we encounter.[64] The incorporation of human situations in theological thinking is also what makes Tillich's approach compatible with liberation theologies, which critically engage the symbols of the Christian faith through the lens of the experience of the oppressed. His use of the concept kairos has found echoes in various liberation theology documents, such as the South African *Kairos Document*, the *Kairos Central America Document*, and *Kairos Palestine*.[65]

In more recent scholarship, Tillich has influenced theologians with a rich variety of interests and approaches. For example, Tillich's desire to rewrite his theology in light of what he had learned about other world religions, which he expressed toward the end of his life, finds expression in John Thatamanil's utilization of Tillich's hamartiology in Christian–Hindu conversation.[66] Pentecostal theologians like Nimi Wariboko and Amos Yong have highlighted the importance of Tillich's pneumatology, an aspect of his thought that had previously been neglected by Tillich scholars.[67] Other theologians, arguing against the opinion that Tillich is "safe and dated," have focused on the radical elements of his thought.[68] His political theology is reflected in theologians who are critical of the excesses of capitalism and of neoliberalism, such as Francis Yip and Mark Lewis Taylor.[69] In fact, in recent years there has been a growing interest in Tillich's political thought, as evidenced by panels at the meetings of the North American Paul Tillich Society (and its German and French counterparts), as well as the American Academy of Religion's "Paul Tillich: Religion, Theology, and Culture" group.

Perhaps most important, as Adam Pryor notes, Tillich endures because he encourages others to be their own theologian, because what existential theology encourages us to do is this: "rework, rephrase, and reconstruct meaningful answers to the changing nature of our existential questions." The method of correlation, seeking as it does to probe again and again the new questions that arise, is at the heart of Tillich's continuing appeal. Tillich himself always remained open to new questions and new insights. "What I had found as a Tillich scholar," writes Pryor, "and sense in other contemporary Tillich scholars around me, is that commitment to correlational theology is simultaneously a commitment to intellectual wondering."[70]

Notes

1 Paul Tillich, *On the Boundary: An Autobiographical Sketch* (New York: Charles Scribner's Sons, 1966).

2 Wilhelm and Marion Pauck, *Paul Tillich: His Life and Thought, Vol. I: Life* (New York: Harper & Row, 1976), 41.

3 Wilhelm and Marion Pauck, *Paul Tillich*, 49.

4 Wilhelm and Marion Pauck, *Paul Tillich*, 51.

5 Paul Tillich, "Basic Principles of Religious Socialism," in *Paul Tillich: Theologian of the Boundaries*, ed. Mark Kline Taylor (Minneapolis, MN: Fortress Press, 1987), 57.

6 Wilhelm and Marion Pauck, *Paul Tillich*, 283.

7 Paul Tillich, "On the Idea of a Theology of Culture," in *Paul Tillich: Theologian of the Boundaries*, 35–54.

8 Paul Tillich, *Systematic Theology*, Vol. III (Chicago, IL: University of Chicago Press, 1963), 248; *Theology of Culture* (New York: Oxford University Press, 1959), 42.

9 Tillich, *Theology of Culture*, 5–6.

10 Paul Tillich, "Protestantism and the Contemporary Style in the Visual Arts," *The Christian Scholar* 40, no. 4 (1957): 307.

11 Tillich, *Theology of Culture*, 41.

12 Paul Tillich, "The Problem of Theological Method: II," *The Journal of Religion* 27, no. 1 (1947): 25.

13 Tillich, "The Problem of Theological Method," 24.

14 Tillich, *Systematic Theology*, Vol. III, 4.

15 Tillich, "The Problem of Theological Method," 22–3.

16 Wilhelm and Marion Pauck, *Paul Tillich*, 48.

17 Paul Tillich, "Basic Principles of Religious Socialism," in *Paul Tillich: Theologian of the Boundaries*, 54–66.

18 Tillich, "Basic Principles of Religious Socialism," 58.

19 Albert H. Friedlander, "Tillich and Jewish Thought," in *The Thought of Paul Tillich*, ed. James Luther Adams, Wilhelm Pauck, and Roger Lincoln Shinn (San Francisco, CA: Harper & Row, 1985), 176.

20 Robert E. Meditz, *The Dialectic of the Holy: Paul Tillich's Idea of Judaism within the History of Religion* (Boston, MA: De Gruyter, 2016), 2.

21 Paul Tillich, "The Church and the Third Reich," in *Paul Tillich: Theologian of the Boundaries*, 116–18.

22 Mary Ann Stenger and Ronald H. Stone, *Dialogues of Paul Tillich* (Macon, GA: Mercer University Press, 2002), 229.

23 Paul Tillich, "Principles of Religious Socialism," in *Paul Tillich: Theologian of the Boundaries*, 61; *The Interpretation of History*, trans. N. A. Rasetzki and Elsa L. Talmey (New York: Charles Scribner's Sons, 1936), 93.

24 Tillich, *The Interpretation of History*, 119.

25 Paul Tillich, *The Socialist Decision*, trans. Franklin Sherman (San Francisco, CA: Harper & Row, 1977), 10.

26 Tillich, *The Socialist Decision*, 5.

27 Franklin Sherman, "Tillich's Social Thought: New Perspectives," *Christian Century* 90, no. 6 (1976), 168–72.

28 Tillich, *The Socialist Decision*, 162.

29 Ronald H. Stone and Matthew Lon Weaver, eds. *Against the Third Reich: Paul Tillich's Wartime Radio Broadcasts into Nazi Germany* (Louisville, KY: Westminster John Knox Press, 1998).

30 Mark Lewis Taylor, "Tillich's Ethics: Between Politics and Ontology," in *The Cambridge Companion to Paul Tillich*, ed. Russell Re Manning (New York: Cambridge University Press, 2009), 190.

31 Paul Tillich, *The Courage to Be* (New Haven, CT: Yale University Press, 1952, 2000), 35.

32 Tillich, *The Courage to Be*, 190.

33 Paul Tillich, *A History of Christian Thought: From Its Judaic and Hellenistic Origins to Existentialism*, ed. Carl Braaten (New York: Simon & Schuster, 1967), 214; *The Courage to Be*, 164.

34 Paul Tillich, *The Shaking of the Foundations* (New York: Charles Scribner's Sons, 1948), 153–63.

35 Paul Tillich, *Systematic Theology*, Vol. I (Chicago, IL: University of Chicago Press, 1951), 163–289.

36 Tillich, *Systematic Theology*, Vol. I, 235–8.

37 Tillich, *Systematic Theology*, Vol. I, 174–86.

38 Paul Tillich, *Systematic Theology*, Vol. II (Chicago, IL: University of Chicago Press, 1957), 27, 45.

39 Tillich, *Systematic Theology*, Vol. II, 45.

40 Tillich, *Systematic Theology*, Vol. II, 39.

41 Tillich, *Systematic Theology*, Vol. II, 66.

42 Tillich, *Systematic Theology*, Vol. II, 119.

43 Tillich, *Systematic Theology*, Vol. II, 125.

44 Tillich, *Systematic Theology*, Vol. II, 97.

45 Tillich, *Systematic Theology*, Vol. II, 116.

46 Tillich, *Systematic Theology*, Vol. II, 136.

47 Langdon Gilkey, *Gilkey on Tillich* (Eugene, OR: Wipf and Stock, 1990), 164.

48 Tillich, *Systematic Theology*, Vol. III, 107.

49 Tillich, *Systematic Theology*, Vol. III, 269.

50 Tillich, *Systematic Theology*, Vol. III, 264.

51 Tillich, *Systematic Theology*, Vol. III, 245.

52 Hannah Tillich, *From Time to Time* (New York: Stein & Day, 1973).

53 Rollo May, *Paulus: Reminiscences of a Friendship* (New York: Harper & Row, 1973); Alexander C. Irwin, *Eros towards the World: Paul Tillich and the Theology of the Erotic* (Minneapolis, MN: Fortress Press, 1991); Rachel Sophia Baard, "Tillich and Feminism," in *The Cambridge Companion to Paul Tillich*, 273–87.

54 Ann Belford Ulanov, "The Anxiety of Being," in *The Thought of Paul Tillich*, 120.

55 May, *Paulus*, 65.

56 Tillich, *A History of Christian Thought*, 103.

57 Paul Tillich, *The Protestant Era* (Chicago, IL: University of Chicago Press, 1951), 36; "The Two Types of Philosophy of Religion," in *Paul Tillich: Ausgewählte Texte*, ed. Christian Danz, Werner Schüssler, and Erdmann Sturm (New York: Walter De Gruyter, 2008), 300.

58 Paul Tillich, "The Two Types of Philosophy of Religion," in *Paul Tillich: Ausgewählte Texte*, 289.

59 Tillich, *The Courage to Be*, 128.

60 Martin E. Marty, "The Tillich Legacy," *International Christian Digest* 1, no. 6 (1987): 10.

61 Langdon Gilkey, *Naming the Whirlwind: The Renewal of God-Language* (Indianapolis, IN: Bobbs-Merrill, 1969); Richard L. Rubenstein, *After Auschwitz: History, Theology and Contemporary Judaism* (Basingstoke: Macmillan, 1966).

62 Roger Haight, *An Alternative Vision: An Interpretation of Liberation Theology* (Mahwah, NJ: Paulist Press, 1985), 48–9.

63 Mary Daly, *Beyond God the Father: Toward a Philosophy of Women's Liberation* (Boston, MA: Beacon Press, 1973), 200 n. 10.

64 David Tracy, *The Analogical Imagination: Christian Theology and the Culture of Pluralism* (London: SCM Press, 1981), 64.

65 Ronald H. Stone, "Tillich's Kairos and Its Trajectory," in *Why Tillich? Why Now?*, ed. Thomas G. Bandy (Macon, GA: Mercer University Press, 2021), 295–306.

66 John Thatamanil, *The Immanent Divine: God, Creation, and the Human Predicament* (Minneapolis, MN: Fortress Press, 2006).

67 Nimi Wariboko and Amos Yong, eds., *Paul Tillich and Pentecostal Theology: Spiritual Presence and Spiritual Power* (Bloomington, IN: Indiana University Press, 2015).

68 Russell Re Manning, ed., *Retrieving the Radical Tillich: His Legacy and Contemporary Importance* (New York: Palgrave MacMillan, 2015).

69 Francis Ching-Wah Yip, *Capitalism as Religion? A Study of Paul Tillich's Interpretation of Modernity* (Cambridge, MA: Harvard University Press, 2010); Mark Lewis Taylor, "Socialist Spirit in Tillich, Pentecostalism, and the Neoliberal Demonic Today," in *Paul Tillich and Pentecostal Theology*, 203–27; and "Socialism's Multitude: Tillich's *The Socialist Decision* and Resisting the US Imperial," in *Retrieving the Radical Tillich*, 133–57.

70 Adam Pryor, "Needing Tillich Now More than Ever Before," in *Why Tillich? Why Now?*, 4, 6.

Recommended Reading

Primary

Tillich, Paul. *Against the Third Reich: Paul Tillich's Wartime Radio Broadcasts into Nazi Germany.* Edited by Ronald H. Stone and Matthew Lon Weaver. Louisville, KY: Westminster John Knox Press, 1998.

———. *Biblical Religion and the Search for Ultimate Reality.* Chicago, IL: University of Chicago Press, 1955.

———. *The Courage to Be.* New Haven, CT: Yale University Press, 1952.

———. *Dynamics of Faith.* New York: HarperCollins, 1958.

———. *The Interpretation of History.* New York: Charles Scribner's Sons, 1934.

———. *On the Boundary.* New York: Charles Scribner's Sons, 1966.

———. *The Shaking of the Foundations.* New York: Charles Scribner's Sons, 1948.

———. *The Socialist Decision.* Translated by Franklin Sherman. New York: Harper & Row, 1977.

———. *Systematic Theology.* Vols. 1–3. Chicago, IL: University of Chicago Press, 1951–63.

———. *Theology of Culture.* New York: Oxford University Press, 1959.

Secondary

Adams, James Luther, Wilhelm Pauck, and Roger Lincoln Shinn, eds. *The Thought of Paul Tillich.* San Francisco: Harper & Row, 1985.

Bandy, Thomas G., ed. *Why Tillich? Why Now?* Macon, GA: Mercer University Press, 2021.

Gilkey, Langdon. *Gilkey on Tillich.* Eugene, OR: Wipf and Stock, 1990.

Meditz, Robert E. *The Dialectic of the Holy: Paul Tillich's Idea of Judaism within the History of Religion.* Boston, MA: Walter De Gruyter, 2016.

Pauck, Wilhelm, and Pauck, Marion. *Paul Tillich: His Life and Thought.* Vol. 1. Chicago: Harper & Row, 1956.

Re Manning, Russell, ed. *The Cambridge Companion to Paul Tillich.* New York: Cambridge University Press, 2009.

———, ed. *Retrieving the Radical Tillich: His Legacy and Contemporary Importance.* New York: Palgrave MacMillan, 2015.

Stenger, Mary Ann, and Ronald H. Stone. *Dialogues of Paul Tillich.* Macon, GA: Mercer University Press, 2002.

Taylor, Mark Kline. *Paul Tillich: Theologian of the Boundaries.* Minneapolis, MN: Fortress Press, 1991.

Wariboko, Nimi, and Amos Yong, eds. *Paul Tillich and Pentecostal Theology: Spiritual Presence and Spiritual Power.* Bloomington, IN: Indiana University Press, 2015.

The Niebuhrs

Joshua Mauldin

Introduction

Born two years apart, the brothers Reinhold Niebuhr and H. Richard Niebuhr were leading American theologians and ethicists who made a lasting impact in the academy, the church, and the wider society. There are ways to interpret the two Niebuhrs that emphasize their similarity and their contribution to a common project, but there are also ways to interpret them as pursuing strikingly different goals, despite the proximity of their origins. There is, of course, some truth in both interpretations.

Reinhold Niebuhr (1892–1971) and Helmut Richard Niebuhr (1894–1962) were the third and fourth children, respectively, in the household of Gustav and Lydia Niebuhr. Reinhold and H. Richard grew up in Missouri and Illinois in parsonages of the German Evangelical Synod, in which Gustav served as a pastor. Both Reinhold and H. Richard followed their father into ministry in the German Evangelical Synod, a denomination that would later become what is now the United Church of Christ. Reinhold and H. Richard both studied at Elmhurst College and Eden Theological Seminary before finishing their formal educations at Yale, where H. Richard would earn a PhD while Reinhold concluded his studies with an MA degree, electing to enter the ministry in Detroit rather than pursue a doctoral degree.

Reinhold served as a pastor in Detroit for thirteen years before joining the faculty of Union Theological Seminary in New York in 1928, where he would remain even beyond his official retirement from the faculty in 1960. Reinhold Niebuhr's experiences in the industrialized city of Detroit, along with the horrors of World War I and its aftermath, led him to abandon the liberal theological assumptions of his youth for a more measured perspective on human possibilities that came to be called "Christian realism." Across several decades, including the tumult of World War II, the Cold War, and into the 1960s, Niebuhr's Christian realism provided an illuminating perspective on ethics and social issues that was influential not only in theological and academic circles but also among journalists, policymakers, and political leaders.

H. Richard's impact was important as well, though more academic in nature. Following the completion of his PhD at Yale, H. Richard served as president of Elmhurst College and academic dean of Eden

Ford's The Modern Theologians: An Introduction to Christian Theology since 1918, Fourth Edition.
Edited by Rachel Muers and Ashley Cocksworth.
© 2024 John Wiley & Sons Ltd. Published 2024 by John Wiley & Sons Ltd.

Theological Seminary. In 1931 he joined the faculty of Yale Divinity School, where he would spend the rest of his career, influencing generations of scholars in the fields of theology and Christian ethics and establishing a legacy in those fields that continues to the present day.

Survey: Reinhold Niebuhr

Reinhold Niebuhr began his career as the pastor of Bethel Evangelical Church in Detroit, Michigan, in August 1915 with high hopes for social progress in American society. Like other pastors at the time, Niebuhr was involved in unionization, improving race relations, and a range of other social issues related to industrialization and urbanization within Detroit and further afield. These experiences in Detroit led Reinhold to begin to question the assumptions of the Social Gospel. This movement in Protestant Christianity had been popularized in the 1890s by Charles Sheldon, who suggested that social ills could be ameliorated if only everyone lived their daily lives in accord with the question, "What would Jesus do?"[1] Later thinkers in the Social Gospel tradition had begun to undertake a more structural analysis of social ills,[2] and Reinhold took this analysis to its logical conclusion: conflict is unavoidable, even our moral ideals are mired in sin and self-interest, and those in power will not give up power unless forced to do so.

Reinhold was joined by other thinkers in this turn toward realism, broadly understood. An entire generation of theologians on both sides of the Atlantic began to challenge what they now saw as the naïve sentimentality of the Social Gospel, which had seemed so morally inspiring at the turn of the century. Karl Barth witnessed what he saw as the bankruptcy of liberal theology in the support his liberal theological teachers gave to the imperial ambitions of Germany in World War I. Meanwhile, by 1931 H. Richard had begun his teaching career at Yale Divinity School and was beginning to question the prevailing assumptions of liberal Protestant theology. Reinhold's unique contribution was to focus these efforts on social and political critique.

Although Reinhold's first book, *Does Civilization Need Religion?*, foreshadowed many themes to which the author would later return, it was his second book that put him on the theological map. *Moral Man and Immoral Society* was published in 1932, and the book's contents led many to conclude that Reinhold had abandoned his Christian understanding of God, humanity, and the church entirely, such was the historical materialist focus on power in social and political relations. One family friend even proclaimed, "Reinie's gone crazy!"[3] Contemporaries such as Francis Pickens Miller lamented that Reinhold lacked any ecclesiology, a critique that Stanley Hauerwas would resurrect many decades after Reinhold's death.[4] Reinhold conceded at the time that *Moral Man* was indeed not directed at the church but at liberal thinkers in general.[5] Reinhold's next book, *Reflections on the End of an Era*, published two years later in 1934, only confirmed his critics' suspicion that Reinhold had forsaken Christian thought for Marxist materialism. Deep down, however, Reinhold's understanding of history and of politics had roots in the Christian tradition in Martin Luther, and in the history of political philosophy in Thomas Hobbes. Working in this tradition of thought, Reinhold conceived of politics through the lens of a political leader wielding power. This framework would later help him communicate with modern political realists like Hans Morgenthau and other figures in public life.

A realist account of human nature

The Christian realism Reinhold Niebuhr had developed by midcareer involved an interlocking set of claims about human nature, politics, God, and morality. Niebuhr's realism was grounded in an account of human nature, which he articulated most clearly in his magnum opus, *The Nature and Destiny of Man*, originally delivered as his Gifford Lectures at the University of Edinburgh in 1939. Realism about human nature involved considering all the realities in a situation, especially the role of self-interest, which is involved at all levels of human activity. This was the ground for Reinhold Niebuhr's political realism, but it is important to note that Niebuhr's Christian realism was not reducible to a form of political realism. It also involved commitments to theological realism as well as moral realism.[6] As a form of theological realism, Reinhold's Christian realism assumes that the divine reality exists independently of human conceptions of God. Likewise, his moral realism assumes that moral truths exist independently of the moral languages we use to attempt to describe these moral truths. Our apprehension of both divine and moral truth is always inadequate, provisional, and marked by self-interest and self-deception. There is thus a role for a kind of judgment on history that takes place beyond history, as Reinhold elaborated in the second volume of his Gifford Lectures, on human destiny.

According to Reinhold's account of human nature, human beings are characterized by a tension between our finitude as created beings and our capacity for self-transcendence. Not only are we marked by finitude; what is more, we know ourselves to be so. This leads to anxiety, and thus to sin, as we search in vain for ways to escape our finitude through our own power. Our capacity for self-transcendence makes this hope for an escape from finitude seem possible and necessary, but it ends in despair. As Reinhold sees it, the Christian tradition, better than any modern or classical alternatives, speaks to this human tension, particularly in its ideas of the image of God and of the fall into sin. The image of God is a symbol of the human capacity for self-transcendence, whereas original sin and the Fall are symbols for human finitude and the anxiety involved in the prideful human attempt to escape finitude. This escape was "inevitable" though not necessary, Reinhold suggests, attempting to thread a needle to account for both human freedom as well as our bondage to sin.

The Nature and Destiny of Man provides a sweeping tour of ancient and modern thought, in which Reinhold depicts the variety of traditions that have tried and failed to account for this basic tension in human nature. Reinhold argues that the Christian tradition provides the best option we have for taking account of these fundamental aspects of human nature. As is clear from this way of framing the question, Reinhold Niebuhr does not begin with revelation as the Word of God and then from there lay out a theology and ethics, in the manner of a theologian like Karl Barth. Reinhold instead wants to speak to anyone interested in understanding human nature, not only those willing to begin with the truth of the Christian revelation. Reinhold thus begins with an account of human nature that he believes anyone, Christian or not, can accept. He then argues that the Christian tradition, and in particular certain symbols within the Christian tradition, can account for the tensions in human nature better than any other secular or religious alternatives. This was a theological method that Niebuhr would never abandon, and it is the clearest sign of the endurance of liberal theological assumptions in his work throughout his career.[7]

Faith, ethics, and politics

Even as Reinhold published his Gifford Lectures on human nature and human destiny, much of his attention throughout his life was on practical affairs in the political realm. Indeed, he would even deny that he was a theologian at all, somewhat defensively noting in 1956 that "I have never been very competent in the nice points of pure theology; and I must confess that I have not been sufficiently interested heretofore to acquire the competence."[8] Reinhold held a chair at Union Theological Seminary in "applied Christianity" and primarily identified as a social ethicist. Even at his most theological, Reinhold was always interested in religious traditions and systems in terms of their ethical and social implications. If a theological or religious system encourages quietism and supports the status quo, it is found wanting. Likewise, if it builds castles in the air that have no clear bearing on ethics and politics, it is a failed religious and theological system.

In an earlier work from 1935, *An Interpretation of Christian Ethics*, Reinhold developed the argument that the ethics of Jesus represents an "impossible ideal," which, although not achievable this side of the eschaton, serves a practical function by providing a kind of yardstick by which to judge our moral action. In this book, Reinhold speaks characteristically more of "prophetic religion" than of Christianity more generally. Prophetic religion, as Niebuhr sees it, begins with the Hebrew prophets, culminates in the ethics of Jesus, and continues in religious forms and practices that preserve the relevance of an impossible ideal. The teaching of Jesus is the fruit of Hebraic prophetic religion. It indicts all human action, even while maintaining that created life is meaningful. In contrast with mystical religion, Jesus does not enjoin a flight away from the created order into a transcendent realm. His teaching is relevant for the world in which we live, even while it points to an ideal that we can never reach.

The prophetic tradition of the Hebrew Prophets and of Jesus's teaching is to be commended for maintaining the "relevance" of an impossible ideal as a criterion for social criticism, without committing the opposing errors of seeing the ideal either as a simple achievement within history or as irrelevant to human social life. Ever the dialectical thinker, Reinhold sees the first error in liberal Christianity, and the second error is that of what he calls "orthodoxy," which dwells so radically on human sin and finitude that religious ideals come to have no bearing on the moral life. In both instances there are religious and secular forms of the twin errors. Liberalism, whether in the religious form of the Social Gospel, or in secular form in the teachings of contemporaries like John Dewey, falls into the error of viewing moral ideals as achievable in history, if only we try hard enough or provide everyone with a proper education. In this instance, the impossibility of the ideal is lost. Likewise, orthodoxy emphasizes human sin to such an extent that moral ideals cease to have any relevance in practical affairs. According to the framework of one of Reinhold's later works, these twin errors can be seen as those of the Children of Light on the one hand, who are too enamored of their own virtue, and the Children of Darkness, on the other, who know no moral law beyond their own self-interest.[9] In his later work, Reinhold would return to this framework repeatedly to illuminate the global power struggle between the United States and the Soviet Union. Whereas Reinhold's earliest works emphasized the role of power and self-interest at every level of human affairs, by his later works he provided a limited defense of democracy as the best political system available, even though imperfect.

Certain threads run throughout Reinhold's corpus of work, lying dormant for some time only to reemerge in other contexts. One is the idea that the Christian faith properly understood should underwrite both a "critical" and a "responsible" attitude. Against those conceptions of theology that too closely aligned God's transcendent reality with contemporary cultural mores, Reinhold advocated a "critical" attitude. Here, Reinhold pointed to the shortcomings of liberal Protestantism, which naïvely believed we could build God's kingdom on earth if only we tried hard enough. Against conceptions of God that provide a totalizing judgment of the created order such that human choices become meaningless or inconsequential, Reinhold pointed to the need for a responsible attitude. Even while all our moral strivings fall short of the absolute commands of love, we are enjoined to choose the better options available to us. Here is where Reinhold thought the theology of "orthodox" thinkers like Karl Barth fell short, leaving us with no resources for making moral and political decisions, and failing to show how Christian theology bears on these necessary choices.[10]

The "critical attitude," Reinhold famously declared, must be matched with a "responsible attitude," one that does not refuse "to make a decision between political answers to a problem because each answer is discovered to contain a moral ambiguity in God's sight. We are human beings, not God; we are responsible for making choices between greater and lesser evils, even when our Christian faith, illuminating the human scene, makes it quite apparent that there is no pure good in history; and probably no pure evil either. The fate of civilizations may depend upon these choices between systems of which some are more, others less, just."[11] The early Reinhold of *Moral Man and Immoral Society* saw the "critical" task and the "responsible" task as divided between rival groups in a society, with the powerless managing the critical task and the powers that be managing the task of responsibility. In his later work, Reinhold came to see that the two attitudes could be held in dialectical tension by a single individual rather than marking the site of perpetual social conflict. The theological framework Reinhold developed in his later work served in part to make this dialectical tension between the critical and the responsible attitude tenable for a single individual.

Another central thread in Reinhold's work is the idea that "God" is a reference to the unity of values and interests of all people, a unity that transcends what would otherwise be inevitable conflict among persons and groups. That conflict endures within nature and history, but those who believe in God can act in the hope that a final unity is possible.[12] For some critics, this picture highlights the extent to which Reinhold never really escaped the assumptions of Protestant liberalism, beginning with human needs and "projecting" a picture of the divine on that basis. As Stanley Hauerwas would later put the point, "Niebuhr's god is but a reflection of ourselves."[13] Defenders of Reinhold offer the rejoinder that for Niebuhr, the God who serves as a symbol of the harmony of interests is nonetheless a reality, one which indeed transcends even our inadequate attempts to understand the divine reality.

Survey: H. Richard Niebuhr

The younger Niebuhr brother, H. Richard, was a student of the history of Reformed theology as well as a Reformed theologian himself. Throughout his career his work was characterized by this twin mode, both historical and constructive. H. Richard sought to make theological arguments through the mode of historical study of the history of Christianity, and specifically the history of Protestant Christianity. His work bore the imprint of his study of Max Weber and especially Ernst Troeltsch, about whom he wrote his doctoral dissertation. A Troeltschian historical approach to theology is evident in Richard's first book, *The Social Sources of Denominationalism*, published in 1929. H. Richard observed in this study how American denominations are characterized and differentiated not so much by doctrinal disagreements but instead by differences in class, ethnicity, and race. H. Richard noted a repeated pattern in which low status groups formed one denomination, only to later rise in status and join an establishment from which they had once been excluded. H. Richard would later depict a similar pattern in terms of how new movements for reform in the Christian tradition are always under pressure to eventually conform to the wider society and support the status quo, thereby raising again the need for new reform movements to arise.[14]

H. Richard arrived at Yale as a professor in the field of Christian ethics two years after *The Social Sources of Denominationalism* was published and three years after his brother Reinhold took up his teaching post at Union Theological Seminary in New York. Christian social ethics was by that time a burgeoning field in the tradition of the Social Gospel, which sought to employ modern, social-scientific conceptions of modern society in order to reform society in accord with biblical ideas of love and justice. Both of the Niebuhrs continued this work of the field of social ethics even while questioning some of its fundamental assumptions and seeking a broader historical perspective on the Christian moral tradition.

For H. Richard, the next step on this path came to fruition with his book, *The Kingdom of God in America*. A history of Protestant Christian theology in America, the book seeks to show that the idea of remaking the broader society on the basis of theological ideas is not something new that the Social Gospel invented. Beginning with the earliest New England settlements, Richard shows how the initial motif for this new society was one grounded in the sovereignty of God. Later, with the first Great Awakening, the focus shifted to the Reign of Christ. The nineteenth century saw the rise of the idea of the kingdom of God, so central to the Social Gospel. Richard's contention is that we need all of these motifs, as each serves an important role in the Christian tradition and in the church. The ideas build on one another but also support each other, as any one of them alone misses out on much the Christian tradition can offer to society.

The Kingdom of God in America was a book about history, but H. Richard's purposes were not merely historical. He saw the history he provided as a kind of rebuke of the paths Protestant Christianity had taken since the early Social Gospel movement. What had begun with the Social Gospel as a powerful account of the kingdom of God had devolved into various forms of bland moralism. Relating the central creed of this vapid American liberal theology, H. Richard famously wrote: "A God without wrath brought men without sin into a kingdom without judgment through the ministrations of a Christ without a cross."[15] H. Richard's disdain for what Protestant liberalism had become could hardly be more evident.

History and revelation

Karl Barth's challenge to liberal theology's attempt to synthesize Christian theology and culture challenged H. Richard's historical approach to theology. In a later work, *The Meaning of Revelation*, H. Richard responded to the Barthian critique of Protestant liberalism by articulating how history itself can serve as a vehicle for God's revelation. H. Richard drew an important distinction between *external* and *internal* history. External history refers to an objective perspective on events as described by a third-party observer. Internal history, by contrast, is history as described by those who live it. Internal history, unlike external history, can be a vehicle of revelation, as a living community comes to understand how God has acted in their history.

H. Richard would extend this framework ten years later, providing his own kind of internal history of Christianity, in his book *Christ and Culture*. Richard finds in the history of the Christian tradition five ideal types regarding how the Christian faith is related to the surrounding culture. The Christ *of* culture seeks to accommodate the Christian message to the needs of culture and society. At the other end of the spectrum is a Christ *against* culture, the kind of mode Barth advocated of a Christian theology of revelation that rejects culture, especially the culture that produced the horrors of World War I. Richard also points to a Christ *above* culture focused on the love of God, and a Christ and culture in *paradox*, highlighting forms of theology that uphold simultaneously human sin and finitude alongside our salvation through grace. Richard points to historical figures in the Christian tradition who exemplify each of these ideal types, before finally arriving at the final type, Christ *transforming* culture. It is significant that Richard treats this type last, leading some to conclude that he has stacked the deck in its favor. But even while the transformation of culture should be a kind of ultimate hope, Richard sees it as applicable under certain social conditions, and he continues to maintain that all the types have a role to play in the Christian tradition as it develops and changes through various historical and social contexts.

Radical Monotheism and Responsibility

H. Richard would take this basic framework of internal and external history into new directions in his later works. The idea of an internal history had already suggested a radical openness to the realities of the world as the starting point of the moral life. Human beings do not stand outside their history as external observers but rather within the historical fray, groping to see what is going on around them, including what God is doing. Richard developed this account further in his book *Radical Monotheism and Western Culture*, emphasizing how a radically theocentric perspective neutralizes all the loyalties to which human beings are prone to devote themselves. Richard would speak of a "theocentric relativism," which acknowledges the reality of God even while admitting our own limited nature in understanding fundamental realities.

At the time of his death in 1962, Richard had planned a three-volume work on Christian ethics, the first on methods in Christian ethics, the second on principles in Christian ethics, and the third on concrete moral and political issues.[16] The posthumously published book, *The Responsible Self*, hints at what the first volume of that larger project would have accomplished. It also provided a moral theory to accord with the radical monotheism he had developed previously. As in *Christ and Culture*, Richard in *The Responsible Self* provides a typology to outline the various ways human beings have understood ethical agency. "Man-the-maker" points to the human being working to fashion given materials toward some end or goal. This type is found in various forms of teleological ethics, from Aristotle at the beginning all the way to modern utilitarianism. "Man-the-citizen, living under law" prioritizes the right before the good, and is found in various forms of deontology, emphasizing ideas of law, duty, and obligation. The two options of teleology and deontology had set the agenda for the study of ethics for a long time, but H. Richard thinks they are inadequate for moral agents who must act responsibly in interaction with other moral agents, within the changing realities of the world, and in response to God. These realities require a new symbol of moral agency, that of "man-the-answerer," whose actions are measured not merely in terms of goods achieved or rules obeyed, but instead in terms of the fittingness of response to those who respond to our actions. Richard provides an ethics of responsibility as an alternative to the tired debate between teleology and deontology. "Responsibility," Richard suggests, "proceeds in every moment of decision and choice to inquire: 'What is going on?'"[17] Richard thus conceives of ethics in terms of an ongoing pattern of "fitting" response to what is going on, with expectation of a response from others to our original action, calling for yet another response. As ever in Richard's thought, God is active in this situation, always acting as well as calling forth action from human beings.

Influence and Achievement: The Niebuhrian Legacy

H. Richard's legacy as a scholar and teacher is perhaps most evident in the many generations of scholars he influenced as a professor at Yale Divinity School. Among those who studied with H. Richard, James Gustafson developed a "theocentric ethics" over the course of many books, notably on the question of how theology can integrate the findings of the natural sciences. Gustafson himself mentored many generations of students while teaching for many decades at both Yale and the University of Chicago. Furthering the legacy of H. Richard are now the many students of Gustafson, including William Schweiker, Gerald McKenny, and Stephen Pope, to name just a few. William F. May studied with H. Richard Niebuhr and has furthered his capacious conception of the role of ethics, including notably in the area of professional ethics. Stanley Hauerwas arrived as a student at Yale Divinity School shortly after H. Richard's death but was nonetheless influenced by his work and by like-minded colleagues at Yale such as Hans Frei.[18] Hauerwas would go on to develop H. Richard's emphasis on the integrity of the Christian faith into an account of the virtues and into a larger project of ecclesial ethics. That theologians as different as Stanley Hauerwas and James Gustafson could plausibly understand themselves as furthering the legacy of H. Richard Niebuhr says something important about the breadth of his thought.

Reinhold Niebuhr's legacy is less easily delineated, as it extended well beyond the academic sphere into public life more generally, though he certainly had an impact on the academy as well. Among Reinhold's students at Union was a young Dietrich Bonhoeffer on his fellowship year of 1931–32. Bonhoeffer was not particularly impressed by the faculty or students at Union, but a few years later Reinhold was instrumental in helping Bonhoeffer flee Germany in 1939 for the United States, where he would remain only a few weeks before fatefully deciding to return home. Reinhold played a similar role of mentor to Kiyoko Takeda, a Japanese student at Union Theological Seminary who returned to Japan in 1942, despite Reinhold's offer to help her remain in New York during the war.[19] Reinhold's influence is apparent in other of his students, such as Ronald Stone, who has written several books on his famous mentor, as well as in others who did not study with Reinhold but who furthered his theological legacy, notably Robin W. Lovin, Gary Dorrien, and Douglas Ottati. Reinhold's influence has also endured in the work of political theorists, including Jean Bethke Elshtain, Andrew Bacevich, William Inboden, Anatol Lieven, and John Hulsman. Reinhold's work remains influential at the heights of statecraft, with leaders such as President Barack Obama and the late Senator John McCain citing Niebuhr as an important influence on their thinking.

One wonders if Americans have almost learned Reinhold Niebuhr *too* well. When Reinhold wrote *The Irony of American History* in 1952, he contrasted America's naïve self-understanding as a paragon of virtue with the reality of its actual practice, which was more mixed with compromise and self-interest. For Reinhold, this was to America's credit, insofar as a complete purity of virtue was, in his mind, both impossible and dangerous. This was a time when American power was unparalleled in the world and was on the rise. America today perhaps stands closer to where Britain stood in 1952, and China today is perhaps where America was in 1952, enjoying a steady rise in economic, political, and military might that enables the country to ignore its shortcomings. Meanwhile, contemporary American society is afflicted by political polarization, economic stagnation, and social disillusionment.

In addition to facing a rising power in China, in more recent decades, Americans have become far more attuned to the more lamentable aspects of their history, even to the point of losing sight of the moral ideals and virtues that marked the American founding, inspired democratic movements around the world (including in France) and continue to attract immigrants from countless countries around the world, even in spite of America's shortcomings both in the past and today. If Reinhold wrote at a moment when America's self-image was one of naïve purity that called for acknowledgment of the more compromising realities of American social practice, perhaps today we live in a time when our self-understanding as a country of unremitting evil and injustice requires some leavening with attention to America's democratic virtues and ideals that have endured throughout a morally mixed history into the present day.

Debate: Common Causes, Differences, and Reception of the Niebuhrs

We began this chapter with the observation that there are ways to interpret the Niebuhr brothers as undertaking a common project albeit using different methods, and there are also ways to interpret them as engaged in radically different pursuits. A key moment that emphasizes their disagreement was the Niebuhrs' public debate over the Japanese invasion of Manchuria. In response to the Japanese aggression, H. Richard published an essay in the *Christian Century* titled "The Grace of Doing Nothing," in which he outlined a theological justification for doing nothing even in the face of the aggression. He sought in the essay to question the assumption, common among Americans, that in the face of injustice there was always some clear action that had to be undertaken. At times, he argued, doing nothing was the best option available.

Reinhold Niebuhr responded with vigor, in the same pages of the *Christian Century*, publishing a response titled "Must We Do Nothing?" Much of what separated the two brothers in terms of theology and ethics rose to the surface in this debate. Reinhold came to the question with his characteristic starting point in politics and ethics, in which he tended to judge theological systems on the basis of their social and ethical impact. In this, the influence on Reinhold of William James's pragmatism was evident, wherein truth is "what works" and systems of thought are judged by their fruits, by their impact in the real world. For Reinhold, it was above all evident that something must be done in response to Japan's aggression, and the United States had the capability and thus the imperative to act. Any theological framework would have to adjust to this basic moral fact, and rival theological systems would be judged in accord with how well they did so.

For H. Richard, the starting point was different. H. Richard began more within a specified theological framework and sought to interpret worldly realities through that lens. As H. Richard would later put the point, it was always important to begin with the question "What is going on?," remaining attentive to all the realities that bear on any situation. A central reality in this inventory of what is going on is the question of what God is doing in any given situation. At times, H. Richard suggested, it is not clear to us what God is doing, or what we should do, or can do. At such times, there is a certain grace in doing nothing, since we are unsure of what God will do and of the impact of our actions. As H. Richard would declare in a letter to Reinhold a few years later, "I do think that an activism which stresses immediate results is the cancer of our modern life. It is betraying us constantly into interfering with events, pushing, pulling, trying to wriggle out of an impassable situation, and so drawing the noose tighter around our necks. We want to be saviors of civilization and simply bring down new destruction."[20] If Reinhold had a basic moral intuition that something had to be done, and sought a theological framework to account for that intuition, for H. Richard it was the role of a theological perspective to make us question even our most certain moral intuitions.

The debate also raised the question of whether Reinhold saw God as an actor in history at all. In the wake of the publication of *Moral Man and Immoral Society*, H. Richard had once admonished his older brother in a letter:

> You think of religion as a power – dangerous sometimes, helpful sometimes. That's liberal. For religion itself religion is no power, but that to which religion is directed, God.... I think the liberal religion is thoroughly bad. It is a first-aid to hypocrisy. It is the exaltation of goodwill, moral idealism. It worships the God whose qualities are "the human qualities raised to the nth degree," and I don't expect as much help from this religion as you do. It is sentimental and romantic. Has it ever struck you that you read religion through the mystics and ascetics? You scarcely think of Paul, Augustine, Luther, Calvin. You're speaking of humanistic religion so far as I can see. You come close to breaking with it at times but you don't quite do it.[21]

Both Niebuhrs went through a break with the naïve sentimentality that characterized the liberal theology of the previous generation. At times this looked like a turn away from liberal theology more broadly, as the moniker "neo-Orthodox" was meant to attest. But neither completely broke away from the assumptions of Protestant liberalism, with Reinhold arguably maintaining liberal theological assumptions to a greater extent than H. Richard, who combined a Barthian commitment to the Word of God as a source of revelation with an historical approach to the study of theology steeped in the work of Ernst Troeltsch and Max Weber. Even while attacking the sentimentality of "liberalism," Reinhold was aware that he never completely broke from liberal theological assumptions. A kind of internal critic from within liberal theology, Reinhold sought to make theology more attentive to worldly realities, including to the role that power plays in all human endeavors. Simply trying to live out the teachings of Jesus will not magically solve the world's problems, however righteous our intentions. Sin exists at a much more structural level and is not amenable to simple moral suasion. Insofar as social injustice exists at such a deep structural level, liberals had better get used to the wielding of power. The powerful in any social system will rarely voluntarily give up their power, and so the oppressed have to use means of power to overcome their plight. Reinhold sought to establish all of these claims, even while holding on to certain liberal theological assumptions. In this sense, H. Richard's movement away from liberalism was more fundamental.

Despite these differences, others have interpreted the Niebuhrs more in continuity, as engaging in a similar theological project despite their different approaches and perspectives. In the highly regarded book, *Reinhold Niebuhr and Christian Realism*, Robin W. Lovin avails himself of H. Richard's conception of radical monotheism in an effort to elucidate Reinhold's understanding of God. The interpretation suggests that Reinhold and H. Richard held similar views of God, though perhaps H. Richard's analysis was at times more perspicuous and thus can help us make sense of Reinhold's theology. Scott Paeth has also provided an analysis of the Niebuhr brothers that highlights their continuity, even as it acknowledges important points of divergence and disagreement.[22]

In the years after Reinhold's death his reputation waned in theology. His seemingly slow movement on civil rights and his late defense of a Cold War ideology led many to dismiss his work as outdated. Only in the 1980s and 1990s did his star begin to rise again, and even more so in the twenty-first century. In the post-9/11 era, political theorists such as Andrew Bacevich turned to Reinhold Niebuhr as a resource for rethinking American foreign policy in a changing world, and Jean Bethke Elshtain provided a Niebuhrian analysis of a "just war against terror."[23] Among theologians, Robin W. Lovin extended his analysis of Niebuhrian Christian realism for the "new realities" of a globalized world where the power of nation-states was challenged by international governing bodies, multinational corporations, and terrorist groups that easily crossed national borders.[24] More recently, threats posed to the international liberal order by Russia, Iran, North Korea, and a rising China suggest the era of great power conflict has returned, and with it the relevance of Reinhold Niebuhr's political thought.

Late in his career, the liberation theologian James Cone published a strong critique of Reinhold Niebuhr's failure adequately to respond to the issue of racism in America.[25] A few years earlier, Christian social ethicist Traci West had criticized Reinhold for paying too little attention to what was going on in nearby Harlem while he was working at Union Theological Seminary.[26] Others have painted a more complex and nuanced picture of Reinhold's attention to the issue of racism in the United States.[27] Reinhold's early work had some influence on the Civil Rights movement in America, even if in later years he was unable to imagine how effective the movement could be in the short term. Realism requires attention to both human limits as well as possibilities, and human beings can err in either direction, either giving in to wishful thinking in the face of limitation, or failing to see what possibilities exist, because of a too-consistent pessimism. Niebuhrian realism teaches us to expect such failures, even on the part of Niebuhrians themselves.

Today, the influence of the Niebuhrs is evident even in places where we might not expect it. H. Richard Niebuhr has spawned generations of theologians who are more attentive to the distinctiveness of the Christian tradition even while acknowledging the historically embedded nature of Christianity.[28] Indeed, many contemporary theologians are working in fields first cultivated by H. Richard Niebuhr without always remaining aware of his influence. Reinhold's influence is pervasive far beyond the walls of the church and academy, impacting how political issues are debated in American culture as a whole. Reference to "structural injustice" is so ubiquitous in political discussions today that it is easy to miss how groundbreaking Niebuhr's emphasis on structural sin and injustice was at the time. When Reinhold's career began, to be liberal was to assume that social problems could solved by mere moral suasion, or improved education, or even by simply enacting the teachings of Jesus as an individual. By the end of Reinhold's life, progressives had become far more attentive to the role of power in society, and to the facts of structural injustice and sin. Indeed, attending closely to the morality of individual actors is no longer seen as a progressive ideal at all. In order to address social ills we are instead directed to look at the structures in which injustice is embedded, alongside the history that gave rise to these structures. Only by attending to these wider social forces can real change take place. Even then, moral suasion alone will be insufficient. Conflict is inevitable, as those who possess power will not willingly give it up. These ideas represent a major impact of the Niebuhrian legacy, influencing how democratic societies continue to debate and address social problems. Reinhold's way of thinking endures whether we are aware of it or not. In a very real sense, we are all Niebuhrians now.

Notes

1 Charles M. Sheldon, *In His Steps* (Philadelphia, PA: Henry Altemus, 1899).

2 Walter Rauschenbusch, *A Theology for the Social Gospel* (Louisville, KY: Westminster John Knox Press, 1997).

3 Langdon Gilkey, *On Niebuhr: A Theological Study* (Chicago, IL: University of Chicago Press, 2001), 4.

4 Stanley Hauerwas, *With the Grain of the Universe: The Church's Witness and Natural Theology* (Grand Rapids, MI: Brazos Press, 2001), 137.

5 Richard Wightman Fox, *Reinhold Niebuhr: A Biography* (Ithaca, NY: Cornell University Press, 1996), 142–3.

6 Robin W. Lovin, *Reinhold Niebuhr and Christian Realism* (Cambridge: Cambridge University Press, 1995).

7 Hauerwas, *With the Grain*, ch. 4.

8 Reinhold Niebuhr, "Intellectual Autobiography," in *Reinhold Niebuhr: His Religious, Social, and Political Thought*, ed. Charles W. Kegley and Robert W. Bretall (New York: Macmillan, 1956), 3.

9 Reinhold Niebuhr, *The Children of Light and the Children of Darkness: A Vindication of Democracy and a Critique of Its Traditional Defense* (Chicago, IL: University of Chicago Press, 2011).

10 Joshua Mauldin, "Karl Barth," in *The Oxford Handbook of Reinhold Niebuhr*, ed. Robin Lovin and Joshua Mauldin (Oxford: Oxford University Press, 2021), 111–26.

11 Reinhold Niebuhr, *Faith and Politics: A Commentary on Religious, Social and Political Thought in a Technological Age*, ed. Ronald H. Stone (New York: George Braziller, 1968), 56.

12 Lovin, *Reinhold Niebuhr and Christian Realism*, 33–71.

13 Hauerwas, *With the Grain*, 122.

14 H. Richard Niebuhr, *The Kingdom of God in America* (Chicago, IL: Willett, Clark & Co., 1937).

15 Niebuhr, *The Kingdom of God in America*, 193.

16 Donald W. Shriver, *H. Richard Niebuhr* (Nashville, TN: Abingdon Press, 2009).

17 H. Richard Niebuhr, *The Responsible Self* (New York: Harper & Row, 1963), 60.

18 Stanley Hauerwas, *Hannah's Child: A Theologian's Memoir* (Grand Rapids, MI: Eerdmans, 2010).

19 Robin Lovin, "Two Students: Dietrich Bonhoeffer and Kiyoko Takeda," in *The Oxford Handbook of Reinhold Niebuhr*, 625–7.

20 Fox, *Reinhold Niebuhr*, 145–6.

21 Fox, *Reinhold Niebuhr*, 145.

22 Scott R. Paeth, *The Niebuhr Brothers for Armchair Theologians* (Louisville, KY: Westminster John Knox Press, 2014).

23 Andrew Bacevich, *The Limits of Power: The End of American Exceptionalism* (New York: Metropolitan Books, 2008); Jean Bethke Elshtain, *Just War against Terror: The Burden of American Power in a Violent World* (New York: Basic Books, 2004).

24 Robin Lovin, *Christian Realism and the New Realities* (Cambridge: Cambridge University Press, 2008).

25 James H. Cone, *The Cross and the Lynching Tree* (Maryknoll, NY: Orbis, 2013).

26 Traci West, *Disruptive Christian Ethics: When Racism and Women's Lives Matter* (Louisville, KY: Westminster John Knox Press, 2006).

27 For example, see essays by Peter Paris and Yoshibumi Takahashi in *The Future of Christian Realism: International Conflict, Political Decay, and the Crisis of Democracy*, edited by Dallas Gingles, Joshua Mauldin, and Rebekah Miles (Lanham, MD: Lexington Books, 2023).

28 Willliam Werpehowski, *American Protestant Ethics and the Legacy of H. Richard Niebuhr* (Washington, DC: Georgetown University Press, 2002).

Recommended Reading

Primary

Niebuhr, Reinhold. *An Interpretation of Christian Ethics*. New York: Seabury Press, 1979.

———. *Moral Man and Immoral Society*. Louisville, KY: Westminster John Knox Press. 2001.

———. *The Nature and Destiny of Man*. Vol. I. Louisville, KY: Westminster John Knox Press, 1996.

Niebuhr, H. Richard. *Christ and Culture*. New York: Harper and Brothers, 1951.

———. *The Kingdom of God in America*. Chicago, IL: Willett, Clark & Co., 1937.

———. *The Meaning of Revelation*. New York: Macmillan, 1941.

———. *Radical Monotheism and Western Culture*. New York: Harper, 1960.

———. *The Responsible Self*. New York: Harper & Row, 1963.

———. *The Social Sources of Denominationalism*. New York: Henry Holt & Co., 1929.

Secondary

Fox, Richard Wightman. *Reinhold Niebuhr: A Biography*. Ithaca, NY: Cornell University Press, 1996.

Gilkey, Langdon. *On Niebuhr: A Theological Study*. Chicago, IL: University of Chicago Press, 2001.

Hauerwas, Stanley. *With the Grain of the Universe: The Church's Witness and Natural Theology*. Grand Rapids, MI: Brazos Press, 2001.

Kegley, Charles W., and Robert W. Bretall, eds. *Reinhold Niebuhr: His Religious, Social, and Political Thought*. New York: Macmillan, 1956.

Lovin, Robin. *Reinhold Niebuhr and Christian Realism*. Cambridge: Cambridge University Press, 1995.

Paeth, Scott R. *The Niebuhr Brothers for Armchair Theologians*. Louisville, KY: Westminster John Knox Press, 2014.

Shriver, Donald W. *H. Richard Niebuhr*. Nashville, TN: Abingdon Press, 2009.

Werpehowski, William. *American Protestant Ethics and the Legacy of H. Richard Niebuhr*. Washington, DC: Georgetown University Press, 2002.

Western Europe

Philip G. Ziegler

Introduction

Doing theology in Western Europe during the twentieth century meant, among other things, negotiating the complex, weighty, and unresolved inheritances of the previous century. As the framing of this volume suggests, the "long nineteenth century" inaugurated by the French revolution (1789) is often understood to end on the slaughter-bench of World War I (1914–18). The world-historical trauma of that "Great War" shattered many of the political, cultural, and intellectual commonplaces and confidences of old Europe; its experiences ramified and proved deeply corrosive of intergenerational trust, funding a revolutionary climate and movements in all fields of human endeavor – in the arts, philosophy, politics, religion – in following decades. And yet the century that followed the signing of the Treaty of Versailles in 1919 still had much in common with the preceding one and received from it a series of questions and disputes that continued to shape the theological agenda.

For Roman Catholic theology, this first meant continuing to navigate the varied and shifting cultural and political conditions for Catholicism in Western European nations: for example, the program of *Laïcité* and the secularization of political, social, and cultural life in France's Third Republic after 1870; the legacy of Bismarck's *Kulturkampf* – the programmatic effort in Germany, newly unified under Protestant Prussian leadership in 1871, to curtail the political and social power of Catholicism – and its softer echoes in the Netherlands following the formation of Catholic Belgium in 1830–31; the uneven progress of Catholic emancipation in Britain following the *Roman Catholic Relief Act* of 1829, in view of the reality of continued anti-Catholicism and the religious politics of the "Irish question."[1]

More immediately theological were the lasting implications of the "modernist controversy." The dispute – formally opened by Leo XIII in *Providentissimus Deus* (1893) as regards the interpretation of scripture – culminated in the encyclical *Pascendi dominici gregis* (1907) in which Pius X sharply demarcated the bounds of legitimate Catholic theology to exclude scholarship marked by what was styled subjectivism, historicism, immanentism, and methodological agnosticism. The "antimodernist oath" by which theologians, religious, and clerics subsequentially were bound between 1910 and 1967 pressed the consequences of this controversy deep into Catholic theology up to the time of the Second Vatican Council and beyond.

Ford's The Modern Theologians: An Introduction to Christian Theology since 1918, Fourth Edition.
Edited by Rachel Muers and Ashley Cocksworth.
© 2024 John Wiley & Sons Ltd. Published 2024 by John Wiley & Sons Ltd.

But as even the actual text of the antimodernist oath itself makes clear, the anathemas included in encyclicals and oath were but corollaries of the positive reassertion of the validity and rationality of the inherited Catholic dogmatic tradition as republished in the dogmatic constitution *Dei filius* (1870) at the First Vatican Council and *Aeterni patris* (1879), the latter recommending recovery of the "gravity" of scholastic theology generally, and of Thomas Aquinas in particular, in uniting of "the forces of revelation and reason."[2] Significantly, the history of Catholic theology in Western Europe since 1918 unfolds against the horizon of the "century of pontifical Thomism" established in the previous century.[3]

For Protestant theology, the nineteenth century legacy was no less commanding if ecclesiastically and nationally more diverse. In some quarters, theology had developed in national contexts where the Protestant church had been disestablished (as in the Netherlands after 1795) or had never been such (as in France). But in others, Protestant churches continued to enjoy forms of legal establishment, for example in England and (to a lesser degree) in Scotland, as well as in the *Landeskirchen* of Germany during the Second Reich. In each case, but especially where there were established churches, societal configurations entangled Protestant theological endeavor with the ambiguities of European imperialism and the missionary impulses and activities intertwined with it.[4] This legacy positioned subsequent Western European theology – Protestant but also Catholic – in distinct and important ways.

Survey and Debate

All Western European theology of the twentieth century has been undertaken within earshot of the continuing "melancholy, long, withdrawing roar" of the "sea of faith."[5] The ubiquity of the nineteenth-century "crisis of faith" has sometimes been overstated, yet the secularization of life that accompanied modernization and urbanization in Europe during that period confronted the theology that followed it with intellectual challenges both profound and unsettling.[6] Although the course of secularization proved uneven and less comprehensive, the religious landscape of Western Europe has continued to be terraformed by the forces of "detraditionalization" and "pluralistic secularization."[7]

Many of the developments at the heart of the Catholic modernism crisis that were associated with a threatening advance of just such secularization within theology – e.g. higher criticism of the Bible, critical historical study of the development of Christian doctrine, contestation of the viability of the ancient metaphysics of received dogma (not least from Kantian quarters), and a certain "anthropological turn" in theological method – had already become firm features of the ecology of Protestant theology in the period before World War I. Some of the most notable Protestant theologians at the threshold of the twentieth century were those grappling directly with these challenges with honesty and rigor: Louis August Sabatier in France, Adolf von Harnack and Ernst Troeltsch in Germany, and perhaps less radically Charles Gore and the other "liberal catholic" contributors to *Lux Mundi* (1889) in England. The labor of theologians advancing countervailing conservative movements – such as Anglo-Catholicism in England and Lutheran confessionalism in Germany and an analogous Reformed confessionalism in Scotland and the Netherlands – ensured that the new century opened amidst a vigorous *Methodenstreit*, i.e., roiling debate about the methods, sources, and norms of Christian theology itself and their relation to the modern world.[8]

As in the nineteenth century, so also in the twentieth these debates continued to be a properly *academic* affair, in the sense that theology continued to find its most important institutional locations in Western European university faculties of theology and ecclesiastical seminaries. The figure of "the professor" stands out as the primary producer of theological research and writing in this era, with the theological faculty as his – and latterly, also her – base of operations. And while the nineteenth century is often heralded as the era of great modern theological *systems*, the sustained teaching of theology in many European universities continued to fund their production in the twentieth. One thinks, of course, of examples like Karl Barth's massive *Church Dogmatics* (1932–67), G. C. Berkouwer's *Studies in Dogmatics* (1949–72), Michael

Schmaus' six-volume *Dogma* (1972–), Jürgen Moltmann's multivolume "contributions to theology," or latterly the *Dogmatique pour la catholicité évangélique* [*Dogmatics for Evangelical Catholicity*] of Gérard Siegwalt (1987–) as leading examples. Many notable shorter systematic theologies from this era – such as Hendrikus Berkhof's *Christian Faith*, Gerhard Ebeling's *Dogmatik des christlichen Glaubens* [*Dogmatics of the Christian Faith*], John Macquarrie's *Principles of Christian Theology*, Pannenberg's *Systematic Theology* – arose from the labor of recurrent university teaching.

The developments, revolutions, and retrievals that constitute the story of theology in Western Europe since 1918 represent patterns of both extension and deviation, continuity and contradiction vis-à-vis the nineteenth-century legacy.[9] Encompassing as it does diverse Christian confessions, languages, and cultures and a plethora of individual theologians and their work, this story is highly variegated and not easy to render concisely without idiosyncrasy and misrepresentation. A variety of approaches might be ventured in the hope of avoiding both.

One might attempt to tell the story chiefly along national-linguistic lines as parallel tales of theology in the French-, German-, Dutch-, and English-speaking worlds. This approach is perhaps unavoidable because theology in this period had no single *lingua franca*, distinctive linguistic channels are clearly traceable, and university faculties were centers of theological activity: indeed, certain locales – such as Tübingen, Basle, Le Saulchoir, the Louvian – are names by which to conjure theological worlds.[10] Yet, undertaken too consistently this approach would belie the multilingual character of theological labor and exchange, the movement – free or forced – of theologians and their ideas within and across Europe, as well as the transnational character of Christian confessions and theological labor within their traditions. It may also preempt consideration of the possible common "European" quality of such theology.

Alternatively, one might organize the story around the two great confessional blocs of Catholic and Protestant theology. This second possibility is also perhaps unavoidable and has much to recommend it, as my own introduction to this chapter already suggests. For all its diversity, the Catholic theological conversation has an internal coherence and dynamic shaped by inherited dogmatic traditions and resources as well as its responsibilities to the life and work of its ecclesiastical institutions. The preoccupying questions of Catholic theology and their framing reflect this. On the other hand, the dynamic of the Protestant theological conversation is plural – even diffuse – and for reasons internal to its own development is exposed to the challenges of modernity in an aggravated way. Yet, many of the most pressing questions of theology in this era are common to Catholic or Protestant spheres, even if their emergence, framing, and treatment are inflected differently. Moreover, a certain historic ecumenical convergence between these two streams is itself part of the distinctiveness of European theology in this very period, as we shall see.

A third approach might recommend one or more particular doctrines as uniquely important in shaping twentieth-century European theology. An obvious candidate might be the doctrine of the Trinity: the period since 1918 has been marked by resurgent interest in the tenability, centrality, and formative power of the doctrine concerning the triune God in relation to other tracts of Christian teaching. For leading examples in German-language theology, one might look to Protestants like Karl Barth, Jürgen Moltmann, Wolfhart Pannenberg, and Eberhard Jüngel, as well as to Catholics like Karl Rahner, Hans Urs von Balthasar, and Walter Kasper.[11] British theologians like T. F. Torrance, Colin Gunton, John Webster, and Sarah Coakley could also be canvased as exemplars of this trend.[12] Notable in all such cases is how Trinitarian doctrine reshapes thinking about revelation, Christology, soteriology, etc., and in some sense determines the very architecture of theological systems. Equally notable is the way in which reassertion of Trinitarian doctrine involves retrieval of doctrinal resources modern theology had perhaps bypassed or neglected. All this is true and well observed, and previous iterations of this volume – with their discrete chapters treating many of the figures just named – have emphasized this. Yet too fulsome a fixation upon the explanatory power of any single doctrinal "red thread" would inevitably set much else aside, while perhaps also belying the actual plurality, disparateness, and nonlinearity of developments in the field.

Yet another, fourth, approach might present a catalogue of proper names, emphasizing thereby the formative contributions made by individual theologians. Around the names of these great figures would be spun a story of influences, disputes, movements, and "schools." This approach is well tried: the entire first volume of the original edition of this book was devoted to just such an exposition, discharging its task by serial treatment of more than a dozen leading Western European theologians by name.[13] Such lists can be contentious, yet there is something right and compelling about this approach to be sure: it acknowledges the importance of individual theologians as teachers and authors; it emphasizes their role in disrupting and resetting theological practice and shifting common sense; it resists too formal and reductive a view of theological discourse as a mere epiphenomenon of the play of impersonal factors; it recalls the importance of relationships, conversation, and interpersonal exchange in the doing of Christian theology; and it also draws attention to the historico-social situatedness, limitations, and sheer humanity of theological discourse. And yet, concatenating accounts of individual theologians does not as such discern or display the defining contours of the era in which they labored and to which they contributed by their many achievements.

In what follows I want to suggest that a certain justice can be done to the distinctive features of twentieth-century theology in Western Europe by attending to three crucial foci. These are (1) the question of the reality and consequences of eschatological revelation in history, (2) the problem of Christian division and doctrinal unity, and (3) the question of church and synagogue. These three foci are, I believe, of epochal significance, distinguishing the theology of this time and place in important ways. None of these three questions has been the exclusive purview of Western European theologians, to be sure. Yet, they are its especial marks and formative preoccupations, and Western European theologians have been at the heart of these developments, shaping and directing them decisively to global effect.

The question of eschatology and revelation in history

Varieties of "liberal theology" undertaken in the manner of *Glaubenslehre,* i.e., inquiry into the contemporary expression of the religious faith of Christians and reflection upon its presuppositions and entailments, continued well after 1918. Funded by analysis of the believing subject, such theology concentrates upon questions concerning faith's present tenability and articulation as well as its contribution to the ongoing formation of modern society, culture, and nation. In its theorizing of Christianity under the conditions of modernity, the concepts of faith, religion, history, and society regularly prove decisive. In Germany a line that begins in the Weimar years with Horst Stephan and Georg Wobbermin stretches into the present in the work of Friedrich-Wilhelm Graf – and the late-century revival of Troeltsch's program and legacy he has led – and Hans-Martin Barth, for example.[14] Something akin to this theological sensibility also animated the exercise of historical "doctrinal criticism" by figures like Maurice Wiles, G. F. Woods, and others in the United Kingdom. In France, this liberal tradition was carried into *l'Église réformée de France* from its founding in 1938 by André-Numa Bertrand and others downstream from Sabatier who pursued theology as "religious science" with keen interest in theology's connections with culture. The long-standing interest in Paul Tillich's theology – with its focus upon the "religious dimension" of human life and culture – within French Protestant theology later in the century also reflects this legacy.

Yet, the decades following World War I also brought with them a vigorous effort to "change the subject" of Christian dogmatics, as it were, and to break with just this vision of theology. Methodologically, this "revolt" was an effort to surmount historicism without retreat into dogmatism. Materially, it involved reassertion of *God* as the proper object of theological inquiry and speech. These twinned ends were pursued by a theology of revelation, or more precisely a theology of the Word of God. Broadly neo-Reformational in tone and conviction – and accompanied by retrievals of the legacies of both Luther and Calvin – it took the biblical witness as its predominating source and norm, and willfully and purposefully transgressed the hardening boundary between theology and biblical exegesis in pursuit of the traces of divine address and encounter. Its methods were, as was said, "dialectical," and this as a consequence of the acknowledged impossibility of ever doing final justice to the radical transcendence of its living divine object. Eschatology predominated, not however as a discrete *loci* or theme, but rather as a comprehensive environment and saturating tone befitting the effort to think and speak of the miraculous advent of God in the midst of the world, the effective event of the gospel come upon history with salvation from beyond.

This "dialectical theology" was an internally variegated effort to rehabilitate the doctrine of divine revelation making use of conceptual, logical, and discursive strategies to honor its eschatological quality as met in the "strange new world of the Bible." Those associated in the loose movement in the 1920s included Karl Barth, Rudolf Bultmann, Emil Brunner, Friedrich Gogarten, and Eduard Thurneysen, among others.[15] The title of one of Barth's programmatic essays announced their preoccupying theme: "The Word of God as the Task of Theology."[16] That God as Subject speaks – *deus dixit* – that only God can rightly and truthfully speak of God and that such speech constitutes the crisis of everything human – these axioms state the conditions of possibility, the promise, and the peril of Christian theology. Here, it was repeatedly stressed that "history is a predicate of revelation" though revelation never thereby becomes "a predicate of history."[17] Christian theology is ventured in the hope that, as Barth put it, "it might be possible that the Word ... has taken our weakness and perversion, so that our word becomes capable of the Word of God precisely in its weakness and perversion."[18] The "theological critique of religion" ingredient in this program gave sharp expression to the power of these fundamental convictions to disrupt and deflate interest in theology's anthropological presuppositions.[19]

Though emerging in Germany and Switzerland, these impulses resonated among Protestant theologians elsewhere in Western Europe: in France they were received and advanced in various ways over many years by figures such as Jean Bosc, Charles Westphal, and Pierre Maury.[20] In the Netherlands, theologians like Oepke Noordmans, G. C. Berkouwer, and K. H. Miskotte fruitfully pursued their independent theological programs in critical engagement with these same impulses.[21] An extended British reception of these authors and their work saw their ideas refracted in and through the work of figures as diverse as T. F. Torrance, Donald MacKinnon, and Ronald Gregor Smith.[22]

Much Protestant theology pursued in this vein reiterated the Christocentrism of the liberal theology that proceeded it but did so in a firmly eschatological register, looking to the figure of Christ as the decisive and final self-revelation of God, and so the determinative center of all theological reflection and Christian doctrine. This rehabilitation of eschatological revelation fostered renewed interest in the importance and role of the doctrine of the Trinity as an affordance and implicate of the dynamics of divine *self*-revelation in Christ. But it also raised important questions about *mediation*. Subsequent decades saw new generations of theologians asking whether and how to understand the capacity of history, scriptural texts, liturgical and ecclesiastical structures, and cultural forms more generally to serve as sites and media of the eventfulness of transcendent divine revelation. We might trace this along two broad trajectories worked out in European Protestant theology in the decades following World War II.

A first trajectory variously reasserted the *temporal* mediation of revelation and did so by stressing its "future" character. An emphasis on the future as the locus of the full and final disclosure of the truth of God was naturally paired with concern for hope, promise, and expectation as determining themes of Christian life and thought. Reassertion of the futurity of revelation did not vacate the present of the divine but expressed it as the paradoxical "presence of the future" or foretaste of the eschaton. Pannenberg's account of the resurrection as a proleptic realization of the final justification of God that will constitute the end of universal history, Jürgen Moltmann's vision of the immanent unfolding of the *futurum* disrupted by the *adventus* of God's own future into the present, and Gerhard Sauter's pursuit of a comprehensive "eschatological rationality" variously exemplify this program.[23] Such theologies of hope also looked to recover awareness of the universal and cosmic scope of biblical eschatology, often by appeal to the motif of the "kingdom of God." Moltmann's expanding pursuit of ecological themes and the radical political theology of Johann Baptist Metz can rightly be associated with just this recovery.

A second trajectory concerned itself with exploration of the *hermeneutical* questions that attend revelation's linguistic and textual mediation, reasserting their explicit theological treatment as something essential to responsible Christian theology. From the first, this had a notable existential dimension. Bultmann famously asserted that all Christian theological talk of God is fully self-involving, simultaneously disclosing our own self-understanding so as also to make it an object of critical reflection. If we are to speak responsibly of the God who speaks of himself – if we are to hear, discern, and think the gospel *kerygma* today – then the careful labor of textual as well as of cultural and existential hermeneutics must be undertaken.[24] The entanglement of theology proper, fundamental anthropology, and comprehensive theories of interpretation remained a hallmark of work downstream from Bultmann. The "New Hermeneutic" of Gerhard Ebeling and Ernst Fuchs, and in a different way the theological program of Eberhard Jüngel, all exemplify these concerns.[25] In the case of Jüngel, revelation entails an existential and epistemological interruption: God's gracious "coming to language" affords us an "experience with experience," a liberating transcendence of our own situation interpreted anew in faith.[26] What is recovered along this trajectory is a focused theological interest in doing justice to the Word of God as an event of *communication*, and so also to human beings – and their transformation – as *hearers* of the Christian gospel. Like the first trajectory, this one also amplifies theological concern for the public and political dimensions of Christian faith and thought.

Among Catholics, beginning in the 1930s there appeared a collection of mostly francophone theologians who undertook to engage afresh with the sources of the theological past in order to win new and much needed traction on present doctrinal issues. This "new theology" (*nouvelle théologie*) as it was styled by detractors broke ranks with the neoscholasticism that predominated in the wake of the modernist controversy. Though not a bald repudiation of Thomism as such, the work of its advocates – not least publication of new critical editions of patristic and early medieval texts under the rubric of *Sources chrétiennes* – by its very nature undermined the neoscholastic settlement and questioned the reception and interpretation of the tradition it involved. Yet its ambition was fundamentally positive rather than critical: namely, to draw living water from the wells of *la tradition profonde* by which to refresh Catholic theology in light of contemporary challenges—in short, *ressourcement*.[27]

The work of figures such as Marie-Dominique Chenu, Yves Congar, Jean Daniélou, and Henri de Lubac revisited the vexed questions at the heart of earlier debates, not least with their acknowledgment of the inescapably contingent nature of theological reasoning and so also of the conception and expression of church dogma. And for a time in the 1950s this brought formal censure upon some of its leading proponents. Yet, as Chenu explained, the object of theology is "a series of absolute divine initiatives" marked by "the sweet and terrible contingency of a love that needs give no account."[28] This contingency of divine revelation conspires with the further exigencies of the theologian's own existence to limit the reach and aptitude of deductive and propositional reasoning in the work of theology. The dynamic unfolding of this process is the church's Tradition richly manifest in and across its many traditions, as Congar influentially conceived and expressed it during the time of the Second Vatican Council.[29] Recovery of the effective reality of divine transcendence in a concept of contingent revelation at once makes history in all its dynamism the crucial field of theological reasoning even as it makes *historicism* untenable.

The dogmatic challenge at the heart of the *nouvelle théologie* – namely, to conceive and to honor the concrete historical mediation of revelation on the basis of the divine quality of that revelation itself – was of course not its exclusive affair: for example, certain styles of Catholic humanism in France and Germany from these same decades also concentrate upon reconceiving the "mediation of history and culture in the domain of ontology" in the face of both anxious neoscholasticism and complacent bourgeois Christianity.[30] One can aspire to secure eschatological hope in and through ambiguous historical and cultural forms just because, as Erich Pryzwara remarked, "the supernatural order encompasses *and also penetrates* the natural order."[31] As with their Protestant contemporaries, Catholic theologians in this period were concerned in their own ways both to do justice to the eschatological quality of divine revelation and to take responsibility for understanding the complexities, forms, and consequences of its historical mediation.

The question of Christian division and doctrinal unity

The emergence and normalization of *ecumenism* – the committed pursuit of Christian unity by overcoming historic doctrinal and institutional divisions – as a decisive context for Christian thought is a further hallmark of Western European theology in recent times. The ecumenical question provided a formative horizon for theological endeavor throughout most of the century and ecumenical programs and institutions generated unprecedented theological engagement across ecclesial and confessional boundaries. Although some ecumenical motivation came from liberal deflation of the importance of doctrine and so also of historical doctrinal differences, deeper and more significant was the emergence and embrace of a properly theological repugnance at the scandal of Christian disunity in modern Europe and beyond.

The inaugural "World Conference on Faith and Order" in Lausanne (1927) and subsequent gathering in Edinburgh (1937) established comparative doctrinal discussion of church-dividing differences as fundamental to pursuit of the "visible unity" of the Christian church. Their stated purpose was "to register the apparent level of fundamental agreements with the Conference and the grave points of disagreements remaining" as well as to "suggest certain lines of thought which may in the future tend to a fuller measure of agreement."[32] Fundamental topics concerning the nature of the gospel, grace, church, ministry, sacraments, and confessional teaching were subsequently pursued. This theological program of multilateral dialogue to clarify and reduce doctrinal disagreements continued within the structures of the newly founded World Council of Churches at and after its first assembly in Amsterdam (1948).

Although global by nature and design, of course, Western European theologians played an outsized role in the ecumenical movement especially during its early decades, and the importance of their involvement for the direction of Christian theology cannot be overestimated. Many young European theologians were decisively shaped by their formative involvement in national, regional, and global ecumenical organs and events – think only of the young Dietrich Bonhoeffer in Germany, or in France of Marc Boegner and Jean Bosc, all of whom made signal contributions to the ecumenical theology.[33] Especially in the wake of World War II, the role of ecumenical agencies in reopening contact and theological exchange in Western Europe was immense. Some theologians became virtually identified with formal ecumenical work of this sort – for instance, Willem Visser 't Hooft and Suzanne de Dietrich who played key roles in the World Council of Churches (WCC) – and many others contributed substantively to extended bilateral and multilateral dialogues between disparate Protestant traditions, as well as latterly with Roman Catholic and Orthodox theologians.

Indeed, the "arrival" of Orthodoxy in Western Europe was itself an ecumenical and theological event of great importance during this century. Its advent came first by way of flight: one thinks especially of the St Sergius Institute in Paris founded in 1925 by émigré Russian priests (theologians Sergei Bulgakov and Georges Florovsky among them) as perhaps the chief engine of this. It then continued by way of active Orthodox involvement in ecumenical agencies and events. Florovsky himself in particular played a decisive role in the formation and early shaping of the WCC; indeed, "the credibility of the WCC as more than a pan-Protestant organization" has been ascribed to the cooperative efforts of Florovsky, Barth, and the leading Anglican theologian, and future archbishop of Canterbury, Michael Ramsey.[34]

The successful conclusion of the "Agreement between Reformation Churches in Europe" at Leuenberg in 1973 was an ecumenical watershed for European Protestant theology.[35] On the basis of a common theological understanding of the gospel, it authorized full recognition of ministries and sacraments and unimpeded fellowship (notwithstanding continuing confessional differences), thereby overturning long-standing mutual condemnations and theological strife especially between Reformed and Lutheran traditions in Europe. Not only did it spur other similar efforts toward theological *rapprochement*, including between the Church of England and the Protestant churches of Germany realized in the Meissen Agreement (1988).[36] But the "Leuenberg Fellowship" to which it gave rise undertook further important pioneering doctrinal studies, particularly in ecclesiology.[37] Taken together with the teaching of the Theological Declaration of Barmen (1934) – itself the fruit of Protestant ecumenical action – this work arguably provided something like the first fully articulated Protestant doctrine of the church.[38] The ecumenical nexus also nurtured the ecclesiological doctrine of many individual Protestant theologians. Outstanding among these are the Dutch theologians Johannes Hoekendijk and Johannes Blauw, who from positions of responsibility within the ecumenical movement made globally influential contributions to missiology rooted in the idea of the *missio dei*.[39] In Britain, Michael Ramsey's ecumenically important work, *The Gospel and the Catholic Church,* was shaped by insights won from personal encounters with exiled Orthodox theologians.[40] And T. F. Torrance's contributions to theology proper, Christology, and soteriology won their distinctive shape from sustained ecumenical engagements, again, particularly with the Orthodox.[41]

Among Catholics, many representatives of the *nouvelle théologie* – perhaps most notably Yves Congar – were ecumenically engaged, making notable theological contributions to the overall conception of the unity of the church and ecumenical endeavor, as well as to discrete doctrinal dialogues.[42] The "Decree on Ecumenism" – *Unitatis Redintegratio* – issued by the Second Vatican Council in 1964, was a landmark theological development, committing Catholic theologians to ecumenical engagement and orienting them in their dialogue with Protestant and Orthodox theologians ever since. Several of the council's other decrees – *Dei Verbum, Lumen Gentium, Nostra Aetate,* and *Dignitatis Humanae* treating respectively of revelation, the church, non-Christian religions, and religious freedom – also had profound ecumenical and theological significance both within and outside the Catholic Church.[43]

These conciliar texts and their reception were integral to the ongoing reconsideration of long-contested doctrines in the decades that followed. Not only were many of the Western European theologians who served as *periti* (expert theological advisors) to the bishops at the Council – including Congar, Küng, Rahner, Schillebeeckx, Ratzinger, and de Lubac – deeply involved in the formulation and reformulation of its decrees. In the wake of the council, they also became some of its key doctrinal interpreters. The program of the Pontifical Council for Promoting Christian Unity – but also the WCC Faith and Order Commission and many long-standing bilateral dialogues – became crucial fora in which leading theologians like Bernard Sesboüé and Walter Kasper, for example, developed and flourished. Moreover, the newly founded journals *Concilium* and *Communio* became crucial vehicles for theological debate about the council's dogmatic teaching and the implications of its twin dynamics of *ressourcement* and *aggiornamento*. As the high-profile cases of Hans Küng and Edward Schillebeeckx suggest, ecumenically engaged exploration of these dynamics at points raised difficult questions about the proper directions and limits of post-conciliar theological developments.[44] Yet the century's end saw both confirmation of the permanent ecumenical horizon of Catholic theological endeavor in the encyclical *Ut Unum Sint* (1995) and the realization of the *Joint Declaration on the Doctrine of Justification* (1999), the latter funded in no small measure by decades of European bilateral dialogue and theological effort.[45]

Looking forward from the start of the century, few if any would have anticipated the signal importance of ecumenism as a decisive emergent context for theology in Europe: but its pressing tasks generated a commanding theological agenda within which ecclesiological questions and doctrines played a particularly fundamental role; and its ecclesial and academic organs exercised a decisive formative influence upon many of the most prominent theologians of this period, ensuring that ecumenical concerns and sensibilities were integrated into the very form and substance of their dogmatic work to an unprecedented degree.

The question of Judaism and the relation of church and synagogue

Another decisive development in the past century has been the fundamental revaluation within Christian theology of the relationship between Christianity and Judaism. Twentieth-century European theology inherited a tradition of deep antipathy toward Judaism. The view of Judaism as an outdated and fossilized religion, the historic "teaching of contempt," the ascription of deicide to the Jews as a people, the image of the Jew as the proper object of divine retribution, an eschatological vision of the eradication of Jews and

Judaism by way of their exhaustive conversion – all of this was the common deliverance of centuries. Historical-critical biblical scholarship and the theology that tracked with it increasingly struggled to discern the living function of the Old Testament within Christianity: von Harnack famously considered it now entirely "apocryphal" suggesting that "to continue to keep it in Protestantism as a canonical document after the nineteenth century is the consequence of religious and ecclesiastical paralysis."[46] Both Catholic and Protestant theology operated with strongly supersessionist doctrines of the church vis-à-vis Israel which made the very existence of contemporary Jews and Judaism anachronistic, and as such a continuing provocation and challenge to Christian life and teaching. The progress of social emancipation and assimilation of Jews in Western European nations in the nineteenth century did little to ameliorate this *odium theologicum*.

The twentieth century, however, saw slow and hard-won recognition of the entanglement Christian theology in more than a millennium of anti-Judaism and anti-Semitism. From this arose attempts to take account of this doctrinally and to redress it theologically. This was a global development, to be sure, but one in whose vanguard Western European theologians played a most significant role. In the decades before World War II there was very limited interaction between Christian theology and the Jewish thought contemporary with it: only rarely were leading Jewish thinkers like Martin Buber, Leo Baeck, or Franz Rosenzweig studied or engaged by their Christian contemporaries. This situation was to change, but not before – and tragically not without – the virulently anti-Semitic program of the Third Reich and its murderous prosecution of a "final solution to the Jewish problem."[47]

The systematic destruction of European Jewry between 1932 and 1945 was envisaged, willed, and executed by a Nazi party regime whose platform cynically committed it to "positive Christianity." Amidst the regime's imposition of patently anti-Semitic laws and expanding discrimination against Jews in public life, it was chiefly the instrumentalizing of the churches in pursuit of ideological conformity (*Gleichschaltung*) that first provoked concentrated theological reactions. Yet, driven to searching reconsideration of the nature of the church and its proper relation with state and society in this way, the ensuing *Kirchenkampf* in Germany – and then under Nazi occupation also elsewhere in Western Europe – led some Christian theologians to confront "the Jewish question" anew, sometimes with quite radical results.

These "church struggles" proved to be crucibles for the emergence and articulation of revisionist theological thinking about Israel and Judaism. One thinks, for example, of Bonhoeffer's influential movement on these questions.[48] Although an article on the church and the Jews was notoriously absent from the Barmen Declaration itself, inspired by it Dutch theologians Jan Koopmans and K. H. Miskotte penned a confession in 1941 whose fourth article claimed that "we believe antisemitism to be something much more serious than an inhuman racial theory. We believe it to be one of the most stubborn and most deadly forms of rebellion against the holy and merciful God whose name we confess."[49] In France, again in 1941, "The Theses of Pomeyrol," authored by a group of theologians including Madeleine Barot, Roland de Pury, and Suzanne de Dietrich, similarly affirmed the permanence of Israel's election, the mystery of God's fidelity and on that basis raised "a solemn protest against every situation in which Jews are pushed out of the human community."[50] Indeed, the key framer of the Barmen Declaration, Karl Barth, himself came to characterize the division of Christians and Jews as "the most grievous and fundamental schism" and to assert that "there is in the end only one great ecumenical question: our relations with Judaism."[51]

In the immediate aftermath of the war, German theologians were pressed into these matters further by the *Stuttgarter Schuldbekenntnis* (1945) and *Darmstädter Wort* (1947) and the debates about Christian responsibility, collective guilt, and the church's ongoing relation to Jews and Judaism to which they gave rise. These years also saw the first and second conferences of the *International Council of Christians and Jews* in Oxford (1946) and Seelisberg (1947), inaugurating a new and important forum for theological engagement in which Europeans played a leading role.[52] In these sorts of developments are to be found the beginnings of a Christian theological recognition of – and repentance for – the legacies of anti-Judaism and anti-Semitism and so a basis for the emergence "in the lands of the perpetrators" of new and different Christian thinking about Israel, Judaism, the doctrine of election, the place of the Old Testament in Christian doctrine, the interrelation of church and synagogue, etc. Theologians formed by these church struggles and their theological legacies emerged as leading voices in the postwar reconsideration of the "doctrine of Israel" and its entailments. One thinks of signal contributions here by Hans-Joachim Iwand, Helmut Gollwitzer, Eberhard Bethge, K. H. Miskotte, and later by Bertold Klappert, Friedrich-Wilhelm Marquardt, and Andreas Pangritz.[53] These thinkers wrestle at length with questions including the distorting effects of anti-Semitism in the history of Christian dogma, the Jewishness of Jesus, the centrality of Israel in salvation history, the interrelation of law and gospel, the importance of the doctrines of election and covenant, the fundamentality of the Old Testament for Christian doctrine, the church's mission and the place of the Jews therein, and of the theological significance of the founding of the state of Israel.

Catholic theologians undertook a similar journey during this period, one important fruit of which is the distilled teaching found in paragraph four of *Nostra Aetate* issued by the Second Vatican Council, which repudiates the "teaching of contempt," affirms divine fidelity to the "gifts and calls" issued to Israel, decries anti-Semitism, and conceives of the church in explicit positive relation to "Abraham's stock."[54] The quite radical theological transformation involved here is, as Walter Kasper has observed, "irrevocable," being grounded in the fundamentals of conciliar teaching on revelation and ecclesiology.[55] From here Catholic theology is committed to acknowledging that Judaism and Christianity have an intractable common root and, though presently suffering an acute historical estrangement, their relationship is marked by the hopeful promise of its overcoming.

Another contribution fundamental to the reshaping of Christian theological accounts of Jews and Judaism is found in the formulation of explicitly *post-Holocaust* Christian theology. Although not isolated from the kinds of considerations and conversations surveyed here, Christian theologians also reconsidered Judaism and its relation to Christianity by confronting the radical challenge posed to traditional theodicy by the unimaginable horrors of the death camps. What George Steiner once wrote of British theologian Donald MacKinnon aptly describes the motivation of all such efforts, namely, a conviction that "there could be no justifiable future for Christianity so long as Christian theology and practice had not faced up to, had not internalised lucidly, its seminal role in the millennial torments of Judaism and in the Holocaust."[56]

Convicted in this way, several leading postwar European theologians ventured searching revisions of the doctrines of divine impassibility, divine providence and presence, salvation, the understanding of evil, the meaning of human suffering, and the substance of Christian eschatological hope. Johann Baptist Metz and his student Tiemo Rainer Peters stand out among Catholics for their sharp insistence that Christian theology requires radical reorientation "after Auschwitz."[57] Among Protestants, beginning with *The Crucified God*, Jürgen Moltmann, for example, made a new and radical confrontation with suffering central to his account of the Christian God and the work of salvation.[58] Moltmann's later program advanced a specifically *messianic* Christology developed in running conversation with historic and contemporary Jewish sources and explored the Jewish roots of the doctrine of the Trinity.[59] Dorothee Sölle's provocative political theology embraced strong claims of divine co-suffering in and with human suffering funded by a revisionist doctrine of God demanded, she adjudged, by what took place at Auschwitz.[60] And the "tragic vision" and ethical austerity of Donald MacKinnon's theological program involve an unflinching confrontation with the "horror of Golgotha" prompted precisely by acknowledgement of Christianity's complicity in the *Shoah*.

The shift in Christian thinking concerning the place and import of Israel and Judaism reflected in the European theology of the last century is remarkable and of epochal significance. Akin to the case of ecumenism, no one looking forward from the year 1900 could have anticipated just how radical a reconfiguration of the Christian theological posture toward Judaism and "the question of Israel" the new century would deliver. Neither, of course, could they have foreseen the gravity of the "unprecedented crime of the Shoah" that finally provoked and demanded it.[61]

Influence, Achievement, and Agenda

Western Europe was a globally important locus of Christian theological endeavor and development throughout the twentieth century. The globalization of Christianity and Christian theology over the course of this period relativized European theology and unsettled its historic *de facto* normativity. Yet, this same globalization also exported around the world both the constitutive problems of modern European theology – not least those arising from the social, cultural, and intellectual challenges of modernity – and its many, varied, and sophisticated theological strategies, programs, and trialed solutions. The story of European theology in the twenty-first century will undoubtedly also be shaped by its reception of new and differing theological impulses arising from other parts of the global church.

I have argued that the period since 1918 has been decisively marked by three unexpected transformations. First, revelation and eschatology – theological concepts sorely pressed in 1900 – were still operative at century's end having in fact given decisive shape to a variety of theological renewals, retrievals, and striking revisions. The ambition to think and speak truly of God remains central to the theological enterprise as practiced in Western Europe. So too does an ambition to think of Christian thought, doctrine, and practice as decisively determined by the eschatological character of divine revelation, whether this finality is conceived qualitatively or quantitatively, as it were. Can and will this continue to be so?

Sustained exploration of the problem of eschatological revelation and its contingent historical and cultural mediations is therefore a vital bequest to the twenty-first century. How ought theological attention and effort be proportioned here? On the one hand, an intense emphasis upon mediation as such casts theology chiefly as a cultural science whose object is religion – human piety and faith and practice in its manifold expressions – and whose controlling questions concern its presuppositions, sources, forms, and implications, as well as its moral measure and sociopolitical arrangements. Here, intellectual discipline tethers attention to contingent media and may, perhaps, exhaust itself in their careful analysis, criticism, and immanent repair. On the other hand, strict emphasis upon the eschatological subject and source of revelation means contending for theology as a divine science whose object is God encountered in free and sovereign self-giving. With this come decisive questions concerning the identity and agency of deity and the doctrines concerned with this, as well as their manifold implications and affordances. Questions of creaturely media – of human experience, history, scriptural and other texts, religious institutions, rituals etc. – are then approached in ways guided by recognition that they are fundamentally determined in and by their relationship to God. Disciplined and directed in these ways, theological attention will then fix chiefly upon that which is mediated and only derivatively and secondarily upon the structures of mediation themselves. European theology in the twenty-first century will continue to unfold through the development, conversation, and contest of these two distinctive approaches.

Second, I have suggested that the expansion and embrace of ecumenical concerns has been a further distinguishing feature of twentieth-century theology. But can the passion for Christian unity that animated decades of theological dialogue and scholarship in pursuit of doctrinal understanding endure the chill winds of our present "ecumenical winter" and our complacence before perduring ecclesial divisions? Is pursuit of doctrinal agreement of the kind advanced last century still a central concern at all? What does the migration of the center of global ecumenism away from matters of "faith and order" firmly into sustained engagements with burning issues of "life and work" mean for theology? Will inherited ecumenical dispositions and preoccupations last, or will they be overtaken and displaced by other more pressing concerns raised by continuing secularization and the expansion of interreligious pluralism?

Finally, I have suggested that an epochal reassessment of the Christian theological understanding of Judaism and the significance of Jewish–Christian relations represents a third distinctive transformation marking Western European theology in the twentieth century. And yet we must ask: How can the question of Israel, of Judaism, continue to be confronted and made intelligible as a properly ecumenical question, as one internal and proper to Christian theology and self-understanding? What developments in the doctrine of the church and other tracts of Christian theology might in fact encompass and achieve this? Can the question of church and synagogue continue to be asked and answered in ways that resist its dissolution into more general theological reflection on "non-Christian religions"? If all this proves possible, what might Christian theology learn in turn from distinctively Jewish reflections on "the Christian question"? How deeply could such lessons inform the development of Christian doctrine, giving shape to future developments not only in ecclesiology but also in Christology and the doctrine of God?

Notes

1 On these matters see Yolande Jansen, "*Laïcité*, or the Politics of Republican Secularism," in *Political Theologies: Public Religions in a Post-Secular World*, ed. Hent de Vries and Lawrence E. Sullivan (New York: Fordham University Press, 2006), 475–93; Rebecca Ayako Bennette, *Fighting for the Soul of Germany: The Catholic Struggle for Inclusion after Unification* (Cambridge, MA: Harvard University Press, 2012); Peter Jan Margry and Henk te Velde, "Contested Rituals and the Battle for Public Space: the Netherlands," in *Culture Wars: Secular Catholic Conflict in Nineteenth-Century Europe*, ed. Christopher Clark and Wolfram Kaiser (Cambridge: Cambridge University Press, 2003), 129–51, as well as E. R. Norman, ed., *Anti-Catholicism in Victorian Britain* (New York: Routledge, 2016).

2 *Aeterni Patris*, §24 in Heinrich Denzinger, *Compendium of Creeds, Definitions, and Declarations of Matters of Faith and Morals*, 43rd ed., ed. Peter Hünermann, Robert Fastiggi, and Anne Englund Nash (San Francisco, CA: Ignatius Press, 2012), §§3000–45 and §§3135–40 respectively.

3 Terence McGuckin, "A Century of 'Pontifical' Thomism," *New Blackfriars* 72, no. 852 (1991): 377–84.

4 See Jeremy Best, "Godly, International, and Independent: German Protestant Missionary Loyalties before World War I," *Central European History* 47, no. 3 (2014): 585–611, and Hilary M. Carey, *God's Empire: Religion and Colonialism in the British World, c. 1801–1908* (Cambridge: Cambridge University Press, 2011).

5 Famously, from Matthew Arnold, "Dover Beach" in *New Poems* (Oxford: Oxford University Press, 1867), 113.

6 For discussion of the "Victorian crisis of faith" see A. N. Wilson, *God's Funeral* (New York: W. W. Norton, 1999), contested by Timothy Larsen, *Crisis of Doubt: Honest Faith in Nineteenth-Century England* (Oxford: Oxford University Press, 2006), 1–17. On the German and Dutch cases respectively, see Todd H. Weir, *Secularism and Religion in Nineteenth-Century Germany: The Rise of the Fourth Confession* (Cambridge: Cambridge University Press, 2014) and Arie L. Molendijk, *Protestant Theology and Modernity in the Nineteenth-Century Netherlands* (Oxford: Oxford University Press, 2021).

7 See Yves Lambert, "A Turning Point in Religious Evolution in Europe," *Journal of Contemporary Religion* 19, no. 1 (2004): 29–45, and Lieven Boeve, "Religion After Detraditionalization: Christian Faith in a Post-Secular Europe," *Irish Theological Quarterly* 70 (2005): 99–122.

8 Classically expressed in Ernst Troeltsch, "On the Historical and Dogmatic Methods in Theology" (1898), in *Religion in History*, ed. and trans. James Luther Adams and Walter E. Bense (Minneapolis, MN: Fortress Press, 1991), 11–32.

9 On this complex pattern, see Katherine Sonderegger, "Modern Theology in a Scientific, Historical Age," in *The Edinburgh Critical History of Twentieth-Century Christian Theology*, ed. Philip G. Ziegler (Edinburgh: Edinburgh University Press, 2022), 7–25.

10 Examples of such national-linguistic accounts include Günther Wenz, "Das 'kurze' 20. Jahrhundert: Entwicklungstendenzen evangelischer Theologie in Deutschland von 1918–1989," *International Journal of Orthodox Theology* 11, no. 4 (2020): 57–74; John I. Hesselink, "Contemporary Dutch Protestant Theology," *Reformed Review* 26, no. 2 (1973): 67–89; Jean-Daniel Causse, "Systematic Theology in Francophone Protestantism: Some Contemporary Perspectives," *Exchange* 29, no. 3 (2000): 249–63; Gabriel Flynn, "Renaissance in Twentieth-Century Catholic Theology," *Irish Theological Quarterly* 76, no. 4 (2011): 323–38; Rowan Williams, "Theology in the Twentieth-Century," in *A Century of Theological and Religious Studies in Britain, 1902–2002*, ed. Ernest Nicholson (Oxford: Oxford University Press, 2004), 237–52.

11 Indicatively, see Jürgen Moltmann, *The Trinity and the Kingdom of God: The Doctrine of God*, trans. Margaret Kohl (London: SCM Press, 1981); Wolfhart Pannenberg, *Systematic Theology*, Vol. 1, trans. G. W. Bromiley (Grand Rapids, MI: Eerdmans, 1991); Eberhard Jüngel, *God as Mystery of the World: On the Foundation of the Theology of the Crucified One in the Dispute between Theism and Atheism*, trans. D. Gruder (London: T&T Clark, 2014); Walter Kasper, *The God of Jesus Christ*, new ed. (London: T&T Clark, 2012). For

discussion of Barth, Balthasar, and Rahner see elsewhere in this volume.

12   See Thomas F. Torrance, *The Christian Doctrine of God: One Being Three Persons* (London: T&T Clark, 2016); Colin E. Gunton, *The Promise of Trinitarian Theology*, 2nd ed. (London: T&T Clark, 1997); John Webster, *God Without Measure: Working Papers in Christian Theology, Vol. 1: God and the Works of God* (London: T&T Clark, 2016); Sarah Coakley, *God, Sexuality, and the Self: An Essay "On the Trinity"* (Cambridge: Cambridge University Press, 2013).

13   See David F. Ford, ed., *The Modern Theologians: An Introduction to Christian Theology in the Twentieth Century* (Oxford: Blackwell, 1989), Vol. 1, v–vi.

14   See Matthias Wolfes, *Protestantische Theologie und moderne Welt: Studien zur Geschichte der liberale Theologie nach 1918* (Berlin: De Gruyter, 1999); Friedrich Wilhelm Graf, *Der heilige Zeitgeist: Studien zur Ideengeschichte der protestantischen Theologie in der Weimarer Republik* (Tübingen: Mohr Siebeck, 2011); Hans-Martin Barth, *Dogmatik: Evangelischer Glaube im Kontext der Weltreligionen* (Gütersloh: Gütersloher Verlagshaus, 2001).

15   For representative sources, see *The Beginnings of Dialectical Theology: Vol. 1*, ed. James M. Robinson (Richmond, VA: John Knox Press, 1968). Cf. Christophe Chalamet, *The Dialectical Theologians: Wilhelm Hermann, Karl Barth, and Rudolf Bultmann* (Zürich: TVZ, 2005).

16   Karl Barth, "The Word of God and the Task of Theology," in *The Word of God and Theology*, trans. Amy Marga (New York: T&T Clark, 2011), 171–98.

17   Karl Barth, *Church Dogmatics*, vol. I, part 2 (Edinburgh: T&T Clark, 1956), 58.

18   Barth, "The Word of God and the Task of Theology," 197.

19   For discussion, see Hans-Joachim Kraus, *Theologische Religionskritik* (Neukirchen: Neukirchener Verlag, 1982).

20   See Françoise Smyth-Florentin, *Pierre Maury – Prédicateur d'Evangile* (Paris: Labor et Fidès, 2009), and Jean Bosc, *L'office royal du Seigneur Jésus-Christ* (Geneva: Labor et Fidès, 1957).

21   See Karel Blei, *Oepke Noordmans: Theologian of the Holy Spirit*, trans. A. J. Janssen (Grand Rapids, MI: Eerdmans, 2013); G. C. Berkouwer, *A Half-Century of Theology*, trans. Lewis B. Smede (Grand Rapids, MI: Eerdmans, 1977); K. H. Miskotte, *When the Gods Are Silent*, trans. John W. Doberstein (London: Collins, 1967).

22   See D. Densil Morgan, *Barth Reception in Britain* (London: T&T Clark, 2010).

23   See Wolfhart Pannenberg, "Dogmatic Theses on the Concept of Revelation," in *Revelation as History*, ed. Wolfhart Pannenberg, trans. David Granskou and Edward Quinn (London: Sheed and Ward, 1969),

123–58; Jürgen Moltmann, *The Theology of Hope: On the Ground and Implications of a Christian Eschatology*, trans. James W. Leitch (London: SCM Press, 1967) and Gerhard Sauter, *Zukunft und Verheissung. Das Problem der Zukunft in der gegenwärtigen theologischen und philosophischen Diskussion* (Zürich/Stuttgart: Zwingli Verlag, 1965).

24   See Bultmann's classic statement, "What Does It Mean to Speak of God?" in *Faith and Understanding, Vol. 1* (New York: Harper & Row, 1969), 53–66; Cf. David Congdon, *The Mission of Demythologizing: Rudolf Bultmann's Dialectical Theology* (Minneapolis, MN: Fortress Press, 2015).

25   James M. Robinson and John B. Cobb, Jr., eds., *The New Hermeneutic* (New York: Harper & Row, 1964).

26   Jüngel, *God as the Mystery of the World.*   .

27   See Anna N. Williams, "The Future of the Past: The Contemporary Significance of the *Nouvelle Théologie*," *International Journal of Systematic Theology* 7, no. 4 (2005): 347–61.

28   Marie-Dominique Chenu, "Position de la Théologie," as cited by Brian E. Daley, "Knowing God in History and in the Church: *Dei Verbum* and 'Nouvelle Théologie,'" in *Ressourcement: A Movement for Renewal in Twentieth-Century Catholic Theology*, ed. Gabriel Flynn and Paul D. Murray (Oxford: Oxford University Press, 2012), 337.

29   Yves Congar, *Tradition and Traditions: An Historical and a Theological Essay*, trans. Michael Naseby and Thomas Rainborough, (London: Burns and Oates, 1966).

30   Tracey Rowland, *Beyond Kant and Nietzsche: The Munich Defence of Christian Humanism* (London: T&T Clark, 2021), 16.

31   Cited in Rowland, *Beyond Kant and Nietzsche*, 172, emphasis added.

32   "Lausanne. First World Conference on Faith and Order, August 3–21, 1927," in *A Documentary History of the Faith and Order Movement, 1927–1963*, ed. Lukas Vischer (St Louis, MO: Bethany Press, 1963), 27.

33   Marc Boegner, *L'Exigence œcuménique: Souvenirs et Perspectives* (Paris: Albin Michel,1968); Jean Bosc, *Situation de l'œcuménisme en perspective réformée* (Paris: Editions du Cert, 1969).

34   Andrew Louth, *Modern Orthodox Thinkers: From the Philokalia to the Present* (London: SPCK, 2015), 79.

35   *Agreement between Reformation Churches in Europe. Leuenberg Agreement, 1973* (Leipzig: Evangelische Verlagsanstalt, 2013).

36   *On the Way to Visible Unity. A Common Statement*, 18 March 1988, Meissen. https://www.churchofengland.org/media/3320 (accessed 10 September 2023).

37   The core text of which is *The Church of Jesus Christ* (3rd Assembly, Strasbourg, 1987). Leuenberg Texts 1. 5th ed. (Leipzig: Evangelische Verlagsanstalt, 2018).

38 See Douglas S. Bax, "The Barmen Theological Declaration: A New Translation," *Journal of Theology for Southern Africa* 47 (1984): 78–81.

39 Johannes Hoekendijk, *The Church Inside Out* (Philadelphia: Westminster, 1966) and Johannes Blauw, *The Missionary Nature of the Church* (New York: McGraw-Hill, 1962).

40 Michael Ramsey, *The Gospel and the Catholic Church* (London: Longmans and Co., 1935).

41 See Thomas F. Torrance, *Theology in Reconciliation: Essays towards Evangelical and Catholic Unity in East and West* (Grand Rapids, MI: Eerdmans, 1996).

42 See Yves Congar, *Theologian of the Church*, ed. Gabriel Flynn (Leuven: Peeters, 2018).

43 See the Latin and English texts in Denzinger, §§4201–35, 4101–79, 4195–99, 4240–45 respectively.

44 Hans Küng's ecumenically important thesis, *Justification: The Doctrine of Karl Barth and a Catholic Reflection* (London: Burns & Oates, 1964) was followed by controversial studies of *The Church* (London: Burns & Oates, 1968) and in 1971 of the doctrine of the papacy, *Infallible?* 2nd ed. (London: SCM Press, 1994), which led to his being stripped of the right to teach as a recognized Catholic theologian in 1979. Schillebeeckx was recurrently investigated first concerning his 1974 *Jesus: An Experiment in Christology*, Vol. 6 of *The Collected Works of Edward Schillebeeckx* (London: Bloomsbury T&T Clark, 2014) and later concerning the "Protestant" quality of his ecclesiology as expressed in the 1970s in *The Church with a Human Face* and *Church: The Human Story of God* (vols. 9 and 10 of *The Collected Works of Edward Schillebeeckx* (London: Bloomsbury T&T Clark, 2014). Cf. *The Schillebeeckx Case: Official Exchange of Letters and Documents in the Investigation of Fr Edward Schillebeeckx by the Sacred Congregation of the Faith, 1976–1980*, ed. Ted Schoof (New York: Paulist Press, 1980).

45 *Ut Unum Sint. On Commitment to Ecumenism*, Pope John Paul II, 25 May 1995, in Denzinger, §§5000–12. For the latter, see the Lutheran World Federation and the Roman Catholic Church, *Joint Declaration on the Doctrine of Justification*, 20th anniversary ed. (Geneva: LWF, 2019).

46 Adolf von Harnack, *Marcion: The Gospel of the Alien God*, trans. John E. Steely and Lyle D. Bierma (Eugene, OR: Wipf and Stock, 2007), 134, translation altered.

47 Writing in 1952, Paul Tillich gestured at a "changed situation" and meaningful engagement with Buber's *I and Thou* personalism by himself as well as Emil Brunner and Karl Barth – "Jewish Influences on Contemporary Christian Theology," *CrossCurrents* 2, no. 3 (1952): 35–42. K. H. Miskotte's dissertation *Het wezen der Joodse religie* (Amsterdam: H. J. Paris, 1933) represents a rare exception to this rule.

48 See Andreas Pangritz, "Bonhoeffer and the Jews," in *The Oxford Handbook of Dietrich Bonhoeffer*, ed. Philip G. Ziegler and Michael Mawson (Oxford: Oxford University Press, 2019), 91–107.

49 See "An Unofficial Confession of Faith," in *The Struggle of the Dutch Church for the Maintenance of the Commandments of God in the Life of the State*, ed. W. A. Visser 'T Hooft (New York: American Committee for the World Council of Churches, 1945), 80.

50 See Christine Prieto, "Les thèses de Pomeyrol. Une position protestante méconnue," *Autres Temps. Cahiers d'éthique sociale et politique* 63 (1999): 108. Translation from "article seven" my own.

51 Karl Barth, *Ad Limina Apostolorum: An Appraisal of Vatican II*, trans. Keith R. Crim (Richmond, VA: John Knox Press, 1968), 30; *Church Dogmatics*, vol. III, part 3 (Edinburgh: T&T Clark, 1961), 225.

52 See the influential "Ten Points of Seelisberg (1947)," in *More Stepping Stones to Jewish-Christian Relations: An Unabridged Collection of Christian Documents, 1975–1983*, ed. Helga Croner (New York: Paulist Press, 1985), 32–3.

53 See Eberhard Bethge, "Christology and the First Commandment," *Holocaust and Genocide Studies* 4 (1989): 261–72; W. Travis McMaken, "'Shalom, Shalom, Shalom Israel!' Jews and Judaism in Helmut Gollwitzer's Life and Theology," *Studies in Christian-Jewish Relations* 10, no. 1 (2015): 1–22; K. H. Miskotte, *Das Judentum als Frage an die Kirche. Schriftenreihe für christlich-jüdische Begegnung* (Wuppertal: Theologischer Verlag Rolf Brockhaus, 1970); Friedrich-Wilhelm Marquardt, *Die Entdeckung des Judentums für die christliche Theologie. Israel im Denken Karl Barths* (München: Chr. Kaiser Verlag, 1967) and *Von Elend und Heimsuchung der Theologie. Prolegomena zur Dogmatik* (München: Chr Kaiser Verlag, 1988); Bertold Klappert, *Miterben der Verheißung. Beiträge zum jüdisch-christlichen Dialog* (Neukirchener: Neukirchener Verlag, 2000); as well as Andreas Pangritz, *Vergegnungen, Umbrüche und Aufbrüche. Beiträge zur Theologie des christlich-jüdischen Vehältnisses* (Leipzig: Evangelische Verlagsanstalt, 2015).

54 See *Nostra Aetate* §4 in Denzinger, §§4198. On European Catholic theology en route to *Nostra Aetate*, see John Connelly, *From Enemy to Brother: The Revolution in Catholic Teaching on the Jews, 1933–1965* (Cambridge, MA: Harvard University Press, 2008). Rolf Rendtoff, Hans Hermann Henrix, and Wolfgang Kraus, eds., *Die Kirchen und das Judentum*, 2 vols. (Paderborn/Gütersloh: Bonifatius/Gütersloher Verlaghaus, 2001) collects almost two thousand pages of official ecclesiastical texts, the great majority from European churches, ecumenical organs, and academic bodies.

55 Walter Kasper, "Foreword," to *Christ Jesus and the Jewish People Today: New Explorations of Theological Interrelationships*, ed. Hans Hermann Henrix et al. (Grand Rapids, MI: Eerdmans, 2011), x–xviii.

56 George Steiner, *Errata: An Examined Life* (London: Weidenfeld & Nicholson, 1997), 136.

57 See Johannes Baptist Metz, "Facing the Jews: Christian Theology after Auschwitz," in *The Holocaust as Interruption*, ed. Elisabeth Schüssler Fiorenza and David Tracy (Edinburgh: T&T Clark, 1984), 26–33, and Tiemo Rainer Peters, *Nach Auschwitz von Gott sprechen* (Hamburg: Katholische Akademie Verlag, 1995).

58 Jürgen Moltmann, *The Crucified God*, trans. R. A. Wilson. 40th anniversary ed. (London: SCM Press, 2015).

59 Jürgen Moltmann, *The Way of Jesus Christ: Christology in Messianic Dimensions*, trans. Margaret Kohl (London: SCM Press, 1990), and Jürgen Moltmann and Pinchas Lapide, *Jewish Monotheism and Christian Trinitarian Doctrine*, trans. Leonard Swidler (Philadelphia, PA: Fortress Press, 1981).

60 Dorothee Sölle, *Christ the Representative: An Essay in Theology after the Death of God*, trans. David Lewis (London: SCM Press, 1967), and *Suffering*, trans. Everett Kalin (Philadelphia, PA: Fortress Press, 1975).

61 Kasper, "Foreword," x–xi.

Recommended Reading

Primary

Congar, Yves. *The Meaning of Tradition.* Translated by A. N. Woodrow. San Francisco, CA: Ignatius Press, 2004.

Jüngel, Eberhard. *God as Mystery of the World: On the Foundation of the Theology of the Crucified One in the Dispute between Theism and Atheism.* Translated by D. Gruder. London: T&T Clark, 2014.

Kelly, Patricia, ed. *Ressourcement Theology: A Sourcebook.* London: T&T Clark, 2001.

Moltmann, Jürgen. *Theology of Hope.* Translated by M. Kohl. London: SCM Press, 1967.

Ramsey, Michael. *The Gospel and the Catholic Church.* 2nd ed. London: Longman, 1961.

Robinson, James M., ed. *The Beginnings of Dialectical Theology.* Vol. 1. Richmond, VA: John Knox Press, 1968.

Secondary

Dorrien, Gary. *The Barthian Revolt in Modern Theology: Theology without Weapons.* Louisville, KY: Westminster John Knox Press, 1999.

Flynn, Gabriel, and Paul D. Murray, eds. *Ressourcement: A Movement for Renewal in Twentieth-Century Catholic Theology.* Oxford: Oxford University Press, 2012.

Heron, Alasdair. *A Century of Protestant Theology.* London: Lutterworth Press, 1993.

Kerr, Fergus. *Twentieth-Century Catholic Theologians.* Oxford: Blackwell, 2007.

Rowland, Tracey. *Beyond Kant and Nietzsche: The Munich Defence of Christian Humanism.* London: Bloomsbury T&T Clark, 2021.

Karl Barth

Hanna Reichel

Introduction

Born into a notable Basel family of pastors and theologians in 1886, Karl Barth began his own theological studies in Bern, where his father Johann Friedrich (Fritz) taught New Testament. He was quickly drawn to the more liberal schools of Berlin and Marburg. Immersing himself in Schleiermacher and Kant, and impressed by Adolf von Harnack and Wilhelm Hermann, Barth emerged from his studies as a self-proclaimed disciple of the "modern school," which saw the Christian faith as subject to critical investigation, tied up with religious experience, and dedicated to the moral transformation of society.

First signs of disenchantment with that tradition – as well as of Barth's polemical disposition – surface during his time as an editorial assistant for the *Christliche Welt,* the leading journal of Liberal Protestantism in Germany. In his first article, "Moderne Theologie und Reichsgottesarbeit" (1909),[1] Barth critiqued "modern theology" for its comparatively lesser use for pastoral ministry and practical work, producing a heated exchange with his father as well as with leading practical theologians. Barth served in the German Reformed church in Geneva for two years and married Nelly Hoffmann, with whom he would have five children, before taking a call to Safenwil, Aargau in 1911. Pastoring this congregation of factory workers and agrarian labourers, Barth participated in their struggle, joined the Social Democratic Party, and was soon nicknamed "the red pastor of Safenwil."

Barth dates the "twilight of the idols" that finalized his break with liberal theology to Germany's invasion of Belgium in 1914. Appalled by the enthusiasm of his once revered teachers for German warmongering, Barth diagnosed their inability to resist nationalism and militarism as a theological failure, the close identification of the Christian God with cultural and ethical achievements. Together with his fellow pastor-theologian and friend Eduard Thurneysen, Barth turned to the Bible in search for a different theological foundation.

The resultant commentary on Paul's letter to the Romans (1919)[2] represented a startling departure from historical-critical scholarship: rather than speaking *about* Paul's theology, Barth located himself *with* Paul in

Ford's The Modern Theologians: An Introduction to Christian Theology since 1918, Fourth Edition.
Edited by Rachel Muers and Ashley Cocksworth.
© 2024 John Wiley & Sons Ltd. Published 2024 by John Wiley & Sons Ltd.

the same dilemma, beyond historical distance, suffering an in-breaking of God "vertically from above" that could leave no epistemic, ethical, or pastoral standing point. The second edition, revised in light of the debates that quickly ensued, distanced itself even further from Liberal Protestantism and asserted the "wholly Other" God in both judgment and affirmation of humanity.

Famous overnight, the rural Swiss pastor was appointed to an "honorary" position for Reformed dogmatics in Göttingen in 1921. Tasked to teach courses on Reformed confessions and figures without the academic credentials normally required for such a position, Barth built his repertoire as the lone Reformed theologian in a staunchly Lutheran faculty, and as a foreigner funded from abroad in an increasingly nationalistic climate, with economic catastrophe leading to further political turmoil. In these years, momentum built around Barth, Thurneysen, Friedrich Gogarten, Rudolf Bultmann, and Emil Brunner as a group who spoke of "crisis" and advocated a new "Word of God theology." Their emphasis on the radical difference between God and the world became known as "dialectical theology" and found its voice in the periodical *Zwischen den Zeiten*, edited by Georg Merz from 1922 until its dissolution in 1933 when, during the Nazi rise to power, previously existing tensions could no longer be bridged.

In 1925, Barth moved to a professorship in Münster that brought him into close contact with Roman Catholicism. In discussions with his Jesuit colleague Erich Przywara over nature and grace, the role of analogy, and the "scientific" nature of theology, Barth cemented his fundamental disagreement with Roman Catholicism while also being inspired by its interdisciplinary engagement with philosophy of religion, psychology, and sociology. Charlotte "Lollo" von Kirschbaum, a trained Red Cross nurse whom Barth had met in 1924 over shared theological interests, moved into the Barth household in 1929. Officially serving as his secretary and assistant, von Kirschbaum became Barth's partner in life as well as theological work, resulting in an uneasy "triangular" relationship with Nelly.

Called to the University of Bonn in 1930, Barth programmatically restarted the project of a comprehensive systematic theology, which he had twice before begun under different titles. An outspoken critic of National Socialism, Barth became strongly involved in the "Confessing Church" movement, culminating in his role in drafting the *Barmen Declaration* in 1934. Confessing Jesus Christ as "the one Word of God whom we have to hear, and whom we have to trust and obey in life and in death," it denounced the Nazi claim to power over church polity, proclamation, and doctrine as heretical. After refusing an unreserved oath of loyalty to Hitler in 1935, Barth was dismissed from his position and soon prohibited from publishing and speaking in Germany. Basel University offered Barth the post that he would hold until his retirement in 1962.

From Basel, Barth continued to be a public voice with as much pastoral concern as political fervor and often controversial stances. Volunteering for armed service himself, Barth encouraged international military action against Germany. After the war, however, he was one of the first and most ardent advocates of reconciliation with Germany and across Europe. Barth refused to condemn communism in the East outright, while critiquing Western anticommunism as well as NATO rearmament. Barth delivered the opening address for the World Council of Churches' first assembly in Amsterdam in 1948 and was an invited observer to the Second Vatican Council. Barth continued lecturing, writing, and publishing until his death in Basel in 1968. Nelly continued visiting Charlotte von Kirschbaum in the hospital until she died and subsequently buried her in the Barth family tomb.

Survey

Any survey of Barth's work has to reckon with three distinct challenges. Its sheer volume is the most obvious of them. His (unfinished!) *Church Dogmatics* alone extends over more than nine thousand pages, and the *Gesamtausgabe* with his other writings already contains more than fifty volumes at about half of its projected completion. Second, the diversity of sites and genres of Barth's work, as well as differences in their accessibility in print and translation, has led to one-sided appraisals. Finally, Barth had a remarkable willingness and capacity to "begin again" and rethink previous positions, but his public assertions of changes of heart are not always their most reliable chronicle.

Church Dogmatics has been compared to a cathedral due to its monumental architecture, comprehensiveness, systematicity, erudition, and rigor. Read in isolation, this *magnum opus* might give rise to the impression of Barth as a modern scholastic. Yet Barth's theology took place in attentive dialogue with his time, as is evident in the vast number of his public addresses and talks, articles, and essays. Barth was a major public intellectual and a frequent speaker in diverse ecclesial and academic publics. He preached regularly in the State Prison of Basel and maintained vigorous conversations through letters with theologians, church leaders, and ecumenical figures like Emil Brunner, Rudolf Bultmann, Willem Visser 't Hooft, Martin Niemöller, and Josef Hromádka. Barth understood his work to be "fundamentally a theology for pastors,"[3] in service of the church, necessitated both by the human impossibility of proclamation and by the sheer overflowing joy of the gospel.

Barth's fervor and originality grew out of an acute need to speak, as he would say, "with the Bible in one and the newspaper in the other hand." The image captures well his unapologetic rootedness in the scriptures and the attentive contextual witness to which he put the theological tradition. Although both these "texts" were irreducible to him, their relationship also had a very particular shape. Analyzing the context through a distinctly theological lens, he insisted that the text to be proclaimed to this context is time and again the one Word of God in different inflections – formally the scriptures, materially the one Word of God to which they testify: the person of Jesus Christ. Both Barth's contextuality and his aversion to a "system" thus emerged out of a profound theological commitment; the grounding of all theology in the event of divine self-revelation implied a discontinuity and actualism in epistemological terms, a necessity to "every day, in fact every hour … begin anew with the beginning."[4] Not surprisingly, this disposition manifests in some pronounced shifts in emphases and articulations. Yet, the theological "text" with which Barth insisted on beginning time and again – the one Word of God, Jesus Christ – was the anchor of continuity and consistency in Barth's lifelong wrestling, discernment, and dialogical engagement, allowing him to hold complexity without sacrificing decisiveness and versatility.

The development of Barth's thought has been subject to much debate, spurred not only by its temporal distension and changes in language, interlocutors, and theological framing, but also by Barth's own frequent comments on various supposed turns for dramatic effect, which commentators have tended to follow. Special attention has been devoted to dating and characterizing Barth's turn from liberal theology, his move from a dialectical mode of critique to a more positively dogmatic mode, and the material change in his understanding of God through the reconceptualization of the doctrine of election. Although the remarkable consistency in central tenets of Barth's thought has meanwhile been increasingly emphasized, a rough periodization like the following might be useful:[5]

- Until 1915: liberal-theological phase
- 1915/16–19: turn away from liberal theology and to the Bible
- 1920–23: dialectical theology phase
- 1924–mid-1930s: first dogmatic phase, marked by increasing engagement of the Reformed tradition and Roman Catholicism and by first attempts to conceptualize a theological system
- 1930s–68: second dogmatic phase, including new beginnings of a "church" dogmatics, the discovery and reformulation of the doctrine of election, the humanity of Christ, the notion of history, and the political ramifications of the gospel

Some shifts may be attributed less to dramatic conversions than to simple changes in context and audience: finding himself in Calvin's and Beza's historic pulpit, Barth devoted himself to their major works; called into a congregation of workers, Barth spoke the language of socialism. Tasked with teaching Reformed Theology in Göttingen, he delved more deeply into the Reformers; in Catholic Münster, he studied Aquinas and Anselm. During the turmoil of war, Barth preached judgment and divine sovereignty, in its aftermath, reconciliation and humanity.

At the same time, shifts in Barth's theological articulations represent discernment of the Word of God in affirmation and judgment of their respective times: Barth's famous theological rediscovery of the alterity of God in his Romans commentary responded to political and cultural disillusionments in World War I and to challenges encountered in congregational ministry. His insistence on the sovereignty of God and the Lordship of Christ was developed in close contrast to the claims to sovereignty and absolute power in Nazi Germany. In the face of the Nazi takeover of the German church, Barth's famous imperative to "do theology as if nothing had happened" was no quietism but an act of defiance and resistance.[6] In the zero hour after the war, Barth's rediscovery of the humanity of God grounded the humanity of the human being beyond its earthly phenomenology and inevitable disappointments.

Some continuity can be found in two theological "fronts" that map out the space against which Barth developed his theological project: Neo-Protestantism and Roman Catholicism. These categories do not necessarily define or map onto existing ecclesial or doctrinal bodies; rather, they became Barth's labels for specific theological fallacies that he identified as underlying a range of intellectual, ecclesial, and political developments regardless of their denominational affiliation or genealogy.

Barth used the terms "Neo-Protestantism," "liberalism," "modern theology," and "Cultural Protestantism" to refer broadly to an anthropocentric foundation of theology rather than to distinct historical schools. Often identifying this theological "error" with Friedrich Schleiermacher, with whom he had a love–hate relationship, Barth denounced the suspension of theological truth for experience and the centering of human freedom instead of the freedom of God. Such an inversion of the epistemological right relationship of God and human being into the self-consciousness of "religion" instead of the objectivity of revelation lead, according to Barth, to the all-too-easy identification of the divine with human achievements, rationalities, movements, and political systems that he could diagnose in the militarist enthusiasm of his liberal teachers just as much as in overly optimistic forms of religious socialism or in religious pietism.

Barth also militated strenuously against the "natural theology" of Roman Catholicism, which he once pointedly called the "invention of the anti-Christ."[7] Although he could identify the church with the spiritual body of Christ, Barth did so through a conception of Christian existence as witness that resulted in a thoroughly low ecclesiology, utterly uninvested in clerical status, religious institutions, or their difference over and against the surrounding world. But Barth's primary contention against Roman Catholicism was not the Vatican's clerical or sacramental theology, but rather a "natural theology" over which he famously fell out with his Reformed (!) colleague Emil Brunner. Barth considered natural theology's epistemological as well as ethical failure to adequately distinguish between the supernatural-divine and the natural-creaturely as conducive to the theological conflation of contemporary movements and politics with divine revelation that he saw behind German nationalism and the theological validation of the Nazi movement by the German Christians.

Against both Neo-Protestantism and Roman Catholicism, defined thusly as theological issues, Barth insisted on the alterity of God, the epistemological and ontological gap between God and world – a gap that cannot be bridged from the human side – and on the necessarily dispossessive nature of theological inquiry. Most of all, he insisted that the truth of God and the truth of the human being can both be found only in Jesus Christ as God's self-revelation, rather than inferred by human means, whether rational or mystic, philosophical or experiential. This emphasis on revelation in Christ also animates Barth's theological and ideology critiques.

The role of theology is thus ever only a secondary endeavor of tracing that divine movement, of a witness to the Word of God, the humanity of God, the revelation of God in Jesus Christ. Barth was fond of comparing theology to the overlong index finger of John the Baptist in Matthias Grünewald's famous Isenheim Altarpiece, pointing to the crucified Christ. Understanding his theology as such an indexical gesture lent it both its utmost seriousness *and* its self-relativization; its insistence on its *Sache and* its radically dispossessive and self-critical character; its starting point with the divine "yes," and its translations into ideological-critical "no's," its demand for a firm stance *and* its ability to reverse positions as necessary.

Understanding all theology to be self-relativizing witness, pointing away from itself to the Word of God, and out of that commitment critically interrogating the proclamation of the church in service to the execution of its testimonial vocation, Barth saw himself as a lifelong student of theology, time and again asked to return to the site of the event of God's self-revelation. The result is a theology that is unapologetically theological, rooted in the scriptures, developed in rigorous conversation with Reformed doctrine as well as classical, medieval, and modern theology, and committed to a Christian witness and practice in the church. Its articulation in classical terminology should not distract from the fact that Barth's theology is one of the most original and creative, even constructive theological enterprises of recent centuries.

Content

Shifts in language and inflection as well as Barth's reservations against systematicity as a theological form should not distract from central commitments that function almost like axioms. In the mathematical language that especially the early Barth was fond of employing, axioms are propositions whose truth cannot be demonstrated but upon whose assumption complex and sophisticated systems of thinking can be built. Much of Barth's thought, across the wide range of doctrinal loci and diverse contextual engagements, can be described by inflecting, combining, and drawing out the following foundational commitments:

1 God is God.
2 The world is world.
3 God is in the world in God's one word, Jesus Christ.

"God is God" spells out classical notions of divine identity, simplicity, and transcendence while invoking the biblical language of God's self-revelation. In the Romans commentary, this axiom marks God's alterity as "wholly Other" in counterdistinction to the world: "If I have a system, it is limited to the recognition of what Kierkegaard called the 'infinite qualitative distinction' between time and eternity ... 'God is in heaven, thou art on earth.'"[8] However, this wholly Other God is always already God for the world, God revealing Godself to the world, bridging the unbridgeable chasm, as Barth develops extensively in his mature theology: Election, creation, and covenant are expressions of God's faithfulness to be who God is. "The world is world" qualifies the other side of this first axiom: the world in difference to this God. Not God, but not godless, either, the world is loved by God, held by God, and addressed by God who waits for its response and makes space and time for it. "God is in the world in God's one word, Jesus Christ," is spelled out in the doctrines of revelation, incarnation, and redemption. The identification of the Word of God with the person of Jesus Christ both elevates and relativizes the scriptures in Old and New Testaments and the proclamation of the church into testimonies to this one Word of God, which can become the Word of God for us always in only indirect identity with the Word of God in Jesus Christ. Authentic knowledge of God is possible only through divine self-revelation and can never be attained by human means. At the same time, God *has* conclusively revealed Godself in God's Word, as definitive of who God is. There is no *deus absconditus*. The Christ-event, or the person of Jesus Christ, is definitive both for who God is – and for true humanity. The task of the Christian is to listen to this Word, time and again, and to witness to it.

Whereas the first two axioms are formally tautological, the third combines them paradoxically, or maybe dialectically, and dynamizes them. All three axioms boil down to this third – which however turns out to be not an axiom at all, but a name, pointing to a person. Shortly before his death, Barth himself summed up his theological approach:

> The last word which I have to say as a theologian and also as a politician is not a term like "grace," but a name, "Jesus Christ." He is grace, and he is the last, beyond the world and the church and even theology … What I have been concerned to do in my long life has been increasingly to emphasize this name and to say: There is no salvation in any other name than this. For grace, too, is there. There, too, is the impulse to work, to struggle, and also the impulse towards fellowship, towards human solidarity. Everything that I have tested in my life, in weakness and in foolishness, is there. But it is there.[9]

Barth's *Church Dogmatics* too, spells out these three foundational commitments, this divine name. Each of its five volumes presents a Christocentric reformulation of a major doctrinal locus in the history of salvation and develops a theological ethics in corresponding witness to it. This approach leads to highly original reinterpretations within inherited material through recombinations and new internal connections, effecting a dynamization of the systematic structure.

Volume I, *The Doctrine of the Word of God*, holds theological "prolegomena" – usually introductory remarks on epistemology and method. In Barth's case, they contain a full-blown doctrine of the Trinity, grammatically structured around the event of revelation as "God – reveals – Godself." This unusual opening expresses Barth's inner-theological foundation of theology: not principles of rationality nor a formalized methodology, but the event of the living God's self-revelation *is* the presupposition and condition of theology, cutting off all human attempts to reach, understand, master, or possess God by human means – attempts that Barth famously disqualifies as "religion." Grounding the possibility of theology only in divine self-revelation, the volume also defines theology as the church's critical self-reflection of its own proclamation of God's word, necessitating treatments of the incarnation, the Holy Spirit, and scripture.

Volume II, *The Doctrine of God*, identifies God as "the one who loves in freedom." The classical attributes of God are reinterpreted through the dialectical mutual determination of love and freedom: who God is in Godself is thus God *for us*. In what is often considered his most groundbreaking and original theological contribution, Barth incorporates the Calvinist notion of predestination into the doctrine of God as volume II/2, *The Election of God* describes God's self-determination to be both "the electing God" and "the elected human being" in Jesus Christ. Participating in this election and in obedience to God's command, Christians become witnesses to divine election in the world.

Volume III articulates *The Doctrine of Creation* not as a cosmological speculation but as the "external foundation" of the covenant of God with God's people in history, which thus provides the "internal foundation" or inner reason for creation. Constituted toward this covenant, humanity is always already co-humanity, articulated in concrete being-for-others ranging from the parent–child relationship and the spousal encounter to universal humanity. Realized in inseparable unity of body and soul, and circumscribed by temporality, human freedom before God becomes fulfilled in Sabbath, in fellowship, in the affirmation of life, and in acknowledgement of one's own temporal finitude.

The complex architecture of Volume IV, *The Doctrine of Reconciliation*, integrates a classical two-natures Christology with the threefold office into a dialectical movement with several sublayers. The three dogmatic subvolumes unfold this movement as shown in the following table:

	CD IV/1	CD IV/2	CD IV/3
Movement	The Lord as Servant	The Servant as Lord	The True Witness
Being	True God	True Human Being	Unity of the Person
Office	Priest	King	Prophet
Status	*Status exinanitionis*	*Status exaltationis*	Light
Hamartiology	Hybris → fall	Sloth → misery	Falsehood → condemnation
Soteriology	Justification	Sanctification	Vocation
The Work of the Holy Spirit in Community (ecclesiology)	Gathering	Upbuilding	Sending
The Work of the Holy Spirit in the Individual	Faith	Love	Hope

The fourth, ethical subvolume was to spell out the Christian's "free and active answer" to God's reconciling grace. A partial publication, disavowing a sacramental understanding and the practice of children's baptism, caused a last public scandal around Barth. Published posthumously from lectures, a part on the Lord's Prayer framed the Christian zeal for righteousness as active waiting for God's revolt against the "lordless powers" of this world. A part on the Lord's supper, as well as volume V, *The Doctrine of Redemption*, remained unformulated at the time of Barth's death.

If Barth's theology can be read as a radicalization of the Reformers' insights into the sovereign grace of God and the critique of human self-justification in its religious, epistemological, and political inflections against the background of the intellectual and political developments in the nineteenth and twentieth centuries, it does so by spelling out the name Jesus Christ as both God's self-determination and the human being's truest definition. Barth's emphasis is thus only partially captured as a commitment to transcendence (as it is sometimes characterized); it is rather a witness to the living God who determines Godself to be God for the human being and who determines the human being to be for God, in Jesus Christ. Its axiomatic simplicity makes for great consistency and recognizability, while allowing for extreme versatility and generativity. This approach enabled Barth to be both "orthodox and modern,"[10] drawing on central commitments of the theological tradition yet applying them to often surprisingly new effects.

Debate

Barth was a passionate theologian, and he continues to provoke passionate responses. Celebrated by some as a modern church father, a defender of the faith against modernity's onslaughts, reviled by others as a top-down, theocratic thinker firmly opposed to all theological validation of the human being, Barth leaves few unmoved. At the same time, his assessment remains debated even at the most fundamental levels: Was he a modern scholastic or a postmodern thinker? A staunch defender of tradition or a radical innovator? An anti-liberal or a theologian of freedom? A political, apolitical, or antipolitical theologian? Constantly self-relativizing or vexingly self-immunizing? A prophetic witness in an idolatrous world or a self-aggrandizing antagonist?

If Barth's theology has stirred much debate, this starts with his own "life in conflict."[11] Well known for his distaste for apologetics, Barth did not shy away from polemics. As much as he believed in the primacy of the divine "yes," Barth surely executed its resultant "no" fervently. From his first publications in the *Christliche Welt* indicting liberal theology, through his Tambach lecture's deliberate disappointment of his religious socialist audience's hopes, to publicly enacted fallings-out with fellow dialectical theologians, many of Barth's decisive publications constituted contrarian interventions against the assumptions of his immediate context. Although these fights can be read as an ongoing, relentless self-critique of Barth's own tendencies and inclinations, he also picked them with glee and leveraged them rhetorically for dramatic effect at much cost for his opponents. It should thus neither surprise that Barth's epigones have often emulated such public hostilities, nor that Barth's critiques have produced strong counterreactions and aversions.

Of the debates started by Barth but extending after his death, many revolved around theological method as challenged by his theology of revelation: questions surrounding biblical exegesis, scriptural hermeneutics, and historical criticism on the one hand, and questions concerning natural theology and the *analogia entis* on the other. The theological academy in Germany divided itself for several decades over an almost confessional "Barth or Bultmann" question as their historical debate was carried on by their students. Bultmann students like Ernst Fuchs and Gerhard Ebeling saw Barth as neo-orthodox, ahistorical, and lacking hermeneutical sensibility. Influenced by both Barth and Bultmann, Eberhard Jüngel reconciled their systems by reconstructing Barth's Trinitarian theology in functional equivalence to Bultmann's program of demythologization, thus construing both as versions of a critical, hermeneutical theology.[12] Beyond Bultmann, Bonhoeffer's early unease with Barth's "positivism of revelation" was rearticulated in Wolfhart Pannenberg's epistemological critique of Barth, and Paul Althaus's early contentions against Barth's supposed "Christomonism" has repeatedly resurfaced in debates about religious pluralism.[13]

After his death, the interpretation of Barth's thought itself became subject to controversy. In postwar Germany, Marquardt's thesis that "Karl Barth was a socialist"[14] – not only in his early ministry but into the apparently apolitical *Church Dogmatics* – divided right-wing and left-wing Barthians over whether to read him primarily as a dogmatic theologian or as a public theologian of leftist politics. The so-called "Berlin school" of Barth interpretation, among them Helmut Gollwitzer (whom Barth had championed as his successor in Basel) and his students Friedrich-Wilhelm Marquardt and Ulrich Dannemann, advocated for a political and antibourgeois reading of Barth. The so-called "Munich school," spearheaded by Trutz Rendtorff and further developed by Falk Wagner and Friedrich Wilhelm Graf, not only depoliticized Barth but also followed Ernst Troeltsch in reading dialectical theology as an intraliberal reaction that reintroduced liberal theology's defining notion of freedom on the side of the divine rather than the human subject, effectively immunizing itself against the crisis of historicism through a doctrine of revelation.[15] Subsequently, Barth could be reappropriated for a transcendentalized subjectivist theology that would find its fulfillment in a theory of Christianity, with modern society as a space of actualization for Christian freedom. Alternatively, Barth's starting point with the absolute was equated with the totalitarian erasure ("*Gleichschaltung*") of difference. If the Berlin School might be charged with overly heroizing Barth, the Munich School thus declared Barth's explicit doctrinal substance as well as his consistent antitotalitarian advocacy to be a complete and utter self-misunderstanding. Such an openly anti-Barthian interpretation of Barth has consequently been denounced as "a sin against good taste."[16]

For all their stark disagreement, both German schools of interpretation understood Barth as a critical and engaged *modern* theologian. Barth's initial reception in anglophone theology, however, often perceived his pushback against liberalism as a simple pre- or anti-modern repristination of Reformed, classical, or biblicist dogmatics, and often sidelined Barth's theology subsequently as a supposedly reactionary, "neo-orthodox" position. Although this perception has been significantly challenged, Barth's theology is still most often embraced in anglophone theology by those for whom premodern theological commitments find their critically refined expression in the dialectically sophisticated, postmetaphysical, yet unwavering realism of Barth's systematics.

Apart from the overall classification of Barth's theology and the periodization of his work, the specifics of his dogmatic position have of course also been subject to debate. In the early 2000s, Princeton Theological Seminary witnessed a particularly heated debate over the internal relationship between Barth's doctrines of election and Trinity. Headed by Bruce McCormack, one faction found Barth's doctrine of election to imply that even the doctrine of God cannot be conceived *remote Christo*: God's self-determination in Jesus Christ is what effectively constitutes God as triune. The other, headed by George Hunsinger, responded that such an ordering would endanger Barth's ontological divide between creator and creature and, contradicting Barth's fundamental convictions, make God dependent on the human being.[17]

While confident of his influence, Barth himself often joked about self-declared "Barthians," insisting that he was not one of them. Maybe it is the tragedy of Barth's theology that it became so authoritative, as this has often reversed the critical character of his interventions and positions. In postwar Germany, Barthian theology claimed moral superiority as almost the lone theological system untainted by National Socialist cooptation. Although Barth's theological dialectics had been effective against reigning ideologies, and arguably exerted its greatest strengths in the struggle against Christian nationalism and other "possessive" theologies, it could itself become oppressive when articulated from positions of dominance, not just in dogmatics but also in practical theology and church polity. This critique – in variations shared by liberal and feminist theologians – has perhaps been most forcefully articulated by James Cone: "To be sure, as Barth pointed out, God's word is alien to humanity and thus comes to it as a 'bolt from the blue' – but which humanity? For oppressors, dehumanizers, the analysis is correct. However, when we speak of God's revelation to the oppressed, the analysis is incorrect."[18]

Much depends on whose side of the story a theology tells, which movement it effects. In his pushback against human idolatry, Barth's theology moves "top down": from God to the world, from text to context, from dogma to ethics, from revelation to witness. His rejection of subjective or contextual reflection, experience, or culture as theological *starting points* can at times obscure the engaged mode of his own theology. As Barth himself maintained, dialectics are not a superior way of doing theology; they inevitably turn into self-contradictions when fixed methodologically, frozen as the image of the "bird in flight." Barth's theology has thus often been perceived as rather unpastoral (despite his self-understanding as a theology for pastors) and even inhumane (against his insistence on the humanity of God); as crushing liberation and emancipation in their bud (despite his Christologically universalized "royal" human being); as unbearably negative (despite his joyful grounding in the divine "Yes") but also as overly triumphalist (despite all theoretic humility); as antipluralistic (despite all self-critique and self-relativization); and even totalitarian (despite his manifest commitments against fascism and nationalism).

More interesting than debates over Barth's "correct" interpretation or attempts at his vindication are the ones that wrestle constructively with his impulses in their own attempt to point to Christ. When theologians from Southeast Asia sought clarification for their interpretation and contextual application of Barth's theology, he responded:

> Enough pointing toward an understanding of "my" theology! ... Now it is *your* turn. Now it is *your* task to do Christian theology in your new, different and particular situation with head and heart, with mouth and hands. How this ought to happen? In no way can I prescribe this for you. It is truly your own task to respond adequately ... You truly do not have to become "European," "Western" people, let alone "Barthians," in order to be good Christians and good theologians.[19]

Influence, Achievement, and Agenda

Karl Barth's unapologetically theological refoundation of theology after the critical turns of modernity and its prophetic witness in the political turbulences of the time have been pivotal for Western Protestantism in the twentieth century. His influence has extended not only far beyond his own imagination or the stewardship of his theological legacy but also beyond his agenda or endorsement. In fact, the generativity of Barth's thought beyond "Barthianism," often in contradiction or critique, might be one of its most remarkable traits.

Already upon its debut in the 1920s, Barth's theology resonated widely with a feeling of crisis, and his polemical dialectical interventions against liberal Protestantism echoed across a broad theological, ecclesial, and political spectrum. The first dissertation on Barth's theology appeared as early as 1925,[20] and from the 1930s, he attracted international publicity and students. In postwar Germany, Barth's theology quickly became the dominant theological system taught at universities and seminaries, with subsequent generations working out their own profile in relation to and distinction from Barth's theology. Barth has been hugely influential throughout Europe into the present day, especially in the Netherlands, the Czech Republic, France, and Hungary.[21]

Barth has been celebrated as a pioneer of the ecumenical movement, a "*pastor pastorum oecumenicus*" for the impulses his theology provided for it.[22] Barth's Trinitarian formulation of mission inspired Karl Hartenstein's conception of a *missio dei*, which became the new paradigm of missiology for the World Council of Churches. Barth's theology has sparked widespread renewed interest in Trinitarian theology after the nineteenth and early twentieth century's relative silence on the matter. While the English-speaking academic reception of Barth has mostly focused on Barth's *Church Dogmatics*, the wider international and ecclesial reception has drawn much more on Barth's "occasional" writings as translated and circulated by his students into diverse contexts and languages, as well as on the ecumenical significance of the *Barmen Declaration*. Barth's involvement with the World Alliance of Reformed Churches and the ecumenical movement, as well as his public visibility of the "church struggle" years and after, has been influential for confessing theologians and churches in many parts of the world. Next to Bonhoeffer's theology, Barth's was an important resource in the struggle against apartheid in South Africa in the 1980s and 1990s. Ongoing influence – often through his international students – is felt in Japan, Korea, Indonesia, and China.

In the English-speaking academy, the reception was mixed. Barth attracted particular attention in ethics and moral theology (Nigel Biggar, Stanley Hauerwas, John Howard Yoder, Oliver O'Donovan). In Great Britain, his theology was often dismissed on the competing charges of "neo-orthodoxy" or overly liberal interpretation of scripture. In the United States, he was occasionally harnessed as an antidote to cultural emphases on self-actualization or leveraged for a Christian "counterculture." The "postliberal" Yale School drew on Barth's "generous orthodoxy" in their shared concern with the ecclesial function of theology for a particular community and their grammar of articulation (Hans Frei, George Lindbeck). The title "Barth scholar" became descriptive of those who devoted themselves to interpreting Barth's theology and/or applying it in particular extensions (John Webster, Thomas F. Torrance, Bruce McCormack, George Hunsinger).

At times, Barth's theology has been engaged more enthusiastically in Roman Catholic theology than by its Protestant counterparts, starting with the responses to the Romans commentary and Barth's conversations with Erich Przywara, through his reception by Hans Küng and Hans Urs von Balthasar, to more recent Thomist engagements. While relatively little engagement has ensued between Barth and Orthodox theology, he has found widespread interest in evangelical and postevangelical circles. Increasingly, Barth's theology has also been put into conversation with different areas of critical thought, like philosophy of religion, philosophy of language, postmodern interpretation, Jewish thought, gender studies, liberation theologies, postcolonial theologies, and political theologies.

Already during Barth's lifetime, a new generation of systematic theologians developed independent proposals while building on Barth – often rebuked by Barth himself, as in the case of Jürgen Moltmann and Wolfhart Pannenberg. Robert Jenson's narrative Trinitarian theology and Colin Gunton's reckoning with modernity's incoherencies were similarly Barth inspired, yet original proposals. Notable thinkers who carried Barthian impulses in different directions range as widely as Dietrich Bonhoeffer, Dorothee Sölle, José Míguez Bonino, Jacques Ellul, and John Updike.

If there are indications that scholarly interest in Barth as a historical figure or authoritative system is waning, there are also signs that interest in him as a constructive interlocutor might be only just beginning. Barth's rigorous engagement with the tradition combined with a willingness to fundamentally rethink and rearticulate its commitments, and the combination of axiomatic simplicity and constructive versatility offer an appealing toolset for constructive development. The centrality of Christ and the authority of scripture has made Barth's theology compelling to faithful Christians, while the dispossessive and dialectical structure of his thought turns him into a "gateway" from uncritically pre- to hypercritically postmodern articulations of faith. The ecclesial character of Barth's theology and the virtual identification of dogmatics with ethics has resonated with those interested in Christian discipleship, while its "confessing" nature builds bridges to political theology, public witness, and ethics of refusal and resistance. Barth's insistence on the Lordship of Christ has funded resolutely prodemocratic politics and his refusal of theological apologetics lends itself well to an existence in (post)pluralistic societies. Barth's hypercritical theological epistemology and his refusal to essentialize humanity open theology up for fruitful dialogue with different critical theories – decolonial, womanist, queer, crip – even where his material insights fall short of theirs. Barth's eschatology might even present perspectives for Christian hope in a time when politics, theory, and ecology find themselves disenthralled by futuristic conceptions.

Notes

1 Karl Barth, "Moderne Theologie und Reichsgottesarbeit" [1909], in *Vorträge und kleinere Arbeiten 1905–1909*, GA III.21, ed. Hans-Anton Drewes and Hinrich Stoevesandt (Zürich: Theologischer Verlag, 1992), 334–66.

2 Karl Barth, *Der Römerbrief* [1919], GA II.16, ed. Hermann Schmidt (Zürich: Theologischer Verlag, 1992, 1985).

3 Karl Barth, *Final Testimonies*, ed. Eberhard Busch, trans. Geoffrey W. Bromiley (Grand Rapids, MI: Eerdmans, 1977), 23.

4 Karl Barth, *Evangelical Theology: An Introduction*, trans. Grover Foley (Grand Rapids, MI: Eerdmans, 1979), 165.

5 Adapted from Michael Beintker, "Resümee: Periodisierung des Barthschen Denkens," in *Barth Handbuch*, ed. Michael Beintker (Tübingen: Mohr Siebeck, 2016), 232–7. The article also gives a helpful overview over different periodizations of Barth's thought.

6 Karl Barth, *Theological Existence To-Day!: (A Plea for Theological Freedom)* (Eugene, OR: Wipf and Stock, 2012), 9.

7 Karl Barth, *Church Dogmatics*, 14 vols. (Edinburgh: T&T Clark, 1934–76), I/1, xiii.

8 Karl Barth, *The Epistle to the Romans*, trans. Edwyn C. Hoskyns (Oxford: Oxford University Press, 1968), 10.

9 Barth, *Final Testimonies*, 29–30.

10 Cf. Bruce L. McCormack, *Orthodox and Modern: Studies in the Theology of Karl Barth* (Grand Rapids, MI: Baker Academic, 2008).

11 Thus the apt title of Christiane Tietz's biography.

12 Eberhard Jüngel, *Gottes Sein ist im Werden: Verantwortliche Rede vom Sein Gottes bei Karl Barth* (Tübingen: Mohr, 1965).

13 Systematized by Alan Race in *Christians and Religious Pluralism: Patterns in the Christian Theology of Religions* (Maryknoll, NY: Orbis, 1983); Cf. the critique of Sven Ensminger, *Karl Barth's Theology as a Resource for a Christian Theology of Religions* (London: T&T Clark, 2014).

14 Friedrich-Wilhelm Marquardt, *Theologie und Sozialismus: Das Beispiel Karl Barths* (München: Kaiser, 1972).

15 Falk Wagner and Trutz Rendtorff, *Die Realisierung der Freiheit: Beitrage zur Kritik der Theologie Karl Barths* (Gütersloh: Gütersloher Verlagshaus Mohn, 1975). For a detailed account of different inner-liberal interpretations of Barth in German-speaking theology, cf. Stefan Holtmann, *Karl Barth als Theologe der Neuzeit: Studien zur kritischen Deutung seiner Theologie* (Göttingen: Vandenhoeck & Ruprecht, 2007).

16 Eberhard Jüngel, *Barth-Studien* (Zürich: Benziger, 1982), 13.

17 Cf. especially Bruce L. McCormack, "Grace and Being," in *The Cambridge Companion to Karl Barth*, ed. John Webster (Cambridge: Cambridge University Press, 2000), 92–110; George Hunsinger, "Election and the Trinity: Twenty-Five Theses on the Theology of Karl Barth," *Modern Theology* 24, no. 2 (2008): 179–98; Michael Dempsey, ed., *Trinity and Election in Contemporary Theology* (Grand Rapids, MI: Eerdmans, 2011).

18 James H. Cone, *A Black Theology of Liberation*. 50th anniversary ed. (Maryknoll, NY: Orbis, 2020), 30.

19 Karl Barth, "An Christen in Suedostasien," in *Offene Briefe 1945–1968*, ed. Diether Koch (Zürich: TVZ, 1984), 555, my translation.

20 Gottfried Holtz, "Die ethischen Konsequenzen des Gottesgedankens in der Theologie Karl Barths" (PhD diss., Universität Rostock, 1925).

21 For Barth's reception in different European contexts cf. Martin Leiner and Michael Trowitzsch, eds., *Karl Barths Theologie als europäisches Ereignis* (Göttingen: Vandenhoeck & Ruprecht, 2008).

22 Thus Visser 't Hooft's appreciation in Karl Barth, *Gedenkfeier im Basler Münster* (Zürich: EVZ, 1969), 52.

Recommended Reading

Primary

Barth, Karl. *The Church Dogmatics.* 14 vols. Edinburgh: T&T Clark, 1934–76.

———. *Community, State, and Church: Three Essays by Karl Barth.* Eugene, OR: Wipf and Stock, 1960.

———. *Dogmatics in Outline.* Translated by G. T. Thomson. New York: Harper, 1959.

———. *The Epistle to the Romans.* Translated by Edwyn C. Hoskyns. Oxford: Oxford University Press, 1968.

———. *Evangelical Theology: An Introduction.* Translated by Grover Foley. Grand Rapids, MI: Eerdmans, 1979.

———. *Fides Quaerens Intellectum: Anselm's Proof of the Existence of God in the Context of His Theological Scheme.* Translated by Ian W. Robertson. Eugene, OR: Pickwick, 2009.

———. *The Humanity of God.* Richmond, VA: John Knox Press, 1960.

———. "The Word of God as the Task of Theology, 1922." In *The Word of God and Theology.* translated by Amy Marga, 171–98. London: T&T Clark, 2011.

Brunner, Emil, and Karl Barth, *Natural Theology: Comprising "Nature and Grace" by Professor Dr. Emil Brunner and the Reply "No!" by Dr. Karl Barth.* Eugene, OR: Wipf and Stock, 2002.

Secondary

Beintker, Michael, ed. *Barth Handbuch.* Tübingen: Mohr Siebeck, 2016.

Hunsinger, George. *How to Read Karl Barth: The Shape of His Theology.* New York: Oxford University Press, 1991.

Hunsinger, George, and Keith Johnson, eds. *The Wiley Blackwell Companion to Karl Barth,* 2 vols. Hoboken, NJ: Wiley-Blackwell, 2020.

Jones, Paul D., and Kaitlyn Dugan, eds. *Karl Barth and Liberation Theology.* London: Bloomsbury T&T Clark, 2022.

Jones, Paul D., and Paul T. Nimmo, eds. *The Oxford Handbook of Karl Barth.* Oxford: Oxford University Press, 2020.

McCormack, Bruce L. *Karl Barth's Critically Realistic Dialectical Theology: Its Genesis and Development.* Oxford: Oxford University Press, 1995.

Tietz, Christiane. *Karl Barth: A Life in Conflict.* Translated by Victoria J. Barnett. Oxford: Oxford University Press, 2021.

Karl Rahner

Karen Kilby

Introduction: Life

Karl Rahner is one of the giants of twentieth-century theology. He wrote prolifically, lectured widely, and exerted a major influence on theology within and beyond the Catholic Church. He had a tremendous intellectual reach, writing on the full range of traditional theological topics and a good deal more, and produced a body of work consistently marked by a distinctive and often highly creative combination of spiritual depth, fidelity to church tradition, and honest engagement with modern thought.

Rahner's life was, on his own account, rather dull. He was born in Freiburg im Breisgau in Germany, into a middle-class Roman Catholic family, one of seven children. Upon finishing his schooling at eighteen, he entered the Jesuit order and remained a Jesuit until his death in 1984. After completing the novitiate in 1924, Rahner spent most of the next twelve years studying philosophy and theology and then more philosophy and more theology. Following the usual Jesuit pattern, he began with three years of philosophical study and then, after a two-year period teaching Latin, four years of theology. The theology that Rahner learned during these years was the neoscholasticism dominating Roman Catholic seminaries of the time, and one can go a long way toward understanding him by understanding the critical and complex relationship he retained to this system of thought throughout much of his career. After these years of theology there followed a year of tertianship – the final year of a Jesuit's formation – and then Rahner was sent back to Freiburg, the place of his birth, to do a PhD in philosophy.

The intention of Rahner's superiors was to prepare him to teach the history of philosophy to Jesuits in training. Accordingly, Rahner wrote a thesis, eventually published as *Spirit in the World*, on an aspect of the thought of Thomas Aquinas. His official supervisor was Martin Honecker, but a more significant influence was Martin Heidegger, to whose seminar Rahner belonged during his time in Freiburg (1934–6). The thesis, which interpreted Aquinas through the lens of Kant and post-Kantian thinkers, and which showed some influence from Heidegger, was failed by Honecker. Rahner's future had however already been rethought by his superiors, who wished him to replace a retiring Jesuit and teach theology at the University of Innsbruck. Here, within the year, he produced a successful PhD in theology, and in 1937 began teaching.

Ford's The Modern Theologians: An Introduction to Christian Theology since 1918, Fourth Edition.
Edited by Rachel Muers and Ashley Cocksworth.
© 2024 John Wiley & Sons Ltd. Published 2024 by John Wiley & Sons Ltd.

The arrival of the Nazis in Austria in 1938 disrupted teaching in Innsbruck, however. Rahner spent a number of years in Vienna, working in the diocesan Pastoral Institute, and the final year of the war as the parish priest of a Bavarian village. In 1948 he returned to Innsbruck and there began a period of great theological productivity. This was also a time during which Rahner's theology came under official suspicion at a number of points. He was refused permission to publish a long book on Mary in 1951, forbidden to discuss the issue of concelebration in 1954, and told in 1962 that all his writings would have to be read by a Roman censor.

The opening of the Second Vatican Council later in 1962 marked a turning point in Rahner's career, at least as regards his standing in the church. Rahner was brought to the council as a private advisor of Cardinal König of Vienna and given the official role of *peritus*, theological expert. All talk of a special censor for his writings ceased. He was tremendously active during the period of the council and is generally regarded as having had a significant influence on many of its documents. This is difficult to measure precisely, given the complexity of the process by which these documents emerged, and given that elements from Rahner's theology that make an appearance in them can often also be traced to other sources. Rahner himself was agnostic about the exact nature of his impact on the council. Nevertheless, by the end of the Second Vatican Council he had undeniably emerged as a major theologian and had moved from the position of a somewhat suspect theological figure to become the leading representative of what was (at least for a time) a new mainstream.

In 1964 Rahner left Innsbruck to take up a chair in Christianity and the Philosophy of Religion in the philosophy faculty of the University of Munich. He moved again in 1967 to the University of Münster, where he remained until his retirement in 1971. He continued to lecture and write over the next thirteen years and died in 1984.

In many cases one can gain an orientation toward a thinker's work by explaining its relationship to one or two other figures, whether these serve as the source of inspiration or as that which must be reacted against (or both). For Rahner, however, there is no particular intellectual predecessor who serves either as obvious foil or as chief inspiration. He was, as mentioned, a student of Heidegger for a time, and one can find a certain amount of Heideggerian language and concepts and even some Heideggerian strategies in his work. But these are best seen as relatively ad hoc borrowings rather than as a systematic adaptation of Heidegger's thought (in any of its periods) for theology. It is true, again, that lying behind *Spirit in the World*, Rahner's first major work and his most philosophical effort, is the influence of Joseph Maréchal, a Belgian Jesuit philosopher of the previous generation. From Maréchal, who has come to be known as the father of Transcendental Thomism, Rahner learned to read Aquinas through the lens of Kant and post-Kantian philosophy, but it would be a mistake to conclude that the influence of Maréchal was decisive for Rahner's thought taken as a whole. One can place *Spirit in the World* alongside a number of other works of the so-called Transcendental Thomists and see them as developing in different ways the project of Maréchal, but one should not assume that this is therefore an adequate characterization of all of the subsequent work of a man who would later insist that he was not a philosopher and had no philosophy.

There are a number of intellectual figures who played a role in the development of Rahner's thought, then – Aquinas, Kant, Maréchal, Heidegger – but no one who can be singled out as decisive. Indeed, if one is to point to a single "other" who has shaped Rahner and against whom he struggles, it should perhaps not be any individual, but the neoscholasticism that predominated during his years of formation.[1] Neoscholasticism was an intellectual system that claimed allegiance to the thought of the Middle Ages, and of Thomas Aquinas in particular. It was fundamentally hostile toward modern (Kantian and post-Kantian) movements in philosophy. In the second half of the nineteenth century neoscholasticism had succeeded in defeating its rivals and establishing its hegemony as *the* accepted form of Roman Catholic thought. It remained in the ascendency for several generations and became a comprehensive and tidy philosophical and theological scheme, in which the questions were well defined and well understood, the range of acceptable answers could be specified, and the manner in which the answers were to be supported and defended was clear.

Rahner was not alone in having objections to this self-enclosed system of philosophy and theology. A number of thinkers in the previous generation, and nearly all of those who emerged as significant figures in Rahner's generation, struggled against it in one way or another. Hans Urs von Balthasar, Rahner's contemporary, complained that this theology was dry as dust and was reported to have stopped up his ears during lectures in order to read Augustine unhindered. What is significant about Rahner, however, is that he did not simply set aside neoscholasticism in order to do theology in a different way. Instead, Rahner worked to a large extent with the system, probing and questioning it, seeking to bring it into contact with modern philosophy and to open it up from within to the modern world.

Survey

Rahner's first major publication was *Spirit in the World*, the product of his doctoral work in philosophy and a ferociously difficult piece of writing.[2] The next book, based on lectures given in 1937, was *Hearer of the Word* here, Rahner outlined an understanding of philosophy of religion as the study of the conditions of the possibility of the reception of revelation – what must be true about us if we are to be beings capable of hearing a possible revelation from God? These two works are often taken to provide the "philosophical foundations" of all that followed, though Rahner himself distanced himself from them to some degree (he referred to them in an interview, for instance, as "lop-sided works of my youth"). If, as a number of commentators have done, one understands *Spirit in the World* and *Hearer of the Word* as the basis upon which the later work is built, and as therefore to a large degree determining the shape of Rahner's theology, one has a quick way of getting a handle on Rahner, but there is also a danger of reading him reductively, missing the real interest of much of his work. Certainly, many of the same instincts and concerns found in Rahner's later theology make an appearance in these philosophical works, and certainly Rahner would later make use of some of the philosophical material he developed in *Spirit in the World*, but it is inadvisable to read the theology as founded upon or in any simple way flowing from the philosophy.

Rahner's characteristic approach as a theologian was not to write large tomes setting out comprehensive treatments of theology as a whole, nor even to attempt to treat individual doctrines exhaustively. Instead, he wrote primarily, and was at his best in the writing of, relatively short articles, essays probing particular questions from particular angles. For this reason, the single most important place to look for Rahner's theology is not *Foundations of Christian Faith* (an experimental and not entirely successful book he published in his seventies) but the *Theological Investigations*, a collection of essays running to twenty-three volumes in English. Also important are essays in pastoral theology collected in *Mission and Grace*, and the sixteen volumes Rahner authored or coauthored in a series titled *Quaestiones Disputatae*.

In addition to his prolific writing, Rahner undertook an enormous amount of editorial work. The *Quaestiones Disputatae* series was only one of a number of major projects with which he was involved. In some cases he took over the responsibility for new editions of existing works: in the 1950s he brought out several editions of Denzinger's *Enchiridion Symbolorum*, which contains the texts of official church teaching, and between 1957 and 1965 together with a coeditor he published a new edition of Herder's *Lexicon für Theologie und Kirche*. He also launched, usually in conjunction with others, major new projects: he was for instance an editor of *Sacramentum Mundi*, and of the *Handbuch der Pastoraltheologie*, and together with Edward Schillebeeckx and others he founded the international journal *Concilium*.

Rahner's bibliography is not only long, it is also wide. He wrote on an enormous number, and an almost whimsical range, of topics. There are few subjects into which he did not stray. Rahner's works include – to mention some themes almost at random – essays on the Trinity, the incarnation, the church, the sacraments, Mary, angels, indulgences, heresy, the development of doctrine, the diaconate, concupiscence, poetry, childhood, power, leisure, sleep, pluralism, mystery, symbol, old age, death, devotion to the sacred heart of Jesus, devotion to the saints, asceticism, prayer, theological education, eucharistic devotion,

Ignatian mysticism, the relationship of Christianity to Marxism, to evolutionary theory, and to psycho-therapy, the relationship between nature and grace, between scripture and tradition, between exegesis and theology, between the papacy and the episcopate, between the Mass and television.

Rahner sometimes liked to describe himself as a theological dilettante, and this was not sheer modesty. It conveys some sense of the freedom of his theological work and of the fact that he did not usually follow a model of scholarship in which one works in a well-defined field and expounds the whole history of an issue before making one's own contribution. Rahner was also not, essentially, a "systematic" theologian. It is true that his thought has a kind of center – interlocking themes to which he returns again and again – and it is true that if one were to read only *Foundations of Christian Faith* one might be forgiven for supposing he was a highly systematic thinker. But Rahner's essays on particular topics ought not to be read as part of a process of working out a larger system; the essays were occasioned by contemporary theological debates or contemporary pastoral problems, by new pronouncements of church authorities, by invitations to give lectures, lead retreats, or participate in conferences, or simply by Rahner's teaching duties.

Overall, Rahner is a challenging figure to come to terms with: in interviews, published prayers, and the writings in his later years, he is more accessible, but on the whole he is among the most daunting of modern theologians to read. The mixture of scholastic categories and the language of modern German philosophy is one reason for this; Rahner's own caution in exhibiting the orthodoxy of his proposals as a counterweight to their creativity is another. Nevertheless, Rahner's fundamental orientation is not abstract or academic, but pastoral. There is a narrow sense of this word that would describe only some of Rahner's theology – that which is concerned with the specific work a pastor does, with how to organize a parish, preach sermons, counsel individuals, and so on. But there is a broader sense of the word in which almost all of Rahner's theology, even when it is concerned with the Trinity, the incarnation, the notion of heresy, or the significance for theology of the theory of evolution, is pastoral. A recurring concern of Rahner's work is to confront the ways in which modern people, including "good Catholics," can find Christianity alien, something foreign, something that they cannot make sense of, something that they perhaps accept but that has little to do with them, and to seek to understand anew Christian doctrines and the Christian faith so as to overcome this felt foreignness.

If openness to the world, honesty in confronting difficulties in belief, and the desire to reconceive the Christian faith for the contemporary world sound like the typical virtues and characteristics of a theological liberal, it is important to keep in mind that in Rahner's case these are found in a person profoundly steeped in the tradition, and absolutely committed to being faithful to the teachings of the Roman Catholic Church.

Content

Although Rahner is not fundamentally a system builder, there are certain recurrent, and to some degree interlocking, elements in his thinking. To understand them is to be well equipped for the reading of many of Rahner's essays, though one should beware of the danger of taking these notions, abstracted from concrete contexts, as a simple summary of Rahner's theology.

Two closely related ideas that weave their way in and out of many of Rahner's writings are the *Vorgriff auf esse* (often translated as "preapprehension of being") and the supernatural existential. Rahner maintains that in every human act of knowing and willing there is a preapprehension of infinite being, and therefore of God. God cannot be known directly: God is never the object of an act of knowledge in the way that chairs and tables can be; but when the mind knows some particular object, or wills some finite value, it never *merely* knows or chooses the particular but is always at the same time reaching beyond it, towards the whole of being, and therefore toward God. The relationship of this *Vorgriff* to the knowledge of particular objects can be conceived with the help of an image drawn from Heidegger – we are aware of infinite being as the *horizon* for our knowledge of particular things – or one drawn from Aquinas – the *Vorgriff* is the *light* that in illumining the individual objects allows our intellect to grasp them. It can also be understood with the help of Kantian terminology: the *Vorgriff* is, according to Rahner, a transcendental condition of the possibility of knowing and willing. Just as for Kant we do not come across time, space, and the categories of the understanding in the world, do not deduce them from experience, but necessarily bring them to experience, so for Rahner we do not discover infinite being in the world nor subsequently deduce it from what we learn of the world; rather, we are unable to have anything to do with the world at all except against the background of this preapprehension.

The *Vorgriff* is argued for at some length in *Spirit in the World*, and Rahner makes use of it (sometimes under other names) in a variety of ways in his theological writings. The assertion that there is a *Vorgriff* is clearly a bold one: if Rahner is right, then everyone, whether they describe themselves as agnostic or atheist or indifferent, is actually on some level aware of God. Though Rahner is not involved in proving the existence of God, if he is right no such proof is necessary, because anyone who tries to deny the existence of God is in fact in contradiction with herself.

The "supernatural existential" is closely related but distinguished from the *Vorgriff* at least in principle. Just as there is (according to Rahner) a universal apprehension of God, so there is also, he holds, a universal experience of grace, or at least of grace as offered.[3]

"Existential" is a term borrowed from Heidegger; it refers to a fundamental element in human existence, something which is a feature of all our experience rather than one object of experience or one experience among others. This, according to Rahner, is the fundamental character of grace. It is not, or not primarily, something given now and then – the forgiveness of a particular sin, the sudden capacity to overcome a temptation, a particular help in a particular situation, a definitive response to prayer. Instead, grace is an ever-present gift offered to us at such a fundamental and central level that it affects all that we are, and know, and do: "grace … always surrounds man, even the sinner and the unbeliever, as the inescapable setting of his existence."[4]

The supernatural existential is *supernatural* in that it takes human beings beyond their nature. It is not an intrinsic part of what it is to be a human being, not something humanity can claim as its right. This is a rather delicate point, because on Rahner's account human nature has never in fact existed without this supernatural elevation. Human beings *could*, however, have existed on a merely natural level, and so the supernatural existential is genuinely gratuitous, a gift from God beyond the basic gift of creation.

Rahner regards the *Vorgriff*, by contrast, as built into our nature as such – not just built into the way we actually find ourselves to be, our concrete nature, but built into human nature in the abstract theological sense: it is a condition of the possibility of our experience, and without it we would not be human beings at all. The supernatural existential can be thought of as affecting the way in which the *Vorgriff* is experienced – it alters our relation to our horizon. Because of the supernatural existential, God is not just the infinitely distant goal of all our striving, but the goal which, Rahner says, "draws near" and "gives itself." (The images here, it should perhaps be noted, are not easily pinned down: though the goal may give itself, it does not become something *possessed* in our experience, something we can grasp and understand and manipulate like anything else we know. The horizon, even if it draws near, remains the horizon.)

It is worth making clear that in speaking of a universal elevation of human nature, Rahner is not declaring that all are in a state of sanctifying grace and therefore justified. He wants to steer a delicate course, in fact, between maintaining that sanctifying grace is universally present, and everyone is in a state of grace (which would be to say too much), and maintaining that sanctifying grace is universally offered, but *given* only to those who accept the offer (which would be to say too little). His solution is to describe grace as universally present, but present *as offered*. It is, one might say, "there" in all of us, but we have a role in that we accept or reject it, and only if we accept it can we be said to be in a state of sanctifying grace, justified, saved.[5]

It is important to realize that both the supernatural existential itself and its acceptance (or rejection) are according to Rahner "prethematic." The supernatural existential can be present without one being reflexively aware of it – this is, one might say, because it lies so deep within us, because it is an existential, not one distinguishable bit of experience among others, but ever present, impossible to pin down, easily missed.

Rahner suggests that his readers should perhaps be able to recognize what he is talking about: "If this theological and dogmatic interpretation of [a person's] transcendental experience is offered to him by the history of revelation and by Christianity he can recognize his own experience in it."[6] This is, however, very carefully qualified – the experience itself remains ambiguous and introspection on its own would not enable a person to come to such a conclusion.

Closely related to the ideas of *Vorgriff* and supernatural existential is the notion of "transcendental experience." To transcend means simply to go beyond: transcendental experience is the experience of going beyond all the things we know and choose and love, even as we are knowing and choosing and loving them – and when we go beyond all particular things, what we go toward is, on Rahner's account, God.

Just as the awareness of God given in the *Vorgriff* is not ever available on its own, apart from our dealings with the world, and just as the experience of grace is not a separate experience among others but an existential, so transcendental experience is not something occurring in isolation. It is always given only in an experience of the concrete, the particular, the finite. Rahner characteristically expresses this point by pairing "the transcendental" with either "the categorical" (the realm of that which can be put into categories, that which can be pinned down and grasped by concepts) or "the historical."

Rahner's single most famous proposal is that those of other faiths, or of no faith at all, may be considered "anonymous Christians," and his development of this notion also has connections to the ideas of the *Vorgriff* and particularly the supernatural existential. He begins from the fact that Christians believe in the universal salvific will of God on the one hand and in the necessity of faith in Christ and membership of the church for salvation on the other. How can these be reconciled? If church membership is necessary for salvation, then, reasons Rahner, it must be a possibility for all people, and if an explicit church membership is not a real possibility for some people then it follows that there must be some other kind of church membership. Similarly, if faith in Christ is necessary for salvation but explicit, professed faith is not a real possibility for all, then there simply must be something that is *not* explicit and professed and yet that still is faith in Christ. It is only when it comes to suggesting how what *must* be the case *can* be the case that Rahner draws on the notion of the supernatural existential. He proposes that individuals who may never have come across Christianity are nevertheless offered the grace of Christ in the depths of their experience, and may, without ever recognizing it to *be* that, accept it. These then are anonymous Christians.

Laying out these themes one after another in concise form tends to distort the tone of Rahner's theology and fails to give a sense of its depths. So perhaps it is worth pausing briefly, before moving to a second set of ideas, to observe that all the concepts I have so far introduced are for Rahner a way of saying something about a relationship to *mystery*:

> Nothing is more familiar and obvious to the alerted spirit than the silent question which hovers over all that it has attained and mastered. … In his heart of hearts, there is nothing man [sic] knows better than that his knowledge, ordinarily so-called, is only a tiny island in the immense ocean of the unexplored. He knows better than anything else that the existential question facing him in knowledge is whether he loves the little island of his so-called knowledge better than the ocean of the infinite mystery; whether or not he will concede that the mystery alone is self-evident; whether he thinks that the little light with which he illuminates this little island – we call it science – should be the eternal light which shines on him forever (which would be hell).[7]

If the *Vorgriff* and the supernatural existential provide one conceptual starting point for exploring some of Rahner's proposals, his theology of the symbol offers another. A symbol – a real symbol, in any case – is not merely an external sign, according to Rahner: it is intrinsically related to what it symbolizes. One might think of the example (though this is not one that Rahner gives) of a kiss. The kiss as a symbol of love is not simply a pointer, standing in for something essentially different from it, but is intrinsically related to the love; the love expresses itself, and becomes more fully itself, in the kiss. Rahner in fact thinks that all of reality is symbolic, that all being necessarily expresses itself in an "other," and only fully becomes itself, only "comes to itself," in thus expressing itself.

One obvious place where this notion of symbol is useful, and on which it is at least in part based, is the theology of the Trinity. The traditional understanding of the relation of the first and second persons of the Trinity – of the Father to the Son – can be translated neatly into the statement that the Son is the symbol of the Father. Just as a symbol is neither identical with nor simply different from that which it symbolizes, so the Son is distinct from and yet one with the Father. Just as a symbol expresses what it symbolizes, so the "Word" is the self-expression of the Father. And just as a being becomes itself through expressing itself in its symbol, so the Father would not be the Father without the Son, but "is himself by the very fact that he opposes to himself the image which is of the same essence as himself, as the person who is other than himself."[8]

The incarnation too can be understood in symbolic terms. In the incarnation God expressed himself exteriorly, and more particularly, expressed "what God wished to be, in free grace, to the world."[9] There can be a tendency, Rahner suggests, to think of the humanity of Christ as a mere instrument of God, a tool that the second person of the Trinity takes up in order to convey a message to the world. In fact, however, Christ's humanity is not a sign arbitrarily chosen to indicate the presence of God but a real symbol of God. And it is because of this that Jesus himself (and not just what Jesus says or does) can genuinely be the revelation of God – because the humanity is a symbol of the divinity, Christians can say that in Christ they do not just find a pointer to God but actually encounter God himself. The fact that the humanity of Christ is the real symbol of God also has significance for how we are to think about humanity: human beings are not just something that God happened to choose to create; humanity is "that which 'appears' when in his self-exteriorization [God] goes out of himself into that which is other than he."[10]

Rahner has many things to say about the church – in fact, over half of his publications are on ecclesiology[11] – but one central and significant theme here too draws on the theology of the symbol. The church is itself a symbol: it is the "symbolic reality of the presence of Christ, of his definite work of salvation in the world."[12] The role of the church is to continue over time and in a social form the function of the incarnation, of making grace tangible and historically definitive, of symbolizing grace. This is what it means to call the church the "body of Christ." The grace that enters history in a definite way and becomes incarnate in Christ in turn needs to be made concrete in a socially organized community. The church is thus, according to Rahner, the fundamental sacrament. Sacraments in the ordinary sense of the word, the seven sacraments, are also of course to be understood symbolically, and they are to be understood as flowing from the nature of the church as sacrament. The sacraments in the ordinary sense of the word are the particular acts in which the primary sacrament, the church, concretely expresses itself. When the church does what is its business to do, namely make grace concrete and present, symbolize grace, and when it does this as fully and as formally as possible, then there occurs a sacrament in the usual sense of the word.

Debate

A persistent worry about Rahner is that in his efforts to open up Catholic theology to modern philosophy and the modern world, and to reformulate Christian doctrine in a way that will make sense to the contemporary person, he runs the risk of losing sight of the particularity, the historical rootedness, and the concrete shape of Christianity, and forcing it into the procrustean bed of an a priori anthropology.

This worry lies behind objections on a number of levels. There has been a good deal of criticism of *Spirit in the World*, Rahner's first book. The arguments of *Spirit in the World*, viewed as philosophical arguments in their own right, have failed to persuade in some quarters. Because many have seen *Spirit in the World* as a "foundational" work, it is often assumed that if Rahner has gone wrong at this point, all of his subsequent theology will be called into question. If one takes a more cautious a view of the relationship of this youthful work to Rahner's later essays, however, it is not so clear that philosophical weaknesses of *Spirit in the World* need be of such overwhelming significance for his theology.

The same worry is sometimes expressed as an unease with Rahner's "transcendental method" or transcendental approach to theology: by insisting upon the introduction of a Kantian turn to the subject within theology, Rahner is felt to be pursuing an ultimately reductive project. It is in fact not possible to find a single method that unifies all, or even most, of Rahner's writings, but Rahner does at times make programmatic statements, insisting for instance that "theology today must be theological anthropology"[13] and discussing a "method" of transcendental theology.[14] One of the points at which he himself seems to be closest to following this method (the method that "raises the question of the conditions in which knowledge of a specific subject is possible in the knowing subject himself")[15] is in his proposal of a "transcendental Christology," and this has come under particular criticism.[16] Rahner here begins by asking what must be true about human beings if they are to be capable of hearing of Christ and having faith in Christ – "what are the *a priori* possibilities in man which make the coming of the message of Christ possible." It is in our very nature, he argues, to be searching through history for an "absolute savior." Thus, when we do in fact hear of Christ, we are hearing not of something that is utterly strange to us, that seems to have nothing to do with us. Rahner seems to think one can reconstruct the broad outlines of a Christology in this transcendental mode, including the Chalcedonian formula, and that without such a transcendental Christology, traditional Christological formulae are in danger of appearing mythological.[17]

How much weight one gives to worries about the reductive tendencies of Rahner's transcendental approach will be bound up with the question of how one construes the overall shape of his oeuvre. If one sees it as, in spite of all its variety, essentially promoting *a* vision and *a* system of theology, whose essence is captured by the notion of a transcendental method, and whose apogee is reached in a rendition of Christ as essentially knowable in advance, then the problem of reductionism, of the loss of the concrete and historical particularities of the Christian faith, may seem acute.[18] But, as we have already seen, there is another possibility. Rahner's discussion of transcendental Christology is one among several suggestions he had to make in the area of Christology, and not necessarily the most persuasive; Rahner's comments on the transcendental and anthropological nature of theology point to *some* of his interests in the particular context of the need to get away from the dry formality and "extrinsicism" of neoscholasticism. Reductionism in this case may still be seen as a danger that Rahner courts *from time to time*, but not as the fundamental character of a theology that in fact repeatedly begins, not from its own first principles, but from what is concretely given in the faith of the church.

Rahner has most frequently been criticized for the theory of the anonymous Christian, and some of these criticisms reflect once again the concern that Rahner's thought is reductionist. If Christianity can be spoken of as existing in a person apart from any explicit reference to Christ and the cross, then surely it has been evacuated of content: the notion of the anonymous Christian, as for instance Hans Urs von Balthasar presents it, undermines Christianity as a distinctive, particular form of life which exists as a response to the distinctiveness of Christ's love. Balthasar's satirical critique was very effective and caused Rahner's work to be closely identified with the theory of the anonymous Christian, even though Balthasar himself, together with Joseph Ratzinger and nearly every other major Catholic theologian of the period, had, at Stephen Bullivant has shown, "at one time or another, affirmed the existence of an 'implicit,' 'anonymous,' 'unconscious,' 'secret,' or 'hidden' faith as the means by which conscious non-Christians can be saved."[19] What we have in Rahner's anonymous Christianity, then, is not the center or key to his thought, but his own attempt, alongside those of most in his generation, to grapple with a particular spiritual-theological knot confronting the church.

Influence, Achievement, and Agenda

The significance of Rahner's work can be considered on two levels: there is the question of his immediate influence in the Catholic Church, the place of his writings within the ebb and flow of ecclesiastical politics; and there is the slightly different question of his lasting achievement.

Rahner's immediate influence was considerable. As we have seen, his was among – and perhaps preeminent among – the theological voices that shaped to a considerable degree the outcome of the Second Vatican Council. His teaching and his writings also did much to form the thought of the next generation of theologians in the United States, of theologians and bishops in Germany, and to some degree of emerging theological movements such as Latin American liberation theology. On the other hand, fashions in church politics, as elsewhere, change. In terms of ecclesiastical cachet, Rahner's standing was at a high point in the period immediately following the council; under the papacies of John Paul II and Benedict, one was more likely to hear overtones of the thought of Hans Urs von Balthasar (who had been out of favor during the years of the council) in documents from Rome. More recently the mood has shifted again, a little away from Balthasar.

There has been an instinct in postconciliar Catholic theology to look for a single figure to provide an overarching system to replace the figure (Thomas) and system (neoscholasticism) that dominated the preconciliar Catholic landscape. Will this come from Rahner, or Balthasar – or will we turn to another? Perhaps it ought to be de Lubac or Lonergan. There is an unfortunate European provincialism at work here – Rahner himself began to write at the time of the Second Vatican Council of the emergence of a "world church" and of the Western world "in the evening of its existence."[20] Nevertheless the middle portion of the twentieth century was undoubtedly a rich period for Catholic theology in Europe, and out of it comes, not a single great system, but a wide and deep set of resources, challenges, and issues to go on thinking with and about.

Rahner will continue to make an appearance in theological treatments of Trinity, Christology, eschatology, and ecclesiology, as well as in discussion on development of doctrine, on death, on the nature of symbols, on theology and science, and so on. Perhaps the single most important thing Rahner offers subsequent generations, however, is not a contribution on any particular theological locus or topic but the modeling of a way to do theology across many topics. Rahner brings together deep fidelity to tradition with creativity and openness to the contemporary world. And beyond this, he models the practice of theology as a form of spiritual and ecclesial therapy, a steady acknowledgment of the difficulties of church and faith, a serene willingness to reflect on and address them – he is perhaps the greatest exemplar since Thomas Aquinas of a theology whose faith and its hope are exhibited by calmly and confidently bringing difficulties to the surface of our thought.

Notes

1   Another approach would be to look, not to explicitly intellectual influences, but to the influence of the spiritual exercises of Ignatius of Loyola. Rahner himself, especially toward the end of his life, pointed to Ignatius, the founder of the Jesuits, as a decisively important influence on him. See Philip Endean, *Karl Rahner and Ignatian Spirituality* (Oxford: Oxford University Press, 2001) for an interesting and full attempt to explore the significance of such claims.

2   *Spirit in the World* is Rahner's first *major* work, but not his first work: he had already published a number of articles on the history of spirituality.

3   The account of the supernatural existential given here is based on some of Rahner's later writings. In an earlier version of the notion, presented in "Concerning the Relationship between Nature and Grace" (*Theological Investigations*, Vol. 1, trans. Cornelius Ernst [New York: Crossroad, 1982], 29–318), the supernatural existential appeared not as grace nor even its offer, but as the desire for, and the orientation toward, grace and the beatific vision.

4   Karl Rahner, "Nature and Grace," in *Theological Investigations*, Vol. 4, trans. Kevin Smyth (London: Darton, Longman & Todd, 1974), 181.

5   Even this acceptance of grace, Rahner is careful to insist, is "borne" by God, made possible by grace itself.

6   Karl Rahner, "The Concept of Mystery in Catholic Theology," in *Theological Investigations*, Vol. 4., trans. Kevin Smyth (London: Darton, Longman & Todd, 1974), 57.

7   Rahner, "The Concept of Mystery in Catholic Theology," 57.

8   Karl Rahner, "On the Theology of Symbolic Reality," in *Theological Investigations*, Vol. 4, trans. Kevin Smyth (London: Darton, Longman & Todd, 1974), 236.

9   Rahner, "On the Theology of Symbolic Reality," 237.

10 Rahner, "On the Theology of Symbolic Reality," 239.

11 See Richard Lennan, *The Ecclesiology of Karl Rahner* (Oxford: Clarendon Press, 1995).

12 Rahner, "On the Theology of Symbolic Reality," 241.

13 Karl Rahner, "Theology and Anthropology," in *Theological Investigations*, Vol. 9, trans. Graham Harrison (London: Darton, Longman & Todd, 1972), 28, 29.

14 In, for instance, the second part of "Reflections on Methodology in Theology," in *Theological Investigations*, Vol. 11, trans. David Bourke (London: Darton, Longman & Todd, 1974).

15 Karl Rahner, "Reflections on Methodology in Theology," 87. This is of course broadly speaking a Kantian use of the term "transcendental," though it is worth noting that Rahner deviates from Kant's usage in certain ways: in particular, what is to be investigated according to Rahner is not, as with Kant, the conditions of the possibility of knowledge or experience as such, but instead the conditions of the possibility of some quite delimited kind of knowledge – for instance, knowledge of some one particular dogma.

16 This has been criticized — by Balthasar at various points and, in particular, by Bruce Marshall in *Christology in Conflict: The Identity of a Saviour in Rahner and Barth* (Oxford: Blackwell, 1987).

17 Rahner also notes, however, that it is not possible clearly and explicitly to formulate such a transcendental Christology until after the fact, until after a relationship with the actual Jesus Christ is already present (*Foundations of Christian Faith*, 207). Transcendental Christology is a priori only in principle; in actuality it is a retracing of what is already concretely known.

18 If this is the way one envisions Rahner's work, the fact that he frequently insists that the historical as well as the transcendental side of theology must be acknowledged will fail to reassure.

19 Stephen Bullivant, "The Myth of Rahnerian Exceptionalism: Edward Schillebeeckx's 'Anonymous Christians,'" *Philosophy and Theology* 22, no. 1 (2010): 341. Rahner has also misleadingly been characterized as an "inclusivist" and criticized on that score. See chapter 7 of Karen Kilby, *Karl Rahner: Theology and Philosophy* (New York: Routledge, 2004) for a fuller discussion of the debate surrounding anonymous Christianity.

20 Karl Rahner, "Philosophy and Theology," in *Theological Investigations*, Vol. 6, trans. Karl H. and Boniface Kruger (New York: Crossroad, 1982), 81.

Recommended Reading

Primary

Rahner, Karl. *Encounters with Silence*. Translated by James Demske. South Bend, IN: St Augustine's Press, 1999.

———. *Foundations of Christian Faith: An Introduction to the Idea of Christianity*. Translated by William Dych. New York: Crossroad: 1989.

———. *Hearer of the Word*. Translated by Joseph Donceel. New York: Continuum, 1994.

———. *The Practice of Faith: A Handbook of Contemporary Spirituality*. Edited by Karl Lehmann and Karl Raffelt. New York: Crossroad, 1992.

———. *Theological Investigations*. 23 vols. Baltimore, MD: Helicon Press, 1961–9; New York: Crossroad, 1971–92.

Secondary

Dych, William. *Karl Rahner*. Collegeville, MN: Liturgical Press, 1992.

Endean, Philip. *Karl Rahner and Ignatian Spirituality*. Oxford: Oxford University Press, 2001.

Kilby, Karen. *Karl Rahner: Theology and Philosophy*. New York: Routledge, 2004.

———. *The SPCK Introduction to Karl Rahner*. London: SPCK, 2007.

Lennan, Richard. *The Ecclesiology of Karl Rahner*. Oxford: Clarendon Press, 1995.

O'Donovan, Leo J., ed. *A World of Grace: An Introduction to the Themes and Foundations of Karl Rahner's Theology*. Washington, DC: Georgetown University Press, 1995.

Vorgrimler, Herbert. *Understanding Karl Rahner: An Introduction to His Life and Thought*. New York: Crossroad, 1986.

Hans Urs von Balthasar

Mark McInroy

Introduction

God's glorious revelation refracts in myriad forms throughout creation, enrapturing and transforming those with eyes to see. If there is an idea for which Hans Urs von Balthasar (1905–88) is known, it is likely this. His theology, of course, contains much more; as author of approximately 100 books and 500 articles, Balthasar "single-handedly heaved up a huge mountain range of theology," as has been said about his oeuvre, and one does not come to be regarded as the most significant Catholic theologian of the twentieth century based on one idea alone, provocative and potent though it has proven to be.

For all the multifaceted immensity of his theology, however, Balthasar leads with "theological aesthetics" (translated in English as *The Glory of the Lord*)[1] because he thinks it must be the first response the theologian summons to the unconcern with God endemic to modern Western culture. When God is understood as absolute beauty (or "glory," as Balthasar often prefers), encounter with God is powerfully recast as analogous to one's most stirring experiences of beauty in art, music, and the natural world.

Balthasar regards beauty as a transcendental property of being, or an objective feature of reality at its very roots. Like the other transcendentals, goodness and truth, beauty permeates all things; it constitutes the very structure of being. And, in fact, Balthasar insists that beauty performs crucial work that truth and goodness cannot achieve on their own. Without beauty, "the good loses its attractiveness, the self-evidence of why it must be carried out," and truth remains uncompelling; it no longer captivates. Neglect of the "third transcendental" leads to the world itself becoming a mere "lump of existence," manipulable to human interests, rather than a sacred arena in which the "light of Being" shines to the human observer.[2]

Crucially, however, even the most robust and capacious philosophical understandings of beauty are unable to accommodate *theological* aesthetics. In this conviction Balthasar draws from the *maior dissimilitudo* of the principle of analogy, according to which any similarity between God and the world is far outweighed by dissimilarity. To Balthasar, *theological* beauty is paradigmatically expressed by Christ on the cross, which confronts as much as it consoles. This beauty does not in any straightforward way fulfil one's desires and expectations, but instead profoundly challenges them. For Balthasar, the absolute beauty of God is revealed in an event that brings with it its own criteria by which it will be evaluated.

Ford's The Modern Theologians: An Introduction to Christian Theology since 1918, Fourth Edition.
Edited by Rachel Muers and Ashley Cocksworth.
© 2024 John Wiley & Sons Ltd. Published 2024 by John Wiley & Sons Ltd.

Balthasar holds that one ultimately responds to beauty with the conviction that a change of life must follow. As he is fond of saying, the glory of the Lord is not simply something to look at; instead, it moves one to pursue the good, and to inquire into the true – hence the progression from *The Glory of the Lord* to the second portion of Balthasar's trilogy, *Theo-Drama*,[3] and the third, *Theo-Logic*.[4] On this more will be said in a subsequent section.

Balthasar's life

Balthasar came by his interest in aesthetics honestly. He was born on 12 August 1905 in Lucerne, Switzerland, and his childhood was consumed with music. In the summer of 1924 he matriculated at the University of Zürich, where he began his studies in *Germanistik* (a field that primarily examines German language and literature but includes German philosophy as well). He also received a pivotal and enduring influence on his thought through Friedrich Gundolf's "New Germanist" presentation of Goethe. Goethe's notion of form (*Gestalt*) would emerge as a central category for Balthasar, not only for his theological aesthetics but also for his biblical hermeneutics, which resists the atomizing tendency of historical-critical approaches, and which insists instead on seeing the "form" of scripture as an organic whole that must not be broken down into its constituent components.

After a semester he transferred to Vienna, where he spent the next four terms. He published his first book during this time.[5] He would finish his doctoral work under the guidance of Robert Faesi with a dissertation titled *History of the Eschatological Problem in Modern German Literature*. This ambitious study and its revised version attempted to expose the hidden theological convictions of Germany's literary and philosophical giants.[6] Balthasar discerned during his studies that theological questions do not actually disappear during the ostensibly secular modern period; instead, they are transformed, disguised, and reassembled.

Shortly before completing his doctoral studies, Balthasar's path took a decisive turn. Under the guidance of a charismatic Jesuit named Friedrich Kronseder, Balthasar made a thirty-day retreat at Whylen, near Basel. During that time he saw with unanticipated clarity that he should enter the Society of Jesus. Within months of finishing his doctorate, Balthasar entered the south German province of the Jesuits as a novice. After two years of novitiate (back at Feldkirch in Austria), he began his study of philosophy at Pullach, near Munich.

In Pullach, Balthasar encountered Erich Przywara, who was the first of Balthasar's great mentors. Przywara's *Analogia Entis* puts forward a version of the analogy of being that draws from apophatic theology to emphasize God's ever-greater transcendence of creaturely being. Balthasar's work for the remainder of his career would be guided by the notion he took from Przywara that the world is theologically instructive on account of its similarity to God yet insufficient in itself and thereby propels one beyond it (Rom. 1:19–20). After Pullach, Balthasar pursued theology at Fourvière, near Lyons, where he came to know Henri de Lubac, his "friend and master."[7] De Lubac guided Balthasar through the patristic witness, and the two of them would come to be associated with the *ressourcement* movement dubbed (not without irony) *la nouvelle théologie*.

Balthasar was ordained to the priesthood on 26 July 1936 and moved to Basel as a chaplain for students in 1940. Living in Basel provided Balthasar the opportunity to develop a close relationship with Karl Barth, who was by this time internationally regarded as the most significant voice in Protestant theology. Balthasar had previously published on Barth's thought, but their proximity to one another allowed sustained, ever-deepening theological engagement over a period of many years.

In Basel, Balthasar also became acquainted with Adrienne von Speyr, for whom Balthasar served as spiritual director, and who was received into the Catholic Church under his supervision. Speyr was the recipient of exceptionally intense mystical experiences during which she regularly underwent painful, even "hellish" torments, particularly on Holy Saturday. Her experiences profoundly influenced Balthasar's theology, especially his understanding of Christ's descent into hell, so much so that he insisted that his work could never be considered apart from hers. She also received visions concerning the founding of a new kind of Christian community that would be a witness to Christ in the world. The secular institute became known as the Community of St. John, and the founding of it eventually led Balthasar – after repeated efforts at securing support from the Jesuits failed – to leave the order in 1950. He described it as the most difficult decision of his life.

After leaving the Jesuits, Balthasar was viewed askance for some time; no bishop would incardinate him, leaving him unable to preach, hear confessions, or celebrate Mass. Even after he was licensed by the bishop of Chur in 1956, he remained fairly isolated, as evidenced by the fact that he was not invited to be a *peritus* (theological expert) in the lead-up to the Second Vatican Council. His own challenges were worsened by Speyr's deteriorating health. In the midst of these difficulties, however, he did manage to publish a significant number of studies, and the first volume of his theological aesthetics appeared in 1961.

In key respects, the Second Vatican Council was the crowning moment for which Balthasar and his confreres had labored. A hallmark of the council involved the very emphasis on patristic theology and the accompanying turn away from neoscholasticism that Balthasar had been recommending since the 1930s. Most visibly, the fortress mentality that had gripped the church was abandoned, and the church opened itself to the contemporary world. However, in the immediate wake of the council Balthasar grew acutely concerned that engagement with the world had led to an accommodationist mentality that threatened what was distinctively Christian. He published a number of short pieces criticizing this trend, none more acerbic than his satirical attack on Karl Rahner's "anonymous Christianity," *Cordula oder der Ernstfall*. He also cofounded the journal *Communio* as a theological counterweight to the progressive *Concilium*. These developments contributed to Balthasar's rehabilitation, but also to him being regarded as a decidedly conservative theologian, a view that was bolstered by his enthusiastic endorsement by John Paul II and Benedict XVI. He was appointed a cardinal in 1988 but died just days before receiving his cardinal's hat.

Survey of Approach, Works, and Themes

The theologian is the one who prays. One cannot adequately grasp the sort of theology Balthasar puts forward without understanding this fundamental feature of his theological method. To him, theology and spirituality must be reunited, such that the theological task is once again approached "on one's knees."[8] Balthasar is aware that his call for a kneeling theology will strike those invested in the modern theological project as unsettlingly nonacademic. For this reason, in an important essay titled "Theology and Sanctity" he surveys the whole of Christian history in an effort at exposing the roots of the "mischievous cleavage" between theology and spirituality.[9] Echoing de Lubac, Balthasar holds that although patristic theologians regarded the two as intimately intertwined, the introduction of Aristotelianism to theology in the medieval period set in motion a process that ended with the presumed self-sufficiency of philosophy and the sciences (thus giving birth to modern secularism).[10] The postscholastic period witnessed the use of philosophy not merely as a propaedeutic to biblical theology but as judge *over* the claims made in revelation, overturning the relationship Thomas Aquinas had so carefully articulated. Theology thus came to be viewed as sufficiently rigorous only when it submitted itself to criteria privileged in secular philosophy such as detachment and objectivity, and it therefore veered into conceptual abstraction, emptying itself of all life in the process. Balthasar saw neoscholasticism as guilty of this deviation from tradition, but he viewed it as only the most recent in a history of problematic approaches to the theological task.

If theology has endured desiccation as a result of the separation, spirituality may have fared even worse. Unmoored from a theological tradition that could serve as a structuring resource, it puts forward "flesh without bones, that very pious literature that serves up … a porridge that, in the end, becomes indigestible through lack of substance."[11] The problem is not only that what passes for spiritual literature has become drenched with "unctuous, platitudinous piety," but also that it often puts forward subjective inner states as the ends of the spiritual search.[12] In so doing, it does not consistently direct one toward service to God, the church, or one's neighbor.

In that contemporary spirituality places the individual human being at the center of spiritual striving, and in that academic theology attempts to stand outside of and above its objects of study, both place the human in a God-like position in key regards. Balthasar uses different terms for the latter tendency, including Prometheanism, Titanism, and especially Gnosticism, and he tirelessly inveighs against it.[13] To him, the attempt to occupy a position outside of God's revelation is fundamentally misguided, for "with revelation there is no such thing as an objective, uncommitted, scientific 'objectivity,' but only a personal encounter of Word and faith, Christ and Church."[14] The theologian, therefore, always occupies a position *within* the drama of God's relation to the world, never outside of the dramatic action.

From this vantage point, we can appreciate that it is not just sanctity, abstractly considered, that is important for Balthasar, but also specific saints, whose lives serve as witnesses to the disposition he endorses. It would be difficult to locate a figure more significant for him than Ignatius of Loyola. In Ignatius himself and his exercises, Balthasar sees one cultivating "indifference" to the point that one encounters no resistance within oneself to respond to God's call. One becomes wholly receptive, abandoning oneself to God in active obedience to what God has in store. Much of Balthasar's own project can be seen as an effort at developing the theological implications of Ignatius's views.

If a posture of receptivity and obedience is paramount, then Mary will emerge as the exemplary model for the Christian. Mary's *Fiat*, her Yes to God, stands out for Balthasar as the paradigmatic moment of human openness to God's call. Balthasar also contends, not without considerable controversy, that Mary is "feminine" in this receptivity. Mary's *Yes* is "a total faith act, whose hearing and obedient response to the address of God is such that the 'seed Christ' comes to birth from her flesh."[15] Although only Mary gives birth to Christ in a literal sense, each Christian is called by God to be "fruitful" through a distinctively shaped life that will bear witness to God's glory.

The saints, it should be noted, do not merely provide inspiring models for Christian living. Instead, in keeping with the reunification of theology and spirituality that shapes so much of Balthasar's approach, he contends that the saints offer a distinctive and noteworthy religious epistemology. One comes to know God, not by grasping, but by receiving.

Balthasar develops this epistemology in *The Glory of Lord*. In his theological aesthetics Balthasar turns to beauty, to a great extent, because aesthetic experience provides the contemporary person with a familiar touchstone for the receptive posture he endorses. When one beholds beauty, one does so from a stance of generous responsiveness to the beautiful form (*Gestalt*) as it has been given. Amid such experiences, one does not typically assert oneself; instead, one gratefully receives. Beauty puts one on one's heels. Although only the Christ-form is *absolutely* beautiful, the entire creation bears witness in its beauty – to the extent that finite being is capable of doing so – to the glory of God. Balthasar is at great pains to explain that one of the conditions for the perception of the beautiful form is that it must be perceived *as a whole*, and it cannot be apprehended via a critical method that would break it down into its constituent components.

Perceiving the form thus stands out as a crucial task for the reception of divine revelation. Balthasar draws from the "spiritual senses" tradition to explain that this occurs when one adopts a receptive disposition that allows one's perceptual faculties to be transformed by divine grace. For revelation to be recognized, one's sensorium must become "spiritualized" such that one perceives in a super-corporeal register that is intertwined with its bodily counterpart, allowing one to behold the whole of what is revealed.[16]

Content

If, as we observed at the outset of this chapter, the leading edge of Balthasar's theology seeks to awaken the somnambulant through a stirring encounter with God's glorious revelation, the center of his theological vision consists of the absolute self-surrender that lies at the heart of the divine life. Following Sergei

Bulgakov, Balthasar holds that a "primal kenosis" (*Urkenosis*) within the Godhead not only characterizes the divine essence (i.e. what it means to be God); further, this central feature of the Trinitarian relations determines the very structure of the world, such that all of finite being is inherently self-emptying. There is "a fundamental kenosis given with the creation as such."[17] Finite being, then, "bears the marks of its origin," in Rowan Williams' turn of phrase, in that all things move out of themselves kenotically, ek-statically.[18] Balthasar thus grounds his metaphysics in this vision of a perpetually self-emptying God.

It would be difficult to overstate just how extensively *Urkenosis* reaches throughout Balthasar's thought. Much of what is distinctive about his views can be traced back to this foundational commitment, and it constitutes one of his most provocative contributions to theology. *Urkenosis* decisively shapes Balthasar's Trinitarian theology, Christology, doctrine of creation, anthropology, soteriology, and eschatology. To each of these topics we now turn.

Trinity and distance

Balthasar casts the very essence of divinity as dynamic self-dispossession. The Father is God in the act giving himself away in love. In fact, this divestment of self goes so far "back," so to speak, that there simply is no already established, rounded-off individual who precedes it. "The Father must not be thought to exist 'prior' to this self-surrender (in an Arian sense): he *is* this movement of self-giving that holds nothing back ... [He] cannot be God in any other way but in this 'kenosis' within the Godhead itself."[19] The very essence of divinity, then, entails ecstatic movement beyond the self; God is never self-enclosed, but always already giving of God's self.

Precisely because the Father out of boundless love genuinely gives his divinity *away*, he brings forth the consubstantial Son as a distinct person – and decidedly not as an instrument for the Father's own self-actualization. As Balthasar puts this point, "The Father does not 'lose' himself to someone else in order thereby to 'regain' himself; for he is *always* himself by giving himself."[20] The Father's self-giving, then, cannot be reduced to an "investment" in himself made in anticipation of a return. Instead, it is truly a *gift* made in love that does not enter into an economy of exchange.[21] Without calculation or forethought, the Father gives his divinity away so that the Son can in freedom be himself.

The Son, then, as his own person, is "totally distinct" from the Father, and in fact Balthasar characterizes the Son as "infinitely Other." Balthasar suggests that, in the act of the Father wholly giving his divinity away, there arises "an incomprehensible and unique 'separation' of God from himself."[22] He further explains that, among the different persons of the Trinity, "Something like infinite 'duration' and infinite 'space' must be attributed to the acts of reciprocal love so that the life of the *communio*, of fellowship, can develop."[23] Out of his love for the Son, the Father opens up an "infinite distance" between them. This distance is, furthermore, maintained even as it is bridged by the Holy Spirit, the "We" who proceeds from Father and Son.

The unsurpassable "distance" within the Trinity plays a particularly important role in Balthasar's thought, as the infinite separation among the Trinitarian persons grounds, includes, and exceeds all would-be alienation from God – for instance, as enacted by human beings in their refusal of God. The "primal divine drama" within the Godhead "contains and surpasses all possible drama between God and a world."[24] Intra-Trinitarian distance, in other words, outperforms any estrangement from God in the world. Crucially, too, any giving of the self in love is also far exceeded by what eternally takes place among the Father, Son, and Holy Spirit.

The doctrine of the Trinity thus occupies an indispensable, "load-bearing" position in Balthasar's theology; it is not a cumbersome inheritance from the tradition without real import, as it arguably is for a number of modern theologians. Instead, as we shall see, the dynamic kenosis among the Trinitarian persons has direct relevance for the most acutely felt existential realities that Christian theology addresses.

Christology and mission

The *Urkenosis* within the Trinity connects very closely, of course, to Balthasar's Christology. If it is the case that divinity as such necessarily entails self-expropriation, then the Son can only be God in giving himself away, too. This takes the form, in the first place, of thanksgiving (*eucharistia*) to the Father, a "gratitude that is ready to give the utmost in response to the giver."[25] Obedience to the Father is thus framed within a posture of gratitude, and Balthasar even casts the Son as *eager* to "pour *himself* forth in any way the Father may determine."[26] The Son, then, is not coerced into following the will of the Father but instead spontaneously responds to the Father with "generous, eucharistic availability," with a magnanimity that matches the recklessness with which the Father gives himself away.

With the eucharistic kenosis of the Son as the foundation of his Christology, Balthasar is able to make several moves that advance Christological reflection. First, the self-emptying that takes place as the second person of the Trinity becomes incarnate in Jesus Christ in no way constitutes an alteration of God. Instead, the incarnation is simply the expression in time of God's eternal, kenotic character. Second, and most creatively, if divinity involves dynamic self-giving, then humanity – Christ's human nature, specifically – will be one with divinity to the extent that it is also self-emptying. This thought lies at the heart of Balthasar's reframing of the hypostatic union, which he conceives in dynamic rather than static categories.

The term Balthasar uses to develop this line of thinking is mission (*Sendung*). The central distinguishing feature of Jesus Christ concerns his sense of mission; he is, most fundamentally, the One Sent (*der Gesendete*). Jesus's awareness that he has been sent by the Father is so thoroughgoing that it wholly constitutes his person. According to Balthasar, Jesus is not a person who *has* a mission; instead, he is a person who *is* his mission. His personhood and his mission completely coincide with one another.

By using mission in this way, Balthasar is able to recast the conditions that obtain in Jesus's humanity such that it can be regarded as one with God. Jesus's personal identity as Son of God does not depend on, for instance, an abstract attribution of omniscience to his human consciousness. Instead, what it means to be the Son of God is to stand in a relation of filial obedience to the Father. In that the human Jesus stands in that filial relation, he is the Son.[27] Jesus's self-consciousness is confined, then, to a "mission-consciousness," but it is precisely here that "he has a *visio immediata*, and we have no reason to suggest that this *visio* of the divine is supplemented by another, as it were, purely theoretical content, over and above his mission."[28] What is important about Jesus is that in him we see one whose entire life is "marked by the continually unfolding awareness in each situation of *how* to be the Son of the Father."[29]

Jesus's mission inexorably leads to the dereliction of the cross, and it is here that Balthasar's Christology, drawing from the mystical visions of Adrienne von Speyr, reaches its most daring and controversial point, namely, his theology of Christ's descent into hell. In *Mysterium Paschale*, Balthasar resists the claim that Christ "use[d] the so-called 'brief' time of his death for all manner of 'activities' in the world beyond," for instance as expressed in the *Christus Victor* tradition and the harrowing of hell, according to which Christ descends to the dead as a conqueror.[30] In distinction to this position, Balthasar resolutely holds that Christ descends to the dead *as one who is dead*. He is not at all active, but instead utterly passive. On Holy Saturday, Christ's obedience to the Father takes the form of "the obedience of a corpse."[31] Balthasar holds that the kenotic structure of his Christology and Trinitarian theology has as its logical conclusion this final self-emptying, namely the "absolute emptying of life" from Jesus Christ.[32] If it is the case that kenosis is inherent to divinity, then the self-emptying of Jesus Christ will necessarily be stretched to this maximal degree.

Balthasar's theology of Holy Saturday advances a profound account of the deep identification God effects with human beings that unflinchingly embraces suffering, evil, and death. To Balthasar, when Jesus descends to the dead as one who is dead, he lies in *solidarity* with humankind. "In that same way that, upon earth, he was in solidarity with the living, so, in the tomb, he is in solidarity with the dead."[33] And, indeed, one might say that what matters most is *this* solidarity, a joining with the very darkest features of the human condition (death, alienation from God, utter hopelessness). A God who stops short, who endures only some and not all dimensions of human existence, would arguably leave unreconciled the utter distance from God that human beings undergo. In death, Jesus journeys out to the farthest possible point into what is not God, ultimately to transform and redeem that which had been bereft of divine presence.

Creation

One sees just how comprehensive Balthasar's use of kenosis is as one looks to his doctrine of creation, as "self-emptying" appears here in a seemingly unlikely *locus* for theological reflection. For Balthasar, all of finite being bears the marks of its origin, as noted briefly previously, and given that its origin is the God who gives God's self away in love, the creation as such is also engaged in perpetual self-emptying. One thing this means is that "every worldly being is epiphanic," as Balthasar memorably puts it; being *shows* itself because it is constantly *emptying* itself out.[34]

In conducting his metaphysics through Trinitarian theology Balthasar takes an atypical approach, but based on the preceding discussion of his theological method we can see that it follows directly from his unwillingness to countenance a theological approach that begins with matters that can be universally agreed upon by a use of "neutral" reason. If it is the case that "pure nature" is a fiction, and that divine grace permeates the creation, then it will be appropriate to examine the character of created being *through* Trinitarian theology, not treat metaphysics as a prolegomenon to subsequent theological matters.

With clear import for his theological aesthetics, Balthasar maintains that finite being does not display mere surface-level appearance. The "things in themselves" do not remain perpetually hidden behind a veneer of present-able being. Instead, finite being is dynamic in a way that resembles its divine source, and it could therefore be said to possess a "churning" quality that continually dredges its "lower" layers, in so doing manifesting the *whole* of being to the human observer. Finite being gives itself away just as wantonly as does the God who is its self-emptying source.

If this aspect of kenosis thus leads to a remarkable depth that can be displayed through finite being, another dimension of kenosis in Balthasar's hands suggests an equally impressive breadth of expressive possibilities. In that the *Urkenosis* of the Father leads to an uncollapsible distance among the persons of the Trinity, similarly, within finite being *difference* abides. The self-emptying within God can thus be described as an "other-making" kenosis. "There is nothing prior to or beyond difference," as Rowan Williams gives expression to this fundamental Balthasarian commitment.[35] Such a positive regard for difference not only allows for a tremendous diversity of forms throughout the world to manifest the divine (undergirding Balthasar's claims in his aesthetics that God can appear in a wide variety of cultural expressions). It also places an extraordinarily high value on the created order as such. That is, for Balthasar, natural forms are more expressive of God, not as they are dissolved into divinity, but instead precisely as natural forms. The natural does not need to get out of the way for the supernatural to manifest. Instead, it is precisely *through* the natural that God is revealed.

Anthropology

To Balthasar, human beings are most in accord with the structure of reality – ultimately most themselves – when giving themselves away. And, in fact, inasmuch as the Father is utterly "reckless" in his *urkenotic* dispossession of self, human freedom will be misused to the extent that it does not respond in kind. It is precisely when one uses one's freedom for "calculating, cautious self-preservation" that one falls into sinfulness, in Balthasar's view.[36]

Crucially, although true humanity involves giving oneself away, it is through such dispossession of self that one discovers one's mission and ultimately becomes a fully realized person. For Balthasar, living kenotically takes the particular shape of Ignatian indifference. It involves the cultivation of a sensibility that empties the self of all resistance to God and is open to wherever God's call leads. In discerningly following that call, one lives into one's particular mission, the unique role that one is to play in the drama of God's engagement with the world. That drama is "choreographed" by God, but – precisely because of the character of the Trinitarian relations, which allow for difference – there is room for the meaningful exercise of finite human freedom within it.

It is when this use of finite freedom aligns with God's infinite freedom that one becomes a true human person, to Balthasar. What one discovers as one is drawn into the divine life through the incorporative work of the Spirit is that God in God's infinite freedom did not opt for "the infinite self-possession of infinite reality."[37] Although it would be easy to suppose that this would result in "the ultimate satisfaction and blessedness," in Jesus Christ a deeper, "more blessed mystery is revealed, namely, that love – self-surrender – is part of this bliss of absolute freedom."[38] The most profound fulfillment is found only in entering into the filial dynamic between Jesus Christ and the Father, and in so doing giving oneself away in love.

Soteriology

Balthasar's soteriology is intricately intertwined with his theology of Holy Saturday, as it is not only death that stands to separate human beings from God, as examined previously, but also sin. Balthasar applies the kenotic logic of Christ's descent into hell to advance the claim that Jesus stands in solidarity not only with the dead but with *sinful* humanity. Jesus's self-emptying, in other words, involves him standing in the place of sinful human beings, and from that horrific position undergoing for himself the alienation from God, utter hopelessness, and terror that they feel. In so doing, Balthasar maintains that Jesus takes on the sins of humanity not as something external to him, but instead within his very being. Balthasar explains, "The Son bears sinners within himself, together with the hopeless impenetrability of their sin, which prevents the divine light of love from registering in them. In himself, therefore, he experiences, not their sin but the hopelessness of their resistance to God and the graceless No of divine grace to this resistance."[39] Balthasar here shifts the emphasis from Jesus's vicarious punishment satisfying the wrath of God to Jesus's first-hand experience of alienation and hopelessness bringing about reconciliation. As he puts this point, "To be solidary with the lost is something *greater* than just dying for them in an externally representative manner."[40]

On this soteriological model, Christ takes on the sin of humankind to internalize and thereby transform sin itself. Through this approach, Balthasar makes clear that there is no place that will remain untouched by Christ's kenotic mission, which journeys into utter Godlessness in order to heal it and draw it into the divine life.

Eschatology

Following directly from his soteriology, Balthasar controversially holds that the transformation wrought by Christ during his kenotic mission into hell stands to transform even hell itself, and on that basis Balthasar is willing to consider the possibility of universal salvation. As he puts this point, precisely because Jesus's "descent is a priori deeper than the depths any lost person in the world can reach[,] even what we call 'hell' – although it is indeed the place of reprobation – is still even more a Christological place."[41] If, as we observed above in treating Balthasar's Trinitarian theology, the "distance" among persons of the Trinity outperforms any and all attempted alienation from God in the world, then there will be no place that is "outside" of God, and therefore no place that cannot be a locus for salvation.

If such is the rationale that could undergird a doctrine of universal salvation, it is important to note that Balthasar issues caution against full-blown *apokatastasis*. In *Dare We Hope "That All Men be Saved"?*,

Balthasar observes that the New Testament conveys two streams of reflection, one of which claims that only some will be saved (e.g. Mark 16:16), the other of which suggests that salvation will be extended to all (e.g. Rom. 5:18). To Balthasar, neither of these streams can be eliminated out of a desire to produce a "readily comprehensible system;" instead, the tension between them must be allowed to endure. This means, in the first place, that one must recognize that being lost is a real possibility, and there is insufficient foundation for the confident proclamations that all will be saved (as Balthasar sees in Barth's doctrine of election). And yet, in the second place, Balthasar's tension-filled juxtaposition also means that one cannot with absolute assuredness hold that some will be condemned. Ultimately, to Balthasar, "one ought to … limit oneself to that Christian hope that does not mask a concealed knowing but rests essentially content with the Church's prayer, as called for in 1 Timothy 2:4, that God wills that all men be saved."[42]

The Debate

As one might expect of such a bold, creative theological vision, Balthasar's works occasioned controversy from an early date, and although debate about his theology was muted during the pontificates of St John Paul II and (to a lesser extent) Benedict XVI, recent years have witnessed vigorous engagement and criticism once again.

Among the important early criticisms is that of Karl Rahner, who characterizes the Trinitarian theology of both Balthasar and Jürgen Moltmann as "gnostic" in that they betray a "Schelling-esque projection into God of division, conflict, godlessness, and death."[43] Rahner worried, in particular, that Balthasar and Moltmann plunge God into the strife of the world to the point that God remains mired in its pain, and they thereby do not provide sufficient grounds for hope of salvation.

One can certainly question whether Balthasar and Moltmann should cause equal concern in this arena, particularly because Balthasar takes some effort to distance his theology from that of Moltmann on these very grounds.[44] However, recent criticisms of Balthasar have refined aspects of this line of thinking by suggesting that Balthasar does not sufficiently differentiate between distance among the Trinitarian persons and the alienation of sin. By allowing the latter into the former, Balthasar appears to some critics to effectively hypostasize sin and not recognize its parasitic relation to the good.[45]

Such charges stand in an intriguing tension with another line of criticism, which holds that Balthasar actually sorts matters too neatly in his theology. According to scholars such as Ben Quash, Balthasar's emphasis on harmony in his aesthetics and clear resolution in his dramatics "appear[s] to entail the excessive tidying up of loose ends."[46] Whereas one set of critiques holds that Balthasar objectionably allows darkness to persist, the other suggests that he too readily dismisses it. These criticisms do not necessarily stand in an irreconcilable tension with one another, but they do call for continued consideration of this complex feature of Balthasar's thought and attention to the criteria by which such determinations are made.

Accusations of Balthasar being too cavalier with tradition reach their most pitched form in the criticism of his theology of Holy Saturday advanced by Alyssa Lyra Pitstick.[47] Pitstick insists that magisterial teaching regards Christ's descent into hell as glorious and without suffering, and on this basis determines Balthasar's departure from tradition to be so radical as to be outside the bounds of orthodoxy. Similar issues have been raised, from a much earlier date, concerning Balthasar's proximity to universal salvation, with some critics insisting that even restraining his position to one of *hopefulness* is unwarranted. Concerning the former topic, whether there actually is a definite magisterial position on Christ's descent can be questioned, as has been done by Paul Griffiths. If not, then regarding Balthasar as "heretical" would be out of order. What Pitstick's criticism has made clear is that robust, frank discussion is needed concerning what is gained and what is lost in Balthasar's audacious account of Christ's descent and the universalist implications it carries.

From a different theological vantage point, Balthasar's views of sex and gender have provoked worry for what critics see as a troublingly complementarian ascription of receptivity to the feminine and activity to the masculine.[48] Similarly, to Balthasar, whereas man speaks, woman only answers. Some commentators sympathetically observe that, inasmuch as Balthasar's theology actually privileges receptivity, he elevates femininity in important ways. Nevertheless, the position of woman as perpetually second, derived from the ontologically prior man, and even silenced unless addressed, has elicited a great deal of concern from a considerable number of Balthasar scholars. Additionally idiosyncratic and disquieting to some is the pervasive application of sexual difference throughout Balthasar's theology, such that even the Trinity is "sexed" in that Father, Son, and Spirit exhibit "(super)masculinity" and "(super)femininity" in their postures of activity and receptivity, respectively, toward one another.[49]

Balthasar, it seems, receives criticism from all sides, with some viewing him as hopelessly reactionary and others regarding him as dangerously untethered from the theological tradition. To be sure, Balthasar presents a number of theological ideas that are unexpected, and those who understand themselves as traditionalists will view such seeming innovations with suspicion. It is, however, worth noting with Rodney Howsare that when Balthasar departs from familiar doctrinal points, he does so from a profoundly well-informed position, having consulted major theologians and extremely obscure ones (both East and West) from the patristic, medieval, Reformation, and modern periods.[50] This is not to say that Balthasar is always correct in advancing the claims that he does (no theologian is), but it should call one to look closely at what the Christian theological tradition in all of its complexity holds in its capacious storehouses before too confidently proclaiming that Balthasar has departed from it.

In previous decades, many were either wholly dismissive of Balthasar or entirely accepting of his theological vision. One positive fruit of the current climate is that one finds theologians today who are both inspired by Balthasar and critical of him, leading to a judicious use of Balthasarian ideas in a wide variety of settings. To some of those projects we now turn.

Influence, Achievement, and Agenda

There are some states of affairs in contemporary theology for which credit cannot be given to Balthasar alone, but to which he has offered essential contributions along with others. Foremost among these is the current use of patristic theologians for constructive theological projects. Such an approach views these ancient theologians, not as artifacts of the Christian past but instead as viable resources for systematic theology. Although so frequently practiced as to be taken for granted today, this turn to the fathers owes much to the *ressourcement* theologians of the twentieth century, especially Balthasar and de Lubac. Additionally, Balthasar's ascendancy has brought with it an interest in key figures in his intellectual development such as Erich Przywara and Ferdinand Ulrich, each of whose major works have recently been translated into English. Increased awareness of such figures will likely lead to a recharacterization of twentieth-century theology that differs significantly from the regnant paradigm.

Balthasar's most immediately visible legacy concerns his theological aesthetics, which has inspired a veritable movement within contemporary theology that has augmented his treatment of divine glory. Accompanying this interest in beauty and glory is the Balthasarian conviction that the whole of human culture gives expression to the form of Christ, providing opportunities for robustly theological treatments of literature and the arts. Particularly intriguing are the implications of Balthasar's aesthetics for a metaphysically robust phenomenology that further develops his account of the form.

A contentious, but ultimately promising arena for engagement with Balthasar's thought involves the role of kenosis in contemporary theology. A number of feminist theologians have voiced concern about the potential for kenosis (Balthasarian or otherwise) to lead to a harmful insistence on self-abnegation. Recent scholarship, however, has suggested that, although a model of kenosis as blunt *elimination* of the self would indeed be troubling, a fuller account of kenosis can be developed by using Balthasar to augment central insights advanced by Sarah Coakley. Specifically, both Balthasar and Coakley regard "self-emptying" as a cultivation of vulnerability that makes space for the *transformation* of the human being, ultimately into the image of God.[51]

For some time, characterizations of Balthasar as a *ressourcement* theologian obscured the sophistication of his engagement with modern theology. In the current setting, however, one finds increased appreciation of the genealogical work Balthasar does vis-à-vis modernity. Cyril O'Regan, in particular, draws from Balthasar in his treatments of various "Gnostic" strains of thought in the modern period.[52] More broadly, Balthasar has been a powerful ally for questioning the purported secularity of modern modes of inquiry and categories of thought, as one finds for instance in Radical Orthodoxy.

One of the most thought-provoking assessments of Balthasar's theological achievement can be found in Rowan Williams, who suggests that Balthasar's Trinitarian theology, for all of the controversy it provokes, provides resources for the broadly "postmodern" project of conceptualizing otherness so as to resist the "dominance of identity."[53] On Williams' reading, Balthasar's account of intra-Trinitarian distance bears noteworthy affinities with the effort at thinking of otherness as a form of "difference that differs differently" than mere negation.

Summing up, if renewed criticism of Balthasar in recent years has cast doubt on the extent to which he straightforwardly and reliably speaks for magisterial teaching, it has also drawn attention once again to just how very creative and generative his theological vision is.

Ultimately, what must be understood about Balthasar is that he did not see it as his role simply to repristinate the tradition. Instead, he discerned that the contemporary situation in which Christians find themselves calls for the very audacious creativity that he found among patristic theologians. Those figures met their moment by interweaving the Christian witness with the thought forms of their day, and as a result put forward theologies that sought to be simultaneously faithful to the gospel and compelling to their age. It would be difficult to deny that Balthasar's audaciously creative theological vision flirts with danger at numerous junctures. The question for future generations to consider will be whether more is gained than lost in his daring rearticulation of the Christian faith.

Notes

1 Hans Urs von Balthasar, *The Glory of the Lord: A Theological Aesthetics*, 7 vols., trans. Erasmo Leiva-Merikakis, et al. (San Francisco, CA: Ignatius Press, 1982–91). Hereafter *GL*.

2 *GL* I, 19.

3 Hans Urs von Balthasar, *Theo-Drama: Theological Dramatic Theory*, 5 vols., trans. Graham Harrison (San Francisco, CA: Ignatius Press, 1988–98). Hereafter *TD*.

4 Hans Urs von Balthasar, *Theo-Logic: Theological Logical Theory*, 3 vols., trans. Adrian J. Walker (San Francisco, CA: Ignatius Press, 2000–5). Hereafter *TL*.

5 Hans Urs von Balthasar, *Die Entwicklung der musikalischen Idee: Versuch einer Synthese der Musik* (Braunschweig: Fritz Bartels Verlag, 1925).

6 Hans Urs von Balthasar, *Apokalypse der deutschen Seele: Studien zu einer Lehre von letzten Haltungen*. 3 vols. (Salzburg: A. Pustet, 1937–9).

7 Hans Urs von Balthasar, *My Work: In Retrospect* (San Francisco, CA: Ignatius Press, 1993), 48–9.

8 Hans Urs von Balthasar, "Theology and Sanctity," in *Explorations in Theology I: The Word Made Flesh*, trans. A. V. Littledale and A. Dru (San Francisco, CA: Ignatius Press, 1989), 181–209.

9 Balthasar, "Theology and Sanctity," 195.

10 Balthasar, "Theology and Sanctity," 186.

11 Balthasar, "Theology and Sanctity," 193.

12 Balthasar, "Theology and Sanctity," 208.

13 *GL* V, 41; *TD* IV, 460; *Mysterium Paschale: The Mystery of Easter*, trans. Aidan Nichols, OP (San Francisco, CA: Ignatius Press, 1990), 62. Hereafter *MP*.

14 Balthasar, "Theology and Sanctity," 201.

15 David Moss, "The Saints," in *The Cambridge Companion to Hans Urs von Balthasar*, ed. Edward T. Oakes and David Moss (Cambridge: Cambridge University Press, 2005), 79–92.

16 Mark McInroy, *Balthasar on the Spiritual Senses* (Oxford: Oxford University Press, 2014).

17 *MP*, 35.

18 Rowan Williams, "Balthasar and the Trinity," in *The Cambridge Companion to Hans Urs von Balthasar*, 41.

19 *TD* IV, 323, 325.

20 *TD* II, 256.

21 Cyril O'Regan, *The Anatomy of Misremembering: Von Balthasar's Response to Philosophical Modernity: Volume I: Hegel* (Chestnut Ridge, NY: Crossroad, Herder & Herder, 2014), 259.

22 *TD* IV, 325.

23 *TD* II, 257.

24 *TD* V, 245.

25 *TD* V, 245.

26 *TD* IV, 330.

27 Mark A. McIntosh, "Christology," in *The Cambridge Companion to Hans Urs von Balthasar*, 32.

28 *TD* III, 166.

29 McIntosh, "Christology," 32.

30 *MP*, 148.

31 *MP*, 176; quotation from Francis of Assisi.

32 *MP*, 173.

33 *MP*, 148–9.

34 Hans Urs von Balthasar, *Epilogue* (San Francisco, CA: Ignatius Press, 2004), 59.

35 Williams, "Balthasar on the Trinity," 42.

36 *TD* IV, 349.

37 *TD* IV, 349.

38 *TD* IV, 349.

39 *TD* IV, 349.

40 *MP*, 13.

41 Hans Urs von Balthasar, "Eschatology in Outline," in *Explorations in Theology IV: Spirit and Institution*, trans. Edward T. Oakes (San Francisco, CA: Ignatius Press, 1995), 457.

42 Hans Urs von Balthasar, *Dare We Hope "That All Men Be Saved"? With a Short Discourse on Hell*, trans. David Kipp and Lothar Krauth (San Francisco, CA: Ignatius Press, 1988), 44–5.

43 Karl Rahner, *Karl Rahner in Dialogue: Conversations and Interviews, 1965–1982*, ed. Paul Imhoff and Hubert Biallowons (New York: Crossroad, 1986), 126–7.

44 See esp. *TD* IV, 321–3.

45 Joshua R. Brotherton, *One of the Trinity Has Suffered: Balthasar's Theology of Divine Suffering in Dialogue* (Steubenville, OH: Emmaus Academic, 2020).

46 Ben Quash, "Balthasar," in *The Modern Theologians: An Introduction to Christian Theology since 1918*, 3rd ed., ed. David F. Ford, with Rachel Muers (Malden, MA: Wiley Blackwell, 2005), 118.

47 Alyssa Lyra Pitstick, *Light in Darkness: Hans Urs von Balthasar and the Catholic Doctrine of Christ's Descent into Hell* (Grand Rapids, MI: Eerdmans, 2007).

48 Tina Beattie, *New Catholic Feminism: Theology and Theory* (London and New York: Routledge, 2006). Karen Kilby, *Balthasar: A (Very) Critical Introduction* (Grand Rapids, MI: Eerdmans, 2012), 123–46.

49 *TD* V, 91.

50 Rodney Howsare, *Balthasar: A Guide for the Perplexed* (New York: T&T Clark, 2009), 161.

51 See Sarah Coakley, "*Kenōsis* and Subversion: On the Repression of 'Vulnerability' in Christian Feminist Writing," in *Powers and Submissions: Spirituality, Philosophy, and Gender* (Malden, MA: Blackwell Publishers, 2002), 3–39; Aristotle Papanikolaou, "Person, *Kenosis*, and Abuse: Hans Urs von Balthasar and Feminist Theologies in Conversation," *Modern Theology* 19, no. 1 (2003): 41–65; Jennifer Newsome Martin, "The 'Whence' and the 'Wither' of Balthasar's Gendered Theology: Rehabilitating Kenosis for Feminist Theology," *Modern Theology* 31, no. 2 (2015), 211–34; Linn Tonstad, *God and Difference: The Trinity, Sexuality, and the Transformation of Finitude* (New York: Routledge, 2016).

52 Cyril O'Regan, "Balthasar and Gnostic Genealogy," *Modern Theology* 22, no. 4 (2006): 609–50.

53 Rowan Williams, "Afterword," in Lucy Gardner, David Moss, Ben Quash, and Graham Ward, *Balthasar at the End of Modernity* (Edinburgh: T&T Clark, 1999), 173.

Recommended Reading

Primary

Balthasar, Hans Urs von. *Dare We Hope "That All Men be Saved"? With a Short Discourse on Hell*. Translated by David Kipp and Lothar Krauth. San Francisco, CA: Ignatius Press, 1988.

_____. *Explorations in Theology*. 5 vols. Translated by A. V. Littledale et al. San Francisco: Ignatius Press, 1989–2014.

_____. *The Glory of the Lord: A Theological Aesthetics*. 7 vols. Translated by Erasmo Leiva-Merikakis et al. San Francisco, CA: Ignatius Press. 1982–91.

_____. *Love Alone Is Credible*. Translated by D. C. Schindler. San Francisco, CA: Ignatius Press, 2004.

_____. *Mysterium Paschale: The Mystery of Easter*. Translated with an introduction by Aidan Nichols, OP. San Francisco, CA: Ignatius Press, 1990.

_____. *Theo-Drama: Theological Dramatic Theory*. 5 vols. Translated by Graham Harrison. San Francisco, CA: Ignatius Press, 1988–98.

_____. *Theo-Logic: Theological Logical Theory*. 3 vols. Translated by Adrian J. Walker. San Francisco, CA: Ignatius Press, 2000–05.

_____. *A Theology of History*. San Francisco, CA: Ignatius Press, 1994.

_____. *The Theology of Karl Barth: Exposition and Interpretation*. Translated by Edward T. Oakes, SJ. San Francisco, CA: Ignatius Press, 1992.

Secondary

Gardner, Lucy et al. *Balthasar at the End of Modernity*. Edinburgh: T&T Clark, 1999.

Howsare, Rodney. *Balthasar: A Guide for the Perplexed*. New York: T&T Clark, 2009.

Kilby, Karen. *Balthasar: A (Very) Critical Introduction*. Grand Rapids, MI: Eerdmans, 2012.

McInroy, Mark, and Anthony Sciglitano, eds., with Cyril O'Regan, consultant editor. *The Oxford Handbook of Hans Urs von Balthasar*. Oxford: Oxford University Press, forthcoming.

Mongrain, Kevin. *The Systematic Thought of Hans Urs von Balthasar: An Irenaean Retrieval*. New York: Crossroad, 2002.

Nichols, Aidan, OP. *A Key to Balthasar: Hans Urs von Balthasar on Beauty, Goodness, and Truth*. Grand Rapids, MI: Baker Academic, 2011.

Oakes, Edward T., SJ, and David Moss, eds. *The Cambridge Companion to Hans Urs von Balthasar*. Cambridge: Cambridge University Press, 2005.

O'Regan, Cyril. *The Anatomy of Misremembering: Von Balthasar's Response to Philosophical Modernity. Vol. I: Hegel; Vol. 2: Heidegger*. Chestnut Ridge, NY: Crossroad, Herder & Herder, 2014; Vol. 2, forthcoming.

Quash, Ben. *Theology and the Drama of History*. Cambridge: Cambridge University Press, 2005.

Riches, John, ed. *The Analogy of Beauty: The Theology of Hans Urs von Balthasar*. Edinburgh: T&T Clark, 1986.

Dietrich Bonhoeffer

Eleanor McLaughlin

Introduction

Dietrich Bonhoeffer is one of the rare twentieth century theologians whose work has gained an extensive readership both within and beyond the academy. This is partly because the story of his life has captured the imagination of many. Bonhoeffer's life story is significant because, as André Dumas claims, he is above all a "theologian of reality," his thought constantly shaped by his lived experience.[1] Bonhoeffer's theology is written in direct response to what he encounters in the world: for instance, his time leading the seminary at Finkenwalde inspired his book *Life Together*, and his realization during World War II that "people as they are now simply cannot be religious anymore" triggered his thinking on religionless Christianity.[2] It is therefore important to begin by dedicating more space to a discussion of Bonhoeffer's life than might be necessary for a theologian whose lived experience is less foundational for their theology.

Born in 1906 into a large and wealthy family, Dietrich and his twin, Sabine, were among the younger of the eight Bonhoeffer children. The family moved from Breslau (now Wrocław in Poland) to Berlin in 1912 when Bonhoeffer's psychiatrist father, Karl, was appointed to a post at the University of Berlin. The family shared a keen interest in music, and at an early age Dietrich had planned to become a concert pianist. His love of music is apparent throughout his life, from the collection of spiritual records he brought home after his year in New York, to the references to music that feature prominently in the letters he wrote from prison in his final days.

During his early teenage years however, Bonhoeffer decided instead to become a theologian, a decision that propelled him to study first in Tübingen, and then in Berlin. At this time, as Martin Rumscheidt notes, "faith [for Bonhoeffer] was a component of the historical legacy and intellectual tradition to be guarded; it was only later that faith became a matter of discipleship."[3] In 1927, he completed his doctoral thesis, *Sanctorum Communio*, followed by his *Habilitation* thesis *Act and Being* in 1930.

Through his teachers in both Tübingen and Berlin, Bonhoeffer was greatly influenced by liberal theology, which posited faith as akin to knowledge. The theology of Karl Barth, which Bonhoeffer encountered during his studies in Berlin in the mid-1920s, stood in stark contrast to this, highlighting as it did the centrality of God's revelation in Jesus Christ rather than being centered in humanity's efforts to know about

Ford's The Modern Theologians: An Introduction to Christian Theology since 1918, Fourth Edition.
Edited by Rachel Muers and Ashley Cocksworth.
© 2024 John Wiley & Sons Ltd. Published 2024 by John Wiley & Sons Ltd.

God. Barth's distinction between faith and religion, would continue to influence Bonhoeffer until the end of his life, and the two thinkers later became allies in the church struggle of the early 1930s. Barth's emerging theology also allowed Bonhoeffer to read Luther as standing in opposition to Idealism, providing him with the lens of dialectic theology through which to encounter the reformer. Luther's influence on Bonhoeffer's thought is particularly evident in the *Ethics*, where Bonhoeffer proposes a rereading of Luther's two kingdoms doctrine *contra* its appropriation by Nazi ideology.[4]

Between his studies in Tübingen and Berlin, Bonhoeffer traveled to Rome in spring 1924 with his brother Klaus. He was profoundly moved by the universality of the Roman Catholic Church, which made him view his own denomination as bound by national and provincial concerns. He was also inspired by the great number of people attending church for confession. Later, when Bonhoeffer became the director of a Confessing Church seminary, he taught on the subject of confession and encouraged his students to practice private confession.

After a year serving as assistant pastor in the Lutheran church in Barcelona, Bonhoeffer returned to Berlin and in 1930 qualified for teaching at the university. He spent the academic year 1930–1 studying at Union Theological Seminary in New York. There, he met and formed long-lasting friendships with both fellow international students and Americans. His friendship with African American student Albert Franklin Fisher led him to attend the Abyssinian Baptist Church in Harlem, where he worshipped and became a Sunday school leader. As a member of this Black church community, Bonhoeffer became acutely aware of the oppression African Americans were suffering in the United States. This had repercussions for his theology: Bonhoeffer learned to see Christ as a fellow sufferer alongside oppressed people.[5] French student Jean Lasserre's pacifist reading of the Sermon on the Mount challenged Bonhoeffer. This would have an enduring impact on him throughout the 1930s as he sought to convince the ecumenical movement that it had the power to bring about peace, and as he came to write *Discipleship*.[6]

Returning to Germany, Bonhoeffer was ordained in the Lutheran church in November 1931 and took up a role as lecturer at the University of Berlin. Over the following few years, he taught on a range of topics including Genesis 1–3 and Christology. The notes students made in these lectures would later be collated and turned into two books that form part of Bonhoeffer's opus, *Creation and Fall* and *Christology* respectively. In his pastoral role, Bonhoeffer was a students' chaplain and worked with young people in east Berlin. He also cemented his commitment to the ecumenical cause in Europe by becoming the youth secretary for the World Alliance of Churches.

In 1933, with the rise to power of Adolf Hitler and his National Socialist German Workers' Party and the implementation of the Aryan paragraph, which prevented non-Aryan pastors from holding office in the Reich Church, Bonhoeffer and other concerned church leaders formed the Pastors' Emergency League. The league openly challenged the new law and swiftly gained several thousand members. This opposition movement would, the following year, develop into what became known as the Confessing Church. In August 1933, Bonhoeffer participated in the writing of the Bethel Confession. The document's aim was to oppose the movement known as the German Christians, who sought to create a nationalist church in line with Nazi values. During the drafting of the Confession, Bonhoeffer wrote to his grandmother: "The real question is between Germanism and Christianity, and the sooner the conflict comes out into the open the better."[7] The conflict highlighted here would remain a focal point in Bonhoeffer's theology.[8]

In October of the same year, Bonhoeffer moved to London to become the pastor of two expatriate German churches in Whitechapel and Sydenham. Despite being in England, Bonhoeffer remained committed to the ongoing church struggle in Germany, finding new allies in England and fostering his contacts in ecumenical circles throughout Europe.[9] 1935 saw Bonhoeffer return to Germany to lead a seminary, training men to serve as pastors in the Confessing Church. After an initial beginning in Zingst, the seminary found its home in Finkenwalde. The seminary operated for only two years before being closed by the Gestapo in 1937. The following years saw the birth of two of his best-known works: in 1937 he published *Discipleship*[10] and wrote *Life Together* in 1938.

In June 1939, with war looming, Bonhoeffer traveled to New York where friends had arranged for him to work as a pastor and teacher. However, his doubts about removing himself from the danger that his fellow Germans would face during the impending conflict overcame his initial plans to remain in the United States, and he sailed for Europe, arriving in Berlin on 27 July. The sense of responsibility that compelled Bonhoeffer to return to Germany is of a piece with the theology he would develop shortly thereafter: from summer 1940 to until his arrest on 5 April 1943, Bonhoeffer was engaged in writing the essays that were to form his posthumously edited *Ethics*, which has a theology of responsibility, with Christ as "the responsible human being par excellence," at its heart.[11]

It is evident that by the mid-to-late 1930s the Nazi regime viewed Bonhoeffer with deep suspicion. His right to teach at the university was withdrawn in 1936; Finkenwalde seminary was shut down in 1937, and some of the seminarians arrested. He was expulsed from Berlin in January 1938. In 1940 he was banned from public speaking and obliged to report regularly to the police, and the collective pastorates (two small communities of seminarians living and learning together in the wake of the closure of Finkenwalde, which Bonhoeffer visited regularly for teaching) were dissolved by the Gestapo. His right to print or publish was withdrawn in 1941.[12]

Through his brother-in-law Hans von Dohnanyi, Bonhoeffer joined the *Abwehr*, the military intelligence, in October 1940, becoming a member of the group led by Admiral Canaris that was secretly seeking to overthrow Hitler. In this role he traveled within Europe, informing allies of the real situation within Germany and seeking support for the resistance movement. He also continued to fulfil a pastoral role among his former seminarians. During this period, in January 1943, he became engaged to Maria von Wedemeyer.

Bonhoeffer was arrested on 5 April 1943 and incarcerated in Tegel Military Interrogation Prison in Berlin. During his months in prison, Bonhoeffer wrote to his family, his fiancée, and his friend Eberhard Bethge, with whom he shared his increasingly radical theological ideas, as well as his developing forays into theological fiction and poetry. After initial expectations of an early release, Bonhoeffer pinned his hopes for freedom on the plot to assassinate Hitler on 20 July 1944. After this plan's failure, Bonhoeffer looked to the Allied invasion of Germany, but the discovery of secret resistance movement papers in Zossen on 22 September 1944 caused Hitler to order the execution of all those in Admiral Canaris' group. Bonhoeffer was moved to a secure prison on Prinz Albrecht Strasse on 8 October 1944. He was later taken from Berlin, first to Buchenwald concentration camp and then to Flossenbürg concentration camp, where he was killed by hanging with his fellow conspirators Hans Oster and Wilhelm Canaris on 9 April 1945. With the shifting contexts of Bonhoeffer's life in mind, we now turn to the themes emerging throughout his life in his theological work.

Survey

Eberhard Bethge, Bonhoeffer's friend and biographer, suggests that Bonhoeffer's adult life can be viewed in three distinct stages. He terms these "Foundation," "Concentration," and "Liberation" and sees them running from 1927 to 1933, 1933 to 1940, and 1940 to 1945 respectively. He describes them as:

> The dogmatic, the exegetical, and the ethical; or, again, the theoretical period in which he learned and taught at Berlin University, the pastoral period in which he served the Confessing Church in a preachers' seminary, and the political period in which his life became ambiguous.[13]

Bethge states that the first pivot point, in the early 1930s, occurred when Bonhoeffer became a Christian. Noting that "Bonhoeffer always greatly disliked stories of conversion,"[14] Bethge simply points to changes in Bonhoeffer's approach to theological study and in particular his new way of reading the Bible, which now included meditation on the biblical text.[15] The second turning point, in 1940, was when Bonhoeffer began to "lead two lives," as both a theologian and an intelligence officer.[16] Bethge also proposes another way of thinking about these different periods in Bonhoeffer's life, picked up by André Dumas:

> In his twenties Bonhoeffer said to the theologians, your theme is the church. In his thirties he said to the church, your theme is the world. And in his forties he said to the world, your theme, which is forsakenness, is God's own theme; with his theme he is not cheating you out of the fullness of life, but opening it up to you.[17]

This description gives us more of a sense of Bonhoeffer's shifts of focus over the course of his theological career; of who his interlocutors were, and what themes he considered to be of the utmost importance at different points in his life.

Taking Bonhoeffer's theological output as a whole, from his earliest work *Sanctorum Communio* to the fragments we have from his time in prison, it is clear that Christology is the central theme in his work across all three periods identified by Bethge.[18] The central Christological questions, for Bonhoeffer, are about who Christ is and what that means for human relationships and actions.

The theme of human relationality is at the heart of Bonhoeffer's initial work in his first "theoretical" period, his thesis *Sanctorum Communio*. Bonhoeffer brings together sociology and a Barthian theology of revelation to propose an ecclesiology in which he defines the church as "Christ existing as church-community."[19] Bonhoeffer suggests that our relationships are theologically crucial because, as Bethge puts it, we can "think revelation only in social relations."[20] In this text and his *Habilitation* thesis *Act and Being*, Bonhoeffer seeks to engage with Barth's theology of revelation, first by putting it into conversation with sociology, and second by challenging what he perceived as Barth's unsatisfactory model of the relationship between revelation and history: In *Act and Being* Bonhoeffer proposed, against Barth, that God is located within history, and not merely in a nonhistorical "act" of revelation.[21]

Bonhoeffer's lectures on Genesis 1–3 and Christology, discussed in more depth subsequently, mark the transition from the "theoretical" to the "pastoral" period in which Bonhoeffer's primary context was the Confessing Church struggle. In this period, he writes *Discipleship* and *Life Together*. These books show Bonhoeffer's concern for Christians, their daily ethical choices and spiritual practices. In *Discipleship* he outlines the difference between cheap and costly grace, the former being the misunderstanding that "through discovering the gospel of pure grace, Luther proclaimed a dispensation from obeying Jesus' commandments in the world,"[22] whereas the latter is costly because it "calls to discipleship," thus requiring a response of the believer.[23] Bonhoeffer develops this in the second part of the book, a commentary on the Sermon on the Mount, in which he sets out what is required of Jesus's disciples. Although Bonhoeffer's view of discipleship is demanding, he also provides encouragement in the closing section "The Church of Jesus Christ and Discipleship," emphasising the fellowship to be found within Christian community and in relationship with Christ. These ideas are further developed in *Life Together*, discussed more fully later in this chapter.

Turning from the "pastoral" to the "political" period, in which Bonhoeffer focuses on life in the world, we reach Bonhoeffer's final works, which were all edited and published posthumously: *Ethics*, *Letters and Papers from Prison* and *Fiction from Tegel Prison*. In *Ethics*, we see among others the dual themes of Christology and human relationality, mentioned previously, as Bonhoeffer presents Jesus Christ as the "one who concretely enacts God's love"[24] and "the one who seeks to be there not for God's own sake but 'for us.'"[25] Here, the continuation of the importance of ecclesiology in Bonhoeffer's theology is clear, as he writes, "*The church is the place where Jesus Christ's taking form is proclaimed and where it happens.*"[26] Bonhoeffer develops the idea of Jesus being "for" people in both his *Fiction from Tegel Prison*, and in *Letters and Papers from Prison* when he writes "Jesus only 'is there for others.'"[27]

In his prison texts, Bonhoeffer develops a network of interconnected concepts, the most famous of which is probably his idea of religionless Christianity, in which he asks what Christianity might look like if it jettisoned the religious "garb" that it has worn since its beginnings.[28] These several concepts are grounded in

Bonhoeffer's conceit that the world has "come of age,"[29] which he explores imaginatively in his fiction text *Story*.[30] According to Bonhoeffer, the world come of age indicates a new period of history in which humans no longer need to refer to God, or a religious a priori, in order to understand the world around them. Bonhoeffer likens this situation to a person who has reached adulthood and no longer needs a mentor to help with moral decision making.[31] The fact that God no longer fulfills the role of the stopgap, the God that people turn to when they need answers to their questions, does not mean that God no longer has a purpose. On the contrary, Bonhoeffer states that God should be spoken of "not at the boundaries but in the centre,"[32] arguing for what he calls "this-worldliness": living fully in the world and finding oneself there, precisely, "in the arms of God."[33] For Bonhoeffer, when we live wholly in the world, we inevitably see the suffering Christ, thus learning to know more fully who Christ is. Living thus, we also pay closer attention to the people around us and our shared reality.

This brief survey of theological themes shows that while Bonhoeffer was a thinker who tackled a range of topics, from a variety of perspectives, there remained two questions that were of vital importance to him: Who is Jesus Christ, and what does that mean for how we relate to others? It is therefore to these two central questions that we now turn: Who is Christ? What does our relationship with Christ mean for human relationality?

In *Sanctorum Communio* Bonhoeffer is concerned, among other matters, with the person of Christ "existing as church-community."[34] From the outset then, as Clifford Green argues, Christology and theological anthropology are inevitably intertwined in Bonhoeffer's work.[35] His theological anthropology will emphasize the importance of relationality for what it means to be human. In *Sanctorum Communio* and in *Creation and Fall* Bonhoeffer suggests that relationality is necessary for humans to be able to develop a sense of self. He contends that it is only when in relationship with someone else that a person can begin to perceive their own individual identity, and this happens in an absolute way when confronted by the divine person: "The Christian person originates only in the absolute duality of God and humanity; only in experiencing the barrier does the awareness of oneself as ethical person arise."[36] The Christian comes into being when confronted with the divine person.

Bonhoeffer's emphasis on the relation being central to the individual's sense of self is also found in the theological anthropology articulated in *Creation and Fall* in his discussion of Adam and Eve. He makes comparisons between how Adam and Eve relate to each other before and after the Fall, drawing out the differences between a relationship that allows for limitation of the self (before the Fall) and one that does not (after the Fall), in which each individual self tries to impose itself on the other. This model of relationality that includes limitation also extends to God. Before the Fall, humans live within limits set by God: they are not allowed to eat the fruit of the tree of knowledge of good and evil. But after the Fall they resent this limitation. Indeed, it is reflecting on the limitation and judging God's command not to eat the fruit of the tree of knowledge that leads to the fall.[37]

Bonhoeffer's warning against considering God's command as an object of intellectual critique, instead of remaining in relationship with Godself, develops in his *Christology* lectures. If *Creation and Fall* marks a turning point in Bonhoeffer's Christology, moving from considering Christ no longer only in terms of ecclesiology, but as "the cosmic word of God that speaks from the center of world history,"[38] thus speaking from and into our reality as historical beings, his lectures on Christology, delivered at the University of Berlin in 1933, confirm and develop this new direction. Bonhoeffer makes it plain that he is not interested in the "how" of Christ but in the "who" of Christ: "It is therefore an impossible question to ask how the man Jesus, limited by space and time, can be contemporary with us ... The only possible and meaningful question is, 'Who is there, present in time and place?'"[39] This is because Christ cannot be merely an idea, one among many concepts that can be considered intellectually by humans. It is the encounter with Christ that is important, and that dictates how human beings will interact with each other.

Bonhoeffer's contention that the encounter with Christ has a bearing on how humans encounter and relate to each other is fleshed out in his later works, *Discipleship* and *Life Together*. In the former work,

Bonhoeffer emphasizes that to be a disciple of Christ, a person must first hear Christ's call and respond to it. It is impossible, Bonhoeffer maintains, for people to start out on the road to discipleship without first hearing Christ's call: to do so exposes "[t]he gap between the free offer of discipleship and real discipleship."[40] To put this in the language of relationality, the beginning of a relationship between Christ and the individual, a call and a response, is necessary before that person can begin their journey of discipleship and enter into a community of disciples.[41]

In *Life Together*, Bonhoeffer reflects on living in community at the seminary in Finkenwalde and describes two types of community. The first, which he calls "psychic" and "emotional," consists of individuals trying to shape others according to their desires for what the community should be like. Bonhoeffer warns that this type of community can be created even when its members are devout.[42] It is dominated by the powerful and it is not oriented toward Christ. The second he terms "spiritual."[43] Here, individuals orient themselves to Christ and relate to each other via that primary orientation, such that humans are never in direct relationship with one another but relate to each other only through Christ. Bonhoeffer extends his comparison between two types of community to distinguish between two types of love: self-centered love and spiritual love. The latter is the love mediated through Christ: "It knows that it has no direct access to other persons. Christ stands between me and others."[44] Thus, spiritual love between people is never direct but always channeled through Christ, and therefore cannot be coercive. It is clear here that Bonhoeffer's view of who Christ is – someone with whom we are called to be in relation, someone of whom we should ask "Who are you?" – is the foundation for how he thinks people should be in relation with each other.

In his *Ethics*, Bonhoeffer develops his Christology, and its concomitant theology of relationality, for a context in which his readers and the bonds between them will be challenged as never before. The two opening essays, written between summer and mid-November 1940, speak to the interconnected questions of how Christians can know and enact the will of God and how they can withstand the evils of the Nazi regime. In answer, Bonhoeffer provides what might be called a Christology of reality: "*In Jesus Christ the reality of God has entered into the reality of the world.*"[45] To live in accordance with "the reality of Christ," Bonhoeffer tells his readers that they should be "*participating in the reality of God and the world in Jesus Christ today,* and doing so in such a way that [they] never experience the reality of God without the reality of the world, nor the reality of the world without the reality of God."[46] Bonhoeffer thus introduces his idea, later called "this-worldliness" in his prison writings,[47] that Christ's own identity compels us to engage seriously with the world. It is not only an abstract ethical duty that obliges the Christian to act against evil in the world, but it is a theological imperative. Bonhoeffer proposes that it is only through formation to Christ, through participation in the acceptance, judgment, and awakening to new life that God has bestowed on Christ, that Christians can hope to withstand the tide of evil brought about by the Nazis and stand in solidarity with those being persecuted.

Bonhoeffer's constant emphasis on the question "who is Christ?" is perhaps most famously articulated in a letter addressed to Bethge dated 30 April 1944. He writes, "What keeps gnawing at me is the question, what is Christianity, or who is Christ actually for us today?"[48] The question of Christ leads Bonhoeffer to his questioning of the place of religion – more specifically, religiosity – within Christianity, and to his concept of religionless Christianity, perhaps the most debated idea to emerge from Bonhoeffer's work. He suggests that the religionless Christian stands in opposition to the *homo religiosus*, who reaches out toward a God who resides beyond reality. Instead, the religionless Christian recognizes that their context is the world come of age and tries to live as a disciple of Christ in a world in which God is present as a suffering God, allowing this to shape their relationship to Christ and to others.

How we relate to others is a central theme in Bonhoeffer's thoughts on the church's position in Germany after the war. One of the main criticisms he makes about the church's behavior is that it has focused on its self-preservation rather than its mission to communicate God's word to the world. Because of this self-interest and lack of attention to others, according to Bonhoeffer, the church will have to keep silent in the public arena, praying and seeking to do justice until God grants it a new language with which to communicate God to the world.[49]

In Bonhoeffer's later work, particularly in the prison period, he is in a sense considering the relationship between Christology and human relationality in two directions, working both forwards and backwards simultaneously. Who Christ is matters for how we relate to others and operate in the world. But also, what happens in the world *matters* for Christology. Theological reflection does not take place in a context that is removed from the world but must respond to what is happening in ordinary people's ordinary lives. Jesus Christ is the God who suffers in the world and who calls on human beings to suffer alongside him in the world. We may not detach ourselves from others' suffering. Bonhoeffer explains that Christ's plea to his disciples in Gethsemane to "remain here, and stay awake with me" (Matt. 26:38b) is the reverse of what a religious person would expect to hear from God.[50] Here, we have a God who is weak, not a problem-solving God. Instead of the divine calling us into a painless beyond, Bonhoeffer asserts that we find God suffering in the world and that we are called to share this suffering.[51] That Christ, the suffering God, calls us into and affirms the imperative "this-worldliness" draws us into relation with those who are suffering.[52] It also reveals new insights into who Christ is.

We see, then, that Bonhoeffer's theology of relationality and his Christology run throughout his theological writing, spiraling like a double helix to form the structure of his theological DNA. Each concern informs the other, and through them he addresses the multiple theological questions arising from the shifting circumstances of his own life. Thus, these concepts provide the pattern for the body of his theological work.

Debate

Many debates about Bonhoeffer's work could be said to center around the question of how we perceive Bonhoeffer. Do we focus primarily on the inspirational pastor-theologian whose key message is encapsulated in the call to obedience of *Discipleship*? Or do we look at a more complex figure, whose writing can be both foundational for theological reflection as well as disturbing to twenty-first century readers? It is difficult to adopt the second position when Bonhoeffer is widely hailed as a quasi-saintly figure (his statue stands above Westminster Abbey's Great West Door in a lineup of "modern martyrs"), but such a stance is necessary if we are to treat his work as serious theological material for our time.

Linked to this question are two central debates within the field of Bonhoeffer studies: First, on whether there are breaks or ruptures within Bonhoeffer's oeuvre, or whether his thought develops in a continuous arc, from its beginnings in *Sanctorum Communio* to its end in the prison texts. Second, and closely related to it, is the question of whether the prison theology presents such a departure from his previous thought that it indicates Bonhoeffer was suffering from extreme psychological pressure at the time and should therefore not be taken seriously as part of Bonhoeffer's opus. In addition, there is the dilemma of what to do with elements of Bonhoeffer's work that do not appear to sit well with contemporary theological concerns around gender, race, and class.

Regarding the first debate, the emphasis here is not so much on whether a much-admired theologian could have written things that are problematic in today's context, but rather on the extent to which Bonhoeffer's ideas were shaped by his changing circumstances, how much pressure his life in prison exerted on his thinking, and whether he ever turned his back on previously held theological convictions. This debate is triggered in part by Bonhoeffer's own comment in a letter to Bethge from Tegel prison dated 21 July 1944, in which he comments that he now sees the dangers of his book *Discipleship*, although he still stands by what he then wrote. In this letter Bonhoeffer makes the point that in later life he discovered that "one only learns to have faith by living in the full this-worldliness of life," a view that stands in contrast to his previous belief that he could "learn to have faith by trying to live something like a saintly life," which informed his writing of *Discipleship*.[53]

The contrast between Bonhoeffer's work in the prewar years and his wartime writing is visible not only in the contents of the texts but also in their tone. In *Life Together* and *Discipleship*, Bonhoeffer adopts a didactic voice and explains to the reader how to live within a Christian community, and the correct steps one must take in order to become a Christian. He also indicates, in *Discipleship*, what people should do if they are struggling with doubt. He advises them to obey Christ so as to enter into a situation in which faith is possible, for: "Only the believers obey … Only the obedient believe."[54] However, when it comes to the prison texts, Bonhoeffer's tone is exploratory, admitting to interior conflict (see for instance the poem "Who Am I?") and uncertainty. It is also important to note that the forms of these texts are very different. *Discipleship* is a polished, finished text, which Bonhoeffer intended as a resource for Christian readers; he therefore sets out his points in clear way that people will be able to follow easily. The letters, notes, and musings in *Letters and Papers* were not intended for publication. Writing his theological letters to Bethge, Bonhoeffer awaited replies from his friend that would further refine and develop his own ideas; the letters were never intended to be his last word on any of the topics they raise. Likewise, the notes were the basis on which he hoped to develop a book, to be written after his release, and although, like the letters, they address important themes, they do not represent his final thoughts on these matters. The shifts in style and content within Bonhoeffer's work indicate that Bonhoeffer is indeed a "theologian of reality,"[55] a man who writes theology as a direct response to the context in which he finds himself, and the majority of Bonhoeffer scholars agree that although these shifts do indeed exist, they are not great enough to indicate a rupture within the development of his thought.

The second debate, on whether Bonhoeffer's prison texts should be read as the products of a period of intense psychological anguish, and therefore not treated as important within Bonhoeffer's theology, has diminished in importance in recent years. However, in the 1960s and early 1970s the debate was heated, and James Woelfel, among others, pugnaciously rejected the stance of ignoring the prison theology: "To dismiss the 'Christianity without religion' project by psychological innuendo is not only somewhat irresponsibly facile; it is also an unfair and inaccurate portrayal of Bonhoeffer himself."[56] Most Bonhoeffer scholars now accept the prison texts as a valid part of Bonhoeffer's theological work. Interestingly, emerging scholarship is beginning to address the role of trauma, particularly in Bonhoeffer's poetry, but does not thereby question the importance of the prison texts for understanding Bonhoeffer's theology as a whole.

Although much of Bonhoeffer's writing remains fresh and appealing today, some elements within it starkly reflect his background in the patriarchal, *bürgerlich* society of early-twentieth-century Germany. That being so, it is hardly surprising that some of his work relating to gender, race, and class makes for difficult reading in today's context. Indeed, it was not until the twenty-first century that the conversation between Bonhoeffer's theology and perspectives taking gender, race, and class seriously began to emerge.[57] In the case of feminist theology, for instance, this is perhaps partly because Bonhoeffer's writing does not at first glance seem to provide any promising ground for discussion: he uncritically accepts patriarchy and places women firmly in a subordinate position in their relationships with men.[58] Feminist scholars engaging with Bonhoeffer's work have highlighted the obvious sexism in his writing and also made the point that his viewpoint is rigidly androcentric.[59]

However, the feminist readings of Bonhoeffer that first acknowledge that some of his work is problematic from the perspective of gender equality and then work, as Jennifer McBride puts it "beyond Bonhoeffer, with Bonhoeffer" have shown that critical engagement with Bonhoeffer's theology can yield new insights into both feminist theologies and Bonhoeffer's own thought.[60] This work helps us move beyond Bonhoeffer's time-bound assumptions and prejudices, while retaining important insights from his theology. McBride, building on the contributions of other feminist theologians, concludes that Bonhoeffer's prioritisation of the "who" question over the "how" question in Christology, which highlights Christ as a person with whom one enters into relationship, as opposed to an idea that needs to be analyzed, allows for feminist engagement with this topic that has often proved problematic for both feminist and womanist thinkers.[61]

Similarly, given the context in which Bonhoeffer was raised, it is unsurprising that he should start out in life with views on social structures and class that reflect his own privileged position.[62] What is perhaps more remarkable is that this perspective does not seem to alter throughout his life; one might expect that his experiences of travelling and living abroad could shape his *bürgerlich* perspective into something more nuanced. However, although his late work points to a realization that the gospels point to a radical equality between classes that he finds difficult to countenance, there is no evidence of prolonged engagement with this idea.[63] In prison, after writing the fiction in which he explores the idea of shifting social classes he returns to a critique of his fellow inmates' inability to cope with longing for their loved ones. He writes, referring to "the proletarian classes" that it is not good for people to be "beaten up by life early and often," as "[i]n most cases it simply breaks a person."[64] Bonhoeffer is not apportioning blame here, but giving his view on how people from different social backgrounds are subsequently able to cope with challenging situations. Although this aspect of Bonhoeffer's thought has not received sustained scholarly attention, it remains a part of the debate about how to receive his work in the twenty-first century.

The debates surrounding Bonhoeffer, therefore, have much to do with who we want him to be. They point to a reluctance to acknowledge him as a conventional and yet convention-breaking figure, who combined social conservatism with a developing and radical theology.

Influence and Achievement

Although there are clear facts to be ascertained about Bonhoeffer's life and writing, it is also vital to note that his actions and ideas have been interpreted in startlingly diverse ways. For instance, Bonhoeffer's theology was influential in the struggle against the institutionalized racism of apartheid in South Africa[65] but was more recently taken up by prominent American writer and Donald Trump supporter Eric Metaxas, author of a deeply flawed biography of Bonhoeffer in which he contends that Bonhoeffer was fighting against not just Nazism but also liberal Christianity.[66] Although Bonhoeffer scholars have been swift to critique Metaxas' interpretation of Bonhoeffer,[67] the very existence of this attempted appropriation of Bonhoeffer as an inspiration for the right-wing political agenda in the United States points to one of the central facts about Bonhoeffer and his legacy: because of his anti-Nazi stance and his death at the hands of that regime, Bonhoeffer has become a figure of moral authority within popular theology. Even those whose views are incompatible with Bonhoeffer's own seek to present him as supporting their cause, as this lends them theological and moral weight. The desire to appropriate Bonhoeffer in support of a theological argument can be traced from early scholarship to the present day.

Many of Bonhoeffer's books were published in English throughout the 1950s, but his theology came to greater prominence in the English-speaking world in 1963 when John A. T. Robinson used *Letters and Papers* as one of three conversation partners in his book *Honest to God*.[68] In fact, although it brought them into prominence in Britain, Robinson's account did not do full justice to Bonhoeffer's ideas as he advocates the idea of religionless Christianity for an increasingly secular society, without explaining what Bonhoeffer means by "religion."[69] Concurrently, thinkers who became known as the Death of God theologians in the United States were drawing on Bonhoeffer's late theology to support their argument that "there was once a God to whom adoration, praise and trust were appropriate, possible, and even necessary, but that now there is no such God."[70] The Death of God theologians emphasized Bonhoeffer's late writing on the world come of age and his idea that we must live in a world *etsi deus non daretur* (as if God were not a given).[71] They did not, however, pay attention to Bonhoeffer's simultaneous and paradoxical claim that "[t]he world come of age is more god-less and perhaps just because of that is *closer to God* than the world not yet come of age,"[72] thus missing the central point Bonhoeffer makes about new possibilities for humanity's relationship with God in a world come of age.

The Death of God movement shows that it is possible to read Bonhoeffer into different contexts and shape his work to fit a preexisting agenda. Metaxas has gone a step further than the Death of God thinkers and has applied his preexisting agenda to the entirety of Bonhoeffer's life and work. As Clifford Green acutely points out, Metaxas reads Bonhoeffer and his life story through the polarizing lens that wishes to set conservative evangelicals against liberals.[73] This lens allows Metaxas to compare Bonhoeffer with Trump, which he did in a *Wall Street Journal* article in 2016, urging Christians to vote for Trump in the upcoming presidential election.[74] That Bonhoeffer has been coopted into an apologetic for a right-wing, populist, nationalist movement should remind us of a central element in Bonhoeffer's own theology: theology should not be divorced from the real world. If theologians do not engage with the world, and do not allow their theological thinking to be shaped by and in response to the reality around them, sharing insights and knowledge, it becomes easy for theological figures and ideas to be misunderstood and misappropriated.

In light of the interest in Bonhoeffer's late writing on a world come of age in which God is "pushed out of the world and onto the cross,"[75] it is surprising that some texts from the prison period that deal with these themes have been largely ignored. These texts are the fiction fragments that Bonhoeffer wrote in December 1943 and spring 1944: an unfinished play, an unfinished novel, and a completed short story. Although his poetry, collected in *Letters and Papers from Prison*, has received some attention,[76] his fiction has not been widely discussed within Bonhoeffer scholarship. Bonhoeffer uses the fiction to address the future of the church, how society should be ordered, gender roles, the roles of different classes within societal structures, power and corruption, suffering, death, powerlessness, love, and countless other themes that tie into the more well-known texts of the prison period. In addition, Bonhoeffer sets his short story in a context in which God, the church, Jesus, and Christianity are never mentioned. In short, it is a story that plays out in a world come of age. More research into these extraordinary texts would provide a greater insight into Bonhoeffer's thinking during the final months of his life.

Bonhoeffer's work in *Life Together* has recently featured in scholarship on place-based hermeneutics, which broadens Bonhoeffer's writing on how humans should live together into a consideration on healthy interspecies life together in specific geographical locations.[77] Using Bonhoeffer's work in this way is not only fruitful for suggesting solutions to our present climate crisis but also reveals new insights into his theology. To put Bonhoeffer's theology to work in this way does justice to his evident love of the natural world and there is more rich material, both in terms of his own thought and what it can contribute to our situation, to be uncovered here.[78]

Bonhoeffer's lasting achievement is that he addressed his theology firmly to each context in which he found himself. He dedicated his thinking to the questions he met in the world. He remained convinced that theology can, and must, adapt its language, its content, and its mode of delivery to its context in order to speak out clearly the word of God.[79] This flexibility means that rather than being confined to a specific time and place, his work has grown in relevance throughout the twentieth and early twenty-first centuries.

Notes

1 See André Dumas, *Dietrich Bonhoeffer: Theologian of Reality*, trans. Robert McAfee Brown (London: SCM Press, 1971).

2 See Dietrich Bonhoeffer, *Letters and Papers from Prison*, Dietrich Bonhoeffer Works in English (DBWE) Vol. 8, ed. John W. de Gruchy, trans. Isabel Best, Lisa E. Dahill, Reinhard Krauss, and Nancy Lukens (Minneapolis, MN: Fortress Press, 2010), 362, letter dated 30 April 1944.

3 Martin Rumscheidt, "The Formation of Bonhoeffer's Theology," in *The Cambridge Companion to Dietrich Bonhoeffer*, ed. John de Gruchy (Cambridge: Cambridge University Press, 1999), 52.

4 See Dietrich Bonhoeffer, *Ethics*, DBWE Vol. 6, ed. Clifford J. Green, trans. Reinhard Krauss, Charles C. West, and Douglas W. Stott (Minneapolis, MN: Fortress Press, 2009), 56ff. For more detail on the relationship between Bonhoeffer and Barth, see Eberhard Bethge, *Dietrich Bonhoeffer: Theologian, Christian, Contemporary*, ed. Edwin Robertson, trans. Eric Mosbacher, Peter and Betty Ross, Frank Clarke, and William Glen-Doepfel

(London: Collins, 1970), 131–42. For more detail on Bonhoeffer's theological influences, see Rumscheidt, "The Formation of Bonhoeffer's Theology," 50–70.

5 For a detailed exploration of Bonhoeffer's time in Harlem and its influence on his theology, see Reggie L. Williams, *Bonhoeffer's Black Jesus: Harlem Renaissance Theology and an Ethic of Resistance* (Waco, TX: Baylor University Press, 2014).

6 For a discussion of Bonhoeffer, his call for peace, and his engagement with the ecumenical movement, see Keith W. Clements, "Ecumenical Witness for Peace," in *The Cambridge Companion to Dietrich Bonhoeffer*, ed. de Gruchy, 154–72. For a discussion of Bonhoeffer's pacifism and his later decision to become involved in the resistance movement, see Larry L. Rasmussen, *Dietrich Bonhoeffer: Reality and Resistance*, rev. ed. (Louisville, KY: Westminster John Knox Press, 2005).

7 Letter dated 20 August 1933, cited in Bethge, *Dietrich Bonhoeffer*, 232.

8 See Bonhoeffer's letter to Reinhold Niebuhr in which he explains his decision to leave the United States and return to Germany in summer 1939: "Christians in Germany will find themselves faced with a terrible alternative of whether to desire the defeat of their nation in order that Christian civilization may survive or to desire the victory of their nation and thereby the destruction of our civilization." Letter cited in Sabine Leibholz-Bonhoeffer, *Portrait of a Family* (Chicago, IL: Covenant Publications, 1994), 44.

9 Notably, in this period Bonhoeffer began a strong and lasting friendship with Bishop George Bell of Chichester.

10 The book was originally published in English under the title *The Cost of Discipleship*.

11 Bonhoeffer, *Ethics*, 232.

12 For a detailed timeline of Bonhoeffer's life, see Bethge, *Dietrich Bonhoeffer*, 839–41.

13 Eberhard Bethge, "The Challenge of Dietrich Bonhoeffer's Life and Theology," in *World Come of Age: A Symposium on Dietrich Bonhoeffer*, ed. Ronald Gregor Smith (London: Collins, 1967), 25.

14 Bethge, *Dietrich Bonhoeffer*, 156.

15 For more detail see Bethge, *Dietrich Bonhoeffer*, 153–6.

16 Ferdinand Schlingensiepen, *Dietrich Bonhoeffer, 1906–1945: Martyr, Thinker, Man of Resistance* (New York: T&T Clark, 2010), 246.

17 Dumas, *Dietrich Bonhoeffer: Theologian of Reality*, 70. Dumas cites Eberhard Bethge in *Die Mündige Welt*, Vol. I, ed. Eberhard Bethge (Munich: Kaiser Verlag, 1955), 24. This is part of a four-volume collection of essays on Bonhoeffer edited by Bethge and published between 1955 and 1963.

18 For a detailed discussion of Bonhoeffer's Christology across Bonhoeffer's œuvre, see Ernst Feil, *The Theology of Dietrich Bonhoeffer*, trans. Martin Rumscheidt (Minneapolis, MN: Fortress Press, 2007), 59–96.

19 Dietrich Bonhoeffer, *Sanctorum Communio*, DBWE Vol. 1, ed. Clifford J. Green, trans. Reinhard Krauss and Nancy Lukens (Minneapolis, MN: Fortress Press, 1998), 231. For a full discussion of this text, see Michael Mawson, *Christ Existing as Community: Bonhoeffer's Ecclesiology* (Oxford: Oxford University Press, 2018).

20 Bethge, "The Challenge of Dietrich Bonhoeffer's Life and Theology," 34.

21 See Michael P. de Jonge, "Bonhoeffer the Student," in *The Oxford Handbook of Dietrich Bonhoeffer*, ed. Michael Mawson and Philip G. Ziegler (Oxford: Oxford University Press, 2019), 20. This chapter also provides a helpful general discussion of both *Sanctorum Communio* and *Act and Being*.

22 Dietrich Bonhoeffer, *Discipleship*, DBWE Vol. 4, ed. Geffrey B. Kelly and John D. Godsey, trans. Barbara Green and Reinhard Krauss (Minneapolis, MN: Fortress Press, 2001), 49.

23 Bonhoeffer, *Discipleship*, 45.

24 Bonhoeffer, *Ethics*, 232.

25 Bonhoeffer, *Ethics*, 400.

26 Bonhoeffer, *Ethics*, 102. Italics in original text.

27 Bonhoeffer, *Letters and Papers from Prison*, 501.

28 These concepts include the nonreligious interpretation of Christian concepts, unconscious Christianity, the stopgap God, God as *deus ex machina*, arcane discipline, and the taking seriously of God's suffering in the world (see Bonhoeffer, *Letters and Papers from Prison*, 490, 489, 500, 366, 373, and 486 respectively). He first broaches the topic of religionless Christianity in a letter to Eberhard Bethge dated 30 April 1944.

29 See Bonhoeffer, *Letters and Papers from Prison*, 424ff., letter dated 8 June 1944.

30 See Dietrich Bonhoeffer, *Fiction from Tegel Prison*, DBWE Vol. 7, ed. Clifford J. Green, trans. Nancy Lukens (Minneapolis, MN: Fortress Press 2010), 183–94. For a detailed discussion of the fiction and its place in Bonhoeffer's theology, see Eleanor McLaughlin, *Unconscious Christianity in Dietrich Bonhoeffer's Late Theology: Encounters with the Unknown Christ* (London: Lexington Books/Fortress Academic, 2020), 56–60.

31 See Bonhoeffer, *Letters and Papers from Prison*, 425–31, letter dated 8 June 1944.

32 Bonhoeffer, *Letters and Papers from Prison*, 366, letter dated 30 April 1944.

33 Bonhoeffer, *Letters and Papers from Prison*, 486, letter dated 21 July 1944.

34 Bonhoeffer, *Sanctorum Communio*, 121.

35 Clifford Green, *Bonhoeffer: A Theology of Sociality*. Revised edition (Grand Rapids, MI: Eerdmans, 1999), 64.

36 Bonhoeffer, *Sanctorum Communio*, 49.

37 See Dietrich Bonhoeffer, *Creation and Fall: A Theological Exposition of Genesis 1–3*, DBWE Vol. 3, ed. John de Gruchy, trans. Douglas Stephen Bax (Minneapolis, MN: Fortress Press, 1997), 103–10.

38 de Gruchy, "Editor's Introduction to the English Edition of Bonhoeffer," in *Creation and Fall*, 10.

39 Dietrich Bonhoeffer, *Berlin, 1932–1933*, DBWE Vol. 12, ed. Larry L. Rasmussen, trans. Isabel Best and David Higgins (Minneapolis, MN: Fortress Press, 2009), 312–13.

40 Bonhoeffer, *Discipleship*, 60.

41 See Bonhoeffer, *Discipleship*, 57–8, Part 2, "The Church of Jesus Christ and the Life of Discipleship."

42 Dietrich Bonhoeffer, *Life Together* and *Prayerbook of the Bible*, DBWE Vol. 5, ed. Geffrey B. Kelly, trans. Daniel W. Bloesch and James H. Burtness (Minneapolis, MN: Fortress Press, 2005), 38–40.

43 Bonhoeffer, *Life Together*, 38.

44 Bonhoeffer, *Life Together*, 43.

45 Bonhoeffer, *Ethics*, 54. Italics in original text.

46 Bonhoeffer, *Ethics*, 55. Italics in original text.

47 See Bonhoeffer, *Letters and Papers from Prison*, 486, letter dated 21 July 1944.

48 Bonhoeffer, *Letters and Papers from Prison*, 362, letter dated 30 April 1944.

49 See Bonhoeffer, *Letters and Papers from Prison*, 389, in "Thoughts on the Day of Baptism of D. W. R., May 1944."

50 Bonhoeffer, *Letters and Papers from Prison*, 480, letter dated 18 July 1944.

51 Bonhoeffer, *Letters and Papers from Prison*, 480, letter dated 18 July 1944.

52 Bonhoeffer, *Letters and Papers from Prison*, 486, letter dated 21 July 1944.

53 Bonhoeffer, *Letters and Papers from Prison*, 486, letter dated 21 July 1944.

54 Bonhoeffer, *Discipleship*, 67.

55 See André Dumas: *Dietrich Bonhoeffer: Theologian of Reality*.

56 James W. Woelfel, *Bonhoeffer's Theology: Classical and Revolutionary* (Nashville, TN: Abingdon Press, 1970), 294.

57 We discuss questions around gender and class briefly here. For a more detailed discussion on race in Bonhoeffer's work, see Williams, *Bonhoeffer's Black Jesus*; Andreas Pangritz, "Bonhoeffer and the Jews," in *The Oxford Handbook of Dietrich Bonhoeffer*, ed. Mawson and Ziegler, 91–107.

58 See for instance his comments on the respective roles of husband and wife in his sermon for the wedding of Eberhard Bethge and Renate Schleicher, in Bonhoeffer, *Letters and Papers from Prison*, 82–7.

59 See Jennifer McBride, "Bonhoeffer and Feminist Theologies," in *The Oxford Handbook of Dietrich Bonhoeffer*, ed. Mawson and Ziegler, 365–82, in which she discusses the work of Rachel Muers, Lisa Dahill, and Karen Guth.

60 See McBride, "Bonhoeffer and Feminist Theologies," 365. In this phrase McBride is drawing on both Harvey Cox, "Beyond Bonhoeffer: The Future of Religionless Christianity," in *The Secular City Debate*, ed. Daniel Callahan (New York: Macmillan, 1966), 205–14, and John W. de Gruchy, who draws on Cox's phrase expression

"beyond Bonhoeffer" and writes about working "beyond but with" Bonhoeffer, in "A Concrete Ethic of the Cross: Interpreting Bonhoeffer's Ethics in North America's Backyard," *Union Seminary Quarterly Review* 58, no. 1–2 (2004): 43–5.

61 See McBride, "Bonhoeffer and Feminist Theologies," 378–80.

62 See Bonhoeffer, *Fiction from Tegel Prison*, 84–6 for comments on class distinctions in Bonhoeffer's *Novel* that reflect the views of the Brake family, which can be taken to reflect those of the young Bonhoeffers.

63 See Bonhoeffer, *Fiction from Tegel Prison*, 101–8.

64 Bonhoeffer, *Letters and Papers from Prison*, 227.

65 For a summary of Bonhoeffer's influence on the struggle against apartheid in South Africa, as well as examples of his influence in other political contexts, see Christiane Tietz, *Theologian of Resistance: The Life and Thought of Dietrich Bonhoeffer*, trans. Victoria J. Barnett (Minneapolis, MN: Fortress Press, 2016), 116–17. For a more in-depth account of the relevance of Bonhoeffer's theology for the South African context, see John de Gruchy, *Bonhoeffer and South Africa: Theology in Dialogue* (Grand Rapids, MI: Eerdmans, 1984).

66 See Victoria Barnett, review of *Bonhoeffer: Pastor, Martyr, Prophet, Spy: A Righteous Gentile vs. the Third Reich* by Eric Metaxas, *Contemporary Church History Quarterly* 15, no. 3, (September 2010), https://contemporarychurchhistory.org/2010/09/review-of-eric-metaxas-bonhoeffer-pastor-martyr-prophet-spy-a-righteous-gentile-vs-the-third-reich/ (accessed 12 September 2023). Metaxas is also the coauthor of the three-volume children's book series *Donald Drains the Swamp*, *Donald Builds the Wall*, and *Donald and the Fake News*, in which Donald the Caveman protects his people against freedom-haters and swamp-creatures.

67 See for instance Clifford Green, "Hijacking Bonhoeffer," *The Christian Century*, 4 October 2010, https://www.christiancentury.org/reviews/2010-09/hijacking-bonhoeffer (accessed 12 September 2023), and Barnett, review of *Bonhoeffer: Pastor, Martyr, Prophet, Spy*.

68 Despite the publication of Bonhoeffer's *Ethik* in Germany in 1949 (appearing as *Ethics* in English in 1955), it was not until the publication in 1951 of some of his prison material in *Widerstand und Ergebung* (translated into English and published under the title *Letters and Papers from Prison* in 1954) that Bonhoeffer's theology received sustained attention in his home country.

69 See Keith W. Clements, "A Tale of Two Bonhoeffers? Ronald Gregor Smith, J. A. T. Robinson, and the Dissemination of Bonhoeffer in the English-Speaking World," in *Engaging Bonhoeffer: The Impact and Influence of Bonhoeffer's Life and Thought*, ed. Matthew Kirkpatrick (Minneapolis, MN: Fortress Press, 2016), 16.

70 Thomas J. J. Altizer and William Hamilton, *Radical Theology and the Death of God* (Middlesex: Penguin Books, 1968), 13. It should be noted that not all the authors usually associated with the Death of God movement wanted to be grouped together in this way, and neither did they all espouse the same viewpoint. For a more detailed discussion on Bonhoeffer and the death of God theologians, see Eleanor McLaughlin, "Bonhoeffer and the Death of God Theologians," in *Engaging Bonhoeffer*, ed. Kirkpatrick, 25–43.

71 See Bonhoeffer, *Letters and Papers from Prison*, 476, letter dated 16 July 1944.

72 Bonhoeffer, *Letters and Papers from Prison*, 482, letter dated 18 July 1944. Italics mine.

73 See Clifford Green, "Hijacking Bonhoeffer."

74 See Eric Metaxas, "Should Christians Vote for Trump? Trump's Behavior Is Odious, but Clinton Has a Deplorable Basketful of Deal Breakers," *Wall Street Journal*, 12 October 2016, https://www.wsj.com/articles/should-christians-vote-for-trump-1476294992 (accessed 12 September 2023). Seeking to allay the fears of Christians who were disgusted by Trump's outrageous misogyny, Metaxas writes "[t]he anti-Nazi martyr Dietrich Bonhoeffer also did things most Christians of his day were disgusted by," going on to speak of Bonhoeffer's participation in the Resistance plot to kill Hitler. See also Stephen R. Haynes, "Readings and Receptions," in *The Oxford Handbook of Dietrich Bonhoeffer*, ed. Mawson and Ziegler, 472–85, in which he quotes and comments on Metaxas' article.

75 Bonhoeffer, *Letters and Papers from Prison*, 479, letter dated 16 July 1944.

76 Notably in Bernd Wannenwetsch, ed., *Who Am I? Bonhoeffer's Theology through His Poetry* (London: T&T Clark, 2009).

77 See Lisa E. Dahill, "Rewilding Life Together: Bonhoeffer, Spirituality, and Interspecies Community," *Dialog: A Journal of Theology* 61, no. 2 (2022): 166–76.

78 See for instance Bonhoeffer, *Letters and Papers from Prison*, 110, letter dated 24 June 1943.

79 See Bonhoeffer, *Letters and Papers from Prison*, 390, in "Thoughts on the Day of Baptism of D. W. R., May 1944."

Recommended Reading

Primary

Bonhoeffer, Dietrich. *Act and Being*. Dietrich Bonhoeffer Works in English (DBWE) Vol. 2. Edited by Wayne Whitson Floyd, Jr. Translated by H. Martin Rumscheidt. Minneapolis, MN: Fortress Press, 1996.

———. *Berlin, 1932–1933*. DBWE Vol. 12. Edited by Larry L. Rasmussen. Translated by Isabel Best and David Higgins. Minneapolis, MN: Fortress Press, 2009.

———. *Creation and Fall: A Theological Exposition of Genesis 1–3*. DBWE Vol. 3. Edited by John W. de Gruchy. Translated by Douglas Stephen Bax. Minneapolis, MN: Augsburg Fortress, 1997.

———. *Discipleship*. DBWE Vol. 4. Edited by Geffrey B. Kelly and John D. Godsey. Translated by Barbara Green and Reinhard Krauss. Minneapolis, MN: Fortress Press, 2001.

———. *Ethics*. DBWE Vol. 6. Edited by Clifford J. Green. Translated by Reinhard Krauss, Charles C. West, and Douglas W. Stott. Minneapolis, MN: Fortress Press, 2005.

———. *Fiction from Tegel Prison*. DBWE Vol. 7. Edited by Clifford J. Green. Translated by Nancy Lukens. Minneapolis, MN: Fortress Press, 2010.

———. *Letters and Papers from Prison*. DBWE Vol. 8. Edited by John W. de Gruchy. Translated by Isabel Best, Lisa E. Dahill, Reinhard Krauss, and Nancy Lukens. Minneapolis, MN: Fortress Press, 2010.

———. *Life Together* and *Prayerbook of the Bible*. DBWE Vol. 5. Edited by Geffrey B. Kelly. Translated by Daniel W. Bloesch and James H. Burtness. Minneapolis, MN: Fortress Press, 2005.

———. *Sanctorum Communio*. DBWE Vol. 1. Edited by Clifford J. Green. Translated by Reinhard Krauss and Nancy Lukens. Minneapolis, MN: Fortress Press, 1998.

Secondary

Bethge, Eberhard. *Dietrich Bonhoeffer: Theologian, Christian, Man for His Times: A Biography*. Revised and edited by Victoria J. Barnett. Minneapolis, MN: Fortress Press, 2000.

de Gruchy, John W. *The Cambridge Companion to Dietrich Bonhoeffer*. Cambridge: Cambridge University Press, 1999.

Dumas, André. *Dietrich Bonhoeffer: Theologian of Reality.* Translated by Robert McAfee Brown. London: SCM Press, 1971.

Green, Clifford J. *Bonhoeffer: A Theology of Sociality.* Revised edition. Grand Rapids, MI: Eerdmans, 1999.

Mawson, Michael and Philip G. Zielger, eds. *Christ, Church and World: New Studies in Bonhoeffer's Theology and Ethics.* London: Bloomsbury T&T Clark: 2016.

———, eds. *The Oxford Handbook of Dietrich Bonhoeffer.* Oxford: Oxford University Press, 2019.

Schliesser, Christine. *Everyone Who Acts Responsibly Becomes Guilty: Bonhoeffer's Concept of Accepting Guilt.* Louisville, KY: Westminster John Knox, 2008.

Schlingensiepen, Ferdinand. *Dietrich Bonhoeffer, 1906–1945: Martyr, Thinker, Man of Resistance.* Translated by Isabel Best. New York: T&T Clark, 2010.

Wannenwestch, Bernd, ed. *Who Am I: Bonhoeffer's Theology through His Poetry.* London: T&T Clark, 2009.

Williams, Reggie L. *Bonhoeffer's Black Jesus: Harlem Renaissance Theology and an Ethic of Resistance.* Waco, TX: Baylor University Press, 2014.

South Asia

Felix Wilfred

Introduction

South Asia is increasingly drawing worldwide attention as one of the most fertile theological sites. Theologians of the region continue to discover innovative insights and orientations while being critical of theologies in terms of *systems*. There is a *fragmentary* sense to all kinds of South Asian theologies as they try to come to terms with ever new and challenging situations calling forth fresh faith responses.

It is well known that in modern times the discourse on history has occupied a prominent place in philosophical reflections and consequently in the development of theologies. We may recall here the irruption of historical consciousness in the West through the historical-critical method in biblical interpretation, and such theologically significant philosophical work as that of Heidegger's *Sein und Zeit*. If temporality has found a pride of place in this tradition, South Asian theologies, for their part, have tried to place the accent on the other dimension of human existence – *spatiality*, which is so very crucial to the approach to truth, and consequently, also to theology. Hence, South Asian theologies are contextual in spirit, nature, and orientation.[1]

Space or context can be described in various ways – most obviously, in terms of a specific culture, tradition, language, and so forth. This dimension has led South Asian theologies to engage themselves with the issue of so-called *inculturation*. However, context is also characterized by the dominant sociopolitical issues and concerns, all of which shape people's theological mood and orientation. Therefore, within South Asia in the last decades of the twentieth century and the first decades of the twenty-first century, a variety of contextual theologies have emerged; for example, *tribal theology* focusing on the issue of the indigenous peoples; and *Dalit theology* derived from a reinterpretation of the gospel through the experience of oppression by the outcastes of South Asia.[2] The concerns addressed by these various contextual theologies have contributed to shaping the theology of religions and to South Asian liberation theology, theology of mission, etc. In such theologies, the cultures and sociopolitical situation become new sources of theology and *loci theologici*.

Ford's The Modern Theologians: An Introduction to Christian Theology since 1918, Fourth Edition.
Edited by Rachel Muers and Ashley Cocksworth.
© 2024 John Wiley & Sons Ltd. Published 2024 by John Wiley & Sons Ltd.

Survey of Theology and South Asian Religious Traditions

South Asia is a region that shares a common Indic civilization and history. Indic is a civilization concept and not to be equated with the modern nation-state of India, which is one of its constituents, albeit a significant geographical portion of it. When considering theology in India and Nepal, it is crucial to understand Christianity's relationship to Hinduism, similarly in Sri Lanka to Buddhism, and in Pakistan and Bangladesh to Islam. Of course, there are many Hindus in Sri Lanka and Muslims in India, but I am referring here to the dominant religious traditions of the various countries. In the following paragraphs, I inquire into the dynamics of the theological development that results from an encounter with the different religious traditions.

Christian theology through classical Hinduism

Attempts were made to express Christian truths through Hindu categories and, later, to interpret Christian doctrines and practices through Hinduism. The Bengali convert Brahmabandhab Upadhyaya (1861–1907) initiated such an approach.[3] Later on, missionaries like Pierre Johanns (1882–1955) tried to carry forward the impulse of Upadhyaya through a series of writings known as "Christ through Vedanta." The Christian truths taken here for granted were those formulated in neoscholastic terms. The Protestant thinkers initiated a more thoroughgoing approach known as the "Rethinking Christianity in India group," consisting of Vengal Chakkarai, Pandipeddi Chenchiah, and Aiyadurai Jesudasen Appasamy, and others.[4] Thinkers like Raimon Panikkar and Stanley Samartha have carried forward the ideal of dialogue with Hinduism with greater theological depth and vigor in more recent times.

The relationship has also taken on a practical expression, inasmuch as attempts have been made to integrate Hindu symbolism and rituals in creating Christian *ashrams* according to Hindu patterns. The ideal of the *ashram* and the milieu it represents have given birth to a very refreshing kind of mystical and ethereal theology. We may recall here the initiative of the French missionary Jules Monchanin, who started an *ashram* on the banks of the Cauvery at the outskirts of the city of Tiruchirappalli in the southern Indian state of Tamilnadu. This tradition was continued by the mystic Abhishiktananda (Henri Le Saux) and Swami Dayananda (Bede Griffiths). The latter was an Anglican convert to Catholicism, who joined the Benedictines at Prinkash Abbey and then traveled to India and adopted the life of a *sannyasi* (Hindu renouncer) and mystic.[5] The writings of these and others like Vandana Mataji and Sara Grant, associated with Christian *ashrams*, remain an important source of South Asian theology.[6]

Theology and critique of Hinduism

Dalit Christians in South Asia have challenged the type of Christian theology that feeds on classical Hinduism. The oppression and caste discrimination they have undergone down the centuries have been, according to them, legitimized by Hinduism. How could they, then, find the Christian message of liberation in a theology couched in Hindu concepts and symbols? Further, the Dalits point out that Hinduism itself is a modern colonial construct and that it is made up of many divergent streams of South Asian religious traditions. In this sense, they claim to have their own subaltern religious traditions, which cannot and should not be equated with Hinduism. This kind of theological orientation is closely allied to the general political stance of the Dalits vis-à-vis Hinduism. The foremost political representative was the Dalit leader Bhimrao Ramji Ambedkar, who was also the chief architect of the Constitution of India. In more recent times, the political climate of India is configured by Hindu religious nationalism. Growing attacks on Christian churches and institutions have caused considerable alarm among Christian faithful and theologians who would not like to give up the path of dialogue despite many provocations from radical right nationalist groups. Hence, the Christian thinkers clearly distinguish in their dialogue with Hinduism between Hinduism as a religion and spiritual quest on the one hand and Hindutva as an ideology on the other, the latter fomenting enmity among various religious groups and causing violence, division, and social unrest. In short, the current situation has made dialogue with Hinduism more challenging.

Another group of theologians view with suspicion an uncritical *rapprochement* between Christianity and Hinduism that, they believe, is effected at the cost of the liberation of the poor and the oppressed and compromising justice and equality. This stream of thought is represented by theologians like Sebastian Kappen and Samuel Rayan, whose critique applies to Hinduism as much as to institutional Christianity when it comes to the issue of human liberation.[7] In this connection, it needs to be pointed out that an important source of theologizing in South Asia is the involvement of committed individual Christians and groups at the grassroots. The grassroots movements have provided ingenious theological insights stemming from the struggles of workers, daily laborers, fisherfolk, the tribals, the Dalits, exploited and trafficked women, and other marginalized people. They critically question Eurocentric theologies of the past and the present and dispute the adeptness of these theologies to respond to current South Asian issues. In the same vein, people at the grassroots bring church structures and institutions under critical scrutiny.

Theology in relation to Buddhism and Islam

Original insights and orientations are springing forth from various centers of study and dialogue. This is the case concerning the relationship of Christian theology to Buddhism. In Sri Lanka, we have many centers of Christian–Buddhist encounters, like the Study Centre for Religion and Society with its first director Lynn A. de Silva and the Tulana Research Centre directed by the well-known theologian Aloysius Pieris. Other centers try to combine a Christian–Buddhist interreligious approach with a liberational thrust.

For a long time, Buddhism was viewed by Christian missionaries as an atheistic system of philosophy, challenging Christian truths with its negative soteriology. Unfortunately, such views are persistent and have given rise to heated controversy, especially in Sri Lanka, when John Paul II repeated such remarks in his book *Crossing the Threshold of Hope*.[8] There have also been polemics between Christians and Buddhists as to which of the two founders was supreme. Nevertheless, the new development in the relationship is one of mutual discovery of the riches of each other's traditions. Furthermore, convulsions in society, especially the youth revolt of 1971 in Sri Lanka, have drawn together Christians and Buddhists in everyday dialogue with Marxists for the common cause of liberation.

In modern times, there has not been a sustained dialogue with Islam in India comparable to Hinduism. However, we need to single out the exceptional role played by the Henry Martin Institute, initially founded in Lahore (present-day Pakistan) in 1930 and now functioning in Hyderabad, India. Unmistakably, in Pakistan and Bangladesh, the dialogue with Islam has been an important source for developing contextual theologies.

In furthering Christian theology in the Muslim environment, we also need to highlight the contributions by Pakistani theologians like Louis Mascarenhas, Anwar M. Baskat, and Charles Amjad-Ali; centers like the Christian Study Centre in Rawalpindi and the Pastoral Institute in Multan; and journals like *Ali-Mushir* and *Focus*. Similar efforts could be identified in Bangladesh, which is predominantly Muslim, and where the situation is similar to that in Pakistan. In addition, Bangladeshi theologians bring to bear upon their work the long Bengali tradition of Hindu *Bhakti* or loving devotion to God. The dialogue with Islam is not only a matter of doctrinal tenets; it also has – as has become too evident in recent years – a great deal to do with the political climate. In this regard, it may be pointed out how Pakistani Christians stood together with their Muslim neighbors in opposing the US-led war on Iraq in 2003, and Christian leaders brought out a joint pastoral letter expressing their solidarity with Muslims.[9] Such concrete steps and decisions contribute to greater understanding and dialogue among Muslims and Christians.

Theology of Religions

At the beginning of the twentieth century, John Nicol Farquhar and others tried to overcome the (until then) prevailing negative attitudes toward other religions by proposing the theory of fulfilment. This theory recognized positive values in other religions; however, Christianity was the "crown" and fulfilment of them all.[10] This theology of religions continues to have numerous advocates. However, subsequent developments in South Asia have superseded such theories and have opened up new horizons. The experience of interacting and dialoguing with peoples of other faiths has led Christians to a deeper realization of quintessential truths for unity. These truths include recognizing one single universal plan of God for the entire humankind, transcending humanmade religious boundaries; the activity of the Spirit in the institutions, symbols, and expressions of other religions; and on the whole, a much broader understanding of the kingdom of God. These insights have brought about greater clarity in understanding and expressing the mystery of Christ, God, church, and the meaning of salvation.

Asian theologians, for example, believe that the mystery of Christ could be understood without the need to have recourse to such categories as uniqueness; nor would they think that the Chalcedonian formula best expresses the mystery of Christ. The ferment of new thinking in South Asia has found its way to global Christianity through the adoption – not without hesitation – of its positions in official documents, such as those of the Vatican and the World Council of Churches (WCC). It has also found its way to those Western theologians who have lived in or visited India, absorbed this theology, and presented it to the West in their writings, often couched in a Western liberal spirit and terms. Unfortunately, there is no acknowledgment of what they owe to South Asia in their theology of religions.

The theology of religions is an important site of Christological interpretation in South Asia. Contrary to the dominant trend of interpreting Jesus Christ concerning what distinguishes him from others and makes him unique, South Asians interpret Jesus with regard to what *relates* him to others. This is the crucial difference that shapes the nature and orientation of Christology, soteriology, and so forth. It is from this perspective that we understand the significance of a statement like "Jesus is the Christ; Christ is not Jesus only."[11]

Hardly would one find an earnest South Asian theologian espousing an exclusivist position. Nor do the pluralist positions developed by John Hick and Paul Knitter, for example, have many takers in South Asia. South Asian theologies of religions have developed by employing many subtle nuances that steer clear of being categorized as inclusivist or pluralist. This is done with the help of the philosophical category of "*advaita*" – nonduality. The mainline theologies of religions in South Asia are a negotiation between inclusivism and pluralism, to use the familiar typology. This kind of theology denies that all religions are ultimately the same. Nor does it maintain that Christianity alone has the ultimate truth of divine mystery without regard to the religious experience of divine mediations in other religious traditions and the working of the Spirit beyond the confines of the church and Christianity. Raimon Panikkar, Aloysius Pieris, Michael Amaladoss, and Jacques Dupuis could be considered representatives of a highly nuanced South Asian theology of religions.

Christ is not the monopoly of the Christian community, and hence it is not surprising to see that peoples of other faiths have interpreted Jesus through their own religious experiences and from their particular backgrounds. In South Asia, there is what could be described as the "Christology of non-Christians." We might recall here the interpretations and statements of significant figures like Ram Mohan Roy, Mahatma Gandhi, Vivekananda, and others.[12] The great Hindu mystic Ramakrishna Paramahamsa claimed to have had a mystical experience of Jesus Christ and the Virgin Mary. In the monastic order of Ramakrishna, founded by his disciple, Christmas is celebrated very solemnly and meaningfully every year. However, the approaches of neighbors of other faiths to Jesus Christ remains an untapped theological source in South Asia. Some attempts have been made by Madathilparampil Mammen Thomas and more recently by Rasiah Sugirtharajah to highlight the Christology of non-Christians.[13]

Understanding the Church – Casting the Net Wider

The understanding of the church in South Asian theology is not limited to Christian communities or issues like the local and universal church. Instead, the concern is for the *universal community*, which cannot be realized without forging relationships with the larger community of peoples of other faiths and ideologies. That tells the importance of forming truly "human communities" or "kingdom communities." If the understanding of salvation has often been conditioned by the category of causality and theory of satisfaction, South Asians think that salvation needs to be seen in terms of a call, relationship, freedom, and response.[14] It follows that salvation cannot be narrowed down and confined exclusively to any one particular religious tradition; all religions as collective entities could serve as vehicles and mediums of this relationship, and they do have a place in the universal plan of God's salvation.

In this context, a radical question has been raised about the participation in the religious rites of other traditions as well as the participation of peoples of other faiths in the sacramental celebration of the eucharist (*communicatio in sacris*) and reading of the scriptures of other religions in Christian worship. The question includes the issue of adopting religious rites of others in the case of mixed marriages. Such issues have immense practical implications. For, one does not understand the religious experience of one's neighbors unless he or she enters into the ritual world that the neighbors hold as most sacred. An entire research seminar was held on this issue in 1988 in Bangalore, India.[15]

> As a symbolic re-enactment of the primordial experience of believers in Jesus Christ, God and man, Sacraments can have an affinity with similar other symbols and rituals. This affinity makes Christian sacraments related to the symbolic structures of other religions. . . In specifically religious festivals, in which popular religiosity plays a major role, Christians may express their solidarity with their neighbours of other faiths, for example, by sharing the "*prasadam*" or contributing to the collections. As the deity is a manifestation of the divine Mystery, we may participate as Christians as long as our Christian identity is not jeopardised or compromised.[16]

The issue assumes great importance in the context of many people who believe and are committed to the Christian gospel, without, however, joining formally in the institution of the church because of the social and familial alienation it costs. Such believers without belonging to the church are characterized as "*Khrist Bhaktas.*" A legitimate question is whether the eucharist can precede baptism in such a case.

Reconceptualization of Mission

South Asian theology of religions is intertwined with new perspectives on mission. The situation of being a minority religious community and developments in the political, social, and cultural spheres in the region prompted Christians to rethink thoroughly the mission theology handed down from colonial times. A new look at mission and its approach was also necessitated because of growing opposition to Christian conversion from the States in India and right-wing religious nationalists. As a result, conversion has become a burning political issue all over South Asia.

Against this background, mission is no more viewed in terms of salvation or damnation. Modern South Asian theologies have brought about a radical change by their understanding of it as a matter of relationship and hence not in opposition to other religious traditions. It is in this context that we need to situate also the debates on the relationship between mission and dialogue. South Asian theologians have contended with the view of dialogue as an instrument of mission – a position that had gained widespread acceptance in many theological circles in the West. Instead, they have sought to clarify that dialogue and mission have their own distinct features and goals, and one should not be made subservient to the other. Even more, when dialogue is practiced, mission takes care of itself. Dialogue allows mission to happen by bearing witness to what one believes. Furthermore, it pays attention to mutuality and the agency of the partners involved.

At the bottom, the Asian approach to mission is inspired by the sense of the inscrutable divine mystery and the role of the subject in the mission. One does not view mission as a teleologically oriented project where people are viewed simply as objects of mission. On the contrary, people are subjects of mission. It is they who in freedom, appropriate faith, a process set within a definite social, political, and cultural setting of their history.

Further, Asian theological efforts increasingly evince an integral understanding of salvation and liberation – the objectives of mission. It means that salvation (*salus*) is the holistic well-being of persons without any dichotomy of body and soul; it is also the welfare of everyone without discrimination of caste, class, or religious belonging. To be on the way to salvation means progressive liberation from all that maims, corrodes, or negates life in any form. Integral salvation and liberation imply at the bottom that there are not two histories – one history of salvation and the other history of the world, moving on parallel lines. All peoples share a single history across borders and boundaries, testifying to the universality of God's grace and dealings. In fact, the realization of the presence of the Spirit in the tradition, cultures, and religions of neighbors of other faiths has prompted South Asian theologians to critically question classical missiology, its methods, and practice.

Moreover, South Asian theology of mission is infused with the positive affirmation of diversity, and the spirit of pluralism is understood as a value to be fostered and not a mere fact. Few continents have such diversity as Asia in its composition of peoples, cultures, traditions, and the variegated gifts of nature. The traditional recognition of pluralism and the value of a life of harmony resist trends of uniformity and homogenization. Overwhelming is the mystical feeling that all the differences and plurality we experience meet somewhere and are somehow interconnected, though we may not identify the bonds binding them together. Pluralism also derives from the fact that human beings are subjects, and their perception of reality and their judgments are shaped by these differing worldviews, experiences, diverse contexts, histories, etc. This realization has led South Asian theologies to view the diversity of perspectives as a significant enrichment to the life of faith.

South Asian Liberation Theology

To hold that liberation theology in Asia is an adoption of the Latin American variety would be grossly mistaken. The truth is that, even though the expression "liberation theology" was not used, it has been happening in South Asia since the last few decades of the twentieth century. The pioneers were people engaged at the grassroots, with workers' movements, student movements, etc. The number of liberating initiatives undertaken by Paul Casperz and Tissa Balasuriya of Sri Lanka would surprise those unfamiliar with non-Latin-American liberation theology. Michael Rodrigo of that country who was resolutely engaged in inter-religious initiatives for liberation suffered a martyr's death in 1987. South Asian liberation theology is the fruit of such struggles associated with social and political movements. On its part, it became an inspiring force for grassroots activism.

There are numerous examples in India too. Theologians like Sebastian Kappen, Samuel Rayan, Madathilparampil Mammen Thomas, and others derived their inspiration by responding to the people's struggles by reading the scriptures and interpreting them in context. It brought out also a fresh understanding of salvation and an exhilarating image of Jesus. Aloysius Pieris perceives in Jesus God's defensepact with the poor.[17] Instead of emphasizing those attributes and titles characterizing the divine nature of Jesus, these South Asian liberation theologians see the human dimension of the mystery of Jesus, his passion and death, and the hope he offers to the poorest of the poor. Simply reducing Jesus to his divine titles would make him but one more divinity in the Hindu pantheon, for example. The divine humanity of Jesus is what South Asia badly needs.

A distinguishing feature of South Asian liberation theology right from its inception has been the interlinking of liberation with the question of religion and culture[18] – something that the Latin American theology tried to do in the second phase of its development, with a focus on such themes as popular religion and culture.[19] Furthermore, South Asian theology had to face up to the issues of economy and religion and especially caste stratification. It is the Dalit people's encounter with manifold social oppression that led to a rereading of the gospel. As a result, Dalit Christians came to interpret the person and suffering of Jesus through the lens of their own experiences of oppression and marginalization.[20] Marxist tools of analysis could not do full justice to the situation, marked by caste oppression. Hence, South Asian theologies developed an analysis of society going deep into the caste structure and directing its critique against Brahminical hegemony.[21]

Developments in Dalit theology

It is a fact that about 70 percent of Christians in India and 90 percent in Pakistan are Dalits, treated and despised as outcastes and "untouchables." Similar is the situation in other South Asian countries. For example, in Bangladesh, the Dalits are known as "Rishis" and are marginalized and oppressed by mainstream society.[22] It is not surprising then that South Asian theology of liberation has developed its own distinctive branch of Dalit theology, which addresses, in the light of faith, the situation of oppression of the Dalits both inside and outside Christian communities.

In the early years of the emergence of Dalit theology in the 1980s, the theme of identity and the victimhood of Dalits were dominant. This theology tried to deconstruct history and create room for those erased from it. In this context, Dalit theology, like the secular Dalit movements, became highly critical of Brahminism as an ideology of oppression. Reading the Bible through the eyes of the oppressed Dalits has been a significant effort by Dalit theology. This theology proved to be a challenge to mainline South Asian theologies, which, in their efforts to enculturate faith, adopted elements from Brahminic Hinduism for theological concepts, worship, popular practices, etc. Dalit theologians are weary and highly critical of the dominance of Brahminic elements entering Christianity in the name of inculturation, which would mean an endorsement of a system that oppressed the Dalits for millennia.

> The demographic make-up of congregations has impacted their theology and practices in the form of a noticeable rejection of Brahmanic [sic] ideas and concepts in Hindi Christian speech and acts. Unlike many early Christian theologians writing in English who sought to find common ground between their own pre-Christian high-caste backgrounds and elite Hindu interlocutors, Hindi Christian authors rejected Brahmanical forms of Christianity in favour of speech and vocabulary that created conceptual distance from those forms of Christianity.[23]

Further, there is an attempt to recover the Dalit culture, tradition, and history and read through them the person and message of Jesus and his good news to the poor and the oppressed. In this context, there are efforts to focus on popular religions as practiced by the Dalits and tribals rather than on classical Hinduism or Buddhism.

If an earlier generation of Dalit theologians driven by identity politics emphasized the victimhood of the Dalits, a new generation of them speak of "Dalit rage" similar to "Black rage" and foreground the active agency of the Dalits in resisting the current system of oppression.[24] Moreover, Dalit theology has become internationalized in the past two decades and has allied itself with global emancipatory theological movements such as the ones against racism and subjugation of indigenous peoples. In this sense, Dalit theology has become conscious of its potential for mission and for the transformation of society, the world at large, and its contribution to bringing about justice, freedom, and equality. This theology, far from being simply reactionary to mainstream theology, has acquired its own distinctive features and contours and is contributing to reinvigorate Dalit movements.[25]

Theology of minorities

The authoritarian rule in most South Asian nations bolstered by religious nationalism has led to the harassment and oppression of the minority Christian communities. This is often done under the pretext that they are engaged in the work of conversion, or they have offended the majority religion, inviting such draconian laws as "blasphemy law" in Pakistan, for example. The rise of authoritarianism fueled by religious nationalism in South Asia has directed theological attention towards matters of human dignity and rights, placing the issue of minorities within this broader framework. Fundamental questions are raised on the substance and approach to Christian theology in a context where the Christians are an insignificant minority and are discriminated against and harassed. Attention is being paid simultaneously to ensure that the theology of minorities does not become sectarian, fostering withdrawal and isolation. Instead, it should serve as a springboard to pursue larger goals of equality and justice in society, even in conflicting situations.

Some South Asian Theologians

We now turn to some theologians from this region whose thought and method of theology reflect some of the significant South Asian concerns. Obviously, these thinkers do not exhaust the depth and breadth of South Asian theology.

Aloysius Pieris (b. 1932)

Pieris is a trailblazing theologian who draws upon many sources and weaves them into his theological tapestry. In particular, he harnesses his accomplished scholarship of Buddhism to Christian theological thought and interpretation. He proposes a theology of religions that distances itself from the oft-cited typology of exclusivism, inclusivism, and pluralism. His deep knowledge of Asian religious traditions, especially Buddhism, leads him to disengage from this kind of framework, and clamor for another paradigm, more consonant with Asian cultures and traditions. Nor does he advocate the kind of perfunctory comparisons that bring about little progress. Instead, he espouses a core-to-core dialogue among these religious traditions, a dialogue that will be mutually enriching. For example, he shows that, though Buddhism and Christianity give importance to wisdom and love, there is a penchant in Buddhism to highlight wisdom and in Christianity love.[26] The meeting of these idioms will bring out the best in both religious traditions and cause mutual transformation. Hence, Pieris argues for an inter-textual reading of scriptures that will go beyond cursory comparisons and lead the religious traditions to a symbiotic relationship. Pieris's reflections have found great resonance all over Asia, especially where Buddhism has been influential.

Pieris appeared on the international theological scene at the height of liberation theology in Latin America. He showed how that theology was still tied to the Western conceptual world and pointed out the necessity of bringing an intense conversation with the world of religions and cultures into the liberation agenda. This, for him, is crucial, especially in Asia, which, according to him, is characterized by its deep religiosity and abysmal poverty. His theological effort has been to relate these two poles and, in the process, to pave the way for an Asian paradigm of liberation theology.[27] In this paradigm, voluntary poverty, the protest against selfishness and greed advocated robustly by the Indic religious traditions, is pressed into the service of overcoming material poverty through liberative engagement. Thus, the spiritual struggle and the pledge to end material poverty meet and merge to become part of the same liberation agenda.

Raimon Panikkar (1918–2010)

This foundational thinker, who made a highly significant contribution to the theology of religion in the twentieth century, is at home both in the Indian Hindu classical tradition and Western Greek and Latin traditions. However, his Indian theological vision rests on certain philosophical premises. He is critical both of the *longue durée* cosmological worldview of the Indic tradition and the West's anthropocene worldview, bolstered by modern science and technology. While underlining the importance and pitfalls of both, he suggests an inspiring *cosmotheandric* vision of reality, which is holistic, comprising the cosmic, divine, and human dimensions. This holistic outlook also leads him to affirm the radical relativity or relational character of all reality, which is not the same as epistemological relativism.[28] This integral and relational reality expresses itself not simply through the instruments of *logos* and epistemology but more appropriately through *mythos* and the language of poesis.

This theoretical framework leads him to call for a cross-cultural enterprise, of which interreligious dialogue is an integral part. In this regard, his contribution has been remarkable. For Panikkar:

> the different religious traditions of humankind are like the almost infinite number of colours that appear once the divine, or simply the white light of reality, falls on the prism of human experience; it refracts into innumerable traditions, doctrines, and religious systems. Green is not yellow; Hinduism is not Buddhism, and yet at the fringe, one cannot know, except by postulating it artificially, where yellow ends and green begins.[29]

In the light of his cosmotheandric vision, Panikkar interprets the mystery of Christ as a point of convergence and unity of all reality, which is not exhausted in the historical Jesus. Out of his deep knowledge of Hinduism, Panikkar has also been able to produce a new perception and interpretation of the ineffable mystery of the Trinity.[30] No less significant have been his contributions to such current global issues as human rights, ecology, technology, peace, and "cultural disarmament," all of which proceed from his basic vision of reality.[31]

Madathilparampil Mammen Thomas (1916–96)

M. M. Thomas was a leading lay theologian whose influence stretched out all over the Asian continent, primarily through his association with the Christian Conference of Asia. He embodied ecumenism and was extraordinarily active at the WCC as the chairman of its Central Committee during some of the crucial years of its history (1968–75). He often disclaimed the title of "theologian" for himself. His bent of mind was to study the political and social processes taking place in Asia and bring the message of Christ meaningfully to bear upon them.[32] This led him to study the influence exerted by the person and message of Christ on some of the leaders and thinkers of the Indian Renaissance since the nineteenth century and to discover the meaning of Jesus Christ in relation to the secular ideologies of India.[33] His theology, in short, was concerned with Christian involvement in politics and, consequently, with political ethics from a Christian perspective. He expressed his views through the journal *Religion and Society* he launched and collaborated with the other great Protestant Indian theologian Paul Devanandan (1901–62).

In all his theological enterprises, Thomas remained Christ-centered in his approach, though it was perplexing for his friends and critics alike how he could reconcile his "rightist" Christology with his "leftist" social and political thought. He was moved and intellectually provoked by the unfolding of events in India and other parts of the world, to which he responded with great human and theological sensitivity.[34] His thrust and orientation were liberational, much before the advent of liberation theology. Yet, even in those difficult times when the fear of communism gripped the mainline churches, M. M. Thomas was drawn to the concern for justice and emancipation he found in socialist thought and practice. Toward the end of his life, he was appointed as governor of Nagaland, a state at the northeastern borders of India with a large majority of tribal Christians – a recognition of his lifelong concern with social and political issues.

Pandita Ramabai (1858–1922)

Ramabai was a woman theologian who anticipated the concern of present-day South Asian feminist theologians in their struggle against the patriarchy and oppressive traditions. She was born into an orthodox Brahmin family but rebelled against its conventions, learned Sanskrit (forbidden for women), and commenced her own independent spiritual and intellectual journey.[35]

Ramabai's journey led her to Christianity, which was, for her, not an end point. Though she converted to Christianity, she refused to conform to a Christianity cut out for her by missionaries and others but reinterpreted it in unconventional ways due to her continuous spiritual search. She was unsparing in her criticism of Christianity as she knew it from the Anglican tradition. Her devastating critique of church authorities and structures can be gleaned from her interaction and conflict with the community of sisters with whom she stayed in England for some time and from the correspondence with Sister Geraldine, her spiritual mother.[36]

Ramabai's theology was born out of her dedication to the cause of subjugated Indian women, whose plight she tried to improve through such acts as creating homes for young widows.[37] She also had a personal history of great suffering and pain and even tragedies: she lost her parents early in life, was widowed after a very short period of marriage, and saw her only daughter, Manoramabai, die on her lap. Ramabai may come across to many as defiant and freakish, but she paved the way for the future shape of Indian/South Asian feminist theology through her bold options. South Asian Christian women must respond to the double oppression legitimized both by the religious traditions of the region and by Christianity. The present generation of South Asian feminist theologians has a very inspiring forerunner in Pandita Ramabai.

Debates, Influence, Achievements, and Agenda

The preceding overview of South Asian theologies with representative figures is not complete without recalling here, even though briefly, the new frontiers being opened up, and areas of debates and further deepening. We are also led to consider the growing global influence of South Asian theologies and their agenda.

New frontiers

Feminist theology

First, there is an upsurge of feminist theology in South Asia, increasing its impact. As for gender equality, this region is characterized by blatant contradictions. Although there is a phenomenal rise in women's role in public life, economic production, and development, this is not matched by gender parity, exposing many deep-rooted contradictions. Caste is ubiquitous in South Asia, and women in the region must grapple with this source of their oppression. They feel twice alienated and oppressed through the interplay of caste and patriarchy, making their subjugation beyond compare. Fortunately, numerous women's movements in the region challenge the social evils and religious and cultural conditioning that subjugate women and rob them of their dignity and rights. South Asian feminist theology has closely associated itself with these movements and grassroots experiences to reflect on women's emancipation in the light of the gospel. This is accompanied by a fresh rereading and interpreting of the scriptures. South Asian feminist theologians address issues affecting women both in society and the church. A recent empirical study by Kochurani Abraham addresses the "persistent patriarchy" and unveils how Christian women in the state of Kerala come to terms with the intersectionality of caste, class, gender, culture, and religion through "negotiations and subversions" and how they claim active agency for themselves.[38] Through feminist theological associations and other bodies, women take up some of the crucial questions impinging upon their lives.

In recent times, feminist theology in the region has directed its attention to the various vulnerabilities of marginalized sections of the society. Thus, issues of migration/displacement, the intersectionality of sexual violence, gender, and caste – especially in the lives of Dalit women – the concerns of people who are lesbian, gay, bisexual, transgender, queer, questioning, intersex, asexual +, have figured prominently in their reflections. They have also addressed theologically the linkage between gender and ecology relating to ecofeminist spirituality. Feminist theologians have been at the forefront in challenging the clerical abuse in the church and calling church leaders to accountability. The theological voice of the South Asian feminists is growing louder and affecting the larger society, thanks to their transformative praxis. More recently, the concept of synodality has resonated strongly in Catholic feminist theological circles in the region, with a heightened reflection from women's perspective.

Theology and literature

Second, there is a growing realization that the new avenues of theology in South Asia could be opened and creativity fostered by relating theology to the abundance of literature in numerous literary works of rich South Asian languages. A most recent attempt has been by Freya Gupta, who interprets theologically the novel *Our Lady of Alice Bhatti* by Mohammed Hanif, which brings out the dilemmas and challenges Christians face in Pakistan.[39] Another recent dissertation has brought out the implicit theology in Christian Hindi literature.[40] Dalit literary output of the past decades, on its part, has helped give impetus to the Dalit movement of liberation in general. This has also influenced Dalit theologians who have begun to relate to both textual and oral traditions and narrations, including autobiographical ones, of the Dalit people.

Postcolonialism and theology

Third, postcolonial South Asian Theology is pursued mainly by South Asian diaspora theologians like Rasiah Sugirtharajah and Jude Lal Fernando – both from Sri Lanka. It attempts to deconstruct theology of the colonial and missionary era, whose objectives and concerns were conditioned by subjugation, and to rediscover Christian truth and life through a fresh reinterpretation from the life-stream of contemporary South Asia. To rediscover Jesus as Asian is, for example, one of the crucial concerns of postcolonial theology.[41] It goes beyond the project of what is termed as inculturation. Postcolonial South Asian theology is a creative enterprise that respects the subjecthood and agency of the people who try to appropriate Christian faith in their own world, freed from the baggage of an imported colonial model of Christianity and its theology.

Public theology

Fourth, theology has remained, by and large, within Christian communities lacking any impact on the life of the larger society. However, increasing interest in public theology has led to theological reflections starting from issues and questions that affect the people and their lives across religious and ideological boundaries.[42] If, in the past several decades, theology explored issues around culture, today it is seized by the political and public character of its engagement. In South Asia, the project of public theology has, obviously, an interreligious character. This theology helps the church step out and contribute, in collaboration with peoples of different convictions and ideologies, to the cause of common good. However, there lurks the danger that the common good could replace the engagement for justice, and the public identified with the bourgeois public. Aware of this danger, South Asian efforts at public theology focus on the invisible, marginalized, and subaltern public and the need for struggles to establish common good that ensures justice, especially for the subaltern public.[43]

Continuing debates

The dialectics of incarnation and prophecy

Since the context defines the specificity of Christianity and its contours in a particular region, there must be ever greater integration of Christian faith with the sociopolitical process of the locality. However, the question that may immediately be raised is to what extent can Christianity really integrate itself with the context. There is not only the principle of incarnation but also the challenge of prophecy. In fact, integration and immersion could turn out to be a compromise, something that reminds us of Richard Niebuhr's "Christ above Culture" paradigm.[44] Hence, one may argue for the need to stand above culture to raise the voice of prophecy. We face a dilemma, but not Hobson's choice. When Christianity stands above culture and fails to root itself in the soil, given the colonial history of many developing countries of the South, Christians will continue to be viewed and treated as aliens – "one more Christian, one less Chinese," as the axiom goes. On the other hand, if Christians exercise prophetic critique of culture, tradition, and the powers that be, without being rooted in the soil, their prophetic exercise will not have any cutting edge. The challenge is to bring into a dialectical relationship these two dimensions so that the prophetic derives from "rootedness," and rootedness is not at the expense of prophecy. Theology in South Asia and other parts of the Global South have the important task of maintaining this dialectic balance which may be called for at every step.

Church–society relationship

Over the centuries, the attitude of Christians to society and the political realm has conditioned theological orientations; and the converse is also true. However, the South Asian experience leads us to another set of problems and issues in this relationship. South Asian Christianity finds itself in a minority vis-à-vis other religious groups (Muslims in Pakistan and Bangladesh; Buddhists in Sri Lanka; Hindus in India and Nepal). Pakistan, for example, is officially an Islamic country, and the Christian community suffers double oppression of being a minority religious group and for belonging to the lowest caste group. We need only to recall here the protest suicide by Bishop John Joseph of Pakistan against the discriminatory laws in that country, particularly the laws regarding blasphemy.[45]

In this context, Western models such as pope and emperor, the two cities, sacred and secular, may not be able to come to terms with the novelty of the situation and its complexity. For example, the war on Iraq in 2003, interpreted as a "Christian" enterprise of the West reviving the discourse on crusade, led to the harassment and killing of Christians in Pakistan. Moreover, Christianity is so closely associated with the West that Pakistani and Bangladeshi Christians are targeted when a political clash between Western "Christian" countries and Middle East Islamic countries occurs. Further, there are the questions surrounding religious freedom. Although the possibility of conversion would be viewed as an integral part of religious freedom for many Westerners, many Hindus would seriously dispute it. For them, religious freedom would include professing one's faith and propagating it but not converting. One speaks of the right to defend one's faith against the onslaught of conversion. Against this background, theology needs to evolve new paths and paradigms in the relationship between the church and society.

Fundamental theology

Some of the questions and issues we have raised lead us to understand fundamental theology differently. Classical fundamental theology revolves around questions of faith and reason, but the experiences in South Asia show more and more clearly that it has to do with some crucial issues. Classical fundamental theology concerns itself with the *Praeambula fidei* which sets the stage for justifying doctrinal and theological content. What South Asian theologies seem to indicate is that the questions we need to be concerned about are not primarily the *first principles* of theology but rather *primordial features* of life. Even though theology is a *logos* – and hence there is the legitimate question of epistemology – it needs to touch upon the reality of life and serve its promotion and defense. Hence issues of food, water, shelter, equity, freedom, and solidarity become primary for theology in contexts like South Asia, where life is threatened by the denial of these basic human needs; God seems to be absent.

Paradigm shift: Theology of religions

Immersion in the South Asian situation and context tells us that the theology of religions cannot be divorced from the *realpolitik* in the relationship among the various religious groups.[46] Undoubtedly, there have been many efforts to develop a theology of religions in Christianity. However, much of this effort has been directed at waking Christianity from its dogmatic slumber and engaging Christians in a dialogue among themselves about how to come to terms with religious diversity.

The South Asian theology of religions calls for a shift toward the concrete reality of everyday relationships among religious groups and the sociopolitical processes in which these relationships are intertwined. Here is the starting point for a theology of religions through dialogue. Hence the *dialogue of everyday life*, respect, and openness to learning from each other becomes the beginning for a theology of religions – a different approach, indeed, from the attempt to derive a theology of religions from Christian revelation and faith. Once again, we realize how the theology of religions cannot be reduced to such models as exclusivism, inclusivism, and pluralism. Instead, South Asian theology leads us toward a theology of religions in constant dialogue with sociopolitical processes.

Conclusion

The theologies pursued in the South Asian region, in many respects, are little known in the West and the rest of the world. With its unique culture and history, this world is so unfamiliar that many do not dare enter this terrain. On the other hand, where it is known, it is often suspected and misunderstood, as the conflict of some of the South Asian theologians with the Vatican reveals. The general mood among South

Asian theologians is one of relative indifference to the image their theologies project. Instead, they seem to be gripped by the questions they must address – questions that do not have any precedents or models in Christian history to go by.[47] In their venture, they are less attracted by issues of orthodoxy and heterodoxy than by a sense of fidelity to the gospel and the truth as revealed through the realities of their context.

A sincere dialogue with South Asian theology by theologians worldwide is long overdue. Major shifts and new orientations are emerging, which have far-reaching consequences for the future of theology and Christianity as a whole. In these times of crisis of Christianity – in different continents, due to different factors – we need radically new interpretations of Christianity to shape its future course. South Asia, with its great civilizational heritage, may have much to offer for this global project. To reiterate what was mentioned in the introduction, I think that the most fundamental shift in South Asia is the one from temporality characterizing most forms of theology to *spatiality*. Any survey on South Asian theologies and their creativity would be best understood in the light of this radical change.

Notes

1   See Felix Wilfred, *On the Banks of Ganges: Doing Contextual Theology*, rev. ed. (Delhi: ISPCK, 2005).

2   A significant number of South Asian Christians are *Dalits* (formerly known as "Untouchables").

3   See Julius J. Lipner, *Brahmabandahab Upadhyay: The Life and Thought of a Revolutionary* (Delhi: Oxford University Press, 1999).

4   The nomenclature "Rethinking Christianity" derives from a book published under the same name just before the International Missionary Council, Tambaram (1938).

5   See Joshua B. Kulak, "The Strengths and Limitations of Bede Griffith's Christian *advaita* in Tamil Nadu," *Nidān: International Journal of Indian Studies* 4, no. 2 (2019): 43–60.

6   See Jules Monchanin, *Ermites du Saccidananda: Un essai d'integration chrétienne de la tradition monastique de l'Inde* (Tournai: Castermann, 1956); Abhishiktananda, *La Montée au fond du coeur: Le journal intime du moine chrétien-sannyasi hindou 1948–1973* (Paris: OEIL, 1986); Bede Griffiths, *The Cosmic Revelation: The Hindu Way to God* (Springfield, IL: Templegate, 1983); Bede Griffiths, *Return to the Centre* (Springfield, IL: Templegate, 1976).

7   See Sebastian Kappen, *Jesus and Cultural Revolution: An Asian Perspectives* (Bombay: BUILD, 1983).

8   John Paul II, *Crossing the Threshold of Hope* (New York: Alfred A. Knopf, 1994), 84–94.

9   The leaders noted: "As the calamity of war in Iraq looms on the horizon, we recognise that this war will have far-reaching and disastrous consequences for all our region. We share the concern of our Muslim brethren and all people of goodwill in expressing their total condemnation of this pre-emptive strike." See *Lahore Link News Letter* (Lahore Archdiocese, January/February 2003), no. 37.

10 J. N. Farquhar, *The Crown of Hinduism* (Oxford: Oxford University Press, 1913).

11 Raimon Panikkar, "Man and Religion: A Dialogue with Panikkar," *Jeevadhara* 11 (1981): 25; Raimon Panikkar, *Christophany: The Fullness of Man* (Maryknoll, NY: Orbis, 2004), 57–8.

12 Rasiah Sugirtharajah, *Jesus in Asia* (Cambridge, MA: Harvard University Press, 2018).

13 M. M. Thomas, *The Acknowledged Christ of Indian Renaissance* (Madras: CLS, 1970). Sugirtharajah, *Jesus in Asia*; *The Brahmin and His Bible: Rammohun Roy's Precepts of Jesus 200 Years On* (London: Bloomsbury T&T Clark, 2021).

14 See Michael Amaladoss, "The Multi-Religious Experience and Indian Theology," paper presented at the Indian Theological Association meeting held in Bangalore, 24–29 April 2003.

15 The papers and the proceedings of the seminar are published by Paul Puthanangady, *Sharing Worship: Communicatio in Sacris* (Bangalore: NBCLC, 1988).

16 Final Statement of the seminar, in Paul Puthanangady, *Sharing Worship*, 793, 796.

17 Aloysius Pieris, *God's Reign for God's Poor: A Return to the Jesus Formula* (Kelanya: Tulana Centre, 1999).

18 See Ignatius Jesudasan, *A Gandhian Theology of Liberation* (Anand: Gujarat Sahitya Prakash, 1987).

19 See Juan Carlos Scannone, *Weisheit und Befreiung. Volkstheologie in Lateinamerika* (Düsseldorf: Patmos Verlag, 1992).

20 See A. Maria Arul Raja, "Dalit Encounter with their Sufferings: An Emancipatory Interpretation of Mark 15:1–47 from a Dalit Perspective" (PhD diss., University of Madras, 2000); Antony John Baptist, *Together as Sisters: Hagar and Dalit Women* (Delhi: ISPCK, 2012).

21 See James Massey, ed., *Indigenous People: Dalits. Dalit Issues in Today's Theological Debate* (Delhi: ISPCK,

1998); Arvind Nirmal, ed., *A Reader in Dalit Theology* (Madras: Department of Dalit Theology, Gurukul, n.d.); Paul Puthanangady, ed., *Towards an Indian Theology of Liberation* (Bangalore: NBCLC, 1986).

22 See Cosimo Zene, *The Rishi of Bangladesh: A History of Christian Dialogues* (London: Routledge, 2002).

23 Rakesh Peter Das, "Language and Religion in Modern India: The Vernacular Literature of Hindi Christians" (PhD diss., Harvard University, 2016), 225.

24 Samuel Joshua, "Raging for Liberative Reconciliation: Prophetic Anger in Dalit and Black Theologies," *International Journal of Asian Christianity* 4, no. 2 (2021): 209–22.

25 See Sathiananthan Clarke et al., eds., *Dalit Theology in the Twenty-First Century: Discordant Voices, Discerning Pathways* (Delhi: Oxford University Press, 2010).

26 See Aloysius Pieris, *Love Meets Wisdom: A Christian Experience of Buddhism* (Maryknoll, NY: Orbis, 1988).

27 Aloysius Pieris, *An Asian Theology of Liberation* (Maryknoll, NY: Orbis, 1988).

28 Raimon Panikkar, *The Cosmotheandric Experience: Emerging Religious Consciousness* (Maryknoll, NY: Orbis, 1993).

29 Raimon Panikkar, *The Intrareligious Dialogue* (New York: Paulist Press, 1978).

30 Raimon Panikkar, *The Trinity and the Religious Experience of Man: Icon – Person – Mystery* (Maryknoll, NY: Orbis, 1973).

31 Raimon Panikkar, *Cultural Disarmament: The Way to Peace* (Philadelphia, PA: John Knox Press, 1995).

32 M. M. Thomas, *The Secular Ideologies of India and the Secular Meaning of Christ* (Madras: CLS, 1976).

33 M. M. Thomas, *The Acknowledged Christ of Indian Renaissance* (Madras: CLS, 1970).

34 See Samuel Rayan, "M. M. Thomas – Response-ability," in *Christian Witness in Society: A Tribute to M. M. Thomas*, ed. K. C. Abraham (Bangalore: BTESSC, 1998).

35 See Uma Chakravarti, *Rewriting History: The Life and Times of Pandita Ramabai* (Delhi: Kali for Women, 1998); Gauri Viswanathan, *Outside the Fold: Conversion, Modernity, and Belief* (Princeton, NJ: Princeton University Press, 1998), 118–52.

36 See A. B. Shah, ed., *The Letters and Correspondence of Pandita Ramabai – Compiled by Sister Geraldine*

(Bombay: Maharashtra State Board for Literature and Culture, 1977).

37 See Meera Kosambi, "Women, Emancipation, and Equality: Pandita Ramabai's Contribution to Women's Cause," *Economic and Political Weekly* (29 October 1988): 38–49.

38 Kochurani Abraham, *Persisting Patriarchy: Intersectionalities, Negotiations, Subversions* (London: Palgrave Macmillan, 2019).

39 Freya Gupta, "Social Justice through Fiction: Intersectionality of Religion, Caste, and Gender in Mohammed Hanif's Our Lady of Alice Bhatti," *International Journal of Asian Christianity* 4, no. 2 (2021): 223–35.

40 See Das, "Language and Religion in Modern India."

41 Sugirtharajah, *Jesus in Asia.*

42 Felix Wilfred, *Asian Public Theology* (Delhi: ISPCK, 2010); Felix Wilfred, ed., *Theology to Go Public* (Delhi: ISPCK, 2013); Felix Wilfred, "Asian Christianity and Public Life – The Interplay," in *The Oxford Handbook of Christianity in Asia*, ed. Felix Wilfred (New York: Oxford University Press, 2014), 558–74; Gnana Patrick, *Public Theology: Indian Concerns, Perspectives, and Themes* (Minneapolis, MN: Fortress Press, 2020).

43 See Rajbharat Patta, "Towards a Subaltern Public Theology for India" (PhD diss., University of Manchester, 2018).

44 Richard Niebuhr, *Christ and Culture* (San Francisco, CA: Harper Collins, 2001).

45 See Linda S. Walbridge, *The Christians of Pakistan: The Passion of Bishop John Joseph* (London: Routledge 2003); Anwar M. Barkat, "Church–State Relationships in an Ideological Islamic State," *Ecumenical Review* 29, no. 1 (1977): 39–51.

46 For example, the relationship between Muslims and Christians in any particular country in the West has much to do with the state's policy on immigration, asylum, and so on. See David Singh, "Adaptation and Change among Asian Muslims Immigrants in the West," *International Journal of Asian Christianity* 5, no. 1 (2022): 45–68.

47 Felix Wilfred, *Asian Dreams and Christian Hope*, 2nd ed. (Delhi: ISPCK, 2003).

Recommended Reading

Amaladoss, Michael et al., eds. *Theologizing in India.* Bangalore: Theological Publications in India, 1981.

Amjad-Ali, Christine, ed. *Developing Christian Theology in the Context of Islam.* Rawalpindi: Christian Study Centre, 1996.

Boyd, Robin. *An Introduction to Indian Christian Theology.* Delhi: ISPCK, 2000.

Clarke, Sathiananthan et al., eds. *Dalit Theology in the Twenty-first Century.* Delhi: Oxford University Press, 2010.

England, John C. et al., eds. *Asian Christian Theologies: A Research Guide to Authors, Movements, Sources*. Vol. 1. Maryknoll, NY: Orbis, 2002.

Dasgupta, Freya. "Social Justice through Fiction: Intersectionality of Religion, Caste, and Gender in Mohammed Hanif's *Our Lady of Alice Bhati.*" *International Journal of Asian Christianity* 4, no. 2 (2021): 223–35.

McCahill, Bob. *Dialogue of Life: A Christian Among Allah's Poor*. Maryknoll, NY: Orbis, 1996.

Thomas, Madathilparampil Mammen. *The Acknowledged Christ of Indian Renaissance*. London: SCM Press, 1969.

Walbridge, Linda S. *The Christians of Pakistan: The Passion of Bishop John Joseph*. London: Routledge, 2003.

Wilfred, Felix. *Beyond Settled Foundations: The Journey of Indian Theology*. Madras: University of Madras, 1993.

———. *On the Banks of Ganges: Doing Contextual Theology*. Delhi: ISPCK, 2002.

Korea

Sung Bihn Yim

Introduction

Theology is a critical reflection on our lives in the light of the Bible, traditions, and experiences. From this perspective we can understand Christian theology in Korea as critical theological reflections on Korean lives. Thus, no one theology can be defined as "the Korean theology." A study of Christian theology in Korea should take diverse historical contexts and themes, and theological reflections, into consideration inclusively.

Survey

Korean reformed theology

Reformed theology in Korea reflects theological trends from conservative, to moderate, and on to progressive through four Presbyterian denominations and their seminaries. The Presbyterian Church in Korea (hereinafter referred to as KPC) and the General Assembly of Presbyterian Church in Korea (hereinafter GAPCK) represent Conservative Reformed theology. The Presbyterian Church in the Republic of Korea (hereafter PROK) leads liberal theology, including Minjung theology (theology for the people). The Presbyterian Church of Korea (PCK)'s moderate position is to integrate Reformed theology and ecumenical theology together.[1] The early Presbyterian faith introduced to Korea was a conservative, evangelical Christian faith. Pyongyang Theological Seminary, led by missionary Samuel H. Moffett, became the center for nurturing conservative theology and played a significant role in the formation of Korean conservatism. At the same time, and as a unique characteristic of early Korean Presbyterianism, Reformed Dogmatic thought and Pietistic Revivalism were introduced together and were both accepted.[2] The early missionaries who came to Korea were generally considered to draw upon Reformed theology oriented toward moderate and conservative Calvinism, but they were additionally influenced by Old-Princeton theology centered on the Westminster Confession of Faith and Pietistic Revivalism.[3] This conservative Reformed theology

Ford's The Modern Theologians: An Introduction to Christian Theology since 1918, Fourth Edition.
Edited by Rachel Muers and Ashley Cocksworth.
© 2024 John Wiley & Sons Ltd. Published 2024 by John Wiley & Sons Ltd.

contributed to the formation of religious identity and church and to the fulfillment of the church's social responsibility in the face of the national crisis caused by the Japanese imperialist invasion. Unfortunately, it had disappointing results in coping with the tasks of later times, including the division of North and South Korea, the establishment of democratic society, and subsequent developments.

The acceptance of Reformed theology was not restricted to the conservative perspective in Korea. There are noteworthy claims that the liberal tendency emerged during the early days of missionary work in 1889 and has continued to develop since around 1925.[4] Liberal theology developed into the theology of social engagement and of culture. In the 1930s, under the severe challenge of "modernism" or "neoevangelicalism," the Calvinistic Reformed tradition and theology of the early Korean church faced criticism that they were losing their identity between the perfunctory conservative theology and epistemological neo-orthodoxy. Jae-Joon Kim and Nak-Joon Baek criticized Pyongyang Presbyterian theological education.[5] Although the radicality of the liberal Reformed theology came to be in the vanguard of social engagement and democratizing procedure, its lack of fluency in communication with congregations served as a limitation in the ministerial field. In addition, the active political involvement resulted in selective support from church leaders for the progressive regime (and associated vested interests), with participation in public service and even in cabinets. This phenomenon has led to difficulties in maintaining a position of prophetic criticism.

The fatal pain of the Korean church, particularly the Reformed church, is schism, the division of churches. Religious sociologist Won Gyoo Lee has argued that "the conservative religious nature of Korean church contributed to growth, but on the other hand, it produced social problems such as unilateralism, authoritarianism, zero-tolerance, exclusivity, prejudice and discrimination, and formed an antisocial, ahistorical view of the world by paying more account to individual redemption, resulting in a hindrance to ecumenical movement by encouraging individual churchism."[6] However, rather than focusing on the pain of schism, it may be better to focus on the theological legacy of "establishing a united church." In this regard, Kyung Bae Min has applauded the sermon of Samuel Moffett, who was the first president of Pyongyang Theological Seminary, arguing that Moffett's consciousness of the organic unity of the church is no different from the original mainstream of the Great Awakening.[7] The early Presbyterian missionaries with serious interest in cooperation and union unanimously agreed to establish a single "Chosun Christian Church" in Korea at a conference of Presbyterian and Methodist missionaries in 1905. The purpose of establishing the "Korea Evangelical Missionary Council" was to "cooperate in missionary work and ultimately establish an indigenous evangelical church in Korea."[8] Presbyterian University and Theological Seminary (PUTS, the former Pyongyang Theological Seminary) followed this tradition in their development of theology within the Presbyterian Church of Korea. PUTS made it clear through the "2015 Theological Statement" that they are oriented toward ecumenical theology based on biblical and evangelical theology, which is the orthodoxy of the Reformed church.

Korean contextual theology

As noted earlier, Korean theologians have begun appreciating that theology is inextricably related to its context. Striving for an intrinsic understanding of Korean Christianity, from the 1960s onwards, various types of Korean contextual theology have emerged as follows: Korean theology of culture, Minjung theology, and Korean Pentecostal theology. Since the 1960s, theologians who have studied overseas have posed a new challenge to the Korean theological community when they return home. The setting for the emergence of Korean indigenous theology is the worldwide rise of ethnic nationalism, accompanied by the promotion of national consciousness. In addition, there is one more key reason – the awareness that the Christian faith remained in a "formal ritualization" after 1945, during the period of liberation from Japanese imperialism, due to the high reliance on a foreign missionary education system and the Western way of understanding the gospel. The fact that "rediscovery of Korea," "Korean things," and "Korean studies" were of great interest in Korean humanities academia at that time is also noteworthy. Against this backdrop,

Tong-Shik Ryu published a paper on indigenization in October 1962, challenged by the lecture, "Study of Bible and Indigenization Issues," by D. T. Niles, district evangelist of the Methodist Church of Ceylon in India, in August 1962.[9] The key argument of cultural indigenization theology is as follows: specific procla-mation of the transcendent gospel and the declaration of the gospel of the church is bound to be made through the cultural medium of time and space. The missionary work of the church that proclaims the gospel is essentially indigenous. This is because the gospel revealed through Jesus Christ refers to the exist-ence of God in this time and space, that is, the incarnation of God who is transcendent.[10]

In the 1970s, South Korea was in a turbulent political and economic situation. With economic growth and the flow of social reformation symbolized by a struggle for democracy, the church and the theological world also attempted to present a responsible answer. In the 1960s, the theological world of Korea was interested in indigenous theology as a cultural theological response from the perspective of ethnicity and subjectivity. In the 1970s, Minjung theology emerged as a theological response from a political and eco-nomic perspective.

Minjung is a Korean word, but it is a combination of two Chinese characters *min* (民) and *jung* (衆). *Min* can be translated as "people" and *jung* as "the mass." Thus, Minjung means "the mass of the people," or mass, or just the people.[11] The development of Minjung theology itself was accompanied by self-criticism of excessive academic and intellectual characteristics. In addition, Minjung theology is similar to the libera-tion theology of South America, in its relation to human rights and justice movements at the political, economic, and social level. However, Minjung theologians argued for differentiation in that the roots of their theology are based on Korean national history.[12]

In the 1970s, Korea's desire for democratization was rising along with rapid economic development. At the same time, tensions and threats caused by the division of the two Koreas created a growing sense of social crisis, which increased due to communist rule in Vietnam. In the crisis of loss of self-identity experi-enced by many people who migrated from agricultural areas, and the crisis caused by the weakening or destruction of traditional family and local communities, urban churches had a remarkable opportunity for growth as alternative communities. A representative example of this was Full Gospel Central Church, estab-lished by Reverend Yonggi Cho. Cho's experience of recovery from disease, and the vision of Jesus seen during the three days of fasting after his condition deteriorated, have eventually become the core of Full Gospel faith. Full Gospel faith has gained popularity and interest, particularly the idea that cure from dis-ease and wealth as a divine blessing accompany salvation through the Spirit.[13]

Korean feminist theology

Korean feminist theology was established in the context of independence movements in developing coun-tries, the 1968 revolution, the American Civil Rights movement, and the Korean democratization move-ment. We can distinguish two main types of feminist theology in Korea.[14] First, from the perspective of Korean feminist theology for bringing together Christianity, nationality, and gender, the core problem in Korea is the "division situation," so Korean theology should wrestle with the separation of North Korea and South Korea. *Minjung* (the people) is a concept that includes the concept of the nation that was embedded in the human rights concerns held by Minjung theologians in the 1970s. In that sense, the most oppressed women among the Minjung are closely linked to national issues, because class emancipation and women's emancipation cannot occur without resolving national contradictions in relation to the hegem-onic structures of the United States and Japan.[15] Therefore, when considering nation, Minjung, and women, nation takes precedence. From this point of view, the subject of Korean feminist theology is the Korean people, and the core problem of the Korean people is the division issue. Further, they argue that Korean feminist theology should be kept separate from other Korean theologies because "[feminist] theology serves as a guard that prevents theology from turning into a male-dominant ideology."[16]

Second, the intersectional approach to gender, Christianity, and nationality uses the lenses of ethnicity and religion to develop Korean feminist theology. For them, feminist theology should contribute to achieving women's equality in both theology and the church. For this task, Korean feminist theology should avoid romanticizing and idealizing Korean traditional religion and culture in the process of finding alternatives to Western women's theology. They argue that the sexism hidden in Korea's traditional religion and culture should not be overlooked. Korean feminist theology should also pay attention to the multiplicity of women's experiences. For example, the suffering of Jesus and the suffering of Korean women should not be regarded as the same, without gender analysis, as the former was voluntary and the latter compulsory. Therefore, the suffering of Asian women must be overcome and eliminated, unlike the suffering of Jesus.[17]

Unification theology

The loss of sovereignty due to Japanese imperialism from 1910 to 1945 had great significance in Korean social history. After the defeat of Japan, Korea achieved liberation, but soon the division between South and North Korea was created, followed by a fierce war (the Korean War) that lasted from 1950 to 1953. Since then, the armistice on the Korean Peninsula that has continued until today has led to reflection on the important theological themes of peace and the unification of South and North Korea. Minjung-centered unification theology underscores the subjectivity of the Minjung (the people) in the process of unification. It argues that the cause of the national division lies not in the Minjung but in those who hold political power. Therefore, the way to overcome the division and move toward unification inevitably involves correcting the divisive and antiunification judgments and actions of those in authority who long for power. The Minjung who are the subject of unification are not the proletariat, and unification by the Minjung should not be equated with the realization of a world of equality through the universal domination of the proletariat. Minjung theology claims that the theoretical and practical justification of the dictatorship of the proletariat is nothing more than the deception of a specific intellectual group that wants to occupy a dominant position. Due to this, it favors Minjung-oriented Christianity over Minjung-oriented communism. It bases this on Jesus Christ's command to preferentially love the socially disadvantaged, who are the Minjung. It argues that the Minjung orientation of the communists should be replaced by genuine love for the poor as the priority in loving one's neighbor.

Another type of unification theology is argued from an indigenization-centered theological perspective.[18] It applies the motifs of indigenization theology to the issue of unification and theology. The division of Korea reinforced dichotomous separatist thought and practice, such as the division between an ally and an enemy and good and evil in society. This unification theology notes that the political authorities attempted to fix the division by using factors of separation, including region and class, to maintain their power. It argues that this separatist, dichotomous structure and consciousness must be overcome and suggests that the well-integrated structure and spirit within *Shintobuli* (身土不二) theology can make a meaningful contribution. Thus, the priority task of indigenization-centered unification theology is to recover national homogeneity and secure cultural identity, along with implementing "the system of empirical awareness of the nation that arose from the climate of Korea, that is, the inseparable coexistence of life that is embodied in the life of the nation."[19]

There is also a theology of unification representing the form of unification most typically supported by Korean Protestant churches. This takes "Christian state building" while maintaining an anticommunist stance as the critical goal, and holds a negative view of the North Korean regime.[20] Its thoughts on the unification plan reflect a change in emphasis from the "rebuilding the North Korean church" of the 1950s, "promoting North Korean liberalization" of the 1960s and 1970s, and "renewing Korean society and the church" of the 1980s. The methodology has moved from "North Korea reception" theory to "North Korea collapse" theory, and since the end of 1980, the churches have promoted the theory of national reunification followed by national evangelization.[21]

Key Figures

Reformed theologians: Hyung-Ryong Park and others

Hyung-Ryong Park represented the conservative Reformed theology of the early Korean church. He believed that the Bible is the inspired Word of God, and he taught it as the infallible rule of faith and practice. Park held to a theological tradition that was Calvinist and continental European Reformed, laced with Anglo-American Puritanism, such as is reflected in the Westminster Standards. Park claimed to be an orthodox Calvinist and a positive fundamental theologian who opposed the World Council of Churches and protected the fundamental truth of Christianity.[22] The origin of liberal Reformed theology in Korea, which contrasts in nature, content, and orientation from conservative Reformed theology and churches, can be found in Jae-Joon Kim.[23] Under Kim's leadership, the PROK adopted new "Faith Declarations" in 1972. The basis of Jae-Joon Kim's theology of political involvement was Calvin's doctrine of Jesus Christ's sovereignty. Maintaining this focus, Kim's political theology advanced the progressive theological line of engagement with historical reality and enabled political speech and witness along with resistance to the most practical dynamics of political power and distorted use of power. Noting this context, Jong Sung Lee (former dean of PUTS and moderator of PCK) has argued that it was those who led conservative Reformed theology that failed to inherit this spirit of union and rather provided the basis for the division of churches. For example, Hyung-Ryong Park designated Jae-Joon Kim as a neotheologian in the division of the PROK and the PCK in 1953. Park was also blamed as the main cause of the division of the PCK and GAPCK in 1959.[24] Criticizing Park's theology as fundamentalist, Jong-Sung Lee has pursued Reformed theology beyond the limits of fundamentalist theology.

Korean contextual theologians: Tong-shik Ryu and others

In general, cultural theologians who contend for indigenization have underscored the religious perspective along with the subjective perspective of Korea. They have intentionally tried to use the symbolic systems within Korean philosophy, culture, religious traditions, and so on. The characteristics of Tong-Shik Ryu's Pung-Ryu theology are as follows:

1 The Word and the gospel of God are transcendent, so there needs to be a process for understanding and subjective interpretation.
2 The perspective for understanding and interpreting the gospel may differ depending on the historical events and cultures of each ethnic group. At this time, the perspective for interpreting and understanding the gospel is a cultural perspective, and this is the unique spirituality of the people that is rooted in each nation and culture.
3 Because the work of understanding and interpreting the gospel is undertaken by a theologian with a specific identity and spirituality, the gospel and cultural spirituality have an analytical recursive relation.

Adopting this approach, Tong-Shik Ryu defined Pung-Ryu Do as the most fundamental spirituality of Korea, and the basic idea of modern Korean consciousness and culture. He took Pung-Ryu Do to include the educational dimension of Confucianism, Buddhism, and Taoism, which makes humans human beings, and integrated it into his theology.[25]

Sung-Bum Yoon stressed the need to be freed from the Babylonian captivity of Western theology. He stated that the purpose of Korean style theology is "to revive our traditions again by adding Western theological traditions to the Korean cultural and spiritual traditions."[26] Yoon, from this theological point of view, attempted to actively interpret the Dan-gun myth, which corresponds to the birth myth of Korea.[27]

He sought a triune analogy for the divine beings in the Dan-gun myth, and eventually made the argument that "The Dan-gun Myth is 'Vestigium Trinitatis'." Moreover, regarding the blending between Confucianism and Christianity, Yoon attempted to interpret and to make theological use of *Sung* (誠), a core concept of Confucianism.[28] Sung-Bum Yoon emphasized the "independence" of the gospel and insisted that only an independent Korean church and Christians could accept the gospel.[29] On the other hand, Tong-Shik Ryu stressed that the gospel and Korean culture should encounter each other as subject to subject.[30]

The Minjung theologian Nam-Dong Suh claims that Minjung theology is a movement already embedded in the history of the Korean church, ever since its birth as a progressive, millenarian, active Christianity – so there needs to be a Minjung-centered approach to church history. Suh argued that Minjung theology emphasizes the historicity and practicality of theology. Furthermore, Suh emphasized the "theology of testimony" based on the theory of practice's superiority – giving priority to the Minjung's experiences, events, and interpretation of the situation. In conclusion, he emphasized that Minjung theology is a "theology of Minjung's advocacy" that represents Minjung. For Byung-Mu Ahn, another well-known Minjung theologian, the concept of Minjung is undefinable. It is a holistic, dynamic, and changing reality, one that escapes categorization. Once it is subjected to definition, it becomes the victim of ideology and the object of speculation. It is, therefore, unwise to define it. However, for the ease of communicating a general understanding of Minjung, the term commonly refers to those who are politically oppressed, economically exploited, and socioculturally alienated in our day-to-day life. Putting the primary emphasis on the theme of "humanization" beyond nationalism,[31] Byung-Mu Ahn suggested the concept of "people as Minjung."

Pentecostal theologian: Yonggi Cho

The Full Gospel faith of Yonggi Cho has some conservative evangelical characteristics.[32] Cho stresses Pentecostalism and Charismatism. Alongside the emphasis on the four traits of Pentecost (regeneration, divine healing, baptism with the Holy Spirit, and sanctification), glossolalia (gift of tongues) is valued as the evidence of baptism with the Holy Spirit, and divine healing and prayer response as evidence of the Holy Spirit. At the same time, Cho advocated the prosperity gospel or successism, which was inspired by Norman Vincent Peale's and Robert Schuller's positive thinking. Full salvation means health without diseases, and affluence, along with redemption of the soul from sin. The selective affinity with Shamanism, which is Cho's cultural background, is a key factor in his theology. In fact, the beginning of Cho's life as a minister quite closely resembled that of shamans – suffering from illness and then recovering after accepting gods. In addition, the emphasis on direct revelation, prophecy, vision, and illumination through the "fourth dimension" is similar to shamanism. His claim to gain advantage from the "fourth dimension" by talking about the formula of prayer is also analogous to the shamans' rituals of controlling, coaxing, and soothing the spirits. However, this criticism may in fact apply to many Korean churches. It is possible to claim that the emphasis on vigil prayer, concerted prayer with intense emotions, prayer house and mountaintop prayer, benediction, blessings of wealth, and divine healing is also relevant to shamanic elements.[33] Along with shamanism, what attracts attention in Cho's theology is the conflation of Full Gospel faith and Confucianism. Yonggi Cho caused a significant conflict with the conservative Reformed churches while preaching on 30 November 1979 by affirming the ancestral rites and insisting it was not idolatry but courtesy to one's late parents. He argued that one could perform rites for one's deceased parents, as one had prepared a meal for one's parents and bowed to them with courtesy in their lifetime. To some extent, Yonggi Cho's theology can be seen as the expression of the Pentecostal style of indigenization theology. Cho's approach to indigenization is, in typical Pentecostal fashion, experiential. Cho has brought the indigenization issue forward through his experiences of shamanism and filial piety as lived out within the church. The theology of Cho is a clear indication that the earlier issues of Christ and culture are still very much alive in the Korean church.

Feminist theologians: Soon-Kyung Park and others

Representative figures of first-generation Korean feminist theologians are Soon-Kyung Park of the Korean Methodist Church, Woo-Jeong Lee of PROK, and Sun-Ae Joo of PCK. I describe Park's work to introduce the characteristics of Korean feminist theology because she developed her own unique theories of feminism in the context of Korea and has published a number of works on the topic. Her study abroad in the United States, Switzerland, and Germany, and her praxis of doing and teaching theology in Korea, seem to have led to her desire to construct a Korean feminist theology. Park asserts that the European theological tradition requires a "critical reinterpretation."[34] She argues that Korean theology has contributed to the revival of the notion of truth, which has been marginalized in Western theology's postmodern critical reinterpretation.

Soon-Kyung Park's Korean feminist theology focuses on the nation of Korea rather than on women. For Park, the theme of woman belongs under the theme of nation. Feminist theologians might view this as a disappointing approach. However, Park's feminist theology differs from Western feminist theology because her theological work prioritizes the context of Korea at the time when the tragedy of the national division into South Korea and North Korea was the fundamental source of all contradictions. Park's theological methodology is distinctive. Drawing on Barth's theology, she denies the experience-centered method, the theological method that began with Schleiermacher. She argues that women's emancipation should seek "liberation within historical conditions" rather than women escaping into their own world by focusing solely on women's experiences.[35]

Making a good contrast with Park, Nam-Soon Kang was greatly influenced by Western frameworks such as postmodernism, poststructuralism, and postcolonialism. She uses these theories to reflect critically on the modern era, which presupposes a firm foundation for the self, reason, language, and divine revelation. She argues that dismantling this modern foundation can bring about the liberation of women and the natural world, which have been subjugated by modern subjects, primarily men.[36] Kang calls herself a "humanist feminist" rather than a "gynocentric feminist." Feminist theology, in this view, is not a theory and practice that women practice in their own interest but a new paradigm.[37] She notes that "awareness of sexism serves as a window for me that enables me to look at the human reality and the world with new eyes."[38]

Unification theologians: Ik-hwan Mun and others

Ik-hwan Mun claims that it is possible to transcend ideological differences with communism, including North Korean communism, and enter into a way of cooperation and coexistence. He suggests that Korean churches should strengthen their faith in the reconciliation accomplished by Jesus Christ and practice dialogue and coexistence.[39] Mun's unification theology underscores the need to achieve reunification by reconciliation between compatriots in South and North Korea. As early as October 1972, when anticommunist ideology was prevalent in South Korea, he proposed unification theology in an article titled "South–North Unification and the Korean Church." Mun argued that unification theology should move toward a theology of reconciliation, and he highlighted the spirit of reconciliation and peace that is the "heart of love" that he discovered in prison and realized through Jesus Christ. Furthermore, his love for life was based on his love for nature and for human life. Above all else, his theology reflected his passionate love for the Minjung.

Jeong-bae Yi proposed his own type of unification theology by participating in the discourse of unification theology centered on Minjung theology and Korean theology of culture from the indigenization-centered theological perspective.[40] Yi supports the unity of these two approaches, while arguing that Minjung theology and national theology have resulted in a separatist structure that excludes spatiality by focusing exclusively on temporality or historicity in understanding human existence. Arguing for the integration of time and space as well as the need to take a unified approach that considers the two as a whole (or integrative), Yi proposes an indigenous type of Unification theology.

In my own work, I have explored the theological and ethical role of Korean Church in unification. In "The Churches' Role in the Unification of the People: Focusing on a Cultural Integration of South and North Korea," I address the need for "unification of the people" as a cultural and psychological unification beyond "unification of the land" as a political, economic, and military unification.[41] After exploring the North Korean worldview and culture centered on the "Juche idea (self-reliance ideology)" and the South Korean worldview and culture centered on "postmodernism and the capitalist consumer culture," I propose that the church has a role in cultural integration based upon the common good including human dignity, justification of love, and life-centered ecology.[42]

Debate, Achievement, and Agendas

Reformed theology in Korea

As shown in the example of conservative Reformed theology, a specific interpretation of the Calvinist perspective instilled a kind of "biblicism" in Korean Reformed theology. In fact, the linguistic inspiration and inerrancy of sacred scripture are the two pillars of the "biblical" framework that includes both Calvinist orthodoxy and orthodox Reformism. There is, however, an analogy between the view of the Bible in Korean Christianity and that of scripture in Neo-Confucianism. In this regard, it is possible to argue for the selective affinity between the Reformed tradition in Korea and the Korean culture represented by Confucianism and Taoism.[43] Arguably, the Korean church followed a Confucian pattern in its cultural aspect, and a Taoist pattern in its practical aspect.[44]

In spite of historical controversies around Calvin's theology in Korea, it played a major role in the church-centered faith of Presbyterianism and the revival of the church. It is noteworthy that Reformed theology has produced outstanding church leaders in the field of pastoral theology such as Sun Ju Gil, Ik Du Kim, and Kyung Chik Han. In addition, Chi Yil Pang, the last overseas missionary to China, served in China even after the Chinese Communist Party took power, and was one of the fruits of the mission field.[45] Reformed churches in Korea, however, are confronted by internal and external crisis. At the root of the crisis lies privatized spirituality and individual churchism. The cultural perception of the Korean church must be converted into an ethical spirituality based on community and daily life rather than an individualistic and superficial spirituality. Calvin's spirit of the Reformation demands that the Reformed church should pursue communal spirituality and play a public role in civil society. The prior task of Korean Reformed theology is strengthening and embodying the public theological nature of reformed theology through rediscovery and evaluation of Calvin's common good.[46]

The complex impact of Calvinism in the economic realm is worth pointing out; historically, many Korean Christian leaders equated Calvinism with capitalism.[47] Today, given the prevalence of globalization and neoliberalism, finding the way of coexistence and coprosperity in consideration of the poor, and finding the third way that reveals the spirit of community emphasized by Calvin and the early Calvinists, deserves deep consideration.[48]

Korean contextual theology

Korean Indigenous theologians argued for the legitimacy of the indigenization of the gospel in other cultures by distinguishing the essential gospel itself from the nonessential cultural form. From this point of view, they reflected on Korean missionary work over the seventy years preceding 1963 and pointed out the phenomenon of "mixture" with traditional religion as the cause of both the success and failure of Korean missionary work. The pursuit of indigenization theology of first-generation theologians represented by Tong-Shik Ryu and Sung-Bum Yoon provided an opportunity to develop into the religious pluralistic Christian theology of Kwang-Shik Kim and Sung-Hwan Byun and into the second generation of political and economic indigenization theology (Minjung theology). Tong-Shik Ryu has replied to the criticism that the first generation of cultural indigenization theology was indifferent to political and economic situations as follows. "Politics and economy are also culture, but eventually religion is the substance. Thus, religious theology should focus on the religion itself ... Although it is criticized for having no political and economic nature, politicality and sociality can be one phenomenon that stands above it. Theology concerns the substance, not the peripheral adaptation."[49] However, there have been very serious criticisms of this type of indigenization theology. Postindigenization theologians like Sun-Hwan Byun criticized Ryu and Yoon's deviation into exclusivism, related to their development of theology from the positions of Bultmann and Barth. In other words, the first generation of indigenization theologians still had a dialectical dimension and advocated "Bible-centered biblical realism." In the end, the postindigenization stance is bound to radical theological thoughts like religious pluralism, stating, "Jesus Christ is to Christians what Buddha is to Buddhists."[50] It is a perennial agenda for Korean theology to make a balance between theological identity and cultural relevance.

The focus of theological interest of early Minjung theologians was the relationship between the people of the nation and Minjung, and the understanding of God as the subject of mission work. History is a place of divine and human activities, a place where God's salvation is revealed, and this history should be a place of liberation for the people of the nation and for the Minjung. At the same time, what these theologians paid attention to from the perspective of *missio dei* was the situation of dehumanization, especially due to political oppression for economic development. For them, "humanization" was a core existential and theological theme.[51] In the name of nationalism, the people who were always marginalized, exploited, and burdened with the suffering of the nation were not the whole nation, but just Minjung. Minjung theology argued that the object of Christ's salvation is the people of the nation, and that Minjung, the center of the people, should be the specific object of salvation.[52]

However, as Korea's political and economic situation changed rapidly in the twenty-first century, Minjung theology's interest in identity and subjectivity in globalization and postmodern situations became more complex. Theologians of the second and third generations of Minjung theology are now facing their task of solidifying their biblical and theological foundations and securing a relationship with the church. In addition, they are facing difficult challenges of identifying the reality of the "multiple Minjung" emerging in the context of the twenty-first century, and acting in solidarity with them.[53]

Pentecostal theology

Full Gospel faith and theology have had a tremendous impact on Korean church. Representative examples include district gatherings, cell gatherings, afternoon praise services, divine healing, benediction, the emphasis on glossolalia, prayer and fasting, and the prayer house movement. In addition, the Full Gospel movement has made a substantial contribution by providing a theological basis for conducting education and social welfare projects, without distinguishing between spiritual salvation and physical salvation and blessings. However, it is a fatal vulnerability of this movement to be indifferent to social structural evil and to weaken *theologia crucis*, the theology of the cross. In the final analysis, the Full Gospel faith emphasizes the subjectivism, individual salvation and positivity thinking, putting more weight on the individual than on society and espousing "social nominalism." Moreover, faith conflated with positivity thinking in the context of "successism" has tended to lean toward support for corrupt traditional culture and political dictators. The emphasis on positivity thinking was in line with the government-led economic development trend, creating collusion between religion and political leadership. It also was reluctant to participate in social reformation movements and became aligned with political conservatism and anticommunism. In the end, it is not easy to avoid the criticism that Full Gospel theology has contributed to justifying anti-intellectual religious sentiment.

Korean feminist theology

Criticizing the patriarchy, anthropocentrism, and individualism of the Korean church as well as modern Western Christianity, Korean feminist theology seeks to find alternatives in the Indigenous religion and culture of Korea, as well as in Western philosophies such as postmodernism, postcolonialism, and feminism. Feminist theologians try to empathize with the reality of the lives of women in various sectors of society, especially in the most oppressive conservative churches, and lead the way as theoreticians and practitioners of women's liberation. However, one of the agendas that Korean feminist theology has been wrestling with for a long time is that Korean women in the church do not actually support the "feminist" approach. It is true that lay Korean women Christians who uphold mostly the evangelical faith have been reluctant to embrace feminist theology. It is a challenging task for Korean feminist theology to become a field of scholarship in which all women in the church can participate. In order for feminist theology to appeal to women in the Korean church, it may be important to do more than be critical. Some evangelical feminist theologians suggest including recognition of women who adapt to and develop their own capabilities within the church and the family. This, however, may not serve well as an alternative for present and future generations, as the model of the male as the sole wage earner is being challenged due to neoliberalism and the growing number of women in the workforce. It seems that one of the agendas for Korean feminist theology is to suggest a more inclusive model of society for human beings, both men and women, beyond criticizing the status quo.

Unification theology

Minjung-centered unification theology can contribute to the development of unification theology on the issues of recognition and reinforcement of the Minjung's identity in the journey of unification, the establishment of the identity of unification theology as a theology of peace, and the connection with democratization and human rights movements. From a practical point of view, these points are noteworthy because the unification movement is making an effort to shift from being government-centered to people-centered, to expand the establishment of peace on the Korean Peninsula in the context of world peace, and to strengthen mutual exchanges in various fields beyond the military-political approach. It cannot be denied that the nation-centered and indigenization-centered unification theologies are weak in quantitative terms compared to Minjung-centered unification theology. However, these two approaches have deepened the discourse on unification theology. Nation-centered unification theology has expanded the discussion by supporting the union of Minjung-centered and nation-centered unification theologies and linking the agenda of unification with the theme of liberation and transformation of the world and nation. Furthermore, indigenization-centered unification theology attempts a kind of synthesis while critically examining the unification theology of the Minjung-centered and nation-centered approaches. By pointing out that the latter two unification theologies have methodologies and beliefs biased toward temporality (or historicity) under the influence of Western theology, indigenization-centered unification theology emphasizes the need to accept and integrate the principle of integrating temporality and spatiality within unification theology. Church-centered unification theology is the main link between unification and North Korean missions, avoiding an exclusively political approach to unification while taking a critical approach to the communist ideology and system. While taking a cautious stance on the discussion of unification among liberal Christians, the hope is to contribute to the discourse on unification in Korean Christianity through dialogue and communication. In particular, the church-centered approach is helpful in that it is aiming for the unification of people beyond the unification of the land, intends to expand the discourse on unification theoretically and practically, and is producing meaningful research and practical results.

All of these approaches of unification theology should participate in the unification discourse to make up for the weaknesses of each approach and to strengthen each theology through face-to-face dialogue and other exchanges. In addition, it is important to seek a common ground for participating in the unification movement. Efforts should also be made to expand the horizon of unification theology through continuous exchanges and communications with society and with academicians in fields beyond the church and theology.

Conclusion

Putting the Bible and historical context as the crucial poles of their hermeneutics, Korean theologians have reached out to have conversations with others such as Confucianism, Buddhism, Taoism, and shamanism. They have also wrestled with contextual issues such as democratic movements, feminism, and unification. In the twenty-first century, they are facing new agendas such as climate change, digital technology, and post/trans human issues. These agendas are not limited to Korea alone but are global; we need more ecumenical communication and solidarity for the safety and the peace of our *oikumene*. Thus, Korean theologians needs to broaden their context beyond Korean culture and geography. Moreover, while doing theology in the ecumenical context, additional tasks for Korean theology would be to do theological reflection on the K-Culture (such as BTS, "Squid Game," and the Parasites) and on the issues of peacemaking among Korea (South and North)-Japan-China-Taiwan. These theological reflections would generate some insights for global as well as regional peace, and for mutual understanding via cultural media between the East and the West, the developed and the developing countries, and the South and the North.

Notes

1　Sung Bihn Yim et al., "Reformed Theology in Asia and Oceania," in *The Cambridge Companion to Reformed Theology*, ed. Paul T. Nimmo and David A. S. Ferguson (Cambridge: Cambridge University Press, 2016), 301–2.

2　In 1893–1901, among forty Presbyterian Church (USA) missionaries, sixteen were from Princeton, and eleven were from McCormick. Korean church theology was indebted to revivalism with doctrinal reformist elements until the 1920s due to the influence of missionaries who were directly or indirectly influenced by the Great Revival Movement of the State.

3　Jae Juh Seo, "Theological Character and Significance of the Early Korean Church from the Perspective of Reformed Theology," *Journal for the Society of Reformed Theology* 12 (2012): 141–3.

4　Harvie M. Comm, "Studies in the Theology," *Westminster Theological Journal* 29, no. 1 (1967): 138.

5　Seo, "Theological Character," 154.

6　Kwang Mook Kim, "John Calvin's Ecumenical Theology and a Theological Perspective on Ecumenical Movements in Korean Church: Focusing on Korean Presbyterian Church," *Korean Journal of Systematic Theology* 52 (2018): 7–48.

7　Kyoung-Bae Min, *Korean Christian Church History* (Seoul: Yonsei University Press, 1994), 285.

8　Myung Hyuk Kim, "The Theology of World Reformed Church and Korean Presbyterian Church," *Hapshin Theological Journal* 13, no. 2 (1995): 380–429.

9　Jae Yong Joo, *The History of Korean Christian Theology* (Seoul: Christian Literature Society of Korea, 1998), 223–4.

10　Joo, *The History of Korean Christian Theology*, 225–6.

11　Kim Yong Bock, ed., *Minjung Theology: People as the Subjects of History* (Singapore: CTC-CCA Publications, 1981), 16.

12　Kim, *Minjung Theology*, 312.

13　Daniel J. Adams, *Korean Theology in Historical Perspective* (Delhi: ISPCK, 2012), 143.

14　This part is heavily indebted to the suggestion of the feminist theologian Yu-jin Choi. She argues for four types of theological arguments representing Korean feminist theologies. Besides the types presented here, there are more. One is the model of "The Interweaving of Gender, Nationality, and Religion" argued by Eun-Sun Lee. The other is "The Gender Negotiation Model" by Jung-Sook Lee.

15 Soon-Kyung Park, *The Future of Unification Theology* (Paju: Four Seasons, 1997), 272.

16 Soon-Kyung Park, "The Significance and Task of Salvation History in Korean Theology and Korea Women's Theology," in *10 Years of Korean Women's Theology*, ed. Korean Association of Women Theology (Seoul: Woosinsa, 1990), 51–2.

17 Nam-Soon Kang, "Confucian Familism and Its Social/Religious Embodiment in Christianity: Reconsidering the Family Discourse from a Feminists Perspective," *Asia Journal of Theology* 18, no.1 (2004): 362.

18 Jeong-bae Yi, "Minjung Theology and Minjok (nation) Theology Seen in Terms of Indigenization Theology 1: Centering on Issues of Unification and Environment," *Christian Thought* 38 (1994): 90–107.

19 Yi, "Minjung Theology," 116.

20 Seonghan Jeong, "A Study on the Consciousness of 'Peaceful Reunification' of Korean Christians," *Theology and Ministry* 19 (2003): 103–35.

21 Jeong, "A Study on the Consciousness of 'Peaceful Reunification' of Korean Christians," 131.

22 Yohahn Suh, "The Tradition of Reformed Theology and the Presbyterian Church in Korea," *Presbyterian Theological Quarterly* 78 no. 1 (2011): 111–45.

23 Jae-Joon Kim, *Jae-Joon Kim's Collection*, Vol. 1 (Seoul: Hanshin University Press, 1992), 161; Kim Kyoung Jae, "Jang-gong Kim Jae-Jun's Political Theology: Its Theological Principles and Theory of Social and Political Transformation," in *Korean Protestantism and Its Social and Cultural Changes in Modern and Contemporary Korea* (Seoul: Institute of Theological Studies in Academy of Hanshin University, 2000), 279.

24 Myung Yong Kim, "Yesterday and Today of Korean Systematic Theology," *Korean Journal of Christian Studies* 52, no. 1 (2007): 113–37.

25 Berthold Laufer, "Burkhan," *Journal of American Oriental Society* 36 (1916): 390–5, Tong-Shik Ryu recited in *A Journey to Pyung-Ryu Theology* (Seoul: JunMangSa, 1988), 42. The lexicon Pyung-Ryu originated from Puru, which means fire, brightness, light, unity, heaven. Also, Puru was the name of Dan-gun's son.

26 Sung-Bum Yoon, *Korean Theology: The Hermeneutics of Sung* (Seoul: Seoul Culture Company, 1972), 12.

27 Sung-Bum Yoon, "The World-Historical Feature of the Concept of God," *The Realm of Ideas* (1963): 260.

28 Sung-Bum Yoon, *Korean Theology*, 13–16.

29 Sung-Bum Yoon, *Christianity and Korean Thoughts* (Seoul: Korean Christianity Press, 1964), 25–30.

30 Tong-Shik Ryu, *A Journey to Pyung-Ryu Theology*, 215.

31 Joo, *The History of Korean Christian Theology*, 310.

32 Joo, *The History of Korean Christian Theology*, 145.

33 Joo, *The History of Korean Christian Theology*, 152.

34 Soon-Kyung Park, *Korean Nationality and the Tasks of Women's Theology* (Seoul: Christian Literature Society of Korea, 1983), 9.

35 This sentence describes Soon-Kyung Park's critique of Sun-hwa Seon's thesis, "Feminine Theological Illumination of the Goddess Statue in Korean Folk Beliefs" as expressed by Ae-young Kim, "Evaluation and Prospect of Korean Women's Theology in the 1980s – Commemorating the 10th Anniversary of the Founding of the Korean Council of Theologians," in *10 Years of Korean Women's Theology*, ed. Korean Association of Women Theology (Seoul: Woosinsa, 1990), 33.

36 Nam-Soon Kang, "Feminist Theology in the 21st Century: A Critical Study on the Epistemological Horizons and Issues of Feminist Theology, and Its Reflective Tasks," *Theological Thought* 115 (2001): 159–60.

37 Nam-Soon Kang, *Gender and Religion: Religions Reconstruction through Feminism* (Paju: Dongnyok, 2018), 43.

38 Nam-Soon Kang, *Feminism and Christianity* (Seoul: Christian Literature Society of Korea, 1998), 7.

39 Ik-hwan Mun, "South–North Unification and the Korean Church," *Christian Thought* 16 (1972): 50–7.

40 Yi, "Minjung Theology."

41 Sung Bihn Yim, "The Churches' Role for Unification of People: Focusing on Cultural Integration of South and North Koreas," in *Integrative Unification and the Task of Christians II* (Seoul: Yeyeong, 2003), 197–236.

42 Yim, "Churches' Role for Unification of People," 235–6.

43 Sung Bihn Yim et al., "Reformed Theology in Asia and Oceania," 296–9.

44 For example, it is the analogy of "*Pietas et Scientia*" emphasized in the Calvinist tradition and "Geogyeonggungri" (거경궁리, 居敬窮理), which is the basic method of academic cultivation in Neo-Confucianism.

45 Sung Bihn Yim et al., "Reformed Theology in Asia and Oceania," 302.

46 Yong Won Song, "'Economic Democratization' from the Perspective of Calvin's Reformed Theology," *Korea Presbyterian Journal of Theology* 52, no. 1 (2020): 93–121.

47 Ulrich H. J. Körtner, "Calvinism and Capitalism," in *John Calvin's Impact on Church and Society: 1509–2009*, ed. Martin Ernst Hirzel and Martin Sallmann (Grand Rapids, MI: Eermands, 2009), 171.

48 Gon-Taik Park, "Reflective Calvinism," *Presbyterian Theological Quarterly* (2012): 92–119.

49 Tong-Shik Ryu et al., "Special Discussion: Evaluation and Prospects of the Korean Indigenization Theology Controversy," *Christian Thought* 35, no. 6 (1991): 98–9.

50   Kwang Shik Kim, *Indigenization and Hermeneutics: For the Encounter of Indigenization Theology and Theology of Conversation* (Seoul: Korean Christianity Press, 1987), 158.

51   Joo, *The History of Korean Christian Theology*, 310.

52   Joo, *The History of Korean Christian Theology*, 346.

53   Yong Bock Kim, "An Asian Proposal for the Future Directions of Theological Curricula in the Context of Globalization," in *Charting the Future of Theology and Theological Education in Asian Contexts*, ed. David Kwang-sun Suh et al. (Hong Kong: ISPCK, 2004), 249.

Recommended Reading

Primary

Ahn Byeong-mu. *With the People in Front of History*. Seoul: Hangilsa, 1986.

Kang Nam-Soon. *Feminism and Christianity*. Seoul: Christian Literature Society of Korea, 1998.

Kim Jae-Joon. *Jae-Joon Kim's Collection*. Vol. 1. Seoul: Hanshin University Press, 1992.

Park Soon-Kyung, *The Future of Unification Theology*. Paju: Four Seasons, 1997.

Ryu Tong-Shik. *A Journey to Pyung-Ryu Theology*. Seoul: JunMangSa. 1988.

Suh Nam Dong. *Minjung Sinhak-ui Tamgu [In Search of Minjung Theology]*. Seoul: Hangilsa, 1983.

Yim Sung Bihn. "Churches' Role for Unification of People: Focusing on Cultural Integration of South and North Koreas." *Integrative Unification and the Task of Christians II*. Seoul: Yeyeong, 2003.

Yoon Sung-Bum. *Korean Theology: The Hermeneutics of Sung*. Seoul: Seoul Culture Company, 1972.

Secondary

Adams, Daniel J. *Korean Theology in Historical Perspective*. Delhi: ISPCK, 2012.

Nimmo, Paul T., and David A. S. Ferguson, eds. *The Cambridge Companion to Reformed Theology*. Cambridge: Cambridge University Press, 2016.

Suh, David Kwang-sun et al., eds. *Charting the Future of Theology and Theological Education in Asian Contexts*. Hong Kong: ISPCK, 2004.

Joo Jae Yong. *Hankuk Grisdokyo Shinhaksa [The History of Korean Christian Theology]*. Seoul: Daehankidokkyoserhye, 1998.

Kim Kwang Shik. *Indigenization and Hermeneutics: For the Encounter of Indigenization Theology and Theology of Conversation*. Seoul: Korean Christianity Press, 1987.

Kim Kyung Jae. *Hermeneutics and Religious Theology: Encounter of the Gospel and Korean Religions*. Seoul: Korean Theology Research Institute, 1994.

Min Kyoung-Bae. *Korean Christian Church History*. Seoul: Yonsei University Press, 1994.

Oak Sung-Deuk. *The Making of Korean Christianity: Protestant Encounters with Korean Religions 1876–1915*. Waco, TX: Baylor University Press, 2013.

China

Alexander Chow

Introduction

The date 4 May 1919 was a watershed moment for modern China and modern Chinese theology. At the end of World War I, Allied forces decided to give German-occupied lands in China not back to China, which fought with the Allies as a fledgling republic (est. 1912), but to Japan. In what became known as the May Fourth movement, students and intellectuals took to the streets of Beijing and rallied for Western modern ideals of "Mr Science" (*Sai Xiansheng*) and "Mr Democracy" (*De Xiansheng*). The collapse of the Qing dynasty (1644–1912) marked the end of two millennia of Confucian dominance as state orthodoxy and "feudal" rule; but reformers blamed China's continued failings on a prevailing feudal mindset and sought to modernize the country.

The foreign imperial legacy of Christianity – caused by the nineteenth century Opium Wars (1839–42 and 1856–60) and unequal treaties – and the intellectual ferment of May Fourth have left indelible marks on modern Chinese theology. Questions around the role Christians can play in nation-building and in modernizing China were accentuated through the course of the Chinese civil war (1927–37 and 1945–9) and the Second Sino-Japanese War (1937–45). Under the new People's Republic (est. 1949), Chinese Christians were faced with a new dilemma and were called upon to demonstrate their patriotism. But by the time of the Cultural Revolution (1966–76), all public religious worship came to an end.

Deng Xiaoping's reform and opening up era in the late-1970s allowed the Protestant Three-Self Patriotic Movement (TSPM, est. 1954) and the Catholic Patriotic Association (CPA, est. 1957) to be reestablished as the main means for registration of Christian activities,[1] while communities that remained unregistered were described as Protestant "house churches" (*jiating jiaohui*) or Catholic "underground churches" (*dixia jiaohui*). Furthermore, since the 1980s, China has witnessed a "Christianity fever" (*Jidujiao re*) – a rapid growth initially in rural villages, before eventually spreading to urban centers.

Modern Chinese theology has thus navigated a tumultuous century by addressing existential and social questions around Christianity's foreignness and its relevance within Chinese society.

Ford's The Modern Theologians: An Introduction to Christian Theology since 1918, Fourth Edition.
Edited by Rachel Muers and Ashley Cocksworth.
© 2024 John Wiley & Sons Ltd. Published 2024 by John Wiley & Sons Ltd.

Survey

May Fourth was also a significant moment for Chinese Christians. Protestant academics at Yenching University established the Peking Apologetic Group (*Beijing Zhengdao tuan*, later known as Life Fellowship or *Shengming she*), that hoped to offer a "Christian Renaissance" in China by articulating ways Christianity could participate in the regeneration of Chinese society. It attempted the "use of modern conceptions of science and philosophy in order to clear up the religious misunderstandings and doubts of the present generation, and with a view to proving the truth of the claims of Christ."[2] In part shaped by the North American modernist theological movement of the day, these Protestant intellectuals were at the forefront of modern Chinese theological development.

Although the intellectual response of Catholics in this period was quite different, the year 1919 marked the promulgation of *Maximum illud*, which revolutionized the understanding of the Chinese church's relationship with European powers.[3] This was followed by the convening of the First Council of China (1924) to bring reform in the Catholic Church in China and the consecration of six new Chinese bishops in 1926. Prior to this, only one other Chinese bishop had been consecrated, in 1685 – two and a half centuries earlier.

Chinese Christians of every theological persuasion have shared similar theological debates and concerns across this evolving context, ever since May Fourth. Broadly speaking, we may consider two major themes that have preoccupied modern Chinese theologians: Christianity and Chinese culture, and the nature and mission of the Chinese church.

Christianity and Chinese culture

Many Chinese Christians engage Chinese culture, especially as represented by Confucianism, as an important dialogue partner for Chinese theology. We see this in the first Chinese chancellor of Yenching University, Wu Leichuan (1870–1944) who, in his earliest theological writings in the 1920s, explores similarities and dissimilarities between Christianity and Confucianism, comparing the Christian Bible with the Confucian classics, prayer with Confucian understanding of self-cultivation (*xiuyang*), the personalities of Jesus and Confucius, and the Holy Spirit with the Confucian notion of benevolence (*ren*).[4] Other Christian intellectuals focused less on comparisons and more on the epistemological good that can be found in Chinese culture. The Yenching theologian T. C. Chao (Zhao Zichen, 1888–1979) reasoned that the salvation of individuals cannot be achieved apart from the historical society they are a part of, and that the sages of China's spiritual past paralleled the Old Testament prophets.[5] Francis C. M. Wei (Wei Zhuomin, 1888–1976), the first Chinese president of Huachung University, likewise suggested that China's non-Christian traditions were "groping for God" and that Christians need to get "hold of the best in those systems and [incorporate] it into the heritage of the Ecumenical Church."[6] Catholic Bishop Paul Yu Pin (Yu Bin, 1901–78) echoes this, seeing in China's ancient culture greatness for producing an impressive civilization of art, architecture, literature, philosophy, and society. He remarked, "What has been and will be the attitude of the Church towards … culture? It will endeavour to conserve all that is best in it."[7]

These theologians recognized traditional Chinese culture offers resources for the construction of Chinese theology. Yet relying too much on the past, especially mindful of May Fourth and later Cultural Revolution criticisms against Confucianism, can result in a fossilized theology. After Wu Leichuan's initial foray into comparative studies, he acknowledged the naivety of such an approach and reasoned it was futile for Christianity to identify with traditional Chinese culture because it was stagnant and dying. Rather, Christianity and Chinese culture need to work toward the future transformation of Chinese society.[8] Timothy T. Lew (Liu Tingfang, 1892–1947), another Yenching academic, was pleased May Fourth was producing a new modern culture – promoting written Chinese in the vernacular (*baihua*) of the commoner instead of the classical Chinese (*wenyanwen*) of the literati, battling numerous "superstitions," championing mass education, and liberating women.[9] But he also thought Protestantism brought more positive change to China than May Fourth, especially in terms of the family, by promoting monogamy, attacking concubinage, pioneering modern education for women, and creating Christian schools and hospitals.[10] P. S. Tseng (Zeng Baosun, 1893–1978) likewise recognized the importance of Christian missionary schools in educating women well before the end of the Qing,[11] and Ruth Cheng (Cheng Guanyi) in 1922 argued that the church could do more to treat women as equals with men, especially in terms of ordination.[12]

Conservative Protestants have been a bit more mixed in their approach to Chinese culture. There are some who look towards traditional Chinese thought to construct their theologies, such as the fundamentalist Jia Yuming's (1880–1964) use of Confucianism to speak about sanctification as becoming a Christ-human (*Jidu ren*),[13] or the inspiration found in the Chinese cosmological text the *Book of Changes* (*Yijing*) for evangelicals such as Chow Lien-hwa's (Zhou Lianhua, 1920–2016) "theology of changes" (*yi de shenxue*)[14] and Wang Weifan's (1927–2015) "ever-changing God" (*shengsheng shen*).[15] Others such as Wang Mingdao (1900–91), John Sung (Song Shangjie, 1901–44), and Watchman Nee (Ni Tuosheng, 1903–72) – all of whom are remembered as forerunners to the house church movement – have tended to be seen as less embracing of Chinese culture. These evangelists would likely assert that their theologies come from a simple reading of the Bible. However, some commentators have noticed selective engagements with Chinese culture – sayings or ideas that reinforce biblical teachings – and parallels with Confucianism's views on social structures or with Chinese popular religiosity's emphases on charisma, apocalyptic millennialism, sectarianism, and its appeal to women.[16]

By the end of the twentieth century, the place of traditional Chinese culture lost its status within modernizing Chinese society. As the CPA Bishop Aloysius Jin Luxian (1916–2013) gloomily reported, "now, facing the challenge of modernization, of pure materialism, of the idolatry of money, of individualism, I have fears. How to teach [*sic*] the Catholics to live the Gospel?"[17] The non-Christian academic Zhuo Xinping (b. 1955) has made a similar observation, simply explaining: "This is the state of 'original sin.'"[18] Yu Jie (b. 1973), Bei Cun (b. 1965), and others associated with urban house churches have asserted that the best thing for Chinese Christians to do is to "evangelize culture" (*wenhua fuyin hua*) through the pursuit of spiritual and political transformation in Chinese society.[19]

We see an evolving understanding of what Chinese culture means and an evolving understanding of its relationship with Christian theology. These questions are tenacious because of the enduring concerns around Chinese Christian identity and whether Christianity should be regarded as a "foreign religion" (*yangjiao*)[20] – or a Chinese religion connected to a worldwide church.

Chinese church

Along with questions related to Chinese culture, the most visible testimony of whether Christianity is foreign has been in the Chinese church. In the early 1900s, despite the growing number of Chinese clergy, missionary paternalism meant local church governance and finances remained largely in the hands of foreigners. This was further complicated by theological disputes that were imported into the Chinese context. Catholics were dismissed for their "Popery" and "Romanism," and Protestants were accused of simply "tossing Bibles from shipside upon the beach."[21] Protestants had the added confusion of foreign denominationalism with quarrels over the proper mode and meaning of baptism and the Lord's supper, whether to worship on Sunday or Saturday, and the appropriate Chinese translation for "God."[22]

Cheng Jingyi (1881–1939) captured the sentiments of many Chinese Protestants at the 1910 World Missionary Conference in Edinburgh when he declared that Chinese Christians "hope to see, in the near future, a united Christian Church without any denominational distinctions ... [D]enominationalism has never interested the Chinese mind. He finds no delight in it, but sometimes he suffers for it!"[23] For Catholics, the layman Ying Lianzhi (1867–1926) along with missionaries Antoine Cotta and Vincent Lebbe (a naturalized Chinese citizen) fought against the Catholic "spiritual colonies" in China. In particular, Ying found the level of Catholic education embarrassing, commenting, "Will pagans notable for intelligence and knowledge sign up for Catholic instruction, while priests capable of properly drafting a letter are as rare as the morning stars?"[24] Without a proper Catholic education system, how could China have a proper Catholic church?

The 1920s and 1930s saw a gradual shift from foreign to Chinese leadership and the creation of new Protestant Chinese churches and networks. However, missionary paternalism swiftly ended after the establishment of the People's Republic resulted in the expulsion of all foreign missionaries. In May 1950, Y. T. Wu (Wu Yaozong, 1893–1979) led a delegation of Chinese Protestants to meet with Premier Zhou Enlai in Beijing and penned the so-called "Christian Manifesto" that evoked the three-self principle from the nineteenth-century Protestant missionary strategy to develop indigenous churches that were self-governing, self-supporting, and self-propagating. The manifesto underscored a severing of connections with foreign imperialism and the cultivation of a patriotic spirit, which eventually led to the establishment of the TSPM in 1954.[25] Wang Mingdao, in the 1955 article "We, Because of Faith," denounced TSPM leaders as modernists and explained how his church could not be united with "unbelievers" or the "unbelieving faction" (*buxin pai*).[26] Whereas Wang used the categories of fundamentalism and modernism as a theological basis for unity or division, K. H. Ting (Ding Guangxun, 1915–2012), the future head of the TSPM in the 1980s, argued that unity was possible because of the common fight for patriotism and against imperialism.[27] A few months later, Wang was imprisoned as a counterrevolutionary and his church was closed down.

Some Chinese Catholics followed the pattern of their Protestant compatriots, releasing the "Kwanyuan Manifesto" (or Guangyun Manifesto, November 1950) and the "Chunking Manifesto" (or "Chongqing Manifesto," January 1951).[28] Both manifestos likewise spoke of the three-self principle, despite the fact that it was primarily a Protestant missionary strategy and never discussed by Catholic missionaries. In June 1951, Father John Tung (Dong Shizhi) delivered a speech criticizing the developments toward a "schismatic" church, arguing that a separate patriotic church would no longer be "Catholic" in its universal nature. He reminded his hearers of the church's millions of martyrs over two thousand years and appealed to God "to forgive my numerous sins and grant me the unparalleled gift of martyrdom."[29] Tung was arrested the next day and never heard from again. The next year, Pope Pius XII echoed Tung's stance in *Cupimus imprimis* and encouraged Chinese Catholics to remain faithful and to be willing to be martyred themselves.[30]

Many of the debates in the 1950s were repeated in the 1980s and 1990s. Protestant house church leaders spoke about the need to have Christ as their head, not the government, and to uphold the Bible as the foundation of their faith, as opposed to the approach of theological "liberals" and "non-Christians" in the TSPM.[31] In contrast, K. H. Ting continued to maintain that the TSPM existed to unite Chinese Protestants. He was also adamant that he could not dismiss house churches as illegal.[32] Catholic underground churches continued to assert that the CPA separated from the Catholic Church, disobeying the pope, and was no longer Catholic.[33] In contrast, Bishop Jin Luxian argued that the CPA is a political mass organization and not a church. Drawing on the ecclesiology of the Second Vatican Council, Jin further insisted the CPA helps the Chinese church in the process of inculturation and to contribute to the catholic or universal church.[34]

In the 1990s, the debates between registered and unregistered churches, and the education level of many Chinese Christians, offered little space for a new generation of Christian intellectuals who wanted to invest in theological construction for Chinese society. The cultural Christian Liu Xiaofeng (b. 1956) drew from Ernst Troeltsch to argue that the Chinese church exists in three basic forms: the church type (*da jiaohui* or German *Kirche*) represented by the TSPM and the CPA, the sect type (*xiao jiaopai* or German *Sekt*) represented by Protestant house churches and (possibly) Catholic underground churches, and mysticism (*shenmi zhuyi* or German *Mystik*) represented by intellectuals like himself.[35] He concludes that the mystical church emphasizes personal spiritual experience apart from traditional ecclesial communities but also has the potential of offering important insights for creating Chinese theology and Christian culture.[36]

In the early 2000s, a growing number of Protestant intellectuals echoed Liu Xiaofeng's aspirations to have an intellectual faith but did so from within urban house churches – many drawing from Calvinism to address the changing context.[37] Some have described this as a "third church" (*disan jiaohui*) – a new ecclesial model that is able to engage the state and the civil society. Jin Tianming (b. 1968), pastor of Shouwang Church in Beijing, argues that the third church is an alternative to the deadlock that exists between the "illegal" house churches and the "adulteress" TSPM.[38] Another Shouwang leader framed it using Dutch Neo-Calvinist language: "God's word or biblical truth must enter into a culture and, expressing itself in every domain of this culture, become God's common grace in human society. This is the church's cultural mandate."[39] Others, such as Wang Yi (b. 1973), the pastor of Early Rain Church in Chengdu, disagree with this language, seeing urban churches as the next phase in the development of the traditional house churches.[40]

The pursuit of a Chinese church has needed to negotiate the relationship between the church and others – whether it be foreigners or, since the 1950s, the state. Additionally, there is a more fundamental question of the nature of the church and its mission within the broader Chinese society and, ultimately, the world.

Named Theologians

T. C. Chao (Zhao Zichen, 1888–1979)

T. C. Chao is considered by many to be the most important Chinese theologian of the twentieth century. Chao was a professor of theology and philosophy at Yenching University (1926–52), was confirmed Anglican and successively ordained deacon and priest all on the same day in July 1941, and was elected as one of the six presidents of the World Council of Churches in 1948.

Chao is best known for his efforts to develop Chinese theology. He saw it as a process first involving the purification of Christianity. Institutionally, this meant rejecting the confusion of foreign denominationalism, an emphasis on building an indigenous church based on the three-self principle, an urgent need for Christian literature that "is touched by the throbbing Chinese heart," and Chinese expressions of prayer, worship, and liturgy.[41] Controversially, purification also involves removing doctrines that are unscientific or unreasonable – miracles, the virgin birth, and the resurrection. After being purified, Christianity is better suited to engage the Chinese context. As already mentioned, Chao saw a continuity between China's spiritual legacy and Christianity. However, Chinese culture is also limited. The Confucian ethical system offers an aspiration toward harmony with family and society, but does so risking the loss of the dignity of the individual, leading to subordination and blind observance. Rather, China can gain from the social gospel of Christ, which was taught by the apostles and saints and lived out through Christian missionaries in China who offer philanthropy, education, and evangelistic service.[42] After purification and adapting to Chinese culture, China can participate with the West in a "universal spiritual fellowship" – the consummation of the kingdom of God through a catholic realization of the faith.[43]

In the late-1930s, Chao's theology began to shift when he recognized limitations in theological liberalism, seeing it as sacrificing true religion for the sake of humanism and scientific naturalism. His reservations were accentuated during the Second Sino-Japanese War, after Chao was imprisoned by Japanese authorities for six months alongside other Yenching professors. Many years later, he reflected on the pressures of war, captivity, and societal failures and concluded that the academic environment he was involved in was superficial and attempts to merge Christianity with Chinese culture were futile. Chao had a deepening experience with God and, now, rejected his earlier humanistic theology and spoke of human sinfulness and the need for divine grace to receive salvation.[44] Within a few years, the situation drastically changed again. Despite his support of the new regime and TSPM, he was severely criticized and no longer wrote theology. By the end of his life, it is uncertain if Chao remained a Christian.[45]

P. S. Tseng (Zeng Baosun, 1893–1978)

P. S. Tseng was known for her passion for women's education, serving as the founding principal of Yifang Girls' College (est. 1918) and participating in international fora such as the International Missionary Council and representing the Republic of China (Taiwan) in the United Nations in 1952. She did not produce the same kind of literary corpus as T. C. Chao and is perhaps less well known than her great grandfather, the famed statesman and general Zeng Guofan (1811–72). However, P. S. Tseng's life and writings are remarkable, serving as a model of an early Chinese Protestant feminist.

Like other Protestant intellectuals of her generation, Tseng saw much that was complementary between Confucianism and Christianity but thought the latter could invigorate the former.[46] She noted how Christianity was the first tradition in China to offer education to women – including herself. Furthermore, Christ modeled something quite different from other religious teachers. Compared to Buddha, Mohammed, or Confucius, "when Christ came, women began to come into their true inheritance."[47] Tseng notes the many ways Christ respected and upheld women, sending them as special witnesses of theological truths such as Jesus's messiahship (the Samaritan woman who preached about the living Christ) and the resurrection (Mary Magdalene who shared the news to the hiding disciples). She concludes:

> Christ is indeed the emancipator of women! We women, who are given all the privileges and responsibilities, must pray for His grace and power, so that we may not fail to carry out His purpose for us. The duty and work for us to-day is – I cannot do better than quote the celebrated [Giuseppe] Mazzini – to "hasten the redemption of woman … by restoring her to her mission of Inspiration, Prayer and Pity, so divinely symbolised by Christianity in Mary."[48]

Tseng was ahead of her time – in China and in the world – to speak about the revolutionary aspect of Christ towards women.[49]

Wang Mingdao (1900–91)

Wang Mingdao is considered one of the most important Chinese evangelicals of the twentieth century – a self-declared fundamentalist, founder of the Beijing Christian Tabernacle (est. 1937) and the popular *Spiritual Food Quarterly* (*Lingshi jikan*, published from 1927 to 1955), known for his opposition to the TSPM and subsequent arrest, and esteemed as a spiritual forefather for the house church movement.

Foundational to Wang's theology was his use of the Bible. In his autobiography, he explains the ways studying the Bible transformed his perception of teachings he received early on from a Pentecostal church in Beijing.[50] He was taught a form of Christian perfectionism that insisted on a daily pursuit of holiness to receive salvation but was later convinced the Bible held that faith alone was necessary for salvation. He once adhered to strict observance of Saturday Sabbath-keeping but realized the apostles never taught gentile churches to uphold the Sabbath. He also discusses the Pentecostal understanding of first evidence, whereby the speaking in tongues is proof of the Holy Spirit's filling. However, Wang witnessed some who spoke in tongues but were hot-tempered, whereas others without this gift were living holy Christian lives – surely, they too possess the Holy Spirit. He concludes, "What I found in the Bible I received. What I did not find in the Bible I rejected."[51] This determination led to an embrace of fundamentalism and a rejection of modernism. However, this biblicist zeal also resulted in Wang's dismissal of doctrines not found in the Bible, including the Trinity.[52]

Wang is known outside of China for his rejection of the TSPM. But this has to be understood as largely a theological resolve as opposed to a political one. Wang believed the church was full of sin and apostate teachings; to attack the first would provoke Pharisee-like "hypocrites" (*weishan pai*) and to attack the second would provoke Sadducee-like "unbelievers" (*buxin pai*). But he needed to remain faithful to God, recalling the comfort God offered God's prophets in Jeremiah 1:19.[53] His commitment was tested in the midst of the Second Sino-Japanese War when Japanese authorities pressured Wang to join the North China Christian Union, which claimed to adhere to the three-self principle and was therefore independent of foreign powers. But he reasoned they were a political organization led by unbelievers.[54] Although Japanese authorities interrogated and threatened Wang, this was eventually dropped. Then in the 1950s, Wang again resisted the TSPM and criticized its leaders as modernists who rejected the revelatory nature of the Bible and teachings like the virgin birth, substitutionary atonement, and the second coming of Christ. Again, Wang resolved that he could not have unity with unbelievers in the TSPM.[55] Communist authorities were less forgiving and he was imprisoned for twenty-five years.

Wang Mingdao's emphases on the simple preaching of the Bible as the Word of God and the rejection of modernism and the TSPM have left a lasting impression on the house church movement and, in many respects, Chinese Protestant communities in other parts of the world.

Paul Yu Pin (Yu Bin, 1901–78)

Paul Yu Pin was a Catholic priest who was consecrated Vicar Apostolic of Nanjing in 1936 and Archbishop of Nanjing in 1946. After the establishment of the People's Republic, Yu relocated to Taiwan, becoming rector of the reestablished Fu Jen Catholic University and created cardinal in 1969.

Yu saw the establishment of the Republic in 1912 and the Holy See's efforts to build a Chinese church (through *Maximum illud* and the consecration of new Chinese bishops) as pointing toward a growing recognition of equality that exists between nations.[56] However, the Second Sino-Japanese War revealed something insidious: "Japan is not hostile to China. She is, to put it shortly, hostile to the human race."[57] Yu argues that Japanese militarism underscores an egotistical determination. At the time, it was focused on China; but when given the opportunity, Japan would turn their attention to other countries. Yu reasons that Japan launched an unjust war and, referring to the just war theory of Augustine and Thomas Aquinas, argues that Chinese participation in the war was "serving our country" to bring peace and striving towards the ideal of "universal brotherhood."[58]

Yu also addressed one of the most contentious concerns in Christianity within Chinese culture: Chinese ancestral veneration. This was the focal point of the seventeenth- and eighteenth-century "Chinese rites controversy" between various Catholic missionaries, which eventually led to the Papal ban against the practice and the consequent Imperial ban against Catholic missions.[59] It was overturned two centuries later in 1939 by Propaganda Fide, but Chinese Catholics were unable to fully respond due to the ongoing wars. Another half century later in the 1970s, Yu Pin took advantage of Second Vatican Council reforms and created a Catholic liturgy for ancestral veneration, describing it as a process of "Christianisation of China, Sinicisation of Christianity" (*Zhongguo Jidu hua, Jidu Zhongguo hua*).[60]

K. H. Ting (Ding Guangxun, 1915–2012)

K. H. Ting was the first principal of Nanjing Union Theological Seminary (est. 1952), consecrated Anglican bishop of Zhejiang in 1955, and served as head of the reinstated TSPM and the newly formed China Christian Council in the 1980s and 1990s.[61]

In a 1991 speech, Ting argues that Chinese Christians have moved toward a view of the cosmic nature of Christ – a cosmic Christ.[62] First, this underscores the universal extent of Christ's domain and care, as seen in Hebrews 1:3 and Colossians 1:15 and 17. It is not as though God created the world and ceded control to Satan, with Christ rescuing a select few to return to God. Rather, Christ is deeply concerned with the flourishing of all creation. Second, to speak about the cosmic Christ is to underscore the Christlike love that is the greatest of God's attributes. God is the great Lover of humanity.[63]

Ting further laments that Christians too often emphasize solidarity with the fall of Adam rather than solidarity with the work of Christ. An unhealthy preoccupation with sinfulness leads to a distinction between the "sinner" and the "saved" – that is, between the non-Christian and the Christian. Rather, both must be recognized as "not only the sinner, but also the sinned against."[64] Furthermore, Ting argues that Martin Luther's emphasis on "justification by faith" has been misunderstood, leading to a form of antinomianism. Instead, "It was a banner of human liberation. Its goal was never to consign people to hell."[65] Although both the doctrines of sin and justification by faith are seen as foundational for many Chinese evangelicals, Ting claims the ways they have been interpreted have been counterproductive in a society with a Christian minority and many morally good non-Christians – especially communists. He laments, "How can we tolerate the idea that they are now in hell?"[66]

For Ting, Chinese Christians need a theology that is mindful of the harshness of the Cultural Revolution and Tiananmen Square military clash in 1989, but still working from within this context to speak of "the fidelity of God even in the darkest moments of personal and social despairs."[67]

Debate, Achievement, and Agenda

By the 2010s, religious liberties enjoyed since the end of the Cultural Revolution began to wane. A cross-removal campaign affected hundreds of Protestant and Catholic churches in Zhejiang province in 2014 and 2015. Xi Jinping also introduced a campaign for the "Sinicization" or "Chinafication" of religions (*zongjiao Zhongguo hua*).[68] The state-sanctioned Protestant and Catholic organizations held meetings to engage these efforts and issued five-year plans for its development.[69] However, the idea is quite different from theological contextualization or inculturation. Whereas the rhetoric underscored the need for religions like Christianity to shed their foreignness, the state-sponsored campaign promotes an adaption of religions to China's socialist society.

Some Protestants have been outspoken against these developments. In July 2015, Joseph Gu (Gu Yuese), the senior pastor of the TSPM-registered Hangzhou Chongyi Church and the head of the Zhejiang Christian Council, wrote an open letter condemning the cross-removal campaign. However, by January 2016, Gu was removed from his posts and arrested on suspicion of embezzling funds. Despite the timings of these events, government-run *Global Times* published an article criticising "overseas media" for associating Gu's arrest with his open letter and for spreading rumors about government authorities.[70] Among house church Christians, Wang Yi in August 2015 penned ninety-five theses articulating a two kingdoms theology – between the "City of God" and the "City of Man," or the "Kingdom of God" and the government (the "Kingdom of this world") – and expressed why his church rejected the TSPM and any interference by an atheistic government, including the Chinafication of Christianity.[71] Wang Yi was eventually arrested in 2018 and charged for inciting subversion of state power and illegal business operations.

In the midst of these events, the Vatican signed a provisional agreement in September 2018 that offers the Chinese government a role in the selection process of bishops in the Chinese Catholic Church, but giving the Vatican final veto privileges. Pope Francis stated that the agreement was made due to pastoral concerns, moving toward resolving the longtime rift between the CPA and the underground church. Nevertheless, Joseph Zen Ze-Kiun (Chen Rijun, b. 1932), the Shanghai-born cardinal and bishop emeritus of Hong Kong, retorted in *The New York Times* that "The Pope Doesn't Understand China."[72]

Christianity has continued to be challenged about its foreignness, its allegiance to the state, and its relevance within Chinese society. The future of Christianity and Christian theology in China is unclear. But beyond the focus of this chapter on the internal dynamics of the Chinese mainland, we must appreciate that these developments highlight Chinese Christianity's connections beyond the boundaries of the People's Republic – not least with "overseas media," the Vatican, and Christians in Hong Kong, Taiwan, and farther afield. Christianity is a worldwide faith. Furthermore, as Chinese Christians have moved to and developed in other parts of Asia and the world, Chinese Christianity is increasingly a worldwide phenomenon. Many of the "heroes" of Christianity in China continue to capture the theological imaginations of the Chinese diaspora. But these new contexts produce new questions, caused by factors such as anti-Asian racism or differences between various subgroups of Chinese.[73] This dynamic introduces an increasingly complex picture. Beyond this chapter, a fuller discussion of modern Chinese theology would require a more transnational consideration of the kinds of theology being articulated by Chinese theologians around the globe.

Furthermore, it is not simply a matter of Chinese theology for the Chinese sake, but rather how Chinese theology can help shape and be shaped by theologians of other contexts. It is only through this mutual interaction that we will truly understand what T. C. Chao and Paul Yu Pin were speaking of in terms of a "universal spiritual fellowship" or a "universal brotherhood" – a catholic church of every nation, tribe, people, and language, in the already and in the not yet.

Notes

1 The government recognizes five religions: Buddhism, Daoism, Catholicism, Protestantism, and Islam. Catholicism and Protestantism are treated as two religions, and the small size of Orthodoxy is not officially recognized by the state.

2 T.C. Chao, trans., "Christian Renaissance in China: Statement of Aims of the Peking Apologetic Group," *The Chinese Recorder* 51, no. 9 (1920): 636.

3 Pope Benedict XV, "Apostolic Letter *Maximum illud* of the Supreme Pontiff Benedict XV to the Patriarchs, Primates, Archbishops and Bishops of the Catholic World on the Propagation of the Faith Throughout the World" (1919), https://www.vatican.va/content/benedict-xv/en/apost_letters/documents/hf_ben-xv_apl_19191130_maximum-illud.html (accessed 13 September 2023).

4 Wu Leichuan, "Jidujiao jing yu Rujiao jing" [Christian Bible and Confucian Classics], *Shengming* [Life] 3, no. 6 (1923): 1–6; Wu Leichuan, "Lizhi yu Jidujiao" [Rituals and Christianity], *Shengming* [Life] 1, no. 2 (1920): 1–4; Wu Leichuan, "Renge: Yesu yu Kongzi" [Personality: Jesus and Confucius], *Shengming* [Life] 5, no. 3 (1924): 5–11; Wu Leichuan, "Jidujiao zhi 'Shengling' yu Rujiao zhi 'ren'" [The "Holy Spirit" in Christianity and "Benevolence" in Confucianism], *Shengming* [Life] 6, no. 5 (1926): 11–18. See Ng Leeming, "Wu Lei-chuen – From Indigenization to Revolution," *Ching Feng* 20, no. 4 (1977): 200–4; Chu Sin-Jan, *Wu Leichuan: A Confucian-Christian in Republican China* (New York: Peter Lang, 1995), 45–62.

5 T. C. Chao, "Revelation," in *The Authority of the Faith*, ed. International Missionary Council (London: Oxford University Press, 1939), 40–8.

6 Francis C. M. Wei, *The Spirit of Chinese Culture* (New York: Charles Scribner's Sons, 1947), 24.

7 Paul Yu-Pin, *Eyes East: Selected Pronouncements of the Most Reverend Paul Yu-Pin* (Paterson, NJ: St Anthony Guild Press, 1945), 129.

8 Wu Leichuan, *Jidujiao yu Zhongguo wenhua* [Christianity and Chinese Culture] (Shanghai: Shanghai gu ji chubanshe [Shanghai Ancient Books Publishing House], [1936] 2008). See Ng, "Wu Lei-chuen," 205–9.

9 Liu Tingfang, "Xinwenhua yundong zhong Jidujiao xuanjiaoshi de Zeren" [The Responsibilities of Christian Missionaries in the New Culture Movement], *Shengming* [Life] 1, nos. 9–10 (1921): 1–54. See John Barwick, "Liu Tingfang: Christian Minister and Activist Intellectual," in *Salt and Light 3: More Lives of Faith That Shaped Modern China*, ed. Carol Lee Hamrin with Stacey Bieler (Eugene, OR: Pickwick, 2011), 69–70.

10 Timothy Tingfang Lew, "The Family," in *As It Looks to Young China*, ed. William Hung (New York: Friendship Press, 1932), 43–5.

11 P. S. Tseng, "The Chinese Woman Past and Present," in *Symposium on Chinese Culture*, ed. Sophia H. Chen (Shanghai: China Institute of Pacific Relations, 1931), 286.

12 Ruth Cheng, "Women and the Church," *The Chinese Recorder* 53, no. 8 (1922): 539–40.

13 Jia Yuming, *Wanquan jiufa* [Total Salvation] (Hangzhou: Zhejiang Provincial Christian Council, 1945). See Kwok Wai Luen, "The Christ-human and Jia Yuming's Doctrine of Sanctification: A Case Study in the Confucianisation of Chinese Fundamentalist Christianity," *Studies in World Christianity* 20, no. 2 (2014): 145–65; Baiyu Andrew Song, "Jia Yuming (1880–1964) – A Chinese Keswick Theologian: A

Theological Analysis of Christ-Human Theology in Jia's Total Salvation," *Journal of Global Theology* 4, no. 1 (2018): 68–83.

14 Zhou Lianhua, *Shenxue gangyao* [Outline of Theology], 7 vols. (Taipei: Chinese Christian Literature Council, 1979–2009); Zhou Lianhua, "Yi de Shenxue" [Theology of Changes], *Taiwan Baptist Theological Seminary Annual Bulletin* no. 13 (2015): 3–11.

15 Wang Weifan, *Zhongguo shenxue ji qi wenhua yuanyuan* [Chinese Theology and its Cultural Origins] (Nanjing: Nanjing Theological Seminary, 1997); Wang Weifan, "Chinese Traditional Culture and its Influences on Chinese Theological Reflection," *Chinese Theological Review* 13 (1999): 8–18. See Archie Chi Chung Lee, "Contextual Theology in East Asia," in *The Modern Theologians: An Introduction to Christian Theology Since 1918*, 3rd ed., ed. David F. Ford with Rachel Muers (Malden, MA: Blackwell, 2005), 527–8.

16 See Lian Xi, *Redeemed by Fire: The Rise of Popular Christianity in Modern China* (New Haven, CT: Yale University Press, 2010), 14–16, 233–47; Gloria S. Tseng, "Bathsheba as an Object Lesson: Gender, Modernity and Biblical Examples in Wang Mingdao's Sermons and Writings," *Studies in World Christianity* 21, no. 1 (2015): 52–65; Daryl R. Ireland, *John Song: Modern Chinese Christianity and the Making of a New Man* (Waco, TX: Baylor University Press, 2020), 155–7. Melissa Inouye has pushed back on some of these claims as they seem to support more a search for "Chineseness" than the recognition of parallels in Christianity in other parts of the world. Melissa Inouye, *China and the True Jesus: Charisma and Organization in a Chinese Christian Church* (New York: Oxford University Press, 2019), 6–7.

17 Quoted in Richard Madsen, *China's Catholics: Tragedy and Hope in an Emerging Civil Society* (Berkeley, CA: University of California Press, 1998), 114.

18 Zhuo Xinping, "Original Sin in the East–West Dialogue: A Chinese View," *Studies in World Christianity* 1, no. 1 (1995): 84.

19 Part of this is inspired by the Chinese "return missionary" Jonathan Chao (Zhao Tianen, 1938–2004) and his threefold vision for China: the evangelization of China (*Zhongguo fuyin hua*), the kingdomization of the Church (*jiaohui guodu hua*), and the Christianization of culture (*wenhua Jidu hua*). Zhao Tianen, *Fu wo qian xing: Zhongguo fuyin hua yixiang* [Leading Me to Go Forward: Vision of the Evangelization of China] (Taipei: China Ministries International, 1993). See Fredrik Fällman, "Calvin, Culture and Christ? Developments of Faith among Chinese Intellectuals," in *Christianity in Contemporary China: Socio-cultural Perspectives*, ed. Francis Khek Gee Lim (London: Routledge, 2013), 154, 161–2, 166 n. 1; Alexander

Chow, "Jonathan Chao and 'Return Mission': The Case of the Calvinist Revival in China," *Mission Studies* 36, no. 3 (2019): 442–57.

20 This term, literally meaning "religion from the ocean," was coined in the nineteenth century in the midst of the Opium Wars, when missionaries were demonized as "foreign devils" (*yang guizi*) and Chinese Christians were derided as running dogs of imperialism. See Thoralf Klein, "The Missionary as Devil: Anti-Missionary Demonology in China, 1860–1930," in *Europe as the Other: External Perspectives on European Christianity*, ed. Judith Becker and Brian Stanley (Göttingen: Vandenhoeck and Ruprecht, 2014), 119–48.

21 See Jean-Paul Wiest, "Roman Catholic Perceptions of British and American Protestant Missionaries (1807–1920)," *Journal of Cultural Interaction in East Asia* 6, no. 1 (2015): 19–30.

22 There was an early dispute within Catholicism over the use of a neologism *Tianzhu* or the name of an ancient deity *Shangdi*, that was eventually settled in favor of *Tianzhu*. Protestants debated between *Shangdi* and *shen*, the latter being a generic term for spirits or deities. See Irene Eber, "The Interminable Term Question," in *Bible in Modern China: The Literary and Intellectual Impact*, ed. Irene Eber, Sze-kar Wan, and Knut Walf (Sankt Augustin: Monumenta Serica, 1999), 134–61; Alexander Chow, "Finding God's Chinese Name: A Comparison of the Approaches of Matteo Ricci and James Legge," in *Scottish Missions to China: Commemorating the Legacy of James Legge (1815–1897)*, ed. Alexander Chow (Leiden: Brill, 2022), 213–28.

23 World Missionary Conference, *Report of Commission VIII: Cooperation and the Promotion of Unity* (Edinburgh: Oliphant, Anderson, and Ferrier, 1910), 196.

24 Quoted in Ernest P. Young, *Ecclesiastical Colony: China's Catholic Church and the French Religious Protectorate* (New York: Oxford University Press, 2013), 176.

25 "The Christian Manifesto," in *Documents of the Three-Self Movement: Source Materials for the Study of the Protestant Church in Communist China*, ed. Wallace C. Merwin and Francis P. Jones (New York: NCCCUSA, 1963), 19–20.

26 Wang Mingdao, "We, Because of Faith," in *Documents of the Three-Self Movement*, 99–114.

27 K. H. Ting, "Truth and Slander," in *No Longer Strangers: Selected Writings of K. H. Ting*, ed. Raymond L. Whitehead (Maryknoll, NY: Orbis, 1989), 141–6.

28 "Manifesto on Independence and Reform" and "The Chunking 'Manifesto,'" *China Missionary Bulletin* 3, no. 4 (1951): 149–50.

29 John Tung, "Father John Tung's Speech," *China Missionary Bulletin* 3, no. 8 (1951): 680.

30 Pope Pius XII, "Litterae Apostolicae *Cupimus impri-mis*" [Apostolic Letter *Cupimus Imprimis*] (1952), https://www.vatican.va/content/pius-xii/la/apost_letters/documents/hf_p-xii_apl_19520118_cupimus-imprimis.html (accessed 13 September 2023).

31 "Appendix B: Confession of Faith," in David Aikman, *Jesus in Beijing: How Christianity Is Transforming China and Changing the Global Balance of Power*, rev. ed. (Washington, DC: Regnery, 2006), 322–3.

32 Zhao Puchu and Ding Guangxun, "Tan Luoshi zongjiao zhengci wenti" [On the Implementation of Religious Policy], *Renmin ribao* [People's Daily] (9 September 1980): 3.

33 "Thirteen Points," in *The Catholic Church in Modern China: Perspectives*, ed. Edmond Tang and Jean-Paul Wiest (Maryknoll, NY: Orbis, 1993), 142.

34 Aloysius Jin Luxian, "The Role of the Patriotic Association," in *The Catholic Church in Modern China*, 112–13. See Rachel Xiaohong Zhu, "Bishop Jin Luxian and the Chinese Catholic Patriotic Association of Shanghai," in *People, Communities, and the Catholic Church in China*, ed. Cindy Yik-yi Chu and Paul P. Mariani (Singapore: Palgrave Macmillan, 2020), 56.

35 In contrast to the understanding in English parlance, Chinese cultural Christians (*wenhua Jidutu*) are academics in secular universities and think-tanks who look to Christianity for cultivating Chinese society but are less interested in local Christian communities.

36 Tan Xing (pseudonym of Liu Xiaofeng), "Culture-Christians on the China Mainland," *Tripod* no. 6 (1990): 46–55.

37 See Alexander Chow, *Chinese Public Theology: Generational Shifts and Confucian Imagination in Chinese Christianity* (Oxford: Oxford University Press, 2018), 92–114.

38 Jin Tianming, "Tuidong jiaohui dengji dao jintian" [The Promotion of Church Registration], *Xinghua* [Almond Flowers] (Spring 2008): 40–2.

39 Sun Mingyi, "Zhongguo jiaohui chengsheng guan ji wenhua shiming lianxiang" [The Relationship between Sanctification and the Cultural Mandate in the Chinese Church], *Xinghua* [Almond Flowers] (Winter 2008): 31, translation mine.

40 Liu Tongsu and Wang Yi, *Guankan zhongguo chengshi jiating jiaohui* [Observation on China's House Churches in Cities] (Taipei: Christian Arts Press, 2012), 45.

41 T. C. Chao, "The Indigenous Church," *The Chinese Recorder* 56, no. 8 (1925): 496–505.

42 T. C. Chao, "Christianity and Confucianism," *International Review of Mission* 17, no. 4 (1928): 597. See Lee-ming Ng, "An Evaluation of T. C. Chao's Thought," *Ching Feng* 14, no. 1–2 (1971): 31–3.

43 Chao, "The Indigenous Church," 497. See Alexander Chow, *Theosis, Sino-Christian Theology and the Second Chinese Enlightenment: Heaven and Humanity in Unity* (New York: Palgrave Macmillan, 2013), 67–78.

44 Zhao Zichen, "Ji yu ji" [My Experience in Prison], in *Zhao Zichen wenji* [The Works of T. C. Chao], 5 vols., ed. Wang Xiaochao (Beijing: Commercial Press, 2003–10), 2.461. See Chow, *Theosis, Sino-Christian Theology and the Second Chinese Enlightenment*, 78–83.

45 See Winfried M. Glüer, "T. C. Chao Re-visited: Questions about His Later Years," *Ching Feng*, n.s., 11, no. 2 (2012): 171–96.

46 Zeng Baosun, *Confucian Feminist: Memoirs of Zeng Baosun (1893–1978)*, trans. Thomas L. Kennedy (Philadelphia, PA: American Philosophical Society, 2002), 30. She later (107) discusses how Buddhism and Christianity likewise had much in common.

47 P. S. Tseng, "What Christmas Means to Women," *Ch'uen Tao* no. 3 (Christmas 1915): 11.

48 Tseng, "What Christmas Means to Women," 12.

49 See P. S. Tseng, "Christianity and Women: As Seen at the Jerusalem Meeting," *The Chinese Recorder* 59, no. 7 (1928): 443; Kwok Pui-lan, "Chinese Women and Protestant Christianity," in *Christianity in China: From the Eighteenth Century to the Present*, ed. Daniel H. Bays (Stanford, CA: Stanford University Press, 1996), 208.

50 Wong Ming-dao, *A Stone Made Smooth*, trans. Arthur Reynolds (Southampton: Mayflower Christian Books, 1981), 79–84. This is a rough translation of Wang Mingdao, *Wu shi nian lai* [The Last Fifty Years] (New Taipei City: CCLM, [1950] 2012), 93–9.

51 Wong, *A Stone Made Smooth*, 84.

52 See Ying Fuk-Tsang (Xing Fuzang), "Juren ai hen – Wang Mingdao suo renshi de Ni Tuosheng" [Watchman Nee in the Eyes of Wang Mingdao], *Ching Feng*, n.s. 15, no. 1–2 (2016): 135–7.

53 Wang, *Wu shi nian lai*, 113.

54 Wang, *Wu shi nian lai*, 183.

55 Wang, "We, Because of Faith," 99–114. It should be noted that, despite these claims the early TSPM leadership also included evangelicals like Jia Yuming and Marcus Cheng (Chen Chonggui, 1884–1963) who could hardly be called modernists.

56 Yu Pin, "The War in the Far East," in Marius Zanin, Auguste Haouissé, and Yu Pin, *The Voice of the Church in China, 1931–1932, 1937–1938* (London: Longmans, Green and Co., 1938), 48–58. See "His Holiness Pius XI, Message to the Chinese People," in *The Voice of the Church in China*, 1.

57 Yu, "The War in the Far East," 63.

58 Yu Pin, "Christian Patriotism," in *The Voice of the Church in China*, 89–92. See Stephanie M. Wong, "Yu Bin and Vincent Lebbe's Theology of Resistance: Catholic Participation in the Chinese War Effort Against Japan," in *Modern Chinese Theologies I: Mainland and*

Mainstream, ed. Chloë F. Starr (Minneapolis, MN: Fortress Press, 2023), 109–29.

59 See George Minamiki, *The Chinese Rites Controversy from its Beginning to Modern Times* (Chicago, IL: Loyola University Press, 1985). This is still an ongoing debate among Chinese Protestants. See Ying Fuk-tsang (Xing Fuzang), ed., *Zhongguo jizu wenti* [The Chinese Ancestor Veneration Question] (Hong Kong: Alliance Bible Seminary, 2002).

60 Paulin Batairwa Kubuya, *Meaning and Controversy within Chinese Ancestor Religion* (New York: Palgrave Macmillan, 2018), 129–34.

61 The TSPM and the CCC are closely related. The former is a bridge organization with the government whereas the latter is more concerned with pastoral, liturgical, and theological nurturing and development.

62 During the 1980s and 1990s, a number of Chinese theologians spoke about the cosmic Christ. See Alexander Chow, "Wang Weifan's Cosmic Christ," *Modern Theology* 32, no. 3 (2016): 384–96.

63 K. H. Ting, "The Cosmic Christ," in *Love Never Ends: Papers by K. H. Ting*, ed. Janice Wickeri (Nanjing: Yilin Press, 2000), 408–18. See Chow, *Theosis, Sino-Christian Theology and the Second Chinese Enlightenment*, 90–100.

64 K. H. Ting, "Human Collectives as Vehicles of God's Grace," in *Love Never Ends*, 44.

65 K. H. Ting, "On a Profound Christian Question," in *Love Never Ends*, 507.

66 Ting, "On a Profound Christian Question," 508. See Chow, *Theosis, Sino-Christian Theology and the Second Chinese Enlightenment*, 100–109.

67 Edmond Tang, "The Cosmic Christ," *Studies in World Christianity* 1, no. 2 (1995): 141.

68 Although English sources normally render this "Sinicization," I prefer to translate it "Chinafication" or "Chinization" because of the statist emphasis of the campaign.

69 An early TSPM and CCC meeting was held in September 2015, with select papers translated and published in *Chinese Theological Review* 27 (2015).

70 Su Tan, "Religious Activities Not Immune from Regulation," *Global Times*, (1 February 2016), http://www.globaltimes.cn/content/966651.shtml (accessed 13 September 2023).

71 The 95 theses appear to echo Martin Luther's disputation with medieval Roman Catholicism. However, Wang Yi explains his text was written to commemorate the sixty-year anniversary of Wang Mingdao's "We, Because of Faith" and eventual arrest – a reaffirmation of the ecclesial lineage Wang Yi sees within the house church movement. Early Rain Covenant Church, "95 Theses: The Reaffirmation of Our Stance on the House Church," *China Partnership* (30 August 2015), https://www.chinapartnership.org/blog/2015/08/95-theses-the-reaffirmation-of-our-stance-on-the-house-church (accessed 13 September 2023).

72 Joseph Zen Ze-Kiun, "The Pope Doesn't Understand China," *New York Times* (24 October 2018), https://www.nytimes.com/2018/10/24/opinion/pope-china-vatican-church-catholics-bishops.html (accessed 13 September 2023).

73 There are often presumed differences between longer standing populations in Taiwan and Hong Kong when compared to those who later moved from the mainland, after 1949 and 1997, respectively. In other parts of Asia and the West, subgroups are often identified by various linguistic clusters and waves of Chinese immigration.

Recommended Reading

Primary

Chao, T. C. (Zhao Zichen). *Zhao Zichen wenji* [The Works of T. C. Chao]. 5 vols. Edited by Wang Xiaochao. Beijing: Commercial Press, 2003–10.

Merwin, Wallace C., and Francis P. Jones, eds. *Documents of the Three-Self Movement*. New York: NCCCUSA, 1963.

Ting, K. H. (Ding Guangxun). *Love Never Ends: Papers by K. H. Ting*. Edited by Janice Wickeri. Nanjing: Yilin Press, 2000. (Chinese edition: *Ding Guangxun wenji*. Nanjing: Yilin Press, 1998.)

Tseng, P. S. (Zeng Baosun). *Confucian Feminist: Memoirs of Zeng Baosun (1893–1978)*. Translated by Thomas L. Kennedy. Philadelphia, PA: American Philosophical Society, 2002. (Chinese edition: *Zeng Baosun huiyilu*. Hong Kong: Chinese Christian Literature Council, 1970.)

Wang Mingdao. *A Call to the Church from Wang Ming-dao*. Translated by Theodore Choy. Fort Washington, PA: Christian Literature Crusade, 1983.

Wang Yi, et al. *Faithful Disobedience: Writings on Church and State from a Chinese House Church Movement*. Edited by Hannah Nation and J. D. Tseng. Downers Grove, IL: IVP Academic, 2022.

Zanin, Marius, Auguste Haouisé, and Yu Pin. *The Voice of the Church in China, 1931–1932, 1937–1938*. London: Longmans, Green and Co., 1938.

Secondary

Chow, Alexander. *Chinese Public Theology: Generational Shifts and Confucian Imagination in Chinese Christianity.* Oxford: Oxford University Press, 2018.

———. *Theosis, Sino-Christian Theology and the Second Chinese Enlightenment: Heaven and Humanity in Unity.* New York: Palgrave Macmillan, 2013.

Kwok Pui-lan. *Chinese Women and Christianity, 1860–1927.* Atlanta, GA: Scholars Press, 1992.

Lam, Wing-hung. *Chinese Theology in Construction.* Pasadena, CA: William Carey Library, 1983.

Lian Xi. *Redeemed by Fire: The Rise of Popular Christianity in Modern China.* New Haven, CT: Yale University Press, 2010.

Malek, Roman, ed. *The Chinese Face of Jesus Christ.* Vols. 3a–3b. Sankt Augustin: Monumenta Serica, 2005, 2007.

Ng, Lee-ming (Wu Liming). *Jidujiao yu Zhongguo shehui bianqian* [Christianity and Social Change in China]. 3rd ed. Hong Kong: Chinese Christian Literature Council, 1997.

Starr, Chloë F. *Chinese Theology: Text and Context.* New Haven, CT: Yale University Press, 2016.

———., ed. *Reading Christian Scriptures in China.* London: T&T Clark, 2008.

Tang, Edmond, and Jean-Paul Wiest, eds. *The Catholic Church in Modern China: Perspectives.* Maryknoll, NY: Orbis, 1993.

Ecclesial Contexts

Catholic Theology after Vatican II

Paul D. Murray

Introduction

This chapter does not attempt a comprehensive review of all the significant individuals and movements of thought that comprise the world of Catholic theology *since* the Second Vatican Council (aka "Vatican II" and "the council"). The aim rather is to explore the key factors, debates, and diverse, even conflicting, theological instincts and approaches that have shaped the story of Catholic theology as it has been pursued *after* ("in light of") Vatican II as intentional interpretation and reception of it, particularly as that has played out in European and North American contexts.[1] The aim also is to identify what is of continuing significance and where the live issues are for contemporary Catholic theology.

   The first section explores something of the complexity surrounding the diverse ways in which the story of modern Catholicism can be told. The heart of the chapter then consists in three interrelated surveys of key dimensions of change and development in Catholic theology after the council. The first focuses upon some notable changes in the institutional landscape and contexts of Catholic theology. The second deals with various crucial developments in relation to its perceived task, scope, methods, and sources. The third explores a number of the most significant substantive changes in Catholic understanding over recent decades as Catholic theologians have intentionally pursued their task in the light of the perspectives and possibilities opened up by the council. The concluding section draws all this together by reflecting on what appropriate structures, processes, habits, and commitments might enable Catholicism to negotiate the continuing task of discerning the living truth of God in Christ and the Spirit. Although many famous names are mentioned and referenced en route, it is notable that the chapter does not consist in a focused study of any such figures, crucial though they were in the decades leading up to and following the council. By contrast, for over twenty years now Catholic theology has largely been operating in a space post-great names and post-omnicompetent superstar individuals, wherein the task has become both more multiply specific and more collaborative.

Ford's The Modern Theologians: An Introduction to Christian Theology since 1918, Fourth Edition.
Edited by Rachel Muers and Ashley Cocksworth.
© 2024 John Wiley & Sons Ltd. Published 2024 by John Wiley & Sons Ltd.

The Stories of Modern Catholicism

The story of modern Catholicism is considerably more complex than has sometimes been recognized. For a time, it was typically, if variously, told as a drama of two acts, strikingly different in their respective moods, with the Second Vatican Council (meeting in four sessions between 1962 and 1965) depicted as *the* great scene-change and dramatic pivot between.[2]

In such tellings, Catholicism prior to Vatican II had become defined by a series of increasingly oppositional stances, first against the challenge of Protestantism from the sixteenth century, then against what was perceived as the irredeemably anti-Christian spirit of modern liberalism. As the last thesis of the 1864 *Syllabus of Errors* expresses it, "If anyone thinks that . . . The Roman pontiff can and should reconcile and harmonise himself with progress, with liberalism, and with recent civilisation . . . Let him be anathema."[3] In each case the countermove took the form of heightened emphases upon distinctively Catholic practices and beliefs, and upon the Catholic Church's uniquely privileged ability to read reality aright, culminating in the proclamation of papal infallibility in 1870 during the final session of the curtailed First Vatican Council. Within Catholicism such defensiveness was felt most sharply through the policy promoted by Pope Pius X (1903–14) of suppressing any scholars deemed to be infected by the ills of "modernist" commitment, the repressive after-effects of which policy continued long after its actual promotion.[4]

When set alongside this synopsis of modern Catholicism's supposed first act, Pope John XXIII's surprise announcement on 25 January 1959 of a Second Vatican Council concerned to renew Catholicism in the context of the modern world appears as a somewhat discontinuous turn of events. Indeed, if the final thesis of the *Syllabus* is emblematic of the "first act" of modern Catholicism so construed, equally so for the "second" are the opening words of *Gaudium et Spes* ("Pastoral Constitution on the Church in the Modern World," 7 December 1965): "The joys and hopes, the grief and anguish of the people of our time . . . are the joys and hopes, the grief and anguish of the followers of Christ as well. Nothing that is genuinely human fails to find an echo in their hearts."[5] In this spirit of passionate solidarity, generous hospitality, and confident trust in the prevenient ubiquity of God's gracious presence lies, for a "progressivist" telling of the story at least, the great, lasting legacy of Vatican II. But simplistic binaries are seldom adequate conveyors of complex truth.

In the years following the election of Karol Wojtyła as Pope John Paul II in 1978, and continuing throughout the papacy of his erstwhile closest collaborator, Joseph Ratzinger, as Benedict XVI (2005–13), it became necessary to tell a more complicated tale: one requiring, at the very least, a third controverted act or supplementary epilogue.[6] For some, despite his acknowledged development of Catholic social thought, John Paul II's papacy represented a reversal of Vatican II's central movement. For others, it was a necessary corrective to what they regarded as a disastrous misappropriation of the council in the years following it.[7] These differing assessments show that the binary two-phase narratives of modern Catholicism – whether "restorationist" or "progressivist" in orientation – require significant qualification.[8] In turn, at point of writing, Catholic communities around the world are in process of exploring the possibilities and navigating the challenges arising from Pope Francis's intentional promotion of a significant new phase in the reception of the council.[9]

In longer frame, it is as inaccurate to suggest that Pius IX's *Syllabus* and Pius X's antimodernist campaign expressed the universal state of pre-Vatican II theological options as it is to suggest that at Vatican II the bishops were in unanimous agreement on the wording and interpretation of the various documents endorsed. As regards the former, in the nineteenth century the Catholic Tübingen school requires particular mention, as do John Henry Newman and Friedrich von Hügel in England and Antonio Rosmini in Italy. Again, in the early to middle part of the twentieth century, despite the continuing reverberations of Pius X's antimodernist campaign, there were many Catholic intellectuals who courageously, patiently, and imaginatively devoted themselves to seeking to give richer, more vital expression to the faith than the dominant neoscholastic categories allowed: Karl Adam, Romano Guardini, Marie-Dominique Chenu, Yves Congar,

Henri de Lubac, Jean Daniélou, and Karl Rahner, to name but a few. It was their work of *ressourcement* – of returning behind the formulas of neoscholastic manuals to the great sources and expressions of Christian faith – that broke up and tilled the ground for the renewed ways of thinking (*"aggiornamento"*) that came to fruition in the council.[10]

However, these renewed ways of thinking did not meet with universal approval during the council any more than beforehand. A fluctuating minority remained opposed and the final form of the documents reflects the compromises that had to be struck. Even among the approving majority there were differences between those who saw the task of *aggiornamento* as limited to the council – with the postconciliar task viewed purely as one of consolidation and application – and those who regarded it as a necessarily continuing aspect of Catholicism.

Such tensions became significant well in advance of the accession of Wojtyła to the papacy, as symbolized by the breakaway in 1972 of the *Communio* theologians (notably Balthasar, Ratzinger, de Lubac, and Walter Kasper) from those associated with the journal *Concilium* (most notably Rahner, Congar, Schillebeeckx, and Hans Küng), which explicitly sought to extend the work of the council. The tension between these differing traditions of reception has continued as a significant factor in European and North American Catholic theology, not withstanding Pope Francis's call to move beyond any binary factionalism.[11]

It is simplistically wrongheaded to construe this as a tension between opposing stances of *openness to* and *withdrawal from* the world. As the topics covered in the journals indicate, the difference is less one of range than of tone and approach. It relates to the relative emphasis given to the possibility of Catholicism's learning from extraecclesial resources in its ongoing discernment of God's living truth and to the need for the world's sin-dimmed perception of half-truths to be judged and read aright in the light of Catholic tradition. Alternatively, it concerns the balance to be maintained between the need to renew Catholic faith in the light of what can be appropriately learned from the world and the need to offer back a richer understanding than the world can achieve of its own resources. Also relevant, however, is the degree to which the Catholic Church itself is viewed, in the terms of Vatican II's *Lumen Gentium* ("Dogmatic Constitution on the Church," 21 November 1964), as being in need of reform and renewal rather than as the perfect antidote to the world's ills.[12]

A better, although still imperfect, analogy for the relationship between *Concilium* and *Communio* tendencies is the potentially creative tension between revisionist and postliberal instincts in Christian theology more generally. In this regard the comparison sometimes drawn between Rahner as a Catholic Schleiermacher and Balthasar as a Catholic Barth is not entirely without merit; particularly so if taken with Hans Frei's retrieval of Schleiermacher as a genuinely ecclesial theologian.[13] The view espoused here is that the unfortunate ecclesial-political capital frequently made of the supposed irreconcilability of these two instincts would be better invested in viewing them as two sides of a healthy dialectical tension. As the Catholic philosopher, Alasdair MacIntyre, recognizes, "Traditions, when vital, embody continuities of conflict."[14] Equally, as Nicholas Lash reminds us, it is important not to be naïve about the ways in which such conflicts can be skewed by unequal distributions of power, as with Balthasar's elevation as preferred court theologian under John Paul II.[15]

The problem, then, with the binary, two-act presentation of modern Catholicism is not that it is devoid of truth. Whatever one makes of it, Vatican II was an extraordinarily significant event. Nor is it simply that completeness requires both a third act, recounting the subsequent postliberal reaction to the dramatic events of the second, and now a fourth, identifying and reflecting on some of the outflow from Pope Francis's pressing "reset" on the Vatican II agenda.[16] The real problem is with its linear, neatly phased telling of a story considerably more complex in reality, with diverse – even conflicting – dimensions, pressures, drives, and movements throughout. The instincts of the reactionary conservative, the progressive reformer, the creative retriever, the cautious consolidator, and the countercultural critic exist not in temporally sequential relation but as differing yet overlapping parameters of concern. To alter the image, they constitute the diverse modes within which the music of Catholicism has been and is being variously performed, with the possibility of both harmony and dissonance between. The story of Catholic theology after Vatican II is the story or, more accurately, the story of the stories of these various performances.[17]

Survey (I) – Changes in the Institutional Contexts of Catholic Theology

Mindful of Johann-Baptist Metz's stipulation that the "important questions to be asked by theology" are "Who should do theology and where, in whose interest and for whom?"[18] the ambiguity of the phrase "Catholic theologian" should be noted. Officially it refers only to theologians working on behalf of the official Catholic magisterium (understood here as the Pope and the bishops) and/or holding a mandate to teach within a Catholic institution.[19] In a broader empirical fashion, however, it more naturally refers to any member of the Catholic Church engaged in theological work, regardless of context.

In the former sense the degree of change in the institutional context of Catholic theology has been relatively slight but nevertheless significant. Although official Catholic theology continues to be located in the pontifical universities, the seminaries, and the various ecclesial bureaucratic bodies, and continues, in the main, to be pursued by ordained male celibates, it has become increasingly common for lay women and men to be co-opted into such activities, including, most significantly, Pope Francis's opening-up the possibility of leadership of Vatican dicasteries in this manner.[20] As is most particularly evident at time of writing in the work of the Office of the Synod, the extension of perspective and concern this affords is now genuinely contributing to the ongoing shaping of official Catholic discourse. It is no longer the case – as tended to be so throughout John Paul II's papacy – that only those in robust sympathy with existing teaching are allowed such access, with anything less being regarded as damaging "dissent" rather than constructive contribution.[21]

If the picture at the official level is one of relative stability, at unofficial levels it is one of tremendous vitality and diversity, at least in certain regions. With regard to England and Wales, for example, from local catechetical groups, diocesan programs of lay formation, the availability of theology courses in a wide range of institutions, to the higher echelons of research in major international universities, there has been a genuine flowering of lay Catholic theology since the council, in turn influential beyond the Catholic Church.

Particularly significant is the number of Catholic women who, having acquired theological training, have proceeded to employment in pastoral ministry and theological education and research. Given that some, judging Christianity to be irredeemably patriarchal, have subsequently passed beyond any form of Christian commitment, whereas others have moved into a space of prophetic opposition to the Catholic Church as currently configured, all the more notable is the considerable number of feminist theologians who continue to find their home and calling within Catholicism.[22] Instances of women of feminist sympathy entering into full communion with the Catholic Church should also be noted.[23]

In this as in many other respects the vitality and range of unofficial Catholic theology represents a potentially rich resource. Again, however, how to link the official and unofficial in appropriate conversation and structures of discernment remains a real challenge for contemporary Catholicism. This goes to the heart of the concern under Pope Francis to develop more synodal ways of being. The adage "the Catholic Church is not a democracy" is inappropriately intoned when used to legitimate it being something less rather than something more. All with relevant experience and expertise should be able to participate by right rather than by concession in the church's processes of collective discerning (*sensus fidelium*).

Survey (II) – Changes in Understanding of the Task, Scope, Methods, and Sources of Catholic Theology

As noted earlier, the neoscholastic concern for the orderly presentation and defense of Catholic belief in Aristotelian categories, dominant since the latter half of the nineteenth century, had already come under considerable strain prior to the council. Taking their lead from Leo XIII's earlier promotion of Aquinas as the Catholic theologian *par excellence*, historical scholars such as Étienne Gilson and Chenu had recovered Aquinas's distinctiveness compared both with his contemporaries and later scholastic interpreters.[24] Most significant here was the recovery, variously performed by de Lubac, Rahner, and others, of a view of created reality as intrinsically oriented to God as its source, sustainer, and consummation in contrast to the "extrinsicist" tendency to view grace and nature, the sacred and the profane, as utterly distinct.[25]

More generally, studies in historical theology, most notably by Congar, combined with Pius XII's opening of Catholicism to modern biblical study in his 1943 encyclical *Divino Afflante Spiritu*, had begun to show the need for increased hermeneutical sophistication vis-à-vis the historic sources of the tradition. Likewise, liturgical, patristic, and scriptural scholarship had served to give greater emphasis to the lived, ecclesial dimensions of faith and theology as complement to the cognitive, philosophical dimensions dominant within neoscholasticism. In turn, modern philosophical thought had already been used to give fresh articulation to the Thomistic inheritance. Particularly notable here is Joseph Maréchal's Kantian-influenced transcendental Thomism, extended in different ways by, among others, Bernard Lonergan and Rahner. Also significant is Teilhard de Chardin's engagement with the human and natural sciences in his reflections on theological anthropology and created process; as too the diverse influence of phenomenological ideas on thinkers as different as Schillebeeckx and Wojtyła.

Against this background, John XXIII's calling of the council for pastoral reflection and ecclesial renewal rather than dogmatic definition together with the bishops' rejection of the draft documents in favor of documents more scripturally rooted and pastoral in tone gave official sanction to the move beyond neoscholasticism as the only valid mode of Catholic theological reflection.[26] At work in the resulting documents, preeminently so in *Gaudium et Spes*, is a recovery of the grand vision of Catholic theology as concerned to understand the significance of all particular things in relation to God's self-revelation in Christ and as correlatively open to the contributions of the diverse forms of analysis this requires.[27] It is this vision of rooted, practically engaged, disciplinarily-pluriform theological analysis and reflection that has continued to characterize Catholic theology after Vatican II, in turn reinforced by the emerging shift in consciousness to being what Rahner referred to as a truly world church.[28]

Although a range of appropriations of the Thomist tradition still feature as an important part of the Catholic theological scene, they now feature precisely as a part – and an internally differentiated part – rather than as the whole.[29] Informing them are diverse other modes of theologizing typically shaped by similarly close engagement with other significant streams in the broad expanse of Christian tradition and one or more of the natural and social sciences, the various modes of analysis operative in the humanities, and the practices and understanding of other faith traditions and non-European cultural contexts. Suffice to say that the work of Catholic theologians features significantly in each major example of contemporary theology in critical-constructive, expansive-interrogative mode.[30]

This shift is particularly clear in fundamental theology, which has progressed from the attempt to present tight proofs of Catholic belief modeled on deductive modes of reasoning to the use of a broad range of hermeneutical tools in service of more modest attempts to demonstrate its reasonableness.[31] Reinforcing this move has been the assimilation of postfoundationalist understandings of human rationality,[32] a development in some ways anticipated if not consistently carried through by Lonergan in the central role he accorded to "conversion" in theological understanding.

Although this proliferation of methodologies and analytical tools has greatly enriched Catholic theology, it has become increasingly difficult to hold it in gathered, cross-boundary, mutually constructive conversation.[33] It is, consequently, as vital to Catholicism's health to develop and to sustain spaces for richly textured conversation between theologians of varying persuasions and differing expertise as it is to nurture the opportunities for similar conversations between theologians and the hierarchy.

Survey (III) – Changes in Substantive Theological Understanding

No aspect of Catholic thought and practice is untouched by the combined effects of the spirit of *ressourcement* and renewal, the newfound openness to the world, the increased sense of being a genuinely world church, the proliferation of theological approaches and resources, and the multiplication of contexts and perspectives that have together characterized Catholic theology after Vatican II. Reflecting the pastoral, ecclesial orientation of Vatican II and the fact that the specifically doctrinal tensions that have emerged since have frequently been indicative of prior ecclesiological concerns, this section begins with ecclesiology.

Church

Clearly there is more to say regarding the characteristic sense and practice of Catholicism than can be conveyed by focusing on institutional factors alone. Nevertheless, going right to the core of the notion of Catholicity, with profound implications both for the shaping of Catholicism's own internal structures and for the formal, institutional dimension of its witness to the world, are ongoing debates concerning the appropriate relationship between episcopal collegiality and Roman primacy or, alternatively expressed, between the various local churches that together constitute the universal church and the particular local church of Rome as the symbolic and structural organ of the church's unity.[34] In practical terms, until the Francis papacy the degree of actual change had been minimal. Although a strong theology of the episcopate was included in *Lumen Gentium* as a counterbalance to the unqualified papal monarchianism of Vatican I, the precise relationship between the college of bishops and the Pope was left unresolved. This, combined with the lack of any legislative requirement for the reform of the Roman curia until Pope Francis's 19 March 2022 publication of *Praedicate Evangelium*, meant the balance of power long continued to be weighted in favor of Rome with the episcopacy effectively confined to the ranks of subalterns.

Nevertheless, the centrality of this issue to the performance of Catholicism kept it a live focus of attention at the highest levels. Particularly notable here was the published disputation between Ratzinger, when prefect of the CDF, and Kasper, when bishop of Rottenburg, concerning the relationship between the universal church and the local churches, with Ratzinger arguing for the ontological priority of the former over the latter and Kasper arguing for their simultaneity and necessary reciprocity.[35] Quite apart from its role in shaping assumptions at every level of Catholic life concerning appropriate governance and authority, this issue raises in structural form the key question as to the quality of the unity the church is called to reflect—whether one of centralized, acontextual uniformity or one of internally differentiated, contextually specific communion.[36] Further, for all his close working relationship with Ratzinger, it is significant that amidst this public disagreement Pope John Paul II appointed Kasper president of the then Pontifical Council, now Dicastery, for Promoting Christian Unity, and made him a cardinal. Seeking a rebalance on this issue in turn became one of the central concerns of the Francis papacy.

Ecumenism

Clearly related to the preceding discussion is the ecumenical issue placed so firmly on the Catholic agenda by the groundbreaking council document *Unitatis Redintegratio*.[37] Particular highpoints since have been the recognition of the degree of communion that already exists between the divided churches, the progress made in various bilateral discussions (most notably the joint Catholic–Lutheran declaration on justification), and the positive exploration of the idea of "reconciled diversity" by Avery Dulles and Walter Kasper. With this also is Pope John Paul II's affirming inventory in his 1995 encyclical, *Ut Unum Sint* ("On Commitment to Ecumenism"), of the significant progress made since Vatican II, culminating in his remarkable invitation to church leaders and theologians in other Christian traditions to help with the task of reimagining the Petrine office and its associated structures so that it might again become a resource for Christian unity rather than the continuing cause of division it currently is. Persistent tensions have also been in evidence, however, as came to a head in 2000 with the publication by the CDF of *Dominus Iesus*. Its tone, particularly when read together with a note to bishops banning the use of the phrase "sister churches" in reference to other Christian bodies, led many to infer that Roman policy was in reverse. The intervening years have given some cause for hope that it is the more constructive spirit of receptive ecumenism evinced by *Ut Unum Sint* that will prevail.[38]

Ministry

Another key focus after Vatican II has been the relationship between the dignity, vocation, and ministry of the laity and of the clergy. If the context for this has been the massive development of lay ministry since the council, framing it has been an apparent tension within *Lumen Gentium* where, despite structural precedence being given to the common baptismal dignity and priesthood of all over the hierarchical character of the church, it is held that the specific priesthood of the ordained is essentially different from that of the laity.[39] Schillebeeckx, Küng, and others have charged that any notion of an essential or ontological distinction between lay and ordained supports the perpetuation of a separate clerical caste by failing to give due recognition to the Spirit-indwelled, charism-endowed, priestly character of the entire "people of God."[40] In response it has been maintained that it is only by viewing ordained priesthood as a fundamentally different exercise of ministry to that of the laity that one avoids suggesting the first is a better, more intense version of the same thing. Together with this is the recognition that the primacy and dynamism of grace requires ordination to be viewed as pertaining to priests' vocations and being before God and not just the things they do.

The ecclesial-political dimension that is a factor in all theological debate has been a particularly complicating factor here, with strong values such as the desire for a more collaborative, transparent, and accountable church and the concern to articulate a rich, sustaining theology of ordained ministry frequently finding themselves in conflict.[41] There is, consequently, an outstanding need within contemporary Catholicism for an integrated, noncompetitively articulated theology of lay and ordained ministry capable of generating a working consensus.

A possible way forward here is to view the "sacramentality" of ordained priesthood as consisting in the public, officially authenticated, representative performance of the God-given ministry pertaining to the entire Spirit-filled People of God.[42] As such, the distinctiveness of ordained priesthood would be held to lie neither in it being *an essentially different kind of* priesthood to that of the laity, nor in it being *a higher quality version of* the same priesthood. Rather, its distinctiveness would lie in it being *a fundamentally different mode of exercise* (public, official, representative) of the one priesthood of Christ in which all the baptized share; a different mode of exercise, moreover, that defines the specific vocation of the ordained.

One implication is that for the sake of its own authenticity this distinctive exercise of ministry must be performed in genuine service of and accountability to the ministry of the entire church. A further implication might be that if the distinctive sacramentality of ordained ministry consists precisely in its being *representative* of the Spirit-filled, charism-endowed ecclesial body of Christ, then the regulations concerning eligibility for ordination should be altered so as to reflect the actual composition of that body. In this regard the council's decision to admit mature married men to the permanent diaconate – one of the very few structural changes actually made at the council – might be seen as a modest first step in this direction.

Spirituality

Stimulated in part by the council's recommendation that religious orders should reconnect with their respective founding spirit; in part by *Lumen Gentium*'s emphasis on the calling of the entire pilgrim people of God to holiness; in part by the increased emphasis on the need for prayerful reflection on the word of scripture; in part by the influence charismatic renewal has had on many Catholics both lay and ordained; in part by what Rahner recognized as the need for contemporary Christians to have an experiential dimension to their faith if they are to be sustained in a secularized context; and in part also by generally increased Western expectations of personal fulfilment, the net result is that growth toward Christian spiritual maturity is no longer viewed as an esoteric pursuit of the few but as the normal path of Catholic life.

In terms of formal theology this shift is reflected in three ways. First is the growth of scholarship in the classics of spiritual theology and contemporary disciplines that has led to the emergence of spirituality as an academic subject area in its own right.[43] Second is the phenomenon of theologians whose writings, at least in part, take the form of high-level meditative reflection-cum-spiritual-counsel oriented toward the dramatic shaping of Christian life, Balthasar being the most obvious example. Third is an increasing concern to view theologians of even the most rigorously philosophical of appearances as seeking to articulate good habits of thought in the service of Christian discipleship and the life of the church.[44] It is, perhaps, the second and third of these points in particular that help explain the significant interest now frequently shown in notable Catholic theologians by theologians in other Christian traditions.

Moral theology

Reflecting in some ways an implicit tension between the ahistorical, universalist essentialism of neoscholastic natural law theory and the emphasis placed upon the role of the informed conscience in Vatican II teaching, much subsequent Catholic moral theology has been characterized by a profound disagreement between those of an "absolutist" commitment and those influenced by "proportionalist" ways of thinking.[45] It would be inaccurate to view this as a difference between Christocentric and personalist commitments. Catholic absolutists are as concerned for the flourishing of the person as Catholic proportionalists and the proportionalists are as concerned to articulate an ethic that reflects the discerned patterns of God's self-revelation in the incarnate Christ as the absolutists, albeit construed in different ways in each instance.

The difference relates more to whether human nature and the teleology of human acts are understood in fixed, essentialist terms or in historically particular and, hence, intrinsically plural terms requiring discerning judgment in the specificities of particular lives. Where absolutists judge proportionalists as guilty of an indulgent relativism, proportionalists judge absolutists as operating with an outmoded anthropology, particularly regarding human sexuality, that does not reflect the realities of created human life and renders Catholic moral teaching inflexible, incredible, and damaging to faith.[46]

Although now rapidly fading at time of writing, for long the symbolic benchmark took the form of defense of or dissent from the 1968 encyclical *Humanae Vitae* in which, against the majority decision of the consultative commission but supported by then Archbishop Karol Wojtyła, Pope Paul VI reaffirmed the traditional ban on so-called "artificial" means of contraception.[47] This led to an unfortunate climate in which criticism of *Humanae Vitae* was generally but inaccurately read as a rejection of moral absolutism per se.

The renewed appeal to a Thomist-inspired virtue ethic offers a way of overcoming this standoff. Here the emphasis is neither simply upon the observance of rules rightly viewed as absolute, nor upon the requirement that judgments always be made in proportion to one's perceived needs and circumstances. Rather, the emphasis is upon becoming sufficiently skilled in the habits of virtue, through disciplined practice among those already proficient in playing according to the rules, as to be able to make appropriately prudent judgments in the particularities of life.[48] In this understanding, defining rules and creative play are not antitheses but necessary correlates of sound ethical apprenticeship in genuine Christian autonomy.

The disagreement between absolutist and supposedly proportionalist stances can be restated more precisely, then, in terms of the need for the official magisterium to examine whether the various positions it currently holds indiscriminately as absolutely binding laws are indeed all appropriately so regarded.[49] For all the energetically executed countermoves of John Paul II and Ratzinger/Benedict XVI, the Catholic Church has continued to find itself in a dysfunctional situation where the prayerfully discerned judgment of many active members is at odds with the judgment of those controlling the revision of the rule book. Catholic laity were once told they should "Pay, pray, and obey." It seems they are now responding, "It pays to pray about what it means to obey." As Pope Francis recognized in the process around his controversial 2016 postsynodal Apostolic Exhortation, *Amoris Laetitia*, quite apart from its negative impact on Catholic ecclesial life, the danger for Catholicism's viability as a school of virtue is that if left unrepaired this crisis of authority will lead to more wholesale dismissals of the binding force of Catholic moral teaching and so further the kinds of uninformed autonomy it seeks to counter.

Political theology

The altered common sense that *Gaudium et Spes* and the subsequent emergence of Latin American liberation theology promoted is reflected most broadly in an increased concern to treat the various dimensions of Catholic faith in a way that draws out their social and political freight.[50] Significant in a more specific way are the contributions made by Catholics in the many contextual, or issue-based, theologies now generally covered by the phrase "political theology": ecotheology, Black theology, Hispanic theology, gay theology, and as already noted, feminist theology, with the latter itself now more appropriately subcategorized in terms of feminist, womanist, and mujerista theologies. In turn, for those whose specific focus is upon the explicitly economic dimensions of the political, the collapse of state communism in the former Soviet-bloc countries in 1989 and the subsequent globalization of the market economy has required a process of fresh thinking.

Although a desire lingers on in Catholic left circles, fired by a vision of the church as a prophetic community of resistance and counteranticipation, to adopt a stance of fundamental opposition to the capitalist system, the increasing realization of our common implication in and dependence upon the global economy is leading to more subtle negotiations.[51] Of continuing importance here is the recognition of the "preferential option for the poor" as *the* vital lens through which to judge the grossly unjust and dehumanizing failings of the present system and, complementing this, the need for imaginatively enacted, evangelically inspired anticipations – lived parables – of a transformed order.[52] As is also appreciated, however, equally important is the need to apply both intelligence and vision to identifying integral ways in which the existing global system can be made more just, and correlative acumen and pressure to achieving these.[53] Given that the extent of most theologians' engagement with economic theory is generally relatively slight – Lonergan and Küng being notable exceptions[54] – there is a sense in which much of the most important work in Catholic political theology is now being carried out by theologically informed analysts, advocates, and campaign organizers within the Catholic aid and development agencies.

Revelation and fundamental Christology

Intertwined with the various substantive developments thus far reviewed have been a number of key shifts in specifically doctrinal understanding. Issuing, for example, from Vatican II's *Dei Verbum* ("Dogmatic Constitution on Divine Revelation," 18 November 1965) has been a more dynamic, pneumatologically governed understanding of revelation and tradition that has prompted a fresh emphasis upon the historicity of Christian life in much subsequent Catholic theology.[55] In this way of thinking it is inadequate simply to apply the inherited form of Catholic understanding to the specificities of contemporary experience in a secondary manner. Even allowing for Lindbeck's influential critique of the role of experience in theology, the intrinsic dynamism of Christian tradition itself requires a process of integral discerning of genuinely fresh yet authentic articulations in the new circumstances encountered.[56]

These fundamental shifts in perspective combined with the further encouragement given in *Dei Verbum* to the use of critical methods of scripture study prompted massive efforts of doctrinal reformulation, in some ways paralleling the process that Protestant theology had been working through since the nineteenth century.[57] As in that context, a key concern has been how historical-critical methods of analyzing the gospels and other relevant documents are to be reconciled with the traditional doctrine of Christ and appropriately assimilated into its contemporary articulation.

For a period, the dominant approach, motivated both by apologetic concern and by the conviction that it supported significantly fresh understandings of God's self-revelation in Jesus, was to adopt a view, as it were, "from below," and to seek thereby to move inductively on the basis of historical analysis to an account of Jesus, who became recognized as the Christ.[58] Typically accorded a fulcrum role in this process are traces in the New Testament writings of experiences of encounter with the saving, transforming reality of God in the risen Jesus and the Spirit.[59] In reaction, however, to what was felt to be the relative fragility and theologically thin texture of the resulting reconstructions, a renewed concern emerged to read the gospel accounts in a manner explicitly informed by traditional credal understanding of the identity of their central character.[60] As befits the duality that is inevitably at issue in Christian understanding of the person of Jesus, the most astute interpreters recognized that both approaches are in fact necessary, each tending toward imbalance without the other.[61]

Indeed, in mainstream Catholic theology there is an important sense in which any notion of a supposedly irreconcilable tension between these approaches is somewhat artificial. For the vast majority of Catholic scholars adopting an approach "from below," liturgically informed credal faith can be assumed to provide an implicit prior frame of understanding, such that historical-critical methods are all along at the service of seeking to understand the character of God's self-revelation in the incarnate Word, Jesus of Nazareth. Equally, historical analyses represent a vital ancillary resource for the ad hoc testing and potential enrichment of more dogmatically driven Christologies and can help guard against the dangers of indulgent fantasy and constriction of vision. This Christologically focused issue can, then, be viewed as a particular instance of the broader issue, implicit in the work of Catholic scripture scholars such as Raymond Brown, of how to integrate the various critical modes of scriptural analysis within what *Dei Verbum* recognized to be the continuing need for explicitly tradition-informed, canonical readings.[62]

Trinity and soteriology

Accompanying these developments in fundamental Christology have been related developments in the theology of the Trinity and soteriology. With regard to the Trinity, particularly notable is the influence jointly exerted by Rahner's principle of the identity of the "economic Trinity" (the Trinity as disclosed in the economy of salvation) and the "immanent Trinity" (the inner Trinitarian life of God) and the related traditional principle of the interrelated unity in act of the three distinct eternal modes of God's being.[63] Together these principles have promoted a heightened concern to treat as genuinely disclosive of how God is what can be discerned of the patterns, actions, and commitments that characterized the life, death, and resurrection of Jesus and continued to characterize early Christian life in the Spirit.[64] Equally, viewed from a different angle, they have promoted dogmatically intensified readings of these patterns and commitments as the enactment in finite temporal reality of the dynamics that *are* the eternal being in act of God.[65]

More recently, such understandings of the being of God and, specifically, of the role of the Spirit have been put to work in the context of seeking to articulate a theology of religious pluralism that can maintain the reality of God's presence and action in the particularities of other faith traditions – and in ways from which Christians can learn – while also maintaining the traditional claim that there is nothing that can be known of God that will not cohere with what is shown in Jesus, the incarnate Word.[66] Particularly notable here is the move from viewing the covenant in Christ as dissolving the covenant with the Jewish people, as was standard in much pre-Vatican II understanding, to viewing the latter as of permanent validity.[67] This is of real significance to all ecumenical and interfaith theological reflection as it requires a considerably more subtle theology of divine providence and call than is implied by supersessionist accounts of the relationship between the Jewish and Christian covenants.

Turning to matters soteriological, the recurrent tension in recent Catholic theology between more world-receptive and more world-judging tendencies has been played out here in some interesting if unhelpful ways. According to the caricature, from the more world-receptive perspective the world-judging tendency lacks due appreciation for the intrinsic goodness of God's grace-indwelled creation as brought to fulfilment in the incarnation, and so tends toward a form of sub-Christian dualism.[68] Equally, from the more world-judging perspective the world-receptive tendency lacks a realistic understanding of the radical extent and disfiguring effects of sin and the consequent need for its unmasking and redemption in the cross and resurrection.[69] In reality the differences between these two emphases neither are, nor ever could be, as radically opposed as this suggests.

Rahner, for example, does, in a sense, view the incarnation itself as the achievement of human salvation in as much as it represents the absolute self-communication of God being met with absolute responsive openness in a way that recapitulates, fulfils, and redeems the story of creation, grace, and sin.[70] He does not, however, take this as a static fact but as a dynamic reality characterizing Jesus's entire life, climactically so in his death, and a movement, moreover, into which others are in turn drawn. Equally, for all Balthasar's concern to depict the contrast between the disorder of sin and the order of grace in starker terms than he finds in Rahner and, with this, to view God's judgment on sin in Jesus's crucifixion as an event of inner-Trinitarian alienation, he also views the total event of the incarnation as the crowning and fulfilment of creation. Again, despite their apparent greater sympathy with a Rahnerian rather than a Balthasarian/*Communio* orientation, it is a real concern also for politically conscious theologians such as Metz, Schillebeeckx, Gustavo Gutiérrez, and Jon Sobrino that due emphasis be given to the countercultural, transformative dynamic at the heart of Jesus's life, death, and resurrection.

Further, it is possible to integrate this emphasis on the political/cultural dimensions of the soteriological significance of the Jesus event with a robust understanding of the Trinitarian reality of God. The countercultural, transformative dynamic that shapes the particular story of Jesus can be viewed as the dramatic performance within the conditions of temporal human life of the dynamic of life-giving self-giving that *is* the eternal being of God. In turn, if this creative-transforming dynamic constitutes the "objective" dimension to God's saving act in Christ and the Spirit, the "subjective" dimension consists in our being drawn to participate in it and to grow into it even while continuing to exist in a world marked by the contrary self-serving dynamic of sin.[71] In such a perspective the primary calling of the church is to bear convincing, attractive witness to the countercultural, transforming action of God known in the church as at work in the world. Correlatively, it is in the light of this that all aspects of church life and structure, both local and universal, need to be held open to judgment and potential reconfiguration lest they themselves should become countersigns of that which they proclaim. It is hardly surprising that this indicates the locus for many of the continuing challenges within contemporary Catholic theology.

Assessment: A Still Unfolding Story

The institutional (Survey I), methodological (Survey II), and substantive (Survey III) developments that have occurred in Catholic theology since Vatican II each variously reflect the shift to being a truly world church, both one and universal. The fundamental issue of how to handle unity in diversity, how to hold plurality in appropriate communion, is raised in one way by the proliferation of specific theological commitments, methods, and resources and in a more pervasive way by an increased appreciation for the irreducible historicity and particularity of Christian life.

On the one hand, the proliferation of specialisms highlights the dual need to view theology as a collaborative exercise and to nurture structures that promote critically constructive conversation across specialisms and diverse perspectives. On the other hand, increased sensitivity to the historicity of Christian life highlights the need for mutual critically constructive interchange between the official and unofficial levels of Catholic theology, in the dual process of sieving and retrieving the historic tradition and discerning its appropriate performance today. Each of these points, particularly the second, in turn requires that explicit attention be paid – as Pope Francis has recognized with his call for more synodal ways of being church – to core issues concerning the appropriate structures of governance and exercise of authority at the various levels of Catholic life.

Closely related to this and in its service is the need to move toward a more collegial, reciprocal, and less monarchical exercise of the Petrine office and associated curial bureaucracy vis-à-vis the Catholic episcopate.[72] Quite apart from its bearing on the integrity, initiative, and potential contributions of the local churches, this issue is of enormous symbolic significance. It serves to shape the broader Catholic common sense as to the appropriate exercise of the dual ministry of authority and communion in its many other forms, whether episcopal, priestly, or lay. Again, it also bears directly on the ecumenical context, as John Paul II recognized in *Ut Unum Sint*. Interwoven with this is the question of whether Catholicism can be genuinely receptive to what can be learned from the alternative ecclesial forms, structures, and practices of the other Christian traditions and so be held open to its own potential expansion and renewal. Some particular cases in point here are the differing Anglican and Orthodox experiences of synodical structures and the connectional ethos that is so deeply ingrained in Methodism, together with the associated role of Conference in collective decision-making.

In the 2005 third edition of this volume, in the context of recognizing how difficult it is for institutions and bureaucracies to reform themselves, Nicholas Lash was quoted as advocating for Archbishop John Quinn's proposed establishing of a papal commission comprising "perhaps forty or fifty diocesan bishops, drawn from every corner of the world" with both curial officials and "historians, theologians and canon lawyers from outside Rome" acting as advisors. The brief would be "to draw up proposals for the transfer of governance in the Church from pope and Curia to pope and bishops, through the establishment of a standing synod, whose members would be diocesan bishops and whose work would be assisted by the offices of a curia so reformed as to function, not as an instrument of governance, but as a service of administration."[73] Lash's hope was that were such a shift in the culture of Catholic governance to take place, the result might be a cascade of subsidiarity through all dimensions of Catholic life.

In 2005, in the hinge between the long papacy of John Paul II and the successor papacy of Ratzinger/Benedict XVI, that may have seemed an act of hoping against hope. By contrast, at point of working on this revised version, over ten years into the Francis papacy and his unleashing of multiple initiatives in Catholic ecclesial reform, although the actual realization of that hope may still be far from certain its possibility now feels significantly more grounded in reality. Interesting to note as a possible point of connection here is the reported claim that among the reading Jorge Mario Bergoglio took into the 2013 conclave that would elect him Pope was John Quinn's book, as passed to him by his friend Cardinal Cormac Murphy O'Connor, then archbishop emeritus of Westminster.

For sure, the current opening of the Catholic Church to more synodal ways of working in all dimensions of its life has a long way to travel before it becomes received into a new Catholic normal. In the meantime, however, it is already serving to create a climate in which it increasingly appears simply nonsensical to seek to handle contentious issues in the life of the church either by refusing for them to be discussed or by excluding all but those with sworn allegiance to the current state of official understanding from participation in the conversation. On the contrary, although needing to identify appropriate means of duly respecting the particular roles and responsibilities of those in authority in any given context, the assumed Catholic common sense has already moved significantly toward recognizing the need also to make appropriate spaces at both the local and universal levels of church life for those of differing perspectives and areas of expertise to meet with members of the hierarchy, ecclesial bureaucrats, theologians, and others in order to work together at discerning the good of the whole ecclesial body. If it goes the distance, the officially sponsored emergence of structures, processes, and habits for genuine, critically constructive conversation in service of the church's continued learning will represent a significant new phase in the institutional reception of Vatican II. Rather than difference and debate being viewed as its problematic inheritance, they will, as Francis is encouraging, come to be valued as normal and necessary to the health of the whole. This is really to be doing Catholic theology "after Vatican II" for, as Congar noted, the council's legacy lies in no small part in the way in which its very occurrence granted legitimacy to the fact of debate in the church and to the associated need for appropriate structures and practices of shared discernment by retrieving the ancient conciliar dimension of authentic Catholic life.[74]

Notes

1   Also relevant is Paul D. Murray, "The Reception of Vatican II in Systematic Theology," in *The Oxford Handbook of Vatican II*, ed. Catherine E. Clifford and Massimo Faggioli (Oxford: Oxford University Press, 2022), 396–417. As regards other key global contexts, see Shazi George Kochuthara, "Reception of Vatican II in Asia," in *The Oxford Handbook of Vatican II*, ed. Clifford and Faggioli, 638–56; Agbonkhianmeghe E. Orobator, "The Impact, Reception, and Implementation of Vatican II," in *The Oxford Handbook of Vatican II*, ed. Clifford and Faggioli, 657–75; Carlos Schickendantz, "Reception of Vatican II in Latin America and the Caribbean," in *The Oxford Handbook of Vatican II*, ed. Clifford and Faggioli, 676–94; and Ormond Rush, "Receiving the Vision of Vatican II in Oceania," in *The Oxford Handbook of Vatican II*, ed. Clifford and Faggioli, 735–54; also Vimal Tirimanna, "Asian Theology," in *The Oxford Handbook of Catholic Theology*, ed. Lewis Ayres and Medi-Ann Volpe (Oxford: Oxford University Press, 2019), 877–89; and Anthony Akinwale, "Catholic Theology in Africa," in *The Oxford Handbook of Catholic Theology*, ed. Ayres and Volpe, 890–904.

2   For sophisticated versions of this telling, see Edward Schillebeeckx, *Vatican II: The Real Achievement* (London: Sheed & Ward, 1967); Langdon Gilkey, *Catholicism Confronts Modernity: A Protestant View* (New York: Seabury Press, 1975); and for a sociologically informed account, Bill McSweeney, *Roman Catholicism: The Search for Relevance* (Oxford: Blackwell, 1980).

3   Published along with Pope Pius IX's encyclical letter, *Quanta Cura* (8 December 1864), condemning perceived errors of the time, an Italian version is available at https://www.vatican.va/content/pius-ix/it/documents/encyclica-quanta-cura-8-decembris-1864.html (accessed 3 October 2023).

4   The "modernist" position condemned in Pius X's 1907 encyclical, *Pascendi Dominici Gregis*, was a synthetic construct of various ideas entertained by Catholic intellectuals exploring how Catholic faith might be integrated with modern thought; see Nicholas Lash, "Modernism, Aggiornamento and the Night Battle," in *Bishops and Writers: Aspects of the Evolution of Modern English Catholicism*, ed. Adrian Hastings (Wheathamstead: A. Clarke, 1977), 63–4; also Darrell Jodock, *Catholicism Contending with Modernity: Roman Catholic Modernism and Anti-Modernism in Historical Context* (Cambridge: Cambridge University Press, 2000).

5   Austin Flannery, ed., *Vatican Council II: Constitutions Decrees Declarations. A Completely Revised Translation in Inclusive Language* (Northport, NY: Costello; Dublin: Dominican, 1996), 163. Notable is Joseph Ratzinger's reference to *Gaudium et Spes* as "a kind of countersyllabus," in *Principles of Catholic Theology: Building Stones for a Fundamental Theology* (San Francisco, CA: Ignatius, 1987 [1982]), 381.

6   See Adrian Hastings, "Catholic History from Vatican I to John Paul II," in *Modern Catholicism: Vatican II and After*, ed. Adrian Hastings (London: SPCK, 1991), 8–13. In 1981, three years into his long papacy, John Paul II made the distinguished theologian and Cardinal Archbishop of Munich, Joseph Ratzinger, Prefect of the Congregation for the Doctrine of the Faith (CDF) – the then most powerful dicastery within the Roman Curia – followed, in 2002, by also making him dean of the College of Cardinals. Ratzinger continued in both these key roles until his own election as pontiff in the 2005 conclave following the death of John Paul II.

7   For the first, negative, assessment, see Peter Hebblethwaite, "John Paul II," in *Modern Catholicism*, ed. Hastings, 447–56. For the second, more positive, appraisal, see George Weigel, *Witness to Hope: The Biography of Pope John Paul II* (New York: HarperCollins, 1999), 486–90, 502–5, 846–7; also Tracey Rowland, *Culture and the Thomist Tradition after Vatican II* (London: Routledge, 2003), 11–50.

8   For a fine study, see Joseph Komonchak, "Vatican II as an 'Event,'" *Theology Digest* 46 (1999): 337–52; also Giuseppe Alberigo and Joseph Komonchak, eds., *History of Vatican II*, Vols. 1–5 (Maryknoll & Leuven: Orbis & Peeters, 1996–2004); and John W. O'Malley, *What Happened at Vatican II?* (Cambridge, MA: Harvard University Press, 2008). From his time as Cardinal Prefect of the CDF through his papacy, Ratzinger's/Benedict XVI's preferred way to speak of the relationship between pre- and postconciliar Catholicism was in terms of reform within the continuity of tradition; see Benedict XVI, "A Proper Hermeneutic for the Second Vatican Council," in *Vatican II: Renewal within Tradition*, ed. Matthew L. Lamb and Matthew Levering (Oxford: Oxford University Press, 2008), ix–xv.

9   For the effective manifesto, see Pope Francis, "*Evangelii Gaudium*. Apostolic Exhortation on the Proclamation of the Gospel in Today's World" (24 November 2013), http://w2.vatican.va/content/francesco/en/apost_exhortations/documents/papa-francesco_esortazione-ap_20131124_evangelii-gaudium.html (accessed 3 October 2023); and for analysis, see Alana Harris and Duncan Dormor, eds., *Pope Francis, Evangelii Gaudium, and the Renewal of the Church* (Mahwah, NJ: Paulist Press, 2018).

10 See Gabriel Flynn and Paul D. Murray, eds., *Ressourcement: A Movement for Renewal in Twentieth*

Century Catholicism (Oxford: Oxford University Press, 2012); also Fergus Kerr, *Twentieth-Century Catholic Theologians: From Neoscholasticism to Nuptial Mysticism* (Malden, MA: Blackwell, 2007).

11 See Tracey Rowland, *Catholic Theology* (London: Bloomsbury, 2017), 3–5, 91–138, 139–66; also Philip Trower, *Turmoil and Truth: The Historical Roots of the Modern Crisis in the Catholic Church* (San Francisco, CA: Ignatius, 2003).

12 See Flannery, ed., *Vatican Council II*, 10. Here a fascinating cross-type discussion is to be found in Nicholas M. Healy, *Church, World and Christian Life: Practical-Prophetic Ecclesiology* (Cambridge: Cambridge University Press, 2000).

13 See Hans Frei, *Types of Theology*, ed. George Hunsinger and William C. Placher (New Haven, CT: Yale University Press, 1992), 34–8; and Karen Kilby, *Karl Rahner: Theology and Philosophy* (London: Routledge, 2004); also Paul D. Murray, "The Lasting Significance of Karl Rahner for Contemporary Catholic Theology," *Louvain Studies* 29, no. 1–2 (2004): 8–27.

14 Alasdair MacIntyre, *After Virtue: A Study in Moral Theory*, 2nd ed. (Notre Dame, IN: University of Notre Dame Press, 1984), 222.

15 See Lash, "Theologies at the Service of a Common Tradition," in *Different Theologies, Common Responsibility: Babel or Pentecost?*, ed. Claude Geffré, Gustavo Gutiérrez, and Virgil Elizondo (London: SCM Press, 1984), 76. Such complications of patronage and power aside, Kilby dissects Balthasar's theological style as embodying a distorting concern for totality that makes his approach resistant to being a contributor to a wider dialectical process, see Karen Kilby, *Balthasar: A (Very) Critical Introduction* (Grand Rapids, MI: Eerdmans, 2012).

16 See Myriam Wijlens, "Reforming the Church by Hitting the Reset Button: Reconfiguring Collegiality within Synodality because of *sensus fidei fidelium*," *The Canonist* 8 (2017): 235–61.

17 For some interesting African-context perspectives on this, see Agbonkhianmeghe E. Orobator, ed., *The Church We Want: African Catholics Look to Vatican II* (Maryknoll, NY: Orbis, 2016).

18 Johann-Baptist Metz, *Faith in History and Society: Toward a Practical Fundamental Theology* (London: Burns and Oates, 1980), 58.

19 See CDF, "*Donum Veritatis*, Instruction on the Ecclesial Vocation of the Theologian" (24 May 1990), https://www.vatican.va/roman_curia/congregations/cfaith/documents/rc_con_cfaith_doc_19900524_theologian-vocation_en.html (accessed 3 October 2023).

20 See Pope Francis, "*Praedicate Evangelium*. Apostolic Constitution on the Roman Curia and Its Service to the Church in the World" (19 March 2022), §10, https://www.vatican.va/content/francesco/en/

apost_constitutions/documents/20220319-costituzione-ap-praedicate-evangelium.html (accessed 3 October 2023).

21 See John Paul II, "*Veritatis Splendor*. Encyclical Letter on the Church's Moral Teaching" (8 August 1993), §113, https://www.vatican.va/content/john-paul-ii/en/encyclicals/documents/hf_jp-ii_enc_06081993_veritatis-splendor.html (accessed 3 October 2023).

22 In the latter regard Anne Carr, Mary Grey, Elizabeth Johnson, Catherine Mowry LaCugna, Susan Ross, Sandra M. Schneiders, and Lisa Sowle Cahill have been particularly significant.

23 For example, Janet Martin Soskice of Duke Divinity School and Jesus College, Cambridge, and Tina Beattie, formerly of the University of Roehampton.

24 See Étienne Gilson, *The Philosophy of Saint Thomas Aquinas*, 3rd ed. (New York: Dorset Press, 1929); Marie-Dominique Chenu, *Aquinas and His Role in Theology* (Collegeville, MN: Liturgical Press, 2002 [1959]).

25 See Stephen J. Duffy, *The Graced Horizon: Nature and Grace in Modern Catholic Thought* (Collegeville, MN: Liturgical Press, 1992).

26 See Rahner, "The Abiding Significance of Vatican II" (1979), *Theological Investigations XX* (London: Darton, Longman & Todd, 1981), 94–7; and Bernard Lonergan, "Theology in Its New Context" (1968), *A Second Collection*, ed. W. F. J. Ryan and B. J. Tyrrell (London: Darton, Longman & Todd, 1974), 55–67.

27 See Aquinas, *Summa Theologœ*, Ia.I,7; compare *Gaudium et Spes*, §22.

28 See Rahner, "The Abiding Significance of Vatican II," 91–2; also "Basic Theological Interpretation of the Second Vatican Council" (1979), *Theological Investigations XX*, 77–89. Significant here is the new millennium Orbis book series, *Theology in Global Perspective*, with Peter C. Phan as editor-in-chief; also the recent Brill series, *Studies in Global Catholicism*, with Massimo Faggioli and Bryan T. Froehle as editors-in-chief.

29 See Gerald A. McCool, *From Unity to Pluralism: The Internal Evolution of Thomism* (New York: Fordham University Press, 1987) and Fergus Kerr, *After Aquinas: Versions of Thomism* (Malden, MA: Blackwell, 2002); also Fergus Kerr, ed., *Contemplating Aquinas: On the Varieties of Interpretation* (London: SCM Press, 2003).

30 Significant also are fresh retrievals of the tradition within historical theology, particularly recent revisionist readings of the Reformations. See Eamon Duffy, *The Stripping of the Altars: Traditional Religion in England, c.1400–c.1580* (New Haven, CT: Yale University Press, 1992); also *The Voices of Morebath: Reformation and Rebellion in an English Village* (New Haven, CT: Yale University Press, 2001).

31 See Gerald O'Collins, *Fundamental Theology* (New York: Paulist Press, 1981); and Leo J. O'Donovan and T. Howland Sanks, eds., *Faithful Witness: Foundations of Theology for Today's Church* (New York: Crossroad, 1988); and René Latourelle and Rino Fisichella, eds., *Dictionary of Fundamental Theology* (New York: Crossroad, 1994).

32 See Francis S. Fiorenza, *Foundational Theology: Jesus and the Church* (New York: Crossroad, 1984); and Avery Dulles, *The Craft of Theology: From Symbol to System* (New York: Crossroad, 1995), 3–15, 53–68; also Paul D. Murray, *Reason, Truth and Theology in Pragmatist Perspective* (Leuven: Peeters, 2004); and Ormond Rush, *The Reception of Doctrine: An Appropriation of Hans Robert Jauss' Reception Aesthetics and Literary Hermeneutics* (Rome: Gregorian University Press, 1997); and Gregory A. Ryan, *Hermeneutics of Doctrine in a Learning Church: The Dynamics of Receptive Integrity* (Leiden: Brill, 2020).

33 See Rahner, "Reflections on Methodology in Theology" (1970), *Theological Investigations XI* (London: Darton, Longman & Todd, 1974), 72–3.

34 See *Lumen Gentium*, §§21–27, in Flannery, ed., 28–39; also Dulles, *The Catholicity of the Church* (Oxford: Clarendon, 1985), 106–46; and Küng, *The Church* (Tunbridge Wells: Search Press, 1968), 444–80; compare Balthasar, *The Office of Peter and the Structure of the Church* (San Francisco, CA: Ignatius, 1986).

35 See Kasper, "On the Church," *The Tablet* (2001): 927–30; Ratzinger, "The Local Church and the Universal Church: A Response to Walter Kasper," *America* (19 November 2001): 7–11.

36 See Bernard Hoose, ed., *Authority in the Roman Catholic Church: Theory and Practice* (Aldershot: Ashgate, 2002); Rahner, "Unity of the Church – Unity of Mankind" (1978), *Theological Investigations XX*, 154–72; also Schreiter, *The New Catholicity: Theology between the Global and the Local* (Maryknoll, NY: Orbis, 1997).

37 "Decree on Ecumenism" (21 November 1964), Flannery, ed., 499–523.

38 See Paul D. Murray, ed., *Receptive Ecumenism and the Call to Catholic Learning: Exploring a Way for Contemporary Ecumenism* (Oxford: Oxford University Press, 2008); and Paul D. Murray, Gregory A. Ryan, and Paul Lakeland, eds., *Receptive Ecumenism as Transformative Ecclesial Learning: Walking the Way to a Church Re-formed* (Oxford: Oxford University Press, 2022).

39 See *Lumen Gentium*, §10.

40 See Küng, *Why Priests? A Proposal for a New Ministry*, trans. John Cumming (London: Collins, 1972); Schillebeeckx, *Ministry: A Case for Change* (London: SCM Press, 1981).

41 For the latter concern, see John Paul II, *Letters to My Brother Priests: Complete Collection of Holy Thursday Letters (1979–2005)*, ed. J. P. Socias (Chicago, IL: Midwest Theological Forum, 2006); also CDF, "Instruction on Certain Questions Regarding the Collaboration of the Non-ordained Faithful in the Sacred Ministry of Priests" (15 August 1997), http://www.vatican.va/roman_curia/congregations/cclergy/documents/rc_con_interdic_doc_15081997_en.html (accessed 3 October 2023).

42 For an initial account, see Paul D. Murray, "The Need for an Integrated Theology of Ministry within Contemporary Catholicism: A Global North Perspective," in *Ministries in the Church*, ed. Susan Ross, Maria Clara Bingemer, and Paul Murray (London: SCM Press, 2010), 43–54.

43 See Schneiders, "Spirituality in the Academy," *Theological Studies* 50 (1989): 676–97.

44 See Philip Endean, *Karl Rahner and Ignatian Spirituality* (Oxford: Clarendon, 2001); also Nicholas Healy, *Thomas Aquinas: Theologian of the Christian Life* (Aldershot: Ashgate, 2003).

45 Of the first group, Germain Grisez, John Finnis, John Ford, and John Paul II are the outstanding figures. Of the second, Bernard Häring, Joseph Fuchs, and Charles Curran have had particular influence. See Richard A. McCormick, "Moral Theology 1940–1989: An Overview," *Theological Studies* 50 (1989): 3–24; Paulinus I. Odozor, *Moral Theology in an Age of Renewal: A Study of the Catholic Tradition since Vatican II* (Notre Dame, IN: University of Notre Dame Press, 2003).

46 See John Paul II, *Veritatis Splendor*, §§28–83; compare Charles E. Curran, *Toward an American Catholic Moral Theology* (Notre Dame, IN: University of Notre Dame Press, 1987).

47 See Joseph Komonchak, "*Humanae Vitae* and Its Reception: Ecclesiological Reflections," *Theological Studies* 39 (1978): 221–57; and John C. Ford and Germain Grisez, "Contraception and the Infallibility of the Ordinary Magisterium," *Theological Studies* 39 (1978): 258–312; also John Paul II, *Veritatis Splendor*, §80; and "*Familiaris Consortio*. Apostolic Exhortation on the Role of the Christian Family in the Modern World" (22 November 1981), https://www.vatican.va/content/john-paul-ii/en/apost_exhortations/documents/hf_jp-ii_exh_19811122_familiaris-consortio.html (accessed 3 October 2023).

48 See Herbert McCabe, "Manuals and Rule Books," in *Understanding Veritatis Splendor*, ed. John Wilkins (London: SPCK, 1994), 61–8.

49 See Stan Chu Ilo, ed., *Love, Joy, and Sex: African Conversations on Pope Francis's Amoris Laetitia and the Gospel of Family in a Divided World* (Eugene, OR: Cascade, 2019).

50 See, for example, Edward Schillebeeckx, *Christ: The Christian Experience in the Modern World* (London: SCM Press, 1980); and Nicholas Lash, *A Matter of Hope: A Theologian's Reflections on the Thought of Karl Marx* (London: Darton, Longman & Todd, 1981); also Nicholas Lash, *Believing Three Ways in One God: A Reading of the Apostles' Creed* (London: SCM Press, 1992).

51 See Metz, *Faith in History and Society*, 88–99, 200–4; and Anna Rowlands, *Towards a Politics of Communion: Catholic Social Teaching in Dark Times* (London: T&T Clark, 2021).

52 See John Paul II, "*Sollicitudo Rei Socialis*. Encyclical Letter on the Twentieth Anniversary of *Populorum Progressio*" (30 December 1987), https://www.vatican.va/content/john-paul-ii/en/encyclicals/documents/hf_jp-ii_enc_30121987_sollicitudo-rei-socialis.html (accessed 3 October 2023); and "*Tertio Millennio Adveniente*. Apostolic Letter towards the Third Millennium" (11 October 1994), https://www.vatican.va/content/john-paul-ii/en/apost_letters/1994/documents/hf_jp-ii_apl_19941110_tertio-millennio-adveniente.html (accessed 3 October 2023).

53 See Martin Khor, *Rethinking Globalisation: Critical Issues and Policy Choices* (London: Zed, 2001).

54 See Hans Küng, *A Global Ethic for Global Politics and Economics* (London: SCM Press, 1997); and Bernard Lonergan, *Collected Works of Bernard Lonergan 15. Macroeconomic Dynamics*, ed. Patrick Byrne, Frederick Lawrence, Charles Hefling (Toronto: University of Toronto, 1999); also *Collected Works of Bernard Lonergan 21: For a New Political Economy*, ed. Philip J. McShane (Toronto: University of Toronto, 1998).

55 See Flannery, ed., 97–115; compare Yves Congar, "The Pneumatology of Vatican II," in *I Believe in the Holy Spirit* (London: Geoffrey Chapman, 1983), 167–73; also Gerald O'Collins, *Retrieving Fundamental Theology: The Three Styles of Contemporary Theology* (London: Geoffrey Chapman, 1993).

56 See George Lindbeck, *The Nature of Doctrine: Religion and Theology in a Postliberal Age* (London: SPCK, 1984).

57 See Francis Schussler Fiorenza and John P. Galvin, eds., *Systematic Theology: Roman Catholic Perspectives*, 2nd ed. (Minneapolis, MN: Fortress Press, 2011).

58 See Walter Kasper, *Jesus the Christ* (New York: Paulist Press, 1976); Edward Schillebeeckx, *Jesus, an Experiment in Christology* (London: Fount, 1979); also Raymond Brown, *An Introduction to New Testament Christology* (New York: Paulist Press, 1994).

59 See Schillebeeckx, *Jesus*, 320–571, particularly 379–97.

60 Compare Gerard Loughlin, *Telling God's Story: Bible, Church and Narrative Theology* (Cambridge: Cambridge University Press, 1996).

61 See Nicholas Lash, "Up and Down in Christology," *New Studies in Theology 1*, ed. S. W. Sykes and D. Holmes (London: Duckworth, 1980), 31–46; also Elizabeth Johnson, *Consider Jesus: Waves of Renewal in Christology* (New York: Crossroad, 1990).

62 See *Dei Verbum*, §12, Flannery, ed., 105–6; also Pontifical Biblical Commission, "The Interpretation of the Bible in the Church," (Vatican City: Libreria Editrice Vaticana, 1993); and Pope Benedict XVI, "*Verbum Domini*. Post-synodal Apostolic Exhortation on the Word of God in the Life and Mission of the Church" (30 September 2010), https://www.vatican.va/content/benedict-xvi/en/apost_exhortations/documents/hf_ben-xvi_exh_20100930_verbum-domini.html (accessed 3 October 2023); compare Sandra M. Schneiders, *The Revelatory Text: Interpreting the New Testament as Sacred Scripture*, 2nd ed. (Collegeville, MN: Liturgical Press, 1999 [1991]); and Luke Timothy Johnson and William S. Kurz, *The Future of Catholic Biblical Scholarship: A Constructive Conversation* (Grand Rapids, MI: Eerdmans, 2002).

63 See Karl Rahner, *The Trinity* (Tunbridge Wells: Burns & Oates, 1970), 21–4, 34–8, 45–6, 68–73, 76–7; and Lash, *Believing Three Ways in One God*, 30–3.

64 See Catherine LaCugna, *God for Us: The Trinity and Christian Life* (New York: HarperCollins, 1991), 21–52, 209–41, 377–417.

65 Compare Hans Urs von Balthasar, *Mysterium Paschale* (Edinburgh: T&T Clark, 1990 [1970]).

66 See Gavin D'Costa, *The Meeting of Religions and the Trinity* (Edinburgh: T&T Clark, 2000); and Jacques Dupuis, *Toward a Christian Theology of Religious Pluralism*, 2nd ed. (Maryknoll, NY: Orbis, 2001 [1997]); also Michael Barnes, *Theology and the Dialogue of Religions* (Cambridge: Cambridge University Press, 2002); compare CDF, "*Dominus Iesus*. Declaration on the Unicity and Salvific Universality of Jesus Christ and the Church" (6 August 2000), https://www.vatican.va/roman_curia/congregations/cfaith/documents/rc_con_cfaith_doc_20000806_dominus-iesus_en.html (accessed 3 October 2023).

67 See Vatican II, "*Nostra Aetate*. Declaration on the Relation of the Church to Non-Christian Religions" (28 October 1965), §4, Flannery, ed., 580; and Pontifical Biblical Commission, *The Jewish People and Their Sacred Scriptures in the Christian Bible* (12 February 2002), https://www.vatican.va/roman_curia/congregations/cfaith/pcb_documents/rc_con_cfaith_doc_20020212_popolo-ebraico_en.html (accessed 3 October 2023).

68 See Edward Schillebeeckx, *God Among Us: The Gospel Proclaimed* (London: SCM Press, 1983), 91–6.

69 See Hans Urs von Balthasar, *The Moment of Christian Witness* (San Francisco, CA: Ignatius, 1994 [1966]).

70 Among many, see Karl Rahner, "Current Problems in Christology" (1954), *Theological Investigations I* (London: Darton, Longman & Todd, 1965), 165; and "Christology Within an Evolutionary View of the World" (1962), *Theological Investigations V* (London: Darton, Longman & Todd, 1966), 160–1, 174–5; and *Foundations of Christian Faith: An Introduction to the Idea of Christianity* (London: Darton, Longman & Todd, 1978), 181, 197.

71 See Frans Jozef van Beeck, "Trinitarian Theology as Participation," in *The Trinity*, ed. Stephen T. Davis, Daniel Kendall, and Gerald O'Collins (Oxford: Oxford University Press, 1999), 295–325.

72 See Michael J. Buckley, *Papal Primacy and the Episcopate: Towards a Relational Understanding* (New York: Herder & Herder, 1998).

73 Nicholas Lash, "Vatican II: of Happy Memory – and Hope?," in *Unfinished Journey: The Church 40 Years after Vatican II*, ed. Austin Ivereigh (New York: Continuum, 2003), 29, compare John Quinn, *The Reform of the Papacy* (New York: Herder & Herder, 1999).

74 See Yves Congar, "A Last Look at the Council," in *Vatican II: By Those Who Were There*, ed. Alberic Stacpoole (London: Geoffrey Chapman, 1986), 338–42.

Recommended Reading

Alberigo, Giuseppe, and Joseph Komonchak, eds. *History of Vatican II*. Vols. 1–5. Maryknoll, NY: Orbis; Leuven: Peeters, 1996–2004.

Clifford, Catherine E., and Massimo Faggioli, eds. *The Oxford Handbook of Vatican II*. Oxford and New York: Oxford University Press, 2022.

Fiorenza, Francis Schüssler, and John P. Galvin, eds. *Systematic Theology: Roman Catholic Perspectives*. 2nd ed. Minneapolis: Fortress Press, 2011.

Flannery, Austin, ed. *Vatican Council II: Constitutions Decrees Declarations. A Completely Revised Translation in Inclusive Language*. Northport, NY: Costello; Dublin: Dominican, 1996.

Flynn, Gabriel, and Paul D. Murray, eds. *Ressourcement: A Movement for Renewal in Twentieth Century Catholicism.* Oxford and New York: Oxford University Press, 2012.

Harris, Alana, and Duncan Dormor, eds. *Pope Francis, Evangelii Gaudium, and the Renewal of the Church.* Mahwah, NJ: Paulist Press, 2018.

Kerr, Fergus. *Twentieth-Century Catholic Theologians: From Neoscholasticism to Nuptial Mysticism.* Oxford: Blackwell, 2007.

Lakeland, Paul. *A Council that Will Never End: Lumen Gentium and the Church Today.* Collegeville, MN: Liturgical Press, 2013.

Murray, Paul D., Gregory A. Ryan, and Paul Lakeland, eds. *Receptive Ecumenism as Transformative Ecclesial Learning: Walking the Way to a Church Re-formed.* Oxford and New York: Oxford University Press, 2022.

O'Malley, John W. *What Happened at Vatican II?* Cambridge, MA: Harvard University Press, 2008.

Rush, Ormond. *The Vision of Vatican II: Its Fundamental Principles.* Collegeville, MN: Liturgical Press, 2019.

Pentecostal Theology

Sammy Alfaro

Introduction

With over one hundred years of historical presence the Pentecostal-Charismatic renewal movement has become a global force in the twenty-first century.[1] In its origins around the turn of the twentieth century, some labeled Pentecostalism as merely consisting of fanatical fervor that read scripture emotionally and would soon die out as an experiential religious fad. Others went as far as branding Pentecostalism "the latest vomit of Satan," seeking to discredit the movement by associating it with demonic activity.[2] Despite the early negative assessments and continued caricaturing, it has become demonstrably evident that Pentecostalism could very well be the most determining religious movement for the present and future of the Christian church.

Recent estimates calculate that there are roughly 644 million Pentecostal/Charismatic Christians around the world, which means that one in four Christians worldwide identify as what Todd M. Johnson and Gina A. Zurlo label "Spiritempowered."[3] What is more, an overwhelming number of them (554 million or 86%) reside in the majority world (4.5 million in Australia and Oceania, 125 million in Asia, 195 million in Latin America, and 230 million in Africa).[4] Conversely, this means that roughly less than 14% of Pentecostal/Charismatic believers live in what many viewed as the "academic centers" of global Christianity – North America (68 million) and Europe (21 million). With the growing trend being that North America and Europe are becoming increasingly secular and less Christian, the explosive growth of Pentecostalism in the majority world signals a new Christendom emerging with Spirit-led faith as the center of its theology.

Given the dynamic nature of Pentecostal faith and the fragmented postdenominational identity of global Pentecostalism, an exploration of Pentecostal theology should seek to capture the main essence and characteristics of the faith of its adherents. Thus, instead of focusing on the intricacies of unique strands of Pentecostal/Charismatic denominations or organizations that tend to divide, this chapter will focus on the main emphases and contours of Pentecostal theology by aiming to foreground the most salient characteristics of Spirit-led faith. But first, a historical overview of the origins of Pentecostalism will serve to highlight major issues of its theological roots and development.

Ford's The Modern Theologians: An Introduction to Christian Theology since 1918, Fourth Edition.
Edited by Rachel Muers and Ashley Cocksworth.
© 2024 John Wiley & Sons Ltd. Published 2024 by John Wiley & Sons Ltd.

Survey and Debate: Origins and Theological Development

As the name itself suggests, Pentecostalism's foundational emphasis consists in being a back-to-Pentecost movement. Early Pentecostals believed God was restoring the Christian movement back to its original order as was initially established through the outpouring of the Spirit in Acts 2. God's Spirit has always been present in the history of Christianity, but with the rise of Pentecostalism something new was taking place. Pentecostal historian Vinson Synan explains this ethos:

> Over the two thousand years of Christian history, there have been many renewals, revivals, and reforms. Without these *occasional* awakenings, the church might well have drifted into corruption, dead ritualism, and ultimate insignificance. Some of these renewals offered their enthusiastic followers a spiritual experience or ritual that went beyond the usual sacraments of the church.[5]

Early Pentecostalism truly believed God was fully restoring the faith of primitive Christianity with a return to Pentecost.

Grant Wacker describes this type of restorationism as "historical primitivism" in the sense that early Pentecostals believed God was recreating apostolic Christianity through their movement, which sought to reinstate the charismatic gifts of the Spirit in the church.[6] Notably, what set Pentecostalism apart from the preceding healing, revivalist, and holiness movements at the end of the nineteenth century was "the experience of speaking in tongues as the evidence of having received the baptism with the Holy Spirit."[7] Fueled with revivalist missional fervor and the belief that the end of the world was near, it was the understanding of the baptism of the Spirit as an empowerment for witness that gave Pentecostalism the impetus for global growth. Prior to the rise of Pentecostalism, Wesleyan Holiness movements were preaching the importance of sanctification as a subsequent experience to being born again labeling the doctrine "Christian perfection," "entire sanctification," "second blessing," or "a second work of grace." From these seminal ideas, the teaching on the baptism in the Holy Spirit emerged as a "crisis experience" that followed conversion and served to prepare the believer for service and witness within the church.

Rather than mere theological discovery, however, the doctrine of the baptism in the Spirit needs to be understood in connection to the religious affections of Holiness preachers and followers who desired a deeper experience with God. Focus on the doctrine of Spirit baptism was already being taught by Holiness preachers like A. B. Simpson, Phoebe Palmer, Andrew Murray, and R. A. Torrey among others. But it was the action of "tarrying before the Lord," praying for an Acts-like experience of the baptism of the Holy Spirit, that led Pentecostal pioneers such as Charles Parham to search the scriptures for the genuine evidence of having received the baptism in the Spirit.

After having begun a missionary school, Bethel Bible College in Topeka, Kansas, Parham was among the first to formulate the doctrine of the baptism in the Holy Spirit accompanied by speaking in tongues to facilitate worldwide evangelism.

> In December of 1900 we had our examination upon the subject of repentance, conversion, consecration, sanctification, healing and the soon coming of the Lord. We had reached in our studies a problem. What about the second chapter of Acts? . . . I set the students at work studying out diligently what was Bible evidence of the baptism of the Holy Ghost.[8]

What began as an academic assignment quickly led to a late-night vigil praying for the experience of Spirit baptism with tongues. Having prayed and fasted from early on December 31st and through January 1st, a female student, Agnes Ozman, was the first to speak in tongues after Parham laid hands on her. In the next few days, Parham himself and other students would receive the gift of the Spirit with the evidence of speaking in tongues. Such a historical account contains all the hallmarks of a typical Pentecostal encounter as experienced and recounted in the past and present by Spirit-filled believers around the world.

Parham's "Apostolic Faith" movement led him to start another Bible school in Houston, TX where an African American preacher named William Joseph Seymour caught the fire and brought it to Los Angeles, CA sparking the Azusa Street Revival of 1906.[9] News of Azusa Street spread quickly, and visitors came pouring in from throughout North America and around the world. Essentially, Azusa became a revolving door where visitors came to experience Pentecost and then exported its message and charismatic fervor to the ends of the world. Allan H. Anderson encapsulates the significance of Azusa like this:

> [W]hat cannot be denied is that for three years [1906–1908], Seymour's Apostolic Faith Mission was the most prominent and significant centre of Pentecostalism on the continent. That this was a predominantly black church and leadership, rooted in the African American culture of the nineteenth century, is really significant. Many of the early manifestations of Pentecostalism came from African American Christianity and were also found in the religious expressions of the slaves.[10]

Though much can be said about the place of the Azusa Revival with regard to the spread of global Pentecostalism, one has to recognize that early narratives celebrate its prominence at the expense of various other American hubs of Pentecostalism that were ignited almost simultaneously in the early 1900s.[11]

Whereas earlier assessments of the global Pentecostal movement gave more prominence to its beginnings within the United States, it has become more commonplace to speak of the origins of Pentecostalism as being polycentric with multiple independent origination spots. Already the story of Azusa Street signaled interconnectedness and even interdependency with preceding and concurrent Pentecostal revivals around the globe. For example, early chronicler of the Pentecostal Movement, Frank Bartleman (1871–1936), hints at the related web of Pentecostal fires when he wrote: "The present world-wide revival was rocked in the cradle of little Wales, it was 'brought up' in India, following; becoming full grown in Los Angeles later."[12] Bartleman's insightful remarks point of course to the Welsh Revival of 1904–5 and the Indian Pentecost in Mumbai (1905) under the leadership of a woman, Pandita Sarasvati Ramabai. Similarly, the Chilean Pentecostal revival (1909) under the leadership of Methodist minister Willis Collins Hoover was also sparked from the embers of the Indian Pentecostal revival.

The origins of Pentecostal faith around the world attest to an interconnected movement, which can only problematically be imagined as having one central place of birth. Rather than arguing for the supremacy of one reservoir from which all Pentecostal streams flowed, it is best to consider the Pentecostal movement as developing among various centers with assorted expressions of what it means to be baptized in the Spirit and live the Spirit-filled life. For some, the initial evidence of speaking in other tongues (be it human languages or unknown spiritual/angelic tongues) became the hallmark of being Pentecostal. For others, the charismata or gifting of the Spirit cannot be limited to speaking in tongues because scripture provides various lists for other spiritual manifestations and ecstatic experiences (see Romans 12:6–8; 1 Corinthians 12:8–10, 28–30; Ephesians 4:11; 1 Peter 4:10–11). In addition, what characterized early Pentecostals was not merely the occurrence of spiritual experiences, healings, and giftings, for these were accompanied by a genuine desire and empowerment to spread the message of the gospel to the ends of the earth out of a sense of eschatological urgency.

Although some might opine that early Pentecostalism lacked a theological approach that could be systematized, in his magisterial study of this period, Douglas Jacobsen demonstrates the rich tapestry of theological beliefs in the initial phase of the movement.[13] Wolfgang Vondey rightly concludes: "The focus of Pentecostal theology during the first decades can be seen in its recourse to the scriptures and the organization of biblical themes around Pentecostal experiences."[14] Indeed, the main focus of Pentecostal books and articles of the early period centered on outlining a framework for understanding the biblical doctrine of the baptism in the Holy Spirit and the effects such an experience had on the believer and the church.

Pentecostal theology has come a long way from its spiritually formative years in the first half of the twentieth century. The need to prepare ministers with a distinctively Pentecostal ethos led pioneers and later denominations to begin their own Bible training schools and eventually found their own universities and seminaries. Pentecostals soon realized they needed their own ministerial and theological resources to prepare Spirit-led pastors and leaders. In response to this necessity, Pentecostal textbooks focused on biblical doctrines began to appear. In his study of *Types of Pentecostal Theology*, Christopher A. Stephenson examines foundational Pentecostal textbooks that instructed a generation of Pentecostal leaders through a Spirit-filled approach for understanding biblical doctrines.[15] These classic Pentecostal academicians provided the movement with foundational assessments of key doctrines and strategies for biblical interpretation.

Named Theologians: Veli-Matti Kärkkäinen, Amos Yong, Wolfgang Vondey, Frank D. Macchia

Over the last fifty years, Pentecostal theology has flourished globally, providing the movement a voice within the greater theological academy. At first, Pentecostal academics focused primarily on providing a theological defense of key Pentecostal distinctives and spirituality.[16] Eventually, the focus turned to developing a thoroughly Pentecostal approach to theological methodology and themes and embarking on the quest for a truly systematic Pentecostal theology. Although it would be impossible to name and trace the contributions of leading Pentecostal scholars from the past few decades, the following section provides a short analysis of a few prominent Pentecostal theological and their major contributions.

Considering the contribution of Pentecostal theology to the greater religious academy represented in this volume, Terry Cross playfully asked some years ago whether Pentecostals could bring more than just the relish to the rich feast of theology.[17] Moreover, it has been suggested that in times past Pentecostals have many times lowered their own status by borrowing alien "methodological thought structures" to give shape to their Pentecostal reflections.[18] More recently, though, there has been a move to do theology from within a Pentecostal framework: to theologize with a characteristic Pentecostal orientation. Some major theological players who have placed Pentecostal theology on the map with a more global and ecumenical reach are Veli-Matti Kärkkäinen, Amos Yong, Wolfgang Vondey, and Frank D. Macchia.

The sheer volume of output alone would be enough to include Veli-Matti Kärkkäinen and Amos Yong on a list of influential Pentecostal theologians. However, their value to the Pentecostal academy is their fine-tuned sense of ecumenical methodology and global awareness. Together they have stretched Pentecostal theologians to engage in more critical dialogue outside the typical borders of their own theological frameworks. Central to their meticulous approach for doing theology is the sense that theology is best done from the perspective that Pentecostal faith is intertwined with other Christian faith traditions and within the greater religious environments it inhabits. In addition, their theologies embark on distinct but related theological programs that broach interreligious, philosophical, and scientific studies. In recognition of the value of their research, their colleagues and students have collected their essays for the Pentecostal community and abroad.[19]

Slightly less prolific but equally influential due to the depth of their theological contributions are Wolfgang Vondey and Frank D. Macchia. The careers of Vondey and Macchia are marked for their desire for Pentecostal theology to engage directly and be integrated with contemporary evangelical theology. In their own ways, they demonstrate what Pentecostal theology can learn from and contribute to the larger field of Christian dogmatics. Among Macchia's numerous contributions, he places Pentecostal theology in fruitful conversations with Johann and Christoph Blumhardt, Karl Barth, and Paul Tillich, to name a few unusual theological pairings.[20] In addition, Macchia's most recent contribution, *Tongues of Fire*, is being hailed as the most mature Pentecostal systematic theology to date.[21] Eager to embrace the experiential spirituality of Pentecostal origins while integrating it with the larger Christian theological agenda, Vondey embarks on a mission to rehabilitate and strengthen Pentecostal theology by having it engage and contribute to other contemporary Christian confessional theological traditions. In short, what Vondey calls for in *Beyond Pentecostalism* he then delivers in *Pentecostal Theology,* by gifting us a truly Spirit-filled systematic theology of the full gospel.[22]

Though lacking in voluminous output from a singular scholar, the present state of global Pentecostal theology has produced a rich harvest of scholarship from the majority world. A recent four-volume collection of works edited by Amos Yong and Vinson Synan offers a comprehensive assessment of the theological production within global Pentecostal/Charismatic Christianity. This collection is perhaps the most complete and current analysis of global renewal Christianity in the voices of its own scholars.[23] Too numerous and broad ranging to describe compactly in this essay, global Pentecostal theology is well represented by this diverse group of theologians who collaborate to produce a Spirit-infused theology of the movement's faith and practice.[24]

Debates

The Oneness-Trinitarian dialogue

From early in the development of the Pentecostal movement, there have been ongoing debates regarding Pentecostal faith. Some early debates, which are now considered less critical, involved the indispensability of speaking in tongues in relation to the baptism of the Spirit. However, a major doctrinal debate that still preoccupies Pentecostal theology is the ongoing conversation between Oneness and Trinitarian Pentecostals. Early in the history of the Assemblies of God (AG), the controversy caused it to split into two movements. However, in more recent times, the Oneness-Trinitarian dialogue has been approached by formidable theologians on both sides of the debate in academic conferences and journal articles.

The Oneness Pentecostal movement broke off from the AG in 1916 over the issue of the Trinity.[25] Two years after the official establishment of the denomination the schism prompted the "Statement of Fundamental Truths" (the official statement of beliefs of the AG) in order to affirm a Trinitarian understanding of the Godhead. Gary B. McGee describes the development as follows:

> When the Oneness issue threatened to split the General Council [of the Assemblies of God] at its gathering in 1916, church leaders willingly set aside the anticreedal sentiments of the Hot Springs meeting by drawing doctrinal boundaries to protect the integrity of the Church and welfare of the saints. Several leading ministers, led by Daniel W. Kerr, drafted the Statement of Fundamental Truths; it contained a long section upholding the orthodox view of the Trinity.[26]

From the Oneness perspective, David K. Bernard, documents the split in this manner:

> In 1916 the Assemblies of God adopted a strong, detailed trinitarian statement that caused Oneness preachers to leave the two-year-old organization. Some trinitarian preachers left also, because the church had violated its founding principle of adopting no creed other than the Bible. Those that remained in the Assemblies of God felt that the Oneness believers were in doctrinal error, but at no time did they classify them as a non-Christian cult.[27]

That the doctrine of the Trinity was at the center of the split is clear from both sides. What caused the Trinitarian disputes was the distinctive doctrine of the name of Jesus as developed by early Oneness Pentecostal leaders like Frank Ewart, Garfield T. Haywood, and Andrew Urshan. At the center of the controversy was establishing the correct biblical baptismal formula and deciding what to do about the practice of rebaptisms that developed within the denomination. Oneness Pentecostals emphasized the correct baptismal formula as being *only* "in the name of Jesus" referencing Acts 2:38 and 19:5. As a result, their Trinitarian opponents pejoratively labeled them as "Jesus Only." Oneness Pentecostals, however, have defended their understanding of the view of God as "the New Issue" or "Jesus's Name doctrine."

Whereas in the early phase of Pentecostalism Oneness and Trinitarian Pentecostals engaged in heated debates concerning their theological differences regarding their understanding of the nature of God and water baptism, in more recent times the animosity has turned to fruitful open dialogue between the two camps. Perhaps, at a local church member level one might still witness the passionate defenses and disagreements that often surround talk of doctrinal and denominational distinctives, however, within the Pentecostal academe a sustained critical conversation has been taking place for over twenty years with great comradery.[28] A formal dialogue took place within the auspices of the Society for Pentecostal Studies (SPS) annual meetings between 2002 and 2007. Frank Macchia, a key participant in the dialogues, provides the following Lindbeckian summary analysis of the gatherings:

> Oneness and Trinitarian grammars differ, though their language of faith and its expression in life are quite similar. To press the analogy of grammar further, the Oneness and the Trinitarian Pentecostals agree that the "Father, Son, and Spirit" involved in the story of Jesus function as *adverbs* descriptive of God's impartation of life. The Trinitarians, however, maintain that the triadic titles also function in a specialized sense as adjectives descriptive of the eternally-distinct modes of self-relation in God.[29]

In many ways, the continued and growing participation and contributions by Oneness Pentecostal scholars in SPS conferences is a great indicator of the theological maturity of the movement even in the midst of radical differences in belief.

The cessationist critique

In recent years financial scandals associated with the very popular Word of Faith movement have brought Pentecostalism into some disrepute, particularly in the United States.[30] With this concern, it is understandable the popular reformed pastor John MacArthur would call for putting out the *Strange Fire* of Pentecostalism on account of the financial and spiritual abuses that occur within the movement.[31] However, it is quite important to remember that "Word of Faith" Pentecostalism in the United States is not necessarily descriptive of the type of global Pentecostalism that is on the rise. In sharp contrast to the views of evangelical and conservative pastor John MacArthur, the liberal scholar Harvey Cox lauds Pentecostalism as follows: "Something highly significant is going on in the Pentecostal movement. Its main focus was once fixed on a strictly otherworldly salvation, but now the example of Jesus's concern for the impoverished, the sick, and the socially outcast has begun to play a more central role."[32]

MacArthur's attack on Pentecostalism is representative of the typical fundamentalist cessationist critique of the modern experience of the gifting of the Holy Spirit. MacArthur, however, does not engage the ample historical and theological Pentecostal scholarship but rather creates a caricature of the Pentecostal/Charismatic movement by focusing primarily on the Word of Faith movement, or as it might be known more popularly, the Gospel of Prosperity or even the Health and Wealth Gospel. MacArthur's analysis goes on to build its case by putting the Word of Faith movement under the microscope and questioning its biblical interpretations and theological rigor. In the end, by using this strawman strategy, MacArthur questions Pentecostalism's connection to God's Spirit and labels it a modern heretical movement.

Ironically, Pentecostal/Charismatic scholars would agree with much of MacArthur's criticism of the excesses that exist within the movement, in particular when it leads to the exploitation of Spirit-filled believers and center on making preachers wealthy. In addition, MacArthur's fundamentalist oriented critique has historically been informed by a biblicist perspective that aims to preserve a system of Christian faith without room for the contextualization of the gospel, the present charismatic move of the Spirit, and issues of political and social concern. This fundamentalist hesitancy to accept Pentecostalism has its origins in the staunch defense of biblicism, which should not be confused with the principle of *sola scriptura*. Arguably, it is contradictory to interpret scripture against itself in order to deny a present move of the Spirit, which has biblical precedent and theological support.

Tracing back the roots of these fundamentalist approaches, one inevitably arrives at the Reformation. Tom Pennington, in 2013, made two of his main arguments for biblical cessationism by pointing to the testimony of church history and the sufficiency of scripture.[33] Quoting Luther, Calvin, and B. B. Warfield, Pennington aimed at debunking the Pentecostal/Charismatic belief in the continued miraculous work of the Spirit. Martin Luther writes, "This visible outpouring of the Holy Spirit was necessary to the establishment of the early church as were also the miracles that accompanied the gift of the Holy Ghost. Once the church had been established and properly advertised by these miracles, the visible appearance of the Holy Ghost ceased."[34] John Calvin similarly writes, "The gift of healing, like the rest of the miracles which the Lord willed to be brought forth for a time, has vanished away in order to make the preaching of the gospel marvelous forever."[35]

Finally B. B. Warfield writes,

> These gifts were distinctly the authentication of the Apostles. They were part of the credentials of the Apostles as the authoritative agents of God in founding the church. Their function thus confined them to distinctively the apostolic church and they necessarily passed away with it. The miraculous working which is but the sign of God's revealing power cannot be expected to continue and in point of fact, does not continue after the revelation of which it is the accompaniment had been completed.[36]

Luther and Calvin's remarks should be understood with historical appreciation for the Reformers' demonizing of parallel radical reformation groups with charismatic tendencies. In addition, as Vinson Synan points out, Luther and Calvin's cessationism is fueled by the desire to dismiss the Catholic charges leveled against the Reformers alleging Protestantism lacked authenticity due to the absence of miraculous signs.[37] Finally, Warfield's argument hinges on the cessationist clause of 1 Corinthians 13:8, which states that tongues will cease, a cryptic mention that determines how three full chapters of scripture are read. In fact, 1 Corinthians 12–14 focuses on the charismatic activity within the local church precisely because believers were well acquainted with miraculous giftings of the Spirit. Why would Paul cryptically inform the Corinthian congregation that the spiritual gifts would come to an end while correcting the misuse of the spiritual gifts and explaining how they, not the apostles, could make the best use of the spiritual gifts? It is surprising that theological movements like fundamentalism and modern-day conservative evangelicalism, which are focused on the all-sufficiency of scripture, would leave no room for contemporary manifestations of the Spirit by excluding ample biblical evidence in support for the continued miraculous work of the Spirit in the church.

Influence, Achievement, and Agenda

Considering the influence, achievement, and agenda of Pentecostal theology, here are some key contributions that may serve as possible indicators for understanding how it can serve the wider theological community. In thinking about the contours of a Pentecostal theology, this author realizes that in many respects the task ahead is provisional – a sort of out-loud theological reflection on the way. Moreover, due to the distinctiveness of Pentecostal theology one would expect the shape of its methodology to have a less rigid framework and a more dynamic character. In a sense, it seems that a sort of conversion experience from traditional approaches to theological method and how we understand theology overall are needed. Harvey Cox narrates his testimony concerning his rethinking of Pentecostal theology in this way:

> As a theologian I had grown accustomed to studying religious movements by reading what their theologians wrote and trying to grasp their central ideas and most salient doctrines. But I soon found out that with pentecostalism this approach does not help much. As one Pentecostal scholar puts it, in his faith "the experience of God has absolute primacy over dogma and doctrine." Therefore the only theology that can give an account of this experience, he says, is "a narrative theology whose central expression is the testimony." I think that he is right.[38]

Likewise, it would be wise to rethink theological method from a Pentecostal perspective. Although this writer feels that this study has yielded significant findings regarding the Pentecostal theology, it is nonetheless my opinion that there is much ground for us to cover. Thus, I offer the following pages as a provisional proposal for setting an agenda toward embracing a Pentecostal approach for doing theology.

A pneumatic-experiential orientation

A study of theological hermeneutics reveals that for Pentecostals a pneumatic-experiential orientation provides new windows into the text. As early accounts of Pentecostalism demonstrate, the Pentecostal theological imagination was born out of the quest to integrate the biblical narrative with a personal and communal narrative. Kenneth J. Archer describes the process in this way:

> Pentecostals found biblical parallels with their life experiences and would incorporate these into their testimonies. This reinforced the Pentecostal story. Hence, Pentecostals did not see a difference between how God worked in biblical times and how God worked in the present. In addition, they did not recognize any difference in perceived reality due to the changing of time or culture. People have always had similar experiences. Thus, they saw their experiences similar to Bible times. This outlook reiterated the easy accessibility and immediacy of the meaning of Scripture for their Pentecostal community.[39]

It could be said that Pentecostalism since its origins has focused more on the experience of the believer as a source for thinking theologically. In this sense, their testimonies, songs, sermons, and worship practices become an integral part of their theologizing. For Pentecostals, these are the main resources that give shape to their theological imagination; as they speak, sing, and give witness of the continued work of God in their daily lives they are doing theology. What is more, the practice of their religious affections is filtered through an experience that is grounded in a life of struggle and suffering. As they listen to a sermon or sing a song, their theological framework continues to be shaped, for it is the God of their faith who comes to meet them with miraculous power in the midst of their daily struggle. Thus, Pentecostal theology is not learned merely through typical academic formation. Principally, the theological Pentecostal imagination is born out of the triadic engagement between the scriptures, the Spirit, and the Spirit-led experience of the community.[40]

For Pentecostals the scriptures already contain an experiential theology of the Spirit, for men and women of God in biblical times encountered the presence and power of the Spirit in their daily lives. In both the Old and New Testaments, the biblical authors reflect theologically through the agency of the Holy Spirit on their encounters with a wonder-working God. In short, God has manifested his presence in the history of humanity through providential acts on behalf of his people and the world, and the biblical authors guided by the Spirit preserved God's revelation of those divine encounters mostly in narrative form. To understand the Pentecostal imagination at work, one needs to understand that for Pentecostals God continues to manifest his presence through miraculous activity such as a healing or a prophetic utterance in tongues. Considering this, for Pentecostal theologians it is not an option to remain connected to the Spirit-filled community, but rather a theological prerogative.

The doxological approach to doing theology

Another major concern that guides Pentecostal theology is the quest to recover and retain the doxological approach that it had in its beginnings. "We live in an epoch where academic study of Scripture and spirituality do not always inhabit the same spheres of thought; where sermon preparation and biblical studies at times do not have a significant connection with the theological task at an academic level."[41] One might wonder if, especially within Pentecostal circles, the professional theologian has done more to create a wedge between ministry and academia, than is usually taken responsibility for. Could it be that the disregard that the Pentecostal clergy and laity have for the scholarly community is in many ways warranted? Is it not true that many times the miracle-believing church leader who went to seminary, and later entered doctoral study, has now become an antisupernaturalist who has long shed his/her Pentecostal heritage?

Pentecostal scholars would do a great service to the church and the academy if they continued to do theology approaching it as a spiritual discipline. Pentecostalism was birthed after arduous nights of spiritual travail, therefore, if Pentecostal theology is to be a faithful witness of the movement – the scholarly discourse that articulates what Pentecostals think about God – then it needs to imbibe from the same spiritual fountain. There must be a correlation between Pentecostal spirituality and Pentecostal theology, for one cannot theologize from a Pentecostal perspective if one does not share in the Pentecostal way of life.[42] Put differently, one necessarily needs to be rooted in one's religious tradition if one desires to be a true interpreter of his or her community. Recovering the doxological nature of theology will not only bridge the divide between church and academia, but also serve the Pentecostal scholar as a methodological means for advancing their distinctive approach toward theology.

Toward a contextual and global theology

Pentecostalism has certainly come of age in the southern hemisphere. The majority world that experiences great economic, political, and social challenges is where Pentecostal faith is growing immensely. For this reason, scholars of Pentecostalism have risen to the challenge of picking up the mantle of liberation thrust upon them.[43] If, as the popular slogan goes, "Liberation Theology opted for the poor, but the poor opted for Pentecostalism," then Pentecostals still have a great challenge before them to be the voice for the voiceless and to rise in action for their defense.[44] In looking at early accounts of the Pentecostal movement, one inevitably notices the complete affinity that the Pentecostal minister had for the community; sermon and life shared a common sphere of experience. Such contextualization is also much needed in Pentecostal theology. According to Darío López Rodríguez:

> The leveling and equalizing effect of the experience of Pentecost, as well as its personal and communal nature, serves to explain why a growing number of Pentecostal communities in the global south have among its leadership and members those who are marginalized by the greater society and other religious traditions because they do not qualify, according to their social conventions and denominational regulations, to represent them in public life or to be their spiritual guides.[45]

Considering the southern hemisphere accounts for the overwhelming majority of Pentecostals worldwide, it would be significant to consider how their experience of the Spirit from the margins of society serves to enrich and challenge American and European Pentecostalism. In many ways, one can no longer speak (if one ever could) of *a* Pentecostal theology, for its multicultural and multiethnic diversity as a movement leads all Pentecostal adherents to worship and think from a particular context. Yet, this should not be seen as a disadvantage; for within the global Pentecostal community is the opportunity to enrich contextual theologies through a meaningful engagement of what it means to be Pentecostal in other parts of the world. In this regard, Pentecostal theology has the potential to be a catalyst and innovator in the prospect of a truly global theology. Due to the presence of Pentecostal faith in the remotest parts of the world and the widespread reach of Pentecostalism among the most diverse of cultures, Pentecostals are positioned to develop a truly global and ecumenical theology. Amos Yong prophetically challenged the Pentecostal academic community with a prayerful hope for arriving at this promising future:

> Pentecostal theology in the twenty-first century will need to build on developments made during its scholastic phase but also move beyond them and come of age by engaging the broad spectrum of conversations as a full dialogue partner seeking to learn but also able to contribute something fresh.[46]

Notes

1 Although it has become increasingly difficult to define what is and who belongs within the Pentecostal movement, this exploration considers Pentecostalism in its broadest dimensions seeking to identify the core of its faith and theology. With "Pentecostal," one may simply refer to the currents of Spirit-led faith that flow from the classical rivers of Pentecostal revivalism that had its origins toward the end of the nineteenth and beginning of the twentieth centuries. Today one can differentiate and classify the movement with various strands and permutations; for a recent and authoritative general assessment and definition of Pentecostalism see the introductory essay by Michael Wilkinson in *Brill's Encyclopedia of Global Pentecostalism*, ed. Michael Wilkinson (Leiden: Brill, 2021).

2 This continued ridicule is what led Harvey Cox to title his chapter on Pentecostalism "The Last Vomit of Satan and the Persistent List Makers: Pentecostals and the Age of the Spirit," in *Future of Faith* (New York: Harper One, 2009). The title alludes to the disparaging epitaph fundamentalist C. Campbell Morgan pronounced over Pentecostalism in its early days. Harvey Cox, *Fire from Heaven: The Rise of Pentecostal Spirituality and the Reshaping of Religion in the Twenty-First Century* (Reading, MA: Addison-Wesley, 1995), 75.

3 Todd M. Johnson and Gina A. Zurlo, *Introducing Spirit-Empowered Christianity: The Global Pentecostal and Charismatic Movements in the 21st Century* (Tulsa, OK: ORU Press, 2020), 6.

4 "Evangelicals and Pentecostals/Charismatics" in Todd M. Johnson and Gina A. Zurlo, *World Christian Encyclopedia Online* (Leiden: Brill, 2023), http://dx.doi.org/10.1163/2666-6855_WCEO_COM_0406 (accessed 3 May 2023).

5 Vinson Synan, "Pentecostal Roots," in *The Century of the Holy Spirit: 100 Years of Pentecostal and Charismatic Renewal, 1901–2001*, ed. Vinson Synan (Nashville, TN: Thomas Nelson, 2001), 15, emphasis added. Interestingly, the cameo charismatic appearances of the Spirit took place within some questionable Christian movements like those of the second century Montanists and the Jansenists of the seventeenth century. Stanley M. Burgess defines Montanism as "an early Christian group with pentecostal-like traits, including belief in spirit-possession, an imminent parousia, and the leadership of women, as well as the practice of prophecy and glossolalia [speaking in tongues]." From Montanus's opponents we learn of how he lost control and fell into "a sort of frenzy and ecstasy" in which "he raved and began to babble and utter strange things, prophesying in a manner contrary to the constant custom of the church handed down by tradition from the beginning" (Eusebius, *Church History*, 5.16.7). Burgess does, however, distance Montanism from the modern-day Pentecostal movement by pointing to the excesses of Montanus and his followers. Perhaps, though, the main reason that Montanism continues to be spoken of in the history of Christianity is on account of its greatest convert and second century theologian Tertullian. See Stanley M. Burgess, "Montanism," in *The New International Dictionary of Pentecostal and Charismatic Movements*, ed. Stanley M. Burgess and Eduard M. Van Der Maas (Grand Rapids, MI:

Zondervan, 2002), 903–4. Moreover, the Jansenists were Catholic reformers of the seventeenth century who practiced speaking in tongues, prophesied, and sought to introduce a new sacrament called the "consolamentum," which would equate to a sort of baptism of words including the laying on of hands and impartation of spiritual gifts. See Stanley M. Burgess, *Christian Peoples of the Spirit: A Documentary History of Pentecostal Spirituality from the Early Church to the Present* (New York: New York University Press, 2011), 169–70.

6 Grant Wacker, "Playing for Keeps: The Primitive Impulse in Early Pentecostalism," in *The American Quest for the Primitive Church*, ed. Richard T. Hughes (Urbana, IL: University of Illinois Press, 1988), 198, emphasis added.

7 Donald Dayton, *Theological Roots of Pentecostalism* (Metuchen, NJ: The Scarecrow Press, 1987), 176.

8 Sarah E. Parham, *The Life of Charles F. Parham: Founder of the Apostolic Faith Movement* (Joplin, MO: Tri-State, 1930), 51–2.

9 The significance of Azusa Street cannot be underestimated, resulting in continued debates among prominent Pentecostal scholars regarding the origins of classical Pentecostalism in the United States and its association with international outpourings of the Spirit. For a great entry point into the ongoing discussion, see Cecil M. Robeck, Jr., "The Origins of Modern Pentecostalism: Some Historiographical Issues," in *The Cambridge Companion to Pentecostalism*, ed. Cecil M. Robeck, Jr. and Amos Yong (Cambridge: Cambridge University Press, 2014), 13–30.

10 This Pentecostal revival began as a cottage prayer meeting that Seymour started after he had been rejected by the small African American Holiness church he had been invited to pastor. As the son of freed slaves, Seymour had listened to Parham's views on the baptism in the Spirit from outside the door due to the segregationist laws of his time. Through his leadership Seymour would go on to spread the message of Spirit baptism around the world through the publication of the periodical *The Apostolic Faith*, which circulated internationally with 50,000 copies by 1908. Allan H. Anderson, *An Introduction to Pentecostalism: Global Charismatic Christianity* (Cambridge: Cambridge University Press, 2004), 43. For an overview of the Black roots of American Pentecostalism, see Estrelda Y. Alexander, *Black Fire: One Hundred Years of African American Pentecostalism* (Downers Grove, IL: InterVarsity Press, 2011).

11 For an insightful collection of dueling, yet complementary, essays concerning the emergence, centrality, and legacy of the Azusa Street Revival see Allan H. Anderson, "The Emergence of a Multidimensional Global Missionary Movement: Trends, Patterns, and Expressions," and Cecil M. Robeck, Jr., "Launching a Global Movement: The Role of Azusa Street in Pentecostalism's Growth and Expansion," in *Spirit and Power: The Growth and Global Impact of Pentecostalism*, ed. Donald E. Miller, Kimon H. Sargeant, and Richard Flory (Oxford: Oxford University Press, 2013), 25–41, 42–62.

12 Frank Bartleman, *How Pentecost Came to Los Angeles: As It Was in the Beginning* (Los Angeles, CA: self-published, 1925), 19.

13 Douglas Jacobsen, *Thinking in the Spirit: Theologies of the Early Pentecostal Movement* (Bloomington, IN: Indiana University Press, 2003).

14 Wolfgang Vondey, "Theology," in *Brill's Encyclopedia of Global Pentecostalism*, ed. Michael Wilkinson (Leiden: Brill, 2021), 632–3.

15 Among the contributors in this academic burgeoning of Pentecostal systematic theologies, we can include Myer Pearlman, *Knowing the Doctrines of the Bible* (Springfield, MO: Gospel Pub. House, 1937); Ernest S. Williams, *Systematic Theology* (Springfield, MO: Gospel Pub. House, 1953); Guy P. Duffield and Nathaniel M. Van Cleave, eds., *Foundations of Pentecostal Theology* (Los Angeles, CA: L.I.F.E. Bible College, 1983); John R. Higgins, Michael L. Dusing, and Frank D. Tallman, eds., *An Introduction to Theology: A Classical Pentecostal Perspective* (Dubuque, IA: Kendall/Hunt Pub. Co., 1994); Stanley M. Horton, ed., *Systematic Theology: A Pentecostal Perspective* (Springfield, MO: Logion Press, 1994); French L. Arrington, *Christian Doctrine: A Pentecostal Perspective*. 3 vols. (Cleveland, OH: Pathway, 1992–4). For a helpful assessment of these formative years, see Christopher A. Stephenson, *Types of Pentecostal Theology: Method, System, Spirit* (Oxford: Oxford University Press, 2013).

16 Some influential books characteristic of this era are Steven J. Land, *Pentecostal Spirituality: A Passion for the Kingdom* (Sheffield: Sheffield Academic, 1993); Simon Chan, *Pentecostal Theology and the Christian Spiritual Tradition* (Sheffield: Sheffield Academic, 2000); William W. Menzies and Robert P. Menzies, *Spirit and Power: Foundation of Pentecostal Experience: A Call to Evangelical Dialogue* (Grand Rapids, MI: Zondervan, 2000).

17 This becomes especially significant if we consider that the overwhelming majority of Pentecostals, whom our theology should serve, reside in the "two-thirds world" in situations of extreme poverty and marginalization. One must ask then if Pentecostal theologians from the "third world" are allowed to bring more than just the *salsa*, *harissa*, or soy sauce to the great banquet of theology. Terry L. Cross, "The Rich Feast of Theology: Can Pentecostals Bring the Main Course or Only the

Relish?" *Journal of Pentecostal Theology* 8, no. 16 (2000): 28.

18 Christopher A. Stephenson, "The Rule of Spirituality and the Rule of Doctrine: A Necessary Relationship in Theological Method," *Journal of Pentecostal Theology* 15, no. 1 (2006): 84.

19 Veli-Matti Kärkkäinen, *Toward a Pneumatological Theology: Pentecostal and Ecumenical Perspectives on Ecclesiology, Soteriology, and Theology of Mission*, ed. Amos Yong (Lanham, MD: University Press of America, 2002); Veli-Matti Kärkkäinen, *Theological Renewal for the Third Millenium: A Kärkkäinen Compendium*, ed. Andrew Ray Williams and Patrick Oden (Eugene, OR: Cascade, 2022); Amos Yong, *An Amos Yong Reader: The Pentecostal Spirit*, ed. Christopher A. Stephenson (Eugene, OR: Cascade: 2020); Wolfgang Vondey and Martin William Mittelstadt, *The Theology of Amos Yong and the New Face of Pentecostal Scholarship: Passion for the Spirit* (Leiden: Brill, 2013).

20 Frank D. Macchia, *Spirituality and Social Liberation: The Message of the Blumhardts in the Light of Wuerttemberg Pietism* (Metuchen, NJ: Scarecrow Press, 1993); *Baptized in the Spirit: A Global Pentecostal Theology* (Grand Rapids, MI: Zondervan, 2006); *Justified in the Spirit: Creation, Redemption, and the Triune God* (Grand Rapids, MI: Eerdmans, 2010).

21 Frank D. Macchia, *Tongues of Fire: A Systematic Theology of the Christian Faith* (Eugene, OR: Cascade, 2023).

22 Wolfgang Vondey, *Beyond Pentecostalism: The Crisis of Global Christianity and the Renewal of the Theological Agenda* (Grand Rapids, MI: Eerdmans, 2010); *Pentecostal Theology: Living the Full Gospel* (London: T&T Clark, 2017).

23 *Global Renewal Christianity: Spirit-Empowered Movements Past, Present, and Future,* Vol. 1: Asia and Oceania, ed. Amos Yong and Vinson Synan; Vol. 2: Latin America, ed. Amos Yong, Vinson Synan, and Miguel Alvarez; Vol. 3: Africa, ed. Amos Yong, Vinson Synan, and J. Kwabena Asamoah-Gyadu; Vol. 4: Europe and North America, ed. Amos Yong and Vinson Synan (Lake Mary, FL: Charisma House, 2016–17).

24 A select though not exhaustive list of notable representative theologians includes Cheryl Bridges Johns, Kimberly Ervin Alexander, Lisa P. Stephenson, Estrelda Alexander, Daniela C. Augustine, Clifton Clarke, Nimi Wariboko, Opoku Onyinah, Simon Chan, Wonsuk Ma, Eldin Villafañe, Samuel Solivan, Carmelo Alvarez, Néstor Medina, and Daniel Castelo.

25 For a more detailed introduction see D. A. Reed, "Oneness Pentecostalism," in *The International Dictionary of Pentecostal and Charismatic Movements*, ed. Stanley M. Burgess and Eduard M. van der Maas (Grand Rapids, MI: Zondervan), 936–44.

26 McGee, "Historical Background," in Stanley Horton, *Systematic Theology*, 21.

27 David K. Bernard, *The Oneness View of Jesus* (Hazelwood, MO: Word Aflame Press, 1994), 142.

28 Frank D. Macchia, "The Oneness-Trinitarian Pentecostal Dialogue: Exploring the Diversity of Apostolic Faith," *Harvard Theological Review* 103, no. 3 (2010): 329–49; "Oneness-Trinitarian Pentecostal Final Report, 2002–2007," *Pneuma: The Journal of the Society for Pentecostal Studies* 30, no. 2 (2008): 203–24.

29 Macchia, "The Oneness-Trinitarian Pentecostal Dialogue," 349.

30 Eldin Villafañe provides a great analysis and corrective of the problematic association between the Word of Faith movement and Pentecostalism in the sixth chapter titled "¿Fuego santo o fuego extraño?" ["Holy Fire or Strange Fire?"] See, Villafañe, *Manda Fuego Señor*, 147–51.

31 John MacArthur, *Strange Fire: The Danger of Offending the Holy Spirit with Counterfeit Worship* (Nashville, TN: Nelson Books, 2013).

32 Cox, *The Future of Faith*, 204–5.

33 Tom Pennington, "A Case for Cessationism," Strange Fire Conference, 17 October 2013. https://www.gty.org/resources/sermons/TM13-7/a-case-for-cessationism (accessed 19 September 2023).

34 Martin Luther, *Commentary on St. Paul's Epistle to the Galatians*, 4.6.

35 John Calvin, *Institutes of the Christian Religion*, IV.19.18

36 B. B. Warfield, *The Cessation of the Charismata* (New York: Charles Scribner's Sons, 1918), 6.

37 Synan, *The Century of the Holy Spirit*, 20.

38 Cox, *Fire from Heaven*, 71.

39 Kenneth J. Archer, *A Pentecostal Hermeneutic for the Twenty-First Century: Spirit, Scripture and Community* (London: T&T Clark, 2004), 122.

40 Archer, *A Pentecostal Hermeneutic*, ix.

41 The separation between academia and the church is perhaps more prevalent within Pentecostal congregations. Whereas in mainline denominations it might be more likely to have someone in the pastoral team with a master's degree or higher, within Pentecostal congregations this is a rare find. There is no question that as professional thinkers whose main area of research is the Bible more needs to be done on our part to change this unneeded dichotomy. See Sammy Alfaro, "Theological Education and Spiritual Formation," in *Spiritual Formation for the Global Church: A Multi-Denominational, Multi-Ethnic Approach*, ed. Ryan A. Brandt and John Frederick (Downers Grove, IL: InterVarsity Press, 2021.

42 The popular Pentecostal-friendly book by Tony Campolo comes to mind. Its title, *How to Be Pentecostal Without Speaking in Tongues*, begs the question for this discussion: Can one be a Pentecostal theologian without speaking in tongues or one might say without experiencing life in the Spirit?

43 Sammy Alfaro, "Liberating Pentecostal Theologies: a view from the Latina/o and Latin American Pentecostal Contexts," in *Global Renewal Christianity: Spirit-Empowered Movements: Past, Present, and Future*, Vol. 2: Latin America, ed. Amos Yong and Vinson Synan (Lake Mary, FL: Charisma House, 2016).

44 Donald E. Miller and Tetsunao Yamamori, *Global Pentecostalism: The New Face of Christian Social Engagement* (Los Angeles, CA: University of California Press, 2007), 12.

45 Darío López Rodríguez, *Pentecostalismo y Transformación Social: más allá de los estereotipos, las críticas se enfrentan a los hechos* (Buenos Aires: Ediciones Kairós, 2000), 33, author's translation.

46 Amos Yong, *The Spirit Poured Out on All Flesh: Pentecostalism and the Possibility of Global Theology* (Grand Rapids, MI: Baker Academic, 2005), 30.

Recommended Reading

Primary

Abrams, Minnie F. *The Baptism of the Holy Ghost and Fire*. Kedgaon, India: Mukti Mission Press, 1906.

Bartleman, Frank. *How Pentecost Came to Los Angeles As It Was in the Beginning*. Los Angeles, CA: self-published, 1925.

Ewart, Frank J. *The Phenomenon of Pentecost*. Hazelwood, MO: Word Aflame, 1975 [1948].

Lawrence, Bernard F. *The Apostolic Faith Restored*. St. Louis, MO: Gospel Publishing House, 1916.

Taylor, G. F. *The Spirit and the Bride*. Dunn, NC: self-published, 1908.

Secondary

Anderson, Allan. *An Introduction to Pentecostalism: Global Charismatic Christianity*. Cambridge: Cambridge University Press, 2004.

Dayton, Donald W. *Theological Roots of Pentecostalism*. Metuchen, NJ: The Scarecrow, 1987.

Jacobsen, Douglas. *Thinking in the Spirit: Theologies of the Early Pentecostal Movement*. Bloomington, IN: Indiana University Press, 2003.

Macchia, Frank D. *Tongues of Fire: A Systematic Theology of the Christian Faith*. Eugene, OR: Cascade, 2023.

Stephenson, Christopher A. *Types of Pentecostal Theology: Method, System, Spirit*. Oxford: Oxford University Press, 2013.

Vondey, Wolfgang. *Pentecostal Theology: Living the Full Gospel*. London: T&T Clark, 2017.

———, ed. *The Routledge Handbook of Pentecostal Theology*. London: Routledge, 2020.

Yong, Amos. *The Spirit Poured Out on All Flesh: Pentecostalism and the Possibility of Global Theology*. Grand Rapids, MI: Baker Academic, 2005.

Ecumenical Theology

Odair Pedroso Mateus

Introduction

In this essay, I use the term "ecumenical theology" in reference to theological work done in the service of multilateral dialogue undertaken by Christian churches to address their past and present divisions with a view to the restoration of full visible unity. Throughout the twentieth century, no other movement or institution embodied with comparable longevity and persistence the service of theology to the search for Christian unity as the 1910 movement on Faith and Order and its successor after 1948, the World Council of Churches (WCC) Commission on Faith and Order (sometimes referred to here as F&O). This essay offers a narrative that maps almost one hundred years of Faith and Order work as one way of proposing an introduction to modern ecumenical theology.[1] It is presented in four chronological periods that are not to be seen simply as successive stages of Faith and Order work, but rather as layers bearing marks of their time that progressively juxtapose and increasingly interact with each other, making the task of ecumenical theology far more complex at the end of the twentieth century than at its beginning.

Survey

Ecumenical theology and the unity of the churches in the age of colonialism

When the movement for a world conference on Faith and Order was launched in 1910, the European colonial system as well as world missions inspired by the great awakenings of the eighteenth and nineteenth century had already globalized Christianity, as well as globalizing the divisions that marked the history of its long European moment. Anglican thinking on Christian unity had prepared its theological ground,[2] from the Oxford movement in the 1830s and the ecumenical ecclesiology of Episcopalian William Reed Huntington, to the high church ecclesiology of Charles Gore.[3] Those were also the days of internationalism: the awareness of being one humanity inspired both in Europe and in the United States greater resistance

Ford's The Modern Theologians: An Introduction to Christian Theology since 1918, Fourth Edition.
Edited by Rachel Muers and Ashley Cocksworth.
© 2024 John Wiley & Sons Ltd. Published 2024 by John Wiley & Sons Ltd.

to war and the promotion of greater cooperation across national borders and cultures as a progressive move toward world peace.[4]

Under the initiative of Charles Brent, the movement on Faith and Order was launched by the Protestant Episcopal Church in the United States late in 1910 through the following resolution: "that all Christian communions throughout the world which confess our Lord Jesus Christ as God and Saviour should be asked to unite with Protestant Episcopal Church in arranging for and conducting a conference based on a clear statement and full consideration of those things in which we differ, as well as those things in which we are one."[5] Thus, the vision – the very modern vision – was to move from isolation to global, multilateral theological dialogue whose results would persuade the divided churches to take steps toward the restoration of a unity ultimately expressed in the sharing of the eucharist or holy communion.

Following ten years of an epic preparation[6] that transformed the small city of Gardiner – "a backwater New England mill town" in Maine – into what John Woolverton later called the "improbable centre of a worldwide movement,"[7] the preparatory meeting for the world conference was finally held in Geneva, Switzerland, in August 1920.[8] It took place just a couple of days after the publication, by a worldwide Anglican bishops' conference called "Lambeth," of a groundbreaking "Appeal to Christian Unity."[9] The appeal called for the visible unity of the churches based on four principles known as "Lambeth Quadrilateral": scriptures, the ancient creeds, the sacraments of baptism and the Lord's Supper, and a form of episcopal ministry adapted to its context. The movement on Faith and Order was to hold three world conferences before the winds of emancipation, blowing in the world and in the churches in the 1960s as secularization and liberation, would push Faith and Order to enlarge – and make less consensual – the scope of its vision of unity and, consequently, of its theological program.

The first two world conferences were held before World War II, one in Lausanne, Switzerland, in 1927 and the second in Edinburgh, Scotland, in 1937.[10] Each gathered some 400 delegates from more than 100 communions in all continents. Their theological program reflected the dominant Euro-North American, Anglican-Reformation profile of the churches engaged in the movement, which included an important minority of Old Catholic, Eastern, and Oriental Orthodox representatives. In the spirit of the Lambeth Quadrilateral, Anglicans were happy to keep the focus on ancient creeds, the church, and ministry and sacraments; whereas, in the spirit of the *satis est* of the Augsburg Confession's article 7, Reformation theologians insisted on agreement on the proclamation of the gospel, as in the first conference, or on the doctrine of grace, as in the second.

Which were the main ecumenical theological frontiers opened by the 1920 preparatory meeting and the first two world conferences? The first was to describe the core of the ecumenical utopia as "visible unity." Our vision, Bishop Charles Brent noted at the opening session of the 1920 preparatory meeting, "is that of an outward and evident unity of the Church of God."[11] It would not be achieved by simply federating the separated churches; by satisfaction with partial unities; or by one church absorbing the others. We are endeavoring "to bring into the common treasury of a Catholic Church the experience and knowledge which each has gathered locally and in isolation."[12] The goal of God's placing, Brent wrote one day after the end of the Geneva meeting, is that of "a Church, on earth, among men, visibly and organically one."[13]

The Edinburgh conference noted that the unity we seek has two aspects: "(a) the inner spiritual unity known in its completeness to God alone; and (b) the outward unity which expresses itself in mutual recognition, co-operative action and corporate or institutional unity."[14] That conference tried to unpack this vision by describing three "conceptions of church unity" – cooperative action, intercommunion, and corporate union – and by indicating the elements of unity that each of them required: agreement on faith or confession, on nonsacramental worship, on sacramental faith and practice, on order, or on church polity.[15] The 1937 report included a short section, proposed by the F&O North-American Section, on what would later be called "nontheological factors" of disunity. They were of three categories: sociological or political, historical, or cultural. Churches are kept apart, notes the report, by "barriers of nationality, race, class, general culture, and, more particularly, by slothful self-content and self-sufficiency."[16]

The second frontier may often have gone unnoticed. The two world conferences gave clear evidence and legitimacy to the foundational ecumenical experience, awareness, and conviction of a fundamental unity in Christ beneath existing ecclesial division. Although divided by dogmatic differences, wrote the Orthodox delegates in 1927, "we are one with our brethren here in faith in our Lord and Saviour Jesus Christ."[17] The second world conference concluded with an "affirmation of union in allegiance to our Lord Jesus Christ" in which the delegates stated that, "this allegiance takes precedence of any other allegiance that may make claims upon us."[18]

The third frontier was the doctrine of the church or ecclesiology. On the way to the first world conference, a synthesis of responses to a question about the nature of the church and its unity became the first Faith and Order text on this subject.[19] Its aim was to transcend two ecclesiological attitudes that generated indifference toward the search for visible unity. The first was the belief that one's church was the one and only true church; the second consisted in arguing that the true church and its unity are invisible, known to God alone. In due course, the first world conference received a short statement titled "The Nature of the Church," stating that God constitutes the church as witness to the gospel of salvation.[20] The church, as the communion of believers, is the people of the new covenant, the body of Christ, and the temple of God. The church is Christ's instrument of reconciliation through the Holy Spirit. There is and can be but one church, holy, catholic, and apostolic. However, there was disagreement on "the extent and manner in which the Church … finds expression in the existing Churches."[21] For some the invisible church is wholly in heaven; for others it included believers on earth. Some contend that the visible expression of the church was determined by Christ, whereas others argue that the church "may express itself in varying forms."[22] Some hold that one of the existing churches is the only true church, others hold that the only true church is in some or all of the existing communions. For some, a particular form of ministry "has been shown to be necessary to the best welfare of the church" whereas for others "no one form of organisation is inherently preferable."[23]

What can be said about the participation of Orthodox theologians in these early conferences? At the 1920 preparatory meeting, the young theologian Hamilcar Alivisatos offered an introduction to Orthodoxy. The Greek Orthodox local churches "make together the one Holy Catholic and Apostolic Orthodox Church." Its doctrines come from "the fountains of Holy Scripture and apostolic tradition," developed and explained "by the great Fathers and Doctors of the Church in the Ecumenical Councils." Its order "is based on the democratic principles of the Church at the time of the Apostles." Its liturgy is that of St John Chrysostom and St Basilius. History knows "what this Church has done to spread the Christian faith and its struggles against Mohammedanism." The innovations caused separation with the Western Church. "To reach union, we must be willing to know and help each other and we therefore propose a League of Churches till the World Conference reaches its complete result."[24] Archimandrite Chrysostome Papadopoulos noted, in relation to the debates between Anglicans and Protestants on ecclesiology and the authority of the ancient creeds, that those themes would have been better understood "if more attention were paid to the historic bases of Christianity."[25]

The Eastern Orthodox delegates to the first world conference rejected its theological results as a possible basis for the future reunion of the churches. The exception was the Section II report "The Church's Message to the World – the Gospel." The reports conveying agreements on the other subjects, they contended, were in fact verbal agreements that hid real disagreements. They were the result of compromise between "conflicting ideas and meanings" that led to external agreements "on the letter alone." However, in matters of faith and conscience, "there is no room for compromise." Two different meanings, they went on to argue, "cannot be covered by, and two different concepts cannot be deduced from, the same word of a generally agreed statement." In the absence of "the totality of faith … there can be no *communio in sacris*." Reunion can take place "only on the basis of the common faith and confession of the ancient, undivided Church of the seven Oecumenical Councils and of the first eight centuries."[26]

From unity in Christ to the unity of the churches

With the establishment of the World Council of Churches (WCC) in 1948, the experience, awareness, and affirmation of unity in Christ mentioned in the first section of this essay took the unprecedented form of a covenantal relationship among the churches.[27] This covenant relationship expressed itself in the 1938 theological basis of the future WCC – "The World Council of Churches is a fellowship of churches which accept our Lord Jesus Christ as God and Saviour"[28] – and gained a certain ecclesiological density in the 1950 WCC statement on its self-understanding. The covenanting churches, without abdicating their respective understandings of the church and its visible unity, stated that the membership of the church of Christ was more inclusive than their respective membership and recognized in each other (at least) *vestigia ecclesiae* or elements of the one, holy, catholic, and apostolic church.[29]

Alongside this, however, came the recognition by the covenanting churches of a fundamental difference separating them. The report "The Universal Church in God's Design," of the WCC 1948 assembly, had noted quite straightforwardly – under the influence of Karl Barth, and to the great dismay of many in the very Anglican Faith and Order movement – that a "deepest difference" expressed itself in two paradigms of Christian faith called respectively "catholic" and "protestant."[30] According to the report, "the essence of our situation is that, from each side of the division, we see the Christian faith and life as a self-consistent whole, but our conceptions of the whole are inconsistent with each other."[31]

At its Lund 1952 world conference, the newly established Commission on Faith and Order responded in two ways to the churches' move from isolation to an imperfect fellowship expressed in the establishment of the WCC and to the recognition of a "fundamental difference" separating them into two systems of Christian faith and life. First, it called the churches to relate to each other by what became known as the "Lund Principle," that means to "act together in all matters except those in which deep differences of conviction compel them to act separately."[32] Second, it moved beyond the comparative method employed since the 1920 preparatory meeting. "We have seen clearly," notes the conference in its message to the churches, "that we can make no real advance towards unity if we only compare our several conceptions of the nature of the Church and the traditions in which they are embodied." One of the conference reports put it thus: "We seek to penetrate behind the divisions of the Church on earth to our common faith in the one Lord. From the unity of Christ we seek to understand the unity of the Church on earth, and from the unity of Christ and His Body we seek a means of realising that unity in the actual state of our divisions on earth."[33] This "Christological" method, applied to traditional topics of the theology of controversy such as baptism, eucharist, and ministry, would lead ecumenical theology in the following decades to some of its most outstanding achievements.

The first expression of the new way of doing ecumenical theology in the service of ecclesial fellowship was "Christ and the Church," the second chapter of the Lund Report.[34] In a single voice, starting from the center of faith rather than from its denominational or confessional peripheries, theologians representing different ecclesiological traditions noted that "many of our differences arise from a false antithesis between the Church's being in Christ and its mission in the world" and from a failure "to understand the Church in the light of Jesus Christ as God and man, and in the light of His death and resurrection." "Christ, through his Word and Spirit," they go on to state, "calls the Church from the world and sends it into the world." Through this double movement, He builds the church as "the living Temple of God." The church in history, they conclude, "is at once the congregation of sinners and the new creation."

Four themes dominated the ecumenical theological work accomplished by the North American and European sections of F&O during the years that followed Lund 1952. The first was – once again – ecclesiology. Whereas the American section proposed a Christological ecclesiology of the church and its unity in the world,[35] the European section combined more explicitly a Christological and a Trinitarian approach to ecclesiology that included a systematic treatment of the church's attributes, ministry, and mission.[36] The second theme, "institutionalism," was again ecclesiological, but this time breaking new ground, as its ecumenical focus was the church as a human organization approached in an interdisciplinary way. Under the impact of the report *The Non-Theological Factors in the Making and Unmaking of Church Union*,[37] the Edinburgh 1937 world conference had recognized that there were obstacles to church unity that were not restricted to issues of faith and church order.[38]

Tradition and traditions was the third theme. The ancient Western polemic opposing Protestants and Roman Catholics in relation to sources of authority was formulated in terms of a polarization between the Reformation's "Scripture first, tradition second" and the Roman Catholic post-Tridentine's "Scripture and tradition." In the F&O study "Tradition and Traditions," a third voice intervened at the outset. The 1953 discussions on its launching were based on a short memorandum drafted by the Russian Orthodox Georges Florovsky.[39] "Christianity is essentially a historical religion," he noted, and added that "the *kerygma* is preserved and propagated by a faithful and loyal *paradosis*." As its title suggests, the study on "Tradition and Traditions" applied the new F&O method and consequently widened the topic in order to transcend the narrow polarization of the Western divide.[40]

Ways of worship was the fourth theme. The work took the form of three inquiries on worship, in Europe, North America, and East Asia, although the East Asian section was never able to convene as such. The European study formulated theses on worship in relation to creation, redemption, and new creation and recommended further study on the discrepancies between worship and modern culture.[41] The North American section focused on the liturgical practices of American churches in light of scripture and raised questions about the intelligibility of worship language in contemporary culture.[42] The East Asian report reviewed what several conferences, consultations, and ad hoc meetings had said recently about worship in Asia, listing positive emphases – such as the variety of worship traditions and the commonalities they shared – and negative emphases, such as the misunderstandings about indigenization. "There is also laid upon the Church," the report notes, "responsibility to express its faith and life in terms that can communicate to the world, so that the gospel and Christian life are not seen as foreign but as related to human life in particular cultural situations."[43]

The renewal of ecumenical theology and the unity of the churches in times of emancipation

Winds of emancipation were blowing on world history, on global Christianity and, as a result, on the ecumenical movement when Faith and Order held its fourth world conference in Montreal, Canada, in July 1963. The "younger" churches in colonized countries often found it difficult to relate theologically to the critique of colonialism and to liberation struggles in their contexts. Meanwhile, churches in colonial countries, hit by growing dechristianization, found it equally challenging to make theological sense of the emancipation from institutional religion signified by secularization or the emancipation from white supremacy embodied by the civil rights movement in the United States. The ecumenical movement was reaching the zenith of its influence and self-confidence through the remarkable growth and influence of the WCC. The "younger," emancipated churches from Africa, Asia, and the Pacific sought membership in the WCC at the same time as the Orthodox churches of Russia, Bulgaria, Romania, and Poland were being admitted. In December 1961, soon after the first WCC assembly in Asia, Visser 't Hooft, the first WCC general secretary was pictured on the cover of the US *Time* magazine as "World Churchman" leading a "Second Reformation."

In the following years, the Roman Catholic Church, which had said "no" to the Faith and Order movement in 1914 and in 1927, would hold its Second Vatican Council with Christian unity very high on its agenda.[44] This council greeted the 1961 theological basis of the WCC in its decree on ecumenism *Unitatis redintegratio*;[45] and, in the same decree, it built on the WCC 1950 Toronto Statement's reference to the *vestigia ecclesiae*.[46] It revised in 1963 the Tridentine ambivalent language about one or two sources (*duplex fons*) of revelation[47] in convergence with the Section II report of the 1963 Montreal conference "Scripture,

Tradition and Traditions."[48] It stated, in the 1965 constitution *Lumen gentium*, that the church of Christ *subsistit in* (subsists in) rather than simply *is* the Catholic Church, a move that would ground ecclesiologically the flourishing of ecumenical bilateral dialogues in the following decades.[49] The Roman Catholic Church was represented at Montreal 1963 and joined the Commission on Faith and Order in 1968.

The 1963 world conference produced what its chairperson, Oliver Tomkins, quoting a delegate, described as "a most promising chaos."[50] It was far more culturally diverse than previous conferences, with eighty-six participants out of 489 coming from outside Europe and North America. It was more ecclesially diverse with the very active participation of Orthodox theologians – who no longer waited until the end of the conference to complain about its results – and the presence for the first time of Roman Catholic observers and speakers. It saw lively debates on fundamental issues such as the unity of the church in the New Testament. The German Protestant Ernst Käsemann landed a blow on Lund's Christological method by contending, "the historian simply cannot speak of an unbroken unity of New Testament ecclesiology" (what would then be the point of returning to the sources?) whereas his American Roman Catholic counterpart Raymond Brown argued that there is a "unity of belief present in all stages of New Testament thought about the Church."[51] The contemporary relevance of F&O ecumenical theology was questioned. The American Episcopalian William Stringfellow could not be more straightforward: "Modern thinking and unthinking man does not care a hoot about the Faith and Order Movement because Faith and Order apparently does not care about him."[52] In a vivid exchange about the eucharist, a Roman Catholic and a Presbyterian agreed on the following formula: "When *you* celebrate the Eucharist, our Lord is present, and *I* am present with him."[53]

Through the 1960s and 1970s, the ecumenical theological program of Faith and Order was considerably different from the theological agenda of its first three world conferences. If churches' ancient divisions had become confessional cultures, which were now increasingly divided among themselves and within themselves by a wide range of issues related to human emancipation such as racism or systemic poverty, then ecumenical theology could no longer be the same in scope and method.[54] Four themes addressed by F&O during those years deserve a special reference: secularization, unity, the common expression of faith, and the enormously influential work on *Baptism, Eucharist and Ministry*.

Concerning the first, the 1963 world conference had requested a study on creation and redemption.[55] The study was approved in the following year with a more ecumenical title: "Creation, New Creation and the Unity of the Church." It was then linked with another ongoing study in the WCC on "The Finality of Jesus Christ in the Age of Universal History." It was revised in its final stage by historians and natural scientists, and finally reported to the Bristol 1967 meeting of the Commission on F&O with the title "God in Nature and History."[56] Modern people, wrote its authors, have entered into "a new experience and understanding of nature and history": these are no longer static, geocentric, limited entities, but processes – as the theory of evolution suggests – "in an indeterminate space and an almost endless time."[57] Has the God of the Bible any relation to the modern scientific world-view? Our task is "to discover the relations between the biblical message and modern world-view."[58] The present secular movement toward the unification of humankind and its history through science and technology, the study noted, "lays a heavy pressure on all the Christian churches to seek … the world-wide unity of the Christian Church"; and it concluded: "Only the one Church can be the adequate counterpart of the one world."[59]

Concerning the second theme, unity, the 1937 world conference had dedicated a section to the unity of the church in life and worship. The text described "several conceptions of unity" (what we would call today "models of church union"): cooperative action, intercommunion, and corporate union, and identified the requirements of each of them.[60] Our oneness in Christ and our disunity as churches were the main themes of the F&O contribution to the WCC 1954 assembly. Following a New Testament-based exposition on Christ's unifying work and the oneness of the church in its earthly pilgrimage, the text shows "how it is that our disunity as churches contradicts our unity in Christ."[61] The fruits of those initial reflections on the vision of the ecumenical movement were harvested in a concise and positive statement on unity – adopted first by F&O in 1960 then by the WCC New Delhi 1961 assembly – which became "canonical" in ecumenical dialogue:

> We believe that the unity which is both God's will and his gift to his Church is being made visible as all in each place who are baptised in Jesus Christ and confess him as Lord and Saviour are brought by the Holy Spirit into one fully committed fellowship, holding the one apostolic faith, preaching the one Gospel, breaking the one bread, joining in common prayer, and having a corporate life reaching out in witness and service to all and who at the same time are united with the whole Christian fellowship in all places and all ages in such wise that ministry and members are accepted by all, and that all can act and speak together as occasion requires for the tasks to which God calls his people.[62]

The New Delhi statement offered a vision of church unity – all in each place united in a fully committed fellowship by apostolic faith, sacramental life, ministry, mission, and witness – with which was implicitly associated a model of church union: that of organic union, in other words, that of united, postdenominational churches in different regions or countries. The study on concepts of unity and models of church union, launched in Louvain in 1971,[63] added to the local emphasis of New Delhi a universal or catholic dimension by introducing in the vision of unity the notion of conciliar fellowship. Regional or national united churches are in communion with each and express it through a conciliar way of living together at the universal level. According to a consultation held in Salamanca in 1973, "the one Church is to be envisioned as a conciliar fellowship of local churches which are themselves truly united."[64] This expanded description of the ecumenical vision initially formulated in New Delhi was adopted by the Nairobi WCC assembly in 1975.[65]

It was the beginning of a sustained debate,[66] throughout the 1970s, centered on the expression "truly united" understood as a synonym for postconfessional or postdenominational, and nurtured by the remarkable growth of ecumenical bilateral dialogues involving world confessional bodies.[67] Led by the Lutheran World Federation, the world confessional bodies rejected in 1974 the idea that only united or postconfessional churches could live in a universal conciliar fellowship.[68] The unity of all in each place with all in all places and ages in conciliar fellowship was, in their view, fully compatible with a reconciled diversity in which ecclesial identities such as Lutheran, Roman Catholic, Anglican, Reformed, or Orthodox, purified from their divisiveness through the ecclesial reception of the results of multilateral and bilateral ecumenical dialogues, would exchange their unique gifts and grow together in communion locally and universally.

This polemic on the relationship between the goal of unity and the way to unity was also the horizon of a second debate, which was more explicitly related to the task of ecumenical theology in the age of emancipation. The WCC 1968 Uppsala assembly greeted emancipation by choosing as its theme "Behold, I make all things new" and speaking of the church as "the sign of the coming unity of mankind". In response, F&O launched in 1971 – following sustained discussions on the struggle for justice in society, the encounter with living faiths, the struggle against racism, the handicapped in society, and cultural diversity – a study on the need to hold theologically together the search for "the unity of the church and unity of mankind."[69] The study saw the polarization between the vision of unity represented by Orthodoxy through the F&O moderator John Meyendorff and the vision of unity from the conflicting perspective of liberation theologies, represented by the Argentinian Methodist and F&O commissioner José Míguez Bonino.[70] The title of a 1974 summary of this study was eloquent: "Towards Unity in Tension." We believe, the authors wrote, that "the unity of mankind for which we pray and hope, and the just interdependence of free people inseparable from it, cannot be thought of apart from God's liberating activity and an active human response and participation."[71]

Launched in 1971, the study on the common expression of the faith, also known as "Giving Account of the Hope that is in Us," was based on three convictions with methodological implications for ecumenical theology: "(1) churches and Christians have the obligation in every new age to confess afresh, in the language of that age, their faith in Christ; (2) they must strive for expressions of the Christian faith within different cultural worlds and in diversified social, political and religious situations; (3) the divided churches might rediscover their unity by letting themselves be reconstituted by the truth of the Gospel."[72]

The unusual result of this empirical, inductive study on what one could call "the lived faith of the churches today," closed in Bangalore in 1978, was a collection of affirmations, poems, confessions, prayers often gathered according to their regional origins in four volumes.[73] In the preface of the first volume, the Taiwanese theologian C. S. Song raised the following question: "Would it be too ambitious to hope that statements and expressions of faith made in confessing situations collected in this and succeeding volumes may help redirect the ecumenical search for unity to its 'logical' and thus 'primary' place, that is, confessions that Christians today are making in various parts of the world at the risk of their safety and their lives?"[74] Future F&O work on the theme appeared to answer this question with a "Yes."

The landmark text *Baptism, Eucharist and Ministry*, known as BEM, came into existence in Lima in 1982 less as a planned study and far more as an insight, that is, to harvest the fruits of half a century of Faith and Order ecumenical tradition in three key areas of its theological work. BEM became, in the words of Günther Gassmann, "the most widely published, translated, discussed and commented text in the history of the ecumenical movement."[75] It was destined to rekindle hope in the churches' growth toward visible unity, representing as it did a convergence achieved by theologians officially representing churches from the Reformation, Roman Catholic, and Orthodox traditions in F&O as well as in official bilateral dialogues.

As he introduced *Baptism, Eucharist and Ministry* to the 1982 Lima Commission meeting, the Methodist theologian Geoffrey Wainwright noted that it was "a good fortune" that BEM was written in a time in which ecumenical theologians were able to shed new reconciling light on ancient controversies by taking stock of recent developments of biblical, liturgical, and sacramental scholarship.[76] The ecclesiological conviction underlying the composition of BEM – in the words of the Reformed and Roman Catholic Brother Max Thurian from the Taizé Community, one of its senior drafters – is that "when the churches, through their representatives, are gathered together by the WCC, they are no less churches than when making their decisions individually." This ecumenical tradition, he concluded, "is the fruit of a common 'reading' by the various churches of holy scripture and of the great Tradition interpreting God's word, with a view to re-discovering the visible unity willed by Christ."[77] However, although designed "for the conversion of the churches," BEM did not convince any of them to reconsider their self-understanding for the sake of visible unity.

Ecclesiology and the unity of the churches in the age of world Christianity

When F&O gathered ecumenical pilgrims in Santiago de Compostela, Spain, for its 1993 sixth world conference, with focus on ecclesiology,[78] neoliberalism was spreading economic inequalities around the world; the Soviet Empire and the "cold war" no longer existed; some religions were increasingly playing a cultural and political identity role; ecology, ethnicity, and nationalism were important challenges to the unity of humanity and to Christian unity. The ecumenical movement, the future WCC general secretary Konrad Raiser contended, was going through a paradigm shift, which called for new approaches to the search for unity and the generation of new ecumenical space.[79] Christianity's demographic "center of gravity" had moved from Europe to Southern Africa; newly established Independent, Evangelical, Pentecostal, and Neo-Pentecostal denominations in the southern hemisphere found it increasingly difficult or more often unnecessary to make theological sense of what looked to a growing number like the Eurocentric and colonial ecumenical agenda, of the search for the manifestation of the one church of Christ in eucharistic fellowship through agreement on apostolic faith, sacramental life, ministry, and mission made possible by ecumenical multilateral and bilateral dialogues.

The profile of the ecumenical theological work accomplished by F&O during the last two decades of the twentieth century changed considerably when compared with the outlook of the theological program described in the final section of this chapter. From a critical and ecumenical reflection on the life and witness of the churches in the world, facing secularization and liberation and divided among themselves and within themselves by those challenges, Faith and Order ecumenical theology moved back to its initial self-understanding of a service to the overcoming of inherited ecclesial division understood primarily, if not exclusively, as theological division. Studies such as the outstanding "Ecclesiology and Ethics," which sought to hold together what the church is and what the church does as a moral community,[80] and "Ethnic Identity, National Identity and the Unity of the Church" were the exception that, in the last two decades of the twentieth century, confirmed the rule. This move can be discerned through a review of three areas of work corresponding to the period leading to the 1993 Compostela world conference.

The first area was the ecumenical reception of *Baptism, Eucharist and Ministry*. Commentaries and study guides on BEM, favoring its ecumenical reception, were published.[81] More than 180 churches' responses were received, analyzed between 1986 and 1988 and published in six volumes.[82] An extensive summary, published in 1990, identified three theological themes requiring further work: scripture and tradition, sacrament and sacramentality, and ecumenical perspectives on ecclesiology.[83] The three had been addressed by the Faith and Order movement in its first two world conferences.

The second area was the study "Towards the Common Expression of the Apostolic Faith Today," proposed in Bangalore 1978, launched formally in Buenos Aires in 1982 and concluded in 1990. Its predecessor in the 1970s, "Giving Account of the Hope that Is in Us" attempted at eliciting unity, holiness, catholicity, and apostolicity from expressions of *fides qua creditur*, from faith confessed in action in different contemporary contexts and in challenging situations. The new study attempted at presenting the contemporary meaning and the ecumenical potential of an ancient expression of *fides quae creditur* – the Creed of Nicaea-Constantinople (381) – as a judge of the authenticity of contextual expressions of faith. Its main result was *Confessing the One Faith*, an explication of the Nicene Creed structured in sections corresponding to the three articles of the Creed.[84] Each section identifies the main theological themes of its corresponding article, presents the relation between the article and its biblical roots and offers perspectives on its contemporary meaning. The Nicene Creed, wrote the authors in the introduction of *Confessing the One Faith*, "serves to indicate whether the faith as set forth in modern situations is the same faith as the one the Church confessed through the centuries."[85] In reaction, some asked whether God must remain Greek and considered this study a neocolonial expression of a Eurocentric control of the Christian Tradition.

The third area was the 1993 fifth world conference and its theme. Its aim was to bring before the churches the results of recent F&O work on *Baptism, Eucharist and Ministry*, the confession of the apostolic faith today and the unity of the church and the renewal of the human community. Launched in 1982 and initially foreseen to be held in 1987 in connection with the 1200th anniversary of Nicaea II, the seventh ecumenical council, the conference was postponed to 1989 because of the time F&O needed to complete its ongoing studies and then to 1993 due to the WCC calendar. The postponement was providential for the choice of its theme, inspired by promising results of bilateral dialogues.

Following the Roman Catholic Second Vatican Council, bilateral dialogues involving official representatives of two or more churches or Christian World Communions, addressing primarily issues that had traditionally separated them, grew in number and ecumenical importance. The debate on concepts of unity and models of union, described previously, showed the need of coordination and synergy between Faith and Order multilateral work and the blossoming of bilateral dialogues especially during the 1970s. This was done to some extent through the establishment of a Forum on Bilateral Dialogues, which addressed several issues of ecumenical methodology.

In the early 1980s, influential international bilateral dialogues such as the Anglican-Roman Catholic, the Orthodox-Roman Catholic or the Anglican-Orthodox began to explore and realize the ecumenical potential of the understanding of the church as *koinonia* or communion for their growth in fellowship. This was one of the important impulses that led F&O in 1989 to decide that ecumenical ecclesiology would be in the following years not only the overarching focus of its theological work but also one of its main studies, and that – inspired by an address by the Orthodox John (Zizioulas) of Pergamon – the study would focus on the church in the image of the Trinity.[86]

In the same vein, F&O's contribution to the statement on unity adopted by the 1991 WCC assembly made the polysemic term *koinonia* its focus. "The unity of to which we are called is a koinonia given and expressed in the common confession of the apostolic faith; a common sacramental life entered by the one baptism and celebrated together in one eucharistic fellowship." This goal is realized, the text goes on to say by pointing to confessional reconciled diversity as a legitimate expression of the understanding of unity, "when all the churches are able to recognise in one another the one, holy, catholic and apostolic church in its fullness."[87]

At the end of the ecumenical century, Faith and Order remained in continuity with the move described in the present section. The first results of the study on ecclesiology were published in 1998 as *The Nature and Purpose of the Church*.[88] A study on ecumenical hermeneutics,[89] whose aim was "to assist the churches to engage in dialogue across cultures and confessions and to understand the inter-relation between them," had been launched in the aftermath of the 1993 world conference.[90] A third study, on the role of worship in the search for unity, was initiated in 1994. Finally, Faith and Order launched in 1997, in cooperation with the WCC, a study on "Ethnic Identity, National Identity and the Unity of the Church."[91]

Agenda: The Challenge of World Christianity and Moral Issues

The attempt at achieving convergence on the essentials of a basic understanding of the church would remain the "major project" of Faith and Order between 1994 and the 2020s.[92] The WCC responded in 1998 to the ecumenical challenge represented by the sustained growth of a post-Eurocentric Christianity, in which division is often perceived as Christian "biodiversity," by moving toward the establishment of a Global Christian Forum in 2007. Faith and Order, however, was not in a position, until 2015, to address the ecumenical implications of what its convergence text *The Church: Towards a Common Vision* called emerging churches "which propose a new way of being the Church."[93] The first results were not published until late 2022.[94]

Faith and Order proved to be more reactive in responding to the ecumenical challenges raised by intra-church or interchurch controversies concerning moral issues. The role of the so-called "nontheological factors" in disunity and unity has been recognized at least since the 1937 world conference although the methodology of ecumenical dialogue seems to underestimate their importance. Since the last decades of the last century, moral issues have emerged prominently as one of them. Following the WCC 1998 assembly, Faith and Order responded to the growing controversial nature of some moral issues by launching first a study on theological anthropology. On that basis, the commission moved to a descriptive approach to what happens when churches teach on moral issues.[95] At the very final stage of the study, Orthodox and Roman Catholic members of Faith and Order surprisingly decided that the working methodology of text led to "the relativistic approach."[96] The study started from scratch in 2015 by first showing how different traditions teach on moral issues.[97] This was followed by the analysis of situations in which churches have felt the need to reconsider deep-seated views on certain moral issues.[98] It was concluded by making the theological and practical case for an enlightened understanding of the factors that lead to disagreements on moral issues.[99]

Multilateral and bilateral dialogues on these and other controversial topics have arguably remained too much indebted to an Enlightenment-centered notion of truth that lacks continuity with the fact that the foundational "truth" of Christianity is narrative – a person. Dogmatic and doctrinal truth-claims are not hermeneutically autonomous in relation to Jesus of Nazareth's foundational compassion for the crowds.

With this in mind, it is possible to imagine a future of ecumenical multilateral and bilateral dialogues in which textual truth-claims would lose part of their hegemony as the privileged basis of theological convergences preparing the way for ecclesial communion. Dialogue could instead undertake an archaeology of hidden communion – a search for *vestigia ecclesiae* or elements of the true church that do not necessarily find their way into texts about normative textualities but that are no less important as potential bonds of fellowship.

Another possible way forward for ecumenical theology would involve abandoning the search for symmetric lexical equivalences between two or more confessional languages in favor of the search for semantic equivalences between them. The absence of symmetric translations between words from confessional languages need not be seen as an index of ecclesial estrangement. It could be transcended by the charity-based search for semantic equivalences, involving deeper understanding of how different confessional languages communicate similar meanings.

Notes

1. Most F&O texts quoted in this essay can be freely accessed at the "Faith and Order Papers Digital Edition," https://archive.org/details/faithandorderpapersdigitaledition?&sort=-downloads&page=2 (accessed 7 September 2023).
2. Paul Avis, "The Origins of Anglican Ecumenical Theology, the Chicago-Lambeth Quadrilateral, and the Question of Anglican Orders," in *A History of the Desire for Christian Unity: Ecumenism in the Churches, 19th–21st Century, Vol. 1: Dawn of Ecumenism,* ed. Luca Ferracci (Leiden: Brill, 2021), 264–99.
3. Michael Ramsey, *From Gore to Temple: The Development of Anglican Theology between* Lux Mundi *and the Second World War, 1889–1939* (London: Longmans, 1960).
4. Thus John F. Woolverton's biography of Robert H. Gardiner, a driving force of the Faith and Order movement in its first fourteen years, is titled *Robert H. Gardiner and the Reunification of Worldwide Christianity in the Progressive Era* (Columbia, MO: University of Missouri Press, 2005).
5. Faith and Order, *Joint Commission Appointed to Arrange for a World Conference on Faith and Order,* F&O paper 1 (leaflet, reprinted 20 March 1913), 4.
6. Tissington Tatlow, "The World Conference on Faith and Order," in *A History of the Ecumenical Movement 1517–1948,* ed. Ruth Rouse and Stephen Charles Neill (Geneva: World Council of Churches, 1993), 403–41.
7. Woolverton, *Robert H. Gardiner and the Reunification of Worldwide Christianity in the Progressive Era,* 197.
8. Robert H. Gardiner, *A Pilgrimage toward Unity: Report of the Preliminary Meeting at Geneva, Switzerland August 12–20, 1920,* F&O paper 33 (Gardiner, ME: Continuation Committee, 1920).
9. Lambeth Conference Resolutions Archive, resolution 9 https://www.anglicancommunion.org/resources/document-library/lambeth-conference/1920/resolution-9-reunion-of-christendom.aspx (accessed 14 September 2023).
10. H. N. Bate, *Faith and Order: Proceedings of the World Conference – Lausanne, August 3–21, 1927* (New York: George H. Doran, 1927); Leonard Hodgson, *The Second World Conference on Faith and Order Held at Edinburgh, August 3–18, 1937* (London: SCM Press, 1938).
11. Gardiner, *A Pilgrimage toward Unity,* 17.
12. Gardiner, *A Pilgrimage toward Unity,* 20.
13. Gardiner, *A Pilgrimage toward Unity,* 90.
14. Hodgson, *The Second World Conference on Faith and Order,* 259.
15. Hodgson, *The Second World Conference on Faith and Order,* 250–7.
16. Hodgson, *The Second World Conference on Faith and Order,* 258–9.
17. Bate, *Faith and Order,* 385.
18. Hodgson, *The Second World Conference on Faith and Order,* 275.
19. Faith and Order, *Statements by the Subjects Committee of the World Conference on Faith and Order* (Boston, MA: Secretariat, 1927), 9–14.
20. Bate, *Faith and Order,* 463–6.
21. Bate, *Faith and Order,* 465.
22. Bate, *Faith and Order,* 465.
23. Bate, *Faith and Order,* 465.
24. Gardiner, *A Pilgrimage toward Unity,* 62–4.
25. Gardiner, *A Pilgrimage toward Unity,* 62.
26. Bate, *Faith and Order,* 382–6.
27. W. A. Visser 't Hooft, ed., *The First Assembly of the World Council of Churches Held at Amsterdam August 22th to September 4th, 1948* (London: SCM Press, 1949), 9.
28. "Constitution for the World Council of Churches," *Documents of the World Council of Churches* (Amsterdam: WCC, 1948), 11–14.
29. "The Church, the Churches and the World Council of Churches: The Ecclesiological Significance of the World

Council of Churches," *The Ecumenical Review* 3, no. 1 (1948): 47–53.

30   Visser 't Hooft, ed., *The First Assembly of the World Council of Churches*, 51–7.

31   Visser 't Hooft, ed., *The First Assembly of the World Council of Churches*, 52.

32   Oliver S. Tomkins, ed., *The Third World Conference on Faith and Order Held at Lund August 15th to 28th, 1952* (London: SCM Press, 1953), 16.

33   Tomkins, ed., *The Third World Conference on Faith and Order*, 18.

34   Tomkins, ed., *The Third World Conference on Faith and Order*, 17–20.

35   Faith and Order, *Report of the Theological Commission on Christ and the Church*, F&O paper series 2, no. 38 (Geneva: WCC, 1963), 7–34. See also Paul Sevier Minear, ed., *Faith and Order Findings: The Final Report of the Theological Commissions to the Fourth World Conference on Faith and Order, Montreal 1963* (London: SCM Press, 1963).

36   Faith and Order, *Report of the Theological Commission on Christ and the Church*, 35–62. See Minear, ed., *Faith and Order Findings*.

37   Faith and Order, *The Non-Theological Factors in the Making and Unmaking of Church Union*, F&O paper series 1 (New York: Harper & Brothers, 1937), 84.

38   Hodgson, *The Second World Conference on Faith and Order*, 258–9.

39   Faith and Order, *Working Committee – Minutes of the Meeting held at the Château de Bossey, near Geneva 11th to 19th August 1953*, F&O papers, series 2, no. 17 (Geneva: WCC, 1953), 31–3.

40   Faith and Order, *Report on Tradition and Traditions*, F&O paper series 2, no. 40 (Geneva: WCC, 1963).

41   Faith and Order, *Report of the Theological Commission on Worship*, F&O paper series 2, no. 39 (Geneva: WCC, 1963), 7–25. See also W. Vos, ed., *Worship and the Acts of God* (Nieuwendam: Studia Liturgica Press, 1963).

42   Faith and Order, *Report of the Theological Commission on Worship*, 47–62.

43   Faith and Order, *Report of the Theological Commission on Worship*, 29–45.

44   Marie Levant, "The Positioning of the Catholic Church in the Interwar Period: The Encyclical *Mortalium Animos*," in *A History of the Desire for Christian Unity*, ed. Melloni and Ferracci, 703–21.

45   Vatican II, *Decree on Ecumenism Unitatis Redintegratio*, para 1, 20, https://www.vatican.va/archive/hist_councils/ii_vatican_council/documents/vat-ii_decree_19641121_unitatis-redintegratio_en.html (accessed April 29, 2022).

46   Vatican II, *Decree on Ecumenism Unitatis Redintegratio*, para 3, https://www.vatican.va/archive/hist_councils/

ii_vatican_council/documents/vat-ii_decree_19641121_unitatis-redintegratio_en.html (accessed April 29, 2022).

47   Vatican II, *Dogmatic Constitution on Divine Revelation Dei Verbum*, para 7, 8, 10. https://www.vatican.va/archive/hist_councils/ii_vatican_council/documents/vat-ii_const_19651118_dei-verbum_en.html (accessed April 29, 2022).

48   P. C. Rodger and L. Vischer, eds., *The Fourth World Conference on Faith and Order Montreal 1963* (New York: Association Press, 1964), 50–61, para 39, 45, 50.

49   Vatican II, *Dogmatic Constitution on the Church Lumen Gentium*, 8. https://www.vatican.va/archive/hist_councils/ii_vatican_council/documents/vat-ii_const_19641121_lumen-gentium_en.html (accessed April 29, 2022).

50   David M. Paton, "A Montreal Diary," in *The Fourth World Conference on Faith and Order Montreal 1963*, ed. Rodger and Vischer, 7.

51   Paton, "A Montreal Diary," 16–17.

52   Paton, "A Montreal Diary," 18.

53   Paton, "A Montreal Diary," 20.

54   Faith and Order, "Commission on Faith and Order" in *Uppsala to Nairobi 1968–1975, Report of the Central Committee to the Fifth Assembly of the World Council of Churches*, ed. D. E. Johnson (London: SPCK, 1975), 72.

55   Rodger and Vischer, eds., *The Fourth World Conference on Faith and Order Montreal 1963*, 42–3, para 13–15 and footnotes.

56   Faith and Order, "God in Nature and History," *New Directions in Faith and Order: Bristol 1967 – Reports – Minutes – Documents* (Geneva: WCC, 1967), 7–31.

57   Faith and Order, "God in Nature and History," 7.

58   Faith and Order, "God in Nature and History," 9.

59   Faith and Order, "God in Nature and History," 25.

60   Hodgson, *The Second World Conference on Faith and Order*, 250–69.

61   "Faith and Order: Our Oneness in Christ and Our Disunity as Churches," in *The Evanston Report* (New York: Harper & Brothers, 1954), 82–92.

62   "Reports of Sections: Unity," in *The New Delhi Report*, ed. W. A. Visser 't Hooft (London: SCM Press, 1961), 116–34.

63   Faith and Order, *Louvain 1971 – Study Reports and Document*, F&O papers, series 2, no. 59s (Geneva: WCC, 1971), 240–1.

64   Faith and Order, "The Unity of the Church: The Goal and the Way," in *Uniting in Hope: Reports and Documents from the Meeting of the Faith and Order Commission*, F&O paper, series 2, 72 (Geneva: WCC, 1975), 113–14.

65   "What Unity Requires," in David M. Paton, *Breaking Barriers: Nairobi 1975 – The Official Report of the Fifth Assembly of the World Council of Churches, Nairobi, 23 November – 10 December, 1975* (London: SPCK, 1976), 59–69.

66 Harding Meyer, *That All May Be One: Perceptions and Models of Ecumenicity* (Grand Rapids, MI: Eerdmans, 1999), 102–26.

67 Reports of international bilateral dialogues are published in the series *Growth in Agreement*. See also Nils Ehrenström and Günther Gassmann, *Confessions in Dialogue: A Survey of Bilateral Conversations among World Confessional Families 1959–1974*, F&O paper, series 2, no. 74 (Geneva: WCC, 1975).

68 Günther Gassmann and Harding Meyer, *The Unity of the Church: Requirements and Structures* (Geneva: LWF, 1983).

69 G. Müller-Fahrenholz, ed., *Unity in Today's World: The Faith and Order Studies on "Unity of the Church – Unity of Humankind,"* F&O paper, series 2, no. 88 (Geneva: WCC, 1978).

70 O. Pedroso Mateus, "José Míguez Bonino and the Struggle for Global Christianity in the 1970s," in *Globalisierung der Kirchen: Der Ökumenische Rat der Kirchen und die Entdeckung der Dritte Welt in den 1960er und 1970er Jahren*, ed. Katharina Kunter and Annegreth Schilling (Göttingen: V&R, 2014).

71 Faith and Order, "Towards Unity in Tension," in *Uniting in Hope: Reports and Documents from the Meeting of the Faith and Order Commission*, F&O paper, series 2, no. 72 (Geneva: WCC, 1975), 90–4.

72 Faith and Order, "Giving Account of the Hope that Is Within Us – Report of the Conference," in *Uniting in Hope*, 25.

73 Faith and Order, *Confessing Our Faith around the World*, Vol. I: F&O paper 104; Vol. II: F&O paper 120; Vol. III: F&O paper 123; Vol. IV: F&O paper 126 (Geneva: WCC, 1980–5).

74 Faith and Order, *Confessing Our Faith around the World*, 7.

75 Günther Gassmann, ed., *Documentary History of Faith and Order 1963–1993* (Geneva: WCC, 1993), 25.

76 Faith and Order, *Towards Visible Unity: Commission on Faith and Order Lima 1982, Vol. I – Minutes and Addresses*, F&O paper 112 (Geneva: WCC, 1982), 80.

77 Max Thurian, "Baptism, Eucharist and Ministry," in *Dictionary of the Ecumenical Movement*, ed. Nicholas Lossky et al. (Geneva: WCC, 2002), 92.

78 Thomas F. Best and Günther Gassmann, eds., *On the Way to Fuller Koinonia: Official Report of the Fifth World Conference on Faith and Order*, F&O paper 166 (Geneva: WCC, 1994).

79 Konrad Raiser, *Ecumenism in Transition: A Paradigm Shift in the Ecumenical Movement?* (Geneva: WCC, 1994).

80 Thomas F. Best and Martin Robra, eds., *Ecclesiology and Ethics: Ecumenical Ethical Engagement, Moral Formation and the Nature of the Church* (Geneva: WCC, 1997).

81 Max Thurian, ed., *Ecumenical Perspectives on Baptism, Eucharist and Ministry*, F&O paper 116 (Geneva: WCC, 1983); Max Thurian and Geoffrey Wainwright, eds., *Baptism and Eucharist: Ecumenical Convergence in Celebration*, F&O paper 117 (Geneva: WCC, 1983); William H. Lazareth, *Growing Together in Baptism, Eucharist and Ministry: A Study Guide*, F&O paper 114 (Geneva: WCC, 1982).

82 Max Thurian, ed., *Churches Respond to BEM – Official Responses to the "Baptism, Eucharist and Ministry" Text*, Vol. I: F&O paper 129; Vol. II: F&O paper 132; Vol. III: F&O paper 135; Vol. IV: F&O paper 137; Vol. V, F&O paper 143; Vol. VI: F&O paper 144 (Geneva: WCC, 1986–98).

83 Faith and Order, *Baptism, Eucharist & Ministry 1982–1990: Report on the Process and Responses*, F&O paper 149 (Geneva: WCC, 1990).

84 Faith and Order, *Confessing the One Faith: An Ecumenical Explication of the Apostolic Faith as It Is Confessed in the Nicene-Constantinopolitan Creed (381)*, F&O paper 153 (Geneva: WCC, 1991).

85 Faith and Order, *Confessing the One Faith*, 4.

86 Thomas F. Best, *Faith and Order 1985–1989: The Commission Meeting in Budapest 1989*, F&O paper 148 (Geneva: WCC, 1990), 202–19.

87 "The Unity of the Church as Koinonia: Gift and Calling," in *Signs of the Spirit: Official Report – Seventh Assembly*, ed. Michael Kinnamon (Geneva: WCC, 1991), 172–4.

88 *The Nature and Purpose of the Church*, F&O paper 181 (Geneva: WCC, 1998).

89 *A Treasure in Earthen Vessels*, F&O paper 182 (Geneva: WCC, 1998).

90 Faith and Order, *From Canberra to Harare: Activity Report 1991–1998 – An offprint from the Unit I Hearing Report* (Bialystok: Orthdruk, 2000), 6.

91 *Faith and Order at Crossroads: Kuala Lumpur 2004 – The Plenary Commission Meeting*, F&O paper 196 (Geneva: WCC, 2005), 201–48.

92 *The Nature and Mission of the Church* (Geneva: WCC, 2005, F&O paper 198); *The Church: Towards a Common Vision*, F&O paper 214 (Geneva: WCC, 2013); *Churches Respond to the Church: Towards a Common Vision*, 2 vols., F&O papers 231, 232 (Geneva: WCC, 2021); *What Are the Churches Saying about the Church*, F&O paper 236 (Geneva: WCC, 2021); *Common Threads*, F&O paper 233 (Geneva: WCC, 2021); *Global Christianity and the Common Understanding of the Church*, F&O papers 234, 239 (Geneva: WCC, 2022–3).

93 *The Church: Towards a Common Vision*, F&O paper 214 (Geneva: WCC, 2013), para 7.

94 *Global Christianity and the Common Understanding of the Church*, F&O papers 234, 239 (Geneva: WCC, 2022–3).

95   *Moral Discernment in the Churches* (Geneva: WCC, 2013).

96   *Moral Discernment in the Churches* (Geneva: WCC, 2013), 3–4.

97   *Learning from Traditions*, F&O paper 228, *Churches and Moral Discernment: Vol. 1* (Geneva: WCC, 2021).

98   *Learning from History*, F&O paper 229, *Churches and Moral Discernment: Vol. 2* (Geneva: WCC, 2021).

99   *Facilitating Dialogue to Build Koinonia*, F&O paper 235, *Churches and Moral Discernment: Vol. 3* (Geneva: WCC, 2021).

Recommended Reading

Bonino, J. Míguez. "A Latin American Attempt to Locate the Question of Unity." *The Ecumenical Review* 26 (1974): 210–21.

Braaten, Carl E., and Robert W. Jenson, eds. *In One Body through the Cross: The Princeton Proposal for Christian Unity*. Grand Rapids, MI: Eerdmans, 2003.

Commission on Faith and Order of the World Council of Churches. *Baptism, Eucharist and Ministry*. Geneva: WCC, 1982.

———. *The Church: Towards a Common Vision*. Geneva: WCC, 2013.

Congar, Yves. *Divided Christendom: A Catholic Study of the Problem of Reunion*. London: Centenary Press, 1939. Original in French: Chrétiens désunis. Principes d'un oecuménisme catholique. Paris: Cerf, 1937.

Hoedemaker, Bert, and Theo Witvliet. "Christian Unity Reconsidered: Comments on the Dream of the Ecumenical Century." In *Rethinking Ecumenism: Strategies for the 21st Century*, edited by Freek Bakker, 105–20. Zoetermeer: Meinema, 2004.

Institute for Ecumenical Research. *Crisis and Challenge of the Ecumenical Movement: Integrity and Indivisibility*. Geneva: WCC, 1994.

Raiser, Konrad. *Ecumenism in Transition: A Paradigm Shift in the Ecumenical Movement?* Geneva: WCC, 1991.

Tesfai, Yacob. *Liberation and Orthodoxy: The Promise and Failures of Interconfessional Dialogue*. Maryknoll, NY: Orbis, 1996.

Evangelical Theology

Sung Wook Chung

Introduction

Evangelical theology cannot be separated from evangelicalism or the evangelical movement, a global Christian movement committed to and centered on the gospel. In other words, the evangelical movement provides evangelical theology with its context and circumstance wherein evangelicals do their theological work. As such, evangelical theology can only be fully understood hand in hand with a sufficiently broad and deep understanding of the evangelical movement. Conversely, the evangelical movement maintains its identity in its historical development by its essential theological commitments and features.

Many church historians including David Bebbington and Mark Noll have traced the origin of the evangelical movement to the eighteenth-century religious awakenings in Great Britain and New England. However, I agree with Alister E. McGrath who has argued that the sixteenth-century European Reformation should be regarded as the historical origin of the evangelical movement. Nevertheless, if one understands the gospel of Jesus Christ as the core of the evangelical movement, we should trace the origin of the evangelical movement to the first century CE, the so-called apostolic age. It is undeniable that the original apostles of Jesus Christ were men of the gospel, who lived, worked and died for it.

It is still of some historical utility to place the origin of the evangelical movement in the sixteenth-century European Reformation, as it brought about revolutionary changes in the development of the Christian church up to that point through the rediscovery of the gospel. The Reformation mottos including the five *solas* (*sola scriptura, solus Christus, sola gratia, sola fide*, and *soli deo gloria*) and the principle of the priesthood of all believers are crystallizations of the central and essential message of the gospel. The evangelical movement that started in Germany, Switzerland, and Great Britain began to spread throughout Europe in the later sixteenth and early seventeenth centuries. In particular, the Lutheran movement became a dominant presence in northern Germany, Denmark, and Scandinavian countries. The Reformed movement

Ford's The Modern Theologians: An Introduction to Christian Theology since 1918, Fourth Edition.
Edited by Rachel Muers and Ashley Cocksworth.
© 2024 John Wiley & Sons Ltd. Published 2024 by John Wiley & Sons Ltd.

became pervasive all over Europe, especially in Southern Germany, Switzerland, the Netherlands, Hungary, Scotland, and so on. In the seventeenth century, Lutheran and Reformed theologians advanced their own orthodox dogmatic traditions through the employment of the scholastic method. In reaction, pietism and its theology became a renewing force in the German context, and Puritanism and its theology became a revitalizing force in the Reformed churches in England, Scotland, and Ireland. For many historians, Puritanism was a version of pietism in Great Britain and New England.

In the eighteenth century, the Great Awakening led by John Wesley and Jonathan Edwards reignited evangelical commitment and evangelistic fervor among Protestant Christians in Great Britain and New England. These spiritual reawakenings made an indelible and irreplaceable impact upon the English-speaking European Protestant world. For many historians and theologians, these great revivals became a driving force for the recovery of the liveliness of the evangelical movement. Ever since the Great Awakening, the evangelical movement had been a predominantly English-speaking movement until it became a global movement in the twentieth century. In the nineteenth century, both Britain and the United States produced leading evangelical theologians such as J. C. Ryle, Charles Spurgeon, Charles Hodge, and B. B. Warfield and pioneering missionaries such as David Livingstone, William Carey, and Adoniram Judson. Neo-Calvinism in the Netherlands can be viewed as a renaissance of evangelical theology, whose leading figures were Abraham Kuyper and Herman Bavinck.

In the late nineteenth century the evangelical world was divided into two major camps. One is the classical evangelical tradition and the other is the rising fundamentalism. It is not hard to understand why fundamentalism began to form a powerful force against the threats of modernism and liberalism. The fundamentalist movement played a significant role in deterring the expansion of the modernist agenda and defending the essential truths of the Christian faith including the virgin birth, divinity, humanity, atoning death, resurrection and second coming of Jesus Christ. However, the fundamentalist movement was characterized by dogmatism, judgmentalism, separatism, and a militant attitude. In the first half of the twentieth century, neoevangelicalism began to rise as a powerful antidote and alternative to the fundamentalist movement.[1] Leading figures in the rise of neoevangelicalism include Carl F. H. Henry, Harold Ockenga, Vernon Grounds, Edward John Carnell, Bernard Ramm, and Billy Graham. Historians have been emphasizing Henry's contributions to the rise of neoevangelicalism in tandem with the foundation of Fuller Theological Seminary.[2]

In the second half of the twentieth century, the evangelical movement began to become a genuinely global movement. Evangelicalism has been gaining momentum not only in the English-speaking world but also in global South countries in Africa, Asia, and Latin America. The International Congress on World Evangelization held in Lausanne, Switzerland in 1974 crystallized the globalization of the evangelical movement. More than 2300 evangelical leaders from 150 countries gathered together to discuss and pray for the strategies and tactics of the global evangelistic endeavor. The Lausanne Covenant was one particularly fruitful result of this epoch-making congress, which pronounced the theological and missional visions of the global evangelical movement. The second and the third Lausanne congresses were held in Manila, the Philippines in 1989 and Cape Town, South Africa in 2010. The fourth Lausanne congress will be held in Seoul, South Korea in 2024.

In the late twentieth and early twenty-first centuries, the global evangelical movement continued to grow and expand. In particular, the rise and revival of evangelical movements in China, India, Indonesia, South Korea, Nigeria, Brazil, and other countries that scholars consider part of "the majority world" or "the global South,"[3] represents the current reality that the majority constituencies of Christianity and the evangelical movement consist not in the Euro-American world but in Africa, Asia, and Latin America. In short, the centers of Christianity have already moved to these continents from the Western world. Christian revivals in the global South have been largely evangelical in their theological character and Pentecostal or charismatic in their practices.

Survey

David Bebbington identifies four major theological features of the evangelical movement: authority of scripture, centrality of Jesus Christ, necessity of personal conversion, and urgency of evangelism and mission.[4] Alister E. McGrath contributes two additional features to these four: lordship of the Holy Spirit and importance of the church and faith community.[5] I prefer McGrath's taxonomy to Bebbington's because the former correctly, in my view, recognizes the Pentecostal/Charismatic movement as one vital constituent of the global evangelical movement. The following is a detailed explanation of these six major theological emphases of the global evangelical movement.

Authority of scripture

Everyone that identifies himself or herself as an evangelical demonstrates a profound commitment to the authority of scripture as the supreme norm and standard for faith and practice. For most evangelicals, scripture is identified as the Word of God per se, or the Word of God written. When scripture speaks, God speaks. In terms Jesus often employed, "it is written" means "God has spoken." In relation to the authority of scripture, such terminology as inerrancy, infallibility, and inspiration is significant. Most evangelicals confess that scripture is the inerrant and infallible revelation and Word of God inspired by the Holy Spirit.

There were serious debates and disputes over the "inerrancy" of scripture in the United States in the 1960s and 1970s.[6] Nevertheless, many evangelicals still retain their conviction that scripture is inerrant, which means that the original manuscript of scripture has no errors in what it affirms whether theological, ethical, historical, geographical, or scientific. In contrast to US evangelicals, British and Australian evangelicals tend to not use the concept "inerrancy," preferring instead to use the idea of "infallibility" or "total trustworthiness."[7] When they use the word "infallibility," they want to stress that scripture has absolute authority particularly in the matters of faith and salvation rather than also in history, geography, and science. It is intriguing to note in this context that evangelicals in the global South tend to employ the term "inerrant" more often than British and Australian evangelicals.[8] This implies that global South evangelicals have a higher or more conservative view about scripture than Western evangelicals.

Whether one employs the term "inerrant" or "infallible," most evangelicals concur that crude and primitive biblicism is not healthy. By "crude and primitive biblicism" I mean hermeneutically naïve literalism that completely ignores the historical context and literary genres of the biblical text. Thus, many evangelical theologians have been striving to construct a robust and resilient hermeneutical system to drive destructive "bibliolatry" out of the evangelical camp. For example, some evangelical theologians have proposed the idea of "organic inspiration" against the notions of "mechanical inspiration" or "dictation." The idea of "mechanical inspiration" neglects human writers' personal involvement in the process of inscripturation. Human writers are regarded as just impersonal typewriters, recording what God dictates without any personal engagement. In contrast, the concept of "organic inspiration" reinforces the human dimension of scripture, which means that scripture is not a direct product of divine dictation but rather a product of divine engagement with human writers respecting and employing their personal characteristics, professional backgrounds, different writing styles, experiences of suffering and pain, and so on.

In some fundamentalist circles, the idea of "verbal" inspiration is often misconceived as "verbatim" inspiration. Within these circles, a verbatim quotation of biblical verses and passages without any hermeneutical engagement is sufficient to make a truth claim or a final decision on doctrines and religious practices. This view implies that there is no need for serious interpretative endeavor with scripture. In contrast, evangelicals tend to interpret "verbal inspiration" to require a robust engagement with grammatical, historical, and contextual understanding of the text with the help of proper linguistic tools for original languages of Hebrew, Aramaic, and Greek. A balanced and appropriate grammatical interpretation of scripture should consider seriously the grammatical structure, literary genres, and rhetorical distinctives of a given text. A proper and pertinent historical interpretation of the Bible is geared toward a balanced consideration of historical and social background of a given passage.

Furthermore, many evangelicals are convinced that grammatical and historical interpretation of scripture is not the end of the hermeneutical endeavor. For them, theological interpretation should be the next stage in the interpretative engagement with scripture. The rationale for theological interpretation is a belief that ultimately every passage of the Bible aims to reveal something about God including who God is, what God does, and what God requires of human beings. Many theologians including evangelicals have recently been participating in the revival of theological interpretation of scripture, which is a positive trend for strengthening evangelical engagement with scripture.[9]

On top of that, for many evangelicals the final stage of biblical interpretation is application, whether personal or communal. At the stage of applicatory interpretation of biblical text, readers should glean theological, ethical, spiritual lessons and make existential decisions on their application in the context of their personal lives, church ministries, workplace, and the community of faith. For evangelicals, application of what they learn from reading scriptural texts is of paramount importance for their faith and conduct.

Despite evangelicals' commitment to historical and contextual interpretation of scripture, they tend to draw a clear line between their approach and liberal higher criticism of scripture crystallized in historical-critical method. More than anything else, most evangelicals retain their commitment to a biblical, namely, supernaturalistic worldview, whereas liberals do theology under the umbrella of naturalistic presuppositions. Therefore, evangelicals tend to believe that the Old Testament prophetic texts should be interpreted to be genuinely predicting and anticipating fulfillments in the history of Israel and the person of Jesus Christ whereas liberals do not consider the Old Testament texts to be authentically prophetic or predictive. Relatedly, evangelicals have tendencies to employ typological interpretation of the Old Testament, although there are differences of the degree of commitment to typology among evangelicals.[10]

Centrality of Jesus Christ and the cross

The second theological feature of the global evangelical movement is that Jesus Christ is the center of the Christian faith. Most evangelicals are convinced that Christianity is about Christ and the central dimension of the Christian faith is our relationship with Jesus. For evangelicals, Jesus Christ is eternally the Son of God, the second person of the Triune God. Jesus Christ's eternal and infinite divinity is unapologetically affirmed. Most evangelicals pledge to the Nicene Creed, "I believe in one Lord Jesus Christ, the Only Begotten Son of God, born of the Father before all ages. God from God, Light from Light, true God from true God, begotten, not made, consubstantial with the Father; through him all things were made."

Evangelicals have commitment to not only the deity of Jesus Christ but also his true humanity.[11] According to the Nicene Creed, "For us men and for our salvation he came down from heaven, and by the Holy Spirit was incarnate of the Virgin Mary and became man." That is to say, the second person of the triune God took upon full human nature including human soul and body and became the same as us in all things except sin. Most evangelicals would also accept wholeheartedly the Chalcedonian definition, "One and the Same Christ, Son, Lord, Only-begotten; acknowledged in two natures unconfusedly, unchangeably, indivisibly, inseparably; the difference of the natures being in no way removed because of the Union, but rather the properties of each nature being preserved, and (both) concurring into One Person and One Hypostasis; not as though He was parted or divided into two Persons, but One and the Self-same Son and Only-begotten God, Word, Lord, Jesus Christ." Evangelicals enjoy consensus that the person of Jesus Christ, the second person of the Trinity, is the one who determines the content and perimeter of evangelical faith, practice, and spirituality.[12]

It is important to appreciate that not only the person but also the work of Jesus Christ forms the core of evangelical commitment. Most evangelicals would affirm that Jesus Christ was born of the Virgin Mary and led a sinless life of perfect obedience to God the Father. Jesus's ministries were focused on teaching the Word of God, preaching the gospel of the kingdom, healing the sick and having mercy and compassion upon the lost (Matt. 9:35–6). Christ's healing ministry included casting demons away and raising the dead. Jesus also performed numerous miracles to demonstrate his messiahship and the presence of the Holy Spirit with him.[13]

Most important, the culmination of his messianic work was crucifixion, namely, the atoning death upon the cross. John the Baptist declared that Jesus came to the world as the lamb of God taking away the sins of the world (John 1:29). Jesus also proclaimed that he did not come to be served but to serve, giving his life as the ransom for many (Mk. 10:45). Most evangelicals would agree that Jesus Christ died on the cross to atone for their sins as their substitute and sacrificial offering. Thus, despite various alternative theories of atonement, the idea of vicarious and substitutionary atonement has been a dominant conviction among evangelicals throughout church history. Most evangelicals believe that the blood of Jesus Christ has the power to cover all sins including original and actual sins. They believe that Jesus Christ finished the redemptive work for humanity upon the cross by laying down his life, shedding his blood and tearing his body.[14]

On the third day, Jesus Christ was raised from the dead and his glorious resurrection vindicated his complete work of redemption and messiahship.[15] Forty days later, Jesus Christ ascended into heaven and was seated at the right hand of the Father. He received the Holy Spirit from the Father and poured the Spirit upon the church. He is interceding for his followers as the high priest and ruling the church and the world as the exalted king.[16] He is preparing for his second coming as the victor and judge and will bring the new heaven and earth as eternal inheritance for believers.[17] These statements constitute core beliefs for evangelicals. For evangelicals, Jesus Christ's crucifixion consists in the very core of the gospel message and the meaning of crucifixion should be interpreted in the context of his resurrection and second coming.

Lordship of the Holy Spirit

The Holy Spirit has taken a central place in evangelical theological reflection throughout church history, at least ever since the Reformation. For example, Martin Luther and John Calvin emphasized that the Holy Spirit is essential in sinners' converting to Christ and their understanding of the gospel and the Word of God. Many Puritan theologians including John Owen stressed the crucial role of the Holy Spirit in believers' life of faith, especially in the process of sanctification. Jonathan Edwards, the last and foremost Puritan theologian, also emphasized the dynamic and powerful work of the Holy Spirit for conversion, sanctification, and perseverance. John Wesley was another paramount figure in stressing the crucial role of the Holy Spirit for personal and social holiness. The Methodist movement and the Holiness movement in the nineteenth century demonstrated their profound commitment to the person and work of the Holy Spirit.

However, it is the Pentecostal and Charismatic movements that played the largest role in recovering the central role of the Holy Spirit in personal conversion and sanctification as well as communal ecclesial life along with a rediscovery of the important function of charismatic gifts. Despite many cases of misuse and overuse of and disputes over charismatic gifts including gifts involving divine signs and revelations, it is an undeniable consensus among most evangelicals that the Holy Spirit continues to work as dynamically and powerfully as during the early centuries of Christianity. Of course, evangelicals would take a cautious approach when they deal with charismatic gifts. Nevertheless, only a small minority of evangelicals would argue for the cessation of "sign" gifts. Despite differences between the evangelical movement and the Pentecostal/Charismatic movement in terms of their religious practices and spiritual sensibilities, there is significant theological overlap between them, which means that the Pentecostal/Charismatic movement can be regarded as a close relative to the evangelical movement.

Nevertheless, in consideration of theological and practical aberrations in some extreme charismatic circles, evangelical theologians want to place more stress upon the lordship of the Holy Spirit rather than his gifts.[18] Evangelicals recognize that the Holy Spirit is not an impersonal force or influence but rather the third person of the Trinity. Simply put, the Holy Spirit is the Lord and God, a personal being. Believers, therefore, are not to try to control the Holy Spirit for their whims and desires but rather the Holy Spirit as the Lord of the universe should control the lives of believers. Of course, the lordship and sovereignty of the Holy Spirit should not be interpreted to dismiss human freedom and responsibility. Rather, the Holy Spirit's sovereign work establishes the true freedom and responsibility of Christ followers.

In further contrast to the Pentecostal and Charismatic movements, which have placed primary emphasis on the gifts of the Holy Spirit, evangelicals tend to stress more the fruit of the Holy Spirit.[19] For evangelicals, the main ministry of the Holy Spirit is not about dramatic manifestations of dynamic power but rather about the Holy Spirit's sovereign and gracious engagement with believers to become more Christlike, bearing the fruit of Christian virtues such as faithfulness, gentleness, love, and patience. In a nutshell, the lordship of the Holy Spirit is one of the central theological convictions of most evangelicals.

Necessity of personal conversion and regeneration

The fourth central theological conviction of evangelicals is the absolute necessity of personal conversion and regeneration. Evangelicals take seriously biblical teachings about human depravity and the need for regeneration. Scripture proclaims the universal sinfulness of human beings. That is, every human being is born into sin, and human nature is so corrupt that every aspect of human nature is tainted and marred by sin. All human beings are dead spiritually and need to be born again to see and enter the kingdom. By being born again evangelicals mean spiritual regeneration or rebirth. Only by repenting of their sins and putting their personal trust in the Lord Jesus Christ can sinners be born again and experience spiritual rebirth. If sinners do not repent of and turn from their sinful lives, they will not be able to avoid eternal condemnation and separation from God, the wellspring of life. In this context of conversion and regeneration, the Reformation slogan, "by faith alone" (*sola fide*) plays a crucial role. Sinners can be regenerated only through faith in Jesus Christ.

At the moment of conversion and regeneration, evangelicals believe that the event of union with Christ happens.[20] When sinners put their trust in Christ, the Holy Spirit unites them with Christ by indwelling and sealing them. Believers' spiritual union with Christ is closely connected with the biblical portrait and parable of spiritual marriage between believers as the bride and Christ as the bridegroom. This event of spiritual union with Christ plays a role as a bedrock for other salvific events and believers' assurance of salvation.

The events of justification and adoption happen simultaneously at the moment of spiritual union with Christ. The event of justification cannot be separate from the event of union with Christ. John Calvin even argued that justification and sanctification are two benefits of believers' union with Christ through faith.[21] Despite serious disputes over the meaning of justification between the old and the new perspectives on Paul, most evangelicals concur that justification is primarily about vertical reconciliation between the righteous God and sinful human beings. God justifies sinners or declares them to be righteous or "right with him" by imputing or transferring the perfect righteousness of Christ to believing sinners. Justification is not a lifelong process but a once and for all event.[22]

The event of adoption occurs along with the events of regeneration, union with Christ and justification. When sinners come to believe in Jesus Christ, God adopts them as his sons and daughters. Through the event of adoption, believers receive the privilege to become God's children, heirs, and inheritors. Believers begin to enjoy intimate fellowship with God as their spiritual Father and Christ as their older brother. The idea of adoption implies not only privileges, powers, glories, and riches but also responsibilities and duties to lead a life worthy of God's children, a life of holiness, purity, and obedience. Personal conversion and regeneration are the first steps for believers to enjoy all these salvific benefits. For this reason, evangelicals put a great emphasis on their necessity.[23]

Importance and value of the church and faith community

Evangelicals believe that scripture provides them with various parables or portraits of the church.[24] In relation to God the Father, the church is a household or family of God who calls God "Abba, Father." Thus, members of the church are spiritual brothers and sisters who are to love and care for one another. In relation to God the Son, the church is the body and the bride of Jesus Christ. As the body, the church is an organic community rather than an institutional organization. Of course, the church retains its institutional and organizational dimension, but the church is primarily imagined as an organic body, a congregation of disparate elements that are nevertheless unified and through which life flows. Therefore, members of the church are parts of the body and they are to be closely and intimately connected with one another. As the bride, the church is united with Christ and enjoys special benefits and blessings from her bridegroom. Heavenly privileges and powers belong to the church, the bride of Christ. It is very important, however, to appreciate that the church as the bride of Christ has weighty responsibilities to keep her purity and holiness before her bridegroom. Secularization and corruption of the church can be detrimental not only to the church herself but to the larger society.

In addition to these images of the church, the New Testament pictures the church as the mother of all believers. As the spiritual mother, the church conceives and gives birth to new lives. The church feeds and takes care of her children, rears them through training, education, and discipline. The church sends her children out to the world to evangelize and serve. In a nutshell, the church continues to do the works that Jesus Christ did while he was on earth: teaching, preaching, evangelism and mission, healing, mercy giving, discipleship training, and so on.

For evangelicals, therefore, the church is not something optional but necessary and essential. Evangelicals concur with Cyprian of Carthage, "there is no salvation outside the church (*extra ecclesiam nulla salus*)." Of course, the evangelical interpretation of "*extra ecclesiam nulla salus*" is radically different from the Roman Catholic interpretation. Here the church is not about a visible and hierarchical institution but about an invisible, organic, and global community. Evangelicals are convinced that it is automatic for new converts to become members of the invisible church, and its visible and natural manifestation is their being members of a local congregation. Evangelicals would strive to maintain unity, apostolicity, holiness, and catholicity of the church. They want to make the church an uplifting and upbuilding community through mutual love, service, and encouragement. The church serves as an indispensably important lifeline for evangelicals.[25]

The urgency of evangelism and mission

The last theological feature of the global evangelical movement consists in the urgency of evangelism and mission. Evangelicals believe that Jesus came to save the lost and commanded his followers to "go and make disciples of all nations and to be my witnesses to the end of the earth" (Matt. 28:19; Acts 1:8). This great commission characterizes the life of evangelicals. Evangelicals are committed to saving souls through evangelism, the most urgent task that must be completed before the lost are eternally condemned. In other words, evangelicals are evangelistic!

Traditionally, the word "mission" has been connected with overseas or international work of evangelism. With the rise of "missional church" movement,[26] the word "mission" has come to mean "the church's engagement with the specific society and culture for the expansion of the Kingdom," which naturally embraces the work of evangelism. Furthermore, the missional church movement has defined "mission" not as just one of many ministries of the church but rather the church's ontological identity. The church is intrinsically missional because it has been called to participate in *missio Dei*, the triune God's holistic work of redemption of the lost world. Therefore, mission is not only urgent but also unstoppable and uninterruptible.

Evangelical commitment to the urgency of evangelism and mission can be epitomized by the principle of "missionaryhood of all believers," which means that not only full-time and professional missionaries but every ordinary believer is a missionary called and sent by Jesus Christ. During the sixteenth-century European Reformation, the theological slogan of "priesthood of all believers" was restored, making an incalculable and indelible impact upon European churches and society. In light of this, it is my view that the idea of "missionaryhood of all believers" should be rediscovered on a global scale in the twenty-first century as well. The rediscovery of the principle of "missionaryhood of all believers" promises to impact the global expansion of the kingdom on a massive scale.[27]

Named Theologians

British and European evangelical theologians: John Stott, Alister McGrath, G. C. Berkouwer, Helmut Thielicke

In the twentieth century, Great Britain produced several major theologians for the evangelical movement. One of the most well-known figures is John R. W. Stott, a pastor-theologian par excellence. Stott played a tremendously impactful role for global evangelical movement as a representative statesman and influential theological writer. Among his powerful books are the *Cross of Christ*, the *Message of Romans*, *Basic Christianity*, and *the Radical Disciple*. More than anything else, Stott, along with Billy Graham, made an incalculable contribution to the formation of the Lausanne movement and the creation of the Lausanne Covenant. James I. Packer is another leading theologian. As a Reformed evangelical and an expert on Puritan theology, Packer wrote many influential books such as *Knowing God*, *Keep in Step with the Spirit*, *Evangelism and the Sovereignty of God*, and so on. In addition, he maintained a lifelong interest in the themes of holiness and sanctification.

Under the influence of Stott and Packer, Alister E. McGrath has become one of the most influential theologians alive today. McGrath started his academic career as a natural scientist in the area of molecular biology but turned into a professional theologian. He has published numerous influential books on the Reformation theology, systematic/historical theology, apologetics, and even spiritual theology. In his later life, he concentrated his energy on the issue of the proper relationship between the Christian faith and science. He is currently regarded as one of the most erudite theologians of the evangelical persuasion.

Continental Europe is the home of several significant evangelical theologians, including a Dutch Reformed theologian, G. C. Berkouwer (1903–96) and German evangelical theologian Helmut Thielicke (1908–86). Berkouwer's *Studies in Dogmatics* has been regarded as a representative formulation of Christian theology from a Dutch evangelical perspective. Thielicke is viewed as a representative German evangelical theologian who tried to defend the identity of evangelical Christianity against neo-orthodox revision.

North American evangelical theologians: Carl Henry and others

The United States has also produced many influential evangelical theologians. Carl F. H. Henry is regarded as the founding figure of neoevangelicalism in America. One of his masterpieces, the *Uneasy Conscience of Modern Fundamentalism*, signaled the rise of neoevangelicalism as a distinctive movement from fundamentalism. His magnum opus, *God, Revelation and Authority*, paved the way for the consolidation and advancement of American evangelical theology. Millard Erickson is another towering figure who formulated an evangelical theological system in his *Christian Theology* and many other books. Even though he was a

Baptist, he presented a broadly evangelical systematic theology. *Christian Theology* has been attracting readers from many other denominations and traditions. Both Henry and Erickson were conservative evangelical theologians rooted in Baptist tradition.

There are many leading evangelical theologians connected with North American Reformed/Presbyterian tradition. Louis Berkhof and Anthony Hoekema were major theologians rooted in Dutch Calvinism. John Murray, John Frame, and Michael Horton can be regarded as significant theologians in Scottish and American Presbyterian tradition. Donald Bloesch was a Reformed evangelical theologian with an ecumenical slant. In particular, he was passionate to reappropriate positive contributions of neo-orthodox theologians such as Karl Barth,[28] Emil Brunner, and Dietrich Bonhoeffer.

Postconservative evangelical theology arose as a reaction to the shortcomings of traditional conservative evangelical theology. Among leading theologians are Stanley Grenz, Roger Olson, and John R. Franke.[29] These postconservative theologians attempted to revise the traditional evangelical view of scripture into a moderate and instrumental view. Moreover, they accused conservative evangelical theologians of making the mistake of doing theology under the framework of the Enlightenment rationalism or foundationalism. For Grenz, Olson, and Franke, theology is not about building a propositional system of truth based on foundational truths but about transforming people. For them, every theological truth claim is not something eternally fixed but something under continuous scrutiny and revision. Moreover, according to these theologians, postmodernism is not necessarily an enemy but can be a source of positive contribution to evangelical theology.

Global evangelical theologians: Rene Padilla and others

Rene Padilla is one of the most influential evangelical theologians that Latin America has produced. He is renowned for employing the concept "integral mission" to integrate evangelistic endeavor and social action.[30] He has also made a significant contribution to the Lausanne Congress of 1974. Kwame Bediako is a world-renowned African evangelical theologian. He was interested in delving into the mutual relationship between the Christian faith and indigenous religious and cultural contexts in Africa. He discussed this issue in his book, *Theology and Identity*.[31] Vinay Samuel is an Asian evangelical theologian who made an indelible impact upon the consolidation of Asian evangelical theology and missiology. In particular, he promoted holistic theology and mission in Indian context, integrating evangelism and transformational concern for the poor.[32]

Debate

So far, we have focused on the elements of the evangelical movement that bring it together, both in terms of theological commitment and historical development. However, despite these common threads, the global evangelical movement has not been a uniform movement. Rather, it has been a movement characterized by various approaches, perspectives, constituents, and emphases. For example, various theological controversies regarding major issues such as hermeneutical frameworks and soteriological arguments are apparent within the evangelical movement.

Covenant theology vs. dispensationalism

Regarding the hermeneutical framework of the entirety of scripture, we have two major competing systems within the evangelical movement. One is covenant theology[33] and the other is dispensationalism. Covenant theology originated from the sixteenth-century European Reformation. Reformed theologians such as Huldrych Zwingli, John Calvin, and Heinrich Bullinger were the pioneering figures in the covenantal understanding of scripture. Zwingli espoused infant baptism with a covenantal interpretation of the sacraments. Calvin presented similarities and differences between the old covenant and the new covenant in his *Institutes of the Christian Religion*. Bullinger traced God's covenantal dealings with his people from Genesis to Revelation.

In the late sixteenth and early seventeenth century, British and Dutch Reformed theologians promulgated a system of covenant theology grounded upon the concepts of the covenant of works and the covenant of grace. This twofold covenantal hermeneutics expanded into a threefold covenantal hermeneutical system consisting in the covenant of redemption, the covenant of works, and the covenant of grace. The covenantal hermeneutical framework emphasizes God's sovereign and gracious engagement with his people throughout the history of Israel and the church. It also stresses the continuity of God's covenantal dealings with his people. For the covenantal hermeneutical framework, there is only one people of God which includes both the Jews and the gentiles throughout biblical history. In the Old Testament, Israel was a major portion of God's people, but many prominent gentiles such as Tamar, Caleb, Rahab, Ruth, and Bathsheba belonged to the people of God. In the New Testament, gentiles formed a major portion of God's people, but it also included many noteworthy Jews such as the twelve apostles.

For most covenant theologians, the church of the New Testament replaced Israel of the Old Testament. Moreover, the New Testament baptism is the replacement of the Old Testament circumcision and the New Testament Lord's supper is the replacement of the Old Testament Passover meal. As Calvin has argued, the Old Covenant and the New Covenant are different in forms and institutions alone but the same in terms of theological ideas of grace and forgiveness of sins. Recent and contemporary theologians who espouse this view include Michael Horton. Furthermore, for covenant theologians most of the Old Testament prophecies were fulfilled in and through Christ and the church. In terms of eschatology, covenant theologians tend to espouse amillennialism or historic premillennialism.

In contrast, dispensationalism posits two peoples of God, Israel and the church. For dispensationalists, Israel and the church must be distinguished perpetually and God's dealings with Israel are totally distinct from those with the church. Importantly according to dispensationalism, God gives privileges and preferences to Israel over the church. Simply put, the Jewish Israel is superior to the gentile church. For dispensationalists, many of the Old Testament prophecies should be fulfilled in and through the physical Jews and the modern state of Israel, not the gentile church. Recent and contemporary theologians who espouse this view include Charles Ryrie and John Walvoord. In terms of baptism and the Lord's supper, dispensationalists regard them as ordinances that require believers' obedience, not sacraments, signs of mysterious grace. Most dispensationalists do not endorse infant baptism but uphold believers' or adult baptism alone. In terms of eschatology, despite internal disputes between classical and progressive dispensationalism, dispensationalists tend to espouse pretribulational rapture, premillennialism, and the Jewish character of the millennial kingdom.[34]

In spite of major differences in hermeneutical framework between covenant theology and dispensationalism, there are some undeniable commonalities between them. In particular, it is intriguing to appreciate that like most covenant theologians most dispensationalists are Reformed or Calvinistic in their soteriology, emphasizing the total depravity of human nature and God's sovereign grace over human freedom and responsibility. Therefore, it is impossible and irresponsible for both camps to accuse each other of heresy. Both camps are orthodox in soteriological underpinnings even though hermeneutical frameworks are radically divergent. It is a global trend that both camps maintain a conciliatory attitude in mutual engagement.

Calvinism vs. Arminianism

In evangelical soteriological reflection, we have two major contrasting and competing camps. One is Calvinism/Reformed soteriology and the other is Arminianism. Representative proponents of Calvinism/Reformed view include Michael Horton, J. I. Packer, and John Piper. Arminian proponents include Roger Olson and Thomas Oden.

John Calvin is viewed as the father of the Calvinistic interpretation of salvation although there are both continuities and discontinuities between Calvin's own views and the later Calvinism. The Calvinist soteriology is epitomized by the so-called five points of Calvinism, acronymously known as TULIP (total depravity, unconditional election, limited atonement, irresistible grace, and perseverance of the saints).[35] It starts with an affirmation of the total depravity and inability of human nature. Natural human beings are alive biologically but dead spiritually. Every aspect of human nature is defaced and distorted by sin. Therefore, nobody can save himself or herself on their own. Human beings are enslaved by death and the Devil, and their will is bound by sin.

Among the mass of sinful and spiritually dead people, God unconditionally elects some toward salvation and left other in their wretched condition. Throughout its history, the idea of God's salvific election of some has been a puzzling conundrum for many people. However, most Calvinists accept God's sovereign election of some as God's gracious initiative to redeem humanity. Why not elect all? Should the God of love not elect all for salvation? Calvinists believe that God has his own reason and freedom for not electing and saving all human beings even though he can. From the perspective of sinners, God's election of them is the only hope for their salvation.

The third article of the five points of Calvinism is limited atonement. The idea of limited atonement is closely connected with the scope of salvation. By limited atonement, Calvinists mean that Jesus Christ died for the elect alone. In other words, the effect of Christ's atoning death is limited to the elect, that is to say redemption is particular not universal. This article has been sparking internal disputes among Calvinists. Some moderate Calvinists believe that Jesus Christ truly died for all sinners but only the elect respond to the grace of atonement. Whether staunch or moderate, it is clear that all Calvinists believe that only the elect can respond to God's grace and ultimately be saved.

God provides the elect with an irresistible grace in and through Christ. The word "irresistible" tends to connote a kind of mechanical relationship between God and sinners. In response, contemporary theologians employ the word "effectual" as an alternative. God's effectual grace leads sinners to realize their wretched condition, repent of their sins, and redirect their lives by putting their personal trust in Christ. God's effectual grace is amazing grace because sinners do not deserve and cannot merit it. Salvation is a sheer gift from God's unexpected grace and mercy. Sinners who are also believers receive the gift of salvation only by faith, the channel through which the gift of salvation is given.

The final point is the perseverance of the saints. By the perseverance of the saints, Calvinists mean that those who have responded to God's salvific grace through faith will persevere until the end and never lose their salvation given once and for all at the moment of conversion and regeneration.[36] In spite of believers' continuous experience of sins, mistakes, and temptations, God will remain ever faithful in finishing the good work that he has begun. However, it is important to appreciate that perseverance of the saints is not something automatic but believers are to act responsibly and cooperate with the Holy Spirit who dwells and works in them.

In radical contrast to the Calvinistic soteriology, Arminianism emphasizes human freedom, choice, and responsibility rather than God's sovereignty.[37] Arminians tend to use "serious" corruption rather than "total" depravity of human nature. They espouse "conditional" rather than "unconditional" election. For Arminians, God elects some sinners on the basis of his foreknowledge that they would put their personal trust in Jesus Christ in the future. God does not foreordain them to believe but foreknows those who will believe. Arminians believe that the scope of Christ's atoning death is universal, which means Christ died for all without discrimination. Through Christ's atoning death, God makes salvation of sinners possible. Salvation depends on sinners' decision to trust Jesus. Because sinners have not lost their freedom completely, God's grace remains resistible by human free decision. Ultimately, believers can lose their salvation because of their serious spiritual lapses and falls. Therefore, for Arminians, assurance of salvation is not something guaranteed. No one's salvation is eternally guaranteed.

As there are moderate Calvinists who are opposed to the idea of limited atonement like Arminians, we can find moderate Arminians who concur with Calvinists that true believers cannot lose their salvation. In other words, there are various spectrums between hard Calvinism and classical Arminianism. We can find strong Calvinists, moderate Calvinists, so-called "Calminians" or "Arminists," and classical Arminians among evangelicals.[38] Controversies between Calvinism and Arminianism will continue but evangelical consensus is that soteriological issues between Calvinism and Arminianism are not essential but nonessential issues for salvation. Despite interpretative differences, both Calvinists and Arminians believe that sinners are saved in Christ alone, by grace alone and through faith alone.

Conclusion: Achievement and Agenda

In sum, evangelical theology is not something permanently fixed but constantly in flux. Ultimately, it is anchored in the Word of God and the person of Jesus Christ. We have no singular, perfect, and absolute "evangelical theology" but only a variety of evangelical theologies. It is undeniable that radical diversity does characterize evangelical theological formulations. Nevertheless, evangelicals have a broad consensus that they are willing to pursue unity in the essentials, liberty, respect, and generosity in the nonessentials, and charity in all other things. That is, evangelicals all hold to at least some essential theological features. Of course, evangelicals have been debating over what the essentials should be. Still, it is not hard to identify essential doctrines for evangelicals such as the Trinity, deity and humanity of Jesus Christ, his atoning death on the cross and resurrection, lordship of the Holy Spirit, and salvation by grace and through faith alone.

As the evangelical movement becomes increasingly global, it is evident that evangelical theologians in the global South will make increasingly more important contributions to the growth and expansion of the global evangelical movement. Until now, Western evangelical theologians have been playing leading roles on the stage of evangelical theology. From the twenty-first century on, evangelical theologians in the global South have been raising their voices and these will change the landscape of the theological scene of the evangelical movement.

Notes

1 Joel A. Carpenter, "Fundamentalist Institutions and the Rise of Evangelical Protestantism, 1929–1942," *Church History* 49 (1980): 62–75.

2 George M. Marsden, *Reforming Fundamentalism: Fuller Seminary and the New Evangelicalism* (Grand Rapids, MI: Eerdmans, 1987).

3 Philip Jenkins, *The Next Christendom: The Coming of Global Christianity*, 3rd ed. (New York: Oxford University Press, 2011).

4 David Bebbington, *Evangelicalism in Modern Britain: A History from the 1730s to the 1980s* (London: Unwin Hyman, 1989).

5 Alister E. McGrath, *Evangelicalism and the Future of Christianity* (Downers Grove, IL: IVP, 1995).

6 Harold Lindsell, *The Battle for the Bible* (Grand Rapids, MI: Zondervan, 1978).

7 Michael Bird, *Evangelical Theology*, 2nd ed. (Grand Rapids, MI: Zondervan, 2020), 51–5.

8 Philip Jenkins, *The New Faces of Christianity: Believing the Bible in the Global South* (New York: Oxford University Press, 2008).

9 For a robust introduction of theological interpretation from an evangelical perspective, see Daniel J. Treier, *Introducing Theological Interpretation of Scripture* (Grand Rapids, MI: Baker Academic, 2008).

10 See James M. Hamilton, Jr., *Typology-Understanding the Bible's Promise-Shaped Patterns: How Old Testament Expectations Are Fulfilled in Christ* (Grand Rapids, MI: Zondervan, 2022).

11 Millard Erickson, *The Word Became Flesh: A Contemporary Incarnational Christology* (Grand Rapids, MI: Baker, 1991).

12 See Stephen Wellum, *God the Son Incarnate: The Doctrine of Christ* (Wheaton, IL: Crossway, 2016).

13 Wellum, *God the Son Incarnate*, 209–46.

14 For an excellent explication of the doctrine of the cross, see Bruce Demarest, *The Cross and Salvation* (Wheaton, IL: Crossway, 1997), 147–201. John Stott's classic work on the cross remains very helpful. See *The Cross of Christ* (Downers Grove, IL: IVP, 1986).

15 See N. T. Wright, *The Resurrection of the Son of God* (Minneapolis, MN: Fortress Press, 2003).

16 See Peter C. Orr, *Exalted above the Heavens: The Risen and Ascended Christ* (Downers Grove, IL: IVP, 2019).

17 See George E. Ladd, *The Blessed Hope: A Biblical Study of the Second Advent and the Rapture* (Grand Rapids, MI: Eerdmans, 1956).

18 John MacArthur is critical about charismatic chaos. See his *Strange Fire: The Danger of Offending the Holy Spirit with Counterfeit Worship* (Nashville, TN: Thomas Nelson, 2013). For a counterargument against MacArthur, see Michael L. Brown, *Authentic Fire: A Response to John MacArthur's Strange Fire* (Lake Mary, FL: Creation House, 2015).

19 See John Stott, *Baptism and Fullness: The Work of the Holy Spirit Today* (Downers Grove, IL: IVP, 2006).

20 Luther's view of the believer's spiritual union with Christ is presented in his treatise *The Freedom of a Christian* by employing the concept of "holy and great exchange" between Christ and the Christian.

21 For Calvin's idea of union with Christ, see Dennis E. Tamburello, *Union with Christ: John Calvin and the Mysticism of St. Bernard* (Louisville, KY: Westminster John Knox Press, 1994) and Kevin Dixon Kennedy, *Union with Christ and the Extent of the Atonement in Calvin* (New York: Peter Lang, 2002).

22 See Demarest, *The Cross and Salvation*, 345–84.

23 Demarest, *The Cross and Salvation*, 235–312.

24 For an excellent and classical study of the images of the church in the New Testament, see Paul S. Minear, *Images of the Church in the New Testament* (Louisville, KY: Westminster John Knox Press, 2004).

25 For an excellent discussion of evangelical ecclesiology, see Gregg Allison, *Sojourners and Strangers: The Doctrine of the Church* (Wheaton, IL: Crossway, 2012).

26 See Michael Goheen, *A Light to the Nations: The Missional Church and the Biblical Story* (Grand Rapids, MI: Baker, 2011).

27 See Robert Muthiah, *The Priesthood of All Believers in the Twenty-First Century: Living Faithfully as the Whole People of God in a Postmodern Context* (Eugene, OR: Pickwick, 2015).

28 For a comparative discussion of evangelical theology and Karl Barth, see my book, *Karl Barth and Evangelical Theology: Convergences and Divergences* (Grand Rapids, MI: Baker, 2008).

29 See John R. Franke, *The Character of Theology: An Introduction to Its Nature, Task, and Purpose* (Grand Rapids, MI: Baker, 2005).

30 Rene Padilla, *What Is Integral Mission?* (Oxford: Regnum, 2021).

31 Kwame Bediako, *Theology and Identity: The Impact of Culture upon Christian Thought in the Second Century and in Modern Africa* (Oxford: OCMS, 1999).

32 Vinay Samuel and Chris Sugden, eds., *Mission as Transformation: A Theology of the Whole Gospel* (Eugene, OR: Wipf and Stock, 2009).

33 See Michael Horton, *God of Promise: Introducing Covenant Theology* (Grand Rapids, MI: Baker, 2006).

34 For a robust discussion of classical and progressive dispensationalism, see Sung Wook Chung and David Mathewson, *Models of Premillennialism* (Eugene, OR: Wipf and Stock, 2018).

35 For a robust defense for Calvinism, see Michael Horton, *For Calvinism* (Grand Rapids, MI: Zondervan, 2011).

36 For a defense of the doctrine of the perseverance of the saints, see Dongsu Kim, *Perseverance and Apostasy in the New Testament: Unpacking the Dynamic of God's Sovereignty and Human Responsibility* (Bloomington, IN: Westbow Press, 2022).

37 For a solid presentation of Arminianism, see Roger Olson, *Against Calvinism* (Grand Rapids, MI: Zondervan, 2011).

38 Strong Calvinists include Michael Horton and Wayne Grudem. Among moderate Calvinists are Millard Erickson and Bruce Demarest. "Calminians" or "Arvinists" include Craig Blomberg. Among classical Arminians are Roger Olson and William Klein.

Recommended Reading

Bebbington, David. *Evangelicalism in Modern Britain: A History from the 1730s to the 1980s.* London: Unwin Hyman, 1989.

Bediako, Kwame. *Theology and Identity: The Impact of Culture Upon Christian Thought in the Second Century and in Modern Africa.* Oxford: OCMS, 1999.

Bird, Michael. *Evangelical Theology.* 2nd ed. Grand Rapids, MI: Zondervan, 2020.

Erickson, Millard. *Christian Theology.* 3rd ed. Grand Rapids, MI: Baker, 2013.

Henry, Carl F. H. *The Uneasy Conscience of Modern Fundamentalism.* Grand Rapids, MI: Eerdmans, 1947.

Jenkins, Philip, *The Next Christendom: The Coming of Global Christianity.* 3rd ed. New York: Oxford University Press, 2011.

Marsden, George M. *Reforming Fundamentalism: Fuller Seminary and the New Evangelicalism,* Eerdmans, Grand Rapids, 1987.

McGrath, Alister E. *A Passion for Truth: The Intellectual Coherence of Evangelicalism.* Downers Grove, IL: IVP, 1996.

Noll, Mark. *The Rise of Evangelicalism: The Age of Edwards, Whitefield and the Wesleys.* Downers Grove, IL: IVP, 2010.

Packer, J. I. *Knowing God.* Downers Grove, IL: IVP, 1973.

Padilla, Rene. *What Is Integral Mission?* Oxford: Regnum, 2021.

Samuel, Vinay, and Chris Sugden, eds. *Mission as Transformation: A Theology of the Whole Gospel.* Eugene, OR: Wipf and Stock, 2009.

Stott, John. *The Cross of Christ.* Downers Grove, IL: IVP, 1986.

Sweeney, Douglas. *The American Evangelical Story: A History of the Movement.* Grand Rapids, MI: Baker, 2005.

Anglican Theology

Joseph D. Galgalo and Jenny Leith

Introduction

Anglicanism is a contextualized Reformed Catholicism with neither a founder nor a particular statement of faith. The term Anglican reflects the movement's English origin, and "Anglicanism" came into general usage in the nineteenth century. It reflects a creative adaptation to different contextual realities in which the *Ecclesia Anglicana* found itself following extensions beyond its British borders. As the British Empire expanded globally in the eighteenth and nineteenth centuries, the church generally tagged along. In most cases the Bible and the flag went hand in hand and where the church may have preceded, the state followed swiftly. Today, Anglicanism (also called Episcopalianism in some places) is a truly worldwide movement with over 85 million adherents comprising some 42 national or regional churches called Provinces. In addition, there are also five other national churches known as Extra Provincials. Traditionally, each Province is in communion with the See of Canterbury, the senior-most See of the Church of England, though this principle has come under severe strain in practice over recent years. All the Provinces are members of one global family called the Anglican Communion. Although the Communion presents great diversities across contexts, common provenance as well as shared traditions and historic formularies gives it a recognizable, although complex, Anglican identity.

The movement distinctively emerged in the sixteenth century when the Church of England, under close patronage of the English monarchy, initiated a protracted process of separation from the church of Rome. A close intercourse between the church and state served to advance various political, personal, theological, and ecclesial interests. The ramifications were far reaching. Over time, the ancient English church that from around the end of the sixth century had been under the domain of the papacy became autonomous from Rome. Several political, legislative, and religious maneuvers slowly brought about the birth of a separate branch of the Western church, which, drawing on practices and teachings of both Roman Catholicism and the Protestant Reformation, evolved a distinct ecclesial identity. Because of this dual heritage, some Anglican proponents often see Anglicanism as *via media* or the "middle way." In any case, Anglicanism is a true child of the English Reformation, as shaped by multiple inter- and intra-contextual influences and interests.

Ford's The Modern Theologians: An Introduction to Christian Theology since 1918, Fourth Edition.
Edited by Rachel Muers and Ashley Cocksworth.
© 2024 John Wiley & Sons Ltd. Published 2024 by John Wiley & Sons Ltd.

Anglicanism today is diverse in practice and beliefs, perhaps as it was even in the beginning. Technically, we do not have *the Anglican Church,* but rather Anglican Churches. Each Province is autonomous and relates to the Communion on its own terms and can pick and choose levels of participation in the common life of the Communion. At the national or regional level, the church is organized in dioceses under the authority of the bishop who governs through a diocesan synod. A number of dioceses form a Province at which level an Archbishop or a Metropolitan governs through a Provincial Synod, though the situation in England is more complicated. Synods are legislative in function and the resolutions and laws passed are binding at the specific synodical jurisdiction. This has given rise to canon laws and constitutions, which by nature and application can define and enforce doctrine and practice only within a specific diocese or province. The center of Anglican authority, in practice, is situated locally and cannot be applied horizontally across defined jurisdictions such as dioceses or enforced downwards by a Body or any instrument of the Communion. Communion-level decisions, therefore, cannot be implemented within the autonomous jurisdictions unless such decisions are mutually agreed to, adopted, and applied by specific provincial synods. There are churches that are Anglican or Episcopalian in name, heritage, and origin but are not in communion with the See of Canterbury, and therefore are not members of the Anglican Communion. Some of these churches see themselves as "continuing churches," claiming authority and authenticity on the basis of faithful propagation of the gospel and preservation of Anglican traditions and beliefs.

Survey and Debate: Anglicanism, a Global Movement

The Anglican multiple heritage has tended over time to breed a multiplicity of theological and doctrinal traditions. The situation has in turn given birth to varied styles of church life of which three strands, each dominant in its own way, have emerged. Rowan Williams refers to the three strands as the triple "components in our [Anglican] heritage." He identifies these as evangelical Protestantism with emphasis on Biblical priority, Roman Catholicism with strong defense of sacramental life of the church, and religious liberalism preferring greater latitude for contextual appropriation of truth, cultural sensitivity, and intelligibility of faith. Each of these plays a dominant role in the life of the church and has been part of the Anglican synthesis right from the beginning.[1] The naming of these strands may have emerged at different times in the development of Anglicanism but each version has always displayed distinct emphases and made unique contributions to the whole, even as each continually adapts to changing times and circumstances as each strand constantly learns to live one with the other. Such tension in the very nature of being church does not make it easy for the unity of the church. Appreciating this, William asserts: "To accept that each of these has a place in the church's life and that they need each other means that the enthusiasts for each aspect have to be prepared to live with certain tensions or even sacrifices."[2] Such is the nature of being Anglican, as each of these strands flourishes alongside the others.

The Anglo-Catholic strand of Anglicanism, for a long time derogatorily referred to as the "ritualists," made a significant leap forward in the 1920s and 1930s through a series of congresses.[3] The first four congresses (1920, 1923, 1927, and 1930) were particularly instrumental in reinvigorating the life of the movement, securing its place within the larger Anglican family, and afforded helpful clarity on the theology of Anglo-Catholicism – especially on the sacramental life of the church, centrality of Christ's atoning death, and the instrumentality of the sacraments of baptism and the eucharist as a means of appropriating the benefits of Christ's sacrifice. The fourth congress explored the nature of the church; while affirming the four marks of the church – one, holy, catholic, and apostolic – as of essence to ecclesiology, they affirmed the need for ecumenical efforts in the interest of unity of the one, holy, catholic, and apostolic church. It is observable that Anglo-Catholicism constantly seeks, perhaps as its most enduring feature, to make current the marks of the church and the implications of its practical fruitfulness in the lives of the faithful. Some of the thinkers from this period, perhaps best exemplified by Geoffrey Studdert Kennedy, emphasized practical implications of the gospel and, through social preaching, inspiring actions to social and economic justice, works of charity, ministry to prisoners and factory workers, and those who by reason of encumbrances of life could not be part of any congregational life. Kennedy, in many ways, offered his life as a living gospel. In a recent sermon, Alan Amos sums up Kennedy's philosophy of life in one sentence: "It is much easier to do and die than reason why." Through the eyes of those who experienced his inspirational approach to life, Amos narrates:

> I tried to follow his lead in how he dealt with people ... He took his bed to a poor parishioner to the horror of his ... wife. (I could not do that!) He thought outside the box and found the Divine in the hell of The Somme ... His Christianity was practical, compassionate, on fire. He preached with a passion that set souls alight. He ministered with a tender touch that brought Christ's comfort to the poor, the sick and the dying. He was excruciatingly honest, [and] lived out his faith as well as spoke it. He knew the love of God and shared it unstintingly.[4]

The continued impact and lasting influence of Anglican liberalism have today earned it a recognition as a distinct stream, not only standing alongside Anglo-Catholicism and Evangelical Anglicanism but also cutting across both of these other strands. It is worth noting that there are within each strand of Anglicanism internal divergencies on various matters. The conservative parties' level of adherence to traditional positions on such matters as women in ministry, for example, varies considerably. Although the Anglo-Catholics or Evangelicals may not identify themselves as liberals, it is common to see shifting views on some contentious issues, initially rejected but with time, slowly becoming mainstream. Ordination of women, for example, is one case in point. This is a pointer to the reality of a broad overlap and continuous cross-fertilization of ideas within the different strands of Anglicanism. Indeed, every strand of Anglicanism has own ecumenical enthusiasts, charismatics, liberals, traditionalists, or conservatives.

There is a good reason why liberalism cuts across all strands of Anglicanism, even though some of its teachings on the authority of scripture, human experience of revelation vis-à-vis traditional views of inspiration, revisionism or theological reductionism, and moral theology may be unacceptable to some Anglo-Catholics and evangelical Anglicans. The very foundation of Anglicanism going back to its beginning in sixteenth-century England was a revisionist exploration with a liberal spirit. Henry VIII, with the help of Thomas Cranmer, initiated a process that in effect firmly placed the authority to interpret scriptures in the hands of the church. Rome no longer had the monopoly of interpreting the scripture, but the church through seemingly synodical-like processes can build a theological consensus to arrive at a doctrinal decision based on the church's authoritative interpretation of scripture. Such thought, that the meaning of scriptures rests not necessarily with an inherited position but rather is subject to contextual realities and reason, is seminal to liberal views. Anglicanism, generally speaking, is anchored on the insight that the Bible is the source of faithful Christianity. The church gives it life and relevance through varied interpretations based on reason and scientific investigations to determine the meaning of the received texts. Most liberals would hold the view that, whereas the church owns the scriptures, the scriptures do not necessarily and certainly not exclusively own the church. The church unequivocally belongs also to the world. This view limits the power and voice of the scriptures. Essentially, although ultra-liberals would generally endorse the view that the scriptures are living, breathing texts, they nevertheless have no other voice than that which the church gives to them.

Liberal Anglicanism seeks to broaden the understanding of truth. For example, William Temple, Archbishop of Canterbury (1942–4), refuting the traditional belief about revealed truth wrote, "There is no such thing as revealed truth ... There are [contending] truths of revelation."[5] In the decades that followed, Anglican liberalism proved a driving intellectual force for cultural revolution that imbibed secularism's moral revisionism in the West. Liberal Anglicans in the United Kingdom and the United States led the way in reappraising traditional Christian core doctrines including the Trinity, incarnation, virgin birth, uniqueness of Christ, and death and resurrection of Jesus Christ. In 1960, for example, James Pike, a bishop in The Episcopal Church in the United States of America (known also as The Episcopal Church), dismissing the doctrine of the Trinity as irrelevant, called upon the church to end what he termed, "outdated, incomprehensible and nonessential doctrinal statements, tradition and codes."[6] This liberal trend has become characteristic of mainstream Anglicanism particularly in the West with influential teachings undermining the traditional beliefs including the works of Paul van Buren, John Robinson, John Shelby Spong, and David Jenkins, among others. The dominant liberal trend in the North has continued to antagonize the majority conservative in the South who see the liberal trend as scandalous to the gospel. A countermovement of conservative evangelicals comprising twenty-five Provinces mainly from the global South churches has come into formation since 1994. To counter the dominant liberalism from the North, these churches hold annual conferences in which they issue statements called the global South Trumpets. The Sixth Trumpet issued in 2016 affirms the vision of the global South Anglicans "to contend together in the face of false teaching for the faith that was once delivered to the saints (Jude 3)."[7] In this regard, the majority of Evangelicals will affirm the Thirty-Nine Articles as a comprehensive statement of faith – spelling out in summary the biblical faith as received by the church.

Liberalism's generous accommodation of varied and often contradictory views has, perhaps rightly so, earned it the nickname of a "broad church." Its latitudinarian nature is perhaps as old as the church itself, with the characteristic tendency to allow wide range of opinions, spirituality, theology, and diverse views of ecclesiastical authority, and places a premium on individual choices and freedom in all matters of faith and morality. These preferences generally tend to elevate culture above scripture and accord generous leeway to broad understanding and varied interpretations of truth. Such generalities and relativity undermine doctrinal consistency and unity of purpose. Currently, we hardly hear this strand of the church referred to as "broad" in common conversations. The "liberal" tag has become more or less its proper name, perhaps in recognition of its broad synchronization with secularism and social political liberalism characteristics of postmodern times. "Broad" also, in some branches of the church like the American Episcopalians, is associated with Anglican traditions that would prefer a middle path that is liturgically neither high nor low church in any distinctive manner. In many ways, liberalism is no longer just "broad" with regard to its comprehensiveness but is also increasingly becoming mainstream tradition in some parts of the Anglican world. If current trends in most Western churches of the Anglican Communion are anything to go by, it is unlikely that the tide of theological liberalism will ebb anytime soon. Over time, liberalism has become the face of Anglicanism as the dominant tradition particularly among the older churches in the Northern hemisphere.

The most mixed group within the larger Anglican churchmanship is the Evangelical strand. This party is often associated with the Anglican low church tradition, a tag that does not accurately describe the diverse nature of this group. They are rooted in the Protestant Reformed tradition and draw heavily on the theological influences, spirituality, and teachings of puritanism, pietistic movements, as well as the Wesleyan revival in England and the Great Awakening in America. Its emergence as a distinct party within the larger Anglican churchmanship has been gradual, its presence is enduring, and evangelicals are typically good at networking and outreach, impressively able to work with other like-minded groups across denominational boundaries. Evangelicals generally emphasize the importance of evangelism and preaching, inspiration of the scripture, scripture as the source and basis of authority for ethics, spirituality and doctrine, the incarnation and centrality of the cross, conversion experience, prayer and personal relationship with God, Lordship of the Holy Spirit, community, the social dimension of Christian faith, and discipleship.[8] Most Anglican Evangelicals are of low church tradition with a low view of sacraments and practices of church ordinances and government, and most are generally open to ecumenical engagements.

In the beginning, the Anglican Evangelicals mainly distinguished themselves as defenders of biblical faith against what they saw as overly ritualistic and sacerdotal tendencies of the Anglo-Catholics. The eighteenth and nineteenth centuries were particularly a watershed moment for Anglican Evangelicalism in England and The Episcopal Church in America and the missionary churches in other parts of the world.

They distinguished themselves as champions of moral order through social involvements. Individuals and associations, motivated by evangelical convictions, distinguished themselves through movements such as the abolition of slavery, formation of charitable societies to support schools, missionary activities, and other evangelical causes.

The triumph and progress of Anglican evangelicalism are, and perhaps inevitably, largely beset by internal divisions and disagreements. Evangelicals generally hold varied views on any given subject including relation of science to faith, dispensationalism, nature of atonement, doctrine of eschatology, or even social responsibility. Endless categorizations of evangelical groups exist. Varied emphases identify them as classic evangelicals, pietistic, fundamentals, open evangelicals, conservative, progressive or neoevangelicals, including charismatics. In the twentieth century, leading Anglican evangelicals who had great influence in the life of the Communion through their life of faith, work, and study included John Stott, James Innell Packer, Alister McGrath, Peter Akinola, David Gitari, Emmanuel Kolini, John Chew, Stephen Noll, Peter Jensen, Héctor Tito Zavala, and many others.

Influence, Achievement, and Agenda

With varied theological persuasions and church styles, the common life of the Anglican or Episcopalian family of churches is dependent on the goodwill of member churches. Anglicans appreciate that they belong together but are rarely agreed on the essentials that define their identity or that which holds them together as members of the same Communion.[9] Doctrinal and theological diversities have always raised and continues to raise difficult questions and stoke deep divisions. At the heart of this difficulty is a lack of structures effective to resolve disagreements. When the Church of England began churches in the overseas British territories, church leadership in those parts found themselves in the unchartered territory of evolving, undefined boundaries of ecclesial authority. New jurisdictions emerged with no formal link to the English parliament or the Privy Council, raising the question of who legally could settle disputes of ecclesial nature.

By the time of the first Lambeth Conference (1867), some Anglican churches already established in overseas territories, such as The (Protestant) Episcopal Church and the Episcopal Church of Canada, were beginning to grapple with questions of essential doctrines and practice. The most pressing question in this regard was "What would be the necessary basis for the unity of the Christian Churches?" In 1870, William Reed Huntington in *The Church Idea: An Essay Toward Unity* offered a proposal outlining what he deemed as bare essentials for the reunion and unity of Christian Churches.[10] He saw the basis of such unity as "four-square" essentials of the scriptures as the Word of God, the creeds as the rule of faith, the two dominical sacraments of baptism and the Lord's Supper, and the historic episcopate. These proposals were considered and adopted with slight modifications at the 1886 General Convention of The (Protestant) Episcopal Church, which met in Chicago, and were also adopted at the third Lambeth Conference of 1888. The four points have since come to be called the Chicago-Lambeth quadrilateral, generally accepted across the Anglican Communion not only as a basis for ecumenical engagements but a reference point for Anglican identity. Its significance was reiterated and reaffirmed in the Lambeth Conference of 1920. Perhaps because of the clarity that the quadrilateral brings to the question of the basis of unity, the Anglican Churches have made great contributions across the world to ecumenical cooperations and actual unions of churches using the quadrilateral as the framework for engagement. In 1947, for example, the Church of South India was established out of the union between Anglicans and several Protestant denominations. Elsewhere, such other churches as the Spanish Episcopal Reformed Church and the Lusitanian Church of Portugal are members of the Anglican family of churches. It also featured prominently in the Second Vatican Council debates, particularly attracting attention because of its powerful vision of Christian unity on the basis of scripture, creeds, sacraments, and episcopacy.

When Archbishop Charles Longley called the first Lambeth Conference, he cautioned that such episcopal gatherings would not make decisions that will in any way interfere with existing synodical jurisdictions. This has been the spirit and limit of all Lambeth Conferences ever since, with resolutions having no binding force upon the member churches. Appreciating Lambeth's lack of legislative authority, Lambeth 1930 clarified that the Communion is not governed by any legislative body but organized by way of "mutual loyalty sustained through the common counsel of the bishops in conference."[11] Given that internal divisions and disagreements of theological nature continue to abound, the Communion has evolved three other mechanisms alongside the Lambeth Conference to serve as the "Communion's instruments of unity." Long before the beginning of the Lambeth Conferences, the church looked up to the Archbishop of Canterbury as the "focal point of unity," and the *primus inter pares* for the bishops of the church. The other two instruments are the Anglican Consultative Council, which was created by the Resolution of Lambeth 1968 and held its first meeting in Limuru, Kenya in 1971, and the Primates (a Body, which draws together the most senior of the Anglican Bishops in a meeting). None of these instruments possess synodical powers to enforce any of their decisions. In the absence of Communion-wide effective governance structures, the Communion lives with such tension and sometimes in real danger of schism. In the absence of a particular "center" the Communion is held together by "bonds of affection,"[12] mutual fellowship, and historical ties nurtured through these four instruments of Communion, without which it is impossible to talk of any form of Anglican connexion or Communion.

These instruments, by way of their operation, are indicative of the nature of Anglican ecclesiology. Dispersed authority informs, influences, and determines Communion-wide decisions by way of mutual encouragement and consensus building, conscientiously undertaken so as not to impinge on the autonomy of the national churches or stoke a potentially divisive issue. In the absence of structures to enforce common discipline, the Anglican family of churches, at its best, has grown to be one of the most tolerant branches of Christianity accommodating diverse theologies typical only of Anglicanism. This is reflected in the Anglican principle of comprehensiveness with roots in the Elizabethan settlement. In practice, comprehensiveness can be described in the words of Augustine of Hippo as *In necessariis unitas, in dubiis libertas, in omnibus caritas,* that is, unity in essentials, freedom in matters *adiaphora*, and charity in all things. No wonder then, that Calvinists, charismatics, Pentecostals, evangelicals, traditional Anglo-Catholics, and liberals have found a place within a Communion that is broad, high, and low, all at the same time. Internal divergencies even within each of these groups also exists. The evangelicals, for example, do not all agree on women's ordination, sexual ethics, or all aspects of biblical criticism – thereby open to internal comprehensiveness blurring the lines between fundamentals and inessentials. Such theological complexities ironically nurture deep doctrinal convictions and enrich Anglican missions through the principle of subsidiarity, which gives authority and freedom to the local levels. The Anglican principle of subsidiarity, however, does not always function at two levels as it should. In matters of local dispute, the higher Communion level has no residual authority to intervene in the issues of lower levels. In the circumstances, incidents of internal divisions have occasionally resulted in "walking apart," where informal intradiocesan or Provincial cross-border interventions fueled by formations of fellowships, associations, or mission agencies that have arisen from within and complexly coexist with one another. This development even has a name, the Anglican realignment, where new ways of episcopal oversight either by agreement or by dissent have evolved. In the circumstances, Anglicans cannot rely on subsidiarity as a mechanism for church unity and discipline but rather awkwardly look to each other to responsibly exercise interdependence and mutual accountability to uphold doctrinal integrity and biblical faithfulness.

The most divisive issues among the Anglicans are ecclesiastical polity, sexual norms, and women in ministry, both at clerical and episcopal levels. The first female ordination (of Hongkonger Florence Li who ministered to wartime refugees in Macau) happened in 1944 in the rather difficult context of war, where practical need rather than theological consideration carried the day and proved ultimately too controversial for the church at the time. In 1974 and 1975, further ordinations happened, both independent of the earlier ordination and independent of each other – but both rather irregularly conducted by retired bishops and without the sanction of the whole church through the episcopal council or synods as it should be. The matter was debated at the Lambeth Conference 1978, which acknowledged that "the debate about the ordination of women as well as the ordinations themselves have, in some Churches, caused distress and pain to many on both sides" and affirmed, "the autonomy of each of its member Churches, [with] legal right of each Church to make its own decision about the appropriateness of admitting women to Holy Orders." The conference, however, without assuming authority to approve women's ordination, resolved that, "there are either no fundamental or theological objections to the ordination of women to the historic threefold ministry of the Church."[13] There was no similar encouragement, however, on the matter of women in episcopacy. Instead, the conference issued this caution:

> While recognising that a member Church of the Anglican Communion may wish to consecrate a woman to the episcopate, and accepting that such member Church must act in accordance with its own constitution, the Conference recommends that no decision to consecrate be taken without consultation with the episcopate through the primates and overwhelming support in any member Church and in the diocese concerned, lest the bishop's office should become a cause of disunity instead of a focus of unity.[14]

Although the matters of women's ordination and episcopacy have gained general acceptance across the Communion, conservative evangelicals and some Anglo-Catholics, who see it as an innovation undermining orthodoxy and contrary to the traditional apostolic succession of the threefold order of ministry, find it difficult to accept. Established in 1976, the *Evangelical and Catholic Mission* is perhaps the most vocal critic against women's admission to holy orders.

Matters of gay ordination and blessings of same-sex unions have proved even more controversial and divisive. The debate on whether homosexuality is compatible with Christian ethics and doctrine was first discussed at the 1998 Lambeth Conference. Resolution 1:10 upheld the traditional view that homosexuality is "incompatible with Scripture" (1:10d) and resolved that the scripture "upholds faithfulness in marriage between a man and a woman in lifelong union" (1:10b). The conference recommended abstinence for persons differently oriented and/or not "called to marriage." The conference also resolved that it "cannot advise the legitimising or blessing of same sex unions nor ordaining those involved in same gender unions."[15] Since 1998, numerous Anglican churches have developed liturgies for blessings of same sex-unions, ordained practicing homosexuals, and admitted persons with homosexual orientations to full membership of their churches without any restrictions; these churches include those of Brazil, Canada, New Zealand, Scotland, South India, South Africa, America, and Wales. Anglicans had once again to revisit the matter when The Episcopal Church in America changed their canon on marriage and allowed the blessing of same sex unions. The Primates expressed the desire for unity and resolved "to walk together ... as a deep expression of [the need for] unity in the body of Christ."[16] The Primates, however, accepted the recommendation of a task force to suspend The Episcopal Church for a period of three years from participating in the life of the Communion through representation on bodies of the Communion.

The conservatives, in response to what they saw as flagrant disregard for biblical teaching and doctrinal integrity, have taken steps to "retain and restore the Bible to the heart of the Anglican Communion." In 2008, a movement of "confessing Anglicans," the Global Anglican Future Conference (GAFCON) was born. At a parallel meeting designed to coincide with the official Communion gathering during the 2008 Lambeth Conference, GAFCON met in Jerusalem. In a fourteen-point statement named the Jerusalem Declaration, GAFCON defined itself as "a spiritual movement to preserve and promote the truth and power of the gospel of salvation in Jesus Christ as we Anglicans have received it."[17] In principle, the Communion still shares a lot in common including such important identity markers as the Anglican Five Marks of Mission. These include commitment to the proclamation of the gospel, teaching, baptism and nurture of new believers, loving service, advocacy and reconciliation, and protection of creation. The sharing of these common markers, however, does not always reflect the irreconcilable differences that exist in practice.

The Global South churches are well positioned to be the future face of Anglicanism. Large sections of African Provinces, for example, are deeply rooted in evangelical Christianity. A significant stimulus in this regard is the East African Revival Movement with continuing influence particularly in Rwanda, Uganda, Tanzania, Kenya, Burundi, and parts of Democratic Republic of Congo. For over eighty years, the revival movement has continued to affect the life of these regional churches. The revival has particularly nurtured a culture of evangelism, emphasizing renewal of spiritual life, conversion experience, and a deeper commitment to Christian discipleship and personal piety. Deeply entrenched in a thoroughly Bible-based revival tradition, Anglicanism in this region has continued to enjoy unabated growth, a trajectory projected to last well into the future.

Named Theologians

In the chapter so far, we have identified two central qualities of Anglicanism: first, a particularly strong theological diversity within Anglicanism (including ongoing debate about what it means to be Anglican), which animates the life of the Anglican Communion and its constituent churches; and, second, something particular to Anglicanism's relationship with social and political structures – especially the British Empire – which is central to its distinctive denominational character. These two features of Anglicanism orient our discussion of the work of William Temple, Kwok Pui-lan, and Daniel W. Hardy. We ask: how do these theologians make sense of ongoing disagreement within the church, and how do they think the diverse theological strands within Anglicanism should relate to one another? How do they understand Anglicanism to have been shaped by the social and political contexts in which it is set, and what relationship do they believe the churches of the Anglican Communion should have with sociopolitical structures?[18]

Each of these three theologians is differently located – socially, geographically, and chronologically – and these different locations inform their theological priorities. Temple (1881–1944) was the child of an English archbishop who, after a time as headmaster of a prestigious public school, went on to become an archbishop himself. Kwok (b. 1952) meanwhile writes as a lay Anglican in the academy and her work is directly informed by growing up in the Anglican Church in Hong Kong, in ways that shape her relationship with her current ecclesial location within The Episcopal Church. Hardy (1930–2007) grew up in the United States and was ordained into The Episcopal Church but spent much of his career working in universities in the United Kingdom.

William Temple

We begin with Temple, the earliest of these three theologians. Although Temple is much better known for his social theology than for his work on ecclesiology, his understanding of the church's relationship with society is deeply informed by his understanding of the church in itself. Temple was able to affirm the fundamental unity of the church (including the unity of the Church of England) even in the midst of theological diversity and disagreement because of his understanding of the sacramental nature of the universe. Strongly influenced by Aquinas (but with a markedly Platonic flavor), Temple saw a unity at the heart of creation in which all things were being drawn toward ultimate and eternal fulfilment in God – and so also into harmonious unity with the rest of creation.[19]

This sacramental grounding informed Temple's ongoing work to bring about reconciliation in the midst of Christian disunity both within the Anglicanism and across denominations. Anglican disagreements in

Temple's day included the parliamentary Prayer Book crisis of 1927–8 and the protracted attempt to create a united Church of South India. Temple's belief in the fundamental unity of truth, and therefore that every fragment of truth must belong to a whole, shaped his approach to contestation between Anglicans. Temple assumed there to be some truth contained in each strongly held position, and that the task was therefore to discern where this lay and how it might be connected to the other fragments of truth within a given dispute to point to a way forward for the church.

When it comes to the relationship of the church to wider society, Temple believed that Christians are to be actively involved in this work of bringing about unity, orienting society to its ultimate *telos* in God. He understands the church to have a responsibility to communicate to the world: it is, he argues, charged with "guiding society so far as society consents to be guided," on the basis that it "has a special illumination which it is called to bring to bear on the whole range of human relationships."[20] Temple distils this special illumination into three closely intertwined principles for the ordering of society: "freedom," "fellowship," and "service."[21] The church, then, must "announce Christian principles and point out where the existing social order at any time is in conflict with them," but it passes on to Christian citizens "the task of re-shaping the existing order in closer conformity to the principles."[22] Although Temple believes the church should be guiding society, he argues that the work to translate theology into concrete policy and legislation is necessarily collaborative and depends on the knowledge that comes through immersion in the affairs of the world and particularly "in those empirical disciplines that seek to gain a purchase on it," such as the social sciences.[23]

Kwok Pui-lan

Although Temple was born and bred within the "mother church" of Anglicanism, Kwok grew up and became an Anglican in one of the smallest and longest-lasting outposts of the British Empire, Hong Kong. This informs the critical perspective that she brings to bear on Anglicanism. Kwok approaches the question of the desirability of Anglican comprehensiveness by addressing current disagreements about sources of authority, forms of polity, and sexual ethics through a postcolonial lens. This allows her to expose some of the power dynamics at play in these disagreements. For instance, she points to the role played by the history of empire in Anglican disagreements over sexual ethics, suggesting that the views of Anglican leaders in the majority world often replicate the oppression of their former colonizers.[24] Through this lens, Kwok also sets out another possible form of ecclesiology: one that is based upon the experiences and participation of those she names as "the multitudes."[25] This is an approach to Anglicanism that does not rely upon looking back to a single point of origin to find Anglican unity and identity. Instead, Kwok looks at the traditions of the living, exploring the collaborative potential of "cultural hybridity."[26] She has written for example, of her vicar, Jane Hwang Hsien-yuin, becoming one of the first women officially ordained in the Anglican Communion in 1971 and the way this sharpened her sense that the colonial centers of Anglicanism need to learn to receive from and be reshaped by the wisdom of those whom they are accustomed to see as requiring help and guidance.[27]

As with the church, Kwok's Asian feminist postcolonial lens informs her account of the need for critique and reconstruction of wider social and political structures.[28] She highlights, for example, the disproportionate harm borne by global majority women in the ecological crisis.[29] Through engaging theologically from this perspective, she is also able to point to what is necessary for hope be wrought in the relationship between the church and society. It is a hope in which neither side will remain unchanged; an identification of forms of oppression will require change both in the church and in wider society.

Running through both Kwok and Temple's theology is an understanding of the kind of conversation that should be happening in the church for Anglican comprehensiveness to truly be a reality – and of the conversation between the church and its wider sociopolitical contexts. In both these directions, they are concerned not just with the content of that conversation – what is currently lacking in it, where that conversation could go, and what should result from it – but also with the form of the conversation. In keeping with his position at the heart of the Establishment, Temple underlines the need, for example, for policy discussions to be conducted in such a way that the voices of recognized experts can be heard. Kwok, meanwhile, is working with a more expansive understanding of expertise, highlighting experiences that need to be heard, not just socially sanctioned forms of knowledge.[30] She is concerned therefore with the structures of conversation within the Anglican Communion – with what will allow for global majority voices, lay voices, and women's voices to be more fully heard. As she asks, "even when these subaltern speak, who will listen?"[31]

Daniel W. Hardy

For Daniel Hardy, this concern with the form of theological conversation is central. When Hardy is thinking about what it means for God to be at work in the world, and about what it means for Christians to be drawn more deeply into God's ways with the world, he is often raising questions about the form of polity this requires. Hardy's reflections upon diversity and unity within Anglicanism are set within his belief that the "inner" life of the church cannot be understood apart from its relationship with the world. For Hardy, we cannot talk about the gathered life of the church without also talking about the scattered lives of its members, and without considering what he calls the "sociality" of the church – that is, the way in which it is placed socially, geographically, and historically.

The church's fulfilment of its vocation rests, then, upon participation in life in the world. In part, this is because of the way in which Hardy accounts for the movement of the Holy Spirit. He speaks of the Spirit pressing Christians into new understandings through engaging with the demanding issues of life today – with the expectation that we will discover things about God on our journey of interaction in the world that we could not discover otherwise.[32] If we think about the way that doctrinal and ethical disputes in the church are often bound up with social change – as in contemporary discussions over gender and sexuality – Hardy does not see these social changes as a distraction from the way in which God is at work to form the church. Rather, the church's discernment of God's will involves paying attention to the world around us, expecting that the Spirit will either be pointing to wisdom to be received or to something to be resisted. This will change the way we engage with scripture and tradition, involving a dynamic process of interchange between what is encountered in the world and established Christian practice.[33]

This is obviously a dynamic that will also shape how we understand how the church should be in relationship with society.[34] Hardy uses the image of the church being on pilgrimage: discovering its social responsibility by walking about, in imitation of Jesus, on the particular land in which it is placed and by encountering the people of the land.[35] The church's understanding of itself, and so also of its praxis, should be reshaped by ongoing encounters in the world, through which it receives "new images of what this order and unity might be."[36]

Hardy's focus on God's action in the world points us to important continuities and points of departure between these three theologians, as well as helping us to map Anglican theology more generally. Who is God understood to be working through? Which voices are privileged theologically as those reliably able to recognize God's ways with the world? What kinds of institutions are able to perceive and be drawn into God's action? What needs to change for the churches of the Anglican Communion to be drawn into fuller participation in the life of God – and so to also more fully mediate that life to the world?

Conclusion

Anglicanism was born in strife and exists in a fractious yet a tenacious state of being. Torn asunder by internal divergencies and irreconcilable churchmanship, Anglican churches stand distinct as one Communion but many churches. It is difficult to speak of "Anglican theology" because of Anglicans' multiplicity of theological teachings. If it were not for the internal autonomy operative at the local level and somehow holds the Communion together, it would be impossible to talk of Anglicanism as an entity. There are several cross-currents at the moment within the same movement. It is difficult to tell whether the Communion can survive the cross-currents and renew a faithful vision of the gospel or whether it will fragment. The resilience of the Anglican movement is not in doubt. Visible unity can be possible, and many Anglicans believe and prayerfully sing from their heart: "the church is one foundation, with Christ as her Lord, it shall never perish."

Notes

1   Rowan Williams, "The Challenge and Hope of Being an Anglican Today: A Reflection for the Bishops, Clergy and Faithful of the Anglican Communion," http://rowanwilliams.archbishopofcanterbury.org/articles.php/1478/the-challenge-and-hope-of-being-an-anglican-today-a-reflection-for-the-bishops-clergy-and-faithful-o.html (accessed 2 September 2023).

2   Williams, "The Challenge and Hope of Being an Anglican Today."

3   For a comprehensive treatment of this subject, see John Gunstone, *Lift High the Cross: Anglo-Catholics and the Congress Movement* (Norwich: Canterbury Press, 2009).

4   "Giving Thanks for Geoffrey Studdert Kennedy," sermon preached on 14 March 2021 at Holy Trinity Church, https://holytrinitygeneva.org/sermons/giving-thanks-for-geoffrey-studdert-kennedy-canon-alan-amos-11-march (accessed 10 September 2023).

5   William Temple, *Nature, Man and God* (London: Macmillan & Co., 1960, originally published 1934), 317–22.

6   James Pike, *A Time for Christian Candour* (London: Hodder & Stoughton 1965).

7   Communiqué from the Sixth Global South Conference, Cairo 2016 (7 October 2016), https://www.gafcon.org/news/communiqu%C3%A9-from-the-6th-global-south-conference-cairo-2016 (accessed 7 September 2023).

8   Alister McGrath, *Evangelicalism and the Future of Christianity* (Downers Grove, IL: InterVarsity Press, 1995).

9   William Jacob, *The Making of the Anglican Communion Worldwide* (London: SPCK, 1997).

10 William Reed Huntington, *The Church Idea: An Essay toward Unity* (New York: Charles Scribner's Sons, 1899).

11 Resolution 49, Jan Nunley, "Authority versus Autonomy: An Old Debate for Anglicans" (23 February 2001), https://archive.wfn.org/2001/02/msg00245.html (accessed 7 September 2023).

12 A phrase commonly used by Anglicans to describe the links that connect churches of the Anglican Communion across varied geographical settings, culture, and history.

13 LC 1978 Resolution 21, Resolutions Archive: https://www.anglicancommunion.org/media/127746/1978.pdf (accessed 11 September 2023).

14 LC 1978 Resolution 22.

15 LC 1998 Resolution 1:10(e), Resolutions Archive: https://www.anglicancommunion.org/media/127746/1978.pdf (accessed 11 September 2023).

16 LC 1998 Resolution 1:10(e).

17 The Complete Jerusalem Statement, 2008, https://www.gafcon.org/resources/the-complete-jerusalem-statement-2008 (accessed 11 September 2023).

18 Each of these theologians is considering these questions in dialogue with a wide range of theologians, not just Anglicans, and their thought has valence beyond Anglicanism. However, in looking for what it means to name these three as "Anglican theologians" looking at their treatment of these concerns is a helpful starting point.

19 Temple, *Nature, Man and God.*

20 William Temple, *Religious Experience and Other Essays and Addresses* (London: James Clarke, 1958), 244.

21 William Temple, *Christianity and Social Order* (London: Shepheard-Walwyn, 1976).

22 Temple, *Christianity and Social Order,* 63–8.

23 Temple, *Christianity and Social Order,* 47, 98.

24 Kwok Pui-lan, "The Legacy of Cultural Hegemony," *Beyond Colonial Anglicanism,* ed. Ian Douglas and Kwok Pui-lan (New York: Church Publishing, 2001), 64–5. See also Laura E. Donaldson and Kwok Pui-lan, eds., *Postcolonialism: Feminism and Religious Discourse* (Abingdon: Routledge, 2002); and Kwok Pui-lan, "Theology as a Sexual Act?" *Feminist Theology* 11, no. 2 (2003): 149–56.

25 She also explores questions of participation in relation to wider political structures – for example, in Kwok Pui-lan and Francis Ching-Wah Yip, eds., *The Hong-Kong Protests and Political Theology* (Lanham, MD: Rowman and Littlefield, 2021).

26 Kwok, "The Legacy of Cultural Hegemony," 55.

27 Kwok, "The Legacy of Cultural Hegemony," 66.

28 See Kwok Pui-lan, *Postcolonial Politics and Theology: Unravelling Empire for a Global World* (Louisville, KY: Westminster John Knox Press, 2021).

29 See, for example, Kwok Pui-lan, "The Mending of Creation," in *Postcolonial Imagination and Feminist Theology* (London: SCM Press, 2005), 209–30.

30 See for example, Kwok, "Searching for Wisdom: Sources of Postcolonial Feminist Theologies," *Postcolonial Imagination and Feminist Theology*, 52–76.

31 Kwok, "The Legacy of Cultural Hegemony," 61–3.

32 Daniel W. Hardy, *Wording a Radiance: Parting Conversations on God and the Church* (London: SCM Press, 2010), 32–3.

33 Daniel W. Hardy, *Finding the Church: The Dynamic Truth of Anglicanism* (London: SCM Press, 2001), 232–3.

34 Hardy, *Finding the Church*, 159.

35 Hardy, *Wording a Radiance*, 30, 85.

36 Hardy, *Wording a Radiance*, 86–7.

Recommended Reading

Primary

Book of Common Prayer and Administration of the Sacraments 1662, Articles of Religion (1987), http://www.eskimo.com/~lhowell/bcp1662/articles/articles.html.

Book of Common Prayer and Administration of the Sacraments 1662, Original Manuscript. http://justus.anglican.org/resources/bcp/1662/baskerville.htm.

Bray, Gerald, ed. *Documents of the English Reformation 1526–1701*. Cambridge: James Clark & Co., 1994.

Cranmer, Thomas. *The Thomas Cranmer Collection* (10 vols.). Oxford: Oxford University Press, 1829–1906.

Hooker, Richard. *Divine Law and Human Nature: Book I of Hooker's Laws: A Modernization*. Edited by W. Bradford Littlejohn, Brian Marr, and Bradley Belschner. Landrum, SC: Davenant Press, 2017.

Jewel, John. *An Apology of the Church of England*. Edited by Robin Harris and Andre Gazal. Leesburg, VA: Davenant Press, 2020.

Newman, John Henry. *An Essay on Development of Christian Doctrine*. Notre Dame, IN: University of Notre Dame Press, 1994.

Secondary

Avis, Paul. *The Identity of Anglicanism: Essentials of Anglican Ecclesiology*. London: Continuum, 2007.

Chapman, Mark. *Anglican Theology*. London: T&T Clark, 2002.

Neill, Stephen. *Anglicanism*. London: Mowbrays, 1977.

Null, Ashley, and John W. Yates III, eds. *Reformation Anglicanism: A Vision for Today's Global Communion*. Wheaton, IL: Crossway, 2017.

O'Donovan, Oliver. *On the Thirty-Nine Articles: A Conversation with Tudor Christianity*. 2nd ed. London: SCM Press, 2011.

Perham, Michael, ed. *The Renewal of Common Prayer: Unity and Diversity in the Church of England Worship*. London: SPCK/Church House Publishing, 1993.

Secor, William, and Lee Gibbs, eds. *The Wisdom of Richard Hooker*. Bloomington, IN: Authorhouse, 2005.

Sykes, Stephen, John Booty, and Jonathan Knight, eds. *The Study of Anglicanism*. Revised Edition. London: SPCK, 1988.

Wolf, William J., ed. *The Spirit of Anglicanism: Hooker, Maurice, Temple*. Wilton, CT: Morehouse-Barlow, 1978.

Orthodox Theology

CHAPTER 23

Paul Ladouceur and Brandon Gallaher

Introduction: Orthodoxy's Search for an Alternate Modernity

For the last century, Orthodox theology has largely revolved around a search for an alternate modernity that is both in continuity with Orthodox traditions, teaching, worship, and spirituality, and that responds creatively and cogently to the ever-changing challenges posed by modernity and postmodernity. Countries of Orthodox tradition have been profoundly marked by the intellectual, social, economic, political, scientific, and technological innovations arising from the Renaissance, Reformation, Counter-Reformation, and the Enlightenment in Western Europe. In the early twentieth century, challenges to Orthodoxy included the encounter with secularism, materialism, nationalism, and Marxism and other atheistic and nihilist philosophies; with a powerful, if splintered, Western Christianity; and with scientific theories such as evolution, modern cosmology, and psychoanalysis. In the new millennium, other issues generated by modernity have risen high on the Orthodox theological agenda: gender, sexuality, and marriage; the role of women in the church; rapid technological advances in areas such as bioengineering, communications, and artificial intelligence; and the relationship of non-Christian religions to Orthodoxy.

Orthodoxy remained largely untouched by the Reformations that swept Western Europe in the sixteenth century, and it did not implement a modernizing liturgical and pastoral program like that of the Second Vatican Council in the Catholic Church. Instead, the Orthodox Church struggled to maintain the fundamental elements of its premodern religious and cultural tradition. Yet Orthodoxy exists in cultures that have undergone massive changes since the advent of modernity and it has been powerfully influenced by Western intellectual trends. Until recently, Orthodoxy tended to respond defensively rather than creatively to such challenges. The last century has seen attempts to articulate an Orthodoxy that is simultaneously both ancient and modern, attempts resisted by many theologians and church leaders promoting antimodernism, anti-Westernism, and antisecularism, rejecting such core notions such as human rights and democracy. Many theologians discussed in this chapter are noted less for their creative engagement with contemporary issues than for their response to modernity by invoking traditional theology and spirituality to provide a sure and stable doctrinal, spiritual, and ecclesial identity in the face of the secularization and the atomization of Western societies.

Ford's The Modern Theologians: An Introduction to Christian Theology since 1918, Fourth Edition.
Edited by Rachel Muers and Ashley Cocksworth.

Thus, until recently, especially since the fall of communism, Orthodox theology advanced a largely defensive account of Orthodoxy, looking for inspiration primarily in premodern sources, including the Bible, early church fathers, ecumenical councils, liturgy and prayer, icons, and the lives and writings of saints, for its doctrines, rituals, institutions, and overall ethos. The Byzantine rite remains the principal manifestation of the religious and cultural self-consciousness of the Orthodox Church and the hallmark of its theology: belief follows worship and prayer. The Byzantine rite has changed little since the early modern period; indeed, there is no central Orthodox ecclesial mechanism to enact liturgical revision – and little appetite for it. Modern Orthodox theology thus faces the major difficulty of reconciling the ancient and the modern. It must remain premodern in its historical, theological, spiritual, and liturgical sense of itself; yet it must be modern in its encounter with challenges not faced in earlier times and in its coexistence with societies and philosophical and religious outlooks foreign to its underlying ethos.

This chapter traces theological quests to articulate an Orthodox modernity, focusing on theologies arising in and inspired by modern Russian theology. Until the late twentieth century, Orthodox theology was largely a story of Russian theology, in Russia before 1917 and afterwards in the Russian emigration in Western Europe and North America. For most of Orthodox history since the fall of the Byzantine Empire in 1453, the Russian Empire was the only independent traditionally Orthodox land, and the origin of a powerful religious renaissance beginning in the mid-nineteenth century that reached its peak in the decades prior to the Russian Revolution and subsequently in exile. The revolution and the civil war forced most Russian Christian intellectuals into exile, either voluntary or by Soviet expulsion in the early 1920s, such that new centers of Orthodox thought emerged, notably Paris and New York. Theological renewal spread from its Russian base to other centers of Orthodox thought beginning in the 1960s. The transition from a predominantly Russian theological face of Orthodoxy to a more global one was signaled by events such as the deaths in 1983 of Fr Alexander Schmemann and in 1992 of Fr John Meyendorff, the last major theologians formed out of the Russian diaspora experience; and by the publication in English in 1985 of the widely influential book *Being as Communion* by the Greek theologian Metropolitan John Zizioulas (1931–2023). By the end of the twentieth century, movements of theological renewal were dispersed throughout Orthodoxy, in countries of Orthodox tradition such as Greece and Romania, and among Orthodox in Western Europe and North America.

Survey

At the end of World War I, Orthodox theology existed principally in three religious and theological modes. Formal church or academic theology was taught in Orthodox seminaries and theological academies and featured in official church publications. In Russia, Greece, Romania, and other countries of Orthodox tradition, academic theology exhibited strong Western methodological, philosophical, and theological influences, especially scholasticism. Official church theology, reflected in confessions of faith of individual church leaders in the sixteenth century, was marked by the articulation of Orthodox thought in Western doctrinal schema, whether Protestant or Catholic. Fr Georges Florovsky (1893–1979) and his student John Zizioulas refer to this as the "Western captivity" of Orthodox theology. Prominent twentieth-century academic theologians include the Russian Fr Michael Pomazansky (1888–1988) and the Greeks Christos Androutsos (1869–1935) and Panagiotis Trembelas (1886–1977).

The second broad articulation of modern Orthodox theology, often termed the Russian Religious Renaissance, flourished in Russia in the late nineteenth century and until the Bolshevik revolution of 1917, and then in the Russian exile community in Western Europe until the end of World War II. Most of the leaders of this movement were lay philosophers and theologians, as well as artistic and literary figures, outside formal church structures and hence freer to express themselves than academic theologians. Leading figures, mostly nonordained, of the religious renaissance were the philosophers Nikolai Fedorov (1829–1903) and

Vladimir Solovyov (1853–1900), and the novelist Fyodor Dostoyevsky (1821–81); and a younger generation, most of whom went into exile, included Fr Sergius Bulgakov (1871–1944), Nicolas Berdyaev (1874–1948), Symeon Frank (1877–1950), Fr Pavel Florensky (1882–1937), Mother Maria Skobtsova (St Maria of Paris) (1891–1945), Fr Nicholas Afanasiev (1893–1966), and Nicolas Zernov (1898–1980).

This Russian Christian intelligentsia participated actively in the intellectual conflict between positivists-materialists and idealists in late imperial Russia, caught in the turmoil of rapid social and economic development and an antiquated autocratic imperial sociopolitical system. They shared with the rest of the intelligentsia a vivid social conscience, reflected especially in the goal of seeking the end of the imperial regime and the installation of a more equitable society. The religious thinkers advanced a Christian alternative to the revolutionary historical, economic, and social theories of Marxism and other non-Christian and atheistic philosophies popular among the intelligentsia in late imperial Russia. The Christian philosopher-theologians articulated an alternate Orthodox modernity in the face of the challenges of individualism, materialism, nationalism, racism, and Western Christianity. Intermediary between the church and the non-Christian intelligentsia, the religious intelligentsia was hard put to establish its credibility both with the Russian Orthodox Church, which refused to see the religious intelligentsia as loyal "sons and daughters of the church," and with the non-Christian intelligentsia, for whom Christianity had nothing to offer for the future of Russia. The religious intelligentsia never reached deeply into Russian society; it remained a brilliant but elite movement, largely restricted to intellectual and literary circles of Saint Petersburg and Moscow. The spirit of change in Russian Orthodoxy that they represented reached a peak at the All-Russian Church Council of Moscow (1917–18), which was cut short by the Bolsheviks. The council restored the patriarchate (which had been suppressed by Peter the Great in 1721), and elected Metropolitan Tikhon (Bellavin) of Moscow (1865–1925; canonized in 1989) as Patriarch of Moscow. It also encouraged greater participation of the laity in church life, theological creativity in the face of modern challenges, and worship in vernacular Russian instead of traditional church Slavonic. It was a brief moment of unity for the Russian Church, which split into several rival branches after the Bolsheviks triumphed in the civil war.

The third theological mode was the continuity of the Orthodox ascetic and spiritual tradition, represented especially by charismatic elders, mostly monastics, in Russia, Greece, Romania, and Serbia, and on Mount Athos. They practiced and transmitted the mystical theology of hesychastic spirituality, revived by the publication of the Greek, Slavonic, and Russian editions of the *Philokalia* (an important collection of spiritual and ascetic writings). In Russia, this spiritual revival was exemplified by the lives and writings of nineteenth century saints such as St Seraphim of Sarov (1754/1759–1833), the *startsi* (elders) of Optina Monastery (who influenced Dostoyevsky and Solovyov), the bishops St Ignatius Brianchaninov (1807–67) and St Theophan the Recluse (1815–1904), and the popular book *The Way of the Pilgrim* (1881). Major modern Orthodox spiritual theologians include the Serbian bishop St Nicolas (Velimirović) (1881–1956), the French monk Fr Lev Gillet ("A Monk of the Eastern Church") (1893–1980), the Russian monk St Sophrony (Sakharov) of Essex (1896–1993), and the Athonite monks Aimilianos (Vafeidis) (1934–2019) and Vasileios (Gondikakis) (1936–2019).

This chapter focuses primarily on creative theological developments since World War II inspired by the Russian Religious Renaissance. Paris was the center of Russian religious thought in the interwar period. Many exiled Russian theologians and philosophers taught at the St Sergius Orthodox Theological Institute, established by the Russian Church in exile in 1925 and for most of its history affiliated with the Ecumenical Patriarchate of Constantinople, where the exiled Russian Christian thinkers sought to perpetuate their mode of theology in radically different social and religious circumstances from their homeland. By the 1930s, however, younger Russian theologians, dissatisfied with the dependence of their elders' thought on suspected Western sources, especially German Idealism, considered that their religious thinking deviated in important respects from Orthodox tradition and identity. Russian religious thought had arisen as a Christian alternative to non-Christian philosophies in the philosophical and sociopolitical debates in late imperial Russia, a context no longer relevant in the exile situation. Younger theologians were searching for an identity in closer harmony with Orthodox tradition, a theology in continuity especially with the Greek fathers and Orthodox liturgy and spirituality. The leaders of this movement, notably the historian and theologian Fr Georges Florovsky and the medievalists and patristic scholars Myrrha Lot-Borodine (1882–1957) and Vladimir Lossky (1903–58), turned to the Greek fathers, especially the Cappadocians, Maximus the Confessor, Nicholas Cabasilas, and Gregory Palamas, for theological inspiration for an Orthodox *ressourcement* movement, which soon became known (in Florovsky's expression) as the "neopatristic synthesis." Theology, for Florovsky and his followers, is called to be "patristic" because it adopts the patristic spirit and vision ("the mind of the fathers") as a theological method, "neopatristic" because it addresses contemporary issues, and a "synthesis" precisely because it is a creative response inspired by the fathers to the challenges of our age. Other leading neopatristic figures were the liturgical theologian Fr Alexander Schmemann (1921–83), the patristic scholar and Byzantine historian Fr John Meyendorff (1926–92), the Romanian theologian Fr Dumitru Stăniloae (1903–93), and Western converts to Orthodoxy such as Olivier Clément (1921–2009) and Metropolitan Kallistos Ware (1934–2022).

Neopatristic theology was the dominant Orthodox theological mode in the second half of the twentieth century. There was no equivalent of Russian religious thought in other countries of Orthodox tradition, but neopatristic theology became prominent in Greece, where it is often called "the theology of the 60s," under figures such as the Greek-American theologian Fr John Romanides (1927–2001), Metropolitan John Zizioulas (1931–2023) and the philosopher Christos Yannaras (b. 1935). For many external observers, neopatristic theology *was* Orthodox theology in the second half of the twentieth century. Yet academic theology remained important in Orthodox theological education, and the ascetic-mystical tradition was powerfully represented by articulate elders, especially in Greece, Romania, and Serbia, and monasticism enjoyed a vibrant resurgence on Mount Athos beginning in the 1970s and in Eastern Europe after the fall of communism.

In the early twenty-first century, the dominance of neopatristic theology was increasingly challenged as its limitations became more evident, especially its difficulty in addressing adequately modern social, political, cultural, scientific, and technological issues, its defensive and polemical posture toward the West, its "Byzantinism," and its corresponding failure to assimilate the relevant contributions of non-Greek Christian theology (Latin, Reform, Oriental, even Russian). Younger generations of theologians seek to address contemporary issues creatively by deploying the strengths of patristic theology and spirituality and the Orthodox liturgical and iconographic traditions, and by drawing on relevant features of contemporary Western theology, philosophy, the social sciences, and science and technology. Going beyond a hostile and judgmental attitude toward the West and Western Christianity, and an accompanying idealization of a largely romanticized Orthodox sociopolitical-religious past in the Byzantine and Russian Empires, they endeavor to build bridges with Western Christianity and nonreligious movements that reflect Orthodox values in an increasingly materialistic and secularized world. At the same time, scholarship demonstrated that neopatristic theology built directly upon certain themes in the Russian Religious Renaissance, such as the theology of creation, human personhood, and ecclesiology and ecumenism.

Named Theologians

Sergius Bulgakov

Fr Sergius Bulgakov (1871–1944) is increasingly acknowledged as a theological giant of modern Christianity. He wrote on most aspects of systematic theology (including two dogmatic trilogies), political theology, philosophy of economics, idealism, philosophy of language, sacramental theology, and biblical exegesis. Son of an Orthodox priest, Bulgakov lost his faith in seminary, and became a leading Marxist intellectual and academician, specializing in political economy, holding chairs in Moscow and Kyiv. Increasingly dissatisfied with Marxism's philosophical weaknesses, he returned to Orthodoxy by way of idealism, a spiritual journey completed by 1908. He was a leading lay representative at the Moscow Council of the Russian Church in 1917–18; he was ordained to the priesthood in 1918 and exiled by the Bolsheviks in 1922. He made his way with his immediate family from Istanbul to Prague and finally to Paris, where he was professor of dogmatic theology and dean of the St Sergius Orthodox Theological Institute from 1925 to 1944. Bulgakov was a pioneering ecumenist engaged in dialogue with Anglicans, Catholics, and Protestants, and in the Faith and Order Movement, precursor of the World Council of Churches.

The outstanding feature of Bulgakov's theology is the theology of Divine Wisdom ("Sophia") (sophiology), seen as the principle for understanding the relationship between God and the world, the Uncreated Creator and creation. Sophiology is both a way of understanding the relationship of divine and human activity and a meditation on the cosmic nature of Christ as *Bogochelovechestvo* (Godmanhood or divine-humanity). In developing his sophiology, Bulgakov drew from patristic sources (especially Athanasius, Maximus, and Palamas), from liturgy and iconography, esoteric sources (Jacob Boehme and the Kabbala), German Romantic literature (Goethe, Heine, Novalis, and Schiller), and German philosophy (Fichte, von Baader, Hegel, and Schelling). Bulgakov's sophiology was mediated through his critical engagement with the thinking of Vladimir Solovyov and his friend Fr Pavel Florensky.

In his widely influential "Lectures on Godmanhood" (1877–81), Solovyov understands Sophia in terms of an eternal Christology where Christ is the "divine organism" of the Logos and Sophia. Christ as a divine organism consists of an active "producing unity" that reduces the multiplicity of elements to itself as One, and a passive "produced unity" of the All or Godmanhood, the many entities rendered to unity. The producing unity is the Logos as the divine principle and form; Sophia is all-unity and Godmanhood, insofar as she, as the body of God, is continually informed or headed by the Logos. Solovyov understands the divine as Godmanhood insofar as the content of God is continually "Logified" by the Word. All-unity/Sophia is Godmanhood because the essence of a human being is both eternal and all embracing and can thus serve as the form of the unification of material nature with divinity.[1] Solovyov's later thought became more biblically and patristically focused. In *Russia and the Universal Church* (1889), Solovyov understands Sophia as the substance of God (*ousia*), as "all-unity" (*vseedinstvo*), with each of the members of the Trinity possessing consubstantial wisdom in a fashion particular to each hypostasis.[2]

Bulgakov builds on this later Solovyovian sophiology. In his early sophiology, Bulgakov, like Florensky, connected Sophia to the hypostasis/person side of the classic hypostasis/essence (*ousia*) distinction, which opened the door to accusations of creating a "fourth hypostasis" in the Trinity. But after 1925 Bulgakov identified Sophia with the divine essence; Sophia as divine ousia is "not a hypostasis but hypostaticity [*ipostasnost'*], or the Divine Sophia," being/nature as the capacity for loving activity that is personalization or hypostatic activity.[3] Sophia is the basis of hypostatic (interpersonal) relations: the divine persons love and act through Sophia.

Bulgakov's sophiology is also grounded in antinomism, a theological method pioneered by Florensky.[4] Florensky and Bulgakov argue that religious truths, for humans who do not see reality in unity as God does, consist of two positive but seemingly contradictory theological statements (antinomies), which are held together through a *podvig* or spiritual trial of faith (God is One and Three; Christ is divine and human). Sophia is such a living antinomy, existing in two modes, divine Sophia, as the eternal, uncreated *ousia* or substance of God, and creaturely Sophia, the temporal creation as an act of divine love in and as the world. God in himself is the Holy Trinity, Father, Son, and Holy Spirit, bound together in an unending act (perichoresis or circumincession) of free self-giving, self-emptying, and self-receiving love (kenosis). Bulgakov calls this perfect act of divine love, God as love, Divine Sophia. Love as creative activity is being itself, the reality of the divine life. In this sense, all being is divine being, and this divine being can also exist in a self-donated, self-given, and self-emptying form as creaturely being, a movement of divine love in otherness from itself in a new created reality (creaturely Sophia).

Bulgakov's Trinitarian theology draws on a wide range of sources, including Augustine, Maximus, and Palamas. Thus for Bulgakov, the Son is eternally begotten from the Father in a bestowal of his total existence, and the Son reaches out in gratitude to the Father, and in this movement, the Spirit proceeds from the sole source (*monarchos*) of the Father as their common caritative jouissance. In this act of pure love, love as both the content of God's existence and the dynamic act of God's being, Divine Sophia as God's *ousia* is imprinted with the Son's image through the love of the Spirit between the Father and the Son.

God as divine love is not content to remain in himself, to love only eternally as Holy Trinity, and in creating the world, this love "spills out" from God and is expressed in and as creation, a new reality grounded in God, which God loves as other than himself. Creation, in temporality and becoming, exists in perfect free love, just as God exists freely and eternally. Divine Wisdom, as the reality of existence, the wise love of the Trinity, is expressed in everything in the heavens and on earth, including spheres of human existence such as economics, science, politics, and art. Bulgakov emphasizes that there is a fundamental continuity and discontinuity of love between the divine and the creaturely. Continuity is real but never wholly fuses the uncreated and the created, which remain in tension until the eschaton, when God will be "all in all" (1 Cor 15:28), one of Bulgakov's favorite expressions. In engaging every area of knowledge, Bulgakov uses Wisdom as a metaphor for the tension between heaven and earth, an ultimate continuity in difference.

Bulgakov considered his sophiology a further development of the theology of the divine energies of St Gregory Palamas, and as theological *panentheism*: God is in the world and the world is in God (in contrast to pantheism: all is God). But in the eyes of critics, Bulgakov's attempts to harmonize sophiology with the Orthodox tradition were unsuccessful, and in the mid-1930s he was accused of heresy (pantheism, determinism, Apollinarianism, Gnosticism) by two rival Russian churches to his own. Critics, including Florovsky and Lossky, accused him of blurring the distinction between God and creation, effectively fusing the two. In Paris, Bulgakov was exonerated of the accusation of heresy by his own Russian Exarchate under Constantinople, although the allegation remains vivid in some Orthodox quarters.

Until the turn of the millennium, Bulgakov's work was largely neglected in both Orthodox and Western theological circles, partially because of a lack of English translations. Many of Bulgakov's central theological writings are now published in English (some of which are abridged from the Russian originals). Orthodox neglect was also a residue of the controversy concerning his alleged "heterodoxy" and suspicions concerning a "modernist theology" that did not simply appeal to a perennial Orthodox identity founded in Greek patristic sources. Yet a younger generation of Orthodox is attracted to Bulgakov's theology (for example, Antoine Arjakovsky, Brandon Gallaher, David Bentley Hart, and Nathaniel Wood) precisely because it is a modern vision of the integration of the divine and the human in all aspects of church, society, and all creation, and it provides new resources to respond to contemporary issues including sexuality, politics, gender, science, the climate crisis, and religious diversity, while also drawing on the fathers, hesychast spirituality, and the liturgy, even if key aspects of Bulgakov's theology are infused with sophiology, a theology still contested and often poorly understood. Through a more serious critical engagement with Bulgakov in dialogue with Western theologians such as Karl Barth, Karl Rahner, and Hans Urs von Balthasar, Bulgakov's theology can become a central theological resource for global Christianity.

Maria Skobtsova (St Maria of Paris)

Mother Maria (Skobtsova) (St Maria of Paris) (1891–1945) was a most atypical modern Orthodox saint: a poet, playwriter, artist, politician, philosopher, and theologian – and social activist. She was married and divorced twice, had a child by a third man, was active in the Russian Socialist Revolutionary Party, served as the first Russian woman mayor (in a small city on the Black Sea) during the revolution, and was almost executed first by the Bolsheviks then by the counterrevolutionaries. Following the collapse of the counter-revolution, she went into exile with her husband and first child (soon joined by two others), arriving in

Paris in 1924. In the late 1920s, she assisted poor Russian refugees throughout France, and in 1933 she became a nun and founded several social and cultural undertakings. During World War II, she assisted Russian Jews to escape persecution. In 1943 she was arrested by the Gestapo, deported to the Ravensbrück concentration camp in Germany, where she was gassed in March 1945. She was canonized in 2004.

Mother Maria wrote on contemporary social, political, and spiritual themes (not only in prose but also in poetry and poetic plays) and on major figures of the Russian Religious Renaissance. Like Bulgakov, her spiritual father, she retained a sensitive social conscience in exile. Her writings focus extensively on the social and political responsibilities of Christians and can be understood as a creative application of Bulgakov's sophiology. The four foundation stones of Mother Maria's theology are the second gospel commandment, love of neighbor; the Orthodox notion of *sobornost'* as universality and conciliarity, the basis of the church; Godmanhood or Divine-Humanity – from which she derived the notion of "Godmotherhood"; and the eucharist. She advocated, controversially, a monasticism oriented to social works, rather than the more traditional contemplative Orthodox monasticism.

A social reading of the gospel and the fathers lies at the core of Mother Maria's theology. Her essay "The Second Gospel Commandment" argues against a tendency in Orthodoxy to focus on the solitary "path of self-salvation," in contrast with cultivating love of neighbor as the fulfilment of the love of God.[5] She reads the Slavophile concept of *sobornost'*, "catholicity," "conciliarity," or, more broadly, "solidarity," as resting "entirely on love, on lofty human communion," asserting boldly (if questionably) that "the main theme of nineteenth century Russian thought had to do with the second commandment, with its dogmatic, moral, philosophical, social, and other aspects," marshaling an array of arguments supporting her emphasis on the social responsibilities of Christians, from the pluralist language of many Orthodox prayers, writings of the fathers, and ascetic texts in the *Philokalia*.[6]

For Mother Maria, the mere practice of charitable acts solely because "they are accepted as ascetic exercises for the soul" is insufficient. No, she writes, "it was not for this kind of love that Christ was crucified." Rather, the inner disposition of the Christian or motivation toward those being assisted is just as important if not more so than the external act. Christians are called to disinterested love, "as an act in the name of the neighbor," a recognition of "the image of God in him." In the poor and unhappy person, she writes: "Christ is indeed present in a humiliated way, and we receive him or her in the name of the love of Christ, not because we will be rewarded, but because we are aflame with this sacrificial love of Christ and in it we are united with him." She refers to this attitude as "mysticism": "Christianity demands of us not only the mysticism of communion with God, but also the mysticism of communion with man." Our communion with humanity is a communion with God precisely because we are united with our fellows in the Body of Christ, Godmanhood. Each person is made in God's image and "by contemplating that image, we touch the Archetype – we commune with God"; we are called to act as Christ and suffer for others with whom we are united.[7]

Maternity as a religious notion features high in Mother Maria's spiritual theology. For her, the Mother of God is also the "Mother of Godmanhood," the church, not as "a sort of pious lyricism," but as continuing "to co-participate, co-feel, co-suffer," indeed being "co-crucified" not only with Christ on the cross, but "with each human soul." Each person is not only the image of God but also the image of Mother of God and is called to participate in her perception of God and Christ in every human being. The imitation of the Mother of God, the "path of God-motherhood," is participation in human suffering, the "co-crucifixion of oneself ... at the foot of every human cross."[8]

Mother Maria's life and writings provide immense resources for an understanding of religious life and holiness (for example, in Élisabeth Behr-Sigel (1907–2005), Paul Ladouceur, and Fr Michael Plekon), and for social and political theologies relevant to a Christian presence in the secular and modernist environment (Jim Forest, Fr Cyril Hovorun, Fr John Jillions, Sr Vassa Larin), which characterizes not only Western countries but increasingly countries of Orthodox tradition. She inspired many later Orthodox women theologians, attracted to her as a Christian feminist before the time, by her social commitment and her preeminent stature as a woman in her overwhelmingly male-dominated intellectual and social milieux.

Vladimir Lossky

Vladimir Lossky (1903–58), Fr Georges Florovsky, and Metropolitan John Zizioulas are eminent representatives of neopatristic theology. Distancing themselves from Bulgakov and the older generation of the religious renaissance, they looked more explicitly than their predecessors to the Greek fathers and the mystical and liturgical traditions in response to the challenges of modernity. Lossky, son of the philosopher Nicolas Lossky (1870–1965), initially studied mainly Byzantine and Western history in St Petersburg, and, after fleeing the revolution with his father first to Prague then to Paris in 1924, he studied medieval philosophy, theology, and history at the Sorbonne, preparing a doctorate on negative theology and the knowledge of God in Meister Eckhart under the historian and neo-Thomist philosopher Étienne Gilson (1884–1978).

In the mid-1930s, Lossky was deeply involved in the critique of Bulgakov's sophiology and other aspects of Bulgakov's theology. As suggested by Bulgakov himself, Lossky turned to a positive expression of neopatristic theology, culminating in 1944 in the publication in French of *The Mystical Theology of the Eastern Church*.[9] Perhaps the most well-known work of Orthodox theology in modern times, *The Mystical Theology* – its title consciously borrowed from the short but powerful work of Pseudo-Dionysius the Areopagite, and perhaps inspired by the writings of Myrrha Lot-Borodine – showed what neopatristic theology could be in a systematic study. It is both a synthesis of the teaching of the Eastern (primarily Greek) fathers, and, more importantly, a work of constructive theology expressing Lossky's interpretation of the patristic corpus as centered on salvation, in the context of the inseparable union of theology and spirituality or mysticism: "The eastern tradition has never made a sharp distinction between mysticism and theology; between personal experience of the divine mysteries and the dogma affirmed by the church."[10]

In this light, several interrelated themes form the backbone of Lossky's theology and *The Mystical Theology* in particular: apophatism, the unknowability of the divine essence, and more broadly, the inability of human concepts and language to express adequately divine existence; the Palamite theology of divine energies, by which God makes himself known to humanity and throughout creation; deification or theosis as the ultimate purpose of human existence; and personalism, human existence as personal, an image of the mode of existence of the divine Persons. Lossky considered that apophatism and theosis were conjoined in a prayerful ascent to union with God, renouncing "both sense and all the workings of reason ... that which is and all that is not, in order to be able to attain in perfect ignorance to union with Him who transcends all being and all knowledge."[11]

These themes were already present in Russian religious thought before Lossky – for example, apophatism and antinomies in Florensky and Bulgakov, the divine energies in Bulgakov, personalism in Berdyaev and Bulgakov, and theosis in nineteenth-century spiritual literature and in Myrrha Lot-Borodine. Lossky's genius was to integrate these strands in a coherent conceptual structure firmly grounded in patristic theology and the Orthodox ascetic-spiritual tradition. *The Mystical Theology* has been enormously influential both among Orthodox theologians such as Metropolitan John Zizioulas, Metropolitan Kallistos Ware, and Fr Christopher Knight, and in wider Christian circles (notably among Anglican theologians such as Lossky's friend and translator, A. M. Allchin (1930–2010); Rowan Williams, who wrote his doctorate on Lossky under Allchin; Sarah Coakley; and Fr Andrew Louth, an Orthodox convert from Anglicanism), where it is appreciated for both its patristic foundation and its emphasis on the union of theology and spirituality/mysticism, while acknowledging weaknesses, such as an exaggeration of differences and conflicts between Eastern and Western Christianity.

A strong point of Lossky's theology, which has become crucial in the twenty-first century as theologians struggle with new anthropological challenges, especially gender, is his elaboration of a theology of human personhood, drawing heavily both upon his predecessors in the religious renaissance, especially Bulgakov and Berdyaev, and on French personalists such as Gabriel Marcel (1889–1973) and Emmanuel Mounier (1905–50). Lossky applies to human existence the classic distinction between person and essence, *hypostasis* and *ousia*, developed by the Greek fathers of the fourth century to express how God can be One and Three simultaneously. Like Bulgakov, Lossky pithily articulated the essence of human personhood in a formula which may be summarized as "the irreducibility of person to nature": "It will be impossible for us to form a concept of the human person and we will have to content ourselves with saying: 'person' signifies the irreducibility of man to his nature."[12] The human person is called to surpass nature to achieve the full realization of human existence: "It cannot be a question here of 'something' distinct from 'another nature' but of *someone* who is distinct from his own nature, of someone who goes beyond his nature while still containing it, who makes it exist as human nature by this overstepping and yet does not exist in himself beyond the nature which he 'enhypostasizes' and which he constantly exceeds."[13]

For Lossky, in the wake of Bulgakov and Berdyaev, "person" signifies freedom, whereas "nature" is conceived as fundamentally limited and even deterministic: "The idea of the person implies freedom vis-à-vis the nature. The person is free from its nature, is not determined by it."[14] On the other hand, an "individual" (different from a person) is governed by nature, acting out of his natural qualities ("character"), asserting himself against others.[15]

Lossky's theology of the person strongly influenced Christos Yannaras and, through him, John Zizioulas. Personalism is a golden thread running through modern Orthodox theology from the late nineteenth century, through the twentieth century, and into the twenty-first century.

Georges Florovsky

Fr Georges Florovsky (1893–1979), the originator of neopatristic synthesis, was the most influential Orthodox theologian in the second half of the twentieth century. Florovsky studied philosophy in Odessa, and fled the Russian Civil War to Istanbul, then to Sofia and Prague, where he once again studied philosophy and began his teaching career. In 1926, at the invitation of Bulgakov, he moved to Paris to teach patristics, in which he was entirely self-taught, at the newly established St Sergius Orthodox Theological Institute. Florovsky spent World War II in Yugoslavia, returning briefly to Paris before moving to New York in 1948. Florovsky was professor and dean at St Vladimir's Seminary, New York (1948–55), professor of Eastern Church history at the Harvard Divinity School (1956–64), and visiting professor of Slavic Studies and Religion at Princeton University (1964–79).

Florovsky elaborated much of his theology in reaction to Bulgakov's sophiology, which Florovsky saw as deterministic and pantheistic. Tradition is the cornerstone of Florovsky's theological method. In his 1936 paper "Patristics and Modern Theology" proposing his neopatristic project, Florovsky calls on Orthodox theologians to return to the fathers and the liturgy as the basis of Orthodox theology. The fathers, he writes, forged a "new, Christian Hellenism," such that their schemes and formulae were "through and through Hellenistic or Greek." "*Hellenism,*" Florovsky concludes, "*is a standing category of Christian existence.*"[16] Florovsky articulates a dynamic and creative understanding of tradition and warns against "a blind or servile imitation and repetition" of the fathers, advocating instead "a further *development* of this patristic teaching"; Orthodox theologians must "kindle again the creative fire of the Fathers, to restore in ourselves *the patristic spirit*" resulting in "the real continuity of lives and mind, and inspiration."[17]

In Florovsky, tradition is living and contemporary, not a museum. He warned continuously against a simplistic "theology of repetition": "Tradition," he writes, "is the constant abiding of the Spirit and not only the memory of words. Tradition is a *charismatic*, not a historical, principle." Tradition is thus not simply a guarding of the apostolic deposit, conservativism for its own sake, but "primarily the principle of growth and regeneration." To describe the dynamism, creativity, and freedom of the life of the Body of Christ, the church, animated by the Spirit, Florovsky uses a phrase common among his Russian émigré contemporaries – "living tradition" (*zhivoe predanie*).[18]

Florovsky's advocacy of the need to acquire the "mind of the fathers" was not adherence to a mythical *consensus patrum* (an expression that Florovsky disliked), but rather the acquisition of a patristic mode of theology, doing theology as the fathers did. The following elements enter into Florovsky's notion of the "patristic mind" as a theological method: scripture as the foundation of all theology; Christ as the center of theological reflection; a historical awareness, both the history of salvation as revealed in scripture and the history of the church; a "catholic consciousness," theology in the context of the church; fidelity to the Hellenistic-Byzantine theological tradition; a focus on contemporary issues and problems; and the integration of theology with the prayer and sacramental life of the church – the fathers were "Holy Men of Old," not simply "theologians" in an academic sense.[19] For Florovsky, the saints, in particular the ancient fathers, are the preeminent instances of "catholic consciousness," attaining such a fulness of catholicity that their faith is not only personal profession but also "the testimony of the Church; they speak to us from its catholic completeness, from the completeness of a life full of grace."[20]

In 1963 Florovsky told his students that the patristic "vision" (earlier, "the patristic mind") has authority, "not necessarily their words": "The 'authority' of the Fathers is not a *dictatus papae*. They are guides and witnesses, no more ... By studying the Fathers we are compelled *to face the problems*, and then we can follow them but creatively, not in the mood of repetition."[21] Ironically, Florovsky's flexible attitude toward patristic theology is close here to that of Bulgakov, who in 1937 had written that patristic writings "are historically conditioned and therefore limited in their meaning ... the writings of the Fathers are not the Word of God and cannot be compared to it or made equal to it."[22]

Florovsky was the leading Orthodox figure in the ecumenical movement from the late 1930s until the 1960s, and he is one of the founders of the World Council of Churches. The ecumenical theology that he developed – Orthodox ecumenical engagement with other churches as "witness" to the truth of Orthodoxy – became the working ecumenical theology in Orthodoxy. Florovsky's ecumenism presupposes his ecclesiology, which represents both continuity with certain notions of his predecessors concerning the church, as well as a break with them. In his foundational 1933 article "The Limits of the Church," Florovsky, building on Augustine, examines the reception of heretics and schismatics in the early church without the requirement of a new baptism, seeing in this a recognition of divine grace among those visibly separated from the main body of the church.[23] Florovsky concludes that the charismatic and sacramental activity of the church extends beyond the canonical boundaries of the Orthodox Church: "As a mystical organism, as the sacramental Body of Christ, the Church cannot be adequately described in canonical terms or categories alone ... In her sacramental, mysterious being the Church surpasses canonical measurements."[24] Thus non-Orthodox Christians can indeed be members of the church. Here and elsewhere Florovsky retains as an aspect of the church the Slavophile characterization of the church as unity in freedom and love – *sobornost* – while discarding, like Solovyov and Bulgakov before him, the Slavophile identification of the model of the church in Russian peasant communal organization.

The originality of Florovsky's contribution to Orthodox ecclesiology lies in his unflinching focus on Christ as the basis of the unity of the church, a line of thought developed from the Pauline notion of the church as the Body of Christ. Florovsky's longest and most developed writing on the church is "The Body of the Living Christ," prepared for the founding Assembly of the World Council of Churches in 1948.[25] Distinguishing between the Incarnation of the Word of God and the role of the Holy Spirit, Florovsky argues that Christians are united in Christ. Thus ecclesiology should begin with Christ and proceed to "investigate the implications of the total dogma of the Incarnation, including the glory of the Risen and Ascended Lord, who sitteth at the right hand of the Father."[26] "The theology of the Church is only a chapter, and an essential chapter, of Christology ... It is in this Christological framework that the mystery of the Church is announced in the New Testament. It is also within this framework that the Greek and Latin fathers presented the mystery of the Church."[27]

For Florovsky, divisions among the Christian churches are above all dogmatic. He imposes strict conditions on church reunification to the point that "he himself admitted that he had little faith in 'theologians' conferences' and transferred his hope to an 'eschatological twilight,' that is, to the end of history, the moment of the authentic coming together."[28] In this light, Orthodox participation in the ecumenical movement is justified primarily by witness, to witness to other Christians that the truth of Christ subsists *fully* only in the Orthodox Church and that they are called to reunion with the ancient church it embodies. Emphasizing what separates rather than what unites Christians, Florovsky's ecumenical perspective is dogmatic, historical, patristic, canonical, and eschatological.

Florovsky inspired Lossky and later Russian, Greek, Serbian, and Romanian theologians whose work dominated much of Orthodox theology in the second half of the twentieth century. His creative and historically grounded theological approach to the study of patristics and church history is reflected in such figures as Fr Demetrios Bathrellos, George Demacopoulos, Paul Gavrilyuk, Fr Andrew Louth, Ashley Purpura, and former students and followers of Metropolitan Kallistos Ware, notably Fr John Behr, Peter Bouteneff, Fr John Chryssavgis, Marcus Plested, Norman Russell, and Fr Alexis Torrance.

In less creative expressions, neopatristic theology become, as Florovsky warned, a routinized theology of repetition of the fathers, with strongly anti-Western and authoritarian overtones and little responsive to modern issues. Florovsky's theology begins not with a fundamental union between God and creation (Godmanhood, Sophia), but with the church as a mystical organism, whose life is expressed through sacred tradition and its hierarchical, institutional order. Even if the church as the Body of Christ extends beyond the bounds of its canonical limits, and tradition is living and dynamic, Florovsky was little interested in the secular world, which is not understood to be holy in its divine-human roots. It would take a more recent Orthodox theological return to Bulgakov's intuitions of a fundamental sacred quality of creation for more extensive Orthodox engagement with creation and society.

Alexander Schmemann

Fr Alexander Schmemann (1921–1983) drew on all that is best in Bulgakov and Florovsky and others in the last major creative expression of the Russian Religious Renaissance. Schmemann was born in Estonia and his family moved to Paris via Belgrade in 1929. Schmemann was educated in Russian and French schools, then at the St Sergius Institute (1940–45), where he trained first as a priest, then worked on Byzantine church history, on which he lectured from 1946 to 1951. He was influenced by Fr Cyprian Kern (1899–1960), a liturgical theologian and patrologist, and by the liturgical theologian and canonist, Fr Nicholas Afanasiev. Schmemann studied under Bulgakov and, although he had great respect for Bulgakov, Schmemann never warmed to the systematizing aspects of sophiology. However, he retained and expanded on Bulgakov's liturgical vision of the divine presence in creation.

After the war, Schmemann was briefly Florovsky's colleague and shared his appeal to patristic theology and prayer and the sacraments as the animating center of Orthodox theology. In 1951, Florovsky, after becoming dean of St Vladimir's Seminary in New York, invited Schmemann to teach church history at the Seminary. After a dispute with Schmemann and other colleagues, Florovsky was forced to leave St Vladimir's in 1955 and Schmemann became dean in 1962. He was one of the architects of the new Orthodox Church in America (OCA), which was granted autocephaly by the Moscow Patriarchate in 1970. Schmemann spearheaded a eucharistic and liturgical revival in America through his extensive writings, lectures, wide ecumenical work (he was an ecumenical observer at the Second Vatican Council), and appointments as adjunct professor in other institutions; and for several decades he made vastly influential religious broadcasts to the Soviet Union through Radio Liberty.

Schmemann is associated primarily with liturgical theology, of which he arguably can be said to be the "founding father" – "liturgy" in the wide sense of all the rituals, sacraments, and services of the Byzantine rite. The liturgy is both the source of theology and its ultimate primary expression, following the adage *lex orandi, lex credendi* (the law of prayer is the law of belief). For Schmemann, a human is not so much *homo sapiens* or *homo faber* as *homo adorans*, what others call *homo liturgicus*. To be human is thus to be a "priest of creation," offering to God the "world as sacrament," an idea which Schmemann drew from both modern sources such as Bulgakov, and ancient writers such as Maximus the Confessor. Schmemann expressed this notion in vivid imagery in his well-known book *For the Life of the World*:

> The first, the basic definition of man is that he is *the priest*. He stands in the center of the world and unifies it in his act of blessing God, of both receiving the world from God and offering it to God – and by filling the world with this eucharist, he transforms his life, the one that he receives from the world, into life in God, into communion with Him. The world was created as the "matter," the material of one all-embracing eucharist, and man was created as the priest of this cosmic sacrament.[29]

Humanity as priest of creation offers creation to God, recognizing that it is God's from the outset, as Creator, Sustainer, and Finality of all that exists: "For man can be truly man – that is, the king of creation, the priest and minister of God's creativity and initiative – only when he does not posit himself as the 'owner' of creation and submits himself – in obedience and love – to its nature as the bride of God, in *response* and *acceptance*."[30]

Schmemann was the last major theologian of the Russian emigration who had a wide appeal beyond Orthodoxy. His concept of the "priest of creation" has been appropriated by both Orthodox theologians working in ecotheology, notably John Zizioulas and John Chryssavgis, and non-Orthodox, reflected, for example, in the religious dimensions of the environmental crisis in Pope Francis's *Laudato si'* (2015). Schmemann's innovative work in the advancement of Orthodox liturgical theology has made his thinking influential among Orthodox scholars including Nicholas Denysenko, Job Getcha, Christina Gschwandtner, Paul Meyendorff, and Gregory Tucker, and among major Protestant and Catholic thinkers, such as Aidan Kavanagh (1929–2006), Geoffrey Wainwright (1939–2020) and David Fagerberg (b. 1952).

John Zizioulas

In the opening decades of the twentieth-first century, Metropolitan John Zizioulas (1931–2023) was widely considered the senior Orthodox theologian, together with Metropolitan Kallistos Ware. Zizioulas's theological prominence marked the transition from the theologians who emerged from the Russian Religious Renaissance to a broader base of theologians in countries of Orthodox tradition such as Greece and Romania, and Orthodox theologians in Western Europe and North America.

Zizioulas studied in Thessaloniki and Athens before pursuing doctoral studies at Harvard University, where he studied under Georges Florovsky and Paul Tillich. Zizioulas taught briefly at St Vladimir's Seminary, and it was through his contacts with Fr Alexander Schmemann and Fr John Meyendorff that Zizioulas became acquainted with the eucharistic ecclesiology of the Russian émigré theologian Fr Nicholas Afanasiev. In 1965 Zizioulas completed his doctorate for the University of Athens on "The Unity of the Church in the Holy Eucharist and the Bishop during the First Three Centuries." After teaching at the University of Athens, Zizioulas taught in Edinburgh and Glasgow, where he began a deep engagement with British theologians, including T. F. Torrance and Colin Gunton. In 1986, he was elected titular Metropolitan of Pergamon and taught in Thessaloniki and at King's College London. Zizioulas was a major Orthodox figure in ecumenical circles, especially in the World Council of Churches and in the Orthodox-Catholic theological dialogue, which he cochaired until his retirement in 2016.

The core of Zizioulas's theology lies in a harmonious integration of four interrelated spheres: Trinitarian theology, Christology, ecclesiology, and anthropology. Zizioulas built critically on Afanasiev's eucharistic ecclesiology. Afanasiev considered that the eucharist, as Christ's continuing presence on earth, was the heart of the church. Afanasiev looked to the early Christian communities as the model of the church, seeing in them eucharistic communities embodying the fullness of the church in a given locality; the local church was "catholic" in its celebration of the eucharist.

Zizioulas, dissatisfied with Afanasiev's emphasis on the local eucharistic assembly and his apparent minimization of dogmatic differences in an ecumenical context, stresses the importance of unity of faith in the church and the role of the bishop as the head of the local eucharistic community and in the universal church. The bishop is inseparable from the community in which he presides: "There is no Church without the community, as there is no Christ without the Body," writes Zizioulas; "there is no episcopacy without a community attached to it."[31] The bishop expresses in himself the multitude of the faithful in one place, offering the eucharist to God in the name of the church, "thus bringing up to the throne of God the whole Body of Christ."[32] Zizioulas affirms the divine origin and nature of episcopal authority and from there, the essential place of the bishop, as "presiding in love" (Afanasiev's expression, borrowed from Ignatius of Antioch) over the local eucharistic community, and manifesting its catholicity in relation with the other catholic eucharistic communities.[33]

For Zizioulas, eucharistic ecclesiology must echo Trinitarian theology, because God is a communion (*koinonia*) of divine persons, and the church's being must likewise be one of personal communion. Eucharistic ecclesiology must also be Christological in that Christ is the head of his Body, the church, "born and existing in the *koinonia* of the Spirit."[34] Zizioulas's ecclesiology is also personalist. Just as God's being is fundamentally communion or love among the three Persons of the Holy Trinity, so humans are called to realize the fullness of their existence, of their personhood, in communion with God and with each other, through eucharistic communion in the church. Zizioulas calls this aspect of human existence in the church an "ecclesial hypostasis," "something different" from the mere "biological hypostasis"; it is an eschatological reality pointing beyond our present nature to reach out ecstatically to the age to come: "The ecclesial hypostasis is the faith of man in his capacity to become a person and his hope that he will indeed become an authentic person ... The Eucharist is first of all an assembly (*synaxis*), a community, a network of relations, in which man 'subsists' in a manner different from the biological as a member of a body which transcends every exclusiveness of a biological or social kind."[35]

Zizioulas's ecclesiology is closely interwoven with an anthropology, which, as in his predecessors among the Russian religious thinkers and in existentialism, emphasizes the priority of person over nature and the person over the individual. Zizioulas reiterates Lossky's ideas of "the irreducibility of person to nature"[36] and, following Bulgakov and Berdyaev, the theological distinction between person and individual.[37] "I have excluded every possibility of regarding the person as an expression or emanation of the substance or nature of man (or even of God himself as 'nature')"[38] and "Man's personhood should not be understood in terms of ... the human individuum."[39] The personal existence of the Trinity is the model for human personhood, the highest aspect of the divine image in humanity. Zizioulas characterizes this as "being as communion" (the title of his well-known book). Similarly, Christos Yannaras, from whom many of Zizioulas's key ideas were drawn, refers to the personal "mode of existence" and "being-as-person."[40] Zizioulas elaborates: "The perfect man is consequently only he who is authentically a person, that is, he who subsists, who possess a 'mode of existence' which is constituted as being, *in precisely the manner in which God also subsists as being.*"[41] Full personhood can be accomplished only in interrelation with other persons and, as in the Trinity, love is the basis for true interpersonal relations.

The being of God is free personal love because God constitutes his substance by a free act of love: "Love as God's mode of existence 'hypostasizes' God, *constitutes* his being ... Love is identified with ontological freedom."[42] The person, divine or human, is "*otherness in communion and communion in otherness*"; and this otherness constitutes freedom: "*Personhood is freedom* ... Personhood is inconceivable without freedom; it is the freedom of being other."[43] Zizioulas calls the state of ecclesial being "the Christian ethos of otherness," which looks toward the age to come.[44] In this new eschatological mode of life, humanity is no longer constrained by the necessities of its own nature, or history itself, but is called to transcend its creatureliness and even temporality and mutability.[45]

Eucharistic ecclesiology as developed by Afanasiev and Zizioulas rapidly became the preeminent vision of the church in Orthodox thought and had a powerful impact in wider Christian circles, especially in the Catholic Church. But in the early years of the new millennium there emerged a lively debate among Orthodox theologians concerning Zizioulas's ecclesiology and his personalism. The main criticism levied against his ecclesiology is that it overemphasizes the importance of the liturgical role of the bishop in the constitution of the church, to the detriment of the entire people of God, the priesthood, and the pastoral and teaching roles of spiritual elders in Orthodoxy (*gerontes* or *startsi*), who are also channels of grace and teachers, thereby falling into "episcoplatry" (Metropolitan Kallistos Ware's expression). Critics of Zizioulas's personalism, such as Jean-Claude Larchet and Fr Nikolaos Loudovikos, argue that, by considering the person as the supreme ontological category, the carrier of freedom, Zizioulas denigrates nature or essence, negatively identified with determinism and necessity. Nature, instead of being divinely created as "very good" (Gen 1:31), is thus tainted because it is seen as subject to determinism and is associated with degenerate or fallen humanity, destined to return to dust, nonexistence, or hell. Critics argue for a more balanced approach to the relationship between nature and person. Scholars such as Fr Andrew Louth and Lucian Turcescu also argue that, contrary to Zizioulas's claims that his theology was derived from the fathers, especially the Cappadocians, in fact, many of his basic ideas – including existence preceding essence and the person-individual dynamic – had been tacitly adapted from Western existentialism, phenomenology, and personalism.

Zizioulas's theology is pervasive in contemporary Orthodoxy, attracting conservatives because of its emphasis on the hierarchical nature of the church, and progressives (notably Nikolaos Asproulis, Pantelis Kalaitzidis, and Aristotle Papanikolaou) for its personalism. It has also attracted considerable attention from many Protestant and Catholic thinkers because of its eucharistic and Trinitarian centered understanding of personhood and ecclesiology (for example, Douglas Farrow, Colin Gunton, Douglas Knight, Catherine LaCugna, Paul McPartlan, and Miroslav Volf). But because Zizioulas almost entirely ignores the people of God in favor of the ordained clergy, especially the hierarchy, nature in favor of personhood, history in favor of eschatology, there is little room for Orthodox social and political theology, nor for consideration of other major contemporary issues such as gender, sexuality, and the role of women in the church. Despite weaknesses in Zizioulas's theology, he remains one of the most widely influential Orthodox theologians of modern times.

Achievement and Agenda: Orthodox Theology in the Twenty-First Century

At the onset of the new millennium, weaknesses of neopatristic theology became increasingly apparent, especially difficulty in engaging creatively with modern problems, and a conceptual framework which accentuated differences and conflict between East and West. Neopatristic theology, which dominated Orthodox theology since World War II, appeared increasingly ill adapted to deal with emerging issues such as gender identity and sexual diversity, the role of women in the church, nationalism in society and in the church, science and theology, technological developments in communications and artificial intelligence, human enhancement using technology, and the globalization of major religions.

Two important conferences in 2010, at the Volos Academy for Theological Studies in Greece (Pantelis Kalaitzidis and Nikolaos Asproulis) and at the Orthodox Christian Studies Center, Fordham University in New York (George Demacopoulos and Aristotle Papanikolaou), exemplified a critical tendency toward the neopatristic paradigm. The title of the Volos conference was itself provocative: "Neo-Patristic Synthesis or Post-Patristic Theology: Can Orthodox Theology be Contextual?" Papers questioned aspects of the neopatristic project, others dealt with the possibility of Orthodox contextual theology and with modern issues such as historical-critical method, theology and science, liberalism, social theology, ethnotheology, feminism, and non-Christian religions.[46] The Fordham Conference critiqued anti-Western polemics pervasive in much of modern Orthodox theology, seen as intellectually unsound and counterproductive.[47]

The questioning of neopatristic theology and the desire to respond more effectively to contemporary issues is reflected in three trends characterizing Orthodox theology in the new millennium. First is a diminishing preponderance in Orthodox theology of theologians of the two major centers of Orthodoxy, Greece and Russia (including the Russian exile community). The second half of the twentieth century witnessed the emergence of major theologians in other countries of Orthodox tradition, especially Serbia and Romania, and in Western Europe and North America, including both theologians descendant from Orthodox immigrants and converts to Orthodoxy. Theologians who exemplify this tendency include the Romanian Fr Dumitru Stăniloae (1903–93); the Serb Archimandrite Justin (Popović) (1894–1979) (canonized 2010), whose conservative, anti-Western and antiecumenical theology has made him a leading figure in the traditionalist strain of modern Orthodox thought; and the English convert from Anglicanism, Metropolitan Kallistos Ware, whose book *The Orthodox Church* has been the standard general introduction to Orthodox theology, history, and spirituality since its initial publication in 1963.

Fr Dumitru Stăniloae is now particularly important. He united theology and spirituality in a harmonious expression of the Orthodox tradition, reflected in a vast literary production. Stăniloae taught theology in Sibiu and Bucharest and was imprisoned for five years during the communist regime. He is a candidate for canonization in 2025. His major works include studies of St Gregory Palamas and the Incarnation and redemption, a dogmatic theology (three volumes in the original Romanian), a manual of Orthodox spirituality, and a Romanian *Philokalia* in twelve volumes. Stăniloae was a pioneer of the revival of the Palamite theology of the divine energies and of the theology of Maximus the Confessor. He sees Christianity as a divine-human culture, uniting East and West, and his patristically inspired mystical theology is infused with a cosmic vision unifying God, humanity, and the rest of creation in Christ. Stăniloae's stature as a major Orthodox theologian is increasing as more of his works become available in translation.

Another contemporary trend in Orthodox theology is the emergence of many lay Orthodox theologians, accompanied by the establishment of centers of Orthodox theology in universities. Lay theologians dominated the Slavophile movement and the Russian Religious Renaissance, and Greek theological education. With the suppression of theological institutions in the Soviet Union after the Bolshevik Revolution, the locus of Orthodox theology was mainly in a few seminaries and theological institutes in Western Europe and North America, and faculties of theology in countries of Orthodox tradition. Orthodox theologians were typically raised in ethnic Orthodox milieux and often ordained (hence always men). By the opening decades of the twenty-first century, Orthodox theology had moved to a more diffuse model characterized by numerous lay theologians, with a large number of women and many converts to Orthodoxy, often educated and teaching in secular or non-Orthodox religious universities in the West. Both Orthodox lay and ordained theologians in Western universities enjoy greater academic independence than their counterparts in countries of Orthodox tradition, especially Russia, Romania, and Serbia. The French theologian Élisabeth Behr-Sigel (1907–2005), who was from the mid-1970s the main Orthodox figure on the role of women in the church, is a prominent example of the trend toward lay Orthodox theologians.

Many of the lay theologians were themselves converts to Orthodoxy as conversion has became increasingly prominent after World War II, starting as a trickle but becoming a flood. In addition to Metropolitan Kallistos Ware and Élisabeth Behr-Sigel, Orthodox convert theologians include Fr Lev Gillet (1893–1980), Olivier Clément, Philip Sherrard (1922–95), Jaroslav Pelikan (1923–2006), Fr Andrew Louth, Elizabeth Theokritoff, Fr John McGuckin, and David Bentley Hart. Converts to Orthodoxy converge with either the more progressive strand of Orthodoxy, or the more conservative strand, adhering to traditionalist, anti-Western Orthodox thinking, such as Fr Seraphim (Eugene) Rose (1934–82) of Platina Monastery in California, an American convert to Orthodoxy.

The increasing prominence of lay Orthodox theologians and converts has been accompanied by a noticeable shift of creative theological engagement from Orthodox seminaries, institutes, and faculties of theology to academic centers and programs for the study of Orthodoxy in non-Orthodox religious and secular universities, almost all located outside traditionally Orthodox countries.

A trend related to the rise of secular and non-Orthodox institutions focusing on Orthodox theology has been increased study of Orthodoxy in an historical and religious studies perspective, employing typical social science methods drawn from anthropology, sociology, and political science, especially since the fall of communism in the Soviet Union and Eastern Europe and the disintegration of the Soviet Union. The most popular Orthodox countries for religious studies are Russia, Greece, and Romania, and increasing attention is devoted to Orthodox communities in Western Europe and the United States. Religious studies concerning Orthodoxy focus mainly on the religious practices of Orthodox faithful; political influences and involvement (both the collusion of Orthodox churches with governments and political movements, and the involvement of political authorities in church governance and discipline); the relationship of Orthodox churches and theologians with social and political ideologies such as communism, fascism, liberalism, and nationalism; policies and behavior of churches relating to human rights, for example concerning religious, ethnic, and social minorities; the involvement of religious bodies in the public square, especially on social, political, and moral issues; and power and influence within religious institutions. Prominent Orthodox exponents of this area include Effie Fokas, Lucian Leustean, Vasilios Makrides, Elizabeth Prodromou, Vera Shevzov, and Lucian Turcescu, as well as non-Orthodox, such as Kristina Stoeckl.

A third trend in Orthodox theology is the growing collaboration among Orthodox scholars in different institutions and countries, often involving the academic centers mentioned previously. As the center of Orthodox research has moved away from ecclesial institutions to secular and non-Orthodox religious institutions, there has been a corresponding rise in interdisciplinary collaboration between Orthodox theologians, religious studies scholars, and social scientists (especially in political science, anthropology, and sociology) specializing in Eastern Christianity. Facilitated by improvements in communications and the ease of travel, Orthodox theology functions increasingly at an international level, with English as the common language. This international collaboration is reflected in conferences and joint publications on issues relevant to Orthodox theology, multi-institutional and interdisciplinary research projects, and participation in national, regional, and international academic associations.

Leading Orthodox theologians, notably Fr John Chryssavgis, Metropolitan Kallistos Ware, Archbishop Anastasios Yannoulatos of Albania, and Metropolitan John Zizioulas, participated in the Holy and Great Council of the Orthodox Church (the first in many centuries), held in Crete in June 2016. This was preceded by intensive preparatory discussions among lay and ordained Orthodox theologians and followed by conferences analyzing the wide-ranging documents adopted by the council.[48]

After the Crete Council, there emerged multiple international theological collaborations, often led by those who attended Crete or were inspired by its vision. The International Orthodox Theological Association, established by Paul Gavrilyuk, Gayle Woloschak (both attended Crete), and Carrie Frederick Frost, has held widely attended conferences in Iasi (Romania) (2019), and Volos (Greece) (2023). The document *For the Life of the World: Toward a Social Ethos of the Orthodox Church* (2020), approved for publication by the Ecumenical Patriarchate, advances a progressive Orthodox social theology grounded in the Gospel and Orthodox tradition. It was prepared by a group of mostly lay Orthodox theologians led by Fr John Chryssavgis, a leading voice at Crete, and has received wide international attention.[49] A project of the University of Exeter and the Orthodox Christian Studies Center, Fordham University, involving scholars and clergy from many churches and countries and led by Brandon Gallaher (who attended Crete) and Aristotle Papanikolaou, explored the complex Orthodox responses to gender and sexual diversity in Orthodoxy, both in Western countries and traditionally Orthodox lands.[50] In response to the Russian invasion of Ukraine in February 2022, Orthodox scholars from several countries, including Brandon Gallaher, Fr Cyril Hovorun, Pantelis Kalaitzidis, Paul Ladouceur, and Fr Richard René, prepared a "Declaration on the 'Russian World' (*Russkii mir*) Teaching," subsequently signed by several thousand persons, critiquing the religious basis invoked by the Putin regime and the Russian Orthodox Church as justification for the war against Ukraine.[51]

The central thrust of Orthodox theology in the last century has been the search for a creative Orthodox creative response to Western modernity, an "alternate Orthodox modernity," that remains faithful to the Orthodox tradition, avoiding the temptation to abandon apparently archaic forms of the past for forms and values of the present age. This entails an innovative appropriation of the relevant resources of the West, a new definition of how Orthodoxy can harmonize all that is best in both East and West, Eastern and Western Christianity. This is an ongoing process, and the movements and personalities discussed in this chapter manifest this constant search for the "groanings of the Spirit" (Rom 8:26) in the contemporary world, finding new patterns of ideas, in continuity with the "Faith of the Fathers," a living tradition ever ancient and ever new (Rev 21:5).

Notes

1   See Vladimir Solovyov, *Lectures on Divine Humanity* (1877–81) (Hudson, NY: Lindisfarne Press, 1995), passim. For discussion see Brandon Gallaher, "The Christological Focus of Vladimir Solov'ev's Sophiology," *Modern Theology* 25, no. 4 (October 2009): 617–46.

2   See Vladimir Solovyov, *Russia and the Universal Church* (1889) (London: Geoffrey Bles, 1948).

3   Sergius Bulgakov, "Protopresbyter Sergii Bulgakov: Hypostasis and Hypostaticity: Scholia to the *Unfading Light*" (1925), *St Vladimir's Theological Quarterly* 49, nos. 1–2 (2005): 41.

4   See Pavel Florensky, "Contradiction," in *The Pillar and Ground of the Truth* (1914) (Princeton, NJ: Princeton University Press, 1997), 106–23. Compare Sergius Bulgakov, *Unfading Light* [1917] (Grand Rapids, MI: Eeerdmans, 2012), 103–10. For discussion see Brandon Gallaher, "Antinomism, Trinity and the Challenge of Solov'ëvan Pantheism in the Theology of Sergij Bulgakov," *Studies in East European Thought* 64, nos. 3–4 (2012): 205–25.

5   Mother Maria Skobtsova, *Essential Writings* (Maryknoll, NY: Orbis, 2003), 47, 58.

6   Skobtsova, "The Second Gospel Commandment," *Essential Writings*, 58, 59.

7   Skobtsova, "The Mysticism of Human Communion," *Essential Writings*, 83, 79.

8   Skobtsova, "On the Imitation of the Mother of God," *Essential Writings*, 68–73.

9   Vladimir Lossky, *The Mystical Theology of the Eastern Church* (1944) (Crestwood, NY: St Vladimir's Seminary Press, 1967).

10 Lossky, *The Mystical Theology*, 8.

11 Lossky, *The Mystical Theology*, 27.

12 Vladimir Lossky, "The Theological Notion of the Human Person," in *In the Image and Likeness of God* (Crestwood, NY: St Vladimir's Seminary Press, 1974), 120.

13 Lossky, "The Theological Notion of the Human Person," 120.

14 Lossky, *The Mystical Theology*, 122.

15 Lossky, *The Mystical Theology*, 121–2.

16 Georges Florovsky, "Patristics and Modern Theology" (1939), in *The Patristic Witness of Georges Florovsky*, ed. Brandon Gallaher and Paul Ladouceur (London: T&T Clark, 2019), 157. For discussion, see John Chryssavgis and Brandon Gallaher, eds., *The Living Christ: The Theological Legacy of Georges Florovsky* (London: T&T Clark, 2021).

17 Florovsky, "Patristics and Modern Theology," *The Patristic Witness of Georges Florovsky*, 155–6.

18 Florovsky, "Sobornost: The Catholicity of the Church" (1934), *The Patristic Witness of Georges Florovsky*, 265; "Breaks and Links" (1937), *The Patristic Witness of Georges Florovsky*, 172.

19 See Florovsky, "Breaks and Links," *The Patristic Witness of Georges Florovsky*, 159–83; "Introduction," *The Patristic Witness of Georges Florovsky*, 17–20.

20 Florovsky, "Sobornost," *The Patristic Witness of Georges Florovsky*, 263.

21 Florovsky, "On the Authority of the Fathers," *The Patristic Witness of Georges Florovsky*, 238–9.

22 Sergius Bulgakov, "Dogma and Dogmatic Theology" (1937), in *Tradition Alive: On the Church and the Christian Life in Our Time*, ed. Michael Plekon (Lanham, MD: Rowman & Littlefield, 2003), 71.

23 Florovsky, "The Limits of the Church" (1933), *The Patristic Witness of Georges Florovsky*, 247–56.

24 Florovsky, "The Limits of the Church," *The Patristic Witness of Georges Florovsky*, 248–9.

25 Georges Florovsky, "The Body of the Living Christ: An Orthodox Interpretation of the Church" (1948), in Chryssavgis and Gallaher, *The Living Christ: The Theological Legacy of Georges Florovsky*, 437–84.

26 From Matthew Baker, "The Body of the Living Christ: Ecclesiology in the Thought of Father Georges Florovsky," Symposium, Princeton Theological Seminary, 10–11 February 2012.

27 Florovsky, "The Body of the Living Christ," 441.

28 Antoine Arjakovsky, *The Way: Religious Thinkers of the Russian* Emigration (Notre Dame, IN: University of Notre Dame Press, 2013), 359, citing Florovsky's article "The Question of Christian Unity" (in Russian), *Put'* 37 (1933): 8–9.

29 Alexander Schmemann, *For the Life of the World: Sacraments and Orthodoxy* (1963) (Crestwood, NY: St Vladimir's Seminary Press, 1973), 15. The British edition is titled *The World as Sacrament*.

30 Schmemann, *For the Life of the World*, 85.

31 John Zizioulas, *Being as Communion: Studies in Personhood and the Church* (Crestwood, NY: St Vladimir's Seminary Press, 1985), 137.

32 Zizioulas, *Being as Communion*, 153.

33 Zizioulas, *Being as Communion*, 156–7.

34 John Zizioulas, "The Church as Communion," in *The One and the Many: Studies on God, Man, the Church, and the World Today* (Alhambra, CA: Sebastian Press, 2010), 51.

35 Zizioulas, *Being as Communion*, 58, 60.

36 Zizioulas, *Being as Communion*, 59.

37 John Zizioulas, "Person and Individual – A 'Misreading' of the Cappadocians?," in *Communion and Otherness: Further Studies in Personhood and the Church* (London: T&T Clark, 2006), 171–7.

38 Zizioulas, *Being as Communion*, 59.

39 John Zizioulas, "Human Capacity and Human Incapacity: A Theological Exploration of Personhood," *Scottish Journal of Theology* 28, no. 5 (1975): 407.

40 See Christos Yannaras, *Person and Eros* (Brookline, MA: Holy Cross Orthodox Press, 2007), 19.

41 Zizioulas, *Being as Communion*, 55.

42 Zizioulas, *Being as Communion*, 46.

43 Zizioulas, *Communion and Otherness*, 9.

44 Zizioulas, *Communion and Otherness*, 86.

45 Zizioulas, *Communion and Otherness*, 53–8.

46 The proceedings of the 2010 Volos conference have not been published in English. Program: http://orthodoxie.typepad.com/ficher/synthse_volos.pdf (accessed 10 June 2023).

47 Proceedings in George Demacopoulos and Aristotle Papanikolaou, eds., *Orthodox Constructions of the West* (New York: Fordham University Press, 2013).

48 Council documents available at https://www.holycouncil.org/ (accessed 16 June 2023).

49 John Chryssavgis and David Bentley Hart, eds., *For the Life of the World: Toward a Social Ethos of the Orthodox Church* (Brookline, MA: Holy Cross Orthodox Press, 2020). https://www.goarch.org/fr/social-ethos (accessed 10 June 2023).

50 "Bridging Voices: Contemporary Eastern Orthodox Identity and the Challenges of Pluralism and Sexual Diversity in a Secular Age" (2018–20). https://www.fordham.edu/orthodoxy/bridgingvoices/ (accessed 10 June 2023).

51 Brandon Gallaher and Pantelis Kalaitzidis, "A Declaration on the 'Russian World' (*Russkii mir*) Teaching," *Mission Studies* 39, no. 2 (2022): 269–76. Published online 13 March 2022: https://publicorthodoxy.org/2022/03/13/ (accessed 23 November 2023).

Recommended Reading

Primary

Afanasiev, Nicholas. *The Church of the Holy Spirit*. Notre Dame, IN: University of Notre Dame Press, 2007.

Behr-Sigel, Elisabeth. *The Ministry of Women in the Church*. Crestwood, NY: St Vladimir's Seminary Press, 1991.

Bulgakov, Sergius. *The Bride of the Lamb*. Translated by Boris Jakim. Grand Rapids, MI: Eerdmans, 2001.

Bulgakov, Sergius. *The Comforter*. Translated by Boris Jakim. Grand Rapids, MI: Eerdmans, 2004.

Bulgakov, Sergius. *The Lamb of God*. Translated by Boris Jakim. Grand Rapids, MI: Eerdmans, 2008.

Bulgakov, Sergius. *Unfading Light: Contemplations and Speculations*. Translated by Thomas Allan Smith. Grand Rapids, MI: Eerdmans, 2012.

Florensky, Pavel. *The Pillar and Ground of the Truth: An Essay in Orthodox Theodicy in Twelve Letters*. Princeton, NJ: Princeton University Press, 1997.

Gallaher, Brandon, and Paul Ladouceur, eds. *The Patristic Witness of Georges Florovsky: Essential Writings*. London: T&T Clark, 2019.

Lossky, Vladimir. *In the Image and Likeness of God*. Edited and Translated by John Erickson and Thomas Bird. Crestwood, NY: St Vladimir's Seminary Press, 1974.

Lossky, Vladimir. *The Mystical Theology of the Eastern Church*. Crestwood, NY: St Vladimir's Seminary Press, 1976.

Lossky, Vladimir. *Orthodox Theology: An Introduction*. Crestwood, NY: St Vladimir's Seminary Press, 1978.

Meyendorff, John. *A Study of Gregory Palamas.* Crestwood, NY: St Vladimir's Seminary Press, 1964.

Plekon, Michael, ed. *Tradition Alive: On the Church and the Christian Life in Our Time – Readings from the Eastern Church.* Lanham, MD: Rowman & Littlefield, 2003.

Schmemann, Alexander. *For the Life of the World.* Crestwood, NY: St Vladimir's Seminary Press, 1970.

Schmemann, Alexander. *The Eucharist: Sacrament of the Kingdom.* Crestwood, NY: St Vladimir's Seminary Press, 1987.

Skobtsova, Maria. *Mother Maria Skobtsova: Essential Writings.* Maryknoll, NY: Orbis, 2003.

Stăniloae, Dumitru. *The Experience of God: Orthodox Dogmatic Theology.* 6 vols. Brookline, MA: Holy Cross Orthodox Press, 1994–2013.

Stăniloae, Dumitru. *Orthodox Spirituality: A Practical Guide for the Faithful and a Definitive Manual for the Scholar.* South Canaan, PA: St Tikhon's Seminary Press, 2003.

Williams, Rowan, ed. *Sergii Bulgakov: Towards a Russian Political Theology.* Edinburgh: T&T Clark, 1999.

Yannaras, Christos. *Orthodoxy and the West: Hellenic Self-Identity in the Modern Age.* Translated by Peter Chamberas and Norman Russell. Brookline, MA: Holy Cross Orthodox Press, 2006.

Yannaras, Christos. *Person and Eros.* Translated by Norman Russell. Brookline, MA: Holy Cross Orthodox Press, 2007.

Zizioulas, John. *Being as Communion: Studies in Personhood and Church.* Crestwood, NY: St Vladimir's Seminary Press, 1985.

Zizioulas, John. *Communion and Otherness: Further Studies in Personhood and Church.* London: T&T Clark, 2006.

Secondary

Arjakovsky, Antoine, *The Way: Religious Thinkers of the Russian Emigration.* Notre Dame, IN: University of Notre Dame Press, 2013.

Cunningham, Mary, and Elizabeth Theokritoff, eds. *The Cambridge Companion to Orthodox Christian Theology.* Cambridge: Cambridge University Press, 2008.

Gallaher, Brandon. *Freedom and Necessity in Modern Trinitarian Theology.* Oxford: Oxford University Press, 2016.

Gavrilyuk, Paul. *Georges Florovsky and the Russian Religious Renaissance.* Oxford: Oxford University Press, 2013.

Ladouceur, Paul. *Modern Orthodox Theology.* London: T&T Clark 2019.

Louth, Andrew. *Modern Orthodox Thinkers.* London: SPCK, 2015.

Plekon, Michael. *Living Icons: Persons of Faith in the Eastern Church.* Notre Dame, IN: University of Notre Dame Press, 2002.

Plested, Marcus. *Wisdom in Christian Tradition: The Patristic Roots of Modern Russian Theology.* Oxford: Oxford University Press, 2022.

Valliere, Paul. *Modern Russian Theology.* Grand Rapids, MI: Eerdmans, 2000.

Williams, Rowan. *Looking East in Winter: Contemporary Thought and the Eastern Christian Tradition.* London: Bloomsbury, 2021.

Witte, John, and Frank S. Alexander, eds. *The Teachings of Modern Orthodox Christianity on Law, Politics, and Human Nature.* New York: Columbia University Press, 2007.

Zernov, Nicholas, *The Russian Religious Renaissance of the Twentieth Century.* New York: Harper & Row, 1963.

Theological Movements

Feminist Theology

Karen O'Donnell

Introduction

The emergence of women's voices, feminist concerns, and wide-ranging gender analysis has, of course, been significant across the twentieth century, but these themes are given explicit recognition in the work of feminist theology. Feminist theology is not just women doing theology (although this is significant). Nor is it simply the affirmation of the feminine alongside the masculine, which often serves only to underline the dominant gender paradigm already well established within Christian theology. Rather, as Rosemary Radford Ruether argues,

> Feminism is a critical stance that challenges the patriarchal gender paradigm that associates males with human characteristics defined as superior and dominant (rationality and power) and females with those defined as inferior and auxiliary (intuition, passivity).[1]

Feminist theology, therefore, is theology that seeks to question – in a wide range of creative ways – the patterns and modes of theology that justify and perpetuate male dominance and female subordination.

The development of feminist theology, its interests, characteristics, and controversies, are intimately connected to the waves of the feminist movement. Beginning in the mid-nineteenth century, waves of feminism have surged and abated in pursuit of a range of different discourses and developments around the lives of women. The first wave of feminism, usually dated between the 1840s and 1920s, sought the (partial) emancipation of women. It included some of the first attempts to challenge the sexist paradigms of Christian theology. For example, in this period we find work by women such as Lucretia Mott. A Quaker abolitionist, Mott also campaigned for the rights of women especially around divorce, property and custody rights, and the right to vote. Elizabeth Cady Stanton was also a prominent women's rights campaigner and one of the primary authors of *The Women's Bible*, one of the first feminist commentaries on the biblical text.

The second wave of feminism began in the 1960s and was focused predominantly on issues of civil rights and antiwar sentiment (particularly in the United States). In the 1970s, as a result of this feminist wave,

Ford's The Modern Theologians: An Introduction to Christian Theology since 1918, Fourth Edition.
Edited by Rachel Muers and Ashley Cocksworth.
© 2024 John Wiley & Sons Ltd. Published 2024 by John Wiley & Sons Ltd.

ordination began to open up to women in some traditions and more women were studying theology in theological schools. For Catholic women, ordination was (and still is not) open, and yet this was also a period of substantial change for the Catholic Church thanks to the implications of the Second Vatican Council. Many prominent Catholic feminist theologians appeared at this time, for example, Mary Daly, Rosemary Radford Ruether, Elisabeth Schüssler Fiorenza, Elizabeth Johnson, and Susan Ross – to name but a few. It is ironic that this stream of Christianity, which denies women admission to the priesthood, has produced – and continues to produce – so many first-rate feminist theologians.

By the 1980s and the third wave of feminism, feminist theology was becoming firmly established. This decade, in particular, saw the development of feminist liturgies and the women-church movement. These liturgical communities were spaces in which feminist spirituality flourished and became contexts in which more radical feminist theology could be imagined. It is in this period that feminist theologians were challenged on their Whiteness and the extent to which their discourse can speak to women of color. Here we see, then, the development of theologies by women of color (often deeply rooted in liberation theologies) such as womanist, Latina, Asian, Africa, and mujerista theologies.

The fourth wave of feminism, its beginning usually dated to 2012, has been focused on empowering women, attending to intersectionality, and the opportunity that digital technology has offered to the movement. It has been characterized by a focus on sexual violence, misogyny, body shaming, rape culture, and sexual harassment. Attending to intersectionality has meant advocating with, and attending to, the voices of women of color, trans women, women who are economically marginalized, and women who are disabled. The internet has offered women the opportunity to speak about their experiences with projects and discourses such as Everyday Sexism, No More Page 3, and #MeToo (and #ChurchToo). Feminist theologians in this period have followed suit with works focused on purity culture, trauma, trans women, sexual and spiritual abuse, and intersectional approaches to feminist theology.[2]

Throughout the last two centuries, feminist theory has developed alongside these waves of feminism. Feminist theology bears a close relationship with feminist theory and has consistently developed in dialogue with progress in feminist theory. Feminist theology uses the tools of analysis developed in feminist theory in order to critique and transform feminist theological discourse. A significant element in contemporary approaches to feminist theology is grounded in theories of intersectionality.[3] Taking into account intersecting layers and experiences of oppression has been a significant element in more recent feminist theology in response to critiques regarding those earlier works that seem to suggest a universal female experience and a White, middle-class emphasis.

Survey of the Movement

How does one go about *doing* feminist theology? This is a key question in establishing any particular subdiscipline within theology. There is an expectation that a coherent approach to a particular way of *doing* theology can be found, and that this is what characterizes the discipline. This is not the case in feminist theology. Indeed, feminist theology has been accused of, and criticized for, lacking an internal methodological cohesion.[4] This is an accurate accusation but perhaps does not matter quite as much as some might think. One of the reasons for this lack of internal methodological cohesion is that feminist theology, as we have already seen, is really *theologies*. Because of its openness to plurality and the necessity of attending to the vast array of differences between women's experiences, there cannot be one single methodological approach. Indeed, some theologians who are perceived to be feminist might more readily identify themselves with liberation theologies.

However, central to the work of *doing* feminist theology is attending to the experiences of women and bringing these experiences into critical dialogue with the traditions of Christianity, whether that be sacred texts, Christian history, or women's experience within the life of the church today. The aim of this attention is to de/reconstruct theology that has been skewed by patriarchy, to imagine theology and scripture in a more just way, and to produce theological spaces that allow all people to thrive, remembering that patriarchy is a bad deal for more than just women.

There are a number of key themes that have been highlighted through the work of feminist theologians over the last fifty years. The starting point for feminist theology was a focus on Christology and the person of Jesus. For example, Rosemary Radford Ruether asked "can a male savior save women?" in her book *Sexism and God-Talk: Toward a Feminist Theology,* published in 1983. In this text Ruether demonstrates the disconnection between the messianic mission of Jesus, focused on "the vindication of the poor and the oppressed," and the later "patriarchalization of Christology," which ensured that women could not represent Christ because Christ came to be understood as "founder and cosmic governor of the existing social hierarchy and as the male disclosure of a male God whose normative representative can only be male."[5] The patriarchalization of Christology, Ruether argues, made the maleness of Jesus an ontological necessity, which ultimately meant that only male priests could represent Christ. Ruether's resolution here is to return to the Jesus of the Gospels, to return to a Jesus whom she finds remarkably compatible with contemporary feminism. She identifies the ways in which Jesus speaks on behalf of the marginalized and despised groups, his message of the Messiah as servant rather than king, and his rejection of dominant-subordinate relationships in community. The maleness of Jesus, she concludes, has no ultimate theological significance.[6] Where Jesus's maleness is significant is in the ways in which he subverts patriarchal expectations and privilege.

Although Ruether's chapter on this theme is considered a classic and essential reading in feminist theology, it is important to note that many other theologians have picked up the same theme in the intervening decades. For example, Nicola Slee reflects on Christology and the maleness of Jesus in her work *Seeking the Risen Christa* in which she explores, through poetry and art, as well as through academic discourse, the figure of the female Christa and the ways in which She illuminates theological presuppositions and biases within Christology.[7] Furthermore, Kelly Brown Douglas reflects, from a womanist perspective, on who Jesus is for the Black community. Douglas examines the incarnate Christ as one who is publicly executed and explores the meaning of this Christ in dialogue with spiritual elements that define a Christ image associated with Blackness. Similarly, Rita Nakashima Brock offers a feminist theological reading of Christology in her book *Journeys by Heart: The Christology of Erotic Power.* She writes:

> In moving beyond a unilateral understanding of power, I will be developing a christology not centered in Jesus, but in relationship and community as the whole-making, healing center of Christianity. In that sense, Christ is what I am calling Christa/Community.[8]

This radical rethinking of Christology sought to recover the relational nature of reality, long denied by classical Christian theology. Brock drew on the concept of erotic power found in the works of Audre Lorde and Haunani-Kay Trask to break out of death-dealing and hierarchical patterns of life and community and to explore a theology of child abuse. Rethinking Christology from a feminist perspective has broken a wide range of fresh theological ground. These refigurings of Christ bear testimony to the original question Ruether raised; they ask Christians to consider the significance of Christ again, in fresh ways that are relevant to human experience, particularly the varieties of experiences of women, today.

Of course, these Christological reflections are part of a much wider theme within feminist theology that challenges the idolatry of the male Trinitarian God. A key text in this theme is Elizabeth Johnson's work *She Who Is: The Mystery of God in Feminist Theological Discourse. She Who Is* draws traditional Christian doctrine concerning the Trinity into dialogue with women's experiences. She examines the history of Christian language for God and argues for a gender balance (or even gender neutrality) in the language we use to talk about God. Johnson offers a model of the Trinity based on this engagement with classical theology, women's experience, analysis of scripture, and feminist theology. She articulates the Trinity as Spirit-Sophia, Jesus-Sophia, and Mother-Sophia, drawing on the Hebrew framing of Sophia as Lady Wisdom and deliberately putting Spirit-Sophia first. Johnson offers her readers "the vivifying ways of the Spirit, the compassionate liberation story of Jesus Sophia, and the generative mystery of the Creator Mother" as she demonstrates that the "Christian experience of the one God is multifaceted."[9]

Alongside the centrality of Jesus's body in feminist theology, there is also a marked interest in bodies in general. This manifests as a particular interest in the functions and experiences of women's bodies and the ways in which these intersect with or impact upon theological discourse. For example, Serene Jones discusses the experience of miscarriage and stillbirth in her article "Hope Deferred: Theological Reflections on Reproductive Loss (Infertility, Miscarriage, Stillbirth)."[10] Jones argues that the experience of reproductive loss, although having no intrinsic value in itself, can offer theological insight into the nature and relationship of the Trinity. Jones highlights the ways in which the Christian tradition has been limited in its imagination regarding the way in which the living Godhead can hold death in the experience of Jesus's death on the cross.[11] A feminist approach to the same doctrine, but grounded in the narratives of women who have experienced reproductive loss, offers fresh revelation. Here we find a death that happens deep within God – perhaps in the very womb of God – and yet in this death God does not die but lives. Jones wonders if this might offer some kind of divine solidarity to people who experience such loss and if "this rupturing, anti-material tale of the Trinity won't stop their sorrow but [it] might lessen their sense of isolation."[12] Attending to the varieties of experiences of women's bodies offers a rich site for the feminist theological imagination.

Broadening attention to bodies further still, Sallie McFague offers an ecofeminist perspective on theology in her work *The Body of God: An Ecological Theology*. Drawing on her earlier work focused on theological language as metaphor, and the interpretative elements within such a position, McFague recovers the tradition from the early church of understanding the world (or the cosmos) as God's body. McFague understands God as Mother in the sense that God "bodies forth" the creation of the world. McFague thereby offers a more intimate connection between the created and the creator than the traditional *ex nihilo* model does. Developing this further, McFague establishes the metaphor of the world as God's body. By taking this perspective McFague establishes the significance of the human body (and all other bodies) – "we are all made of the ashes of dead stars."[13]

A further central element to the work of feminist theology is the critical rereading of texts, employing feminist methodologies of tending to gaps, silences, and absences. Many feminist scholars have employed this kind of hermeneutic in their engagement with both scripture and other theological texts. A significant example can be found in the groundbreaking work of Delores Williams whose book *Sisters in the Wilderness: The Challenge of Womanist God-Talk* was first published in 1993 and has been a classic text of womanist theology ever since. Williams considered the biblical figure of Hagar who was the mother of Ishmael. Cast into the desert by Abraham and Sarah but protected by God, Hagar is, for Williams, the prototype for the struggle of the African American woman. Hagar is an African slave, a surrogate mother, and a homeless exile and yet she survives. Williams particularly focuses on issues surrounding reproduction and surrogacy in her reading of Hagar in order to highlight the particularity of Black women's oppression. Williams highlights the ways in which womanist approaches to theology bring distinctive emphases that are not highlighted in feminist approaches or in Black liberation approaches. Womanist theology is, therefore, an important and significant theological corrective as it centers Black women's experience.

Away from dealing with scripture in this way, Grace Jantzen also applied a similar methodology to the examination of mystical texts within the Christian tradition. In her book *Power, Gender, and Christian Mysticism*, Jantzen demonstrates both the ways in which patriarchal systems oppressed and controlled women mystics and how the way in which mysticism is understood today, as being based on intense, personal experience, is misguided. Jantzen's work was a groundbreaking approach to the study of mysticism and the first attempt to read through the patriarchal systems and modes of obscuring, in order to reveal the underlying dynamic of power at work in mystical experiences and the ways in which they are received and interpreted by the wider church.

Ultimately, the overarching themes of feminist theology have been twofold. First, feminist theology has established loud and clear that there is no such thing as a neutral theology. Theologies that claim to be objective and neutral are theologies that, feminist theologians claim, have been written by men who *assume* that their position is one of neutrality. Feminist theology has exposed the fact that there is no neutrality and that theology is always born of and shaped by the body and experiences of the theologian. With that in mind, the second significant overarching theme in feminist theology is that when we attend to experience, particularly women's experience that has so long been absent from and ignored by "classical" theology, we find rich sites of theological discourse that offer theologies shaped in marked different, liberative, and life-oriented ways.

Named Theologians

It is difficult to select a small number of named theologians who are outstanding representatives of the work of feminist theology. Not because there are none to choose from – indeed, there are a great many examples of outstanding and genre-defining work within the field – but because to do so is contrary to some of the tenets of feminist theology and the mode of doing this kind of work. Many feminist theologians do their work in communities, either communities of scholars or communities of faith. They collaborate and produce work together. They meet to share their thoughts and lives together and produce collections out of those conversations. They produce resources for communities of faith. Feminist theologians are, often, community theologians. As such, raising up particular examples of outstanding representatives feels contrary to the ways in which much feminist theology is done. Nonetheless, the following four feminist theologians are all brilliant and influential representatives within the field of feminist theology.

Kelly Brown Douglas

Kelly Brown Douglas is an African American Episcopal priest and the inaugural dean of the Episcopal Divinity School at Union Theological Seminary in New York. Her book *The Black Christ* was republished in 2019 as a twenty-fifth anniversary edition, marking the ongoing relevance of this particular work and the impact of Douglas' womanist theology in general. First published in 1994, *The Black Christ* asked who Jesus is for the Black community. This question is emblematic of Douglas' theological interests. Her work has consistently drawn attention to the oppressive, homophobic, White nationalist, and anti-Black discourses that have shaped the North American psyche in particular. She notes that "[A]ny theological discourse that takes seriously the crucifixion-resurrection event must partner with God to mend the world of crucifying violence, such as white supremacy."[14] In *The Black Christ*, Douglas challenges the incarnational approach to understanding who Jesus is. She argues that this approach "does not necessitate, therefore, that Christian theology highlight Jesus's ministry as a standard for a Christian's response to injustice."[15] Douglas emphasizes, instead, a liberation approach and the imperative to understand Jesus through his liberating ministry to the oppressed. Highlighting the ways in which previous engagements with the Black Christ have had an exclusively male focus, Douglas identifies the ways in which Black women's experience has been ignored and devalued even within the Black church community itself. She carried this concern for those who are marginalized and devalued within the Black church community forward into her next major piece of research. Douglas' book *Sexuality and the Black Church: A Womanist Perspective* was the first research into the homophobia and heterosexism that characterized the Black church.[16] Having exposed these discourses within the Black Christian community, Douglas then sought to offer a sexual discourse of resistance from her womanist theological perspective.

Douglas' work has continued to be pertinent and relevant. Deeply grounded in academic research, her work has, nonetheless, been accessible and oriented toward supporting the life and flourishing of the Black community. For example, in the wake of recent attacks on Black people Douglas wrote *Stand Your Ground: Black Bodies and the Justice of God*.[17] More recently, in the aftermath of the killing of George Floyd and other Black victims of injustice, Douglas wrote *Resurrection Hope: A Future Where Black Lives Matter*.[18] In this book Douglas identifies the persistence of White supremacy and the White epistemology that dominates American identity and shapes the consciousness of American Christians. She turns to an exploration of her own faith, in dialogue with the faith of Black folks in articulating a resurrection hope for a more just future. Deeply rooted in her own experience, Douglas demonstrates the ways in which womanist theology spreads its arms wide and seeks the flourishing of Black communities in the face of the particular circumstances of injustice.

Douglas has consistently sought to examine and analyze the challenges facing the Black community (especially in the United States) from the holistic and life-oriented perspective of womanist theology. Her work embodies the marked difference between womanist and feminist theological work. Whereas feminist theology focuses on women's experience as the corrective to traditional forms of theology, womanist theology – as exemplified by Douglas' oeuvre – has a focus on the empowerment of all African Americans, women and men, in their quest for life and freedom in all its fullness.

Kwok Pui-lan

Kwok Pui-lan is a Hong Kong-born feminist theologian with particular interests in Asian feminist theology and postcolonial theology. Her research has particularly focused on the experiences of Asian women and the extent to which Christianity – in its postcolonial form – can offer new hope in the life of Asian women. To do this, she argues, Christianity must wrestle with both its inherited patriarchy and sexism. Kwok argues that traditional feminist theory (and thus White Western formulations of Christian feminist theology) has paid insufficient attention to the experience of women of color and the impact of colonialism on their experiences. She is deeply grounded in theologies of liberation and an acute global consciousness. As such she "leads the vanguard of feminist theologians who utilize tools and insights provided by post-colonial theory and criticism."[19] Her 2000 book *Introducing Asian Feminist Theology* is considered an essential text in feminist theology and Kwok has developed this work further still in books such as *Post-Colonial Imagination and Feminist Theology* and *Hope Abundant: Third World and Indigenous Women's Theology*.

Kwok notes that "as Asian Christian women, we have our own story, which is both Asian and Christian. We can tell this story only by developing a new hermeneutics: a hermeneutics of double suspicion and reclamation."[20] The task, therefore, of postcolonial feminist theology is threefold. It requires "resignifying gender, requeering sexuality, and redoing theology."[21] Drawing postcolonial and feminist theology into critical dialogue, Kwok applies a postcolonial imagination to biblical interpretation. In seeking to create an epistemic shift, this engagement with the postcolonial becomes a way of unmasking colonial epistemological frameworks of Christology, religious difference, creation, ecology, and hope. This is achieved through a pluricultural dialogue that seeks to overcome gender binaries in theology and to integrate queer sexualities into theological discourse. It also requires the place of oral history within theology, in recognition of the story telling traditions in Asia (and other parts of the world) that do not usually find epistemological acceptance in theological discourse. Ultimately, Kwok's method of postcolonial criticism engaged with feminist theology offers us an "ethical paradigm for a systematic critique" of global suffering and anguish.[22]

Kwok's work has been groundbreaking. Her book *Post-Colonial Imagination and Feminist Theology* was the first work to draw postcolonial theory into dialogue with feminist theology. As an Asian feminist scholar, Kwok has consistently drawn attention to the lingering impact and ongoing reality of colonialism in the Asian context.

Marcella Althaus-Reid

Argentinian born, Marcella Althaus-Reid became the first woman appointed professor of theology at New College, University of Edinburgh. A feminist theologian, deeply rooted in liberation theologies and equally interested in queer theologies, Althaus-Reid defies easy categorization. She has woven together feminist, queer, postcolonial, and liberation theologies into something distinctive and distinctly shocking. Her book *Indecent Theology* certainly shocked its readers with its explicit, sexual language when it was first published! For Althaus-Reid, all theology is sexual theology. She identifies vanilla (as opposed to BDSM or fetish) Christian sexual theology as oppressive and developed her perspective of indecent theology as a challenge to these oppressive theologies; a challenge that was both counterpatriarchal and heterosexist.[23] Althaus-Reid argues that sex has been constructed by a patriarchal worldview and that theology needs to be *indecented* in order to speak more authentically about sex and into people's real lives. For example, she argues that the virginity of the Virgin Mary needs to be indecented because it hides the real lives of many poor women who are, she argues, rarely virgins. Similarly, Jesus needs to be indecented as well. Althaus-Reid notes that Jesus "has been dressed theologically as a heterosexually oriented (celibate) man. Jesus with erased genitalia; Jesus minus erotic body."[24] She posits, instead, a bisexual Christ who offers an inclusive understanding of the Incarnation. Althaus-Reid brought class and economic analysis into dialogue with feminist theology and challenged feminist theologians to move away from the relatively safe ground of gender and to start considering women's bodies as sexual as well. She notes:

> The right not to be normal and to be able to rethink Christ from a sexual dissident position is the right to claim what Michael Warner calls "the trouble with normativity." This normativity is in reality abnormal; it disenfranchises the real life experience of people by forming them to adapt to an idealized discourse. As it is on earth, so in heaven theology becomes a distorting praxis, far from liberating, it itself enslaves even more.[25]

In her work *The Queer God*, Althaus-Reid extended a call to theologians to be unfaithful to sexual ideological constructions of God in order to "liberate God – a queer God who also needs to come out the closet of theologians of the status quo."[26]

Althaus-Reid wrote prolifically, always with a passion for radical inclusion and attention to those who are excluded from both theological discourse and from Christian practice. Her theological discourse has been significant not only in feminist theologies but also in queer theologies and theologies of the body.

Nicola Slee

Nicola Slee is based at the Queen's Foundation in the United Kingdom, and professor of feminist practical theology at the Vrije Universiteit, Amsterdam. With a career in feminist theology spanning almost forty years, Slee contributed chapters to influential and ground-breaking early collections of writings such as *Feminist Theology: A Reader* and *Swallowing a Fishbone: Feminist Theologians Debate Christianity*. Since then, Slee has established herself as a leading figure in feminist practical theologies. Her 2003 book *Faith and Feminism: An Introduction to Christian Feminist Theology* is a widely used introductory text on the subject. However, the distinctive and significant contribution that Slee makes to the discourse in feminist theology is as much in the way in which she *does* theology as it is in the results of her discourse.

Slee is a liturgist and a poet. You are as likely to see, in her work, poetry exploring key theological doctrines as you are to see chapters of academic prose. Slee weaves poetry, storytelling, and autoethnographic reflection together as she seeks to develop ways of doing theology that are authentic and that do justice to the experience of women. For Slee, this mixed mode approach to feminist theology is deeply rooted in her exploration of women's faith lives and spirituality. Indeed, her PhD research on women's faith development exposed some of the gender biases and inadequacies in work by people like James Fowler on the stages of faith.[27] When exploring faith lives with women, the patterns and processes that Slee uncovered were far more complex and iterative than Fowler's five stages made space for.

Slee has committed her academic work to understanding the faith and spirituality of women. She has convened a long-running research group focused on the faith lives of women and girls, producing a number of edited collections focused on these themes and establishing key methodological processes for researching female faith.[28]

As a feminist theologian with an interest in liturgy, Slee has also made significant and contemporary contributions to the growing set of feminist liturgies and rituals. These are always grounded in her poetic theological research and arise as a natural instinct out of this work. For Slee, her theological reflection must have an outworking; it must make an impact. This has often found expression in terms of liturgical innovation and creative spiritual practice. Books such as *Praying Like a Woman*,[29] *Presiding Like A Woman: Feminist Gesture for Christian Assembly*,[30] and *Abba Amma: Improvisations on the Lord's Prayer*[31] have provided many women (and men) with fresh revelation in liturgical practice, grounded in feminist approaches to theology.

Debate

"Controversies are the life-blood" of feminist theology according to Marcella Althaus-Reid and Lisa Isherwood.[32] This is because it is through internal disagreement and debate that feminist theology continues to push forward in its work. There have been a number of debates within and around feminist theology that, for the most part, are not resolved. For example, there is significant debate within feminist theology over what should be done about gender dualisms. Some feminist scholars argue that we should accept gender dualisms outright and seek to position women as fundamentally and essentially different to men. Other scholars have argued that feminist theology should reject gender dualisms outright. Another group still seek to reform the gender dualisms we have inherited into something more positive for women, seeking to reinscribe what it means to be female away from the passivity and receptivity of the Christian tradition.

A further key debate surrounds the ways in which feminist theology reappropriates characters and symbols of the tradition into feminine or gender-neutral positions. For example, feminist theologians have made much of the feminine noun used for God's Spirit in scripture, consciously depicting the Holy Spirit in feminine terms. We might, for example, mention the work of Elizabeth Johnson on Spirit-Sophia here.[33] Similarly, the Wisdom of God, characterized by Lady Wisdom in the Wisdom literature has been figured as female. Or we could turn to the work by people such as Carol Christ who have sought to present the Goddess – a female deity in contrast to the typical masculine-depicted God of Christian tradition.[34]

Ironically, given her status as the most significant woman within the Christian tradition, the person of Mary the mother of Jesus has long been a point of internal debate within feminist theology. Some feminist scholars have sought to make Mary a feminine icon, a powerful female spiritual figure who complements the perceived masculinity of the Triune God. In this mode, Mary has been much explored by feminist theologians who have sought to center Mary as a model for all Christians – women and men – who played a significant role in the early church (along with other women such as Mary Magdalene).[35] In contrast, however, some feminist scholars have abandoned Mary the mother of Jesus as of little or no benefit to the feminist cause. Highlighting her lack of choice in the Annunciation, her submissiveness and silence, and the way in which her image has been used to reinforce natality and motherhood as the ideal (often only) roles for women, these scholars have found Mary to be a lost cause with nothing positive to contribute to feminist theology.[36]

Perhaps the most significant internal debate, however, is around the word "feminist" itself. Who is "feminist"? And what does it mean to take a "feminist" approach to theology? As I highlighted earlier, the lack of internal methodological cohesion has long been pointed to as a critique of the feminist theological perspective. But internally, scholars have often queried – for a variety of reasons – whether the term "feminist" is the right one to use. Some scholars whose work is seeking to attend to the experience of women and to promote the full flourishing of women prefer, as we have already seen, other terms such as womanist, mujerista, Latina, among others. Indeed, this volume is open to critique in this sense too. We include within the volume a chapter on feminist theology alongside chapters on liberation theology, Black theology, and African women's theologies. But there is no discrete chapter on womanist theology – arguably a significant, creative, and developing movement within contemporary theology. Instead, womanist theology is included as a type of feminist theology. Although this might be the case, there are certainly those scholars who would argue that womanist is not simply a type of feminist. Indeed, Alice Walker (who coined the term "womanist") writes that "womanist is to feminist as lavender is to purple."[37] In this sense, it might make more sense to have a chapter on womanist theology with a subsection on feminist theology. Walker makes the point that feminism is incorporated into womanism, that womanism is a broader category than feminism. Womanism is instinctively pro-humankind and concerned not simply with gender inequality but rather with race- and class-based forms of oppression too. Douglas notes that "womanist theology attempts to empower African-American women and men in their quest for life and freedom as it makes clear that the God of Jesus Christ opposes the interlocking system of oppression that denies their humanity."[38] Given the focus on race- and class-based oppression within womanist theology, incorporating it into Black and/or liberation theologies might do more justice to the differences between feminist and womanist, many of which have been artificially flattened for the sake of brevity in this chapter.

Influence, Achievement, and Agenda

Feminist theology has exerted some important influence in theological discourse. In particular, feminist theology has established theological reflection on experience as a valid epistemological foundation for thinking theologically. Similarly, feminist theology has paid attention to the body, the located embodiedness of all theological work, and the ways in which the body must be attended to in theological thinking. Bodies matter and we have feminist theologians to thank for this move forward.

Similarly, feminist theology was, in its early years, at the forefront of theological discourse concerning women's ordination and women's ecclesial leadership across a range of denominations. Progress has, of course, been made in this area around the world. Part of this discourse was centered around conversation regarding the extent to which women were able to fully image the Divine, a key theme in feminist theology.

What has feminist theology achieved in the last sixty years? In the 1990 book *Feminist Theology: A Reader* – one of the earliest edited volumes on feminist theology – editor Ann Loades writes about the situation of feminist theology at that time. She notes that "the Christian tradition is fundamentally ambivalent for women."[39] She highlights the ways in which Christianity has offered women unhelpful gender constructions, the ways in which the symbolic system gives pride of place to male-related symbol and metaphor, the challenges in feminist theology to attend to the difference of experience in terms of class and ethnicity, and the optimism of feminist theology. She hopes that old stories can be retold, and new ones narrated, to articulate God in a more inclusive way.[40] Thirty-two years later, the same things are still true. Christianity still gives pride of place to male-related symbol and metaphor, as many who have tried to use female imagery for God in prayers in a local church context will tell you. Feminist theology is still conscious of the ways in which it does not always do well at attending to the intersectionality of experience. There are still conversations taking place regarding complementarianism, women as leaders within the church, and the patriarchal nature of Christianity. The androcentric fallacy is still alive and well in the current symbols and language of the church. Women have been ordained and are now, in some denominations at least, appointed as bishops. However, the patriarchal systems, structures, and symbols of Christianity remain largely intact. Much of what Loades articulated in 1990 still stands.

In the academic sense, there is a continued marginalization of feminist theology. Many students have little opportunity to engage with the richness of the tradition of feminist theology. Courses, for example on Christology, might include just one session engaging with feminist approaches to Christology. Similarly, feminist theology often remains as an optional module (if offered at all) in the same vein as other contextual kinds of theologies, gathering only a self-selecting group of people already interested in the area of study.

Perhaps this stagnation in progress and achievement is due to the problem of the optimism in feminist theology. Loades specifically notes that feminist theologians are optimists.[41] Some ground has been gained in the work of feminist theology – for example in the ordination of women – but that gaining of ground has the paradoxical effect of halting momentum.[42] Perhaps feminist theologians need to be a little bit more pessimistic and hopeless in order to see further advances in the dismantling of patriarchy, the liberation of women from oppressive systems, and the full flourishing of all peoples.

A key question to ask, both in retrospect and in terms of future agenda, is to what extent has feminist theology produced liberative change in real lives? All of the named examples of theologians offered in this chapter have written and developed feminist theology that is rooted in both their own experience and pays genuine attention to the lived experience of the women with whom they are working and for whom they are writing. Their work has had profound impact on both the lives of Christian women (and men) and on the ways in which theologians *do* theology. At the forefront of the agenda for feminist theology over the next sixty years must be broadening the impact feminist theology has on those training for ministry, on lay people, and on the dialogue within the church as a whole. Furthermore, this agenda must include countering the violent and regressive assaults on women's bodily autonomy and rights that are taking place across the world in the name of Christianity. Returning, sadly, to the fight of the second wave feminists, feminist theologians will need to articulate theologies that re-enshrine these principles as core to Christian theology as a whole if women, and indeed all people, are to flourish in the twenty-first century. As one sign held by an elderly woman at the 2017 Women's March on Washington after Donald Trump was elected president read, "I can't believe I'm still protesting this shit."[43] Amen, sister.

Notes

1 Rosemary R. Ruether, "The Emergence of Christian Feminist Theology," in *The Cambridge Companion to Feminist Theology*, ed. Susan Frank Parsons (Cambridge: Cambridge University Press, 2004), 3.

2 See, for example, Susannah Cornwall, *Sex and Uncertainty in the Body of Christ: Intersex Conditions and Christian Theology* (Oakville, CT: Equinox, 2010); Susannah Cornwall, *Un/Familiar Theology: Reconceiving Sex, Reproduction and Generativity* (London: Bloomsbury T&T Clark, 2017); Christina Beardsley and M. O'Brien, eds., *This Is My Body: Hearing the Theology of Transgender Christians* (London: Darton, Longman & Todd, 2016); Katie Cross, "'I Have the Power in My Body to Make People Sin': The Trauma of Purity Culture and the Concept of 'Body Theodicy,'" in *Feminist Trauma Theologies: Body, Scripture and Church in Critical Perspective*, ed. Karen O'Donnell and Katie Cross (London: SCM Press, 2020), 21–42; Karen O'Donnell and Katie Cross, eds., *Feminist Trauma Theologies: Body, Scripture, and Church in Critical Perspective* (London: SCM Press, 2020); Emily Joy Allison, *#ChurchToo: How Purity Culture Upholds Abuse and How to Find Healing* (Minneapolis, MN: Broadleaf Books, 2021); Shannell T. Smith, "'This Is My Body': A Womanist Reflection on Jesus' Sexualized Trauma during His Crucifixion from a Survivor of Sexual Assault," in *When Did We See You Naked? Jesus as a Victim of Sexual Abuse*, ed. Jayme R. Reaves, David Tombs, and Rocío Figueroa (London: SCM Press, 2021), 278–86.

3 Intersectionality is a term first used in Kimberle Crenshaw, "Demarginalizing the Intersection of Race and Sex: A Black Feminist Critique of Antidiscrimination Doctrine,

Feminist Theory and Antiracist Politics," *University of Chicago Legal Forum* 1989, no. 1 (1989): 139–67.

4 Marcella Althaus-Reid and Lisa Isherwood, *Controversies in Feminist Theology* (London: SCM Press, 2007), 1.

5 Rosemary Radford Ruether, *Sexism and God-Talk: Toward a Feminist Theology* (Boston, MA: Beacon Press, 1983), 120, 121, 123–6.

6 Ruether, *Sexism and God-Talk*, 135–7.

7 Nicola Slee, *Seeking the Risen Christa* (London: SPCK, 2011).

8 Rita Nakashima Brock, *Journeys by Heart: A Christology of Erotic Power* (Eugene, OR: Wipf and Stock, 2008), 52.

9 Elizabeth A. Johnson, *She Who Is: The Mystery of God in Feminist Theological Discourse* (New York: Crossroad, 2017), 201.

10 Serene Jones, "Hope Deferred: Theological Reflections of Reproductive Loss (Infertility, Miscarriage, Stillbirth)," *Modern Theology* 17, no. 2 (2001): 227–45.

11 Jones, "Hope Deferred," 242.

12 Jones, "Hope Deferred," 242.

13 Sallie McFague, *The Body of God: An Ecological Theology* (Minneapolis, MN: Augsburg Fortress, 1993), 44.

14 Kelly Brown Douglas, "A Womanist Looks at the Future Direction of Theological Discourse," *Anglican Theological Review* 100, no. 3 (2018): 582.

15 Kelly Brown Douglas, *The Black Christ: 25th Anniversary Edition* (Maryknoll, NY: Orbis, 2019), 585.

16 Kelly Brown Douglas, *Sexuality and the Black Church: A Womanist Perspective* (Maryknoll, NY: Orbis, 2018).

17 Kelly Brown Douglas, *Stand Your Ground: Black Bodies and the Justice of God* (Maryknoll, NY: Orbis, 2015).

18 Kelly Brown Douglas, *Resurrection Hope: A Future Where Black Lives Matter* (Maryknoll, NY: Orbis, 2021).

19 M. Shawn Copeland, "Kwok Pui-lan's Postcolonial Feminist Method," in *Theolgoies of the Multitude for the Multitudes: The Legacy of Kwok Pui-lan*, ed. Rita Nakashima Brock and Tat-siong Benny Liew (Claremont, CA: Claremont Press, 2021), 390.

20 Kwok Pui-lan, "Claiming a Boundary Existence: A Parable from Hong-Kong," *Journal of Feminist Studies in Religion* 3, no. 2 (1987): 122.

21 Kwok Pui-lan, *Postcolonial Imagination and Feminist Theology* (Louisville, KY: Westminster John Knox Press, 2005), 128–37.

22 Leela Gandhi, *Postcolonial Theory: A Critical Introduction* (New York: Columbia University Press, 1998), 176.

23 BDSM is an acronym for bondage, domination, sado-masochism and is shorthand for sexual practices that are kink-orientated rather than vanilla, i.e. plain, basic, conventional sexual practices.

24 Marcella Althaus-Reid, *Indecent Theology: Theological Perversions in Sex, Gender, and Politics* (London: Routledge, 2002), 114.

25 Marcella Althaus-Reid, *From Feminist Theology to Indecent Theology* (London: SCM Press, 2004), 64.

26 Quoted in Robert E. Shore-Goss, "'So Get Your Heels on for Liberation, and Walk!': Some Reflections in Memory of Marcella Althaus-Reid," *Theology & Sexuality* 15, no. 2 (2009): 141.

27 Nicola Slee, *Women's Faith Development: Patterns and Processes* (Hampshire: Ashgate; MPG Books, 2004).

28 See, for example, Nicola Slee, Fran Porter, and Anne Phillips, *The Faith Lives of Women and Girls: Qualitative Research Perspectives* (London: Routledge, 2016); Nicola Slee, *Fragments for Fractured Times: What Feminist Practical Theology Brings to the Table* (London: SCM Press, 2020).

29 Nicola Slee, *Praying Like a Woman* (London: SPCK, 2004).

30 Nicola Slee and Stephen Burns, eds., *Presiding Like a Woman: Feminist Gesture for Christian Assembly* (London: SPCK, 2010).

31 Nicola Slee, *Abba Amma: Improvisations on the Lord's Prayer* (London: Canterbury Press, 2022).

32 Althaus-Reid and Isherwood, *Controversies in Feminist Theology*, 3.

33 Johnson, *She Who Is*.

34 Carol P. Christ, *Rebirth of the Goddess: Finding Meaning in Feminist Spirituality* (London: Routledge, 1997).

35 See, for example, Ally Kateusz, *Mary and Early Christian Women: Hidden Leadership* (Cham: Palgrave Macmillan, 2019); Beverley Roberts Gaventa and Cynthia L. Rigby, eds., *Blessed One: Protestant Perspectives on Mary* (Louisville, KY: John Knox Press, 2002).

36 See, for example, Marina Warner, *Alone of All Her Sex: The Myth and Cult of the Virgin Mary* (London: Picador, 1990).

37 Alice Walker, *In Search of Our Mother's Gardens: Womanist Prose* (London: Phoenix, 2005), xii.

38 Douglas, "A Womanist Looks at the Future Direction of Theological Discourse," 588.

39 Ann Loades, "Introduction," in *Feminist Theology: A Reader*, ed. Ann Loades (London: SPCK, 1990), 4.

40 Loades, "Introduction," 1–10.

41 Loades, "Introduction," 10.

42 Claire Colebrook, "Toxic Feminism: Hope and Hopelessness after Feminism," in *Hope and Feminist Theory*, ed. Rebecca Coleman and Debra Ferreday (New York: Routledge, 2011), 11–24.

43 Joseph Hurley, "I Can't Believe I'm Still Protesting This Shit" Sign. Women's March on Washington, 21 January 2017, Photograph, 21 January 2017, Georgia State University Library Exhibitions, https://exhibits.library.gsu.edu/bridging-communities/protests-for-change-in-atlanta/womens-march/ (accessed 20 September 2023).

Recommended Reading

Primary

Daly, Mary. *Beyond God the Father*. London: The Women's Press, 1986.

Douglas, Kelly Brown. *The Black Christ*. Maryknoll, NY: Orbis, 2019.

Fiorenza, Elisabeth Schüssler. *In Memory of Her: A Feminist Theological Reconstruction of Christian Origins*. New York: Crossroad, 1994.

Isasi-Díaz, Ada-Mariá. *Mujerista Theology: A Theology for the Twenty-First Century*. Maryknoll, NY: Orbis, 1996.

Johnson, Elizabeth A. *She Who Is: The Mystery of God in Feminist Theological Discourse*. New York: Crossroad, 1992.

Kwok Pui-lan. *Postcolonial Imagination and Feminist Theology*. Louisville, KY: Westminster John Knox Press, 2005.

Ruether, Rosemary Radford. *Sexism and God-Talk: Toward a Feminist Theology*. Boston, MA: Beacon Press, 1983.

Secondary

Althaus-Reid, Marcella, and Lisa Isherwood. *Controversies in Feminist Theology*. London: SCM Press, 2007.

Fulkerson, Mary McClintock, and Sheila Briggs, eds. *The Oxford Handbook of Feminist Theology*. Oxford: Oxford University Press, 2012.

Isherwood, Lisa, and Dorothea McEwan. *Introducing Feminist Theology*. Sheffield: Sheffield Academic Press, 2001.

Loades, Ann, ed. *Feminist Theology: A Reader*. London: SPCK, 1990.

Parsons, Susan, ed. *The Cambridge Companion to Feminist Theology*. Cambridge: Cambridge University Press, 2002.

Watson, Natalie. *Feminist Theology*. Grand Rapids, MI: Eerdmans, 2003.

Postcolonial Theologies

Susan Abraham

Introduction: Postcolonial Theology of the Ampersand

Is postcolonial theology really theology? And can a constructive proposal that considers the complex ways in which theory and theology intertwine in the postcolonial context create a theological framework, thus denying the lure of binary thought that separates theory and theology? Christian theology has historically attempted such a constructive and complex move as it integrated Jewish, Greek, and Roman philosophical and cultural thought into its metaphysics, an original theology of the ampersand. This chapter attempts to track some of the multiple strands of postcolonial theology circulating around the world by surveying some of the influential thinkers in the field today.

In an overview of postcolonial theory and theology identifying competing and complementary strands of development, I attempt to show that postcolonial theology arising in formerly colonial contexts continued to be "the study of Christian witness, a testimony of those who have been captivated by God."[1] Although some contextual particularities of postcolonial theology create a specific framework for doing theology, there are universal elements resonant with the work of theological reflection. Competing claims of postcolonial theology need to be understood in relation to these particularities and attempts to universalize theologically. Postcolonial theology draws on the vibrant field of postcolonial theory, which arose in "the colonial aftermath, marked by a range of ambivalent cultural moods and formations which accompany periods of transition and translation."[2] Here, Christian theology is sometimes indistinguishable from the colonial enterprise. In other cases, religion is itself a suspicious category, denying the particularity of cultural contexts. Yet, for many postcolonial contexts, religion remains a vital force, often for the good, leading to new articulations of postsecular and postcolonial imaginations.

Postcolonial theology encompasses a form of political spirituality that consists of epistemic and theological practices that challenge the idea of oppositional relationships and focus instead on decolonizing the binaries of self and other. Hence, I seek to present this study as an exercise of a theology of the ampersand, aided by political spiritual practices. Of course, in one manner of speaking, Christian theology has been a consummate exemplar of a theology of the ampersand, in which the "and" of the Christological dogma

Ford's The Modern Theologians: An Introduction to Christian Theology since 1918, Fourth Edition.
Edited by Rachel Muers and Ashley Cocksworth.
© 2024 John Wiley & Sons Ltd. Published 2024 by John Wiley & Sons Ltd.

balancing the divinity and humanity of Jesus hints at a unique Christian episteme. A theology of the ampersand deliberately eschews the partisan politics of divides between religion/secular, theory/practice, and either/or. Advocating a both/and, such a constructive theological idea challenges the sheerly secular analyses of many postcolonial theoretical perspectives.

The complexity of postcolonial thinking can be tracked in two early anticolonial resistance movements: Mahatma Gandhi in India resisting British colonialism and Frantz Fanon in Algeria resisting French colonialism. The particularity of contexts created different strategies of resistance:

> If (Mahatma) Gandhi speaks in an anachronistic religio-political vocabulary [*sic*], Fanon's idiom is shot through with Sartre's existential humanism. If Gandhi's encounter with British imperialism generates a theology of non-violence, Fanon's experience of French colonialism produces a doctrinaire commitment to the redemptive value of collective violence. And if Gandhi enters Indian national politics in middle age, the more impetuous Fanon is dead, after a career of anti-colonial resistance, at the age of thirty-six.[3]

Postcolonial theory is explicitly not a simple opposition to Western modernity but a complex interweaving of some aspects of Western modernity with cultural particulars, including cultural premodernities. Such a counterintuitive contrariness of the postcolonial mood arises from the rueful realization that there is an "ambivalent and symbiotic relationship between colonizer and colonized."[4] Both Fanon and Mahatma Gandhi also were "modern" thinkers; both were acutely aware of the psychological effects of colonialism, a very modern stance toward understanding the postcolonial subject; both were very clear that colonized contexts needed to disavow nativist and cultural colonialism. Hence their anticolonial efforts were directed at cultural transformation and not necessarily an overturning of Western modernity. As Leela Gandhi aptly describes: "In their categorical disavowal of cultural colonialism, both thinkers attempt, albeit through very different strategies, to transform anti-colonial dissent into a struggle for creative autonomy from Europe. And it is this quite specific emphasis on creativity rather than authenticity which ultimately prevents both from espousing a nostalgic and uncritical return to the 'pre-colonial' past."[5] It is such creativity that led eventually to the development of postcolonial theology, which is expressly not a return to some form of imagined homogenous and nativist past.

In an early introduction to postcolonial theological method, biblical scholar Musa Dube asserts that even though the term "postcolonial" became common only in the last decade of the twentieth century, it is quite an ancient phenomenon. Biblical literature for example, often defined as "preexilic, postexilic," or as "First Temple and Second Temple," chronicles Israel's encounters with imperial powers.[6] The genre of "epic" in Western literatures, she observes, similarly deals with imperial encounters and struggles for liberation and independence. In the past five hundred years however, colonialism was foisted on the rest of the globe by Spanish, Portuguese, German, French, British, Russian, and North American imperial and military powers in the form of territorial and cultural expansion. Many genres of texts chronicled these incursions, according to Dube: "the novel, anthropology, natural history, map making, ethnography, travel narratives and biography."[7] Religion and theology were never far from these enterprises: "Studies of imperialism show that from ancient to contemporary times three main factors have repeatedly motivated and justified imperialism – God, Glory and Gold."[8] She recounts a popular story of how colonialism came to Africa: "When the white man came to our country he had the bible and we had the land. The white man then said to us: 'Let us pray.' After the prayer, the white man had the land, and we had the bible."[9] Dube's own practices of feminist postcolonial reading of the Bible engage such a complex of cultural and critical ideas.

A term associated with "postcolonial" is "decolonial." Decolonization deals with the historical aftermath of the colonial experience, in the wake of the departure of European colonial authority. In every corner of the globe touched by colonialism, however, decolonization did not bring the promise of true independence and freedom. Hence, scholars make distinctions between the historical reality of decolonization, referring to the newly "independent" state or nation, and the habits of thought, mind, writing, speaking, and doing in the years following independence. In the mid-1990s, drawing on liberation theologies and methodologies, Latin American thinkers began explicitly to use the term "decolonial" instead of postcolonial. In so doing, they drew closely on the methods of liberation theology and cultural and critical theory. However, African and Asian critical thinkers were already speaking of decolonization in the early 1980s to challenge the ways in which former colonies still remained in thrall of European frameworks and ways of thinking. The most influential of thinkers in this regard was Ngũgĩ wa Thiong'o, whose book *Decolonizing the Mind: The Politics of Language in African Literature* spoke about the hold the English language had on various forms of human knowledge. Whereas Thiong'o explicitly rejected writing in English for a countertextual practice, others persisted in their use of the English language arguing that critical thinking needs to have multiple dimensions to it rather than rejection and exclusion.

Similarly, theologian Robert Heaney asserts that postcolonial theology must "overturn the binaries of opposition."[10] Challenging binary and either/or thinking is essential in the spiritual and theological work of "finding each other" in postcolonial spaces. It is also a mistake to think that colonization and decolonization happened only in parts of the world other than Europe. Robert Heaney asserts that the Irish context is equally postcolonial and that in the literature of Ireland, especially in the poetry of W. B. Yeats, we can note the resistance to Empire and imperial power within Europe. Ireland can and should be considered a colonial settler society. In Yeats' poetry, "resistance to the hegemonic intent and cultural dominance of England toward Ireland since at least the twelfth century with themes of otherness, inferiority, liberation, identity, hybridization, resistance and decolonization" are themes that are resonant for postcolonial theology.[11] In situating postcolonial theology in the particular of Irish ethnic identity, Heaney, like others, is arguing that postcolonial theology is a form of resistant theology, especially resistant to hegemonic and Western ways of doing theology. However, precisely because Irish society is a hybrid one, Irish postcolonial theology wrestles with cultural, gender, and other particularities of identity, agency, coloniality, and hybridity simultaneously.[12]

It is difficult to provide a panoptical view of the growth of postcolonial intellectual inquiry and its effect on theological reflection; indeed, there is little unification of thought in the work of contemporary postcolonial thinkers and theologians. Hence, this essay cannot be considered a comprehensive view of postcolonial theology. Rather, it presents a constructive analytical perspective of current postcolonial theological writing, by highlighting three large geographical contexts and the theoretical perspectives developed out of these contexts, to propose that these perspectives have relevance for a theology of the ampersand. Critical here is the transdisciplinary nature of postcolonial theology. Thus, sociology, psychology, history, philosophy, literary theory (especially poststructuralism), and critical race theory all inform postcolonial theology. Postcolonial theology demonstrates an invigorating ability to think with forms of secular theory marking a postsecular renaissance for contemporary theological reflection.

Survey

Postcolonial and decolonial thought from South Asia

Cultural and contextual theologies from the mid-eighties pointed to the significance of "culture" for theology. Intercultural theology and enculturating theology have continuing salience for theological reflection. Postcolonial theory brought a renewed focus on "culture" and cultural particularity as a locus for theology, nuanced now with the history of colonial occupation. West and South Asian postcolonial theoretical debates sparked an intense interest in how language, spatiality, temporality, history, bodies, and human thought wrestled with the experience of colonialism. Interesting here are the disciplinary innovations that led to the development of postcolonial theology and a theology of the ampersand.

In political and cultural theory, "postcolonialism" emerged as an intellectual movement in the 1980s and early 1990s consolidating and developing around the ideas of Edward Said, Homi Bhabha, and Gayatri

Spivak. However, their body of work drew on earlier forms of anticolonialism, including Frantz Fanon, M. K. Gandhi, and others. These thinkers could be classified as providing a "cultural" frame for various fields in the humanities. In contrast, a stream associated with a world systems theory emerged with the sociologists Anibal Quijano, Maria Lugones, and Walter D. Mignolo, emphasizing decolonial strategies. Gurminder K. Bhambra, a sociologist, writes in this regard that "postcolonial and decolonial arguments have been most successful in their challenge to the insularity of historical narratives and historiographical traditions emerging from Europe. This has been particularly so in the context of determining the parochial character of arguments about the endogenous European origins of modernity in favor of arguments that suggest the necessity of considering the emergence of the modern world in the broader histories of colonialism, empire and enslavement."[13] As Bhambra elucidates, the "cultural" frame in the theoretical perspectives of Edward Said, Homi K. Bhabha, and Gayatri C. Spivak emphasized the diasporic contexts of these thinkers – West Asia (Palestine) and South Asia, focusing on the nineteenth and twentieth centuries. Decolonial thought on the other hand, while also dealing in the main with Europe, situates itself in a longer time frame, with "European incursions upon lands that came to be known as the Americas from the fifteenth century onwards."[14]

Said's most influential argument that European forms of knowledge production actively "orientalized" the non-West was developed in his book *Orientalism* and gave rise to the field of contemporary postcolonial studies. Orientalizing the non-West implied that it was not modern as the West was and was lagging in progress. Said thus laid the foundation for a postcolonial critique of Western knowledge, Western disciplines, and the way cultural identities are recognized by the West. "Identity" for Said, "whether of Orient or Occident, France or Britain, while obviously a repository of distinct collective experiences, is finally a construction of opposites and 'others' whose actuality is always subject to the continuous interpretation and re-interpretation of their differences from 'us.'"[15] Hence, instead of the separation of geographical and temporal spaces and times, he advocated for an understanding of the "intertwining and overlapping" histories of Europe and the Rest of the World. As Said demonstrated, knowledge production by the West depended on the universalizing of European perspectives by sidelining other forms of cultural production and knowledge.

Said's admonition to guard against the indifference in scholarship is clear in the work of Latin American decolonial theology. Reinerio Arce-Valentín, a Cuban theologian, asserts that the late 1990s heralded the explicitly decolonial turn in Latin American theology because decolonial thought is "a new approach, new in name and in theoretical elaboration but not in acts... useful in making us more critical about the use of theories, conceptions, ways of thinking and intellectual products that still contain implicit colonialist or colonizing contents."[16] The attention to the framework that creates these complex interweavings is termed "coloniality" and explained in the work of philosophers like Aníbal Quijano. Quijano had argued that Latin American thinkers were particularly attuned to the epistemic violence of coloniality, because Latin America "is without a doubt, the most extreme case of cultural colonization by Europe."[17]

Another aspect of cultural analysis is developed by Homi Bhabha in *The Location of Culture*. Bhabha's major concern is to articulate subject formation under conditions of colonialism. For Bhabha, postcolonial theory was never about cultural diversity. Instead, it focuses on the mechanisms of domination and subordination that create cultural difference. Thus, postcolonial theory was never about contributing to the requirement of the Western academy for "diversity." Instead, postcolonial theory centers the theories, practices, histories, discourses, and aesthetics of the colonized to challenge Western modernity. As Bhabha asserts, "Postcolonial perspectives... intervene in those ideological discourses of modernity that attempt to give a hegemonic 'normality' to the uneven development and the differential, often disadvantaged, histories of nations, races, communities, peoples."[18] This phenomenon, then, gives rise to the "survival" of culture, which depends on strategies of translation that articulate cultural difference, not as absolutes, but as a form of hybridity.

Cultural hybridity as a strategic and innovative practice to aid survival is a characteristic of many South Asian and African postcolonial thinkers. Bhabha argues that in the very act of domination, the colonizing culture "loses" its certitude and attempts to translate using colonial language. In fact, the very act of domination calls into question the legibility of colonizing techniques; for Christian colonial authorities, it became clear that "the Word of God," which they presumed to have universal recognizability, needed to be molded, shaped, and formed differently in the colonial context.[19] The resulting ambivalence around cultural signs, that is the simultaneous recognition of its power and limit, demonstrates that claims of cultural supremacy rests ultimately on the creation of cultural difference: "the concept of cultural difference focuses on the problem of the ambivalence of cultural authority, the attempt to dominate in the *name* of cultural supremacy is itself produced in the moment of differentiation."[20] Hybridity thus is central to thinking with the ampersand.

These ideas find their way into theological reflection as well, even if a theology of the ampersand is not as clearly spelled out. Robert Heaney in *Postcolonial Theology* asserts that hybridity is "a strategy employed toward decolonization that subverts the power of colonial authority and culture by mixing it with, for example, cultural practices, language, philosophy and texts from the colonized culture."[21] Hybridity therefore is often initiated by colonial power and is proof that the oppositional binary of colonizer and colonized is not an absolute binary. Of course, hybridity is also performed under colonial conditions by those colonized as well. In another of his postcolonial theological reflections, Heaney explains how hybridity works, explaining that the metaphysics of modern thought depends on mutually exclusive and discrete categories. These categories overemphasize difference: "Same/Other, Spirit/Matter, Religion/Politics, Subject/Object, Inside/Outside, Pure/Impure, Rational/Chaotic, Civilized/Primitive, Christian/Pagan, Transcendence/Immanence, Sacred/Profane, Native/Alien, White/Black, Male/Female, Rich/Poor, Whole/Disabled."[22] Postcolonial theology, following postcolonial theoretical thinkers, argues that the epistemological certitude of absolute difference garnered by these oppositional categories is not secure. Additionally, it examines the historical archive of Christian theology and has been able to show that Christianity has always been a "great hybrid, intermixing metaphysics, philosophies, and identities at the urban crossroads of the Roman Empire,"[23] reflecting of course, the basis for a theology of the ampersand.

Finally, the third protagonist in the field of postcolonial studies is Gayatri Chakravorty Spivak. Spivak is a secular feminist, Marxist, and deconstructionist who brought her considerable theoretical acumen to the field to challenge what she saw was the coopting of third world subjects and subjectivity into a regime of knowledge construction in which their voices were silenced. Her essay "Can the Subaltern Speak?"[24] was a stunning indictment of Western philosophy and its ventriloquism of third-world subjects, especially women. Hers is a critique of representation, and resistance to Western stereotypes of non-Western identity. In a manner of speaking, many feminists and Marxists are the most resistant to forms of hybrid thought, because the greatest violence of cultural erasure is done to women and to the marginalized poor.

Spivak displays an acute attention to the ethical dilemmas posed by representing women, the disenfranchised and marginalized from within the relative comfort and stability of the Western academy. Here she draws on conventions of disciplines such as anthropology and ethnographic studies of the non-West and eviscerates them for their "foreclosure" of the third-world subject or "subaltern." Spivak asserts that the central problem in European philosophy is the tendency of European thinkers to label any knowledge from the non-West as "marginal." Eurocentric thinkers simply presume that Europe is the center of the world. Consequently, Spivak's constructive proposal protects the ways in which subalterns, especially women, act and speak to resist all forms of hegemonic stereotyping, even as they are not accorded legibility and recognizability by dominant strands of Western knowledges. For a feminist postcolonial perspective, Homi Bhabha's notion of hybridity is not useful as women need to make claims *as* women. However, feminist postcolonial *theologians* explore epistemological and theological hybridities as they think with secular postcolonial feminist theory and theological possibilities for liberative thought. In Africa, for example, the postcolonial context is religious. Hence, if one is attempting to decolonize, or attempting to remove colonial apparatus from philosophical, cultural, social, and economic systems, one necessarily has to deal with religion. For Christian feminist theologians in Africa, this means battling both domestic and colonial patriarchal systems. Hence, "culture," for African feminist theologians is a field of intense violence in the domestic context, deepened by religious institutions. Maaraidzo Mutambara writes in this regard that "culture is to African women liberation theologians what race relations are to African American theologians."[25] This is a theology of the ampersand in a new key. African feminist postcolonial theologians deal with multiple contexts of oppression. Hence theological imagination of God, Jesus, creation, and church takes on an intersectional identity.

In Mutambara's analysis, "decolonial culture" is not nuanced enough in the work of (male) African theologians. Thus, images such as "Jesus as Chief, elder brother, and master of initiation are drawn from a hierarchically organized patriarchal system," that is indistinguishable from conditions of colonialism for women.[26] Following the Christianization of many parts of Africa, Christianity and Christian theology became even more culturally African, repeating existing cultural dynamics of gender violence, erasure, and oppression. Mutambara identifies the central hermeneutics informing African women's theology: "the dignity of every human being and the sacredness of life."[27] Yet, this principle too has its limits for African theology, for, as she asserts, "a cultural critique that is informed by a hermeneutical principle that is anthropocentric cannot adequately address African women's experience of environmental degradation."[28] Critical here is the intersectional nature of African Christian theology. African feminist theology shows up the poverty of feminist postcolonial theory that does not consider religion and theology, while simultaneously providing a critique of masculinist African intercultural theology that colonizes African women. Further, postcolonial African feminist theology must be intersectional; women's lives embedded not only in cultural contexts but also in natural and environmental ones are the source of African feminist theological reimagining.

As can be seen in this section, the impetus provided by postcolonial theoretical thinkers has opened a creative theological space for theologians from other parts of the world. Particularly on the African continent, "the moment of colonialism as well as its aftermath (the postcolonial) were profoundly marked if not driven by the conjunctural dialectic of religious and political motives through which it operated and was constituted."[29] Thus, African postcolonial theology adds to postcolonial theoretical perspectives in its insistence that "culture" as a category of analysis is both where colonialism succeeded, and also the site where "Christianity imposed a new moral consciousness and new forms of identity."[30] In the section that follows, another strand of postcolonial thinking, from Latin America, provides a different and self-avowedly "new" strand of postcolonial thought.

Postcolonial and decolonial thought from Latin America

Latin American postcolonial and decolonial thought was inaugurated in secular sociological studies, unlike the Western, South Asian, and African emphasis on cultural and literary studies. Here, a theology of the ampersand is found in the way Latin American theologians weave sociological insights with the cultural critical theory from Latin American sources. That move has had resonance with theologians around the world as well.

In the first book in English presenting the work of the sociological research collective from South America and the United States, Walter Mignolo asserts that "the decolonial option is an option among existing ones both in the academy and in the spheres of political theory, political economy and social practice."[31] Mignolo's perspective is decidedly secular. In drawing the "radical difference between postcolonial and decolonial projects" he deepens the alleged difference between the "postcolonial" and "decolonial," as "forking paths." Decolonial projects therefore are not the "first," as he acknowledges, but track something quite different: globalization since the 1500s in Latin America. Decolonization is an "epistemological reconstitution," with diverse participants around the world.[32] Mignolo further points out that decolonial thought ought not to be collapsed into Marxist thought, despite the strong economic analysis that attends decoloniality. Marxism, Mignolo argues, developed "in a relatively homogenous community where workers and factory owners belonged to the same ethnicity and, therefore, Marxism relied on class oppression and the exploitation of labor."[33] Decolonial thinking, conversely, focuses on racial discrimination and class exploitation in the colonies because Europe's "modern" project depended on the exploitation of those people of color. In this sense, it is not that decolonial project are subsumed under Marxism; Marxism is subsumed under decolonial thought. Decolonial projects, Mignolo argues, "dwell in the borders, are anchored in double consciousness, in mestiza consciousness."[34]

Arturo Escobar, another doyen of decolonial thought, argues that one of the distinctive features of Latin American decolonial thought is the idea of "borders." Borders are the occasion for new epistemologies, thinking and discourse. In this view, any Eurocentric frame, including that of deconstruction, is not border thinking, because border thinking begins with the fact of colonial difference. "Colonial difference" is a term that highlights "the knowledge and cultural dimensions of the subalternization processes effected by the coloniality of power."[35] Such a discourse then interrupts and interrogates "modernity" as a solely European phenomenon that is spurred on in different parts of the world through globalization.[36] Enrique Dussel and others dismiss the globalizing notion of modernity in favor of transmodernity, with its starting point in the perspective, knowledges, and discourses of subaltern others as constitutive of modernity itself.

The issue of gender and its colonial frame is the focus of Latin American feminist analyses of coloniality. María Lugones asserts that men who are racialized remain "indifferent" to the ways in which masculinism perpetuates violence and oppression against women both in everyday situations as well as in the discourses of liberation. Whereas the coloniality/modernity collective emphasized the exclusion of the other (male persons) in Eurocentric systems, Lugones' focus is on the much more complex lived reality of women laboring under multiple oppressions. In one essay, she asserts that the coloniality of power reveals that there are no women or men in the colonies: "I understand the dichotomous hierarchy between the human and the non-human as the central dichotomy of colonial modernity."[37] When the only "real" humans in the religion, culture, and politics of European colonial logic were bourgeois White Europeans, the colonized, both men and women, were relegated to the status of "animal." Christian colonial missionizing was among the worst structures employing the gender/sex logic. Western style feminism also, is very much guilty of similar tactics of erasure and demonization of women from colonized contexts. Lugones advocates for alliances to be formed at the "fractured locus" of erasure and alienation. The very starting point should be the capacity to form alliances and coalitions as resistances, a constructive rather than deconstructive approach.

Contemporary postcolonial Latin American theologians draw on the ideas of the coloniality/modernity research collective with great success. One area of generative conversation in theological reflection is that of biblical studies. Fernando Segovia provides a view into the ways in which postcolonial and decolonial thought affected his biblical scholarship. In his book *Decolonizing Biblical Studies*, Segovia writes:

> I can no longer describe myself solely as a biblical critic, despite my specific hiring, assignment and location in a department of New Testament and Early Christianity within the context of the highly compartmentalized academic divisions of a graduate department of religion based in a liberal Protestant divinity school. At the very least, I must describe myself as a constructive theologian as well, not only because I presently regard the traditional distinctions between critic and theologian as having altogether collapsed, but also because I see myself as engaged in the task of discoursing about the "this-world" and the "other-world" in the light of my own sociocultural and sociohistorical context in the diaspora, both as a child of the non-Western world and a child of a minority group within the West.[38]

The decolonization of biblical studies, as he points out, was the result of development as an academic discipline in the early nineteenth century, culminating in the development of liberation and decolonial perspectives at the end of the twentieth. In his assessment there was the sequential unfolding of four paradigms in biblical criticism: the development and eventual waning of historical criticism; the rise and consolidation of literary, cultural, and social criticism; the interventions of sophisticated cultural analyses and studies beginning in the late 1980s and early 1990s; and, visible in the academy today, the competing and battling of the three paradigms. These methods, all of which continue to be in circulation in the academy, have led to a plethora of competing discourses and dizzying variety of scholarly positions.

The collapsing of disciplinary binaries, an addition to the challenge of epistemic binaries that Robert Heaney had identified, creates a fruitful complex for contemporary postcolonial biblical thought around the world. For example, Ericka Dunbar, an Africana biblical scholar, situates her "interpretations of Genesis 16 and Esther 1–2 in the context of the transatlantic slave trade in order to better understand the interconnecting relationship between colonialism, diasporization, and sexual trafficking and their deleterious impact on Africana girls' and women's identities."[39] For Dunbar, decolonization and postcolonial critique are intersectional and polyvocal, emphasizing the economic frame of culture and its effects on women. Thus, in her postcolonial reading of the virgin girls in the book of Esther are salient insights on how sexual trafficking affects Black and Brown female bodies more than White female bodies:

> What is often overlooked in traditional interpretations of Chapter 2 [of the book of Esther] but stands out with the foregrounding of polyvocal Africana hermeneutics is that many of the virgin girls come from geographical locales that are predominantly inhabited by Black and Brown girls today: Africa and India. Analogously, Black and Brown females are disproportionately vulnerable to and targeted by sexual traffickers in contemporary contexts.[40]

Dunbar's essay speaks to the entanglement of oppressions in the postcolonial African context. The anthology of essays in which her work appears also underscore the importance of decentering the *anthropos* in postcolonial theology. As the editors assert, the intersection of the themes of colonialism, gender, religion, the earth, and liberation coalesce in African women's postcolonial theology, issues of direct concern to Latin American postcolonial theorists. These constructive theological interventions reveal the contours of the postcolonial theology of the ampersand. From Latin American thought postcolonial theologians adopt a stance of intersectionality, polyvocality, and multiplicity, all characteristics of the theology of the ampersand. Postcolonial biblical scholars thus maintain a delicate balance between the poles of cultural identity, religion, faith communities, gender, and exploitative economic realities.

Postcolonial and decolonial thought from Africa and the African Diaspora

In what is one of the most challenging articulations of postcolonial theological thinking, Cameroonian philosopher Achille Mbembe provides a deconstructive reading of Western Christian theology. It is primarily a criticism of the received Christian theology of colonial Europe. In this essay, Mbembe provides a psychological reading of Christian monotheism, arguing that it "based itself on the idea of universal dominion in time as well as in space."[41] The universality of Christian monotheism created part of the ideological context for colonialism and conquest. He writes:

> The realm in which Christ's lordship was exercised was the world as a whole, in all its activities and its full extent. From Christ's status as head of humanity followed Christianity's claim to a universal empire. In other words, Christ's power to rule was inseparable from his right of property, a right of property exercised, naturally, over so-called Christian lands. His sovereignty and his domination extended "from sea to sea as far as the ends of the earth." From this it followed that the property of the infidels belonged to him, by virtue of the universality of his reign; this conclusion opened the way to assertion of the right of conquest.[42]

Such an analysis of the power of Christian theology in the apparatus of colonization seems to be an indictment of all religion for postcolonial thought. However, Mbembe's indictment of the psychic wounding of colonialism is more balanced in recent work on decolonization.

Decolonization in Mbembe's view is an "active will to community, a will to life."[43] Decolonization is oriented to a future, as yet unwritten, and arrived at through experimentation, innovation and originality. As he argues, decolonization in Africa occurred in the aftermath of the colonization of Africa, a consequence of European imperial designs and ambitions following the "active imperialism of European modern history" occurred in three waves: First, the Iberian and Dutch conquests in the New World and Asia between 1520 and 1620; second, between 1760 and 1830 when European empires seized territories in South and Southeast Asia, North America, and Australasia, marked by the transatlantic slave trade; and third the Partition of Africa after 1878, the Russian conquest of central Asia and the battle for trade concessions in China.[44] Mbembe's presentation of the colonial and postcolonial experience is by far the most astute, benefiting of course from the decades-long studies on colonialism from Asian and South American thinkers.

One of the ways in which this is clear is his exposition on how decolonization was a "decentering" moment. In many parts of Africa, decolonization was "granted, rather than won."[45] Thus, his understanding of colonization is that it was in many ways "a coproduction of colonizers and colonized." From different positions of power, a past was created by both entities, which cannot be called a shared past. Following the departure of colonial powers from the continent, there was a period of destruction of institutions and organizations that were deemed colonial. In the wake of this destruction was a period of "reassemblage" into a complex and multiple plurality. However, his incisive analysis provides yet another dimension to postcolonial theoretical understandings. Decolonization is not just the attribute of the formerly colonized. Former colonizers also must engage in processes of decolonization. In the essay titled "Proximity without Reciprocity," Mbembe argues that decolonization in the former colony (both the colonizing and colonized colony) must take the form of a "radical critique of the totalizing thought of the Same,"[46] an idea that is resonant with the idea of "colonial difference" articulated by Latin American postcolonial and decolonial thinkers. In this chapter, he elucidates the ethics of the postcolony, which have to do with three figures: the neighbor, the enemy, and the foreigner. Drawing on the work of Etienne Balibar, and addressing the French situation, Mbembe writes:

> I am starting from the idea that the problematic of the democracy to come is profoundly linked to the specific institution of the *border* – by which must be understood both the relation between the constitution of political power and the control of spaces, and the more general question of knowing who is *my neighbor*, how to treat *an enemy*, and what to do with *the foreigner*. The difficulty one experiences in taking responsibility for these three figures has mostly been linked to what existing democracies have done with the problem of race. By having so long considered the French republican model to be the perfect vehicle for inclusion and for the emergence of individuality, the Republic has ended up becoming an imaginary institution, and its originary capacity for brutality, discrimination and exclusion has been underestimated.[47]

In the chapter titled "Disenclosure," Mbembe asserts that decolonization has remained an abstract and academic term in Africa. In the postcolony, the term simply meant "the transfer of power from the metropolis to former colonial possessions at the moment of independence." Thus, in Africa, decolonization was the result of struggles for freedom. Freedom, and the reconstituting subjectivity it demanded, was a colossal task, presupposing "enormous epistemological, psychic and even aesthetic work."[48] This is because Western European modern imperialism has left a profound mark on the world. Its cultural, political, economic, and social frameworks were shot through with notions of White superiority. This is best seen in what he terms a "theory of decolonization" in the work of Frantz Fanon:

> Frantz Fanon is one of the very few thinkers to have risked something that resembles a theory of decolonization – a theory that is at the same time a hermeneutics (who the self, the ontological being,

or the subject of this process is) and a pedagogy (how and through what kind of praxis decolonization is to be achieved and for what aims that could be described as a universal). Fanon's theory of decolonization rests almost entirely on a political theory of property and ownership, which is at the same time and ethics of struggle. For Fanon, struggles for ownership are first and foremost about self-ownership ... Racism, in this sense, us fundamentally a technology of dispossession. "To own oneself" is nothing other than a step toward the creation of new forms of life that could be genuinely characterized as fully human.[49]

As he goes on to remind us, calls to decolonize are not new, pointing to Ngũgĩ wa Thiong'o's *Decolonizing the Mind*. In other words, the Latin American critiques of colonialism borrowed from these earlier African strands, as did the South Asian ones.

Like the forms of postcolonial thought presented here, analyses by African diaspora thinkers present complicated strands of histories of colonialism, anticolonialism, European modernity, racism, and complicity. Olúfémi Táíwò, for example, in an incisive analysis of Africa's future, presents an equally incisive analysis of Africa's colonial past. Colonialism in Africa, as he asserts, is inseparable from European modern Christianity. He is resistant of the popular idea that Christianity was a simple excuse for European racists in Africa. "Missionaries," he writes "are probably the most misunderstood of all the groups in the colonial situation in Africa."[50] In the introduction to his work he asserts that "the credit for introducing Africans to modernity must go to missionaries."[51] Thus he challenges African scholars who seem to collapse into one the three kinds of colonial entities that arrived in Africa: missionaries, administrators, and traders.[52] Missionaries were different than administrators, in Táíwò's opinion, because in his understanding, missionaries were enjoined to create Christian churches and Christian agents in Africa, especially before the eighteenth and nineteenth centuries. Marked racist behaviors and policies attended later missionizing, especially following the advent of the colonial administrator, but archival research reveals that earlier missions supported African agency and subjectivity to create "self-supporting, self-propagating and self-governing" African Christians.[53] He alleges that an anti-Christian view dominates the perspectives of scholars (such as Valentin Mudimbe) to condemn European missionaries.[54] Although it is true that the European missionaries did not see these native Christians as equal to them, the particular Christian hierarchical organization that was in play in Africa was an autonomy model of hierarchy, the goal of which was to help native Christians become self-reliant as soon as possible. Far more destructive, in Táíwò's view, is the "aid" model of hierarchy in which the native Christians were forced into a dependency relationship with colonizing Europeans.

Táíwò's focus is the "lag" between European and African modernities, echoing Edward Said's insights in *Orientalism*. The more serious colonial consequence for Africa was the way in which modernity is stunted in Africa.[55] Táíwò is also careful to say that the regional differences in Africa should be taken into consideration. Anglophone West Africa is markedly different in terms of the lag of modernity than other parts of Africa as native agency was far more visible in West African contexts. Critical here is Táíwò's notion that the collision between the missionaries and colonial administrators centered around anthropology: "the administrators' views that Africans were not members of the human family were the source of much tension between them and even the missionaries who subscribed to similar views of the humanity of Africans. After all, the missionaries could not escape the quandary of, on one hand, preaching the gospel of the oneness of all humanity in God, and on the other, suggesting that Africans might not apply. In contrast, because the administrators did not deign to answer to any power higher than the Colonial Office in London, they were not caught in any contradiction between that theory and practice."[56]

Decolonization in such a view is not a simple opposition of cultural identities. Similarly, Kwasi Wiredu, in his essay titled "Toward Decolonizing African Philosophy and Religion," argues: "Decolonization has nothing to do with the attitude which implies that Africans should steer clear of those philosophical disciplines that have at this particular point in history received their greatest development in the West."[57] Instead, what African thinkers need to do is to identify points of continuity rather than exclusion in the way they construct a decolonial future for Africa, another strand of a theology of the ampersand. Wiredu's complex argument calls for a form of decolonization that attempts to remove "undue" elements from African thought, even as African philosophers and theologians bring a form of "double criticism" to their work.[58] Such a double criticism eschews simplistic identity politics of exclusion, while simultaneously emphasizing the unique cultural gifts of African thought.

Achievement and Agenda

For a postcolonial theology of the ampersand, other complex theological conversations that reimagine decolonization as a work of dissolving the binary of colonizer/colonized press through the toxic logic of the "self and other" binary. For example, Choi Hee An, in her excellent proposal reframing postcolonial relationships from a practical theology perspective, maintains that the work of constructive theology is to develop nonbinary relationships by emphasizing the "third other." She writes:

> A postcolonial relationship is not just a nonbinary relationship in opposition to a binary relationship. Being the third other is produced from binary relations, but their third otherness is not recognized in these binary relationships because binary relationships do not allow the existence of being the third other, as they emphasize the existence of the binaries only.[59]

Choi's constructive proposal blends and hybridizes a sociological theoretical analysis of the "third-otherness" of Asian immigrant relationships in the United States with a practical theological perspective. Asian immigrant groups in the United States practice a postcolonial process of "deconstructing the current dominant discourses and structures of colonial/neocolonial and postcolonial constructions and reconstructing/reimagining the past, present and future with the power of people's resistance and challenges."[60] A practical political spirituality attends her sociological analysis. Drawing on Thich Nhat Hanh's idea that forgiveness is an act of making the heart big provides her with the ability to enhance processes of sociological deconstruction with spiritual practices. Another idea is hospitality. In Choi's presentation, hospitality can be enacted and received by anyone, including from and toward a colonial oppressor. This is a transformative postcolonial political spirituality of hospitality that highlights the Christian narrative of Jesus as both host and guest in the world. A final aspect of her political spirituality is the reemphasis on food as it relates to both forgiveness and hospitality. The work of postcolonial theologians is to bring such a spiritual dimension into the work of decolonial theology.

Remarkably, the sustained critiques of secular postcolonial theory have resulted in many postcolonial theorists revising the role of religion in their work. For example, the second edition of Leela Gandhi's critical introduction to postcolonial theory has some significant ideas that await further development by postcolonial theorists and theologians. A genuine postcolonial stance is the ability to critically appraise and perhaps even renounce the trappings of secular modern identity formations, especially nationalist ones. Tracking the use of religion in secular nationalist identity formation is a task of critical postcolonial theory and tracking the way in which faith communities strategize resistance is a task of postcolonial theology. Here, thinkers from Fanon to M. K. Gandhi to contemporary antiracist thinkers reveal how complex reformations of identity, cultural and religious, create complex coalitions and alliances. Resistance to nativist nationalist politics often comes from marginalized religious and theological perspectives. In India, Buddhism became a refuge for those who were and are the continuing victims of caste violence. Thus, the Buddhist idea that one is under an ethical obligation to exit a dangerous or harmful situation is one that B. R. Ambedkar used in India to great effect to counter the imperialist policies of the newly created Indian republic.

A similar moment attends the constructive framework of theology of the ampersand. Although it does not mean a simple opposition to the colonial enterprise, it also does not mean a simple acquiescence to the cruelty of colonialism and racism. Instead, it attends to the complex possibilities of alliance and cooperation to be discovered in history, traditions, religious and faith communities, and secular theory, all for the sake of liberation. Isabel Wilkerson, in *Caste: The Origins of Our Discontents,* tracks the journey of Ambedkar as he arrived in New York City from Bombay in 1913. Her words develop the arc of a theology of the ampersand:

> Many decades later, in the summer of 1946, acting on news that black Americans were petitioning the United Nations for protection as minorities, Ambedkar reached out to the best known African American intellectual of the day, W. E. B. Du Bois. ... Du Bois wrote back to Ambedkar to say that he was, indeed, familiar with him, and that he had "every sympathy with the Untouchables of India." It had been Du Bois who seemed to have spoken for the marginalized in both countries as he identified the double consciousness of their existence. And it was Du Bois who decades before, had invoked an Indian concept in channeling the bitter cry of his people in America: Why did God make me an outcast and a stranger in my own house?[61]

As Wilkerson explains, antiracism movements in the United States have much to learn from the history of the caste system in India, and anticaste activists in India have much to learn from African American activists in the United States. Only alliances and coalitions between the two can do the work of liberation in the two postcolonies. In both, the complex interlacing of religion with liberation politics leads to decolonizing structures. A future theology of the ampersand will develop how such decolonization took place historically and continues today in the work of countless postcolonial theologians attempting to decolonize by grounding their work in a Christian heuristic of thinking with both/and.

Notes

1   Robert Heaney, *Post-Colonial Theology: Finding God and Each Other amidst the Hate* (Eugene, OR: Cascade, 2019), 1.
2   Leela Gandhi, *Postcolonial Theory: A Critical Introduction* (New York: Columbia University Press, 2019), 5.
3   Gandhi, *Postcolonial Theory*, 18. Gandhi's characterization of Mahatma Gandhi's use of religion as "anachronistic" reveals her implicit bias against religion and belies the concluding comments in her book.
4   Gandhi, *Postcolonial Theory*, 11.
5   Gandhi, *Postcolonial Theory*, 20.
6   Musa W. Dube, *Postcolonial Feminist Interpretations of the Bible* (St. Louis, MO: Chalice Press, 2000), 48.
7   Dube, *Postcolonial Feminist Interpretations*, 48.
8   Dube, *Postcolonial Feminist Interpretations*, 47.
9   Dube, *Postcolonial Feminist Interpretations*, 3.
10 Heaney, *Post-Colonial Theology*, 34.
11 Heaney, *Post-Colonial Theology*, 13.
12 Heaney, *Post-Colonial Theology*, 10.
13 Gurminder K. Bhambra, "Postcolonial and Decolonial Dialogues," *Postcolonial Studies* 17, no. 2 (2014): 115–17.
14 Gurminder K. Bhambra, *Connected Sociologies* (London: Bloomsbury, 2014), 117–39.
15 Edward Said, *Orientalism* (New York: Vintage Books, 1978), 332.
16 Reinerio Arce-Valentín, "Towards a Decolonial Approach in Latin American Theology," *Theology Today* 74, no. 1 (2017): 41–8.
17 Aníbal Quijano, "Coloniality and Modernity/Rationality," in *Globalization and the Decolonial Option,* ed. Walter D. Mignolo and Arturo Escobar (London and New York: Routledge, 2010), 24.
18 Homi K. Bhabha: *The Location of Culture* (London: Routledge, 1994), 171.
19 Bhabha, *The Location of Culture*, 34.
20 Bhabha, *The Location of Culture*, 34, emphasis in the original.
21 Heaney, *Post-Colonial Theology*, 5.
22 Robert Heaney, *From Historical to Critical Post-Colonial Theology: The Contribution of John S. Mbiti and Jesse N. K. Mugambi* (Eugene, OR: Pickwick, 2015), 28.
23 Heaney, *From Historical to Critical Post-Colonial Theology*, 28.
24 Gayatri C. Spivak, "Can the Subaltern Speak?" in *Marxism and the Interpretation of Culture*, ed. Cary Nelson and Larry Grossberg (Chicago, IL: University of Illinois Press, 1988), 271–313.
25 Maaraidzo Mutambara, "African Women Theologies Critique Inculturation," in *Inculturation and Postcolonial Discourse in African Theology*, ed. Edward P. Antonio (New York: Peter Lang, 2006), 174.
26 Mutambara, "African Women Theologies Critique Inculturation," 180.
27 Mutambara, "African Women Theologies Critique Inculturation," 176.

28 Mutambara, "African Women Theologies Critique Inculturation," 185.

29 Edward P. Antonio, "Inculturation and Postcolonial Discourse," in *Inculturation and Postcolonial Discourse in African Theology*, ed. Antonio, 9.

30 Antonio, "Inculturation and Postcolonial Discourse," 12.

31 Walter Mignolo, "Coloniality of Power and Decolonial Thinking," in *Globalization and the Decolonial Option*, ed. Mignolo and Escobar, 15.

32 Walter Mignolo, "Coloniality of Power and Decolonial Thinking," 16.

33 Walter Mignolo, "Coloniality of Power and Decolonial Thinking," 16.

34 Walter Mignolo, "Coloniality of Power and Decolonial Thinking," 18.

35 Arturo Escobar, "Worlds and Knowledges Otherwise: The Latin American Modernity/Coloniality Paradigm," in *Globalization and the Decolonial Option*, ed. Mignolo and Escobar, 39.

36 Arturo Escobar, "Worlds and Knowledges Otherwise," 35.

37 María Lugones, "Toward a Decolonial Feminism," *Hypatia* 25, no. 4 (2010): 743.

38 Fernando F. Segovia, *Decolonizing Biblical Studies: A View from the Margins* (Maryknoll, NY: Orbis, 2000), 120 n. 2.

39 Ericka Dunbar, "Sisters of the Soil…Surviving Collective Cultural Traumatization: Intertextualities between Hagar, the Ethiopian Virgin Girls in the Book of Esther, and Mother Africa," in *Mother Earth, Postcolonial and Liberation Theologies*, ed. Sophia Chirongoma and Esther Mombo (New York: Lexington, 2021), 35.

40 Dunbar, "Sisters of the Soil," 42.

41 Achille Mbembe, *On the Postcolony* (Berkeley, CA: University of California Press, 2001), 226.

42 Mbembe, *On the Postcolony*, 227.

43 Achille Mbembe, *Out of the Dark Night: Essays on Decolonization* (New York: Columbia University Press, 2021), 2.

44 Mbembe, *Out of the Dark Night*, 2.

45 Mbembe, *Out of the Dark Night*, 4.

46 Mbembe, *Out of the Dark Night*, 106.

47 Mbembe, *Out of the Dark Night*, 91, emphases in the original.

48 Mbembe, *Out of the Dark Night*, 44.

49 Mbembe, *Out of the Dark Night*, 53.

50 Olúfémi Táíwò, *How Colonialism Preempted Modernity in Africa* (Indianapolis, IN: Indiana University Press, 2010), 51.

51 Táíwò, *Out of the Dark Night*, 7.

52 Táíwò, *Out of the Dark Night*, 49.

53 Táíwò, *Out of the Dark Night*, 7.

54 Táíwò, *Out of the Dark Night*, 57.

55 Táíwò, *Out of the Dark Night*, 4.

56 Táíwò, *Out of the Dark Night*, 11.

57 Kwasi Wiredu, "Toward Decolonizing African Philosophy and Religion," in *Inculturation and Postcolonial Discourse in African Theology*, ed. Antonio, 299.

58 Wiredu, "Toward Decolonizing African Philosophy and Religion," 291.

59 Choi Hee An, *A Postcolonial Relationship: Challenges of Asian Immigrants as the Third Other* (Albany, NY: New York University Press, 2022), 133.

60 Choi, *A Postcolonial Relationship*, 8.

61 Isabel Wilkerson, *Caste: The Origins of Our Discontents* (New York: Random House, 2020), 26–7.

Recommended Reading

Augustine, Sarah. *The Land Is Not Empty: Following Jesus in Dismantling the Doctrine of Discovery*. Harrisonburg, VA: Herald Press, 2021.

Bhambra, Gurminder K., and John Holmwood, eds. *Colonialism and Modern Social Theory*. Medford, MA: Polity Press, 2021.

Diagne, Souleymane Bachir, and Jean-Loup Amselle, eds. *In Search of Africa(s): Universalism and Decolonial Thought*. Medford, MA: Polity Press, 2020.

Go, Julian. *Postcolonial Thought and Social Theory*. New York: Oxford University Press, 2016.

González-Justiniano, Yara. *Centering Hope as a Sustainable Decolonial Practice: Esperanza en Práctica*. New York: Lexington, 2022.

Hong, Christine. *Decolonial Futures: Intercultural and Interreligious Intelligence for Theological Education*. New York: Lexington, 2021.

Lushombo, Léocadie. *A Christian and African Ethic of Women's Political Participation: Living as Risen Beings*. New York: Lexington, 2022.

Mongia, Padmini. *Contemporary Postcolonial Theory*. London: Routledge, 2021.

Patta, Raj Bharat. *Subaltern Public Theology: Dalits and the Indian Public Square*. London: Palgrave Macmillan, 2023.

Ramone, Jenni. *The Bloomsbury Introduction to Postcolonial Writing: New Contexts, New Narratives, New Debates*. London: Bloomsbury Academic, 2018.

Queer Theology

Patrick S. Cheng

Introduction

Since the mid-twentieth century, the voices of lesbian, gay, bisexual, transgender, intersex, and queer (LGBTIQ+) theologians have "come out" of the margins and shadows of Christian theology and moved to the center of the conversation. This emergence of queer theology parallels the emergence of Black, feminist, Latin American, Asian, and other contextual theologies since the 1960s. However, queer theology is more than just another type of identity-based or contextual theology. Queer theology is also about weaving together Christian theology with the academic discipline of queer theory. As a result, queer theology not only challenges traditional categories of sexuality and gender, but it also challenges the underlying assumptions and foundations of theology itself.

What is queer theology? Simply put, queer theology is "queer talk about God."[1] This definition, however, raises the further question of what is meant by the word "queer." On the one hand, "queer" is used as a shorthand term for referring to lesbian, gay, bisexual, transgender, intersex, and queer persons. Thus, queer theology can be understood simply as LGBTIQ+ persons – and our allies – talking about God. However, "queer" also refers to an interconnected series of ideas relating to the fundamental instability of categories, including those relating to sexuality and gender. These ideas include resisting ideas of categorization, challenging the idea of essentialism, questioning what is "normal," deconstructing binary thinking and presumptions, and exposing and disrupting power relations or hierarchies.[2] Thus, queer theology is not just about LGBTIQ+ persons talking about God, but it is also about "God talk" that engages with these interconnected ideas arising out of queer theory.[3] Indeed, it has been argued that "queer" might be "offered as a name for God," because both "queer" and "God" signify an "identity without an essence."[4]

This chapter provides an overview of queer theology as well as key voices and debates with respect to this field of study. First, it discusses the emergence since the mid-twentieth century of four key strands of queer theology: homosexual apologetic theology, gay liberation theology, lesbian relational theology, and queer (including transgender and nonbinary) theology. Second, it explores the work of five individuals who have shaped the discipline of queer theology: Marcella Althaus-Reid, Carter Heyward, Mark D. Jordan, Virginia

Ford's The Modern Theologians: An Introduction to Christian Theology since 1918, Fourth Edition.
Edited by Rachel Muers and Ashley Cocksworth.
© 2024 John Wiley & Sons Ltd. Published 2024 by John Wiley & Sons Ltd.

Ramey Mollenkott, and Robert E. Shore-Goss. Third, this chapter describes some internal critiques, or debates, about queer theology and its shortcomings. Fourth, this chapter concludes by looking at the influence and achievements of queer theology to date as well as suggesting a number of possible future directions for this discipline.

Survey

Four key strands of queer theology have emerged since the mid-twentieth century. They are, in roughly chronological order, (1) homosexual apologetic theology, (2) gay liberation theology, (3) lesbian relational theology, and (4) queer (including transgender and nonbinary) theology. This fourfold schema is consistent with a number of works that have traced the evolution of queer theology over time, including Elizabeth Stuart's *Gay and Lesbian Theologies: Repetitions with Critical Difference* (2003).[5]

Although naming these four strands of queer theology can be useful from a pedagogical perspective, it is important to recall that – as noted previously – queer theology resists the notion of fixed or unchanging categories. As such, these four strands should not be understood as the *only* way in which a survey of queer theology might be organized.[6] Furthermore, we should resist the temptation to view these strands as a linear "progression." That is, the earlier strands should not be viewed as less developed than the later ones.[7] Indeed, each of these strands remain present in the works of contemporary queer theologians.

Homosexual apologetic theology

Homosexual apologetic theology, which can also be described as "Gay Is Good" theology, emerged in the 1950s. This strand emerged in conjunction with attempts in the United States and the United Kingdom to abolish centuries-old secular laws that criminalized consensual sodomy between adults. As the late Yale University history professor John Boswell noted in his groundbreaking book *Christianity, Social Tolerance, and Homosexuality* (1980), there had been a "virulent hostility" in Western Christianity against same-sex-attracted individuals since at least the latter half of the twelfth century.[8] The adherents of homosexual apologetic theology argued that such condemnation was misplaced and that such individuals should not be condemned from either an ecclesiastical or a legal perspective.

One of the earliest works of homosexual apologetic theology was *Homosexuality and the Western Christian Tradition* (1955), written by Derrick Sherwin Bailey, a heterosexual priest and theologian in the Church of England who wrote extensively about theological matters relating to Christian marriage and sexuality. Bailey's book was revolutionary to the extent that it argued that the traditional Christian condemnation against homosexual acts was grounded in a misreading of the applicable biblical passages (including, for example, the Sodom and Gomorrah narrative in Genesis 19). As such, Bailey concluded that this tradition "can no longer be regarded as an adequate guide by the theologian, the legislator, the sociologist, and the magistrate."[9]

Five years later, Robert W. Wood, a gay minister with the Congregational Christian Churches, published his book *Christ and the Homosexual* (1960), which many consider to be the first theological work that spoke directly to the Christian homosexual in an empathetic and affirming manner. Wood argued that the practice of homosexuality by itself is "not necessarily a sin." Rather, the true sin is the "failure adequately *to adjust to being a homosexual* and in this failure permitting oneself *to grow out of harmony with God*."[10] In other words, rather than instructing Christian homosexuals to be celibate or to otherwise suppress their same-sex desires, Wood urged them to integrate their homosexuality with their relationship with God.

These works were followed in the 1970s by John J. McNeill's book *The Church and the Homosexual* (1976). McNeill, a gay Jesuit priest, argued that the Roman Catholic Church should view homosexual relationships as morally good and should also provide adequate pastoral care to lesbians and gay men. McNeill was expelled from his religious order in 1987 for refusing to stop his ministry to this community.

Although the homosexual apologetic theology strand of queer theology might seem unduly cautious – and perhaps even regressive – in its refusal to speak out more forcefully in support of LGBTIQ+ persons in the church, theologians such as Bailey, Wood, and McNeill were deeply courageous in their refusal to accept the status quo condemnation of such persons.

Gay liberation theology

Gay liberation theology, the second key strand of queer theology, emerged in the 1970s following the Stonewall Riots of 1969 in New York City. Unwilling to settle for "Gay Is Good," this strand brought front and center the demands by gays and lesbians to be liberated from their suffering and oppression. Gay liberation theology emerged from two interconnected movements. The first movement was the emergence of Black and Latin American liberation theologies in the 1960s. These theologies, articulated by theologians such as James H. Cone and Gustavo Gutiérrez, viewed liberation as a "religious quest."[11] Not only were such liberation theologies contextual – that is, "tied to the experiences and needs of concrete communities" – but such theologies were also "political in nature and religious in commitment."[12]

The other movement from which gay liberation theology emerged was the gay liberation movement. That movement was born out of the Stonewall Riots that occurred in New York City, during the early morning hours of 28 June 1969. The patrons of the Stonewall Inn, a gay bar in Greenwich Village – as well as other members of the LGBTIQ+ community – fought back against the police officers who were conducting a routine raid of that establishment. The Stonewall Riots led to the broader gay liberation movement, which was supported by a number of Protestant church organizations, as the queer religious historian Heather R. White has documented.[13]

One of the earliest works of gay liberation theology was the anthology *Loving Women/Loving Men: Gay Liberation and the Church* (1974).[14] The editors of that anthology, Sally Gearhart and William R. Johnson, wrote that, from the perspective of lesbians and gay men, "the institutional church must be understood to be an oppressor" as a result of its "fear and ignorance" that dehumanizes lesbians and gay men.[15] Other important works of gay liberation theology included J. Michael Clark's *A Place to Start: Toward an Unapologetic Gay Liberation Theology* (1989)[16] and Gary David Comstock's *Gay Theology Without Apology* (1993).[17] As the titles of these books made it clear, both Clark and Comstock distanced themselves from homosexual apologetic theology in favor of doing theology as a "liberating praxis"[18] that acknowledges the "overcoming and transforming [of] pain, suffering, and death" through the stories of the "Exodus and the life, death, and resurrection of Jesus."[19]

Perhaps the sharpest articulation of gay liberation theology was Robert Goss' powerful book *Jesus ACTED UP: A Gay and Lesbian Manifesto* (1993).[20] *Jesus ACTED UP* was written out of Goss' grief and rage in watching his beloved companion Frank Ring die of HIV/AIDS. Goss, an ordained Jesuit priest who resigned from the order after falling in love with Ring, critiqued the "social practices" of institutional Christianity as "unjust, exclusionary, and violent" and challenged such institutions to continue the "struggle for justice" and the "hope for liberation from oppressive exclusion and violence."[21]

The gay liberation theology strand of queer theology marked an important turning point with respect to the affirmation of LGBTQ lives. Mere toleration by the institutional church was not sufficient; ecclesiastical organizations were called to liberate gays and lesbians from suffering and oppression – an oppression that such organizations were complicit in creating in the first place.

Lesbian relational theology

Lesbian relational theology, the third key strand of queer theology, emerged in the 1980s as a result of the glaring absence of lesbian and other women's voices in the strands of homosexual apologetic theology and gay liberation theology. Indeed, as the lesbian theologian Mary E. Hunt observed, in surveying the field of queer theology for the *Dictionary of Feminist Theologies* (1996) in the mid-1990s, queer theology was "primarily male and not necessarily [a] feminist phenomenon."[22] Hunt did note, however, the existence of a number of lesbian feminist voices, such as those of Carter Heyward, Virginia Ramey Mollenkott, and herself.[23]

Carter Heyward, an Episcopal priest and theologian, was a key exponent of lesbian relational theology. For Heyward, God is not found above or beyond us, but rather *in between* us – that is, *within* our relationships. Heyward drew upon Audre Lorde's notion of the "erotic" and how it is present whenever we are fully engaged with another person or activity – whether it is in our "poems, music, lovemaking, dancing, meditation, friendships, and meaningful work."[24] In her book *Touching Our Strength: The Erotic as Power and the Love of God* (1989),[25] Heyward argued that God is found in the erotic – that is, wherever there is a yearning or longing for "embodied/incarnate mutuality." In other words, God is found whenever "two or more people are struggling to share power between/among ourselves."[26]

A similar lesbian theology of relationality can be found in Elizabeth Stuart's *Just Good Friends: Towards a Lesbian and Gay Theology of Relationships* (1995).[27] For Stuart, lesbian and gay relationships teach us that the "dynamics of sexuality and passion are experienced in *all* our relationships" and that we should not view our sexual relationships as being separate from our other relationships. In other words, those of us who are Christians are called to be "shamelessly, hopelessly, promiscuous in our love." That is, we are called not only to be "passionate friends to each other" but also to God who is our "Passionate Friend."[28]

Lesbian relational theology not only changed the trajectory of queer theology, but has also fundamentally changed how we think about feminism, gender, and theology.[29] As lesbian theologian Lisa Isherwood has observed, relational theologies "turn traditional Christian theologies on their head" by asserting that it is "between us and through our experiences" that we come to understand God. Furthermore, because this paradigm "gives agency to all living things and the cosmos itself," it places theology – as well as our conception of the divine – "within a new frame for reflection."[30]

Queer (including transgender and nonbinary) theology

The fourth key strand of queer theology is itself called queer theology, which emerged in the 2000s and includes, among other things, transgender and nonbinary theologies. As noted previously, the word "queer" is not just a shorthand for LGBTIQ+ people. Rather, the term refers to a constellation of ideas that destabilize categories and norms – especially with respect to sexuality and gender. These ideas include (1) identity without essence, (2) transgression, (3) resisting binaries, (4) social construction, and (5) multiplicity.[31] Each of these ideas are present in the various works that make up this strand of queer theology.

One mark of queerness is "identity without essence." That is, a key characteristic of queerness is its resistance to stable identity categories.[32] To that end, an important moment for queer theology was the publication in 2007 of the anthology *Queer Theology: Rethinking the Western Body*. This work, which was edited by Gerard Loughlin, explored the close connections between queerness and theology – and, in particular, the notion that queerness is an "identity without essence." In his introductory essay, "The End of Sex," Loughlin cites Thomas Aquinas for the proposition that God is "indubitable but radically unknowable." This is basically another way of stating that God is an "identity without essence." Because of this, God can be called "queer."[33]

A second mark of queerness is "transgression," or whatever is at odds with the "normal."[34] To that end, another important moment for queer theology was the publication of Marcella Althaus-Reid's *Indecent Theology: Theological Perversions in Sex, Gender and Politics* in 2000.[35] Althaus-Reid shocked the theological academy with her transgressive book about "Sexual Political Theology." Through provocatively titled sections such as "Mary, *Queer* of Heaven and Mother of Faggots . . . " and "French kissing God: the sexual hermeneutical circle of interpretation,"[36] Althaus-Reid critiqued the failure of liberation theologies to address the intersections between sexuality and poverty. In 2002, Robert E. Shore-Goss published *Queering Christ: Beyond Jesus ACTED UP*, in which he addresses similarly transgressive topics such as "Finding God in the Heart-Genital Connection."[37] More recently, queer theologians such as Laurel Schneider and Chris Greenough have written about transgressive topics ranging from a christology of promiscuity to a Christian theology of bondage, domination, and sadomasochism (BDSM).[38]

A third mark of queerness is "resisting binaries," or challenging the gender binary system in which there are only the two options of male and female.[39] In 2001, Virginia Ramey Mollenkott published the important work *Omnigender: A Trans-Religious Approach*,[40] which was one of the earliest articulations of a transgender and nonbinary theology. This was followed in 2003 by Justin Tanis' book *Trans-Gendered: Theology, Ministry, and Communities of Faith*, which articulated a "Transgendered Body Theology" as well as reflected upon "Transgendered Theological Thought."[41] In 2011, I published *Radical Love: An Introduction to Queer Theology*, which argued that Christian theology is fundamentally nonbinary – and thus fundamentally queer. In other words, Christianity arises out of a love that is "so extreme that it dissolves all existing boundaries, including those boundaries relating to sexuality and gender."[42]

A fourth mark of queerness is "social construction," which argues that there is "nothing natural, universal, or fixed" about contemporary categories of sexuality and gender.[43] One of the key exponents of this mark of queerness is Mark D. Jordan. Drawing extensively upon queer theory, Jordan's work focuses on the socially constructed nature of both Christian speech and sexuality. In 1997, Jordan published his groundbreaking book *The Invention of Sodomy in Christian Theology*,[44] in which he argued that the medieval term "sodomy" is not only "untranslatable," but that the "last thing we should do is to translate 'Sodomy' as 'homosexuality.'" Jordan's subsequent works of queer theology continue to address questions relating to social construction.[45]

A fifth and final mark of queerness is "multiplicity," or the refusal to accept what Laurel C. Schneider calls the "logic of the One" – that is, a mode of thinking that is characterized by oneness, indivisibility, and totality.[46] A logic of multiplicity, by contrast, is characterized by the boundary-blurring themes of fluidity, porosity, and interconnection.[47] For example, instead of classifying or reducing individuals to a single marker of difference (for example, sexuality), a logic of multiplicity affirms the "mutually co-constituted" nature of identities and oppressions such as race, gender, and sexuality.[48] As I have argued, multiplicity is a key theme in the works of queer of color theologians, who often find ourselves at the intersections of multiple identities and oppressions.[49]

Named Theologians

Since the mid-1950s, many individuals have contributed to the development of queer theology.[50] However, five individuals have played a particularly significant role in the evolution of this field: Marcella Althaus-Reid, Carter Heyward, Mark D. Jordan, Virginia Ramey Mollenkott, and Robert E. Shore-Goss. We now turn to an in-depth look at each of these theologians and their works.

Marcella Althaus-Reid

Marcella Althaus-Reid (1952–2009) was a self-described "indecent, Latina, bisexual theologian."[51] Her first book, *Indecent Theology: Theological Perversions in Sex, Gender and Politics* (2000),[52] is a foundational text in queer theology. According to Althaus-Reid, *Indecent Theology* was a "critical continuation" of feminist liberation theology, and it challenged liberation theology's "normative theological views" on gender and sexuality. *Indecent Theology* contained provocatively named sections such as "Talking obscenities to theology: theology as a sexual act" and "Black leather: doing theology in corsetlaced boots." For Althaus-Reid, the gap between feminist liberation theology and indecent theology was ultimately one of "sexual honesty."[53]

Born in Argentina in 1952, Althaus-Reid earned her PhD at the University of St Andrews in Scotland. A prolific writer and editor, Althaus-Reid served in a number of academic positions, including professor of contextual theology at New College, University of Edinburgh. In addition to *Indecent Theology*, she authored *The Queer God* (2003)[54] and *From Feminist Theology to Indecent Theology* (2004).[55] Althaus-Reid also edited many volumes on queer theology.[56]

Althaus-Reid used a multidisciplinary approach in her theological work, weaving together feminist liberation theology, queer theory and theology, postcolonial criticism, Marxist studies, continental philosophy, and systematic theology.[57] Following Althaus-Reid's death in 2009 after a long illness, her colleagues honored her legacy with the book *Dancing Theology in Fetish Boots: Essays in Honour of Marcella Althaus-Reid* (2010).[58] As Lisa Isherwood wrote in that volume's introduction, Althaus-Reid believed that theology had to be "built on earthquakes and that its job was not to heal the ruptures ... but rather to engage with and encourage the discontinuity." To that end, Althaus-Reid left a theological legacy of "complexity, challenge, instability, performativity and courageous love."[59] And this legacy lives on in volumes such as *Indecent Theologians: Marcella Althaus-Reid and the Next Generation of Postcolonial Activists* (2016).[60]

Carter Heyward

Carter Heyward (b. 1945) is an Episcopal priest and theologian who has described her own theological perspective as "liberal, feminist, LGBTQ, and liberationist."[61] In her groundbreaking book *Touching Our Strength: The Erotic as Power and the Love of God* (1989), Heyward argued that theology is about "making connections" – sensual, erotic, and conceptual – and that God should be understood as "erotic power." As such, God is not "above sex or gender" but is rather "immersed in our gendered and erotic particularities," including lesbian and gay relationships.[62] Looking back on her work over thirty years later, Heyward described *Touching Our Strength* as making the "theological case for sexual diversity as good and right."[63] In addition to *Touching Our Strength*, Heyward has written or edited at least fifteen other books, including *When Boundaries Betray Us: Beyond Illusions of What Is Ethical in Therapy and Life* (1993) and *Saving Jesus from Those Who Are Right: Rethinking What It Means to Be Christian* (1999).[64]

Born in North Carolina in 1945, Heyward earned her PhD in systematic theology at Union Theological Seminary in New York City. She was one of the "Philadelphia Eleven," the first group of women to be ordained as priests in the Episcopal Church on 29 July 1974. Although these ordinations were not conducted in accordance with canon law, they were subsequently regularized by the General Convention of the Episcopal Church. In 1975, Heyward was appointed to the faculty of Episcopal Divinity School, where she served in a number of positions, including the Howard Chandler Robbins Professor of Theology, until she retired in 2006. In 1979, Heyward was one of the first mainstream religious leaders in the United States to come out publicly as lesbian.

As noted in the "Lesbian relational theology" subsection, Heyward's theology of relationality and mutuality was key to the emergence of lesbian relational theologies in the 1990s. Perhaps even more significant, however, is Heyward's view that sexual pleasure should be experienced as "good, morally right, [and] without need of justification." Heyward contends that if we should justify anything theologically, it should be the pain and suffering that exist in our lives. Furthermore, as heirs to a "body-despising, woman-fearing, sexually repressive religious tradition," we Christians are called to engage in a "revolutionary transformation" of how sexual pleasure is understood.[65] Heyward's voice continues to be an important one in the field of queer theology.[66]

Mark D. Jordan

Mark D. Jordan (b. 1953) is a professor and theologian who has written extensively about queer theology. Author of the groundbreaking book *The Invention of Sodomy in Christian Theology* (1997), which examined how the theological category of "sodomy" was constructed by medieval Christendom, Jordan's scholarly interests have focused on how language is used to construct both sexualities and Christian theology. According to Jordan, the central question that underlies his writings is "how human language shapes us, shapes our bodily lives, especially in relation to things that exceed us, like the divine."[67] For Jordan, queer theology is not just about overcoming "exclusionary language" or interrupting "homophobic discourse." Rather, queer theology is about creating or "mak[ing] language" that lies "outside the forms of speech by which present power sustains itself."[68]

Born in 1953, Jordan earned his PhD at the University of Texas at Austin. Having taught at a number of different institutions, including Emory University, Jordan retired from active teaching as the Richard Reinhold Niebuhr Professor of Divinity at Harvard Divinity School in 2021. Jordan has written or edited works about a variety of theologians and philosophers across the centuries, ranging from Augustine of Hippo[69] to Thomas Aquinas[70] to Michel Foucault.[71] In addition to *The Invention of Sodomy in Christian Theology*, Jordan's books on queer theology include *The Silence of Sodom: Homosexuality in Modern Catholicism* (2000) and *Recruiting Young Love: How Christians Talk About Homosexuality* (2011).[72]

Jordan has influenced queer theology not only through his scholarship but also through his mentorship and support of future generations of queer theologians and scholars of religion. In November 2022, three program units of the American Academy of Religion honored Jordan through a panel discussion titled "Celebrating and Challenging the Convulsions of, and Beyond, Queer and Trans Studies in Religion and Theology: Honoring the Work of Mark Jordan."[73] In the words of one of the panelists, Jordan's work calls us into "a new way of becoming" and to "imagine new possibilities and futurities not just for academia, but for ourselves and the world."[74]

Virginia Ramey Mollenkott

Virginia Ramey Mollenkott (1932–2020) was an English professor and the author or coauthor of thirteen books, including several important works relating to the LGBTIQ+ religious experience.[75] As noted in the "Queer (including transgender and nonbinary) theology" subsection, Mollenkott published the groundbreaking work *Omnigender: A Trans-Religious Approach* in 2001. Mollenkott's goal in writing *Omnigender* was to challenge the "cognitive prison of *either-or*, a male versus female dualism" and to propose a "new gender paradigm" that would offer "liberation to everyone who has been oppressed by the old model."[76] In so doing, Mollenkott carefully examined what the Bible, church history, and science had to say about transgender people. Two years after the publication of *Omnigender*, Mollenkott revealed her own "gender-variant journey" as a "masculine woman" in a coauthored work, *Transgender Journeys* (2003), with Vanessa Sheridan.[77]

Born in Pennsylvania in 1932 to a deeply religious family, Mollenkott was sent to a Christian boarding school at the age of eleven when her mother discovered that she was in a lesbian relationship. While at boarding school, Mollenkott attempted suicide due to an overwhelming sense of sinfulness. Despite attending college at the fundamentalist Bob Jones University, marrying a fellow Bob Jones student (who was a cisgender man), and giving birth to a son, Mollenkott's same-sex attraction did not go away. Mollenkott eventually earned a PhD from New York University, separated from her husband, and began a forty-four-year career of teaching at William Patterson University in New Jersey.

In 1978, Mollenkott coauthored with Letha Dawson Scanzoni the classic book *Is the Homosexual My Neighbor?: Another Christian View* (1978). This book – based upon a thorough review of scripture and science – urged Christians to love and accept gay and lesbian people. In 1992, Mollenkott wrote *Sensuous Spirituality: Out from Fundamentalism* (1992) in order to demonstrate how sexuality and Christian spirituality did not have to be in conflict. Mollenkott died in 2000, but her memory lives on through the Virginia Ramey Mollenkott Award, which is awarded by the LGBTQ Religious Archives Network to young queer scholars in religion for outstanding scholarship in LGBTIQ+ history.

Robert E. Shore-Goss

Robert E. Shore-Goss (b. 1948) is a United Church of Christ minister and theologian who has published extensively about queer theology since the early 1990s. Shore-Goss' first book, *Jesus ACTED UP: A Gay and Lesbian Manifesto* (1993), is a foundational text in queer theology. Written while his companion was dying of HIV/AIDS, the book was a sharp critique of institutional Christianity's failure to listen to "the truth of gay and lesbian lives, the truth of their sexuality, and the truth of their Christian witness." As such, *Jesus ACTED UP* was a call to action for queer Christians to be in touch with their "holy anger" and to "follow Jesus' lead in his Stop the Temple action" as well as to "follow the lead of ACT UP and Queer Nation in their Stop the Church actions."[78] This was a far cry from the homosexual apologetic theologies of the 1950s.

Shore-Goss was born in 1948 and grew up in a Roman Catholic household. He was ordained a Jesuit priest in 1976, but he left the order in 1978 after falling in love with Frank Ring, a fellow member of the order. It was Ring's subsequent diagnosis of being HIV positive – and ultimate death from HIV/AIDS – that led to Shore-Goss' writing of *Jesus ACTED UP*. Shore-Goss received his ThD in comparative religion from Harvard University in 1993, and he taught in the religious studies department of Webster University in St. Louis, Missouri, from 1994 to 2004. Shore-Goss was licensed as a minister with the Universal Fellowship of Metropolitan Community Churches in 1995, and he transferred his credentials to the United Church of Christ in 2013.[79]

Following *Jesus ACTED UP*, Shore-Goss wrote or edited a number of works relating to queer theology and religious studies.[80] In 2002, he wrote *Queering Christ: Beyond Jesus ACTED UP*, a sequel to *Jesus ACTED UP*. With respect to queer biblical exegesis, he was a coeditor of *Take Back the Word: A Queer Reading of the Bible* (2000) as well as *The Queer Bible Commentary* (2006).[81] Other works written or edited by Shore-Goss included books on queer kinship,[82] gay Roman Catholic priests and the sexual abuse crisis,[83] grief narratives in religious traditions,[84] and queer ecotheology.[85]

In 2014, the Gay Men and Religion Group of the American Academy of Religion held a panel to celebrate the twentieth anniversary of *Jesus ACTED UP*. One of the panelists, Mark D. Jordan, said that *Jesus ACTED UP* followed in the tradition of the "best feminist and liberation theolog[ies]" because it called for the formation of "micro-communities of learning" that will result in "unforeseeable discoveries."[86] Shore-Goss' work continues to be relevant today because of this weaving together of queer theory and praxis.

Debate

During the past few decades, queer theologians have wrestled with a number of internal critiques, or debates, with respect to queer theology. One such debate relates to the failure of gay and lesbian theologies to address adequately the concrete suffering of LGBTIQ+ persons from a theological perspective.

For example, Elizabeth Stuart, in *Gay and Lesbian Theologies: Repetitions with Critical Difference* (2003), critiqued the failure of gay and lesbian theologies to address the AIDS pandemic from an eschatological perspective. Stuart wrote that such theologies "stuttered, stumbled and crumbled over the graves of those lost to AIDS,"[87] particularly in light of their failure to address issues of the afterlife in light of their liberal theological perspectives. Stuart's critique is not limited to liberal theologies; it can be argued that the post-structuralist underpinnings of queer theologies have failed to address these issues adequately as well.

Susannah Cornwall, in her book *Controversies in Queer Theology* (2011), has raised a number of other important debates relating to queer theology. One debate relates to the fundamental tension between LGBTIQ+ identities and queer theology. That is, to what extent does recognizing LGBTIQ+ categories of sexualities and gender identities undermine the instability of queer theology? Another debate relates to the overwhelming whiteness of queer theology and its adherents. What does it mean that voices and perspectives of color are often absent from queer theological discourse?[88] Other significant debates identified by Cornwall include whether queer theology is too "self-indulgent" in its linking of sexuality with transcendence, whether queer theology is too far removed from "theology on the ground" (particularly with respect to issues such as "preaching, praxis and pragmatism"), and whether queer theology is too "apolitical" in nature.[89]

One final debate relates to the relationship between traditional Christian doctrines and queer theology. Some queer theologians have used such doctrines as a means of demonstrating the fundamental queerness or instability of Christian discourse. For example, I have articulated a queer systematic theology – that is, engaging with classical theological doctrines from revelation to eschatology – through the lens of nonbinary thinking in my book *Radical Love: An Introduction to Queer Theology*.[90] Other queer theologians, however, have critiqued the use of Christian doctrine as apologetics and not going far enough in terms of embracing the underlying commitments of queer theory.[91]

Influence, Achievement, and Agenda

Queer theology has come a long way from the 1950s. The recognition and acceptance of queer theology by the academy (including the inclusion of this new chapter in the fourth edition of this work) has paralleled the broader societal acceptance of same-sex-attracted and gender-variant persons. Most mainstream Christian denominations and industrialized nations have stopped using theology as an explicit justification for the criminalization (including the imposition of the death penalty) of same-sex acts. Furthermore, a growing number of ecclesiastical denominations and governmental jurisdictions have recognized the legality of same-sex marriages as well as the existence of nonbinary gender identities under both civil and ecclesiastical law, often due to an implicit acceptance of the underlying commitments of queer theology.

However, the work of queer theology remains unfinished. Indeed, given the ambivalence of certain queer theologians to the idea of a queer *telos* (or end) or queer eschatology,[92] it could be argued that the work of queer theology should never be finished. As noted previously, one key shortcoming of queer theology is its overwhelming whiteness and failure to recognize the voices and experiences of queer persons of color. In response to this failure, a number of queer of color theologies have emerged in the 2010s and 2020s, including Pamela R. Lightsey's *Our Lives Matter: A Womanist Queer Theology* (2015), Jarel Robinson-Brown's *Black, Gay, British, Christian, Queer: The Church and the Famine of Grace* (2021), and Miguel H. Díaz's *Queer God de Amor* (2022). To that end, I have articulated a queer of color theology in *Rainbow Theology: Bridging Race, Sexuality, and Spirit* (2013) that is grounded in works of queer Black theologies, queer Asian American theologies, queer Latinx theologies, and Two-Spirit Indigenous scholarship.

Another shortcoming of queer theology is the relative absence of transgender, nonbinary, and intersex voices. A number of works have emerged in the 2010s and 2020s with respect to engaging with scriptural passages that have been used against such individuals, including Susannah Cornwall's *Intersex, Theology, and the Bible: Troubling Bodies in Church, Text, and Society* (2015), Teresa J. Hornsby and Deryn Guest's *Transgender, Intersex, and Biblical Interpretation* (2016), Austen Hartke's *Transforming: The Bible and the Lives of Transgender Christians* (2018), and Shannon T.L. Kearns' *In the Margins: A Transgender Man's Journey with Scripture* (2022). However, there remains a great need for more transgender, nonbinary, and intersex theologies, particularly from an ecclesiological or denominational context.

In addition to the aforementioned queer of color, transgender, nonbinary, and intersex theologies, there are a number of additional possible future directions for queer theology. These include queer postcolonial theologies,[93] queer ecotheologies,[94] queer theologies grounded in temporality and affect,[95] queer interfaith theologies,[96] and queer disability theologies.[97] In light of this multiplicity of topics, the future (in)directions and (im)possibilities of queer theology as a discipline seem exciting indeed.

Notes

1 Patrick S. Cheng, *Radical Love: An Introduction to Queer Theology* (New York: Seabury, 2011), 2.

2 See Chris Greenough, *Queer Theologies: The Basics* (Abingdon: Routledge, 2020), 26–8; see also Patrick S. Cheng, "Contributions from Queer Theory," in *The Oxford Handbook of Theology, Sexuality, and Gender*, ed. Adrian Thatcher (Oxford: Oxford University Press, 2015), 154–9.

3 It should be noted that this chapter focuses on theology – traditionally understood as "faith seeking understanding" from *within* the Christian tradition – as opposed to religious studies, which is generally written from a nonconfessional perspective. For a helpful overview of queer and transgender studies in religion, see Melissa M. Wilcox, *Queer Religiosities: An Introduction to Queer and Transgender Studies in Religion* (Lanham, MD: Rowman & Littlefield, 2021).

4 Gerard Loughlin, "Introduction: The End of Sex," in *Queer Theology: Rethinking the Western Body*, ed. Gerard Loughlin (Malden, MA: Blackwell, 2007), 10.

5 Elizabeth Stuart, *Gay and Lesbian Theologies: Repetitions with Critical Difference* (Aldershot: Routledge, 2003). Other helpful overviews include Mary E. Hunt, "Theology, Queer," in *Dictionary of Feminist Theologies*, ed. Letty M. Russell and J. Shannon Clarkson (Louisville, KY: Mowbray, 1996), 298–9; Robert E. Goss, "From Gay Theology to Queer Sexual Theologies," in *Queering Christ: Beyond Jesus ACTED UP* (Cleveland, OH: Resource, 2002); Daniel T. Spencer, "Lesbian and Gay Theologies," in *Handbook of U.S. Theologies of Liberation*, ed. Miguel A. De La Torre (St. Louis, MO: Chalice Press, 2004); Robert E. Shore-Goss, "Gay and Lesbian Theologies," in *Liberation Theologies in the United States: An Introduction*, ed. Stacey M. Floyd-Thomas and Anthony B. Pinn (New York: New York University Press, 2010); and Cheng, *Radical Love*, 25–42.

6 Indeed, there are multiple ways in which such a survey could be organized – including by theological doctrine,

theological controversy, or theological field of study. See, for example, Cheng, *Radical Love* (organized by theological doctrine); Susannah Cornwall, *Controversies in Queer Theology* (London: SCM Press, 2011) (organized by theological controversy); and Greenough, *Queer Theologies* (organized by theological field of study, such as contextual theologies and biblical studies).

7 Cornwall, *Controversies in Queer Theology*, 44–5.

8 John Boswell, *Christianity, Social Tolerance, and Homosexuality* (Chicago, IL: University of Chicago Press, 1980), 334.

9 Boswell, *Christianity, Social Tolerance, and Homosexuality*, 173.

10 Boswell, *Christianity, Social Tolerance, and Homosexuality*, 211 (emphasis added).

11 "Introduction," in Floyd-Thomas and Pinn, eds., *Liberation Theologies in the United States*, 1.

12 "Introduction," in Floyd-Thomas and Pinn, eds., *Liberation Theologies in the United States*, 1.

13 Heather R. White, *Reforming Sodom: Protestants and the Rise of Gay Rights* (Chapel Hill, NC: University of North Carolina Press, 2015).

14 Sally Gearhart and William R. Johnson, *Loving Women/Loving Men: Gay Liberation and the Church* (San Francisco, CA: Glide, 1974).

15 "Introduction," in *Loving Women/Loving Men*, x.

16 J. Michael Clark, *A Place to Start: Toward an Unapologetic Gay Liberation Theology* (Dallas, TX: Monument Press, 1989).

17 Gary David Comstock, *Gay Theology without Apology* (Cleveland, OH: Pilgrim Press, 1993).

18 Clark, *A Place to Start*, 12.

19 Comstock, *Gay Theology without Apology*, 10.

20 Robert Goss, *Jesus ACTED UP: A Gay and Lesbian Manifesto* (San Francisco, CA: HarperSanFrancisco, 1993).

21 Goss, *Jesus ACTED UP*, xv.

22 Mary E. Hunt, "Theology, Queer," in *Dictionary of Feminist Theologies*, ed. Russell and Clarkson, 298.

23 Hunt, "Theology, Queer," 298.

24 Carter Heyward, "Notes on Historical Grounding: Beyond Sexual Essentialism," in *Sexuality and the Sacred: Sources for Theological Reflection*, 2nd ed., ed. Marvin M. Ellison and Kelly Brown Douglas (Louisville, KY: Westminster John Knox Press, 2010), 12.

25 Carter Heyward, *Touching Our Strength: The Erotic as Power and the Love of God* (San Francisco, CA: Harper & Row, 1989).

26 Heyward, *Touching Our Strength*, 104–5.

27 Elizabeth Stuart, *Just Good Friends: Towards a Lesbian and Gay Theology of Relationships* (London: Mowbray, 1995).

28 Stuart, *Just Good Friends*, 213, 215, 246 (emphasis added). See also Mary E. Hunt, *Fierce Tenderness: A Feminist Theology of Friendship* (New York: Crossroad, 1991).

29 Rachel Muers, "Feminism, Gender, and Theology," in *The Modern Theologians: An Introduction to Christian Theology Since 1918*, 3rd ed., ed. David F. Ford with Rachel Muers (Malden, MA: Blackwell, 2005), 444–5.

30 Lisa Isherwood and Elaine Bellchambers, "Introduction," in *Through Us, with Us, in Us: Relational Theologies in the Twenty-First Century*, ed. Lisa Isherwood and Elaine Bellchambers (London: SCM Press, 2010), 2.

31 Cheng, "Contributions from Queer Theory," 154–9.

32 Cheng, "Contributions from Queer Theory," 155.

33 Loughlin, "Introduction" to *Queer Theology*, 10.

34 Cheng, "Contributions from Queer Theory," 156.

35 Marcella Althaus-Reid, *Indecent Theology: Theological Perversions in Sex, Gender and Politics* (London: Routledge, 2000).

36 Althaus-Reid, *Indecent Theology*, 63–71, 125–6.

37 Goss, *Queering Christ*, 56–71.

38 Laurel Schneider, "Promiscuous Incarnation," in *The Embrace of Eros: Bodies, Desires, and Sexuality in Christianity*, ed. Margaret D. Kamitsuka (Minneapolis, MN: Fortress Press, 2010), 231–46; Chris Greenough, *Undoing Theology: Life Stories from Non-Normative Christians* (London: SCM Press, 2018).

39 Cheng, "Contributions from Queer Theory," 157.

40 Virginia Ramey Mollenkott, *Omnigender: A Trans-Religious Approach* (Cleveland, OH: Pilgrim Press, 2001).

41 Justin Tanis, *Transgendered: Theology, Ministry, and Communities of Faith* (Cleveland, OH: Pilgrim Press, 2003), 161–75, 176–86. Although Tanis used the term "transgendered," the preferred term used by the transgender and nonbinary community today is "transgender."

42 Cheng, *Radical Love*, 139.

43 Cheng, "Contributions from Queer Theory," 158.

44 Mark D. Jordan, *The Invention of Sodomy in Christian Theology* (Chicago, IL: University of Chicago Press, 1997).

45 See, for example, Mark D. Jordan, *Recruiting Young Love: How Christians Talk about Homosexuality* (Chicago, IL: University of Chicago Press, 2011); Mark D. Jordan, *Convulsing Bodies: Religion and Resistance in Foucault* (Stanford, CA: Stanford University Press, 2015).

46 Laurel C. Schneider, *Beyond Monotheism: A Theology of Multiplicity* (Abingdon: Routledge, 2008) x, 1.

47 Schneider, *Beyond Monotheism*, 164.

48 Patrick S. Cheng, *Rainbow Theology: Bridging Race, Sexuality, and Spirit* (New York: Church Publishing, 2013), 101.

49 Cheng, *Rainbow Theology*, 97–109; Patrick S. Cheng, "Multiplicity and Judges 19: Constructing a Queer Asian Pacific American Biblical Hermeneutic," *Semeia* 90/91 (2002): 119–33.

50 For an online listing of many of such individuals, see the profiles gallery of the LGBTQ Religious Archives Network, https://www.lgbtqreligiousarchives.org/profiles (accessed 8 September 2023).

51 See https://lgbtqreligiousarchives.org/profiles/marcella-althaus-reid (accessed 8 September 2023).

52 Althaus-Reid, *Indecent Theology*.

53 Althaus-Reid, *Indecent Theology*, vi, 6–7.

54 Marcella Althaus-Reid, *The Queer God* (London: Routledge, 2003).

55 Marcella Althaus-Reid, *From Feminist Theology to Indecent Theology* (London: SCM Press, 2004).

56 These works include Marcella Althaus-Reid and Lisa Isherwood, eds., *The Sexual Theologian: Essays on Sex, God, and Politics* (London: A&C Black, 2004); Marcella Althaus-Reid, ed., *Liberation Theology and Sexuality* (Aldershot: Ashgate, 2006); Marcella Althaus-Reid, Ivan Petrella, and Luiz Carlos Susin, eds., *Another Possible World* (London: SCM Press, 2007); Marcella Althaus-Reid and Lisa Isherwood, eds., *Controversies in Feminist Theology* (London: SCM Press, 2007); Marcella Althaus-Reid and Lisa Isherwood, eds., *Controversies in Body Theology* (London: SCM Press, 2008); and Marcella Althaus-Reid and Lisa Isherwood, eds., *Trans/formations* (London: SCM Press, 2009).

57 Althaus-Reid, *Indecent Theology*, 7.

58 Lisa Isherwood and Mark D. Jordan, eds., *Dancing Theology in Fetish Boots: Essays in Honour of Marcella Althaus-Reid* (London: SCM Press, 2010).

59 Lisa Isherwood, "Introduction," in *Dancing Theology in Fetish Boots*, ed. Isherwood and Jordan, xvi.

60 Nicolas Panotto, ed., *Indecent Theologians: Marcella Althaus-Reid and the Next Generation of Postcolonial Activists* (Alameda, CA: Borderless Press, 2016). See also Thia Cooper, *Queer and Indecent: An Introduction to the Theology of Marcella Althaus-Reid* (London: SCM

Press, 2021) and Lisa Isherwood and Hugo Córdova Quero, eds., *The Indecent Theologies of Marcella Althaus-Reid: Voices from Asia and Latin America* (Abingdon: Routledge, 2021).

61 Carter Heyward, *She Flies On: A White Southern Christian Debutante Wakes Up* (New York: Church Publishing, 2017), xviii.

62 Heyward, *Touching Our Strength*, 90–1, 103, 105.

63 Carter Heyward, *The Seven Deadly Sins of White Christian Nationalism: A Call to Action* (Lanham, MD: Rowman & Littlefield, 2022), 236 n. 5.

64 Carter Heyward, *When Boundaries Betray Us: Beyond Illusions of What Is Ethical in Therapy and Life* (New York: HarperCollins, 1993); Carter Heyward, *Saving Jesus from Those Who Are Right: Rethinking What It Means to Be Christian* (Minneapolis, MN: Fortress Press, 1999). Other books by Heyward include Carter Heyward, *A Priest Forever: The Formation of a Woman and a Priest* (New York: Harper & Row, 1976); Isabel Carter Heyward, *The Redemption of God: A Theology of Mutual Relation* (Lanham, MD: University Press of America, 1982); Carter Heyward, *Our Passion for Justice: Images of Power, Sexuality, and Liberation* (Cleveland, OH: Pilgrim Press, 1984); Carter Heyward, *Keep Your Courage: A Radical Christian Feminist Speaks* (London: SCM Press, 2010); Heyward, *She Flies On*; and Heyward, *The Seven Deadly Sins of White Christian Nationalism*.

65 Carter Heyward, "Notes on Historical Grounding: Beyond Sexual Essentialism," in *Sexuality and the Sacred: Sources for Theological Reflection*, 2nd ed., ed. Marvin M. Ellison and Kelly Brown Douglas (Louisville, KY: Westminster John Knox Press, 2010), 12–13.

66 For additional biographical information about Heyward, see https://lgbtqreligiousarchives.org/profiles/carter-heyward (accessed 8 September 2023). See also Stephen Burns and Bryan Cones, "Carter Heyward (1945–)," in *Twentieth Century Anglican Theologians: From Evelyn Underhill to Esther Mombo*, ed. Stephen Burns, Bryan Cones, and James Tengatenga (Hoboken, NJ: Wiley-Blackwell, 2021).

67 See "Following the Questions Wherever They Lead: A Conversation with Mark D. Jordan (SF73)," St. John's College website (24 March 2022), https://www.sjc.edu/news/following-questions-wherever-they-lead-conversation-mark-d-jordan (accessed 8 September 2023).

68 Mark D. Jordan, "*Jesus ACTED UP* and Any Possible Future of 'Queer Theology,'" *Theology & Sexuality* 21, no. 3 (2015): 202.

69 Virginia Burrus, Mark D. Jordan, and Karmen MacKendrick, eds., *Seducing Augustine: Bodies, Desires, Confessions* (New York: Fordham University Press, 2010).

70 Mark D. Jordan, *Rewritten Theology: Aquinas after His Readers* (Malden, MA: Blackwell, 2006).

71 Jordan, *Convulsing Bodies*.

72 Mark D. Jordan, *The Silence of Sodom: Homosexuality in Modern Catholicism* (Chicago, IL: University of Chicago Press, 2000); Jordan, *Recruiting Young Love*. Other books written or edited by Jordan include Mark D. Jordan, *The Ethics of Sex* (Oxford: Wiley, 2002); Mark D. Jordan, *Telling Truths in Church: Scandal, Flesh, and Christian Speech* (Boston, MA: Beacon Press, 2003); Mark D. Jordan, *Blessing Same-Sex Unions: The Perils of Queer Romance and the Confusions of Christian Marriage* (Chicago, IL: University of Chicago Press, 2005); and Mark D. Jordan, ed. with Meghan T. Sweeny and David M. Mellot, *Authorizing Marriage?: Canon, Tradition, and Critique in the Blessing of Same-Sex Unions* (Princeton, NJ: Princeton University Press, 2006).

73 The three units cosponsoring the panel were the Christian Systematic Theology Unit, the Gay Men and Religion Unit, and the Queer Studies in Religion Unit.

74 Kori Pacyniak, "Queer Calling: Imagination & Becoming in the Work and Teaching of Mark D. Jordan" (paper presented at the annual meeting of the American Academy of Religion, Denver, CO, 20 November 2022), 6.

75 For more information about Mollenkott's life, see https://lgbtqreligiousarchives.org/profiles/virginia-ramey-mollenkott-ph-d (accessed 8 September 2023). See also David E. Weekly, "Becoming Grateful Allies: An Interview with Dr. Virginia Ramey Mollenkott," *Journal of Feminist Studies in Religion* 34, no. 1 (2018): 25–36.

76 Virginia Ramey Mollenkott, *Omnigender: A Trans-Religious Approach* (Cleveland, OH: Pilgrim Press, 2001), vii.

77 Virginia Ramey Mollenkott and Vanessa Sheridan, *Transgender Journeys* (Cleveland, OH: Pilgrim Press, 2003), 38–52. This chapter honors Mollenkott's use of the pronoun "her" to describe herself.

78 Goss, *Jesus ACTED UP*, xvii, 177.

79 For more biographical information about Shore-Goss, see https://lgbtqreligiousarchives.org/profiles/robert-e-shore-goss (accessed 8 September 2023).

80 See, e.g. Robert E. Shore-Goss, Thomas Bohache, Patrick S. Cheng, and Mona West, eds., *Queering Christianity: Finding a Place at the Table for LGBTQI Christians* (Santa Barbara, CA: Praeger, 2013); and Robert E. Shore-Goss and Joseph N. Goh, eds., *Unlocking Orthodoxies for Inclusive Theologies: Queer Alternatives* (Abingdon: Routledge, 2020).

81 Deryn Guest, Robert E. Goss, Mona West, and Thomas Bohache, eds., *The Queer Bible Commentary* (London: SCM Press, 2006). The second edition of *The Queer Bible Commentary* was published in 2022.

82 Robert E. Goss and Amy Adams Squire Strongheart, eds., *Our Families, Our Values: Snapshots of Queer Kinship* (Binghamton, NY: The Haworth Press, 1997).

83 Donald L. Boisvert and Robert E. Goss, eds., *Gay Catholic Priests and Clerical Sexual Misconduct: Breaking the Silence* (Binghamton, NY: The Haworth Press, 2005).

84 Robert E. Goss and Dennis Klass, *Dead But Not Lost: Grief Narratives in Religious Traditions* (Walnut Creek, CA: AltaMira Press, 2005).

85 Robert E. Shore-Goss, *The Insurgency of the Spirit: Jesus's Liberation Animist Spirituality, Empire, and Creating Christian Protectors* (Lanham, MD: Lexington, 2020); Robert E. Shore-Goss, *God Is Green: An Eco-Spirituality of Incarnate Compassion* (Eugene, OR: Cascade, 2016).

86 Jordan, *"Jesus ACTED UP,"* 202.

87 Jordan, *"Jesus ACTED UP,"* 75.

88 Conversely, queer voices and perspectives often are missing from works by theologians of color. See Renee L. Hill, "Who Are We for Each Other? Sexism, Sexuality and Womanist Theology," in *Black Theology: A Documentary History, Vol. II, 1980–1992*, ed. James H. Cone and Gayraud S. Wilmore (Maryknoll, NY: Orbis, 1993), 345–51.

89 Cornwall, *Controversies in Queer Theology*, 43–71, 72–113, 224–50.

90 Cheng, *Radical Love*. See also Patrick S. Cheng, *From Sin to Amazing Grace: Discovering the Queer Christ* (New York: Seabury, 2012), proposing a queer hamartiology, or theology of sin, that is also grounded in queer Christology; Andy Buechel, *That We Might Become God: The Queerness of Creedal Christianity* (Eugene, OR: Cascade, 2015).

91 Linn Marie Tonstad, *Queer Theology: Beyond Apologetics* (Eugene, OR: Cascade, 2018).

92 Stephen D. Moore, Kent L. Brintnall, and Joseph A. Marchal, "Introduction – Queer Disorientations: Four Turns and a Twist," in *Sexual Disorientations: Queer Temporalities, Affects, Theologies*, ed. Kent L. Brintnall, Joseph A. Marchal, and Stephen D. Moore (New York: Fordham University Press, 2018), 2–4.

93 See Kwok Pui-lan, "Race, Colonial Desire, and Sexual Theology," in *Postcolonial Politics and Theology: Unraveling Empire for a Global World* (Louisville, KY: Westminster John Knox Press, 2021).

94 See Whitney A. Bauman, ed., *Meaningful Flesh: Reflections on Religion and Nature for a Queer Planet* (North Haven, CT: Punctum, 2018).

95 See Brintnall et al., eds., *Sexual Disorientations*.

96 See Frederick Roden, ed., *Jewish/Christian/Queer: Crossroads and Identities* (Farnham: Ashgate, 2009).

97 Such theologies would build upon works in queer disability studies such as Robert McRuer and Anna Mollow, eds., *Sex and Disability* (Durham, NC: Duke University Press, 2012).

Recommended Reading

Primary

Althaus-Reid, Marcella. *Indecent Theology: Theological Perversions in Sex, Gender and Politics*. London: Routledge, 2000.

Althaus-Reid, Marcella, and Lisa Isherwood, eds. *Trans/Formations*. London: SCM Press, 2009.

Brintnall, Kent L., Joseph A. Marchal, and Stephen D. Moore, eds. *Sexual Disorientations: Queer Temporalities, Affects, Theologies*. New York; Fordham University Press, 2018.

Cheng, Patrick S. *Radical Love: An Introduction to Queer Theology*. New York: Seabury Press, 2011.

Goss, Robert. *Jesus ACTED UP: A Gay and Lesbian Manifesto*. San Francisco, CA: HarperSanFrancisco, 1993.

Heyward, Carter. *Touching Our Strength: The Erotic as Power and the Love of God*. San Francisco, CA: Harper & Row, 1989.

Jordan, Mark D. *The Invention of Sodomy in Christian Theology*. Chicago, IL: University of Chicago Press, 1997.

Lightsey, Pamela R. *Our Lives Matter: A Womanist Queer Theology*. Eugene, OR: Pickwick, 2015.

Loughlin, Gerard, ed. *Queer Theology: Rethinking the Western Body*. Malden, MA: Blackwell, 2007.

Mollenkott, Virginia Ramey. *Omnigender: A Trans-Religious Approach*. Cleveland, OH: Pilgrim Press, 2001.

Rogers, Eugene F., Jr., ed. *Theology and Sexuality: Classic and Contemporary Readings*. Oxford: Blackwell, 2002.

Secondary

Burns, Stephen, and Bryan Cones. "Carter Heyward (1945–)." In *Twentieth Century Anglican Theologians: From Evelyn Underhill to Esther Mombo*, edited by Stephen Burns, Bryan Cones, and James Tengatenga, 175–84. Hoboken, NJ: Wiley-Blackwell, 2021.

Cheng, Patrick S. "Contributions from Queer Theory." In *The Oxford Handbook of Theology, Sexuality, and Gender*, edited by Adrian Thatcher, 153–69. Oxford: Oxford University Press, 2015.

_____. *Rainbow Theology: Bridging Race, Sexuality, and Spirit*. New York: Church Publishing, 2013.

Cooper, Thia. *Queer and Indecent: An Introduction to the Theology of Marcella Althaus-Reid*. London: SCM Press, 2021.

Cornwall, Susannah. *Controversies in Queer Theology*. London: SCM Press, 2011.

Greenough, Chris. *Queer Theologies: The Basics*. Abingdon: Routledge, 2020.

Shore-Goss, Robert E. "Gay and Lesbian Theologies." In *Liberation Theologies in the United States: An Introduction*, edited by Stacey M. Floyd-Thomas and Anthony B. Pinn, 181–208. New York: New York University Press, 2010.

Spencer, Daniel T. "Lesbian and Gay Theologies." In *Handbook of U.S. Theologies of Liberation*, edited by Miguel A. De La Torre, 264–73. St. Louis, MO: Chalice Press, 2004.

Stuart, Elizabeth. *Gay and Lesbian Theologies: Repetitions with Critical Difference*. Aldershot: Routledge, 2003.

Tonstad, Linn Marie. *Queer Theology: Beyond Apologetics*. Eugene, OR: Cascade, 2018.

Wilcox, Melissa M. *Queer Religiosities: An Introduction to Queer and Transgender Studies in Religion*. Lanham, MD: Rowman & Littlefield, 2021.

Postliberal Theology

Ben Fulford

Introduction

Postliberal theology takes its name from the subtitle and final chapter of George Lindbeck's *The Nature of Doctrine* (1984). There is no coherent school or movement. Rather, the label is applied to a group of theologians who share a set of similar traits, many of whom are also connected by having been taught or deeply influenced by the Yale theologians Hans W. Frei, George A. Lindbeck, and David H. Kelsey, the Yale-trained theological ethicist, Stanley Hauerwas, and their students. The most influential works of those founding figures were published in a period beginning with Frei's *The Eclipse of Biblical Narrative* in 1974 and extending through the publication and reception of *The Nature of Doctrine* to Kelsey's *Eccentric Existence* in 2009. Many of those connections derive from generations of graduate students trained at Yale's department of Religious Studies from the early 1970s onwards. Thinkers like Charles Wood, William Placher, George Hunsinger, Ronald Thiemann, David Ford, Kathryn Tanner, James Buckley, Bruce Marshall, Eugene Rogers, Kendall Soulen, and Katherine Sonderegger do not all identify as "postliberal" and do not share a common program but do, in different ways, pursue agendas shaped by that formation to some extent, and their ways of doing theology evince certain family resemblances, though not in any uniform way. The same could be said of several of Hauerwas's students, such as William T. Cavanaugh.

Survey

In broad terms, postliberal theology represents a collection of creative efforts to renew academic Western Christian theology (and theological ethics) for its practical service of Christian communities in increasingly post-Christian, pluralist contexts, following the decline of the postwar influence of neo-orthodox and *ressourcement* theologies in Catholic and mainstream Protestant theology. Taking their lead from Frei's *Eclipse of Biblical Narrative* and his *The Identity of Jesus Christ*, postliberal thinkers largely resource that renewal by attending to (or gesturing toward) normative narrative patterns in canonical scriptural stories, variously construed as an interconnected whole, centered upon the New Testament's Christological stories. Frei's

Ford's The Modern Theologians: An Introduction to Christian Theology since 1918, Fourth Edition.
Edited by Rachel Muers and Ashley Cocksworth.
© 2024 John Wiley & Sons Ltd. Published 2024 by John Wiley & Sons Ltd.

Eclipse is also paradigmatic of postliberal endeavors to repair or circumvent distorted modes of theological practice characteristic of both liberal and conservative reactions to the challenges posed by modernity to Christian traditions in Europe and North America. Like Frei, many postliberals draw constructively (and sometimes eclectically) on premodern sources for this reparative exercise. Following some of Frei and Lindbeck's later ruminations, some thinkers in this lineage have sought to diagnose deeper sources of malaise in Christian tradition, especially its toxic supersessionary and anti-Jewish tendencies, further back into its early centuries. Postliberal theologies thus may produce proposals at once radical and revisionist, whether in relation to theological hermeneutics, Christology, ecclesiology, or the doctrine of marriage.

Frei's felicitous phrase to describe his own project, the search for "a generous orthodoxy," fitly sums up a common ethos of thinkers who have often sought to transcend conservative–liberal polarities and articulate visions of faithfulness to what they take to be Christianity's core logic as the bases for a distinctive, socially engaged, even progressive ecclesial witness to God's inaugurated and coming kingdom. Lindbeck's ecumenical commitments and agenda most fully and formally express the ecumenical orientation of postliberal theology, though he envisaged a grassroots ecumenism beyond the projects of formal doctrinal reconciliation. That spirit is also evident in the way postliberals have sought to find commonalities between figures often set in opposition (like Aquinas and Barth), though they often have also pursued polemical polarities of their own and sometimes reduced the objects of their critiques to caricature.

Postliberals tend to see theology as a practice primarily concerned with the belief and practices of Christian communities, at once ecclesial yet also academic in its institutional setting and its commitments to public conceptual description and evaluation of Christian and secular practices against scriptural and traditional norms, resourced by ad hoc deployment of theoretical resources from a range of disciplines, literary, historical, social scientific, and philosophical. They tend to imagine the church, after the model of biblical Israel, as a visible people – visibly distinctive in changing practices that embody (or should embody) a similar or common basic logic normed by scriptural narrative. In this way the church bears a frail witness to the presence of God in Christ by the Spirit in its practices and community but also in creation, society, and history. The church is at once the people of God in this sense and an irreducibly particular religious community whose visible forms are open to public description. For this reason, postliberal theologians often show a preference for theoretical resources that assist in the description of practices and traditions of practice.

Scriptural narrative identifications of God, Jesus Christ, the Spirit, the people of Israel and the church, humanity, and creatures guide their theological reflections; they also draw on conceptual resources for describing identities, and more literary approaches to biblical texts. They tend to observe a distinction between, on the one hand, the form of doctrinal or theological claims and positions and, on the other hand, the underlying force, logic, or grammar orienting theological or doctrinal responses to contextual issues, which facilitates constructive, generative theological retrieval and conversation. Although not always overtly theological when writing methodologically, they often work out of a logic of the noncontrastive, noncompetitive relation of divine agency to creaturely action, as described by Kathryn Tanner.[1] They seek to take seriously the historical character of creation and the church; to resist individualism while attempting to uphold the particular significance of the individual in community; and to resist totalizing accounts of history and idealistic accounts of God and human persons, even while endeavoring to identify a flexible, basic common Christian identity underlying the great diversity of Christian theologies, practices, and lived experiences.

Named Theologians

Hans W. Frei (1922–88)

Frei's only substantive work of constructive theology is his *The Identity of Jesus Christ*, largely a republication of an essay he wrote on "The Mystery of the Presence of Jesus Christ", published in 1966. The argument of *Identity* is best understood against the background of Frei's rejection of what he took to be the mainstream project of modern Western theology, including in his own day – to commend the plausibility and meaning-fulness of Christian faith in Jesus Christ as the unique revelation of God by showing the potential for such faith in human existence. Frei sought a normative, nonperspectival basis for understanding Christianity and the logic of Christian belief in the structure of the Synoptic Gospels, especially in those sequences where Jesus is presented in and through what he does and what happens to him; he is given to be known in the story, not discovered behind it by speculative historical reconstruction or existential analysis. To attend to that meaning, theologians would need to allow that the singularity of the character depicted would elude comprehensive, systematic conceptualization in any scheme.

Frei found a common basic pattern across the different narratives told by the Synoptic Gospels such that they can be said to render the same main character, so singular in the narrative structures that identify him as to be unsubstitutable. Indeed, Frei underlines that unsubstitutability in *Identity* by showing how various fictional Christ figures fail to reproduce the unified combination of characteristics that identify Jesus in the gospels' stories. Those stories render the theme of redemptive action in and through a narrative structure that is identical with who he is, that is, his story. Frei describes who Jesus is in those stories in two ways. First, he looks for episodes that depict Jesus in actions that are typical of him, which answer the question, "What is he like?" Second, he looks for the embodied and named continuity of the person across the whole Christological narratives told by the gospels.

The first way of describing identity helps Frei identify the characteristic intention whereby Jesus, in the gospel narratives, holds together and makes his own the qualities of saving power and powerlessness before the events that led to his death. Frei finds hints of abiding initiative at moments of helplessness, by which Jesus unites and shapes his power with powerlessness, enacting his consistent intention to save humanity out of love for humankind and in love and obedience to the God who sent him. Out of that twofold love and obedience he exercises his power and undergoes helpless suffering, holding them together in the transi-tion and coexistence between them. Enacting this love and obedience, Jesus identifies with human beings in their helplessness before sin and death, vicariously bearing their guilt as one who is innocent, with a sav-ing power coincident with his powerlessness.

Frei's second mode of description tracks a transition in the depiction of Jesus in the Synoptics of increas-ing individuation and concrete specificity: from a figure identified entirely with the people of Israel in the prebirth and infancy narratives of Matthew and Luke; to an individual more identified by the kingdom he proclaims than the other way around; to someone who emerges as a fully focused individual through the events leading up to and constituting his destiny to suffer. This sequence of the cumulative manifestation of a concretely singular individual culminates in the resurrection appearances, which are also the culmina-tion of a pattern in which God's hidden agency comes to the fore, at first hidden in other forces acting on him, but now veiled and unveiled in Jesus's risen body. At the moment where Jesus is most fully manifest as an unsubstitutable individual, he is manifest as the embodiment of God's presence. His specific identity is inseparable from his being the divine presence and conversely, God's identity is revealed to be inseparable from him. The gospels' complex narrative identification of Jesus as a concrete individual in a social setting in a specific time and place involves the claim that he was raised from the dead and that he cannot be thought not to be alive, to be present. In this way it makes a factual, historical claim of a unique kind, beyond all analogical historical judgments of probability. It also represents God's vindication and redemp-tion of Jesus from death (on our behalf, we may infer), makes sense of the vicarious, cosmic saving power Frei ascribes to him, and secures for all human beings an unalienated identity in virtue of their inclusion in his. This analysis of Jesus's identity as entailing his living presence and the freedom to turn and share it with us provides Frei with the key to interpreting Christian belief in Christ's presence today, in Word, Sacrament, Christian community, and human history. Especially noteworthy is Frei's claim that the history shared by the church and the rest of humanity has a mysterious pattern, to be completed in an eschatological sum-ming up in a future mode of Christ's presence. This pattern is providentially ordered in Jesus Christ's own life, death and resurrection, in a manner that "mysteriously … coexists with the contingency of events."[2]

Something of this pattern can be discerned dimly in light of certain parables, one of which is the salvific pattern of exchange that marks Jesus's vicarious identity. We may tentatively identify figures of Christ's providential presence in events where there are hints of union through the agonized exchange of radical opposites, whose pattern looks toward reconciliation, redemption and resurrection, such as the US Civil War and the subsequent conflicts over the civil rights of African Americans against the background of slavery, segregation, and oppression. *Identity* is a remarkable sketch toward a high Christology grounded in the description of the patterns of the gospel narratives and so attentive to Christ's historical humanity, without leaning heavily on an incarnational frame or the doctrinal categories of Chalcedon.

Frei's best-known work, which complements *Identity*, is *The Eclipse of Biblical Narrative*. Here Frei identifies, in effect, a minimal, historical essence to Western Christianity and offers an analysis of how it came to be distorted, diminished and subverted in modern theologians' hermeneutical responses to a changing epistemic context. That essence has three components: the literal reading of history-like biblical narratives, the joining of those narratives into a canonical framework by figural interpretation, and the interpretation of events and experiences in their own time as figures of the world those stories depicted. Literal reading took the events depicted to be the meaning of the stories and took them to be historical because depicted in a history-like way. Figural interpretation found a coherence between two such stories so read, such that (when done carefully) the later fulfilled the meaning pattern of the earlier, which in turn signified itself and the later event it prefigured. These connected stories set forth, in varying ways, the real world for readers, whose structure, plot, and characters provided the means by which to understand their own circumstances and destinies. The coherences readers found between stories, and between them and the world of the reader, rested, for them, on belief in the unity between God's speech in scripture, God's governance of history, and the work of the Spirit in the hearts of readers. In *Eclipse*, Frei describes the dissolution of those coherences, as scholars came to construe history apart from the narratives, and to distinguish what they described from what they thought had actually happened; they also tended to construe the narratives' meaning in terms of authorially intended references to single events, rational ideas or states of consciousness, rather than vehicles of divine speech depicting a providentially ordered world. Theologians' apologetic concerns led them to accept this basic hermeneutical orientation that privileged subject matter over verbal form, whether they defended the historicity of the stories or not. Wherever interpreters took this approach, the meaning constituted by the structured texture of the stories – the interaction of characters and circumstances – was "eclipsed" when the stories were taken to be about something beyond or behind the text. Crucially, Frei argues that ignoring that narrative meaning was a contingent and, he implies, reversable mistake; the literal and figural reading of biblical narrative might once again orient Christian living in the public sphere.

George Lindbeck (1923–2018)

Many of the enduring concerns and themes of George Lindbeck's theology emerge in the account he gave of the direction of Roman Catholic theology, as indicated by the presence of new theological emphases in the documents of the Second Vatican Council. The council's texts were, he argued in *The Future of Roman Catholic Theology*, transitional documents in a movement toward a new vision of history and the church. Lindbeck's approving exposition of this emerging vision and his use of it to critique a "classical" paradigm of Catholic and Protestant theology and church order, as well as the limitations of the council documents, clearly indicate his own alignment with it.

At the heart of that new vision of history was a realistic, futurist eschatology, drawn from the New Testament: the expectation of the future, full manifestation of the kingdom of God begun in Christ's first coming. That full manifestation will be the transformation and climactic summation in union with Christ of our historical world of time and space: a salvation of humanity and the cosmos. It gives to our history a purpose and goal. This final manifestation will be God's doing, bursting into history from above, but God is guiding the processes of nature in history in preparation for this fulfilment. This vision thus offered a Christian interpretation of the modern historical worldview and, as it transcended confessional boundaries, represented a new framework within which to reexamine traditional doctrinal differences. In an earlier article, Lindbeck had already argued that the health of the church depended "on the recovery of this eschatological perspective."[3]

For Lindbeck, the new ecclesiology emerging in the Council's documents correlated with this new eschatological view of history: it was a renewal of the biblical and early Christian vision of the church as "the messianic pilgrim people of God, the sacramental sign … to the kingdom which has begun and will be consummated in Christ."[4] The church is a people on the move toward God's inaugurated future, impelled forward by their memories and hopes, whose purpose and distinctive being lies in its mission, to point toward and anticipate Christ and the kingdom in its words, its service of the world, and the quality of its communal life. It promised a less clericalist, ecclesiocentric, and isolationist vision of the church, oriented toward the service of the world. In a contemporary article, Lindbeck commended a sociologically sectarian future for churches in rapidly secularizing societies.[5] Lindbeck imagined churches as socially and racially diverse, creative minority communities, after the model of biblical Israel, witnessing to Christ in anticipating his return, which would help prevent open societies lapsing into dogmatic repressiveness of one kind or another by their sacrificial commitment to universal principles of love, brotherhood, and justice. Indeed, Lindbeck argued that the vision of the church as an eschatological people bearing witness to the coming kingdom through its service of humanity depended on the gentile church recognizing itself as engrafted into the people of Israel.[6] This emerging ecclesiology made ecumenical unity missionally imperative, enabling the church to be a sign of God's reconciling grace in its own life, centered on the laity and collegially structured.[7] Lindbeck imagined a worldwide network of churches, sectarian in the intimacy of their communal life but ecumenical "in their inclusion of rich and poor, black and white, educated and uneducated, alien and native," as in the early church. This vision would be framed by the realistic eschatology sketched earlier and the faithful, suffering servant role of the church, in imitation of its Lord, in solidarity with the poor and oppressed and against their oppressors.

Lindbeck was already reflecting on how to conceive of such doctrinal reconciliation at this stage, while he was being drawn into ecumenical dialogues between Roman Catholics and Lutherans in the United States and internationally. His most extensive reflection and best-known work on that subject is *The Nature of Doctrine*. Here he sought to account for instances in recent ecumenical dialogue in which doctrinal reconciliation without capitulation had been achieved, as it would later be on justification. He did so by developing an analogy with rules of grammar, within a cultural-linguistic theory of religion. Religions, he argued, are "comprehensive interpretive schemes, usually embodied in myths or narratives and heavily ritualized, which structure human experience and understanding of self and world."[8] These stories identify and describe what is of maximal importance and organize all of life in relation to it. Like a language, a religion is made up of a symbolic vocabulary (both discursive and nondiscursive) and a distinctive grammar or logic by which it can be meaningfully used by those who have acquired the requisite skills.[9] All this symbolic system and its use is integrally related to a form of life comprising rituals, experiences, recommended actions, and institutional forms. As interpretive schemes or frameworks, religions shape adherents' subjectivities, the way they describe reality, formulate beliefs, and experience attitudes and feelings.[10]

On this view, the story a religion tells, and the grammar that informs how it is told and used, are what abides in a religion, across historical change and variations in "vocabulary." Many different socially constructed human worlds can be inscribed within this story in accordance with this grammar. The interpretive scheme will change each time, but the basic story and grammar remain the same. The grammar is therefore what is significant for church doctrines, understood as communally authorized teachings about beliefs and practices essential to its identity and welfare. For these doctrines gain their force insofar as they reflect that grammar. They are historically contextualized decisions, as before, but decisions with the force of rules, determining legitimate vocabulary, guiding its use, specifying who or what certain terms refer to in religious usage. Sometimes they state regulative principles (like the Lutheran doctrine of justification), sometimes they illustrate correct usage. For Lindbeck, doctrines *qua* doctrines are purely regulatory: they are "second-order" propositions about the grammar of religious language and practice, as distinct from "first-order" propositions about reality. Thinking of doctrines as rules, he argued, could account more adequately for several qualities attributed to doctrines by Christian churches and for doctrinal reconciliation without capitulation than could thinking of them as first-order propositions or symbols expressing or evoking religious experiences.

Lindbeck took one further step beyond rule theory in *The Nature of Doctrine*. In the final chapter, he offered an account of theological method consistent with a cultural-linguistic approach to religion, which he called "postliberal theology." Such theology would describe for its adherents the meaning of religious faith by interpreting the uses of religious language, practice, and behavior within the context of the whole system of such interconnected, purposeful signs ("intratextually"), rather than by how those uses might refer to some objective reality or express a religious experience. In the case of religions with fixed canons of writing taken as exemplary or normative instances of those cultural systems, the literary structures of the texts supply the interpretive framework for all reality and experience. Here, theology describes the meaning of the religion by redescribing reality within this framework, absorbing the world into the text. Frei's account of the literal reading and figural uniting of realistic biblical stories into an overarching narrative framework, and the figural interpretation of history and experience in terms of that story, varying from context to context and making possible internal disagreements, exemplifies this process for Lindbeck.

Lindbeck proposed, then, as a first criterion for postliberal theology its degree of fit with the scriptural framework. As a second, he put forward how far it was able to shape present action by discerning "those possibilities in current situations that can and should be cultivated as anticipations or preparations for the hoped-for future, the coming kingdom," as described in the religious cultural system.[11] In the long term, Lindbeck still thought, religious minorities that preserve their distinctiveness and integrity, and stress service rather than domination, might be essential to the vitality of civilizations like the West, by cultivating concern for others and responsibility for wider society. In such a de-Christianized society, effective catechesis might again become a viable means to exhibit the intelligibility and possible truth of the religious message to interested outsiders. A religion's long-term capacity to keep making "practically and cognitively coherent sense" of "relevant data," on its own terms, through major changes, would be the measure of its reasonableness.

In the latter part of Lindbeck's career, his writings pick up again the ecclesiological theme of the church "as the messianic pilgrim people of God typologically shaped by Israel's story," only now more in terms of his postliberal approach, with a more radical proposal for renewal.[12] He continued to believe that post-Christian societies, particularly dangerous amidst the collapse of Enlightenment ideologies and modernity's erosion of communal commitments, would need strong Christian communities capable of sustaining traditions of personal virtue, common good, and ultimate meaning. The capacity of increasingly diasporic post-Christendom Christian churches to fulfil this role would depend on the spread of a postcritical renewal of premodern biblical reading practices, restructuring churches into pre-Constantinian organizational patterns (with reformed unifying episcopal structures), and "the development of an Israel-like understanding of the Church."[13] If Christians could apply Israel's story to themselves, to see themselves included in that people as the beginning of the eschatological renewal of humanity, as early Christians did, but without the supersessionism or triumphalism of the past two millennia, the realistic narrative rendering of the church's identity would give a renewed sense of being a Christian community and greater cohesion amidst its theological plurality. It would give concrete specificity to their unity, a vocation to witness through the quality of its communal life and service, grounded in its unconditional divine election, and the ability to confer meaning on "the vicissitudes and contradictions of history."[14] It would enable Christians of all churches or denominations, from different parts of the world, to develop a strong intercontinental, interconfessional communal life, able to make a contribution to peace, justice, and the environment.[15] To this end he envisaged a reconceived unitive ecumenism reconstituting Christian community from the bottom up.

Stanley Hauerwas (b. 1940)

Stanley Hauerwas studied theology at Yale, relatively early in the careers of both Frei and Lindbeck, before going on to teach at Notre Dame and then Duke Divinity School. In his work, he carries forward their emphases on the ecclesial location of theology and the decisive significance of the story of Jesus Christ for Christian identity, among other influences, into a distinctively postliberal approach to Christian ethics, one that rests heavily on a narratively formed ecclesiology.

Like Frei's and Lindbeck's theologies, Hauerwas's theological ethics tends to be framed in opposition to a construal of a mainstream liberal paradigm. Liberal Christian ethics, as Hauerwas describes it, was an apologetic enterprise, which aimed to secure the meaningfulness and universality of Christian convictions, and the political participation of Christian ethicists, by translating those beliefs into the terms of a putatively unqualified, objective ethic such as deontological or teleological ethics. In this way, Christian ethics marginalized beliefs essential to Christian identity, bifurcating ethics and theology into separate disciplines, and negated the contribution Christian ethics can make to reflection on contemporary moral issues (including in counter-cultural ways). This approach ignored the essentially tradition-based character of ethics and the importance of narratives for ethics.

According to Hauerwas, narratives, by connecting actions and sufferings in the unfolding of an understanding of a situation, according to a certain set of expectations or "grammar," account for patterns of events as intentional actions in terms of the development of agents' characters. They offer ways of making sense of the lives of communities and individuals in history and offer possibilities for developing skills of moral perception and understanding and for shaping character, to inform how we relate to the world and our destinies. Mainstream Christian ethics, Hauerwas charges, concentrates on the procedure for resolving difficult moral dilemmas between competing moral goods while ignoring the dependency of moral notions, understood as skills of perception, on narratives that specify their institutional contexts and purposes. It thus neglects the way a community's stories, convictions, and dispositions shape character and situations and so determine the moral questions we face. It fosters the formation of primarily rational selves distanced from their desires, emotions, interests, and projects, from their own pasts. Like Frei and Lindbeck, Hauerwas saw the marginality of the church in a post-Christendom culture as an opportunity for renewal: in this case, the renewal of Christian morality.

The church and its central stories are of crucial significance for Hauerwas's ethics. For Hauerwas, the church is formed by a distinctive set of narratives about Israel and Jesus Christ, forming one overarching story, which is its tradition and which it embodies. The story narrates central Christian beliefs about God's relationship to us, as creator and savior, who gives existence as a gift, and who invites human creatures to share in the work of God's kingdom through the history God is creating. This participation in the kingdom is an adventure that completes our nature and created purpose and our particular history: it is the goal of creation. Christians come to know the God they worship, the world they inhabit, and themselves, in interconnected ways through this story, as they enact it through Christian practices like the sacraments and preaching. To understand core Christian convictions is to understand them in the setting of this story and its communal embodiment, to which doctrines and theological concepts are secondary and subordinate aids. It is this content of Christian belief, narratively set forth, which sets Christian ethics apart from other kinds of ethics.

Christians appropriate this knowledge through their faithfulness to Jesus Christ's life, death, and resurrection, discovering their lives, the identity of Jesus, and the meaning of the kingdom in God's story as they learn to be his disciples. Discipleship involves imitating Jesus's characteristic embodiment of the peaceable kingdom that he proclaimed against the background of Israel's tradition. It is a training in dispossession of control and in hospitality to the stranger, which begins with learning to accept forgiveness in light of Christ's resurrection. This discovery involves learning, by means of the narratives, to see our existence and that of the world the way it is – fundamentally contingent, historical, and sinful and yet redeemed by Christ's work – and to share this vision with others. It involves acquiring the character and virtues necessary for living according to God's action in Christ's life, death, and resurrection. Indeed, to acquire a character in this way, through formation in this truthful story, frees Christians to claim their actions and lives as their own, without illusion and without resentment, at peace with themselves and others, through the categories and dispositions learnt through the story in the context of the community. Hence, for Hauerwas, the authoritative hermeneutic of the story, indeed the mediation of its meaning and authority, lies in its embodiment in the lives of those recognized by the community as living most nearly according to its demands.

The church community is thus the primary ethical agent for Hauerwas. Its distinctive manner of life, one transformed by listening to and enacting God's story, constitutes its social ethic. As one of Hauerwas's most famous images has it, the church is a transnational, transcultural colony of resident aliens whose citizenship is in heaven, an island of one culture, nurtured, and transmitted in the middle of another; a social-political alternative to the world that can be made known to it only in this way. Its life is thus its contribution to politics as a sign set up in (and in contradistinction from) the world in order to influence and save it: a truthful and visible foretaste and prefigurement of God's kingdom. Hence one of Hauerwas's best known and most controversial claims, that the social ethical task of the church is not to make the world more peaceful or just, but to be the church. It is to be itself so the world might know what peace and justice look like and learn to recognize itself as the world, as God's good creation freely persisting in being distorted and divided by sin despite its redemption in Christ, in the mirror of the church's life. This stance gives rise not only to Hauerwas's well-known polemics against Christian captivity to mainstream forms of modern Western ethical reflection, political liberalism, and US imperialism, but also to reflections on communities that witness to an alternative, peaceful, patient politics, such as L'Arche, and practices that witness to an alternative ethos.

Debate

Postliberals and public theology

The polemical focus of Frei, Lindbeck, and especially Hauerwas, on the ways in which liberal and conservative theologies and theological ethics have been deformed by their apologetic agendas, provoked criticism in kind. Thinkers committed to renewing traditions of liberal Christian theology and ethics saw in postliberalism a new form of a familiar danger, that of fideism. The charge is that postliberal fideism involves self-isolation from public conversation and critical questioning from others, the retreat to unassailable basic commitments, and the relativistic insistence that others share those commitments as a condition of conversation with them.[16] To their critics, Frei's and Lindbeck's insistence on the basic normative framework of the meaning of the biblical narratives, and their rejection of those who approach the text through extracanonical lenses, courts that charge. At best they do not clarify the relationship of this "intratextuality" to "extratextual" meanings; at worst they delegitimate external perspectives. In a similar way, critics charge postliberals with evading the question of what it means for them to claim that the Christian story is true, which, again, seems like the refusal to have a conversation in which their claims can be scrutinized.[17]

All the postliberal thinkers we have examined are committed to the normativity of patterns identifying God, human creatures, Israel, Jesus Christ, and the church in various scriptural narratives, which they treat as providing a framework within which all reality and experiences may be interpreted. They recognize that their appeals to the logics and formative power of those stories will not be compelling for those who do not recognize or experience their authority. They tend to be wary, however, of the plausibility of foundational or general explanatory theories as a basis on which to ground accounts of the truth of these narratives. They suggest, moreover, that the application of those theories to those stories tends to locate their subject matter elsewhere than the characters and world they depict, not least the central character of Jesus Christ.

Frei offers the most developed realist account. It illustrates the way postliberals' commitment to the primacy of the gospel story at once compels them to talk of truth and to talk of it in strange ways that may disturb expectations about rational conversation but do not seem to preclude or refuse such conversations. His argument that the identity of Jesus Christ, as rendered by the gospels, culminating in his resurrection, entails his living presence makes a unique and strange kind of claim. It presents what Frei calls a "mystery indefinitely penetrable by reason."[18] It can, in principle, be falsified by historical discovery. Yet it exceeds the possibility of any analogy with other historical events and so any judgment of probability. Under our present conditions of finitude the coherence of this rational mystery can be partially described, borrowing concepts from other academic disciplines in an ad hoc manner, bending their meaning in this application, to the point where they are exceeded and the story can only be narrated. This kind of borrowing might afford the possibility of ad hoc analogies, correlations and comparisons with the other uses of these concepts, which might allow for critical conversations about the relative adequacy or coherence of those different uses.[19] Something similar could be said about the figural interpretation of historical events and experiences.

These dynamics apply to talking about the truth of the gospel story, which, Frei argues, involves a strange combination of borrowings and adaptations from three normally rival accounts of truth. The logic of Christ's identity entailing his living presence is like a correspondence claim but in respect of a reality exceeding human categories and the analogies they frame. In the end you have to talk, not so much about the fit between language and reality, as about the gracious condescension of the subject of the stories to their narrative form so that their witness is true. In the absence of any mode of showing this graced "fit," the truth of the stories is more like a coherentist claim, admitting critical scrutiny on those terms. Yet it goes beyond that account of truth, for to describe what it means for the story to be true also requires self-involving and pragmatic dimensions. Accepting the authority of the story is warranted by the church's experience of the fruitful use religious people have made of it in ways that enhance their lives and those of others. To believe it is identical with responding with love and gratitude to God and love for neighbor. Its truth involves its coherence with its effects in believers' lives and its power to hold the world to account by its own measure.

Lindbeck and Hauerwas offer fuller accounts of this pragmatic dimension of truth. For Lindbeck, the religions as cultural systems are idioms for expressing reality, and their truth is a matter of the adequacy of their categories for that purpose, of the extent to which they shape their adherents to conform to the ultimately real (to God's being and will, in Christian terms). It is not so much a question of the correspondence of referential uses of religious language, as of the adequation to the real of the self who is shaped in the use of the stories, concepts, and practices of a given religious idiom and the adequacy of that idiom to that end. Within that total performance, discrete religious utterances may be true insofar as the totality is true in that way, provided they cohere with it. This approach allows for the public testing of that coherence but also the evaluation of religions as comprehensive interpretive schemes within which to live and understand the world. They can be assessed, Lindbeck argues, in terms of their capacity to provide adherents with an intelligible interpretation of situations across change and over the long term.

Similarly, Hauerwas's emphasis is on truthfulness as a quality of believers' perceptions and behavior, their ability to see things (and themselves) as they are, their whole lives as making claims about the way the world is. Stories and the beliefs grounded in them are true primarily in terms of their capacity to shape such lives. Although for Hauerwas there is no available neutral, universal rational standard by which to evaluate Christian beliefs and practice, his position makes two kinds of evaluation possible. First, it affords a coherentist evaluation: the public testing of the coherence of practices and behavior with basic, narrative-based convictions and the exemplary lives that embody them. Second, given its realistic character, there can be a pragmatic evaluation through the practical implications and experiences of communities who live by them, in terms of how far Christian convictions prove habitable in practice, especially in face of suffering and tragedy. This same realism, rooted in the conviction that the world is God's world, means Christian convictions are open also to external challenges of this kind. Others' lives may demonstrate a fruitfulness or suffering that runs counter to what Christians' convictions lead them to expect. Indeed, challenge and persuasion are possible in both directions. For by their practices and lives, Christians may demonstrate the liveability and fruitfulness of their own convictions, counter to prevalent beliefs and practices. Much of Hauerwas's writing on medical ethics, for example, presupposes this public persuasive possibility, rooted in the doctrine of creation.[20]

Faith and history

Frei's approach offers an unusual and controversial approach to the vexed modern question of faith and history, centered on the person of Jesus Christ and the New Testament accounts of his resurrection. Frei is sympathetic to Van Harvey's critique of modern theologies that invoke norms of historical criticism only to bend their rules when it comes to Jesus Christ or salvation history in general.[21] Yet his articulation of the identity of the risen Christ as at once fact-like and yet unique and beyond analogy has seemed, to his critics, to fall foul of a similar equivocation about the historicity of the resurrection accounts and the applicability of modes of historical judgment to what he appears to take to be a historical event.[22]

Frei's posthumously published *Types of Christian Theology* is his most extensive response to this worry. Here he explored different ways in which modern Western theologians negotiated the demands of Christian theology's academic and ecclesial contexts, through the way they related it to other academic disciplines and their standards of public inquiry and argument, including the study of Christianity as a religion. These he evaluated by a criterion for their capacity to attend to the particularity of Christianity as a religion, namely its basic consensus prioritization of the way New Testament Christological stories set forth the character of Jesus of Nazareth as their subject matter. There is not space to do justice to Frei's analysis here, but essentially he thought that the procedures most fully hospitable to the literal sense are those that borrow eclectically and ad hoc from more descriptive disciplines to describe conceptually the logics of Christian practice, including its attention to the scriptural portraits of Jesus Christ. In respect of faith and history, Frei held that the modes of reasoning of historical inquiry are not a good fit for the literal sense, for the stories the literal sense prioritizes, at the very point where they make a historical claim, identify their subject finally by his relation to God. A literary-like procedure is more appropriate for attending to this subject. However, Frei's earlier proposals for the figural reading of history in light of Christ's identity also suggest the possibility of something like a historical consciousness analogous to that which informs historical inquiry but centered around the identity and providential presence of the risen Christ, which might permit theologians' ad hoc borrowing of historical critical tools.[23]

Church, public theology, and politics

These positions on truth indicate how postliberals can address another closely related and well-worn criticism, namely that the alleged tendency of postliberal theologians to isolate themselves from criticism parallels an advocacy of a sectarian sharp separation of the Christian community from the world.[24] This charge, as classically advanced by James Gustafson, was made in respect of Lindbeck and Hauerwas and is most commonly associated with Hauerwas's ecclesiology, because of his claim that the social ethical task of the church is to be the church and his rhetoric distinguishing the church sharply from the world. Yet, as we have seen, Hauerwas and Lindbeck are concerned for the distinctiveness of the church's virtues and practices in some contrast to wider society precisely for the sake of their witness or service to the world. For Hauerwas, who expounds this calling more fully, the calling of the church to be itself for this purpose includes tactical engagement and affirmation of aspects of society, as well as withdrawal and nonviolent resistance, depending on the circumstances. His writings on topics like peacemaking, abortion, suicide and euthanasia, children, medicine, and disability exemplify this kind of socially engaged witness, grounded in Christian distinctiveness and assuming shared fallen creatureliness and redemption at the hands of a gracious God. In such arguments, the church, in the contrastive witness of its practices and virtues, offers something attractive that the world lacks, such as a way of narrating lives with meaning and lamenting inexplicable suffering. The prospect of persuasion holds out the possibility that Christian witness may, in some circumstances, influence institutions, professions and communities. Because of his belief in the redemption of the world and the presence of God's kingdom beyond the church, Hauerwas also acknowledges the possibility that Christians may encounter non-Christians who display Christ's peace superbly and find common ground with them.

Frei's account of Christ's presence to the world seems to take him a little further in arguing that the church receives enrichment from the world as its neighbor and that, from time to time, historical events dimly prefiguring the eschatological redemption and reconciliation of all things in Christ may be identified in light of the pattern of union through the agonized exchange of opposites at the heart of his identity. On that basis, Frei could indicate a partial figural reading of the threads in the history of the United States as a way to a hopeful but realist perspective on the present. This might frame more full-hearted engagement in humanistic projects and movements for social justice, guided by Christ's identification with the marginalized, than Hauerwas's ecclesiology can fund.[25] In his treatment of joyous hopefulness, especially, David Kelsey's *Eccentric Existence* furthers Frei's realistic yet hopeful and progressive political thinking, including in more fully liberative directions.[26]

Romand Coles's careful interrogations of Hauerwas and others probe in a much more subtle and constructive way.[27] Coles worries about a postliberal monological strategy of controlling boundaried territories, of nonviolent rule by outnarration, keeping possession of a larger story and incorporating others' stories into it. The gospel story, he suggests, can be read as inviting Christians to be open to cede the initiative. He commends strategies of radical, receptive patience when interrupted by the surprising textures of the world we encounter and in engagement with others. The church, he suggests, should be open to supplemental enhancement from other bodies of the light it bears.

Coles's critique echoes that of Kathryn Tanner. Tanner has criticized postliberals for the way they invoke a stable cultural essence for the church, located in an underlying framework of rules whose meaning is self-contained and intelligible on its own terms, and which precedes and is independent of its interactions with its wider cultural setting.[28] Such a picture is unrealistic, she argues, for it ignores the way Christian identities, like all cultural identities, are formed from the beginning through the borrowing and transformation of cultural elements from their contexts. It excerpts these rules of practice from the historical processes that produce and change them and overestimates how far they are sufficient to shape action in a situation, and underestimates their diversity and contestation within and across contexts. In seeking a consistent underlying logic to Christian practices, postliberals project a vision of wholeness on to them and privilege their perspective as academic theologians over those of ordinary Christians. In consequence, she adds, they tend to reify and absolutize Christian practices and minimize their own constructive role in selecting and interpreting Christian cultural materials.[29] The move seems to be a way to guarantee the dominance of Christianity in interaction with the wider world and other religions. It reproduces the colonial dynamics at work in the cultural anthropological theories on which they rely and limits the grace and freedom of God's action and reliance on God's Word as guarantor of Christian identity. Rather, she argues, Christian identity is established by the distinctive and consistent style with which, from the beginning, Christians construct their way of life by using borrowed cultural materials in diverse ways, guided by the Spirit, and so is always hybrid or mixed.[30] Lindbeck is perhaps the most vulnerable to these charges, but they challenge Frei and Hauerwas also and indicate how little postliberal theologians have, in general, been attentive to issues of power in the production and practice of theology and in the church.

Postliberal emphases on the distinctiveness of the church resting on its culture and practices can lead to the assumption that when the church betrays itself, it is corrupted by some external contagion. The tendency to think that way allows for prophetic critique of the church but, as Coles argues, may discourage reflection on sources of distortion internal to the church, its story, and its practices, which the church might need to stand ever ready to recognize and resist.[31] In similar vein, Lauren Winner has argued that Christian practices can be deformed in ways that are characteristic of them, for which they have a propensity, which Christians can be alert to. In some cases, she contends, the practices themselves can generate the awareness needed.[32] These arguments do not defeat a postliberal focus on distinctive Christian practices but they do deflate some more optimistic, idealizing accounts of their performance and effects. They present corrections that may make them less prone to legitimate or promote subtle forms of coercion and less likely to overlook internal propensities for violence, exclusion, exploitation, and abuse.

Influence, Achievement, and Agenda

Postliberal theologians have had a wide influence in theological debates, even among those who disagree profoundly with them. Their influence is, I suggest, often felt wherever themes of attending to Christian practices, to the lived reality of Christian communities, to the narrative shapes and particulars of scriptural identifications of God, Christ, the Spirit, the church, and human beings in different contexts, the nature of doctrine, character, the relationship between church and world, are explored or addressed in academic theology and the more theologically oriented forms of biblical studies. Postliberal theology has also had significant influence on the theology of religions through the reception of Lindbeck's work, and on Jewish-Christian-Muslim relations, for example through the growth of Scriptural Reasoning.[33]

There are areas where more work might be done, however. There has, to my knowledge, been relatively limited postliberal engagement with questions of gender, especially in recent years.[34] Postliberal theology has been largely silent about thinking theologically about race, though there are notable postliberal affinities in the work of Willie James Jennings.[35] David Kelsey's *Eccentric Existence* has expanded the canonical and generic range of scriptural stories with which postliberals work.[36] Katherine Sonderegger's *Systematic Theology* extends that expansion still further into the genre of biblical law.[37] However, there has been little postliberal engagement with prophetic or apocalyptic texts. Kelsey's theological anthropology and Sonderegger's doctrine of God also represent the most substantive systematic treatments of doctrinal loci with debts to postliberal method and insights and illustrate its capacity to generate significant and innovative dogmatic contributions – but such examples are rare. Methodologically, postliberals have made big claims about incorporating lived experience and attending to practice but little attempt to do so in depth or detail with actual people or communities. Kelsey's anthropology is a unusual example of incorporating scientific knowledge into the narrative frames of a postliberal theology.[38] John Swinton's work is a relatively rare example of practical theology influenced by postliberal approaches.[39] Both methodologically and in terms of political theology there is a conversation to be pursued with liberation theologians in several traditions and contexts.[40]

Overall, postliberal theologians have had an enormous influence on academic theology. They have developed accounts of Christ and the church of abiding significance and promise and offered renewed avenues for dogmatic theological articulation *and* attention to the concrete reality of churches and their practices, and of ordinary holy lives and holy organizing. With the exception of Kelsey's monumental theological anthropology, the postliberal theology of its founders is an unfinished project – by design, perhaps, in Hauerwas's case: Frei died without completing a major project on modern Christology; Lindbeck never completed his projected Israel-like account of the church. These gaps remain. Other areas of their thought have underexploited promise. To some extent, those whom they taught and students of their work are setting the agenda for taking forward these achievements and this potential.

Notes

1 See, for example, Tanner's *God and Creation in Christian Theology: Tyranny or Empowerment?* (Minneapolis, MN: Fortress Press, 1988).
2 Hans Frei, *The Identity of Jesus Christ: The Hermeneutical Bases of Dogmatic Theology* (Eugene, OR: Wipf and Stock, 2013), 163.
3 George Lindbeck, "The Jews, Renewal and Ecumenism," *Journal of Ecumenical Studies* 2, no. 3 (1965): 473.
4 George Lindbeck, *The Future of Roman Catholic Theology* (London: SPCK, 1970), 27.
5 George Lindbeck, 'Ecumenism and the Future of Belief', *Una Sancta* 25 (1968): 3–17; reprinted in *The Church in a Postliberal Age*, ed. James J. Buckley (London: SCM Press, 2002), 92–105.
6 Lindbeck, "The Jews," 473.
7 Lindbeck, *Future*, 87.
8 George Lindbeck, *The Nature of Doctrine: Religion and Theology in a Postliberal Age* (Louisville, KY: Westminster John Knox Press, 1984), 32.
9 Lindbeck, *Nature*, 35.
10 Lindbeck, *Nature*, 36–9.
11 Lindbeck, *Nature*, 125.
12 George Lindbeck, *The Church in a Postliberal Age*, ed. James J. Buckley (London: SCM Press, 2002), 146.
13 Lindbeck, *Postliberal Age*, 7, 155, 160–5.
14 Lindbeck, *Postliberal Age*, 7, 150–1, 154–60, 202–22.
15 Lindbeck, *Postliberal Age*, 8–9.
16 Terence Tilley, "Incommensurability, Intertextuality and Fideism," *Modern Theology* 5, no. 2 (1989): 87–8; David Tracy, "Lindbeck's New Program for Theology," *Thomist: Speculative Quarterly Review* 49, no. 3 (1985): 468–70.
17 See, for example, Gary Comstock's "Truth or Meaning: Ricoeur versus Frei on Biblical Narrative," *Journal of Religion* 66, no. 2 (1986): 117–40.
18 Hans Frei, *Theology and Narrative* (New York: Oxford University Press, 1993), 32–7; *Types of Christian Theology* (New Haven, CT: Yale University Press, 1990), 80–90.
19 See William Werpehowski, "Ad Hoc Apologetics," *Journal of Religion* 66, no. 3 (1986): 282–301.
20 For a fuller account of the postliberals' approach to publicness and truth, see Fulford, "Postliberal Positions in Public Theology," in Christoph Hübenthal and Christiane Alpers, eds., *The T&T Clark Handbook of Public Theology* (London: Bloomsbury, 2022), 179–99.

21 See Van A. Harvey, *The Historian and the Believer: The Morality of Historical Knowledge and Christian Belief* (New York: Macmillan, 1966).
22 See, for example, N. T. Wright, *The Resurrection of the Son of God* (London: SCM Press, 2003).
23 To develop a conclusion of my *Divine Eloquence and Human Transformation: Rethinking Scripture and History through Gregory of Nazianzus and Hans Frei* (Minneapolis, MN: Fortress Press, 2013), 261–70.
24 See James Gustafson, "The Sectarian Temptation: Reflections on Theology, the Church and the University," *Proceedings of the Catholic Theological Society of America* 40 (2013): 83–94.
25 For a fuller account of the political dimension of Frei's theology, see Ben Fulford, *God's Patience and our Work: Hans Frei's Theology and the Ethics of Hope* (London: SCM Press, 2024).
26 See David Kelsey, *Eccentric Existence: A Theological Anthropology*, Vol. 1 (Louisville, KY: Westminster John Knox Press, 2009), 512–23.
27 See Romand Coles and Stanley Hauerwas, *Christianity, Radical Democracy and the Radical Ordinary* (Eugene, OR: Cascade, 2008).
28 Kathryn Tanner, *Theories of Culture: A New Agenda for Theology* (Minneapolis, MN: Augsburg Fortress, 1997), 104–19, 138–43, 147–9.
29 See also Nicholas Healy, *Hauerwas: A Very Critical Introduction* (Grand Rapids, MI: Eerdmans, 2014), 73–99.
30 Tanner, *Theories of Culture*, 112–18, 144–7.
31 Coles and Hauerwas, *Christianity, Radical Democracy and the Radical Ordinary*, 38–9.
32 Lauren Winner, *The Dangers of Christian Practice: On Wayward Gifts, Characteristic Damage, and Sin* (New Haven, CT: Yale University Press, 2018).
33 See Chapters 41 and 45 in this volume by Randi Rashkover and Jenny Daggers.
34 See Kathryn Greene-McCreight, *Feminist Reconstructions of Christian Doctrine. Narrative Analysis and Appraisal* (New York: Oxford University Press, 2000); and Kathryn Tanner, "Social Theory Concerning the 'New Social Movements' and the Practice of Feminist Theology," in *Horizons in Feminist Theology. Identity, Tradition, and Norms*, ed. R. S. Chopp and S. G. Daveney (Minneapolis: Fortress Press, 179–97. There are postliberal affinities in Serene Jones, *Feminist Theory*

and Christian Theology. Cartographies of Grace (Minneapolis: Fortress Press, 2000).

35 Willie James Jennings, *The Christian Imagination: Theology and the Origins of Race* (New Haven, CT: Yale University Press, 2011). See also Jonathan Tran, *Asian Americans and the Spirit of Racial Capitalism* (New York: Oxford University Press, 2022).

36 David Kelsey, *Eccentric Existence*, 2 vols (Louisville, KY: Westminster John Knox Press, 2009).

37 Katherine Sonderegger, *Systematic Theology, Vol. 1: The Doctrine of God; Vol. 2: The Doctrine of the Holy Trinity:*

Processions and Persons (Minneapolis. MN: Fortress Press, 2015, 2021).

38 Kelsey, *Eccentric Existence,* Vol. 1, 242–69.

39 John Swinton, *Dementia. Living in the Memories of God* (London: SCM Press, 2012); *Becoming Friends of Time: Disability, Timefullness, and Gentle Discipleship* (London: SCM Press, 2021).

40 The key text pursuing that conversation remains David Kamitsuka's *Theology and Contemporary Culture: Liberation, Postliberal and Revisionary Perspectives* (New York: Cambridge University Press, 1999).

Recommended Reading

Primary

Frei, Hans W. *The Eclipse of Biblical Narrative*. New Haven, CT: Yale University Press, 1974.

Frei, Hans W. *The Identity of Jesus Christ. The Hermeneutical Bases of Dogmatic Theology*. Eugene, OR: Wipf and Stock, 2013.

Hauerwas, Stanley. *The Peaceable Kingdom: A Primer in Christian Ethics*. Notre Dame, IN: University of Notre Dame Press, 1991.

Kelsey, David H. *Eccentric Existence*. 2 vols. Louisville, KY: Westminster John Knox Press, 2009.

Lindbeck. George A. *The Nature of Doctrine: Religion and Theology in a Postliberal Age*. Louisville, KY: Westminster John Knox Press, 2009.

Secondary

DeHart, Paul J. *The Trial of the Witnesses: The Rise and Decline of Postliberal Theology*. Oxford: Wiley-Blackwell, 2006.

Healy, Nicholas M. *Hauerwas: A (Very) Critical Introduction*. Grand Rapids, MI: Eerdmans, 2014.

Higton, Mike. *Christ, Providence and History: Hans W. Frei's Public Theology*. London: T&T Clark, 2004.

Practices of Engagement

Practical and Pastoral Theology

Katie Cross

Introduction

Practical and pastoral theology are located at the intersection between religious tradition and human experience. The primary reference of practical theology is the lived life in all its contemporary forms. Historically, it has sought to address disparities between theoretical understandings of God and the lived experiences and practices of people, religion, and society. As such, it often enters into areas of dissonance between the "safe" confines of academic theology and the messy, complex, and all too often turbulent realities of human life. Practical theology attends closely to particularities of context and so often steps over into the boundaries of other disciplines, drawing on human conversations and subject matter that require more than one approach to knowledge. Pastoral theology is related, but tends to focus on questions and issues that arise from the practice of caring for people. Although it has traditionally been dominated by clerical and therapeutic considerations,[1] its scope continues to broaden. Pastoral theology takes social and political issues into consideration, as well as questions that affect religious and nonreligious communities.

Both practical and pastoral theology span a breadth of perspectives, denominations, and religions. Within their ever-shifting boundaries, they encompass diverse approaches and methodologies. They are home to academics and practitioners from different cultures and perspectives, who are shaped by encounters with people and places, systems and circumstances. This applies to the construction of all theology, though in practical and pastoral theology these considerations are often emphasized or given methodological precedence. Neatly defining practical and pastoral theology can be challenging. The complexities and varying dynamics of these disciplines arise (in part) due to their emphasis on engagement with lived experience. No two people doing practical or pastoral theology will respond to the multidirectional conversation between doctrine and practice in exactly the same manner.[2] Those who count themselves as practical and pastoral theologians may have similar tasks and interests, but will handle them in diverse ways according to history, tradition, geography, and lived experiences of privilege and oppression.

This chapter outlines the fields of practical and pastoral theology and considers some of the ambiguities, tensions, debates, and conversations that exist within both. It includes key voices and ideas and reflects on both the history and the future of the discipline.

Ford's The Modern Theologians: An Introduction to Christian Theology since 1918, Fourth Edition.
Edited by Rachel Muers and Ashley Cocksworth.
© 2024 John Wiley & Sons Ltd. Published 2024 by John Wiley & Sons Ltd.

History

Certain issues arise when defining and charting a history of practical and pastoral theology. Firstly, what is the scope of this history? Broadly conceived, both forms of theology have long been a part of religious traditions. If we are to count practices of theological reflection or guidance on pastoral issues and concerns, then traces of pastoral theology are evident within some of the earliest Christian communities and writings.[3] For example, in his four-volume *Pastoral Care*, Pope Gregory I (Gregory the Great) considered the importance of pastoring well and of being a "physician of the heart."[4] In some sense at least, there is a long history of pastoral care. However, it is important to note with some caution that this has been wide ranging in scope and has ultimately been informed by concerns characteristic of the period in question. Whether all instances of "pastoral care" across the centuries fall within the scope of contemporary understandings is a question to be considered carefully. Secondly, more modern descriptions of practical theology emerging from the eighteenth century onwards have largely been dominated by White North American and Western European scholars, and frequently by Protestants.[5] As will become clear in this chapter, the monopolies of power and influence that have come to underpin the field are still being challenged and negotiated. Related to this, the professionalization of practical theology has brought about questions regarding the inclusion of nonacademic practitioners. "God talk" takes place in many different spaces outside the ivory tower, yet this has not always been recognized. Because of this, the history of pastoral and practical theology is one that promotes certain voices to the exclusion of others. It is important to be aware of this as we consider how practical theology has developed and how it might continue to evolve in future by including previously marginalized voices.

Practical theology was first formally identified and theorized as a discipline in the eighteenth century. The term "*die praktische Theologie*" emerged in the writings of German Protestant theologian Friedrich Schleiermacher (1768–1834), particularly in his "Brief Outline" of the theological curriculum that was to be taught in the University of Berlin.[6] In this new institution, which was state run as opposed to church run, there was an emphasis on teaching shaped by research. Schleiermacher's outline is the first reflection on the place and nature of practical theology in the modern university. Notably, his configurations of practical theology were characterized by their "general applicability." He suggested that practical theology should have a clear point of application and hinted at the dual placement of practical theology both within the academy and among church practitioners. However, Schleiermacher's conceptualization of practical theology has since been critiqued for being one-directional and applicationist. In emphasizing the importance of practical theology as the concretization of theological knowledge, Schleiermacher's framework was derived solely from philosophical and historical theology. It moved from the theoretical to the application of practice, without any critical engagement with or reference to lived human experience. As such, Schleiermacher's approach, although a helpful starting point, is deductive and limited.

In the twentieth century, practical theology developed from an applicationist model into a more critical and autonomous field of study. Having historically been understood as applied theology, practical theology began to expand and solidify its own methods and approaches and in doing so began to move away from a dependence on other theological disciplines. American theologian Don Browning is often cited as one of the primary architects of practical theology as we have come to understand it.[7] Browning was critical of the thinkers, such as Schleiermacher and Karl Barth, who adhered to classical perceptions of theology as the systematic interpretation of God's self-disclosure. He argued that this methodological framework was too one-directional from theory to practice and that it left no room for human understanding or action in determining God's will and purpose. In this model, theology can become practical only once theory is applied to practice, and as such, practical theology can only ever be "applied." Contrary to this approach, Browning argued that theology must be practical "from beginning to end."[8] He proposed that practice must therefore inform theory as well, allowing the two to "reinterpret" one another. Browning's model, known as Mutual Critical Correlation, was intended to allow for a two-way conversation between experience and theological understanding.[9]

In more recent decades, practical and pastoral theology have both been affected by a wider academic turn toward anthropocentric considerations, which has placed issues of human experience at the forefront of research. This has been the case in the social sciences and anthropology, where fieldwork and empirical methods have long been used to study social problems. Similarly, in the field of psychology, the "living human document" has been emphasized as a valid way of understanding key issues and ideas. Practical and pastoral theology have moved in a similar direction, adopting empirical and social-scientific methods to further explore the intersections of religion, pastoral issues, and human experience. John Swinton and Harriet Mowat have contributed to this conversation in their text *Practical Theology and Qualitative Research*,[10] and Elaine Graham, Heather Walton, and Frances Ward have explored theological reflection across several volumes of work.[11] Qualitative research is now practiced and taught globally within the context of practical theology. The Theology and Action Research Network connects researchers and practitioners involved in a variety of action and participative research with a theological perspective, and the Network for Ecclesiology and Ethnography gathers and publishes widely on an international scale. More recently, creative research methods have come to occupy a vital position within the discipline, resulting in new opportunities for practical theologians.[12]

The Association for Practical Theology, the International Academy of Practical Theology, the British and Irish Association for Practical Theology, and the Association of Practical Theology in Oceania remain important networks for connecting practical and pastoral theologians on a global scale. These groups hold space for academics, practitioners, and church workers to exchange ideas. From this has stemmed a wider conversation around the professionalization of practical theology, because those who are able to engage in debates and shape the field are generally middle class, White, and educated. This has, of course, had an impact on the way in which the discipline has developed over time. New initiatives, such as the Practical Theology Hub, seek to broaden conversations and disseminate a wide range of voices. Early articles explored the place of colonial terminology, the construction of a Hindu Black theology, and Jewish Mitzvah.[13] Although its academic roots are Christian, these developments suggest that practical theology is no longer the preserve of one single religion.

Questions remain around the boundaries of practical and pastoral theology. In particular, there is an ongoing sense of nervousness around their "worth" among other theological disciplines. This debate will be dealt with in due course. At this point in their history, practical and pastoral theology have both grown and expanded into established, recognized disciplines in their own right. They have developed a deeper and more sophisticated sense of the relationship between theory and practice. Both are practiced in multiple contexts, in religious communities, the academy, and in wider society. For better or worse, practical and pastoral theologies cannot be boxed in, but rather are lived and breathed in many different places and circumstances.

Survey: What Is Practical and Pastoral Theology?

What characterizes practical and pastoral theology? In mapping the shape of these approaches, it is helpful to begin by considering the relationship between the two. Practical and pastoral theology are similar, but not synonymous. There are some significant differences that underpin each. The remit of pastoral theologians tends to be focused on the life and work of the church and the experiences of those who practice pastoral ministry within it. The questions and concerns that shape pastoral theology emerge from the practice of pastoral care; for example, caring for someone who is experiencing pregnancy loss, and the theological questions and issues that might arise in relation to this. Generally, the focus of practical theology is broader. Although the framework of religious life can still be an important starting point, practical theology also addresses a wide range of issues and experiences that stretch beyond the remit of the individual pastoral carer. Examples of this, some of which are examined in this chapter, include systemic issues related to gender inequality, disability, racism, classism, and poverty. Practical theologians generally (though not all) are committed to engaging with religious (primarily, but not always Christian) traditions. However, as Stephen Pattison and Gordon Lynch rightly point out, more recent pastoral care literature contains a greater awareness of the kind of social issues dealt with in practical theology.[14] As such, although it is valid to distinguish between practical and pastoral theology, the two share some important similarities as well as differences.

There has been a lot of debate around what practical theology is and what it entails. There is also the question of who counts as a practical theologian. In a sense, practical theology is an academic pursuit, which takes place within the confines of university departments. However, it is not bound to the academy. It can be argued that questions of a practical theological nature are being asked and explored in public spaces, without the aid of academics. In addressing the debate around the boundaries of the discipline, Eric Stoddart conceives of practical theology as an "imagined community."[15] To say that this community is "imagined" is not to say that it is created *ex nihilo*. Rather, this imagination is constructed from the concepts, worldviews, and plausibility structures of its practitioners. Practical theology, according to Stoddart, is a community in our "minds and behavior" that is generated by our common interests. To say that practical theology is an imagined community, then, leaves in place certain parameters, while allowing for a diversity of approach and holding tension in difference.

Yet, although this tolerance of one another's work in community is a hopeful idea, it does not address the issue of power dynamics that continue to underpin the discipline and its methods. Tom Beaudoin and Katherine Turpin draw attention to the "privilege and narrowness that Whiteness has afforded practical theology."[16] Whiteness is defined by Willie Jennings not simply as "people of European descent" but rather as "a way of being in the world and seeing the world that forms cognitive and affective structures able to seduce people into its habitation and its meaning making."[17] By this, Jennings is referring specifically to ways of being that privilege the bodies and perspectives of people of people with a pale skin tone. More specifically, the pursuit of practical theology has developed within a context of imperialism, colonialism, and White supremacy. Different parts of the world have differing histories of Whiteness and its impact, but practical theology, which was formed largely within North America and Western Europe, has developed through the gaze of majority White, educated scholars, including those who have been named previously. The discipline has also been rooted in the context of university structures, which are themselves plagued by issues of race, gender, and class representation. Rather than being a neutral or universal pursuit, as it imagines itself to be, practical theology is instead culturally White.[18] Warnings about this have been in place for some time,[19] but Black theologians have found that their stories "lack listeners" among their White counterparts.[20] In recent years, practical theology has experienced something of a self-described *kairos* moment.[21] The brutal and violent murder of George Floyd in Minneapolis on 25 May 2020, which was streamed on social media, provoked a wider consideration of Whiteness in the church and theology. However, it is important to point out that this "collective awakening" was revelatory only for some, and certainly not for Black people, who have long suffered under White supremacist structures and the deadly effects of White supremacy.[22] The pursuit of critical White theology, a term attributed to White theologian Al Barrett, reveals a multidimensional racism particularly in church institutions. Although considerations around Whiteness and the particular power dynamic of race in practical theology remain in a nascent stage, it is hoped that these will signal the beginning of further, future developments.

In surveying practical theology and dynamics of power and influence, it is also necessary to consider the different approaches to practical theology from around the world. In European contexts, practical theology continues to present as a scientific examination of Christian church leadership and education, centering Schleiermacher's understandings of the field. In the United Kingdom, where church and religion are growing less influential in a (debatably) postsecular context, practical theology is not limited in focus to the values, beliefs, and issues of the church. Instead, it includes a consideration of meaning making and values in contemporary culture. Meanwhile, in the United States, the discipline is practiced by a wide range of academics and professionals, but within a culture that continues to remain overtly religious in ways that affect legislation, politics, and public life. Although practical theology may have been born within White majority European academia, it is no longer ring-fenced by it. Now, it is a truly global pursuit, informed by the systems, contexts, and situations that its practitioners find themselves in. Global practical theologies can be found, for example, in liberation and mujerista theologies in Latin America. The writings of Cuban-American theologian Ada María Isasi-Díaz have been particularly formative in exploring the intersection between liberation theology and issues of gender discrimination.[23] Emmanuel Lartey's intercultural pastoral theology stems from his experience as a Ghanian theologian from West Africa.[24] The critical postcolonial theologies of thinkers such as Chung Hyun Kyung,[25] Choan-Seng Song,[26] and Kwok Pui-lan[27] are shaped by their lives in places marred by Western colonialization (South Korea, Taiwan, and Hong Kong respectively).

Practical and pastoral theology historically stem from debates around Christian practice and care, though, as previously mentioned, there has recently been more discussion around their place in different religions.[28] Tarek Badawia suggests that practical theology, although not derived from the context of Islamic theology, has always been very close to core ideas of charitable religiosity in Islam.[29] He equates it to the Islamic concept of *waqf*, meaning "to stop, contain, or to preserve."[30] Both practical theology and *waqf* emphasize social justice and the importance of ensuring the welfare of others. From a Buddhist perspective, Bhikshuni Lozang Trinlae considers the generalization of traditionally Christian academic practical theology models. She suggests that a more academic, critical reflection on praxis could be beneficial in a wide range of Buddhist contexts, including Buddhist congregations, clergy, teachers, and scholars.[31] For Kathleen Greider, the "momentous" question of whether practical theology is inherently a Christian concern or may have "resonance with other religious traditions" should be addressed through multireligious discussions.[32] This may well be the case, and some steps have already been taken in this direction. However, Katja Stuerzenhofecker highlights a particular point of tension here: "If the field's roots in Western practice and academia are Christian but current growth is international and multi-traditional, then how is this development best supported?"[33] According to Stuerzenhofecker, the issue does not lie with the inheritance of practical theology by non-Christians but rather with ongoing Christian hegemony that is both historical and continues to exist within institutional circumstances.[34] This is something, she suggests, that has not yet been considered in detail in academic work. It is an issue to be aware of as we consider the expansion of the field and seek to welcome and amplify different voices and contexts.

Having briefly surveyed the fields of practical and pastoral theology, one particular issue presents itself. If practical and pastoral theology are truly and global pursuits that are practiced in different contexts, across various religions, and considered through the lens of personal experience, is it possible to provide one single, all-encompassing definition? This particular debate will be returned to later in the chapter. For now, it is worth noting that despite the religious, geographical, and methodological differences that exist, there are some general characteristics that unite practical and pastoral theologians. Ultimately, lived contemporary experience is a primary lens of understanding. Critical dialogue between this experience and theological and doctrinal ideas drives much of the interdisciplinary work, qualitative research, and reflective practice that takes place in the field. Because of this emphasis on and contact with human life, practical and pastoral theologians tend to favor liberal or radical models of theology, such as liberation, Black, feminist, Womanist, and disability theologies (as opposed to more conservative approaches, which promote tradition and its application). Finally, the work of practical and pastoral theology is done with a view to theoretical and tangible transformation in the contexts and communities where practitioners are located.

Named Theologians: The Creative Challenges of Heather Walton and Courtney Goto

In what follows, the work of some outstanding representatives of practical and pastoral theology is highlighted and detailed. The task of selecting a small number of representatives of the discipline is a difficult one, not least because of practical theology's aforementioned "definitions problem." Heather Walton and Courtney Goto are two scholars who represent the field in different places and contexts. I have chosen to highlight Walton and Goto for their creative, challenging, and radical theologies. Both are attentive to voices that are marginalized in the discipline and are oriented toward future imagination and hope.

Heather Walton

The Scotland-based theologian Heather Walton has contributed deeply to the discipline, challenging practical theologians to consider the immense possibilities of creative methods for research. Her work has spanned themes including (but not limited to) life writing and spirituality, theopoetics, gender, and sexuality, as well as methods for theological research and reflective practice. Walton pays particular attention to the experience of the everyday and is concerned with ensuring that theology is not "a static resource" but a "creative response to the enchantment, wonder and terror of the present age."[35]

Walton's emphasis on creative work and theopoetics is not merely illustrative. It is intended to lead those who encounter it to an "epiphanic" state of understanding. By way of explanation, she writes that "art embodies fundamental questions and, given form, re-formed, they approach us as revelation."[36] However, she also points out that practical theologians have yet to name and explicitly acknowledge the way in which their work draws on, and owes a debt to, culture.[37] This may be because theopoetics, like practical theology, is underpinned by different approaches and understandings. It is an active process that involves multiple ways of knowing and encountering theological knowledge; for example, through an expanded understanding of primary texts to include music, visual art, and poetry or through social engagement and transformation. It can be practiced by academics and nonacademics alike and is therefore theistic and, in some senses, nontheistic. It is centered around bodies and the way in which we understand our carnal relationship with the world.[38] Much of the same can be said for autoethnography, a form of life writing about the personal and particular that pays attention to located, embodied experience. Walton's work on autoethnography links this practice to liberative movements including feminism, postcolonialism, and queer theory, all of which have "emphasised the importance of the standpoint from which we view the world."[39]

Walton is concerned that practical theologians have misunderstood creative practice and that this has resulted in a reluctance to draw theologically on creative methods. Indeed, practical theologians have been wary of these methods, continuing to "shelter behind secure boundaries" and avoid using approaches that might further "disinherit" or distance them from more traditional forms of theology.[40] However, Walton's engagement with creative practice points to new opportunities for the discipline. Autoethnographic writing and reflection pose a challenge to those who distance themselves from context and seek to observe and write theology from a neutral position. Walton reminds us that "where we stand determines what we see."[41] In other words, engaging with life writing practices can help us to decide whether we have an "epistemic advantage" in an issue of concern. This is especially crucial in ensuring that practical theology is active rather than static and that it can deliver insights for change and transformation, particularly for those most affected and marginalized by structures of power and privilege.

Walton's work has challenged the discipline of practical theology in radical ways. She critiques its reliance on a narrative of disinheritance, as well as the way in which it can become too tightly circumscribed by lines of religion, secularity, and traditional expectation. Her work on theopoetics, life writing, and other creative approaches generates deeper perceptions of lived experiences, from spirituality and identity to suffering and trauma.[42] It has created a crucial and much needed space for voices marginalized within and outwith the discipline. Walton's legacy will stretch beyond her work in this area, but it is hoped that her emphasis on creative practice will inspire and guide new generations of practical theologians as they seek further inclusion and authentic representation in the field.

Courtney Goto

The work of Japanese-American scholar Courtney Goto has been influential in shaping current conversations around practical theology. In her writing, Goto addresses the intersections of racism, culture, and faith, as well as theological teaching. Her 2018 work, *Taking on Practical Theology: The Idolization of Context and the Hope of Community*, examines the field's emphasis on context and the "taken for granted" use of paradigm. This has become an influential and even dominant method within the discipline. For Goto, this is deeply problematic. It reinforces both historic and modern structures of privilege and power and in doing so affects the way in which practical theology is created, researched, and taught. At the heart of Goto's work is a challenge to fellow practical theologians to understand their collusion within this system and an invitation to contemplate their individual habits and rituals.

In particular, Goto takes issue with the way in which paradigms, widely used within practical theology, are coded for the majority of people. Scholars who are favored by the paradigm (typically those who are White, North American, Western European, and Protestant) benefit, while their research communities and students are adversely affected. Issues arise where practical theologians consider their own "cultural, theological, gendered, and/or disciplinary" backgrounds as normative, even where they believe that their work is explicitly attentive to "context."[43] Practical theologians such as Don Browning, Richard Osmer, and Johannes van der Ven (among others; these are Goto's examples) propose frameworks and methods that are not culturally neutral, and yet they do not acknowledge this.[44] Rather, they offer their concepts and ideas as though they should apply theologically to all situations. For Goto, all practical theologians have been guilty of idolizing context in one form or another. "Taking on" context involves not only the critical task of exposing idols, but also exposing theologians as idol makers.

Goto suggests several ways in which structures of power and oppression might be challenged. The first involves the adoption of "prophetic tactics." Using the images of "prophet" and "tactician," Goto shows how practical theologians might nurture a greater perception and understanding of what the dominant culture looks like, and how they may be complicit in it in a variety of ways. Prophetic imagination can shed light on these blind spots. It can create space for practical theologians to be tactical, meaning that they can operate as both "an insider and an outsider to multiple groups in order to challenge oppression." Further, Goto suggests that practical theologians require a "critical intersubjective approach" that would allow all participants in the research process an opportunity to "practice critical awareness of themselves, others, and other interaction as they discern "context.'" She also turns her attention toward pedagogy and considers how "idols" in theological teaching may be identified and revised. Goto is critical of traditional pedagogies, which deflect the attention of students away from dynamics of power and oppression and add only "token diversity" to the teaching syllabus. Instead, she imagines a collaborative teaching space, in which the instructor becomes a "co-learner," empowering students to break idolized symbols and expose the paradigm.

Goto's work highlights some distressing issues at the heart of practical theology, its creation, and the ways in which it is taught. She acknowledges that although there is difficult and uncomfortable critical work to do in response, there is hope for the discipline. The solutions that Goto suggests are intended to unite a somewhat disparate field and remind practical theologians of what is at the heart of their "prophetic tradition." As Goto herself explains, "I tell these stories to lend you hope."

Practical and Pastoral Theology: The Debates

At this point, it is clear that practical theology faces a number of internal discussions and debates. Here, the usual caveat applies; there are many approaches to the discipline, and the perspectives of all practical theologians cannot be represented here. Two recurring issues that have been referenced within this chapter are as follows: the essence of practical theology, what it is and what it involves (the "definitions problem"), and the question of whether practical theology is "theological enough" (we might call this the "identity problem"). In what follows, both debates are outlined.

The definitions debate

Practical theology has been described as a "rich and diverse,"[45] "intricate and complex" discipline.[46] To some extent, the same may be said for all of the theological disciplines, but there is a particular level of complexity that comes with tracing the boundaries of practical theology. This is noted by some key voices within the field. Bonnie Miller-McLemore describes practical theology as "a term with loaded and overlapping meanings."[47] Eric Stoddart claims that practical theology is binary and that no two people engaged in the discipline will respond to the conversation between doctrine and practice "in exactly the same way."[48] Richard Osmer adds that members of the field have similar "tasks and interests" but points out that these are handled in diverse ways.[49] The field contains a multitude of theological denominations, religious outlooks and approaches. Self-defined practical theologians can be found both within and outwith the academy. Indeed, examining various university departments, courses, and degrees in practical theology brings us no closer to a common definition. Every department employs a different approach, which is in turn shaped by the interests of their academics and students. Those who call themselves practical theologians are interested in practice but do not necessarily agree on what "practice" entails or how it should be engaged with. Nor is there a single methodological approach or set of methods. Though there are recognizable approaches and frameworks, these remain diverse. For all of these reasons, practical theology is ambiguous and difficult to define.

Practical theologians have been highly concerned about defining the field and about getting it right. In some ways, this relates to the "identity debate" that will be discussed in due course. Perhaps if practical theologians can clearly understand what their role and discipline involves, they will feel less "disinherited" from the wider field. The pursuit of seeking a universal definition is one in which many practical theologians participate (see the opening paragraphs of this chapter), although there is some recognition that this is a misguided enterprise. John Swinton draws attention to the way in which the "meaning and content of the term 'practical theology' is determined by the *practical,* as opposed to the conceptual use of the term." In other words, we can come to know what practical theology is only by engaging in it. The meaning of the discipline is dependent on the interests and formation of the particular theologian. Just as Stoddard puts forward the idea of practical theology as an "imagined community," Swinton references Wittgenstein's idea of "family resemblance," suggesting that there may be some general features that are shared by those within the field. However, he emphasizes that practical theology is "action-oriented;" its identity and its form are dependent on the *actions* performed under the name "practical theology."[50]

So how might practical theology be defined? Bonnie Miller-McLemore is concerned that both extremes, "either declaring practical theology undefinable as a discipline or easily defined,"[51] are problematic. She recognizes some of the complexities of the debate and acknowledges that reaching a definition that is both concise yet expansive is an arduous task. However, Miller-McLemore still thinks that a definition is necessary in order to capture the numerous responsibilities of practical theology. Although practical theology *does* concern the relationship between beliefs and practices, "abbreviated mantras" like this, which are commonly the preserve of academics, do "leave much unsaid."[52] It is worth considering that both overly complex and overly condensed definitions can make the field seem inaccessible and impervious. This, in turn, reflects some of the education-based barriers to practical theology that still exist.

Although it is the case that definitions present a concrete problem concerning accessibility and understanding, there is perhaps a degree of freedom in ambiguity. Those who are marginalized in the discipline can define the field for themselves in ways that are not reliant on a White, European, male frame of reference, stemming from Schleiermacher's one-directional application. To bind practical theology too tightly within a single, universal structure or definition is to do a disservice to those whose work is often overlooked for not immediately fitting with, or at least paying lip service to, the White European "masters" and other makers of tradition. As practical theologians begin to challenge their reliance on these narratives and to examine critically White supremacy, patriarchy, ableism, and other systems that have supported their thinking, unstable definitions are to be expected. Like all theology, practical theology involves a degree of autobiography. As such, it is necessarily experience-driven. Practical theology is written by people living within particular contexts and systems that shape, privilege, and oppress them. It is a reflexive recognition of this that creates some of the debates around definition in the first place. The same recognition should free practical theologians from the task of seeking a single, universal definition.

The identity debate

The second debate for consideration here concerns the "identity" of practical theology. Like the "definitions debate," it thrives on a sense of unease and anxiety about the place of practical theology within the wider discipline. It is characterized by what Heather Walton calls "the ghostly presences of long centuries of intellectual humiliation and marginalisation within the Academy."[53] The question of whether practical and pastoral theology are truly theological has indeed haunted its practitioners.

In part, this stems from the interdisciplinary nature of practical theology. As we have seen in this chapter, practical theologians often employ social-scientific methodologies and frameworks. Swinton and Mowat suggest that these "outside" sources of knowledge can be welcomed into the practical theological inquiry and drawn upon in order to gather information and shed new light on situations. They are, however, concerned that practical theologians might lose sight of their grounding in theology, becoming purely sociologically driven.[54] Their perspective is not one shared by all practical theologians, and there is an ongoing debate (primarily within European practical theology) as to whether practical theology should be seen as confessional or as a "pure science."[55] While these debates are taking place, others have put in place important frameworks for the use of qualitative and social-scientific methods in answering theological questions. The question of whether interdisciplinary movement renders theology "less theological" is connected to how theology is understood and defined more widely and how its aims are imagined.

Practical and pastoral theology have provided space for critical reflection on lived experiences of faith. At their best, they have enabled people in and beyond faith communities to make sense of their experience and the traditions they have been exposed to in constructive ways. However, this has not always been valued by other "logic-centered" disciplines of theology. Connecting theology with lived experience is, by necessity, a context-bound project, but this also means that the outcomes of practical and pastoral theological studies are particular, less generalizable, and in some ways less likely to contribute to wider conversations about theory. This has led to practical theology being perceived as a less sophisticated and theoretical pursuit. Pattison and Lynch warn that practical theology needs to find ways of continuing to generate theoretical work or else it "risks becoming detached from the wider activity of academic theology and its contribution to the construction of theological concepts, symbols, and narratives may be weakened."[56]

This is an important critique and should not be discounted. The question as posed previously is: what does this wider activity of theology constitute? In this chapter, the concept of theology as autobiography has been considered. Although practical theology is anxiously reflexive and encourages practitioners to consider their biases as a matter of methodological importance, this is not always the case in other theological disciplines. Yet these disciplines are constructed in much the same way, representing the particular interests of those who participate in them. Theology in other disciplines is not a disembodied, disconnected occupation, but one that is shaped and informed by its members. Further, should practical theology try to acquiesce and seek to become "more theological," when the pursuit of theology (beyond "God talk") is so varied and multilayered? How can we meaningfully measure what it means to be "theological enough" when the creation of theology across denominations, religions, and continents is so different?

Issues of identity remain as practical theologians are paying closer attention to issues of homogeneity in the discipline. Practical theology is always reshaping itself to include a diversity of perspectives. In creating space for more varied voices that have been marginalized in the discipline, there will be inevitable (and legitimate) critiques of traditional theological structures, which have been created largely by White, male, European academics. If practical theology desires to be truly liberative, to represent the marginalized, and to critique theology through the lens of lived experience, it must remain disenfranchised to an extent from the wider theological project. Its supposed "Cinderella" status is also its power.[57]

Achievement and Agenda: The Future of Practical and Pastoral Theology

To engage in practical and pastoral theology in contemporary times is to do so against a backdrop of global instability. This has, perhaps, always been the case. Certainly, this is not the first time in history that theologians have faced a volatile future, though theologians of today and of the future are, thanks to technological advances, more exposed to global issues than ever before. In approaching these, practical and pastoral theology will inevitably face tensions between a focus on local concerns and worldwide conversations. At its most liberative, it must question not only how to transform the immediate context, but how global and international structures and relationships might be reformed to create a better world.

Discussions around climate change are particularly pertinent, and there is a real and growing anxiety about the future of human life. As the earth rapidly continues to warm, causing famine, fires, drought, and displacement, there will be implications for the practice of pastoral care, and questioning of religious beliefs.[58] Communities in the global South are already suffering the effects of climate change disproportionately, and intersections between the climate crisis and race, gender, disability, and socioeconomic status must be attended to.[59] Theological work in this area is ongoing, but activism and everyday practice have proven just as crucial for tackling climate change.

Meanwhile, the COVID-19 pandemic exposed deep-rooted vulnerabilities in individualistic, capitalist structures. COVID-19 was not a great equalizer; the social and economic impacts of the crisis have been significant.[60] Almost half of the projected new poor will be in South Asia, and more than a third in Sub-Saharan Africa. This is significant for practical and pastoral theology as they seek to include voices from the global South. If done carefully, this will bring a much-needed sense of perspective to discussions around inequality. The pandemic has also affected religious communities, who have been unable to gather and worship together. The impact of this and of the mass movement to online worship is still being interpreted. How it will affect congregational structures and attendance is a question for pastoral reflection.

Previously in this chapter, the impact of the Black Lives Matter movement and the (debatable) kairos moment of 2020 was discussed. White supremacy remains a worldwide issue, deeply embedded in the structures of our daily lives. Important theologies of lived experience, including those from Anthony Reddie, Azariah France-Williams, and Jarel Robinson-Brown in the United Kingdom[61] and Phillis Sheppard, J. Kameron Carter, and Emilie Townes in the United States,[62] have drawn attention to the implicit and explicit impacts of racism and White supremacy in religious contexts. It is important to hear from Black theologians, whose voices and experiences should be elevated. The work of critical White theology must take place concurrently, as a crucial form of active allyship and resistance to racism in all its forms.

Gender-based rights are an ongoing topic of global conversation, and in recent years, the inclusion of transgender and gender-variant voices has been an important step forward. Historically, transgender, gender-variant, and intersex people have existed in all ages and societies. It can therefore be assumed that transgender experience and practice has a long religious history, yet religious groups continue to conceptualize the lives of gender-variant people as an ethical problem or "issue." Much of trans theology is written by allies such as Susannah Cornwall and Megan DeFranza,[63] but in recent years transgender and gender-variant theologians have begun to carve out space to tell their own stories. Alex Clare-Young,[64] Tina Beardsley,[65] and Justin Sabia-Tanis,[66] among others, provide vital insights into the intersections between gender identity, religious faith, spirituality, and discrimination. Practical theology lends itself to liberative and transformative conversations, through methods which uphold the importance of lived experience. It will make a natural home for transgender, gender-variant, and intersex theologies as they continue to expand and grow.

The question of who will engage with these issues is a pertinent one. Who is the future practical theologian? In this chapter, we have established that they may represent any religious or spiritual background, not just Christianity. As some parts of the world (Western Europe and the Asia Pacific in particular) become less religious and more secularized, we should also consider the importance of nonreligious practical theologians. Theological discussions and "God talk" take place in a wide range of social settings. Theoretically, religious institutions understand themselves as separate from wider society. In practice, the two become enmeshed in our daily lives and understandings. Those who are religious are, inevitably, influenced by both; their worldviews are not simply a reflection of their religious beliefs, but of their experiences within wider families, social circles, and societies. Arguably, the practices of the church and of the world are not ontologically separate, because both occur within God's creation.[67] A logical next step would be to include the lives, habits, and rituals of those who exist outside religious communities in theological reflection. There has not been a great deal of work on this yet, though Elaine Graham has written of practical theology as critical reflection on the beliefs and values of communities, with this attention not being restricted to religious communities of faith.[68] Gordon Lynch has outlined a "postreligious" approach to practical theology, which is "open to being practised by those who do not have a commitment to any one particular faith tradition" and seeks practical moral wisdom for living constructively.[69] In doing so, he is careful to suggest that a postreligious approach is no better than a pastoral theological one; these are simply different frameworks that suit the commitment and needs of different people.[70] There is no expectation that the inclusion of a postreligious practical theology would prevent, for example, Christian pastoral theologians from drawing on their religious beliefs. The answer to whether postsecular practical theology will flourish lies in the future, but these are certainly issues worth consideration.

Conclusion

Practical theology faces a future fraught with both internal and external challenges. Internally, it remains divided on issues of focus, methodology, self-interpretation, and identity. Externally, it will be written, taught, and discussed against an unstable backdrop of accelerated global change and misinformation. It is still considered the "Cinderella" of the wider discipline for its enduring attention to lived experience as a lens for critical reflection on religion and doctrine. There are future discussions to be had about the ways in which practical theology can contribute theoretically and methodologically to theology. At the same time, it must be celebrated as a discipline underpinned by liberative practices, which, at their best, are radical, inclusive, and transformative. These qualities ground practical theology in the material, invite new and vital conversations, and uphold marginalized voices. The future of the discipline is full of potential. Perhaps future practical and pastoral theologians will wear the glass slippers with pride.

Notes

1 Elaine Graham, *Transforming Practice: Pastoral Theology in an Age of Uncertainty* (Eugene, OR: Wipf and Stock, 2002), 3.

2 Eric Stoddart, *Advancing Practical Theology: Critical Discipleship for Disturbing Times* (London: SCM Press, 2014), xii.

3 For examples, see William Clebsch and Charles Jaekle, *Pastoral Care in Historical Perspective* (New York: Harper & Row, 1967) and Gillian R. Evans, ed., *A History of Pastoral Care* (London: Cassell, 2000). In *Classical Pastoral Care,* Thomas Oden compiles passages from early church writers concerning pastoral care, including Augustine, Irenaeus, Athanasius, Tertullian, Ambrose, Aquinas, Aelred of Rievaulx, Catherine of Siena, and others. See Thomas C. Oden, *Classical Pastoral Care, Vol. 3: Pastoral Counsel* (Grand Rapids, MI: Baker Books, 1987).

4 Gregory the Great, *The Book of Pastoral Rule,* trans. George E. Demacopoulos (Crestwood, NY: St. Vladimir's Seminary Press, 2007), 29.

5 Courtney Goto, *Taking on Practical Theology: The Idolization of Context and the Hope of Community* (Leiden: Brill, 2018), 6.

6 As I note within this chapter, much of practical theology has evolved from Schleiermacher's original framework, but this can be problematic. It has contributed to the creation of a discipline that is often racially and culturally homogenous. John Swinton recalls a comment made by Ghanaian theologian Emmanuel Lartey at the International Academy of Practical Theology in 2003. "After several papers had traced practical theology's history back to Schleiermacher, Emmanuel commented: 'You know, many of you are critical of African ancestor worship. Perhaps you should take a look at yourselves!' We laughed. . .awkwardly. His point was a fair one." John Swinton, "What Comes Next? Practical Theology, Faithful Presence, and Prophetic Witness," *Practical Theology* 13, nos. 1–2 (2020): 165.

7 See Don Browning, *A Fundamental Practical Theology: Descriptive and Strategic Proposals* (Minneapolis, MN: Fortress Press, 1996).

8 Browning, *A Fundamental Practical Theology,* 7.

9 Carol Lakey Hess takes this a step further, suggesting that practical theology should involve a "mutually critical and mutually enhancing conversation" between the academy and wider society and culture. See Carol Lakey Hess, "Religious Education," in *The Wiley Blackwell Companion to Practical Theology,* ed. Bonnie J. Miller-McLemore (Oxford: Wiley-Blackwell, 2012), 299.

10 John Swinton and Harriet Mowat, *Practical Theology and Qualitative Research,* 2nd ed. (London: SCM Press, 2016).

11 Elaine Graham, Heather Walton, and Frances Ward, *Theological Reflection: Methods,* 2nd ed., ed. Katja Stuerzenhofecker (London: SCM Press, 2019); Elaine Graham, Heather Walton, and Frances Ward, *Theological Reflection: Sources* (London: SCM Press, 2007).

12 In particular, see Wren Radford, "Creative Arts-based Research Methods in Practical Theology: Constructing New Theologies of Practice," *Practical Theology* 13, nos. 1–2 (2020): 60–74.

13 Vishal Sangu, "The Place of Colonial Terminology within Religious Studies – Sikhi, 'Sikhism,' Sikhism, or Sikhi(sm)," *Practical Theology Hub,* 21 July 2022, https://practicaltheologyhub.com/?p=157 (accessed 28 July 2022); Ashkay Gupta, "Constructing a Hindu Black Theology," *Practical Theology Hub,* 11 July 2022, https://practicaltheologyhub.com/?p=153 (accessed 28 July 2022); Harrie Cedar, "Mitzvah – Making the Place More Holy: The Ultimate in Practical Theology," *Practical Theology Hub,* 11 July 2022, https://practicaltheologyhub.com/?p=198 (accessed 28 July 2022).

14 Stephen Pattison and Gordon Lynch, "Pastoral and Practical Theology," in *The Modern Theologians: An Introduction to Christian Theology Since 1918,* 3rd ed., ed. David F. Ford with Rachel Muers (Oxford: Blackwell, 2005), 410.

15 Stoddart, *Advancing Practical Theology,* 12.

16 Tom Beaudoin and Katherine Turpin, "White Practical Theology," in *Opening the Field of Practical Theology: An Introduction,* ed. Kathleen Cahalan and Gordon Mikoski (Lanham, MD: Rowman and Littlefield, 2014), 251.

17 Willie Jennings, *After Whiteness: An Education in Belonging* (Grand Rapids, MI: Eerdmans, 2020), 9.

18 Beaudoin and Turpin, "White Practical Theology," 253.

19 In particular, see Phillis Isabella Sheppard, "Raced Bodies: Portraying Bodies, Reifying Racism," in *Conundrums in Practical Theology,* ed. Bonnie J. Miller-McLemore and Joyce Mercer (Boston, MA: Brill, 2016), 219–49; Jaco S. Dreyer, "Knowledge, Subjectivity, (De)Coloniality, and the Conundrum of Reflexivity," in *Conundrums in Practical Theology,* 90–109; Emmanuel Lartey, *Postcolonialising God: An African Practical Theology* (London: SCM Press, 2013); Anthony Reddie, *Theologising Brexit: A Liberationist and Postcolonial Critique* (London: Routledge, 2019).

20 Michael Jagessar, review of *Rejection, Resistance and Resurrection: Speaking Out on Racism in the Church,* by Mukti Barton, *Black Theology* 4, no. 2 (2006): 233.

21 Al Barrett and Jill Marsh, "Critical White Theology: Dismantling Whiteness?" *Practical Theology* 15, nos. 1–2 (2020): 1.

22 Barrett and Marsh, "Critical White Theology," 1.

23 Ada María Isasi- Díaz, *Mujerista Theology: A Theology for the Twenty-first Century* (Maryknoll, NY: Orbis, 1996).

24 Emmanuel Lartey, *In Living Colour: An Intercultural Approach to Pastoral Care and Counselling*, 2nd ed. (London: Jessica Kingsley Publishers, 2003).

25 Chung Hyun Kyang, *Struggle to Be the Sun Again: Introducing Asian Women's Theology* (Maryknoll, NY: Orbis, 1990).

26 Choan-Seng Song, *Tracing the Footsteps of God: Discovering What You Really Believe* (Minneapolis, MN: Fortress Press, 2007) and *The Believing Heart: An Invitation to Story Theology* (Minneapolis, MN: Fortress Press, 1999).

27 Kwok Pui-lan, *Postcolonial Politics and Theology: Unravelling Empire for a Global World* (Louisville, KY: Westminster John Knox Press, 2021) and *Postcolonial Imagination and Feminist Theology* (Louisville, KY: Westminster John Knox Press, 1995).

28 It is worth noting here that the Professional Doctorate in Practical Theology, awarded by a number of institutions in the United Kingdom including the Universities of Roehampton, Chester, Birmingham, Anglia Ruskin, and Glasgow, has supported the research of professionals from UK-based and international Christian backgrounds, as well as those who are Buddhist, Muslim, and Jewish.

29 Tarek Badawia, "Islamic Practical Theology: waqf and zakāt as Theological Foundations," in *Exploring Islamic Social Work: Between Community and the Common Good*, ed. Hansjörg Schmid and Amir Sheikhzadegan (Cham: Springer, 2022), 152.

30 Khairunnisa Musari, "Waqf-Sukuk, Enhancing the Islamic Finance for Economic Sustainability in Higher Education Institutions," *World Islamic Countries University Leaders Summit* 2016, 4.

31 Bhikshuni Lozang Trinlae, "Prospects for a Buddhist Practical Theology," *International Journal of Practical Theology* 18, no. 1 (2014): 7.

32 Kathleen J. Grieder, "Religious Pluralism and Christian-Centrism" in *The Wiley Blackwell Companion to Practical Theology*, 464.

33 Katja Stuerzenhofecker, "Pluralising Practical Theology: International and Multi-traditional Challenges and Opportunities," *Practical Theology* 13, nos. 1–2 (2020): 123.

34 Stuerzenhofecker, "Pluralising Practical Theology," 123.

35 Heather Walton, "We Have Never Been Theologians: Postsecularism and Practical Theology," *Practical Theology* 11, no. 3 (2018): 225.

36 Heather Walton, "A Theopoetics of Practice: Reforming in Practical Theology," *International Journal of Practical Theology* 23, no. 1 (2019): 7.

37 Walton, "A Theopoetics of Practice," 7.

38 For an in-depth exploration of bodies and Christian memory and theology, see Mayra Rivera, *Poetics of the Flesh* (London: Duke University Press, 2015).

39 Heather Walton, "What Is Autoethnography and Why Does It Matter for Theological Reflection?" *Anvil: Journal of Theology and Mission* 36, no. 1 (2020): 6.

40 Walton, "We Have Never Been Theologians," 226.

41 Walton, "What Is Autoethnography?," 6.

42 Walton includes, for example, issues such as "bullying, bereavement, work challenges, consciousness of ethnic identity, migration, sexual practice, abuse, childbirth, abortion, [and] cancer treatment." Walton, "What Is Autoethnography?," 7.

43 Goto, *Taking on Practical Theology*, 5.

44 Goto, *Taking on Practical Theology*, 26, 95, 111–12.

45 Bonnie J. Miller-McLemore, *Christian Theology in Practice: Discovering a Discipline* (Grand Rapids, MI: Eerdmans, 2012), 157.

46 Swinton and Mowat, *Practical Theology and Qualitative Research*, xi.

47 Bonnie J. Miller-McLemore, "Five Misunderstandings about Practical Theology," *International Journal of Practical Theology* 16, no. 1 (2012): 20.

48 Stoddart, *Advancing Practical Theology*, xii.

49 Richard Osmer, "Practical Theology: A Current International Perspective," *HTS Teologiese Studies/ Theological Studies* 67, no. 2 (2011): 3.

50 Swinton, "What Comes Next?," 164.

51 Miller-McLemore, "Five Misunderstandings about Practical Theology," 19.

52 Miller-McLemore, "Five Misunderstandings about Practical Theology," 19.

53 Walton, "We Have Never Been Theologians," 224.

54 Swinton and Mowat, *Practical Theology and Qualitative Research*, 24.

55 Swinton, "What Comes Next?," 169.

56 Pattinson and Lynch, "Pastoral and Practical Theology," 422.

57 Pattinson and Lynch, "Pastoral and Practical Theology," 422.

58 Ryan LaMothe, "This Changes Everything: The Sixth Extinction and its Implications for Pastoral Theology," *Journal of Pastoral Theology* 26, no. 3 (2016): 179.

59 See Hannah Malcolm, ed., *Words for a Dying World: Stories of Grief and Courage from the Global Church* (London: SCM Press, 2020).

60 Katie Cross, Wren Radford, and Karen O'Donnell, "Fragments from within the Pandemic: Theological Experiments in Silence, Speech, and Dislocated Time," *Practical Theology* 14, nos. 1–2 (2021): 144–58.

61 Anthony Reddie, *Theologising Brexit* and *Introducing James H. Cone: A Personal Exploration* (London: SCM Press, 2022); Azariah France-Williams, *Ghost Ship: Institutional Racism and the Church of England*

(London: SCM Press, 2020); Jarel Robinson-Brown, *Black, Gay, British, Christian, Queer: The Church and the Famine of Grace* (London: SCM Press, 2021).

62 See Phillis Isabella Sheppard, "Raced Bodies"; J. Kameron Carter, *Race: A Theological Account* (Oxford: Oxford University Press, 2008); Emilie Townes, *A Troubling in My Soul: Womanist Perspectives on Evil and Suffering* (Maryknoll, NY: Orbis, 1993).

63 Susannah Cornwall, *Theology and Sexuality* (London: SCM Press, 2013), *Intersex, Theology and the Bible: Troubling Bodies in Church, Text and Society* (New York: Palgrave Macmillan, 2015); Megan DeFranza, *Sex Difference in Christian Theology: Male, Female, and Intersex in the Image of God* (Grand Rapids, MI: Eerdmans, 2015).

64 Alex Clare Young, *Transgender. Christian. Human.* (Glasgow: Wild Goose Publications, 2019).

65 Tina Beardsley and Michelle O'Brien, eds., *This Is My Body: Hearing the Theology of Transgender Christians* (London: Darton, Longman & Todd, 2016).

66 Justin Sabia-Tranis, *Trans-Gendered: Theology, Ministry, and Communities of Faith* (Eugene, OR: Wipf and Stock, 2018).

67 Alistair Campbell, "The Nature of Practical Theology," in *Theology and Practice*, ed. Duncan B. Forrester (London: Epworth, 1990), 16.

68 See Graham, *Transforming Practice*.

69 Gordon Lynch, "Developing 'Post-Religious' Practical Theology," *Contact* 142, no. 1 (2003): 26.

70 Lynch, "Developing 'Post-Religious' Practical Theology," 26.

Recommended Reading

Primary

Goto, Courtney. *Taking on Practical Theology: The Idolization of Context and the Hope of Community.* Leiden: Brill, 2018.

Graham, Elaine, Heather Walton, and Frances Ward. *Theological Reflection: Methods.* 2nd ed. Edited by Katja Stuerzenhofecker. London: SCM Press, 2019.

Lartey, Emmanuel. *In Living Colour: An Intercultural Approach to Pastoral Care and Counselling.* 2nd ed. London: Jessica Kingsley Publishers, 2003.

Mercer, Joyce, and Bonnie J. Miller-McLemore. *Conundrums in Practical Theology.* Leiden: Brill, 2016.

Sheppard, Phillis Isabella. *Self, Culture, and Others in Womanist Practical Theology.* New York: Palgrave Macmillan, 2011.

Swinton, John, and Harriet Mowat. *Practical Theology and Qualitative Research.* 2nd ed. London: SCM Press, 2016.

Secondary

Beaudoin, Tom, and Katherine Turpin. "White Practical Theology." In *Opening the Field of Practical Theology: An Introduction.* Edited by Kathleen Cahalan and Gordon Mikoski, 251–70. Lanham, MD: Rowman and Littlefield, 2014.

Miller-McLemore, Bonnie J. "Five Misunderstandings about Practical Theology." *International Journal of Practical Theology* 16, no. 1 (2012): 5–26.

Moschella, Mary Clark. *Ethnography as a Pastoral Practice: An Introduction.* 2nd ed. London: SCM Press, 2022.

Radford, Wren. "Creative Arts-based Research Methods in Practical Theology: Constructing New Theologies of Practice." *Practical Theology* 13, nos. 1–2 (2020): 60–74.

Slee, Nicola. *Fragments for Fractured Times: What Feminist Practical Theology Brings to the Table.* London: SCM Press, 2021.

Swinton, John. "What Comes Next? Practical Theology, Faithful Presence, and Prophetic Witness." *Practical Theology* 13, nos. 1–2 (2020): 162–73.

Philosophy and Theology

Nicholas Adams

Introduction

The relationship between philosophy and theology since 1918 is marked by two significant forces. The first is the immense generativity in English-, French-, and German-language philosophy from the period of the Reformation (which often provoked this generativity) until the period after the French Revolution in 1789. The second is the catastrophe of World War I (1914–18), which destroyed the younger bearers of this rich tradition. It both forced the rapid reconstitution of knowledge and brought death and catastrophe into sharp focus as contexts for human action.

The period before 1914 bequeathed roughly three patterns of reasoning, three criteria for truth. They have a complex relation to each other. The first is a turn to the subject. This found an intense focus in Luther's "Here I stand," with an interpreter of the Bible free of external control and an institutionally independent relation to God. It also has an intense focus in the prefatory "I am myself the matter of my book" of Montaigne's *Essais*. The turn to the subject thus has both Protestant (Luther) and Catholic (Montaigne) lineage. It appears as an agent with meaningful freedom and independence and as an object for reflection. The turn to the subject is associated with freedom, independence, spontaneity, activity, and productivity.

The second is a turn to language. It found an intense focus in Reformation interpretation of the Bible and the desire to identify constraints on the freedom of the interpreter. The capacity of words not only to represent existing affairs but to have effects in the world becomes an increasingly important theme. The linguistic turn finds philosophical focus around the time of Kant in the work of figures like Herder and Hamann, the German Romantics (and those influenced by them, such as Coleridge), and the early nineteenth-century linguists such as Wilhelm von Humboldt who reflect on the plurality of languages. Tradition, grammar, and cultural identity all operate as constraints on the idea of free subjectivity; and judgments of experience are in a fundamental way culturally and linguistically shaped.

The third is a turn to art. This had an intense focus for many hundreds of years in the European tradition from Greek drama, through medieval art, to the modern novel: Sophocles' *Antigone*, Michelangelo's *Pietà*, Jane Austen's *Sense and Sensibility*. It becomes philosophically significant for those who recognize that the

Ford's The Modern Theologians: An Introduction to Christian Theology since 1918, Fourth Edition.
Edited by Rachel Muers and Ashley Cocksworth.

ground of conceptual articulation cannot itself be conceptually articulated, that nonverbal artistic objects cannot be satisfactorily captured in verbal forms, and that meaningful artistic action is often the creation of something new more than representing what already exists.

The significance of art can be shown by attending to the simultaneity of philosophical and artistic artefacts. To echo and expand a point made recently by Andrew Bowie, Cervantes' *Don Quixote* (1605) and George Herbert's *The Temple* (1633) are close in time to Descartes's *Discourse on Method* (1637).[1] Both Cervantes' protagonist and Descartes's authorial self are on quests, but of quite different kinds. Don Quixote's quests are marked by illusion, frustration, and painful failure. Descartes's "quest for certainty" (John Dewey) seeks a foundation that will be proof against skepticism. Herbert's poetic voice articulates a delight in the flexibility of language and its capacity to evoke a world in and beyond everyday life. All are formative for modern self-consciousness, but in contrasting ways. Likewise Goethe's *Sorrows of Young Werther* (1774) is close in time to Kant's *Critique of Pure Reason* (1781). Goethe's protagonist works through the experience of suffering and failure and his life ends in a lonely and protracted death. Kant's authorial self seeks to establish the objectivity of experience by identifying its universal conditions. Proust's *In Search of Lost Time* (1913) and Stravinsky's *Rite of Spring* (1913) are almost exactly contemporary with Russell and Whitehead's *Principia Mathematica* (1910–13). Proust offers reflections on loss and meaninglessness and Stravinsky explores violently dissonant juxtapositions and the breakdown of tonality. Russell and Whitehead propose a method precise enough to solve the toughest paradoxes. An education in the mainstream histories of philosophy and theology without a parallel education in plays, novels, poems, paintings, ballets, sculptures, symphonies, and opera gives a ruinously misleading picture of European cultural development: the apparent purity of philosophical goals contrasts forcefully with the artistic confrontations with uncertainty, anxiety, and failure. They accompany each other at every step.

These three turns – to the subject, to language, to art – are not mutually exclusive; by 1914, each relates to the others. All leave their mark on theology and in many cases shape its form and its substance. They are in many cases marked by an engagement with modern Jewish philosophy, especially the work of Martin Buber, Franz Rosenzweig, Walter Benjamin, Theodor Adorno, Hannah Arendt, Emil Fackenheim, Emmanuel Levinas, and Jacques Derrida. The relationship between theology and philosophy has tended to be, and continues to be, disproportionately dominated by White male voices.

Under the turn to the subject we shall consider Barth and Kirschbaum on the Trinity and God's sovereign freedom, Bultmann on the decision of faith, neoscholasticism as movements resisting the turn to the subject, *nouvelle théologie* on the significance of historical judgments, Rahner on transcendental experience and on grace, Moltmann on suffering, Lash on everyday experience, Reformed epistemology on belief.

Under the turn to language we shall consider Moltmann on hope and the influence of Gadamer, the analytic turn and its presumption that language is stable, the turn to Wittgenstein and the analogy between grammar and doctrine, and postliberalism on tradition (including Frei, Lindbeck, Ricoeur). Under the turn to art we shall consider Tillich on symbols, Balthasar on glory, and those who draw on the sources that animate this strand of the tradition.

Survey

The turn to the subject

The main idea is that knowledge is not just reception (of teaching, of experience, or whatever). The thinking subject is active. It can be confident of the fact that it is thinking (Descartes), that its experiences belong to it (Locke, Hume, Lessing), that it unifies its field of perception, and that any judgment about an object is a judgment that it makes (Kant), that its consciousness is grounded in its own activity (Fichte), that meaningful faith is a matter of its own passion (Kierkegaard). The modern subject is marked by freedom, independence, and a degree of self-mastery and sovereignty. This intensifies after the American (1765–91) and French (1789) revolutions, in which the themes of liberty and self-governance are amplified.

Dialectical theology

Karl Barth and Charlotte von Kirschbaum make two fundamental claims that draw on the European philosophical tradition. The first is that one of the marks of modern philosophy is an excessive confidence in the freedom and autonomy of the modern subject and a correspondingly diminished picture of the scope and power of God's action. This is especially true, they claim, of Hegel.[2] The second is that this is to be corrected by proclaiming God's freedom and sovereignty

Barth and Kirschbaum invert the modern subject and use the modern language of human subjectivity to describe God. It is God who is sovereign, free, self-determining. In their Trinitarian theology Barth and Kirschbaum further say that God as Trinity is three ways of being (*Seinsweise*) in one subject (*Subjekt*).[3] Barth and Kirschbaum say that God is one. This is qualified by how God is one, namely three ways of being (*Seinsweise*) that are distinctive and mutually related. Barth and Kirschbaum then say that God is Lord. This is qualified by understanding God as the "you" (*Du*) who meets the human "I" and unites himself as "the indissoluble subject." The subject is Chalcedonian in that it cannot be dissolved into separate divine and human components, and also inflected by Martin Buber's *I and Thou – Ich und Du –* which was influential in theology after its publication in 1923 and English translation in 1937.

The term subject has two distinct uses in philosophy. The first appears in the pair subject and object. "Helen reads the book." Helen is the subject and the book is the object. The second use appears in the pair subject and predicate. The book is long: the book is the subject and long is the predicate. This is confusing for an obvious reason. In the sentence "Helen reads the long book," in the first sense Helen is the subject and the long book is the object, but in the second sense the book is a subject and long is its predicate. Depending on which sense one is using, the book is either an object or a subject.

When Barth and Kirschbaum say that God is a subject, they are using the pair subject and object, not subject and predicate. Barth and Kirschbaum refuse to cast God as an object like things in the world. This is in continuity with the long tradition, but it becomes urgent when God becomes in some philosophies an object of knowledge, where it becomes commonplace to ask "does God exist?" and "how can we know God?" Barth and Kirschbaum's strategy of stressing God as subject, as sovereign, as free, is intended to rescue theology from this kind of "objectivity." That strategy is unthinkable without the model of the modern subject as sovereign and free.

Rudolf Bultmann is acutely aware of a problem arising within his discipline of New Testament study. From the late 1700s onwards it had become thinkable that the Bible is a historical source and that one should evaluate its claims in the same way as claims about Greek and Roman ancient history. The Bible became like Homer's *Odyssey* or Livy's *History of Rome,* just as the historicity of these works was being publicly questioned. By the 1930s when Bultmann was writing, this was compounded by the problem that the Bible appeared to make statements discredited by modern science, for example in Psalm 104, which appears to insist that the earth does not move. If knowledge of God comes from scripture, and if scripture is historically and scientifically unreliable, then knowledge of God is proportionally unreliable. Following a well-established pattern in New Testament scholarship, Bultmann suggests that one must distinguish between the message and the "mythology" in which that message is expressed. The "one" who does this distinguishing is the modern subject, using its own criteria.[4]

Drawing on the work of his contemporary Martin Heidegger, Bultmann suggests that the crucial category is not knowledge, and the crucial question is not, "how do I know?" but "decision" (*Entscheidung*), and "how do I relate to things?" Heidegger's refusal of epistemology (knowing) in favor of phenomenology (doing) together with his insistence that the horizon of human action is not eternity but human finitude is linked by Bultmann with theological accounts of human limitedness as creatures. He shares with Barth and others the project of outlining the ways in which the subject does not judge God (God's existence, God's attributes, or whatever) but is confronted by God, above all in scripture, and must respond by making a decision. This twentieth-century "existentialist" project tends to play down God's eternity and the idea that human knowledge should mirror it in favor of a model of human action as a response to what confronts it. This then shapes an account of God as the one who confronts us, above all in the life, death, and resurrection of Jesus Christ, as mediated by scripture.

Bultmann becomes famous for saying that one can discard the mythology of the Bible — its world of miracles, of demons, of a three-storied universe (hell below, earth here, and heaven above) — and becomes a champion for a later "liberal" theology that seeks to escape from the apparent unbelievability of Christian claims. This is not his focus. His project is less to create a believable theology and more to embrace the existential challenge of being a finite subject confronted by God, by Jesus's challenge that we must decide, where everything turns on that decision.

Barth and Kirschbaum and Bultmann thus offer responses to the turn to the subject. Where Barth and Kirschbaum take the modern free subject and in a Calvinist way invert it into an account of God's subjectivity, Bultmann takes Heidegger's finite human subject and in a Lutheran way inverts Heidegger's relentless focus on death as the horizon of being into an encounter with God's offer of salvation that forces a decision of faith.

Neoscholastic retrieval of Aquinas

Neoscholasticism names a range of Roman Catholic refusals of what its official documents call "modernism." In the twentieth century the important documents include Pope Pius X's decree *Lamentabili sane* of 1907. Its "syllabus concerning the errors of the modernists" opens as follows:

> With truly lamentable results, our age, casting aside all restraint in its search for the ultimate causes of things, frequently pursues novelties so ardently that … it falls into very serious errors, which are even more serious when they concern sacred authority, the interpretation of Sacred Scripture, and the principal mysteries of Faith.[5]

The commendation of the work of Thomas Aquinas by Pope Leo XIII in 1879 led nearly forty years later to the formal requirement in Canon 1366 of the Code of Canon Law of 1917, from Title 21 "on seminaries":

> § 2. Professors shall treat studies in rational theology and philosophy and the instruction of students in these disciplines according to the system, teaching, and principles of the Angelic Doctor and hold to them religiously.[6]

This is one of the most important documents in the history of the relationship between philosophy and theology in the twentieth century. After 1917, official Roman Catholic philosophical curricula in seminaries were patterned after Thomas, the "angelic doctor." This produced neo-Thomist Latin works of the kind published by Édouard Hugon (*Cursus philosophiae thomisticae*, 1913), Henri Grenier (*Cursus Philosophiae*, 1944), and Réginald Garrigou-Lagrange (*De Revelatione per Ecclesiam Catholicam proposita*, 1945), as well as vernacular works such as *God, His Existence and Nature: A Thomistic Solution of Certain Agnostic Antinomies* (Garrigou-Lagrange 1914, in French) and *The History of Scholastic Method* (Grabman 1909–11, in German).

There are many "versions of Thomism" (Kerr), including non-Aristotelian or more-than-Aristotelian interpretations of Aquinas. These include *Thomism: Introduction to the Philosophy of St Thomas Aquinas*

(Gilson 1922) and *Elements of Philosophy* (Maritain 1920, 1923), both of which are inflected by a deep knowledge of Descartes, or *The Starting Point of Metaphysics: studies in the historical and theoretical development of the problem of knowledge* (Maréchal 1922–47), which shows a strong post-Kantian reading of Aquinas.

The official role of neoscholasticism can be described either as a response to the modernist crisis with a welcome defense of realism against idealism[7] or an engine to resist challenges to ecclesial authority.[8] Since the 1860s there had in Germany been a new strand of thought called neo-Kantianism. It is today primarily associated with Hermann Cohen, Paul Natorp, and Ernst Cassirer (in Marburg), and Wilhelm Windelband, Heinrich Rickert, and Ernst Troeltsch (in Heidelberg). Their core insight, derived from taking the natural sciences as the preeminent model for truth, was that the question of how we know is prior to the question of what kinds of thing there are to know. In a technical slogan: epistemology precedes metaphysics. This is a good specimen of the turn to the subject: to make epistemology dominant is to place the judging subject front and center. It is the observing and judging subject who determines what is true. On one view of neoscholasticism, neo-Kantianism reproduces the evils of idealism, that is, the view that the representation of the world depends on the representing mind and represents a methodologically entrenched denial of realism, that is, a commitment to a truth independent of how humans see things. On another view, the rise of neo-Kantianism presents obvious challenges to any institution that claims the right to determine what is true. It is conceivable that both views are valid. Either way, the reactive slogan of neoscholasticism was thus: metaphysics precedes epistemology. There is in this view an "objective" truth, grasped in metaphysics, and epistemology is the derivative business of reflecting on how this truth comes to be known. The neoscholastic answer to the question, "what is this objective truth?" is: what Aquinas taught. To the skeptical question, who determines what Aquinas meant, the answer is less certain. There was scope for competing interpretations.

Alongside the requirement for seminaries to teach Thomism, there remained the censorship of books by Catholic intellectuals and the associated list of prohibited books ("The Index"), whose content was considered not merely errant but contrary to the teaching of the church.[9] This sounds drastic, but the final publication of the Index of 1948 can be browsed and it is not long. It contains some eye-catching philosophical works, including by Locke, Hume, Kant, and – added in 1914 – Bergson. It is, however, much less extensive than one might suppose, and although one might expect an increase in activity after 1917, when the new curriculum was enforced, this is not the case.

There are at least four aspects of Aquinas' work that make him useful for combating the skepticism caused by a turn to the subject that makes epistemology central. First, he does not acknowledge any threat of skepticism, unlike his contemporaries who do.[10] Refutations of skepticism generally do not work, so the fact that Aquinas does not even attempt one is attractive: one can proceed confidently without threat. Second, he gives a major role to sensory experience in knowledge, but without being the kind of empiricist who says that all knowledge is acquired in this way. Third, Aquinas sometimes says that there is innate in us a cognition of first principles. This is ambiguous. It could mean, as he says explicitly, that we possess a light of reason (*rationis lumen; Quaestiones disputatae de veritate*, q.11, a.1). That would mean that we innately have the capacity to discover first principles. But it could mean we already have innate knowledge of first principles themselves. That interpretation may be less readily compatible with his other views, but as a weapon against modern skepticism it is a deeply attractive reading.[11] Fourth, he speaks of a preparation of the human will for good (*praeparatio voluntatis humanae ad bonum; Summa theologiae*, 1a2ae.109.6). This is also ambiguous. It could mean that we have natures without grace, ready to receive it. Or it could mean that the gift of grace means we can see that we are already ready to receive that grace. The first interpretation is attractive to those who claim that human knowledge needs to be added to by God, and thus by the church.

Dialectical theology and neoscholasticism are both responses to the turn to the subject. Both see the threat posed by privileging epistemology: if the primary question is, "how do I know?" then any source of knowledge (be it scripture or official church teaching) is automatically placed under the judgment of the thinking subject. It is important to see that neither neoscholasticism nor dialectical theology primarily answer epistemological questions. Of course, the question, "how do I know?" can still be asked, and then the answer will often seem to be "Aquinas!" or "scripture!" This obviously does not scratch the epistemological itch: one can ask, "how do I know what Aquinas says?" or "how do I judge between rival interpretations of scripture?" The answer to these questions is neither Aquinas nor scripture but forces another turn to the subject, this time the subject who interprets Aquinas or scripture. Rather, these movements are better understood as refusals to make epistemology central, alongside "phenomenological" or "existential" philosophies that do the same. They begin in the middle of a nexus of texts and interpretations, although each tradition has a different nexus, and work their way outwards, practically. There are disagreements about the levels of certainty and clarity that are achievable, and this too reflects a response to the turn to the subject. Earlier figures like Descartes and Spinoza (and sometimes Leibniz) had supposed that a high level of certainty could be achieved by thinking clearly. This then applies pressure to the theological tradition to offer comparable clarity and certainty, whether or not this is attainable. A high level of certainty is not attainable, either for philosophy or theology.

When the aspiration to certainty collides with skepticism about epistemology (the normal state of philosophies that make epistemology central) this tends to provoke a crisis of theological confidence. In the twentieth century this also coincides with a wider loss of cultural confidence: World War I provoked fundamental political and economic realignments, and mass slaughter forced the issue of human finitude to take center stage. In the arts there is in Europe from this point onwards an abundance of expressionist, absurdist, surrealist, nihilist, atheist, and existentialist work. The content is often ugly and troubling, but the tone is often confident and strident. Figures like Barth, Bultmann, Balthasar, and leading neoscholastic theologians likewise adopted a tone that was bold, confident, alarming, like the art they were consuming, and like the strong man (Hannah Arendt) political leaders who soon strode onto the stage: Mussolini, Hitler, Stalin, Franco, Churchill, de Gaulle. This is also reflected in the stridently confident tone adopted by many philosophers, including Russell, Moore, Heidegger, Sartre, Wittgenstein, Ryle, Ayer. This may account for such theologians becoming so important so quickly: theirs was a tone that suggested certainty amidst cultural chaos. The relationship between theology and philosophy in this period is often disappointingly macho.

Nouvelle théologie

The neoscholastic movement in Roman Catholic theology can be understood not only as reactive but reparative. The approach was authoritarian but modern developments in philosophy were a problem for theology: the idea of the freely judging subject, the idea of history (and the accompanying insight that what seems true in one era comes to seem false in another), the refusal of eternity in favor of a more limited temporality, and above all the relentless focus on epistemology (which was a problem for philosophy itself). There had been accompanying attempts to negotiate these difficulties: Kant had refused the focus on epistemology in his practical philosophy (where he had also located orientation to God); Hegel had embraced the historical turn and had experimented with a historically inflected concept of God; Kierkegaard had argued (albeit pseudonymously) that religious claims were less a matter of reasoning smoothly from A to B and more a matter of a decision, even a leap of faith; Nietzsche had sown the disquieting idea that even the most well-established beliefs have a "genealogy" that reveals their historical contingency; John Henry Newman had embraced the idea of history somewhat differently in an account of the development of doctrine. The twentieth-century developments can be seen as an attempt to ease the contradictions of modern thought (above all its self-undermining skepticism) in a double movement: to reach back to periods before those contradictions arose and to identify and avoid the developments that seem to lead to those contradictions.

The appeal to Aquinas in Roman Catholic theology was the official route back behind modernity. It was accompanied by an unofficial movement of *ressourcement* associated with Henri de Lubac, Henri Bouillard, Hans Urs von Balthasar, Marie-Dominique Chenu, Jean Daniélou, Louis Charlier, and Yves Congar, concentrated institutionally in France and Belgium. Methodologically and philosophically they used modern techniques in historiography and philosophy to retrieve premodern sources to avoid modern contradictions and especially to circumvent forms of thought that were toxic to an embrace of the long theological tradition. Their willingness to use modern methods led to the accusation, despite their focus on patristic and medieval sources, that they were creating a "new theology" (in a bad sense), giving the movement its name, *nouvelle théologie*.

It is a disparate group and it is questionable whether there are genuinely common threads that connect their work: for the most part they were grouped together by their opponents. Philosophically, they tended to embrace the virtue of thinking historically. The thought of Aquinas was thus placed by many of them (and especially Bouillard and Chenu) in a wider historical trajectory of doctrinal development, rather than being treated as a single point of brilliant light. Patristic thought served for many of them (especially de Lubac and Daniélou) as a way to recover the tradition of philosophy as contemplation and relational against certain modern tendencies to treat philosophy as a means of observation and control. They used philosophy to illuminate the meaning of grace. De Lubac famously argued that it is a mistake to view nature as something that makes sense without grace, because this lays the theological ground for a convincing (but false) secular view of things: grace is not added to nature as something wholly separate from it; rather the completion of nature by the free gift of grace is already implied by the kind of nature it is.[12] One could in a compelling way narrate the story of theology and philosophy in the twentieth century entirely through the theme of grace: it is a site of intense philosophical contestation.

Neopatristic synthesis

Associated with Sergius Bulgakov, Nicholas Berdyaev, Georges Florovsky, Vladimir Lossky, Alexander Schmemann, John Zizioulas, and others, and originally used as by Florovsky to describe the work of Lossky, the "neopatristic synthesis" now often names a *ressourcement* in twentieth-century Eastern Orthodox theology. These figures share a common orientation to a retrieval of patristic texts and their interpretation in order to avoid problems associated with modern European philosophy. Many of its figures had a thorough education in the European philosophical tradition, which was then deployed to draw out a vision of patristic thought that could renew Orthodox intellectual traditions. This renewal often fuses philosophical, political, economic, and mystical lines of inquiry in ways that contrast with tendencies in many Western traditions toward their separation.

Rahner's transcendentalism

Karl Rahner's use of the term "transcendental" in his *Theological Investigations* and his *Foundations of Christian Faith* can be understood as a critical reception of the turn to the subject.[13] As Karen Kilby has noted, Rahner uses this term in two ways: first to describe how our experience points beyond itself (drawing on a traditional meaning of transcendent), and second to describe what makes human knowledge and action possible (drawing on Kant's transcendental idealism).[14] Reading Rahner can be confusing because he argues that (transcendental) investigation into the conditions for human knowledge and action results in discovering that human action reaches out (transcendentally) beyond itself. The two kinds of "transcendental" uses are entangled, not by accident or confusion, but as part of a distinct argument that Rahner makes.[15]

Rahner is fundamentally concerned with the question of how we know God, and that means investigating the conditions for knowledge. To investigate the conditions for knowledge is a turn to the subject, to acknowledge that the world is not merely given to us, to recognize ourselves as subjects who make judgments about the world. To make a judgment requires three things: something to judge, criteria for judging, and the subject who judges. Rahner, in common with many twentieth-century figures, presupposes that we are judges and the purpose of much of his writing is to elaborate what kinds of judgment he supposes that Christians might make. More controversially, he is interested in the kinds of judgment that *anyone* might make, because he supposes (and argues) that these kinds of judgment show that human action points beyond itself.

Rahner demonstrates debts to Schelling, which are, however, not presented as such because Rahner probably gets his Schellingian insights via Heidegger, in which they are somewhat obscured. Commentators on Rahner typically do not mention Schelling. Kilby supposes that the relevant philosophical focus is Kant's transcendental idealism,[16] and in part this is because Rahner's critics suppose that. Rahner is in fact indebted to the post-Kantian tradition, especially Fichte and Schelling. He has a strong and explicit sense of the restless, striving subject. In modern philosophy this has its origins in Spinoza's idea of the *conatus* in his *Ethics*.[17] It reaches a particular point of intensity in Fichte's claim that the striving activity of the I is the ground of consciousness.[18] This enters Catholic theology through Maréchal's *Le Point de Depart de la Metaphysique* (Maréchal 1922–47) with its Fichtean correction of Catholic Kantianism.[19] Rahner is heavily influenced by Maréchal.[20] Heidegger appropriates Schelling's correction of Fichte.[21] Rahner is also heavily influenced by Heidegger.[22] Rahner goes beyond Maréchal and thus beyond Fichte into Schelling's positive philosophy, via Heidegger.

For Rahner the Christian will judge that their subjectivity points to God, but this is not straightforwardly informative because God is a mystery. One may deepen one's engagement with that mystery, through worship and through study, but it resists conceptual clarity. To this extent Rahner also demonstrates his debt to the turn to art in modern philosophy, with its insistence that the ground of conceptual articulation cannot itself be conceptually grounded, an insight from Schelling's positive philosophy.[23] But it is not only the Christian reasoner that Rahner is concerned with. The non-Christian, even anti-Christian, reasoner may judge at least that their subjectivity points beyond its own finite reach, and this is Rahner's invitation to any reasoner to take seriously Christian claims about this "beyond." This is a thoroughly post-Kantian approach, correcting not just the neoscholasticism of post-First Vatican Council theology but also the Kantianism of its critics.

Other responses to the turn to the subject

The "suffering" subject in Jürgen Moltmann's *The Crucified God* makes suffering central to human subjectivity followed by a proposal to modify the doctrine of the Trinity, such that its own subjectivity (its being and its action) is understood to incorporate suffering.

The centrality of everyday action in Nicholas Lash's *Easter in Ordinary* begins with a rejection of William James' ideas that religious experience is unusual and that people who have such intense experience are exceptional. (This is arguably exactly the sort of thing de Lubac warned about – the damaging idea that the "normal" state of affairs is nonreligious.) Lash then develops the idea, drawing on the poetry of George Herbert, that it is precisely in the ordinariness of everyday life that grace most intensely appears. Lash's study was unusual at the time for tackling a major figure in the tradition of American Pragmatism and using poetry as a philosophically significant means, thus also displaying a turn to art.[24]

The idea of a "reformed epistemology," especially in the work of Nicholas Wolterstorff and Alvin Plantinga, develops the kind of subject who appears in Calvin's *Institutes*, namely one who has a natural intuition of God, via an embrace of Scottish common-sense realism, where the subject "naturally" believes certain things, without needing to give reasons for them. This approach is a variant of the wider set of twentieth-century philosophical refusals to make epistemology central, but instead of privileging decision

(Barth) or Thomism (neoscholasticism) it privileges assumptions. Against those who make epistemology central, rather than asking "how do I know?" it is assumed that I know certain things, including that God exists, and asks, "what follows from this knowledge?"[25] Like other variants of the refusal to make epistemology central, it appears unsatisfactory if one requires its practitioners to answer the "how do I know?" question, but as with its dialectical, neoscholastic, *nouvelle théologique*, and Rahnerian cousins, part of its purpose is to suggest that this question should not be made central. Like them, it arguably makes contemplation more fundamental than information.

The turn to language

The turn to language names a concern with cultural identity, tradition, and grammar as conditions for and constraints on meaningful action. The thinking subject is indeed free, but free within bounds that themselves may change, and indeed may change because of the action of thinking subjects.

The analytic turn

Analytic philosophy names a set of concerns around logic, philosophy of language, a certain kind of metaphysics, epistemology, and ethics, all of which have a focus on the structure of claims or "assertions" or "propositions." Figures as diverse as Russell, Carnap, Ryle, Quine, Ayer, and Strawson developed arguments whose purpose is to clarify what makes claims true, especially propositions made in ordinary language. They share, with some exceptions, a belief that religious claims cannot be true. Religious claims are for this group variously badly formulated, unverifiable, and even meaningless. These criticisms arise from prior notions about what makes a well-formulated, or verifiable, or meaningful claim. Others, such as Wittgenstein and Anscombe, produce more sympathetic and generative accounts of what became known as "philosophy of religion." Wittgenstein's *Philosophical Investigations* and especially his *On Certainty*, and various essays by Anscombe now collected in *Faith in a Hard Ground* (including "What is it to believe someone?") are classics from the postwar period.[26]

The relation between theology and philosophy under these conditions is strained. Russell and Wittgenstein, and Ryle and Ayer, had considerable stature in Cambridge and Oxford respectively. Their attacks on religious language posed a challenge to philosophically-minded theologians in Cambridge and Oxford. The Regius Professors of theology (Nairne, Raven, Michael Ramsey et al. in Cambridge, and Goudge, Quick, Hodgson et al. in Oxford) were themselves well established, often holding posts as head of college and/or archbishop of Canterbury, and for the most part were not philosophically inclined. They were able to ignore the challenge (although Ramsey's older brother was one of the translators of Wittgenstein's *Tractatus*). Those whose names are familiar today are remembered for things other than their theology professorships.

More widely, however, there emerged a need for professors of philosophical theology. Oxford created its Nolloth Professorship of the Philosophy of the Christian Religion in 1920 (Webb, Grensted, Ian Ramsey et al.) and Cambridge's Norris-Hulse Professorship was philosophically repurposed in 1949 (Farmer, MacKinnon, Lash). For the most part these figures and others such as Austin Farrer did not tackle the analytic attack directly but drew on literature, drama (especially tragedy), scripture, Eastern Orthodoxy, Aquinas, Pascal, and Kant to develop alternative ways of thinking philosophically. In some ways the continental traditions of philosophy, which were edged out of the faculties of philosophy at Oxford and Cambridge (although Wittgenstein read widely in German philosophy), were kept alive in the theology faculties. The analytic philosophical attack on religious language was partly parried but it left its mark as an estrangement or uneasiness between the faculties of philosophy and theology.

Responses to the analytic turn

The effects of the analytic turn were varied. In Britain they include the influence of the later Wittgenstein in the work of Roman Catholic figures like McCabe, Ernst, and Kerr (Oxford), and Lash and Soskice (Cambridge), in whose work the categories of grammar, analogy, and metaphor play a central role. Their core shared insight is that the theological tradition furnishes the conditions for meaning-making in the same way that a language's grammar furnishes the conditions for linguistic meaning. They also include analytic philosophy of religion in the work of Basil Mitchell, I. M. Crombie, William Alston, Eleanore Stump, Normal Kretzmann, Brian Leftow, and others[27] and has led in more recent years to the development of analytic theology.[28] Whereas the long Christian tradition had supposed that God is stable, and human language must conform as best it can, the analytic traditions mostly suppose that language is stable and God must conform to it. This puts the analytical approaches into a tense relationship with the long tradition but which is rarely the focus of mutual engagement.[29]

In the United States a distinct turn to language developed in postliberal theology associated with Hans Frei, George Lindbeck, Paul Ricoeur, and others, with an institutional focus in Yale and Chicago. Frei's focus on scripture as a narrative rather than propositional medium, Lindbeck's casting of doctrine as a "cultural-linguistic" expression, Ricoeur's privileging of narrative, memory, and scripture, are all variants of the late eighteenth-century insight that linguistic forms both constrain and generate the forms of freedom exercised by the thinking subject.[30] Their shared rejection of the idea that religious claims are primarily propositional (especially prominent in Frei and Lindbeck) is a distinctive refusal of the analytical turn and an alternative embrace of the turn to language. Its core insight is that Christian tradition functions like a language in furnishing the conditions and the limits within which meaningful action unfolds.

The work of the Oxford Catholics (Ernst et al.) and of Oxford Anglicans (Farrer et al.) is refracted in the work of Rowan Williams and John Milbank. Williams' historical study of Arius and his work on spirituality, including *The Wound of Knowledge,* are not overtly philosophical, in the sense of naming contemporary philosophies, but they are explicit attempts to recover a tradition of contemplation and, in the case of *Arius*, to make a substantial contribution to the philosophical turn to language in so far as it addresses the assumption (shared by Williams) that language and culture are the condition of meaning. Williams shows how differentiated and uncertain the Christian "culture" of the early church was. He develops the insight that the better one knows one's tradition, the more ambiguous its character. The horizon of culture is indeed determinative for theological meaning. However, it does not merely change: at any particular point, including major authoritative periods such as the Council of Nicaea in 325 CE, it is itself unstable.[31] Williams' theological oeuvre displays two significant differences from the American postliberal approaches. The first is his emphasis on instability; the second is the generativity for his theology of a wide range of literary sources from John of the Cross and Teresa of Ávila to Dostoevsky and David Jones, where postliberal theologians in the United States tends to see tradition as a relatively stable condition for action, with a narrower textual focus on scripture.

Milbank's *Theology and Social Theory* is on the face of it concerned with sociology but its subtitle, *Beyond Secular Reason,* shows it to be just as much an account of the relation of theology and philosophy. Milbank offers a variation on Hegel's analysis of secular thought in "The Enlightenment Struggle Against Superstition" from *Phenomenology of Spirit*, although without attribution. Hegel suggests that the secularising pressure of the Enlightenment, against religion, itself has its origins in religion, and especially within minority developments within Protestantism. For Hegel the secularizing impulse of the Enlightenment is a struggle against itself, within theology, where antireligious parties conceal from themselves their religious origins.[32] Milbank's unmasking of modern secular thought as itself theological follows Hegel's basic pattern, but whereas Hegel's analysis treats historical inquiry as the primary model for truth, Milbank self-consciously affirms the turn to language, especially in debts to Herder and Hamann.[33]

Moltmann and Gadamer

At the heart of Jürgen Moltmann's *Theology of Hope* of 1964 is an engagement with Gadamer's *Truth and Method* of 1960 and Ernst Bloch's *Principle of Hope* of 1938–47. Bloch, an East-German Marxist philosopher, gives Moltmann an eschatological language with a sharp political edge: images of a transformed future, often in works of art, act transformatively on action in the present and help to bring about that which is imagined. Gadamer suggests that in interpreting a text from the past the interpreter brings their own questions and concerns (an insight he credits to R. G. Collingwood). When interpreting a text's parts the interpreter has an idea of what the whole means, and although this "anticipation of completion" changes as the interpreter engages with the text, it is active as soon as interpretation begins. Moltmann connects this with Bloch's idea of utopian anticipation to produce a vision of Christian action in which the kingdom of God is both the image of a transformed future (Bloch) and an anticipation of completion (Gadamer) that furnishes a Christian horizon of meaning (something absent in Bloch) and a sharp political critique of present conditions (something absent in Gadamer). The Christian agent thus works to transform the present by anticipating God's future in concrete ways.[34]

The turn to art

The core insight is that the ground of thought and action is not fully graspable by the thinking and acting subject and cannot be captured conceptually in language. It thus explicitly inflects the turn to the subject and the turn to language in ways that question subjectivity and language in fundamental ways: the subject is not grounded in itself, and language is not transparent. The language of grasping is often corrected through the language of gift, and the actions of giving and receiving.

In philosophy the turn to art is especially associated with Schelling, Hölderlin, Nietzsche, Benjamin, Heidegger, and Adorno, with the earlier figures making a case for art as a means of expressing what cannot be captured conceptually, and the later figures making a case for art as a means of defying forms of cultural reproduction that seek to coerce and control.[35]

Tillich's appeal to God as "ground of being" and Balthasar's appeal to glory as a guiding theological category display the turn to art. The ground of being is, in German philosophy from Schelling onwards, a term for exploring the insight that although it is possible to articulate things in the world (beings), it is not possible to articulate what gives rise to them, their ground or their reason (the German *Grund* means both). To say that God is the ground of being is thus not a rhetorical flourish but a direct quotation of the early nineteenth-century tradition. This is particularly clear in Tillich's accompanying claim that God, as ground of being, finds human expression not in concepts (which apply to things in the world) but in symbols, especially the symbol of the crucified Christ.[36] His core theological contribution is that terms from Schelling like "ground of being" can repair problems caused by what is often called the "univocity of being," namely the idea that God exists in the same sense that objects in the world exist, or that God is an object of knowledge like things in the world. Although God cannot be grasped conceptually there can nonetheless be meaningful expressions of that ground through art, symbols, and other forms that resist being reduced to general concepts.

Balthasar seeks to respond to Protestant complaints (especially by Barth) that the so-called "analogy of being" in Catholic theology amounts to "laying hands on God."[37] The analogy of being (*analogia entis*) is a set of debates about how to understand God's similarity and dissimilarity to creation. Drawing on the turn to art (*The Glory of the Lord* is a "theological aesthetics") Balthasar answers the Protestant charge that this "analogy of being" is too close. In Jesus Christ and in scripture God appears in a "form" that can be encountered and known, without being captured and conceptually grasped. Drawing on a long tradition of negative theology, God's invisibility appears in what is visible but without abolishing that invisibility; God's infinity appears in what is finite without ceasing to be infinite, and other claims with this structure.[38]

The Lutheran (Tillich) and Roman Catholic (Balthasar) turn to art is extended and critiqued in work by Rowan Williams, Denys Turner, David Bentley Hart, Cyril O'Regan, Ben Quash, Susannah Ticciati, Natalie Carnes, Catherine Pickstock, and others.[39] Their shared insight is, negatively, that no language can capture God or furnish a perspective that captures the whole of things, time, history, etc. and, positively, that part of the role of language including art is to deepen an engagement with God and to transform those who produce and meditate on such expressions.

Debate, Achievement, and Agenda

European philosophical developments do not for the most part happen outside theology: its developments have been a negotiation within and between theological traditions. The turn to the subject can be seen in Luther and Montaigne. The turn to language was to a significant extent motivated by engagements with biblical interpretation and a desire to highlight differences between Catholic and Protestant traditions. The turn to art, especially its core insight that speech (about God) simultaneously fails and yet is meaningful, has its origins in the negative theological traditions of the high Middle Ages. These philosophical developments do, however, often break free of their theological origins and return in forms that seem alien and even threatening to the theology that originally produced them. To take one example, the debate about grace and nature in the high Middle Ages produces a "natural" humanity with its own integrity, which arguably leads to an emphatic sense of the finiteness of the human, which finds an exaggerated articulation in Nietzsche and Heidegger, which then confronts twentieth-century theological explorations of grace.

The relationship between theology and philosophy has to a significant extent divided into two somewhat independent streams. The first stream favors a strong link between truth and beauty, between finding and making meaning, between attentiveness to objects and the transformation of the subject, between articulation and elusiveness, between scripture and a wide range of literature including plays, novels, and poetry in a variety of languages. The second stream favors a strong link between truth and representation, between observation and inference, between articulation and clarity, between science and religion, between scripture and propositions, mostly in English. The future of the relation between theology and philosophy depends to a significant extent on the fate of the humanities in the contemporary university. The first, more literary, stream will very likely suffer heavily from a collapse in the humanities. The second, more scientific and propositional, stream may benefit from a realignment of funding in favor of the hard and social sciences. Time will tell.

Notes

1 Andrew Bowie, *Aesthetics and Modern Subjectivity: From Kant to Nietzsche*, 2nd ed. (Manchester: Manchester University Press, 2013), 12.

2 Karl Barth, *Protestant Theology in the Nineteenth Century*, trans. B. Cozens and J. Bowden (London: SCM Press, 1972). From 1929 to 1966 Karl Barth collaborated closely with Charlotte von Kirschbaum. They cowrote much of the *Church Dogmatics*. In that period it was common under such circumstances for men to receive sole authorial credit and Barth's works were all published under his name alone.

3 Karl Barth, *Church Dogmatics*, vol. I, part 1 (Edinburgh: T&T Clark, 1975).

4 Rudolf Bultmann, *New Testament and Mythology: And Other Basic Writings,* ed. and trans. Schubert M. Ogden (London: SCM Press, 1985).

5 Pius X, *Lamentabile sane* (1907), https://www.papalencyclicals.net/pius10/p10lamen.htm (accessed 26 February 2023).

6 Edward Peters, *The 1917 or Pio-Benedictine Code of Canon Law: In English Translation with Extensive Scholarly Apparatus* (San Francisco, CA: Ignatius Press, 2001).

7 Francesca Aran Murphy, "Thomism 1870–1963," in *The Oxford Handbook of Catholic Theology*, ed. Lewis Ayres and Medi Ann Volpe (Oxford: Oxford University Press, 2017), 653–70.

8 Fergus Kerr, *Twentieth-Century Catholic Theologians* (Oxford: Blackwell, 2007).

9 Murphy, "Thomism 1870–1963," 653–70; Kerr, *Twentieth-Century Catholic Theologians.*

10 Martin Pickavé, "Human Knowledge," in *The Oxford Handbook of Aquinas*, ed. Brian Davies (Oxford: Oxford University Press, 2012), 311–26.

11 Pickavé, "Human Knowledge," 316.

12 Henri de Lubac, *Surnaturel. Études historiques*, ed. Michel Sales (Paris: Desclée de Brouwer, 1991).

13 Karl Rahner, *Foundations of Christian Faith: An Introduction to the Idea of Christianity* (New York: Crossroad, 1989).

14 Karen Kilby, *Karl Rahner: Theology and Philosophy* (London: Routledge, 2004), 32–3.

15 Kilby, *Karl Rahner*, 34.

16 Kilby, *Karl Rahner*, 36ff.

17 Steven Nadler, "Baruch Spinoza," revised 16 April 2020, *The Stanford Encyclopedia of Philosophy* (Summer 2022 edition), ed. Edward N. Zalta, https://plato.stanford.edu/archives/sum2022/entries/spinoza/, 2.4 (accessed 19 September 2023).

18 Dan Breazeale, "Johann Gottlieb Fichte," revised 18 February 2022, *The Stanford Encyclopedia of Philosophy* (Spring 2022 edition), ed. Edward N. Zalta, https://plato.stanford.edu/archives/spr2022/entries/johann-fichte/, 4.1 (accessed 19 September 2023).

19 Anthony M. Matteo, *Quest for the Absolute: The Philosophical Vision of Joseph Maréchal* (DeKalb: Northern Illinois University Press, 1992).

20 Kilby, *Karl Rahner*, 36 and elsewhere.

21 Sonya Sikka, "Heidegger's Appropriation of Schelling," *Southern Journal of Philosophy* 32, no. 4 (1994): 421–48.

22 Kilby, *Karl Rahner*, 134–5.

23 Andrew Bowie, *Schelling and Modern European Philosophy: An Introduction* (London: Routledge, 1993), 147ff.

24 Nicholas Lash, *Easter in Ordinary: Reflections on Human Experience and the Knowledge of God* (Charlottesville, VA: University Press of Virginia, 1988).

25 Alvin Plantinga, *God and Other Minds: A Study of the Rational Justification of Belief in God* (New York: Cornell University Press, 1967); Nicholas Wolterstorff, *Reason within the Bounds of Religion* (Grand Rapids, MI: Eerdmans, 1976).

26 G. E. M. Anscombe, *Faith in a Hard Ground: Essays on Religion, Philosophy and Ethics*, ed. Mary Geach and Luke Gormally (Exeter: Imprint Academic, 2008).

27 William Hasker, "Analytic Philosophy of Religion," in *The Oxford Handbook of Philosophy of Religion*, ed. William J. Wainwright (Oxford: Oxford University Press, 2009), 421–46.

28 William Wood, "Philosophy and Christian Theology," 15 October 2021, *The Stanford Encyclopedia of Philosophy* (Spring 2022 edition), ed. Edward N. Zalta, https://plato.stanford.edu/archives/spr2022/entries/christiantheology-philosophy/ (accessed 19 September 2023).

29 Wood, "Philosophy and Christian Theology," §3.2.

30 Hans W. Frei, *The Eclipse of Biblical Narrative: A Study in Eighteenth and Nineteenth Century Hermeneutics* (New Haven, CT: Yale University Press, 1974); George A. Lindbeck, *The Nature of Doctrine: Religion and Theology in a Postliberal Age* (Philadelphia, PA: Westminster Press, 1984); Paul Ricoeur, *Essays on Biblical Interpretation*, ed. Lewis S. Mudge (Philadelphia, PA: Fortress Press, 1980).

31 Rowan Williams, *Arius: Heresy and Tradition*, 2nd ed. (London: SCM Press, 2001).

32 G. W. F. Hegel, *Phenomenology of Spirit*, ed. and trans. Terry Pinkard and Michael Baur (Cambridge: Cambridge University Press, 2018 [1807]), §§541ff; Jürgen Stolzenberg, "Hegel's Critique of the Enlightenment in 'The Struggle of the Enlightenment with Superstition,'" in *The Blackwell Guide to Hegel's Phenomenology of Spirit*, ed. Kenneth R. Westphal (Oxford: Wiley, 2009), 190–208.

33 John Milbank, *Theology and Social Theory: Beyond Secular Reason*, 2nd ed. (Oxford: Blackwell, 2006), 148–53.

34 Jürgen Moltmann, *Theology of Hope*, trans. J. Bowen (London: SCM Press, 1967).

35 Bowie, *Aesthetics and Modern Subjectivity.*

36 Paul Tillich, *Systematic Theology*, Vol. 1 (London: Nisbet, 1953).

37 Hans Urs von Balthasar, *The Theology of Karl Barth: Exposition and Interpretation*, trans. Edward T. Oakes, (San Francisco, CA: Ignatius Press, 1992), 52.

38 Hans Urs von Balthasar, *The Glory of the Lord: A Theological Aesthetics, Vol. 1: Seeing the Form*, ed. Joseph Fessio and John Riches, trans. Erasmo Leiva-Merikakis (San Francisco, CA: Ignatius Press, 1982), 233.

39 Denys Turner, *The Darkness of God: Negativity in Christian Mysticism* (Cambridge: Cambridge University Press, 1995); David Bentley Hart, *The Beauty of the Infinite: The Aesthetics of Christian Truth* (Grand Rapids, MI: Eerdmans, 2004); Ben Quash, *Theology and the Drama of History* (Cambridge: Cambridge University Press, 2005); Rowan Williams, *Grace and Necessity: Reflections on Art and Love* (London: Continuum, 2006); Cyril O'Regan, *The Anatomy of Misremembering (1): Balthasar's Response to Philosophical Modernity. Vol. 1: Hegel* (New York: Crossroad, 2014); Susannah Ticciati, *A New Apophaticism: Augustine and the*

Redemption of Signs (Leiden: Brill, 2015); Natalie Carnes, *Image and Presence*: A *Christological Reflection on Iconoclasm and Iconophilia* (Stanford, CA: Stanford University Press, 2017); Catherine Pickstock, *Aspects of Truth: A New Religious Metaphysics* (Cambridge: Cambridge University Press, 2020).

Recommended Reading

Balthasar, Hans Urs von. *The Glory of the Lord: A Theological Aesthetics, Vol. 1: Seeing the Form.* Edited by Joseph Fessio and John Riches. Translated by Erasmo Leiva-Merikakis. San Francisco: Ignatius Press, 1982.

———. *The Theology of Karl Barth: Exposition and Interpretation.* Translated by Edward T. Oakes. San Francisco: Ignatius Press, 1992.

Barth, Karl. *Protestant Theology in the Nineteenth Century.* Translated by B. Cozens and J. Bowden. London: SCM Press, 1972.

Bultmann, Rudolf. *New Testament and Mythology: and Other Basic Writings.* Edited and translated by Schubert M. Ogden. London: SCM Press, 1985.

Frei, Hans W. *The Eclipse of Biblical Narrative: A Study in Eighteenth and Nineteenth Century Hermeneutics.* New Haven, CT: Yale University Press, 1974.

Garrigou-Lagrange, Réginald. *Dieu, Son Existence et Sa Nature: Solution Thomiste des Antinomies Agnostiques,* Paris: Beauchesne, 1914.

Peters, Edward. *The 1917 or Pio-Benedictine Code of Canon Law: In English Translation with Extensive Scholarly Apparatus.* San Francisco, CA: Ignatius Press, 2001.

Rahner, Karl. *Foundations of Christian Faith: An Introduction to the Idea of Christianity.* New York: Crossroad, 1989.

Tillich, Paul. *Systematic Theology,* Vol. 1. London: Nisbet, 1953.

Williams, Rowan. *Arius: Heresy and Tradition,* 2nd ed. London: SCM Press, 2001.

Biblical Interpretation

Susannah Ticciati

Introduction

Biblical interpretation in the academy continues to be ineluctably shaped by the disciplinary chasm between constructive Christian theology ("systematic theology") and biblical studies, which remains determinative, as Lewis Ayres remarked in 2004, even for those who "[lament] it and [try] to seek ways to bring the 'two' together."[1] The split has a history, bound up with the changing status of the Bible, and is narrated, with a view to the fate of biblical interpretation, in different ways by Hans Frei, in *The Eclipse of Biblical Narrative*, Jonathan Sheehan, in *The Enlightenment Bible*, and Michael Legaspi, in *The Death of Scripture and the Rise of Biblical Studies*.[2] The exchange that took place between Karl Barth and Adolf von Harnack in 1923 continues to be highly illuminating of the nature of the split, Harnack arguing that an understanding of the Bible can be reached only by historical research and scientific method, and Barth for the "utter contrast" between the world and the Word of God, on which all human methods are shattered.[3]

Although biblical studies, as I will show, is a thoroughly heterogeneous discipline (or set of disciplines), it nevertheless exhibits in its diversity a common denominator, and one that is adumbrated by Harnack: a bent for the methodological.[4] On the side of systematic theology, although Barth's influence looms large, it is far from all-pervasive. Nevertheless, it is notable that Barth is the most significant forerunner for many of the Christian theologians who seek to make biblical exegesis an integral part of their theology (e.g. Robert W. Jenson, John Webster, R. Kendall Soulen, and Katherine Sonderegger), among whom are also those who seek to overcome, or at least trouble, the disciplinary split (e.g. David F. Ford, Douglas Harink, and David H. Kelsey). Indeed, as theological exegete and scriptural theologian *par excellence*, Barth himself might be thought, in respect of the split, precisely to represent its overcoming. Historically, however, this does not seem to have been his legacy, which, if anything, has entailed a cementing of the disciplinary dividing lines: Barth and Barthian exegesis are almost exclusively the province of Christian systematic theologians.

The reasons for this are no doubt multifarious. In what follows, however, I offer and test a diagnosis of the state of biblical interpretation in the academy that accounts not only for the persistence of the disciplinary chasm, and for the impotence of a Barthian resolution, but also for the deepening divisions within

Ford's The Modern Theologians: An Introduction to Christian Theology since 1918, Fourth Edition.
Edited by Rachel Muers and Ashley Cocksworth.
© 2024 John Wiley & Sons Ltd. Published 2024 by John Wiley & Sons Ltd.

biblical studies. I argue, to anticipate, that biblical interpretation in the academy is subject to a broader cultural dichotomy between description and normativity, fact and value, in the context of which a communal pursuit of the truth through engagement with scripture is rendered almost impossible.

Survey

In this section I offer an account of the contemporary options for biblical interpretation within the academy, using the dichotomy between the descriptive and the normative as a way to frame them. I begin with the division within biblical studies between traditional biblical criticism, associated with what is often referred to as the historical-critical method, and ideological criticism, or more broadly, readings that draw attention to their locatedness.

Traditional biblical criticism versus "located" readings

The hallmarks of biblical criticism typically include the attempt to reconstruct a text's original historical context of production, to mark out the limits of what it could have meant for its original audience, and to hypothesize what the author's or editor's intention in writing or redacting it might have been (however problematized the notion of intention has become). Although defenders of biblical criticism in any pure form are increasingly rare, the set of practices and methods that have come to characterize it are still overwhelmingly dominant within biblical scholarship. Indeed, they remain a litmus test of scholarly rigor and authority.[5] Against the tide of mounting criticism, John Barton offers a thorough and coherent defense of biblical criticism within a tradition that dates at least as far back as Baruch Spinoza.[6] Adopting Spinoza's distinction between the meaning of a text and its truth, Barton develops his two-stage account of reading, in which the reader first brackets her truth commitments so that the text's meaning can be ascertained without prejudice, and only then evaluates this meaning. Only thus can the reader be confronted by something that is not at her disposal.

That "something" Barton names the "objective" meaning of the text. And it is just here that the hackles of his antagonists are raised. Since Gadamer and Jauss, let alone Foucault and Derrida, it has surely become impossible to believe in objective meaning. The rejection of an objective meaning in favor of a plurality of readings from different locations is what loosely unites those biblical interpreters who have variously been grouped, over against traditional biblical criticism, under the banner of "ideological criticism," "advocacy readings," or more broadly, "located" or "contextual" readings.[7] Such grouping is itself a symptom of the problem that many of those so grouped are variously seeking to address – and it serves to entrench that problem only further. I indicate how it does so by way of two examples of interpretative approaches that are typically pigeonholed in this way.

In a methodologically oriented companion volume to Sheffield Academic Press's *Feminist Companion to Reading the Bible* series, Athalya Brenner and Carole Fontaine characterize historical-critical scholarship in terms of its goal of value neutrality or objectivity and its concomitant blindness to the very particular "social location" of its elite, male guild: the "malestream."[8] To group feminist interpretation with "located" approaches over against objective biblical criticism is clearly to belie the goal of feminist criticism of exposing the locatedness of all reading, and the male cast of biblical criticism in particular. This is brought home more concretely by Brenner's own essay in the volume.[9] Reading Isaiah 50:4–11, one of the well-known servant poems of Second Isaiah, through the lens of the preceding verses (vv. 1–3), she hears the voice of the servant, traditionally gendered male, as that of the divorced wife-mother-slave of vv. 1–3, thus (as Fontaine points out in her response essay[10]) exposing the ambivalence of the "salvation" wrought by the Lord – as restoration to a life of oppressive submission. Following in the footsteps of Phyllis Trible's naming of "texts of terror," Brenner does not shy away from a moral critique of the Bible that has typically been circumvented by those who seek to offer objective, historicized readings.[11] Rather than submitting to the Bible as external norm, she operates with an internalized normativity gained from the particular experience of gendered oppression. This is, in Brenner's words, to be "*more* than subjective," exposing from a particular vantage point a pervasive structural evil (and thus bringing into question an opposition between subjectivity and objectivity).[12]

Esau McCaulley's *Reading While Black* seeks to unfold "a Black ecclesial interpretive model" that liberates the Bible from its European domination.[13] In keeping with a feminist emphasis on interpretative locatedness, he affirms that his reading "arises out of the particular *context* of Black Americans." Not only, however, does he expose the contrasting locatedness of the White slave master readings geared toward "White degradation of Black bodies," he implicitly makes the case that not all locations are equal.[14] Against relativism, McCaulley's "located" reading seeks a potentially "universal" hearing.[15] In his reading of Romans 13 in chapter 2, rather than aiming, as some biblical commentators do, simply to describe what he finds, he starts out from a particular question, one that is pressing for Black Americans: of how the police should treat citizens. As R. G. Collingwood argues, research should never be done "without any definite question to which an answer was being sought."[16] The results of such aimless research are likely to yield little. While not any question will be appropriately posed of any particular text, a new context (such as being Black in the United States) may give rise to questions that unlock new aspects of an overly familiar text. As Collingwood says, an act of thought "must always happen in some context, [but] the new context must be just as appropriate to it as the old." A reader must come "prepared with an experience sufficiently like [the writer's] own to make [the writer's] thoughts organic to it."[17]

Paul's stipulation in Romans 13:3–4 that the authorities pose no fear to those who do good speaks powerfully to Black people in the United States (for whom this is manifestly not the case), inciting a hope that should galvanize structural change. But what McCaulley hears in Paul is precisely not something only for him, or even African Americans more widely: calling to account especially those in power, Paul speaks to all who are caught up in such fear-instilling structures. Like Brenner's, McCaulley's interpretation has normative and not just descriptive force, holding its wider audience morally accountable. Branding such readings "contextual" and ranging them in a series frames them according to a relativist pluralism that limits their purchase to those who share their (thus parochialized) context, undermining their normative force. As Moore and Sherwood remark, "the moral and political force of feminist biblical criticism has become hamstrung by the trope of 'reading as' ... contained (in both senses of the term) within collections of readings 'from the margins' or from assorted 'social locations.'"[18]

The discipline of biblical studies is, I suggest, in thrall to a wider cultural divide between description and normativity, fact and value – a divide in which description has the monopoly.[19] Whereas the public sphere deals in descriptions (backed by scientific and technological evidence and expertise), values are relegated to the private sphere, norms becoming matters of opinion and preference. The terms of the split foreclose the possibility of public normative discourse. Thus, when norms are detected as being operative in the public sphere, they are quickly identified with an oppressive status quo, and one that needs to be unmasked as such. Within the dichotomy between fact and value, traditional biblical criticism takes up the place of "fact" – having all the hallmarks of scientific objectivity. "Located" readings are consequently assigned to the "value'" side of the divide, in their disavowal of objectivity being hailed as (merely) subjective.[20] By the same token they are privatized, becoming a series of options for the reader.

However, something yet more insidious occurs. Reconceived as an assortment of recognizable and respectable methods (location being problematically conflated with method[21]), contextual approaches are lent their own (pseudo-)scientific validity and objectivity. In this way the subjectivities they display themselves become objective facts to be described and catalogued. What located readings thereby gain in public recognition they lose in normative purchase. Their objectification is their neutralization; their fate a symptom of the wider cultural lack of public normative discourse.

The theological interpretation of scripture[22]

I turn now to another strand within biblical interpretation in the academy: the theological interpretation of scripture. This is the name for a distinctive scholarly movement, with a loose but nevertheless identifiable programmatic agenda (and thus to be distinguished from theological interpretation more broadly).[23] Stephen Fowl describes it as the Christian practice of reading of scripture "to guide, correct, and edify their faith, worship, and practice as part of their ongoing struggle to live faithfully before the triune God."[24] He uses the phrase both descriptively of something to be retrieved, most notably from "premodern" scriptural interpretative practice, and programmatically to name an approach to scripture that resists the disciplinary fragmentation of the modern university, helping, more specifically, bridge the chasm separating theology and biblical studies. It has subsequently developed according to a distinctive set of commitments.[25]

Above all, despite its location in the academy, it is conceived as an ecclesial practice in service of the church. Its proponents point out the fact that the Christian Bible does not exist as a unified book apart from the church, such that the bracketing of its ecclesial context by biblical critics in the modern university undermines the *prima facie* rationale for its study.[26] Several related but distinct commitments follow. In keeping with ideological critics and "located" readers, and in contrast with those biblical critics who aim for objective neutrality, theological interpreters self-consciously embrace the presuppositioned character of all reading. Unlike ideological critics, however, they adopt toward the Bible a posture of trust, or in Paul Ricoeur's terms, a hermeneutic of restoration rather than suspicion. Standing within the Christian tradition, they read the Bible as scripture, receiving it as God's Word. For some, this means discerning behind the multiple and diverse human authors the one divine author, without whom the Bible, rather than a unity, would be a collection of disparate fragments.[27] But the emphasis remains on interpretative plurality, in keeping both with the medieval "fourfold sense of scripture" (and premodern interpretation more generally), and with a postmodern sensitivity to readerly context; and in contrast with belief in a single, "original" meaning.[28]

Interpretative plurality gives rise to the need for interpretative limits. These are found in the ancient church's "rule of faith," which as a condensed summary of Christian credal belief, brings coherence to the Bible as a unity, in which the Old Testament is read in the light of the New, and vice versa.[29] In the context of a wider retrieval of premodern exegetical practice, theological interpreters appeal – as a concrete way of discerning the Bible's unity – specifically to typological reading, in which, paradigmatically, Old Testament events are understood to prefigure Christ and his church.[30] A significant forerunner of theological interpretation is the canonical criticism inaugurated by Brevard Childs, in which the interpretative focus is on the final, canonical form taken by the biblical texts.[31] Some of the same challenges arise. How is it possible to do justice to the diversity of voices within the canon while interpreting them as part of an overriding unity? More specifically, does a reading of the Hebrew scriptures as the Christian Old Testament necessarily involve a supersessionist theology according to which the old covenant is fulfilled in and replaced by the new, or Israel in and by the church?[32] This concern, to which I return later, is arguably heightened by typological reading.

An arguably more fundamental problem for the theological interpretation of scripture concerns the character of its normativity. Although, like ideological critics, it embraces "interested" interpretation, its tendency is to externalize its interpretative presuppositions in the rule of faith, church tradition, and even scripture itself. This tendency goes together with the acceptance of an external (biblical and ecclesial) authority, which as a presuppositional starting point is also the end of argument. Despite a pervasive emphasis on the importance of reading with others, theological interpreters thus face the threat of insularity and fideism: their readings will simply be incommensurable with those who do not accept the same authority. Contrast this situation with that of the feminist critic who interprets in the light of "women's experience." This, at its best, is not an external norm but an internalized gauge in relation to which the Bible will be heard and tested; it is neither static nor necessarily incommunicable to others, and thus, unlike an external norm, invites further critical inquiry in the light both of unfolding experience and encounter with scripture.

In sum, the danger of the approach of theological interpreters is that it renders what are in fact fluid, vague, and mostly unarticulated internal presuppositions external and static. As a result, although these presuppositions can still guide rational inquiry, they can no longer be subject to it. The insularity that results precludes a genuinely common pursuit of the truth through engagement with scripture. While embracing the normative pole of the fact/value divide, theological interpreters remain captive to the divide insofar as their norms become externalized objects ("fact"). Like the two antagonistic poles of biblical studies, therefore, the theological interpretation of scripture is not well placed to foster public normative discourse.

In what might be described as a hermeneutical epilogue to the first volume of her *Systematic Theology*, Katherine Sonderegger offers an appraisal of canonical criticism – which might (in some ways at least) be extended to the theological interpretation of scripture movement – that resonates strongly, albeit in a different idiom, with the critique I have offered here.[33] She articulates a very different kind of "theological" interpretation, retrospectively describing what she has engaged in over the course of the volume. Like the theological interpreters of scripture discussed here, her reading of scripture assumes that God is to be encountered there; but she downplays the notions of God as author or referent of scripture, let alone as character within it, in favor of God's invisible presence within scripture: God is made manifest within it as the one who is hidden within its pages. This is, to anticipate, not unlike the sacramental exegesis articulated by Hans Boersma in his retrieval of patristic interpretation. Indeed, Sonderegger operates with the kind of freedom one finds in patristic exegesis, not bound by modern questions of historical setting and literary genre and ready to find the living God "in the sinews of the text."[34] This freedom goes hand in hand with the necessity of discerning the hidden God, whose presence cannot be equated with scripture as external norm.[35] With Sonderegger we arguably find someone whose practice is not constrained by the fact/value divide.

Retrieving premodern modes of biblical interpretation[36]

Overlapping with the theological interpretation of scripture movement is another trend within recent approaches to biblical interpretation in the academy: a positive reevaluation and retrieval of premodern modes of interpreting the Bible. This trend is distributed among biblical scholars, doctrinal theologians, and patristic scholars. It is thus another area in which the problems of overrigid professional specialization might be addressed. Some of the same motivations identified among theological interpreters can be discerned here, too. Among these are a dissatisfaction with the limits of biblical criticism, with its focus on original context, and a corresponding acknowledgment of multiple possible meanings. The influence of developments in literary theory can be felt here, as well as of increasing interchange between patristic and rabbinic scholars, and a resultant increasing Christian appreciation of midrashic interpretation. Further, a positive reappraisal of the role of tradition is at work, one that is also evident in the rise of reception history. Rather than being conceived merely as an unwanted accretion that inhibits the Bible from speaking on its own terms, or worse, an oppressive authority structure from which the text and its readers should be liberated, tradition is reconceived as the living context within which the Bible is mediated to us. Within this context, an emphasis on reading for (spiritual) transformation replaces an understanding of reading disinterestedly for information (whether of an historical or another kind).[37]

A good indication of the shift that has taken place in the appraisal of patristic interpretation can be gained by comparing the patristic scholarship of R. P. C. Hanson, writing in the 1950s and 1960s, and Frances Young's study of early Christian culture, undertaken in the 1990s. Judging it by modern exegetical standards, Hanson dismisses Origen of Alexandria's allegorical exegesis as arbitrarily importing doctrinal conclusions into biblical texts to which they are alien.[38] Young departs radically from Hanson's assessment, appraising the interpretative practices of Origen and other patristic writers by carefully situating them in their antique cultural context and thereby arriving at a much finer-grained description of their interpretative strategies.[39] No longer judged by alien modern standards, the sophistication of patristic exegetical practices in their own terms is clearly displayed.

Despite her appreciative assessment, Young's work remains descriptively historical rather than generative of norms for biblical interpretation today. Even those writing with a normative theological agenda have, until more recently, stopped short of presenting premodern exegesis as a model for imitation today.[40] Thus it is suggestive of another shift in sensibility when the historical theologian Brian Daley, and more recently still, Hans Boersma, argue that premodern (and specifically patristic) exegesis can, and even should, provide a model for biblical interpretation today.[41] They are accompanied in this advocacy, as we saw in the last section, by theological interpreters of scripture. Going beyond most others in the extent to which he puts premodern (and specifically, figural) modes of reading into practice is Ephraim Radner.[42] I comment later on why he remains a relative outlier.

Those aspects of patristic interpretation held up for imitation include the following, most of which we have met before. First, scripture is a unity, its diverse parts to be read as part of a coherent whole. Young refers to this as the "mind" of scripture, translating the widespread appeal to its *skopos*.[43] Second, and part of the way in which this is achieved, is that scripture is to be read according to the rule of faith, which one might think of as a liturgically rooted, explicit articulation of scripture's *skopos*. Third, to read scripture is to be drawn into the presence of the living God, its ultimate author. Fourth, it follows that the purpose of interpretation is the transformation of the reader, who is addressed by scripture as divine revelation.[44]

A highly contested aspect of premodern exegesis, especially when it comes to its imitation, is allegory. John David Dawson has recently made a theologically motivated case for a sharp distinction between allegory and typology, arguing in favor of the latter.[45] Whereas allegory, on his rendition, is a conceptual translation of literal figure into spiritual meaning without remainder, typology, rooted in history, understands historical figure to point forward to its historical fulfilment without being superseded by it. He interprets Origen's "allegorical" reading as, properly speaking, typological: a matter not of replacement but of spiritual transformation. A precursor to Dawson's argument can be found in Jean Daniélou,[46] whom Young critiques for his anachronistic use of the category of typology.[47] Young's fine-grained mapping of patristic exegesis makes the binary distinction much harder to swallow as a lens through which to read it.

Whether or not Dawson is convincing in his argument for typology over allegory, he joins the growing ranks of those who make a normative case for the recovery of premodern modes of biblical interpretation. In the face of this impetus, it is surprising to find that the translation of this advocacy into practice is still relatively meagre. I hypothesize as a reason for this, in extension of my earlier critical diagnoses, that the treatment of premodern exegesis is caught between historical description (of which Young's work is exemplary) and external norm (as framed with exemplary clarity by Daley). The norms (as summarized previously) remain external to the extent that their rationality has not been internalized and thus made our own, in our very different, contemporary contexts. Attempts to inhabit and thereby exhibit their rationality are nevertheless beginning to emerge. Boersma's *Scripture as Real Presence* and Radner's *Time and the Word* (both, albeit very different, formidable attempts) have been joined even more recently by Mark Randall James's *Learning the Language of Scripture*, a detailed study of Origen's exegetical practice in order to discern its followable logic.[48] On James's account, Origen's is a wisdom hermeneutic: scripture hangs together less by way of a unifying theme or plot than by way of the wisdom it embodies, its *logos*; and the role of the interpreter is to learn to speak as scripture speaks, and thus according to its wisdom.

What works like these highlight is the limits of the language of imitation – insofar as it implies the continued externality of that which is to be imitated. The goal should rather be to think with and after the premodern authors, embodying their wisdom by making it one's own, and by extension to embody the wisdom of scripture.

Debate: A Case Study of Christian Relations with Jews

A promising thematic site for this kind of wisdom is the nexus of questions concerning Christian relations with Jews, past and present.[49] These are pursued, differently but in interconnected ways, in a variety of disciplinary settings. As a case study of contemporary biblical interpretation and its future potential, I comment on the following scholarly loci, drawing out their interconnectedness: postsupersessionist theological literature; biblical study of Paul's writings in their Jewish context; the history of Judaism and Christianity in the early centuries CE; and Jewish–Christian dialogue in the context of interreligious relations, with a focus on the practice of Scriptural Reasoning. The promise of this thematic site lies not least in the fact that it is a point of convergence for theological, exegetical, and historical study. A root problem for modern biblical interpretation has been the coming apart of historical and theological inquiry along a fact/value divide, biblical criticism locating itself on the fact side, leaving value to a theology bereft of its own biblical idiom. A site such as this – at which history matters for theology, and vice versa, and at which neither can do without scriptural interpretation – thus promises to make way for a remapping of the field.

Postsupersessionist theology is the Christian theological critical engagement with the legacy of historic Christian supersessionism – the view that the church replaces Israel in the purposes of God – being aimed at its overcoming. This work has been and is being energetically pursued in a variety of Christian denominational contexts. The Second Vatican Council's declaration *Nostra Aetate* is a landmark reckoning with the Christian tradition's damaging legacy in terms of anti-Judaism and anti-Semitism.[50] Much more recently, the Church of England's 2019 document, *God's Unfailing Word*, has been produced to set the parameters for Anglican teaching on the Christian church's relation with Jews.[51] Tackling this question, there are corresponding, and growing, bodies of literature within academic theology. I focus on the postsupersessionist literature associated with Christian postliberalism, partly because of its thoroughgoing scriptural engagement.[52]

A milestone work within this literature is R. Kendall Soulen's *The God of Israel and Christian Theology*, and it is exemplary of a theological argument worked out through scriptural interpretation.[53] Its goal is to recast the narrative frame within which scripture is read, putting Israel back at its center and thereby overcoming an historic Israel-forgetfulness. Learning from, and reconfiguring, Christian traditional reading, it inhabits rather than imitates the tradition, reading with a view to transforming contemporary Christian attitudes toward Jews. Soulen writes in the wake of the postliberal theologians George Lindbeck and Robert Jenson, as well as Katherine Sonderegger, and is followed (in a subtly new direction) by Tommy Givens.[54]

It is noteworthy that a towering figure that stands behind this theological trajectory (and continues to be an important dialogue partner within it) is Karl Barth, mediated in significant ways by Hans Frei. Postsupersessionist postliberal theologians are an important aspect of Barth's legacy as a *scriptural* theologian, and their relatively exceptional success in this regard has to do, first, with the unavoidably scriptural character of their subject matter. First, supersessionism and its overcoming have to do with the way in which Christians read Old and New Testaments in relation to one another. Second, Christians encounter Jews or their forebears both within their scriptures and as readers of overlapping scriptures. How they relate to Jews is bound up with how they relate to the scriptures they in part share with Jews. Third, scriptural teaching, and especially the *locus classicus*, Romans 9–11, is centrally informative of how Christians understand the church's relation to Israel, and relatedly (but not identically) to the Jewish people. In keeping with this, the Jewish philosopher Peter Ochs, in his landmark work, *Another Reformation*, interprets supersessionism as a fundamentally hermeneutical issue.[55]

A second reason postsupersessionist theologians are poised to make good on Barth's legacy is that their work is framed (in Collingwood's terms, and like McCaulley's work discussed previously) in response to "a question that arises": the problem of Christian anti-Judaism. Thus, in their accountability to a world they share with others (and Jews in particular), they have the potential to overcome a Barthian fideism. However, there is a tendency within the literature for theologians to devote their energies to thinking about how Jews figure *within* a Christian vision, rather than engage with Jewish thinkers and Jewish thought beyond the bounds of a Christian vision, in ways that might challenge that vision. This tendency perpetuates the insularity that might otherwise be overcome. Ellen Charry, working broadly within this theological area, is a good example of someone whose work avoids this insularity.[56]

Another significant locus within which supersessionism and its relatives, anti-Judaism and anti-Semitism, are at stake is the study of Paul in his Second Temple Jewish context. This scholarship forms a clear trajectory, in which, in the wake (among other works) of a seminal article by Krister Stendahl, and the milestone studies of E. P. Sanders,[57] there emerges "the New Perspective on Paul,"[58] subsequently to be superseded by the "Paul within Judaism" movement.[59] The New Perspective's target is a "Lutheran" reading of Paul according to which the object of Paul's critique is a legalist Judaism. Proponents of the New Perspective argue that Paul is concerned rather with the status of gentiles in relation to the people of God, the object of his critique being an ethnocentric Judaism that excludes gentiles as gentiles. Those writing from within the "Paul within Judaism" movement seek to undermine the (false) opposition between Paul and "Judaism" that is presupposed by both "old" and "new" perspectives and thus to overcome the anti-Judaism both equally (albeit differently) ascribe to Paul. On their alternative reading, not only does Paul argue as a Jew with other Jews, but more pointedly, his critique is concerned not with Jews as Jews, but with the manner in which gentile Christ-followers are to live in relation to the traditions of Paul's forefathers. In readings that are quite different in their details, they converge on a radically nonsupersessionist Paul.

Given their different routes to it, this consensus is noteworthy, arguably revealing a shared ideological agenda. Although this whole body of literature, from the New Perspective on, is historically framed, the problem of Christian supersessionism lies barely beneath the surface as a motivating concern. There is a tendency among biblical critics first to critique previous waves of biblical scholarly research by exposing its cultural and ideological situatedness, and then (more or less implicitly) to claim for their own work the ability (however falteringly) to transcend such bias.[60] Such a claim, I argue, is disingenuous – and unnecessary. If postsupersessionist theology benefits from its scriptural orientation, then conversely, the biblical scholarly literature concerned with supersessionism is given a distinct advantage by its theologically freighted agenda. It is undertaken in response to "a question that arises." Furthermore, as we saw in McCaulley's case, new contexts may awaken past contexts in illuminating ways. Thus it is no surprise that each era of biblical scholarship is shaped by its own distinctive concerns, illuminating different aspects of different texts. The problem comes when scholarship that is necessarily interested is presented as disinterestedly objective, giving rise to talk of the "real" Paul, whom others that have come before have failed to find. More troublingly, it is then that the norms covertly operative are assumed by default to be universal, being imposed upon, and marginalizing, others who do not share them. Within the discipline of biblical studies, these norms have historically been, and in many unexamined ways continue to be, Christian. In terms that should by now be familiar, such norms, insofar as they become visible, are presented as "fact," foreclosing debate. By contrast, an overtly normative agenda is one that invites public normative discussion.

In sum, biblical scholarly literature concerned with supersessionism is promising in its character as a response to a pressing problem. It is troubling insofar as it conceals this problem as something that shapes its agenda. The theological literature can, by exposing it, help make it available for discussion. Both the theological and the biblical scholarly literature are bound up, moreover, with a third scholarly locus: constructions of the history of the emergence of Christianity over against Judaism in the first few centuries CE. An old supersessionist theology has tended to go together with an historical narrative according to which Christianity emerges out of and replaces an older Judaism.[61] More recent historical reconstructions hold Judaism and Christianity (as discrete religions) to emerge simultaneously, mutually created and defined over against one another, perhaps as late as the fourth century CE. Daniel Boyarin's landmark work *Border Lines* consolidates an important new paradigm.[62] While nonsupersessionism does not necessarily follow, a crude supersessionism is undermined. This special entanglement of theology and history gives the historical work of Pauline scholars (which both informs and is informed by the broader historical reconstructions of the early centuries CE) unusually direct theological purchase. The disciplinary convergence is thus one in which the influence goes in all directions.

Historical reconstructions of the early centuries not only bring into question a preconceived binary between Judaism and Christianity (not least in light of the recognition that as "world religions" these are modern phenomena) but also confound assumed contrasts between religion and ethnicity and between universality and ethnic particularity.[63] The reworking of such (ideologically loaded) binaries displays both how history is ineluctably crafted by the categories we have to hand and how it challenges and recasts them. The manifestness of this dual truth at this particular historical locus makes it a welcome point of mediation between a potentially insular Christian theological discourse, and a potentially historically reductive biblical criticism. The wider historical canvas holds theological discourse accountable to a shared historical world and invites biblical criticism to recognition of its ineluctable ideological framing.

I turn, finally, to our fourth scholarly locus: study in interreligious relations. There are various umbrellas under which this is pursued, including comparative religion and comparative theology. I focus on Scriptural Reasoning, as a practice in which Jews, Christians, and Muslims study their sacred texts together, and as a body of theoretical reflection on this practice.[64] Without this fourth locus, each of the first three is left potentially (and arguably in fact) wanting.

First, I remarked above on postsupersessionist theology's tendency to insularity. Scriptural Reasoning is an antidote to this problem insofar as it brings Christians into encounter with Jews who reason differently, and sometimes out of the same scriptural texts. Seasoned by such encounters, postsupersessionist theologians can no longer insulate their Christian norms from wider public discussion. They are turned from private values into public norms. Scriptural Reasoning also has something to offer in relation to the other two scholarly loci. As historical, the danger for both (in the context of the modern academy) is toward historical reductionism: the "fact" side of the fact/value divide. Scriptural Reasoning models an unusual normativity insofar as it engages its practitioners in their idiomatic reasoning but in dialogue with others who reason differently, inviting both attentive description of the reasoning employed by others, and normative consideration of it as it challenges one's own. It is nonconfessional insofar as traditional axioms cannot be taken for granted; but it is truth-seeking insofar as practitioners do not disengage from those axioms, nor from the sacredness of their scriptures. It is, as such, an intensified embodiment of public normative discourse: normative as it actively engages one's own axioms or presuppositions, and public insofar as these are open to interrogation in the light of the axioms of others. To undertake historical research in a way that learns from Scriptural Reasoning is to be alert to the normative stakes, ready for surprise, and prepared for attentive description. The fact/value divide is undermined.

Christian biblical interpretation shaped by Scriptural Reasoning can be found in David Ford's *Christian Wisdom* as well as in his more recent *The Gospel of John: A Theological Commentary*, and rather differently, in Mike Higton and Rachel Muers's *The Text in Play*.[65] These offer good examples of descriptively attentive scriptural interpretation that is explicitly Christianly normative but that holds itself open to alternative (specifically Jewish and Muslim) wisdoms. The same might be said both of Ellen Charry's Psalms commentary and of Ellen Davis's *Opening Israel's Scriptures* (specifically, in their engagement with Jewish readings).[66] Highlighted by each is the importance of traditioned but public normativity, shaped in conversation with, and opened to interrogation by, differently traditioned others.

Agenda

I have argued that the fundamental problem besetting biblical interpretation in the modern academy is the fact/value divide. Biblical interpreters are caught on the horns of a dilemma. The traditional biblical critic brackets out his private values and presents his findings as objective fact, unwittingly imposing his concealed (by and large Christian) norms on others. The "located" reader (as framed by this opposition) reads self-consciously according to her "private" values, which thereby lose normative purchase for those who do not share them. Or these values are objectified within a series of options for the reader. Theological interpreters of scripture and postsupersessionist postliberal theologians have a tendency towards insularity – or the privatization of their values (in what might be considered a postmodern version of Barthian fideism). The former tend in this direction by externalizing their norms, unwittingly turning them into "fact," and thus insulating them from critique, and the latter by absorbing the public world into their (private) Christian vision. In both cases the tendency is to undermine public normative discourse, obscuring the truth as that which can be sought in common with others.

I have indicated various sites of biblical interpretation at which the fact/value divide has begun to be eroded. Considered together, these yield a constructive agenda for future biblical interpretation. On this agenda, biblical interpretation will take the following shape. First, as for many of the interpreters branded "contextual," it will involve reading in response to "questions that arise" in a shared world. Second, as does the feminist critic (among others), it will engage an internalized normativity that invites further critical inquiry. Third, as in the context of Scriptural Reasoning, such normativity will be self-consciously open to transformation in the light of encounter with those who, differently normed, inhabit and shape the shared world differently. Fourth, the result will be an interpretative freedom like that of the patristic writers, in which the Bible is approached not as heteronomous norm but as source of wisdom to be inhabited, interrogated, and made one's own. In this way, the Bible will become a site for the common pursuit of the truth – as that which cannot be possessed by anyone but (by the same token) can be inhabited by all.

Notes

1 Lewis Ayres, *Nicaea and its Legacy: An Approach to Fourth-Century Trinitarian Theology* (Oxford: Oxford University Press, 2004), 398.

2 Hans W. Frei, *The Eclipse of Biblical Narrative: A Study in Eighteenth and Nineteenth Century Hermeneutics* (New Haven, CT: Yale University Press, 1974); Jonathan Sheehan, *The Enlightenment Bible: Translation, Scholarship, Culture* (Princeton, NJ: Princeton University Press, 2005); Michael C. Legaspi, *The Death of Scripture and the Rise of Biblical Studies* (New York: Oxford University Press, 2011).

3 H. Martin Rumscheidt, *Revelation and Theology: An Analysis of the Barth-Harnack Correspondence of 1923* (Cambridge: Cambridge University Press, 1972), 29–53.

4 As is forcefully argued in Stephen D. Moore and Yvonne Sherwood, *The Invention of the Biblical Scholar: A Critical Manifesto* (Minneapolis, MN: Fortress Press, 2011).

5 Both Dale B. Martin, in *Biblical Truths: The Meaning of Scripture in the Twenty-first Century* (New Haven, CT: Yale University Press, 2017) and David G. Horrell, in *Ethnicity and Inclusion: Religion, Race, and Whiteness in Constructions of Jewish and Christian Identities* (Grand Rapids, MI: Eerdmans, 2020), continue to practice what they critique. R. S. Sugirtharajah's ruefully titled *Still at the Margins: Biblical Scholarship Fifteen Years after the Voices from the Margin* (New York: T&T Clark, 2008) witnesses to the continued dominance of what Sugirtharajah calls "mainstream" biblical scholarship.

6 John Barton, *The Nature of Biblical Criticism* (Louisville, KY: Westminster John Knox Press, 2007).

7 One manifestation of this grouping is edited volumes that range such readings in a series alongside more "traditional" approaches. See, for example, John Barton, ed., *The Cambridge Companion to Biblical Interpretation* (Cambridge: Cambridge University Press, 1998), Part One, "Lines of Approach."

8 Athalya Brenner and Carole Fontaine, eds., *Feminist Companion to Reading the Bible: Approaches, Methods and Strategies* (Sheffield: Sheffield Academic Press, 1997), 11–13. The term "malestream" was introduced to biblical studies by Elisabeth Schüssler Fiorenza in *Bread Not Stone: The Challenge of Feminist Biblical Interpretation* (Boston, MA: Beacon Press, 1985).

9 Athalya Brenner, "Identifying the Speaker-in-the-Text and the Reader's Location in Prophetic Texts," in *Feminist Companion*, ed. Brenner and Fontaine, 136–50.

10 Carole Fontaine, "Response to Brenner's Speaker-in-the-Text," in *Feminist Companion*, ed. Brenner and Fontaine, 151–3.

11 Cf. Moore and Sherwood, *Invention*, 59–62. A similar willingness is subtly operative in Tat-siong Benny Liew's essays in Tat-siong Benny Liew and Erin Runions, eds., *Psychoanalytic Mediations Between Marxist and Postcolonial Reading of the Bible* (Atlanta, GA: SBL Press, 2016), 99–170, which modulate the wider critical approach of Marxist and postcolonial interpretation. The 40th anniversary edition of Phyllis Trible's field-defining classic has recently been published: Phyllis Trible, *Texts of Terror: Literary-Feminist Readings of*

Biblical Narratives, 40th anniversary ed. (Minneapolis, MN: Fortress Press, 2022).

12 Brenner, "Identifying," 140.

13 Esau McCaulley, *Reading While Black: African American Biblical Interpretation as an Exercise in Hope* (Downers Grove, IL: IVP Academic, 2020), 22.

14 McCaulley, *Reading*, 17.

15 McCaulley, *Reading*, 21–2.

16 R. G. Collingwood, *An Autobiography and Other Writings, with Essays on Collingwood's Life and Works*, ed. David Boucher and Teresa Smith (Oxford: Oxford University Press, 2013), 122. In this context his argument concerns archaeological research, but the principle applies more widely. See his logic of question and answer, *Autobiography*, 29–43.

17 R.G. Collingwood, *The Idea of History, Revised Edition with Lectures 1926–1928*, ed. with an introduction by Jan van der Dussen (Oxford: Oxford University Press, 1994; originally edited by T. M. Knox and published in 1946), 300. This principle is explicitly at work in the essays in Fernando F. Segovia, ed., *Interpreting Beyond Borders* (Sheffield: Sheffield Academic Press, 2000).

18 Moore and Sherwood, *Invention*, 118–19.

19 This divide plays an important role in Alasdair McIntyre's diagnosis of the fate of morality in modern culture; Alasdair MacIntyre, *After Virtue: A Study in Moral Theory* (London: Duckworth, 1985). For a thorough account of the legacy of the fact/value divide in modern Western Jewish and Christian thought, see Randi Rashkover, *Nature and Norm: Judaism, Christianity, and the Theopolitical Problem* (Boston, MA: Academic Studies Press, 2020).

20 As Brenner and Fontaine ruefully note in *Feminist Companion to Reading the Bible*, 13. Some embrace subjectivity in opposition to a (false) objectivity. See, for example, David M. Gun and Danna Nolan Fewell, *Narrative in the Hebrew Bible* (Oxford: Oxford University Press, 1993), 9.

21 A tendency present in, for example, A. K. M. Adam, "Integral and Differential Hermeneutics," in *The Meanings We Choose: Hermeneutical Ethics, Indeterminacy and the Conflict of Interpretations*, ed. Charles H. Cosgrove (London: T&T Clark, 2004), 35.

22 For this section I am indebted to Lewis Edwards, "The Place of Historical Criticism in the Theological Interpretation of Scripture: A Critical Assessment" (Master's thesis, King's College London, 2013).

23 The movement has spawned several theological commentary series: *The Two Horizons Old Testament* Commentary, ed. J. Gordon McConville and Craig Bartholomew (Grand Rapids, MI: Eerdmans, 2008–); *The Two Horizons New Testament Commentary*, ed. Joel B. Green (Grand Rapids, MI: Eerdmans, 2005–); and the *Brazos Theological Commentary on the* Bible, ed. R. R. Reno (Grand Rapids, MI: Brazos, 2005–).

24 Stephen Fowl, ed., *The Theological Interpretation of Scripture: Classic and Contemporary Readings* (Oxford: Blackwell, 1997), xiii.

25 Fowl sets these out in his introduction; Fowl, ed., *Theological Interpretation of Scripture*, xii–xxx. They are also concisely articulated in Ellen F. Davis and Richard B. Hays, "Nine Theses on the Interpretation of Scripture," in *The Art of Reading Scripture*, ed. Ellen F. Davis and Richard B. Hays (Grand Rapids, MI: Eerdmans, 2003), 1–5 (and are variously borne out in the volume as a whole).

26 See Robert Jenson, "Scripture's Authority in the Church," in *The Art of Reading Scripture*, eds. Davis and Hays, 27–37 [27]; R. W. L. Moberly, "Biblical Criticism and Religious Belief," *Journal of Theological Interpretation* 2, no. 1 (2008): 71–100 [86–7].

27 A strong version of this claim is developed in Kevin J. Vanhoozer, *Is There a Meaning in this Text? The Bible, the Reader, and the Morality of Literary Knowledge* (Grand Rapids, MI: Zondervan, 1998), ch. 5.

28 Cf. David C. Steinmetz's 1980 article, "The Superiority of Pre-Critical Exegesis," included in Fowl, ed., *Theological Interpretation of Scripture*, 26–38.

29 See Daniel J. Treier, *Introducing Theological Interpretation of Scripture: Recovering a Christian Practice* (Grand Rapids, MI: Baker Academic), ch. 2.

30 See Christopher R. Seitz, *Figured Out: Typology and Providence in Christian Scripture* (Louisville, KY: Westminster John Knox Press, 2001).

31 See Brevard S. Childs, *Introduction to the Old Testament as Scripture* (Philadelphia, PA: Fortress Press, 1979).

32 Cf. Ellen Charry's reservations about a Christological reading of the Psalms in Ellen T. Charry, *Psalms 1–50: Sighs and Songs of Israel*, Brazos Theological Commentary on the Bible, ed. R. R. Reno (Grand Rapids, MI: Brazos Press, 2015).

33 Katherine Sonderegger, *Systematic Theology, Vol. 1: The Doctrine of God* (Minneapolis, MN: Fortress Press), 505–30.

34 Sonderegger, *Systematic Theology*, Vol. 1, 517.

35 Such freedom is arguably even more evident in her second volume, Katherine Sonderegger, *Systematic Theology: Vol. 2, The Doctrine of the Holy Trinity: Processions and Persons* (Minneapolis, MN: Fortress Press, 2020).

36 For this section I am indebted to Jeremy Hudson, "New Perspectives on Patristic Readings of the Bible: A Critical Discussion" (Master's thesis, King's College London, 2011).

37 See K. J. Torjesen, *Hermeneutical Procedure and Theological Method in Origen's Exegesis* (Berlin: De Gruyter, 1985).

38 R. P. C. Hanson, *Allegory and Event: A Study of the Sources and Significance of Origen's Interpretation of Scripture* (London: SCM Press, 1959).

39 Frances M. Young, *Biblical Exegesis and the Formation of Christian Culture* (Cambridge: Cambridge University Press, 1997).

40 See Henri De Lubac, *Mediaeval Exegesis: The Four Senses of Scripture*, 2 vols. (Grand Rapids, MI: Eerdmans, 1998, 2000) (original French edition published in 1959); and more recently in de Lubac's footsteps, Anderw Louth, *Discerning the Mystery: An Essay on the Nature of Theology* (Oxford: Oxford University Press, 1989).

41 Brian E. Daley, SJ, "Is Patristic Exegesis Still Usable? Reflections on the Early Christian Interpretation of the Psalms," *Communio: International Catholic Review* 29, no. 1 (2002): 185–216. Hans Boersma, *Scripture as Real Presence: Sacramental Exegesis in the Early Church* (Grand Rapids, MI: Baker Academic, 2017). They are anticipated by Steinmetz. See his 1980 article reprinted in Fowl, ed., *Theological Interpretation of Scripture*.

42 See Ephraim Radner, *Time and the Word: Christian Figural Readings of the Christian Scriptures* (Grand Rapids, MI: Eerdmans, 2016).

43 Young, *Biblical Exegesis*, 29.

44 See Daley, "Patristic," who offers a related set of characteristics.

45 John David Dawson, *Christian Figural Reading and the Fashioning of Identity* (Berkeley, CA: University of California Press, 2002).

46 Jean Daniélou, *From Shadows to Reality: Studies in the Biblical Typology of the Fathers*, trans. W. Hibberd (London: Burns & Oates, 1960).

47 Young, *Biblical Exegesis*, 193.

48 Mark Randall James, *Learning the Language of Scripture: Origen, Wisdom and the Logic of Interpretation* (Leiden: Brill, 2021). I have made my own attempt, with Augustine as my interlocutor, in *On Signs, Christ, Truth and the Interpretation of Scripture* (*Reading Augustine*) (London: Bloomsbury, 2022).

49 The reason for phrasing this asymmetrically is that some of the literatures I survey are concerned more with Christian ways of thinking about (and relating to) Jews, and much less with Jewish ways of thinking about (and relating to) Christians. I will critique this tendency.

50 *Nostra Aetate*. Declaration on the Relation of the Church to Non-Christian Religions, Second Vatican Council, 1965, https://www.vatican.va/archive/hist_councils/ ii_vatican_council/documents/vat-ii_decl_19651028_ nostra-aetate_en.html (accessed 26 April 2022).

51 *God's Unfailing Word: Theological and Practical Perspectives on Christian–Jewish Relations*, The Faith and Order Commission (London: Church Publishing House, 2019), https://www.churchofengland.org/ sites/default/files/2019-11/godsunfailingwordweb. pdf (accessed 26 April 2022).

52 There is also a burgeoning Roman Catholic literature. As a snapshot, see Didier Pollefeyt and Marianne

Moyaert, eds., *Never Revoked: Nostra Aetate as Ongoing Challenge for Jewish-Christian Dialogue* (Louvain: Peeters, 2010).

53 R. Kendall Soulen, *The God of Israel and Christian Theology* (Minneapolis, MN: Fortress Press, 1996).

54 See George Lindbeck, "The Church as Israel: Ecclesiology and Ecumenism," in *Jews and Christians: People of God*, ed. Carl E. Braaten and Robert W. Jenson (Grand Rapids, MI: Eerdmans, 2003) 78–94, and Robert W. Jenson, "Toward a Christian Theology of Judaism," in *Jews and Christians*, ed. Braaten and Jenson, 1–13, for more recent contributions. Katherine Sonderegger, *That Jesus Christ Was Born a Jew: Karl Barth's "Doctrine of Israel"* (University Park, PA: Pennsylvania State University Press, 1992). Tommy Givens, *We the People: Israel and the Catholicity of Jesus* (Minneapolis, MN: Fortress Press, 2014).

55 Peter Ochs, *Another Reformation: Postliberal Christianity and the Jews* (Grand Rapids, MI: Baker Academic, 2011).

56 See Charry, *Psalms*.

57 Krister Stendahl, "The Apostle Paul and the Introspective Conscience of the West," *Harvard Theological Review* 56 (1963): 199–215. See esp. E. P. Sanders, *Paul and Palestinian Judaism: A Comparison of Patterns of Religion* (London: SCM Press, 1977).

58 Of which James Dunn (who coined the name) and N. T. Wright are central representatives. See James D. G. Dunn, *The New Perspective on Paul: Collected Essays* (Tübingen: Mohr Siebeck, 2005).

59 See Mark D. Nanos and Magnus Zetterholm, eds., *Paul within Judaism: Restoring the First-Century Context to the Apostle* (Minneapolis, MN: Fortress Press, 2015).

60 This tendency is evident, for example, in Matthew Thiessen, "Conjuring Paul and Judaism Forty Years After *Paul and Palestinian Judaism*," *Journal of the Jesus Movement in Its Jewish Setting* 5 (2018): 6–20.

61 Paradigmatic of an unremittingly anti-Jewish version of this narrative is Adolf von Harnack's *Das Wesen des Christentums*, originally published in 1900. See Adolf von Harnack, *What Is Christianity?*, trans. T. B. Saunders, 5th ed. (London: Ernest Benn, 1958).

62 Daniel Boyarin, *Border Lines: The Partition of Judaeo-Christianity* (Philadelphia, PA: University of Pennsylvania Press, 2004). Cf. also the indicatively titled Annette Yoshiko Reed and Adam H. Becker, eds., *The Ways That Never Parted: Jews and Christians in Late Antiquity and the Early Middle Ages* (Tübingen: Mohr Siebeck, 2003). In their Introduction, Reed and Becker illuminatingly narrate the historical paradigm shifts.

63 See Denise Kimber Buell, *Why This New Race? Ethnic Reasoning in Early Christianity* (New York: Columbia University Press, 2005). Buell brings into question both binaries. Cf. Shaye Cohen, *The Beginnings of Jewishness:*

Boundaries, Varieties, Uncertainties (Berkeley, CA: University of California Press, 1995), whose argument trades on the binary between religion and ethnicity.

64 See David F. Ford and C. C. Pecknold, *The Promise of Scriptural Reasoning* (Oxford: Blackwell, 2006).

65 David F. Ford, *Christian Wisdom: Desiring God and Learning Love* (Cambridge: Cambridge University Press, 2007); David F. Ford, *The Gospel of John: A Theological Commentary* (Grand Rapids, MI: Baker Academic, 2021); Mike Higton and Rachel Muers, *The Text in Play: Experiments in Reading Scripture* (Eugene, OR: Cascade, 2012).

66 Ellen F. Davis, *Opening Israel's Scriptures* (New York: Oxford University Press, 2019).

Recommended Reading

Boersma, Hans. *Scripture as Real Presence: Sacramental Exegesis in the Early Church.* Grand Rapids, MI: Baker Academic, 2017.

Charry, Ellen T. *Psalms 1–50: Sighs and Songs of Israel*, Brazos Theological Commentary on the Bible. Grand Rapids, MI: Brazos Press, 2015.

Davis Ellen F., and Richard B. Hays, eds. *The Art of Reading Scripture.* Grand Rapids, MI: Eerdmans, 2003.

Davis, Ellen F. *Opening Israel's Scriptures.* New York: Oxford University Press, 2019.

Dawson, John David. *Christian Figural Reading and the Fashioning of Identity.* Berkeley, CA: University of California Press, 2002.

Ford, David F. *The Gospel of John: A Theological Commentary.* Grand Rapids, MI: Baker Academic, 2021.

Ford, David F., and C. C. Pecknold, *The Promise of Scriptural Reasoning.* Oxford: Blackwell, 2006.

Fowl, Stephen, ed. *The Theological Interpretation of Scripture: Classic and Contemporary Readings.* Oxford: Blackwell, 1997.

Givens, Tommy. *We the People: Israel and the Catholicity of Jesus.* Minneapolis, MN: Fortress Press, 2014.

Higton, Mike, and Rachel Muers. *The Text in Play: Experiments in Reading Scripture.* Eugene, OR: Cascade, 2012.

James, Mark Randall. *Learning the Language of Scripture: Origen, Wisdom and the Logic of Interpretation.* Leiden: Brill, 2021.

Legaspi, Michael C. *The Death of Scripture and the Rise of Biblical Studies.* Oxford: Oxford University Press, 2011.

McCaulley, Esau. *Reading While Black: African American Biblical Interpretation as an Exercise in Hope.* Downers Grove, IL: IVP Academic, 2020.

Moore, Stephen D., and Yvonne Sherwood. *The Invention of the Biblical Scholar: A Critical Manifesto.* Minneapolis, MN: Fortress Press, 2011.

Ochs, Peter. *Another Reformation: Postliberal Christianity and the Jews.* Grand Rapids, MI: Baker Academic, 2011.

Radner, Ephraim. *Time and the Word: Christian Figural Readings of the Christian Scriptures.* Grand Rapids, MI: Eerdmans, 2016.

Sonderegger, Katherine. *Systematic Theology: Vol. 1, The Doctrine of God.* Minneapolis, MN: Fortress Press, 2015.

———. *Systematic Theology: Vol. 2, The Doctrine of the Holy Trinity: Processions and Persons.* Minneapolis, MN: Fortress Press, 2020.

Soulen, R. Kendall. *The God of Israel and Christian Theology.* Minneapolis, MN: Fortress Press, 1996.

Ticciati, Susannah. *On Signs, Christ, Truth and the Interpretation of Scripture.* (*Reading Augustine*). London: Bloomsbury, 2022.

Trible, Phyllis. *Texts of Terror: Literary-Feminist Readings of Biblical Narratives.* 40th anniversary edition. Minneapolis, MN: Fortress Press, 2022.

Spirituality and Theology

Andrew Prevot

Introduction: Rethinking the Standard Story

Since roughly the middle of the twentieth century, a story has been told about the relationship between spirituality and theology. These are its basic plot points. In antiquity, spirituality and theology were so deeply united that no one would have thought to separate them. They developed in concert, shaping the church's doctrine and practice from the period of the New Testament through the early Middle Ages. Then fissures started to appear with the advent of the university, on the one hand, and the emergence of the "self," on the other. Over time, these cracks widened to form a great chasm. Theology became an arid, rationalist discipline with little connection to human life, and spirituality became a self-absorbed recounting of inner experiences detached from communal wisdom and norms. However – so the story goes – this divorce need not be permanent. Spirituality and theology can be reconciled. Their original unity can be restored through a retrieval of the sources (*ressourcement*) and through various hermeneutical, postmodern, or liberationist efforts to reintegrate theory and practice. Fragmentation can be overcome through a renewed commitment to wholeness. Versions of this story have been told by theologians such as Hans Urs von Balthasar, Gustavo Gutiérrez, Mark McIntosh, Sarah Coakley, and Philip Sheldrake. Whatever their differences, these Christian thinkers share a belief that spirituality and theology ought to go together.[1]

This story about spirituality and theology can be situated within a larger set of stories about modernity, which seek to assess what it has damaged and achieved. Philosophers and cultural theorists such as G. W. F. Hegel, Michel Foucault, Luce Irigaray, Charles Taylor, and Walter Mignolo, to name only a few, have penned influential meta-narratives that detail major epochal shifts.[2] These thinkers agree that something about the construction of reason, knowledge, and subjectivity in the last several centuries of the "West" (a vague region encompassing Germany, France, Italy, Britain, Spain, and other European and Euro-dominant contexts) has fundamentally changed the conditions of human life and meaning. The consequences have been dramatic for science, politics, the arts, and religion. Set within this larger collection of "modernity stories," the story about spirituality and theology offers specific comments about what has happened to religion and recommendations about what to do about it.

Ford's The Modern Theologians: An Introduction to Christian Theology since 1918, Fourth Edition.
Edited by Rachel Muers and Ashley Cocksworth.
© 2024 John Wiley & Sons Ltd. Published 2024 by John Wiley & Sons Ltd.

Although this spirituality-theology story is not merely a tale about secularization (a disputed theme in its own right), these topics are related. A break between spirituality and theology can be interpreted as symptomatic or explanatory of a decline in faith. If one does not think about God (i.e. do theology) in a way that connects God to self-implicating experiences and practices (i.e. spirituality), then the idea of God no longer "functions" as it once did. Conversely, if one pursues a way of life (i.e. spirituality) that is not informed by well-developed thoughts about God (i.e. theology), then one's lifestyle evinces a similar decrease in the relevance of religious belief. Theological rationalism and spiritual subjectivism are two sides of the same secularizing coin. Responding to this situation, theologians have recognized a need for more integrated, relational, and energizing approaches to the contemplation of God, which build on earlier Christian models and develop them for contemporary contexts.

Although theologians have good reasons to argue that there has been a separation of spirituality and theology, this claim makes sense, as it were, only from the "outside" – that is, from a modern epistemological standpoint that understands spirituality and theology as historical constructs that merge or separate based on contingent human choices and behaviors. According to a more "interior" spiritual-theological logic, attuned to the activity of God in hearts and minds, the supposed separation of spirituality and theology could have only ever been a misunderstanding or distortion. Those who have been thinking rightly of God and have deserved to be called "theologians" – ones whose words and thoughts (*logoi*) are of God *(tou Theou)* – have always been, up through modernity and beyond, shaped deeply in their embodied lives by true experiences of contemplation. They have prayed, loved, perceived, and acted as finite, fallen, and graced creatures caught up in a divine and redemptive mystery greater than they could conceive. The Christian ones have been followers of Jesus and witnesses to the gospel, and every authentic theologian, whether Christian or not, has been guided by the Holy Spirit and participated in the sanctification of the world. Their words and thoughts about God have flowed from and strengthened their relationships with God. To reach the original unity that the story of a modern separation between spirituality and theology seeks to recover, there is thus a real sense in which one must refuse to believe this story. Understood rightly, there could never have been a strict separation. Spirituality and theology are one by their very essence.[3]

Yet the need to reconnect with the earlier, unified form of spirituality-and-theology is real. Doing so requires more than a backward-looking, nostalgic gaze. It means seeking and finding the living God in the world now. It means interacting with this living God in all one's quotidian and structural entanglements. It means a million contextually specific things that have, at their center, a dynamic interplay of divine and human freedoms. From this perspective, much that passes for "spirituality" and "theology" in this era of their apparent estrangement may not be deserving of these lofty titles. By the same token, much that goes unnoticed in current conversations around these terms – including the devotions, thoughts, and experiences of non-Western Christians and human beings of various gender performances and cultural backgrounds – may reveal that the essential unity of spirituality and theology has never been lost provided that one has known where to look.

Instead of simply separating spirituality and theology, it may be more accurate to say that modernity has generated a plurality of different spirituality-theology constellations, which call for further investigation. For example, rather than assume that a neoscholastic treatise is a spirituality-free expression of theology, it might be more illuminating to ask what features of (a perhaps specifically neoscholastic) spirituality might be implied or stated in such a text and what prayers, experiences, and actions shaped the life of its author.[4] By the same token, instead of presupposing that a personal memoir is a theology-free expression of spirituality, it might be more clarifying to ask what theological images, ideas, or traditions operate within it.[5] These questions discourage perfunctory judgments on either side, while prompting more important and challenging conversations about how to adjudicate between different combinations of spirituality and theology.

In addition to the problem of overstated separations, there is also a problem in the other direction related to underappreciated distinctions. The standard story deemphasizes the value that some scholars find in the invention of spirituality as an interdisciplinary field of study distinct from theology, and that some theologians find in a type of analytical clarity whose immediate purpose is not to integrate thought and life but to differentiate concepts for the sake of greater understanding.[6] Although such pragmatic distinctions between spirituality and theology may be valuable in certain contexts, these need not cause one to abandon the search for wholeness.

Finally, one must interrogate the Eurocentrism of the standard story. This story's nearly exclusive focus on "the West" is arguably unjust. It lets one racialized geographical region set the terms of a supposedly universal knowledge or history and thereby reifies a center-periphery colonial power structure. However, this epistemic injustice is not the only problem. The very truth of one's spirituality-and-theology is also at stake. The danger is that one will not really know God because one will not recognize where God is at work in history and will not live in close contact with this incarnate divine mystery. Although the very words "spirituality" and "theology" may have colonial baggage, they can still be used beneficially to name and receive the highly significant spiritual-and-theological contributions of non-Western sources, whether they be Christian, belong to another religion, or constitute a creative mixture.[7]

To some degree, the same cultural forces that have appeared to drive a wedge between spirituality and theology are also behind the dehumanizing violence of colonial modernity. A technocratic, objectifying effort to master the world through knowledge and power and an imperious subjectivity that cares only about its own self-serving desires and ambitions have conspired against true Christianity, against the sacredness of the human being, and against the mysterious wholeness of God's presence in creation. The seemingly parochial attempt among a small set of academics to restore the unity of spirituality and theology and the massive, worldwide struggle to right the wrongs of modern colonial history may, in the end, be part of the same fight – in a word, for our souls. Whatever its challenges, the standard story of the spirituality–theology relationship has prepared the way for a renewed search for the living God in the midst of this troubled world.

Survey: Diverse Senses of "Spirituality"

What is spirituality? Although its meaning is not limited to how the word "spirituality" has been used, a consideration of this lexical question may provide some helpful clues. The term is derived from the Latin *spiritualitas*, an abstract noun that is closely connected with the more common *spiritus* (spirit) and *spiritualis* (spiritual). Early Latin Christians used these terms to translate the Apostle Paul's Greek *pneuma* and *pneumatikos*. The earliest known mention of *spiritualitas* occurs in a fifth-century letter from an anonymous Christian author who employs it as an abbreviated name for a way of life in accordance with the Holy Spirit. For this biblical and early Christian tradition, "spirituality" is not opposed to materiality or embodiment per se but rather to what Paul calls *sarx* (*carne*, flesh): a habit of sinful, community-disruptive behavior contrary to the guidance of the Spirit and the mind of Christ. A more philosophically dualistic understanding of "spirituality" as referring to the immateriality or incorporeality of a disembodied soul appears here and there in the Platonically inflected Christian tradition from the ninth century onwards but gains prominence only after it is used in early modernity by philosophers such as René Descartes.[8]

For much of the church's history, the collection of practices, experiences, texts, communities, and ways of life that today would be studied under the category of "spirituality" would not have been given this appellation. The present widespread usage of this term has its origins in the early decades of the twentieth century. Anglophone conversations about philosophical Hinduism (or Vedānta) adopted it to gesture toward a transcendental mode of experience supposedly lying beyond religious difference or at least beyond modern Western materialism. At the same time, Francophone studies of the history of Christian ascetical and mystical doctrines employed the French word *spiritualité* as a shorthand for their field of interest. By the 1950s, translations of some of these French works propelled an increase in English usage. These two lineages – transcendental and interreligious, on the one hand, and Christian historical-theological, on the other – point to disciplinary tensions that remain in the twenty-first-century discourse of spirituality.[9]

Walter Principe, whose careful account of the history of the term "spirituality" I have followed here, reflects these tensions by proposing two definitions of "spirituality." In a general, not-specifically-Christian sense that could be appropriate for interreligious or even secular contexts, he suggests that "spirituality" refers to "the way in which a person understands and lives within his or her historical context that aspect of his or her religion, philosophy or ethic that is viewed as the loftiest, the noblest, the most calculated to lead to the fullness of the ideal or perfection being sought."[10] Sandra Schneiders offers a similarly broad and flexible definition of "spirituality" as "the experience of conscious involvement in the project of life-integration through self-transcendence toward the ultimate value one perceives."[11] Exalted ideals, practices of integration, and ultimate values can vary significantly from one person or group to another and do not presuppose Christian faith. The advantage of such definitions is how accommodating they can be of different religious perspectives and even of the increasing number of (especially younger) people who identify as "spiritual but not religious."[12]

However, the disadvantage of these definitions – from both pluralist and Christian theological perspectives – has to do with their apparent forsaking of particularity. These formulations seem simultaneously to say too little and too much about what "spirituality" means: too little, because they leave pivotal questions unanswered (e.g. what is the highest value?) and too much, because their concepts, however vague, reflect specific histories and choices (e.g. those of modern transcendental philosophy) that can obscure the particular lives and traditions they are meant to cover.

Principe's other, Christian theological definition of "spirituality" is a narrower, Trinitarian formulation tethered to his reading of the Apostle Paul. He argues that, for Christians, "spirituality" names a way of life that is "influenced, as Paul taught, by the Holy Spirit or Spirit of God incorporating the person into Jesus Christ as Head, through whom he or she has access to the Father in a life of faith, hope, love, and service."[13] Although Christian theologians may appreciate this definition's doctrinal specificity, its details would not be beyond dispute. For any given definition, questions can be asked about whether its selected elements are the best ones to emphasize (e.g. Christ's headship as opposed to Christ's friendship, the Pauline corpus as opposed to the gospels or other biblical texts, service as opposed to solidarity, etc.). The plurality of Christian spiritualities across contexts, denominations, religious orders, and even individuals can spark disagreements in which important principles may be at stake, but it also reveals the rich abundance of ways that the Spirit of God touches and molds human lives.[14]

When thinking theologically about what "spirituality" means, it can be helpful to consider phenomena that this neologism was meant to translate, such as the objects of the branch of theology once called "ascetical and mystical" and of early Christian treatises and letters "on prayer" and related topics. In this sense, spirituality would include instructions about how to pray, stories of martyrs and repentant sinners, methods of reading scripture to find deeper meanings, monastic rules and spaces, practices of bodily and psychological self-discipline, communal forms of worship, ecstatic trances and visions, works of erotic poetry, edifying sermons, ecclesiastical teachings and condemnations, guidebooks for retreatants and ordinary laypeople, acts of compassion and social justice, and much more.

It is best to consider these materials, not only as they appear in a supposedly linear occidental development – which often unfortunately passes for the whole of the Christian "tradition" or "canon" – but also as they emerge differently in other contexts, including on the undersides of colonial modernity. For example, in addition to exploring the theology that might be derived from Origen's *On Prayer*, as Coakley does, I find it valuable to think with James Cone about the theological aspects of the prayers of enslaved Black Christians, which they enacted through culturally particular styles of song and dance.[15] Likewise, in addition to seeking Christological insights in medieval hagiographical works, such as Bonaventure's life of St Francis, as the Swiss theologian Balthasar does, it is beneficial to think with the Brazilian theologian Leonardo Boff and the Argentinian pontiff, Pope Francis, about the ecological and social conversions that Franciscan spirituality could inspire in our crisis-ridden, technocratic age.[16] In a similar vein, one might look to the work of Glen Scorgie, who analyzes the reception of Rhineland and Quietist mystical traditions among English-speaking evangelical Protestants and the further development of these traditions by persecuted Chinese Christians such as "Watchman" Nee Tuosheng (1903–72).[17] There are countless analogous cases of intercultural, transhistorical connection that warrant attention in this era of the church's globalization and fragmentation.

Although "spirituality" means many different things to many different people, one should not hastily conclude that it has no integrity or intelligibility as a term. The work to understand it, particularly as a mystery deeply united with authentic theology, requires not only a charitable openness to its varied manifestations but also a discerning effort to perceive the perennial human strivings and divine graces that thread them together. From the perspective of a unified spirituality-and-theology, the point is to discover the living God in our dazzlingly messy web of human vulnerabilities and activities. The goal is to know God *through* and *within* our lives, with their specific yet opaque memories, encounters, communities, and other "everyday" realities. These are the only means, this side of the *eschaton*, that permit us to know anything about that unknown fullness of love that we want to know most of all.

Named Theologian: Howard Thurman

Although the Reverend Howard Thurman (1899–1981) was a professor for many years at Boston University's School of Theology and although he was recognized, by no less an authority than James Cone, as "one of the great theologians of the twentieth century,"[18] he is perhaps better known as a spiritual writer, orator, and mentor than as a theologian per se. Yet his spirituality – in its many forms of embodied and linguistic expression – has made important contributions to theological areas such as theological anthropology, Christology, ecotheology, biblical hermeneutics, interreligious dialogue, and Christian social ethics. I can think of no better example of the promise of a unified spirituality-and-theology.

Raised in a Black Christian community in the Southern part of the United States – specifically, Daytona Beach, Florida – during a period of racial segregation, discrimination, and lynching, Thurman grew up to become a major spiritual leader of the Civil Rights movement, a pioneer in efforts to integrate the American church, and a global ambassador representing African American religious experience and the philosophy of nonviolent resistance. He was a person sensitive to the energizing presence of God in nature, in the depths of the heart, and in communal life, and his spirituality was all about embracing and surrendering to this presence. The theology implicit in his spirituality and that might be developed in accord with it is a Christian theology for the whole world; a theology forged through suffering, joy, and relationship; a theology steeped in eternal mystery and the hope of historical transformation.

Thurman's earliest spiritual experiences were nurtured by wonders of his natural environment: the ocean, thunderstorms, a beautiful oak tree, and above all the deep tranquility of the night. In his autobiography, he recalls, "Nightfall was meaningful to my childhood, for the night was more than a companion to me. It was a presence, an articulate climate. There was something about the night that seemed to cover my spirit like a gentle blanket."[19] Another early influence on his contemplative soul was his formerly enslaved grandmother, Nancy Ambrose, who told the young Thurman and other Black Sunday school children about a sermon that a slave preacher from a neighboring plantation used to preach to her community. The sermon focused on the saving mystery of Christ's passion and then concluded with the line: "You are not slaves! You are God's children!" Thurman explains, "When my grandmother got to that part of her story, there would be a slight stiffening in her spine as we sucked in our breath. When she had finished, our spirits were restored."[20] These early experiences gave Thurman a sense of inner dignity and profound ecological and communal connection. They opened his heart to an awareness of God's nearness in all things and God's revelation in the person of Jesus. They set him on a spiritual path that would develop the traditions of Black Protestant Christianity and, at the same time, expand in ecumenical, interreligious, and cosmic directions.

In 1935, Thurman and his wife Sue Bailey visited India on a pilgrimage of friendship sponsored by the World Student Christian Federation. Many Muslim and Hindu people of color he encountered on this journey questioned his allegiance to Christianity, because they viewed it as a racist and colonialist religion. He was at pains to distinguish the violent Christianity of White slaveholders and British imperialists from the true religion of Jesus. Earlier that year, he had given a lecture addressing this topic called "Good News for the Disinherited." He would later expand this lecture into a book titled *Jesus and the Disinherited* (1949), which Martin Luther King, Jr. is said to have carried in his briefcase. In this book, Thurman emphasizes that Jesus was Jewish, poor, and marginalized and that he preached a Spirit-led movement of resistance against the corrupt values of the Roman empire. Thurman suggests that only those actively engaged in movements against racial oppression, imperial domination, and similar evils really know the true meaning of Jesus. Ultimately, Thurman's dialogues with persons who were suspicious of Christianity because of its historical track record did not weaken his Christian faith. They sharpened it. They helped him get clearer about the central message of any Christian theology or spirituality worthy of the name: Jesus did not reveal love in a generic or sentimental sense, which might be permissive of injustice – rather, he revealed that particular sort of love that overcomes violent forces of social separation and forms inclusive, inwardly free communities.[21]

As much as Thurman's trip to India refined his understanding of his Christian faith, it also allowed him to discover resonances with other spiritual traditions. In conversation with a learned Hindu man named Dr Singh, who was a professor at the university in Shantiniketan, Thurman had two contrasting experiences. In their first tête-à-tête, Singh and Thurman were defensive, each guarding his own religious perspective and seeking to prove its merits. At the end of the morning meeting, both felt dissatisfied and agreed to resume their exchange in the afternoon with a more open disposition. Thurman reports, "That afternoon I had the most primary, naked fusing of total religious experience with another human being of which I have ever been capable. It was as if we had stepped out of social, political, cultural frames of reference, and allowed two human spirits to unite on a ground of reality unmarked by separateness and differences."[22] On his trip to India, Thurman embodied both a particular, Christian sense of "spirituality" and a more universal, transcendental sense.

This balance was also evident in Thurman's meeting with Mahatma Gandhi, which was a beautiful experience of mutual sharing and understanding. Thurman welcomed Gandhi's decision to embrace the "untouchables" of the Hindu caste system and to call them by a new name, "'Harijan,' a word that means 'Child of God.'" Gandhi's humanizing instincts in this instance were the same as the slave preacher's in the story told by Thurman's grandmother. At the end of their time together, Gandhi asked Thurman and his party to sing a spiritual, "Were You There When They Crucified My Lord," explaining, "I feel that this song gets to the root of the experience of the entire human race under the spread of the healing wings of suffering." As the words of this hymn composed by Black Christian slaves washed over Gandhi and his companions, they bowed their heads in prayer.[23] A dozen years later, Thurman reflected on the universal significance of the slave spirituals in his classic lecture, delivered at Harvard Divinity School, called "The Negro Speaks of Life and Death" (1947).[24]

A voyage to Nigeria in 1963 gave Thurman an opportunity to find connection with traditional African spiritual practices and the ways they have been integrated into African Christian worship, especially through sacred drums and dance. Although these experiences were uplifting for him, they were also tinged with the pain of loss and separation. The haunting memory of the Middle Passage prompted Thurman to write some of the most poignant words he ever set to paper. While approaching the West African coast by ship, he penned these lines to his ancestors: "Oh my fathers, what was it like to be stripped of all supports of life save the beating of the heart and the ebb and flow of fetid air in the lungs? In a strange moment when you suddenly caught your breath, did some intimation from the future give to your spirit a wink of promise? In the darkness, did you hear the silent feet of your children beating a melody of freedom to words which you would never know?"[25]

Thurman's questioning meditation about whether there might have been an impossible glimmer of hope for those in the belly of the slave ship, an inkling of the distant freedom of their descendants, does not diminish his sense of the crushing absurdity and horror of their situation but rather accentuates it all the more. His unmistakable point is that these are *human beings*, with dreams and interiorities – not mere chattel. He carries the memory of their battered souls in his body, as an inescapable weight. He is one with them and wants to give some portion of the freedom he now enjoys – and still fights for in the early 1960s – to these annihilated ancestors who could never have conceived it. This is his prayer to and for the dead. Just as his spirituality retains its Christian particularity even as he ventures into spaces of interreligious encounter, so too his spirituality remains marked by the particularities of Black diasporic existence even as he strives for racial integration and universal understanding.[26]

Thurman's spiritual struggle for common ground was on full display in his leadership of the unprecedented interracial and interdenominational Church for the Fellowship of All Peoples in San Francisco, California from its founding in 1944 until his departure for Boston University in 1953. Thurman and other leaders of this church planned liturgies, study groups, periods of quiet meditation, and other spiritual activities meant to foster a sense of oneness with others and with God. In all these practices, Thurman's goal was to find "the *moment* when God appeared in the head, heart, and soul of the worshipper. This was the moment above all moments, intimate, personal, private, yet shared, miraculously, with the whole human family in celebration."[27] In addition to Black and White Christians of various backgrounds, he reached out to Japanese people who had been violently displaced, incarcerated, and persecuted as part of the American war effort; the large population of Filipino laborers in the city; members of the Jewish community; and activists seeking radical social change. He invited all to find renewed strength and fellowship in the presence of God.

Early in his career, Thurman had considered pursuing a PhD in theology, but he feared that "if I were to devote full time to the requirements of a doctoral program, academic strictures would gradually usurp the energy I wanted so desperately to nourish the inner regions of my spirit."[28] Despite this trepidation, he was a lover of knowledge. After completing collegiate and postcollegiate degrees at Morehouse College and Rochester Theological Seminary, with a brief stint at Columbia University, he still wanted to deepen his understanding of the Christian mystical tradition and to satisfy the needs of both his head and heart. In lieu of a doctorate, he arranged to do an independent course of study with the Quaker scholar and mystic Rufus Jones, then a professor at Haverford College, with whom he explored the writings of great Christian contemplatives such as Meister Eckhart, Francis of Assisi, and Madame Guyon.

These sources helped Thurman hone his early intuition that the human soul could find its true standing and purpose only through a complete surrender to God. Although his spirituality was communal and social in character, it was grounded in an inner commitment and detachment meant to free one to be a Christlike beacon of love for others. Without such divinely liberated interiority, he surmised, one would lack the strength needed not merely to act nonviolently but also to sustain nonviolent thoughts and feelings about one's fellow human beings and to experience one's fundamental oneness with them.[29]

Thurman was convinced that human beings are united with God and one another – and, indeed, with the whole created world – at a very deep, interior, and essential level that all patterns of entrenched hostility and division grievously violate. Although he started to grasp this idea at a young age, he cultivated it throughout his life and let it grow into a rich forest of words, rhythms, and experiences. It is a theological insight drawn from his readings of scripture and tradition and his reflection on their meaning in diverse contexts, just as much as it is a spiritual principle shaping his practices of prayer, preaching, and social action. It is a vision of unity that not only preserves the unbreakable bond between theology and spirituality but also pulls down barriers between human communities, even while acknowledging their religious and cultural particularities. Thurman's perspective flows from the life and teachings of Jesus, while simultaneously – and on this very basis – critiquing Christianity's historical involvement in sinful structures of slavery, segregation, and oppression. More than forty years after his death, his witness remains a guiding light to scholars of spirituality and theology, to Christians throughout the world, and to all people of good will.

Debate: Questions of Gender

Gender remains a controversial topic in theology, as it does in culture writ large. The academic conversation about spirituality and theology engages this area of debate in a variety of ways, some more auspicious than others. On the positive side, appreciating the unity of spirituality and theology has enabled Elizabeth Dreyer, Wendy Farley, and other theologians to retrieve theological contributions from women writers, martyrs, saints, and mystics who were denied formal (i.e. university-based) theological education and who have been remembered mainly as figures of spirituality.[30] Grace Jantzen, Barbara Newman, and other scholars studying gendered aspects of the Christian tradition argue that spirituality has been a way for women to gain authority in patriarchal contexts. They also note that it has been a domain of imaginative gender fluidity: e.g. the early Christian martyr Perpetua receives a vision of herself transformed into a male gladiator, and the Spanish Carmelite poet John of the Cross depicts himself as a bride pining after her divine Bridegroom. Amy Hollywood contends, further, that the spiritual detachment one finds in the texts of Marguerite Porete and Meister Eckhart may have more liberative potential even than images of gender fluidity, insofar as it permits detachment from oppressive gender norms.[31] In these ways, recent discussions surrounding spirituality and theology have begun to reveal spiritual bases and implications of feminist, queer, and other critical gender theories.

Along similar lines, Coakley argues that a Spirit-led form of prayer could be the key to overcoming the root causes of patriarchy, phallocentrism, and sexual violence. She notes that such a pneumatologically guided contemplative practice has the potential to free the creature from sinful conditions of masculine dominance and feminine submission and to usher in a third possibility of mysterious gender plasticity, which may – if Gregory of Nyssa is right – even take one beyond gender altogether. Perhaps more important, Coakley maintains that this sort of spiritual practice has the power to chasten, reorient, and transform corrupted human desires, such that they align with the loving will of God. She contends that gender oppression is fundamentally caused by a misaligned desire for mastery over others. To resist this oppression, it is necessary to seek a spiritual therapy for our erotic selves by letting the Spirit guide us into union with the divine *Eros* that is revealed in Christ.[32] Some sort of divinely intended gender liberation may, therefore, be one of the great benefits of a reunified practice of spirituality-and-theology.

However, some theologians and church leaders continue to advance male-dominant, heteronormative, and rigidly binary accounts of the gendered aspects of spirituality, even while drawing on spiritual sources that feature women or experiment with gender fluid imagery. In the Catholic context, Balthasar remains an influential and highly contested example, as feminist theological critics such as Tina Beattie show.[33] On the one hand, his support for a great chorus of women's voices, including his friend Adrienne von Speyr's, and his willingness to welcome the bridal soul's love for God as a spiritual disposition that all Christians are called to embody suggest that there is an admirable inclusiveness and complexity in his thought. On the other hand, none of this alters his commitments to a male-only priesthood and his problematic definition of "woman" as essentially secondary and receptive.[34]

The freedom from gender oppression that spirituality seems to promise, according to Dreyer, Farley, Jantzen, Newman, Hollywood, Coakley, et al. is thus far from secure in all theological projects that make a point of reconnecting with spirituality. These tensions suggest a need, not merely to "respiritualize" theology, but also to think more critically about how it is constructed in relation to gender and other fraught determinants of our bodily, psychological, and social comportment. The achievements of the aforementioned critically gender-conscious theologians and scholars indicate that one has to be intentional about pursuing such lines of interrogation. This sort of intentionality does not imply that questions about fixities and variabilities in the meanings of bodies, desires, and intimacies come exclusively from a secular "outside." On the contrary, these questions emerge to a large extent from the spiritual-and-theological sources themselves.

The debate about gender's relation to spirituality and theology is made more complex by the fact that theories and practices of gender vary across cultural contexts. What seems life giving in one place or time may be perceived as harmful in another. There are also disagreements within local cultural groups about how to interpret the gendered aspects of spiritual traditions that they cherish. For example, the ethnographic work of Maria Del Socorro Castañeda-Liles demonstrates that some Mexican American women favor traditional depictions of Our Lady of Guadalupe as a chaste, maternal figure, whereas others welcome artistic reimaginings that portray her in more erotic and subversive ways.[35] To some degree, these variations depend on generational differences, with older interviewees tending to prefer more conservative representations of this miraculous, darkly hued Marian apparition. But these variations also have to do with personal stories, experiences, and inclinations about which it is difficult to generalize. Each participant in Castañeda-Liles's study expressed a unique spiritual perspective shaped by her own life narrative.

Gender cannot be considered in a vacuum. It intersects with and is structured by other social factors such as race and class. This is a point emphasized by womanist theologians in the African American community, including those such as Emilie Townes and Diana Hayes who have written groundbreaking works on womanist spirituality. Townes and Hayes draw on the spiritual narratives of nineteenth-century Black women evangelists such as Jarena Lee; twentieth-century Black women novelists such as Alice Walker; and everyday Black women who strive to flourish in their homes, societies, and churches. Interweaving these sources, they describe womanist spirituality as an embodied and divinely empowered practice of resistance against intersecting gender, racial, and class oppressions. Townes suggests that it is a way for Black women to experience the presence of God in their very "is-ness" – that is, in their breathing, their flesh, and their whole relational existence. Hayes adds that it is a way for Black women to experience the twists and turns of life as a "deep river" flowing from and returning to God.[36] The womanist tradition achieves a powerful integration of spirituality and theology, which responds to questions of gender by contesting any forms of theological or cultural production that deny the workings of the Spirit in Black women's incarnate lives.

A unified spirituality-and-theology cannot afford to ignore the debate about gender, as if it were a mere worldly concern unrelated to sacred and godly pursuits. Nor can it afford to accept uncritically whatever prejudices or judgments have been handed down in this or that cultural context or tradition. As ever, it is necessary to discern the movements of the Holy Spirit in history, as it blesses and sanctifies those embodied loves and practices that build up inwardly free selves and knit together diverse and inclusive communities. If we call upon it – "Come, Holy Spirit" – the hypostatic breath of God will draw us into an intimate relationship with the gender-nonconforming Jesus, making us members of his motley band of gender-diverse followers, and it will lift us up into the unoriginated God beyond gender and beyond every name, who creates our mysterious body-souls in the image of its invisible nature. Praying in this Spirit may indeed make everything new – including, among other things, the practice of theology.

Influence, Achievement, and Agenda: Seeking the Living God

At the start of this chapter, I outlined the standard story about the relationship between spirituality and theology – namely, the story of an original union, a modern separation, and an emerging reunification. Although this story is persuasive and helpful in many respects, particularly with its emphasis on wholeness, I suggested that it overstates the degree to which a separation was ever possible in principle and has happened in fact, that it disregards the value of pragmatic distinctions between spirituality and theology in particular contexts, and that it is compromised by Eurocentrism. In the next section, I sketched a brief history of the usage of the term "spirituality" (drawing largely on Principe's account) and discussed the challenges and opportunities presented by its multiplicity of meanings. In particular, I encouraged efforts to find connections between spiritual materials from the Western "canon" and sources from the undersides of colonial modernity.

I then turned to Thurman to illustrate the benefits that come, not merely from a unified spirituality-and-theology, but from one rich with biblical, historical, intercultural, interreligious, ecological, sociopolitical, and introspective significance. My point was not to insist that others follow Thurman's lead on every precise point, though it would be hard to go wrong if one did. Rather, my aim was to highlight the sorts of *integration*, in many senses, that are possible if we but seek them: head and heart, particular and universal, psychological and social, humanity and nature, peace and struggle, voice and silence, the truly Christian and the globally religious, the memory of the ancestors and the hope for the future. Finally, in the section preceding this one, I summarized a debate surrounding gender that has developed in recent scholarly literature on spirituality and theology. Although I only skimmed the surface of these complex conversations, especially as they vary across contexts, I at least provided some prima facie reasons to believe that a unified spirituality-and-theology may be a key ingredient to liberative transformations in this area.

I hope that the path ahead for spirituality and theology will continue to strengthen their essential unity (which I have indicated with the hyphenated form "spirituality-and-theology"). Above all, I hope that those engaged in such efforts will concentrate on the most vital thing – that is, the gracious presence of the living God in the fragile contexts of our world. Although I used the word "path," I do not imagine a single line of progress that all must follow. Rather, I am picturing a luminous cloud of dynamic trajectories. I anticipate the interactive movements of communities and persons striving to live in the Spirit and to clarify what this inspirited existence means through embodied words and actions, whether in the classroom, the pulpit, the picket line, the library archive, the found place of quiet, or the forested wilderness.

Notes

1 Hans Urs von Balthasar, "Theology and Sanctity," in *Explorations in Theology*, Vol. 1, *The Word Made Flesh*, trans. A. V. Littledale and Alexander Dru (San Francisco, CA: Ignatius Press, 1989), 181–209; Gustavo Gutiérrez, *A Theology of Liberation: History, Politics, and Salvation*, 15th anniversary edn, trans. Caridad Inda and John Eagleson (Maryknoll, NY: Orbis, 1988), 3–12 and 106–20; Mark A. McIntosh, *Mystical Theology: The Integrity of Spirituality and Theology* (Malden, MA: Blackwell, 1998); Sarah Coakley, *God, Sexuality, and the Self: An Essay "On the Trinity"* (Cambridge: Cambridge University Press, 2013); and Philip F. Sheldrake, *Explorations in Spirituality: History, Theology, and Social Practice* (Mahwah, NJ: Paulist Press, 2010), 54–74.

2 G. W. F. Hegel, *Introduction to the Philosophy of History*, trans. Leo Rauch (Indianapolis, IN: Hackett, 1988); Michel Foucault, *The Order of Things: An Archaeology of the Human Sciences* (New York: Vintage Books, 1994); Luce Irigaray, *Speculum of the Other Woman*, trans. Gillian C. Gill (Ithaca, NY: Cornell University Press, 1985); Charles Taylor, *A Secular Age* (Cambridge, MA: Harvard University Press, 2007); and Walter D. Mignolo, *The Darker Side of Colonial Modernity: Global Futures, Decolonial Options* (Durham, NC: Duke University Press, 2011).

3 Andrew Prevot, *Thinking Prayer: Theology and Spirituality amid the Crises of Modernity* (Notre Dame, IN: University of Notre Dame Press, 2015), 6, 18, 31.

4 In addition to appreciating the spirituality in classic scholastic sources – as Jean-Pierre Torrell, OP does in his *Christ and Spirituality in St. Thomas Aquinas*, trans.

Bernhard Blankenhorn, OP (Washington, DC: Catholic University of America Press, 2011) – one might consider a noted neoscholastic such as Réginald Garrigou-Lagrange who authored spirituality-related works such as *Christian Perfection and Contemplation according to Thomas Aquinas and John of the Cross* (St. Louis, MO: B. Herder, 1937).

5 Scholars have discovered theology in medieval women's visionary texts often categorized as spirituality – e.g. Denys Turner, *Julian of Norwich: Theologian* (New Haven, CT: Yale University Press, 2011). A similar discovery is possible in modern spiritual sources, such as the memoir of the Black woman preacher Zilpha Elaw, which appears in William L. Andrews, ed., *Sisters of the Spirit: Three Black Women's Autobiographies of the Nineteenth Century* (Bloomington, IN: Indiana University Press, 1986), 49–160. Elaw's narrative develops a rich Pauline and Wesleyan theology.

6 Mary Frohlich, RSCJ, "Spiritual Discipline, Discipline of Spirituality: Revisiting Questions of Definition and Method," in *Minding the Spirit: The Study of Christian Spirituality*, ed. Elizabeth A. Dreyer and Mark S. Burrows (Baltimore, MD: Johns Hopkins University Press, 2005), 65–78 and Jean-Yves Lacoste, *From Theology to Theological Thinking*, trans. W. Chris Hackett (Charlottesville, VA: University of Virginia Press, 2014), 24–9.

7 Susan Abraham, "Purifying Memory and Dispossessing the Self: Spiritual Strategies in the Postcolonial Classroom," *Spiritus: A Journal of Christian Spirituality* 13, no. 1 (2013): 56–75.

8 Walter Principe, "Toward Defining Spirituality," *Studies in Religion/Sciences Religieuses* 12, no. 2 (1983): 130–2.

9 Principe, "Toward Defining Spirituality," 133–4.

10 Principe, "Toward Defining Spirituality," 136.

11 Sandra M. Schneiders, "Religion vs. Spirituality: A Contemporary Conundrum," *Spiritus: A Journal of Christian Spirituality* 3, no. 2 (2003): 166.

12 Linda A. Mercadante, *Belief without Borders: Inside the Minds of the Spiritual but Not Religious* (New York: Oxford University Press, 2014).

13 Principe, "Toward Defining Spirituality," 135.

14 There are also academic disagreements about how to name the discipline that investigates such things, whether as "spirituality studies" or "spiritual theology." For a recent discussion of these approaches, which loosely correlate with scholarship in English and Latin-derived languages, respectively, see Diana L. Villegas, "Evolving Methodologies Conference: Reflections on Christian Spirituality Studies vs. Spiritual Theology," *Spiritus: A Journal of Christian Spirituality* 20, no. 1 (2020): 25–30.

15 Coakley, *God, Sexuality, and the Self*, 111–44 and James H. Cone, *The Spirituals and the Blues: An Interpretation* (Maryknoll, NY: Orbis, 2008). Note that although these traditions of Christian spirituality are distanced by centuries and circumstances, they are both "African," in a loose geographic and diasporic sense, from which one should not infer any essential sameness of racial identity.

16 Hans Urs von Balthasar, *The Glory of the Lord: A Theological Aesthetics*, Vol. 2, *Studies in Theological Style: Clerical Styles*, trans. Andrew Louth, Francis McDonagh, and Brian McNeil, CRV, ed. John Riches (San Francisco, CA: Ignatius, 1998), 260–362; Leonardo Boff, *Cry of the Earth, Cry of the Poor*, trans. Phillip Berryman (Maryknoll, NY: Orbis, 1997); and Pope Francis, *Laudato si'* (Vatican City: Libreria Editrice Vaticana, 2015).

17 Glen G. Scorgie, "The Diffusion of Christian Mysticism: From the Medieval Rhineland to Contemporary China," *Spiritus: A Journal of Christian Spirituality* 20, no. 1 (2020): 1–24.

18 Howard Thurman, *A Strange Freedom: The Best of Howard Thurman's Religious Experience and Public Life*, ed. Walter Earl Fluker and Catherine Tumber (Boston, MA: Beacon, 1998), 6.

19 Howard Thurman, *With Head and Heart: The Autobiography of Howard Thurman* (San Diego, CA: Harcourt Brace, 1979), 7.

20 Thurman, *With Head and Heart*, 21.

21 Howard Thurman, *Jesus and the Disinherited* (Boston, MA: Beacon, 1996) and Thurman, *With Head and Heart*, 103, 114, 218–19, 255.

22 Thurman, *With Head and Heart*, 129.

23 Thurman, *With Head and Heart*, 134.

24 Included in Thurman, *A Strange Freedom*, 55–79.

25 Thurman, *With Head and Heart*, 194.

26 Howard Thurman, *The Luminous Darkness* (Richmond, IN: Friends United, 1989), x–xi.

27 Thurman, *With Head and Heart*, 159.

28 Thurman, *With Head and Heart*, 76.

29 Howard Thurman, *Disciplines of the Spirit* (Richmond, IN: Friends United, 2003), 22, 115, and 122.

30 Elizabeth A. Dreyer, *Accidental Theologians: Four Women Who Shaped Christianity: Hildegard of Bingen, Catherine of Siena, Teresa of Avila, and Thérèse of Lisieux* (Cincinnati, OH: Franciscan, 2014) and Wendy Farley, *The Thirst of God: Contemplating God's Love with Three Women Mystics* (Louisville, KY: Westminster John Knox Press, 2015). In androcentric scholarly contexts, it is not uncommon to find spirituality associated with the feminine, insofar as it is supposedly affective and private, and theology with the masculine, insofar as it is meant to be more intellectual and publicly authoritative. The work of Dreyer, Farley, and others to name women's contributions *as* theology troubles this gendering of the spirituality-theology relationship.

31 Grace Jantzen, *Power, Gender, and Christian Mysticism* (New York: Cambridge University Press, 1995); Barbara Newman, "Gender," in *The Wiley-Blackwell Companion to Christian Mysticism*, ed. Julia A. Lamm (Malden, MA: Blackwell, 2013), 41–55; and Amy Hollywood, *The Soul as Virgin Wife: Mechthild of Magdeburg, Marguerite Porete, and Meister Eckhart* (Notre Dame, IN: University of Notre Dame Press, 1995), 173–206.

32 Coakley, *God, Sexuality, and the Self*, 13–15, 55–9, and 308–20.

33 Tina Beattie, *New Catholic Feminism: Theology and Theory* (New York: Routledge, 2006).

34 Hans Urs von Balthasar, *The Glory of the Lord: A Theological Aesthetics*, Vol. 5, *The Realm of Metaphysics in the Modern Age*, trans. Oliver Davies et al. (San Francisco, CA: Ignatius, 1991), 48–140; Hans Urs von Balthasar, *New Elucidations*, trans. Mary Thersilde Skerry (San Francisco: Ignatius, 1986), 187–198; and Adrienne von Speyr, *Handmaid of the Lord*, trans. E. A. Nelson (San Francisco, CA: Ignatius, 1985).

35 María Del Socorro Castañeda-Liles, *Our Lady of Everyday Life: La Virgen de Guadalupe and the Catholic Imagination of Mexican Women in America* (New York: Oxford University Press, 2018), 192–205.

36 Emilie M. Townes, *In a Blaze of Glory: Womanist Spirituality as Social Witness* (Nashville, TN: Abingdon, 1995), 48, and Diana L. Hayes, *No Crystal Stair: Womanist Spirituality* (Maryknoll, NY: Orbis, 2016), 31.

Recommended Reading

Primary

Balthasar, Hans Urs von. "Theology and Sanctity." In *Explorations in Theology, Vol. 1: The Word Made Flesh*, 181–209. Translated by A. V. Littledale and Alexander Dru. San Francisco, CA: Ignatius, 1989.

Coakley, Sarah. *God, Sexuality, and the Self: An Essay "On the Trinity."* Cambridge: Cambridge University Press, 2013.

Principe, Walter. "Toward Defining Spirituality." *Studies in Religion/Sciences Religieuses* 12, no. 2 (1983): 127–41.

Sheldrake, Philip F. *Explorations in Spirituality: History, Theology, and Social Practice*. Mahwah, NJ: Paulist Press, 2010.

Thurman, Howard. *A Strange Freedom: The Best of Howard Thurman's Religious Experience and Public Life*. Edited by Walter Earl Fluker and Catherine Tumber. Boston, MA: Beacon, 1998.

Townes, Emilie M. *In a Blaze of Glory: Womanist Spirituality as Social Witness*. Nashville, TN: Abingdon, 1995.

Secondary

Ashley, J. Matthew. *Renewing Theology: Ignatian Spirituality and Karl Rahner, Ignacio Ellacuría, and Pope Francis*. Notre Dame, IN: University of Notre Dame Press, 2022.

Cocksworth, Ashley. *Prayer: A Guide for the Perplexed*. London: Bloomsbury T&T Clark, 2018.

Dreyer, Elizabeth A., and Mark S. Burrows, eds. *Minding the Spirit: The Study of Christian Spirituality*. Baltimore, MD: Johns Hopkins University Press, 2005.

Lamm, Julia A., ed. *The Wiley-Blackwell Companion to Christian Mysticism*. Malden, MA: Blackwell, 2013.

Prevot, Andrew. *Thinking Prayer: Theology and Spirituality amid the Crises of Modernity*. Notre Dame, IN: University of Notre Dame Press, 2015.

Robinson, Timothy. "He Talked to Trees! 'Thinking Differently' about Nature with Howard Thurman." *Spiritus: A Journal of Christian Spirituality* 21, no. 1 (2021): 1–19.

Liturgical Theology

Stephen Burns

Introduction

This fourth edition of *The Modern Theologians* is the first to have a chapter on liturgical theology. That might suggest the "youth" of the discipline, now joining with the likes of pastoral and practical theology which was included for the first time in the third edition (2005).[1] Whereas other forms of liturgical study, particularly historiography – the study of liturgical texts – have an older pedigree, liturgical theology, which is emphatically not to be correlated with historiography, is very much a twentieth-century development. It has a firm footing in some mainland European and North American universities but less so in the case of Britain, the primary context from which this book emerged.

That being said, earlier exclusion of liturgical theology might also have to do with perspective, given that previous editions of *The Modern Theologians* recognized some theological approaches as "particularizing" whereas others (notably all by European males in more or less "systematic" mode) were deemed "classics" – Barth, Rahner, Tillich, and company.[2] Because liturgical theology brings a strong outlook on what kind of theology is "primary" it presents some questions to the category of "classic." Even as certain kinds of systematics accent a doxological mode – including the work of the editor of the first three editions of this book, David F. Ford – liturgical theology occupies a somewhat different space, focused in one way or another on liturgical celebration.[3] To use a minimal description offered by the Russian Orthodox Alexander Schmemann (1921–83), it is concerned with "the elucidation of the theological meaning of worship." As Schmemann elaborates, its "special subject" is "the liturgical tradition of the church."[4] However, because styles and forms of liturgical celebration are different across (and within) ecclesial traditions and diverse settings, *how* liturgical theology engages celebration is not agreed. Bluntly put, some liturgical theology has tended to use the definite article (as in "the liturgy," "the liturgical tradition") whereas others are cautious of this. The difference points to a very important line of tension within the discipline.

Ford's The Modern Theologians: An Introduction to Christian Theology since 1918, Fourth Edition.
Edited by Rachel Muers and Ashley Cocksworth.
© 2024 John Wiley & Sons Ltd. Published 2024 by John Wiley & Sons Ltd.

Survey

A survey of the landscape of liturgical theology requires attention to both the liturgical movement and the ecumenical movement (which have sometimes come to be conflated as "the ecumenical liturgical movement").[5] The former is commonly traced back to 1909 and a certain speech at a Catholic Works Conference in Mechelen, Belgium. The speech, by the Roman Catholic monk Lambert Beauduin (1873–1960), referred to liturgy as "the true prayer of the church," taking a term that Pope Pius X had in 1903 applied to Gregorian chant – "active participation" – and relating it to a wide range of liturgical actions. Beauduin's subsequent book *The Piety of the Church* (1914) is still sometimes considered a "manifesto" for liturgical theology.[6] At any rate, Beauduin's key term, "active participation," has for more than a century held as the main concern of the liturgical movement.

The Catholic Works Conference of 1909 was close in time with another strand important for liturgical theology, the Edinburgh Missionary Conference in 1910. That conference is widely regarded as the start of the ecumenical movement. It stirred energies toward the formation of the World Council of Churches (WCC) in 1948, and various forums on worship in Edinburgh's wake provided important loci for reflection on liturgy by a broad range of churches. Initially, numerous Protestant traditions were present, and latterly so too have been Orthodox. They have long involved Catholic "observers."

Less commonly noted is a third movement more or less coterminous with the "birth" of the liturgical and ecumenical movements, and that is the Pentecostal. Its "birth" is oftentimes identified with the revival at Azuza Street, Los Angeles, California, in association with the ministry of William J. Seymour (1870–1922). But other stirrings can also be found, such as a "charismatic" strand within the established Church of England at the same time, around St Gabriel's, Sunderland, where Alexander Boddy (1854–1930) was priest. If, as has been suggested, the liturgical movement needs to be seen "against the background of an incipient dechristianization of the European homelands and a simultaneous spread of overseas missions," it might be that the future of the liturgical movement will involve engagement with Pentecostal impulses to an extent as yet unseen.[7] But this is by no means the only agenda it needs to pursue.

Within Roman Catholic contexts, numerous monastic figures contributed alongside Beauduin to shaping the emerging way of thinking. Among the most significant is Odo Casel (1886–1948), a German who popularized the term "paschal mystery" as well wording the dynamic of participation in divine presence that liturgical celebration invites. Although the term paschal mystery has not always carried over into Protestant liturgical theology, the main lines of Casel's insights have, and across the ecclesial spectrum reception of Casel's ideas has helped to keep open dialogue with theology of sacraments in the "systematic agenda."[8]

The years between World War I and World War II saw the establishment of centers concerned with liturgical renewal (e.g. German Liturgical Institute, Trier from 1947; L'Institut Supérior de Liturgie, Paris from 1956) and saw the beginnings of new journals to support it. Very important was the transportation of the movement to North America, via Virgil Michel (1890–1938), a monk of St John's Abbey, Collegeville, Minnesota, home of the journal *Worship* (prior to 1951 called *Orate Fratres*).

In Britain, the growth of Parish and People movement – associated with Anglican A. G. Herbert (1886–1963) – made for settings in which at least some of the ideas coming forward on the continent could be explored.[9] Anglicans were also among those involved in Faith and Order conferences that followed on from beginnings in Edinburgh and that provided opportunity for Protestant convergence. Perhaps the most significant was one in Lund, Sweden in 1952 with its document, "Ways of Worship." This evoked widespread affirmation of the centrality of word and sacrament and "a new realisation of a needed integration" between them.[10] Also of major significance, church union in India in 1947 embodied ecumenism and suggested some liturgy to express it (for eucharist in 1954) – the Church of South India uniting those of Anglican, Methodist, Presbyterian, and Congregationalist background.[11] Notably, in 1963 the Montreal, Canada, Faith and Order Conference for the first time consciously looked beyond North Atlantic regions with attention to East Asia. It also spoke of "*Tradition* (with a capital T), *tradition* (with a small t), and *traditions*" – a triplet that complicates Schmemann's sense of liturgical theology's special subject, and a portal into what would come to be called "indigenization."[12]

Also in 1963 came the first document of the Second Vatican Council (1962–5) – on liturgy. *Sacrosanctum concilium* (SC) boldly harnessed ideas that had been encouraged by the liturgical movement. Although the council revolutionized worship in the Roman Catholic Church, it has also strikingly been identified as "the most radical thing to affect the Protestant traditions in the twentieth century."[13] The *peritus* of the reforms that followed was the Italian Annibale Bugnini (1912–82) and Bugnini's own sense of the council's liturgical priorities provide a distillation of SC's key ideas.

The first is that liturgy is "an exercise of the priestly office of Jesus Christ." So SC #7: "Christ is always present in His Church, especially in her liturgical celebrations." Second, liturgy is a "making present" of paschal mystery. So SC #5–7: "by baptism men are plunged into the paschal mystery of Christ .... as often as they eat the supper of the Lord they proclaim the death of the Lord until He comes" (#6). Third, liturgy is "source and summit" of the church's life. So SC #10: "the liturgy is the summit toward which the activity of the Church is directed; at the same time it is the font from which all her power flows." Indeed, liturgy "manifests" the church (SC #26). Then, focus on what so concerned Beauduin: "full and active participation by all the people" (SC #14); in Bugnini's own evocative words, "a people God has made his own to praise his wonders." Finally, "substantial unity" (SC #38) but not "rigid uniformity" (SC #37), just as "sound tradition" (SC #23) allows for "legitimate progress" (SC #23).[14]

Each of these highlights from SC shapes subsequent liturgical theology, albeit while sometimes being fiercely contested according to different determinations of what SC called liturgy's "immutable elements divinely instituted, and ... elements subject to change" (SC #21). Indigenization (the word is not used but the idea is the burden of SC #36–40) has been a particular flashpoint. Within later Roman Catholic scholarship, the prolific work of Filipino Anscar J. Chupungco (1939–2013) is highly engaged with such matters.[15]

In its own turn, the WCC's *Baptism, Eucharist, and Ministry* (BEM, 1982), much influenced by British Methodist Geoffrey Wainwright (1939–2020), both invited and contributed to further impact of insights of the liturgical movement on Protestantism. Important too has been that over time the Common Lectionary (1983, so shortly after BEM) and the Revised Common Lectionary (RCL, 1992) – based on the Roman Catholic Lectionary for Mass (1970) – have come to attract widespread assent. Hence lectionary has become a substantial ecumenical symbol in celebration.

Taken together, the result of such developments has been that Catholic worship has been "protestantized" as it has reemphasized scripture – liturgical celebration at "the table of God's word" (SC #51) – while many Protestant traditions have been "catholicized" by increased frequency and convergence in style of eucharistic celebration. A measure of the convergence that was incrementally proposed and has piecemeal been attained can be made by contrasting BEM's somewhat disparate list of aspects of celebration (long, prefaced with "the following elements in varying sequence and of diverse importance ..." Eucharist #27) and a 1995 initiative in which US Lutheran Gordon W. Lathrop (b. 1939) was a leading light, the "Fundamental Pattern (Ordo) of the Eucharistic Service." It spoke of "gathering"; then a "Word Service" of reading both Testaments, proclaiming Christ, and interceding for the needy; then a "Table Service" consisting of "giving thanks" over and "eating and drinking" bread and cup; then finally dismissal in mission in the world.[16]

So, on the one hand, from late last millennium the revision of many ritual books has reflected this "fundamental pattern." Moreover, those who embrace it have been likely also to hold very similar patterns of scripture reading. And yet, there are numerous signs of fraying. A weighty case in point is the Roman Catholic Church's 2010 "new translation" of texts for prayer – based on the 2001 *Liturgiam Authenticam*, on "right implementation" of aspects of SC. This has meant that sharing of common texts, which had also sometimes appeared, is now going backwards. Unsurprisingly, then, the twenty-first century has seen increasing fragmentation in liturgical theology. This has been so even as proponents have in their own ways remained keenly concerned with the "meaning" of active participation in paschal mystery. Differences are most intense about unity and uniformity, tradition and progress.

Agenda

The very question "what is liturgical theology?" has foregrounded some shared resources for exploration without leading to uncontested answers. One such resource is an ancient adage of Prosper of Aquitaine (390–455), *legem credendi lex statuat supplicandi*. Prosper's phrase has been variously interpreted as situating matters of belief in relation to practices of praying. A distinction particularly associated with Aidan Kavanagh (1929–2006), a US Roman Catholic, has been widely followed. Kavanagh's *On Liturgical Theology* (1984) puts space between "primary theology" and "secondary theology." By the former term, he means liturgy in practice, the celebration itself, and so writes of liturgy as "theology being born, theology in the first instance."[17] Subsequently, articulations of the "meaning" of the celebration are "secondary theology." It should further be noted that, by extension, secondary theology includes all other theology as well. Neither sacramental theology nor the work of those whom *The Modern Theologians* once deemed "classic" are primary.

After Kavanagh, many others have highlighted the "law of prayer" (*lex orandi*), proposing that worship yields "meaning" from which doctrine flowers. Yet it is clearly the case that liturgical theologians make different things of this shared conviction, not least depending upon if their traditions incline toward ready use of the definite article. Broadly speaking, those who tilt toward talk of "the liturgy" may assume more than others whose liturgical celebration, while perhaps enjoying a common lectionary and reflecting the ordo, is still marked by "ordered liberty."[18] Yet challenging interaction between prayer and belief becomes crucial in reform in whatever tradition reform might be mooted.[19] Gordon Lathrop's turning of Kavanagh's terms helps some here, for he distinguishes "primary," "secondary," and a third, "pastoral liturgical" theology. He means by the former "the communal meaning of the liturgy expressed by the gathering itself" whereas secondary theology "speaks of God as it speaks about the ways the assembly speaks of God" – though it always has "something of a critical, reforming edge." Lathrop's third term concerns reform "turned towards specific problems of our time."[20]

Questions abound about how to conceive and study "participation," the leading notion. Attention to the *actions* of celebration is one key, as the verbs in the WCC's distillation of the ordo: gathering, reading, and the rest. Focus falls not so much on texts that may or may not be in use but on the "full and active participation" of the assembly, the bodies in the room, those celebrating. This has led to various assertions about the assembly as "the primary symbol,"[21] "the primary thing,"[22] "the basic document."[23] But this emphasis sits alongside sensitivity to paschal mystery manifest in the event for which the assembly gathers. This has led to further work on different "levels" of participation. The British-born, US-based, Roman Catholic Mark Searle (1941–92) proposes a schema that moves from surface to depths. Near the surface is "participation in ritual behaviour." Deeper than that is appreciation of "participation in the liturgy of the church as the work of Christ." When one is plunged further again, Seale holds that one may participate "in the life of God" as God graciously enables people's sharing in paschal mystery.[24] Similarly, US Methodist Don Saliers (b. 1937) distinguishes participation "in the phenomena" – singing, reading, praying, "doing the rite" – from participation in the rite "as church": that is, participating "as a solidarity, as belonging to one another." Beyond both, at greater intensity again, Saliers suggests may be "participation in the very divine life itself," sharing "in the mystery of God."[25] In Searle and Saliers, we find pathways into assertions in SC #5–7.

Such insights in turn invite questions of method. Although no single approach reigns, Gordon Lathrop's is arresting. He develops the idea that liturgy learns its method from the Bible.[26] Just as lectionaries involve "at least two words," one portion next to another, so liturgical theology concentrates on "juxtapositions," to use his keyword. In liturgy, juxtapositions extend far beyond the different readings that form part of celebration; there is also that of thanksgiving and lament, reading and preaching, silence and song. And there are many more, which crucially include the "central things" of word next to table, teaching next to water-bath. So in Lathrop's suggestion, liturgical theology always keeps different foci in view, "side by side" – as he memorably puts it, "like two candles near the altar or the two cherubim on the ark of the covenant."[27] It is through exploring juxtapositions that meaning unfolds, attending to how people may participate in liturgy's "pairs."

Lathrop also makes vivid connections with what SC calls paschal mystery. He elaborates how "the patterns of the liturgy root in Jesus Christ,"[28] Christ who read the scriptures, ate with sinners, and whose death and resurrection are the fountainhead of baptism.[29] Lathrop stresses how Christ always "points to a tension-laden duality"[30] and is an "upending of any talk about deity or holiness, an upending that comes to expression in language about the 'Trinity': God, indeed, but God in a way we had not expected."[31] And also, Christ's name "carries along also all those who are identified with Christ": the liturgical assembly *and* "the world's outsiders."[32] While always keenly attentive to assembly – the primary thing – Lathrop's vision is profoundly centripetal, involving the assembly being pushed ever beyond itself.[33] Consequently, some of Lathrop's most fierce writing is against what he labels "anti-liturgica" – the assembly made sick by inward turns, drumming up a "closed circle," or, as grim, oppressed by "hierarchical distortions."[34] In Lathrop's account, celebration of the presence of Christ at the heart of the liturgy protects against such inversions. Such methods of juxtaposition have met questions, as is to be expected with influences that travel so widely. One objector is Melanie Ross, invoking Free Church evangelical optics to suggest that different sensitivities need to be in play to better account for worship in traditions she represents; among them, less emphasis on structure in the search for meaning and more emphasis on "dialogue" with personal stories rather than reference to "liturgical co-efficients" within a service.[35] Another is Cláudio Carvalhaes, whose work is sketched in the next section.

Named Theologians

Gail Ramshaw (b. 1947)

Gail Ramshaw is a Lutheran theologian who taught at a Catholic university, La Salle, in Philadelphia, Pennsylvania. Her teaching post did not name liturgy – she was professor of religion – though for four decades she made liturgical theology her focus, and she is a past president of the North American Academy of Liturgy. Her studies at Valparaiso University, Indiana, University of Wisconsin, Madison and Sarah Lawrence College and Union Theological Seminary (UTS), both in New York City, included a thesis on the Triduum supervised by Alexander Schmemann. By her own account, her liturgical interests were piqued as a university student when prompted by the chaplain to prepare intercessions for worship – a preoccupation she has never put aside. At the same time, she has never been shy of revising her thinking, placing "second thoughts" next to earlier writing, so underscoring the provisionality of secondary theology.[36]

Ramshaw is remarkable as a liturgical theologian who perhaps more than any other at the present time has shaped ritual resources used in liturgical celebration. Her texts for prayer are found not only in *Evangelical Lutheran Worship* (2006) and resources of the Lutheran World Federation, but they also appear in Anglican, Methodist, Presbyterian, and United Church resources, and she has contributed to publications of the WCC.

Over time Ramshaw's writings have covered an impressive range, from textbooks apt for the "3900 students who wanted, or did not want, to take my courses,"[37] through to numerous books on the RCL, on which *Treasures Old and New* (2002) is magisterial. There is also a shelf on liturgical spirituality, including companion books on baptism, eucharist, and Easter Vigil to work on saints, with a patent affection for Catherine of Siena (1347–80) and Julian of Norwich (1343–ca. 1416).[38] Ramshaw has furnished leading constructive and reforming ideas, particularly relating to what she calls "the myth of the crown" riddling the Bible with "pyramidical assumptions" and "triumphalist tone." Ramshaw does not advocate for abandonment of the myth. Rather she thinks it needs to be "re-rendered" and so made to speak of divine mercy: "If God as the crown of the universe chose to be born in a stable, the myth of the crown has to be radically revised. The crown is now on the serving maid."[39] And, "What if the church were to proclaim the crown by boldly, in all its affairs, crowning the poor and the dispossessed?"[40]

Ramshaw's texts for prayer exemplify expansive language, multiplying metaphors – not least from the lectionary – in naming toward God. Part of her concern is undoubtedly in quest of "God beyond gender." She describes herself as a "feminist minimizer," that is, without denying differences between sexes, prioritizing sexual equality – and invoking "baptismal equality."[41] She is sure that "even feminists are in need of what Christ might mean and the Spirit gives."[42]

As her method employs expansive language, she speaks of both "Yes" and "No."[43] In other words, always two words side by side. Saying "yes," she commends "assembl[ing] on the day of the resurrection[,] to practice once again our insertion into the metaphors of grace." But sometimes saying "no," given that "some words can no longer hold trinitarian mercy very well."[44] Enlivened by deft doublets in reformations-era texts for prayer,[45] she does much of her own work in conscious complement by crafting *triplets* – vessels for that "trinitarian mercy," of which her "Triple Praise" is an outstanding example.[46] Sometimes Ramshaw's triplets of images are given their biblical footing, as in a set of Eastertide collects found in US Methodist resources: light, beauty, rest; bread, milk, honey; shepherd, lamb, gate; grove, lover, well, and more – with, for example, the first set of triplets ("O God, our light, our beauty, our rest") touching on Psalms 27:11, 27:4 and Matthew 11:29.[47]

Perhaps the key image Ramshaw has relished is the tree of life. She explores its biblical resonance and employs it to "find occasion for praise" not only for creation but also for redemption, with tree juxtaposed to the cross: "the fertile tree in the garden of God, but also the crossbeam on the pole stuck into Golgotha's hill."[48] Importantly, she also testifies to a practical outcome of "exhuming" the image: "I came to care for living trees because I first cared for the tree of life. Metaphor pulled me into matter."[49]

Teresa Berger (b. 1956)

Teresa Berger is a German Roman Catholic, who after studies in both Germany (Mainz, Heidelberg, and Münster universities) and the United Kingdom (St John's College, Nottingham) has been a long-term resident in the United States. She is professor of Catholic theology and of liturgical studies at Yale University, a role that has given her a guiding hand in a number of anthologies out of Yale's Institute of Sacred Music.[50] Her own writing has been in both German and English and is rich, with an early interest in hymnody – notably Methodist, reflecting something of her strong ecumenical interests[51] – and more recently exploring liturgy's "digital worlds," now especially significant for appearing just ahead of the Coronavirus pandemic with its lockdowns.[52] Newer work again is on creation.

Extensive though her work is, it is most marked by long engagement with gender theory. In this regard there are major publications in English, with more in German. Among the reasons they matter is Berger's scrutiny of the liturgical movement – the context for the emergence of liturgical theology – and then her pursuit of method that picks forceful arguments regarding tradition and progress.

Women's Ways of Worship (1999) is concerned with twentieth-century developments first in the liturgical movement and then what Berger dubs the "Women's Liturgical Movement" arising via second-wave feminism. She makes abundantly clear the dearth of women's voices in the former but also identifies how, nevertheless, women did contribute in some ways, against odds. Importantly, Berger's contentions upset any "simple juxtaposition" that the liturgical movement was "patriarchal" while the Women's Liturgical Movement was "liberating."[53] On the one hand, she observes that the liturgical movement "did not challenge the basic gender divisions and performances of gender in worship," yet was "midwife" for feminist liturgies from the 1960s.[54] On the other hand, she suspects women's liturgies of embedding a binary that is quite unhelpful – a reserve that fares well amidst more commonplace recognition of gender fluidity in third-wave feminism.

Berger's writings also give great insight into what Ramshaw calls "second thoughts." *Gender Differences and the Making of Liturgical History* (2011) functions as a certain kind of second thought about *Dissident Daughters* (2001). Berger's earlier book collates portraits of initiatives in women-church, experiments on the edges of denominations, sometimes among women who had separated from ecclesial traditions. There is no other study quite like it, taking in such a broad view across traditions and with such global reach – and it represents not least a commendable feat in Berger's own scholarship given that *Women's Ways of Worship* had noted that women "in the so-called Third World" deserve attention but needed "a more competent narrator" than herself.[55] Then *Dissident Daughters* ends by invoking a comment by Kathryn Tanner that feminist theology is "strengthened" to the extent that it can "wrestle constructively with the theological claims that have traditionally been important in Christian theology." Tanner continues, cited with approval by Berger: "the more traditional the material with which it works, the greater the influence of feminist theology."[56] Berger takes up this conviction for herself to talk about "tradition-friendliness" that claims neglected elements of the tradition then "reconfigur[es] what is authorized as 'Tradition.'"[57] In her work a decade later, *Gender Differences* neither mentions *Dissident Daughters* nor invokes feminism as a keyword. Rather it attends to "gender separations in liturgical space," showing how early shifts from household gatherings to "public sanctuaries" were gendered developments. Berger writes of what she calls "gender on and under the table," looking at "Jesus as both guest and host," "breast milk as eucharistic metaphor," and reevaluating early documents that explicitly indicate that a woman could "eucharistize" bread. And she explores male and female "bodily flows" – menstruation, ejaculation, birth-giving – and their influences on "liturgical anxieties" and how such flows have affected women's participation and presidency. The 2011 book skilfully invokes Mary's "priestly womb and priestly breasts" to which the tradition attests, albeit marginally compared with other eucharistic tropes. Quite obviously, Berger's work unsettles supposed norms in contemporary practice – a very powerful example of discovering tension in "tradition."

Although "juxtaposition" is by no means a keyword for Berger, there is a sense in which she places side by side different possible ways of pursuing feminist concerns in liturgy. *Gender Differences* especially is an excellent example of the kind of approach Ann Loades calls "searching for lost coins."[58]

Ann Loades (1938–2022)

Ann Loades was the first woman to be president of the Society for the Study of Theology in the UK and the first woman to be honored with a CBE medal for services to theology. Educated at Durham University in northern England and McMaster University, Canada, she lived in Scotland in retirement after a long career at her alma mater, Durham. She was undoubtedly best known as a feminist theologian (she wrote the chapter on it in the first two editions of *The Modern Theologians*), and her teaching positions (in philosophy of religion, latterly professor of divinity) never highlighted liturgy – and nor she did ever belong to a liturgical guild. Her wide-ranging writing spanned philosophical and Anglican theology, among other things.[59] She did, however, have a long-term concern with sacraments – initially via Simone Weil's disturbing preoccupations with eucharist and sacrifice.[60]

From the mid-1990s Loades's work had a strong focus on "sacramental spirituality," initially in conjunction with colleague David Brown.[61] Both Brown and Loades represent connection to the systematic agenda and sacraments in "classic" theology, though Loades was quite insistent on the unsystematic nature of her own work and adamant that wide resources should contribute to theological reflection.[62] No doubt this opened her to liturgical theology's emphasis not only on texts but dynamics of liturgy.[63] In any case, a sermon offers revealing insights into her sense of coming into liturgical awareness.[64]

Much of Loades's writing on liturgy was published piecemeal, assembling ("putting together what we already know") insights from her open-eyed approach.[65] Her ever-present ethical concerns shaped her emphasis on not just material elements of liturgy, and practice at it, but always "striv[ing] to live the imperatives of scripture proclaimed in word and sacrament to be a 'gift' for the world."[66] Patterning life by sacramental practices must always flow into grasping opportunities for courage in our "risky, mistake-ridden, very complex world." While such concerns by no means make her unique among liturgical scholars, her reflection on Christian worship after the Shoah is a powerful rebuke to liturgical theology done with little thought beyond the assembly itself. Although not using the term "anti-liturgica," Loades had clear ideas about what is involved.

Loades learned from her Anglican forebears not only to accent adoration (as did Evelyn Underhill)[67] but to challenge status quos (as did Dorothy L. Sayers with her Christological cathedral and radio plays).[68] She pursued both "sacramental continuities in practices we can identify" and "sacramental discontinuities of unsuspected opportunity." The latter mean at least that forms of celebration are not to be "fixed and frozen," and benefit from care about "the temporary and the throwaway."[69] More, a recurrent streak throughout her writing is about surprises that come from a sacramental spirituality anticipating that God might "appear in any guise." Although in part her perspective is informed by clear appreciation of Rahner's thought on "divine depths of ordinary life," it is turned in her own way to strongly emphasize the public and political, arenas in which she consistently insists that sacramentality must manifest.

Loades's work envelops some powerful juxtapositions. For example, her thinking on child sexual abuse – on some of the worst experiences children may endure – has a "pair" in work on children in liturgy, searching for best case scenarios of children's participation in celebration, children themselves being "living prayers."[70] And without direct dependence on Lathrop she articulates sacramental spirituality in terms of various "imaginative juxtapositions," not least by exploring how "sacrament" and "spiritual" may be "made adjectival to one another."[71] Her thinking also sometimes proceeds in pairs: the natural world next to human making, parenting next to work, music and movement, stillness and silence – with the range meant again to suggest that "sacramentality is fluid across the distinctions between 'church' and 'world'" – finally arriving at "Christ as sacrament," the one whom, focused upon, makes God "sayable."[72] In the context of this chapter, Loades represents how liturgical theology might be acquired even where – unlike parts of mainland Europe and North America – it has not taken hold in the academy. And she indicates the fruitfulness of doing so, with a largesse of perspective that can follow when the struggle to engage is entered.

Cláudio Carvalhaes (b. 1969)

Cláudio Carvalhaes is a Brazilian Presbyterian who by his own account grew up with close experience of poverty, working as a shoeshine boy, and whose local church gave him his first toy. Educated at Independent Presbyterian Theological Seminary and Methodist University, both in São Paulo, Brazil, and then UTS, New York, he has been much influenced by the Brazilian Anglican Jaci C. Marischin (1929–2009), as well as the Roman Catholic Janet Walton, SNJM, herself one of several Catholic religious women to make a distinguished contribution to liturgical theology in the post-Second Vatican Council period. Carvalhaes's writings are published in Portuguese and English, with the influence of – and affection for – eminent liberation theologian Ivone Gebara (b. 1944) also strong. On (undocumented) migration to the United States, Carvalhaes worked as a pastor – in a migrant community whose stories of injustice appear in his writing[73] – and he moved through work at various seminaries before returning to UTS.

Carvalhaes' first book in English was on eucharist and globalization, advocating "borderless borders."[74] His subsequent work includes pushing first signs of postcolonial perspectives on liturgy into interfaith terrain,[75] itself an expression of moving beyond borders. There are several anthologies of his essays, with a strongly iterative feel, having chapters carried over from one to the next as the importance of certain themes enlarge – one way of showing his second thoughts. In this and other ways, his writing has the quality of field notes – indeed, *Ritual at World's End* (2021) uses "itinerary" to introduce its contents – capturing excitement from his journeys of discovery.

Although full of movement, Carvalhaes's thought is imbued with a steady focus on justice. This is gestured in the structure of *What's Worship Got to Do with It?* (2018), with three parts, on "liturgy of the church," "liturgy of the neighbour," and "liturgy of the world."[76] Opening chapters deal with "worship: loving madly," seasons and baptism, while later ones concern the like of "praying with Black people for darker times" and "praising God between the world and the altar." An essay in the anthology becomes the gateway to the next one, giving it its name. In *Praying with the World at Heart* (2020), Carvalhaes then extends work on darkness – "praying with the night" – and offers a complement to his earlier essay on "a hermeneutic of the knees" in another on praying "with a lump in the throat." It also entails reflection on "praying with a plant," which is a herald of his later "eco-liturgical liberation theology" awake to "the loss of the critical zone (the space between the top of the trees and the few miles above where complex interactions between air, rocks, water, soil, and living organisms control and keep the equilibrium of life on earth)" and conveying his "befriending" of a tree (given a name, Wonder). Carvalhaes conceives his latest moves – more second thoughts – as a "conversion," as well as both "wishful thinking and a call to action."[77]

Along the way are many important insights, from Carvalhaes's construction of a "decolonial history of liturgy" lamenting how worship has "served" as a "weapon of mass destruction" through to criticism of a specific liturgical resource, the Presbyterian Church (USA)'s 2018 *Book of Common Worship*. In both cases, though in different ways, he challenges prevailing notions of "common" worship.

At least sometimes Carvalhaes uses the idea of juxtaposition, but distinctively involving "external" juxtapositions to do with "not only what is within a given shape of liturgy" but putting side by side, for example, prayers and race, or baptism and civil disobedience.[78] It is in the shadow of this that Lathrop comes in for critique.[79] It may also be that Carvalhaes could take more encouragement from Lathrop's emphasis on society and the poor, but either way Carvalhaes's seeking to expand the "commons" is a vivid liberation theology-inspired preferential option for the poor.[80] Carvalhaes is candid: "There is no need for Christian faith to exist if the liturgy of this faith is not a ritual of liberation," so liturgical theology must start where people are wounded, where life is threatened.[81] Exploration of the ambiguities of his aspirations is not the least vital part of Carvalhaes's contribution, for example showing how "praying for 'those who are lost'" – which might imply "that 'we' are not lost" – is not so simple.[82] Whatever, he audaciously conveys commitment to explore uncomfortable feelings and to wrestle with difficult problems, the result of which is a critical jolt to more widespread ways of supposing how "laws" of prayer and belief relate. Carvalhaes's unfinished "attempt to stay closer to decolonial knowledges" echoes in a "continuous movement" he insists is essential from "prayer in the heart" to standing in solidarity and using hands to help.[83]

It might not pass without notice that there is little on the surface of Carvalhaes's work on Christ, bar the occasional invocation of Christ's "dangerous memory."[84] Latterly, Carvalhaes is entirely upfront: "No more is my God made of a singular, male, anthropomorphic, one, disembodied, humanoid."[85] A revealing "Afterword" to one of his books suggests a person "carr[ying] remnants of his Christian past into ... the New Diaspora," "the place where exiles from every religious tradition, culture, and geographic region find themselves once they realize their inheritance has no future as a whole or, even in part, by itself."[86] Even so, Carvalhaes's "itinerary" involves strong incentives to unravel and rework the question of who may "participate" in making liturgical "meaning," with vim about meaning that needs to be made.

Debate

This has been a brief exploration of developments in liturgical theology, with fleeting accounts of perspectives from just a few persons. It nevertheless might suggest how a common agenda has emerged and where debate is animated. Most notably, perhaps Aidan Kavanagh gave a name to an imagined "primary" theologian, one whose "faith is carried ... in the vastly complex vocabulary of experiences had, prayers said, sights seen, smells smelled, words said and heard and responded to, emotions controlled and released, sins committed and repented, children born and loved ones buried."[87] His "person in the pews" is a woman: "Mrs Murphy." By contrast, in far too many accounts of liturgical theology, even now, few main movers are women – persons who, even now, may in many settings *only* be in a pew rather than in a pulpit or behind an altar-table, the locations from which a flood of male liturgical theologians have thought away.[88] The list of theologians in the preceding section therefore consciously includes a majority of women. Almost inevitably, they are close contemporary rather than voices long past. It is also intentional that an ecumenical range is represented.[89] Only one, though, is not of North Atlantic origins, and three are currently located in North America. For better or worse, the discipline has its centers of gravity. My choices about whom to represent might begin to suggest broadening out – even turning away – from aspects of dominant dynamics in the discipline, signposting directions that need to be found in the future. But more is needed.[90]

There are many matters of debate. Who may do liturgical theology? Who may lead liturgical celebration? Whose "meaning"-making matters most? How can liturgical theology embrace and express ecumenical commitment – even in shifting ecclesial sands? Does "primary" theology trump the "classic" kind? Is liturgical theology stuck in the North and West? Where are the lines between unity and uniformity, and what triggers the difference? Can ordo be free from ideology?[91] Who decides what aspects of T/tradition/s are in play? How much "progress" does a particular liturgical theologian represent? How to welcome Pentecostals to the conversation? Why bother with any liturgical theology that does not evidently put energies toward what the Orthodox call "the liturgy after the liturgy," the "'gift' to the world"?[92] Which liturgies best approximate justice, maybe even draw it forward? What might Christologies from liberation theologies offer to this discipline? How can liturgical theology be learned – and tested – if it is not taught?[93]

Notes

1   Stephen Pattison and Gordon Lynch, "Pastoral and Practical Theology," in *The Modern Theologians: An Introduction to Christian Theology Since 1918*, 3rd ed., ed. David F. Ford with Rachel Muers (Oxford: Blackwell, 2005), 408–225.

2   See Part 1, "Classics of the Twentieth Century," and Part 5, "Particularizing Theology," in *The Modern Theologians*, 17–127, 427–552.

3   For example, Daniel W. Hardy and David F. Ford, *Jubilate: Theology in Praise* (London: Darton, Longman & Todd, 1984).

4   Alexander Schmemann, *Introduction to Liturgical Theology* (New York: SVS Press, 1966), 16.

5   Topographical imagery has proved appealing in the discipline, e.g. Dwight W. Vogel, "Liturgical Theology: A Conceptual Geography," in *Primary Sources in Liturgical Theology: A Reader*, ed. Dwight W. Vogel (Collegeville, MN: Liturgical Press, 2000), 3–14.

6   Joris Geldhof, *Liturgical Theology as a Research Program* (Leiden: Brill, 2020), 32.

7   Geoffrey Wainwright, "Ecumenical Convergences," in *The Oxford History of Christian Worship*, ed. Geoffrey Wainwright and Karen B. Westerfield Tucker (Oxford: Oxford University Press, 2006), 724.

8   This nomenclature as *The Modern Theologians: An Introduction to Christian Theology in the Twentieth Century*, Vol. 1, ed. David F. Ford (Oxford: Blackwell, 1989), 4.

9   For an excellent ecumenical survey, albeit largely limited to Atlantic isles, see Gordon Wakefield, *An Outline of Christian Worship* (Edinburgh: T&T Clark, 2000).

10 See Wainwright, "Ecumenical Convergences," 734.

11 See Robert Gribben, "The Formation of the Liturgy of the Church of South India," *Studia Liturgica* 30 (2000): 129–42.

12 See Michael Kinnamon, ed., *The Ecumenical Movement: An Anthology of Key Texts and Voices*, 2nd ed. (Geneva: WCC, 2015), 123–7.

13 Don E. Saliers, "Christian Spirituality in an Ecumenical Age," in *Christian Spirituality III: Post-Reformation and Modern*, ed. Louis Dupre and Don E. Saliers (London: SCM Press, 1989), 538.

14 See Annibale Bugnini, *The Reform of the Liturgy 1948–1975* (Collegeville, MN: Liturgical Press, 1990), 39–41.

15 Not only in, for example, Anscar J. Chupungco, *Cultural Adaptation of the Liturgy* (Mahwah, NJ: Paulist Press, 1978), but in his influence ecumenically, most notably through involvement in the Lutheran World Federation's Nairobi Statement. See Gláucia Vasconcelos Wilkey, ed., *Worship and Culture: Foreign Country or Homeland?* (Grand Rapids, MI: Eerdmans, 2014).

16 See Thomas Best and Dagmar Heller, eds., *Eucharistic Worship in Ecumenical Contexts: The Lima Liturgy – and Beyond* (Geneva: WCC, 1998), 34.

17 Aidan Kavanagh, *On Liturgical Theology* (Collegeville, MN: Liturgical Press, 1984), 74.

18 See Uniting Church in Australia, *Uniting in Worship 2* (Sydney: Uniting Church Press, 2005), 13–14.

19 On Roman Catholic contexts, see Massimo Faggioli, *True Reform: Liturgy and Ecclesiology in* Sacrosanctum Concilium (Collegeville, MN: Liturgical Press, 2012).

20 Gordon W. Lathrop, *Holy Things: A Liturgical Theology* (Minneapolis, MN: Fortress Press, 1993), 5, 7. Just as Kavanagh had dedicated his *On Liturgical Theology* to Schmemann (v), Lathrop says that his *Holy Things* is "a homage of thanks" (ix) to the Orthodox elder. But *Holy Things* is dedicated to Gail Ramshaw (v) – see the Named Theologians section.

21 Robert Hovda, *Strong, Loving and Wise: Presiding in Liturgy* (Collegeville, MN: Liturgical Press, 1976), 55–6.

22 Lathrop, *Holy Things*, 57.

23 See Bryan Cones, *This Assembly of Believers: The Gifts of Difference in the Church at Prayer* (London: SCM Press, 2020).

24 Mark Searle, *Called to Participate: Theological, Ritual and Social Perspectives* (Collegeville, MN: Liturgical Press, 2006), 15–45.

25 Don E. Saliers, "Sounding the Symbols of Faith: Exploring Non-verbal Languages of Christian Worship," in *Music in Christian Worship*, ed. Charlotte Kroeker (Collegeville, MN: Liturgical Press, 2005), 23–4.

26 Gordon W. Lathrop, *Saving Images: The Presence of the Bible in Christian Liturgy* (Minneapolis, MN: Fortress Press, 2017), 38.

27 Gordon W. Lathrop, "At Least Two Words: The Liturgy as Proclamation," in *The Landscape of Praise: Readings in Liturgical Renewal*, ed. Blair Gilmore-Meeks (Valley Forge, PA: Trinity Press International, 1996), 183.

28 Lathrop, *Holy Things*, 173; cf. Lathrop, *Saving Images*, 137.

29 Cf. Gordon W. Lathrop, *Holy Ground: A Liturgical Cosmology* (Minneapolis, MN: Fortress Press, 2003), 75.

30 Lathrop, *Holy Ground*, 74, 75.

31 Lathrop, *Holy Ground*, 74, 75.

32 Lathrop, *Holy Ground*, 75.

33 For a striking example, see Gordon W. Lathrop, "Liturgy and Mission in the North American Context," in *Inside Out: Worship in an Age of Mission*, ed. Thomas Shattaur (Minneapolis, MN: Fortress Press, 1999), 203.

34 Lathrop, *Holy Ground*, 179–99.

35 Melanie A. Ross, *Evangelical versus Liturgical? Defying a Dichotomy* (Grand Rapids, MI: Eerdmans, 2014).

36 See Gail Ramshaw, *Reviving Sacred Speech: The Meaning of Liturgical Language* (Akron, OH: OSL Publications, 2000).

37 Gail Ramshaw, *What Is Christianity? An Introduction to the Christian Religion* (Minneapolis, MN: Fortress Press, 2013), vii. Also *Christian Worship: 100,000 Sundays of Symbols and Rituals* (Minneapolis, MN: Fortress Press, 2009).

38 Gail Ramshaw, *Words around the Font* (Chicago, IL: Liturgy Training Publications, 1994); *Words around the Table* (Chicago, IL: Liturgy Training Publications, 1991); *Words around the Fire* (Chicago, IL: Liturgy Training Publications, 1990); *Saints on Sunday: Voices from the Past Enlivening Our Worship* (Collegeville, MN: Liturgical Press, 2018).

39 Gail Ramshaw, *God beyond Gender: Christian Feminist God Language* (Minneapolis, MN: Fortress Press, 1995), 68.

40 Ramshaw, *God beyond Gender*, 69–70.

41 Ramshaw, *God beyond Gender*, 4.

42 See Gail Ramshaw, *Under the Tree of Life: The Religion of a Feminist Christian* (New York: Continuum, 1999/2002).

43 E.g. Ramshaw, *Under the Tree*, 65–8; *Reviving Sacred Speech*, 32–5.

44 Ramshaw, *Reviving Sacred Speech*, 37, 39.

45 Ramshaw, *Saints on Sunday*, 137–42 (on Cranmer).

46 For example, Gail Ramshaw, *Pray, Praise, and Give Thanks* (Minneapolis, MN: Augsburg Fortress, 2017), 54–6.

47 United Methodist Church, *United Methodist Worship Book* (Nashville, TN: UMPH, 1992), 399–400.

48 Ramshaw, *Beyond Gender*, 119.

49 Ramshaw, *Under the Tree*, 129. On "exhuming," see Ramshaw, *Under the Tree*, 30. Also *Treasures*, 393–400; Gail Ramshaw, *40 Days and 40 Nights* (Minneapolis, MN: Augsburg Fortress, 2006), 58–9; Ramshaw, *What Is Christianity?*, 1, 80, 187, and Christian worship described as a "vaulting elm tree" in Gail Ramshaw, *A Metaphorical God: An Abecedary of Images for God* (Chicago, IL: Liturgy Training Publications, 1995), 1.

50 For example, Teresa Berger and Bryan D. Spinks, eds., *The Spirit in Worship – Worship in the Spirit* (Collegeville, MN: Liturgical Press, 2009), and Teresa Berger, ed., *Liturgy in Migration: From Upper Room to Cyberspace* (Collegeville, MN: Liturgical Press, 2012).

51 Teresa Berger, *Theology in Hymns?* (Collegeville, MN: Liturgical Press, 1995).

52 Teresa Berger, *@Worship: Liturgical Practices in Digital Worlds* (Abingdon: Routledge, 2017), but with early hints of interest in Teresa Berger, *Women's Ways of Worship: Gender Analysis and Liturgical History* (Collegeville, MN: Liturgical Press, 1999), 153.

53 Berger, *Women's Ways*, 111.

54 Teresa Berger, "Women in Worship," in *Oxford History of Christian Worship*, 764.

55 Berger, *Women's Ways*, 69.

56 Teresa Berger, *Dissident Daughters: Feminist Liturgies in Global Context* (Louisville, KY: Westminster John Knox Press, 2001), 229, quoting Kathryn Tanner, "Social Theory Concerning the 'New Social Movements' and the Practice of Feminist Theology," in *Horizons in Feminist Theology: Identity, Tradition, and Norms*, ed. Rebecca S. Chopp and Sheila Greeve Davaney (Minneapolis, MN: Fortress Press, 1997), 192.

57 Berger, *Dissident Daughters*, 229–30.

58 Ann Loades, *Searching for Lost Coins: Explorations in Christianity and Feminism* (London: SPCK, 1987).

59 E.g. Ann Loades, *Explorations in Twentieth Century Theology and Philosophy: People Preoccupied with God*, ed. Stephen Burns (London: Anthem Press, 2023).

60 See e.g. Loades, *Lost Coins*, 39–60.

61 David Brown and Ann Loades, eds., *The Sense of the Sacramental* (London: SPCK, 1995); David Brown and Ann Loades, eds., *Christ the Sacramental Word* (London: SPCK, 1996).

62 For example, Loades, *Lost Coins*, 5.

63 See Ann Loades, *Grace is Not Faceless: Reflections on Mary*, ed. Stephen Burns (London: Darton, Longman & Todd, 2021), 49–61; Ann Loades and Bridget Nichols, "The Liturgical Body and the Gift of Presence," in *Theology, Aesthetics, and Culture: Responses to the Work of David Brown*, ed. Robert MacSwain and Taylor Worley (Oxford: Oxford University Press, 2012), 252–65.

64 Ann Loades, *Grace and Glory in One Another's Faces: Preaching and Worship*, ed. Stephen Burns (Norwich: Canterbury Press, 2020), 25–6.

65 Ann Loades, "Sacramentality and Christian Spirituality," in *The Blackwell Companion to Christian Spirituality*, ed. Arthur Holder (Oxford: Blackwell, 2005), 255. Cf. Loades, *Grace and Glory*, 90.

66 Loades and Nichols, "Liturgical Body," 264.

67 See Ann Loades, *Evelyn Underhill* (London: Fount, 1997).

68 See Ann Loades, ed., *Dorothy L. Sayers: Spiritual Writings* (London: SPCK, 1993).

69 Ann Loades, "Finding 'New Sense' in the Sacramental," in *The Gestures of God: Explorations in Sacramentality*, ed. Geoffrey Rowell and Christine Hall (London: Continuum, 2004), 161–72.

70 See Ann Loades, *Feminist Theology: Voices from the Past* (Oxford: Polity Press, 2000), 140–65; "Children Are Church," in *The Lively Oracles of God: Perspectives on the Bible and Liturgy*, ed. Gordon Jeanes and Bridget Nichols (Collegeville, MN: Liturgical Press, 2022), 206–26.

71 Loades, *Grace and Glory*, 101; cf. Loades, "Sacramentality," 254.

72 Loades, "Sacramentality," 255, 257.

73 Cláudio Carvalhaes, *Ritual at World's End: Essays on Eco-Liturgical Liberation Theology* (York, PA: Barbers Son Press, 2021), 24.

74 Cláudio Carvalhaes, *Eucharist and Globalization: Redrawing the Borders of Eucharistic Hospitality* (Eugene, OR: Pickwick, 2013).

75 Cláudio Carvalhaes, ed., *Liturgy and Postcolonial Perspectives: Only One Is Holy* (New York: Palgrave Macmillan, 2015).

76 Cláudio Carvalhaes, *What's Worship Got to Do with It?* (Eugene, OR: Cascade, 2018).

77 Carvalhaes, *World's End*, 14.

78 Cláudio Carvalhaes, *Praying with Every Heart: Orienting Our Lives to the Wholeness of the World* (Eugene, OR: Cascade, 2020), 56.

79 Carvalhaes, *What's Worship Got to Do with It?*, 146–7.

80 Carvalhaes, *Praying with Every Heart*, 47.

81 Carvalhaes, *What's Worship Got to Do with It?*, 236–7.

82 Carvalhaes, *Praying with Every Heart*, 51.

83 Cláudio Carvalhaes, "Praying with the Unwanted People at the End of the World," in *T&T Clark Handbook of Christian Prayer*, ed. Ashley Cocksworth and John C. McDowell (London: Bloomsbury T&T Clark, 2022), 696.

84 In making this observation, I am conscious that I have only touched on Berger's writing on Christ. See especially "Christmas: 'And Became Hu/man'" in her *Fragments of Real Presence* (New York: Crossroad, 2005), 127–34.

85 Carvalhaes, *World's End*, 12.

86 Marc H. Ellis, "Afterword," in *Praying with Every Heart*, 253.

87 Kavanagh, *On Liturgical Theology*, 146–7.

88 Note Geldhof, *Research Program*: of more than three hundred notes, around twenty refer to women, and of those some are second references to the same person, while others are to women working in other disciplines.

89 Note again Geldhof's book, tilted toward Roman Catholic tradition: see 73, n. 223.

90 See Stephen Burns, "Explorations in Decolonial Liturgy: 'Many Voices,' 'From Below,'" *International Journal for the Study of the Christian Church* 22, no. 3 (2022): 183–194.

91 See Gordon W. Lathrop, "Bath, Word, Prayer, Table: Reflections on Doing the Liturgical Ordo in a Postmodern Time," in *Ordo: Bath, Word, Prayer, Table*, ed. Dirk G. Lange and Dwight W. Vogel (Akron, OH: OSL, 2006), 216–28.

92 See Ion Bria, "The Liturgy after the Liturgy," in *The Ecumenical Movement*, 285–6; Loades and Nichols, "Liturgical Body," 264.

93 My thanks to Ann, Cláudio, Teresa, Gail and Gordon, for their feedback on a draft of this chapter.

Recommended Reading

Berger, Teresa. *Gender Differences and the Making of Liturgical History: Lifting a Veil on Liturgy's Past.* Aldershot: Ashgate, 2011.

Carvalhaes, Cláudio. *What's Worship Got to Do with It?* Eugene, OR: Cascade, 2018.

Kavanagh, Aidan. *On Liturgical Theology.* Collegeville, MN: Liturgical Press, 1984.

Lathrop, Gordon W. *Holy Things: A Liturgical Theology.* Minneapolis, MN: Fortress Press, 1993.

Ramshaw, Gail, *Treasures Old and New: Images in the Lectionary.* Minneapolis, MN: Fortress Press, 2002.

Vogel, Dwight W., ed. *Primary Sources in Liturgical Theology: A Reader.* Collegeville, MN: Liturgical Press, 2000.

Contemporary Theology and Its Challenges

Theology, Arts, and Sciences

Theology and Music

Jeremy S. Begbie

Introduction

Until recently, music has attracted relatively little attention in modern theology. In some respects this is puzzling, given the supposedly limitless concerns of theology, the presence of music in every known human culture, the availability through recording of virtually every type of music, the persistence of music in the church's worship, and the growing literature on the politics, sociology, and psychology of music. Moreover, illustrious theological figures from the past have offered penetrating musical reflections – Augustine, Luther, and Calvin among them. Nevertheless, over the last hundred years it is fair to say that the theologian's stance toward music has been characterized more by hesitation than close interest. Doubtless, there are factors at work here that apply to virtually all the arts: the church's fear of idolatry, an anxiety about music's materiality and emotional power, the seeming triviality of music compared to modernity's more pressing life-and-death challenges. Not least, there is the sheer difficulty of speaking about music in ways that do justice to its appeal and genuinely shed new light upon it. As George Steiner observes: "In the face of music, the wonders of language are also its frustrations."[1]

Survey and Representative Figures

There are, however, two major exceptions to this trend in the twentieth century – Karl Barth and Dietrich Bonhoeffer – whom we discuss here. Moreover, in the last twenty years or so there has been something of a burgeoning of interest in music among theologians (matched by a willingness on the part of at least some scholars of music to enter theological territory). Several prominent streams of writing have emerged.

1   There have been a variety of attempts to "read" music through the lenses of scripture and the central confessions of the Christian church, to ask how patterns and frameworks of belief can be seen to "play out" in both the making and reception of music.[2] Some of these focus on particular composers and

Ford's The Modern Theologians: An Introduction to Christian Theology since 1918, Fourth Edition.
Edited by Rachel Muers and Ashley Cocksworth.
© 2024 John Wiley & Sons Ltd. Published 2024 by John Wiley & Sons Ltd.

their output,[3] others on a musical genre[4] or historical period,[5] or on the music of particular contexts (e.g. music in worship, or music's role vis-à-vis social injustice).[6]

2   Others, while working within a Christian theological orientation, have explored the benefits of music for theology, how music might contribute to and enrich theological discovery, enabling theologians to be at once more rigorous and faithful to the substance of Christian faith.[7]

3   Still others have seen in music a way of enabling a theological narration of a particular historical period, believing that music bears a distinctive witness to the theologically charged impulses of a culture.[8]

4   A number of scholars have been attracted to music for the possibilities it opens up for conversations about theological matters in a post- or late modern culture, in a society that has arguably become increasingly impatient, disillusioned with, and perhaps even hostile to religious language and confessional claims. It is urged that "rumors of transcendence" can be discerned in music far beyond any church or religious setting, that music with no explicit or conscious theological intent can nonetheless give voice to searching questions and deeply felt existential drives that very naturally call for theological responses. All this, it is said, presents unique opportunities for a form of theological-cultural engagement that is hard to achieve by other means.[9]

Karl Barth

We begin, however, with the first of the two exceptions to the general neglect of music among theologians, the Swiss Reformed theologian Karl Barth (1886–1968). Although well versed in the music of many periods, Barth harbored a devotion to one composer in particular, amounting almost to an addiction: "I even have to confess," he writes, "that if I ever get to heaven, I would first seek out Mozart, and only then inquire after Augustine, St Thomas, Luther, Calvin, and Schleiermacher."[10]

Why did Barth believe the prodigy from Salzburg deserved a central place in theology, "especially in the doctrine of creation and also in eschatology"?[11] Why was he so convinced that when the angels praise God they play only Bach, but that together *en famille* they play Mozart and God listens with special pleasure?[12] What is probably the main theological reason becomes clear in Barth's treatment of the composer in *Church Dogmatics* III/3, where he asks us to hear Mozart's music as embodying and giving voice to creation's praise of God, and creation's praise precisely *as* created – limited and finite. The context is a discussion of the "shadowside (*Schattenseite*)" or negative dimension of the created world.[13] Comparison with a later passage suggests he is here thinking of finitude and its manifold effects (including death), the quality of having been created out of nothing and therefore always being on the verge of collapsing back into nonexistence.[14] This shadowside must be distinguished from evil (*Das Nichtige*); failure to do so risks eliding the destructive nature of evil as well as suggesting that finite reality is itself intrinsically fallen. The shadowside is the expression of God's "positive will, election and activity."[15] In this light, Mozart's music is presented as singing the praise of the cosmos in its "total goodness," *including* its shadowside. The music does indeed contain a "No," but this is the "No" of the shadowside, not evil.[16] What does it matter if Mozart died in misery like an "unknown soldier," Barth asks, "when a life is permitted simply and unpretentiously, and therefore serenely, authentically and impressively, to express the good creation of God, *which also includes the limitation and end of man*?"[17] Mozart heard in creation a harmony in which "the shadow is not darkness, deficiency is not defeat, sadness cannot become despair, trouble cannot degenerate into tragedy and infinite melancholy is not ultimately forced to claim undisputed sway."[18] Mozart even acknowledges the limit of death, but he discerned the negative only in and with the positive: the overriding impression conveyed by his music, for Barth, is God's almighty "Yes" to creation.

Congruent with this, Barth later expands on the difference between the shadowside and *Das Nichtige* – when the creature "crosses the frontier" of finitude, when "nothingness achieves its actuality in the created world."[19] This is just what Mozart's music does not do. It does not strain for divinity. And Mozart himself does not thrust his ego before us in some "mania for self-expression,"[20] or try to impose a "message" on the listener. In fact, he does not "*will*" to proclaim the praise of God. He just does it – precisely in that humility in which he himself is, so to speak, only the instrument with which he allows us to hear what he hears: what surges at him from God's creation, what rises in him, and must proceed from him."[21] "He simply offered himself as the agent by which little bits of horn, metal and catgut could serve as the voices of creation."[22] This more than anything else, for Barth, is what gives Mozart's music its effortless, light quality.[23]

These reflections can be understood more fully if we turn to the much disputed passages on "parables of the kingdom" and the "lights" of creation in *Church Dogmatics* IV/3.[24] Here Barth proposes that Christ, as the one true Word of God, can testify to himself and to his work of reconciliation by calling forth "parables" that witness to his glory – not only in the Bible and the church but also in spheres where God is not explicitly recognized or acknowledged. Such "signs" and "attestations" are provisional, secondary, and eschatological, pointing to the uniqueness and primacy of revelation and reconciliation in Christ. David Moseley has convincingly argued that the unmentioned figure haunting this discussion is Mozart.[25] Barth was writing the material on parables at roughly the same time as he was working on his Mozart Bicentenary pieces, where he explicitly uses the phrase "parables of the kingdom" of Mozart's music. Further, reading Barth's comments on Mozart along with his treatment of parables of the kingdom confirms that he was not turning against his earlier strictures on "natural theology": no one's music (not even Mozart's) can of itself become an independent, let alone normative source of divine revelation. Although Barth could speak of Mozart's music as "theology," a "miraculous" phenomenon akin to "revelation," "mediating" the constant praise of the cosmos, he understood this to be possible only insofar as it is in conformity with scripture and the gospel to which scripture testifies.

Thus, without any lessening of his passion for methodological rigor, Barth invited his readers to hear music (Mozart's above all) as enacting the grace of God in Jesus Christ, "performing" the dynamics of creation's praise in sound, and thus as exemplary of a radically self-forgetful creativity. (In this, Barth provides a notable example of theology engaging with music according to type (1) discussed previously.)

Dietrich Bonhoeffer

Rather different perspectives are opened up by the German theologian Dietrich Bonhoeffer (1906–45), a highly accomplished musician whose written works contain numerous references to music.[26] Bonhoeffer was especially well educated in the classics of European music, although his encounter with Black spirituals during his visits to New York also proved especially formative for him. It is in his final writings that music comes into special prominence. Imprisoned for his part in a plot to assassinate Hitler, as World War II in Germany nears its cataclysmic end, Bonhoeffer ponders what shape practical obedience to Christ might take amid the tumults of his time. In this context his writing frequently takes musical turns.

Apart from music heard very distantly in and beyond the prison, Bonhoeffer is aware only of the music embedded in his memory: "It's strange how music, when one listens with the inner ear alone and gives oneself up to it utterly, can be almost more beautiful than when heard physically."[27] In November 1943, he writes to his parents:

> For years [Bach's *Mass in B Minor*] has been part of Remembrance Day for me, just as the *St. Matthew Passion* is part of Good Friday. I remember quite clearly the evening I heard it for the first time. I was eighteen years old, was coming from the Harnack seminar in which he had discussed my first seminar essay very graciously and had expressed the hope I would someday become a church historian. I was still quite full with this when I entered the Philharmonic Hall; then the great "Kyrie Eleison" began, and at the moment everything else sank away completely. It was an indescribable impression. Today I am moving through it by memory, section by section, and rejoice that the Schleichers are able to listen to what for me is Bach's most beautiful music.[28]

However, music does more than provide memories to sustain Bonhoeffer in his meager life in jail. It speaks of a way or pattern of life that according to him the church sorely needs to rediscover. In his earlier work, Bonhoeffer had spoken of Christ's relation to the world in terms of four divine "mandates" or commands – labor, marriage, government, and the church – and music is counted under the mandate of labor.[29] Now he locates music in "the broad area of freedom," which embraces art, culture, friendship, and play.

> I wonder whether it is only from the concept of the church that we can regain the understanding of the sphere of freedom (art, education, friendship, play). This means that "aesthetic existence" (Kierkegaard) is not to be banished from the church's sphere; rather it is precisely within the church that it would be founded anew.[30]

The key mark of this "aesthetic existence," it seems, is gratuitousness, a freedom from necessity. We pursue those things belonging to the realm of freedom not because we have been commanded to do so, because we *must* pursue them; we do them simply for the joy of doing them.

This could of course be read as escapist, a relinquishment of responsibility in a broken world. That Bonhoeffer has nothing like this in mind becomes clear when we turn to his deepest engagement with music in these final years, those places where he allows music to generate fresh theological discourse: indeed, he often seems to be *thinking* musically. Now that he is removed from the political maelstrom, this important dimension of his life, internalized through memory, is freed to play a key role in shaping his language and thought.

Bonhoeffer ponders the fractured and dispersed character of wartime Germany and the church's fierce struggle to find a way of living responsibly in the maelstrom: "The longer we are uprooted from our professional and personal lives, the more we experience our lives – in contrast to our parents' lives – as fragmented."[31] But this

> may … point to a higher fulfilment, which can no longer be achieved by human effort. This is the only way I can think, especially when confronted with the death of so many of my best former students. Even when the violence of outward events breaks our lives in pieces, as the bombs do your houses, everything possible must be done to keep in view the way all this was planned and intended to be.[32]

Likening a person's life to a fragment, Bonhoeffer writes: "What matters, it seems to me, is whether one still sees, in this fragment of life we have, what the whole was intended and designed to be, and of what material is made. After all, there are such things as fragments that are only fit for the garbage heap (even a decent "hell" is too good for them)." But there are others "which remain meaningful for hundreds of years, because only God could perfect them, so they must remain fragments – I'm thinking, for example, of the *Art of Fugue*."[33] The reference here is to J. S. Bach's polyphonic *tour de force* that he never lived to complete. This notion of the "unfinishedness" of life also links up with comments Bonhoeffer makes on a hymn by Heinrich Schütz (1585–1672). He asks: "Isn't this passage something like the "restoration" of all earthly desire?" – the allusion here is to the bringing together of all things in Christ envisaged in Ephesians 1:10. Bonhoeffer's own adult life, now heading toward death, and the broken-up quality of his prison writings resonate poignantly with this theme. He takes heart from God's promise of a final recapitulation. Speaking of the *Art of Fugue*, he writes:

> If our life is only the most remote reflection of such a fragment, in which, even for a short time, the various themes gradually accumulate and harmonize with one another and in which the great counterpoint is sustained from beginning to end – then it is not for us, either, to complain about this fragmentary life of ours, but rather even to be glad of it.[34]

The musical imagery is developed further by Bonhoeffer when he coins the term "polyphony of life" to describe the way in which multiple loves and desires can be held together through a coordinating theme, a *cantus firmus* (the principal or central theme that gives many pieces of medieval polyphony their coherence).

> What I mean is that God, the Eternal, wants to be loved with our whole heart, not to the detriment of earthly love or to diminish it, but as a sort of cantus firmus to which the other voices of life resound in counterpoint. One of these contrapuntal themes ... is earthly love. Even in the Bible there is the Song of Solomon, and you really can't imagine a hotter, more sensual, and glowing love than the one spoken of here (cf. 7:6!). It's really good that this is in the Bible, contradicting all those who think being a Christian is about tempering one's passions.[35]

If the *cantus firmus* (our love for God) is secure, the other voices (our other loves) will find their place. "When the cantus firmus is clear and distinct, a counterpoint can develop as mightily as it wants."[36] Bonhoeffer relates this interweaving of the *cantus firmus* and its surrounding counterpoint to Christ's divinity and humanity:

> The two are "undivided and yet distinct," as the Definition of Chalcedon says, like the divine and human natures in Christ. Is that perhaps why we are so at home with polyphony in music, why it is important to us, because it is the musical image of this christological fact and thus also our *vita christiana*?[37]

A diversity of loves and desires can thus flourish around the *cantus firmus*, provided the *cantus firmus* is solidly in place. Writing to his close friend Eberhard Bethge (speaking of Bethge's relationship with his wife), he says:

> I wanted to ask you to let the cantus firmus be heard clearly in your being together; only then will it sound complete and full, and the counterpoint will always know that it is being carried and can't get out of tune or be cut adrift; while remaining itself and complete in itself. Only this polyphony gives your life wholeness, and you know that no disaster can befall you as along as the cantus firmus continues.[38]

In a letter of the next day Bonhoeffer speaks of sorrow and joy as two elements in life's polyphony.[39] And to Bethge, who is enjoying far more in the way of freedom and opportunity, he writes: "I do want you to be *glad* about what you have, which is truly the polyphony of life."[40]

It is hard not to think of Bonhoeffer's own life at this time as polyphonic. He is engaged to his beloved Maria, in regular contact with friends and family, staff and inmates. And in addition to theology, he is also writing fiction, drama, and poetry and reading history, poetry, science, novels, philosophy, and much else besides. And the fact that he can speak of both sorrow and joy in the polyphony of life obviously relates to the darkness of his own situation.

In sum, Bonhoeffer's love of music seems to have had a key part in spawning and giving contours to the vision of the Christian life he was struggling so hard to articulate in his prison years – one that is intensely Christological, that refuses any evasion of the concrete and practical, where a huge diversity of interests, concerns, passions, and activities flourish around a *cantus firmus*, the love of God. Furthermore, Joanna Tarassenko has recently contended that yet another key theological dimension is present in this musical metaphor: Bonhoeffer's appeal to polyphony, she argues, manifests a latent doctrine of the Holy Spirit running through his theology (despite the frequent charge that Bonhoeffer lacks a pneumatology), one that is in fact pivotal for his understanding of Christian formation in Christ.[41]

In all this, it is clear that Bonhoeffer is taking a step further than Barth, in that music is being employed not only as a concrete witness to a major theological dynamic (in Barth's case, authentic praise and creativity) but as the source of fresh conceptuality and language that together enable a deeper theological discernment and articulation. Music has become much more than a sign, and certainly more than a decorative (or emotive) embellishment. In this way, according to the types of musical-theological engagement we outlined previously, Bonhoeffer's late "musical theology" serves as an example of type (2).

Two recent contributions

In recent years, by no means all the theologians engaging music have followed the kinds of paths opened up by Barth and Bonhoeffer. A very different approach, for example, can be found in the work of David Brown and Gavin Hopps of the University of St Andrews, as set out in their jointly authored book *The Extravagance of Music*.[42] Brown and Hopps situate their treatment of music against the canvas of a broad and inclusive conception of religious experience, in a manner reminiscent of leading currents of nineteenth-century Protestant theology. We are invited to see music's theological potential in light of the notion of "excess," or superfluity. Music is capable of mediating an affectively charged experience that by its very nature impels us beyond linguistic and conceptual categories, while still being thoroughly coherent and compelling: "We wish to defend," the authors say, "the ability of music … to engender an awareness of something 'other,' (transcendent), which is at the same time incapable of complete description."[43] Music's stubborn uncontainability by thought or language, its momentum toward surpassing limits, gives it a distinctive theological capacity: to elicit an awareness of divine transcendence and thus facilitate a sense of God's extravagant self-giving presence to the world. Brown and Hopps defend this vision (which, it is worth noting, has many historical precedents) against the widespread suspicion that transcendence necessarily implies escapism or other-worldliness. Indeed, they are eager to stress the concrete and "earthed" character of musical experience: music is to be regarded first and foremost as a range of concrete, socially and culturally embedded practices (in line with the so-called "new musicology" of the 1980s and 90s), not primarily as a series of disembodied "works" enshrined in written scores. At the same time, the immanent properties of musical sounds are intrinsic to music's meaningfulness: for they provide a material "affordance structure" that draws the hearer in, contributing to the possibility of an encounter with the divine.

In commending this theo-musicological outlook, the authors are pushing against a number of tendencies they discern in contemporary theological discourse surrounding music, in particular what they see as a narrowness of vision on the part of many, a grudging unwillingness to acknowledge the breadth of music's revelatory capacities and the largesse of God's activity in the world (they speak of their account of music as "optimistic").[44] They press theologians to venture into spheres of musical culture too often ignored – most notably popular music, and music without overt or intended theological connections. This is in line with a leading thrust in David Brown's writing over many years: the need to pay to attention to "religious experience" in the creative arts at large, far beyond the church: "If God is really our Creator, then the urge to deepen contact with him is likely to permeate human creativity in whatever form it is found."[45]

Allied to this is the authors' keenness to allow music "room" to be a medium of divine revelation in its own right, and thus to set aside where necessary theological prejudgments that might lead us to neglect its revelatory possibilities. By being overconcerned with fidelity to scripture and ecclesiastical tradition, much theology has closed itself off to the possibility of fresh discovery through music, too easily assuming that music's greatest theological value is its ability to confirm preestablished belief. Especially harmful has been the notion that music is of worth only insofar as it provides illustrations or analogues of the divine; music needs to be taken seriously not merely as a *witness to* the divine, but as a vehicle of *encounter with* the divine, a nonverbal conduit of God's own living presence.

Brown and Hopps' theological reading of music will undoubtedly raise questions for many about the norms and criteria with which we might assess this or that experience as a *bona fide* encounter with "the divine." It is not entirely clear how far they wish their account of music to be read as depending upon commitments that most would regard as pivotal to classical Christian theology, not least with respect to the person of Christ and the self-revelation of God. In this regard, the writings of theologian and musician Jeremy Begbie (the present writer), currently at Duke University, stands in some contrast.[46] No less eager to do justice to God's presence and activity in musical cultures at large, to explore music not directly associated with theological belief or discourse, to honor the irreducibility of music as concretely experienced, to allow music a unique role in theological discovery, and to give the category of "excess" a prominent place, I nonetheless wish to pay rather more attention to how the concrete specificities of Christian faith might affect the way these and related concerns are advanced. In particular, I have been concerned to do justice to the witness of the church's scriptures and classical Nicene theology to the triunity of God as disclosed in Christ, and to the highly idiosyncratic metaphysical landscape this witness invites the theologian to inhabit.

I have argued that much depends on setting music within a creation-wide context, specifically one that turns upon the New Testament's focus on what has been concretely enacted in Jesus of Nazareth. The one who has been made flesh (Jn. 1:14) is the one by whom and in whom all things were made (Jn. 1:14; Col. 1:15–20), the one eternally loved by God the Father (Jn. 1:18). The created world has been loved into existence, and is unconditionally upheld and sustained by this same divine love *ad intra*. This carries immense encouragement for the musician to treat it as a proper, meaningful environment to enjoy and explore, worthy of attention, cultivation, and adornment. Making music can be seen as part of humankind's vocation, as God's image-bearer, to "voice creation's praise," to extend and elaborate the praise that creation already sings to God. Sinful humanity's bizarre refusal to praise God is answered climactically in the Son's incarnation: Christ as human uniquely offers the praise due to God, submits to the consequences of our refusal of praise, and on the third day, is raised to a new mode of created being, prefiguring a final "new heaven and a new earth" (Rev. 21:1). By virtue of this "new creation" already forged in Christ, a vocation of renewal and re-creation opens up for the creative musician: through the Holy Spirit, the material realities of sound are not only to be acknowledged and respected, but enabled to take on fresh, richer, meaningful forms, foreshadowing the final re-creation of all things.

In such a vision, I contend, music can be regarded first and foremost as a distinctive way of returning praise to God. Making music will involve respecting the physical integrities of sounds and their dynamic interrelatedness. It will mean taking seriously the rootedness of music in physical bodies, as well as the acute dangers of musical idolatry. There will be a resistance to any tendency to reduce evil to an appearance or subsume it smoothly into a harmonious whole, and yet, because of what has been "performed" in the crucifixion and resurrection, music can (potentially) be a way of sharing in God's renewal of a spoiled creation in anticipation of the world to come.

In addition, I have explored what happens when the traffic moves in the other direction, from music to theology (type (2) discussed previously).[47] While still oriented ultimately to the self-revealing God of Jesus Christ, and thus to the normative texts on which that orientation depends, I have sought to demonstrate that the making and hearing of music can yield striking conceptual and linguistic media for the theologian, forms of thought and discourse that go far beyond mere illustration or apologetic décor. One example I have returned to a number of times concerns the triunity of God.[48] Unlike three colors, which cannot be visible in the same space *as* three colors, sounds can be heard in and through each other while remaining perceptually distinct. Three notes will share and fill the same aural "space" yet can be heard *as* irreducibly different. I have suggested that a large part of the church's chronic tendency to treat the threeness of God as essentially problematic, little more than an intellectually embarrassing conundrum, has been fueled by an excessive reliance on visual conceptions of space, according to which the co-presence of irreducible threeness and oneness is a near impossibility. The hearing of a three-note chord facilitates an imagination of

Father, Son, and Spirit "in" and "through" one another that appears to be far more authentic to, for example, the "in-one-anotherness" of the divine life as testified in John's Gospel, and indeed to the principal lines of mainstream Trinitarian theology.

Debate and Agenda

Although it is hard to foresee how the expanding conversation between theologians and musicians will play out in the future, if present discussions are anything to go by, a number of key issues and questions are likely to be high on the scholarly agenda in the years to come.

First, there will likely be attention given to *clarifying theological norms*. Insofar as there are substantial disagreements in the current music-theology arena, these nearly always concern the major theological alignments that are being presumed, far more than issues surrounding music per se. The matter of theology's normative positioning, where it regards its ultimate responsibilities as lying, is often simply bypassed. This can lead to considerable confusion. So for example, a number of key terms regularly crop up in the literature – "transcendence," "immanence," "sacrament," "the sacred," "the spiritual," "beauty," "presence," "ineffability," "the infinite," and so forth – and it is often assumed that the basic import of these is widely agreed, and that different theological or religious traditions can simply provide their own appropriate "filling" as necessary, leaving the basic sense of the term in play wholly intact. But a modern Muslim's conception of, say, "transcendence" is likely to turn on radically different axes from those of, say, a biblically informed Christian; and it is not at all clear that music is equipped to penetrate beneath all such differences and reveal a commonly held understanding of transcendence on the basis of which theological discussion can proceed. Much the same could be said of the other terms discussed here. This is not to imply that there can be no fruitful discussion between different traditions or that these commonly used terms are to be dismissed as redundant, only to suggest that if the music-theology interaction is to advance fruitfully a greater degree of transparency will required about theology's primary or determinative cues.

This need becomes especially evident in the kind of music-theology conversation we highlighted as type (4): when music is appealed to in order to open up exchanges with those who find themselves increasingly suspicious of religious claims or conventional faith commitments but who nonetheless sense in musical experience a quasireligious aura or dimension. It may well be that for many the experience of music has unusual powers to destabilize a naturalistic, post-Enlightenment "immanent frame" (Taylor), to crack open the hard shell of contemporary secularism, and theologians would be foolish to turn their backs on such intuitions. But drawing upon musical experience in this way always carries the danger of adopting theological assumptions that, paradoxically, may turn out to be highly dissonant with the theological outlook being commended.[49]

Second, and related to the last issue, it is probable that *the relation of music to language* will be a prominent topic in future writing. A considerable literature in the psychology, philosophy, and anthropology of music has arisen on this theme over the last two decades, shedding fresh light on ancient debates. Despite the disagreements, a fairly wide consensus on a number of issues has developed. It seems that music and language probably share a distant ancestor in evolutionary history: a primeval, emotionally charged form of vocal expression ("musilanguage") from which there emerged what we would now call "music" and "language."[50] The primary purpose of this musilanguage, it would seem, was to generate social cohesion, interpersonal bonding. As Iain McGilchrist observes, it would have been far more like what we would now call music than referential language: it would have relied upon pitch, intonation, volume, rhythm, and phrasing but would not yet have used terms that designate or denote. In this sense at least, we can say that language as we know it today (with its immense denotative powers) grew out of music.[51] "If language began in music," then, "it began in … functions which are related to empathy and common life, not competition and division; promoting togetherness … 'betweenness.'"[52] Brain research suggests that even the most formal and strictly referential language depends and draws upon these embodied, communal, and empathetic dimensions of human life.[53] And in any case, a vast amount of the language that we use today is not of the naming, designative type; figurative language (e.g. metaphor) is one way in which we are reminded of the bodily and social roots of our linguistic powers.[54]

If these findings are along the right lines, the consequences for theologians at work in music (and vice versa) are considerable. It will mean eschewing common but erroneous distinctions between music and language, as well as the often-dubious theology that depends upon them. So, for example, we will avoid claiming that whereas music entails a bodily indwelling of the physical world that enables relations with others, the significance of language does not rely on any such indwelling because its core function is to name and describe, and typically in the interests of control and mastery. This kind of distinction might well lead us to imagine that music is more theologically privileged than language, in that it avoids the supposed cramping tyranny of words, the idolatrous desire to exhaustively describe and control God. There would seem to be a triple error here: (1) treating a highly specialized form of language (the designative assertion) as paradigmatic for truthful language use; (2) forgetting that both language and music rely on bodily engagement with the world's materiality, and that at the deepest level both are socially embedded and oriented; and (3) assuming that from a theologian's point of view, language is to be regarded as something to be escaped as far as possible, that it is inescapably distortive and manipulative, and essentially a human tool without any intrinsic or integral role in divine revelation. (Another line of argument moves in the opposite direction, this time in favor of language: it is said that only verbal, descriptive assertions can be "meaningful" and truth bearing, making music impotent with regard to matters of truth – including theological truth. This trades on the same paradigmatic view of language but deploys it to dismiss music as merely decorative or emotive.)

These matters at stake here are weighty and carry significant practical consequences for how we come to terms theologically with a nonverbal medium like music, for what we believe music might bring to theology, and – not least – for how we regard the role of music in the church's worship. Dialogue with those in other disciplines at work on the music–language relation is likely to yield much fruit, pressing theologians to honor the distinctive and irreducible capacities of both music and language but recognizing their common root in enabling bodily-social interaction. At the same time, theologians will need to do justice to the kind of primacy that language possesses in a text-based faith such as Christianity. If human speech-acts have been assumed directly into the communicative and reconciling activity of God (a basic assumption, it seems, of all the biblical authors), although this need not lead to a denigration of music, it will certainly set it in a quite distinctive perspective.

Third, even if recent years have seen a steady growth in theological studies of popular music,[55] a major, extended treatment of the field has yet to appear. Part of the problem is that the very category "popular" is highly fraught and contested; another is that popular music scholarship, though flourishing, has a relatively short history. A further difficulty is that the theoretical tools associated with conventional musicology have been developed not only with a radically different type of music in mind but with a different conception of what is entailed in hearing or listening to music: contrast the silent classical concert attender with the eighteen-year-old at a rock concert. A critically important agenda is opening up here for theologians, but its future shape is by no means clear.

Fresh Voices

Along with these issues, a larger set of questions is being raised with respect to the range of those participating in the music–theology discussions. What scholarship there has been in theology and music over the past hundred years has been undertaken very largely by White males, principally in European and North American academic institutions, and focused mostly on Western (European and North American) music. In recent years there are signs of a greater diversity of interlocutors, speaking from a wider variety of settings and addressing a broader range of musics. There is every likelihood this trend will continue as the centers of theological gravity worldwide shift, and the compass of themes addressed by theologians diversifies.

Heidi Epstein's feminist theology of music, *Melting the Venusberg*,[56] broke fresh ground in 2004 by drawing on major themes in feminist musicology to reconfigure the music–theology interface. She argues that by means of a gamut of musical conventions, composers stimulate, shape, and direct our desires, reinforcing (and often subverting) cultural norms of sexuality and gender construction in ways that challenge the practice of much Christian theology. Epstein mounts a stinging exposure of what she believes have been the baleful effects of masculinist rhetoric and assumptions in Western theologies of music – evident not only in modern and contemporary texts but in many of the classic readings of music to be found in the Western Christian tradition at large. In particular, Epstein is critical of a pernicious tendency to shun or suppress the embodied – and especially erotic – character of musical practices. Music, she insists, is ineluctably rooted in the physical body, engendered, and enmeshed in the dynamics of power. In contrast, the dominant metaphysical sensibility in most Western theologies of music has been one that constantly veers toward disembodied abstraction, with a fixation on a supposedly divinely given order (hierarchically conceived), linked to overharmonized teleologies of salvation that have little place for disruption and dissonance. Countering all this, and referencing women composers and performers from Hildegard of Bingen to Diamanda Galas, Epstein offers what she calls a "very modest, gender-sensitive rearticulation of music's theological import,"[57] appropriating in particular the concept of incarnation and aspects of the "imitation of Christ" tradition.

Given the pointedness of her critique, it is perhaps surprising that Epstein's book has received relatively little scholarly attention, either by musicians or theologians. Feminist musicology has poured forth a flood of writing, but little of it has so far engaged with theology at any depth. Another topic that has received only limited theo-musicological discussion is the way in which music functions with respect to race – for example, to confirm and subvert patterns of racial difference in the life and worship of churches. The literature so far is fairly sparse[58] but is likely to expand rapidly in light of the intense concern in contemporary theology with the dynamics of race.

Related to the repeated emphasis in current musicology on music as embodied practice, mention should be made of the swift growth over the last few decades of ethnomusicology (broadly, the anthropology of music). Questioning the narrow preoccupation of Western scholars with notated "works," and on sound patterns supposedly disengaged from material concerns, early ethnomusicologists focused attention almost exclusively on non-Western music ("world") music. But their perspectives and insights have come to be applied much more widely.[59] It was inevitable that ethnomusicology would come to deal with theological or religious matters, given the integral role that musical practices play in most of the faith traditions of the world.[60] Some of the most fruitful work in this regard has taken the form of studies in congregational music-making, in both Western and non-Western settings. Without assuming that the dynamics of theological belief can be explained wholly in terms of immanent forces, a steady current of scholarship, drawing not only on ethnomusicology but also media studies, psychology and religious studies, has shed a flood of light on how music in particular worship contexts can foment and shape a "lived theology."[61] This has considerable implications, not only for liturgical studies but for how the practices and beliefs of the church – including the way it does theology – are to be understood at the most fundamental levels.

Notes

1 George Steiner, *Errata: An Examined Life* (London: Faber and Faber, 1997), 65.

2 E.g. Jeremy S. Begbie, *Resounding Truth: Christian Wisdom in the World of Music* (Grand Rapids, MI: Baker Books, 2007).

3 E.g. Karol Berger, *Bach's Cycle, Mozart's Arrow: An Essay on the Origins of Musical Modernity* (Berkeley, CA: University of California Press, 2007); Andrew Shenton, *Messiaen the Theologian* (Farnham: Ashgate, 2010); Carol Harrison, *On Music, Sense, Affect, and Voice*

(New York: T&T Clark, 2019); Jonathan H. Harwell, and Katrina E. Jenkins, *Theology and Prince* (Lanham, MD: Fortress Academic, 2019).

4   E.g. James H. Cone, *The Spirituals and the Blues* (Maryknoll, NY: Orbis, 1998); Richard H. Bell, *Theology of Wagner's Ring Cycle* (Eugene, OR: Cascade, 2020); William Edgar, *Supreme Love: The Music of Jazz and the Hope of the Gospel* (Downers Grove, IL: IVP Academic, 2022).

5   E.g. Chiara Bertoglio, *Reforming Music: Music and the Religious Reformations of the Sixteenth Century* (Berlin: De Gruyter, 2018).

6   E.g. Steven R. Guthrie, "The Wisdom of Song," in *Resonant Witness: Essays in Theology and Music*, ed. Jeremy S. Begbie and Steven R. Guthrie (Grand Rapids, MI: Eerdmans, 2011), 382–407; Michael O'Connor, Hyun-Ah Kim Michael, and Christina Labriola, eds., *Music, Theology, and Justice* (Lanham, MD: Lexington Press, 2017); Monique Marie Ingalls and Amos Yong, eds., *The Spirit of Praise: Music and Worship in Global Pentecostal-Charismatic Christianity* (University Park, PA: Pennsylvania State University Press, 2015).

7   E.g. Jeremy S. Begbie, *Theology, Music and Time* (Cambridge: Cambridge University Press, 2000); Maeve Heaney, *Music as Theology: What Music Has to Say about the Word* (Eugene, OR: Wipf and Stock, 2012).

8   E.g. Jeremy Begbie, Daniel K. L. Chua, and Markus Rathey, eds. *Theology, Music, and Modernity: Struggles for Freedom* (Oxford: Oxford University Press, 2021); Chelle Stearns, *Handling Dissonance* (Eugene, OR: Pickwick, 2019).

9   See e.g. David Brown and Gavin Hopps, *The Extravagance of Music* (Basingstoke: Palgrave Macmillan, 2018); Kutter Callaway, *Scoring Transcendence: Film Music as Contemporary Religious Experience* (Waco, TX: Baylor University Press, 2013).

10 Karl Barth, *Wolfgang Amadeus Mozart,* trans. Clarence K. Pott (Grand Rapids, MI: Eerdmans, 1986), 16.

11 Karl Barth, *Church Dogmatics*, III/3, trans. and ed. G. W. Bromiley and T. F. Torrance (Edinburgh: T&T Clark, 1960), 298.

12 Barth, *Wolfgang Amadeus Mozart*, 23.

13 Barth, *Church Dogmatics*, III/3, 297–9.

14 Barth, *Church Dogmatics*, III/3, 349–50.

15 Barth, *Church Dogmatics*, III/3, 350.

16 Barth, *Church Dogmatics*, III/3, 296–7.

17 Barth, *Church Dogmatics*, III/3, 298–9; my italics.

18 Barth, *Church Dogmatics*, III/3, 298.

19 Barth, *Church Dogmatics*, III/3, 350.

20 Barth, *Church Dogmatics*, III/3, 298.

21 Barth, *Wolfgang Amadeus Mozart*, 37–8. Italics original.

22 Barth, *Church Dogmatics*, III/3, 298.

23 Barth, *Wolfgang Amadeus Mozart*, 47–8.

24 Karl Barth, *Church Dogmatics*, IV/3, trans. and ed. G. W. Bromiley and T. F. Torrance (Edinburgh: T&T Clark, 1961), §69.2.

25 David Moseley, "'Parables' and 'Polyphony': The Resonance of Music as Witness in the Theology of Karl Barth and Dietrich Bonhoeffer," in *Resonant Witness: Conversations between Music and Theology*, ed. Jeremy Begbie and Steven Guthrie (Grand Rapids, MI: Eerdmans, 2011), ch. 10.

26 For two fine treatments of Bonhoeffer on music, see Andreas Pangritz, *The Polyphony of Life: Bonhoeffer's Theology of Music*, ed. John W. de Gruchy and John Morris, trans. Robert Steiner (Eugene, OR: Cascade, 2019); Joanna C. Tarassenko, "A Musico-Pneumatology for Christian Formation: Dietrich Bonhoeffer's Polyphony of Life in the Spirit" (PhD diss., University of Cambridge, 2021).

27 Dietrich Bonhoeffer, *Letters and Papers from Prison*, Dietrich Bonhoeffer Works in English, Vol. 8. (Minneapolis, MN: Fortress Press, 2010), 332.

28 Bonhoeffer, *Letters and Papers*, 177.

29 Dietrich Bonhoeffer, *Ethics* (London: Macmillan, 1965), 179.

30 Bonhoeffer, *Letters and Papers*, 268.

31 Bonhoeffer, *Letters and Papers*, 305.

32 Bonhoeffer, *Letters and Papers*, 301.

33 Bonhoeffer, *Letters and Papers*, 306.

34 Bonhoeffer, *Letters and Papers*, 306.

35 Bonhoeffer, *Letters and Papers*, 394.

36 Bonhoeffer, *Letters and Papers*, 394.

37 Bonhoeffer, *Letters and Papers*, 394.

38 Bonhoeffer, *Letters and Papers*, 394.

39 Bonhoeffer, *Letters and Papers*, 397.

40 Bonhoeffer, *Letters and Papers*, 397.

41 Tarassenko, "A Musico-Pneumatology for Christian Formation."

42 David Brown and Gavin Hopps, *The Extravagance of Music* (Basingstoke: Palgrave Macmillan, 2018).

43 Brown and Hopps, *The Extravagance of Music*, 5–6.

44 Brown and Hopps, *The Extravagance of Music*, 27–8.

45 David Brown, *God and Grace of Body: Sacrament in Ordinary* (Oxford: Oxford University Press, 2007), 222.

46 For representative writings, see Jeremy S. Begbie, *Resounding Truth; Music, Modernity, and God: Essays in Listening* (Oxford: Oxford University Press, 2013); *A Peculiar Orthodoxy: Reflections on Theology and the Arts* (Grand Rapids, MI: Baker Academic, 2018).

47 See esp. Jeremy S. Begbie, *Theology, Music and Time* (Cambridge: Cambridge University Press, 2000).

48 See e.g. Jeremy S. Begbie, "'A Semblance More Lucid?' An Exploration of Trinitarian Space," in *Essays on the Trinity*, ed. Lincoln Harvey (Eugene, OR: Cascade, 2018), 20–35.

49 See Jeremy S. Begbie, *Redeeming Transcendence in the Arts: Bearing Witness to the Triune God* (Grand Rapids, MI: Eerdmans, 2018), ch. 1.

50 See e.g. Steven Brown, "The 'Musilanguage' Model of Music Evolution," in *The Origins of Music*, ed. Nils L. Wallin, Björn Merker, and Steven Brown (Cambridge,

MA: MIT Press, 2001); Ian Cross, "The Evolutionary Basis of Meaning in Music: Some Neurological and Neuroscientific Implications," in *The Neurology of Music*, ed. Frank Clifford Rose (London: Imperial College Press, 2010), 1–15; Iain Morley, *The Prehistory of Music: Evolutionary Origins and Archaeology of Human Musicality* (Oxford: Oxford University Press, 2013).

51 Iain McGilchrist, *The Master and His Emissary: The Divided Brain and the Making of the Western World* (New Haven, CT: Yale University Press, 2012), 102–3.

52 McGilchrist, *The Master*, 102–3

53 Ian Cross, "Music and Communication in Music Psychology," *Psychology of Music* 42 (2014): 814–15.

54 McGilchrist, *The Master*, 115–18. Cf. Rowan Williams, *The Edge of Words: God and the Habits of Language* (London: Bloomsbury Continuum, 2014), 27–8, and ch. 4.

55 See e.g. John S. McClure, *Mashup Religion: Pop Music and Theological Invention* (Waco, TX: Baylor University Press, 2011); Jeffrey F. Keuss, *Your Neighbor's Hymnal: What Popular Music Teaches Us about Faith, Hope, and Love* (Eugene, OR: Cascade, 2011); Clive Marsh and Vaughan Roberts, *Personal Jesus: How Popular Music Shapes Our Souls* (Grand Rapids, MI: Baker Academic, 2012); Mike Grimshaw, *The Counter-Narratives of Radical Theology and Popular Music: Songs of Fear and Trembling* (New York: Palgrave Macmillan, 2014); Gavin Hopps "Theology, Imagination and Popular Music," in *The Bloomsbury Handbook of Religion and Popular Music*, ed. Christopher Partridge and Marcus Moberg (London: Bloomsbury Academic, 2017), 77–89. For treatments of popular music favoring a more generalized vocabulary of "religion," representative examples include Georgina Gregory and Mike Dines, eds., *Exploring the Spiritual in Popular Music:*

Beatified Beats (London: Bloomsbury Academic, 2021); Scott D. Calhoun, ed., *U2 and the Religious Impulse: Take Me Higher* (London: Bloomsbury Academic, 2018).

56 Heidi Epstein, *Melting the Venusberg: A Feminist Theology of Music* (London: Continuum, 2004). See also her essay, "My Beloved Is a Bass Line: Musical, 'De-colonial' Interventions in *Song* Criticism and Sacred Erotic Discourse," *The Bible and Critical Theory* 13, no. 1 (2017): 54–83.

57 Epstein, *Melting the Venusberg*, ix.

58 Adam Gussow, *Whose Blues? Facing up to Race and the Future of the Music* (Chapel Hill, NC: University of North Carolina Press, 2020); Teresa L. Reed, *The Holy Profane: Religion in Black Popular Music* (Lexington, KY: University Press of Kentucky, 2003); Cory Hunter, "Thy Kingdom Come: Racial-Ethnic Oneness in African American Gospel Music," *The Musical Quarterly* 105, no. 1–2 (2022): 7–43.

59 See Timothy Rice, *Ethnomusicology: A Very Short Introduction* (Oxford: Oxford Uiversity Press, 2014).

60 See e.g. Jeffers Engelhardt and Philip V. Bohlman, *Resounding Transcendence: Transitions in Music, Ritual, and Religion* (New York: Oxford University Press, 2016); Philip V. Bohlman, Edith Waldvogel Blumhofer, and Maria M. Chow, eds. *Music in American Religious Experience* (New York: Oxford University Press, 2006).

61 E.g. Monique M. Ingalls, Carolyn Landau, and Tom Wagner, eds. *Christian Congregational Music: Performance, Identity and Experience* (Farnham: Ashgate, 2013); Ingalls, *Singing the Congregation: How Contemporary Worship Music Forms Evangelical Community* (New York: Oxford University Press, 2018).

Recommended Reading

Barth, Karl. *Church Dogmatics*, III/3. Translated and edited by G. W. Bromiley and T. F. Torrance. Edinburgh: T&T Clark, 1960.

———. *Wolfgang Amadeus Mozart*. Translated by Clarence K. Pott. Grand Rapids, MI: Eerdmans, 1986.

Begbie, Jeremy S. *Resounding Truth: Christian Wisdom in the World of Music*. Grand Rapids, MI: Baker Books, 2007.

———. *Theology, Music and Time*. Cambridge: Cambridge University Press, 2000.

Bertoglio, Chiara. *Reforming Music: Music and the Religious Reformations of the Sixteenth Century*. Berlin: De Gruyter, 2018.

Blackwell, Albert L. *The Sacred in Music*. Cambridge: Lutterworth Press, 1999.

Bonhoeffer, Dietrich. *Letters and Papers from Prison*. Dietrich Bonhoeffer Works in English, Vol. 8. Minneapolis, MN: Fortress Press, 2010.

Brown, David, and Gavin Hopps. *The Extravagance of Music*. Basingstoke: Palgrave Macmillan, 2018.

Epstein, Heidi, *Melting the Venusberg: A Feminist Theology of Music*. London: Continuum, 2004.

Harrison, Carol. *On Music, Sense, Affect, and Voice*. New York: T&T Clark, 2019.

Heaney, Maeve. *Music as Theology: What Music Has to Say about the Word*. Eugene, OR: Wipf and Stock, 2012.

O'Connor, Michael, Hyun-Ah Kim, and Christina Labriola, eds. *Music, Theology, and Justice*. Lanham, MD: Lexington Press, 2017.

Page, Christopher. *The Christian West and Its Singers: The First Thousand Years*. New Haven, CT: Yale University Press, 2010.

Pangritz, Andreas. *The Polyphony of Life: Bonhoeffer's Theology of Music*. Translated by Robert Steiner. Eugene, OR: Cascade, 2019.

Hawkey, James, Ben Quash, and Vernon White, eds. *God's Song and Music's Meanings: Theology, Liturgy, and Musicology in Dialogue*. London: Routledge, 2019.

Saliers, Don E. *Music and Theology*. Nashville, TN: Abingdon, 2007

Scruton, Roger. *The Soul of the World*. Princeton, NJ: Princeton University Press, 2014.

Stoltzfus, Philip E. *Theology as Performance: Music, Aesthetics, and God in Western Thought*. New York: T&T Clark, 2006.

Stone-Davis, Férdia, ed. *Music and Transcendence*. Farnham: Ashgate, 2015.

Theology and Literature

Kevin Hart

Introduction

The academic field of Theology and Literature is formally distinct from that of Bible and Literature, Religion and Literature, and Mysticism and Literature, although there are significant overlaps among them. It is also separate from "theological fiction," examples of which include Dante's *Divina Commedia* (ca. 1321), John Bunyan's *Pilgrim's Progress* (1678), Shusaku Endo's *Silence* (1966), and, more problematically, Geoffrey Hill's sonnet sequence "Lachrimæ" (1978). Theology and Literature sometimes considers theological fiction as its object, although it is also attentive to theological themes, especially covert ones, that run through other sorts of imaginative writing. The best approach to seeing what the field does is to begin by reflecting on the two nouns used to name it.

Roughly since the twelfth century, the word "theology," which was derived from Greek, has come to denote the λόγος of ὁ θεός, namely, reasoning about the God whom Jesus of Nazareth called "Father" and who revealed Jesus as his son. In the early church, the word "theology" was avoided – θεολογία denoted an archive of myths and was accordingly regarded as pagan through and through – and Christian thinkers preferred to think of themselves as engaging in their own version of φιλοσοφία. Their task was to bring their beliefs and acts into harmony and thereby guide themselves and others in what they called "the Way." With European modernity, the λόγος of ὁ θεός came to bespeak reflection on Christian religious thought and practices, some of which involve the reading (and liturgical performing) of scripture as well as the pondering of postbiblical sacred texts. Expressions such as "Jewish theology" and "Islamic theology" derive from Christian usage and inevitably contain tensions that need to be acknowledged.

By contrast, the Latinate word "literature" appears in the early fifteenth century. There is a progression from the Latin *littera* ("letter of the alphabet"), the plural of which, *litteræ*, denotes "written communication," to the English word "literature"; it goes by way of the Latin *litteratura* ("learning," including grammar and language use) and the Old French *letre* ("written character"). Only in the late eighteenth century does "literature" begin to name writing in the genres of poetry, narrative fiction, and the drama, an early instance being found in the first sentence of Samuel Johnson's "Life of Cowley" (1777), the first author considered

Ford's The Modern Theologians: An Introduction to Christian Theology since 1918, Fourth Edition.
Edited by Rachel Muers and Ashley Cocksworth.
© 2024 John Wiley & Sons Ltd. Published 2024 by John Wiley & Sons Ltd.

in his *The Lives of the Poets* (1779–81).[1] (It is worth noting that "literature" partly subsumes the older word "poetry," which goes back to the seventh-century Latin word *poetria* and which is taken to be the oldest literary genre.) No later than 1778, in his "Life of Waller," Johnson declared himself firmly against religious verse. "Contemplative piety, or the intercourse between God and the human soul, cannot be poetical. Man admitted to implore the mercy of his Creator, and plead the merits of his Redeemer, is already in a higher state than poetry can confer."[2] On reading Johnson's remark, three important things become apparent.

First, these two sentences might plausibly be taken to inaugurate the modern field of Theology and Literature in a gesture intended to close it down at the outset. Johnson admired the sublime in poetry, since it does not preclude invention, but he resisted poetry as prayer or as theology because no poet can or should invent anything concerning the relations of God and humanity. These relations are already authoritative in scripture, have been clarified by dogma, and far too much hangs on them for an individual's imagination to be involved. Second, "theology," as used in Theology and Literature, does not presume the involvement of a professional theologian. Many a literary critic becomes an amateur theologian when commenting on poetry, narrative fiction and the drama (or, these days, film and popular culture as well). In the same way, theologians sometimes become amateur literary critics when they turn to Theology and Literature. Third, appeals to the different modernities of "theology" and "literature" should not blind us to earlier partial formations of the field. To give just one example, St Basil of Caesarea (330–79) commended to the young men of his age that they read Greek λόγων – poetry, history, and philosophy – with all due care, for some of it could usefully aid them in acquiring virtue.[3] When λόγων is translated these days as "literature" we may reflect that the choice is as inevitable as it is anachronistic.

Survey

Background

By and large, then, Theology and Literature is announced with the advent of Romanticism, and although when it develops it readily extends its feelers back into history, it remains marked indelibly by affirmations of and reactions to Romantic writing. To be sure, seventeenth-century poetry comes to play a key role, and the feelers I have mentioned are sensitive to medieval poems, not to mention earlier hymns and psalms. Yet when these feelers touch medieval literature they tend not to cling very tightly: so much of the writing is religious that Theology and Literature has less reason to linger there than with other bodies of writing. Also, it must be said that literary-historical markers such as "Romanticism" are not always helpful or even able to bear much critical pressure. For as soon as one isolates a trait that seems to capture something distinctive about Romanticism, one is likely to think of a work that also features it in medieval or classical writing. The same holds true of other so-called literary periods. That said, it is in Queen Victoria's England that the modern academic field begins recognizably to form itself. It does so under the aegis of Protestantism, with little influence from the Catholic Literary Revival (1860–1960). Catholic influence was to come only later and mainly from theology, not literary criticism. A plausible starting-point to consider the birth of the academic field would be in the cultural criticism of Matthew Arnold (1822–88).

Arnold's principal concern in his writings on religion was to register discontent with the Bible as a firm base for theology. In several works of enduring significance – *Literature and Dogma* (1873) and *God and the Bible* (1875) being the most important of them – Arnold set himself against scripture scholars and theologians for whom biblical language could be read in a quasi-scientific manner. Not so: scripture is originally closer to what we call "literature" than theologians might like to think; its appeal is emotive, not factual. In retrospect, we can see the work as heralding what became known as "theological modernism." In a bold introduction to T. H. Ward's anthology *The English Poets* (1880), Arnold shifts his attention from the language of scripture to poetry itself. In this introduction, later called "The Study of Poetry," he insists that creed and dogma cannot withstand the recognition that scripture better presents emotion, not fact, and that scripture's supposed facts cannot all survive biblical criticism. He begins by quoting something he had written in 1879: "Poetry attaches its emotion to the idea; the idea is the fact. The strongest part of our religion today is its unconscious poetry." He then goes on to make a daring prediction: "most of what passes with us for religion and philosophy will be replaced by poetry."[4] In saying so, he leans heavily on Wordsworth. Sixty-two years later a nuanced version of the same theme will be struck by Wallace Stevens in one of the finest longer poems of his century, "Notes Towards a Supreme Fiction" (1942). The Supreme Being is to be replaced by a Supreme Fiction, which one knows full well to be a fiction. Theology and Literature begins, we might say, by placing a heavy accent on "literature" at the expense of "theology."

Before Arnold, though, we can find Stopford A. Brooke's lectures, delivered in 1872, and later gathered together in *Theology in the English Poets: Cowper, Coleridge, Wordsworth and Burns* (1874). It is worth noting that eight years after delivering his lectures, Brooke, who had always been latitudinarian, left the Church of England, finding himself unable to accept even its core dogmas. His liberal version of Christianity now revolved around "The Kingdom Within," as one of his pivotal sermons, delivered in 1901, was titled. The Kingdom, for him, has no eschatological aspect; it is just "the consciousness of a personal union between God and us."[5] A decade later he devoted himself to raising funds to purchase Dove Cottage so that Wordsworth's house might be a site that his admirers could visit. In his lectures Brooke announced, "The poets of England ever since Cowper have been more and more theological, till we reach men such as Tennyson and Browning, whose poetry is overcrowded with theology."[6] In his introduction Brooke observes that the lectures were an experiment, testing the hypothesis that if "God were in Christ" then all human life had been sanctified, and so there was "no subject which did not in the end run up into Theology" and which might not thereby become religious. The theology of the poets is not that of the church, however; it is not propositional but heartfelt. Independent creatures, poets free themselves from dogma; and to some extent the study of Romantic English poetry allows us to glimpse how religion must have been before the church formalized it in creeds and debated details of the nature of Christ and the Trinity. As Brooke makes clear at the outset, he will not restrict himself to particular poems, but will take the letters of the poets as well as their everyday talk into consideration.

The New Criticism and beyond

Looking outside the text for biographical and historicist cues to the meaning of a poem was frowned upon for the extended middle part of the twentieth century in which the New Criticism held sway. That critical movement slowly begins in the 1930s, with the publication of William Empson's *Seven Types of Ambiguity* (1930) and the anthology edited by Cleanth Brooks and Robert Penn Warren, *Understanding Poetry* (1938). Somewhat to the side of this movement is T. S. Eliot (1888–1965) whose signal essay "Religion and Literature" (1935) nonetheless influenced the New Criticism. Although Eliot was not himself a New Critic, his emphasis, like theirs, was on the poem itself, not literary biography or literary history, as the vehicle of literary greatness; and for him the best literature was the very means by which intellectual laziness and the increasing vulgarity of popular culture could be combatted. Eliot does not address himself to "religious literature" but rather to "the application of our religion to the criticism of any literature." He has no time for those, like Arnold, who in effect dissolve the scriptures into literature. The Bible "has had a *literary* influence upon English literature *not* because it has been considered as literature, but because it has been considered as the report of the Word of God." Great poetry seeks "to affect us wholly, as human beings," and not to consider the religious element of poetry would be to deny a vital part of that affect. All of modern literature, high as well as low, has been corrupted by secularism; and "the primacy of the supernatural over the natural life" needs to be affirmed. However, this does not mean that we should thereby extol religious poetry – Vaughan, Southwell, Crashaw – which tends to be "*minor* poetry." Eliot will go so far as to relegate that most beloved of English religious poets, George Herbert, to the status of a minor poet.[7] It is only in 1962 that he is redeemed as a major poet.[8] The distinction between minor and major poetry is of very limited use in literary criticism, and one may suspect that Eliot himself had doubts about regarding religious poetry as irredeemably minor. It is noteworthy that when he placed "Ash-Wednesday" in his *Collected Poems 1909–1935* (1936) it was not in the section titled "Minor Poems."

Eliot's immense prestige as poet and critic meant that his view of religious poetry as hopelessly minor because it responds to only one facet of human life became, if not a dogma of the New Criticism, then certainly a subsidiary doctrine that was adhered to in many lectures and tutorials. It fell to critics to see religious impulses in poetry, narrative prose, and drama as one element in complex characters or utterances, and not to prize poems, novels, or plays that isolated the religious as a theme. One response to this was to avoid the word "religious." In his *Poetry and the Sacred* (1968), Vincent Buckley (1925–88) prefers the word "sacred" because it countenances a wider range of poetry than the word "religious" does, and he reminds us time and again of difficulties encountered when specifying a poem as "sacred" or "religious." Buckley ranges from Wyatt to Eliot, admirably concerning himself with examples of particular poems. Unlike J. Hills Miller in *The Disappearance of God* (1963), a study of the effects of divine transcendence in nineteenth-century imaginative writing, Buckley speaks of the persistence of God in post-Romantic poetry. He discerns two distinguishable traditions, that of Whitman, Lawrence, Thomas, and Roethke, on the one hand, and that of Hopkins, Eliot, and Auden, on the other. The first group tends to see, sometimes uncritically, the whole of life as a hierophany, whereas the second seeks to discover the shape one's salvation might take.[9] Buckley eschews charting any movements from the sixteenth to the twentieth centuries. A version of that task was undertaken by Hoxie Neale Fairchild in his six-volume *Religious Trends in English Poetry* (1939–68). There we find him trying to correlate the "poetic element in religion" and "the religious element in poetry" from the eighteenth through to the twentieth centuries.[10] Like Eliot, Fairchild was Anglo-Catholic and, like him, had little tolerance for romantic religion, which he regarded as self-worship. Reading the two of them side by side we see that Theology and Literature shows itself perfectly capable of disliking the Romanticism out of which it was born.

Also ill at ease with the consensus of the New Criticism, Nathan A. Scott (1925–2006) pursues a path through religious literature other than that offered by the historical survey. For him, the New Criticism requires correction by way of recovering authorial beliefs. Perhaps "ultimate concerns" would suit Scott's vision better than "beliefs." For his guide is Paul Tillich (1886–1965) whose theology of culture tends to erase the boundary between the sacred and the secular. Criticism, Scott thinks, "is, at bottom, that of deciphering the given work at hand in such a way as to reveal the ultimate concern which it implies."[11] Accordingly, one finds God almost everywhere in literature, although not always the God of orthodox Christianity or Judaism. It is "the ineffable mystery of the Ground of Being" that interests Scott; and he finds it in narrative prose and drama – Samuel Beckett, Saul Bellow, Fydor Dostoyevsky, Graham Greene, Herman Melville, Flannery O'Connor – as well as in poetry.[12] Attention to this mystery is less to do with creedal beliefs than with "*an imagination* of what is radically significant." Eliot was skeptical that poets be regarded as thinkers. Scott agrees that there is seldom a system of beliefs in place in any poet's mind. He thinks, rather, that the poet holds his or her beliefs *per modum inclinationis*, by way of inclination, not *per modum cogitionis*, by way of thought.[13]

In its origins Theology and Literature was mainly a preserve of Christians, some liberal and others conservative; and its focus was more often on poetry than narrative fiction or the drama. Once established, however, the field has also been shaped by others, including a neopagan, an atheist, and a gnostic, as well as by Catholic theologians of the first water. It has also expanded to include works written by Buddhists, Jews, and others. Although poetry has been a major focus of the academic area, there have been rich contributions to prose fiction and the drama as largely opened by Tillich and Scott. Tom F. Driver (1925–2021) inaugurated the field of theater and theology, which has been deepened and refined by Larry D. Bouchard (b. 1952), especially in his *Theater and Integrity: Emptying Selves in Drama, Ethics and Religion* (2011). Prose fiction, most notably that of Flannery O'Connor (1925–64) and J. R. R. Tolkien (1892–1973), has been the topic of formative works by Ralph C. Wood (b. 1942).[14] In some ways, the novel has been the most "this-worldly" of all the genres of imaginative writing, yet this very fact has led some readers to look all the more hard at it.[15]

Named Thinkers

Martin Heidegger

Martin Heidegger (1889–1976) is not known for having a high regard for either Christian theology or literary criticism. Whereas his guiding concern was always with the ways in which being discloses itself, theology, he thought, had a regional aim: to talk of the highest being, God. And so it remains within the orbit of Western metaphysics. His view of things was entirely different: God is not a being at all. "You may wander through all beings," he writes, "nowhere does the trace of the god show itself."[16] Literary criticism also abides within the realm of aesthetics, which is a barely hidden branch of metaphysics.[17] It is only when Heidegger discusses German poetry, especially that of Hölderlin (1770–1843), that he speaks of the sacred, and he is led to do so because the poet's hymns fall outside metaphysics.[18] Where Eliot distrusted the idea of poets as thinkers, Heidegger regards Hölderlin as the most thoughtful of poets. This does not mean that the German poet, youthful friend of Hegel and Schelling, is taken to be an undercover philosopher, but that in his poetry he contemplatively encounters a non-metaphysical understanding of being, what Heidegger came to call *Seyn* ["beyng"], the older form of *Sein* ["being"], in the 1930s. "The poet," he says, "is the one who grounds beyng."[19] Heidegger mentions Greek drama (*Antigone*) but the genre of the novel does not seem to have interested him.

For Heidegger, Hölderlin's poetry [*Dichten*] is far more than a "cultural achievement"; it preserves the essence of poetry by rendering it poetic. The "essence" at issue here is not a timeless εἶδος, as though if one reads the German writer one also captures what animates Homer, Dante, Shakespeare, Pope, and Baudelaire. Rather, Hölderlin allows us to see what is essential to poetry that is written "in lean years" [*in dürftige Zeit*], viz., an historical essence, one that bespeaks a concrete time to come.[20] The lean time is the age when the Enlightenment is drawing to a close and when Romanticism is just beginning. Hölderlin takes himself to write in the period of God's default, when people no longer richly worship the Christian God (and accordingly the deity turns away from the world), and before the advent of the new gods. In this dark period, the poet stands between the gods and human beings, at once joining them in verse that underwrites the possibility of community while also separating them, because only the poet can discern the approach of the new divinities.

The very purest poem on the essence of poetry, Heidegger thinks, is the unfinished hymn "Wie wenn am Feiertage ..." (1800). Here Hölderlin extolls "Die mächtige, die göttlichschöne Natur" [that which is "God-like in power and beauty, Nature"], and, in a paper first read in 1939, he asks himself what Nature, which he assimilates to the Greek notion of φύσις, truly is and how it originates.[21] Taking a clue from Hölderlin's meditation on Pindar, Heidegger observes that Nature is "the all-mediating mediatedness," and that this is the law all creatures must obey. However, Nature herself is begotten "aus heiligem Chaos" ["of holy Chaos"]; she comes from that which is anterior to all law. Hence Heidegger affirms, "What is always former is the holy [*Heilige*]" (or, as he sometimes prefers to say, "beyng"). Hölderlin's poetry bears witness to the holy, which is why the poet considers the writing of verse to be at once harmless and terrible: it is a simple game, though one that allows beings to manifest themselves, and it has the potential to make a poet lose his selfhood and live in madness after encountering the holy. This self-manifestation of beings is not straightforward, however, for there is no unveiling without a veiling. So when a being is uncovered in a poem, the mystery of beyng is also disclosed *as mystery*. Truth and mystery belong together.

It is in two lines of "Wie wenn am Feiertage ..." that Hölderlin specifies what has become a salient claim in the field of Theology and Literature: "Jetzt aber tagts! Ich harrt und sah es kommen, / Und was ich sah, das Heilige sei mein Wort" ["But now day breaks! I waited and saw it come, / And what I saw, the hallowed, my word shall convey"]. What is witnessed here is the moment before dawn when the sun's rays shine over the horizon. The light that precedes the sunrise is the holy or, if we follow Heidegger's phrasing, the holy is anterior to any divinity. So poetry discloses the holy. We might add that, for Heidegger, only *some* poetry has this property: Hölderlin's above all but also particular lyrics by Stefan George, Georg Trakl, and Rilke's *Duineser Elegien* (1923). Perhaps Heidegger would have included, among his contemporaries, René Char (1907–88) and Paul Celan (1920–70). It is an open question how extensively English-language theology and literary criticism can draw on Heidegger's insights when discussing poetry, let alone prose narrative and the drama. Would Wordsworth's *The Prelude* or G. M. Hopkins's sonnets respond well to this treatment? Would Eliot's play *Murder in the Cathedral* (1935) or Marilynne Robinson's novel *Gilead* (2004)?

Maurice Blanchot

It is in his Bremen lectures of 1949 that Heidegger begins to speak of the "Fourfold" [*Geviert*], the interplay of earth, sky, divinities, and mortals; and we might well diagnose an attraction to neopaganism in his later writings, including those on poetry.[22] If we turn to Maurice Blanchot (1907–2003), who plainly learned a great deal from Heidegger, we find neither Christianity nor neopaganism involved in his approach to literature. Instead, he writes from a settled conviction of the truth of atheism. Nevertheless, he too finds literature drawing from a sense of the sacred. Blanchot engages Heidegger's reading of Hölderlin's hymn "Wie wenn am Feiertage ..." in *La Part du feu* (1949). There he pushes Heidegger's exegesis of Hölderlin a little further than the German thinker does: "the Sacred is speech and speech is sacred," he writes. "But how can that be? How can the Sacred, which is 'unexpressed,' 'unknown,' which is what opens provided only that it is not discovered, which reveals because unrevealed – how can it fall into speech, let itself be alienated into becoming, itself pure interiority, the exteriority of song?" The answer is expected: "In truth, that cannot really be, that is the impossible." Then comes a twist that is completely unexpected: "And the poet is nothing but the existence of this impossibility, just as the language of the poem is nothing but the retention, the transmission of its own impossibility."[23] That is, in uttering a poem a poet sacrifices himself, loses his "I," only to become a "he," "she," or "it."

The theme is continued and deepened in *L'Espace littéraire* (1955), this time more generally, and is introduced by posing the question, "Why is art so intimately allied with the sacred?" The answer is to be found in understanding the relation of art and the sacred, as one of manifestation and that which does not manifest itself. This is not a constant relation, for each of art and the sacred both reveals and reveils itself. This endless double movement supplies the artwork with "the profound *reserve* which it needs."[24] In other words, without the divine, the artwork as we have known it would struggle to survive. For all that, in our time, in which Blanchot thinks we have no sense of the divine whatsoever, not even a regret for its absence, art must find another way of coming into being. That way is through "the experience of its origin," which he takes to be the encounter with what he calls the Outside or Neutral.[25] We begin to experience the approach of the Outside when we become aware of how being continually passes into image and back again. As soon as a phenomenon appears, it can become an image of itself: not the striking visual images promoted by modernists such as Ezra Pound (1885–1972), T. S. Eliot, and William Carlos Williams (1883–1963) but rather "a vague and vacant outside, a neutral existence, nil and limitless."[26] We become fascinated by the sheer otherness of the imaginary; we find ourselves passing from a supposedly secure sense of being to a non-world of nothingness and are quite unable to free ourselves from its dark gaze. Only when we can break with this grip of fascination can we snap back into the world about ourselves only for it to begin again, perhaps in another way. What Blanchot takes to be the exemplary literature of our times – Samuel Beckett, René Char, and Franz Kafka – answers to this approach of the Outside. It is a ghost of the sacred.

Karl Rahner

Running parallel in time to the neopagan and atheist contributions to Theology and Literature, and perhaps unintentionally running against them, is an essay by the eminent Catholic theologian Karl Rahner (1904–84). "Poetry and the Christian" appeared in the fourth volume of his *Schriften zur Theologie* (1967). It is not an attempt, as most other work in the area has been, to find theology secreted in literature but rather an investigation into how poetry can make the Christian more faithful to his or her calling. Rahner begins by pointing out "that the starting point is a *theological* one"; indeed, it is "theological reflection on man as he should be if he wishes to be a Christian."[27] The believer knows that Christianity is the religion of the proclaimed word and that scripture has a special relationship with the poetic word. However, divine grace does not wait for the proclamation of the gospel; it comes to prepare the heart for the Word of God, and so we may think of God anticipating the gospel in the human culture that precedes it (and, we might add, succeeds it). There are four prerequisites, Rahner thinks, for being able to hear the gospel and each one is associated with poetry.

First, one must be open to the Word of God that contains "the silent mystery." Now "mystery" usually denotes a property of divine love, both the Trinitarian life of God and the divine motivation for creation and atonement; it also alerts one to the divine permission that evil be allowed; and finally it points to the theological virtues of faith, hope, and charity. When Rahner uses the word "mystery," though, he has principally in mind the incomprehensibility of the transcendent deity. Each word points to this mystery and the thoughtful reading of poetry enables us to be open to it. "The word puts individual things in order, and so always points to a fundamental background order which cannot itself be ordered but remains the perpetual a priori antecedent to all order."[28] This is quite different from the non-theological use of "mystery" in literature, which Blanchot, for example, discusses with respect to Jean Paulhan's *Entretien sur des faits-divers* (1930, augmented in 1945). When we say "A penny is a penny" we utter an irrefutable expression. But there is a "silent double" that accompanies the remark: "A penny is a lot more than a penny." The second meaning "is not expressed, and it comes to distort the logical exactness of the first meaning by forcing one to infer (without saying it) that a penny is not at all a penny."[29] Such is mystery in literature. Rahner does not say that literary mystery educates us to hear theological mystery. Instead, he affirms that the reading of poetry will lead us to respond more deeply to scripture and to the rich silence beyond words.

Second, the reading of poetry teaches us to hear words that touch the heart, not just the intellect. When reading poetry, the whole person, body and soul, is engaged; and this is essential preparation for hearing the gospel which addresses us in the same way. The divine mystery is not merely an intellectual abstraction; it comes to us in "the 'striking' word" such as we find when reading great poetry.[30] Third, reading poetry prepares us to hear the word that unites. Not all words do this; many are mere chatter. The poet chooses words, however, that overcome our isolation: "they speak of *one* death and we taste the death of all."[31] Without being trained to hear this common experience, we cannot adequately receive the gospel. And fourth, reading poetry encourages us to recognize inexpressible mystery *in* the word: not simply a mystery beyond the world but one that is actually incarnate in flesh and blood. "In every word, the gracious incarnation of God's own abiding Word and so of God himself can take place, and all true hearers of the word are listening to the utmost depths of every word to know if it becomes suddenly the word of eternal love by the very fact that it expresses man and his world."[32] God confronts us not from beyond the stars but on the same earth on which we all stand. Indeed, "great poetry only exists where man radically faces what he is"; and in acknowledging "guilt, perversity, hatred of self and diabolical pride," Rahner thinks, one becomes more ready to encounter God in the world, the God who can save us from all that drags us down to the grave.[33]

Hans Urs von Balthasar

Rahner's contemporary, the equally august Catholic theologian Hans Urs von Balthasar (1905–88), is more fully concerned with poetry. His orientation leads him to see the interaction of beauty and grace as it variously manifests itself in theologians and artists alike. That the transcendentals "being" and "one" are convertible was argued by Boethius (d. 524), who also maintained the convertibility of "being" and "good"; and Thomas Aquinas (1225–74) adds that "true" and "being" are also convertible.[34] Aquinas seems to countenance "beauty" as a possible transcendental in his commentary on Pseudo-Dionysius's *The Divine Names* 4.5 and also in the *Summa theologiæ* 1a q. 39 art. 8, although in 1a q. 5 art. 4 ad 1 he gives a reason why that cannot be the case. Modern Thomists, especially Étienne Gilson (1884–1978) and Jacques Maritain (1882–1973), have regarded beauty as a transcendental, but it is Balthasar who is most noted for insisting that everything said in theology about divine unity, being and truth can be restated with reference to divine beauty. To do so is to present a "theological aesthetics," which is the burden of his seven-volume *Herrlichkeit* (1961–7). This project is at the antipodes of an "aesthetic theology," which would be a Romantic venture, one that would fit beauty to the terms of humanistic canons. Of particular interest to scholars in the field of Theology and Literature is the volume translated into English as *Studies in Theological Style: Lay Studies* (1986), which deals with Dante, St John of the Cross, Pascal, Hamann, Soloviev, Hopkins, and Péguy. His long reflection on G. M. Hopkins exemplifies his approach.

Balthasar sharply sees what is central to Hopkins's vision. He states it in two phases. First, he sets in conjunction the sestet of Hopkins's sonnet "As kingfishers catch fire, dragonflies draw flame" (1877) and a brief passage from Hopkins's reflections on the *Spiritual Exercises* (1881–2). The poem ends with the beautiful evocation, "For Christ plays in ten thousand places, / Lovely in limbs, and lovely in eyes not his / To the Father through the features of men's faces." And in the later commentary on the *Exercises*, he reflects on grace, pointing out that "so far as it is looked at *in esse quieto* it is Christ in his member on the one side, his member in Christ on the other. It is as a man said: That is Christ playing at me and me playing at Christ, only that it is no play but truth; That is Christ *being me* and me being Christ."[35] Balthasar observes, "This then is the theological center from which we can develop the laws of Hopkins' aesthetics." He draws out what is at issue: "The principle lies in the fact that all truth is grounded in Christ ('Christ is truth') and that all beauty belongs to him, is related to him, is yielded to him in the 'great sacrifice' and must rest with him ('give beauty back, beauty, beauty, beauty, back to God, beauty's self and beauty's giver')."[36] The "great sacrifice" is of course the Son's self-emptying in the act of incarnation, which is consummated on the cross.

"The great sacrifice" is returned to a few pages later when Balthasar considers Hopkins' poetic language. The Romantics were right, he thinks, to affirm the need for a communion between themselves and the spirit of nature. But Christianity pitches things higher. The believer "must raise himself to this in his faith, in the great sacrifice; his enthusiasm may have no other source than does his faith. It is of this exaltation as the whole man's engagement and effort that the poetic form must speak." Then Balthasar makes a trenchant point: "Hopkins' language is a theological phenomenon and can be understood only in this way."[37] In other words, aesthetics or poetics can go only so far in dealing justly with the language of "The Wreck of the Deutschland" (1876) or the great sonnets of 1877; we gain insight into the poems only when we acknowledge that the vivid metaphors, the sprung rhythm, the inscape and instress, are properly theological, "able to express in a plausible and fine way the unique and the extraordinary, even if not everyone will go along with it at first."[38] This is expression, not self-expression; and what is ultimately uttered, Balthasar wishes to say, is "the inextricable linkage of Christ and Mary."[39] Once again, it is a matter of seeing the deep unity of the divine and the human sides of life, of grace being offered and grace being received in all humility. To grasp this requires, as Hopkins recognizes, seeing contemplatively, *in esse quieto*; only then can one approach "the mystery of Christ" which penetrates "all the levels of being from flesh to spirit and beyond into the abyss of the Trinity."[40]

Debate, Achievement, and Agenda

Although Harold Bloom (1930–2019) largely confined his attention to the Western canon of literature, he severely questioned many of the assumptions that other literary critics had made regarding it and, in principle, expanded the field of Theology and Literature. He approached the canon from the viewpoint of a Jewish Gnostic. Jewish Kabbalah, for him, offers "a *vision of belatedness*," and Gnosticism gives us "a theory of misprision," the two things being cornerstones of his theory of literary influence.[41] His *Ruin the Sacred Truths: Poetry and Belief from the Bible to the Present* (1989) runs from the Hebrew Bible to Milton and then to Kafka and Beckett, all the while challenging orthodoxies of the academic field under consideration. The importance of Jewish authors, including Sigmund Freud (1856–1939), is asterisked throughout. Early in the book, Bloom distances himself from the popular "secularization thesis" – the view that adherence to Enlightenment norms, apparent in much modern literature, has diminished the roles of religious beliefs – which has animated much work in the field. He observes, "I myself do not believe that secularization is itself a literary process. The scandal is the stubborn resistance of imaginative literature to the categories of sacred and secular." Then he states the main thesis of his study: "If you wish, you can insist that all high literature is secular, or, should you desire it so, then all strong poetry is sacred. What I find incoherent is the judgment that some authentic literary art is more sacred or more secular than some other."[42] His concern, then, is with the status of critical judgments about works, and this goes to the heart of much work in the field of Theology and Literature. Certainly Bloom, like Johnson, has little time for devotional poetry: neither George Herbert nor G. M. Hopkins stands high in his canon. And plainly he has no sympathy with T. S. Eliot's distaste for reading the Bible as literature.[43]

Bloom's principal interest is in negativity in literature. A ready awareness of Christian apophatic theology has been in evidence in much work in Theology and Literature.[44] Bloom, however, prefers Jewish and Gnostic models of negativity. His exemplary contrast is between Hegel's view of negation, which "culminates European rationalism and aggressively sets that rationalism against British empiricism, with its contempt for universals," and Freud's *Verneinung*, which is "dualistic, mingling ambivalently a purely cognitive return of the repressed and a continuation of the repression of all affect, of the flight away from forbidden and yet desired images and memories." Where Hegelian negativity is an idealization, Bloom thinks, Freud's always "reenacts the ambiguities of the Second Commandment."[45] Not that Freudian negativity covers the entire field of literature. "Kafka's negative, unlike Freud's, is uneasily and remotely descended from the ancient tradition of negative theology, and perhaps even comes from that most negative of ancient theologies, Gnosticism."[46] A strong literary critic, for Bloom, must formulate and prosecute a radical negativity as a reader.

Attention to apophatic theology in Theology and Literature has mostly been motivated by epistemic concerns. However, apophaticism is less concerned with knowledge than with love. One passes to God in the darkness of ἀγάπη, even if this mode of love is highly eroticized, as it is in the writings of many Christian mystics, above all those influenced by the Canticle. One must be careful using the word "mysticism," which since the late nineteenth and early twentieth centuries has tended to prize psychological categories when considering intimate human relations with God. There is reason to prefer the older word, *contemplatio*, which not only denotes how the soul moves when hovering before God – in straight lines, circles, and spirals, as Pseudo-Dionysius the Areopagite writes[47] – but also indicates how many poems are written and read. For poets do not usually write by way of propositions or even argue a case in poems, but rather proceed by way of entertaining ideas, considering aspects of them, developing them in one or another direction, and then circling back to rethink them in another way. W. B. Yeats is relevant here: "The purpose of rhythm," he writes, "is to prolong the moment of contemplation, the moment when we are both asleep and awake, which is the one moment of creation, by hushing us with an alluring monotony, while it holds us waking by variety."[48] Readers of poems often brood on poems in a similar manner. We do not always follow the hermeneutic of suspicion, in which we seek meanings hidden far beneath the surface of the text. We do not always hunt for marginal signs that reveal hidden power structures and that, if not addressed, will diminish our lives. Instead, we sometimes read by passing from part to part, from part to whole, and often back again; we trace modalizations of belief or commitment as they occur; we dwell on gaps in perception or argument or evaluation; and we tend to look at what is before us, not through it. We expose ourselves to mysteries, in either the literary or theological sense of the word, and sometimes we are granted *dilatio mentis*, the expansion of the mind, such as Richard of St Victor talks about in his treatise on contemplation, *On the Ark of Moses* (composed by 1162). Theology and Literature can be reimagined by way of a spacious, contemplative reading practice, one that is based on understanding, not interpretation narrowly defined.[49]

Debates in Theology and Literature are characterized, as already noted, by whether the field is best served by attending to theological dramas, narratives, or poems or by reading other texts and uncovering hitherto unnoticed theological motifs. Heat has been generated by the question of whether scripture can itself be read as literature. In its formative years, the field focused largely on poetry, partly because of the field's Romantic heritage and partly because the novel is more concerned with the everyday. But that has changed: scholars have examined both the drama and the novel, theological narratives as well as others that would seem not to fit with the interests of the field. Once wholly Christian in its range of concerns and texts, Theology and Literature has expanded to include a wide range of unorthodox religious positions, as well as a wonderful range of Jewish texts and hermeneutical approaches. Now the field is being opened further in order to include adventurous comparative work in theology. Francis X. Clooney's *His Hiding Place Is Darkness: A Hindu-Catholic Theopoetics of Divine Absence* (2014) is exemplary in this regard, and it is very likely that others will find their own religious and literary comparisons and contrasts. Fifty years ago, Theology and Literature was a minor branch of literary studies. Increasing distrust in the secularization thesis, along with major authors in both theology attending to literature and literary critics taking religious and theological issues with all due seriousness, have meant that the field is slowly being absorbed into the mainstream of critical thought in both Theology and Literary Criticism.

Notes

1 Samuel Johnson, *The Lives of the Poets*, 3 vols., ed. John H. Middendorf, *The Yale Edition of the Works of Samuel Johnson*, XXI (New Haven, CT: Yale University Press, 2010), Vols. 1, 5.

2 Johnson, *The Lives of the Poets*, Vol. 1, 314.

3 See N. G. Wilson, ed., *Saint Basil on the Value of Greek Literature* (London: Duckworth, 1975).

4 Matthew Arnold, "The Study of Poetry," in *Essays in Criticism: Second Series* (London: Macmillan, 1905), 1–56. The title of the essay was used only when the introduction was included in this volume.

5 Stopford A. Brooke, "The Kingdom Within," in *Liberal Religious Thought at the Beginning of the Twentieth Century*, ed. W. Copeland Bowie (London: Philip Green, 1901), 305.

6 Brooke, *Theology in the English Poets: Cowper, Coleridge, Wordsworth and Burns* (1874; rpt. New York: AMS Press, 1970).

7 Iman Javadi, Ronald Schuchard, and Jayme Stayer, ed., "Religion and Literature," *The Complete Prose of T. S. Eliot: The Critical Edition. Vol. 5: Tradition and Orthodoxy, 1934–1939* (London: Faber and Faber, 2021), 218, 219, 225, 220.

8 See Eliot, "George Herbert," in *The Complete Prose of T. S. Eliot*, Vol. 8, 498–528.

9 See Vincent Buckley, *Poetry and the Sacred* (London: Chatto and Windus, 1968), ch. 3.

10 Hoxie Neale Fairchild, *Religious Trends in English Poetry. Vol. 1: 1700–1740, Protestantism and the Cult of*

Sentiment (New York: Columbia University Press, 1939), vii.

11 Nathan A. Scott, Jr., *Negative Capability: Studies in the New Literature and the Religious Situation* (New Haven, CT: Yale University Press, 1969), 133.

12 Scott, *Negative Capability,* 107.

13 Scott, *Negative Capability,* 129.

14 See, in particular, Ralph C. Wood, *Flannery O'Connor and the Christ-Haunted South* (Grand Rapids, MI: Eerdmans, 2004) and *The Gospel According to Tolkien: Visions of the Kingdom in Middle-Earth* (Notre Dame, IN: University of Notre Dame Press, 2003).

15 See, for example, Richard Rosengarten, *Henry Fielding and the Narration of Providence: Divine Design and the Incursions of Evil* (New York: Palgrave Macmillan, 2000) and J. Russell Perkin, *Theology and the Victorian Novel* (Montréal: McGill's-Queen University Press, 2009).

16 Martin Heidegger, *The History of Beyng,* trans. William McNeill and Jeffrey Powell (Bloomington, IN: Indiana University Press, 2015), 52.

17 See Heidegger, *Hölderlin's Hymn "The Ister,"* trans. William McNeill and Julia Davis (Bloomington, IN: Indiana University Press, 1996),

18 See Heidegger, *Hölderlin's Hymn "The Ister,"* 18.

19 Heidegger, *Hölderlin's Hymns "Germania" and "The Rhine,"* trans. William McNeill and Julia Ireland (Bloomington, IN: Indiana University Press, 2014), 31.

20 The quotation is from Hölderlin, "Brot und Wein," section 7. See Friedrich Hölderlin, *Poems and Fragments,* trans. Michael Hamburger (London: Anvil Press, 1994), 271. All translations from Hölderlin are taken from this volume.

21 See Hölderlin, *Poems and Fragments,* 395, and Heidegger, "As When on a Holiday ...," *Elucidations of Hölderlin's Poetry,* trans. Keith Hoeller (Amherst, NY: Humanity Books, 2000), 83–5.

22 See Heidegger, "The Thing," in *Bremen and Freiburg Lectures: Insight into that Which Is and Basic Principles of Thinking,* trans. Andrew J. Mitchell (Bloomington, IN: Indiana University Press, 2012), 5–22.

23 Maurice Blanchot, "The 'Sacred' Speech of Hölderlin," in *The Work of Fire,* trans. Charlotte Mandell (Stanford, CA: Stanford University Press, 1995), 126. Also see "The Great Refusal," in *The Infinite Conversation,* trans. Susan Hanson (Minneapolis, MN: University of Minnesota Press, 1993), 39–40. For more detail, see Kevin Hart, *The Dark Gaze: Maurice Blanchot and the Sacred* (Chicago, IL: Chicago University Press, 2004) and *Maurice Blanchot on Poetry and Narrative: Ethics of the Image* (London: Bloomsbury, 2023).

24 Blanchot, *The Space of Literature,* trans. Ann Smock (Lincoln, NE: University of Nebraska Press, 1982), 233.

25 Blanchot, *The Space of Literature,* 233, 241.

26 Blanchot, *The Space of Literature,* 243.

27 Karl Rahner, "Poetry and the Christian," in *Theological Investigations, IV: More Recent Writings,* trans. Kevin Smyth (London: Darton, Longman & Todd, 1974), 357.

28 Rahner, "Poetry and the Christian," 359.

29 Blanchot, "Mystery in Literature," *The Work of Fire,* 57.

30 Rahner, "Poetry and the Christian," 360.

31 Rahner, "Poetry and the Christian," 361.

32 Rahner, "Poetry and the Christian," 362.

33 Rahner, "Poetry and the Christian," 365.

34 See Aquinas, *Summa theologiæ,* 1a q. 16 art. 3. Also see his *An Exposition of the "On the Hebdomads" of Boethius,* trans. Janice L. Schultz and Edward A. Synan (Washington, DC: Catholic University of America Press, 2001).

35 Hans Urs von Balthasar, *The Glory of the Lord: A Theological Aesthetics. Vol. III: Studies in Theological Style: Lay Styles,* trans. Andrew Louth et al. (San Francisco, CA: Ignatius Press, 1986), 385.

36 Balthasar, *The Glory of the Lord,* III, 385–6.

37 Balthasar, *The Glory of the Lord,* III, 392.

38 Balthasar, *The Glory of the Lord,* III, 392.

39 Balthasar, *The Glory of the Lord,* III, 390.

40 Balthasar, *The Glory of the Lord,* III, 394.

41 Harold Bloom, *Kabbalah and Criticism* (New York: Continuum, 1984), 17, 62.

42 Harold Bloom, *Ruin the Sacred Truths: Poetry and Belief from the Bible to the Present* (Cambridge, MA: Harvard University Press, 1989), 4.

43 See Harold Bloom, *The Shadow of a Great Rock: A Literary Appreciation of the King James Bible* (New Haven, CT: Yale University Press, 2011), 22.

44 See, for example, William Franke, *On What Cannot Be Said: Apophatic Discourses in Philosophy, Religion, Literature, and the Arts,* 2 vols. (Notre Dame, IN: University of Notre Dame Press, 2007).

45 Bloom, *Ruin the Sacred Truths,* 150–1.

46 Bloom, *Ruin the Sacred Truths,* 181.

47 See Pseudo-Dionysius the Areopagite, *The Divine Names,* 4.9, in *The Divine Names and Mystical Theology,* trans. and intro. John D. Jones (Milwaukee, WI: Marquette University Press, 1980).

48 W. B. Yeats, "The Symbolism of Poetry," in *Early Essays,* The Collected Works of W. B. Yeats, Vol. 4, ed. George Bornstein and Richard J. Finneran, (New York: Scribner, 2007), 117.

49 See Kevin Hart, *Lands of Likeness: For a Poetics of Contemplation* (Chicago, IL: University of Chicago Press, 2023).

Recommended Reading

Primary

Balthasar, Hans Urs von. *The Glory of the Lord: A Theological Aesthetics. Vol. III: Studies in Theological Style: Lay Styles.* Translated by Andrew Louth et al. San Francisco, CA: Ignatius Press, 1986.

Bloom, Harold. *Ruin the Sacred Truths: Poetry and Belief from the Bible to the Present.* Cambridge, MA: Harvard University Press, 1989.

Javadi, Iman et al., eds. "Religion and Literature." In *The Complete Prose of T. S. Eliot: The Critical Edition. Vol. 5: Tradition and Orthodoxy, 1934–1939,* 218–29. London: Faber and Faber, 2021.

Heidegger, Martin. *Elucidations of Hölderlin's Poetry.* Translated by Keith Hoeller. Amherst, NY: Humanity Books, 2000.

Rahner, Karl. "Poetry and the Christian." In *Theological Investigations. IV: More Recent Writings,* 357–67. Translated by Kevin Smyth. London: Darton, Longman & Todd, 1974.

Secondary

Bouchard, Larry D. *Theater and Integrity: Emptying Selves in Drama, Ethics and Religion.* Evanston, IL: Northwestern University Press, 2011.

Buckley, Vincent. *Poetry and the Sacred.* London: Chatto and Windus, 1968.

Hart, Kevin. *Lands of Likeness: For a Poetics of Contemplation.* Chicago, IL: Chicago University Press, 2023.

Scott, Nathan A., Jr. *Negative Capability: Studies in the New Literature and the Religious Situation.* New Haven, CT: Yale University Press, 1969.

Wood, Ralph C. *The Gospel According to Tolkien: Visions of the Kingdom in Middle-Earth.* Notre Dame, IN: University of Notre Dame Press, 2003.

Theology and Popular Culture

Clive Marsh

Introduction

The exploration of theology and popular culture is a particular way of recognizing the contextual nature of all theology. Theology always emerges from a context and is constructed for, and directed into, a particular context as it tries to speak of God, whose reality is both within and beyond the specifics of local circumstances. The main challenge brought by popular culture is to ensure that God-talk relates to the ordinary, the everyday, the local, the accessible in any given context, lest theology's content be controlled by the culture and cultures of the few (e.g. religious leaders, privileged upper-class aesthetes, or wealthy controllers of media channels).

Theology is, of course, already embedded in or articulated in and through popular culture, for only in this way can words from and about God be made readily available in daily life. Forms of popular culture therefore already are, or can be, theology. Even if, realistically, much popular culture is neither explicitly or implicitly theological, and is not trying to be, at least in the global North-West, theology's interweaving with popular culture is vital for its accessibility and comprehensibility. The need for this chapter, however, highlights the fact that theology is not usually popular, popular culture is often not anything to do with religion or theology, and society has increasingly taken multiple different secular forms. The chapter's presence shows too that there is work to be done in the exploration of what "everyday culture" is doing, how faith takes shape and God-talk happens, and what theology as a discipline might make of all of this. What people do *with* popular culture requires careful examination.

Survey

"Theology and popular culture" in the primary sense intended in this chapter has a specifically modern history. Taking as its lead the growth of mass communication, the development of new forms of popular art and entertainment (especially radio, film, television, recorded music, video games), the existence of

Ford's The Modern Theologians: An Introduction to Christian Theology since 1918, Fourth Edition.
Edited by Rachel Muers and Ashley Cocksworth.
© 2024 John Wiley & Sons Ltd. Published 2024 by John Wiley & Sons Ltd.

multiple new forms of popular art, pastimes, means of communication and diverting activities, popular culture has, since the early twentieth century, and then rapidly so from the second half of the century onwards, expanded the range of what is available for theology's content to interweave with and be informed by. If theatre (passion and mystery plays), public art (church murals, altar pieces, sculptures), and literature (poetry and stories passed on in oral form) may always have dovetailed with theology's ways of working, then new forms of artistic expression, worked out in increasingly secularized Western societies, both presented theology with a new challenge and provided opportunities for fresh thinking and innovative engagement. Should theology resist the influence of such culture, work with it, engage critically, only attend to explicitly religious material? If people (religious or not) are going to be influenced by it, and even immersed within it, how should theology respond?

Such forms of popular culture, though often deriving from Western sources, or deeply influenced by Western forms and media industries, have not been only Western. Although the focus of this chapter is on Western forms of later twentieth and early twenty-first century popular culture, the insights it produces are pertinent to the question of how theology takes local, contextual shape anywhere. And as Western popular culture increases in its influence, the twenty-first century platforms of access (social media, streaming) mean that multiple forms of popular culture can influence belief and theology in vastly differing places. Theology is never contextless, but in contemporary electronic forms the roots of its content are often not visible. If, at its simplest, what this chapter examines is seen as a continuum from producer, through product, to receiver (e.g. director – film – viewer), where "product" can be any kind of cultural "text," then it will become clear that the different points on the continuum receive different emphases, for different reasons and purposes, at different times.

In this briefest of surveys, three types of theological engagement with popular culture may be discerned. The types have not emerged straightforwardly as a chronological development and remain inextricably interwoven, although a basic trajectory is visible.

Approach 1: Popular culture as illustrative

The most obvious manifestation of popular culture in theology is as provider of illustrations. Similar to the way in which a preacher may refer to soap operas, novels, news stories, or sporting events in order to make theological points and observations comprehensible and to come alive, a wide range of popular cultural material can function as theologically explanatory. Hence, much work in the field of theology and film mined the world of film for scenes and plot-lines that connected with doctrine and belief. Such work often functioned as discipleship training or devotional material in so far as it was intended to enable the development of faith through what was seen about theology in the course of daily life. In so doing, it would train a believer's capacity to "read" a film.[1] William D. Romanowski's interpretation of *Titanic* (dir. James Cameron, 1997) is not offered merely and straightforwardly as an exposition of redemption. Many other layers of meaning are disclosed, not least as "an epic version of the American dream centred on the self-realization of Rose."[2] Nevertheless, "redemption" is still one of the frames of interpretation in Romanowski's reading and it is for this reason that the film is deemed theologically interesting. Bryan P. Stone locates a suite of films under the headings of the Apostles' Creed, exploring the doctrine of the Holy Spirit through *Star Wars*, for example.[3] Such thoughtful reflection on film is, for many theological interpreters, not simply a sharpening of the mind or an aesthetic pursuit: "A deeper focus leads to more active discipleship."[4] Popular music can be held to function similarly. Gillard's study of popular music's role in the "quest for ontological security" is much more sophisticated than being a catalogue of examples of where pop songs illustrate Christian insights. And yet his desire to locate the songs he studies within an overarching "Christian story," even if approached from a range of (eight) themes "that must help frame the telling of the Christian story," veers close to this illustrative approach to theological engagement with popular culture.[5]

More direct is David Dark's reading of Radiohead's "Spinning Plates" as an expression of apocalypse – the task of which is "to proclaim, by whatever medium is available, who and what are being left behind in the path of 'progress' while insisting that it doesn't have to be this way."[6] And Darren Sarisky sees Eminem's work as exploring the themes of salvation, holiness, and mission.[7]

Following such an approach it is always tempting to suggest that theology is thereby disclosing what a film or a song is "really about" or what lies "behind" whatever cultural product is being interpreted. Here the language of "use" is often appropriate, for the needs of theology are uppermost. Even if a theological interpretation can be shown to be true to a film or song as a "work" (or text), and even if evidenced in the intention of a songwriter, composer, or film director, it is still the theological purpose and reading that is significant. A piece of popular culture, in being illustrative of a theological point or insight, could in fact be left behind. It is the theological insight that matters, and to such an extent that the work of popular culture is arguably not being respected in its own right. The language of "plundering" could even be deemed apposite for how, on this understanding, popular culture is being approached.

That said, it is clear why such points of connection are being sought. At the same time as being a strategy for accentuating the relevance of theology for the present day, the connection made at least invites popular culture to be taken seriously. Furthermore, by use of popular media and art forms – and in the case of film, for example, pointing to the value and significance of popular blockbusters and not just art-house films for theological articulation – a missiological aspect to this form of cultural theology can be acknowledged. If some of the links made may seem forced or superficial at times, highlighting the significance of interweaving popular arts and meaning-making remains important. Vital too is the fact that illustrative material is not drawn solely from religious films. The theological point here is that God's activity as creator and Spirit is widely dispersed and experienced in many ways.[8]

The drawback to the illustrative approach is that priority is given to what is being said theologically as a result of the engagement. Despite the recognition of "God's wider presence," the extent to which it is often already known in advance what is being looked for renders the degree of openness to newness, novelty, fresh revelation not as broad as might have been hoped, or as open to challenge as may be implied. Ultimately, despite the theology–popular culture interaction in theory being able to respect the particularities of multiple cultures and contexts, theological claims may in effect be being detached from the cultures in and through which they are being expressed.

This illustrative use does, however, begin to identify a dominant role played by the receiver (interpreter, user) of popular culture. In turning further attention upon the receiver, theology and popular culture discussion would go on to attend more to the interaction between product and receiver in the next phase of its development.

Approach 2: Popular culture as resource material for participative engagement

"Reader Response" criticism had long recognized that meaning is found or made *between* a text and the reader, and so what the reader was making of a text is as important as the text itself from the perspective of analysing how a reading happens. The context of reading and the identity and background of the reader are crucial factors in interpretation. Meanings cannot simply be whatever an interpreter wants them to be, as a "text" (book, poem, film, song, play, TV program) may constrain the range of possible interpretations. But equally, what the interpreter *brings to* a "text" is crucial for how they are going to interpret the work/ product in question. Personal factors will be influential, even determinative, within the interpretative process, and may assist or distort the process of reading/listening/watching. But they are vital and need careful scrutiny. Reader response approaches were quickly matched across artistic and popular cultural media with viewer and audience response approaches.[9] By definition, such approaches take the medium of what is being interpreted more seriously. Film is no longer just stories with images. Popular music is to be explored not just for its lyrics but how it actually works (as sound). The crucial input of popular culture for theology lies in the fact that the range of resources being taken seriously in theological circles is expanding. The process of interaction between "text" and "receiver" can therefore be explored in multiple ways. But the "what" being viewed, listened to, or played, as well as read – and seen as potentially theologically significant – might be a video game, a musical, a pop song, a comedy sketch, or a TV soap. The theological significance of a popular cultural product lies not simply within a text itself, but in what it might be doing to and for the receiver. In this way the aesthetic quality of a "text" might be less than had been supposed to be necessary for it to be theologically significant.

Many examples of the interaction between receiver and "text" can be given from the world of TV. *Breaking Bad* proved a compelling drama over five series from 2008–13. Though not explicitly theological, many viewers found its treatment of human frailty and of the downward spiral of evil of its main character, Walter White, provocative for theological exploration in a number of ways.[10] Popular music likewise provides multiple examples of genres and songs that evoke responses from listeners that create contexts within which theology cannot but offer contributions in the process of reception. Country music is sometimes explicitly religious, though often not. Tex Sample's work shows how it engages the life experience of White working-class Americans.[11] Coldplay are prolific and have produced many modern anthems, as well as meditative work. Their theological significance may be as much about the communal experience that they bring about, and the often hymn-like sound through which they achieve this, as any words that they have written.[12]

Important here is the recognition that listeners and viewers are not passive. There may well be different levels of engagement, and attention has to be paid to *how* the interactions are happening and what – in addition to the content of a popular cultural product – proves significant in the interpretative process. But vital is that theological insights and moments of revelation occur *between* "text" and receiver. They are contained not in a text alone – though must be given a prompt by the product in some way – and not simply in what a receiver brings and already knows or believes. God's self-revelation is deemed to occur through what happens in the interplay. Explicit participation (listen actively, read emotionally, watch passionately, play your sport fully embodiedly) is needed for theological encounter to be discerned.

If an extraecclesial theological resource no longer needs to be a piece of classical music, an opera, a well-honed poem, a work of fine art of some age and distinction, but could be a much more recent and more popular product – even kitsch or populist – and proves theologically interesting because of its reception as much as (or more than) its content, then this takes the theological task away from the theologian's control to some degree. Hard questions still need to be asked (Is God here in this interaction? How do we know that? On what basis is the claim being made?). But the very need to probe the interplay further and more deeply is itself a challenge to theology to explore new ways in which the creativity and the presence of God might be grasped in the contemporary world. The fact that nothing may be ruled out at the outset as of potential theological significance is an important insight from this second approach. As soon as the receiver is taken with utmost seriousness – and that means anyone from any background, in any context – then what is consumed culturally and why (whether it is high art or not) becomes potentially significant.[13] As we shall see later, this shift of focus from text to receiver accentuates the question of where authority lies in theology.

Approach 3: Popular culture as performative contextual theology

If the second approach to theology and popular culture shifted attention to the receiver, and to what happens between receiver and "text," there is still the sense that the theological task of discerning what is deemed theologically significant lies "outside" of the interplay. Theologians are the external interpreters who offer a suggestion of what is happening in the interaction between a text and a receiver. Pushing exploration of the interplay between text and receiver a stage further brings us to a stage where we are reminded that theology (though "words about God") is inevitably bound up with that which is beyond words. In the same way that worship, transcendent experience of nature, or indescribable aesthetic encounters with art and music are examples of what may be termed an irreducible form of theology (for words often fail), so also popular culture provides examples of cultural products and experiences which in themselves may be said to *be* theology. Although this third approach cannot remove the sense that theological conclusions are drawn "outside" of the encounter (otherwise there can be no "theology and ..."), the approach begins to accept popular cultural artifacts, products, and encounters with them as sites of theological experience and not just engagement.[14] It is not only when the theologians do their work that theological encounters occur. The interaction of receiver and text *is* the work of theology because God is at work not as words, even if always, in Christian understanding, God is deemed to be present as (the) Word, that which enables all to live, move, and have its being. In human terms, however, the Word of God is noted to be embodied, felt, a source of energy, uplift, or inspiration, of questioning and self-discovery, or a channel of identity clarification. Seeing forms of popular culture as performative, contextual theology notes that receivers are even less passive and binds them to an event in and through which God is disclosed to them.[15]

The distinction between the first, second, and third approaches may be expressed as follows. Rather than the theological content of a theological encounter being identified as *within* a work/product – as and when pointed out by a theological interpreter (the first approach), or residing in the interaction *between* a product/work and an interpreter – and disclosed through reflection on the encounter *after* an event (the second approach), the third approach identifies what God has already done to and for the one enjoying a particular life-enhancing or self-disclosing experience in and through participation in popular culture.

This third approach, then, invites identification of experiences through which viewers, listeners, or gamers are left with a positive response, a sense of uplift, and even a strong affirmation of their self-understanding and personhood. It is too weak to say that a warm feeling results, as all sorts of activities (rock concerts, compelling dramas, demanding videogames, reality TV) may generate powerful emotions. But the significant point here is that emotional response takes precedence over cognitive processing, at least initially. Unlike the second approach, which might draw on a wide variety of resource material including work that is challenging, even shocking, but proves fruitful because of what happens between text and receiver, the third approach leaves the receiver with a fresh affirmation of who they are, even if these responses happen in multiple different ways. Fans of Bruce Springsteen are not just enjoying his music when attending his concerts. They are participating in a community and their sense of transcendence and belonging engages them at the depth of their beings.[16] TV comedy or drama can work, at its best, when providing a strong sense of identity for its viewers. If much in the West has favored and related to the White middle class (*Friends* worked for vast numbers of White middle-class viewers making discoveries about who they were, what they valued in life, and how they formed lasting relationships), there are exceptions.[17] Alan Bleasdale's *Boys from the Blackstuff* (1982) and Steve McQueen's *Small Axe* (2020) are two series handling tough and at times tragic developments in British society – working-class unemployment and the postwar experiences of Caribbean immigrants to Britain. Yet they are important examples of the portrayal of groups that, despite the difficult subject matter of the dramas, are affirmed in their identities. The means by which life enhancement and affirmation may occur cannot always easily be predicted.

Why are such examples important for theology? They present deep examples of what contexts and materials that theology has to work with and within. They invite theology not to work simply with religious subject matter, or with the obvious and ready-to-hand examples of theology-friendly material, but to dig into the contexts out of which its doctrinal work emerges and within which it has constantly to be reworked. Which works of culture are helping society to see who is present in that society, and especially who might be being pushed to its edges? Where, across the whole of society, are identities being discovered and forged and what is theology to make of this in relation to all of the themes with which it works? If James K. A. Smith is right that theology has to attend to the "cultural liturgies" by which people are shaped, then this third approach to popular culture is identifying what these cultural liturgies are.[18]

What is being described here is not necessarily different in kind from experiences of natural beauty or intense emotion in response to fine art. At issue is which cultural products or encounters generate such experiences and what theology might learn from the type of products, the nature of the encounters, and the experiences had. New things may potentially be happening at rock concerts, in video games, at sporting spectacles, or in response to TV dramas and music videos that do not simply replicate in every respect similar experiences from the past. Furthermore, with respect to experiences in the West it is very often the assumed, implied, or overt secularity (or religious indifference) of the texts/products doing the work that may cause surprise. The conviction that God is able to self-reveal in the midst or through people's participation in cultural experiences of very many kinds thus becomes, at root, the contribution of this subfield of theological inquiry. Theology does not add something in itself to what has happened, but its interpretative role informs understanding and repetition of an experience being described.

Named Theologians

Kelton Cobb and Gordon Lynch

Nearly twenty years ago Blackwell published two excellent but quite different books at roughly the same time, both of which became standard textbooks in higher education on the subject of theology and popular culture. The US-based Kelton Cobb's *The Blackwell Guide to Theology and Popular Culture* provided a two-part introduction, with four chapters of theory and five thematic chapters nudging toward a (Christian) "systematic theology" of popular culture through some worked examples. By contrast, UK-based Gordon Lynch's *Understanding Theology and Popular Culture* supplied a study of the different vantage points that theologically inclined readings of popular culture could adopt – akin in some ways to the three approaches presented earlier in this chapter – alongside a recognition of theology's "normativity" when entering the debate about what forms of popular culture are actually doing in everyday life. The two different stances reflected the interests, convictions, institutional commitments, and locations of the respective writers. Aspects of the politics of publishing may well also have contributed to the shaping of the two distinct projects. They do, though, help us understand the shaping of discussion over the past two decades, how the currents of inquiry reach back behind 2005, and how they have diversified through the period.

Cobb's project invites consideration of how Christian-specific engagements with the subfield have developed. Cobb himself engaged with many resources that some may not have considered popular enough to be "popular culture," raising the question as to whether there lurks all the time an assumption that culture needs to have a particular quality or form to merit theological reflection. But the thematically driven trajectory to which he contributed – in his case, looking at images of God, human nature, sin, salvation, and life everlasting – serves as a reminder, as Lynch recognized, that a religiously committed shaping of what was being encountered would always occur to some extent. At issue is whether such shaping would always distort even while always informing what one "sees."

By contrast, Lynch's seeking to step back from normativity, which has continued in his later work, within which he has helpfully and powerfully explored the problematic and damaging aspects of religion, invites a greater opportunity to critique the normative lens. Perhaps being aware of a "shape" to theology's interests is already too restrictive in enabling a committed theologian to read culture in as disinterested a way as possible. There can, of course, be no neutrality of reading. The different vantage points of Cobb and Lynch leave us asking whether all theological reading of popular culture will end up being illustrative (Approach 1) despite intending to be otherwise.

The "Fuller School"

The work of what has, in effect, become a kind of "Fuller School" of engagement with popular culture enables us to explore this question further. Robert K. Johnston, Craig Detweiler, Barry Taylor, Catherine Barsotti, and Kutter Callaway are, or have been, active at some time at the Fuller Theological Seminary in Pasadena, California.[19] Their work is reflected in a string of pertinent publications stretching from Johnston's *The Christian at Play* (1975) through Callaway's projects on film music and TV, Detweiler's work on film, digital technology, and video games and multiple multiauthored works on film, the latest of these appearing in 2019. It has been an astonishingly productive channel of valuable work, institutionally supported through the Brehm Center for worship, theology, and the arts and by a Baker "Engaging Culture" book series.[20] Inevitably because of its scale and variety their work does not fit easily or straightforwardly into the three approaches identified here. However, the fact that even the most recent work addresses what lies "beneath the surface" of film suggests a continuing interest in what a text delivers over and above what goes on between a text and the receiver. To claim that the entire work of the school slots simply into Approach 1 would, however, do it a disservice and would need to be qualified by the range and expertise of the scholars mentioned. Much attention is paid to the ways in which different forms of popular culture function. The communal, public settings (not just ecclesial) in which popular culture needs to be explored and critically reflected upon are also emphasized.

Heidi Campbell

A significant development in popular culture over recent decades is the way in which resources are accessed and discussed. People still go to the cinema and attend live gigs and sporting events. But at the same time, patterns of access are changing. Films are watched on phones on train journeys. Music on YouTube or Spotify is listened to through earphones while jogging. Live gigs are watched at a distance in cinemas, as if the cinemagoers are "actually there." And then the processing of such experiences happens in multiple ways and is then reflected upon, or at least reacted to, through social media. As Heidi Campbell has been exploring in her work, these practices change the ways in which theological exploration happens and religious communities develop. In particular, the question arises of who the authoritative voices are when a wider range of resources than authoritative scriptures interpreted by recognized and authorized leaders begin to have influence in faith and theology. Joining our conversation from a different angle than is represented by the three approaches presented here, Campbell's work presses the issue of how, and by whom, new developments in theological thinking and belief take shape. After all, theology "is done by all who draw upon their experience of Christian community and includes dialoguing with others outside established theological guilds and engaging the wider Christian tradition as desired."[21]

Clive Marsh

I have made contributions personally to the field of "theology and popular culture" over many years, with respect to film, popular music, and television.[22] In my study of the doctrine of salvation I made clear that the popular culture materials used, alongside other cultural resources, were "not to be seen as definitive or in any way unique in their juxtaposition." They were "examples, individually and together, of the ways in which cultural consumption evokes aesthetic and affective response and thereby prepares the ground for explicit theological engagement."[23] What I sought to do was encourage acknowledgement that a very wide range of material indeed could contribute substantively to theological reflection. Furthermore, I was inviting readers to think through *their own* cultural consumption not simply in search of the obvious, and explicitly religious, material to assist theological work. It is, though, inevitable that all are likely to be culturally constrained, even if not culturally bound, in the choices they make and the identification of resources they find helpful. We may talk of people having "broad tastes" or "wide sympathies." And an openness to new styles of music, different genres of films, sports other than one's favorites can all be life expanding as well as life enhancing. Although it is not possible to be able to consume and respond equally to all forms of cultural expression, it *is* possible to learn from outside, even as we are bolstered and shaped by that which is familiar. Theology has to wrestle with what shapes identity and derives from and speaks to the experiences and contexts that are well known to us, and with which we are comfortable, even as the discipline of theology invites us to be challenged by those who are different from us and are also engaging with the same (doctrinal) themes – whether explicitly or not.

Robert Beckford, Anthony Pinn, Noel Leo Erskine, and Cheryl Kirk-Duggan

The work of Robert Beckford, Anthony Pinn, Noel Leo Erskine, and Cheryl Kirk-Duggan provides examples of theological exploration that draws deeply on a wide range of Black music (including dub, rap, reggae, hip-hop) to make clear the extent to which Black music *is* spiritual self-expression and may need no further reflection in order to "become" theology.[24] At the same time, their own reflections on the musical forms extend and deepen understanding of what the music achieves and how it works. In consolidating and affirming aspects of Black experience the results of this interaction between (or is it a fusion of?) theology and popular culture challenges many of the approaches to theology *and* popular culture that are inclined to see more of a separation than Black theology wants there to be.

Beckford's approach is less a set of sustained reflections on types of music than the production of a body of work reflecting theology on Black experience from an activist's perspective in a way that will therefore inevitably be informed by music (reggae, dub, dancehall, for example). In the case of dub, the musical form informs his theological method rather than simply being a resource of expounding Black experience.[25]

Pinn's personal shift from Methodism to atheist humanism does not deflect him from recognizing the spiritual importance of music, causing him to note in rap in particular a form of music that graphically presents life struggles. Having moved from a position in which he might have expected constructive theological responses he now believes that "human ingenuity and creativity are what are needed, as there can be no reliance on a doctrine of God."[26] One of the challenges for Black theology, then, will be the disentangling and critiquing of a range of religious and nonreligious articulations of Black experience, given the generational challenges, particularly within Pentecostalism, of some younger members' doubts about the adequacy of past generations' theologies. Music may still move, but will the words surrounding the musical experience, powerful in itself as it is, still sustain?

Erskine's work brings Jamaica and the United States together in recognizing in ways that resonate more widely the significance of both location and identity in reggae and rap. Erskine discloses sharply key aspects of the specificity of context in a manner that questions more theoretical, academic approaches to "contextual theology." Respect for the particularity of place, and the challenges to male dominance that are required in the critical handling of both rap and Black church traditions, expose and accentuate the necessity of theology's interaction with popular culture.[27]

Kirk-Duggan offers both an invaluable survey of sacred and secular streams and genres of Black music and (with Marlon Hall) a detailed study of hip-hop.[28] Her work witnesses the persistent intertwining of secular and sacred in Black music as "it emerges out of the lived realities of the souls of Black folk."[29] As such, it lays out before the world of theology as a whole, in musical form and with a particular intensity, a challenge to theology borne of Black experience.

Influence, Achievement, and Agenda

The lasting and continuing legacy of the cumulative exploration of theology's presence within and interaction with popular culture in all its varied forms can be summarized in a set of prominent themes.

First, emotion. Popular culture has accentuated the extent to which theology as human work is not simply concerned with cognition and propositions. Though theology's engagement with the arts has long recognized this, the class/social location element in theology's work has often led to an underplaying of affective elements in theology, preferring attention to aesthetic aspects alone. Recognition of theology's emotional elements, however, also enables the spiritual aspect of the theological task to be respected. When film and music, even in popular forms, delve into and evoke attention to the inner life then a first step toward theology's holistic task is taken.

Concerns are raised about the ease with which attention to emotion can lead to preoccupation with sentimentality – uncomplicated, lazy, and potentially untruthful versions of emotional experience.[30] Attention to sentiment does not, however, inevitably lead to melodrama or oversimplicity and remains an important element in theology wherever its origins lie.[31]

Second, embodiment. Emotions are experienced as bodies and thus the attention to embodiment that engagement with popular culture provokes is to be welcomed. Even as embodiment has become an emphasis in theological inquiry from many angles (feminist, liberation, Black, womanist, Asian, trauma theologies, for example) it is prompted here too. Popular culture can admittedly promote inattention or even neglect of the body: static TV or film-viewing, sport-watching rather than active participation leading to theology on the sofa. More positively, attention to the importance of the body and embodiment is promoted through many popular social practices (e.g. dance, sport). Theology is thus reminded that it is a "whole person" practice.[32] Potential alliances can at this point be seen between disability theologies and emphasis upon the significance of embodied spiritual practices and opposition to ableism and overspiritualization (or overemphasis upon the cognitive) in theology as a result of these engagements with popular culture.

Third, participation. Participation has proved a prominent theme in much recent Western theology.[33] Steered both by a conviction that theology is a self-involving, existential discipline of which the content is not simply to be delivered in propositional statements, and by a rediscovery (in the West, at least) of the doctrine of the Trinity, which leads to perceptions of our "joining the dance" of the Trinity in relating to the One who is relational in their very being, participation in God is topical. Popular culture may not in any direct sense be in the list of reasons why this has occurred. But a shift of attention from the passive to the active viewer/hearer/listener does highlight the role of involvement in the task of discovering or making meaning, and fosters an attentiveness to participation. Reservations about the scale and nature of the experiential component in theology will always remain. (Theology is not wholly objective, but how subjective can its content be?) But exploration of what occurs between a popular cultural "text" and a receiver demonstrates theology's interstitial character. God self-reveals in the space between a cultural object and its reception and can do so in relation to many more cultural materials than is often supposed. For a glimpse of revelation to occur, however, then the receiver needs to participate in the communicative act.[34]

Fourth, identity. Closely allied to the recognition of the importance of participation is how the practice of consuming popular culture links to identity. It is much too simple to say "we are what we consume," but there is a close relationship between what we choose to watch, listen to, play, who we undertake these activities with, and what kind of people we are seeking to be, or in practice become.[35] We do not wholly control what we consume, and some of what may prove theologically challenging is when we are caught short, surprised, or confronted by material that is different from what we normally consume and expect to be bolstered by. Consistent patterns of consumption – not just listening to "favorite music" or watching a particular genre of film but also ensuring that we engage with only what we are likely to agree with, or which confirms our politics – can amount to avoidance. More positively, as noted, self-affirming and self-enhancing consumption of popular culture can foster a strong sense of identity. Where a person or group feels excluded from what may be seen as "mainstream" or "normative" theology, then it can be through engagement with popular culture that a significant corrective to a sense of exclusion may occur. Theological reflection on and through TV drama offering accurate portrayals of working-class life may correct common middle-class biases in Western theology. Diverse styles and genres of popular music may connect with a wide range of groups of people who feel disconnected from any theological community. At root, then, we see here a potential alliance between the practice of theologically engaging with popular culture and an intersectional approach to theology. Forms of culture that enable people to discover and express their identities if they do not normally see themselves represented within theology and religious life are vital. Popular culture, at its best, can do this and thus serves as a vital tool to expand the reach of theological exploration and discourse.

Fifth, community. The communal aspect of participation in popular cultural consumption should be noted. Who one participates with – when attending a gig, for example, or dancing, or being caught up in a sporting event – can be a significant indication of an aspect of identity. The concept of fandom is helpful here, and its religion-like qualities are evident.[36] Fan communities may, in Christian perspective, look like alternative churches. But acknowledging the intensity of fandom, group-belonging, and communal participation can make some popular cultural contexts seem and become more than alternative churches. Perhaps they *are* churches if it is true that people can say of a communal popular cultural encounter: "this is where I feel truly me."[37] It can be here where a theological experience may begin, even if not initially as a theological question.

Conclusion: A Systematic Theology of Popular Culture?

Can, then, a systematic theology of popular culture be written? In any neat, straightforward sense, no. The five headings just used do not fit neatly into the categories and themes of a systematic theology. From a different perspective, however, popular culture has a great deal to offer to the systematic theologian who wants to be contemporary as well as traditional. In a very creative take on the practice of videogaming, Frank Bosman has offered "a new systematic theology of video games" in *Gaming and the Divine*.[38] Not all of the classical themes are explored, but Bosman demonstrates in a deeply informative and creative way that goes beyond mere illustration how the practice of gaming – with an emphasis clearly on participation and not just observation – sharpens contemporary thinking about theological topics (creation, Christology, anthropology, evil, ethics, death, sacraments). Bosman's work challenges theologians to consider how different media or forms of culture might likewise be thought through systematically.

Using helpful words about systematic theology's importance from Timothy C. Tennent, we can therefore approach the potential achievement of serious engagement with popular culture from the opposite end: "Theological reflection must arise out of the particularities of each new generation and within each new context. No single systematic theology can be held up as universally adequate for all Christians."[39] This being so, the question arises as to how the "particularities of each new generation and ... each new context" are being articulated and explored in relation to which theology does its systematic work. Exploration of the multiple forms of popular culture are one channel through which this work happens. This chapter has sought to show that such endeavors are not simply *pre*theological or preamble for theology. Theology is tangled up with what is explored in much more complex and embedded ways than is often supposed.

The systematic theologian is therefore invited to consider each of the topics of theology in relation to popular culture. For example, in considering creation, who is writing songs or producing TV documentaries which address concerns about climate change? When exploring Christology, what is the latest thinking about embodiment, about attention to marginalized communities (where Christ is today), and how is this being engaged with in popular culture? In anthropology, what explorations of what it means to be human are appearing in film? How is such material also connecting with eschatology in terms of exploring human finitude and visions of the future?

These are examples of the open-endedness of the engagement between theology and popular culture. Theological traditions carry their themes with them. But contemporary carriers of the traditions (theologians) need to look around themselves on many sides to understand the worlds in which they seek to do their work. Popular culture can help them do this.

Notes

1   For example, Sara Anson Vaux, *Finding Meaning at the Movies* (Nashville, TN: Abingdon, 1999); William D. Romanowski, *Cinematic Faith: A Christian Perspective on Movies and Meaning* (Grand Rapids, MI: Baker Academic, 2019).

2   Romanowski, *Cinematic Faith*, 111.

3   Bryan P. Stone, *Faith and Film: Theological Themes at the Cinema* (St. Louis, MO: Chalice Press, 2000), ch. 10.

4   Robert K. Johnston, Craig Detweiler, and Kutter Callaway, *Deep Focus: Film and Theology in Dialogue* (Grand Rapids, MI: Baker Academic, 2019), 227.

5   David J. Gillard, *Restless: Popular Music, the Christian Story, and the Quest for Ontological Security* (Eugene, OR: Pickwick, 2022).

6   David Dark, *Everyday Apocalypse: The Sacred Revealed in Radiohead, The Simpsons and Other Pop Culture Icons* (Grand Rapids, MI: Brazos Press, 2002), 75.

7   Darren Sarisky, "Despair and Redemption: A Theological Account of Eminem," in *Everyday Theology: How to Read Cultural Texts and Interpret Trends*, ed. Kevin J. Vanhoozer, Charles A. Anderson and Michael J. Sleasman (Grand Rapids, MI: Baker Academic, 2007), ch. 3.

8   Robert K. Johnston, *God's Wider Presence: Reconsidering General Revelation* (Grand Rapids, MI: Baker Academic, 2014).

9   Clive Marsh, "Audience Reception," in *The Routledge Companion to Religion and Film*, ed. John Lyden (London and New York: Routledge, 2009), 255–74.

10 Clive Marsh, *A Cultural Theology of Salvation* (Oxford: Oxford University Press, 2018), 95–105; David K. Goodin and George Tsakiridis, eds., *Theology and Breaking Bad* (Lanham, MD: Lexington Books/Fortress Academic, 2022). The latter appears in an ambitious Theology, Religion and Pop Culture book series.

11 Tex Sample, *White Soul: Country Music, the Church, and Working Americans* (Nashville, TN: Abingdon Press, 1996).

12 As such this may well be an example of the "collective effervescence" spoken of by Émile Durkheim with respect to social and religious groups.

13 This explains why cultural, media, and TV studies, despite their frequent neglect or dismissal of the significance of religion, become theologically important.

14 Theology may do the labeling, but it is not the theological labeling that makes the encounter theological. Doing theology in interaction with popular culture reminds the discipline that theological inquiry is, for most people, a luxury. For many there is little time for reflection. Life has to be got on with even if a moment of transcendence or deep sense of belonging has occurred.

15 In a telling quotation from film director Steve McQueen, even the language of "performance" may need to be challenged. With respect to the TV drama *Lovers Rock*, McQueen notes that when filming the music scenes: "It was a spiritual experience. It wasn't performative." David Olusoga, "These Are the Untold Stories that Make Up Our Nation," *Sight and Sound*, 13 November 2020, https://www.bfi.org.uk/sight-and-sound/interviews/steve-mcqueen-small-axe-black-britain-david-olusoga (accessed 21 September 2023).

16 Daniel Cavicchi, *Tramps Like Us: Music and Meaning among Springsteen Fans* (New York: Oxford University Press, 1998).

17 *Friends* aired originally as ten seasons of half-hour episodes from 1994 to 2004, 236 episodes in all.

18 The first volume of James K. A. Smith's trilogy is especially relevant here: *Desiring the Kingdom: Worship, Worldview and Cultural Formation* (Grand Rapids, MI: Baker Academic, 2009). Unlike Smith, however, I am not suggesting that theology's task is to work out a counterliturgy. I think its task has to be more sophisticated: neither hypercritical nor simply accepting but interrogative and interacting with the materials in and through which people are shaped, shape themselves, and forge identities and political directions. Theology already has material to work with, but how are its content and reservoir of resources evolving?

19 The work of William A. Dyrness, *Poetic Theology: God and the Poetics of Everyday Life* (Grand Rapids, MI: Eerdmans, 2011), Dean Batali's collaboration with Kutter Callaway in *Watching TV Religiously: Television and Theology in Dialogue* (Grand Rapids, MI: Baker

Academic, 2016) and Richard Vance Goodwin, *Seeing Is Believing: The Revelation of God through Film* (Downers Grove, IL: IVP Academic, 2022) should also be mentioned.

20 For example, Craig Detweiler and Barry Taylor, *A Matrix of Meanings: Finding God in Pop Culture* (Grand Rapids, MI: Baker Academic, 2003); Robert K. Johnston, *Reel Spirituality: Theology and Film in Dialogue*, 2nd ed. (Grand Rapids, MI: Baker Academic, 2006).

21 Heidi A. Campbell and Stephen Garner, *Networked Theology: Negotiating Faith in Digital Culture* (Grand Rapids, MI: Baker Academic, 2016), 86.

22 Clive Marsh, *Cinema and Sentiment: Film's Challenge to Theology* (Milton Keynes: Paternoster Press, 2004); *Theology Goes to the Movies: An Introduction to Critical Christian Thinking* (London and New York: Routledge, 2007); with Vaughan S. Roberts, *Personal Jesus: How Popular Music Shapes Our Souls* (Grand Rapids, MI: Baker Academic, 2012).

23 Marsh, *A Cultural Theology of Salvation*, 107.

24 As such, Black music is a good example of the third approach to the relationship between theology and popular culture, and sharpens the questions of whether the music has to be religious to work theologically (e.g. gospel or spirituals) or what strategies are needed to theologize around secular Black music. In this regard the range of forms of Black music have gone well beyond James H. Cone's still valuable study *The Spirituals and the Blues* (New York: Seabury Press, 1972).

25 Robert Beckford, *Jesus Dub: Theology, Music and Social Change* (London: Routledge, 2006) is the most pertinent example of Beckford's work.

26 Anthony B. Pinn, "'Handlin' My Business': Exploring Rap's Humanist Sensibilities," in *Noise and Spirit: The Religious and Spiritual Sensibilities of Rap Music*, ed. Anthony B. Pinn (New York: New York University Press, 2003), 99–100.

27 Noel Leo Erskine, "Rap, Reggae and Religion: Sounds of Cultural Dissonance," in *Noise and Spirit: The Religious and Spiritual Sensibilities of Rap Music*, 71–84.

28 Cheryl Kirk-Duggan, "Sacred and Secular in African-American Music," in *The Oxford Handbook of Religion and the Arts*, ed. Frank Burch Brown (New York: Oxford University Press, 2014), 498–521; Cheryl Kirk-Duggan and Marlon Hall, *Wake Up: Hip Hop, Christianity and the Black Church* (Nashville, TN: Abingdon, 2011).

29 Kirk-Duggan, "Sacred and Secular," 518.

30 Jeremy S. Begbie, "Beauty, Sentimentality and the Arts," in *The Beauty of God: Theology and the Arts*, ed. Daniel J. Trier, Mark Husbands, and Roger Lundon (Downers Grove, IL: IVP, 2007), 45–69.

31 As I sought to argue in *Cinema and Sentiment*.

32 An emphasis in Richard Bourne and Imogen Adkins, *A New Introduction to Theology: Embodiment, Experience and Encounter* (London: T&T Clark, 2020).

33 Among many examples, see Paul S. Fiddes, *Participating in God: A Pastoral Doctrine of the Trinity* (London: Darton, Longman & Todd, 2000); Pete Ward, *Participation and Mediation: A Practical Theology for the Liquid Church* (London: SCM Press, 2008); Michael Gorman, *Participation: Paul's Vision of Life in Christ* (Cambridge: Grove Books, 2018); Andrew Davison, *Participation in God: A Study in Christian Doctrine and Metaphysics* (Cambridge: Cambridge University Press, 2019); and Michael Nausner, *Eine Theologie der Teilhabe* (Leipzig: Evangelische Verlangsanstalt, 2020).

34 James Carey's drawing of a distinction between "transmission" and "ritual" views of communication, in which the latter emphasizes the participative dimension, is invaluable here: *Communication as Culture: Essays on Media and Society*, rev. ed. (New York: Routledge, 2009).

35 Smith, *Desiring the Kingdom*.

36 Matt Hills, *Fan Cultures* (London: Routledge, 2002); Marsh and Roberts, *Personal Jesus*, 134–5, 170–2.

37 Again in relation to the making of *Lovers Rock*, Steve McQueen comments: "For me, it was about ritual. The process is just as important as what it ends up being. To take you on that journey where it gets to a point where it transcends, even beyond the people in the room. It becomes church" (Olusoga, "These Are the Untold Stories ...").

38 Frank G. Bosman, *Gaming and the Divine: A New Systematic Theology of Video Games* (New York: Routledge, 2019).

39 Timothy C. Tennent, *Theology in the Context of World Christianity* (Grand Rapids, MI: Zondervan, 2007), 258.

Recommended Reading

Bosman, Frank G. *Gaming and the Divine: A New Systematic Theology of Video Games*. New York: Routledge, 2019.

Bradley, Ian. *You've Got to Have a Dream: The Message of the Musical*. London: SCM Press, 2004.

Callaway, Kutter, with Dean Batali. *Watching TV Religiously: Television and Theology in Dialogue.* Grand Rapids, MI: Baker Academic, 2016.

Campbell, Heidi A., and Stephen Garner. *Networked Theology: Negotiating Faith in Digital Culture.* Grand Rapids, MI: Baker Academic, 2016.

Deacy, Christopher. *Screening the Afterlife: Theology, Eschatology and Film.* London and New York: Routledge, 2012.

Ellis, Robert. *The Games People Play: Theology, Religion, and Sport.* Eugene, OR: Wipf and Stock, 2014.

Ford, Dennis. *A Theology for a Mediated God: How Media Shapes Our Notions about Divinity.* London: Routledge, 2016.

Gillard, David J. *Restless: Popular Music, the Christian Story, and the Quest for Ontological Security.* Eugene, OR: Pickwick, 2022.

Goodwin, Richard Vance. *Seeing Is Believing: The Revelation of God through Film.* Downers Grove, IL: IVP Academic, 2022.

Kirk-Duggan, Cheryl. "Sacred and Secular in African American Music." In *The Oxford Handbook of Religion and the Arts,* edited by Frank Burch Brown, New York: Oxford University Press, 2014, 498–521.

Lyden, John C., ed. *The Routledge Companion to Religion and Film.* London and New York: Routledge, 2009.

Lyden, John C. and Eric Mazur, eds. *The Routledge Companion to Religion and Popular Culture.* London and New York: Routledge, 2015.

Marsh, Clive. *Cinema and Sentiment: Film's Challenge to Theology.* Milton Keynes: Paternoster Press, 2004.

Marsh, Clive, and Vaughan S. Roberts. *Personal Jesus: How Popular Music Shapes Our Souls.* Grand Rapids: Baker Academic, 2012.

———. *Theology Goes to the Movies: An Introduction to Critical Christian Thinking.* London and New York: Routledge, 2007.

Theology and Film

Jolyon Mitchell

Introduction

Is the church in conflict with the cinema? There is a well-known, and often quoted scene in *Cinema Paradiso* (1988) in which a middle-aged priest sits alone in the picture house of a small Italian town.[1] He is watching a film and every time a couple embrace, he angrily rings a small bell. The projectionist then marks the offending frames on the reel and later edits out these cinematic kisses. Later in *Cinema Paradiso* the small boy who witnesses this censoring returns as a middle-aged film director and is given an old reel of film to watch. To his amusement, he finds that it is all the excised material spliced together into a chain of kisses.

Theologians currently engaged in film criticism often look back at Catholic and Protestant attempts at censorship with a mixture of bemusement and fascination. Although ecclesiastical protests against the cinema have become much more sporadic, the image of Christians morally outraged by a particular film remains a recurring news story. Demonstrations against films such as *Monty Python's Life of Brian* (1979) or *The Last Temptation of Christ* (1988) reinforced the popular perception that many Protestants and Catholics remain deeply uneasy about film's perceived capacity to corrupt viewers.[2] Protests against motion pictures are not a new phenomenon. As early as 1907, in the New England city of Worcester, the *Catholic Messenger* denounced films as "the Devil's Lieutenants," while Swedish evangelical church ministers in the same city condemned attendance at the movie theatre as a serious sin. So strong was their anticinema rhetoric that "some youngsters developed a morbid fear just walking by a movie theatre."[3]

To suggest that the churches have always been in conflict with the cinema is to ignore the full history of their interactions. There have certainly been moments of intense opposition, such as in 1910 when Pope Pius X prohibited the showing of films in Catholic churches or when the Legion of Decency "totally condemned" particular movies.[4] By contrast, there have been periods of mutual involvement, which go back to the very start of moving pictures. From the first decade of film, far from being in conflict with the industry, some Christians creatively used or indeed helped to create movies. For instance, dramatized passion plays took on a cinematic lease of life following the advent of motion pictures in the late nineteenth

Ford's The Modern Theologians: An Introduction to Christian Theology since 1918, Fourth Edition.
Edited by Rachel Muers and Ashley Cocksworth.
© 2024 John Wiley & Sons Ltd. Published 2024 by John Wiley & Sons Ltd.

century. A French religious publishing house, La Bonne Presse, financed one of the first ever films to focus on the life of Jesus. *La Passion* was made in Paris in the summer of 1897. This silent, black and white motion picture lasted five minutes but was popular enough to allow La Bonne Presse to become a film production company. Sadly, like many films from the earliest days of cinema, it has not survived.

There are numerous other early examples of cinematic passion plays. Nearly seventy silent films were produced between 1897 and 1930 relating to the New Testament, of which the majority were made in the United States (thirty-seven) or France (seventeen).[5] Many focused upon the life of Jesus and particularly the passion narratives. Films based on scenes from the life and death of Christ were sometimes even made by evangelists to attract audiences and illuminate their message. For instance, at the start of the twentieth century in Australia, Herbert Booth, son of the founders of the Salvation Army, used specially filmed scenes of martyrdoms and Christ in agony on the cross as part of his "multimedia" presentation *Soldiers of the Cross*. The event received commendations from both the secular and the religious press.[6]

During the first twenty years of cinema many became absorbed by the potential of the evolving medium of film. One of the most prolific Christian advocates for film was the Reverend Herbert Jump, a Congregationalist minister, whose pamphlet *The Religious Possibilities of the Motion Picture* (1910) is one of the earliest theological apologia for film. He uses the parable of the Good Samaritan for the foundation of his argument. This exciting "robber-story" rooted in experience and realistic representation of violent crime, provides a precedent for using film didactically. Jump playfully suggests that the only thing needed to transform this parable into a successful motion picture is a new title: "The Adventure of the Jerusalem Merchant." Films can make the gospel vivid, like the word-pictures of great preachers, illustrated slide lectures, and cathedral art. The motion picture is "the most wonderful invention that has come into existence since the invention of the printing press in the fifteenth century." Although he recognizes some dangers in the medium, overall Jump perceives it as an ally of the church, which can help as an entertainment device, a tool of religious instruction at Sunday school, an informer about missionary work both at home and abroad, a teacher to socially educate the needy, and a powerful illustration for the preacher.[7] During these first decades of the "seventh art," film may not have received sustained theological analysis, but Jump is a leading representative of those who outlined pastoral and apologetic rationales for the uses of film.

At this early stage, as so obviously in film's later history, it was economic necessity that played a highly significant role in how films were made and marketed. Film producers became increasingly sensitive to their potential audiences' different desires. Several of the earliest film catalogues provide purchasers with a choice of the number of scenes from cinematic passion plays. Some went further, ensuring that Catholic exhibitors were offered versions of passion plays that had more scenes centering on Mary.[8] The episodic nature of the gospel narratives particularly suited early styles of filmmaking, which offered audiences short scenes. In later silent films these were connected by title cards. The audience's knowledge of the biblical stories allowed producers to cut directly from scene to scene without having to provide overexplicit narrative links.

Significantly, portraying biblical stories (like filming versions of Dickens or Shakespeare) provided a ready means of respectability in a period when many filmmakers were eager to shed film's more sordid associations. The aim was to demonstrate that film could be edifying rather than merely titillating. Another factor was the desire to experiment with the new medium and create unexpected spectacles. An early film based on the Bible that did not rely on the passion play model was made by Georges Méliès, one of the fathers of French cinema and a groundbreaking director in terms of his development and use of special effects. *Le Christ Marchant Sur Les Flots* (1899/1900) may last only thirty-five seconds, but Méliès used trick photography (a simple double exposure) to astonish audiences by showing a miracle occur in front of their own eyes: Jesus walking across the Sea of Galilee. As just one in a whole series of magical "effects" from the Méliès stable, some viewers believed that such showing debased a divine miracle. The vast majority of Méliès' work does not treat religious themes explicitly, but the responses to his work demonstrate how audiences could be mesmerized by what they saw on the silver screen. The sheer novelty of the spectacle engaged, delighted, and surprised. In this chapter I first outline three significant interpretative practices, investigating how Christians have responded to film over the last century. Through this framework I provide a historical survey that offers a point of entry into a rapidly expanding literature.

Survey: Theological Criticism of Film

Over the last hundred and twenty years, no mutually agreed pattern of theological engagement with films has emerged. The landscape is marked by fragmentation and a diversity of approaches. This is not surprising given the multiplicity of theological beliefs, methods, and practices reflected through much of this volume of *The Modern Theologians*. Mainstream film studies have largely ignored theological and religious film criticism.[9] Nevertheless, there already exist several useful taxonomies setting out the different ways in which theology and film can interact. John May, for example, believes that over the last forty years there has been a shift in how theologians have engaged with film. This has moved through five stages: first, discrimination, which concentrates on the morality of specific portrayals; second, visibility, which focuses on how religious figures or themes are represented; third, dialogue, which promotes theological conversations with particular films; fourth, humanism, which examines how film can promote human progress and flourishing; and, fifth, aesthetics, which ultimately explores how the transcendent may be manifested at the cinema.[10] As May concedes, there is inevitably blurring between these categories.

Rob Johnston's matrix, set out with clarity in *Reel Spirituality*, intentionally offers a complementary framework. Recognizing the parallels with May's work, he also provides five basic categories to reflect the theological responses by the church to moviegoing: avoidance, caution, dialogue, appropriation, and divine encounter.[11] These groupings highlight the range of perspectives offered by various theologians. This includes the whole spectrum of writers, from those who espouse withdrawal from the cinema to those who advocate that watching a film may actually be an occasion of divine encounter. Johnston observes that many theologians who promote a highly critical response to film begin the dialogue from the womb of theology and often judge films on the ethical presuppositions that they bring to the movie. By contrast, those who celebrate the revelatory potential of movies tend to immerse themselves in the world of the film and its aesthetic qualities before drawing upon theological resources for interpreting the film. Johnston's own approach to the cinema is made clear in the text and through the book's subtitle: *Theology and Film in Dialogue*.

More recently, Brent Plate outlined three "waves" of study. For Plate, the first wave started in the 1960s, "particularly grounded in Paul Tillich's 'theology of culture,'" where some theologians explored how film revealed aspects of the human condition. Up to the early 1980s studies tended to focus on European auteurs such as Bergman, Bresson, Dreyer, and Pasolini, as well as Japanese filmmakers such as Ozu and Kurosawa. During the late 1980s a second wave emerged, who largely left behind art house films to more popular Hollywood movies. In the late 1990s and into the 2000s a third wave emerged that eschewed literary ways of reading films toward focusing upon audience interactions with film. Several scholars have identified a fourth wave emerging over the last two decades. For example, in *The Dardenne Brothers' Cinematic Parables* (2023) Joel Mayward identifies this fourth wave as reflecting a "growing appreciation of world cinema beyond American and Eurocentric views," "a renewal of phenomenology by giving greater attention to viewer's emotional and bodily responses," "an increase in religious and theological considerations of cinema beyond hegemonic Christian perspectives," and "an emphasis upon audiovisual aesthetics." Mayward is seeking to lay the foundations for a new "cinematic theology" within a postsecular context, in order to explore how "non-religious films may disclose theological insights and potentially generate revelatory experiences." These observations, relating to the fourth wave of criticism, resonate with my own description of three recent turns in the study of film and theology – "the global turn" toward world cinema, "the cultural turn" toward understanding cultural contexts and audience reception, and the "audiovisual" turn toward recognizing film as a distinct audiovisual form of communication.[12]

The presuppositions behind several of the approaches described by May, Johnston, Plate, Mayward, and myself are inevitably diverse. Some critics have shunned the cinema as a medium that can corrupt morally, socially and doctrinally, whereas others have embraced it as a catalyst for theological exploration or even an art form with transcendent potential. Corruption, exploration, and illumination provide the structure for the following discussion. This leads to a consideration of different film directors' visions and the variety of responses by audiences to film.

Film corrupts?

Suspicion of film grew in the 1920s, heightened by a series of scandals in Hollywood, confirming fears that the industry was inherently decadent. In 1923 the evangelist Jack Linn asserted the movies are the "devil's incubator," which are not "conducive to morality or spirituality." For Linn, "a Christian cannot even darken a movie theatre, and at the same time fellowship with Christ."[13] Linn's was by no means a lone voice. John Rice's *What Is Wrong with the Movies?* (1938) remains one of the most outspoken Protestant polemics against cinema. He attempted to demonstrate that the "commercial cinema is an unmitigated curse" and like Linn he believes "it is so vile in its influence that no Christian should ever set foot in a movie theatre." He believes "the movie is the rival of schools and churches, the feeder of lust, the perverter of morals, the tool of greed, the school of crime, the betrayer of innocence."[14] Unlike some of the earliest Protestant enthusiasts for film, such as Herbert Jump, this masculine duo of Linn and Rice provides examples of those who saw the cinema in direct conflict with the church.

Anxiety about the power of film to corrupt viewers is also expressed in Burnett and Martell's *The Devil's Camera* (1932) (see Figure 36.1), which is dedicated to the "ultimate sanity of the white races" and betrays anti-Semitic sentiments. They assert that the "cinema, taken as a whole, is the greatest lie of our time because it is grossly misrepresenting life."[15] As with many other early critical accounts of film they highlight what they perceive to be satanic influence, "the devil is in full, spiritual control of modern film production." They also see idolatry portrayed on the screen, "the golden calf is god of the cinema."[16] The dominant motif of *The Devil's Camera* is that "film-poison" is doing "unimaginable harm," feeding the worst passions and seducing the "imaginations of the peoples of the world." Burnett and Martell are critical of church leaders who ignored or dismissed the cinema. In contrast to some of the most vitriolic accounts of movies they nevertheless, in their final chapter, celebrate film technology as "a marvelous instrument," which has the potential to educate, to entertain, and to build up the churches.[17]

The belief that film corrupts morals and perverts theological vision is also particularly prevalent in the earlier Catholic documents considering film. For instance, the first papal encyclical letter on film, Pope Pius XI's *Vigilanti Cura* (29 June 1936), reflects a deep anxiety that the motion picture could be a "school of corruption," that "destroys the moral fiber of the nation."[18] The encyclical assumes that films have considerable power in changing people's behavior and beliefs: "There does not exist today a means of influencing the masses more potent than the cinema." This can be for good or for evil. There is a celebratory and hopeful tone in some of the statements about film's potential for good. Although bad motion pictures can damage the soul and be "occasions of sin," "good motion pictures are capable of exercising a profoundly moral influence upon those who see them." For this reason "the motion picture should not be simply a means of diversion, a light relaxation to occupy an idle hour; with its magnificent power, it can and must be a bearer of light and a positive guide to what is good." Addressed in the first instance to the Catholic hierarchy in the United States and then to other bishops around the world, it celebrates the success of the Legion of Decency, which encouraged Catholics to sign a pledge "binding themselves not to attend any motion picture which was offensive to Catholic moral principles or proper standards of living."

More than twenty years later Pope Pius XII's encyclical letter on motion pictures, radio, and television, *Miranda Prorsus* (8 September 1957), develops several of the themes in *Vigilanti Cura*. For instance, it

Figure 36.1 Front cover of *The Devil's Camera: Menace of a Film-ridden World* (London: Epworth Press, 1932).[19]

outlines the significant role of Catholic film critics for setting out the moral issues and instructing their readers in terms of the moral position to be adopted. Alongside reviewers, spectators themselves have a "duty of conscience," similar to when casting a vote, each time they "buy a ticket of admission." Both documents contain within them what might be described as a Christian rigorist response to film, which assumes that motion pictures have considerable power to shape the moral and theological horizons of their viewers. The practical aim was to encourage Christians to be vigilant about films, to view suspect films cautiously, and to avoid some films entirely.

At the height of the Legion's influence, if a film broke the production code's guidelines, it could find itself receiving much worse than negative reviews: thousands of Legion members would stay away from its screenings. In pre-World War II America, virulent anti-Semitism heightened the perception that Hollywood was dominated by Jews, lay well beyond the control of the Christian churches, and therefore needed to be resisted.[20] Deep-rooted suspicion toward film as potentially an evil influence, Hollywood as the new Babylon, and filmmakers as the corrupters of children continues to this day, with some religious leaders encouraging their constituencies to avoid suspect films. In parts of North America or Southern India, a single example of nudity, bad language, sexual innuendo, or unnecessary violence can ensure that a film receives a warning notice, communicated by email or websites strongly advising against viewing. In many cases the force of the cinematic narrative is eclipsed by an unacceptable scene: a moment deemed to be ethically unacceptable such as the "unnecessary nudity" in *Schindler's List*.[21]

Film explores?

Some theologians came to recognize that while film has the potential to amuse, to entertain, and to distract, it also has great potential to explore profound theological questions and moral dilemmas. The result of this understanding was that, particularly in the second half of the twentieth century, a number of less negative Christian responses to film developed. The applause that Pasolini's *The Gospel According to Saint Matthew* (1964) received from the 800 bishops gathered in Rome for the Second Vatican Council is symptomatic of the growing enthusiasm for the theological uses of film. Even in some of the most critical Catholic writings discussed here there is an understated ambivalence about film.[22] Some more recent official Catholic documents reflect a less suspicious attitude toward film in general. For instance, the pastoral instruction *Communio et Progressio* (23 May 1971) celebrates films as works of art that can compellingly treat subjects that concern "human progress or spiritual values." Moreover, certain institutions within the Catholic Church became involved in both the production and the funding of films, which sometimes included scenes that the Legion of Decency would have found deeply problematic (e.g. *Romero*, 1989). The Office [later, Organisation] Catholique International du Cinéma (OCIC) was founded in 1928 at an international Catholic congress on cinema in the Hague. Its founding was supported by Pope Pius XI, and initially it was intended to promote "moral films" and support Christians working in the film industry. After World War II it set up an international film prize. Here was a Catholic body that had moved beyond censoring cinema and was now keen to celebrate some films, particularly those "most capable of contributing to the moral and spiritual elevation of humanity."[23] The OCIC award has been conferred on directors such as John Ford and Francis Ford Coppola. OCIC (now SIGNIS) not only supports the awarding of prizes and the development of national film offices, but it also organizes Catholic film juries, which continue to serve alongside ecumenical juries at the world's major film festivals. There are no restrictions on the kind of films that can receive awards. This has sometimes led to conflict between juries and the Catholic hierarchy. The most celebrated case was Pasolini's *Teorema* (*Theorem*), which was offered the grand prize at the 1968 Venice film festival, only for the film and the jury to be later condemned by the Vatican. In spite of such disagreements, film juries remain autonomous and are allowed to bestow their prizes upon whomsoever they deem fit. Numerous other religious prizes were awarded to films by Bergman, Bresson, and Fellini.[24] Pasolini may have been an atheist Marxist, but *The Gospel According to Saint Matthew* was named best religious film of the year in 1964 by OCIC (see Figure 36.2), who admitted that although Pasolini "did not share our faith," he had produced a "Christian film that produces a profound impression."[25] There is now an increased recognition, by some, that films can explore with great depth, power, and artistry moral dilemmas and theological questions.

Peter Malone, an Australian Jesuit, has devoted much of his writing and teaching career to the enterprise of showing how films are often redolent with theological and moral meaning. Malone's *Film and Values* (1984) is "based on the assumption that contemporary films, the vast majority of them, are not corrupting"; in fact, through storytelling, films often explore and express the heart of the human condition. He suggests that films can function as transformative parables and as such have the potential to "challenge the stands we take, test the values we profess to act by."[26] Malone's work tends toward careful analysis of films and the characterizations they present. This can be seen clearly in *Movie Christs and Antichrists* (1990), which is one of the first books to make the distinction between the Jesus-figure and the Christ-figure in films. The former was the representation of Jesus himself on screen, such as in *The King of Kings* (1927) or *The Greatest Story Ever Told* (1965) and the latter was the portrayal of characters whose depictions resonate with the life or death of Christ, such as the protagonist in *Cool Hand Luke* (1967) or *Pale Rider* (1985). Several other writers have made extensive use of this distinction between Jesus-figures and Christ-figures in films, such as Lloyd Baugh in *Imaging the Divine* (1997). As Baugh and other critics acknowledge, identifying a film's protagonist as a Christ-figure may reveal more about the interpreter than illuminate the actual narrative.

Figure 36.2 Advertisement promoting *The Gospel According to St Matthew* (Dir. Pier Paolo Pasolini, 1964). Everett Collection Inc/Alamy Stock Photo.

Malone is an exception in the early days of theological film criticism, as the majority of exploratory work in the 1960s and 1970s was by North American scholars. Writers such as Neil Hurley, John May, and James Wall led this exploration.[27] Hurley's three books on film demonstrate a fascination with both the specific content of numerous movies and the directorial influence on what is shown. In *Theology Through Film* (1970) Hurley sets out a "cinematic theology." He begins by asserting that "movies are for the masses what theology is for an elite."[28] He attempts, for example, to trace transcendence through a number of contemporary films, suggesting that it is possible to identify signs of grace on the screen. Like Hurley, Wall's method of reading films theologically has evolved over a number of years, in particular while he worked as editor of the *Christian Century*, writing reviews and editorials. In *Church and Cinema* (1971) Wall concentrates on the director's vision of the world as a channel of revelation. May, like Hurley and Wall, emphasizes the role of the director in shaping each film's distinctive perspective. For example, in his later discussion of *The Godfather* trilogy he uses director Coppola's intentions as the touchstone for his interpretation of these classic films. By putting considerable emphasis upon the director's vision, Hurley, May, and Wall show themselves to be sympathetic to elements of the *auteur* theory. This roughly refers to the approach in film criticism that privileges the perspective of the director as the "author" or the organizing genius behind the film.

Film illuminates?

Film may have the potential to provoke theological and ethical questioning, but do movies have an inherent capacity to illuminate scriptural texts? In the last few decades, a number of biblical scholars have answered this question affirmatively. Adele Reinhartz uses *Scripture on the Silver Screen* (2003) to assist in the development of "biblical literacy," while the diverse essays in *Screening Scripture* (2002) demonstrate how "intertextual connections between scripture and film" are possible. These books have earlier precedents. For example, although Larry Kreitzer is by training a biblical scholar, he has made his name through exploring the ways film and fiction can illuminate biblical texts. To date, Kreitzer has produced four books that aim to enable "a dialogue to take place between the biblical text, great works of literature, and that most persuasive of modern art forms, the cinema." He describes this process as "reversing the hermeneutical flow." In essence, this triadic approach means using classic works of literature and their cinematic interpretations as a way of shedding fresh light on biblical passages. For instance, Kreitzer provides a careful reading of different versions of Bram Stoker's *Dracula*, both the novel (1897) and the Coppola film (1992), to illuminate the blood motif in Paul's first letter to the church at Corinth. Kreitzer's case studies usually concentrate upon classic novels and films such as *Dr Jekyll and Mr Hyde*, *Spartacus*, and *Ben Hur*. He brings the skills of a New Testament scholar to bear upon such texts. Kreitzer's three-way or triadic approach is becoming increasingly well known, though it has been criticized for its preoccupation with authorial intent.[29] Nevertheless, Kreitzer's books have made a significant contribution to the rapidly evolving research areas related to theology and film.

Robert Jewett is another biblical scholar who has immersed himself in the world of film criticism. His stated motivation and method are different from Kreitzer's. In his first two books on film he uses St Paul as a conversation partner with specific movies, claiming that, given Paul's missionary desire to be all things to all people, if there had been film in his day, Paul would also have engaged with film criticism. Instead of Kreitzer's triadic approach Jewett uses a two-way "interpretive arch," which intends to treat both biblical and cinematic texts with exegetical respect. He often moves the reader from the world of the film text to the world of the biblical text and back again.[30] One concern raised about both Jewett and Kreitzer's approach is the perceived tendency to rely upon literary models of film criticism, rather than embracing the rich resources of film theory, such as various psychoanalytic-based or spectator-led approaches.[31] The danger is that the attempt to "read" a film turns it into something that it is not: a written text. Films cannot be reduced to mere words to be analyzed.[32] Other skills, such as visual sensitivity, are required to analyze a film. Several writers on theology and film go even further than Kreitzer and Jewett, suggesting that movies can act sacramentally. In *Images of the Passion* (1998) Peter Fraser examines the films that in his opinion best portray Christ's passion, describing them as sacramental films. For Fraser, "the sacramental film allows for the appropriation of spiritual presence sought by the devotional writers, but in a public experience."[33] Each chapter offers an interpretation of a specific film, such as *Gallipoli* (1981), *The Mission* (1986), and *Black Robe* (1991), and Fraser suggests that if the *Diary of a Country Priest* (1950) is embraced as the director Bresson intends, then viewers "will be brought into a sacramental experience with the living God."[34] This is a hard claim to verify, but it does exemplify a belief that film can illuminate the viewer. For Fraser, the sacramental film can become an object of "mystical contemplation," and he correctly predicts that in the future films may well become "more prominent in popular practices of Christian piety."[35] These approaches further reflect how film is now perceived by some as a potential catalyst for prayer, a place of devotion, and a source of revelation.

Catholic author and film critic Andrew Greeley supports such a view, claiming that film as part of "popular culture" is a *locus theologicus*, a theological place – "the locale in which one may encounter God."[36] For Greeley, God "lurks in the places in which the 'stories' of popular culture occur."[37] He developed these points more explicitly in *God in the Movies*, where he claims that cinema is a place where viewers can encounter the divine.[38]

Although other recent writers claim to look for and even find "God in the movies," they invariably admit that this is an arduous task, similar to trying to catch light.[39] Director and screenwriter Paul Schrader provides a sophisticated account of the revelatory function of film. On the basis of a study of three non-Hollywood directors (Ozu, Bresson, and Dreyer), Schrader suggests that through their realistic and sparse filmic style it is possible to encounter the sacred.[40]

"Named Theologians": Directorial Theology

Films can offer alternative views of reality. George Lucas, creator of the *Star Wars* films, made it clear that he does not want to invent a religion or offer answers through his films, but he does want to make young people think about mystery and to ask: "Is there a God? What does God look like? What does God sound like? What does God feel like? How do we relate to God?" He claims to have put the Force into the *Star Wars* movies in order to "try to awaken a certain kind of spirituality in young people," so that they might begin to ask questions about what he describes as "the mystery."[41] Lucas hopes that his *Star Wars* films will lead audiences to ask questions about the existence and nature of God.

Few directors have studied theology in depth and few consciously attempt to articulate theological themes through their work. Their intention is rarely, if ever, explicitly theological. Rose Glass, the director of the well-received surreal horror movie *Saint Maud* (2019), drew on her own religious and convent school background, rather than carrying out new theological research, to explore distorted aspects of Christian practice through portraying the story of a Catholic nurse who believes that she is hearing the voice of God. By attending to specific scenes, films, or directorial statements it is possible, however, to discern how even directors can express themselves like creative theologians. Directors can be seen as visual storytellers grappling with theological issues in new and original ways. Their craft is neither primarily text based nor rooted in logical arguments but rather partly dependent upon the skillful juxtaposition of images, sounds, and dialogue to create a narrative. "I've turned from an image maker into a storyteller," German director Wim Wenders claims. "Only a story can give meaning and a moral to an image."[42]

Directors work not in a closed study or quiet library but among a large group of industry professionals. For example, the team that Krzsztof Kieślowski (1941–96) used to create *The Decalogue* (1988), a series of short films made initially for Polish television and loosely based upon the Ten Commandments, reflects his belief that filmmaking is essentially a collaborative practice. By concentrating upon the work of directors I am not suggesting that the role of other members of the team, such as the screenwriter, producer, director of photography, film editor, composer, casting director, or actor, can be ignored. To focus upon the director's work, writings, and background is not to ignore the inherently communal nature of their profession, nor the economic constraints or social pressures faced by filmmakers, but it is one valuable approach to reflecting critically upon the theological significance of film production and content.

Ingmar Bergman

One specific director provides a useful example to consider the complex nature of directorial theology. The Swede Ingmar Bergman (1918–2007) is widely recognized as a cinematic master-craftsman. He appears to have been intrigued by the legend of Chartres, which told how the cathedral was burnt down, then rebuilt by thousands of anonymous craftsmen. In his introduction to the script of *The Seventh Seal* (*Det Sjunde Inseglet*, 1956) he identifies himself with those nameless builders:

> If I am asked what I would like the general purpose of my films to be, I would reply that I want to be one of the artists in the cathedral on the great plain. I want to make a dragon's head, an angel, a devil – or perhaps a saint – out of stone. It does not matter which; it is the sense of satisfaction that counts. Regardless of whether I believe or not, whether I am a Christian or not, I would play my part in the collective building of the cathedral.[43]

As the son of a Swedish Lutheran pastor, Bergman was brought up in a pious home, which shaped his self-understanding and theological questioning, which in turn influenced his filmmaking.

Bergman "contributed vividly to the cinema of alienation, the cinema of the dispossessed individual, the post-Christian fallen world" of the second half of the twentieth century.[44] Films such as his bleak trilogy about people living in search of comfort and guidance in the absence of God, *Through a Glass Darkly* (1961), *Winter Light* (1962), and *The Silence* (1963), and his Passion film *Cries and Whispers* (1973), explore several of these themes. In *Winter Light*, for example, a Swedish pastor continues to worship even though he has lost his own faith and is faced by the death of God all around him. On the one hand, Bergman saw himself as someone like this pastor who had lost his faith and now confesses that the artist "considers his isolation, his subjectivity, his individualism almost holy."[45] The artist is trapped in his own loneliness, walking in circles, unable to recognize the existence of the other. On the other hand, it appears that during the 1950s and early 1960s Bergman could not easily dispense with his understanding of God's place in the creative process. Earlier, in the introduction to *The Seventh Seal*, he not only bemoans the individualism of the artist, but also claims that "art lost its basic creative drive the moment it was separated from worship."[46]

Bergman was far from unknown when he wrote this introduction. *The Seventh Seal* was the seventeenth film that he had directed and remains one of the most commonly cited. At several moments the star of this film is not the knight (Block) or his squire (Jöns), but death personified. The backdrop to the film is the plague. The film is permeated by the theme of death, exploring how different characters respond to their own impending death. Returning from the Crusades the knight may try to escape death by playing it at chess, but he will never win nor escape (see Figure 36.3). Bergman admitted that this cinematic exploration was cathartic, in that after making this film, although he still thought about death, it was no longer an obsession. Bergman is a director who repeatedly expresses his theological angst on screen, especially during the first two decades of his filmmaking. Block's journey in *The Seventh Seal* resonates with Bergman's own experience: a search for a silent God in the face of both death and human love.[47] Although he may not have

Figure 36.3 *The Seventh Seal* (Dir. Ingmar Bergman, 1957), Svensk Filmindustri production with Bengt Ekerot as Death and Max von Sydow as the Knight. LANDMARK MEDIA/Alamy Stock Photo.

explicitly dedicated his work to the "glory of God," his ability to create and to explore through the screen was clearly a gift that provokes profound theological questions.

Scorsese, Glass, and Bergman are examples of directors who sometimes acknowledged some basis in theological thinking; DeMille did so more rarely, whereas the majority of directors tend to express theological themes without formally naming them as such. The theme emerges from the narrative because it is expressive of primal fears, aspirations, and predispositions, not because it has been consciously planted there. My contention in this section is that to speak of directorial theology does not exclude the possibility of acknowledging the wider role of both the production team and the audience in creating theological meaning around specific films.

Debate, Achievement, and Agenda

There has been a marked increase of literature published on theology and film over the last twenty years. During the last decade well over twenty books, alongside many articles, have been published relating to film and religion, many explicitly theological. Some of these reflect the global and cultural turns in the field described earlier and include *World Cinema, Theology and the Human* (2015) by Antonio Sison, *Transcendence and Spirituality in Chinese Cinema: A Theological Exploration* by Kris Chong (2022), *The Holy Fool in European Cinema* (2016) by Alina Birzache, and *Theology and Survival Movies: An Orthodox Christian Christian Perspective* (2023) by Ioan Buteanu. Nevertheless, compared to many lines of theological inquiry, theological film criticism is still in its early days. One significant change of emphasis over the last one hundred and twenty years is a shift from pastoral concern about the impacts or benefits of film to more sustained critical analysis by theologians who are often writing for a narrower readership. Increasingly, theologians are using film as a source to illustrate rich theological themes or debates.

Examples of this practice include L. Gregory Jones' extended use of *Unforgiven* (1992) in *Embodying Forgiveness* (1995), David Brown's brief analysis of Jesus films in *Tradition and Imagination* (1999), Graham Ward's discussions of *The Matrix* in *Cities of God* (2000), David Cunningham's use of film to illuminate the Apostles' Creed in *Reading is Believing* (2002), Gerard Loughlin's analysis of the *Alien* films in *Alien Sex* (2003), David Jasper's consideration of films of the desert in *The Sacred Desert* (2004), and Francesca Murphy's characterization of narrative theology as "movie like" in *God Is Not a Story* (2007). In these books film is used to illustrate and to support a broader thesis. The cinema is now often portrayed not as a problem to be negotiated but more as a resource to be mined. These theologians are going far beyond moral criticism to engage with the theological issues provoked by different films. They demonstrate how some of the most theologically interesting films are not necessarily explicitly religious in content.

The fact that many Christians regularly now go to the cinema and watch films online, and read and write film reviews, has ensured that in several accounts the censorious role of the churches has taken on the air of a distant half-forgotten memory. There is a sense in which iconoclastic approaches to the cinema are acknowledged but ultimately ignored. Theological exploration of films has taken on a far more confident role both in the academy and in the church. Theological film criticism has moved beyond defending the appropriateness of going to the cinema or watching particular films and now analyzes in some detail how films actually explore moral issues and theological themes. The return to the cinema raises a number of significant questions for Christian theologians. For example, is there a distinctively theological way of analyzing films or do Christians simply draw upon elements of film criticism for their own theological purposes? Many theologians appear to be immersed in either textual analytical discussions or authorial approaches to film. "It is somewhat disappointing to find that writing on film which does take religion seriously has largely ignored the broader social, cultural, and historical contexts within which films are made and consumed."[48] Films such as *It's a Wonderful Life* (1946), *On the Waterfront* (1954), *Ordet* (1955),

Andrei Rublev (1966), *Au Hasard Balthazar* (1966), *The Exorcist* (1973), *Babette's Feast* (1987), *The Decalogue* (1989), *Dead Man Walking* (1995), *Dogma* (1999), *A Serious Man* (2009), *The Tree of Life* (2011), *Ida* (2013), *Calvary* (2014), and *The Whale* (2022) are not only useful for provoking theological questions, they can also be valuable as thermometers of a culture's *Zeitgeist* at a particular moment in time. What, for example, does the continued delight in alternative cinematic worlds as found in the Marvel Universe, the DC Universe, the *Middle Earth* films, the *Harry Potter* movies, and the *Star Wars* franchise show about this current age?

Many theological responses to the cinema are founded on the belief that movies work like the moment from Edwin Porter's *The Great Train Robbery* (1903), where Barnes, leader of the outlaw band, points his gun out toward the audience and fires point blank into their faces. Film legend has it that the result was extreme: some viewers are believed to have screamed, ducked, or put their fingers in their ears, and others supposedly even ran out of the cinema. This is probably a romanticized retrospective view of early cinema: there may have been flinching at the Lumière brothers' showing in 1895, but audiences were already becoming canny and skeptical spectators by 1903. Nonetheless, the unstated assumption in several of the approaches discussed in earlier sections is that through films the bullet of narrative content fires out at the viewers and has a powerful impact on audiences. This "magic bullet theory" of communication is now rarely explicitly defended, but the idea of a passive audience soaking in the messages that are fired at them remains surprisingly tenacious in many Christian documents and theological reflections about film. One way of enriching the evolving theology and film debate would be to leave behind a passive receptor paradigm and replace it with a more sophisticated understanding of audiences as active spectators. In other words, to investigate not only what films do to the audience, but also what audiences do with films.[49]

Until relatively recently theological film criticism has largely emerged from the West and tended to assume a Western audience.[50] This ignores a significant element of current film consumption. For example, a packed cinema or video house in Accra, with a full house watching a locally produced Ghanaian or Nigerian film rich in religious symbolism, brings new meaning to the term "active audience." The viewers are rarely silent, and often they actively cheer, boo, or pray out loud for the characters.[51] This experience stands in sharp contrast with sitting in a Western multiplex watching a Hollywood film, where the audience tends to be far quieter. Except for the occasional cough, rustle of candy wrappers, or munching on popcorn, any talking is normally "shushed" and exclamations are rare, the exceptions being laughter or gasps or screams of surprise in horror movies and thrillers. The silencing of the Western audience is a fascinating story well told elsewhere.[52] Appearances can be deceptive. This silence does not mean that audiences are entirely passive. For well over thirty years researchers have explored how viewers actively weave complex patterns of meaning on the basis of the films, and other media, that they consume. This could go further: how precisely do audiences in different cultural contexts make theological meaning from what they see? How important a factor is their local church, practice of prayer, or understanding of theology in helping them make sense of a specific film? To what extent does this network of experiences shape and color the way they process what they view? Few scholars have actually tested the claim that films have replaced the institutional church as the provider of religious symbols and theological meaning. There is clearly a need for both empirical investigation and greater conceptual clarity around the claim that films can act as points of transcendence or even channels of revelation.

Cultural resistance in the face of films that exploit, stereotype, or damage comes in many forms. For example, Cheryl Exum's consideration of cultural representations of biblical women in *Plotted, Shot and Painted* (1996) proposes a strategy of resistance, which self-consciously "takes seriously the gender politics of both representation and interpretation."[53] Approaches such as this emphasize how the male gaze tends still to dominate both the production and reception of many films. Other writers look for the building up of Christian communities, distinct linguistic and interpretive communities, in the face of the perceived onslaught of the global culture industries that produce films.[54] But this may simply be another form of cultural withdrawal that draws a sharp divide between secular, profane films and holy, sacred believers. It ignores the possibility that films such as *All Quiet on the Western Front* (1930 and 2022) can themselves articulate a sharp cultural critique. Films can interrogate theology. The church has much to learn from specific prophetic films.

Film and theology may appear to approach the world in very different ways. Film, as a form of entertainment, commonly relies on fast moving images and atmospheric sounds, whereas theology, an academic discipline, tends to rely on texts and arguments to explore religious beliefs and practices. There have sometimes been tensions or even hostility between film and different kinds of theology. As we have seen, films commonly also raise theological questions and draw upon theological insights to enrich their narratives and characterizations. Theologians, religious studies scholars, and religious leaders approach films in a number of different ways: autobiographically,[55] experientially,[56] ethically,[57] apologetically,[58] aesthetically,[59] contextually,[60] comparatively,[61] historically, [62] pastorally,[63] biblically,[64] prayerfully,[65] evangelistically,[66] Christologically,[67] redemptively,[68] dialogically,[69] psychologically,[70] and globally.[71]

Nevertheless, there remains a need for nuanced critiques of the film industry itself. How far has it become an agent of capitalism and consumerism? How far has the film industry become an alternative kind of church, with its own sacred times and spaces, its own viewing rituals and canonization ceremonies? How far does it promote the accumulation of wealth and individual celebrity over the formation of character and caring communities? How far does the industry create cinematic distractions from the real and endemic violence in the world? These questions are complicated by the fact that, although many films celebrate the myths of heroic individualism or romantic love or redemptive violence, others function counterculturally, challenging the status quo in a way reminiscent of some of Jesus's most provocative teaching. The global increase in the viewing of films, as well as the crossover of movies to social media, television, and streaming online heightens the significance of these questions. Seeing with the help of film can be encouraged not through the endless censoring enacted in *Cinema Paradiso*, but through communal worship, caring practices, and reflective education.

Notes

1   See, for example, Frank Walsh, *Sin and Censorship: The Catholic Church and the Motion Picture Industry* (New Haven, CT: Yale University Press, 1996), 1. For further discussions of censorship, see Gregory D. Black, *Hollywood Censored: Morality Codes, Catholics, and the Movies* (New York: Cambridge University Press, 1994) and Matthew Bernstein, ed., *Controlling Hollywood: Censorship and Regulation in the Studio Era* (New Brunswick, NJ: Rutgers University Press, 1999).

2   For contrasting accounts of the protests against *The Last Temptation of Christ*, see Michael Medved, *Hollywood vs. America* (New York: Harper, 1992), 38–49 and Margaret R. Miles, *Seeing and Believing: Religion and Values in the Movies* (Boston, MA: Beacon Press, 1996), 33–40. For both films, see L. Baugh, *Imaging the Divine: Jesus and Christ-Figures in Film* (Kansas City, MO: Sheed and Ward, 1997), 48–71.

3   Roy Rosenzweig, "From Rum Shop to Rialto: Workers and Movies," in *Moviegoing in America: A Sourcebook in the History of Film Exhibition*, ed. Gregory A. Waller (Oxford: Blackwell, 2002), 36–7.

4   See Ronald Holloway, *Beyond the Image: Approaches to the Religious Dimensions in the Cinema* (Geneva: World Council

of Churches, 1977), 26 and James M. Skinner, *The Cross and the Cinema: The Legion of Decency and the National Catholic Office for Motion Pictures, 1933-1970* (Westport, CT: Praeger, 1993), figs. 10 and 11 and 193–4.

5   See Charles Musser, "Passions and the Passion Play: Theatre, Film, and Religion in America, 1800–1900," *Film History* 5, no. 4 (1993): 419–56. See also Caroline Vander Stichele, "Silent Saviours: Representations of Jesus' Passion in Early Cinema," in *The Ancient World in Silent Cinema*, ed. Pantelis Michelakis and Maria Wyke (Cambridge: Cambridge University Press, 2013), 169.

6   See Robert K. Johnston, *Reel Spirituality: Theology and Film in Dialogue* (Grand Rapids, MI: Baker Academic, 2000), 32.

7   Herbert Jump, "The Religious Possibilities of the Motion Picture," in *The Silents of God: Selected Issues and Documents in Silent American Films and Religion 1908–1925*, ed. Terry Lindvall (Lanham, MD: Scarecrow Press, 2001), 55–78. See also *Film History* 14, no. 2 (2002).

8   See Baugh, *Imaging the Divine*, 7–8.

9   For an exception, see Krzysztof Jozajtis, "Religion and Film in American Culture: The Birth of a Nation" (PhD diss. University of Stirling, 2001), 98.

10 John R. May, "Religion and Film: Recent Contributions to the Continuing Dialogue," *Critical Review of Books in Religion* 9 (1996): 105–21. See also John R. May and Michael Bird, eds., *Religion in Film* (Knoxville, TN: University of Tennessee Press, 1982). John R. May, ed., *Images and Likeness: Religious Visions in American Film Classics* (Mahwah, NJ: Paulist Press, 1991); John R. May, ed., *New Image of Religious Film* (Kansas City, MO: Sheed and Ward, 1997); John R. May, *Nourishing Faith through Fiction: Reflections of the Apostles' Creed in Literature and Film* (Franklin, MA: Sheed and Ward, 2001).

11 Johnston, *Reel Spirituality*, 41–62.

12 S. Brent Plate, *Religion and Film: Cinema and the Re-Creation of the World*, 2nd ed. (New York: Columbia University Press, 2017), 1–18; Joel Mayward, *The Dardenne Brothers' Cinematic Parables: Integrating Theology, Philosophy, and Film* (Abingdon: Routledge, 2022), 20.

13 C. H. J. Linn, "The Movies – the Devil's Incubator," in *The Silents of God*, ed. Lindvall, 279.

14 John R. Rice, *What Is Wrong with the Movies?* (Wheaton, IL: Zondervan, 1938), 14. See also Tamar Lane, *What's Wrong with the Movies?* (Los Angeles, CA: Waverly, 1923).

15 R. G. Burnett and E. D. Martell, *The Devil's Camera: Menace of a Film-Ridden World* (London: Epworth Press, 1932), 71.

16 Burnett and Martell, *The Devil's Camera*, 108–9.

17 Burnett and Martell, *The Devil's Camera*, 116–17.

18 For *Vigilanti Cura* and other Catholic documents cited in this section, see either the Vatican website (https://www.vatican.va/content/vatican/en/search.html?q=encyclicals) or Franz-Josef Eilers, ed., *Church and Social Communication: Basic Documents*, 2nd ed. (Manila: Logos, 1997).

19 Every effort has been made to obtain copyright clearance for all images in this chapter. The publisher will gladly receive any information enabling them to rectify any error or omission in subsequent editions.

20 See Steven Alan Carr, *Hollywood and Anti-Semitism: A Cultural History up to World War II* (Cambridge: Cambridge University Press, 2001).

21 See US Federal Communications Commission's final judgment (11 January 2000), rejecting Thomas B. North's complaint that the pre-10:00 p.m. nudity contained in the network presentation of *Schindler's List*, 23 February 1997, was actionably indecent.

22 See, for example, Pius XI, *Vigilanti Cura* (1936), II.

23 See Gaye Ortiz, "The Catholic Church and Its Attitude to Film as an Arbiter of Cultural Meaning," in *Mediating Religion: Studies in Media, Religion and Culture*, ed. Jolyon Mitchell and Sophia Marriage (London: T&T Clark, 2003), 179–88.

24 Holloway, *Beyond the Image*, 29.

25 Baugh, *Imaging the Divine*, 97.

26 Peter Malone, *Film and Values* (New York, 1984), 3, 43.

27 For a fuller critical exposition of these and several other approaches, see Steve Nolan, "Towards a New Religious Film Criticism: Using Film to Understand Religious Identity Rather than Locate Cinematic Analogue," in *Mediating Religion*, ed. Mitchell and Marriage, 169–78. For more on "Christ-figures" see Paul Coates, *Cinema, Religion and the Romantic Legacy* (Aldershot: Routledge, 2003), 79–82.

28 See Neil P. Hurley, *Theology through Film* (New York: Harper & Row, 1970); *The Reel Revolution: A Film Primer on Liberation* (New York: Orbis, 1978); *Soul in Suspense: Hitchcock's Fright and Delight* (London: Scarecrow Press, 1993).

29 See L. Joseph Kreitzer, *The New Testament in Fiction and Film* (Sheffield: Sheffield Academic Press, 1993); *The Old Testament in Fiction and Film* (Sheffield: Sheffield Academic Press, 1994); *Pauline Images in Fiction and Film* (Sheffield: Sheffield Academic Press, 1999); *Gospel Images in Fiction and Film: On Reversing the Hermeneutical Flow* (Sheffield: Sheffield Academic Press, 2002). For criticisms of an overliterary approach see Melanie J. Wright, *Religion and Film: An Introduction* (London: Bloomsbury, 2005), 20–2. For other approaches relating the Bible to film, see also George Aichele and Richard Walsh eds., *Screening Scripture: Intertextual Connections between Scripture and Film* (Harrisburg, PA: Trinity Press, 2002); Bruce Francis Babington and Peter William Evans, *Biblical Epics: Sacred Narrative in the Hollywood Cinema* (Manchester: Manchester University Press, 1993); Terry Lindvall, J. Dennis Bounds, and Chris Lindvall, *Divine Film Comedies: Biblical Narratives, Film Sub-Genres, and Comic Spirit* (New York: Routledge, 2016); Adele Reinhartz, *Scripture on the Silver Screen* (Louisville, KY: Westminster John Knox Press, 2003); Erin Runions, *How Hysterical: Identification and Resistance in the Bible and Film* (New York: Palgrave Macmillan, 2003); Bernard Brandon Scott, *Hollywood Dreams and Biblical Stories* (Minneapolis, MN: Fortress Press, 1994). For work on Jesus and early film, see David Shepherd, ed., *The Silents of Jesus in the Cinema (1897–1927)* (Abingdon: Routledge, 2019); Richard Stern, Clayton N. Jefford, and Guerric DeBona, *Savior on the Silver Screen* (New York: Paulist Press, 1999); and Stichele, "Silent Saviours."

30 See Nolan, "Towards a New Religious Film Criticism," 169–78. See also Robert Jewett, *Saint Paul at the Movies: The Apostle's Dialogue with American Culture* (Louisville, KY: Westminster John Knox Press 1993); and *Saint Paul Returns to the Movies: Triumph over Shame* (Grand Rapids, MI: Eerdmans, 1999).

31 See Thomas M. Martin, *Images and the Imageless: A Study in Religious Consciousness and Film* (Lewisburg, PA: Bucknell University Press, 1981), 122.

32 Peter Fraser, *Images of the Passion: The Sacramental Mode in Film* (Westport, CT: Praeger, 1998), 5.

33 Fraser, *Images of the Passion*, 11.

34 Fraser, *Images of the Passion*, 6. See also Joseph Cunneen, *Robert Bresson: A Spiritual Style in Film* (New York: Continuum, 2003).

35 Fraser, *Images of the Passion*, 1–12.

36 Andrew M. Greeley, *God in Popular Culture* (Chicago, IL: Thomas More Press, 1988), 9.

37 Greeley, *God in Popular Culture*, 121.

38 See Albert J. Bergesen and Andrew M. Greeley, *God in the Movies* (New Brunswick, NJ: Transaction, 2000).

39 See Roy M. Anker, *Catching Light: Looking for God in the Movies* (Grand Rapids, MI: Eerdmans, 2004), and Catherine M. Barsotti and Robert K. Johnston, *Finding God in the Movies: 33 Films of Reel Faith* (Grand Rapids, MI: Baker, 2004). By contrast, see John Pungente and Monty Williams, *Finding God in the Dark: Taking the Spiritual Exercises of St. Ignatius to the Movies* (Ottawa: Pauline Books & Media, 2004).

40 Paul Schrader, *Transcendental Style in Film: Ozu, Bresson, Dreyer*, 2nd ed. (Berkeley, CA: University of California Press, 2018).

41 George Lucas interview with Bill Moyers in *Time*, 26 April 1999.

42 Quoted in Anton Kaes, "The New German Cinema," in *The Oxford History of World Cinema*, ed. Geoffrey Nowell-Smith (Oxford: Oxford University Press, 1996), 625.

43 See Ingmar Bergman, introduction to *The Seventh Seal* script (London, 1968, revised 1984).

44 Melvyn Bragg, *The Seventh Seal*, BFI Classics (London: BFI, 1993), 11.

45 Bergman, introduction to *The Seventh Seal*.

46 Bergman, introduction to *The Seventh Seal*.

47 See Jesse Kalin, *The Films of Ingmar Bergman* (Cambridge: Cambridge University Press, 2003), 57–67. See also Arthur Gibson, *The Silence of God: Creative Response to the Films of Ingmar Bergman* (New York: Harper & Row, 1969).

48 Jozajtis, *Religion and Film in American Culture*, 98.

49 See Clive Marsh, *Cinema and Sentiment: Film's Challenge to Theology* (Carlisle: Send the Light, 2004).

50 For exceptions see S. Brent Plate, ed., *Representing Religion in World Cinema: filmmaking, Mythmaking, Culture Making* (New York: Palgrave Macmillan, 2003); Jolyon Mitchell and S. Brent Plate, eds., *The Religion and Film Reader* (London: Routledge, 2007); Antonio D. Sison, *World Cinema, Theology and the Human: Humanity in Deep Focus* (New York: Routledge, 2012); Alina G. Birzache, *The Holy Fool in*

European Cinema* (Abingdon: Routledge, 2016); and Kris H. K. Chong, *Transcendence and Spirituality in Chinese Cinema: A Theological Exploration* (Abingdon: Routledge, 2022).

51 See Jolyon Mitchell, "From Morality Tales to Horror Movies," in *Belief in Media*, ed. P. Horsfield et al., (Aldershot: Ashgate, 2004), 107–20.

52 See Lawrence W. Levine, *Highbrow/Lowbrow: The Emergence of Cultural Hierarchy in America* (Cambridge, MA: Harvard University Press, 1988).

53 J. Cheryl Exum, *Plotted, Shot and Painted: Cultural Representations of Biblical Women* (Sheffield: Sheffield Academic Press, 1996), 53.

54 See Michael Budde, *The (Magic) Kingdom of God: Christianity and Global Culture Industries* (Boulder, CO: Perseus, 1997).

55 See Gareth Higgins, *How Movies Helped Save My Soul* (Lake Mary, FL: Relevant, 2003).

56 See Kutter Callaway, *Scoring Transcendence: Contemporary Film Music as Religious Experience* (Waco: Baylor University Press, 2012).

57 See Jolyon Mitchell, *Media Violence and Christian Ethics* (Cambridge: Cambridge University Press, 2007).

58 See William D. Romanowski, *Eyes Wide Open: Looking for God in Popular Culture* (Grand Rapids, MI: Brazos, 2001) and Tim Cawkwell, *The Filmgoer's Guide to God* (London: Darton, Longman & Todd, 2004).

59 See C. Downing, *Salvation from Cinema: The Medium Is the Message* (London: Routledge, 2016). Downing explores the religious significance of film technique.

60 See Les and Barbara Keyser, *Hollywood and the Catholic Church: The Image of Roman Catholicism in American Movies* (Chicago, IL: Loyola Press, 1984).

61 See John C. Lyden, *Film as Religion: Myths, Morals, and Rituals* (New York: New York University Press, 2003); and Marsh and Ortiz, eds., *Explorations in Theology and Film*.

62 See Lindvall, *The Silents of God*.

63 See Barsotti and Johnston, *Finding God in the Movies*.

64 Robert K. Johnston, *Useless Beauty: Ecclesiastes through the Lens of Contemporary Film* (Grand Rapids, MI: Baker, 2000).

65 E. McNulty, *Praying the Movies I and II: Daily Meditations from Classic Films* (Louisville, KY: Westminster John Knox Press, 2001 and 2004).

66 See David S. Cunningham, *Reading is Believing: The Christian Faith through Literature and Film* (Grand Rapids, MI: Brazos, 2002).

67 See, for example, Eric S. Christianson, Peter Francis, and William R. Telford, eds. *Cinéma Divinité: Religion, Theology and the Bible in Film* (London: SCM Press, 2005); Christopher Deacy, *Screen Christologies: Redemption and the Medium of Film* (Cardiff: University of Wales Press, 2001). Roy Kinnard and Tim Davis,

Divine Images: A History of Jesus on the Screen (New York: Citadel Press, 1992). Peter Malone, *Movie Christs and Antichrists* (New York: Crossroad, 1990); Robin Riley, *Film, Faith and Cultural Conflict: The Case of Martin Scorsese's The Last Temptation of Christ* (Westport, CT: Praeger, 2003). W. Barnes Tatum, *Jesus at the Movies: A Guide to the First Hundred Years* (Santa Rosa, CA: Polebridge Press, 1997). R. Walsh, *Reading the Gospels in the Dark: Portrayals of Jesus in Film* (Harrisburg, PA: Trinity Press, 2003).

68 David Rankin, *Film and Redemption: From Brokenness to Wholeness* (Abingdon: Routledge, 2022).

69 See Anthony J. Clarke and Paul S. Fiddes, eds., *Flickering Images: Theology and Film in Dialogue* (Macon, GA: Smith & Helwys, 2005).

70 See Martin, *Images and the Imageless.*

71 See Plate, ed., *Representing Religion in World Cinema;* Matthew P. John, *Film as Cultural Artifact: Religious Criticism of World Cinema* (Minneapolis, MN: Fortress Press, 2017).

Recommended Reading

Bandy, Mary Lea, and Antonio Monda, eds. *The Hidden God: Film and Faith.* New York: Museum of Modern Art, 2003.

Barnett, Christopher B., and Clark J. Elliston, eds. *Theology and the Films of Terrence Malik.* Abingdon: Routledge, 2017.

Blake, Richard A. After Image: *The Indelible Catholic Imagination of Six American Filmmakers.* Chicago, IL: Loyola University Press, 2000.

Buteanu, Ioan. *Theology and Survival Movies: An Orthodox Christian Perspective.* Abingdon: Routledge, 2023.

Deacy, Christopher. *Faith in Film: Religious Themes in Contemporary Cinema.* Aldershot: Ashgate, 2005.

Desilets, Sean. *Hermeneutic Humility and the Political Theology of Cinema: Blind Paul.* Abingdon: Routledge, 2016.

Mayward, Joel. *The Dardenne Brothers' Cinematic Parables: Integrating Theology, Philosophy and Film.* Abingdon: Routledge, 2022.

Mills, Anthony. *American Theology, Superhero Comics, and Cinema: The Marvel of Stan Lee and the Revolution of a Genre.* Abingdon: Routledge, 2018.

Mitchell, Jolyon, Giselle Vincett, Theodora Hawksley, and Hal Culbertson, eds. *Peacebuilding and the Arts.* New York: Palgrave Macmillan, 2020.

Nayar, Sheila J. *The Sacred and the Cinema: Reconfiguring the "Genuinely" Religious Film.* London: Bloomsbury, 2012.

Plate, S. Brent, and David Jasper, eds. *Imag(in)ing Otherness: Filmic Visions of Living Together.* Atlanta, GA: Scholars Press, 1999.

Rankin, David. *Film and the Afterlife.* Abingdon: Routledge, 2019.

Romanowski, William D. *Reforming Hollywood: How American Protestants Fought for Freedom at the Movies.* Oxford: Oxford University Press, 2012.

Sanders, Theresa. *Celluloid Saints: Images of Sanctity in Film.* Macon, GA: Mercer University Press, 2002.

Settle, Zachary, and Taylor Worley, eds. *Dreams, Doubt, and Dread: The Spiritual in Film.* Eugene, OR: Cascade, 2016.

Stone, Bryan P. *Faith and Film: Theological Themes at the Cinema.* St. Louis, MO: Chalice Press, 2000.

Wall, James M. *Church and Cinema: A Way of Viewing Film.* Grand Rapids, MI: Eerdmans, 1971.

Theology and the Visual Arts

Chloë Reddaway

Introduction

Christianity is sometimes described as a "religion of the book," but visual art has long been used by Christians alongside and in addition to words, to express their experiences of and reflections about God. Its particular significance within some Christian contexts is Christologically justified and based on the power of the image for those who believe that the divine Word became visible, tangible flesh. Although art is a fundamental form of human expression, not a specifically Christian construct, for many Christians, visual art can be theologically expressive, capable of illuminating and influencing, and can be a theological medium describable in sacramental and epiphanic terms.

Christians have used visual art as a means of glorifying God and communicating belief since at least the second century. Despite iconophobic periods within some denominations, art has served didactic, commemorative, and inspirational purposes for much of Christian history, shaping experiences and coloring imaginations. From simple symbols, roughly executed in cheap materials, to exquisitely fashioned masterpieces, art has been a formative and transformative power in Christian lives.

The history of Christian interaction with art, and the history of *theological* engagement with art, are intertwined but not identical. Recorded theological reflection on art has been exceptional rather than continuous. The principal episodes in the history of theological discussion about images occurred in the early Christian period, during the Byzantine conflict between iconophiles and iconoclasts (iconomachy) in the eighth and ninth centuries, during Reformation iconoclasm, and – to a lesser extent – in the Catholic Reformation. The theological commentary, debate, and polemic that arose at these times focused on questions of legitimacy and proper use. The passion with which such questions were argued – and the violence of iconoclasm – speak to the power of art, while its presence or absence in churches and domestic settings reflects both official theological and liturgical trends and popular lay usage.

Ford's The Modern Theologians: An Introduction to Christian Theology since 1918, Fourth Edition.
Edited by Rachel Muers and Ashley Cocksworth.
© 2024 John Wiley & Sons Ltd. Published 2024 by John Wiley & Sons Ltd.

Survey

Following this sporadic and controversy-driven history, in the twentieth century a gradual growth in theological interest in the visual arts led to the development of the discipline of "theological aesthetics" or "theology and the arts" including "theology and the visual arts." The terms cross over considerably, although "theological aesthetics" may relate more to wider discussions of beauty, or the arts in general.[1] Recently the term "visual theology" has emphasized the visual material itself, and theological engagement with it as a form of theology in its own right, although this remains rare.[2]

By definition, the sources for studying theology and the visual arts are both theological and artistic, each potentially opening into wider disciplinary groups. Beginning with the artworks, sources extend to art history and on to history, church history, and cultural history; art theory and criticism; studies of material culture; and aesthetics and philosophy. The theological starting point may broaden out to biblical studies, especially reception history,[3] theological anthropology, and explorations of the physical and spiritual senses.[4]

Art historical literature on Christian artworks is, understandably, often inadequate in its treatment of theological content. The legitimate didactic, inspirational, commemorative, and decorative functions of Christian art have frequently been treated in somewhat simplistic terms, whereas more complex aspects, such as the way in which the coherence of form and content in images can become sacramental, revelatory, inspirational, and transformative in the encounter between viewer and artwork, have been largely overlooked.[5]

The term "Christian art" should be treated with caution. It is a reasonable way to describe the art that has been produced throughout much of Christian history, whose content and context are explicitly religious. With the increase in "nonreligious" art from the sixteenth century onwards and the development of modern and contemporary art, the label "Christian art" can exclude a diverse range of artworks that resonate with Christian thought and experience, without being explicitly or overtly Christian.

The interdisciplinarity of theology and the visual arts requires scholarly flexibility. Theologians are rarely trained in art history or visual analysis but need to take account of art historical scholarship. Art historians often consider theology, particularly contemporary, constructive theology, beyond their remit. Indeed, art historians and critics addressing modern and contemporary artworks can seem oblivious to or antagonistic toward Christian influences, themes, and references. Recent theological scholarship has questioned the assumption that religion has no place in contemporary art, arguing that it is often critics and curators, rather than artists, who have overlooked or rejected Christian or "spiritual" elements in contemporary art.[6]

Early Christian art

Despite the Old Testament prohibition of "idols" and "graven images," textual evidence for Christian images dates from the second century and visual evidence to the third.[7] The earliest survivals are representations of biblical scenes and popular Christian symbols, such as the vine and fish, in Roman catacombs. Usually adapted from pagan imagery, these were used as coded communication under persecution and as a response to the difficulty of directly representing some aspects of Christian belief. With the Edict of Constantine in 313 CE, Christian artistic presence became overt and increasingly narrative and representational.

The extensive art historical literature about early Christian art shows some theological awareness and insight.[8] Theological commentary on art written during this period, however, is limited, although elements of theological aesthetics appear in the patristic authors in relation to the nature of God, Christology, or creation, often within commentary on the "transcendentals" of goodness, beauty, and truth or reflections on divine and human creativity.[9]

Historical justification for the visual arts in Christianity

Questions of visuality and visibility are embedded in the Bible and in a theological understanding of the senses, both physical and spiritual. Sight is established as "good" in the creation narrative, in which God creates light and sees that it is good. Nevertheless, seeing can be a complex matter and theological engagement with the visual arts has to navigate the relationships between biblical passages such as the creation of humans in God's image (Gen 1:26–7), the account of Moses hiding his face because he is afraid to see God (Ex 3:1–5), Jesus's statement that whoever has seen him has seen the Father (Jn 14:9), the celebration of God's own craftsmanship (Is 64:8) and divine inspiration of artists (Ex 25; 31:1–6), and the prohibition of idols and graven images (Ex 20:4; Deut 5:8).

A full theological defense of images appeared in the eighth century, during the controversy in the Eastern Church, which began ca. 730 under the iconoclast emperor Leo III. An iconophile/iconodule position was adopted in 787 by the Second Council of Nicaea but iconoclasm resumed from 814–42. In 843, the regent empress, Theodora, restored icons (the "Triumph of Orthodoxy"). Their legitimacy was further confirmed by the Fourth General Council of Constantinople (869–70), which pronounced the veneration of images of Christ on a par with the honor due to the gospels and the image of the cross.[10]

Iconophobic arguments were based on the dangers of idolatry, whereas iconophiles appealed to the tradition of using images to venerate the holy person represented. Theologians including John of Damascus and Theodore the Studite were instrumental in articulating the theological nature of such images.[11] John of Damascus (ca. 675–749) argued that they are beneficial because they reveal the invisible and manifest the divine presence. He made three key points.[12]

First, he emphasized the authority of the church's tradition of venerating icons, likening this to the tradition of bowing to the cross. Second, he employed the Platonic idea that every image originates in the essence of its prototype and is related to it like a shadow to a body or an impression to a seal. Here he drew on the writings of the fourth-century St Basil the Great who argued that image and model are unified without being identical, distinguishable without being separate.[13] Their relation is like that between the Son and the Father, and therefore divinely sanctioned. The correct attitude to the images is veneration (a kind of submission), not of the material representation, but of the person. Veneration takes the form of adoration when directed to God, and reverence when directed to saints.

John's third and most important argument derives directly from the Incarnation. Although the uncircumscribable nature of the invisible God cannot be portrayed, the Old Testament image was, in his view, partly due to the idolatrous behavior of the Israelites and partly to the impossibility of depicting God. However, since Christ became incarnate, Christians can portray the incarnate Christ who is the image of God the Father. These images remind the viewer of Christ and in Christ we see God as through a glass darkly.

Images in the Western Church

The Western church also encountered differences of opinion regarding images but in general had a less complex approach to them, and they caused fewer problems until the Reformation. The different attitudes of the churches eventually became embroiled in larger issues that led to the great schism of 1054.

In the late sixth century, Pope Gregory the Great argued that adoration of images is indeed wrong but that images allow the illiterate to see what they cannot read, enabling the ignorant to learn, and their use was a tradition sanctioned by the church fathers.[14]

Following the iconoclastic council of 754 and iconophile council of 787, the Emperor Charlemagne commissioned a report on decisions about images taken by the Eastern church. This report criticized both councils, partly due to a poor translation of the original Greek into Latin, but also for political reasons. Known as the *Libri Carolini*, it stated that images were suitable for decoration, instruction, and the commemoration of past events, but emphasized that they were not to be adored (which was, in fact, the Eastern position too). Discussions continued into the ninth century but iconophilia predominated.[15]

The Western church assumed a lesser degree of identification between the image and its model than the Eastern, and though relics and miracle working images abounded, the primary purpose and justification of most images (unlike relics) was didactic, although they also had inspirational and commemorative purposes. Nevertheless, the production of religious art caused controversy in medieval monastic circles, in part over the appropriate materials and concerns about luxury versus asceticism, but also over fears of spiritual distraction.[16]

Against the restrained aesthetic preferred by St Bernard and the Cistercians, the Benedictine Abbot Suger (ca. 1081–1151) saw the creation of beautiful art and architecture as a form of worship. He oversaw the creation of the Gothic cathedral of St Denis in Paris, describing its interior as somewhere between earth and heaven and capable of transporting him, anagogically, from the one to the other. His delight in stained glass and jewels was framed in terms drawn from a Pseudo-Dionysian, Neoplatonic, metaphysics of light in which mundane, earthly light can lead the mind to divine light that illuminates it.[17]

Throughout medieval times and into the Renaissance, church patronage of the visual arts and the production of devotional artworks for domestic use proliferated. Private patrons also commissioned ecclesiastical works, often left as bequests along with stipulated masses for their souls. Although the Renaissance is commonly associated with the rise of the "artist" as a figure of individual genius, in contrast to the – often unnamed – craftsmen and artisans of earlier generations, artistic production involved workshops and the combining of various skills. Artists frequently worked to specific requirements, and sometimes with theological advisors, especially for church commissions.

With the Reformation came a new period of iconoclasm, fueled by arguments about image misuse and idolatry and bound up with attitudes to relics and the saints. Among the reformers, Luther stands out for his moderation and tolerance regarding images. Initially opposed to images as useless and encouraging idolatry he nevertheless argued that, rather than destroying them, people should be persuaded of their inefficacy. Later he came to see images as neutral, neither sacred and efficacious nor prohibited. The Old Testament prohibition applied only to idols, made and used as such: what mattered was how people used images. As ever, Luther emphasized the primacy of the Word of God in scripture and saw a role for images in the illustrated Bibles used even by some iconoclast reformers. He expressed the desire to paint the Bible narrative "word for word on houses" so that everyone might see it and learn about Christ and carry his image in their hearts. He approved of adding scriptural quotations to images and advocated painting the Last Supper above altars, along with inscriptions from the psalms.[18]

In contrast, Karlstadt and Zwingli were iconoclasts, and Calvin later extended arguments against images, criticizing the Byzantine iconophile position and blaming the church for failing properly to educate ignorant people who desire images. He allowed that artistic skill could be a God-given gift but only when used to create things that human eyes are able to see. In this he articulated the movement in the Low Countries away from religious subjects and toward genre paintings, still lives, historical subjects, and portraits, although some of these still contained moral commentary.

Responding to the Reformers, the Roman Catholic Council of Trent (1545–63) reaffirmed the veneration of legitimate images that it decreed should be displayed in churches not because they are efficacious but because (as the Eastern church had argued) the reverence shown to them transfers to the holy persons represented. The council decreed that the faithful should be instructed and strengthened by images reminding them of divine providence and encouraging gratitude for the miracles of the saints, whom they would be inspired to emulate.

Writing in 1582, Cardinal Paleotti defended this position, advocating images based on traditional models, although he accepted that even legitimate sacred images could be treated as profane. He listed specific conditions for calling an image "sacred" and appears to draw on St Bonaventure's understanding of the way in which "sensible images" aid the intellect and memory.[19]

Catholic Reformation strictures on, for example, nudity, superstition, and extravagance in art led to a movement away from the High Renaissance interest in the nude human form, and the sophistication and exaggeration of late Renaissance works. The Baroque art of the sixteenth and seventeenth centuries turned to drama and devotion and to new subjects in the lives of the saints and new iconographies, including the Immaculate Conception. Baroque art was also exported to Asia and the Americas through missionary activity and adapted by local artists. The eighteenth century saw a reduction in church patronage, the looting of art from churches by French armies after the Revolution, and the sale of art from suppressed religious institutions. Many artworks were placed in museum collections and thus moved into the preserve of art history and curatorship.

Modern and contemporary art and aesthetics

Between Protestant zeal for the word rather than the image, and the development of an Enlightenment rationalism that made freedom from religious norms a central principle, art in the West during the seventeenth, eighteenth, and nineteenth centuries shifted toward "secular" subjects such as landscapes. Leading artists could work independently of the church in an expanding art market, driven by demand from the prosperous middle classes. Meanwhile, the style and content of (mainly Catholic) church commissions were distinct, and increasingly divergent, from the work that was critically celebrated in the mainstream art establishment.[20]

From the mid-eighteenth century, the philosophy of aesthetics dominated discussions of the visual arts, with beauty – rather than legitimate forms and uses of art in Christianity – as a central concept. Kant's (1724–1804) attempt in his *Critique of the Power of Judgement* to consider "beauty" disinterestedly, and independently of "goodness" and "truth," had a crucial influence on later philosophers.

Among them, Hegel (1770–1831) diagnosed both art and religion as precursors of a purer philosophical stage in world history. This new stage, unencumbered by the "picture thinking" in which absolute reality had previously been intuited, would provide the conditions for authentic freedom. His theory of "symbolic art" stretched far beyond Christian forms (though it favored them), yet in significant ways Hegel was an inheritor of the Lutheran prioritization of word over image. He saw the high point of art's vocation as a thing of the past, while acknowledging that it remained important for human self-understanding.[21]

German Romanticism reacted to Enlightenment rationalism and materialism with a commitment to both beauty and the "sublime" (in nature and art) as fundamental to human existence and shaping it in all areas. As well as inspiring new art, the advocates of Romanticism often approached medieval and renaissance artworks with an awe for their artistry and expression of religious feeling. Although Schleiermacher (1768–1834) argued that the "feeling" or intuition by which people are oriented toward God was overlooked in Kantian philosophy, with its emphasis on reason and will, he also questioned whether the nonverbal arts could express actual ideas and meanings. Schleiermacher's aesthetics engaged particularly with hermeneutics, which remains an underexplored aspect of theological approaches to the visual arts.

Romantic attitudes were critiqued – even parodied – by Kierkegaard (1813–55) as irresponsible and self-deceiving. Kierkegaard argued that Romanticism reduced religion to aesthetics and replaced God with human creativity. Arguably, Kierkegaard's assertion of the inability of art to take full account of reality, including suffering, has echoes in the modern and contemporary art that rejects art as comforting, seeking to engage with pain and death without offering reassurance.[22]

In the eighteenth century, despite Romanticism's critics, the Gothic revival movement sought a return to medieval artistic forms and values, and by the nineteenth century there was a plethora of highly decorated neo-Gothic churches, particularly in England, France, and the United States. Interlinked with the neo-Gothic aesthetic was an espousal of symbolism and sacramentalism in which the material and circumscribed could be a medium for the immaterial and infinite, and in which art might mediate grace and revelation. In various forms, these ideas can be traced in the writings of the poets Coleridge (1772–1834) – himself influenced by German Romanticism – and Wordsworth (1770–1850), and the art critic and theorist, Ruskin (1819–1900), who argued that human artistic creativity imitated divine creativity.[23] A sacramental outlook was also influential in the development of groups of nineteenth-century painters including the German Nazarenes and the English Pre-Raphaelites. It continued in other forms in the twentieth century, including in the writings of Jacques Maritain, the artistic approaches of, for example, Eric Gill, David Jones, and Georges Rouault, and the commissioning work of Marie-Alain Couturier and Pie-Raymond Régamey.

The twentieth century saw both a continued reduction in overtly Christian art and a new interest in church commissioning post World War II. Some artists continued to engage directly with the long heritage of Christian art. Thus, Cerri Richards' *Supper at Emmaus* (1958) for St Edmund Hall, Oxford, draws on Caravaggio's *Supper at Emmaus* (1601) in the National Gallery, London, and Graham Sutherland's *Noli me tangere* (1960) for Chichester Cathedral looks to Titian's version (ca. 1514), also in the National Gallery. Others converse with a Christian artistic tradition in a broader sense. The stained-glass artist Thomas Denny, for example, joins a line of British visionary artists whose work reveals a transfigured world. Like Stanley Spencer, who reimagined biblical stories in a mundane but Spirit-filled version of life in his own village, Denny's is often a familiar world seen, both literally and metaphorically, in a different light.[24]

His glass is deeply scripturally informed and highly theologically sensitive. Three windows for St James' Grafton Underwood, for example, are inspired by multiple scriptural references to light and by light itself as an agent of transformation. One shows the transformative origins of light in the creation of the sun and moon. Another depicts an illuminated figure with a cloud of butterflies – creatures of dramatic bodily transformation – while a group of people gaze at him intently, uncertain of who he is, and others stand hunched in darkness (Figures 37.1–37.3). There is a sense of what might be, of the possible, of faith hovering, almost within reach. A third window shows "works of light," encounters graced with generosity and openness, lit in golden tones, drawing those still in darkness toward their warmth (Figures 37.4 and 37.5).

Figure 37.1 Jesus and the cloud of butterflies.

Figure 37.2 Figures hunched in darkness.

Figure 37.3 Figures looking toward Jesus. Thomas Denny, details from a triple lancet on the south wall of the chancel, St James' Grafton Underwood, Northamptonshire. © Thomas Denny. Photograph: Alex J. Wright.

Figure 37.4   Woman giving bread to a man.

Figure 37.5   Men helping people into a boat with a lantern. Thomas Denny, details from a double lancet on the north wall of the chancel, St James' Grafton Underwood, Northamptonshire. © Thomas Denny. Photograph: Alex J. Wright.

Identifiable local landscapes are transformed by an intense, color drenched, glowing radiance; peopled by figures who are half portrait, half archetype, both recognizable and dreamlike; and abundant in natural detail – in plants, insects, and stones – things with very specific forms, textures, and surfaces, that belong to very particular places. And although the scope of reference within and around the work is remarkably dense, both scripturally and visually, Denny's treatment has a lightness of touch that combines dignity and delight.

The standard secular narrative that modern art outside Christian contexts is either uninterested in religion or opposed to it is challenged by twentieth century artists from Cecil Collins and Stanley Spencer to Francis Bacon and Paula Rego and by contemporary artists such as Tracey Emin, Chris Ofili, and Cornelia Parker. The presence of Christian themes and motifs is not, however, always apparent to viewers. Andy Warhol's *Death and Disaster* series, for example, may be ironic, but its very irony can be seen as a cutting moral commentary on the dark side of capitalism that says much about biblical themes of vanitas and human frailty;[25] whereas the degree to which viewers of Cornelia Parker's *Thirty Pieces of Silver* (1988–89) appreciate its potential Christian resonance may vary, despite its overtly biblical title.[26] Even contemporary artwork that is antagonistic toward Christianity often explores themes of Christian concern. The disconnection between contemporary art and Christianity is aggravated by each party's limited understanding of the other. Bridging it is partly in the hands of theologians, who are now more willing to engage with art that, although not necessarily explicitly religious, speaks to matters central to Christian faith. There is an increasing openness to seeing and reflecting on such resonance in theological ways.[27]

Global perspectives

Christians have always adapted to their own purposes the art-forms of the cultures in which their faith has established itself. From the earliest use of Greco-Roman motifs to medieval Coptic and Ethiopic textiles to Indo-Portuguese ivories from Goa, and from Japanese woodblock techniques to contemporary Australian art influenced by Maori culture, Christians have drawn on local artistic styles. Nevertheless, European art played a dominating role in some missionary activity, and both anti-Semitism in Christian art and the predominance of a White Jesus are increasingly recognized as problematic. European art has also dominated the study of theology and the visual arts in European and North American academia, reflecting attitudes toward the global South more generally, and perhaps exacerbated by the relative difficulty for scholars from the global North of gaining access to artworks that are not in European or North American collections and that are less likely to be available digitally. It is possible that a degree of prejudice against religion has also restricted interest in these art forms from art historians and critics. This chapter itself has been written from a predominantly Western perspective, in large part because summative, encyclopedic, introductory, and handbook-style studies of non-Western works are scarce, and more likely to focus on art history or material culture than theology. The visual arts of Christianity in the global South and Australia remain an underexplored area, despite growing interest.[28]

Named Theologians

Karl Barth (1886–1968)

Although Karl Barth's attitude to the arts was ambivalent, his theology of divine beauty and glory remain relevant to theological aesthetics. Barth approaches beauty within the context of "the perfections of divine freedom" and what it means to say that God is beautiful. He describes how divine beauty radiates from God and is experienced by his creatures through the attraction and delight with which they receive his freedom and love. This radiated divine beauty is the basis on which we judge the beauty of other things. Although Barth sees no "independent" role in the Bible for beauty, he argues for its importance in relation to God's glory, which we experience as a joy and pleasure, for which we yearn. Beauty is not the primary divine attribute by which we understand God (any attribute taken alone would bring us to a distorted view of God) nor is it the essence of God's glory. Rather, God's glory has form, and that form is attractive to us, and therefore we call it beautiful. Where we recognize the glory of the divine form, we recognize it *as* beautiful. The persuasive power of God's glorious revelation is God's beauty.

While strenuously denying the possibility of knowing God other than through God's own revelation in Christ and denying that art could be in any way revelatory, in later life Barth accepted that Christ's humanity had brought human culture into the context of the revelation of God. He never found a place in this theology for the visual arts in the way that he did for music (especially Mozart), claiming that the humanity of God, being an "event," could never be "fixed" in an image. This suggests a questionable understanding of the nature of visual art and of a viewer's interaction with artworks that is, arguably, a dynamic and ongoing process rather than something "fixed" or definitive.[29]

Paul Tillich (1886–1965)

Paul Tillich's essays on art and theology are among the most influential of the twentieth century, not least because he approached works that were not specifically or overtly "religious" in a spirit of theological inquiry, seeking to overcome the gap he saw between theology and culture and to establish a theology *of* culture. By "normalizing" art and theology as dialogue partners, his lectures and essays contributed to the development of theology and the visual arts as a discipline.

Having experienced intense joy and spiritual understanding looking at Botticelli's Raczinski Tondo (1477) in Berlin in 1918, Tillich later focused on modern and contemporary art as he sought bridges between the religious and secular spheres. He characterized "religious" art as that which speaks about the contemporary context to contemporary people and expresses fundamental meaning or the ground of reality, which he called "ultimate concern." Without suggesting that art could reveal more than scripture, it could bring revelation to the viewer's attention and evoke a response to it. In assessing the nature of art that is religious in this way, Tillich distinguished between form, content, and depth or substance. The combination and organization of these three elements would determine the "style" of the artwork, and Tillich claimed that different artistic styles could be mapped onto various types of religious experience. He found greatest value in a category that he called "the ecstatic-spiritual," which he considered corresponded to an "expressionistic" style in art, and which was not limited to modern art (he argued that there are "expressionist" elements in a wide range of artistic styles from the catacombs through the Byzantine, Romanesque, Gothic, and Baroque periods and in modern art from Cézanne onwards) but he saw it most clearly in modern works, especially by van Gogh and Picasso.[30]

Tillich was, unusually, a theologian with credibility in the artistic and cultural world. He gave influential lectures at the Museum of Modern Art in New York, and was closely involved in the 1954 exhibition, *Masterpieces of Religious Art*, at the Art Institute of Chicago. The theologian John Dillenberger, and art historian Jane Dillenberger edited a collected volume of his writings on art and architecture, and he was a founding member of the Society for the Arts, Religion, and Contemporary Culture, which they directed.

His work has been criticized, however, for being more concerned with fitting artworks into theological schemes than with the artworks themselves. He overlooked art historical and art critical insights, and his dismissal of swathes of explicitly Christian art appears overly influenced by his own cultural and theological conditioning in Weimar Germany, before emigrating to the United States.[31] Despite this justifiable criticism, and recent neglect of his work, Tillich remains one of the most influential figures in the development of theology and visual art as a field of study, and one of its most significant voices.

Jacques Maritain (1882–1973)

The French Roman Catholic convert and neo-Thomist philosopher Jacques Maritain drew on Aquinas in his discussions of beauty and the relationship between the human artist and the divine creator. In particular, he understood artistic creation as a continuation of divine creation. Human creation makes use of created matter, with the artist making beauty as an "associate" of God, and, in the same way that the *imago dei* is imprinted in humans, so the human imprint appears in the artwork, which bears not only the mark of the hands but also of the soul of its maker. Maritain praised art that has the effect of producing an emotion in the viewer but contrasted this critically with art which manipulates the viewer, seducing her subconsciously and imposing emotions on her, in order to produce a particular affective response.

Maritain discussed the relationship between art and beauty, purity, morality, and gratuity, and his descriptions of the nature and purpose of religious art are full of references to grace, delight, and the integrity of the artist. Although he explicitly condemned the elevation of art to the status of eucharistic bread and wine,[32] he described a sacramentality in the gratuitous overflowing of grace in art: "Things are not only what they are; they constantly pass beyond themselves, and give more than they have."[33] He argued for the value of the work itself and claimed that religious art has neither a particular style nor prescribed content. Nevertheless, he thought that for "good" Christian art to be produced, certain "general directions" are – spontaneously – present to the artist, and argued that such works should retain a degree of "ideographical symbolism."[34]

Maritain's writing suffers from sweeping generalizations and questionable artistic judgments that declare large amounts of artistic output unworthy, while idealizing others. Like many apologists for Christian art, or theology and the visual arts more generally, Maritain's lack of engagement with individual artworks means that it is often difficult to see how his theories might apply in concrete rather than abstract situations. There are also inconsistencies in Maritain's approach, for example in his attitude to the freedom of art and the nature of the artist, who seems – despite Maritain's claims – to vary between a genius, a saint, and a simple worker, and in his insistence that there are no rules governing the freedom of art, while imposing criteria for artistic judgment. The value of Maritain's writings for theology and the visual arts today may well lie in his vocabulary of grace and gratuity, in his articulation of the value of artistic *making*, and in his influence on artists such as David Jones. Rowan Williams' sympathetic and expansive reading of Maritain introduced him to a wider audience and revived interest in his work and may serve both to rehabilitate it and stimulate further critical discussion.[35]

Hans Urs von Balthasar (1905–88)

The Roman Catholic theologian Hans Urs von Balthasar's theological aesthetics examine the relationship between beauty and revelation and between form and splendor. He describes beauty – in the sense of divine glory and splendor – as a "form" from which light breaks out, and the church's role as radiating that glory. Balthasar believed that beauty (aesthetics) – the "third transcendental" alongside truth (considered as "theo-logic") and goodness (ethics) – had been overlooked, although it could be transfiguring.

> The form as it appears to us is beautiful only because the delight that it arouses in us is founded upon the fact that, in it, the truth and goodness of the depths of reality itself are manifested and bestowed ... being something infinitely and inexhaustibly valuable and fascinating. The appearance of the form, as revelation of the depths, is an indissoluble union of two things. It is the real presence of the depths, of the whole of reality, *and* it is a real pointing beyond itself to these depths.[36]

He warned, however, against confusing the beauty of the world with the beauty of God (though analogous they are not identical), and against conflating theological aesthetics (applying theological methods to aesthetics) and aesthetic theology (which he saw as betraying theology to transient aesthetic ideas).

The Debate

Historically, the main debates in theology and the visual arts were about legitimacy and usage. In the twentieth century, theologians interested in the visual arts have primarily concerned themselves with a form of apologetics in which the value of the visual arts for theology and the church is analyzed and promoted (often in largely theoretical terms and with minimal comment on specific artworks),[37] with concerns over distinctions between "high" and "low" art and matters of taste,[38] with discussions of particular themes in art (usually aimed at a wide audience),[39] and with church commissioning.

A wave of post-World War II church commissions raised questions about the interaction of churches and contemporary artists. The French priests, Pie-Raymond Régamey (1900–96) and Marie-Alain Couturier (1897–1954) – a Dominican and stained-glass designer – coeditors of the review *L'Art Sacré*, promoted numerous modern church commissions, including by non-Christian artists. Régamey believed that artworks could "speak for themselves" and that self-professedly Christian artists often produced sentimental art of no real value.[40] Indeed, it might fail because it is "artificially manipulated for the good of the cause" and betrays what it intended to serve.[41] Régamey concludes that "sacred art only requires a sacred character of the actual artistic creation, of the artist's exercise of his art" and not of his faith.[42] In the United Kingdom, similarly pioneering work was undertaken by George Bell and Walter Hussey, who commissioned artists including Henry Moore and Hans Feibusch.

From the 1990s, the work of Art and Christianity Enquiry (later Art + Christianity), established by Tom Devonshire Jones, furthered interest in church commissions and created a space for interaction between theology and the visual arts before this was readily available within universities. In the United States, the journal of the Society for the Arts in Religious and Theological Studies published interviews with practicing artists and reflections on practical elements of the arts in churches.

Controversies about church commissions and congregational taste aside, there has been little genuine *debate*, with sustained critical discussion, of the arts within twentieth and twenty-first century theology. The potential for debate now lies more in theological engagement with art history, art criticism, and curatorship and in shifting the focus from discussing the role of modern and contemporary art in Christianity to exploring the role of Christianity in modern and contemporary art.[43]

Recently, and in line with rapidly growing concerns about diversity within the arts and humanities, scholars have begun to take a greater interest in the relationship of theology to visual art from parts of the world other than Western Europe or the global North, and by artists of diverse origins, as well as looking for a greater diversity of scholarly voices. To a lesser extent, theology and the visual arts is beginning to engage with feminist, queer, and postcolonial theology, and with theologies related to contemporary challenges including race, gender, social justice, and environmental crisis. To date these areas have been insufficiently explored, but all are increasingly pressing issues.

Influence, Achievement, and Agenda

The greatest achievement for theology and the visual arts in the twentieth and twenty-first centuries is arguably its acceptance as a valid subject within theology and its growing parameters in terms of publications and conferences, student numbers, and interdisciplinary conversations with artists, art historians, and curators. Its greatest challenge might be described in the same terms: at an institutional level its foothold is still precarious, it is increasingly popular but underresourced, there are very few dedicated teaching and research posts, and opportunities for undergraduate study are minimal.

Certain scholars have contributed greatly to the positive elements of this situation. Tillich's lectures, and the Dillenbergers' books, along with their directorship of the Society for the Arts, Religion, and Contemporary Culture, helped to put theology and the visual arts on the academic map in the United States.[44] In the United Kingdom, Rowan Williams has both deepened and popularized theological engagement with the visual arts from the Western and Eastern traditions. In 2000, Jeremy Begbie and Trevor Hart were influential in creating the St Andrews Institute for Theology, Imagination, and the Arts, along with David Brown. Jeremy Begbie then created Duke Initiatives in Theology and the Arts within the Divinity School at Duke University, NC. In 2008, Ben Quash was appointed as the first professor of Christianity and the Arts at King's College London, and established the Centre for Arts and the Sacred at King's. Its work has been characterized by dialogue with artists and museum professionals, a partnership with the National Gallery, London that includes a unique MA program in Christianity and the arts, and close relationships with other major museums. These have led to increased credibility for theology within art historically dominated environments and have expanded interdisciplinary conversations between theology and art history. The center also houses the Visual Commentary on Scripture, an open-access online publication providing theological commentary on the Bible in dialogue with works of art, whose interdisciplinary, conversational form is exploring a new hermeneutic in theology and the arts.[45]

The establishment of courses in theology and the arts in some prestigious university theology and religious studies departments, and a growing number of theological colleges, indicates progress. Research and teaching in theology and the arts are extended to a wider audience by networks such as Art + Christianity, the Society for the Arts in Religious and Theological Studies, Christians in the Visual Arts, and the Association of Scholars of Christianity in the History of Art.

Nevertheless, many books that should form part of the "canon" of theology and the visual arts have yet to be written. There is particular scope for defining the foundations of theology and the visual arts, as well as expanding its reach and exploring its horizons. Publishers and dedicated journals are increasingly open to proposals from this field, although very few can include high-quality images. With this established, if small, presence, theology and the visual arts needs to continue to move beyond apologetics. In addition to the issues of diversity already mentioned, two areas of study particularly require further attention. First is the question of methodology or hermeneutics: what does a theological approach to the visual arts – and particularly to their interpretation – look like; how can it avoid both a naivety that unquestioningly accepts religious "content" in art, and the cynicism of some art historical and art critical approaches; how can it assert the inspirational and transformative nature of Christian art within a constructive, imaginative, and critical assessment of art?[46] Furthermore, how might it engage with art that is not explicitly Christian, particularly modern and contemporary works that may be seen as divorced from, or even hostile to, Christianity?[47] Second is the issue of engaging directly with particular artworks, artists, schools, periods, and themes — a delightfully broad field of potential discovery.

Notes

1   E.g. David Bentley Hart, *The Beauty of the Infinite, the Aesthetics of Christian Truth* (Grand Rapids, MI: Eerdmans, 2003); Aidan Nichols, *Redeeming Beauty, Soundings in Sacral Aesthetics* (Aldershot: Ashgate, 2007).

2   E.g. Chloë R. Reddaway, *Transformations in Persons and Paint: Visual Theology, Historical Images, and the Modern Viewer* (Turnhout: Brepols, 2016).

3   E.g. Christine E. Joynes, ed., *Perspectives on the Passion: Encountering the Bible through the Arts* (London: T&T Clark, 2007).

4   E.g. Paul L. Gavrilyuk and Sarah Coakley, eds., *The Spiritual Senses: Perceiving God in Western Christianity* (Cambridge: Cambridge University Press, 2012).

5   See Hans Belting, *Likeness and Presence: A History of the Image before the Era of Art*, trans. E. Jephcott (Chicago, IL: University of Chicago Press, 1994); Celia M. Chazelle, "Pictures, Books and the Illiterate: Pope Gregory's Letters to Serenus of Marseilles," *Word and Image* 6 (1990): 138–53; Richard Viladesau, *Theology and the Arts* (New York: Paulist Press, 2000).

6   E.g. Jonathan Anderson and William Dyrness, *Modern Art and the Life of a Culture: The Religious Impulses of Modernism* (Downers Grove, IL: IVP, 2016); Aaron Rosen, *Art and Religion in the 21st Century* (London: Thames and Hudson, 2015); Thomas Crow, *No Idols: The Missing Theology of Art* (Sydney: Power Publications, 2017); James Elkins, *On the Strange Place of Religion in Contemporary Art* (New York: Routledge, 2004); Daniel A. Siedell, *God in the Gallery* (Grand Rapids, MI: Baker Academic, 2008).

7   See Clement of Alexandria on pagan imagery and images on Christian signet rings as discussed in Paul Corby Finney, "Images on Finger Rings and Early Christian Art," *Dumbarton Oaks Papers* 41 (1987): 181–6.

8   E.g. Robin M. Jensen, *Face to Face: Portraits of the Divine in Early Christianity* (Minneapolis, MN: Augsberg Fortress Press, 2005); Robin M. Jensen,

Understanding Early Christian Art (New York: Routledge, 2000); Jeffrey Spier, ed., *Picturing the Bible, the Earliest Christian Art* (New Haven, CT: Yale University Press, 2009).

9   For a selection of sources see Gesa Elsbeth Thiessen, ed., *Theological Aesthetics: A Reader*, 2nd ed. (Grand Rapids, MI: Eerdmans, 2005), 15–48.

10   For summaries of the Byzantine image debates see, for example, Belting, *Likeness and Presence*, 102–208, 491ff.

11   Theodore of Studios made very similar arguments. Theodore the Studite, *On Holy Icons*, trans. Catherine P. Roth (Crestwood, NY: St Vladimir's Seminary Press, 1981).

12   John of Damascus, *On the Divine Images: Three Apologies against Those Who Attack the Divine Images*, trans. David Anderson (Crestwood, NY: St Vladimir's Seminary Press, 1980).

13   Basil the Great, *On the Holy Spirit*, trans. Stephen Hildebrand (Yonkers, NY: St Vladimir's Seminary Press, 2011), ch. 18, section 45.

14   Chazelle, "Pictures, Books and the Illiterate."

15   Belting, *Likeness and Presence*, 533–5.

16   Conrad Rudolph, *Artistic Change at St-Denis: Abbot Suger's Program and the Early Twelfth-Century Controversy over Art* (Princeton, NJ: Princeton University Press, 1990), esp. 48–63.

17   Erwin Panofsky and Gerda Panofsky-Soergel, eds., *Abbot Suger: On the Abbey Church of St-Denis and its Art Treasures*, 2nd ed. (Princeton, NJ: Princeton University Press, 1979), 18–26, 64–5. See also Rudolph, *Artistic Change at St-Denis*.

18   Belting, *Likeness and Presence*, 545–50.

19   Belting, *Likeness and Presence*, 554–6. Bonaventure, "The Soul's Journey into God," in *Bonaventure: The Soul's Journey into God, The Tree of Life, The Life of St Francis*, ed. and trans. Ewert Cousins (Mahwah, NJ: Paulist Press, 1978).

20   My thanks to Ben Quash for contributions to this section.

21   See Nicholas Adams, George Pattison, and Graham Ward, eds. *The Oxford Handbook of Theology and Modern European Thought* (Oxford: Oxford University Press, 2013), esp. 1–14, 419–33.

22   On Kierkegaard and Romanticism, see George Pattison, *Art, Modernity, and Faith* (London: SCM Press, 1998), 21–9.

23   See David Brown, "Sacramentality," in *The Oxford Handbook of Theology and Modern European Thought*, 614–31.

24   See Josie Reed, ed., *Glory, Azure and Gold: The Stained Glass Windows of Thomas Denny* (London: Lund Humphries, 2023).

25   See Chloë Reddaway, "Philosophy, Pleasure, and Folly," in *The Visual Commentary on Scripture*, ed. Ben Quash (London: The Visual Commentary on Scripture Foundation, 2019). https://thevcs.org/philosophy-pleasure-and-folly (accessed 19 December 2022).

26   See Christine Joynes, "Optical Allusions? Exploring the Ambiguity of Biblical Texts in Modern and Contemporary Art," in *Theology, Modernity, and the Visual Arts*, ed. Ben Quash and Chloë Reddaway (Turnhout: Brepols, forthcoming).

27   See note 6.

28   E.g. Anand Amaladass and Gudrun Löwner, *Christian Themes in Indian Art: From the Mogul Times Till Today* (New Delhi: Manohar Publishers & Distributors, 2012); Nicholas J. Bridger and John Picton, eds., *Christian Art and African Modernity* (Glienicke: Galda Verlag, 2021); Gawdat Gabra, "Coptic Art, a Multifacted Artistic Heritage," in *The Coptic Christian Heritage: History, Faith, and Culture*, ed. Lois M. Farag (London and New York: Routledge, 2014); Vrej Nersessian, *Treasures from the Ark: 1700 Years of Armenian Christian Art*, (Los Angeles, CA: Getty Publications, 2001); Maseo Takenaka, *Christian Art in Asia* (Tokyo: Kyo Bun Kwan, for the Christian Conference of Asia, 1975).

29   Karl Barth, *Church Dogmatics*, Vol. 2, Part 1, ed. G. W. Bromiley and T. F. Torrance (Edinburgh: T&T Clark, 1957), 647–77.

30   See Paul Tillich, "Art and Ultimate Reality" in *On Art and Architecture* (New York: Crossroad, 1987), 139–57.

31   See, for example, Russell Re Manning, "Tillich's Theology of Art," in *The Cambridge Companion to Paul Tillich*, ed. Russell Re Manning (Cambridge: Cambridge University Press, 2009), 164–9.

32   Jacques Maritain, *Art and Scholasticism*, trans. J. F. Scanlon (London: Sheed and Ward, 1946), 29.

33   Jacques Maritain, "Poetic Experience," *The Review of Politics* 6, no. 4 (1944): 397.

34   Maritain, *Art and Scholasticism*, 113.

35   Rowan Williams, *Grace and Necessity: Reflections on Art and Love* (London: Continuum, 2005).

36   Hans Urs von Balthasar, *The Glory of the Lord: A Theological Aesthetics, Vol. 1: Seeing the Form*, trans. Erasmo Leivà-Merikakis (Edinburgh: T&T Clark, 1982), 118.

37   E.g. John W. Dixon, *Art and the Theological Imagination* (New York: Seabury Press, 1978); Viladesau, *Theology and the Arts*; Keith Walker, *Images or Idols? The Place of Sacred Art in Churches Today* (Norwich: Canterbury Press, 1996).

38   E.g. Frank Burch Brown, *Good Taste, Bad Taste, and Christian Taste, Aesthetics in Religious Life* (Oxford: Oxford University Press, 2000).

39   E.g. Richard Harries, *The Passion in Art* (Aldershot: Ashgate, 2004); Richard Viladesau, *The Beauty of the Cross* (Oxford: Oxford University Press, 2006).

40 Pie-Raymond Régamey, *Religious Art in the Twentieth Century* (New York: Herder & Herder, 1963), 178.

41 Régamey, *Religious Art in the Twentieth Century*, 184.

42 Régamey, *Religious Art in the Twentieth Century*, 189.

43 See Hans Rookmaaker, *Modern Art and the Death of a Culture* (Downers Grove, IL: IVP, 1970); Anderson and Dyrness, *Modern Art and the Life of a Culture*; Elkins, *Strange Place of Religion*; Rosen, *Art and Religion in the 21st Century*; Siedell, *God in the Gallery*.

44 Jane Dillenberger, *Style and Content in Christian Art* (London: SCM Press, 1965); John Dillenberger, *A Theology of Artistic Sensibilities* (London: SCM Press, 1986).

45 www.thevcs.org (accessed 9 September 2023). See also Ben Quash, "The Visual Commentary on Scripture: Principles and Possibilities," in *Transforming Christian Thought in the Visual Arts: Theology, Aesthetics and Practice*, ed. Sheona Beaumont and Madeleine Thiele (London: Routledge, 2021).

46 Reddaway, *Transformations in Persons and Paint*, 15–41. Further work in this area is urgently needed.

47 E.g. Ben Quash and Chloë Reddaway, eds., *Theology, Modernity, and the Visual Arts* (2024). For projects addressing these issues, see Centre for Arts and the Sacred at King's.

Recommended Reading

Anderson, Jonathan, and William Dyrness. *Modern Art and the Life of a Culture: The Religious Impulses of Modernism.* Downers Grove, IL: IVP, 2016.

Apostolos-Cappadona, Diane. *Dictionary of Christian Art.* New York: Continuum, 1994.

Balthasar, Hans Urs von. *The Glory of the Lord: A Theological Aesthetics, Vol. 1: Seeing the Form.* Translated by Erasmo Leiva-Merikakis. San Francisco, CA: Ignatius Press, 2009.

Belting, H. *Likeness and Presence: A History of the Image before the Era of Art.* Translated by E. Jephcott. Chicago: University of Chicago Press, 1994.

Exum, J. Cheryl, and Ela Nutu, eds. *Between the Text and the Canvas: The Bible in Art and Dialogue.* Sheffield: Sheffield Phoenix Press, 2007.

Hart, David Bentley. *The Beauty of the Infinite: The Aesthetics of Christian Truth.* Grand Rapids, MI: Eerdmans, 2003.

John of Damascus. *On the Divine Images: Three Apologies against Those Who Attack the Divine Images.* Translated by David Anderson. Crestwood, NY: St Vladimir's Seminary Press, 1980.

Maritain, Jacques. *Art and Scholasticism.* Translated by J. F. Scanlon. London: Sheed and Ward, 1946.

Nichols, Aidan. *The Art of God Incarnate: Theology and Image in Christian Tradition.* London: Dorton, Longman and Todd, 1980.

Pattison, George. *Art, Modernity and Faith: Restoring the Image.* 2nd ed. London: SCM Press, 1998.

Rahner, Karl. "Theology and the Arts." *Thought: Fordham University Quarterly* 57, no. 224 (1982): 17–29.

Reddaway, Chloë R. *Strangeness and Recognition: Mystery and Familiarity in Renaissance Images of Christ.* Turnhout: Brepols, 2019.

Romaine, James, and Linda Stratford, eds. *Revisioning: Critical Methods of Seeing Christianity in the History of Art.* Eugene, OR: Cascade, 2013.

Rosen, Aaron. *Art and Religion in the 21st Century.* London: Thames and Hudson, 2015.

Schiller, Gertrud. *The Iconography of Christian Art.* 2 vols. London: Lund Humphries, 1971.

Thiessen, Gesa Elsbeth, ed. *Theological Aesthetics: A Reader.* 2nd ed. Grand Rapids, MI: Eerdmans, 2005.

Tillich, Paul. *On Art and Architecture.* New York: Crossroad, 1987.

Theology and the Physical Sciences

David Wilkinson

Introduction

At the turn of the twentieth century the physical sciences were not seen as an exciting area for theological engagement or indeed for science itself. The controversies of the Copernican revolution and the Galileo affair were no longer theological center stage. Instead, Darwin had subverted reliance on the design argument. In addition, questions of the status and uniqueness of human beings were no longer focused on the earth being the center of the universe, but on whether humans had common ancestors with apes. Geologists had shown that the earth was far older than the thousands of years that a literal reading of Genesis 1 might suggest, resonating with a majority theological tradition that had not looked for scientific dating of the creation within the text. The main problem for theologians was the legacy of the mechanistic universe of Newton, a predictable and picturable universe of clockwork. Although the simplicity of these physical laws had been employed for evidence of a designer, it brought with it the problem of how God interacted with the universe beyond the initial act of creation in providence and miracle.

Survey

The subtlety and suppleness of time

Newton's universe was one where space and time were rigid, separate, and universal. In thinking about God's relationship to time, although there was a genuine distinction for us between past, present, and future, God towered above all time and space. Boethius saw the flow of time as an army marching below the tower, at a constant and disciplined pace, with God seeing all of the past, present, and future. With the advent of Albert Einstein's theories of special and general relativity, such an understanding of time was revolutionized, and its philosophical and theological consequences remain complex and disputed. In a remarkable intuitive insight Einstein suggested that the speed of light in a vacuum was the same however you measured it.[1] This led to the conclusion that the measurement of time depended on motion. This

---

Ford's The Modern Theologians: An Introduction to Christian Theology since 1918, Fourth Edition.
Edited by Rachel Muers and Ashley Cocksworth.
© 2024 John Wiley & Sons Ltd. Published 2024 by John Wiley & Sons Ltd.

special theory of relativity was followed by his general theory that took gravity into account.[2] Here the mass and distribution of matter determine the geometry of space and the rate of flow of time. This complex interaction of matter and space-time was described by a set of equations, whose solution gave the geometry of space-time and showed how bodies moved within it. Thus, not only was time coupled to space but also to its location and movement in the universe. The Newtonian model of the absolute nature of space and time was superseded.

However, relativity poses several intriguing questions for the nature of time and God's relation to time and space.[3] Some have used it to defend God's omniscience and foreknowledge in a classical sense.[4] In the equations of relativity, as Einstein wrote to the grieving family of Michelangelo Besso in 1955, "the separation between past, present and future has only the meaning of an illusion, though a persistent one."[5]

But we need to be careful in arguing that relativity supports a determined future. In particular we are not sure how it fits with our understanding of an arrow of time.[6] This is not only our psychological experience of a flow of time, but we also see distinction between past and future in the second law of thermodynamics, where the disorder in a closed system, characterized by a property known as entropy, increases with time. Indeed, the universe itself expands in size with time and therefore a flow of time is seen. It is not clear how these different experiences of time can be reconciled. The arrow of time may arise in complex systems, or may emerge when a theory is found that combines relativity with quantum theory.[7] And then Einstein's equations imply other bizarre possibilities, such as time travel into the past. Although the practicalities of doing this seem to rule it out, nevertheless it indicates that time is far more subtle and supple than our everyday experience indicates.[8] Far from time marching forward at a uniform and universal pace, time may be better thought of as the flow of a river reacting to the riverbed with many eddy currents and the river flowing at different speeds in different places.

There have been those such as McTaggart who have argued that because of inconsistencies and contradictions, time cannot be real.[9] We need to be careful in employing relativity in supporting this claim, or the claim that our perceptions of time are simply socially determined. Relativity works in an astonishing way, not least in its prediction and subsequent discovery a century later of gravitational waves produced by the collision of two black holes some 1.3 billion light-years away.[10] However, T. F. Torrance was right in pointing out that because we cannot perceive the structure of space-time by our senses, it encourages a humility toward surprising aspects of our experience of the universe as a whole. Torrance was one of the few modern theologians to take Einstein's work seriously. Bringing incarnation and resurrection into dialogue with it he argued "the Incarnation does not mean that God is limited by space and time, it asserts the reality of space and time for God in the actuality of His relations with us, and at the same time binds us to space and time in all our relations with Him."[11]

The glimpses that this gives us into the complexity of our understanding of time in this creation may make us pause in thinking about God's eternity. We shall return to this later in this chapter when thinking about eschatology, but relativity has suggested that the rigidity of Newton's universal time should not be the dominant theological paradigm. To see God as "outside time" often follows from this view of time. But there are a number of problems with such a view of eternity as atemporal. As Lucas comments, "We should not think of it as timeless or changeless, but as free from all those imperfections which make the passage of time for us a matter of regret."[12] Further, it is our involvement and God's involvement with time that allow petitionary prayer and human responsibility to be taken seriously. God's experience in Trinity and acting in the world suggests experiencing time as a personal agent.[13] Some have suggested therefore God has both eternal and temporal poles to his nature in order to maintain both transcendence and immanence with regard to time. Others speculate that God is timeless without creation, and temporal subsequent to it.

Here some of the most recent speculation in the physical sciences might help us. Some of the models of the early universe suggest that there may be more dimensions of space and time than the four represented by Einstein's space-time. Thus, it may be better to think of God experiencing and working in more dimensions of space-time than the four-dimensional space-time that we experience. This might allow God to act in time without being limited by time in the way that we are.[14]

Subverting a mechanistic common-sense universe

In the previous section I borrowed the words "subtle" and "supple" from John Polkinghorne's characterization of the world described by quantum theory and chaos.[15] In this section we once again see a world far more subtle and supple than the clockwork mechanism of Newtonian physics.

Quantum theory is one of the most powerful theories of modern physics, giving the world lasers, nuclear power, the transistor, and the electron microscope. However, since its formulation in the early part of the twentieth century it remains surprising, disturbing and has a number of questions that remain as elusive as the particles it describes.[16]

It led to an understanding of the world at the atomic level that was radically different from the everyday world where Newton had reigned supreme. The Newtonian world was picturable, reliable, and predictable, where mechanical windup models of the planets of the solar system adorned Victorian sitting rooms. In contrast the quantum world of photons and electrons described a reality that was unpicturable, unpredictable, and uncertain. At this level of reality, the Heisenberg uncertainty principle says that you cannot know precisely both the position and the momentum of a particle. You can know one or the other but not both. One can only describe probabilities of position and momentum. Such a situation is impossible to picture in everyday terms, and to talk of causes becomes irrelevant.

Einstein was so uneasy with a picture where God seemed to play dice with the universe that, with collaborators Podolsky and Rosen, he attempted to construct a paradox to show that quantum theory was flawed. This EPR paradox did not undermine quantum theory but led to an even more bizarre and experimentally verified aspect of the theory; two quantum particles, such as electrons, once they have interacted with each other, retain the ability to influence each other even though extremely large distances separate them. This is sometimes termed "quantum entanglement" or "nonlocality" or in Polkinghorne's phrase "togetherness in separation."

Before moving to the theological implications, it is worth noting the uncertainties of understanding the theory itself. The first, the measurement problem, is how the uncertain quantum world gives certain answers when interrogated by our everyday world. Here a number of suggestions have been made. The Copenhagen interpretation favored by most physicists suggests that the intervention of macro world measuring instruments "collapses" the probability of the quantum world into a definite measurement. Yet the very measuring instruments are themselves composed of atoms that have quantum behavior. To solve this problem, Wigner and Wheeler suggested that it is the intervention of a conscious observer that leads to a measurement. This raises the same problem of the brain being composed of atoms, but it might be argued that the complex relationship between mind and brain might provide a solution. A completely different solution to the problem was proposed by Hugh Everett III in his many worlds interpretation, where in every act of measurement, each possibility available is realized and at that point the universe splits into separate universes corresponding to the realized possibilities.[17] This has been popular with countless science fiction writers, but also with some cosmologists who want to apply quantum theory to the beginning of the universe where there is no human observer. However, it leads to unimaginable countless universes where every possibility is fulfilled.

The second unanswered question of quantum theory is: what does quantum theory tell us about the nature of reality? What is the relationship between epistemology and ontology? Most physicists take that view that uncertainty is in the nature of reality, rather than the belief that it is just a limit on our knowledge. A smaller minority including David Bohm believe that there must be a deeper theory that explains the apparent uncertainty of quantum theory.

The theological implications have been both profound and the arena of speculation for many modern theologians.[18] The most profound is that quantum theory shows the limits of the Newtonian worldview as a description of reality. Just as in relativity, quantum theory cautioned that our experience of the everyday modeled by Newton's clockwork universe is far from the nature of reality at its fundamental level. It is an awkward moment of history when, at the same time that quantum theory was overturning our view of the universe, Rudolf Bultmann on the basis of the Newtonian universe was arguing: "We cannot use electric lights and radios and in the event of illness avail ourselves of modern medical and clinical means and at the same time believe in the spirit and wonder world of the New Testament."[19] Much later in the twentieth century there were still some theologians wedded to this Newtonian paradigm leading to arguments against God's particular actions in the world.[20]

Quantum theory does not endorse that "all is mystery," but it does challenge predictability and picturability in everyday terms as a way of understanding. Here it resonates with those such as Bernard Lonergan who suggest that intelligibility is the clue to reality.[21]

There have been other avenues of more speculative thinking. For example, a number of thinkers have suggested that it is in the uncertainty of the quantum world that freedom of action is located. John Eccles argued that the openness of quantum processes could explain human free will,[22] whereas William Pollard saw it as the location of God's providence.[23] God finds space to work in a way that does not break laws and remains hidden. More recently, Robert Russell sees the possibility of God working at the quantum level, especially when in the early stages of the universe processes were all in the realm of the quantum world.[24] Unfortunately, the problem of this suggestion is that it involves one of the big unanswered questions of quantum theory that we noted earlier. How does the quantum world relate to the everyday world? It is difficult to see how God working at the uncertainty of the quantum level would affect the everyday level. Nevertheless, it remains a possibility for a type of divine action that can enable God's freedom to act in the universe while remaining consistent with the laws of physics.

A more promising possibility for God's action to remain hidden but significant in the everyday world is another aspect of contemporary physics that in the latter part of the twentieth century undermined the Newtonian mechanistic paradigm. In 1961, Ed Lorenz showed that complex systems such as the atmosphere exhibit a great sensitivity to initial conditions, with very different outcomes arising from infinitesimally different starting points.[25] These chaotic systems obey immutable and intelligible laws but due to their sensitivity their outcomes cannot be fully predicted. Lorenz characterized this as "the butterfly effect," that is, systems such as the weather are so sensitive that the flapping of a butterfly's wing in Rio could lead to a hurricane in New York.

This insight provided by chaotic systems became more significant than quantum theory for John Polkinghorne in locating divine action. Polkinghorne argued that God could work in the hiddenness of chaotic systems and this action would be significant in the everyday world. As a critical realist, Polkinghorne makes a strong link between epistemology and ontology, and further argued that the unpredictability of chaos (and quantum theory) indicated that the future was undetermined or open to human beings and to God.[26] Indeed, it was in the interaction of God's freedom to act, human free will, and an inherent openness in physical process that questions of prayer, providence, and the problem of evil could be considered.

The response to Polkinghorne asks the question of whether chaos implies a limitation on our knowledge rather than a genuine ontological openness. Chaos does not rule out the possibility that an infinitely intelligent being with perfect senses would be able to predict the system. More important, is God's activity so self-limited to chaotic systems and in a way that is hidden?

Nevertheless, here the physical sciences began to resonate with theological insights reacting against the clockwork universe. Process theology became a popular theological movement and was favored by another of the pioneers of theology and the physical sciences, Ian Barbour.[27] Although rejected by many theologians, it opened a theological space for the development of a more complex understanding of God's relationship with time and the physical processes of the universe. It certainly resonated with those who saw God's creative love always accompanied by vulnerability.[28] In kenosis, God self-limits, giving to humans and the universe a degree of freedom to explore their own potentiality, meaning that the future is not fully determined.

This openness to the future has caused some controversy, not least in evangelical theology.[29] Pinnock argued that in contrast to "the unmoved mover" of classical theism, the Bible uses images of God as a free personal agent who acts in love, cooperates with people, and responds to prayer. God creates a world where the future is not yet completely settled and takes seriously our response.[30] There are significant similarities here with process theology, but with a greater stress on God's transcendence and a claim to be motivated more by scripture than by philosophy.[31] Yet it is interesting that there is little engagement with the insights of the physical sciences, summing up a century where many biblical theologians have not engaged with the revolutions in physics.[32]

Our understanding of the universe has significantly moved from Newton's clockwork model. There are of course some systems that obey Newton's laws and are predictable. But it is a mistake to generalize that to a model of reality that limits God's activity. The cloudiness of the worlds of quantum theory and chaos may give God space to interact with the physical universe, but they may not be the whole story. The signs and wonders of the New Testament are not about God's hidden action. They are in fact quite the opposite, drawing attention directly to God's special actions in the world for specific purposes. God is the God who gives the gift of freedom, but God is also the one who is free to raise Jesus from the dead.

Creation and new creation

The understanding of the origin, structure, and evolution of the universe in the development of the model of the Big Bang attracted huge public and theological interest. Alexander Friedmann, a Russian cosmologist and mathematician, and independently Georges Lemaître, a Belgian physicist and Roman Catholic priest, saw that Einstein's equations of general relativity could be understood to show that the universe was expanding. Lemaître proposed that the recession of the galaxies, observed by Slipher and Hubble, was due to the expansion of the universe from a single point, a "primeval atom."[33]

This interpretation of the Einstein equations and the observational evidence, however, did not lead to universal acceptance of a point of beginning of the universe. Many were hesitant about the philosophical and theological implications of a model of cosmology in which a Big Bang needed someone to set off the explosion. This culminated in the steady state model of the universe proposed by Fred Hoyle, Tom Gold, and Herman Bondi, where new matter in a series of "little bangs" fueled the expansion of an eternal universe. Yet from the 1960s onwards Big Bang cosmology triumphed because of new observations of the microwave background radiation and the abundance of helium in the universe.

Some theologians were quick to baptize the Big Bang. First, some saw a contemporary resurrection of the cosmological argument in temporal form, that is, there needs to be a cause of the Big Bang itself. In an address to the Pontifical Academy of Sciences given in 1951, Pope Pius XII claimed,

> Thus with that concreteness which is characteristic of physical proofs, it [science] has confirmed the contingency of the universe and also the well founded deduction as to the epoch when the cosmos came forth from the hands of the Creator. Hence, creation took place in time. Therefore, there is a Creator. Therefore God exists.[34]

Science, however, had a problem with the "primeval atom." As the universe became smaller and smaller its density increased toward infinity, the so-called singularity. General relativity at this point broke down and further when the universe was very small general relativity and quantum theory were inconsistent. This led Stephen Hawking to a lifelong pursuit of a quantum theory of gravity, a unification of relativity and quantum theory. This "theory of everything" would explain the initial conditions of the universe and remove the need for the intervention of a Creator God.[35]

Hawking never discovered this quantum theory of gravity. He explored applying quantum theory to the universe using string theory, M-theory, and multiverse.[36] His attempt and the current work of cosmologists who followed him is important for theologians. As Hawking noted:

> So long as the universe had a beginning, we could suppose it had a creator. But if the universe is really completely self-contained, having no boundary or edge, it would have neither beginning nor end: it would simply be. What place, then, for a creator?[37]

This is a note of caution for theologians to avoid a "God of the gaps" argument. More positively, this speculation by cosmologists can be an important reminder of the Christian view of theism rather than deism. Theism does not see God hiding in the gaps of a mysterious first cause. Rather God is creator and sustainer of all space-time, as much involved in all events and laws as in the initial conditions. If the universe arises because of a quantum field fluctuation, then the theist can rightly ask "where does quantum theory itself come from and how is it sustained?" To ask where the laws of physics themselves come from is not God of the gaps, rather it is a question that goes beyond science. Science simply assumes the existence of laws. The physical sciences raise a metaphysical question in their success of exploring the universality and intelligibility of the physical laws. Indeed, Hawking's universe may also resonate with *creatio ex nihilo,* in a far more satisfying way than a god who makes some preexisting matter go bang!

If the attempted resurrection of the cosmological argument failed, but in doing so raised some fruitful theological questions, the same could be said for those who attempted to use the Big Bang to reenergize the design argument. From the 1960s onwards there was a growing appreciation that the laws and circumstances of the universe seemed to be astonishingly fine-tuned for the existence of carbon-based life. Not only did some theologians see this as a possible way back into the design argument, but more significantly scientists such as Paul Davies and Fred Hoyle, who had vested interest in faith communities, began speaking of a deeper story to the universe.[38]

One possible understanding of the fine-tuning problem is that we see such a universe because it is selected by the fact that it must be consistent with our existence. That is, we see because we are here. In other universes where there is no fine-tuning there would be no observers. This proposal comes under what has been called the anthropic principle. However, this understanding of fine-tuning comes from a proposal that there is a selection effect out of a multiverse. As we have already seen, multiverse has become part of contemporary culture as well as contemporary cosmology. And indeed, there are multiple theories of many universes. Everitt's interpretation of quantum theory says that whenever a measurement is made of the quantum world the universe fulfils all quantum possibilities forming a new universe with each possibility. This leads to literally billions and billions of independent universes all slightly different from each other. Another scenario suggests that we may be one universe out of a sea of bubble universes all with different physical laws.

However, this coupling of the anthropic principle with a theory of many universes is more a metaphysical suggestion than a physical theory. The question must be asked: in what sense do other universes exist if they have no observable consequences? There are many who argue, with some justification, that talk of many universes goes beyond physics, to the extent that it becomes an explanation of the way the world is on the same level as philosophical and theological explanations.

Multiverse can be fruitful for theological thinking. It is a reminder that the design argument cannot be brought back through cosmology. In biology, the design argument fell because Darwin proposed the alternative explanation of natural selection to the explanation of a divine watchmaker. The possibility of multiverse in cosmology acts in a similar way. It cautions against trying to prove the existence of God from fine-tuning. More positively, just as early observation of the vastness of the universe by astronomers such as Richard Bentley and Christiaan Huygens led to a sense of awe at the extravagance of God in creation and a sense of humility for the place of human beings in the cosmos, multiverse speculation can be welcomed in the same way. This sense of awe, the intelligibility of the physical laws, and fine-tuning of the laws and circumstances of the universe should not be discounted. As Polkinghorne rightly stressed, they cannot be used as proofs for a creator, but they may be pointers to questions that lie beyond the physical sciences, and they certainly find a natural explanation in the Christian view of the universe as creation.[39]

Whereas much of the theological attention has been on the origin of the universe, a very important but not widely recognized contribution of the physical sciences in the last decade of the twentieth century was models of the future of the universe. The astonishing result of new observations is that far from the universe slowing down, the expansion of the universe was speeding up. This was completely unexpected and indicated some type of force that led to an "accelerating Universe."[40] The nature of this "dark energy" remains unknown. The consequence of its existence, however, is the universe is destined to futility with all structure ripped apart or at the very least suffering a cold, lifeless heat death. This ultimate futility of the universe portrayed by the physical sciences subverts the myth of human progress where there is a long march to Utopia created by the power of human beings.[41]

This scenario raises some fruitful questions for Christian theology. Biblical eschatology is about new creation, a transformed new heaven and new earth. There is not the sense that this creation will continue for ever. This good but fallen creation will be redeemed through the power of the creator who has not given up on it. The work of redemption through Christ is not just for human beings but for all things and the resurrection of Jesus is the first fruits of that which is to come.

The centrality of new creation to biblical thought means that God's plan is not to throw away this universe and start again. As Polkinghorne notes,

> the new creation is not a second attempt by God at what he had first tried to do in the old Creation. It is a different kind of divine action altogether, and the difference may be summarized by saying that the first creation was *ex nihilo* while the new creation will be *ex vetere*. In other words, the old creation is God's bringing into being a universe which is free to exist "on its own," in the ontological space made available by the divine kenotic act of allowing the existence of something wholly other; the new creation is the divine redemption of the old.[42]

It is here that the physical sciences can be brought into dialogue with bodily resurrection.[43] The resurrection of Jesus is both the evidence for and model of God's work of new creation. The resurrected body of Jesus is not less than physical but has been transformed. Jesus eats fish and has the marks of the nails, but he does not need to eat fish to survive, and the marks of crucifixion are now marks of glory rather than suffering. In this the Christian understanding of eucharist points toward this continuity and discontinuity of matter, the bread and wine being a foretaste of the heavenly banquet.

The resurrection therefore raises some significant questions about God's relationship with space, time, and matter both in this creation and in new creation. Torrance uses the language of redemption, healing, and restoration.[44] The redemption of time may not be atemporal existence. Rather, could it be a fuller experience of time that is not coupled to decay or is limiting in the same way that it is in this creation? Thus theology proposes a different way of thinking about the future, seeing hope beyond futility.

Named Theologians

John Polkinghorne

Some scientists such as Ian Barbour and John Polkinghorne moved from physics into the theological academy, the phenomenon of the "scientist-theologians."[45] Polkinghorne, former professor of mathematical physics at Cambridge University, became an Anglican priest and then returned to the Faculty of Divinity. His early trilogy of books on science and theology expressed key themes in his thinking and were foundational for those influenced by him.[46] He argued that the basis of fruitful dialogue of science and theology was first continuities in their methodology, and second understanding science and theology as critical realist activities provisionally describing a common reality. As we have seen, he also argued for a

God at work in the world in the midst of complex chaotic systems, and this meant that the universe was open or that the physical process was given a freedom in creation in addition to human freedom. It was a creative and at times controversial proposal attempting to engage an emerging scientific insight with Christian theology.

Through all of his work he proceeded on the basis of two fundamental convictions. First, he advocated the value of bottom-up thinking in the engagement of science and theology. This became part of his Gifford Lectures.[47] He preferred beginning with specific insights into the world such as quantum theory, chaos, the Big Bang, or the end of the universe and then bringing these into theological dialogue. This became a dominant form of theological work with the physical sciences, and laid the foundation of science-engaged theology. Second, he was deeply rooted in the Anglican theological tradition that had shaped his life, based on scripture, tradition, and reason. He reflected the overall perspective of a Creator God who had spoken and acted in the life, death, and resurrection of Jesus of Nazareth. Thus although he took seriously anthropic balances and the intelligibility of the physical laws, he saw them as pointers to, rather than proofs of, a Creator God. This was in part due to the manifold problems that such simplistic attempted proofs had exhibited over history, but mainly due to his conviction that God was known first through God's self-revelation in Jesus Christ.

Wolfhart Pannenberg

Wolfhart Pannenberg was a crucial theological voice in critiquing Barth's decision to refrain from any reference to scientific insights in the doctrine of creation in his preface to *Church Dogmatics*. Pannenberg then advocated that theology must pay careful attention to the physical sciences.[48] At the same time, unless God is properly considered, a scientific theory cannot fully comprehend the world it seeks to explain, as it is creation:

> If the God of the Bible is the creator of the universe, then it is not possible to understand fully or even appropriately the processes of nature without any reference to that God. If, on the contrary, nature can be appropriately understood without reference to the God of the Bible, then that God cannot be the creator of the universe.[49]

While seeing theology and science as needing one another, he goes further, to think of theology as scientific as it adopts the same method and deals in part with the same finite reality. He sees theology as the "science of God" with each theological assertion having the logical structure of a hypothesis, which is subject to verification. Assertions are then tested by their implications. Thus, assertions about God can be tested by their implications for understanding the whole of finite reality, a wholeness that is implicitly anticipated in the ordinary experience of meaning. The idea of God becomes the hypothesis raised by Pannenberg to provide the most adequate explanation for the experience of meaning.

This was a significant move within the theological arena and gave science an important place in a post-Barth world. Pannenberg's ambition was impressive but he struggled to fulfil it, especially in specific interaction with science, from the initial conditions discussed by Hawking through to scenarios of the end of the universe.[50] Fellow theologians such as T. F. Torrance, Philip Clayton, Robert Russell, and Ted Peters have been far more successful in turning their considerable theological expertise to the specific issues of the physical sciences.[51]

His particular emphasis on the importance of the resurrection and God's self-disclosure, although lying at the end of history, being proleptically present in Jesus becomes an important contribution for the physical sciences. In terms of the future, Pannenberg states that "all reality is referred to the future and is experienced as eschatologically oriented."[52] The challenge for those who would follow Pannenberg is how to take seriously the picture described earlier that goes beyond Newtonian determinism and an openness to the future. If God is the power of the future, how does God relate to both the predictability and the uncertainty?

Where Pannenberg gave specific contributions was in his belief that science can help to shape our theological thinking. For example, he suggested that the work of the Spirit can be described in terms of the force of a field, as an immaterial force causes physical changes. While running the risk of depersonalizing the Spirit, it nevertheless is an interesting use of the physical sciences. In addition, he opened up a dialogue with cosmologist Frank Tipler on the future of the universe and eschatology.[53] Pannenberg is to be commended for both stimulating and participating in the dialogue.

Debate, Achievement, and Agenda

Although many theological questions remain on the nature of time, God's action in the world, and eschatology, perhaps the next phase of physical sciences and theology will be in the contribution to the central contemporary question of what it means to be human. This question can be seen in technological areas such as artificial intelligence, but at heart it is the theological issue of the relationship of human beings to God and to the nonhuman creation. Other chapters in this book pick this up in biological and environmental sciences. Yet it is important to note the contribution of the physical sciences, not least in the exploration of space and the atmosphere.

The iconic "Earthrise" image taken from Apollo 8 gave energy to the early stages of environmental concern and action.[54] Atmospheric physics, not least through remote sensing satellites that provided much of the data, was foundational to the key work of the Scientific Assessment Group of the Intergovernmental Panel on Climate Change who concluded that global warming was produced by emissions of greenhouse gases.[55]

Although the physical sciences will continue to contribute to humans combatting climate change through nuclear power, renewable energy sources, and carbon capture, they will also provide new ethical and theological challenges in the decades ahead. Already there are discussions in private business and national governments about the mining of the moon or Mars. What is servant stewardship of those bodies beyond the earth? The long-term possibility of this trajectory is colonization of other planets and terraforming, that is the changing of a planet's atmosphere to make it hospitable to human life.[56] Although terraforming might give the human race a safeguard against possible disasters affecting the earth, how should this be done in a way that stops other planets and other life forms simply being exploited for human gain?

This discussion has been prompted by the recognition that the earth is vulnerable, not only to human abuse but also in its cosmic context. The death of the dinosaurs in a mass extinction some 65 million years ago was the result of a comet impact on the earth. Currently NASA is monitoring over 2000 asteroids whose orbits cross the orbit of the earth. Smaller asteroids not leading to extinction events may be expected every 0.3 million years and larger ones capable of mass extinction every 100 million years. Schemes to nudge these asteroids away from impacting the earth are possible, but the question is who will pay and take responsibility for defending the whole earth. At even longer timescales of billions of years, the sun itself will come to the end of its life, swelling up and "crispifying" the earth in its outer layers. At this point it is envisioned that human being will have already become space travellers, but the ethical questions of colonising other worlds become extremely important. The insight that the earth is not an eternal home for humans is nontrivial.

This leads to perhaps one of the biggest challenges that the physical sciences provide for theology, and that is the possibility and search for extraterrestrial life. The discovery in the past two decades of exoplanets, that is planets around other stars, has encouraged such a search. Thousands of planets have been identified, with some like the earth, being small and rocky with their orbit in a habitable zone around their star.[57] If most of the 100 billion stars in the Milky Way galaxy have planetary systems, then many will argue that the possibility of life and intelligent life on other worlds is likely. This has become of such importance to the scientific community that one of the central roles of the new James Webb telescope will be to observe the atmospheres of exoplanets looking for signs of life.

If extraterrestrial life, never mind extraterrestrial intelligence, is discovered it could happen in the far future or it could be around the corner. The possibility of discovery poses many questions from the media and the public. There is an urgent need for what Peters calls "exotheology," that is, speculation on the theological significance of extraterrestrial life.[58] The search for extraterrestrial intelligence (SETI) is a new and rapidly emerging field for theologians.[59] Yet speculation about other worlds has a long tradition in Christian theology, with theology often encouraging such speculation.[60] Although questions of human uniqueness, the origin of sin, and the universality of the work of Jesus on the cross have sometimes been used to support the position that we are alone in the universe, several key theological insights have pointed the other way. First, God's freedom in creating cannot be limited by our perspective and experience. God has the freedom to create in whatever way God wants and thus other worlds should not be ruled out. Second, if God is the foundation and sustainer of the universal laws of physics, the physics that leads to human intelligence may lead to intelligence elsewhere. Third, and perhaps most important, Nicholas of Cusa in the fifteenth century made a key theological move suggesting that the special nature of human beings is defined by the gift of intimate relationship with God rather than us being at the center or alone in the universe.[61] This forms a strong theological foundation that encourages SETI.

The questions raised by SETI engage some long-standing theological issues. First, does humanity have to be unique to be special? In questions of the nature of human beings, it may be therefore that we can begin to see human beings as intimately related to God, but not unique as intelligent life in the universe. Sharing much with other life forms, even perhaps intelligence and self-consciousness, human beings are embedded in the story of God's particular acts. This is not an appeal to human superiority. It is about special relationship but not exclusive relationship. Human beings can be special without denying God's love and concern for other intelligent beings. This can be a positive area for theology.

The same could be said for questions of revelation, incarnation, sin, and redemption. SETI can ask questions that explore the universality and particularity of the death and resurrection of Jesus Christ. An openness to multiple incarnations was suggested by Tillich, Pittenger, Mascall, and more recently O'Meara.[62] Yet there has also been theological caution about multiple incarnations. If God's nature is to reach out in love in embodied form, why should there not have been multiple incarnations in different cultures on the earth? Although Christian theology has always recognized that other faith communities have insights into truth, the incarnation of God in Jesus is still held to be supreme. God does not only reveal through incarnation. It may not be necessary for revelation to require multiple incarnations. This is particularly the case when we note that in the case of human beings, the incarnation is about both revelation and salvation. Until we encounter ETI we may not have definitive answers. However, engaging with the questions that are posed by SETI is a useful theological exercise. Certainly, thinking through issues of the uniqueness of revelation and salvation feeds into theology's important and immediate concern of how to relate to those of other faiths and none.

These contemporary questions continue the huge revolutions in the way the physical sciences describe the world. Yet in these revolutions, far from strengthening the outdated conflict model of science and theology, science has gained humility and openness to dialogue. The modern theologian can be encouraged that many physical scientists want to grapple with the big questions and can be engaged in partnership if the theologian takes time to listen and understand, and graciously brings to the table the insights of a tradition that has often had a fruitful, if at times not well-known, engagement with the physical sciences.

Notes

1   Albert Einstein, "Zur Elektrodynamik Bewegter Körper," *Annalen der Physik* 17 (1905): 891.

2   Albert Einstein, "Die Grundlage Der Allgemeinen Relativitätstheorie," *Annalen der Physik* 49 (1916): 771.

3   Iain Paul, *Science and Theology in Einstein's Perspective* (Edinburgh: Scottish Academic Press, 1986); Robert John Russell, "Time in Eternity: Special Relativity and Eschatology," *Dialog* 39, no. 1 (2000): 46–55; Alister E. McGrath, *A Theory of Everything (That Matters): A Short Guide to Einstein, Relativity and the Future of Faith* (London: Hodder & Stoughton, 2019).

4   William Lane Craig, *Divine Foreknowledge and Human Freedom: The Coherence of Theism-Omniscience* (Leiden: Brill, 1991).

5   Albert Einstein and Michele Besso, *Correspondence 1903–1955* (Paris: Hermann, 1972), 537–8.

6   Peter Coveney and Roger Highfield. *The Arrow of Time: The Quest to Solve Science's Greatest Mystery* (London: Flamingo, 1991).

7   Charles H. Lineweaver, Paul C. W. Davies, and Michael Ruse, *Complexity and the Arrow of Time* (Cambridge: Cambridge University Press, 2013).

8   Kip S. Thorne, *Black Holes and Time Warps: Einstein's Outrageous Legacy* (London: Picador, 1994).

9   John M. E. McTaggart, *The Nature of Existence* (Cambridge: Cambridge University Press, 1927).

10   B. P. Abbott et al. (LIGO Scientific Collaboration and Virgo Collaboration). "Observation of Gravitational Waves from a Binary Black Hole Merger," *Physical Review Letters* 116 (2016).

11   Thomas F. Torrance, *Space, Time and Incarnation* (London: Oxford University Press, 1969), 67.

12   J. R. Lucas, *A Treatise on Time and Space* (London: Methuen & Co, 1973), 307.

13   Ted Peters, *God as Trinity: Relationality and Temporality in the Divine Life* (Louisville, KY: Westminster John Knox Press, 1993).

14   David Wilkinson, *Christian Eschatology and the Physical Universe* (London: T&T Clark, 2010).

15   John Polkinghorne, *The Quantum World* (Princeton NJ: Princeton University Press, 1984).

16   Tim Maudlin, *Philosophy of Physics: Quantum Theory* (Princeton, NJ: Princeton University Press, 2019).

17   David Wallace, *The Emergent Multiverse: Quantum Theory according to the Everett Interpretation* (Oxford: Oxford University Press, 2012).

18   Diarmuid Ó Murchú, *Quantum Theology: Spiritual Implications of the New Physics* (New York: Crossroad, 2004); John Polkinghorne, *Quantum Physics and Theology: An Unexpected Kinship* (London: SPCK, 2007); Robert J. Russell, *Quantum Mechanics: Scientific Perspectives on Divine Action* (Notre Dame, IN:

University of Notre Dame Press, 2002); Ernest L. Simmons, *The Entangled Trinity: Quantum Physics and Theology* (Minneapolis, MN: Fortress Press, 2014).

19   Rudolf Bultmann, *New Testament and Mythology and Other Basic Writings*, trans. Schubert M. Ogden (Philadelphia, PA: Fortress Press, 1984), 4.

20   For example, Maurice Wiles, *God's Action in the World: The Bampton Lectures for 1986* (London: SCM Press, 1986).

21   Bernard Lonergan, *Insight: A Study of Human Understanding*, Collected Works, Vol. 3, ed. Frederick E. Crowe and Robert M. Doran (Toronto: University of Toronto Press, 1992).

22   John C. Eccles, *How the Self Controls Its Brain* (Berlin: Springer, 1994).

23   William G. Pollard, *Chance and Providence: God's Action in a World Governed by Scientific Law* (New York: Charles Scribner's Sons, 1958).

24   Robert J. Russell, "Quantum Physics and the Theology of Non-Interventionist Objective Divine Action," in *The Oxford Handbook of Religion and Science*, ed. Philip Clayton (Oxford: Oxford University Press, 2006), 579–95.

25   Edward N. Lorenz, "Deterministic Nonperiodic Flow," *Journal of the Atmospheric Sciences* 20 (1963): 130–41.

26   John Polkinghorne, *Science and Providence* (London: SPCK, 1988).

27   Ian Barbour, *When Science Meets Religion: Enemies, Strangers or Partners?* (London: SPCK, 2000). See also John B. Cobb and David Ray Griffin. *Process Theology: An Introductory Exposition* (Philadelphia: Westminster Press, 1976); David A. Pailin, *God and the Processes of Reality: Foundations of a Credible Theism* (London: Routledge, 1989).

28   W. H. Vanstone, *Love's Endeavour, Love's Expense* (London: Darton, Longman & Todd, 1977); Jürgen Moltmann, *God in Creation: An Ecological Doctrine of Creation*, trans. Margaret Kohl (San Francisco, CA: Harper & Row, 1985).

29   D. Stephen Long and George Kalantzis, *The Sovereignty of God Debate* (Eugene, OR: Cascade, 2009); William Hasker, *Providence, Evil and the Openness of God* (London: Routledge, 2004).

30   Charles H. Pinnock, *Most Moved Mover: A Theology of God's Openness* (Grand Rapids, MI: Baker, 2001).

31   See John Sanders, *The God Who Risks: A Theology of Providence* (Downers Grove, IL: IVP, 1998).

32   See as an exception Thomas Jay Oord, *Creation Made Free: Open Theology Engaging Science* (Eugene, OR: Pickwick, 2009).

33   Georges Lemaître, "A Homogeneous Universe of Constant Mass and Increasing Radius Accounting for

the Radial Velocity of Extra-Galactic Nebulæ," *Monthly Notices of the Royal Astronomical Society* 91, no. 5 (1931): 483–90.

34 Pius XII, "The Proofs for the Existence of God in the Light of Modern Natural Science," An address of Pope Pius XII to the Pontifical Academy of Sciences, 22 November 1951, https://www.intratext.com/IXT/ENG1242/ (accessed 9 September 2023).

35 Stephen W. Hawking, *A Brief History of Time: From the Big Bang to Black Holes* (London: Bantam, 1988); David Wilkinson and David Hutchings, *God, Stephen Hawking and the Multiverse: What Hawking Said, and Why It Matters* (London: SPCK, 2020).

36 Stephen Hawking and Leonard Mlodinow, *The Grand Design* (London: Bantam, 2010).

37 Hawking, *A Brief History of Time*, 160–1.

38 Fred Hoyle, *The Intelligent Universe: A New View of Creation and Evolution* (London: Michael Joseph Ltd., 1983); Paul Davies, *The Goldilocks Enigma: Why Is the Universe Just Right for Life?* (London: Penguin, 2007).

39 John Polkinghorne, *Science and Creation: The Search for Understanding* (London: SPCK, 1988).

40 Robert P. Kirshner, *The Extravagant Universe: Exploding Stars, Dark Energy, and the Accelerating Cosmos* (Princeton, NJ: Princeton University Press, 2016).

41 Richard Bauckham and Trevor Hart, *Hope Against Hope: Christian Eschatology in Contemporary Context* (London: Darton, Longman & Todd, 1999).

42 John Polkinghorne, *Science and Christian Belief: Theological Reflections of a Bottom-Up Thinker* (London: SPCK, 1994), 167.

43 Robert J. Russell, "Bodily Resurrection, Eschatology and Scientific Cosmology," in *Resurrection: Theological and Scientific Assessments*, ed. Ted Peters, Robert J. Russell, and Michael Welker (Grand Rapids, MI: Eerdmans, 2002), 3–30; Wilkinson, *Christian Eschatology and the Physical Universe*.

44 Thomas F. Torrance, *Space, Time and Resurrection* (Edinburgh: Handsel Press, 1976), 90.

45 John Polkinghorne, *Scientists as Theologians: A Comparison of the Writings of Ian Barbour, Arthur Peacocke and John Polkinghorne* (London: SPCK, 1996).

46 John Polkinghorne, *One World: The Interaction of Science and Theology* (London: SPCK, 1986); Polkinghorne, *Science and Creation*; Polkinghorne, *Science and Providence*.

47 John Polkinghorne, *The Faith of a Physicist: Reflections of a Bottom-Up Thinker* (Princeton, NJ: Princeton University Press, 2014).

48 Wolfhart Pannenberg, *Towards a Theology of Nature: Essays on Science and Faith*, trans. W. C. Linss, ed. Ted Peters (Louisville, KY: Westminster John Knox Press, 1993), 50–71; "The Doctrine of Creation and Modern Science," *Zygon* 23 (1988): 3–21.

49 Wolfhart Pannenberg, "Theological Questions to Scientists," *Zygon* 16 (1981): 65.

50 Keith Ward, review of *Toward a Theology of Nature*, by Wolfhart Pannenberg, *Zygon* 30 (1995): 343; Robert J. Russell, "Contingency in Physics and Cosmology: A Critique of the Theology of Wolfhart Pannenberg," *Zygon* 23 (1988): 23–43.

51 Philip Clayton, *Explanation from Physics to Theology: An Essay in Rationality and Religion* (New Haven, CT: Yale University Press, 1989); Robert J. Russell, William R. Stoeger, and George V. Coyne, eds., *Physics, Philosophy, and Theology: A Common Quest for Understanding* (Notre Dame, IN: University of Notre Dame Press, 1988); Ted Peters, *Cosmos as Creation: Theology and Science in Consonance* (Nashville, TN: Abingdon Press, 1989); Philip Clayton, "Theology and the Physical Sciences," in *The Modern Theologians: An Introduction to Christian Theology since 1918*, ed. David F. Ford with Rachel Muers, 3rd ed. (Oxford: Blackwell 2011), 342–56.

52 Wolfhart Pannenberg, "The God of Hope," in *Basic Questions in Theology: Collected Essays*, Vol. II, trans. George H. Kehm (Philadelphia: Fortress Press, 1971), 237.

53 Frank J. Tipler, "The Omega Point as Eschaton: Answers to Pannenberg's Questions for Scientists," *Zygon* 24 (1989): 217–53; Frank J. Tipler, *The Physics of Immortality* (London: Weidenfeld & Nicolson, 1994); Wolfhart Pannenberg, "Theological Appropriation of Scientific Understandings: Response to Hefner, Wicken, Eaves and Tipler," *Zygon* 24 (1989): 255–71; Wolfhart Pannenberg, "Breaking a Taboo: Frank Tipler's *The Physics of Immortality*," *Zygon* 30 (1995): 309–14.

54 Editorial, "Earthrise at 50," *Nature* 564 (2018): 301.

55 J. T. Houghton et al., eds., *Climate Change 2001: The Scientific Basis* (Cambridge: Cambridge University Press, 2001).

56 Michio Kaku, *The Future of Humanity: Terraforming Mars, Interstellar Travel, Immortality, and Our Destiny Beyond Earth* (London: Allen Lane, 2018).

57 Donald Goldsmith, *Exoplanets: Hidden Worlds and the Quest for Extraterrestrial Life* (Cambridge, MA: Harvard University Press, 2018).

58 Ted Peters, *Science, Theology, and Ethics* (Aldershot: Ashgate, 2003), 121.

59 David Wilkinson, *Science, Religion, and the Search for Extraterrestrial Intelligence* (Oxford: Oxford University Press, 2017); Ted Peters, Martinez Hewlett, Joshua M. Moritz, and Robert J. Russell, eds., *Astrotheology: Science and Theology Meet Extraterrestrial Life* (Eugene, OR: Cascade, 2018); Andrew Davison, "Christian Systematic Theology and Life Elsewhere in the Universe: A Study in Suitability," *Theology and Science* 16, no. 4 (2018): 447–61.

60 Karl Rahner, "Sternenbewohner II," in *Lexikon für Theologie und Kirche*, ed. Michael Buchberger, Josef Höfer, Karl Rahner, and Suso Brechter (Freiburg: Herder, 1957), 1061–2; Michael J. Crowe, *The Extraterrestrial Life Debate 1750–1900: The Idea of a Plurality of Worlds from Kant to Lowell* (Cambridge: Cambridge University Press, 1986); Michael J. Crowe, *The Extraterrestrial Life Debate, Antiquity to 1915: A Source Book* (Notre Dame, IN: University of Notre Dame Press, 2008); Steven J. Dick, *Plurality of Worlds: The Origins of the Extraterrestrial Life Debate from Democritus to Kant* (Cambridge: Cambridge University Press, 1982).

61 Thomas F. O'Meara, *Vast Universe: Extraterrestrials and Christian Revelation* (Collegeville, MN: Liturgical Press, 2012), 76.

62 Paul Tillich, *Systematic Theology*, Vol. II (London: Nisbet, 1953), 96; W. Norman Pittenger, *The Word Incarnate* (London: Nisbet, 1959), 249; E. L. Mascall, *Christian Theology and Modern Science: Some Questions in Their Relations* (London: Longmans, 1956), 39–40; O'Meara, *Vast Universe*, 247.

Recommended Reading

McGrath, Alister E. *A Theory of Everything (That Matters): A Short Guide to Einstein, Relativity and the Future of Faith.* London: Hodder & Stoughton, 2019.

McLeish, Tom. *Faith and Wisdom in Science.* Oxford: Oxford University Press, 2016.

Pannenberg, Wolfhart. *Toward a Theology of Nature: Essays on Science and Faith.* Edited by Ted Peters. Louisville, KY: Westminster John Knox Press, 1993.

Polkinghorne, John. *One World: The Interaction of Science and Theology.* London: SPCK, 1986.

———. *The Faith of a Physicist: Reflections of a Bottom-Up Thinker.* Princeton, NJ: Princeton University Press, 2014.

Wilkinson, David. *Christian Eschatology and the Physical Universe.* London: T&T Clark, 2010.

———. *Science, Religion, and the Search for Extraterrestrial Intelligence.* Oxford: Oxford University Press, 2017.

Theology and the Biological Sciences

Celia Deane-Drummond

Introduction

From the 1970s there has been a growing awareness that inequitable consumerism, industrialization, and rising human population levels are well beyond the carrying capacity of the planet, which, added to escalating climate change, threatens the survival of humans, particularly in the most vulnerable regions of the world, and leads to mass extinction of other species.[1] Added to those threats, the increasing use of technological means to achieve fundamental changes in life through, for example, what is now commonly known as gene editing, poses important questions about the relationship of the biosciences with theological anthropology and eschatology, human being and becoming. Such threats have served to reinforce that one of the most popular areas of public debate in the third millennium is the promise and dangers of applied biological sciences.[2] Over half a century ago, there was a quiet revolution in the concept of biological life, following the discovery of the genetic code by James Watson and Francis Crick in 1953. Theologians concerned with pastoral and practical matters could no longer afford to ignore the relationship between theology and the biological sciences. Yet the way life and nature should be understood from a theological perspective has had a checkered history. Contemporary inquirers might still tend to ask: what has theology to do with biology?

Envisioning the hand of God as in some sense operative in the natural world has a very long history. In the early patristic period, the entire natural world was viewed as symbolic of the heavenly realm, pointing to theological truths. The Middle Ages introduced the concept that nature was a book to be read alongside the book of holy scripture. This opened the way for closer observation of the natural world, reinforced by the rediscovery of Aristotelian philosophy in writers such as Thomas Aquinas. However, it was only once experimental science became fashionable in the seventeenth century that a new kind of natural theology emerged, one that viewed the experimenter as discovering the design of God in creation. The botanist John Ray's *The Wisdom of God Manifest in the Works of Creation*, published in 1695, was popular for over a century and went through ten editions by 1835. Unlike other authors who had interpreted their observations in the light of religious concepts, Ray was determined to establish natural history on an empirical basis.

Ford's The Modern Theologians: An Introduction to Christian Theology since 1918, Fourth Edition.
Edited by Rachel Muers and Ashley Cocksworth.
© 2024 John Wiley & Sons Ltd. Published 2024 by John Wiley & Sons Ltd.

His motivation for natural history was not just scientific curiosity; it became a *religious* duty to search for the empirical truth in the natural world so it could be used to serve humankind and ultimately give glory to God. Instead of viewing nature as a threat, Francis Bacon, among others, believed that the natural world needed to be brought under control of scientific reasoning. Questions surfaced that continue to engage those committed to a theistic understanding of the natural world. In what sense is God visible in the natural world? How does one explain the suffering apparent in natural processes? How does empirical science come to terms with the miraculous? What is the role of humanity?

An even more challenging scientific development was to await the Christian religious community with the publication of Charles Darwin's *Origin of Species* (1865), which outlined his theory of evolution. This, in brief, states that variety exists in a population and that those individuals who are best suited to the environment will live longer and hence have more offspring. This ensures that the favored characteristics of these individuals are passed down to the next generation through a process known as natural selection. Gradually, over long periods, new species emerge. His theory posed a significant challenge to existing natural theologies. Now it seemed that new species were no longer fixed in a preconceived divine plan but could emerge autonomously. Is a theological ontology that presumes creation out of nothing, *creatio ex nihilo*, ever reconcilable with evolutionary naturalism? Humanity in Darwin's theory no longer had a special place; rather, it was perceived as just one species from a sub-branch of successful hominins within a densely branched tree of life. Even the origin of life itself became subject to empirical explanations. Theologians became adept at redesigning their theological explanations to take account of evolutionary theory.

Theological justification could take different possible routes. One might be to reject Darwinism outright as in direct opposition to Christian belief in a divine creator. The rise of creationist ideas, alongside purported "scientific" explanations from the scriptural accounts, represents one form of popular accommodation that is rejected by theologians and scientists alike. Alternatively, some form of theistic evolution is accepted, combining evolutionary ideas with belief in a creator. In this scenario there are two alternatives. Either, according to the deist alternative, God simply started the process of evolution and then left nature to itself, or God is intricately involved in the process from the beginning, suffering in and with the processes of the natural world, which is perceived as creation that is not yet finished. If the terminology of "nature" signaled secular alternatives, "creation" flagged a theological understanding of creator and creation. The idea of secondary causation is somewhere between Deism and more participatory alternatives, though it is usually combined with a more general sense of God's immanence in the natural world. Deism tries to avoid the problem of associating God directly with suffering and natural evil. God's involvement in evolutionary change, or variations on it, are rather more influential in the twentieth and twenty-first centuries, which are the focus of this chapter.

Survey

The scientific community largely accepts Darwin's theory of evolution, although with some qualifications. Darwin had no clear concept of how inherited variations were passed down between generations or how such variations arose. The rediscovery of Gregory Mendel's plant breeding experiments highlighted the significance of discrete mutagenic changes. Experimental research showed that the environment could influence mutation rates. In the 1930s and 1940s most biologists came to accept neo-Darwinianism, combining the insights of Darwin with genetic theories about mutation in what has been termed the modern synthesis (MS), a term first used by Julian Huxley. The full explanation as to the way genetic inheritance worked at the molecular level awaited the discovery of the structure of deoxyribonucleic acid (DNA) by James Watson and Francis Crick.[3]

The balance of genes in a population would change if some individuals with a given mutant gene were able to survive better compared with other individuals in the same population. This is the genetic corollary to Darwin's theory of natural selection. There are other ways that gene pools may change, such as through more random processes, also known as genetic drift. The evolutionary biologists John Eldredge and Stephen J. Gould proposed an evolutionary process of punctuated equilibria, where rapid phases of evolutionary change are interspersed with much slower phases. Their results, though challenged by other prominent evolutionary biologists including Simon Conway Morris, supplemented the theory of evolution through natural selection. New combinations of genes may lead to variations, and differences in physical appearance (phenotype) may appear even with the same genetic makeup (genotype). It is also somewhat misleading to speak of mutations as "chance" events, because microscopic events that seem random are a result of physical and chemical changes and lead to law-like properties at the macroscopic level.

Changes in gene *regulation* affect the overall structure or morphology of an organism and hence diversity. The importance of gene regulation has become a topic of increasing concern to contemporary biologists, so much so that even the definition of what a gene means is now subject to debate. Rather than viewing the gene as a "blueprint" for coding the organism there is an increasing awareness of the need to take into account complex regulatory processes, most of which are still not properly understood.[4] The relative importance of environmental and ecological factors in the overall process of evolutionary change is also subject to intense debate, with newer extended evolutionary synthesis (EES) theories putting more stress on the ability of organisms to actively construct their niche within a dynamic interchange between an organism and its environment. If the MS tended to see fixed genetic traits in an organism selected for a given environment, EES perceives that environment as part of a dynamic system.

Pioneers of the twentieth century, on discovering the structure of DNA, claimed they had found the "secret of life." The mushrooming of numerous branches of molecular biology and medical genetics, culminating in the multimillion-dollar Human Genome Project, with its aim to give a full chemical sequence of the human genome, speaks of the future potential of genetic technology. Supporters frequently highlight the medical advantages of the technologies and the possible alleviation of human suffering and pain. Similar arguments have been used to support human cloning.[5] Contemporary discussion has shifted toward debates on heritable human gene editing, a term more commonly used now compared with "germ line therapy," since the latter is permissible in most jurisdictions in early embryos.[6] Gene editing relies on new genetic editing tools that are available, including the highly publicized CRISPR-Cas 9, which uses specific bacterial genes to excise genetic material of target species in specific places, which is followed by inherent repair mechanisms in the cells.[7] At this juncture theology can no longer remain detached from ethical and pastoral concerns. If God is the author of creation, are there limits to the genetic manipulation of nature? What is the role of humanity in evolution? Are we becoming "fabricated" through our own inventions, or are we cocreators with God working for a better future? Who is to gain most from the technology? Does the desire for genetic change disguise a more sinister trend toward normalizing a population to preset ends, that is, eugenics?

A key issue in human genetics concerns the extent to which humanity is determined by its genetic structure, reminiscent of the long-standing nature–nurture debate. A popular view is that we are simply genetically programmed, that the discovery of our genetic composition is all that is really required to define the "self." Theologians generally challenge this so-called "gene myth," and they believe that such misconception leads to unwarranted fears about the dangers of genetic manipulation. Ted Peters, for example, is a strong advocate of human freedom; although we may be genetically constrained in our choices, this does not amount to genetic "programming." Hence, he argues that the use and application of genetics are more likely to be a gift of God to humanity, but only if used responsibly.[8]

Transhumanist philosophers believe that we should use all the technological means available to take control of human destiny. Transhumanism is associated with a desire for human life extension, where gene manipulation is just one of the tools in the toolbox of potential technologies that could be used. More radical transhumanists press for a different definition of life, with speculation that so-called "information" coding for specific persons could become digitized then uploaded into "chips" that could persist in different environments. Theologians, as in the case of heated discussions on genetics, are divided on this topic, some supporting transhumanism as representative of a nascent eschatology, whereas others are far more skeptical of its basis for valuing a truly human life.[9]

The application of genetics to the nonhuman sphere also raises important issues, such as animal welfare, potential environmental damage, and more general questions such as how far and to what extent humanity is warranted in reordering the natural world. Another question arises as to the relative value of humanity compared with nonhumans. Whereas in secular analysis the consequences are normally the measure that judges whether an action is right or not, other values come into play from the perspective of theology, including, from the Genesis account, the idea that all creation is good and belongs to God. The interpretation of the command to humanity to "have dominion" is ambiguous in its history of interpretation, leading to a desire for manipulation, as in Francis Bacon, or, alternatively, leading to a greater sense of human care and responsible stewardship.

The philosophical tension between a stress on the value of either humans (anthropocentrism) or all biological species (biocentrism) is reflected in debates about how far it is right to use animals in experimental science, including medical science, and the relative weight given to protecting endangered species, and so on. Peter Singer believes that animals deserve protection because they are sentient.[10] Theologians have taken issue with Singer in that he seems to imply that humans lacking sentience are dispensable and have no moral worth. Tom Regan campaigns for animal rights and argues that animals are individual "subjects" of a life.[11] The theologian Andrew Linzey justifies his theos-rights approach by suggesting that because God created animals vulnerable to human domestication, they deserve equivalent protection to children.[12] Should we use biological characteristics to define moral worth, or is human dignity beyond comparison with nonhumans? Authors like Singer are nervous about any justification for giving higher priority to humans, dubbing this "speciesism."

As evolutionary science and its varied applications continues to grow and develop, theologians working at the interface with biology have devoted considerable attention to meeting its particular challenges. The palaeontologist and Jesuit priest Pierre Teilhard de Chardin (1881–1955) was one of the pioneers in this field. He believed that it was possible to create a synthesis between evolutionary ideas and Christian theology, culminating in a grand vision for the Christification of the universe. Those theologians of the process theology school, such as Ian Barbour and John Haught, adapt a process vision of reality drawn from the work of the philosopher Alfred North Whitehead. Other theologians are less convinced that scientific theories about the evolution of nature can be fully incorporated into Christian theological frameworks without leading to their distortion. Thomas F. Torrance argued for a Barthian approach to theology but still adhered to the methodology of scientific empiricism. Alister McGrath also claims to aim at a scientific and theological synthesis; however, it soon becomes clear that the vagaries of science are too precarious to give him any real confidence, so instead he opts for attachment to scientific empiricism as essential to theological insight.[13] How far such a methodology is universal in science is somewhat open to question; for example, the falsification hypothesis common in physical science is not used in ecological science at all.

Many theologians have responded to the challenges posed by the work of Richard Dawkins and other biologists sometimes known as the New Atheists who are not just promoting evolutionary ideas as the explanation for life, but who are also rejecting religious experience in the name of scientific "realism." Although Dawkins claimed that he was using the phrase *The Selfish Gene* to stress the tendency for gene conservation through each generation, the moral overtones were obvious. Mary Midgley was quick to point out the rhetoric in what Dawkins was attempting, by elevating "a humble piece of goo within cells to a malign and all-powerful agent."[14] She argues that attitudes will affect the form in which symbolism and imagination take shape. Although Dawkins' attempt to describe cultural evolution through meme theory has largely been superseded in evolutionary biology, biologists remain confident that evolutionary tools help to clarify cultural change. The precise relationship between biological and cultural evolution remains a topic for further debate and consideration. Counterattacks on the New Atheists by theologians such as Michael Hanby and Conor Cunningham stress the incongruence of much evolutionary theory philosophically, such as the tautology of "survival" of the "fittest," arguing instead that theologians, to be true to the ontological presuppositions of Christian tradition, need to understand science as ultimately parasitic on theological beliefs, for without belief in God as distinct from the world there would be no science.[15]

Keith Ward characterizes three areas of philosophical challenge posed by classic evolutionary theory. The first is that there is no ultimate purpose in the universe, the second is that life evolves simply through competitive ruthlessness, and the third is that mind just happens as an "adjunct" to gene survival.[16] He believes that natural selection on its own cannot *guarantee* the emergence of complex conscious life forms. He also shares with Stephen Clark the doubt as to why intelligent life emerged, as there is nothing to suggest that such a capacity would *inevitably* lead to greater survival rates compared with those with no rationality.[17] Of course, other "higher" human cultural characteristics are not simply explicable through reproductive advantage, though the challenge relates to how biological and cultural aspects are intertwined. If we accept that the natural probability of mind emerging is very low, and then invoke divine purpose, then we are left with a God of the gaps, who fills in where science has failed. Simon Conway Morris is a good example of a biologist who is less hostile to religion compared with Dawkins, but who still argues that convergence in evolution implies that human-like species are less the result of "chance" and more the result of an inevitable process.[18] The fate of the earth through science alone portrays a somewhat chilling eschatology. However, this does not mean that our limited understanding of evolutionary science needs to import God either.

Alternative biological models based on mutualism are receiving attention among theologians.[19] Instead of the Darwinian images of competitiveness, biological processes such as symbiosis, cooperation, and integration of processes in ecological systems become inspirational models for human behavior. Feminists have been particularly influential through ecofeminism, including prominent feminist writers such as Rosemary Radford Ruether and Sallie McFague in the United States and Anne Primavesi, Ruth Page, and Mary Grey in the United Kingdom.[20] Page is concerned about the extent of suffering in evolution, so prefers God's immanence to be expressed as *with* creation, rather than *in* creation. Most ecofeminists believe that there is a link between oppression of the earth and oppression of women, though the possible advantage of identifying women with the earth is hotly debated. Carolyn Merchant has linked the Baconian urge to control nature with oppression of women, arguing instead for a relational approach to the natural world.[21] As a corollary to the link between science and sexism, feminist authors have urged a new kind of science, one that focuses more on care rather than control. Ruether has included images of Gaia in her reconstruction of theology and nature.[22] Primavesi has taken up James Lovelock's model of the earth functioning as a single organism (Gaia) to argue for a reformulated theology.[23]

More recent work on scientific ecology has shown that the idea of ecology in terms of stable, interconnected systems is no longer accepted. Ecologists now are more likely to focus on flux, dynamic interchange, and the involvement of humans in ecological change. Theologians tempted to draw on models of ecology in terms of stable interrelationships need to be aware that this is an idealized philosophy rather than ecological science. Global biodiversity loss is a specific area of the biosciences that is receiving more public attention given the drastic changes taking place alongside climate change and other environmental problems. Biodiversity points to something about the variety of life and its richness that scientists have identified as worthy of both scientific and sociopolitical focus. Biodiversity can be defined to mean richness within a species or variability and variety of species or ecosystem diversity.[24] *Genetic diversity* is about that genetic variation of life between individuals of a population and between populations. *Organismal diversity* refers to differences between individuals and between populations that make up subspecies and species, enlarging outwards to include genera, families, and phyla. Variations in habitats, ecosystems and so on comprise *ecological diversity*.

Healthy forests and ecosystems rich in biodiversity harbor less disease and shed fewer viruses. Conservation biologist Enric Sala claims that a healthy natural world will protect humanity from future zoonotic pandemics.[25] He points to our broken relationship with the natural world as one of the underlying causes of many human ills and points to a type of *implicit theology*. Wild places rich in natural biodiversity are, as Sala suggests, like humanity's life support system. They generate the air we breathe, they produce the food we need and clean the water we drink; they are also capable of absorbing half of the carbon dioxide we put into the atmosphere.

Named Theologians

Pierre Teilhard de Chardin (1881–1955)

Pierre Teilhard de Chardin was a brilliant Jesuit scientist whose paleontological research challenged Darwin's assumption that cranial capacity in evolution emerged prior to toolmaking. He argued instead that evolution and toolmaking evolved together. Like the sociobiologists of a later generation, he believed that evolution was responsible not only for physical characteristics but also for all sociocultural history. Yet it was the way he combined his scientific ideas with his theological vision that caused the most controversy.[26] He did not adhere to the materialism characteristic of Darwin's original thesis; instead, he suggested that matter was increasing in spiritualization. *The Human Phenomenon* (1940), possibly his most influential work, urged a unity of matter and spirit, thought and action, personalism and collectivism, plurality and unity. His earlier work, *The Divine Milieu* (1920), was more focused on Christian mysticism informed by an evolutionary account. His commitment to ontological monism is very clear; God's immanent nature is interpreted in terms of the cosmic Christ. His law of complexity/consciousness attempted to explain the emergence of consciousness. Teilhard stressed the significance of human evolution, so that humans could not only influence but also direct evolution; wars were simply growing pains of adolescent humanity that would ultimately grow up through the achievements of science and technology. He understood each phase of evolution to represent distinct jumps over a critical threshold: first, the formation of elementary corpuscles of the cosmos; second, the formation of a biosphere; third, the formation of human species. At death an immortal center of consciousness in human beings united to form a planetary layer of superconsciousness around the earth, eventually to be united with God as Omega, the end of evolution.

Teilhard's grand synthesis was bold, optimistic, daring, and mystical rather than systematic. Teilhard argued that just as theology needed science, so science needed theology if it is to have a "heart" as well as a "head." It is not difficult to criticize his work from a scientific point of view, even though he was a well-respected paleontologist and elected to the French Academy of Sciences in 1947. The place and significance he gave to humans are not evident in Darwin's theory, which posited a branching evolutionary path.[27] David Sloan Wilson has argued that Teilhard needs to be reclaimed by evolutionary biologists for what he contributed to a holistic scientific vision of evolution and his potential for engaging an evolutionary naturalism with religious believers, which was ahead of his time.[28] From a theological perspective his vision is optimistic and anthropocentric in a way that finds rather fewer supporters in contemporary contexts, although his holistic integrated vision of spirituality has contemporary resonance. His focus on process and final goodness is also characteristic of process theology. His attention to the importance of consciousness has become an area of increasing debate. The unity of mind and brain, the relationship to the soul, and the way in which consciousness emerges from our primate ancestors are still unresolved.

Arthur Peacocke (1924–2006)

Arthur Peacocke devoted the early part of his career to working on the chemical structure of DNA. As a biochemist turned theologian, he helped to raise the public profile of issues in biology and theology, especially his reworking of theological ideas. Like Torrance, he envisages scientific method as being critical in its engagement with theology. However, he is prepared to take any article of faith as provisional, unless proved otherwise by scientific "evidence." He argues that the experience of working as a scientist helps humanity understand God's interaction with the world. Understanding does not come through faith in the traditional way, but the other way round. Unlike Teilhard, who believed in rudimentary forms of consciousness in the world, Peacocke prefers the idea of emergence, that at increasing levels of complexity we find new properties emerging that are not predictable at lower levels of organization. He is wary of saying that humankind is just another animal; rather, there are unique characteristics of human species, just as in any other species. In other words, he argues for a holistic approach to life on earth, one that does not simply isolate the genes but explores wider parameters of behavior, sociology, psychology, and religion.

Peacocke's Christology is liberal in its conception of Christ as a perfect human being, though he is also attracted to more abstract ideas such as the divine Logos incarnate in the world. God, for Peacocke, works through the interplay of chance and necessity in allowing the earth to evolve. He distances himself from those authors who wish to locate God's action in evolution at the microscopic level; rather, the action of God is through "top-down" or "whole–part" interaction, so that the influence is indirect, through a chain of levels acting in a "downward" way. Like process theologians, he argues for pan-en-theism, though he retains the idea of a sacramental universe. He rejects classical ideas such as the fall of humanity, preferring reinterpretation in terms of failure to achieve potential given by God. Drawing on the theology of Jürgen Moltmann, he is attracted to the idea of a suffering, pathetic, self-emptying God, one who shares in the suffering of all creatures, as well as humans. Humanity is cocreator, coworker, and coexplorer with God in creation.

Few scientists object to the way in which Peacocke has formulated his theology, though his sharp rebuttal of sociobiology may come as a surprise. His theological position is more controversial, especially his claim that God can be envisaged through scientific exploration. Nicholas Lash believes that presuming that science is a mediator of the truth of theology through scientific observation is false, as it rests on the shift toward the spectator model of human engagement with reality that came to dominate the Western imagination along with the rise of modern experimental science.[29] His critique would also make him part company with more conservative theologians such as Torrance or McGrath, who incorporate scientific empiricism into theological discourse. Lash believes that a diversity of approaches to God, with their fragmentary insights, is more characteristic of God compared with any grand order independent of self. However, although scientific theories may have the appearance of such independent reality, in practice science is more fluid than Lash attests, especially in its most creative and open aspects. Peacocke, like contemporary scientists who work at the interface with theology, such as Tom McLeish, is drawn more to the latter, creative science, which has more in common with music or art than Lash implies.[30] However, whether one is still committed to the way of achieving theological knowledge through scientific discourse is a matter of debate. The natural world is an ambiguous place in which to find God. It seems more likely, then, that only with the eye of faith can wonder in the natural world appear to be truly reflective of the glory of God.

John Zizioulas (1931–2023)

John Zizioulas is an Eastern Orthodox theologian of some distinction who devoted considerable energy to translating Orthodox ideas into a language that can be readily understood in the West. He is also characteristic of a larger movement within the Orthodox community that believes in the importance of caring for the earth as God's gift to humanity. The Orthodox perspective is one that sees "nature" as inclusive of human beings, and a radical distinction between God and creation. How can God and the world be linked without losing the radical distinction between the two? Zizioulas argues that the link between God and the world is possible through humanity. However, he rejects the emphasis on rationality as a basis for human superiority, as evolutionary research presents other animals having this capacity, and it can also be the basis for a rationalization of the world for selfish exploitation. He argues, instead, that human freedom is the most important dimension of human beings. Freedom may be used in ways that are distorting, as is clear from the story of the Fall. Humanity "liberates creation from its limitations and lets it truly be."[31] Christ acts as the model for the perfect relationship between humanity and the world, so that as the bread and wine are offered in the eucharist, so the source of all creation as a gift from God becomes clear. It is through the liturgical act that God and creation are once again drawn into right relationship. Nature as sacred is no longer under the threat of death, but through the free choice of human beings enters life. This sacramental life, faithful to the teaching of the church, engenders an ethos, a way of life that counters the selfishness that Zizioulas believes is at the heart of the ecological crisis.

Zizioulas' writing is traditional in its biblical interpretation without ignoring the discoveries of modern evolutionary biology and science. He is prepared to listen to the insights of evolutionary ideas, without making these paradigmatic. He calls for a specifically liturgical vision, one whose language and narrative is distinct from that of scientific reasoning with its modern tendency toward fragmentation and specialization. His stress on the importance of freedom would have resonance with other authors working at the interface between biology and theology, especially in areas such as genetics. The concept of humanity as priest of creation is more problematic.

The Debate

A controversial but rapidly expanding area of public debate in the medical biosciences concerns human gene editing. The clinical, ethical debate on human gene editing relates to how far it is justified as "therapy" for those who want to bear children but carry diseases. Scientific consensus in the West intends to restrict its use to lethal diseases such as Tay-Sachs.[32] However, there are crucial issues of global governance to work out that remain extremely difficult to implement.[33] All such genetic editing tools rely on artificial reproductive technologies for their implementation and in many cases preimplantation genetic diagnosis, though the latter is complicated by what is termed genetic mosaicism, where only some, rather than all, of the cells in the zygote are transformed genetically. The specificity allows for greater accuracy, though it is still not sufficient to be approved for human use.[34] The scientific importance of such new technologies obscure important social, political, theological, and ethical issues that are ongoing subjects of debate.

Theologians joining the fray of public debates such as these need to be aware that what is at stake are wider theological and philosophical issues of how human life is valued and understood. At the background of such discussions are deep-seated beliefs about the importance and significance of Darwin's theory, that influence human meaning and becoming. In contemporary evolutionary biology developmental systems theory (DST) is one end of the spectrum, whereas what is known as the MS is at the other end, and EES in between. Public understanding has not really caught up with the trends toward DST and holism more generally in biology, as exemplified in the way reductionism about the human person, be it genes, brains, or intelligence, is often assumed. Reclaiming a different public voice for an alternative way of understanding the task of evolutionary biology has practical implications, and the newer theories such as the EES arguably are more compatible with theological thinking.[35] There are heated debates among evolutionary biologists as to how "new" such theories are relative to the originating neo-Darwinian paradigm. The EES concepts championed by biologists such as Jeremy Kendal[36] or Kevin Layland[37] show the importance of ecology in evolution but without losing all sight of the contribution of natural selection. What is still left of MS is a humbled and pruned variety of that hypothesis.

One area that is particularly fascinating and relevant for theological engagement is that there are influential anthropologists and other thinkers now who are beginning to challenge truncated biological views of what it means to be human in favor of a different more holistic approach to anthropology that recognizes how human lives are entangled with other beings and each other in interspecies relationships. Cultural evolution is distinct from biological evolution in important ways, but many anthropologists prefer to speak of *biocultural evolution*, combining insights from both the biological and social sciences. Social anthropologists have often been suspicious of quantitative methods, as they seem to miss out the rich and dense textured lives of real people living in specific communities. Biological anthropologists, on the other hand, have understood qualitative approaches as missing out on empirically based research, meaning that conclusions reached by more qualitative methods are limited, at least as far as they can be termed "scientific." In practice, of course, the situation is even more complicated than this division implies.

In evolutionary terms religions and religious institutions are very recent in human history. But that does not mean that an experience of the transcendent is confined to such a time frame, or that hints in the evolutionary record cannot point to the possibility of experiences of the transcendent. In some fascinating work with macaques, evolutionary anthropologist Agustín Fuentes has shown that on some, but repeated, occasions macaques will be arrested by a scene that can only be described as stunningly beautiful, and there seems to be no other explanation for why they stood still in their tracks.[38] Similar examples of chimpanzees watching waterfalls have been noted by Jane Goodall.[39] There needs to be some care, of course, in interpreting such observations. What it does show is that the possibility of a deep phylogenetic origin to the capacity to experience wonder is likely. What it does not show is whether these experiences are necessarily identical with the kind of wonder-filled experiences humans feel when confronted with beautiful imagery. And wonder, of course, is also distinct from religious awe, even if the two are related.[40]

The puzzle of why religion emerged at all is another area of intense debate, and a difficult one for biologists to come to terms with on a purely evolutionary level. Rather than dismiss religion as a "spandrel" arising out of a complex brain, an alternative, rather more positive explanation, at least in evolutionary terms, is that religion helps to solve the problem of how to deal with free riders in densely cooperative societies.[41] However, there is something dissatisfying about this theory, especially when it comes to reflection on hunter-gatherer groups. There is no evidence, for example, in small-scale societies that there is a need to control free riding through more authoritative means using moralizing gods. Shame associated with "cheating" on other group members is sufficient to curtail antisocial behavior.[42]

Tim Ingold is an anthropologist, trained in evolutionary and biological sciences, who has engaged in a significant way with the arts, the humanities, and theology alongside his studies of different indigenous communities.[43] His radical intellectual freedom to draw on sources that are not necessarily considered respectable by the secular guild in his search for the truth frames his work as prophetic, influencing a wider public beyond the academy. Ingold's argument for conceiving social communities as a meshwork rather than a network is integral to his desire to focus on actual lifeways, rather than what he terms the *inversion* that converts activity of agents to focused bounded points. Entering a meshwork offers a more radical basis for consideration of human-ecological and multispecies relationships, for it allows for direct perception and encounter with a world of animate and inanimate objects. His emphasis is on how organisms, including humans, find their way in the world through the meandering movement of life, rather than what he terms "short circuit" representative thinking that seeks to colonize how humans perceive their world. Central to this argument is a "way of being that is alive and open to a world in continuous birth," giving rise to "astonishment" rather than "surprise."[44] In the world of becoming, in contrast to the surprise of unfulfilled predictions characteristic of standard empirically based science, astonishment is common even in the ordinary events of life. A life suffused by astonished wonder is also resonant with a life attuned to sensing God's immanence in the world, where God's presence, as the mystics understood only too well, can become evident in the ordinary events of the everyday rather than just confined to the out of the ordinary or the surprise of the miraculous. He is, nonetheless, heavily influenced by process thinking, arising from his engagement with indigenous communities but also from the influence of Henri Bergson's theories of creative evolution and the process philosophy of Whitehead.

Influence, Achievement, and Agenda

Biology as a discipline is promiscuous; at its most creative it does not just keep to its own boundaries but spreads into other areas of research such as medicine, anthropology, or engineering, where biological insights are both significant and potentially transformative. One of the ongoing difficulties for any theologian working at the interface with the biological sciences is keeping abreast of scientific discoveries and trends. Theological concentration on history, rather than nature, is understandable in the wake of the plethora of knowledge and information in the sciences, including the biological sciences. Many of the key contributors to the field have had some training in natural science. Yet if biological science is to be taken as a serious issue for debate in theology as such, rather than just by an elite who happen to have combined both careers, then there is a need for more theologians to take biological issues seriously. Such a possibility may come about only if theology becomes a shared task, where mutual encounter and engagement can take place. Theologians need more confidence in what they have to offer to debates about the place of science and technology. It is easy for theologians either to be timid when confronted by science's enormous practical success or to dismiss that science as bent on a philosophically naive empirical imperialism. Instead, respectful listening, paying attention, that needs to be at the heart of all theological enterprise, should serve to shape the way different theologians and their respective traditions approach biological discoveries. However, this need not lead to endorsement or appropriation of ideas emerging from scientific analysis. Rather, it is through careful reflection and discernment that the insights of science can be drawn upon in a creative process of exchange and interpretation. It is no longer possible to ignore the biological horizon of understanding, but the way biblical and theological interpretation intersect requires an ongoing effort.

One way of achieving this task is through more corporate ways of working, so that exchange is facilitated between those with expertise in different fields. The humanities in general have been relatively slow to initiate such practices, whereas in the biological sciences teamwork is taken for granted. In addition to this listening process, some readiness to contribute to practical issues that are of concern to citizens in general becomes part of a theologian's brief when working at this interface. Engaging in theological ethics is inherent in topics such as genetics, environmental issues, and the advances associated with new developments in medicine. There is always the temptation to leave practical issues behind and just formulate theories of God and evolution remote from any pressing social concerns. Such theorization has little more impact than the theologies that it seeks to replace. In other words, it is a misplaced concreteness to claim that because scientific realism is operative in dealing with the world, a theology that takes account of such realism is practical in nature.

The various areas of systematic theology that encounter biological sciences are not simply restricted to theologies of creation. Rather, the full range of possibilities inherent in working through the implications of the biological sciences on theology in its broadest sense needs to be addressed. The resurrection of Jesus, for example, would be impossible from a secular biologist's perspective, which would claim death is irreversible. This dilemma has taxed even the most able of theologians.[45] Yet this does not mean that faith in the resurrection is now no longer possible or that Christ did not rise from the dead. The physical form in which he was raised is obscure from the gospel accounts; he could both eat and also pass through doors. It seems that we are dealing with a reality that is not normally predicated by science. Theologians need to show readiness to accept the challenge of the biological sciences in all areas of theology, without simply accepting biological empiricism as the final arbiter.

There is a danger that once the biological sciences become companions to theology, the insights of theology for science and the practice of science are attenuated. Theologians who have been inducted into the sciences through long training or association need to be aware of the gift that theology can bring to the sciences, as well as the other way round. This is true in decision making, about which aspects of biological science need to be developed, as well as the application of biological science in biotechnology. Hence, discerning priorities for scientific research becomes the task of all citizens, including theologians. Although theologians cannot change the content of science and it would be wrong for them to try and do so, they can influence funding policy. Consultation documents on cloning, use of genetic change to produce drugs, and the status of the embryo have all led to considerable debate on public policy in these areas.

There are also wider social issues to consider in the wake of possible applications of the biological sciences in genetics and ecological science. The former reflects the confident edge of biology, whereas the latter is more aware of human limitations. This implies that particular areas call not just for theorization about the philosophical difficulties in engagement but greater awareness of those who are on the receiving end of injustices as an indirect result of the applications of biotechnology. The colonizing tendency latent within Western cultures under the guise of either religion or science cannot be denied. Transhumanism's grand aim is the full flowering of the Baconian and Enlightenment dream to control the natural world for human ends. This is not to suggest that all biotechnology is oppressive, but rather the task of the theologian is to recognize where this is the case, and work to alleviate the situation within his or her means to do so. Hence, a fifth goal might be a readiness to recognize those situations where applications of biology have led to social injustices and work for their amelioration.

Other possible scenarios might be named, so the list is far from exhaustive. However, it shows the scope of the work to be done that is still very much an ongoing and expanding field of inquiry. Even though theology has expanded its horizons considerably through its engagement with the biological sciences, there is still the need to delve into the rich resources of its tradition and to seek wisdom wherever it may be found, but a wisdom that is ultimately grounded in knowledge and love of God and God's creation.

Notes

1 See chapter 49 of this volume. This chapter was introduced in this fourth edition, demonstrating its clear contemporary significance for theology, not just in terms of engagement with ecological sciences, but in terms of wider political and social debates. Approaches to such global challenges require a holistic integration of all areas.

2 The 2005 (3rd edition) version of this chapter for *The Modern Theologians* has been republished with minor modifications in John Slattery, ed., *The T&T Clark Handbook of Christian Theology and the Modern Sciences* (London: Bloomsbury T&T Clark, 2020), 237–48. This chapter has been significantly revised for this fourth edition.

3 See Christopher Southgate, ed., *God, Humanity and the Cosmos*, 3rd ed. (London: T&T Clark, 2011), 162–203.

4 For an excellent survey of this topic, see Denis Alexander, *Genes, Determinism and God* (Cambridge: Cambridge University Press, 2017).

5 Tradition in the Roman Catholic and Eastern Orthodox churches rejects all forms of human cloning and embryonic research as showing insufficient respect for human dignity.

6 Other terms that flag differences are somatic gene therapy (body cells) and adult stem cells as opposed to embryonic stem cells. In some environments adult stem cells can be manipulated to behave like embryonic stem cells and become pluripotent, that is, capable of growing into any tissue, with the implication that such terms are placeholders only.

7 Erik Parens and Josephine Johnston, eds., *Human Flourishing in an Age of Gene Editing* (Oxford: Oxford University Press, 2019).

8 See Celia Deane-Drummond, *Creation through Wisdom: Theology and the New Biology* (Edinburgh: T&T Clark, 2000).

9 Calvin Mercer and Tracy J. Trothen, eds, *Religion and Transhumanism: The Unknown Future of Human Enhancement* (Santa Barbara, CA: Praeger, 2015).

10 Peter Singer, *Animal Liberation: A New Ethics for Our Treatment of Animals* (New York: HarperCollins, 1975).

11 See, for example, Tom Regan, *The Case for Animal Rights* (Berkeley, CA: University of California Press, 1983).

12 For critique, see Celia Deane-Drummond, *The Ethics of Nature* (Oxford: Blackwell, 2004).

13 See, for example, Alister McGrath, *A Scientific Theology, Vol. 1: Nature* (Edinburgh: T&T Clark, 2001), 45–9.

14 Mary Midgley, *Evolution as a Religion* (New York: Methuen, 1985), 123.

15 Michael Hanby, *No God, No Science: Theology, Cosmology, Biology* (Oxford: Blackwell, 2013); Conor Cunningham, *Darwin's Pious Idea: Why the Ultra-Darwinists and Creationists Both Get It Wrong* (Grand Rapids, MI: Eerdmans, 2010).

16 See Keith Ward, *God, Chance and Necessity* (Oxford: Oneworld, 1996), 64.

17 Stephen Clark, *Biology and Christian Ethics* (Cambridge: Cambridge University Press, 2000).

18 Simon Conway Morris, "The Paradoxes of Evolution: Inevitable Humans in a Lonely Universe?" in *God and Design: The Teleological Argument and Modern Science*, ed. Neil A. Manson (London: Routledge, 2003), 329–47.

19 Andrew Davison, "Christian Doctrine and Biological Mutualism: Explorations in Systematic and Philosophical Theology," *Theology and Science* 18 (2020): 258–78.

20 Celia Deane-Drummond, "Creation," in *The Cambridge Companion to Feminist Theology*, ed. Susan Parsons (Cambridge: Cambridge University Press, 2002), 190–207.

21 Carolyn Merchant, *The Death of Nature: Women, Ecology, and the Scientific Revolution* (New York: Harper & Row, 1983).

22 Rosemary Radford Ruether, *Gaia and God: An Ecofeminist Theology of Earth Healing* (San Francisco, CA: Harper San Francisco, 1992).

23 Anne Primavesi, *Sacred Gaia: Holistic Theology and Earth System Science* (London: Routledge, 2000).

24 Kevin J. Gaston, "Biodiversity," in *Conservation Biology for All*, ed. Navjot S. Sodhi and Paul R. Ehrlich (Oxford: Oxford University Press, 2010), 27–44.

25 Enric Sala, *The Nature of Nature: Why We Need the Wild* (Washington, DC: National Geographic, 2020).

26 He was influenced by Henri Bergson, *Creative Evolution* (first published in 1907), who argued that all spirit in nature emerges as an *élan vital*.

27 Whether intelligent life is inevitable from an evolutionary perspective, or highly improbable, is a matter of ongoing debate.

28 David Sloan Wilson, "Reintroducing Pierre Teilhard de Chardin to Modern Evolutionary Science," *Religion, Brain and Behaviour*, published online 2 February 2023, https://doi.org/10.1080/2153599X.2022.2143399 (accessed 14 September 23).

29 Nicholas Lash, *The Beginning and End of Religion* (Cambridge: Cambridge University Press, 1996), 79–80.

30 Tom McLeish, *The Poetry and Music of Science: Comparing Creativity in Science and Art* (Oxford: Oxford University Press, 2019). For theological engagement, see Tom McLeish, *Faith and Wisdom in Science* (Oxford: Oxford University Press, 2014).

31 John D. Zizioulas, "Preserving God's Creation: Three Lectures on Theology and Ecology," *King's Theological Review* 13, no. 1 (1990): 5.

32 National Academy of Sciences, *Heritable Human Genome Editing* (Washington, DC: National Academies Press, 2020).

33 World Health Organization, *Report of the First Meeting, WHO Expert Advisory Committee on Developing Global Standards for Governance and Oversight of Human Genome Editing* (Geneva: World Health Organisation, 2019).

34 A scientist named Hi Jiankui ignored even his own ethical guidelines to manipulate embryos who were at risk of contracting HIV in order to provide so-called resistance. His desire for scientific recognition backfired in this case, and he has been castigated by the scientific community at large for his attempts. His action was also illegal. David Cyranoski, "What's Next for CRISPR Babies?" *Nature* 566 (2019): 440–2.

35 Celia Deane-Drummond, *The Wisdom of the Liminal: Evolution and Other Animals in Human Becoming* (Grand Rapids, MI: Eerdmans, 2014).

36 Jeremy Kendal, Jamshid J. Tehrani, and F. John Odling-Smee, "Human Niche Construction in Interdisciplinary Focus," *Philosophical Transactions of the Royal Society B: Biological Sciences* 366 (2011): 785–92.

37 Kevin N. Laland, F. John Odling-Smee, and Marc W. Feldman, "Niche Construction, Biological Evolution, and Cultural Change," *Behavioral and Brain Sciences* 23, no. 1 (2000): 131–46.

38 Agustín Fuentes, *Why We Believe: Evolution and the Human Way of Being* (New Haven, CT: Yale University Press, 2020).

39 Celia Deane-Drummond, "Wonder and the Religious Sense in Chimpanzees," in *The Jane Effect: Celebrating Jane Goodall*, ed. Dale Petersen and Marc Bekoff (San Antonio, TX: Trinity University Press, 2015), 225–7.

40 Celia Deane-Drummond, *Wonder and Wisdom: Conversations in Science, Spirituality and Theology* (London: Darton, Longman & Todd, 2004).

41 Dominic Johnson, *God Is Watching You: How the Fear of God Makes Us Human* (Oxford: Oxford University Press, 2014).

42 Christopher Boehm, *Moral Origins: The Evolution of Virtue, Altruism and Shame* (New York: Basic Books, 2012).

43 Tim Ingold, *Imagining for Real: Essays on Creation, Attention and Correspondence* (London: Routledge, 2022).

44 Tim Ingold, *Being Alive: Essays on Movement, Knowledge and Description* (London: Routledge, 2011), 63.

45 Wolfhart Pannenberg's theology shows this tension clearly.

Recommended Reading

Primary

Fuentes, Agustín. *Why We Believe: Evolution and the Human Way of Being*. New Haven, CT: Yale University Press, 2020.

Ingold, Tim. *Imagining for Real: Essays on Creation, Attention and Correspondence*. London: Routledge, 2022.

Pannenberg, Wolfhart. *Towards a Theology of Nature: Essays on Science and Truth*. Edited by Ted Peters. Louisville, KY: Westminster John Knox Press, 1993.

Peacocke, Arthur. *Creation and the World of Science: The Re-shaping of Belief*. Oxford: Clarendon Press, 1979.

Teilhard de Chardin, Pierre. *The Human Phenomenon*. Translated by Sarah Appleby-Weber. Brighton: Sussex University Press, 1999.

Zizioulas, John D. "Preserving God's Creation: Three Lectures on Theology and Ecology." *King's Theological Review* 13, no. 1 (1990): 1–5.

Secondary

Alexander, Denis. *Genes, Determinism and God*. Cambridge: Cambridge University Press, 2017.

Clark, Stephen. *Biology and Christian Ethics*. Cambridge: Cambridge University Press, 2000.

Davison, Andrew. "Christian Doctrine and Biological Mutualism: Explorations in Systematic and Philosophical Theology." *Theology and Science* 18 (2020): 258–78.

Deane-Drummond, Celia. *Theological Ethics through a Multispecies Lens: Evolution of Wisdom, Vol. I*. Oxford: Oxford University Press, 2019.

———. *The Wisdom of the Liminal: Evolution and Other Animals in Human Becoming*. Grand Rapids, MI: Eerdmans, 2014.

Haught, John F. *God after Darwin: A Theology of Evolution*. Boulder, CO: Westview Press, 2001.

McGrath, Alister. *A Scientific Theology, Vol. 1: Nature*. London: T&T Clark, 2001.

McLeish, Tom. *Faith and Wisdom in Science*. Oxford: Oxford University Press, 2014.

Mercer, Calvin, and Tracy J. Trothen, eds. *Religion and Transhumanism: The Unknown Future of Human Enhancement*. Santa Barbara, CA: Praeger, 2015).

Parens, Erik, and Josephine Johnston, eds., *Human Flourishing in an Age of Gene Editing*. Oxford: Oxford University Press, 2019.

Ruse, Michael. *Can a Darwinian Be a Christian? The Relationship between Science and Religion*. Cambridge: Cambridge University Press, 2001.

Sala, Enric. *The Nature of Nature: Why We Need the Wild*. Washington, DC: National Geographic: 2020.

Southgate, Christopher, ed. *God, Humanity and the Cosmos*. 3rd ed. London: T&T Clark, 2011.

———. *Theology in a Suffering World: Glory and Longing*. Cambridge: Cambridge University Press, 2018.

Theology and the Social Sciences

Luke Bretherton

Introduction: What Is Social Science?

We cannot survive, let alone thrive, without others. We come to be, both individually and collectively, through social interactions over time. Within social science, differences abound as to how these social interactions are conceptualized. However, in general, the social sciences inquire as to the nature, form, and extent of these interactions; the significance ascribed to them; what they produce; and how natural things are put to social uses (for example, the symbolic and monetary value attached to gold rather than its density or ductile properties). Contrary to behaviorism, such inquiry cannot be merely a cataloguing of human behaviors and social practices. It must also inquire as to the beliefs and meanings humans generate about their relations with each other and the world around them. And to provide coherence to and make sense of all this, the social sciences must give an account of these interactions through broader generalizations and social theories that seek to explain and interpret human behaviors and beliefs. So a distinction can be made between the qualitative and quantitative methodologies used for social scientific investigation (its tools), the speculative social theories derived from and drawn on to interpret the findings (all data require interpretation), and the various disciplines that determine what kinds of interaction are investigated (economics, social anthropology, social psychology, human geography, sociology, political science, science and technology studies, media studies, etc.).

The formations and dynamics social science investigates are no less real than physical processes, but they do operate differently. For example, basketball is an irreducibly social reality. It exists only through social interactions and the meanings we assign it. If we could erase the practice of basketball and all thought about it, it would cease to exist. This is not to say humans would not play games, but these would not be the social construct we call basketball. The same applies to phenomena as diverse as class, the nation-state, jazz, and science as itself a social practice. So the phenomena that social science investigates are real but contingent, change through time, and their significance is inherently contestable.[1] There are no impersonal, mechanistic causes that determine social interactions. As will be seen, social scientists often forget this and imagine themselves to be doing something like natural science, elucidating unchanging, universal laws. Economists

Ford's The Modern Theologians: An Introduction to Christian Theology since 1918, Fourth Edition.
Edited by Rachel Muers and Ashley Cocksworth.
© 2024 John Wiley & Sons Ltd. Published 2024 by John Wiley & Sons Ltd.

are particularly prone to this fallacy, becoming unmindful of the constitutively social character of what they study and the inherently interpretative, value-laden nature of their accounts of social realities.

Social science is clearly not a form of theological inquiry. But contrasting the guiding assumptions of each is instructive. When theology – in all its myriad forms and genres – seeks to give either descriptive or prescriptive accounts of human interactions, these are envisaged as taking place in creation and in relation to God. By contrast, for social scientists, human interactions are imagined as taking place under their own steam, without reference to anything other than immanent social and material processes. While not necessary and contested, most social science operates under the auspices of scientific naturalism, positing a metaphysical claim whereby reality is perceived as a closed system in which there are no nonnatural or "supernatural" entities, experiences, or causes (ontological naturalism), and in some cases presumes that only the scientific method should be used to investigate all areas of reality, including social relations (methodological naturalism).

There are harder and softer versions of naturalism in play in the social sciences. Constituting an expression of methodological naturalism, harder versions subscribe to forms of materialism and empiricism that, in the name of being "scientific," reject anything other than empirically based explanations and favor quantitative over qualitative forms of research. Softer versions may well be immanent in focus but recognize the limits of the scientific method for investigating human social relations, favor qualitative forms of research, and foreground the inherently interpretive, and thence contingent and contestable character of the social sciences (often referred to as hermeneutic or interpretative traditions of social science). These differences between hard and soft versions are often built into different disciplines and subdisciplines: for example, evolutionary anthropology represents a harder form and social anthropology a softer one.

Interpretive traditions of social science have generated pathways beyond naturalism. Indeed, if naturalism envisions culture in terms of nature, Bruno Latour and others reverse the flow of traffic by envisioning nature in terms of culture.[2] They wrestle not only with how science itself depends on analogy, metaphor, and symbol and, as a social practice, is itself socially constructed but also with how, as what evolutionary biologists call "ultrasocial" or "hypercooperative" animals, humans must sustain shared meanings across generations to survive and thrive. This requires mimesis, play, telling stories, creating rituals, imagining other possibilities, and developing enduring symbolic and figurative frames of reference.[3] There are now an increasing number of approaches to social science that operate outside of a naturalistic framework. The advent of such things as "new materialism," existential anthropology, and the recovery of animist ontologies represent this kind of development. A good example of these is Marisol de la Cadena's work on mountains as other-than-human earth beings involved as political agents in Quechua struggles over land rights and mining access in the Andes.[4] Cadena develops an ethnographically driven conception of "cosmopolitics" that disrupts modernist, secularizing, and naturalistic conceptions of politics, whether of the left or the right.

The dominant strands of social science do still operate under naturalistic assumptions, understanding the cosmos in mechanistic, wholly material, and morally neutral terms. Such a view assumes the cosmos cannot disclose any sense of how we should live. Indeed, instead of the world around us giving us a sense of meaning and value, we ascribe meaning and value to it. The cosmos is a universe: that is, a flat, meaningless, and inert thing on which we impose meaning. Social scientific frameworks that assume this way of describing the world operate with a fact–value distinction and envisage social science as about imposing meaning on a morally neutral universe (a realm of facts) that in and of itself can reveal nothing about how to live well and sets no limits to what humans can or cannot do to nature.

Putting to one side their inherent anthropocentrism, such views generate forms of attention that operate not with participatory modes of reasoning such as practical reason. Instead, they operate with what the philosopher Charles Taylor calls "disengaged reason," adopting the standpoint of an "impartial spectator" who sees but is not seen.[5] More often than not, such disengaged social scientists reproduce their own cultural biases and assumptions in their research – but these are then labeled scientific discoveries and thereby naturalized. In a parallel operation, contingent categories such as "culture," "class," and "religion," after being constructed, are then taken to be natural, universal substances to be investigated, under which actual social relations are subsumed. That these categories and classifications are themselves interpretive frameworks is forgotten. There are moves to counter the standpoint of the impartial spectator and the pathologies this generates. This work emerges from those social scientists already more attuned to humanistic concerns in the soft rather than hard social sciences. However, such work can itself shift over into reductive forms of constructivism and relativism.

How then should the relationship between theology and social science be understood? And why might it be important to understand it? From what I have said so far, it would seem the relationship between theology and social science is at best fraught. That said, constructive theological anthropology demands some engagement with social science. As Paul Fiddes puts it: "Since faith is embodied in worldly forms, and these forms exist within the relational life of God, the theologian exploring them must draw on the insights of the various sciences that set out to analyze the world. The concern of the theologian . . . is to find the theological dimensions within the worldly forms of community, to be able to reflect on the presence, nature, purpose, and activity of the triune God that can be perceived within and through the form."[6] This is the case even for theologians who derive their conceptions of, say, the human, society, or the church wholly from doctrine. Such conceptions are still at some point overlaid on a particular cultural manifestation of human life, which itself requires an account. However, as the imbrication of modern theology in the formation of a racist social imaginary illustrates, such deductive theologies too often simply reproduce the norms and prejudices of their cultural milieu. Systematic theological reflection on, for example, the humanity of Christ must go hand in hand with self-reflexivity about our context and its tacit constructions of the human (and who does and does not count as fully human). This dynamic is even more acute when we look beyond systematic concerns to those of moral and political theology. Can moral and political questions be meaningfully addressed without reference to descriptions of the ways these questions are manifested and responded to through social interactions beyond the conceptual models derived from dogma? If something more than anecdote is to be relied upon, social science cannot be avoided. My thesis explored here is that social science needs modern theology for its own critical self-understanding, and modern theology needs social science – particularly its more humanistic and interpretive strands – as part of its attunement to, participation in, and descriptions of the ongoing work of Christ and the Spirit in creation. Yet both have good reasons for being suspicious of the other and each is prone to render the other illegible within its own conceptual apparatus.

Overview: Overlapping Stories

Modern theology and the social sciences have overlapping origin stories. The first point of overlap is that their formation shares a geographic and historical context. They are both born out of and responses to processes of modernization in the Atlantic world that connects Europe, the Middle East, Africa, and the Americas. Whether it is the Reformation and Counter-Reformation, the Atlantic slave trade and its legacies, modern imperialism, a fossil-fueled, industrialized, and consumerist way of life, the Westphalian order of nation-states, or the creation of modern banking and monetary systems, arguably what we call modernity emerges through the interactions shaping the Atlantic world from the fifteenth century onwards, interactions that led to the creation, destruction, and reformation of whole cultures across the Atlantic basin. Modern theology and the social sciences emerge as attempts to make sense of the seismic changes in how humans interact, generated by processes of modernization such as industrialization. And it is within this world that both theology and social science become specialized and professionalized academic disciplines operating in the modern university – specialization and professionalization themselves being processes of modernization. This shared institutionalization story is the second point of overlap.

A third point of overlap is that both are focused on "society" and the nature and form of social relations. These were "discovered" as objects of inquiry in the nineteenth century. For theology, the concern was normative: there was a need to defend and tend social relations – whether for emancipatory or reactionary purposes – against either commodification by capitalism, instrumentalization by the modern nation-state, or being subsumed into forms of determinism. This is exemplified in the names of movements central to the institutional development of *both* modern theology *and* social science; namely, Christian *social*ism, the *Social* Gospel, and Catholic *social* teaching. All of these sought to respond to the rise of industrial capitalism, modern bureaucratic states, the destruction of nature, an atomized mass society, and the formation of totalizing systems, whether these be Fordist or totalitarian. A focus on society and social relations is obviously constitutive of the development of something called *social* science. In addressing the social nature of human life, theology and social science also entered a shared philosophical terrain. Echoing long-standing debates, both wrestled with how to relate the particular and universal, the necessary and contingent, and the simultaneously free and determined character of human agency and sociality.

More often than not, social science became aligned with prosecuting rather than resisting state and market driven projects of modernization. Building on the work of social theorists Michel Foucault and James C. Scott, social science can be seen as a knowledge regime through which to count, tax, educate, inoculate, and generally surveil and manage "populations" within the emerging market–state nexus.[7] Despite its critical currents (Marxian, DuBoisian, poststructuralist, etc.), applied social science was utilized by governing and colonizing regimes around the world (whether of the left or the right) to render newly minted modern individual subjects governable. In doing so, it superseded theology as a primary episteme of governmentality even as many of the categories and concerns of theology were sublated within the social sciences. The gaze of both the bureaucrat and advertiser, who see but are unseen through means of social science, displace the ear of the confessor. In the age of the panoptical state, surveillance capitalism, and big data, this has intensified beyond a gaze to an instrumentalizing and commodifying manipulation of our thoughts, emotions, and relationships through marrying social science to information technologies.

A fourth point of overlap is the bifurcated temporal-social division between "tradition" and "modernity" that much modern theology and social science adopted. This division is exemplified in the work of foundational figures of European sociology: namely, Ferdinand Tönnies's distinction between *Gemeinschaft* and *Gesellschaft*; Emile Durkheim's distinction between mechanical and organic solidarity, the former associated with traditional societies, the latter with modern ones; and Max Weber's distinction between traditional and capitalist societies. On such accounts, community is understood as either a static or inherited social formation that is subject to inevitable dissolution through processes of modernization such as industrialization and urbanization. By and large this division is assumed to be oppositional and characterizes different kinds of social relations, which are then indexed in moral terms. For example, traditional relations are seen as good by many theologians in contrast to modern ones, which are seen as inherently atomized and alienated. In contrast, for many social scientists, traditional relations are of the past and thereby judged reactionary. Given that the majority world is deemed traditional, the colonial and racist logic of this view is not hard to see: European social science serving the interests of modernization was deemed emancipatory when in actuality it reinscribed westernization and racial capitalism.

This temporal-social division is also exemplified in the "secularization thesis," which assumes a move from medieval sacrality to modern secularity, with an inherent incompatibility between what it means to be modern and what it means to be religious, with religion understood as a form of traditional relation. This can be overheard in the following quote from the American sociologist C. Wright Mills. Writing in 1959, he stated: "Once the world was filled with the sacred – in thought, practice, and institutional form. After the Reformation and the Renaissance, the forces of modernization swept across the globe and secularization, a corollary historical process, loosened the dominance of the sacred. In due course, the sacred shall disappear altogether, except possibly, in the private realm."[8] Within the secularization thesis, what is religious is epiphenomenal, whereas what is modern and thereby secular is reality stripped of its superstitious and irrational garb. Notions of secularization are also an example of social science superseding and sublating theological concerns: in this case, the eschatological category of the secular as that-which-is-not-eternity becomes the social scientific category of the secular as that-which-is-not-religious.

In the theological version of this temporality, the role of the church is to shore up or protect community from the depredations of modernity. Lurking behind the mistaken theological adoption of a temporal division between tradition and modernity are two assumptions. The first is a Neoplatonic view of an organic harmony and hierarchy of interests and ends ("the great chain of being") that modernity undermines and dissolves into a conflict of each against all. The second is a certain reading of Augustine. Modernity, with its technological prowess, commercial spirit, and will-to-power represents the antithesis of the city of God and a reiteration of the *libido dominandi* of the earthly city. But contrary to Augustine, for whom the *saeculum* was a field of wheat and tares, this modernity-critical stream of Augustinianism – some authoritarian, some democratic – introduces a temporal division that sacralizes the past and falsely demonizes the present, forgetting that the Spirit can make Christ present to all times and places.

The division between tradition and modernity is not a theological distinction. Neither is it a necessary sociological one. An influential American stream of sociology exemplified in the work of Robert Park and Ernest Burgess, and in their wake a host of more contemporary sociologists, points in a different direction. Park and Burgess were the founders of urban ethnography and, influenced by George Herbert Mead, their philosophy was pragmatist and antipositivistic. Unlike Tönnies, they saw community as an ongoing work of institution building and symbolic interaction through which people form meaningful relationships and develop a collective sense of identity and place over time. Any such process involves both conflict and conciliation. The role of social science is to chart particular configurations of conflict and consensus, power and resistance. Modernization can lead to new and better configurations of community as well as oppressive and decadent ones. This would seem to be a truly Augustinian orientation, one that attempts to understand our social and political life as an order of love, albeit one disfigured and disordered by idolatrously loving the right things the wrong way, yet always open to change and conversion. It also serves an Augustinian sense of what it means to truly confess who we are in time before God.

All forms of solidarity, organic or mechanical, can be prone to domination and idolatry. No one form is intrinsically better than another. And every solidarity is at the same time a mode of exclusion, so all need deliverance and redemption. Just and compassionate forms of life together and common objects of love in the earthly city must always be discovered through processes of conflict and conciliation that transect competing solidarities and loyalties. Of necessity, if this process of discovery is to be faithful, it entails humility and rendering ourselves vulnerable to God and neighbor. The crucifixion is the condition and possibility of our conversion and movement into more just and loving kinds of relationship with God and neighbor. Yet this conversion demands that we orientate ourselves in a particular way to living in time and the experience of flux, change, and transition that is constitutive of being temporal creatures. Becoming "church" in any period of history is about discovering, with these people, in this place, at this time, how communion amid our differences might be experienced and embraced through shared social and spiritual struggle. If the Spirit makes Christ present in all periods of history, albeit in different ways, then every historical era is a field of wheat and tares in which the work of Christ and the Spirit must be discerned and discovered.

To anticipate a later argument, social science can aid theology in the process of better attunement to, participation in, and description of the work of Christ and the Spirit in creation. In part this works through drawing academic theology down from its speculative heights and breaking open its self-referential (and often idolatrous) enclosure through attending to life as lived and the empirical, material conditions of divine–human relations. Conversely, theology calls social science to more nonreductive, symbolically rich, transcendent, and we might add, loving and just conceptions of the human than social science is wont to offer. I turn now to how theology has made sense of social science within theological frameworks.

Main Approaches and Key Figures

As the adoption of the categories "modern" and "traditional" by theologians indicates, modern theology frequently forgets its proper task and deploys social scientific categories as if they were theological descriptions. A common example is how Ernst Troeltsch's distinction between "church" and "sect" is used to mark certain theological positions as unsavory by designating them "sectarian." However, modern theology has also configured social science in ways that help generate distinctively theological claims. Sarah Coakley's repurposing of Troeltsch's distinctions to reflect on the relationship between Trinitarian doctrine and social and institutional embodiment is a case in point.[9]

A characteristic way in which social science is configured within both modern Protestant and Catholic theology is as a way to understand the culture, society, or context that is then reflected on theologically. More often than not, this approach to social science operates within a kernel and husk paradigm: there is some timeless, universal, wholly cognitive theological kernel that is transmitted by or needs to be communicated within an epiphenomenal and transitory cultural husk. Social science becomes a way to identify and describe the "context," with theology elucidating the ahistorical kernel. The German Lutheran historian Adolf von Harnack lays a foundation for this kind of view, himself coining the kernel and husk metaphor.[10] For Harnack, after the first three centuries of maturation in which Christianity borrowed from and incorporated cultural, philosophical, and religious practices from across the Mediterranean, it became a coherent body of belief and practice that could be transmitted historically. The gospel had a permanent validity for all times and places, but this essential gospel could be distinguished from its contingent cultural trappings. Thus, periodic reformation was needed to strip away false accretions that distorted its purity. Contemporary calls for inculturation, contextualization, and indigenization, emerging from a concern for how to coordinate "Christ" and "culture" and a sense that theology needs to take its cultural embeddedness seriously, may seem at variance with Harnack. But even these tend to operate with a parallel framework.[11] The same can be said for most introduction to theology courses that set out a golden thread of ideas and topics transmitted from text to text through history independent of any material and social histories of reception. The dogmatic enterprise is somehow unaffected by and independent of ongoing processes of material and social reproduction. Conversely, social science is viewed as independent of theology and can be used as a neutral tool to excavate a culture.

Karl Barth directly opposed Harnack and what he saw as the cultural captivity of German liberal Protestantism expressed through the support of Harnack and others for Germany's entry into World War I. Beginning with his commentary on Romans he envisioned the otherness of divine self-revelation given in Jesus Christ as a crisis to all human ways of knowing and being in the world. Within this framework, little could be learned from social science for making sense of what it means to be human, let alone for understanding divine–human relations. Although not a difficulty Barth himself would recognize, the problem with Barth's conception is that it tends to either cut off revelation from human processes of cultural production or smuggle such an account into theology unawares. His contemporary Paul Tillich represents the polar opposite of Barth. For Tillich, materiality, history, and culture are the crucibles of divine–human encounter. Within this framework, social science becomes a vital component in determining what in human experience constitutes revelation. However, for all its attention to "ultimate concerns," the problem with Tillich's approach is that it tends to collapse revelation into processes of cultural production.

Some modern theologians seek to integrate the concerns of Barth and Tillich. In a European context, Dietrich Bonhoeffer's *Sanctorum Communio* is an underdeveloped example of an attempt to draw on sociology in the service of a theology that prioritizes the Word of God. However, much modern theology oscillates between Barth and Tillich. This is illustrated by the early work of Black liberation theologian, James Cone. On the one hand, Cone recognizes the salience of Barth's emphasis on the priority of divine revelation: "The real temptation is to identify our own interests with God's and thus say that he is active in those activities which best serve our purposes. Karl Barth pointed out this danger in a convincing way in his

Romans commentary."[12] And elsewhere he states that "whatever is said about the nature of God and his being-in-the-world must be based on the biblical account of God's revelatory activity. We are not free to say anything we please about him."[13] On the other hand, drawing on Tillich, Cone contends that all theology is contextual, "written for particular times and places" and "defined by the human situation that gives birth to it."[14] For Cone it is the Black experience of oppression that is the determinative context in which to truly hear the Word of God and this experience is made sense of theologically in Black forms of cultural production, namely the blues and the spirituals, and the Black Power movement. As Cone puts it: "Black Power, then, is God's new way of acting in America."[15] Social science can help name this experience, unveiling both the oppression African Americans undergo and how they respond to it culturally and politically. Cone contends he moves beyond both Barth and Tillich in his emphasis on participating in the liberation of the oppressed. Whether he does so methodologically is another matter.

David Tracy offers an account of the relationship between theology and social science that draws on Tillich rather than Barth. He advocates for a critical correlation between "Christian texts" and "common human experience," with human experience being described through social scientific or other means.[16] Correlationist approaches like that developed by Tracy posit a relative autonomy between different modes of knowledge such as theology and social science, an autonomy that must then be correlated. On this account, the social sciences are simply a means of delineating human experience that theology then reflects on. However, the complex and multifarious exchanges between theological and political, economic, or social categories makes implausible any such autonomy; Christian discourses and common human experience cannot be disentangled so clearly.

Latin American liberation theology offers a parallel approach to that of Tracy, but it is the social analysis of class relations and the social theory of Marxism that is the primary point of reference. In his foundational book, *A Theology of Liberation* (1971), Gustavo Gutiérrez speaks of theology's "direct and fruitful confrontation with Marxism." He goes on to say that, "it is to a large extent due to Marxism's influence that theological thought, searching for its own sources, has begun to reflect on the meaning of the transformation of this world and human action in history."[17] Gutiérrez and other liberation theologians, in their initial formulations, attempted to use a Marxist conception of class as a way to give an account of the unjust social order in Latin America. As Gutiérrez put it: "Only class analysis will show what is really at stake in the opposition between oppressed lands and dominant peoples."[18] Liberation theology drew on particular streams of nondeterministic Marxist analysis as tools for articulating how and why faithful Christian witness entailed solidarity with the poor. For Latin American liberation theology, the church and its forms of worship perpetuate the dominance of elite groups and reinforce social divisions if they fail to confront injustice, of which the class system is a symptom.[19] Hence its most influential insight: God has a preferential option for the poor and we encounter God most fully in solidarity with the poor. As with Cone, the epistemological implication of this insight for modern theology is that the initial step toward right reflection on God and reality in general is solidarity with and involvement in the struggles of the poor, and dialogue with the experience and knowledge about their situation that the poor produce of and for themselves. Social science aids this dialogue.

While its proponents came to recognize that there were many forms of oppression, including those based on gender, sexuality, and race, for the first wave of Latin American liberation theologians it remained the case that socioeconomic class was the primary and paradigmatic form of oppression. Subsequent generations challenged this focus and made social scientific analysis central to their challenge. Combining an emphasis on liberation and the prioritization of the social over and against capitalism and modern statecraft, Latinx and womanist Christian social ethics focused on the quotidian as a vital aspect of theological reflection, particularly when trying to discern what liberation for marginalized people might look like.[20] This is because the ordinary and everyday world is the site at which forms of domination, and the precarity and oppression they produce, are most acutely displayed. This is exemplified in Katie Cannon's contribution to womanist social ethics that made the folklorist and anthropologist Zora Neale Hurston a key interlocutor in her turn to the ordinary and everyday as sites for generating theological wisdom about liberation.[21] The mujerista theology of Ada Maria Isasi-Díaz develops one of the fullest expressions of such a move, a move that was based in part on her innovative use of qualitative research.[22] Isasi-Díaz's conception of the common people as *mestizaje-mulatez* attends to the mixed ethnic, racial, as well as economic histories that inform the everyday experiences of Latino/as living in the United States and elsewhere.[23] Isasi-Díaz retains liberation as a normative criterion for evaluating whether something is good or bad, but rather than focus on structural problems – as the first wave of liberation theologians did – she focuses on *lo cotidiano* or quotidian experiences, particularly of "Hispanas/Latinas."[24] *Lo cotidiano* is not merely the reproduction of habit but experiences that have been analyzed to generate "folk wisdom" about how to survive and thrive amid daily struggle.[25] And attention to *lo cotidiano* leads to questioning and even subverting established traditions and customs, especially when these reinforce structures of oppression, but these traditions and customs are still vital sources of wisdom.[26] Isasi-Díaz's mujerista theology represents both an extension and a break with prior forms of liberation theology and illustrates a constructive example of how combining theology and qualitative research generates new conceptual possibilities.

In response to Latin American liberation theology and correlationist accounts such as those of Tracy, John Milbank and William Cavanaugh criticized any overreliance on Marxist social theories, and the social sciences more generally, as tools of analysis. Their constructive move was to restate how the church itself is a *polis* and theology is itself a social theory.[27] For them, theology is the only truly social science as it speaks from the only truly peaceable society – the city of God – in which social relations are characterized by love rather than domination. To draw insights for living faithfully from social scientific descriptions of the earthly city is to simply reproduce the violent ontologies at work this far east of Eden. This operation is exemplified in Cavanaugh's critique of liberation theology in which he proposes that the liturgy constitutes a counterperformance to the politics of domination and oppression in Latin America. The paradigmatic contrast for Cavanaugh is not between state socialism and capitalism but between torture and eucharist. Torture as a practice disaggregates and disciplines bodies so that society becomes subject to the control and manipulation of the state. The eucharist, by contrast, congregates and forms an alternative physical regime that liberates bodies for communion with each other.[28] As he puts it: "The liturgy does more than generate interior motivations to be better citizens. The liturgy generates a body, the Body of Christ . . . which is itself a *sui generis* social body, a public presence irreducible to a voluntary association of civil society."[29] For Cavanaugh, the Catholic Church, through its worship practices, constitutes a form of social interaction that witnesses to a distinctive, peaceable vision of social, political, and economic life. A problem with Milbank and Cavanaugh's accounts is that beyond statements about the fall, they offer few resources for narrating the ongoing and institutionalized violence that constitutes the church as lived.

Roman Catholic social teaching develops a different set of concerns in response to Marxist analyses of class and the turn to social scientific analysis among liberation theologians. Against the backdrop of scientific naturalism, Marxist and many social scientific accounts tend to subordinate social relations to material ones, seeing them as epiphenomena of material processes. Herein lies an important aspect of the magisterial critique of recourse to scientific Marxist modes of analysis.[30] Pope John Paul II argued that civil society, and society more generally, has priority over politics and economics as that which drives historical change and is the true sphere of human freedom.[31] For John Paul II, it is through our shared social/cultural life that humans become persons through the pursuit of transcendent, nonmaterial goods. The contrast here is with political ideologies on the left *and* right that wish to define social and political relations solely in terms of the exercise of unilateral power and reduce what it means to be human to material concerns alone. Christian theological appropriations of social sciences, Marxist or otherwise, need to question therefore any materialist and deterministic views of social relations that characterize scientific Marxism and much of the social sciences more generally.

The magisterial critique is not a wholesale rejection of social science as either antitheology or a sublimated form of liberal Protestant theology (as in Milbank's work). Social science (even its most positivist and generalizing forms) is helpful insofar as it aids discernment of the form and nature of social relations. But it must recognize its limits and be open to the inherently transcendent ends of what it means to be a person. A measure of it being deemed helpful is that John Paul II established the Pontifical Academy of Social Sciences in 1994. The academy investigates and evaluates the insights of Catholic social teaching, drawing in a wide array of social scientists to do so.

Within the purview of Catholic social teaching, social science contributes to the "see, judge, act" approach initially developed by Joseph Cardijn, the Belgian cardinal and founding figure of the democratic movement, Catholic Action. Cardijn's approach has its roots in Thomistic moral theology and was adopted into Catholic social teaching as a way to frame the relationship between theology and practice,[32] and provided the basis for the Second Vatican Council's "Pastoral Constitution on the Church in the Modern World" (*Gaudium et Spes*, 1964). It also directly influenced the threefold paradigm of becoming aware of reality, taking responsibility for reality, and transforming reality developed by Latin American liberation theologians and subsequently mujerista theology.[33] Here social science serves becoming aware of reality.

Debate, Achievement, and Agenda

The role of social science in Catholic social teaching points to the inadequacy of theologies that view social science with unremitting suspicion. It is not sufficient to position theology as an independent sphere of knowledge that can disregard political and social theory or social scientific kinds of analysis as either antitheology or irrelevant to theological claims. While a critique of antitheological presuppositions and the methodological atheism and individualism informing much social scientific work is necessary, attention also needs to be given to how theology itself is a product of material and social processes. Moreover, as Catherine Pickstock argues, theology, in all its forms, is inherently interdisciplinary: "It is not as if one first enthrones theology as a pre-linguistic pristine edifice, and then asks, how do I communicate this? Rather, its earliest formation, integrity and canonical bases presumed mediation by means of other discourses and bodies of learning. And theology must perforce have recourse to literary and linguistic forms, philosophical analysis, poetry, music and many other disciplines and idioms of expression, in order to express herself as herself."[34] Pickstock unveils how both correlationist and competitive accounts of the relationship between theology and social science fail to reckon with the interpenetration of interpretations and the mutually constitutive nature of church and world. To be a "sister," "brother," or "citizen" requires conceptualizations of those terms in relation to actual sisters, brothers, and citizens and their histories and our encounter with each other as sisters and brothers in Christ and citizens of the kingdom of God.

The social sciences offer disciplined ways of excavating the intersection of ecclesial with other social practices. The various disciplines thereby provide differing ways to generate conceptualizations attentive to the ways church and world are interdependent and mutually constitutive yet also not the same. Furthermore, they highlight the kinds of ad hoc and contingent commensurability between theology and other ways of naming and making judgments about life with others and the different ways of being alive these generate. Through such disciplined modes of listening to the church and/or the world, conceptions of ourselves in relation to God and others can undergo a deepening moral conversion. Such conversion heals our practical reasoning so that we may make increasingly just, wise, and faithful judgments and become more open to receiving and responding to the work of the Spirit.

A nuanced and constructive relationship between theology and social science may be more visible to those who can embrace the insight that theology is discovered, not made, and received rather than mastered. We do not impose meaning on the world by an act of will. Contrary to clunky fact–value distinctions, the universe is not a blank slate passively waiting to receive the meaning humans assign it. Rather, it is pregnant with the meanings and purposes given to creation by God. Theology must discern these meanings and purposes, and needs all the help it can get in doing so. Conversely, the truth of revelation is neither reducible to nor verified by whether we espouse this or that statement of faith or dogma. The truths of revelation are neither things to be possessed nor problems to be solved, but participative events and relationships to be encountered and inhabited. Moreover, the accuracy of our apprehension of God's self-revelation in Jesus Christ is known by the quality and depth of our love of God and neighbor (1 Jn 3:11–24): the one who loves realizes a better understanding than the one with a cold heart but a cogent systematic theology of love. Indeed, to name the workings of love in time rather than merely repeat formulas about love in sentences, theological reasoning needs help describing the Word made flesh.

Just as we discover friendship as we give an account of it, so we discover creatureliness and redemption and their meanings and purposes through a process of participating in and naming them. This discovery and articulation take place through immersion in and through the interlaced pathways, places, and events that form our lifeworld. This lifeworld is one that generates us, and that we help generate, in an ongoing process of communication. It is through this meshwork of physical, biotic, social, and spiritual relations and the communicative webs between them that we hear and respond to the Word of God and within which we are constituted. As Jürgen Moltmann puts it:

> To be alive means existing in relationship with other people and things. Life is communication in communion. And, conversely, isolation and lack of relationship means death for all living things and dissolution even for elementary particles. So if we want to understand what is real as real, and what is living as living, we have to know it in its own primal and individual community, in its relationships, interconnections and surroundings.[35]

When directed to participation in Christ, the aim of such integrating and holistic thinking is "to generate the community between human beings and nature which is necessary and promotes life. And here 'nature' means both the natural world in which we share, and our own bodily nature. As a network and interplay of relationships is built up, a symbiotic life comes into being."[36]

On this kind of account, we do not develop a concept of friendship that is then either applied to people we meet or merely demonstrated by the friendships we form. Rather, friendship is a social reality God makes possible that we in turn discover together with others, how we name it emerging through that discovery in an iterative way. Likewise, we cannot try to get our theology or worldview straight in the abstract and then apply it to the world around us. Nor can we begin with the church, as if the church is a distinct social reality wholly separate from the world. Nor can we investigate the world using social science and then reflect on that "reality" theologically, as if theology was a wholly second-order activity and the world had an autonomous existence independent of the flow of divine communication and the ongoing historical impact of Christian institutions and practices. Rather, reflection on God and reflection on social and political life, and the implications of one for the other, emerge together as we discover their reality through participating in both. For example, the New Testament writers drew on political terms to articulate what it meant to be the church: the Greek word *ekklēsia*, which came to mean *church*, originally meant a political assembly. This and many other political terms proved crucial to saying something about the nature and form of divine–human relations. Conversely, participation in ecclesial practices enabled new kinds of social interaction and generated new understandings of what it means for humans to flourish as inherently social animals. Theology must display how divine–human relations and social, economic, and political life are mutually constitutive and refract each other, and how, for better or worse, this interrelationship shapes *both* the church and the world. Social science, in so far as it contributes to this task, is a vital adjunct.

The potential for a mutually reparative and coproductive relation between theology and social science can be illustrated by a range of contemporary work in the social sciences.[37] It should also be noted that the account of a synergistic relationship between theology and social science sketched here is consonant with developments within the social sciences, particularly in sociology and social anthropology.[38] That said, a coproductive relationship is premised on the conversion of social science so that it serves loving ends.

By way of a case study for how to envisage a synergistic relation I focus here on ethnographically informed *theological* reflection. As a methodology, ethnography is at least tacitly committed to an epistemology in which knowledge of the world comes primarily through participation and apprenticeship and not through abstraction and disengaged observation. It is thus more consonant with an incarnational understanding of truth: that the truths of revelation are participative and relational. Ethnography as a method is well suited to diagnosing and analyzing lived forms of belief and everyday practices that are mediated not only via texts but also by language in use, material exchanges, and a world of acoustic, visual, olfactory, and other physical affects and modes of communication. As part of the interplay of the descriptive and the normative there is an iterative relationship between fieldwork and theology as a mode of theorization, constructive theology providing a normative point of reference for ethnographic description, thereby bringing accountability beyond the emic and the immanent. Sarah Coakley's proposal for a *théologie totale* reaches for an account of constructive theology that models this approach.[39] And it has parallels with the sociologist and theologian Jean-Marc Ela's "shade tree" theology of revelation. Holding that the gospel speaks only dialect, his approach begins with immersion in a particular place and history. Through a process of *palabra évangélique,* a community discovers new ways to speak forth the self-revelation of God in Jesus Christ.[40]

What I am advocating does not render theology answerable to an autonomous and independent philosophical framework, social theory, or social reality described by means of social science. Neither does it propose a dialectical relation, with theology entering like a bolt of lightning from a clear sky. Rather, I propose letting theology be informed by ethnography in three different ways. There is a need for *ethnographically driven theology* whereby the conclusions reached emerge from the ethnographic research process and would not be possible without it. Such a theology begins inductively, with broader conceptualizations emerging from a synergistic process that moves from the particular to the universal, and from practical to theoretical reasons. Working inductively involves observing something over a period of time, thinking backwards from experience (either one's own or that of others), drawing from multiple archives and sources, and learning from contingent events and examples, which includes learning from failure and folly. Learning by induction is itself a way of being formed in prudential theological reasoning. It is also a way we may hear God's Word made flesh among these people, in this place, at this time. There is also a need for *ethnographically informed theology*, where there is an interplay of inductive and deductive elements in its construction. However, most theology will continue to be almost wholly deductive. Yet such theology needs to be *ethnographically haunted*; that is, done with self-reflexive attention to the meshwork of peoples, places, political economies, histories, and intercultural, interspecies, and biological exchanges within which the theologian is entangled, for better and worse, and that are the condition for the possibility of the questions addressed, texts exegeted, and conclusions drawn.[41] All three types are ways of rendering theology accountable to and serving what it means to live, here and now, as a disciple of Christ in community with others, including nonhuman others.

A constructive theology whose imagination is either shaped by social scientific modes of attention or haunted by its material and social conditions can produce writing that summons us to contemplation and conversion. Such writing calls for open attention to and reception of a lifeworld we did not make, do not control, and cannot predetermine the meaning and purpose of by means of a theoretical blueprint. Going beyond the anthropologist Clifford Geertz's influential notion of "thick description," such work generates *iconic description*: what it signifies exceeds its immediate representational conditions in such a way that it can germinate new ways of understanding and convert our forms of seeing, hearing, and talking about the world around us. As an icon pointing beyond itself, the particular is not subsumed within the universal, nor the part within the whole. Rather, an iconic case study invites and allows for a dynamic and imaginative interplay between its particularity and other historical and contemporary contexts. The kind of iconic deployment of ethnography or other forms of granular, social scientific description in relation to theory generation and the articulation of normative theological commitments constitutes a form of witness. It is not the witness of the third party who impartially observes and speaks out on behalf of another. Rather, it is a form of testimony: the confession of one who has seen and heard the events described and challenges others to come together with them to tend something of worth or create something new. Such iconic descriptions can be a vital part of the ongoing argument within Christianity about what it means to bear witness to the divine self-revelation given in Jesus Christ, and how all history and cultures are constituted from a meshwork of ongoing divine, human, nonhuman, and ecological communication.

Notes

1 This point echoes a range of philosophical analyses of social science, particularly those by Peter Winch, Alasdair MacIntyre, Charles Taylor, and Jürgen Habermas, and those that draw on Roy Bhaskar's critical realism.

2 See, for example, Bruno Latour, *We Have Never Been Modern*, trans. Catherine Porter (Cambridge, MA: Harvard University Press, 1993).

3 See Robert Bellah, *Religion in Human Evolution from the Paleolithic to the Axial Age* (Cambridge, MA: Belknap Press, 2011).

4 Marisol de la Cadena, *Earth Beings: Ecologies of Practice across Andean Worlds* (Durham, NC: Duke University Press, 2015).

5 Charles Taylor, *A Secular Age* (Cambridge, MA: Harvard University Press, 2007), 232.

6 Paul Fiddes, "Ecclesiology and Ethnography: Two Disciplines, Two Worlds?" in *Perspectives on Ecclesiology and Ethnography*, ed. Pete Ward (Grand Rapids, MI: Eerdmans, 2011), 29–30.

7 James C. Scott, *Seeing like a State: How Certain Schemes to Improve the Human Condition Have Failed* (New Haven, CT: Yale University Press, 1998); Michel Foucault, *Security, Territory, Population: Lectures at the Collège de France: 1977–78* (Basingstoke: Palgrave Macmillan, 2007).

8 C. Wright Mills, *The Sociological Imagination* (Oxford: Oxford University Press, 1959), 32–3.

9 Sarah Coakley, *God, Sexuality and the Self: An Essay "On the Trinity"* (Cambridge: Cambridge University Press, 2013).

10 Adolf von Harnark, *What Is Christianity?*, trans. Bailey Saunders (Philadelphia, PA: Fortress Press, 1986 [1900]), 55.

11 Ross Kane, *Syncretism and Christian Tradition: Race and Revelation in the Study of Religious Mixture* (Oxford: Oxford University Press, 2021), 86–95.

12 James H. Cone, *Black Theology and Black Power* (Maryknoll, NY: Orbis, 1997 [1969]), 49.

13 James H. Cone, *A Black Theology of Liberation* (Maryknoll, NY: Orbis, 2010 [1970]), 64.

14 Cone, *A Black Theology of Liberation*, xv.

15 Cone, *Black Theology and Black Power*, 61

16 David Tracy, *Blessed Rage for Order: The New Pluralism in Theology* (Chicago, IL: University of Chicago Press, 1996).

17 Gustavo Gutiérrez, *A Theology of Liberation: History, Politics, and Salvation*, rev. ed. (Maryknoll, NY: Orbis, 1988), 8.

18 Gustavo Gutiérrez, *The Power of the Poor in History* (Maryknoll, NY: Orbis, 1983), 46.

19 Gutiérrez, *Theology of Liberation*, 145–61, and Enrique Dussel, *Beyond Philosophy: Ethics, History, Marxism, and Liberation Theology*, ed. Eduardo Mendieta (New York: Rowan & Littlefield, 2003), 41–52.

20 See, for example, Ada María Isasi-Díaz, *Mujerista Theology: A Theology for the Twenty-First Century* (Maryknoll, NY: Orbis, 1996), 66–72.

21 Katie Cannon, *Black Womanist Ethics* (Atlanta, GA: Scholars Press, 1988).

22 Ada María Isasi-Díaz, *La Lucha Continues: Mujerista Theology* (Maryknoll, NY: Orbis, 2004), 92–106.

23 Isasi-Díaz, *Mujerista Theology*, 64.

24 Isasi-Díaz, *Mujerista Theology*, 69–70.

25 Isasi-Díaz, *La Lucha Continues*, 96.

26 Isasi-Díaz, *Mujerista Theology*, 72.

27 John Milbank, *Theology and Social Theory: Beyond Secular Reason* (Oxford: Basil Blackwell, 1990).

28 William Cavanaugh, *Torture and Eucharist: Theology, Politics, and the Body of Christ* (Oxford: Blackwell, 1998).

29 William Cavanaugh, *Theopolitical Imagination: Discovering the Liturgy as a Political Act in an Age of Global Consumerism* (Edinburgh: T&T Clark, 2002), 83.

30 See *Laborem Exercens* (1981), §11; Congregation of the Doctrine of the Faith, *Libertatis Nuntius* (1984); and *Libertatis Conscientia* (1986). Gutiérrez makes clear he entirely rejects this aspect of Marxist analysis and concurs with the magisterial critique of it (*The Truth Shall Make You Free*, 76–77); likewise, Enrique Dussel agrees with the magisterial critique of historical materialism but contends this was never an aspect of Marxism on which liberation theology drew ("Theology of Liberation and Marxism," 85–102).

31 John Paul II, *Centesimus Annus* (1991).

32 *Mater et Magistra* (1961), §236.

33 See for example, Ignacio Ellacuría, *Ignacio Ellacuría: Essays on History, Liberation, and Salvation*, ed. Michael E. Lee (Maryknoll, NY: Orbis, 2013), 80; and Isasi-Díaz, *La Lucha Continues*, 98–101.

34 Catherine Pickstock, "The Confidence of Theology: Frontiers of Christianity in Britain Today," *ABC Religion and Ethics Online*, 15 April 2016, https://www.abc.net.au/religion/the-confidence-of-theology-frontiers-of-christianity-in-britain-/10097104 (accessed 11 September 2023).

35 Jürgen Moltmann, *God in Creation: A New Theology of Creation and the Spirit of God*, trans. Margaret Kohl (Minneapolis, MN: Fortress Press, 1993), 3.

36 Moltmann, *God in Creation*, 3.

37 See, for example, the work of José Casanova, Korie Edwards, Grace Yukich, Christian Smith, Philip Gorski, Valentina Napoli, and Joel Robbins.

38 See, for example, Bent Flyvbjerg, *Making Social Science Matter: Why Social Inquiry Fails and How It Can Succeed Again*, trans. Steven Sampson (Cambridge: Cambridge University Press, 2001); Christian Smith, *What Is a Person?* (Chicago, IL: University of Chicago Press, 2011); Tim Ingold, *Anthropology: Why It Matters* (Cambridge: Polity Press, 2018); Joel Robbins, *Theology and the Anthropology of Christian Life* (Oxford: Oxford University Press, 2020).

39 Coakley, *God, Sexuality and the Self*, 33–92.

40 Jean-Marc Ela, *African Cry*, trans. Robert R. Barr (Maryknoll, NY: Orbis, 1986); Ela, *My Faith as an African*, trans. John Pairman Brown and Susan Perry (Maryknoll, NY: Orbis, 1988); Philip Gibbs, *The Word in the Third World* (Rome: Gregorian University Press, 1996), 97–157.

41 My own work provides examples of all three types. *Resurrecting Democracy* (2015) is driven by ethnographic research, *Christianity and Contemporary Politics* (2010) is directly informed by the ethnographic and social scientific work of others, and *Christ and the Common Life* (2019) is haunted by ethnographic concerns even though it draws on social scientific studies only on occasions.

Recommended Reading

Bevans, Stephen B. *Models of Contextual Theology*. Rev. ed. Maryknoll, NY: Orbis, 2002.

Bonhoeffer, Dietrich. *Sanctorum Communio: Theological Study of the Sociology of the Church*. Dietrich Bonhoeffer Works in English, Vol. 1. Edited by Clifford J. Green. Translated by Reinhard Krauss and Nancy Lukens. Minneapolis, MN: Fortress Press, 2009.

Bretherton, Luke. *Resurrecting Democracy: Faith, Citizenship and the Politics of a Common Life*. Cambridge: Cambridge University Press, 2015.

Coakley, Sarah. *God, Sexuality and the Self: An Essay "On the Trinity."* Cambridge: Cambridge University Press, 2013.

Ela, Jean-Marc. *African Cry*. Translated by Robert R. Barr. Maryknoll, NY: Orbis, 1986.

Fiddes, Paul. "Ecclesiology and Ethnography: Two Disciplines, Two Worlds?" In *Perspectives on Ecclesiology and Ethnography*, edited by Pete Ward, 13–35. Grand Rapids, MI: Eerdmans, 2011.

Gutiérrez, Gustavo. *A Theology of Liberation: History, Politics, and Salvation*. Revised edition. Maryknoll, NY: Orbis, 1988.

Isasi-Díaz, Ada María. *Mujerista Theology: A Theology for the Twenty-First Century*. Maryknoll, NY: Orbis, 1996.

Milbank, John. *Theology and Social Theory: Beyond Secular Reason*. Oxford: Basil Blackwell, 1990.

Tracy, David. *Blessed Rage for Order: The New Pluralism in Theology*. Chicago, IL: University of Chicago Press, 1996.

Theology Between Faiths

Judaism

Randi Rashkover

Introduction

More than any other period, the past one hundred years of Christian theology have reshaped the long and often painful history of Christian perspectives of Judaism. As is widely recognized, Karl Barth's *Israellehre* marks the beginning of this new chapter with its recognition of God's eternal election of Israel. For Barth, as Katherine Sonderegger explains, "the God the Bible speaks of is the God of Israel. There is no other."[1] In the pre-1945 period, other notable Christian thinkers such as Dietrich Bonhoeffer and Edith Stein also incorporated concern for Jews into their understanding of Christian witness. Unfortunately, these pre-1945 positions failed adequately to challenge key elements of Christian anti-Judaism.[2] For Barth, Israel and by extension Judaism, is the dehistoricized, creaturely witness to sin. Similarly, Bonhoeffer remained steadfastly tied to the traditional supersessionist idea that Jewish suffering is punishment for the rejection of Jesus as Messiah. In "The Church and the Jewish Question," Bonhoeffer states that, "the Church of Christ has never lost sight of the thought that the 'chosen people,' which hung the Redeemer of the world on the cross, must endure the curse of its action in long-drawn out suffering."[3] It is not until after the Holocaust that Christian theologians and Christian institutions reconsidered this identification of the Jews as the object of God's punishment. Arguably, there are four major intellectual stages in Christianity's post-Holocaust reflections upon Judaism: (1) linguistic reformulation, (2) total revolution, (3) redescription, and (4) logical repair. Much has already been written about the first three of these stages.[4] Consequently, in what follows I provide a brief review of the first three stages and then focus on the last phase of "logical repair" because it is the most current area of constructive theological effort by Christian theologians as they work together with Jewish theologians and philosophers to make room for the ongoing validity and self-understanding of the Jewish tradition by Jews throughout history.

Ford's The Modern Theologians: An Introduction to Christian Theology since 1918, Fourth Edition.
Edited by Rachel Muers and Ashley Cocksworth.
© 2024 John Wiley & Sons Ltd. Published 2024 by John Wiley & Sons Ltd.

Survey

In 1947, a Jewish French historian and Holocaust survivor named Jules Isaac published a book titled *Jesus and Israel* that examined the New Testament roots of Christian anti-Jewish contempt. In that same year, Isaac participated in a conference in Seelisberg, Switzerland designed to identify the most anti-Jewish elements of the New Testament and introduce a ten-point proposal to guide the Catholic Church in correcting its anti-Jewish rhetoric. Included in these ten points were the recognition that (1) Jesus, Mary, and the apostles were Jewish; (2) not all Jews were responsible for Jesus's death; (3) Jesus had forgiven his Jewish murderers; and (4) Jesus taught a gospel of love for all. In 1960, Pope John XXIII met Isaac and was inspired by the ideas of the Seelisberg conference. As Gregory Baum explains, after the visit, John XXIII "asked the Secretariat for Christian Unity to prepare a statement for the Council to renew the Catholic Church's relationship to the Jews. After a long discussion at the Council, this statement became Chapter 4 of the Declaration *Nostra Aetate*."[5] *Nostra Aetate* introduced a paradigm shift in Christian rhetoric around Judaism. In addition to incorporating many of the Seelisberg conference proposal points, the declaration challenged the long-standing notion of God's rejection of the Jewish people. Instead, the declaration reformulated the Catholic view and stated that, "although the Church is the new people of God, the Jews should not be presented as repudiated or cursed by God ... All should take pains, then, lest in catechetical instruction and in the preaching of God's Word they teach anything out of harmony with the truth of the gospel and the spirit of Christ."[6]

From a practical standpoint, the Second Vatican Council's overt rejection of the language of contempt represented a critical intervention into centuries of harmful discourse about Jews and Judaism. Nonetheless, changes in rhetoric alone do not address the theological roots of Christian anti-Judaism. As noted, the declaration supports the notion that "the Church is the new people of God" and replaces Israel in this role. When compounded by the belief that salvation and restoration of the covenant relationship is possible through Jesus alone, a direct contradiction emerges between the Catholic attempt to offer positive rhetoric about Judaism and the implications of the church's theological commitments. As Gregory Baum explains,

> [when the church deals] specifically with the Jewish people, then they pursue the new position and defend the ongoing validity of the ancient covenant in Israel; but when they deal with the central Christian teaching on Christ and redemption they fall quite spontaneously into the traditional way of speaking which presupposes that the Jews no longer exist.[7]

In the wake of the Second Vatican Council, a wave of Christian theologians inaugurated a second stage in post-Holocaust Christian reflections on Judaism. Appropriating the term introduced by Roy Eckardt, we may characterize this as the "total revolution" stage represented most notably by the work of Eckardt, Paul Van Buren, and Rosemary Radford Ruether. Proponents of the total revolution view maintain that Christian anti-Judaism not only emerges directly out of the New Testament but is constitutive of and inseparable from the gospel. In *Faith and Fratricide*, for example, Ruether argues that anti-Judaism is "the left hand of Christology."[8] According to Ruether, the "most fundamental affirmation of Christian faith is the belief that Jesus is the Christ."[9] However, to say that Jesus is the Christ is to say that Jesus is the Messiah for the Jews, or the one through whom Jewish history and covenantal reality is completed and fulfilled. If Jesus is the Jewish Messiah, then only those who proclaim this are the covenant people and those who do not are enemies of God.

Moreover, according to Ruether, Christology is anti-Jewish when it views Jesus as the one who proclaims an ultimate or future "eschatological horizon impinging on history,"[10] and the one whose proclamation and person exemplifies this eschatology. When, Ruether says, "this experience and person in the past ... becomes the final eschatological event of history, [it places] all history before that time in an obsolescent and morally inferior relation to itself or invalidat[es] the access to God of those who go forward on other grounds."[11]

For Ruether, therefore, anti-Judaism is "an expression of Christian self-affirmation … [and] rethinking anti-Judaism has become … an internal task of Christian theological reconstruction."[12] It is not enough for the church to critique problematic anti-Jewish discourse. Christians must "think [themselves] back into a framework in which Christianity was within, not outside of Judaism."[13] This rule Ruether asserts applies equally to the church's scriptural hermeneutics and its Christology. When applied to the latter, the rule translates into a call to demythologize Jesus and to challenge the aforementioned tendency to associate his person and his proclamation with God's final eschatological event. As Ruether states,

> the idea that the final messianic Advent has already happened in Jesus must be reformulated through an empathetic encounter with the way this idea originally arose in its Jewish context. Here we discover a historical Jesus as a faithful Jew within the Mosaic covenant, who did not set out to replace Judaism by another religion, but who lived in lively expectation of the coming of God's Kingdom and judged his society in its light.[14]

It is one thing, Ruether argues, "to reaffirm Jesus' [eschatological] hope in his name" and another "to claim that in Jesus this hope has already happened, albeit in in invisible form."[15] Moreover, identifying Jesus as one who proclaims this hope does not imply that "it is now only in his name that this hope can be proclaimed."[16] Rather, identifying Jesus as the one who proclaims this hope is, she says, the "Christian story," which like the story of the Exodus, represents "an experience of salvation that is remembered by the heirs of that community which experienced it as an expression of ultimate hope."[17]

Perhaps the greatest virtue of the total revolution approach to Christian theology is its call for Christians to listen to Jewish descriptions of their relationship to God. Even so, many theologians have suggested that the total revolution approach sacrifices key elements of the Christian message. In his *Church and Israel after Christendom*, Scott Bader-Saye expresses this concern and says,

> these theologians who have thought extensively about how to reconstruct Christian theology without its anti-Jewish elements have been markedly lacking in their willingness to affirm … the Christological claims …. In short, Christianity can be salvaged, but what will remain of Christology remains unclear.[18]

Bader-Saye's *The Church and Israel after Christendom* charts a new course in post-1945 Christian theological responses to Judaism or what we may refer to as "redescription." By "redescription" I mean the attempt to present the Christian soteriological story and its canonical narrative in a way that includes a positive and ongoing role for "Israel." Committed to advancing what he takes to be a non-supersessionist picture of "how the Church's own identity and life is grounded in Israel's election,"[19] Bader-Saye argues that the church is engrafted on to the material, political body of Israel and joins with Israel in the one covenant with God to bring peace and blessing to the world.

This does not mean that the church is not unique or that it does not see itself in relation to a "new covenant" for all people. To explain, Bader-Saye turns to Paul's letter to the Romans. Drawing from Jeremiah, Paul identifies the "new covenant" as the covenant "written on the heart" and available to all, Jews and gentile alike. Even so, Paul insists, God's invitation to the gentiles does not create a new people of God but grafts them on to the community of Israel and their inherited promises. As such, the people Israel, in Bader-Saye's account, includes both believing Jews and believing gentiles, together with nonbelieving Jews since all are part of the divine economy. According to his reading of Romans, God has purposely hardened the heart of nonbelieving Jews in order to make room for gentiles, but in the end, "together with the 'full number of Gentiles … all Israel will be saved' (Romans 11:25–32)."[20]

With this redescription of the one people of Israel, Bader-Saye believes he has formulated a non-supersessionist picture of the new covenant. Unlike the Second Vatican Council, Bader-Saye understands that non-supersessionism requires more than rhetorical change. Unlike Ruether, Bader-Saye seeks to avoid demythologization. The Jewish and gentile story of Israel is not merely a subjective representation of a community's experience but an expression of a divine economy and "one that reflects in its basic structure the inter-working of Father, Son and Holy Spirit."[21] For Bader-Saye, the doctrine of the Trinity is "the conviction that the very nature of God corresponds to, is faithful to, the ways God engages the creation."[22] God the Father enlists the activity of both the Holy Spirit and the life of Jesus "to redeem the covenant with Israel."[23] Together, "Christ and the Holy Spirit … trace the outlines of Israel's redemption on the body of the Church."[24] Jesus's miraculous life and charitable deeds "make redemption visible"[25] and his death redeems Israel from sin, but the Holy Spirit supports the unity of Israel in its efforts to realize its political purpose as a "community of peace and plenty."[26] This is not, Bader-Saye contends, "to say that the Torah is rendered obsolete, only that the Torah is now read through the lens of the cross" and in relation to God's triune relationship with the created order.[27]

Bader-Saye's work offers a strong example of the attempt by Christian theologians to construct a theologically rich redescription of the soteriological narrative of the church that includes a positive and ongoing role for biblical Israel.[28] However, in an essay titled, "Israel and the Cosmic Christ: A Non-Supersessionist Reading of Ephesians," Susannah Ticciati makes the following critical observation regarding attempts like Bader-Saye's to redescribe Israel.

> Definitions go with the creation of boundaries: to define Israel is to mark out membership criteria (however elusive these may be) …. If [for example] Ephesians is understood to be affirming the inclusion of gentiles in Israel, enlarging its boundaries, a definitional approach to Israel can only conclude that a *re*definition of Israel is entailed …. And however one might stress the inclusivity of the new criteria, redefinition cannot but involve supersession: the replacement of one people by another. The widening of boundaries in one place (to include gentiles) entails narrowing of it in another place.[29]

Elsewhere, Ticciati explains how supersessionism is not merely a matter of the content of Christian claims, but more so, an expression of a particular logic or rule concerning propositional truth and validity. Supersessionist claims, she argues, take the form of a binary or "true or false" logic that takes for granted the fixed opposition between the two. If, in the case at hand, "we assume we know who biblical Israel is, we are very likely to end up with a supersessionist dynamic" because such knowledge is said to represent uncontested "truth."[30] Christian attempts to distinguish between two different Israels, i.e. the church as the true, spiritual Israel and biblical Israel as the false legal or carnal Israel offer a good example of this logic. As we have seen, Bader-Saye also rejects this bifurcation of Israel into two separate and opposing communities. Even so, Bader-Saye's redescription of Israel as one community of Jews and Gentiles elected by God manifests the same binary logic as the two Israel description since he presents it as an absolute claim rather than one valid *interpretation* of the concept "Israel." Both the two-Israel account and Bader-Saye's redescription reject the opportunity to entertain arguments about the concept of Israel and deny what Peter Ochs calls a logic that "turns contradictions into contraries."[31] This sort of logical reorientation is necessary, however, if post-Holocaust Christianity theologians want to learn how to appreciate ongoing Jewish interpretations of the meaning and value of Israel.

Named Theologians

Gregory Baum

In a 1973 essay, "The Jews, Faith and Ideology," the late Canadian Catholic theologian Gregory Baum asks, "How is it possible that the Christian Church, professing love as the highest value never to be surpassed, could generate a profound bias against a certain people, embody this concept in its teaching, and promote unjust social practices?"[32] Baum's answer is somewhat surprising today and certainly novel for its time. "In many cases, if not most," he says, "the tendency to spread contempt for the Jews and berate their religion was produced by [thinking] processes that … [are appropriately referred to as] ideological."[33] Ideology, he continues, "is the … tendency present in any group, to produce views and values that legitimate and reinforce the present order and protect it against competing groups."[34] Elsewhere, Baum defines ideology as "the distortion of truth for the sake of social interest."[35] With this turn to an analysis of ideology, Baum's thought introduces a fourth and what I argue is the most advanced phase in Christian theological responses to Judaism, or what we may refer to as the "turn to logic."

In what respect is a focus on "ideology" a logical turn? As described by Baum, ideological ideas are ideas promoted by certain groups to meet their own social interests. However, because ideological ideas serve to legitimate or secure certain social interests, those who hold them have a vested interest in sustaining these ideas regardless of challenges to them and/or argumentative contestation. As such, ideological ideas thwart attempts to question them by people who do not share the same social interests. Ideologues usurp the rational agency of others who are entitled to participate in processes of the rational determination of ideas and in so doing, act irrationally or illogically.

According to Baum, Christian anti-Judaism is a product of ideological thinking. Like Ticciati, Baum recognizes the connection between supersessionism and binary logic or what Peter Ochs explains is the tendency to "define one's position as the logical contradictory of a position one is criticizing."[36] As Ochs further details, binary logic presupposes that,

> an offending [position] displays a class character that can be defined according to a finite set of propositions, or … reduced to a relatively simple propositional function P and [that one's preferred position can] also be defined according to a finite set of propositions ["Q"] … so that "intentionally or unintentionally [one presupposes] that Q and P are logical contradictories.[37]

In his work, Ochs frequently notes the utility of binary logic in circumstances when the claim or claims at hand are commonly accepted and infrequently contested. However, Ochs also argues that when applied to highly contested claims, binary logic works as a "hermeneutics of war."[38] This is because binary logic treats divergent claims as invalid or as "the logical contradictory" of the supported claim.[39] Like Ochs and Ticciati, Baum understands the damaging effects of the application of binary logic. Ideological rhetoric, he says, is

> a rhetoric of exclusion … if unchecked, it has devastating consequences. It will eventually taint the entire culture of the group [that deploys it], produce spontaneous yet untruthful judgments about others, [and] lead to the creation of institutions that embody widespread contempt.[40]

Also like Ticciati and Ochs, Baum recognizes the false character of ideological claims since unlike many ordinary binary claims that are commonly held and infrequently contested, ideological claims are binary claims held regardless of ongoing challenges and contesting positions. Ideological positions suppress opportunities for falsification and prohibit processes of inquiry required by the search for truth.

For Baum, therefore, it is impossible to understand supersessionism without understanding its logical character as ideology. Baum's analysis of supersessionism is not only valuable because it illuminates how supersessionism is a matter of how claims are held and not just a matter of their content. Rather, Baum's account of anti-Judaism is also valuable because like other critical theorists, he recognizes the link between binary or ideological logic and the social interests of particular social groups who seek to secure the legitimacy of their own ideas and limit the input of any and all others who might contest them. This is why ideological expressions of binary logic are a perpetual threat to societal and cultural well-being. It is far easier for a ruling group seeking power to advance ideological notions that secure its own interests than it is for the same group to defend its particular ideas in and through processes of argumentation. According to

Baum, the church's own ideological tendencies are rooted in the period of Christian origins when it relied on binary determinations of itself as the people of God and the Jews as the people rejected by God in order to shore up its legitimacy. As he explains,

> in the Christian church, this rhetoric of exclusion was operative against the Jews almost from the beginning. It began when the Jews as a whole refused to acknowledge Jesus as the Messiah and was aggravated when the Christians regarded themselves as replacing the Jews as God's chosen people .... This discovery of the anti-Jewish trends in Christian preaching has profound consequences for the Church's self-understanding. We have come to realize, possibly for the first, time in an overwhelming fashion, that the Christian church is subject to ideology.[41]

As a form of *Ideologiekritik*, Baum's post-Holocaust Christian thought makes a substantial contribution to Christian theological efforts to challenge supersessionism. Even so, Baum's greatest contribution is diagnostic since he does not offer a clear picture of what a nonideological Christian theology looks like and how it is achievable. To do this, Baum would need to show how Christians have historically exercised and continue to exercise the ability to welcome and not fear the need to offer reasons for their claims.

Susannah Ticciati

Earlier, we discussed Susannah Ticciati's contribution to the diagnosis of supersessionism as a logical problem. However, Ticciati's work also attempts to offer a positive account of nonideological Christian reflection. In an article titled, "The Future of Biblical Israel: How Should Christians Read Romans 9–11 Today," Ticciati argues in favor of a theological and exegetical appropriation of the fruits of historical studies. There she states that scriptural readings that have not been

> put through the mill of historical askesis run ...... the strong risk of falling prey to a theologically troubling essentializing logic, and more specifically in the case of Romans 9–11, an anti-Judaic logic .... History is a particularly powerful debunker of parochial, and potentially harmful assumptions.[42]

What does Ticciati mean by this and how does Ticciati's invocation of history prompt nonideological theological reflection?

In Ticciati's estimation, historical studies of first- and second-century Judaism document the argumentative activity within different communities, each making some claim to call itself "Israel." More specifically, these historical investigations illuminate how different communities aspired to achieve historical impact (i.e. preserve themselves in view of their account of who and what they were) in complex modes of contest with one another. As Ticciati says, historical studies expose "the contest over the future of biblical Israel ... in the early centuries."[43] More specifically, this history reveals how (1) supersessionist accounts of the replacement and therefore death of Judaism through the emergence of the church are historically false, and (2) the plurality of communities advancing claims regarding the meaning of "Israel" shows that there was no single account of what "Israel" meant but rather, different "interpretations" of this category and different arguments presented by these communities as they sought to gain adherents and preserve themselves in history. To support the first claim, Ticciati draws from the work of Annette Yoshiko Reed and Adam H. Becker who claim that historical shifts

> in the relations between Jews and Christians in the early centuries ... [show] how the crudely supersessionist model according to which Christianity as a new religion founded by Jesus himself, suspended an old Judaism which persisted only in ossified form, was succeeded in the postwar period by the

"Parting of the Ways" model .... By contrast with the now thoroughly outdated supersessionist model (in which a new Christianity supersedes an old Judaism), the "Parting" model suggests that rabbinic Judaism is just as much a contingent and constructive historical development as the Christianity over against which it was defined, making both valid claimants to continuity with biblical Israel. As Robert Jenson as put it, both are forms of "Israel-after-Israel."[44]

In other words, history confirms what Jews have long known: that rabbinic Judaism constitutes a dominant means by which a certain interpretation of biblical Israel continues after the destruction of the second temple.

With regard to the second point, Ticciati maintains that,

according to the emerging [historical] picture, postbiblical Israel is all the more underdetermined ... taking on multiple forms in complicated interaction with one another (and not settling into any neat and *uncontested* [emphasis mine] configuration at any identifiable point).[45]

Both points illustrate the role that historical studies can play in challenging the ideological logic of Christian anti-Judaism. On the one hand, history exposes the falsehood of ideological positions that deny the reality of contesting positions, and on the other hand, history illuminates the alternative to ideological logic, namely the argumentative context of the relation between multiple interpretative positions. No doubt, the historical preservation of one community over and another is not necessarily a result of one community's argumentative success. Often, communities perdure as a result of ideological force, particularly when the ideology is generated by an economically or militarily backed ruling power. In the case at hand, however, history presents a window into a fluid environment where one community's interpretation is not (yet) backed by social forces that would allow for ideological domination and where by contrast, different communities preserved themselves in contest with other communities and did so on the grounds of the rational (i.e. persuasive) strength of their ideas.

Unlike Baum, Ticciati shows how reflection upon the fruits of historical studies can offer an alternative to the binary logic of supersessionism. As she argues, "recent historical paradigm shifts should surely be definitive enough to overcome these supersessionist habits and their accompanying caricatures."[46] Christian laypersons and theologians alike ought to be able to appreciate these historical findings and recognize the extent to which they debunk ideological notions and call the church to recognize its claims as subject to, and only defensible through, practices of human rational argumentation, particularly in times of internal or external challenge or contestation. However, despite this confidence in the fruits of historical studies, Ticciati also appreciates the importance of a *theological* basis for the idea that religious claims, like other claims we hold, require justification and are contestable, even if many of the religious claims we hold have stood the test of time and do not currently need immediate justificatory review.

In the second section of her essay, Ticciati uses the findings of historical studies to guide a reading of chapters 9–11 of Paul's Letter to the Romans. On the one hand she encourages readers to appreciate Paul's positions as one voice in the historical contest of first-century interpretations of the meaning of "Israel." On the other hand, she uses the results of historical studies as a framework for understanding Paul's theology. The goal of the analysis is to offer an account of a non-supersessionist, nonbinary Christian theology that not only grounds an ongoing critique of Christian tendencies toward ideology but also grounds a picture of Christianity as argument.

The key to Ticciati's theological rereading of chapters 9–11 rests on the claim that, "Paul is not offering a whimsical redefinition of Israel (in keeping with binary logic), but instead, a theological characterization of Israel's identity through constructive engagement with Israel's scriptures in light of Christ."[47] More specifically, Ticciati reads Romans 9.6b, "For not all from Israel are Israel," as Paul's way of signaling the role of divine election in the constitution of Israel and not as his binary effort to "distinguish between Israel according to the flesh (however defined), and 'Israel within Israel,' or a 'true Israel.'"[48] Romans, she argues, advances a profile of the one, not two "Israels" of God's elective determinations as the fruits of those determinations appear in history. In her view, Paul hopes to persuade gentiles recently invited into the community of "Israel," to recognize that they should not disown nonbelieving Israelites from their "new Israel" because only God can determine who is and is not Israel.

In Ticciati's estimation, this (Pauline) account of divine election parallels the outcomes of historical studies. Each confers the same logical effect, or the reminder that attempts to issue fixed or absolute judgments are ideological since these judgments resist falsification by either history or God. This is not the case, however, because historical studies not only serve to guard believers and theologians against ideology but also illuminate a framework for a positive, nonbinary logic. As discussed earlier, historical studies signal the fact that communities and their ideas preserve themselves when they ground the actions of those who hold them. In turn, these actions materialize these ideas and thereby sustain the role of "x" tradition in history. Moreover, as we have noted, people act on ideas under two primary conditions. Either (1) the ideas are supported by good reasons, when by good reasons, we mean, they serve a positive function for those who hold them, or (2) ideas are ideologically or coercively maintained by a group whose interests they serve. In the short term, it may seem that traditions are more often preserved ideologically. However, in the long term, ideological ideas inevitably burn out either from polemical contest or from falsifications that expose their untruth. By and large, history shows that traditions preserve themselves over time through argumentative adaptation. As such, history not only serves as a form of *Ideologiekritik* but as a reminder of the positive value of a nonbinary logic.

Unfortunately, Ticciati's *theological* account of divine election does not explain how Christianity can issue claims in a nonideological way. This is because in her view, divine election is the primary agent of historical determination and not the argumentative activity of the communities who claim to be "Israel." Indeed, Ticciati confirms this point when she invokes Barth and says, "if essentialised belief in Christ is historically questionable, then Barth's theological critique in Romans subjects it to a devastating blow from which there is no recovery."[49]

Ticciati specifically references Barth when she argues that a Pauline theology of divine election guards against fast and loose "mappings" of Paul's (unbelieving) Israel with today's Jews and Paul's believing community with today's church. Not only does the church need to recognize other claimants to Israel, but it needs to "recognize that … it will not be long…. before it recognizes that it has itself become hardened Israel."[50] If what Ticciati means here is that throughout the course of history, Christians can and ought to expect to get things wrong and be subject to both valid internal and external criticisms, then, no doubt, she is correct. As well, if by "hardened" Ticciati means that the church runs the risk of falling prey to binary or ideological thinking, she is also right. However, Ticciati's invocation of Barth goes beyond this since as she says, Barth's theology distinguishes "between the Gospel of Jesus Christ as 'the impossible possibility of God,' and the Church as 'the last human possibility.' In their confrontation, the one dissolves the other … belief in Christ as a divine possibility is not something the Church can lay claim to, either as such, or by contrast with other human bodies."[51] Despite her attempt to provide an account of the theological grounds of a nonideological Christianity, Ticciati issues an overly powerful Barthian "Nein" to any and all Christian claims. As such, Christian theology is reduced to a perpetual theology of suspicion rather a positive, nonideological expression of religious claims.

The implications of such a view for Christian attitudes toward Judaism are also significant, since if Christians cannot trust in the provisional validity of their own claims, they cannot trust in the provisional validity of postbiblical Jewish claims either. Thus, Ticciati concedes that "Barth flattens out all human history in its contrast with the impossible possibility of God. This she says, "has the negative consequence … of evacuating the term Jew of any particular significance" and offers no grounds to appreciate an ongoing and non-ideological, Jewish interpretation of God's word.[52]

Peter Ochs

Historical studies are not the only source of evidence of how traditions present claims as arguments. As Jewish philosopher Peter Ochs shows, evidence of nonbinary logic appears throughout religious traditions and in a contemporary, post-Barthian, school of Christian theology that he refers to as postliberalism. According to Ochs, postliberal Christian theologians such as George Lindbeck, Robert Jenson, David F. Ford, and others have stumbled on the benefits of a nonbinary logic in the course of their efforts at internal religious reform.

Reform, Ochs explains, is a hybrid intellectual activity that combines the impulse to critique problematic claims and norms presented by one's tradition without advancing a position of critique whose critical standards are external to and are used solely to determine the validity of the tradition's claims. Thus, in his view, Christian reform challenges "the hegemonic paradigms of reason" characteristic of modern, Western philosophical accounts.[53] If, as Ochs suggests, these accounts had "their sphere and time of usefulness," they now work at cross-purposes with reformers' desire to combine critique with the preservation of tradition.[54] From a reformer's perspective, modern accounts of human reason as the absolute and self-evident standard of truth and rationality perpetuate a binary logic that ultimately pits religion against reason. Postliberalism, by contrast seeks, "reaffirmation and correction ... [and] seeks to criticize certain institutions from within ... according to norms embedded within the practices and histories of those institutions, but not necessarily visible to contemporary practitioners and leaders."[55] By contrast, absolute notions of reason as critique perpetuate a "hermeneutics of war" that prohibits critique from achieving any positive ends.[56] Externally derived, absolute critique destroys the objects of its critique and provides no resources for the reestablishment of positive content.

As an expression of binary logic, modern philosophical critique outlives its usefulness and guarantees its own tragic self-destruction. According to Ochs, this is because, even before it turns into a hermeneutics of war, binary logic functions as a "logic of suffering." When we suffer, we see only two possibilities: the continuation of our suffering by the object of our critique or the elimination of our suffering through the elimination of the object through critique. Unfortunately, the binary logic of suffering and critique that sees one's position as the logical contradictory of a position one is criticizing also leaves the sufferer without a pathway beyond the destruction of the object of her critique, unable to "reintegrate ... into a given order of creation."[57]

In their efforts to reform, correct, and reaffirm, postliberal Christian theologians in Ochs' account recognize that modern critique cannot support sufferers in their attempts to challenge existing ideas or norms without alienating themselves them from the positive resources of their tradition, those resources that these same sufferers affirm and use as the contents of their "*Lebenswelt*." Sufferers need a lifeworld in order to correct the object of their critique and then reposition themselves in the world in the wake of their critique. As Ochs says, suffering temporarily alienates us from our world or "refers ... to an event of separation within the relational continuum that characterizes a given order of creation."[58] However, because lifeworlds are the ideas and inferential habits we perform when we use the ideas that shape "our everyday practices,"[59] they are also the ideas and inferential habits that can help us "repair ... how one does this or that."[60] Thus, like John Dewey, postliberal theologians offer essentially "pragmatic analyses of [their] institutions [or see them] as progressively ordered to serve the relative ends of repairing suffering, then of repairing the repair of suffering, and so on."[61] Not surprisingly, the process of enlisting a tradition's working norms and ideas to guide the attempt to contend with a point of suffering is a layered one. One first enlists the most immediate solutions to one's problem (e.g. a particular text appears troubling and one appeals to an understanding of how that text relates to other proximate texts and their common readings) and only upon the failure of such an attempt proceeds to dig deeper to enlist the aid of the increasingly secure norms, practices or principles that over time have proved most helpful to members of a community.

Consequently, unlike the binary logic of critique, the exercise of internal traditional reform deploys lifeworld elements in and for specific problems in specific contexts and does not absolutize the working solutions applied in these particular contexts. As agents of internal reform, postliberal theologians show how traditions work as arguments rather than as ideological assertions of fixed truths. Instead of appealing to Christian norms, practices, and ideas as history transcending claims used to undermine the potential validity of either Christian or non-Christian (in this case, "Jewish") norms and ideas, they provisionally invoke and defend these norms and ideas to resolve context-specific problems. As such, postliberal theologians

> argue against the *a prioricity* of any universal canon of human reason. They argue that the only reason we share as a species is God's reason, and God's reason is embedded in the orders of creation and the words of Scripture in a way that enables us to observe that it is there but not to articulate its universal character through any finite set of humanly constructed propositions.[62]

Thus, as Ochs argues, the postliberal appreciation for the nonbinary character of reformist reflection presupposes an awareness of a reason we can observe, but never fully master; that is to say, it presupposes a theo-logic dimension of nonbinary reformational activity. Always present, the theo-logic dimension of nonbinary reformational activity becomes most apparent in times of grave crises that challenge even the most tried and true lifeworlds. During these times, sufferers and those who seek to help them find it difficult to imagine how any lifeworld resources can be enlisted to help the sufferers make sense of their suffering and thus, on these occasions, as Ochs explains, Jews and Christians (and no doubt others) look to God to feel justified in their attempts to continue with the highly strenuous work of repair. As Ochs explains,

> Charles Peirce argued that while many … failings may be repaired by common sense, there are classes of failings that common sense [everyday lifeworlds] cannot repair … a … self-evident class of failings is the class of societal and civilizational failings, when "things fall apart" and received systems of language and meaning are sources of more suffering than repair.[63]

Under these crisis circumstances, it becomes difficult for human beings to imagine where they may find a source of new lifeworld contents. This is why for Peirce, as Ochs explains, the continuation of pragmatic impulses and drives in times of crisis points to the activity of "musement" or consideration of the created order as a product of a generative God who offers it as infinite set of possibilities for the formation and development of new lifeworlds.

From here, Ochs extends Peirce's focus on God's word in the created order to an appreciation of God's word in revealed texts. As he argues, "pragmatism's reparative reasoning is thus a species of scriptural reasoning," since there are times when even the created word cannot provide the imaginative resources necessary for renewing and/or constructing lifeworlds.[64] Thus, Ochs maintains, scripture "is the prototype as well as the primary book of instruction in how to compose new diagrams of repair" and Scriptural Reasoning is the practice of illuminating scripture as the site of reasoning possibilities.[65]

For postliberal Christian theologians, pragmatic appeals to the revealed word constitute the deepest and ultimate source of pragmatic wisdom. Although in their view, internal problems can often be resolved through the nonscriptural resources of the tradition, these resources are rooted in and are products of ongoing acts of scriptural interpretation. Reformist activities in other words, follow the model of a Scriptural Reasoning process whereby readers,

> bring the suffering of some single group of people to the attention of some particular community of Israel, and bring that community to some particular texts of Scripture, and those texts to the context of that suffering, and that communion of texts, interpreters, and sufferers to some series of inquiries, actions, and testing that continues until the suffering is relieved.[66]

In sum, Ochs' analysis of postliberal Christian thought illustrates how the primary feature of contemporary work in Christian theologies of Judaism consists in an appreciation and deployment of nonbinary forms of logic. Christian theology need not offer a particular narrative concerning Judaism or Jews but only recognize the relationship between anti-Judaism and ideology. Logical form is more important than content. This is why in *Another Reformation*, Ochs maintains that postliberal Christian theologies "provide the most reliable protection against formal or de facto supersessionism" and not, he argues, because "postliberal Christianity … first arise[s] out of a concern for the Jews" but because the nonbinary logic it deploys is freed from the absolutist tendencies that permit the church to make fixed determinations regarding Judaism that deny the validity of the Jewish relationship to the Hebrew scriptures.[67] Instead, postliberal Christian theologians recognize the surplus of hermeneutical possibilities presented through processes of interpreting the revealed Word and recognize the pragmatic provisionality of these interpretations and their indebtedness to a divine source that cannot be managed or contained. As Ochs explains, "once engaged in this movement, postliberal theologians discover that these activities of recovery lead them … to a new relationship with the Old Testament, with Israel's ancient covenant with God, and with the Jews as a religious people during the time of Jesus and into the rabbinic period that continues today."[68] Stated differently, postliberal scriptural pragmatism invites an appreciation for the potential validity of Jewish readings of the Hebrew scriptures as these readings have achieved vitality in and through the rabbinic tradition.

Ongoing Debates

Ochs' *Another Reformation* offers the leading account of how and why logical reorientation constitutes a promising pathway for improving Christian theology's relationship to Judaism. As Ochs announces, "the premise of this book is that the movement I will label 'postliberal Christian theology' … offers a way to reaffirm classical Christology while eliding its supersessionism … [or] is inseparably associated with the rejection of supersessionism."[69] Nonetheless, Ochs' hypothesis stands in some tension with the position presented by Robert Jenson in his essay, "Toward a Christian Theology of Judaism." There Jenson notes the following:

> that there should be any difficulty in understanding Judaism's claim to be Israel may, of course, seem preposterous to Jews. But for Christian theology it is not merely a difficulty but a torment … That the vast majority of Abraham and Sarah's descendents maintain a claim to be faithful Israel without acknowledging Jesus' resurrection, must indeed give the church furiously to think … From a certain angle of vision, the mere existence of Judaism looks much like a refutation of Christianity – and may indeed be just that.[70]

Jenson's comment is an important reminder that the philosophical entailment of a non-supersessionist position is not enough to guard against anti-Jewish ideology. Like Jenson, Christian theologians need to recognize the ongoing temptation of anti-Jewish ideology and develop Christian theologies of Judaism that explicitly challenge them. Like Jenson and Baum, Christian theologians need to recognize that anti-Jewish ideology is, like other ideologies, an attempt by a particular community to silence the interpretive freedom of communities that do not support and/or legitimize their unique social interests. Ochs' account downplays this feature of ideological thought insofar as Ochs links ideology to suffering such that one could reasonably expect ideological proponents to abandon their fixed positions if presented with reparative options that alleviate their suffering. If, however, one understands ideology as driven by social interests, it becomes clear why more often than not, ideologues remain unwilling to forfeit their binary positions, despite the prospect of reparative possibilities.

In addition to these lingering concerns over the place of anti-Jewish ideology in Christian theology, Christian theologians must pay particular attention to its role in nonofficial forms of Christian discourse including preaching, Bible study, and Christian education. As Gregory Baum explains, all too frequently,

> ordinary Christian preaching provides an evolutionary picture of world history which assigns Jewish religion to an early phase and Christian religion to the later, mature and possibly final phase ... [unfortunately] ... the theology of substitution is so much part and parcel of the Christian imagination that it operates in the minds of theologians even after they have decided to adopt a more positive approach to the Jewish religion.[71]

As the developments in Christian theology over the course of the past century have shown, there is no magic bullet that can finally reorient Christian theological reflection upon Judaism. Minimally speaking, Christian theology must be aware of and learn how to exercise nonbinary modes of reflection. Maximally speaking, it needs to sustain ongoing vigilance concerning the prevalence of anti-Jewish ideology in not only its theological discourse but also its ordinary rhetoric, its sermons, its educational materials, and its media expressions. Ideology is a formidable and persistent foe that requires an equally persistent and formidable exercise of theologically inspired pragmatic reflection and response to the suffering of those perpetually affected by it.

Notes

1   Katherine Sonderegger, *That Jesus Christ Was Born a Jew* (University Park, PA: Pennsylvania State University Press, 1992), xxi.
2   See Leora Batnitzky, "The Holocaustum of Edith Stein," *Liberties* 3, no. 1 (Autumn: 2022).
3   Dietrich Bonhoeffer, "The Church and the Jewish Question," in *No Rusty Swords: Letters, Lectures and Notes 1928–1936* (New York: Harper & Row, 1965), 226.
4   Peter Ochs, "Judaism and Christian Theology," in *The Modern Theologians: An Introduction to Christian Theology Since 1918*, ed. David Ford F. with Rachel Muers (Oxford: Blackwell, 2005), 645–62.
5   Gregory Baum, "The Fiftieth Anniversary of *Nostra Aetate*," *Journal of Ecumenical Studies* 50, no. 4 (2015): 525.
6   Pope Paul VI, *Nostra Aetate* (1965), https://www.vatican.va/archive/hist_councils/ii_vatican_council/documents/vat-ii_decl_19651028_nostra-aetate_en.html (accessed 11 September 2023).
7   Gregory Baum, *Christian Theology after Auschwitz* (London: The Council of Christians and Jews, 1976), 10.
8   Rosemary Radford Ruether, "Anti-Semitism in Christian Theology," *Theology Today* 30, no. 4 (1974): 365.
9   Rosemary Radford Ruether, *Faith and Fratricide: The Theological Roots of Anti-Semitism* (Eugene, OR: Wipf and Stock, 1997), 246.
10   Ruether, *Faith and Fratricide*, 248.
11   Ruether, *Faith and Fratricide*, 248.
12   Ruether, *Faith and Fratricide*, 248.
13   Ruether, *Faith and Fratricide*, 248.
14   Ruether, *Faith and Fratricide*, 249.
15   Ruether, *Faith and Fratricide*, 249.
16   Ruether, *Faith and Fratricide*, 249.
17   Ruether, *Faith and Fratricide*, 249.
18   Scott Bader-Saye, *The Church and Israel after Christendom: The Politics of Election* (Eugene, OR: Wipf and Stock, 2005), 78.
19   Bader-Saye, *The Church and Israel after Christendom*, 2.
20   Bader-Saye, *The Church and Israel after Christendom*, 101.
21   Bader-Saye, *The Church and Israel after Christendom*, 103.
22   Bader-Saye, *The Church and Israel after Christendom*, 104.
23   Bader-Saye, *The Church and Israel after Christendom*, 105.
24   Bader-Saye, *The Church and Israel after Christendom*, 104.
25   Bader-Saye, *The Church and Israel after Christendom*, 106.
26   Bader-Saye, *The Church and Israel after Christendom*, 106.
27   Bader-Saye, *The Church and Israel after Christendom*, 106.
28   For another example of this approach, see R. Kendall Soulen, *The God of Israel and Christian Theology* (Minneapolis, MN: Fortress Press, 1996).

29 Susannah Ticciati, "Israel and the Cosmic Christ: A Non-Supersessionist Reading of Ephesians," delivered at the Society of Biblical Literature, San Diego, CA, November 2019, 1.

30 Susannah Ticciati, "The Future of Biblical Israel: How Should Christians Read Romans 9–11 Today?" *Biblical Interpretation* 25, no. 4–5 (2017): 502.

31 Peter Ochs, *Religion without Violence: The Practice and Philosophy of Scriptural Reasoning* (Eugene, OR: Wipf and Stock, 2019), 37.

32 Gregory Baum, "The Jews, Faith and Ideology," *The Ecumenist* 10 (1972): 71.

33 Baum, "The Jews, Faith and Ideology," 72.

34 Baum, "The Jews, Faith and Ideology," 75.

35 Gregory Baum, "The Impact of Sociology on Catholic Theology," *The Proceedings of the Catholic Theological Society of America* 30 (2012): 21.

36 Peter Ochs, *Another Reformation: Postliberal Christianity and the Jews* (Grand Rapids, MI: Baker Academic, 2011), 6.

37 Ochs, *Another Reformation*, 7.

38 Ochs, *Another Reformation*, 7.

39 Ochs, *Another Reformation*, 66.

40 Baum, "The Jews, Faith and Ideology," 74.

41 Baum, "The Jews, Faith and Ideology," 74.

42 Ticciati, "The Future of Biblical Israel," 498.

43 Ticciati, "The Future of Biblical Israel," 504.

44 Ticciati, "The Future of Biblical Israel," 503.

45 Ticciati, "The Future of Biblical Israel," 504.

46 Ticciati, "The Future of Biblical Israel," 504.

47 Ticciati, "The Future of Biblical Israel," 508.

48 Ticciati, "The Future of Biblical Israel," 508.

49 Ticciati, "The Future of Biblical Israel," 515.

50 Ticciati, "The Future of Biblical Israel," 513.

51 Ticciati, "The Future of Biblical Israel," 515.

52 Ticciati, "The Future of Biblical Israel," 516.

53 Ochs, *Another Reformation*, 6.

54 Ochs, *Another Reformation* 7.

55 Ochs, *Another Reformation*, 6.

56 Ochs, *Another Reformation*, 7.

57 Ochs, *Another Reformation*, 14.

58 Ochs, *Another Reformation*, 14.

59 Ochs, *Another Reformation*, 15.

60 Ochs, *Another Reformation*, 11.

61 Ochs, *Another Reformation*, 11.

62 Ochs, *Another Reformation*, 5.

63 Ochs, *Another Reformation*, 12.

64 Ochs, *Another Reformation*, 13.

65 Ochs, *Another Reformation*, 15.

66 Ochs, *Another Reformation*, 14.

67 Ochs, *Another Reformation*, 4, 17.

68 Ochs, *Another Reformation*, 17.

69 Ochs, *Another Reformation*, 2.

70 Robert W. Jenson, "Toward a Christian Theology of Judaism," in *Jews and Christians: People of God*, ed. Carl E. Braaten and Robert W. Jenson (Grand Rapids, MI: Eerdmans, 2003), 3.

71 Baum, *Christian Theology after Auschwitz*, 9.

Recommended Reading

Baum, Gregory. *Christian Theology after Auschwitz*. London: The Council of Christians and Jews, 1976.

Bader-Saye, Scott. *Church and Israel after Christendom: The Politics of Election*. Eugene, OR: Wipf and Stock, 2005.

Braaten, Carl E., and Robert W. Jenson, eds. *Jews and Christians: People of God*. Grand Rapids, MI: Eerdmans, 2003.

Ochs, Peter. *Another Reformation: Postliberal Christianity and the Jews*. Grand Rapids, MI: Baker Academic, 2019.

Ruether, Rosemary Radford. "Anti-Semitism in Christian Theology." *Theology Today* 30, no. 4 (1974): 365–81.

———. *Faith and Fratricide: The Theological Roots of Anti-Semitism*. Eugene, OR: Wipf and Stock, 1997.

Sonderegger, Katherine. *That Jesus Christ Was Born a Jew: Karl Barth's Doctrine of Israel*. University Park, PA: Pennsylvania State University Press, 1992.

Soulen, Kendall. *The God of Israel and Christian Theology*. Minneapolis, MN: Fortress Press, 1996.

Ticciati, Susannah. "The Future of Biblical Israel: How Should Christians Read Romans 9–11 Today." *Biblical Interpretation* 25, no. 4–5 (2017): 497–518.

Islam

Joshua Ralston

Introduction

The theological challenges that the Islamic tradition presents to Christianity cut to the heart of a number of the most prominent questions in Christian theology. Muslims inquire how confession of the One God is not contradicted by the Christian worship of a triune God. For Muslims, God's unity and uniqueness (*tawhid*) is the preeminent theological claim and the Christian idea about God being one in nature and three in person/hypostasis is viewed as a compromise of God's unity. The Islamic tradition extols Jesus as a prophet sent by God, and even as a word from God (*kallimatullah*), but the Qur'an reports Jesus asking Christians to "not exceed their religion" and to not worship him but God alone (Qur'an, 4:171). The Islamic view of Muhammad as a prophet and messenger that is sent by God as a mercy to the world and to call humanity back to God, in part by correcting errors in Christian and Jewish theology and practice, challenges Christian claims about the culmination of revelation in Jesus Christ. The Qur'an depicts itself in continuity with biblical revelation, narrating God's dealings with Abraham, Noah, David, Mary, and others; and yet, its depictions of these stories diverge in important ways from Christian understandings. Muslims also recognize the Islamic religion or *dīn* as a holistic way of life that integrates faith and works, prayer and politics, this world and the next, theology and law, and external ritual and the internal heart.

An astute student of Christian theology will recognize that these questions echo many of the recurring preoccupations of modern Christian thought. Modern theology has included (1) a revival of Trinitarian thought since Barth and Rahner, (2) important debates on Christology carried out in light of historical critiques of the Gospels' depictions of Jesus and contestation over the legacy of the Council of Chalcedon, (3) debates on natural theology and nature and grace that have import for understandings of revelation and religions, (4) arguments about supersessionism and Christianity's relationship with Judaism, and (5) the emergence of liberation, feminist, and womanist theologies that critique dominant forms of Christian theology's approaches to power. Put differently, although the critiques of Muslim thinkers to Christian theology are particular to the Islamic tradition and Christian–Muslim dialogue, the broader concerns are relevant to all Christian theologians. Christian engagement with Islamic thought can be a journey into the core of Christian theology.

Ford's The Modern Theologians: An Introduction to Christian Theology since 1918, Fourth Edition.
Edited by Rachel Muers and Ashley Cocksworth.
© 2024 John Wiley & Sons Ltd. Published 2024 by John Wiley & Sons Ltd.

Viewing the Islamic tradition and Muslim thinkers as significant and serious interlocutors in the work of Christian theological reflection is not, however, the historically dominant approach to the religion in either the Latin West or the Greek East.[1] Until the last few decades, Christian theology has largely engaged with Islam as a political threat, a corrupted version of biblical religion, an object of missionary concern, or a trope for intra-Christian controversy. Although these tendencies are still present, the twentieth and twenty-first centuries have been marked by significant social and political changes that have challenged Christian churches and theologians to reassess their relationship with Muslims and Islam. The end of both the Ottoman Empire and European colonialism, rising migration and globalization in a technological age that increases interreligious and cross-cultural encounter, and 9/11 and the so-called war on terror have all contributed to an urgent demand for Christian theologians and churches to engage in more in-depth ways with Muslims. These Christian approaches to Islam have varied widely, from those theologians who seek to find commonality and common ground between Christians and Muslims to those theologians who emphasize the fundamental differences between the two traditions, be this in irenic or more competitive ways.

Survey

Second Vatican Council: A turning point in Christian views of Islam

The Second Vatican Council (1962–5) proved a watershed moment in Christian approaches to Islam as a religion and Muslims as people. It names many of the most fundamental issues in Christian–Muslim debate, such as the unity of God, worship, Abraham, social justice, Mary, and most of all the divinity of Jesus. However, Muslims have also pointed out how it fails to engage with many vital aspects of the Islamic tradition like the Qur'an, the prophet Muhammad, and *sharī'a*. As such, it serves as a useful fulcrum to examine Christian theological views, both before and after the council, as well as many of the issues that have dominated Christian approaches to Islam in the twentieth and twenty-first century.

Paragraph 3 of *Nostra Aetate* begins by depicting the resonances between Catholic and Muslim views on God, creation, Abraham, the final judgment, and piety. The text celebrates how Muslims revere God and honor Abraham, particularly how Muslims and Christians both share and diverge in our views of Jesus and Mary. The council writes of how Muslims "do not acknowledge Jesus as God" but do "revere Him as a prophet. They also honour Mary, his virgin Mother."[2] In *Lumen Gentium,* the council even appears to affirm a place for Muslims in the economy of salvation. "But the plan of salvation also includes those who acknowledge the Creator. In the first place amongst these there are the Muslims, who, professing to hold the faith of Abraham, along with us adore the one and merciful God, who on the last day will judge mankind."[3] While these two texts offer a nuanced account of a shared scriptural legacy and common theological concerns on the one hand, and also name important differences, *Nostra Aetate*'s discussion of Islam ends by suggesting a shift away from theology to social and political themes. It concludes by recognizing how Christians and Muslims have had "quarrels and hostilities" over the centuries but asks "us all to forget the past and to work for mutual understanding" by promoting "social justice and moral welfare, as well as peace and freedom." These two short and dense chapters present us with a helpful framework for surveying the most pressing questions and contested approaches to Islam in the last century.

Islam in the economy of salvation

Islam claims a biblical heritage in Abraham, Moses, Mary, and Jesus, but understands itself as correcting Christian errors. Many of the earliest Christian discussions of Islam wrestle with how to make sense of the rise of Islam within Christian understandings of history and God's economy of salvation. For instance,

Pseudo-Ephrem the Syrian deployed apocalyptic imagery to depict the rise of Islam; John Bar Penkaye, an East Syrian, interpreted Islamic armies conquering Jerusalem, Damascus, and Alexandria as an instrument of divine judgment; and John of Damascus listed Islam as a Christian heresy.[4] Christian theologians and missionaries have continued for centuries to wrestle with the challenge of a new religious tradition that claims continuity with the God of creation and Abraham and yet offers stringent critiques of Christian theology and practice.

Christian theology in the twentieth and twenty-first centuries has continually debated how to understand a claim to divine revelation after Christ, including substantial reflection on the Qur'an and the prophet Muhammad. The dominant approach, as evident in Protestant missionaries and scholars like Hendrik Kraemer (1888–1965) and Samuel Zwemer (1867–1952) is to view the prophet and Islam as either a corruption of Christianity or a dim reflection of natural knowledge of God. Islamic monotheism may be affirmed, but there is no divine origin in Islam. The most fundamental evidence for this, and the dividing line between Christians and Muslims, is found in the life, death, and resurrection of Jesus. No matter what unity might be seen between the two traditions, the Christian commitment to God's presence in the manger and salvation through the cross means that Islam cannot be understood as part of the divine economy.

By contrast, theologians and Christian scholars of Islam such as Louis Massignon (1883–1962) and Montgomery Watt (1909–2006) sought to offer a positive account for Islam within religious history by affirming the prophet's experience of God. This did not amount to a full affirmation of Islam or a turn to pluralism like in later thinkers like Wilfred Cantwell Smith (1916–2000) or Hans Küng (1928–2021), but a more moderating position. In the past decades, there has been an increased focus on thinking about the prophethood of Muhammad and the nature of the Qur'an on their own terms, especially through reflection on how Christians might affirm the prophet without denying core Christian theological commitments. This work extends some of the insights of the Second Vatican Council, but moves them in new directions through liberation theology or comparative theology.

Islam as Abrahamic religion

One of the key frameworks for considering Islam within Christian theology is through the person of Abraham. Islam claims biblical lineage through Abraham, but in particular through Hagar and Ishmael. In the Islamic tradition, Abraham remains present with Ishmael and Hagar traveling back and forth between his family in Hebron and his family that settles in the Arabian desert. According to Islamic tradition, the Kab'a in Mecca was built by Abraham and Ishmael. Given Islamic understandings, as well as the biblical promise to Hagar and Ishmael in Genesis 17, it is no surprise to see the many Christian approaches to Islam center on Abraham.

Abraham is often mentioned by theologians like Massignon and Youakim Moubarac, as well as in church statements on Islam, or in popular forms of Christian–Muslim dialogue including feminist reading groups like the Daughters of Abraham. Two dominant approaches to Abraham are apparent, one the seeks rapprochement through a broad shared commitment to monotheistic faith and the other that positions Abraham as both a figure of unity and division. The later position, especially as it is explicated by Moubarac, interprets Christianity and Islam as joined by Abraham but also divided, like Isaac and Sara are with Ishmael and Hagar.[5] As we will see later in the chapter, this Abrahamic reading of history aims to balance the commonality named in the Second Vatican Council and the rivalries and divisions that emerge between Christians and Muslims.

Abraham is called by the One God, creator and sustainer of the universe, the One who has sent revelation through the law and prophets. On this, Christians and Muslims agree. Christians and Muslims diverge, however, on God's relationship to Jesus and what Jesus and the Holy Spirit entail for theologies of God's (tri)unity. Does the Christian confession of the Trinity and Christ's divine identity mean that other shared philosophical, theological, and scriptural depictions of God between Muslims and Christians are only superficial? Theologies of Abraham, then, are also theologies that engage with the God that he followed and the legacies of interpretation of God in the history of Christianity and Islam.

Spirituality and worship

Part of the appeal of Abraham is the concept of faith in the one God before the revelations at Sinai, in Christ, or in the Qur'an. Abraham appears to experience a form of worship, piety, and reverence that is in some ways pre-Christian or pre-Islamic. Of course, later traditions interpret Abraham through Christian ideas, especially in light of the Apostle Paul's writings, or Islamic categories of prophethood, but some argue that this does not negate the shared experience of worship.

Islamic spirituality, especially through prayer, ritual, and Sufi practices, has been a source of fascination for many Christian theological engagements with Islam. A number of the theologians examined in this chapter, such as Massignon, Cragg, Burrell, and Stosch, were drawn to the study of Islam in part because of their encounter with the depths of Islamic spirituality. Even critics of Islam like Zwemer find Islamic ritual and prayer admirable. Moreover, spirituality and Sufi apophaticism appear to offer a way to move beyond the theological recriminations over the doctrine of God previously mentioned. If God is the transcendent one, source of all that is, may worship of God and appreciation of spirituality provide an alternative grounding for Christian reflection on Islam than dogmatic theology? Still, as Gavin D'Costa has pointed out, Christian prayer is infused with the Trinity and Christology and thus appeals to prayer and spirituality are not as simple a solution to theological divisions as they might appear.[6]

Ethics and social justice

In addition to appeals to mystery and prayer, *Nostrae Aetate*'s call for shared social action and care for humanity remains one of the most recurrent arguments for how Christians and Muslims can overcome their theological and scriptural differences about God. The most well-known advocate of this position is the Catholic theologian, Hans Küng, who has argued for religions to seek out a shared global ethic. In a more theologically measured fashion, Miroslav Volf has argued that commitment to the One God can issue in political shared communities of Christians and Muslims. The global challenges of climate change, economic injustice, migration, and failed political leadership, then, are all areas where Christian and Muslims might engage more deeply together.[7]

Ethics and social justice, however, also areas of disagreement. Pope Benedict XVI, Lamin Sanneh, and John Milbank have all astutely noted how Christians and Muslims differ on understandings of law, politics, and power, in part because of diverging theologies of revelation. George Khodr and Kenneth Cragg forcefully critiqued the rise of political Islam as twisting the ethical and spiritual core of the religion, while also tracing back many of these problems to events in the early history of Islam. Appeals to social justice, then, return us to questions of theology, scripture, and history. It seems that we cannot simply forget the past, we must find theological ways to address and heal it.

Named Theologians

Louis Massignon and Kenneth Cragg: Western Christians transformed by living in the Middle East

Until recently, the vast majority of Western Christians had very little knowledge of Islam and minimal concrete encounters with Muslims. This led to a tendency in Christian theology to present Islam in broad brush strokes, dependent on secondhand knowledge or common tropes of a false religion, a violent prophet, and a corrupted book. Encounter is the one of the best antidotes to stereotypes. Two of the most influential theologians of Islam in the twentieth century, the French Catholic Louis Massignon and the English Anglican Kenneth Cragg (1913–2012), were transformed in part by their experiences of living, working, and ministering in the Arab speaking world, both with Muslims and Christians.

The Second Vatican Council's statements on Islam and Muslims would not have been possible without the life and scholarship of Louis Massignon. His work pressed preconciliar Roman Catholic theology to engage in a more nuanced and sympathetic way with the Islamic tradition, seeking spiritual solidarity and community together. After a childhood in France, Massignon's visits to French colonies in Algeria sparked an interest in Islamic Studies. Initially his interest in Islam was primarily academic with no concern for Christian–Muslim dialogue or theology, especially since he had renounced his own Catholic faith in his teenage years. During a visit to Iraq in his mid-twenties, Massignon had a profound spiritual experience that changed the course of his life. He suffered a serious illness and was cared for by a Muslim family, during which he had an overwhelming experience of encountering Christ in the form of a stranger. The combination of Muslim hospitality and spiritual encounter with God would come to shape his theological approach to Islam and Muslims.

Massignon's most important contribution to Christian theological engagement with Islam is found in his study of Sufism, especially his four-volume work on Mansur al-Hallaj. Al-Hallaj was a controversial early Persian Sufi, known for his teachings on cultivating awareness of God's presence in all things, commentaries on God's names and the inner meaning of rituals. Al-Hallaj was executed for blasphemy for reportedly saying, "Ana al-Haqq," or I am the truth. Massignon viewed al-Hallaj's teachings on God and his death as echoing the gospel and Christ's death.

Much of Massignon's work grapples with how to account for God's presence with Muslims on the one hand and with the limitations of Islamic traditions on the other. For Massignon, Islam struggled between its inner spiritual core that was a gift from God and its outer limitations as an apologetic, political, and legal tradition – the very same forces that killed al-Hallaj. Massignon fosters a deeper appreciation of Islam as a mystical tradition, both for Muslims and Christians. Daniel Brown notes, "Massignon's positive vision of Islam, and his engagement with it as a Christian, was almost exclusively through the lens of Sufism."[8]

Massignon describes Islam as an "Abrahamic Schism." Viewing Islam as schismatic and not heretical provided scriptural recognition of a shared lineage but also important theological and historical divergences. Muslims remain part of God's covenant with Abraham but are separated from Christianity through accidents of history and theological disagreements. These differences do not override the central power of God's transcendent unity or the spiritual power and presence of God with Muslims. Thus, unlike heresy that needs to be condemned, schism demands engagement, hospitality, and the quest to understand.

Within this lens, Massignon sought to interpret Islam and the Qur'an as part of God's economy. Massignon provocatively claims that the Qur'an "can be considered as a truncated Arabic edition of the Bible" that serves a divine role to "catch up the descendants of Ishmael" with God's work in the world.[9] The Qur'an comes from the same wellspring as the Bible and aims to include Muslims into the divine economy. Still. Islam is not Christianity and cannot be equated with the fullness of the Triune God in Christ and Spirit, the church, and sacraments. He thus describes Islam as on the theological way toward God, even if it is not the fullness of theology as found in the Christian gospel. Admirably, he sought a way to affirm Islam as more than just an expression of natural theology or religiosity, wanting to recognize Muslims' own self-understanding as being grounded in an event of divine revelation.

These theological claims emerged in part due to Massignon's abiding commitment to creating spiritual community alongside Muslims in way that honored spirituality but emphasized the primacy of Christ. The core of the church is not the institution but a communion of saints, which may include those beyond the bounds of the visible church. To express this commitment, Massignon and the Egyptian Christian Mary Khalil founded a society of prayer and spiritual exploration, the Badaliya, which aimed to nurture a Christian presence alongside and for Muslims. Badaliya means substitute or substitution in Arabic and is meant to express Massignon's and Khalil's vision of Christians offering prayer and spiritual practices for the sake of others. Like Christ, and al-Hallaj in Massignon's reading, Christians are meant to give their lives over to God for the sake of Christ and others. Badaliya enacted this spiritual vision through hospitality, presence, and prayer in the Arab world. The aim was not conversion to the church, but toward Christ, and to assist Muslims to experience how Christ was already present with them.

Kenneth Cragg spent the majority of his life working between his native England and his ministry in Lebanon, Jerusalem, and Egypt. As an Anglican with evangelical leanings, Cragg initially traveled to the Middle East as a missionary but his experience with Muslims, Christians, and Jews in the region transformed his vocation to focus on understanding and interpreting Islam as a Christian bishop and theologian. He taught and preached across the Middle East and England and wrote prolifically, including influential works like *The Call of the Minaret* (1956), *The Event of the Qur'an* (1971), *Muhammad and the Christian: A Question of Response* (1984), and *Jesus and the Muslims: An Exploration* (1985).

Whereas Massignon's work focused primarily on Sufism and Islamic spirituality, Cragg's scholarship engaged with more modern and reformist Muslims and considered questions of the Qur'an and the prophethood of Muhammad. That said, his own shift to Christian theological reflection on Islam was occasioned in large part by the power of Islamic piety expressed in the call of the minaret. He takes the invitation to prayer called out five times a day to be "the epitome of Muslim belief and action" and considers what the call of the minaret demands of Muslims and also of all of humanity.[10] His work, then, attempts not only to understand Islam within a Muslim framework but also to explore the implications of Islamic theology and practice on Christianity.

Cragg's most lasting, and controversial, contribution to Christian reflection on Islam comes in his studies of the Qur'an and the prophethood of Muhammad. Cragg positively affirms Muhammad's religious consciousness and commitment to God, community, and justice during the first 12 years of his prophetic ministry in Mecca. He extols the Qur'anic call to worship the One God and likens Muhammad to a prophet of Israel with his focus on God's glory, judgment, and mercy. Muhammad is persecuted, reviled, and rejected, enduring this due to his abiding faith in God. Possibly learning from Fazlur Rahman's study of the Qur'an, Cragg views the Qur'an as inspired by God but also Muhammad's own words. *Contra* the Muslim view of the Qur'an as God's speech, Cragg writes how there is no doubt that "the voice in the Book is authentically the voice of the prophet."[11]

These provisionally positive depictions of both the prophet and the Qur'an are counterbalanced by Cragg's critique of the political turn of the prophet and Islam. For Cragg, the *Hijra* or flight to Medina in 622 CE was not a necessity that would allow the burgeoning Muslim community to survive, but a turn from prophetic ministry to political leadership. Cragg admits that his critique of Muhammad, and by extension portions of the Medinan revelations of the Qur'an, is informed by his own Christian theology of the cross and suffering. Thus, Cragg laments the military dimensions of Muhammad's life and argues that this is the chief hindrance for a positive Christian account of the prophet. Even with this critique, however, Cragg still sees an overriding divine dimension permeating the Qur'an and the prophet, "a consciousness of God, His claim, His creating, his Sustaining, His ordaining" that justify a "shared theism warranting community across disparity."[12]

Youakim Moubarac and George Khodr: Christian theology in the Middle East

For centuries, Christians have lived, worked, prayed, and theologized in the "shadow of the mosque,"[13] as numeric minorities in Muslim majority contexts. Unfortunately the contributions of these Christian theologians have too often been overlooked by Western scholars engaged in Christian–Muslim dialogue. Christian thinkers writing in Syriac and Arabic in the medieval era such as Theodore Abu Qurrah, Yahya ibn 'Adi, 'Ammar al-Basri, and Bar Hebraeus offer some of the most sophisticated theological engagements with Islamic thought in the history of Christianity. Through translation projects and the work of historical theologians such as David Thomas, Sidney Griffith, Salam Rassi, Sandra Keating, and others, these classical approaches have now increasingly been engaged with as a resource for modern theologians. This long tradition of Christian–Arab theological and political dialogue with Islam continues in the modern period. Two theologians from Lebanon reflect this long tradition of nuanced critical engagement with Islam: the Maronite priest Youakim Moubarac (1924–95) and the Greek Orthodox Metropolitan George Khodr (b. 1923).

Youakim Moubarac was born in northern Lebanon, but moved to Paris to study with Louis Massignon who had a significant impact on his approach to Islam.[14] He wrote a number of studies on the Maronite Church, the history of Islam, the Arab–Israeli conflict, a theological analysis of the prophet Muhammad, and a five-volume study on Christian–Muslim relations.

Moubarac insists that Middle Eastern Christians have a unique vocation and approach to Muslims and Islam. Christians in the region have a unique cultural and spiritual connection with Muslims. Dialogue with Muslims is a central demand of Christian witness in the Middle East, and according to Moubarac involves attending to history, engaging theology, and exploring ways of coexistence. Dialogue's ultimate aim is not itself, but the flourishing of humanity. "Christianity will be more likely to last and develop in the Middle East when the fight there is no longer for Christians against Islam, but instead for humanity – for each human, and the whole human."[15] Christian witness to and with Muslims is not primarily for the sake of proselytization but for the flourishing of abundant life, including spiritual well-being and social harmony.

Like Massignon, Moubarac understood Judaism, Christianity, and Islam as part of a shared and contested Abrahamic heritage. More so than Massignon, however, and indicative of his Arab and Eastern Catholic identity, Moubarac emphasized how the three religions and the figure of Abraham exist first and foremost within the culture and history of the Middle East. For Moubarac, the Abrahamic fraternity of Jews, Christians, and Muslims is a mutually corrective challenge, one that calls Middle Eastern Christians especially to recognize their cultural affinity with Muslims. He affirms that Islam is the fulfilment of God's promise to Ishmael and a sign that God has not abandoned either Hagar or Ishmael. Drawing on Genesis 17, Moubarac interprets Muslims specifically and Arabs more generally as part of God's irrevocable covenant; as such, the Qur'an and Islam can be interpreted as in some sense part of God's revelation and economy of salvation.

Moubarac does not stop with this simple biblical affirmation, but goes on to probe how the Ishmaelite identity of Islam offers a corrective to errors in both Jewish and Christian understandings of Isaac. According to Moubarac's reading of history, which contains traces of anti-Judaism, Islam presents a challenge to the particularistic reading of election in Judaism and the universalizing hegemony of Western Christianity.[16] Islam is a challenge to Jews and Christians, especially to remember their calling to serve God and humanity and not to hoard the promises of God. At the same time, as part of the Abrahamic covenant, Christianity and Judaism also present challenges and reminders to Muslims and Islam to reclaim their spiritual heritage and the inner core of Islamic faith in the one God. For Moubarac, the Abrahamic paradigm is not aimed at negating differences between the three traditions or finding a common core, but as a means to explore theology, history, and spirituality in a dialectic and historically nuanced fashion.

If Islam is in some sense part of God's economy, then it is necessary to understand and engage its central revelation, the Qur'an. Moubarac's approach to the Qur'an is nuanced and focuses primarily on engagement with the Qur'an's content and aesthetic form, not theoretical reflection upon it. Christians in the region, especially as speakers of Arabic, are shaped by the Qur'an in ways they both know and are unaware of. Thus, a Christian reading and engagement with the Qur'an is authorized. On the one hand, he affirms the ways that the Qur'an is part of a broader scriptural milieu and revelation. As such, Christians are encouraged to engage with the Qur'an, both as a text for Christian reflection and as a way to better understand Muslims. At the same time, he recognizes the fundamental variances between the Christian Bible and the Qur'an, as well as how Christians and Muslims will invariably read these texts differently. Moubarac writes, "a Christian reading of the Qur'an is as normal as a Christian reading of the Old Testament ... Inevitably, there will be significant differences between Christians and Jews on the subject of the Old Testament, and between Christians and Muslims on the subject of the Qur'an."[17] Although Moubarac does not fully carry out such a Christian reading, he does draw attention to the important insights that can be found for Christians in Qur'anic Christology, the link between divine unity and social justice, and the theological and spiritual import of the apophatic mystery of God.

George Khodr was born in 1923 in Tripoli in North Lebanon, before studying in Beirut where he originally was focused on law and politics. During the 1940s, Khodr was involved in a number of youth renewal movements aimed at reviving Eastern Orthodoxy in Lebanon and Syria and resisting French colonialism. This experience was part of a shift that led him into theological education work, ordained ministry, and eventually to the role of Greek Orthodox Metropolitan of Mount Lebanon in 1970.

His contributions to Christian theological engagement with Islam are eclectic and occasional, found in sermons, newspaper articles, public lectures, and short essays, and not sustained monographs like his Maronite contemporary, Moubarac. Nonetheless, his role as a bishop coupled with his important roles in the World Council of Churches (WCC) in the 1970s onward, and his willingness to speak out during a tumultuous time in Lebanese and Arab politics, has meant that his theological perspectives have far-reaching import. He also was instrumental in founding the Centre for Christian–Muslim Studies at the University of Balamand in Northern Lebanon, a premier institution for Orthodox studies of Islam and Christian–Muslim relations.

Central to Khodr's engagement with Islam are two key features of his Orthodox theology and spirituality: the work of the Spirit and divine mystery. Khodr's most well-known contribution to theological reflection on Islam is not actually an essay on Islam specifically, but a paper on theologies of religion presented at the central committee meeting of the WCC in 1971 in Addis Ababa. Khodr argues for the importance of Orthodox understandings of the Spirit being sent by the Father as core for interpreting the mystery of the divine economy and overcoming the limitations of Western notions of Christology and mission. For Khodr, the presence of the Spirit in religion is not dependent on confession of Christ, because the Spirit of God is present in the world and even in religions. Drawing on Irenaeus's understanding of the Son and Spirit as two hands of God, alongside biblical concepts of divine hiddenness in Acts 14 and 17, and critiquing the *filioque* clause, Khodr affirms the possibility of God's work in religions apart from confession of Christ or involvement in Christianity. The divine economy or *okionomia* "cannot be reduced to its historical manifestation" because the work of God is a mystery that cannot be contained by theology or structures alone.[18] God's covenants with humanity are all related to Christ, but they are not exhausted by Christianity. Confession of Christ and the mysteries of the church remain important as signs or sacraments of God's presence and mission in the world, but Christians are called to engage with other religions in expectations of the Spirit's presence already at work.

Khodr's commitment to discerning the work of the Spirit in other religions is evident in his ongoing engagement with Muslims and commentary on Christian–Muslim relations. He adopts a stance of critical openness to the Islamic tradition, one that seeks to affirm areas of genuine divine presence while refusing to shy away from Christian critiques of Islam. One recurring aspect of Khodr's commentary on Islam is to draw a distinction between the original revelation of Islam on the one hand and subsequent Islamic theology, law, and politics on the other. For instance, he positively affirms the Qur'an, especially its Mariology and reverence for Christ, going so far as to suggest that the book is a "humble house" that Christ has revealed himself in.[19] The problems of Christian–Muslim relations arise in part because of later traditions, which wrongly critique Christian views of Christology, the Trinity, and ethics to show Islamic superiority. Khodr claims that the Islamic tradition misunderstood the Qur'anic view of Christianity because of later military conflict with Christian empires in Byzantium and Europe.[20] For an Orthodox theologian, deeply committed to the import of early Christian tradition, it is ironic that Khodr draws a sharp distinction in Islam between the original revelation which is affirmed and what he perceives to be the corruption of the

Qur'an in early Islamic tradition. Although this move may allow Khodr to affirm positively the Qur'anic message of Christ, it does lead to an evasion of significant Islamic critiques of Christian theology and a failure to name explicitly how differences in Christology prove to be a fundamental dividing line for much Christian–Muslim dialogue.

Daniel Madigan, SJ and Building Bridges

The Building Bridges Programme has been one of the most sustained sites of theological dialogue in the English-speaking world over the last two decades. The yearly seminar gathers Christian and Muslims scholars from all over the world for a week of in-depth study, lectures, debate, and dialogue. The initiative was started by then Archbishop of Canterbury George Carey in 2002, before being taken over in 2003 by the theologian and new Archbishop, Rowan Williams. The aim is not agreement or superficial commonality, but a quest to engage and understand one another well in order to strengthen the character of disagreement. The model includes a series of keynote public lectures, followed by four days of intense study of a shared theme or topic with Christian texts one day and Muslim texts the other. Meetings have been held in places like United States, Bosnia, Singapore, Qatar, Italy, and Germany with topics explored including prophets, justice, monotheism, the Word of God, and grace.

Since 2012, the seminar has been spearheaded by Daniel Madigan, SJ and David Marshall with significant support from Lucinda Mosher. Although all three have made important contributions to Christian theological engagement with Islam, the work of Madigan exemplifies new trajectories and approaches to Islam by Christian theologians. Trained as a Jesuit priest and scholar of the Qur'an, Madigan's experience of living and working in Pakistan and teaching in Rome pushed his work into more explicitly theological directions. During his tenure teaching at Georgetown, Madigan developed an approach that he dubbed Christian theology responsive to Islam. Madigan's own work in this area centers around examining shared and diverging concepts about the Word of God in Christianity and Islam.

In a series of influential articles on the first chapter of John, Madigan has offered a compelling argument that attending closely to the place of the Word, both in John and the broader theological accounts of God's communication with humanity, allows us to note common patterns of thinking and to "develop a common language to express our disagreements."[21] Madigan argues that Islamic theology, particularly in the Sunni tradition, develops something akin to a Johannine pattern of discussion of God's unity, speech, and a distinction within God. "God's speech is an essential attribute of God, neither identical with God, nor other than God. It is unthinkable that there would have been a time when there was no speech of God, because that would imply that God once had nothing to say for Godself – and a mute God is no god at all. Or it would imply that God had undergone a change from being silent to speaking, and the idea of such a change in God is no more satisfactory."[22] Madigan goes on to discuss how this notion might be developed through a closer reading of John and Jesus as the "body-language of God."

Instead, Madigan argues that even when Christians do not share in Muslim convictions regarding the Qur'an's centrality and finality, their own understanding of Christ's existence as the Word of God and Christian scripture's importance for theology better equips them to follow the reasoning of Islamic arguments that appeal to the Qur'an's status as divine Word. The comparison, then, is not between Jesus and Muhammad or the Bible and the Qur'an, but between the Word of God incarnate as Jesus of Nazareth for Christians and God's Word recited in an Arabic book for Muslims. Madigan's approach does not offer a definitive position on how Christians can theologically understand the Qur'an within the Christian economy of salvation à la Cragg or Moubarac. Instead, Madigan examines questions of God's transcendence and communication in order to engage sympathetically with Islam in modes that respect the internal logics of Christianity and Islam without denying their differences.

Klaus von Stosch: Comparative theology

Sympathetically attending to difference and commonality is a hallmark of the emerging field of comparative theology. Comparative theology is a method of writing Christian theology in and through conversation with non-Christian religions, theologians, and practices. The German Catholic Christian Klaus von Stosch (b. 1970) has been one of the most influential in advancing Christian reflection on Islam through the method of comparative theology. He has established centers for comparative theology in both Paderborn and Bonn, and his work has been translated into English, Arabic, and Farsi. Central to Stosch's work is a desire to interpret and understand Islam both on its own terms, but also within his Catholic theological worldview. This includes a focus on questions of theology, especially on interpreting and understanding the Qur'an as a word of and from God and Muhammad as a prophet. The question for Stosch is whether or not it is possible to affirm the Qur'an without denying central tenets of Catholic teaching on God, Jesus, Mary, and salvation. He lays out his broad theological arguments for affirming the Qur'an and Muhammad in his book *The Challenge of Islam. Christian Approaches*, before concretizing this through two books on Jesus and Mary in the Qur'an[23] According to Stosch, Islam can be received as a divine gift that might strengthen Christian faith and clarify Christian theology.[24]

Drawing on the work of the eminent German Qur'an scholar Angelika Neuwirth and through coauthorship of two books with Muslim colleagues, Stosch lays out an innovative historical, theological, and exegetical reading of Jesus and Mary in the Qur'an. He argues that Qur'anic Christology and Mariology texts must be interpreted in light of late antique Christianity, especially Syriac and Byzantine theology and politics. He claims that the recurrent refrain in the Qur'an that Jesus and Mary must eat (Qur'an 5:75) should be read as critique of Julianism and that Islamic accounts of Christology in later Medinan suras are challenges to Heraclius's imperial theology. From this, he makes the provocative claim that Islamic critiques of Christian theologies are not primarily concerned with high Christology but are focused on recovering Christ's humanity and challenging Byzantine political Christologies of dominance. The Qur'an's challenges to Christian Christology, then, are invitations to recover the humanity and humility of Jesus and to resist Christian political hegemony. Although questions must surely be asked of Stosch's reading and whether or not his appeal to historical readings of the Qur'an evade later Islamic Christologies, his courageous work shows a willingness to not only think about Islam but to engage the Qur'an and Islamic theology as a genuine source of Christian theology.

Debate

Christian debates about Islam often center on the relationship between particularity and universality, commonality and difference. There are certain trajectories of Christian theology that focus primarily on overcoming differences through an emphasis on commonality through appeals to the one God, Abraham, scripture, or shared social action. By contrast, another approach to Islam focuses on the fundamental areas of divergence such as the triunity of God, salvation and Christology, and religion and politics. These governing assumptions about commonality and difference come to shape some of the most significant debates about God, the Qur'an, and Muhammad in Christian theology. They also affect the aim of Christian theological engagement. Is dialogue with Muslims and reflection on Islam oriented toward finding areas of agreement or is engagement focused on exploring differences, either for the sake of mission or improved understanding? Returning to the Second Vatican Council, we can see how this tension remains apparent in its discourse on biblical characters. Is a shared reverence for Mary or appreciation of Abraham's faith a ground for agreement? Or do the interpretations of these figures within the broader framework of Christian and Islamic theologies actually mean that even shared figures are sources of conflict?

For instance, one of the recurring arguments within Christian theological reflection on Islam is whether or not Christians and Muslims worship the same God. Historically, there has been a tendency to answer this question in the negative, with Muslim critiques of the Trinity and Christology being marshaled as evidence. Early twentieth-century Christian missionaries such as Samuel Zwemer, Hendrik Kraemer, and others tended to view the Islamic account of God as a pale imitation of the Christian God or a dim reflection of natural knowledge of God. Karl Barth writes, "It is unthinking to set Islam and Christianity side by side, as if in monotheism at least they have something in common. In reality, nothing separates them so radically as the different way they appear to say the same thing – that there is only one God."[25] By contrast, we have seen how theologians such as Cragg, Massignon, and Burrell point to shared understandings of divine transcendence, creation, and attributes to justify the claim that Muslims and Christians speak of the same God, even if they understand God differently. Miroslav Volf's *Allah: A Christian Response* seeks to articulate a clear theological justification for affirming Christians and Muslims worship the same God, even as he attends to fundamental differences about the Trinity.

While these debates will continue, and often have profound political import, the more prominent current debates about the doctrine of God center around explorations of God's names, attributes, and Word. This approach, exemplified in Madigan, holds in abeyance the question of whether or not Christians and Muslims worship the same God, and instead probes how Christians and Muslims understand, theologize, and speak about the one God. This opens up further possibilities to explore theologies of God that might attend to both similarities as noted by Burrell and Volf and differences as emphasized by Barth and Pope Benedict XVI. Debates about the doctrine of God are vital because they come to shape other recurring theological debates between Christians and Muslims, especially around views of divine revelation in scripture, understandings of prophethood, faith and salvation, Christology, and political theology.

Influence, Achievement, and Agenda

While the twentieth century witnessed growing interest in Islam among Christians theologians, the twenty-first century has seen a proliferation of theological engagements with Islam by Christian thinkers, communities, and churches. Thanks in large part to the trailblazing work of theologians like Louis Massignon, Kenneth Cragg, Youakim Moubarac, and David Burrell, as well as the call for renewed engagement from the Second Vatican Council, Christian engagement with Islam has moved up the agenda of Christian theology. Islam is no longer viewed as a distant curiosity but as a significant challenge that demands coherent Christian reflection and engagement. This is evident in the growing number of church documents focused on the question of Islam, from the WCC, Conferences of Bishops, or even in national protestant churches in Germany.[26] Major Christian theologians that are not experts in Islam such as Miroslav Volf, John Milbank, Rowan Williams, Pope Benedict XVI, James Cone, and Letty Russell have written significant books or essays on Islam. Churches, seminaries, and universities across the globe have invested in courses on Islam and Christian–Muslim relations or centers of study like the Lamin Sanneh Institute in Ghana, The Christian–Muslim Studies Center in Lebanon, the Center for Theology and Social Issues in Germany, and the Christian–Muslim Studies Network in Scotland. Importantly, this engagement with Islam has increasingly shifted from discourse about a distant or stereotyped other to concrete dialogue with and even theologizing alongside Muslim neighbors.

Christian theologians and churches take the theological, scriptural, political, and spiritual challenges that Muslims present to the Christian tradition with increasing seriousness and urgency, especially in terms of the Qur'an. Christians like Pim Valkenburg, Gabriel Said Reynolds, and the al-Kalima Christian community in Lebanon have written commentaries on parts of the Qur'an; Martin Whittingham has studied Muslim views of the Bible and Qur'an; Daniel Madigan and Cornelia Docktor have explored Islamic theological understandings of the Qur'an in comparison to Christ; Klaus von Stosch has rethought the Qur'an in light of Christian late antiquity. Yet there remains much more to be done on the Qur'an's relationship to broader issues in Christian–Muslim dialogues. Four areas stand out as demanding further Christian engagement.

First, hadith (teaching and practices of Muhammad and early Muslims), and sira (biographies of Muhammad). As we have seen, questions about the prophethood of Muhammad are recurring features of Christian reflection on Islam. Although there have been important theological attempts to make sense of Muhammad within a Christian theology of salvation history, especially by Anna Moreland and David Kerr who offer tentative affirmation of the prophethood of Muhammad, these often engage with Muhammad in the abstract.[27] Muhammad is not a living figure but a theological puzzle to be solved. For instance, Moreland's book cites Thomas Aquinas far more than any Islamic sources on the prophet, be they hadith or the major siras. This is a significant lacuna, not simply in Moreland's work, but in Christian theology in general. In his important survey on recent Christian writings on Islam, David Marshall notes how focus on the Qur'an has come at the cost of engagement with the Sunna. "Hadith, in contrast, receive so little attention, despite their great importance in Islam."[28] The life and teachings of the prophet are fundamental to Islamic practice, law, and even theology, shaping how prayers are carried out, the Qur'an is read, and community is formed. Future Christian theological work on the Qur'an and also on the place of the prophet within Christian theologies of religion would be well served to engage with the sunna and hadith.

Second, gender. Christian theological engagement with Islam has largely been the preoccupation of men, with very little attention given to feminist or gender critical perspectives on theology and history. This has begun to change with the work of Anja Middlebeck-Varwick and Anna Moreland, both of whom write on more classical theological issues with only passing references to gender.[29] When questions of patriarchy, gender justice, and the history of female figures in Islam are discussed in most Christian scholarship, this is most often done as a means to critique Islam and valorize Christianity. Muhammad's marriages are demonized or Islamic law is shown to favor men. There is no denying that patriarchy has permeated Islamic history, but the same has been true of Christianity. Christian scholarship on gender and patriarchy is required that explores questions of theology, exegesis, and law in ways that are nuanced and critical of both the Christian and Islamic tradition. This demands attention to the ways that Islamic scholars such as Saba Mahmood, Lila Abu-Lugoud, and others have challenged Western feminist biases about Muslim women. Importantly, some of the most significant Muslim thinkers writing on Christianity and Islam, such as Jerusha Tanner Rhodes, Mona Siddiqui, and Muna Tatari, are women and often include aspects of gender or feminist perspectives in their comparative theologies. Muslim feminists have increasingly offered new readings of the Qur'an that challenge patriarchal histories. Christian theologies of Islam and with Muslims might discover new modes of thinking about God, the Qur'an, and theology in conversation with Muslim scholarship on gender.

Third, political theology and law. Christian theological engagement with Islam and Muslims has always been influenced by power and politics. Muslim battles with Byzantium, Christian Crusades in the Holy Land, Ottoman advances on Europe, European colonialism, and the rise of Political Islam have all influenced Christian views of Islam and Muslims views of Christianity. Even Christian reflections on Muhammad have often been dominated by concerns over the relationship between politics and religion. Kenneth Cragg's negative assessment of the Medinan period of Muhammad's prophetic mission, Pope Benedict XVI's Regensburg address, and George Khodr's critique of Islamic traditional views on political power are all focused on perceived problems in Islamic political theology. These approaches often take an implicitly secular or at least church–state separation bias that upholds the merits of Christianity and the West. Even Hans Küng's call to engage in a shared global ethic between Jews, Christians, and Muslims depends on distinguishing between ethics, which he perceives as good, and law and jurisprudence, which he interprets as problematic legalism. This approach has a tendency to evade engaging with the variety of Islamic political theologies, the long legacies of Islamic jurisprudence, and Islamic critiques of Christian political theology. Christian theology has begun to engage more significantly with Islamic political theology and law; for instance in my work on *sharīʿa* and Felix Körner's on political religion.[30] There remains a vast area of study that remains unexplored, especially on the varieties of Islamic governance in history, the transformations caused by the modern nation state, and the global dynamics of political theology.

Finally, Christian–Muslim theological engagement needs to be set in a global context. Christianity is not European; Islam is not Arab. The center of Christian geographical gravity is no longer the West, but Africa and the global South. Islam remains a dominant force in the Arab world, but the majority of Muslims are not Arab but from South Asia, Southeast Asia, and West Africa. The encounters between Christians and Muslims are between two global religions, not between Europe and the Middle East. Too often, however, the relationship between Christians and Muslims is depicted through the longer legacy of rivalries and wars between the West and the Middle East. As we saw in our discussion of both Moubarac and Khodr, however, Christian theological reflection on Islam is still hindered, even in the Arab world, by assumptions about Christianity being inherently European. Future Christian theological reflection on Islam and with Muslims will increasingly need to take these realities seriously and attend to the unique histories, theologies, and practices of Christians and Muslims across the world and in their specific local. Engagement is never with Islam as a whole but a particular manifestation or form of Islam, be that Sunni or Shiʿa, reformist or Salafi, South Asian Deobandi or West African Tijaniyya.

If Christian theological engagement with Islam is to avoid abstraction, it is necessary to ground dialogue and theological reflection in specific thinkers, traditions, and locals that recognize both the Christian and the Muslims own particularities. Recognizing the global dimensions of both Christianity and Islam requires attention to both universalities and particularities, commonalities and differences. In some ways, the global dimensions of Christianity and Islam return us to one of the recurring challenges of Christian reflections on Islam. How do Christians take seriously the deep commonality and the shared history between Muslims and Christians on the one hand, but attend to the significant theological differences and history of rivalry on the other? This remains the enduring challenge of Christian–Muslim theological engagement.

Notes

1 The churches and theologians living in Muslim majority contexts are an exception to this, as we will see later in the chapter.
2 Vatican II, "*Nostra Aetate*. Declaration on the Relation of the Church to Non-Christian Religions" (28 October 1965), §3.
3 Vatican II, "*Lumen Gentium*. Dogmatic Constitution on the Church" (21 November 1964), §16.
4 Stephen J. Shoemaker, *A Prophet Has Appeared: The Rise of Islam through Christian and Jewish Eyes: A Sourcebook* (Berkeley, CA: University of California Press, 2021), 80–92, 185–201.
5 For more on Moubarac's position, see Mouchir Basile Aoun, *The Arab Christ: Towards an Arab Christian Theology of Conviviality* (London: Gingko Library, 2022), 135–44.
6 Gavin D'Costa, "Interreligious Prayer between Christians and Muslims," *Islam and Christian–Muslim Relations* 24 (2013): 1–14.
7 Miroslav Volf, *Allah: A Christian Response* (San Francisco, CA: Harper Collins, 2011); Hans Küng,

Islam: Past, Present, and Future (Oxford: OneWorld, 2004).
8 Daniel Brown, "Islamic Origins and Christian Theological Engagement," *IslamoChristiana* 48 (2022): 50.
9 Louis Massignon, *Les trois prières d'Abraham* (Paris: Cerf, 1997), 89.
10 Kenneth Cragg, *The Call of the Minaret* (Oxford: OneWorld, 2000), x.
11 Cragg, *The Call of the Minaret*, 88.
12 Kenneth Cragg, *Muhammad and the Christian* (Oxford: OneWorld, 1984), 145.
13 Sidney Griffith, *The Church in the Shadow of the Mosque* (Princeton, NJ: Princeton University Press, 2008).
14 A recent study of Moubarac's work is included in *The Arab Christ*.
15 Youakim Moubarac, *La chambre nuptiale du coeur. Approches spirituelles et questionnements de l'Orient, Syriani, coll. "Libanica"* (Paris: Cariscript, 1993), 98.
16 Youakim Moubarac, *La Pensée Chrétienne et l'Islam* (Beirut: Université libanaise, 1986).

17 Youakim Moubarac, *L'Islam et le dialogue islamo-chrétien* (Beyrouth: Éditions du Cénacle libanais, 1972), 192.

18 George Khodr, "Christianity in a Pluralistic World: The Economy of the Holy Spirit," *Sobornost* 6 (1971): 170.

19 George Khodr, *Thoughts and Opinions on Christian–Muslim Dialogue and Common Life, Vol. II* (Jouneih: Al-Maktaba al-Bulusiyya, 2000), 141 (translated from the Arabic).

20 The power of politics to shape negatively Christian–Muslim encounter is a recurring theme in a number of Khodr's speeches. He laments how Christianity has come to be associated with the West and political power through the Crusades and colonialism, as well as ongoing anti-Muslim discourse in Europe, even as he critiques Islam for failing to disentangle spiritual and earthly rule.

21 Daniel Madigan, SJ., "People of the Word: Reading John with Muslims," *Review and Expositor* 104 (2007): 82.

22 Madigan, "People of the Word," 86.

23 Klaus von Stosch, *Herausforderung Islam. Christliche Annäherungen* (Paderborn: Ferdinand Schöningh, 2019).

24 Stosch, *Herausforderung Islam*, 176.

25 Karl Barth, *Church Dogmatics*, vol. II, part 1 (Edinburgh: T&T Clark, 1957), 449.

26 Douglas Pratt, "The World Council of Churches in Dialogue with Muslims: Retrospect and Prospect," *Islam and Christian–Muslim Relations* 20 (2010): 21–42.

27 Anna Moreland, *Muhammad Reconsidered: A Christian Perspective on Islamic Prophecy* (Notre Dame, IN: University of Notre Dame Press, 2020).

28 David Marshall, "Christian Theological Engagement with Islam," *The Ecumenical Review* 73 (2021): 909.

29 Anja Middlebeck-Varwick, *Cum Aestimatione. Konturen einer christlichen Islamtheologie* (Münster: Aschendorff, 2017).

30 Joshua Ralston, *Law and the Rule of God: A Christian Engagement with Sharīʿa* (Cambridge: Cambridge University Press, 2000) and Felix Körner, *Politische Religion: Theologie der Weltgestaltung – Christentum und Islam* (Freiburg: Herder, 2020).

Recommended Reading

Primary

Cragg, Kenneth. *The Call of the Minaret*. 3rd ed. Oxford: OneWorld, 2000.

Daou, Fadi, and Nayla Tabbara. *Divine Hospitality: A Christian–Muslim Conversation*. Geneva: World Council of Churches, 2017.

Madigan, Daniel. "People of the Word: Reading John with Muslims." *Review and Expositor* 104 (2007): 81–95.

Moreland, Anna. "Analogical Reasoning and Christian Prophecy: The Case of Muhammad." *Modern Theology* 29 (2013): 62–75.

Ralston, Joshua. *Law and the Rule of God: A Christian Engagement with Sharīʿa*. Cambridge: Cambridge University Press, 2020.

Siddiqui, Mona. *Christians, Muslims, and Jesus*. New Haven, CT: Yale University Press, 2012.

Tatari, Muna, and Klaus Von Stosch. *Mary in the Qur'an: Friend of God, Virgin, Mother*. Translated by Peter Lewis. London: Gingko, 2021.

Tieszen, Charles, ed. *Theological Issues in Christian–Muslim Dialogue*. Eugene, OR: Wipf and Stock, 2018.

Secondary

Accad, Martin. *Sacred Misinterpretations: Reaching across the Christian–Muslim Divide*. Grand Rapids, MI: Eerdmans, 2019.

Aoun, Mouchir Basile. *The Arab Christ: Towards an Arab Christian Theology of Conviviality*. Translated by Sarah Patey. London: Gingko, 2022.

Goddard, Hugh. *A History of Christian–Muslim Relations*. 2nd ed. Edinburgh: Edinburgh University Press, 2020.

Krokus, Christian S. *The Theology of Louis Massignon: Islam, Christ, and the Church*. Washington, DC: The Catholic University of America Press, 2017.

Marshall, David. "Christian Theological Engagement with Islam." *The Ecumenical Review* 73 (2021): 892–911.

Renard, John. *Islam and Christianity: Theological Themes in Comparative Perspective*. Berkeley, CA: University of California Press, 2011.

Buddhism

Michael Barnes

Introduction

For centuries contacts between Christians and Buddhists were limited to a handful of references in patristic writings and the reports of travellers and missionaries. The contemporary encounter can be traced back to the early nineteenth century and the post-Enlightenment fascination with Europe's "silent other." First judgments were curtly dismissive; it was only in the middle of the century that the first of the great European buddhologists, Eugene Burnouf, could speak of this "brilliant light" as a "page from the origins of the world."[1] His friend and contemporary, Jules Barthélemy Saint-Hilaire, was less impressed. Buddhist moral teaching he found in many ways quite admirable, but he was blunt in his criticism of "strange and deplorable doctrines" that have contributed "so little to the happiness of mankind."[2] In a few short decades the visionary revelation that so fascinated the Romantics had morphed into something altogether more challenging and problematic. The German philosophical and cultural elite were stimulated by the novelty of what they read. Schopenhauer found a ready support for his pessimistic account of human history as dominated by a sort of blind cosmic will. Under his influence Nietzsche became thoroughly steeped in Buddhist ideas, particularly the notion of transmigration, the counterintuitive concept of *Nirvana* and the *bodhisattva* ideal of heroic human living. And Wagner's last opera, *Parsifal*, structured around motifs taken from the ancient Grail myth, began life as a Buddhist take on love and renunciation and still retains a central hero who is "enlightened through compassion." At the other end of the religious spectrum, Christian evangelicals found Buddhist teaching disturbingly nihilistic. They were also nervous about the figure of the Buddha who emerged as an all too plausible alternative to Jesus himself. In Edwin Arnold's *Light of Asia*, he is portrayed as the exemplar of Victorian values, a gentlemanly ascetic to set against Nietzsche's Indian Übermensch and Wagner's mythic Heldentenor.[3] Such caricatures say more about "the West" than "the East," but arguably they have dominated the dialogue between the two traditions ever since.

In what follows I have retained the terminology of "conceptual," "interior," and "socially engaged" dialogues from the chapter that appeared in the last edition of this book. These distinctions are still helpful in mapping out the enduring questions that can be traced back to the nineteenth century encounter,

Ford's The Modern Theologians: An Introduction to Christian Theology since 1918, Fourth Edition.
Edited by Rachel Muers and Ashley Cocksworth.
© 2024 John Wiley & Sons Ltd. Published 2024 by John Wiley & Sons Ltd.

particularly the concept of Ultimate Reality, the nature of the human person and human transformation, and different approaches to religious language. After giving space to a range of modern theologians, both those whose contributions have acquired a "classic" status and some more recent names, I attend to shifts of perception, both of Buddhism itself and within interreligious dialogue more generally. My main concern, however, is to foreground those areas that have proved most fruitful in promoting what I call interreligious learning.[4] This chapter is thus less a survey than a series of reflections on the experience of "being in dialogue." I argue that what holds Buddhism and Christianity together is their intrinsically "cross-cultural" dynamic. Although there is a normative orthodoxy in both traditions, it is at the level of "orthopraxis" they can be most fruitfully compared. Both follow canonical narratives – the enlightened *bodhisattva* and the crucified and risen Christ respectively – in the name of which they are committed to speaking truth in a pluralist world. Buddhism like Christianity is a "missionary" tradition – not just because the *Buddhadharma* is intended for the welfare of all sentient beings, but because it comes properly alive and transformative only when it is *communicated* or translated into a form that particular individuals and groups – indeed whole cultures – can assimilate and understand.

The Dialogue: Theology and Theologians

It was not until 1965, with the Second Vatican Council's *Nostra Aetate*, that a Christian church ventured an official comment. "The Declaration on the Relationship of the Church to Non-Christian Religions" began life as a brief theological statement about Judaism; as its vision expanded, it incorporated the discourse of the history of religions with its focus on cross-religious themes and existential questions about "the unsolved riddles of human existence."[5] The reference to the Asian religious traditions is decidedly tentative. After a thin description of Hinduism, it says that Buddhism testifies to "the essential inadequacy of this changing world" and proposes a way of life "by which people can, with confidence and trust, attain a state of perfect liberation and reach supreme illumination either through their own efforts or by the aid of divine help."[6] That irenic little summary did not come out of nowhere, of course. For centuries Jesuit missionaries, from Ricci in China and Desideri in Tibet to their many successors in contemporary Japan, such as Hugo Enomiya Lassalle and William Johnston, had been fascinated by the impact Buddhism made on religious culture. When one of the great apostles of the council, Henri de Lubac, was put under a cloud of official disapproval in the early 1950s, there is some irony in the fact that he turned to Buddhism. This great master of Catholic *ressourcement* had developed an interest in the religions of Asia from his earliest teaching days and was fascinated by the Pure Land tradition with its focus on the grace manifested by the compassionate Buddha. By the end of the council the Catholic Church had moved decisively into the interreligious landscape embraced by the World Council of Churches in the wake of the great missionary conferences of the first half of the twentieth century. Whereas many leading theologians from the Protestant tradition, such as Paul Tillich and Jürgen Moltmann, were concerned with both conceptual and existential questions that arose directly from conversations with Buddhists,[7] their Catholic compatriots, notably Karl Rahner and Hans Urs von Balthasar, were exploring broader issues to do with the church's relationship to culture in all its forms.[8] Rahner's thesis of the "anonymous Christian" led to him being referred to by the Japanese philosopher Keiji Nishitani as an "Anonymous Buddhist" – a title that Rahner accepted with a humble graciousness.

What can be loosely summarized as Protestant and Catholic "instincts" – the one focused on the relationship between "The Word" and the multiple religious voices that are sounded beyond the Christian tradition, the other on a sacramental sensibility that seeks to discern the signs of grace manifested in the world more generally – is reflected in the growing subdiscipline of theology of religions. The familiar framework of the threefold paradigm retains a certain pedagogical usefulness but quickly breaks down when confronted with the complexity of the questions Buddhism raises for Christianity. John Ross Carter acknowledges his debt to Wilfred Cantwell Smith's personalist pluralism as well as taking a stand on the "Protestant Principle" that "consistently protests against the practice of holding the penultimate as ultimate, stopping short with the *idea* of God for God, halting prematurely the investigation of the mind and the devotion of the heart."[9] The prolific Pentecostalist theologian Amos Yong is even more difficult to place. There are plenty of touches of pluralism in his inquiry into "the possibility of a Christian theology 'after' Buddhism" and his conviction that the ways of the Spirit and the Middle Way are in some way convergent. But this is a wide-ranging synthesis that opens up a number of comparative categories and includes the Orthodox spirituality of *theosis* as well as notions of the demonic other, whatever resists God's intentions for the world.[10] Even established figures such as John Cobb, Winston King, Raimon Panikkar, Donald Mitchell, and Frederick Streng do not fit easily within anything but the most bland versions of "inclusivism."[11] Others, such as John Keenan, Leo Lefebure, and Lynn de Silva, are less interested in "Christianity-centered" questions than with crafting Christian theology in Buddhist terms.[12] What all hold in common is a close reading of Buddhist texts and traditions and a generous hospitality to what Buddhists and Christians can learn from each other for the sake of the wider world. Thus, Perry Schmidt-Leukel finds in his experience of the dialogue a "hermeneutic maxim" that can be applied more globally to all interreligious relations, while Aloysius Pieris builds his Asian liberation theology out of a profound scholarly as well as pastoral engagement with the Theravada Buddhism of his native Sri Lanka.[13]

For none of them is Buddhism "a problem." If there is a post-Second Vatican Council ecumenical consensus, it is marked by a growing shift away from an account of a Buddhism characterized as atheistic, or even nontheistic, and toward a more open-ended exploration of the theological and cultural "space" between what has been *given* in Christian revelation and what a Buddhist critique of language sees as tantalizingly "beyond." Various forms of identification with the other seek to establish what it seems appropriate to call a theological Middle Way, whether Cobb's "mutual transformation," King's "sympathetic interpenetration," or Panikkar's "mutual fecundation." That is not to deny the truth in a range of familiar divergences, even oppositions. Christians understand God in personal terms, whereas Buddhists regard an impersonal process of coming to be and falling away; for Christians the person possesses unique individuality, whereas Buddhist teaching is dominated by *anatmavada* or the teaching of "no self"; Christian spirituality insists that true liberation comes only through a response to grace, whereas Buddhist practice emphasizes the overcoming of ignorance and desire.[14] Nevertheless, a growing sensitivity to what others say about themselves (perhaps the most important principle of authentic dialogue) sets the parameters for meaningful conversation. The paradox is that, once two very different ways of thinking and religious practice are taken with as much seriousness as possible, the very difference between them opens up a great deal of potential for a fruitful dialogue.

If the relationship with Judaism sets the initial terms for Christianity's encounter with "the other," the comparatively recent Buddhist encounter has emerged as the most significant, and arguably most rewarding, experience of interreligious learning. Debate about the "macro-problem" of Buddhist atheism has given way to a more precise focus on "micro-studies" or readings of texts – whether comparatively or for their own sake as a fund of religious wisdom. The practice of Scriptural Reasoning that began as an extension of forms of Talmudic study to include Jews and Christians, and subsequently Muslims, has now been extended in China to Taoists, Confucianists, and Buddhists.[15] Comparative theology, with its roots in a pedagogy of the interreligious reading of canonical texts, has crossed further boundaries and produced a number of highly sophisticated studies – not least a remarkable collection by Peter Feldmeier.[16] At the same time, more difficult existential questions are being raised by the phenomenon of dual belonging. The best known comes from Paul Knitter with his autobiographical exploration of a hybrid Buddhist–Christian identity.[17] This and a number of possible forms of dual belonging are examined in an edited collection of essays, many of which offer case studies of broadly conceived themes such as creation, salvation, and suffering.[18] The underlying premise is that religions will always be "other" but not so incommensurable that they cannot provoke deeper learning of the "home" tradition. Classic texts encapsulate the wisdom of a people but exercise a certain authority over other readers by provoking the religious imagination. The aim, as Feldmeier insists, is not to construct an interreligious metanarrative but to make possible fresh religious insights into familiar and revered truths.

Shifts of Perception – Learning from Dialogue

Once the move is made from religions as systems to religions as communities of persons, distinctions between the way people think and the way they live in an increasingly pluralist world seem artificial. For some time it has been commonplace in interreligious relations to speak not just of the dialogue of theological exchange or the "dialogue of specialists," but the dialogues of religious experience, common life, and common action.[19] Although these distinctions have proved helpful in moving beyond the textbook stereotypes of "the religions," they are no longer adequate in shaping the dialogical imperative itself. They tend to avoid the crucial issue that affects all interreligious relations, namely how theory and practice, tradition and experience, even old and new, meld – in short: how communities of faith and conviction grow and adapt through contact with each other. This is particularly important where the Buddhist–Christian encounter is concerned. Within the overarching category of what Aloysius Pieris calls *metacosmic* religiosity, Buddhism and Christianity are to be distinguished not in terms of religious "essences" but *idioms* – the "gnostic" and "agapeic" respectively. As ways of life and thinking each has developed sophisticated intellectual structures that are to be understood not as "variations on a theme" but as distinct modes of engagement that depend less on the terms of an inherited tradition than the dynamics of learning from the ever-shifting process of interpersonal encounter.[20]

In Christian terms, of course, dialogue begins with the paradox of the call of one man, Abraham, in whose descendants the promise of "God with us" to the whole of humankind is to be realized. However one understands the relationship between the Jewish people and the church – a question that is beyond the scope of this chapter – it makes sense to distinguish a prior dialogue that is instantiated in God's covenant with the Jewish people and subsequent dialogues in which Christians seek to build further relationships with "other others."[21] Just as that originating relationship with Judaism, in which Christianity is deeply implicated, recognizes in the other a living tradition, so the contemporary encounter with Buddhists is sensitive both to scholarly work that has deepened appreciation of the ancient roots and philosophical integrity of the *Buddhadharma* and to historical encounters that have shifted attention to the social and ethical dimensions of the dialogue. No longer is it possible to speak of a binary distinction between early and later traditions, between Theravada as the only surviving school of the pejoratively titled Hinayana or "small vehicle" and Mahayana, the "great vehicle," with its focus on nonmonastic "popular" practices of devotion, imitation, and cult. The received wisdom is now that different schools grew up together and it therefore seems more appropriate to think in terms of a number of "Buddhisms," in the plural.[22] A third variation has long been identified, designated as Vajrayana, the "diamond vehicle," with its visualization practices and Tantric liturgies of initiation. More recently, a new diffusion of Buddhist teaching, aided by the process of immigration, has built on the post-1960s fad of "oriental mysticism" and given rise to various versions of a fourth "turning of the wheel," including postmodern readings and more globally disseminated versions of "Engaged Buddhism" in which practices aimed at individual transformation meld into the social and political arenas.[23]

A more unlikely development within the discipline of religious studies is "Buddhist theology," which takes the ancient commentarial tradition of monastic training into the modern academy. In borrowing a term from the Christian world, it highlights an important dimension of the Buddhist tradition, its strict avoidance of "unskilful" forms of purely metaphysical speculation.[24] It also suggests that, if there is to be a theological dialogue with Buddhism, it has to focus on more than a comparison of orthodoxies. Although it may make sense to speak of the religious language of theistic traditions like *bhakti* Hinduism and Islam as a sort of "natural theology" pointing to a proper fulfilment in terms of an explicitly Christian faith, such a move cannot work with Buddhism – if only because Buddhist philosophy is highly skeptical about the possibility of inferring ultimate principles or values from the manifold of experience. The intricate dialectics of the Madhyamaka are primarily concerned with spiritual liberation and only secondarily with metaphysical theory about ultimate states. The object of the analysis, a more sophisticated version of the meditative principles of enumeration inscribed in the earlier Abhidharma texts, is to develop that typically Buddhist "skill in means," which recognizes the contradictions of ordinary experience, particularly the belief that there is some ultimate reality "behind" our everyday perceptions. Schmidt-Leukel is surely right to argue that the reference of religious language is not transcendent reality *in itself* but the "various forms and aspects of human *experiences* with transcendence."[25] The Mahayanist ideal of the *Bodhisattva* – popularly understood as "postponing" enlightenment until everyone else has been enlightened – is more exactly emblematic of the virtues necessary to build a "unity of life" that prepares the ground for enlightenment.

Buddhists tend to place an emphasis on normative patterns of experience rather than normative ideals. Arguably for Christians it is the other way round. Both, however, are concerned with the conditions – from the cultural-religious to the social-psychological – which make experience possible in the first place. In turning now to the three forms taken by the dialogue – identified earlier as conceptual, interior, and social – I want to focus on orthopraxis rather than orthodoxy, on ethos rather than logos. The distinction is, of course, difficult to hold with consistency as the one is inevitably created by and fades into the other. This very fluidity, however, is not the least important aspect of a dialogue between two traditions that, for all their differences, foreground practices of attention and listening.

Conceptual Dialogue: Silence and the Language of "Ultimates"

Buddhism may no longer be Europe's "silent other," but neither is it a nonreligious alternative to religious commitment appropriate for life in contemporary "post-everything" Western culture. In the first place, the Buddha was reacting against the religion of the brahmanical sacrifice, its sheer "wordiness," and the desire for hard and fast solutions to the human condition that it embodied. There is, however, something more significant at stake. He was born into the heavily ritualized world of the sixth century BCE, a world dominated by a pantheon of variously named *devas* – "gods" or literally "shining ones." He did not reject them. Indeed they remain as guardians and intercessors, the lords of other worlds who continue to play a part in everyday religious life. When the Buddha gains enlightenment, his instinct is to remain silent; it is only because of the intervention of the *deva* Brahma that he resolves to preach the Dharma out of compassion for the lot of suffering sentient beings. The question is not whether "the gods" exist, but whether they have any sort of *ultimate* significance. To that extent he shared the concern of a number of ascetical movements and philosophical schools, namely the revaluing of ritual. The Vedic sacrifice, an external liturgy of movement toward a high point of intense religiosity, is *interiorized,* to be understood as an inner pilgrimage, a structured journey toward the center of the self. In the classical Upanisads, the "end" or the essence of the Veda, that self or *Atman* is homologized with the single transcendent reality of *Brahman,* the source and object of personal integration. But, whereas the Upanisadic speculative texts think in terms of an objective state of affairs to which humankind is subject, Buddhism is much more reticent. To dare to speak of what is strictly beyond speech is to risk reducing the ultimate to something less than ultimate, a projection of human needs and desires.

It is not, therefore, that the Buddha denies the significance of questions about ultimate truth and value. Rather he attempts to overcome the tendency to reify images or constructs by awakening people to a sense of their own contingency. Consistently the proliferating range of "Buddhisms," from the Theravada dialogues that foreground the three jewels of Buddha, Dharma, and Sangha, to more engaged forms of Buddhist practice, the primary focus is not on the goal itself but on the *way* to the goal. Buddhism is called the "Middle Way" not just because it seeks to avoid extremes of self-indulgence and self-hatred but because it encourages an equanimity with regard to the goal. To attend to life "in the middle" overcomes more metaphysical extremes, whether the "eternalism" of Upanisadic speculation or "annihilationism," forms of materialism and ascetical fatalism. Yet equanimity does not imply the silence of an ignorant indifference (which would shift the focus in the direction of the nihilist end of the spectrum) but a clear-sighted openness or attention to the way things are. The Dharma, what the Buddha taught, is not another version of the search for *moksha*, release or liberation, but a question mark raised over the tendency to overobjectify the source of religious meaning. His well-known image of the raft supports the view that Buddhism is pragmatic; the teaching of the Way is to be adapted to needs and circumstances. The Buddha himself comments: "I have taught the Dharma compared to a raft, for the purpose of crossing over, not for the purpose of holding on."[26] Although it sounds plausible to make the Dharma purely provisional, to be silenced when the goal has been reached, that is to risk missing a more subtle point. The Dharma includes both truths about the human condition, suffering, and impermanence *and* the means to get there, the practices known as the Noble Eightfold Path that structure a way of life. To be abandoned is not teaching as such but any *inadequate understanding* of the teaching. To invoke another familiar Buddhist analogy, the Buddha is like the physician whose first task is to identify the nature of the illness and prescribe the correct remedy. Whatever takes away from the capacity to see things as they really are is to be put to one side in favor of the cultivation of virtue and the purification of consciousness.

What gives continuity and coherence to the Middle Way is an habituated wisdom that echoes through language of all kinds, from liturgical performance to the records of personal experience. Raimon Panikkar points out how silence has a constructive role to play within all ritual, a role that sets it in a dialectical play with "word," the language that in some sense can be said to "command" the traditions that give shape to religious life. Ritual is, of course, based on a response that is expressed in words and actions, but it relies for its effectiveness on the silence that it encourages and to which ultimately it leads. No religion, as Panikkar reminds us, can afford to ignore the religious significance of silence that "not only hushes word, but also, and especially, thought."[27] Compared with Christianity, the Middle Way is not normally thought of as a ritual, but it is impossible to ignore many ritual-like elements, not just the central practice of meditation but the taking of the refuges and precepts. In both, silence opens up a space within which attention to what is seen and heard and felt can be cultivated. Christians and Buddhists take that key insight in different directions. Nevertheless, they share a *reflexive awareness* not only that words reify and therefore condition our perceptions, but that it is impossible to step outside the "webs" of language. To put it in Buddhist terms, Silence and Word are always "dependently co-arisen"; they depend on and enfold each other.[28] Christianity is nothing if not a tradition in which revealed words and images always maintain a privileged status. But that is not to reduce Buddhism's role in the dialogue to that of apophatic critic to Christianity's kataphatic ethos. The Buddhist account of the person as essentially *anatman* – lacking a substantive sense of self – is nothing if not a reminder that Christianity too is based on a sense of personhood that is only ever found by being lost. In both traditions the fundamental "problem" of the human condition is the fragility, if not transience, of our experience of things. The paradox is that in understanding that truth correctly lies the solution. For the Christian it means the embrace of suffering, loss, and death in hope of resurrection "in Christ." For a Buddhist it demands an "awakening," what Stephen Batchelor calls "the opening up of a way of being-in-this-world that is no longer determined by one's greed, hatred, fear, and selfishness."[29]

Within an attentive silence can be heard resonances of sameness-in-difference. If Buddhism, especially in its more critical Theravada and Zen forms, always privileges silence over words, Christianity, with its roots in the call of a people, insists that silence is never enough. Rowan Williams, in a discussion of the postmodern fixation with "absence," points to the difference between Buddhism and Christianity. The latter, he says, refuses Buddhist reticence by giving what he calls a "pivotal place" to the "language of *gratitude*." "The absent other in language is there-and-not-there because we are always already spoken *to*."[30] Christian theology always begins as response to an encounter with the unremitting otherness of God who yet speaks a Word. Where Buddhism exercises a judicious caution about the language of ultimacy, Christianity dares to name the source of the meaning of things. As David Tracy puts it, where the mystic gives voice to an experience of personal interiority, the prophet speaks a word that is not his or her own.[31] No such Eternal Word is voiced in Buddhism; the Buddhadharma is never given that level of significance. On the other hand, it does not follow that Buddhism has no place for contemplative attention, devotion, and wonder before the *sheer givenness of things*. Before learning how to speak a different language, one has to *listen* to the way that language is spoken. The prophetic "here I am" is not that far removed from the "act of faith" that the searcher after truth places in an enlightened teacher.[32] If the former is rooted in the leading of the Spirit who teaches Christians to pray "Abba Father" – a conscious address to God after the manner of Jesus – the latter reflects virtues of *Prajña* and *Karuna*, wisdom and compassion, which cultivate an enlightened sensitivity to the suffering of other sentient beings.

Interior Dialogue and the Spiritual Imagination

To foreground the paradox of a silence that is given form by words makes the point that a conceptual dialogue between Buddhism and Christianity is not circumscribed by an unwavering binary of atheism and theism but depends on a more existential choice that is inseparable from the language that has formed different religious worlds. If Christianity cannot be understood without reference to the world of Second Temple Judaism, then Buddhism needs to be related to the ancient Brahmanical tradition where it has its roots. Religious languages are always historically and socially instantiated. This is not to reject the quest for cross-cultural themes but a plea to recognize their provisionality – the need for a critique of how religious language is *used*. In all interreligious encounter, conceptual issues that are nonnegotiable dimensions of the "home" tradition exist in tension with questions that arise in the course of engagement with the other. This is the great strength of John Cobb's *Beyond Dialogue,* a brilliantly lucid survey of Western interpretations of Nirvana and a persuasive account of contemporary interreligious practice. What Cobb advocates is a practice of "passing over" into another religious world that will lead to a transformation of both traditions. Carefully avoided is any tendency to reduce one tradition to another. On the contrary, he commends an openness to a wisdom that intensifies the inner experience of both Christian and Buddhist. For Cobb even the Zen tradition, where he feels most at home, is part of a broader religious discourse that takes its rise from a radical opposition to Brahmanical thought. Nirvana is not a metaphysical "ground of Being" that is to be identified with an inner eternal principle or *Atman*. With its connotations of the "blowing out" of the *causes* of rebirth – ignorance, hatred, delusion – it is a refusal to speak of ultimate concepts of all kinds. Buddhist meditation, says Cobb, "is not in quest of the ground but of the dissolution of all grounds."[33]

That sounds at first disturbingly nihilistic but, understood in terms of enlightenment as a process (what Christians, following an insight of William Johnston, might term conversion),[34] raises an important distinction between *nothingness* and *emptiness*. This is the theme of Hans Waldenfels' intense engagement with the Madhyamaka dialectics of Nagarjuna and the Zen-based philosophy of Keiji Nishitani. Published in German nearly half a century ago with the forbidding title of *Absolutes Nichts,* the book is much more than an analytic exercise in conceptual dialogue.[35] Waldenfels shares with various members of the Kyoto school, especially Masao Abe, a concern for the place of religious thought in a world dominated by "scientism" and various forms of reductionist materialism. Applauding Abe's concept of "dynamic *Śunyata*" or emptiness, a more positive correlate to the early Buddhist teaching of "no self," in terms of the interpenetration of all things, Waldenfels himself works within the framework of the famous Zen "ox-herding pictures." The search for enlightenment begins with glimpses of the truth of things that can be understood only in negative terms, "naught, nothing, simple and unqualified nothingness," but leads to "emptiness in the positive sense as radical openness; air, sky, heavens, space, void." The distinction is hardly consistent – if only because the Zen "Great Doubt" hangs over everything that is said – but the interior dialogue that goes on between denial and assertion brings with it a clarity of vision and compassion for all sentient beings. Waldenfels acknowledges a "spectrum of meanings" between the nothingness of sheer ignorance to "what is *unspeakable* and *unknowable*," that which challenges the power to understand and which asks for an attitude of vulnerability and utter selflessness. The spectrum thus reaches from "the despair of nothingness to that emptiness in which man, having come to the end of the ox path, steps into the marketplace with open hands."[36]

As Feldmeier has shown, Christian mystical writers such as Meister Eckhart and Ignatius of Loyola, and Buddhist compatriots like Buddhaghosa and Śantideva, continue to exercise a significant influence on conceptual issues that arise from the contemplative experience not just of facing the unspeakable but daring to shift attention from the interior realm to exterior relations. These themes shape a fascinating project by two Catholic mystical theologians to interrogate the fourteenth-century Flemish mystic, Jan van Ruusbroec.[37] The conviction of Paul Mommaers and Jan van Bragt is that a writer who so much influenced European mystical literature could do the same for the growing dialogue with Buddhism. Van Bragt begins with a question he refers to as a *koan* he has carried around while living in Japan for many years. "How can such a natural affinity in religiosity result in such an incurable disjunction in doctrine?"[38] Mommaers, rather more guardedly, confesses in an afterword to have moved beyond his initial scepticism that Buddhism "would finally land itself in the sort of quietism and social apathy that the best tradition of Christian mysticism has always railed against."[39] What is at stake in their study is not a dialectic of theory and practice but a phenomenology of mystical experience that is bound up with, but not determined by, the language of tradition. They explore the paradox that can be understood in Christian terms as an experience of God without the mediation of divine grace, in Buddhism as the enlightenment that is anchored in the ordinary everyday experience of life in *samsara*. That Christians and Buddhists speak of that paradox in different ways – Johnston's enlightenment/conversion homology – does not detract from a profound affinity, that element of critical attention to whatever is given to consciousness. Mystical texts are not concerned to give an account, let alone analysis, of discrete paranormal experience but to narrate what Mommaers calls a "particular kind of awareness" that arises from the immediacy of the given moment.[40]

How to narrate the particular "shape" of an awareness that arises from the dialogue with Buddhism? Tracy's mystic–prophet distinction reminds us that practices of Buddhist mindfulness not only generate an intense sensitivity to the way things appear in human consciousness; they also challenge the Christian prophetic imagination to see the external world differently and to act more generously. If there is one voice in the dialogue who fits that description it is Thomas Merton. On the day he died in a tragic accident, in Bangkok on 10 December 1968, Merton had delivered a lecture on the unlikely topic of "Marxism and Monastic Perspectives," finishing with the conviction that in openness to the great religions of Asia "we stand a wonderful chance of learning more about the potentiality of our own traditions, because they have gone, from the natural point of view, so much deeper into this than we have."[41] For years the dialogue with Buddhism had been a constant preoccupation for Merton, conducted largely through correspondence, not least with the great Zen teacher, D. T. Suzuki.[42] Despite his growing conviction that in its fundamental psychological honesty, Zen is "inseparable from the interior poverty and sincerity Christ asks for,"[43] he had never felt the need to make Buddhist practice part of his contemplative practice. Yet on that first and last journey to Asia, a new sense of the significance of a disarming sameness-in-difference begins to emerge. When contemplating the great Buddha statues in Polonnaruwa in the north of Śri Lanka, he is knocked off his guard by an unexpected aesthetic experience, a "holy vision" that has an integrity all of its own – and demands a response. His description of what he sensed there has become something of a "classic" in its own right. It stands witness to Merton's conviction, shared by many Christian contemplatives who have entered deeply into the Buddhist meditative experience, that in being grasped by the Word, a more vital and chastened speech about God becomes possible.

Engaged Dialogue: Fidelity and Responsibility

In much of the commentary on the interior dialogue it is impossible to miss resonances of Karl Rahner's often quoted remark that Christians of the future will be mystics or they will not exist at all. Unlike Merton, of course, Rahner was not thinking about Christian dialogue with Buddhism. Rather, as an experienced pastoral theologian, he was asking how the experiential mediates between the conceptual and the ethical. In *Absolute Nothingness* Waldenfels refers to a typically dense essay of Rahner's called "Christian Humanism," which warns against concepts of the human person that are not sufficiently sensitive to the risk of being "swept away into the intractable, nameless mystery of God."[44] Buddhists and Christians speak out of religious languages that are rooted in very different perceptions of the relationship between finite and infinite, but both are committed to avoiding a reduction of the one to the other. Put more positively, both share a fundamental concern for the multiple ways in which the search for inner wholeness and harmony underpins practices of virtuous relations within wider community. In turning to engaged dialogue, therefore, the appropriate question to ask is not how Buddhist and Christian ethical and social practices differ (not surprisingly, perhaps, they reflect very similar values and ideals about what makes for human flourishing) or even how such practices are justified philosophically, but how the *ethos that generates practices* grows out of and reflects those values.

Buddhism is usually understood as a meditative practice, with its origins set firmly within the Indian "renouncer" movement. And there is no doubt that a Buddhism without mindfulness would lose one of its essential dimensions – just as the current fad for secularized versions of mindfulness, for all that it is extraordinarily effective within institutional settings from prisons to board rooms, risks missing out on the deeper dynamics of Buddhist wisdom.[45] The growing academic interest in the relationship between normative doctrine and ethics has nuanced that perspective.[46] A "virtue ethics" approach to the dialogue between Christians and Buddhists takes the emphasis away from purely philosophical considerations and toward the dispositions that sustain human beings in their pursuit of the good. This focus on the ethos generated by foundational narratives does not make for moral relativism or incommensurability; it simply reminds us that ethics and religion are related as practice to the source of motivation. Religion is not an alternative to ethics; nor does it provide a list of sanctions, still less a series of moral imperatives. It is, rather, a source of that energizing power, vested in symbols, stories, and traditional imagery, which sustains a community of faith, enabling it to respond creatively to the dilemmas and exigencies of everyday practical existence. Christianity sustains one such vision of "the good life" by building up the ethos of a life lived after the manner of Christ; Buddhism is the record of a different way, one that traces its provenance back to another story – the Buddha's enlightenment and preaching of the Dharma. The dialogue between the two is made all the richer for being conducted at the level of both orthodoxy and orthopraxis.

The nineteenth-century fascination with legendary archetypes has long given way to closer comparison of the historical figures of Gotama the Buddha and Jesus the Christ. Two immensely popular Buddhist works have given the dialogue a distinctly devotional tinge.[47] At the more scholarly level, a growing interest in the power of narrative and rhetoric is taking both Christian and Buddhist commentators back to the originating stories.[48] Stephen Batchelor, for instance, seeking to retrieve the exemplary status of the Buddha tells us that he is "searching for a gospel-like narrative that can weave the threads of teaching together with those of the life."[49] In recalling the perennial interest in the "historical Jesus" for Christian faith and living, Batchelor is drawing attention to the complexity of the question of how an originating experience or insight about the deep meaning of things, the object of human desire and hope, continues to inspire contemporary religious practice. Such a move complements enduring examples of an intradoctrinal dialogue between Christology and Buddhology, not least Keenan's account of Christ the Wisdom of God as inherently "self-emptying" and Buddhist readings of the Philippians hymn by the likes of Abe and Nishitani.[50] Although the Buddhist silence always seeks to critique and deconstruct the pretensions of language, it never fades into a cynical nihilism. On the contrary, it opens up a different level of engagement where, to repeat Panikkar's point, silence and word are mutually enfolding. This does not take away from but rather reinforces a deep conviction – the theme of Rahner's dense argument about a humanity formed in relation to Holy Mystery – that foundational narratives and founding figures are always organically connected. Thus for a Christian, the Word is not just revealed through words but through the images crafted by narrative and all manner of interpersonal relations. After delving into abstract questions about the limits of what can and cannot be said about anything (let alone nothing or "no-thing") Waldenfels finishes his book by commending a "leap" that Christians and Buddhists are called to take together. Enlightenment and love are not so much correlates as mutually enforcing forms of virtuous living which face each other through the contrasting figures of the smiling Buddha and the tortured Christ. "Enlightenment that radiates love and love that is enlightened and gripping, condition one another."[51]

This Buddhism-inspired insight is reflected in Pieris's plea for Buddhists and Christians to recognize the difference yet complementarity of their respective religious "idioms": Christian "agapeic gnosis" and Buddhist "gnostic agape." Both are modes of an intrareligious dialogue that lead into an extrareligious engagement with the wider world.[52] Where the ethos of Christianity is rooted in Jesus's response to the God who calls for justice and love, Buddhists live out of a tradition formed by the Buddha's practice of virtues of wisdom and compassion that arise from a growing sensitivity to suffering in all its forms. Opinion is divided about whether engaged Buddhism is best understood as a further "turning of the wheel" suitable for the West or as the renewal of the traditional motivations of Buddhist practice.[53] But in many respects it has strong affinities with the liberation and political dimensions of contemporary Christian theology. Western engaged Buddhists like Ken Jones and Joanna Macy find their source of motivation not just in concepts of *anatmavada* and emptiness (which, while they build a sense of selflessness, all too easily privilege a gnostic sense of the emptiness of all things – and people) but in versions of what Thich Nhat Hanh memorably speaks of as InterBeing, with its connotations of a liminal state that demands movement and change.[54] It thus provides inspiration for many "dual belonging" Christians who take spiritual energy from their experience of Buddhist meditative practice. Paul Knitter, for instance, confesses to what he has learned from the Buddha. "If, as Christians insist," he says, "we must all be agents of social change that will bring this world closer to the Reign of God, we will not be able to bring about such change around us unless we are also, even a priori, working on change within ourselves."[55]

Achievement and Agenda

The encounter between Buddhists and Christians has produced a number of variations on the conceptual, interior, and engaged pattern. Most likely this will continue, if only because Buddhism, as it makes further impact outside its more traditional homelands, appeals primarily to individuals searching for meaning and support in the midst of a rootless postmodernity. There are, however, signs that groups gathered for prayer, meditation, and mutual support are making a significant challenge to forms of "privatized religion." Psychologists and physicists who follow a Buddhist path, for instance, find that the analysis of the various forms of "craving" implicit in the teaching of "no self" and holistic concepts like *Pratityasamutpada* encourage a dialogue across their specialist boundaries rather than being obscured by them. For both Buddhists and Christians "orthopraxis" acts not as a comforting spiritual pragmatism but as a corrective to the all too human tendency to erect – and cling to – grand narratives that explain everything. Before enlightenment or conversion lies a way of life rooted in the religious worlds of two quite distinct founder figures. And after enlightenment or conversion follow engagements with the wider culture that create new but again quite distinct modes of relation to "the other." Strictly speaking, of course, there is no "before" and "after," only a single continuum of experience marked by a whole range of foundational and existential "moments" that two vast traditions of canon and commentary handle in their own particular way.

That, however, is not to prevent the "reading" of one tradition by the other giving inspiration to both – whether in the particular sense intended by Scriptural Reasoning and comparative theology or in the broader terms implied by the dialogues of common life and common action. Christianity and Buddhism are not rivals in a competition for shared space. I have argued that both are "cross-cultural" of their very nature and have much to learn from each other in terms of engaging from different – yet, in important ways, complementary – perspectives across a wide variety of philosophical and ethical questions. There is no "essence" that can be neatly extracted from two ways of life that become properly alive only when being translated or adapted to new challenges. What guides them both are accounts of virtuous living, whether understood in terms of wisdom and compassion or faith, hope, and love. A dialogue that started by comparing common ideas and concepts, often to the detriment of one or the other, has grown into something more humane. To what extent it can make a distinctive contribution to more intractable issues to do with the ecological crisis and geopolitics remains to be seen. "The religions," however, are not public manifestos but communities of persons seeking a sound basis for virtuous living. Toward the end of his explorations of faith and understanding "in the company of friends" Carter concludes by commending the transcendent quality of compassion as "our grounded center of value in living." Buddhists and Christians are thereby enabled to form community with each other: "we become capable of trusting each other, of placing our faith in each other, and also we become enabled to be recipients of each other's faith as both fidelity and responsibility to each other."[56]

Notes

1   Quoted in Stephen Batchelor, *The Awakening of the West: The Encounter of Buddhism and Western Culture* (London: HarperCollins, 1994), 239–40.

2   Quoted in Guy Richard Welbon, *The Buddhist Nirvana and Its Western Interpreters* (Chicago, IL: University of Chicago Press, 1968), 69.

3   Batchelor, *Awakening*, 261.

4   Michael Barnes, *Interreligious Learning: Dialogue, Spirituality, and the Christian Imagination* (Cambridge: Cambridge University Press, 2012).

5   *Nostra Aetate* 1. Translation from Giuseppe Alberigo (ed.) with English translation edited by Norman Tanner, *Decrees of the Ecumenical Councils,* Vol. II, Trent-Vatican II (London: Sheed and Ward, 1990).

6   *Nostra Aetate* 2.

7   Paul Tillich, *Christianity and the Encounter with the World's Religions* (New York: Columbia University Press, 1963). Jürgen Moltmann, *The Church in the Power of the Spirit* (New York: Harper & Row, 1971).

8   References to Rahner's contested thesis of the Anonymous Christian are scattered throughout his collected *Theological Investigations* (London: Darton, Longman & Todd, 1966–), especially volumes 5, 6, and 12. Balthasar's reflections on Buddhism are well informed and never less than thought provoking. See especially an edited collection of articles in *Communio* 15, no. 4 (1988).

9   John Ross Carter, *In the Company of Friends: Exploring Faith and Understanding with Buddhists and Christians* (Albany, NY: State University of New York Press, 2012), 220.

10 Amos Yong, *Pneumatology and the Christian-Buddhist Dialogue: How the Spirit Blows through the Middle Way* (Leiden: Brill, 2012), 24–7.

11 John B. Cobb, *Beyond Dialogue: Toward the Mutual Transformation of Christianity and Buddhism* (Philadelphia, PA: Fortress Press, 1982). Winston L. King, *Buddhism and Christianity: Some Bridges of Understanding* (Philadelphia, PA: Westminster Press, 1962). Raimundo Panikkar, *The Silence of God: The Answer of the Buddha* (Maryknoll, NY: Orbis, 1989). Donald W. Mitchell, *Spirituality and Emptiness* (Mahwah, NJ: Paulist Press, 1991). Frederick J. Streng, *Emptiness: A Study of Religious Meaning* (Nashville, TN: Abingdon Press, 1967).

12 John P. Keenan, *The Meaning of Christ: A Mahayana Theology* (Maryknoll, NY: Orbis, 1989); Leo D. Lefebure, *The Buddha and the Christ: Explorations on Buddhist and Christian Dialogue* (Maryknoll, NY: Orbis, 1993). Lynn de Silva, *The Problem of the Self in Buddhism and Christianity* (New York: Barnes and Noble, 1979).

13 Perry Schmidt-Leukel, *Transformation by Integration: How Inter-Faith Encounter Changes Christianity* (London: SCM Press, 2009). Aloysius Pieris, *Love Meets Wisdom: A Christian Experience of Buddhism* (Maryknoll, NY: Orbis, 1988)

14 Paul Williams, brilliant interpreter of the Mahayana and practicing Gelugpa Buddhist until his conversion to Catholicism, sets out many of the key doctrinal and existential distinctions in "Catholicism and Buddhism,"

in *The Catholic Church and the World Religions: A Theological and Phenomenological Account*, ed. Gavin D'Costa (London: T&T Clark, 2011), 141–77.

15 See the work of the Institute of Comparative Scripture and Inter-religious Dialogue at Beijing's Minzu University.

16 Peter Feldmeier, *Experiments in Buddhist–Christian Encounter: From Buddha-Nature to the Divine Nature* (Maryknoll, NY: Orbis, 2019). Comparative theology originated with the comparative reading of Hindu and Christian texts by Francis X. Clooney. For examples of comparative theological reading of Christian and Buddhist texts, see especially James L. Fredericks, *Faith among Faiths: Christian Theology and Non-Christian Religions* (Mahwah, NJ: Paulist Press, 1999) and Michael Barnes, *Ignatian Spirituality and Interreligious Dialogue: Reading Love's Mystery* (Dublin: Messenger, 2021).

17 Paul Knitter, *Without Buddha I Could Not Be a Christian* (New York: Oneworld, 2009).

18 Gavin D'Costa and Ross Thompson, eds., *Buddhist-Christian Dual Belonging: Affirmations, Objections, Explorations* (Basingstoke: Ashgate, 2016).

19 The fourfold distinction originated in the work of the Roman Catholic Federation of Asian Bishops' Conferences and is first noted in the 1984 document from the Secretariat for non-Christian Religions, "The Attitude of the Church Towards the Followers of Other Religions," *Bulletin* [of the Secretariat] 1/2 (1984): 126–41.

20 See Aloysius Pieris, *Fire and Water: Basic Issues in Asian Buddhism and Christianity* (Maryknoll, NY: Orbis, 1996), especially ch. 7, "Does Christ Have a Place in Asia?"; and *Love Meets Wisdom*, especially ch. 11, "Christianity in a Core-to-Core Dialogue with Buddhism."

21 This theme is developed at length in Michael Barnes, *Waiting on Grace: A Theology of Dialogue* (Oxford: Oxford University Press, 2020).

22 See for example the excellent synthesis of tradition and contemporary teaching in John S. Strong, *Buddhisms: An Introduction* (London: Oneworld, 2015).

23 "Engaged Buddhism" is usually attributed to the work of the Vietnamese Zen activist Thích Nhat Hạnh and is often understood as a mainly Western phenomenon. See for example Christopher S. Queen, *Engaged Buddhism in the West* (Boston: Wisdom, 2000). However, the term now covers a wide range of more traditional practice and commentary, including B. R.Ambedkar, Venerable Walpola Rahula, and Bhikkhu Buddhadasa. See, for example, Charles S. Prebish and Martin Baumann, eds., *Westward Dharma: Buddhism Beyond Asia* (Berkeley, CA: University of California Press, 2002), and Christopher Queen, Charles Prebish and Damien Keown, eds., *Action Dharma: New Studies in Engaged Buddhism* (London: RoutledgeCurzon, 2003).

24 See Roger Jackson and John Makransky, eds., *Buddhist Theology: Critical Reflections by Contemporary Buddhist Scholars* (London: Curzon Press, 2000).

25 Schmidt-Leukel, *Transformation by Integration*, 123.

26 See *Alagaddupama Sutta* (*Majjhima Nikaya* 22).

27 Panikkar, *The Silence of God*, 156.

28 The teaching of no self, *anatmavada*, or emptiness, *śunyatavada*, is given a more positive philosophical framework through the concept of *pratityasamutpada*, the "nexus of conditioned origination," based on the axiom that whatever arises is dependent on what has gone before.

29 Stephen Batchelor, *Secular Buddhism: Imagining the Dharma in an Uncertain World* (New Haven, CT: Yale University Press, 2017), 163.

30 Rowan Williams, *Lost Icons: Reflections on Cultural Bereavement* (Edinburgh: T&T Clark, 2000), 182

31 See David Tracy, *Dialogue with the Other: The Inter-Religious Dialogue* (Louvain: Peeters Press, 1990), 17–26.

32 See the *Samaññaphala Sutta* and other dialogues of the *Digha Nikaya* that follow the same pattern of the path to enlightenment that begins with trust being put in the person of the enlightened teacher.

33 Cobb, *Beyond Dialogue*, 89.

34 See William Johnston, *Christian Zen: A Way of Meditation* (New York: Harper, 1971).

35 Hans Waldenfels, *Absolute Nothingness: Foundations for a Buddhist-Christian Dialogue*, trans. J. W. Heisig (New York: Paulist Press, 1980), 3. See also Waldenfels, *Buddhist Challenge to Christianity* (Bangalore: Dharmaram Publications, 2004).

36 Waldenfels, *Absolute Nothingness*, 65.

37 Paul Mommaers and Jan van Bragt, *Mysticism: Buddhist and Christian* (New York: Crossroad, 1995).

38 Mommaers and van Bragt, *Mysticism*, 3.

39 Mommaers and van Bragt, *Mysticism*, 289.

40 Mommaers and van Bragt, *Mysticism*, 12.

41 *The Asian Journal of Thomas Merton*, edited from the original notebooks by Naomi Burton, Patrick Hart, and James Laughlin (London: Sheldon Press, 1974), 343.

42 Thomas Merton *Mystics and Zen Masters* (New York: Farrar, Straus and Giroux, 1967), ix.

43 In *A Search for Solitude: The Journals of Thomas Merton*, Vol. 3, ed. Lawrence S. Cunningham (San Francisco, CA: Harper, 1995), 139.

44 Waldenfels, *Absolute Nothingness*, 137; see Karl Rahner, *Theological Investigations*, 9 (London: Darton, Longman & Todd, 1972), 193–4.

45 See Barnes, *Ignatian Spirituality*, ch. 7: "Signs of the Times."

46 See the groundbreaking work of Damien Keown, especially *The Nature of Buddhist Ethics* (London: Macmillan, 1992).

47 Thich Nhat Hanh, *Living Buddha, Living Christ* (London: Rider, 1995). The Dalai Lama, *Good Heart* (London: Rider, 1996)

48 In addition to Lefebure, *The Buddha and the Christ,* see also Ulrich Luz and Axel Michaels, *Encountering Jesus and Buddha* (Minneapolis, MN: Fortress Press, 2006). Rita M. Gross and Terry C. Muck, eds., *Buddhists Talk about Jesus, Christians Talk about the Buddha* (New York: Continuum, 2000). Paul Knitter and Roger Haight, *Jesus and Buddha: Friends in Conversation* (Maryknoll, NY: Orbis, 2015).

49 Batchelor, *Secular Buddhism,* 191–2.

50 For a very full account of the debate occasioned by Abe, see John B. Cobb and Christopher Ives, eds., *The Emptying God* (Maryknoll, NY: Orbis, 1990). See also discussion of Nishitani's "Pauline *koan*" of the

"Emptiness of God" in Waldenfels, *Absolute Nothingness,* 155–62.

51 Waldenfels, *Absolute Nothingness,* 162.

52 Pieris, *Love Meets Wisdom,* 118.

53 For an excellent summary of the debate surrounding the contested question of Buddhist contributions to the environmental crisis, see Christopher Ives, "A Mixed Dharmic Bag: Debates about Buddhism and Ecology," in *The Routledge Handbook of Religion and Ecology,* ed. Willis Jenkins, Mary Evelyn Tucker, and John Grim (London: Routledge, 2017), 43–51.

54 Ken Jones, *The New Social Face of Buddhism* (Boston, MA: Wisdom, 2003); Joanna Macy, *World as Lover, World as Self* (Berkeley, CA: Parallax Press, 1991).

55 Quoted in D'Costa and Thompson, *Double Belonging,* 43.

56 Carter, *The Company of Friends,* 222–3.

Recommended Reading

Batchelor, Stephen. *The Awakening of the West: The Encounter of Buddhism and Western Culture.* London: HarperCollins, 1994.

Carter, John Ross. *In the Company of Friends: Exploring Faith and Understanding with Buddhists and Christians.* Albany, NY: SUNY Press, 2012.

Cobb, John B. Beyond Dialogue: *Toward the Mutual Transformation of Christianity and Buddhism.* Philadelphia, PA: Fortress Press, 1982.

D'Costa, Gavin, and Ross Thompson, eds. *Buddhist-Christian Dual Belonging: Affirmations, Objections, Explorations.* Basingstoke: Ashgate, 2016.

de Silva, Lynn. *The Problem of the Self in Buddhism and Christianity.* New York: Barnes and Noble, 1979.

Feldmeier, Peter. *Experiments in Buddhist-Christian Encounter: From Buddha-Nature to the Divine Nature.* Maryknoll, NY: Orbis, 2019.

Johnston, William. *Christian Zen: A Way of Meditation.* New York: Harper, 1971.

Jones, Ken. *The New Social Face of Buddhism.* Boston, MA: Wisdom, 2003.

Keenan, John P. *The Meaning of Christ: A Mahayana Theology.* Maryknoll, NY: Orbis, 1989.

Knitter, Paul. *Without Buddha I Could Not Be a Christian.* New York: Oneworld, 2009.

Lai, Whalen, and Michael von Brück. *Christianity and Buddhism: A Multi-Cultural History of their Dialogue.* Maryknoll, NY: Orbis, 2001.

Lefebure, Leo D. *The Buddha and the Christ: Explorations in Buddhist and Christian Dialogue.* Maryknoll, NY: Orbis, 1993.

Merton, Thomas. *Mystics and Zen Masters.* New York: Farrar, Straus and Giroux, 1967.

Panikkar, Raimundo. *The Silence of God: The Answer of the Buddha.* Maryknoll, NY: Orbis, 1989.

Pieris, Aloysius. *Love Meets Wisdom: A Christian Experience of Buddhism.* Maryknoll, NY: Orbis, 1988.

Schmidt-Leukel, Perry, ed. *Buddhism and Christianity in Dialogue: The Gerald Weisfeld Lectures 2004.* Norwich: SCM Press, 2005.

———. *Transformation by Integration: How Inter-Faith Encounter Changes Christianity.* London: SCM Press, 2009.

Waldenfels, Hans. *Absolute Nothingness: Foundations for a Buddhist-Christian Dialogue.* New York: Paulist Press, 1980.

Yong, Amos. *Pneumatology and the Christian-Buddhist Dialogue: How the Spirit Blows through the Middle Way.* Leiden: Brill, 2012.

Hinduism

Julius Lipner

Introduction

India remains the focus of Hinduism in the world with regard to history, numbers, and sociopolitical change – there are nearly a billion people, close to one sixth of the world's population, who are identified as "Hindus" in India today. Appreciable numbers of Hindus also live in the diaspora around the world (over 70 million people, according to one estimate). Further, as is well known, India is taking its place in the forefront internationally: it is reputed to have the world's sixth-largest economy, it is an established nuclear power, and it is situated in one of the most consequential geopolitical regions of our times. These statements demand more contextualized analysis, no doubt; nevertheless, since India remains inextricably linked to the development of Hinduism, they are properly indicative of the importance of Hinduism today. As for Christians in India, they number about 26 million and belong mostly to Roman Catholic or Protestant denominations. Thus, "Hinduism" and "Christianity" are very large terms in context, their referents comprising a plethora of sects and denominations.[1]

In *The Meaning and End of Religion*, Wilfred Cantwell Smith pointed to the way such abstractions as "Hindu*ism*" and "Christian*ity*" *standardize* and *reify* our understanding of the faiths they represent (invariably through the diktat of some accepted authority).[2] *Standardizing* a faith implies that there is a privileged form of that faith and that other forms are of lesser importance. The problem here is that in the context of the faiths we are considering there is inevitably a range of competing authorities; this gives rise to contestation and dissent. Nevertheless, it is also an occasion for renewed understanding and dialogue. *Reifying* a faith, that is, making a bloc-reality of it, gives the impression that there is a semantic hard core to this faith that remains, or should remain, intact and unchallenged throughout the course of history. Both assumptions are theologically and religiously misleading, if not false. Though verbal markers of a faith may persist, as, for example, in some enduring creed, their meaningful content is constantly changing over time through reinterpretation via various kinds of transaction across cultural and verbal boundaries. After all, this is what keeps a faith alive and relevant.

Ford's The Modern Theologians: An Introduction to Christian Theology since 1918, Fourth Edition.
Edited by Rachel Muers and Ashley Cocksworth.

Such changes occur all the more in what is today called a "globalized" world, where the phenomenon of globalization, that is, the *intensified* exchange of ideas, goods, peoples, and languages – through debate, technology (including the printing press), travel, migration, economic development, cosmopolitan living, etc. – is both irreversible and accelerating. Endeavoring to transform the broad, changeable meanings of key religious terms into the currency of everyday interaction with other faiths under the watchful eye of religious authority in a globalizing world has been the nub of meaningful interreligious encounter.

So what counts for a valid form of a global religion on the basis of which one may establish some significant theological engagement with another faith? It is a matter of observation that each of the current primary faiths – "primary" in the sense of enduring historical, religious influence – comprises a cluster of denominations that share, at least in large part, a nexus of ideas and practices that identify that faith as such – with "outliers," more or less "wacky" minorities distant in doctrine and practice, in sometimes eccentric orbit around that cluster. Among some analysts, the binding characteristics in this network of component elements have been likened to those that constitute a "family resemblance" among a dispersed group of individuals, some showing more, others less, pronounced evidence of this resemblance. Be that as it may, it is from the stances of our two faiths that are generally agreed by both insiders and outsiders to belong inalienably to the Hindu and Christian family groupings that we must consider the theoretical outreaches that figure in this essay. A final observation: I am engaging in a phenomenological, not a theological, exercise. That is, I am commenting on what different Christian theologians/theoreticians have *said* about the salvific viability of Hinduism (whether in part or in whole), *not* on whether they are *right* to have said what they have. My aim is not to adjudicate issues of truth or falsity but rather to explore how those concerned or tasked with protecting Christian "truth/s" have approached other faiths as possible partners in dialogue.

Survey

Background

There is no such thing as "*the* Christian" approach to Hinduism (or vice versa); such generalizations collapse not only methodologically but also under historical scrutiny. De facto, then, up for consideration are only approaches of salient forms of Christianity to salient forms of Hinduism, or rather, *thinkers rooted in those forms,* each form characterized by a noticeable group of adherents and a notable place in history. In what follows, we are concerned with thinkers who fall into the categories described.

This chapter considers the interactions between the two faiths from about the end of World War I. By then, significant British presence had been established in India for over a century and a half. The intellectual effects of this presence had begun to blossom in the first quarter of the nineteenth century with the rise of the *bhadralok,* i.e. the "cultured" male Hindu elite from the upper castes and classes of Bengali society, especially in and around Calcutta, the capital of British India at the time. With Rammohan Roy (1772–1833) and a number of other individuals as leading lights of this loose movement,[3] there was a surge in establishing English education in India at least among the elite classes, encouraged by Thomas Babington Macaulay's famous Education Minute of 1835, which favored the teaching of English, over Arabic and Sanskrit, for progress in education in India.

The *bhadralok* were the catalyst for ushering what became a modern mentality into the subcontinent. When established, this modern mentality valued the dominion of reason over the supremacy of passion and the imagination, that is, it emphasized the heritage of the Enlightenment over that of the Romantics. By the beginning of the twentieth century, this rationalist ethos was well entrenched among the upper classes of India. In this context, what passed for Christianity – the broad religious background with which scientific advancement in the world was associated – came under scrutiny, either as a potential religious home in its own right or as an inspiration for an active social ethic, or, indeed, as a hostile target for its capacity to "denature" Hindu identity by way of conversion or uncritical accommodation. It was largely through the brokerage of *bhadralok* culture that the Indian Christian elite were primed to come to terms, in one way or another, with their ancestral Hindu faith. This did not mean that Hindus from less privileged socioeconomic backgrounds (generally those from the "lower castes") were not converted to various Christian denominations; that continued regardless. But such converts lacked the influence the *bhadralok* possessed to directly affect attitudes between Christianity and Hinduism.

Concomitant with this anglicizing development, interaction of various kinds between Christianity and Hinduism was well under way. Both Protestant Christianity in its various forms and Roman Catholicism were well established. Converts to the Protestant and Catholic faiths (irrespective of whether the convert was generational or new) were, at least at the turn of the nineteenth century, invariably expected to abandon all vestiges of their former religious affiliation, whether creedal or liturgical, and accept the *mores* of the adopted faith.

In short, a powerful and often painful rift, psychological if not wholly cultural, arose between converts and their traditional ethnic communities. The Hindu pandit, Nīlakaṇṭha Goreh (1825–85), famous at first for his defense of Hinduism and his vigorous denunciation of Christianity, shocked his former coreligionists when he converted to the Protestant faith, taking the name "Nehemiah," and denounced Hindu religious thinking in turn. As a convert, his inability to come to terms with his native Hindu roots plunged him in anguish. He is reported to have said, as a consequence, that he often "felt like a man who has taken poison" so alienated had he become as an Indian Christian.[4]

Approaching the dialogue

Nehemiah Goreh's experience as a disenfranchised Hindu is a telling indicator of the cultural and theological divides that obtained at the time between Christian and Hindu. By the first decade or so of the twentieth century, as India and other regions of the world were becoming more interconnected through the effects of widespread colonialism and its legacy of shared if imposed languages as well as more efficient means of communication, Christian theologians had developed various approaches to other faiths including Hinduism, largely dependent on the Christian commitment they themselves had espoused.

These approaches have been grouped in the literature under three headings: "exclusivist," "inclusivist," and "pluralist."[5] In the wake of continuing discussion, these labels are now regarded as somewhat wanting at best. Various scholars have commented on them and/or sought to extend them in some way.[6] Nevertheless, in my view they are still useful *methodologically as starting points* for the discussion at hand. In what follows I look at each category in turn, in its stark form, so as to isolate its main points, while commenting on the adequacy or otherwise of this division.

Key Approaches and Key Figures

Exclusivists: Hendrik Kraemer

The exclusivist approach, sometimes also called the absolutist approach, is based largely on the conviction that religious faiths, denominational though they are, are nevertheless sociologically "organic wholes," and that their constitutive concepts and doctrines, and the resulting practices, are so inextricably interrelated both structurally and semantically, that it is not possible to tease out individual components to act as a proper basis for constructive interfaith dialogue. Thus, the nature of *agape* or altruistic love in Christian doctrine is so distinctive, notwithstanding its various implementations, that it is futile to seek meaningful comparison with Hindu *bhakti* or "devotion to God." In fact, the exclusivists argue, there is really more to contrast these themes than to compare them. Both *agape* and *bhakti* are tied to the history, emotions, and doctrinal developments of their respective faith stances so indelibly that trying to detach them from context in order to compare them is not only a wrongheaded exercise but also a misleading one, for it generates misunderstanding and false hopes – in short, it is theologically futile. These concepts belong to integrated wholes whose component interweavings cannot be relativized through any meaningful comparative exercise calculated to generate insights that constitute helpful interfaith knowledge.

The Dutch theologian Hendrik Kraemer (1888–1965) of the Netherlands Reformed Church, who worked as a lay missionary in Java, Indonesia, from 1922–28, and became professor of the history and phenomenology of religion in the University of Leiden, serves as a classic exemplar for this uncompromising approach in our period.[7] Invited to produce a discussion document for the International Missionary Council at Tambaram in Madras (now Chennai) in 1938, he published a highly influential work, *The Christian Message in a Non-Christian World*, in which he first stated his position at length.[8]

Reiterating his fundamental stance in *Religion and the Christian Faith* (1956), he could affirm:

> When we try to define the relation of the Christian message ... to the spiritual world manifest in the whole range of religious experience ... we cannot account for it by an unqualified conception of "fulfilment" or continuity. We must, out of respect for the proper character of the Christian Faith and the other religions, begin by pronouncing emphatically the word "discontinuity" – *Totaliter aliter* [Completely different], with emphasis on both words.[9]

Allegiance to Hindu faith falls under this general critique, though this allegiance has its particular drawbacks:

> In spite of all Hinduism's splendid piety and effusion of deep religious emotion and experience, the harsh word must be said that this is sheer religious utilitarianism or *hybris* [spiritual pride] .... [The] tolerance [that] is also one of the traits of Hindu spirituality ... in fact [is] spiritual latitudinarianism, indifference to the august and severe authority of Truth.[10]

This is fundamentally an *a priori* judgment. It is not based on some *a posteriori* evaluation of theological belief and practice in one or other of the Hindu denominations in order to judge whether it may in any way act as an instrument of salvation from a Christian viewpoint, but on a blanket rejection, from the outset, of the salvific viability of Hinduism in particular and non-Christian faiths in general. Any apparent similarity of doctrine or concept between the Christian and "other"/Hindu faith is no more than a delusive veneer of compatibility, masking the real and deep-set salvific incommensurability between them.

For Kraemer, the non-Christian faiths have no effective means of overcoming the structural *hubris* that permeates human reason and that acts as a natural block to God's saving outreach. Kraemer also subjects "empirical" Christianity, that is, the denominational Christianity of everyday belief and practice around the world, to this dialectical stricture, to the continuous *yes* of God's invitation to saving faith on the one hand and the continuous prevarication of the human response on the other, for over time it too has been subject to the distortive ravages of human sin from which it continually needs purification: "Christ, as the ultimate standard of reference, is the crisis of all religions, of the non-Christian religions and of empirical Christianity too."[11] But empirical Christianity has the potential for effectively mediating saving grace because only Christianity harbors the *structural orientation*, through its historical beliefs and practices, that can successfully transmit the saving power of the Christian message.[12]

Kraemer singles out the Advaita Vedānta (the "absolute monistic Idealism") of Sarvepalli Radhakrishnan (1888–1975) – sometime president of India, and perhaps the most well-known Hindu thinker of Kraemer's generation – as a stance representative of Hinduism. He writes:

[the Hindu] spiritual quest ... aims at one goal: man must realize his deepest truth, his spiritual essence or being, which – and this is an axiom – is identical with the ultimate divine principle .... This quest for ultimate reality, for self-realization, which consists in its fullness in reaching the goal of eternal oneness with it and the struggle for release from *saṃsāra* [the world of karma and rebirth], pervades all Indian [= Hindu] thinking and aspiration as salt pervades the sea.[13]

This is not the place to contest this dubious assimilative pronouncement. According to Kraemer, Radhakrishnan's thinking embodies this view in the monistic idiom of his times.[14] But, for Kraemer, this stance is entirely anthropocentric, and as such is pervaded by "insincerity"/*hubris* because "Release, liberation" into this state, "are [said to be] realized by the gradual developments of man's *natural faculties.*"[15] There is no room here for the effective action of that which mediates true liberation, God's grace, through "genuine prophetical religion, of which biblical religion is the only authentic representative."[16]

All the philosophies of religion devised by Hindus over the centuries, a number of which Kraemer mentions, fall under this same condemnation. They are void as means of salvation. Interestingly, Kraemer says relatively little about the two facets of Hindu religion often regarded as distinctive of the faith – image worship (which many Christian exclusivists usually describe as a combination of "polytheism" and "idolatry") and "caste," whether understood as the four-tiered system of *varṇa* (consisting of Brahmins, Kshatriyas, Vaishyas, and Shudras) or as the innumerable *jāti*s or "birth-groups," including the outcastes (now referred to as *dalits,* the "oppressed ones"), that derive from it. Nor does Kraemer have much to say – and this is not surprising for the culture of the period – about the status of women in Hinduism.

What might be said in brief critique of the exclusivist standpoint, with special reference to Kraemer? One can begin by undermining Kraemer's starting point, shared by many exclusivists, that the different world religions constitute self-contained wholes that are unable to interrelate in any meaningful way. Surely this is not the case. Because all languages are capable, *qua* language, of being humanly intelligible (even though historically they may have been put to particular contextual use), their constitutive ideas cannot but function as potential semantic bridges between the different religions and cultures of the world. How many Greek, Latin, and Jewish ideas have gone into the very making of the Christian faith!

If Kraemer and his exclusivist colleagues are right that the God of the Bible wants all humans to be saved, how could this God confine his saving action to but one web of religious linguistic discourse, especially if, as Kraemer readily admits, humans from the different religions have striven throughout history to know and describe the one Supreme Being? If God were to act in this restrictive way, he would be lacking in compassion and the will to effect universal salvation. The world faiths, then, are not *"totaliter aliter,"* completely cut off from each other both as linguistic realities and as conduits of divine grace, but, in so far as they are, at least potentially, interrelated webs of meaning generally inhabited (one must assume) by people of good will in their search for God, they must be envisaged as participants in the divine plan of universal salvation in which each faith plays its part in bringing God's plan to fruition. This can be achieved only by interfaith dialogue through which points of contact, conceptual or otherwise, between the faiths can be discerned and developed. Here Christianity and Hinduism can be no exception, not least with regard to our example earlier of *agape* and *bhakti.* This does not mean that decisive elements of God's saving message are necessarily *equally* distributed in all the faiths, but it does mean that each faith is duty bound to share what it does have of this message with the others. Such a stance undermines the whole exclusivist project.

Today, a number of Indian Christian Churches of various denominations, often described as fundamentalist, have adopted the exclusivist approach toward their Hindu (and other non-Christian) compatriots. Except for retaining their indigenous forms of attire, and using local languages for rituals, prayer, Sunday schools, the dissemination of tracts, etc., they maintain little if anything in their religious forms of life that can be described as deriving from Hindu sources. Though their children usually attend educational and other institutions with Hindus and other non-Christians, religiously most regard the Hindu faith as hardly more than a welter of polytheism and idolatry so that the non-Christian in this respect becomes "un-Christian," if not "ungodly."[17] Nevertheless, the Christian exclusivists are generally tolerated by their Hindu compatriots, though voices have been raised in protest.[18] But many Indian Christians do not subscribe to this uncompromising stance.

Inclusivists: Brahmabandhab Upadhyay, Abhishiktananda, Raimundo Panikkar, Hans Küng, Francis X. Clooney

As their name indicates, the inclusivists are prepared to enter into genuine dialogue with Hinduism with a view to real adaptive change of their theological position. This is based on the principle that the primary non-Christian faiths, at least, have been "prepared" in some real sense, under the guiding hand of Providence, for the reception of the gospel in the course of their historical development.[19] Whereas Christian exclusivists emphasize "discontinuity" between their faith and that of non-Christians, the inclusivists acknowledge the possibility of a real "continuity" between decisive features of their faith – conceptual and/ or structural – and those of their non-Christian interlocutors, notwithstanding the obduracies of human nature. This important difference between the exclusivist and inclusivist standpoints gives added incentive for the give and take of genuine interfaith dialogue.

A well-known pioneer of the inclusivist view in the period under discussion was the Scottish missionary, John Nicol Farquhar (1861–1929). In his famous work, *The Crown of Hinduism* (1913), Farquhar proposed a "fulfillment" theology with regard to Christian approaches to Hinduism. Though Farquhar claims at the end of his book that it is Christ, as God incarnate, who is the crown of Hinduism – "In Him is focused every ray of light that shines in Hinduism. He is the crown of the faith of India"[20] – he muddies the waters earlier by consistently substituting Christianity for Christ in this apex role. So, he states: "This hard, unyielding [Hindu] system must fall into the ground and die, before the aspirations and the dreams of Hindu thinkers and ascetics can be set free to grow in health and strength .... Hinduism must die in order to live. It must die *into* Christianity."[21] And again: "It is one of the chief aims of this volume to show that Christianity is the Crown of Hinduism."[22]

This unfortunate confusion places undue emphasis on cultural idiom, that is, the outward apparatus represented by "Christianity," rather than on the person who is supposed to lie at the heart of this structure, and bedevils on occasion the clarity of Farquhar's stance. As the book progresses, Farquhar moves toward the decisive focus of his fulfillment theology: the comparison between the Christ of the New Testament and the Krishna – as Vishnu's avatar – of the *Bhagavadgītā*. Hindus will appreciate the real purpose of Krishna as avatar, claims Farquhar, only when they acknowledge that he prefigures Christ, who is the true incarnation of God. This comparison had already been the subject of Farquhar's earlier book, *Gita and Gospel* (1903, 1906), where Farquhar gives a clear statement of his fulfillment view. The *Gītā*, he avers, is not a "fresh revelation" but is "the concentrated essence of Hinduism .... Rightly read, the Gita is a clear-tongued prophecy of Christ, and the hearts that bow down to the idea of Krishna are really seeking [Christ] the incarnate son of God."[23]

On consideration, Farquhar is not particularly sympathetic to Hinduism in his work; there is something of the glib and dismissive in his approach. One might even label him a superficial inclusivist. A more engaged and daring exponent of the Christian inclusivist stance toward Hinduism is the Bengali Brahmin nationalist, Bhabani Charan Bandyopadhyay (1861–1907) who, after becoming a Roman Catholic at the age of thirty, adopted the religious name Brahmabandhab Upadhyay.[24] Upadhyay has had a major impact, especially among Catholic thinkers, in shaping the Indian Christian inclusivist theology of our times. His theology dug deep into Hindu ideas and practice, especially with reference to Advaita Vedānta. In the various journals he founded, he reinterpreted, among other terms, the Advaitic words *māyā* (which refers to the world's "reality" in relation to the Supreme Being), *avidyā* (or ignorance of our true relationship with this Being), and *nirguṇa Brahman* (which Upadhyay translated, literally, as "God without essential ties to anything") as superior to any European counterpart for their capacity to express Christian doctrine. In short, according to Upadhyay, Advaita, judiciously handled, was a better vehicle for communicating the Christian revelation than any current (non-Hindu) medium. The natural–supernatural divide of Thomism remains: words are to be "elevated" in their outreach toward Christian meanings, but in arguing for this Upadhyay shows a clear bias toward the superiority of Sanskrit terms as the medium.

As for caste, Upadhyay consistently defends his idealized understanding of this practice on the grounds that it is a natural expression of the Hindu genius and as such does not militate against the supernatural religion of Christ, which is confined to beliefs that transcend but do not contradict reason:

> No mistake could be more fatal to progress than to make the Indian Christian community conform to European social ideals .... So long as the Christians of India do not practise their faith on the platform of Hindu life and living and Hindu thought and thinking, and elevate the national genius to the supernatural plane, they will never thrive.[25]

Upadhyay favored the education of women: "Let us educate our women, develop their susceptibilities, give free scope to their aptitudes ... and then only we shall be fit to achieve greatness." This may be regarded as somewhat "progressive" for the age, but scrutiny of Upadhyay's writings on the subject shows that it was a progressiveness that did not challenge the patronizing and role-directed expectations that Hindu society had of its women at the time. Further, his support of the caste system, however idealized, tended to overlook the great evils of discrimination that it actually shielded.

Two other features of Upadhyay's legacy continue to resonate with current Indian Christian practice: (1) his experiment of founding a Hindu-Catholic ashram or "monastery" (*maṭha*) at Jabalpur, a city in the state of Madhya Pradesh, and (2) his composition of the now well-known Sanskrit hymn, *Vande Saccidānandam*.

As to the first, Upadhyay proclaimed that the monastery would house and school "itinerant missionaries" who "should be thoroughly Hindu in their mode of living. They should, if necessary, be strict vegetarians and teetotalers and put on the yellow *sannyasi* [ascetic] garb."[26] From their hub at Jabalpur, these ascetics would travel around India preaching by word and example the Christian revelation in a Hindu idiom. But this experiment soon petered out, for want, yet again, of adequate application by Upadhyay, and proper ecclesiastical support. The idea, however, of a Hindu-Christian *maṭha* lived on and subsequently gave rise to similar attempts, with more or less successful outcomes.[27]

In the hymn *Vande Saccidānandam*, Upadhyay "converts" the well-known Advaitic compound, *sac* [Being]-*cid* [Consciousness]-*ānanda* [Bliss], which describes the Advaitic Absolute in human terms, into a description of the Christian Trinity: "I hail [the Trinity] as Being/Father, Consciousness/Son, and Bliss/Holy Spirit." The hymn is sung regularly in Indian Christian, especially Catholic, churches today.[28]

Upadhyay remains highly significant for Christian, especially Catholic, attempts at the "inculturation" of Hinduism. It might even be argued that his *fin de siècle* attempts at indigenizing Christianity had a bearing, at least indirectly (through the thinkers he influenced), on the Second Vatican Council's positive reference to Hinduism in its encyclical *Nostra Aetate* ("The Declaration on the Relationship of the Church to Non-Christian Religions"), where the council speaks approvingly of contemplation of the divine mystery in Hinduism and the search therein to express this mystery "through an unspent fruitfulness of myths and through searching philosophical inquiry," and of Hinduism's attempts to "seek release from the anguish of [the human] condition through ascetical practices or deep meditation or a loving, trusting flight toward God."[29]

A number of Christians seeking dialogue with Hinduism have followed in Upadhyay's footsteps, explicitly citing his lead. Here we may consider but two: the Frenchman, Henri le Saux (1910–73), who came to India in 1948 as a Benedictine monk, and who, without falling out with his church, followed his lights as a *sannyāsī* under the title, Swami Abhishiktananda ("The Bliss of the Anointed"), by steeping himself especially in Advaitic thought and practice; and the Indo-Spanish theologian, Raimundo (sometimes Raimon, Raymon[d]) Panikkar (1918–2010), who adopted a more discursive approach.

Abhishiktananda followed a mystical path, and after meditating for some time on the sacred mountain Arunachala (in Tamil Nadu), he went on to explore, as he put it, the mystery of "the One in the cave of the heart," which he then sought to express through various writings and interfaith encounters. We give here a threaded sample of his insights from various letters; both the Advaitic bent of his thinking and his scant respect for the verbal convolutions of conventional "theology," come through in these quotations:

> The essential thing is to penetrate the *interior mystery* to which India bears witness so intensely .... I think no real theology of the Trinity-Incarnation is possible as long as we do not turn back to the fundamental *anubhava* [experience] they express .... The Hindu discovery of [the Upanishadic] "*I am,*" [is] the only support that abides when everything collapses – everything that was founded on knowing [rather than on experiencing]. How the theology of Europe ... finally rings hollow *here* .... Yes, when you have discovered this *I am,* scorching, devastating, then no longer even (can you say) *God is* – for who *is* there to dare to speak of God .... Can a "Christian symbolic" [creed] emerge from the *anubhava* [experience of the One]? The whole Jewish-Christian systematization of Christianity will explode at that point.[30]

Attentive reading of this passage will show that Abhishiktananda can be described as an "inclusivist" or "fulfillment theologian" only hesitantly, for though Hindu insights were incorporated into his Christian starting point, the result seems to have been an experience describable in language that points to the limitations of Hindu and Christian terminology.

Raimundo Panikkar came to prominence as an innovative thinker on our topic through his book, *The Unknown Christ of Hinduism* (1964). Although Panikkar agrees here with all Christians of faith, exclusivists and inclusivists alike, that it is only through Christ that one can be saved, like other inclusivists (but unlike the exclusivists), he argues, with special reference to Hinduism, that in the non-Christian faiths Christ has a hidden, salvific presence through his Spirit.

> The relationship between Hinduism and Christianity ... does not express relationships such as falsehood-truth, darkness-light ... damnation-salvation .... One tends more to associate it with such pairs as potency-act, seed-fruit ... symbol-reality .... [T]here is a certain relationship belonging to the Christian dynamism of death and resurrection.[31]

Whereas Farquhar speaks of Hinduism's need to "die into Christianity" (see earlier), Panikkar speaks of the need for Hinduism to die and be resurrected with Christianity. The interior, divine impulse toward transforming Hinduism's unknown Christ into a recognizable, risen Christ, Panikkar explains in Trinitarian terms, where God acts through creation and incarnation: the Father is the unspeakable Source, the Son (*īśvara*) is "Being, the *Thou*" (the Father *qua* manifest among us), and the Spirit is the divine "we" that draws us into the unity of this "cosmotheandric" reality (Panikkar revels in compound neologisms).[32] There is potential in all the major faiths to participate, through dialogue, in this cumulatively redeeming process, though Panikkar focuses on Hindu resources vis-à-vis the Christian revelation. Finally, in *Myth, Faith and Hermeneutics* (1983), Panikkar explores the meaning of sacrificial death through Hindu myth and the witness of faith in a transcendent Reality consummated in an *advaita* of love that is:

> loving you really as you, a love that both discovers and effects the identity of lover and beloved .... It is not authentic and ultimate unless it is a sacrament – a real symbol of the divine identity discovered in two pilgrim sparks fusing themselves in order to reach the single divine Fire.[33]

But – to complicate matters (and Panikkar was a complex thinker) – Panikkar, especially in late career, described himself as a Christian "pluralist" (while claiming never to have abandoned his commitment as a Christian). This is another instance where the neatness of the threefold categorization (inclusivism etc.) for our thinkers breaks down. Panikkar's pluralist stance is explored in a collection of essays entitled *The Intercultural Challenge of Raimon Panikkar* (1996). In this connection, Beverly Lanzetta writes:

> Pluralism becomes the expression best suited to convey the profound mutual interdependence and mutual distinction inherent in the mystery of the Trinity. Pluralism is not just a goal to reach or the mere searching for common ground, but the fundamental nature of things. Panikkar clarifies that in using the term *pluralism* he is not referring to plurality, which implies difference; or pluriformity, in the sense of variety; or to diversity, which connotes an unattainable harmony. Instead he sees *pluralism* as "an awareness leading to a *positive* acceptance of *diversity* – an acceptance which neither forces the different attitudes into an artificial unity, nor alienates them by reductionistic manipulations."[34]

Two Roman Catholic thinkers played significant roles in preparing the ground for the Catholic inclusivist approach to Hinduism. The first was the German theologian Karl Rahner (1904–84), whose idea of "anonymous Christians," which parallels Panikkar's more specific notion of "unknown Christ" (of Hinduism), made of the sincere non-Christian (including the atheist) a genuine candidate for salvation. On the basis of the theological assumption that human nature is intrinsically oriented toward salvation, because of the Creator's desire for the salvation of all, Rahner argued that non-Christian religions, as products of human thought, must in principle act, under God's providence and through the indwelling Spirit of Christ, as social vehicles of an authentic revelation that may lead to salvation.[35] In effect, these faiths harbor what we may call "anonymous Christians," who also belong in some real if not clearly visible way to the salvific reality that is the Catholic Church.[36]

The Swiss theologian Hans Küng (1928–2021) considered Hinduism in his book, *Christianity and the World Religions* (English edition, 1986). Acknowledging the enormous diversity of views in Hinduism, Küng nevertheless characterizes Hinduism as a "mystical" faith, that is, as a faith that at its deepest level holds to a notion of time that is essentially "circular/cyclical" (while Christianity as a "prophetic" faith regards time as essentially "goal directed"), and that seeks ultimately to resolve existential difference into some form of ultimate unity.[37] But this is something of a false contrast, as we have already indicated.

Küng gives special consideration to Krishna in the *Bhagavadgītā*, in the light of which he acknowledges that there is in Hinduism a prominent notion of a "thoroughly secular piety" (i.e. a piety affirming action *in* the world) as well as of a God that is "both immanent in and superior to the world," which in his estimation makes most Hindus monotheists.[38] He believes that the point of departure for a "vigorous" Hindu–Christian dialogue would be "the concrete Jesus of the Sermon on the Mount and the Way of the Cross, whom many Hindus greatly respect as a revelation of perfect inwardness and unique closeness to God."[39] Christians of all denominations in India, continues Küng, "must send down roots of their Christianity into their native soil" by way of (1) Indian (= Hindu) forms of meditation, dance, decoration etc., (2) the traditional Indian incorporation of nature into Christian worship (through flowers, light etc.), and (3) "liturgical reading of, and personal meditation on, Indian sacred scriptures: [viz.] of appropriate texts from the Vedas."[40]

Finally, under this heading, I turn to Francis X. Clooney (1950–), whose views are still unfolding. Clooney (currently a professor at Harvard) has been inspired by the insights of a pioneer of engaged Christian–Hindu understanding in the seventeenth century, the Jesuit missionary priest, Roberto de Nobili. In *Seeing through Texts* (1996) and *Hindu God, Christian God* (2001), Clooney endorses an "integral" approach to Hinduism, whereby comparative theology "remains rooted in one tradition while seriously engaging another tradition and allowing that engagement to affect one's original commitments."[41] With deep sensitivity and scholarship, Clooney engages with the Tamil devotional songs of the ninth century *ālvār*,

Śaṭakōpan and their later Śrīvaiṣṇava commentaries, and seeks to initiate "an extended conversation between the Hindu and Christian theological traditions on [four topics] ... God's existence, the true God, divine embodiment, and the measuring of religions by revelation."[42]

So, how should we assess Christian inclusivism? To put it bluntly from the "receiving" end: the "knowing" Christian, when this approach is adopted crudely, seems to be making two points from the vantage point of the Christian's appropriation of the "truth": (1) that it is the Christian who understands better than the non-Christian which parts of the latter's sacred texts are the more important religiously, and (2) that it is the discerning Christian rather than the non-Christian who can grasp the hidden, salvific meanings of these texts. All that non-Christian exegetes have said about their own texts in the course of history has, with regard to these texts' true religious significance, been only superficial: the non-Christian must await the unveiling of these texts' deeper import through Christian hermeneutics.

More sensitive exponents of this approach, such as Clooney, point out that focusing on what is important to interlocutors in conversation is a natural part of human discourse – so there is nothing untoward about this – and that religious dialogue is really a process of *dispelling ignorance and learning respectfully,* through which what each side holds dear must first be appropriately acknowledged before any dialogic transaction can occur.[43] There is no room here for arrogant appropriation. Nevertheless, on the theoretical level, non-Christians may well object to a form of condescending church-speak that is prepared to co-opt them into the Christian fold as "anonymous" Christians.

Pluralists: John Hick, Perry Schmidt-Leukel

I turn now to a third approach, that of the pluralists. Here the starting point seems obvious: the highly influential stance of the philosopher of religion, John H. Hick (1922–2012), who often had recourse to Hinduism in expounding his views. Though some of his adversaries doubted his Christian credentials – so radical was his pluralist stance – and though Hick's personal faith "was of a more universal than *exclusively* Christian kind" – he came across, and was generally known, as a Christian pluralist.[44]

Hick rests his pluralist stance on certain basic statements: that religion is essentially "fact asserting," namely, that it is the fundamental intention of religious language to state *what is the case* rather than to speak through metaphor and myth (though there is plenty of scope for figurative language in religion); that God (or, in Hick's later writings, "the Real" or "the Transcendent," which is conceived religiously by way of various "personae" such as Jahweh, Krishna, Jesus, as well as "impersonae" such as Brahman, Nirvana, etc.) exists; that the world religions function as vehicles of salvation, each in its own right; and that a viable, incomparable ethical path can be derived from the teachings of Jesus. Religious believers, affirmed Hick, must transform their hitherto "Ptolemaic" stance of regarding their own faith as the salvific center of the universe of faiths (and subject continually to "epicyclic" adjustments so as to accommodate the salvation of others) into a stance of seeing *the Real* as the salvific center of the universe of faiths. This is the "Copernican Revolution in Theology."[45] Hick quoted the Ṛg Veda's rationalization of its multiple gods (in 1.164) in support of this paradigm-shift:

> They call it Indra, Mitra, Varuna, and Agni, and also heavenly, beautiful Garutman. The real is one, though sages name it variously. We might translate this thought into the terms of the faiths represented today .... They call it Jahweh, Allah, Krishna, Param Atma, and also holy, blessed Trinity. The real is one, though sages name it differently.[46]

Hick augments this example by citing another: that of the blind men and the elephant. Here, several blind men who have had no experience of an elephant are each allowed to touch a different part of the animal. One grasped the tail and said the elephant was like a rope; another held the trunk and said the elephant was like a large snake; a third felt a leg and said it was like a pillar, and so on. "And then they all quarreled together, each claiming that his own account was the truth and therefore all the others false. In fact .... they were all true ... each referring to only one aspect of the total reality and all expressed in very imperfect analogies."[47]

Thus, to speak of Jesus as "God incarnate" is to speak in the language of analogy or transformative myth. The meaning is: follow Jesus's way of loving self-sacrifice that reveals the enabling presence of the Real in our lives. Hick also made a detailed analysis of the "eschatological" teachings of Hinduism and Buddhism, i.e. those teachings describing the path to the ultimate goal and the nature of this state, and of Hindu and Buddhist doctrines of karma and rebirth, on which he concludes: "There are forms of reincarnation doctrine which *may* be broadly true pictures of what actually happens," but this does not substantiate the *popular* conception that the same ego has lived before and will live again, reaping in the course of its present life what it has sown in the past, and sowing fresh karmic seeds for future lives.[48]

Finally, we can mention the pluralist, Perry Schmidt-Leukel (b. 1954). In his knowledgeable references to Hinduism, Schmidt-Leukel points to the diversity of Hindu approaches to Christianity during our period, which include "the inclusivist and semipluralist tendencies that can be discerned in Ramakrishna and Vivekananda and the exclusivist tendencies as represented by Dayananda [Saraswati] [which] still exert their influence on the interpretation of religious diversity in contemporary India."[49]

He also discusses the "contemporary Hindu pluralist ... Anantanand Rambachan, a native of Trinidad and Tobago," and an Advaita Vedantin.[50] According to Schmidt-Leukel, Rambachan "subscribes to the fundamental insight that all human expressions are inadequate to express ultimate reality ... [and that] they need a theology of religions that encourages them to be self-critical .... This is the function of dialogue."[51]

As for Radhakrishnan, discussed by us earlier, Schmidt-Leukel argues that this thinker maintains that each religion enables us to attain the same goal. However, Schmidt-Leukel continues, this statement can mean *either* that the "Neo-Hindu's" mission is "to raise all other religions to the same high level that is exclusively found in Hinduism" *or* it can mean (more equitably) that "the major religions are indeed able to rise above their exclusivist or inclusivist superiority claims by means of their own religious potential." Schmidt-Leukel concludes: "[T]his ambiguous perspective ... realistically mirrors where Hinduism stands in relation to the question of religious pluralism."[52]

Now to a brief critique of the pluralist stance. Many find this position attractive, as an equitable treatment of the various faiths as separate pathways to the final goal for humans. Others, however, have argued that a proper concept of truth in religion transcends such a notion of fairness. Religions contradict one another in many, even profound, ways, and these contradictions cannot all be true. Here the analogy of the blind men and the elephant does not have more than superficial validity: if one of the men had been granted even a partial vision of the whole animal (= God/the Real), he would be closer to grasping the nature of the ultimate Being than the others.[53] This is precisely the claim of a "final Revelation" in a religious tradition, according to which it is perfectly open to God (or "the Ultimate") to grant such a revelation in one or more faiths as and when He/It pleases. This is indeed what most adherents of the various religions believe has occurred in the universe of faiths.

Debate, Achievement, and Agenda

Religious traditions, especially the so-called "world religions," are continually on the move. Not only do these faiths manifest an internal plurality (for who could count the number of Christian and Hindu denominations that are active in the world, not least because new formations keep coming into being, while a number of existing ones wither away?), but the relationships within and across the two faiths are constantly changing, depending on the social, political, and theological conditions that prevail. In this vortex of continuous change, it is well-nigh impossible to determine universal voices that have the authority to speak from within as well as across the divides. This is why, as noted earlier, it is not possible to determine *the* Christian approach to Hinduism (and vice versa). All one can do – and this has been my aim in this essay – is to highlight the *kinds* of approach that have obtained, in terms of named theologians who may be regarded as exemplifying the attitudes concerned. For this exercise, we have found our well-known threefold categorization of exclusivist, inclusivist, and pluralist useful as methodological starting points, though we have also indicated where the apparent neatness of this grouping seems to break down.

With regard to Christian approaches to Hinduism in the future, two points in particular come to mind as the world continues to globalize its peoples, cultures, and resources. First, with a greater emphasis on *ecumenicity* between the Christian denominations – one hopes the reverse will not occur! – the Christian message will come across to non-Christians in general and Hindus in particular as a less fractured and fractious witness of the gospel proclamation. For this, the dispersed doctrinal authorities of the various Christian churches, hitherto so prone to dissension amongst themselves, will have to implement a more effective vision of mutual cooperation and respect, and particularly of *learned* appreciation of the theological riches that reside in the Hindu traditions.

Second, however, Christian ecumenicity is not enough. This must be given dynamic impetus by a continued and sensitive process of Christian indigenization of Hindu ideas, themes, and practices, as indeed some of the Christian theologians we have reviewed have recommended. The aim here is not crass appropriation or imitation, but fertile exchange.

Both these qualities are the criteria of a real conversation between the two faiths, where wisdom will be offered and received in a mutually enriching relationship that is the mark of true interreligious dialogue.

Notes

1 We must distinguish Hinduism from Hindutva (translated as "Hinduness") and neo-Hindutva: the latter represent forms of a Hindu fundamentalism tied to race, religion, territory, and history. On Hindu fundamentalism, see Julius Lipner, "Hindu Fundamentalism," in James Dunn, ed., *Fundamentalisms: Threats and Ideologies in the Modern World* (London: I. B. Tauris, 2016), 93–116. On neo-Hindutva, see Deepa S. Reddy, "What Is Neo- about Neo-Hindutva?" in Edward Anderson and Arkotong Longkumer, eds., *Neo-Hindutva: Evolving Forms, Spaces, and Expressions of Hindu Nationalism* (London: Routledge, 2020), ch. 9. These concepts throw into sharp contrast the status of Indian Muslims and Christians who, according to Hindutva ideology, have taken on borrowed and hence alien identities. It is important to note that – as yet – a great many Hindus, if not the majority, do not subscribe to the limiting criteria of Hindutva proclamation. In this essay, we are concerned with the concept of Hinduism as a diverse tradition, and not with (the homogenizing implications of) "Hindutva" in its various forms.

2 Wilfred Cantwell Smith, *The Meaning and End of Religion* (Minneapolis, MN: Fortress Press, 1991). See especially ch. 3.

3 On Rammohan Roy (various spellings) and his *bhadralok* context, see David Kopf, *The Brahmo Samaj and the Shaping of the Modern Indian Mind* (Princeton, NJ: Princeton University Press, 1979) and Dermot H. Killingley, *Rammohun Roy in Hindu and Christian Tradition: The Teape Lectures 1990* (Newcastle: Grevatt & Grevatt, 1993).

4 Richard Fox Young, *Resistant Hinduism: Sanskrit Sources on Anti-Christian Apologetics in Early Nineteenth-century India,* Publications of the de Nobili Research Library, Vol. VIII (Vienna: Institut für Indologie der Universität Wien, 1981), 171.

5 Ever since Alan Race introduced this threefold grouping in his *Christians and Religious Pluralism: Patterns in the Christian Theology of Religions* (Maryknoll, NY: Orbis, 1983).

6 See Paul Hedges and Alan Race, eds., *Christian Approaches to Other Faiths: An Introduction* (London: SCM Press, 2008) and Elizabeth J. Harris, Paul Hedges, and Shanthikumar Hettiarachchi, eds., *Twenty-First Century Theologies of Religions: Retrospection and Future Prospects* (Leiden: Brill, 2016).

7 Jan A. B. Jongeneel, "Kraemer, Hendrik," in *Biographical Dictionary of Christian Missions,* ed. Gerald H. Anderson (Grand Rapids, MI: Eerdmans, 1998), 375: "From 1938 to 1961 Kraemer dominated the scene in mission theology."

8 Wesley Ariarajah offers a useful review of Christian attitudes toward Hinduism before Tambaram in terms of the

World Missionary Conferences at Edinburgh (1910) and Jerusalem (1928). See S. Wesley Ariarajah, *Hindus and Christians: A Century of Protestant Ecumenical Thought* (Grand Rapids, MI: Eerdmans, 1991), ch. 2 and 3.

9 Hendrik Kraemer, *Religion and the Christian Faith* (London: Lutterworth Press, 1956), 224.

10 Kraemer, *Religion and the Christian Faith*, 112.

11 Hendrik Kraemer, *The Christian Message in a Non-Christian World* (London: The Edinburgh House Press, 1938), 110.

12 Kraemer has reservations about some forms of Christianity. Thus, he is doubtful of the Roman Catholic Church as a vehicle of salvation because of its doctrinal reliance on the distinction between nature and grace attributed to Thomism.

13 Kraemer, *Religion and the Christian Faith*, 102–4.

14 For Kraemer on Radhakrishnan, see especially *Religion and the Christian Faith*, ch. 5.

15 Kraemer, *Religion and the Christian Faith*, 110, emphasis added.

16 Kraemer, *Religion and the Christian Faith*, 117.

17 It is interesting to note that many of these Christian groups observe, by default or otherwise, caste distinctions and related practices, particularly in respect of marriage.

18 See Arun Shourie's impassioned critique of Christian missions in India, largely from a Hindu viewpoint, in Arun Shourie, *Missionaries in India: Continuities, Changes, Dilemmas* (New Delhi: ASA Publications, 1994).

19 This process has been described as a *praeparatio evangelica* (to use the Latin expression).

20 J. N. Farquhar, *The Crown of Hinduism* (London: Oxford University Press, 1913), 458.

21 Farquhar, *The Crown of Hinduism*, 51, emphasis added.

22 Farquhar, *The Crown of Hinduism*, 55.

23 J. N. Farquhar, *Gita and Gospel*, 2nd ed. (London: CLS, 1906), 73.

24 "Brahmabandhab": "Friend of *Brahman*/God." Upadhyay compared it to "Theophilus." On Upadhyay, see Julius J. Lipner, *Brahmabandhab Upadhyay: The Life and Thought of a Revolutionary* (Delhi: Oxford University Press, 1999). One of the reasons Upadhyay gave for becoming a Roman Catholic rather than a Protestant was that he did not wish to join the dominant faith of the colonizers of his land.

25 From Upadhyay's journal, the weekly *Sophia*, 27 October 1900.

26 Cf. Lipner, *Brahmabandhab Upadhyay*, 206.

27 For an account of one such attempt, the founding of *Saccidānanda* ashram at Shantivanam near the Kaveri river, see Jules Monchanin, *Swami Parama Arubi Anandam: [Fr J Monchanin], 1895–1957: A Memorial* (Tiruchirapalli: United Printers, 1959).

28 For a discussion of the hymn, see Lipner, *Brahmabandhab Upadhyay*, 191ff.

29 See *The Documents of Vatican II*, 1966, 661–2.

30 James Stuart, *Swami Abhishiktananda: His Life Told through His Letters* (Delhi: ISPCK, 1995), 235, 245, 271, 293.

31 Raimundo Panikkar, *The Unknown Christ of Hinduism* (London: Darton, Longman & Todd, 1964), 35.

32 See Raimundo Panikkar, *The Trinity and the Religious Experience of Man* (London: Darton, Longman & Todd, 1973), 68.

33 Raimundo Panikkar, *Myth, Faith and Hermeneutics* (Bangalore: Asian Trading Corporation, 1983), 287.

34 Beverly Lanzetta, "The Mystical Basis of Panikkar's Thought," in *The Intercultural Challenge of Raimon Panikkar*, ed. Joseph Prabhu (Maryknoll, NY: Orbis, 1996), 97.

35 See Karl Rahner, *Foundations of Christian Faith: An Introduction to the Idea of Christianity*, trans. William V. Dych (London: Darton, Longman & Todd, 1978), especially 311–21.

36 See Karl Rahner, "Anonymous Christians," in *Theological Investigations*, Vol. 6, trans. David Bourke (New York: Crossroad, 1982), 390–8.

37 Hans Küng, *Christianity and the World Religions: Paths to Dialogue with Islam, Hinduism, and Buddhism*, trans. Peter Heinegg (Garden City, NY: Doubleday, 1986), 176.

38 Küng, *Christianity and the World Religions*, 207, 227, 260.

39 Küng, *Christianity and the World Religions*, 280.

40 Küng, *Christianity and the World Religions*, 280–3.

41 Francis X. Clooney, *Seeing through Texts: Doing Theology among the Śrīvaiṣṇavas of South India* (Albany, NY: State University of New York Press, 1996), 37.

42 Francis X. Clooney, *Hindu God, Christian God: How Reason Helps Break Down the Boundaries between Religions* (Oxford: Oxford University Press, 2001), 8.

43 Cf. Francis X. Clooney, *The Future of Hindu–Christian Studies: A Theological Inquiry* (London: Routledge, 2017).

44 John Hick, *John Hick: An Autobiography* (Oxford: Oneworld, 2002), 323, emphasis added.

45 John Hick, *God and the Universe of Faiths: Essays in the Philosophy of Religion* (London: Palgrave Macmillan, 1973), chs. 9 and 10. Hick elsewhere uses Kantian language to express this distinction, paraphrased by Gavin D'Costa as follows: "The 'Divine Reality,' 'Eternal One' or the 'Real' ... occupied the centre of the universe of faiths and was analogous to the *noumenal* realm. The varying *phenomenal* responses within the different religious traditions, both theistic and nontheistic, were to be viewed as authentic but different responses to this noumenal 'Divine Reality.'" Gavin D'Costa, *Theology and Religious Pluralism: The Challenge of Other Religions* (Oxford: Basil Blackwell, 1986), 39.

46 Hick, *God and the Universe of Faiths*, 140. See also John Hick, *God Has Many Names: Britain's New Religious Pluralism* (London: Palgrave Macmillan, 1980), 33.

47 Hick, *God and the Universe of Faiths*, 140.

48 John Hick, *Death and Eternal Life* (Louisville, KY: Westminster John Knox Press, 1994), 391.

49 Perry Schmidt-Leukel, *Religious Pluralism and Interreligious Theology* (Maryknoll, NY: Orbis, 2017), 65–8.

50 Schmidt-Leukel, *Religious Pluralism and Interreligious Theology*, 69f.

51 Schmidt-Leukel, *Religious Pluralism and Interreligious Theology*, 69.

52 Schmidt-Leukel, *Religious Pluralism and Interreligious Theology*, 70.

53 See Schmidt-Leukel, *Religious Pluralism and Interreligious Theology*, 71–4 for a more detailed discussion of this popular but rather patronizing analogy in respect of the unsighted.

Recommended Reading

Anderson, Edward, and Arkotong Longkumer, eds. *Neo-Hindutva: Evolving Forms, Spaces, and Expressions of Hindu Nationalism*. London: Routledge, 2020.

Ariarajah, S. Wesley. *Hindus and Christians: A Century of Protestant Ecumenical Thought*. Grand Rapids, MI: Eerdmans, 1991.

D'Costa, Gavin. *Theology and Religious Pluralism: The Challenge of Other Religions*. Oxford: Basil Blackwell, 1986.

Dunn, James D. G., ed. *Fundamentalisms: Threats and Ideologies in the Modern World*. London: I. B. Tauris, 2016.

Farquhar, J. N. *Gita and Gospel*. 2nd ed. London: CLS, 1906.

———. *The Crown of Hinduism*. London: Oxford University Press, 1913.

Harris, Elizabeth J., Paul Hedges, and Shanthikumar Hettiarachchi, eds. *Twenty-First Century Theologies of Religions: Retrospection and Future Prospects*. Leiden: Brill, 2016.

Hedges, Paul, and Alan Race, eds. *Christian Approaches to Other Faiths: An Introduction*. London: SCM Press, 2008.

Killingley, Dermot H. *Rammohun Roy in Hindu and Christian Tradition: The Teape Lectures 1990*. Newcastle: Grevatt & Grevatt, 1993.

Kopf, David. *The Brahmo Samaj and the Shaping of the Modern Indian Mind*. Princeton, NJ: Princeton University Press, 1979.

Kraemer, Hendrik. *Religion and the Christian Faith*. London: Lutterworth Press, 1956.

———. *The Christian Message in a Non-Christian World*. London: The Edinburgh House Press, 1938.

Lipner, Julius J. *Brahmabandhab Upadhyay: The Life and Thought of a Revolutionary*. Delhi: Oxford University Press, 1999.

Panikkar, Raimundo. *Myth, Faith and Hermeneutics*. Bangalore: Asian Trading Corporation, 1983.

———. *The Trinity and the Religious Experience of Man*. London: Darton, Longman & Todd, 1973.

———. *The Unknown Christ of Hinduism*. London: Darton, Longman & Todd, 1964.

Prabhu, Joseph, ed. *The Intercultural Challenge of Raimon Panikkar*. Maryknoll, NY: Orbis, 1996.

Rahner, Karl. *Foundations of Christian Faith: An Introduction to the Idea of Christianity*. London: Darton, Longman & Todd, 1978.

Schmidt-Leukel, Perry. *Religious Pluralism and Interreligious Theology*. Maryknoll, NY: Orbis, 2017.

Smith, Wilfred Cantwell. *The Meaning and End of Religion*. Minneapolis, MN: Fortress Press, 1991.

Stuart, James. *Swāmī Abhishiktānanda: His Life Told through His Letters*. Delhi: ISPCK, 1989.

Theology and Religious Plurality

Jenny Daggers

Introduction

In the opening year of the period covered in this book, the colonial era was still in full swing, though the recent trauma of World War I was to hasten its demise. In this contemporary moment, it is timely to reassess our postcolonial legacy. Christian theology was implicated in colonialism then, and is caught up in postcolonial struggles now. The question of theology and religious plurality was pressing during the colonial period and is pressing now in our current postcolonial moment.

By the start of the period covered in this book, Christian theological understanding of religious diversity was indelibly marked by developments during the preceding four centuries of European colonialism and modernity. As our period opens, strong cultural connections forged between North America and Europe had created a Euro-American arena in which theological understandings of religious diversity had already taken shape.[1] Key aspects considered here are first, *religion and the religions* as a new conceptual framework for understanding religious diversity; second, *developmental theories of religion*, with Christianity placed as pinnacle, other text-based traditions ranked in the middle, and oral religious practices of Indigenous peoples at the base; and third, expansive European and American Protestant Christian missions, aiming at aggressive *displacement* or gradualist *fulfillment* of existing ritual practices by Christianity.

To point up this first development, some brief comments on premodern notions of Christian theology and religious plurality may be helpful. Although Judaism and paganism preceded Christian origins, Augustine's notion of Christianity as *vera religione* – the one true religion – was to shape long-standing Christian dismissal of other practices and beliefs, including Islam, as heresy, unbelief, or paganism.[2] By a related logic, Judaism was seen to have served its purpose as preparation for the gospel fulfilled in Christ. In this Augustinian perspective, Christianity alone emerged as a missionary religion, capable of transcending cultural boundaries. Late medieval Catholic Christian orders engaged afresh with Muslims and Jews, but none of those involved saw these intercultural encounters as dialogues between distinct "religions."

Ford's The Modern Theologians: An Introduction to Christian Theology since 1918, Fourth Edition.
Edited by Rachel Muers and Ashley Cocksworth.
© 2024 John Wiley & Sons Ltd. Published 2024 by John Wiley & Sons Ltd.

During the modern period, this Christian monopoly of the term "religion" was subject to serious challenge, as new notions emerged of *religion* as a generic category, to be studied in the plurality of historical positive *religions*. Colonizing Europeans encountered a range of ritual traditions, both oral and textual. Western Orientalist scholarship of these traditions gave rise to the founding disciplines of religious studies: history of religions and comparative religion. As this chapter shows, these forms of scholarship could be used for radically different ends. On one hand, knowledge of religious traditions and practices was viewed as a missionary tool to facilitate conversion of adherents to Christianity, in the expectation that all traditions would wither away following Christian missionary contact; on the other, such knowledge was used to challenge any notion of Christianity as the only true religion.

Developmental theories of religion manifest the European racism that justified the centuries-long slave trade of Africans to work colonial plantations, at a time when modern notions of human rights were being articulated for White European peoples: notions of white superiority and race-based White supremacy underlay such starkly contrasting human destinies. Premodern ideas of Christianity as the one true religion were perpetuated when Christianity was held up as the most developed form of religion. Missionary expectation that Christianity would *displace* Indigenous religions, or *fulfill* more complex textual traditions, once again manifested this premodern notion. In contrast, there was fierce resistance to even dignifying African ritual traditions as forms of religion. Developmental theories of religion perceived Christianity as the superior religion of modern colonial Europeans, who saw themselves as the most highly developed peoples. Secularizing narratives of progress likewise affirmed European superiority but asserted secular European modernity as destiny for the world. In this contrasting developmental view, Christianity was perceived as redundant.

In colonial contexts, then, conflicting European visions were in play. Secularists anticipated the replacement of precolonial cultures with Euro-American modernity; Christian missions assumed conversion would ensure all other forms of religion would wither away during this modernization process; and Orientalist fascination with the range of religions allowed for Christianity to be transcended by the generic category "religion," in the expectation that religious diversity would persist, and Christianity would be seen anew as one religion among others.

Survey: Four Moments for Theology and Religious Diversity Since 1918

This chapter identifies four moments in the relation of Christian theology and religious diversity since 1918. Although the opening of each moment can be identified historically, these moments are best understood as continuing into the present day, rather than as completed or even superseded. First, during the waning decades of the colonial era, mission, and the "young churches" established through mission, provided the main Protestant context for theological debate on persisting religious diversity.[3] Protestant mission conferences in this period offer a window on these debates. These conferences also provided a vehicle for the formation of the World Council of Churches (WCC) in 1948, where these debates continued.

The Second Vatican Council in the early 1960s opened a significant second moment in the relation of Christian theology and religious diversity. The council gave rise to a distinct Catholic impetus toward hospitable interreligious dialogue. One effect of this new direction was to facilitate ecumenical engagement between Catholic and Protestant advocates of dialogue.

A third moment emerged from the 1960s, in response to continuing hostility in some quarters toward respectful Christian engagement with other religions. New theologies of religions were articulated, offering a pluralist method of hospitality between religious traditions as an alternative to existing displacement and fulfilment methods, which were defined and critiqued in new terms as respectively exclusivist and inclusivist. Pluralist challenge deploys the "religion and the religions" map to place Christianity as one religion among others, so demoting its claim to Christian uniqueness.

The fourth moment evolved from the 1990s, in light of emerging postmodern and postcolonial criticism of pluralist theology of religions as a modernist White liberal movement, inflected with persisting colonial attitudes. Postmodern critique – a postscript to White colonial European modernity – challenges notions of fixed, clearly bounded religious traditions, emphasizing instead their dynamism, their internal variety, and their interconnections: the practice of official interreligious dialogue between authorized representatives is therefore problematized. Postcolonial perspectives – spearheaded by theologians of colonized heritage – interrogate the power relations between Christian mission churches and the religious plurality of (post) colonial contexts, often offering theologies of religious diversity or difference in place of theology of religions. The debate in recent decades is prefigured in the contribution of theologians of Asian heritage, who had long advocated peaceable coexistence of Christianity amid Asian religious diversity.

Within this fourth moment, hospitable engagement between religious traditions has been an enduring legacy of two distinct theological strands: a neglected and disregarded strand in Asian Christian theologies throughout our period, continued in postcolonial theologies; and the innovative and much-discussed Euro-American pluralist contribution. Both strands offer a vision of peaceable coexistence of Christianity with enduring religious traditions. Their substantial challenge to – often aggressive – Christian displacement attitudes to religious diversity has stimulated hospitable Christian theological projects that offer an alternative to the pluralist method, by simultaneously holding both to incommensurable difference between religious traditions and to the particularity of Christian theology. Trinitarian theologies of religion and projects such as Scriptural Reasoning and comparative theology exemplify an acceptance of religious diversity and a commitment to hospitable engagement, on Christian terms, with those who share this hospitable impetus, but on grounds drawn from their own religious traditions. Both pluralist and particularist grounds for hospitality offer a significant alternative to interreligious violence, bringing Christian theology closer to the peaceable interreligious living proposed by Asian theologians. Where pluralist approaches effectively employ religious studies methodologies, particularism enables Christian openness to religious diversity to be articulated on theological grounds.

Mission versus dialogue: Protestant World Missionary Conferences and the World Council of Churches

Records of world missionary conferences during the late colonial period provide a window on Christian attitudes to religious diversity in the twentieth-century missiological context.[4] The predominant mood of the first World Missionary Conference (WMC) in Edinburgh – held in 1910 at the zenith of the modern missionary movement – had been a confident expectation that radical displacement of other religions by Christianity was imminent. Participants at the Edinburgh conference were overwhelmingly White male missionaries. At the following event in Jerusalem in 1928, nearly one third of those gathered were participants from the "young churches" founded by mission but now under indigenous leadership. Despite this, the conference was dominated by Euro-American concerns and perspectives. The certainties of the long nineteenth century had underwritten the tone and content of the Edinburgh conference, but these had faltered in the aftermath of World War I. A fading confidence in the link between the gospel and Western civilization is evident in the 1928 conference proceedings.[5]

At the 1938 WMC at Tambaram, despite the majority of delegates being from the young missionary churches, discussion was focused on a debate between two Euro-American theologians: William E. Hocking, an American Harvard professor, and Hendrik Kraemer, professor of history of religions at Leiden, in the Netherlands. Hocking, author of *Rethinking Missions*, advocated a synthesis or reconception of religions. In this vision, the particularity of each tradition would be transcended by a single religion, which would therefore replace religious plurality. In contrast, Kraemer presented the thesis from his book, *The Christian Message in a Non-Christian World*, to argue for a radical discontinuity between Christianity and other religions, so that aggressive Christian mission intent on their displacement is the only theological option.[6]

Missing from this polarized debate is the gentler position of Christianity as fulfillment of other traditions, which encouraged respectful engagement and a deep appreciation of their inherent truth and value. Predating Tambaram, a minority Christian practice of respectful dialogue is found in some nineteenth-century mission and is evident in the 1910 Edinburgh conference papers.[7] However, this minority position was entirely squeezed out of the Tambaram discussion, with Kraemer dismissing it as abhorrent.

Although both Hocking and Kraemer's positions were debated at Tambaram, Christian theologians and missiologists opted strongly for Kraemer in the polarized debate in subsequent years, with the result that Christian engagement in interreligious dialogue was treated with suspicion for decades to come. It is significant that Kraemer drew on Karl Barth's theology in making his case, so implicating Barth in debates on religious diversity, which were largely absent in his *Church Dogmatics*. Kraemer's positioning of Barth was to be significant for critiques of the latter in pluralist theologies of religions.

Paul Tillich, too, began to address the question of persistent religious plurality in the final decade of his life. Although there is no direct link between Hocking and Tillich, they each brought their Western philosophical training to bear on, respectively, Christian mission and Christian theology, in relation to the recently coined term of universal generic religion. Tillich reconceived secularism as a religion. This enabled him to reposition his long-standing engagement of systematic theology with secularism, as a form of theological engagement with history of religions: his three-volume *Systematic Theology* could therefore be read in this new way.[8] Both Hocking and Tillich conceive of forms of universal religion that transcend Christianity. This move recurs in pluralist theologies of religions.

Christian attitudes articulated by White Euro-American theologians within the International Missionary Council (IMC) persisted within the WCC once the IMC was integrated within the WCC during the 1960s. Asian delegates at Tambaram spoke on both sides of the debate, but it is significant that many Indian theologians, notably Pandipeddi Chenchiah at Tambaram, and Paul Devanandan and M. M. Thomas in subsequent debate, argued strongly for a respectful engagement with Asian religious traditions, which – counter to Edinburgh conference expectations – were renascent under colonialism. This principled argument for the enduring theological worth of religious diversity was to reemerge in later postcolonial theologies.

Euro-American theologians defined dominant themes in the Protestant ecumenism of the WCC, where nascent postcolonial thinking was distrusted. However, through the patient insistence of Asian theologians such as Russell Chandran of India and Lynn de Silva of Sri Lanka at the 1975 WCC Nairobi conference, the Indian theologian, Stanley Samartha, as first director of a WCC subunit on interfaith dialogue, was empowered in 1977 to organize a significant interfaith consultation at Chiang Mai. Samartha's compatriot, S. Wesley Ariarajah, as a subsequent director of the subunit, continued the work begun by Samartha. However, this project was carried forward in the face of considerable Euro-American opposition, grounded in a frequently expressed fear that dialogue would lead to syncretism.

The Second Vatican Council: Catholic dialogue with other faiths and ecumenical interfaith engagement

The staunch opposition to interreligious dialogue arising from the IMC is in stark contrast with the revised theology of mission emerging at this time in the post-Second Vatican Council Catholic Church. As one expression of a wider *aggiornamento*, openness to interfaith dialogue became the authorized position of the Catholic Church, in contrast to strong support for Kraemer's resistance to dialogue in Euro-American Protestant mission circles. The 1965 document, *Nostra Aetate*, affirmed "Non-Christian Religions" and opened a path toward interreligious dialogue. Although there was no change to the Catholic Church being conceived as the sole means of salvation, interreligious dialogue was conducted alongside conversations with ecumenical and secular partners. It is significant that Msgr Petro Rossano was appointed to a Secretariat for Non-Christians, where he forged a path for dialogue, in 1966 speaking on this subject at a joint WCC-Catholic working group. Rossano and Samartha worked as ecumenical partners, with Rossano invited to make closing remarks at Chiang Mai.

Karl Rahner and Hans Küng made substantial contributions to Second Vatican Council Catholic theologies of religious diversity. Rahner's "supernatural existential" allowed him to perceive adherents to other religions as "anonymous Christians." While asserting Christ as the sole cause of salvation, Rahner saw Christ's salvific grace as mediated within history beyond the Catholic Church. His willingness to explore the action of grace beyond the sacraments of the Catholic Church was of great significance within the reorientation of Catholicism through the Second Vatican Council. Küng was committed to long-term engagement in interreligious dialogue. However, when he posited other religions as "ordinary ways of salvation," in contrast to the Catholic Church as "extraordinary way of salvation," he invited censure from the Catholic hierarchy. Both Rahner and Küng were subject to critique in pluralist theologies of religions.

The Second Vatican Council's openness to adherents of other faiths created significant paths for interfaith engagement in conformity with authorized Catholic doctrine. Catholic theologians, notably the American Jesuit, Francis X. Clooney, have pioneered committed forms of comparative theology. Lay American theologian Catherine Cornille makes a significant contribution to theologies of religious plurality, involving interreligious engagement with partners who each see their own faith tradition as a "place of return."[9]

It is significant to note that the impetus for the Second Vatican Council – with its ensuing openness toward dialogue – came from the Western church. The council expressed a newfound willingness to engage Western modernity and, through positive ecumenical relations, to heal the long-standing Catholic-Protestant splits of European history, and their wider ramifications. In contrast with Protestant Asian theologies that – contra dominant Western displacement missiologies – asserted the value of religious diversity and advocated respectful dialogue, postcouncil interfaith hospitality did not arise from a postcolonial appreciation of renascent religious diversity.

However, in the ensuing decades, a specifically Asian form of liberation theology arose in the Federation of Asian Bishops' Conferences (FABC), with a marked focus on interreligious living. FABC theologies contribute to the fourth moment in Christian theology and religious diversity. These debates are reflected in the mature work of the Sri Lankan Jesuit theologian, Aloysius Pieris. The Belgian Jesuit, Jacques Dupuis, is significant among White Catholic theologians for his careful engagement with Asian perspectives on interreligious living. This is evident in his book *Toward a Christian Theology of Religious Pluralism*, where he argues for the complementarity and convergence of the religions with the church. As with Küng, Dupuis's positing of the religions as paths of salvation contravenes the authorized Catholic view. The Congregation for the Doctrine of the Faith required a notification to this effect be added as appendix to the second edition of his book.

Dupuis also comments in this text that the postconciliar magisterium is "marked by a certain ambiguity."[10] The notable authorized Catholic volume *Catholic Engagement with World Religions* does a great deal to lend clarity.[11] The four parts of the book deal extensively with the history of Catholic understanding of religion, securely established truths of the Catholic faith, a synthetic theology of the uniqueness of Christianity and the meaning of other religions, and comparative science of the religions. Coeditor Morali shows a gentle graciousness toward Dupuis, affirming his "tenacious desire to remain firmly anchored in the faith."[12] However, no reference to FABC documents or to Pieris is made in *Catholic Engagement*: constituent authors do not discriminate between Asian Catholic perspectives – which are ignored – and Euro-American pluralist theologies of religions, which are subject to critique.

Christian theologies of religions: Theological pluralism and theological countermoves

It is important to recognize the distinction between the fact of religious pluralism or plurality and the method of hospitable Christian interreligious engagement that constitutes pluralist theologies of religions. Debates concerning Christian theology and religious plurality over the last forty years have relied on a schema for theologies of religions that defines exclusivist, inclusivist, and pluralist categories, often presented as exclusivism, inclusivism, and pluralism. First named by Alan Race, exclusivist and inclusivist categories are defined, then critiqued, so preparing the ground for the pluralist alternative.[13] However, these terms have been so widely used that their origin in pluralist theologies of religions is frequently overlooked. One reason for this is that Christian theologians have been willing to appropriate the terms exclusivist and inclusivist as self-descriptions, and so to work within the pluralist typology: in effect, earlier displacement and fulfilment positions are thus perpetuated.

John Hick and Paul Knitter are the two major architects of pluralist theologies of religions. Hick was a British philosopher of religion of Protestant formation who crafted the pluralist typology; Knitter is a lay Catholic American theologian who subsequently developed a pluralist liberation theology of religions. Hick and Knitter coedited a landmark text, *The Myth of Christian Uniqueness*, which had a major impact on subsequent debate.[14]

Hick's motivation for his pluralist turn was impeccable. Appointment to a chair in theology at the University of Birmingham in 1967 brought him to a British multicultural city, where he encountered people of diverse faiths. Hick undertook leading roles in several interfaith organizations in the city. His related theological project expresses the same commitment to harmonious relations between the diverse faith communities of postcolonial Britain. The political sensitivity of his context was demonstrated when, in 1968, the politician, Enoch Powell, delivered near Birmingham his notorious "rivers of blood" speech, predicting a violent outcome of this multicultural challenge to a White British identity. Knitter, in contrast, wrote as a lay theologian within a Second Vatican Council context, drawing strongly on Latin American liberation theology.

The pluralist method has appealed strongly to progressive Euro-American theologians who seek to promote interreligious justice and peace, while sitting lightly to authorized versions of the received doctrinal tradition. Thus, feminist theologians Rosemary Radford Ruether and Marjorie Suchocki contributed chapters to Hick and Knitter's *Myth*, while the religious studies scholar, Rita Gross, strongly recommended the pluralist method as the only option for a feminist theology of religions.[15]

A significant counter move to Hick and Knitter was made in the essay collection, *Christian Uniqueness Reconsidered: The Myth of a Pluralist Theology of Religions*, edited by lay Catholic theologian Gavin D'Costa.[16] Most contributors shared with advocates of the pluralist method an attitude of Christian respect and hospitality toward other religions. The dominant theme of this collection is a theological willingness to combine hospitality with a continuing commitment to Christian particularity, so creating an alternative option for Christian interreligious hospitality to that offered by the pluralist method.

The Trinitarian direction begun in *Christian Uniqueness Reconsidered* is followed by theologians who are deeply committed to Christian interreligious hospitality, based on their conviction that ongoing religious diversity has theological significance.[17] Dupuis argues in Trinitarian terms for an eschatological hospitality, envisaging the complementarity and convergence of the religions with the church.[18] The American Baptist theologian, S. Mark Heim, advances a highly original thesis of distinct religious ends, attempting to make these commensurate within a Trinitarian map.[19] The work of Asian theologians who take a Trinitarian approach is surveyed in the following section.

Theologians who wish to escape the confines of the exclusivist/inclusivist/pluralist paradigm have contested the retrospective designation of significant theologians as exclusivist or inclusivist. Thus, a challenge is made to readings of Barth as exclusivist, which continue Kraemer's deployment of Barth, and of Rahner's much-criticized notion of the "anonymous Christian" as inclusivist.[20] Post-Second Vatican Council Catholic theologians for a time debated whether the authorized Catholic position was better described as inclusivist or exclusivist, though more recent debate is not confined by these pluralist-defined terms.

It is also important to note that the displacement position is continued by evangelical theologians who retain explicit exclusivist affiliations. Daniel Strange re-presents earlier Reformed missiological scholarship to counter theological acceptance of ongoing religious diversity.[21] Keith Johnson also proceeds on the assumption that the sole function of religious diversity is *praeparatio evangelica*.[22] Both maintain that the only purpose of interreligious dialogue is to foster mission and Christian conversion.

Some distinctive Christian theological projects are hospitable to sustained interreligious engagements but choose not to engage further in debates on theologies of religions. Such initiatives assume the received Christian tradition as a place of return, while holding fast to the continuing integrity and incommensurability of distinct, though internally diverse and dynamic, religious traditions. Christian comparative theologians make deep scholarly engagement with texts belonging to other religious traditions.[23] The movement of Scriptural Reasoning, pioneered by David F. Ford, creates a form of interreligious dialogue between partners committed to different religious traditions, with a strong lead given by Ford in dialogue with Jewish and Muslim partners.[24] These provide examples of hospitable outreach without missionary intention.

By the final decade of the twentieth century, pluralist theologies of religions were subject to mounting critique of the modernist and colonialist mindset. As postmodern critique became a dominant theme in Euro-American universities, advocates of the pluralist method adapted with a strong countercritique against particularist reassertion and with adjustments to the original exclusivist/inclusivist/pluralist typology.[25] Graham Adams offers useful remapping of this complex field.[26] Amid these readjustments, an additional category of "particularism" was added to the original typology: pluralists charge particularists with seeing religious traditions as distinct cultural islands, strongly bounded and fortress like; this ascribed fixity contrasts with the dynamic remaking of traditions through pluralist-recommended interaction.[27] In my own work I argue for a particularist theology of religions that assumes dynamic cultural interaction at the boundaries and so accepts that incommensurable – though culturally dynamic – traditions persist. Theological hospitality to ongoing religious diversity is thus prioritized, as advocated by Asian theologians.[28]

Postmodern and Asian postcolonial critique of pluralist theologies of religions

In a postmodern perspective, the internal diversity of each tradition comes to the fore. Euro-American feminist participation in interreligious dialogue became more prevalent in the twenty-first century, often focused on individual interreligious conversations where women's religious commitments are explored as an aspect of broader complex, crosscutting and hybrid identities. Jeannine Hill Fletcher and German theologians Manuela Kalsky and Katherina von Kellenbach explore the implications of such hybrid identities.[29]

When D'Costa commented that pluralists minimize religious differences, because the pluralist "lives out of a history of western guilt about colonialism [and] imperialism," he exemplified a form of postcolonial critique, which sits within a lineage of critical Asian voices on religious plurality articulated throughout the twentieth century.[30] Some prominent examples appear in the preceding account given of IMC and WCC debates. Postcolonial critique, articulated by theologians of colonized descent, makes urgent criticism of the continuing impact of racism in postcolonial societies and brings to the fore alternative traditions and insights. As one aspect of this shift in perspective, during the twenty-first century, Asian Christian perspectives on religious plurality have gained more attention within Euro-American theologies.

Asian women theologians play a significant part. Korean feminist theologian Chung Hyun Kyung made an innovative presentation at the 1991 WCC conference in Canberra. Chung took WCC criticism of syncretism head on, offering an alternative principled syncretism in her performance as a woman shaman in

Korean Indigenous religion, accompanied by drums and dance. By this means, Chung made an invocation of the Holy Spirit, and a litany of spirits of named human beings, creatures, and the liberator Jesus, all of whom had suffered violent abuse.[31] It is important to recognize Chung's broader context of ecumenical Asian women's spirituality, which had been articulated in published theologies from the late 1970s. This network was facilitated by the Ecumenical Association of Third World Theologians and by the journal *In God's Image*; the characteristic openness to religious plurality, already noted in the Christian theologies of Asian men, here found distinct expression in women's theologies.[32]

Since the 1990s, Asian American theologians have articulated Asian theological priorities and so helped to shape wider theological debates in Euro-American contexts – where populations increasingly reflect the global diversity of our postcolonial world. This is fertile ground for Christian theology, which can look forward to a deep enrichment of received Euro-American theological traditions by insights drawn from Asian cultures. Kwok Pui-lan has been a leading exponent of theologies of religious diversity, or difference, over against theologies of religion. Together with other Asian feminist theologians, notably Grace Ji-Sun Kim and Wonhee Anne Joh, Kwok explores themes of syncretism, hybridity, and difference, as she contests the colonial imposition of White Euro-American cultures as the only legitimate forms of Christianity and Christian theology. Kwok argues that Asian feminist theologians envision a hybridized Christ, capable of destabilizing the colonial distinction between Asian wisdom traditions and Christianity.[33] The hybrid Christ offers an alternative to the repressive legacy of the colonial Christ.

In parallel with Asian American women's theologies, Asian American male theologians continue the Asian tradition surveyed here as a second moment following the Second Vatican Council. Notably Vietnamese American lay Catholic theologian, Peter Phan, has written prolifically on Christian theology and religious plurality, referring to dialogue with (poor) Asian peoples, their cultures and religions, as the "modality" of the Asian church: a way of "being religious interreligiously" from which Euro-American Christian theology can learn.[34] Phan argues for perception of the religions as creations of the Trinitarian Word and Spirit.[35] In a comparable vein, Malaysian American Pentecostal theologian, Amos Yong, reflects Asian concern with religious diversity in his theology of religions. His work is informed by African American perspectives, including womanist theologies. Yong adopts a "robust trinitarianism" that goes well beyond a Pentecostal correction of the tendency for Christology to overwhelm pneumatology, in a Trinitarian move that offers a promising way forward beyond the enduring legacy of the colonial Christ.[36]

Named Theologians

Gavin D'Costa (b. 1958)

Gavin D'Costa is a British lay Catholic theologian of Kenyan Asian descent, who took a leading role in countering pluralist theology of religions while extending Christian hospitality to other religions on Trinitarian grounds. As an undergraduate student at the University of Birmingham, D'Costa was taught by John Hick, which facilitated D'Costa's long-standing engagement with Hick's work. D'Costa's critique of Hick's pluralist theology of religions was developed in a number of publications, initially taking up an "inclusivist" position as defined by Hick's schema but discarding this in later work.

D'Costa's position on theology and religious plurality is firmly grounded in post-Second Vatican Council Catholic commitment to interreligious dialogue. By asserting the theological significance of religious plurality, while rejecting the view that "non-Christian religions" are vehicles of salvation, D'Costa steers a course within the bounds of authorized Catholic theology. This is evident in his invitation to coedit the authorized Catholic volume, *Catholic Engagement with World Religions*, and to act as advisor to the Pontifical Council on Interreligious Dialogue.

John Hick (1922–2012)

John Hick was a British philosopher of religion, of Protestant formation. Before Hick turned his attention to religious plurality, he gained wide attention for his controversial edited collection, *The Myth of God Incarnate*.[37] However, for Hick, religious plurality was the pressing issue facing twentieth-century Christian theology. He played a leading role in developing pluralist theologies of religions. This intervention was an aspect of his irenic attempt to promote peaceful relations between Christianity and peoples of other faiths, following postcolonial immigration to Britain. This commitment was also evident in his tireless work for interfaith collaboration in Birmingham, UK.

Hick initially presented his pluralist theology of religions as a "Copernican revolution," challenging Christian theologians to step back from asserting the uniqueness of Christ and thus the superiority of Christianity over differing religious traditions. Instead, he advocated a pluralist "theocentrism." Following his long collaboration with lay Catholic theologian, Paul Knitter, in his later work Hick shifted ground away from a philosophy of religion framework. He showed an openness toward Knitter's pluralist liberation theology of religions, with its soteriological focus, open to diverse religious vehicles of salvation.

Paul Knitter (b. 1939)

An American Catholic lay theologian, Paul Knitter played a significant role in developing pluralist theology of religions, with a pluralist liberation theology as hallmark of his own contribution. By collaborative work with John Hick, Knitter helped to develop theological debate on religious plurality in terms of the exclusive/inclusive/pluralist schema. Knitter's own pluralist positioning is informed by Latin American liberation theologies. He thus attends to oppression of the poor in his soteriological pluralist theology of religions.

Knitter has also helped to map the developing debate in theology of religions by naming a theological particularism, committed to recognizing boundaries between ongoing traditions.[38] In his later work, Knitter advocates interreligious meeting in "the commons," beyond the "backyards" of distinct religious traditions.[39] Knitter practices and articulates a Christian-Buddhist form of multiple religious belonging.

Kwok Pui-lan (b. 1952)

An Asian American theologian of Hong Kong Chinese heritage, Kwok is a pioneering Anglican theologian. She brings a postcolonial perspective, which is critical of the colonial Christ, where religious plurality is valued and power relations within theology and church are critiqued. Kwok works collaboratively with theologians of differing cultural backgrounds who share these priorities. With Rita Nakashima Brock, Kwok cofounded the Asian American feminist theology network, Pacific Asian North American Asian Women in Theology and Ministry. Kwok also draws on the insights of East Asian women theologians.

Kwok argues for theologies of religious difference over against theologies of religion. Shifting attention from the Atlantic to the Asia Pacific, she urges theologians to take seriously the multicultural, multilingual, and multiracial, as well as multireligious differences of Asian nations, and also to engage the increasing diversity and plurality within Western nations. Her attention to religious plurality is therefore cited within a broader theological attention to the implications of postcolonial diversity. Kwok is a leading figure in seeking out transnational and multicultural origins and genealogies for a political theology that is capable of moving beyond Eurocentrism.[40]

Stanley Samartha (1920–2001)

An Indian Protestant theologian from Karnataka, in the south of India, Samartha gained his degree at the United Theology College, Bengaluru, where Paul Devanandan was among his teachers, then was appointed as lecturer in theology and religions at a mission seminary in Mangalore, now Karnataka Theological College. Samartha then completed postgraduate studies at Union Theological Seminary in New York, where he was supervised by Paul Tillich, followed by a doctorate at Union Theological Seminary. After a year in Basel, where he attended lectures by Barth and encountered Kraemer, Samartha returned to become principal of the seminary.

In 1968, Samartha accepted an invitation to work for the WCC, and in 1971 he was appointed as director of a newly founded WCC subunit for Dialogue with People of Living Faiths and Ideologies. The work of the subunit faced considerable opposition within the WCC, mainly from White theologians who followed Kraemer's theology of rejecting Christian participation in interreligious dialogue. Samartha's deep knowledge of Hindu religion, and his commitment to engagement between people committed to different faiths, provided a basis for promoting dialogue in the face of this opposition. The 1977 Chiang Mai interfaith consultation was a significant breakthrough moment, but the standoff continued between Christian mission aimed at displacement and respectful interfaith dialogue. Samartha advocated a shift from a missiological to a theological framework for discerning a Christian response to religious plurality, so opening the question of its theological significance.

Debate

Key debates in the area of Christian theology and religious plurality surveyed here can be summarized under the following seven points.

1   There is a debate between the view that the purpose of Christian encounter with other religious traditions is *mission alone* – with religions valued solely as *praeparatio evangelica* – and the view that *religious plurality has theological significance* and ongoing value. On one hand, both aggressive displacement and more respectful fulfilment missionary attitudes in the colonial era anticipated that Christianity as superior religion would replace existing religious traditions. These approaches are continued by theologians who choose to adopt exclusivist or inclusivist positions, as defined by pluralist critique. In contrast, respectful interreligious engagement between persisting traditions may be valued by Christian theologians, either on pluralist or particularist grounds.

2   Displacement/exclusivist approaches *resist interreligious dialogue*, expressing fear of syncretism. Approaches that demonstrate *openness to interreligious dialogue*, by contrast, may express fulfilment/ inclusivist, pluralist, or particularist positions. All of these share a hospitable Christian attitude toward other religious traditions, fostering peaceful relations between adherents of different religious traditions.

3   Interreligious engagement may be regarded as a form of *alethic contest* between incommensurable truth claims that Christian theologians expect Christianity to win. This can be contrasted with the view that the question of religious truth is an *eschatological matter* that cannot be resolved within history. Where alethic contest brings to the fore incommensurable differences between traditions, eschatological deferral allows for irenic dialogue between partners, despite irreconcilable differences. *Catholic Engagement* expresses this form of hospitable eschatological deferral, which is also found in George Lindbeck's influential work on doctrine.[41]

4   There is an ongoing debate between *pluralist* and *particularist* theologies of religions. Both approaches place a high value on peaceable interreligious relations in postcolonial ethnically and religiously diverse Euro-American societies, but by employing contrasting methodologies. Hick claimed his pluralist

method as a "Copernican revolution," moving theology away from the Christocentric uniqueness of Christ asserted by exclusivist mission theologies, to a theocentric view that sees all religions as vehicles of salvation.[42] Knitter made a further soteriocentric move to a kingdom-centered pluralist liberation theology.[43] Both versions of the pluralist method place all religious traditions in a common field of generic religion, where Christian notions of salvation and humanity gathered into the coming kingdom of God may be realized. Later pluralist work shows a willingness to synthesize new forms of shared religion through interreligious engagement.[44]

In contrast, the particularist method accepts the ongoing incommensurability of religious traditions but finds theological grounds for building irenic relations with adherents of other traditions, who find warrants within their own traditions for their own interreligious engagement. Particularist theologies are centered on doctrine, but neither are they exclusivist nor do they assume rigid boundaries and fixed traditions: interreligious engagement can enrich and renew dynamic Christian tradition, in a similar way to a wider pattern of borrowing cultural materials for Christian use.[45] Theologians such as Hedges and Adams craft sophisticated theological methodologies that attempt to move beyond both pluralist and particularist approaches.[46] However, the question arises as to whether in this move they effectively replace theological with religious studies methodologies.

5 There are various approaches to the use of *religious studies methodologies* and approaches in theologies of religions. Although Hick's moves were made in Christian philosophy of religion, and Knitter's were informed by liberation theology, their method effectively adopted a religious studies methodology based around "religion and the religions," and explicitly rejected theological insistence on the uniqueness of Christ. Thus, theological particularity gives way to generic criteria, so repeating a pattern already found in Tillich and Hocking. Discussion in this chapter has highlighted irenic theological alternatives to the pluralist generic religion method.

Hick's "Copernican revolution" attempted to counter excessive missional Christological exclusivism; theological strategies that resist his "revolution" use the theological method of locating Christ within a renewed Trinitarian framework, and so moderate exaggerated Christocentrism in a theological way. Similarly, all forms of religious engagement where participants see their home traditions, as per Cornille, as a place of return, retain a Christian theological approach to their interreligious encounters, whether through comparative theology, Scriptural Reasoning, or other projects.

6 An important difference of emphasis is seen in the focus on *interreligious dialogue* in Euro-American contexts and *interreligious living* in Asian contexts – the latter being named by Phan as the modality of the Asian church. Such interreligious living is distinct from notions of generic religion forged during colonial modernity. Asian perspectives challenge the mindset of theologians whose tradition is European Christendom and provide models of peaceable interreligious living for contemporary Euro-American contexts.

7 Debates around theologies of religions have brought into focus, in previously colonized contexts, the tension between the *colonial Christ* of missionary theology and the imperative to *see Christ afresh*. For Pieris, Christ is seen with the Asian poor as covenant partners bringing in the Reign of God;[47] for Chung and Kim in forms of principled syncretism; and for Kwok in the hybrid Christ, capable of drawing on Asian wisdom traditions to combat the power relations that constitute our shared postcolonial legacy, shaping relations between those of contrasting colonizer/colonized heritage.

Influence, Achievement, and Agenda

Religious plurality invites Christian theology to locate itself in relation to the "religion and the religions" framework employed by religious studies. Christian theology within ancient and medieval Christendom maintained a self-understanding of Christianity as the one true religion, and a version of this tenet was continued in colonial missionary expectation that Christianity would displace or fulfill all other religious practices. Enduring religious plurality challenges this assumption, raising the question of whether theology should sit lightly to its received doctrinal traditions and favor religious studies methodologies, or whether theology can articulate its own distinct grounds to embrace enduring religious plurality.

Within the Euro-American Christian tradition, the question of enduring religious plurality follows theology's long engagement with secularizing modernity, where theologians articulated Christian "truth" in relation to emergent secularizing, scientific and technological "truths." Thus, Tillich's systematic theology was deeply engaged with Enlightenment philosophy and carefully correlated with secularism. Only by locating secularism as a religion could Tillich redirect his work toward a theology of religious pluralism. Post-Second Vatican Council Catholic theology can similarly be seen as to extend its novel outreach toward secular society to include "non-Christian religions," through Catholic openness to interreligious dialogue.

In the period covered by this textbook, the axis of theological challenge has shifted from modern theology's debates with Enlightenment thought alone, to broader cultural dialogue, including a current priority to address the postcolonial legacy left by colonial modernity. For Euro-American theologies, this involves engaging with ongoing religious plurality within majority White Euro-American contexts. Within this shift, Asian theologies of religious plurality, grounded in Asian interreligious living, have a growing importance for Christian theology.

In the face of ongoing aggressive displacement theologies, pluralist theologies of religion forged an alternative path to the common ground of generic religion as a place of hospitable interreligious encounter. This move invites theology to find its place within a religious studies framework. The pluralist initiative also stimulated creative theological responses from theologians who refused the pluralist invitation. The excessive Christocentrism that informed displacement – or exclusive – mission could instead be countered by hospitable systematic Trinitarian theologies. Textual scholars in comparative theology and Scriptural Reasoning have also pioneered tradition-based interreligious hospitality. Whether through pluralist or tradition-based projects, we must count as an achievement the creation of interreligious networks of friendship, dialogue and scholarly endeavor, amid the tensions of postcolonial societies, where those of colonizer and colonized descent live alongside.

Enduring religious plurality effectively changes Christian theology's subject of debate. Already in process is a shift toward theological engagement with the Euro-American interreligious living that is part of our postcolonial legacy, so unsettling theological preoccupation with Euro-American secularizing modernity. Hick's principled intervention to promote harmonious "interfaith" relations in 1960s Birmingham, UK, was a response to White British hostility toward those of colonized descent who had accepted the invitation to come "home." Half a century later, the colonizer heritage of White theologians is gradually emerging into their view. Meanwhile, Asian theologians continue to offer theologies of peaceable interreligious living. They also make visible the problematic colonial Christ, in contrast with richer theological alternatives that better suit the global postcolonial legacy. Issues raised by theologians of Asian descent are crucial for theology, as theologians of diverse cultural backgrounds – whether of colonized or colonizer descent – reappraise our postcolonial legacies, as we remake our postcolonial world.

Notes

1 I use "Euro-American" as a shorthand term in this chapter to refer to a dominant form of White Western culture that is reflected also in dominant White modern theologies.

2 Augustine's *De vera religione* is cited in Peter Henrici, "The Concept of Religion from Cicero to Schleiermacher: Origins, History, and Problems with the Term," in *Catholic Engagement with World Religions: A Comprehensive Study*, ed. Karl Becker et al. (Maryknoll, NY: Orbis, 2010), 5.

3 This decline preceded the gradual process begun in the mid-twentieth century of colonized nations asserting their political independence.

4 See Jenny Daggers, *Postcolonial Theology of Religions: Particularity and Pluralism in World Christianity* (Abingdon: Routledge, 2013), 74–9.

5 See Report of the Jerusalem Meeting of the International Missionary Council as cited by Wolfgang Günther in "The History and Significance of World Mission Conferences in the 20th Century," *International Review of Mission* 92, no. 367 (2003): 525.

6 For discussion of the Tambaram debate, see E. C. Dewick, *The Christian Attitude to Other Religions* (Cambridge: Cambridge University Press, 1953), 44–5.

7 See Kenneth Cracknell, *Justice, Courtesy and Love: Theologians and Missionaries Encountering World Religions, 1846–1914* (London: Epworth Press, 1995), 35–106 regarding this minority tradition, which he finds expressed in an unpublished report written prior to the 1910 conference, *The Missionary Message in Relation to Non-Christian Religions*.

8 Key texts authored by Tillich in the final decade of his life are *Christianity and the Encounter of the World Religions* (New York: Columbia University Press, 1963) and "The Significance of the History of Religions for the Systematic Theologian," in *The Future of Religions*, ed. Jerard J. Brauer (New York: Harper & Row, 1966), 80–94.

9 Catherine Cornille, *The Im-possibility of Interreligious Dialogue* (New York: Crossroad, 2008), 72.

10 Jacques Dupuis S.J., *Toward a Christian Theology of Religious Pluralism* (Maryknoll, NY: Orbis, 2001), 179.

11 Becker et al., eds., *Catholic Engagement with World Religions*.

12 Ilaria Morali, "Overview of Some Important Francophone and Italian Trends," in *Catholic Engagement with World Religions*, 325.

13 In Alan Race, *Christians and Religious Pluralism: Patterns in Christian Theology* (London: SCM Press, 1983).

14 John Hick and Paul F. Knitter, eds., *The Myth of Christian Uniqueness: Toward a Pluralistic Theology of Religions* (Maryknoll, NY: Orbis, 1987).

15 Rita Gross, "Feminist Theology as Theology of Religions," *Feminist Theology* 26 (2001): 83–101. See Daggers, *Postcolonial Theology of Religions*, 119–22 for my critical engagement with Gross.

16 Gavin D'Costa, ed., *Christian Uniqueness Reconsidered: The Myth of a Pluralistic Theology of Religions* (Maryknoll, NY: Orbis, 1990).

17 Thus Rowan Williams in "Trinity and Pluralism," in *Christian Uniqueness Reconsidered*, 3–16, engages the Trinitarian thought of the unique Catholic theologian, Raimundo Pannikar, informed by Pannikar's deep engagement with Hinduism, whereas Gavin D'Costa in his *Meeting of the Religions and the Trinity* (Maryknoll, NY: Orbis, 2000), 110, maintains the Spirit at work in the religions is "intrinsically trinitarian and ecclesiological."

18 Dupuis, *Toward a Christian Theology of Religious Pluralism*, 356–7.

19 S. Mark Heim, *The Depth of the Riches: A Trinitarian Theology of Religious Ends* (Grand Rapids, MI: Eerdmans 2001).

20 See Daggers, *Postcolonial Theology of Religions*, 97–102, for critique of these characterizations of Barth and Rahner.

21 Daniel Strange, *Their Rock Is Not Our Rock: A Theology of Religions* (Grand Rapids, MI: Zondervan Academic, 2015).

22 Keith E. Johnson, *Rethinking the Trinity and Religious Pluralism: An Augustinian Assessment* (Downers Grove, IL: IVP Academic, 2011). See Daggers, *Postcolonial Theology of Religions*, 188–9 and 192f. for my critical engagement with Johnson.

23 Francis X. Clooney, *Comparative Theology: Deep Learning across Religious Borders* (Oxford: Wiley-Blackwell, 2010).

24 David F. Ford, "An Interfaith Wisdom: Scriptural Reasoning between Jews, Christians and Muslims," *Modern Theology* 22, no. 3 (2006): 345–66.

25 The ecumenical theologian, George Lindbeck defines a cultural-linguistic model of doctrine as alternative to a cognitive-propositional model, which is important in the emergence of particularist methods. George Lindbeck, *The Nature of Doctrine: Religion and Theology in a Postliberal Age* (Louisville, KY: Westminster John Knox Press, 2009).

26 Graham Adams, *Theology of Religions: Through the Lens of "Truth-as-Openness"* (Leiden: Brill, 2019).

27 See, for example, Paul Hedges, *Controversies in Interreligious Dialogue and the Theology of Religions* (London: SCM Press, 2010), 176.

28 Daggers, *Postcolonial Theology of Religions*.

29 See Jeannine Hill Fletcher, *Monopoly on Salvation? A Feminist Approach to Religious Pluralism* (London: Continuum, 2005); and Manuela Kalsky and Katharina von Kellenbach, "Interreligious Dialogue and the Development of a Transreligious Identity: A Correspondence," *Journal of the European Society of Women in Theological Research* 17 (2009): 41–58.

30 Gavin D'Costa, "Pluralist Arguments: Prominent Tendencies and Methods," in *Catholic Engagement with World Religions*, ed. Becker et al., 344.

31 Chung Hyun Kyung, "Come Holy Spirit – Renew the Whole Creation," in *Signs of the Spirit: Official Report of the Seventh Assembly of the WCC, Canberra, 1991*, ed. Michael Kinnamon (Geneva: WCC, 1991), 37–47.

32 See Ursula King "Introduction," in *Feminist Theology from the Third World: A Reader*, ed. Ursula King (London: SPCK, 1994), 12–15; Aruna Gnanadason, "Women and Spirituality in Asia," in *Feminist Theology from the Third World*, 340–50 and Kwok Pui-lan "The Future of Feminist Theology: An Asian Perspective," in

Feminist Theology from the Third World, 63–76; Chung Hyun Kyung, *Struggle to Be Sun Again: Introducing Asian Women's Theology* (Maryknoll, NY: Orbis, 1990); *Faith Renewed II: A Report on the Second Asian Women's Consultation on Interfaith Dialogue, November 1–7, 1991* (Seoul: AWRC, 1991); Choi Man Ja, "A Feminist Theology of the Korean Goddesses" in *Faith Renewed II*, 180–91; Mary John Mananzam and Sun Ai Park, "Emerging Spirituality of Asian Women," in *With Passion and Compassion: Third World Women Doing Theology*, ed. Virginia Fabella and Mercy Amba Oduyoye (Maryknoll, NY: Orbis, 1988), 77–88. It is important to recognize that African women theologians, particularly through the Circle of Concerned African Theologians, with Mercy Amba Oduyoye as founder member, were also involved in interreligious dialogue and solidarity at this time. However, the focus of this chapter is on Asian theologians, given the long history of Asian religious plurality.

33 Kwok Pui-lan, *Postcolonial Imagination and Feminist Theology* (Louisville, KY: Westminster John Knox Press, 2005), 183.

34 Peter Phan, *Being Religious Interreligiously: Asian Perspectives on Interfaith Dialogue* (Maryknoll, NY: Orbis, 2004), 238.

35 Phan, *Being Religious Interreligiously*, 118.

36 Amos Yong, *Beyond the Impasse: Toward a Pneumatological Theology of Religions* (Grand Rapids, MI: Baker Academic, 2003), 43.

37 John Hick, ed., *The Myth of God Incarnate* (London: SCM Press, 1977).

38 See Paul F. Knitter, *Introducing Theologies of Religions* (Maryknoll, NY: Orbis, 2002) for his revised schema of pluralist-defined categories including particularity.

39 See Paul F. Knitter, "Is the Pluralist Model a Western Imposition? A Response in Five Voices," in *The Myth of Religious Superiority: Multifaith Explorations of Religious Pluralism*, ed. Paul F. Knitter (Maryknoll, NY: Orbis, 2005), 32–3.

40 See Kwok Pui-lan, *Postcolonial Politics and Theology: Unravelling Empire for a Global World* (Louisville, KY: Westminster John Knox Press, 2021).

41 See Karl J. Becker and Ilaria Morali, "Conclusion: Looking Backward and Forward," in *Catholic Engagement with World Religious*, 510 for an authorized Catholic statement of this position, and Lindbeck, *The Nature of Doctrine*, 33, 39–41.

42 John Hick, "The Non-Absoluteness of Christianity," in *The Myth of Christian Uniqueness*, 22.

43 Paul F. Knitter, "Toward a Liberation Theology of Religions," in *The Myth of Christian Uniqueness*, 187.

44 See essays in Knitter, ed. *The Myth of Religious Superiority*, as a significant example, and Daggers, *Postcolonial Theology of Religions*, 171–3 for my critical engagement with this text.

45 See Daggers, *Postcolonial Theology of Religions*, 167–71 for discussion of this point, which is informed by Kathryn Tanner's notion of cultural borrowings, across fluid and permeable boundaries between Christian and other ways of life, in Kathryn Tanner, *Theories of Culture: A New Agenda for Theology* (Minneapolis, MN: Fortress Press, 1987).

46 Hedges, *Controversies in Interreligious Dialogue and the Theology of Religions*; Adams, *Theology of Religions: Through the Lens of "Truth-as-Openness."*

47 Aloysius Pieris, "Christ Beyond Dogma: Doing Christology in the Context of the Religions and the Poor," *Louvain Studies* 25, no. 3 (2000): 207.

Recommended Reading

Primary

Becker, Karl J., Ilaria Morali, with Maurice Borrmans and Gavin D'Costa, eds. *Catholic Engagement with World Religions: A Comprehensive Study*. Maryknoll, NY: Orbis, 2010.

Clooney, Francis X. *Comparative Theology: Deep Learning across Religious Borders*. Oxford: Wiley-Blackwell, 2010.

D'Costa, Gavin, ed. *Christian Uniqueness Reconsidered: The Myth of a Pluralistic Theology of Religions*. Maryknoll, NY: Orbis, 1990.

Fletcher, Jeannine Hill. *Monopoly on Salvation? A Feminist Approach to Religious Pluralism*. London: Continuum, 2005.

Hedges, Paul. *Controversies in Interreligious Dialogue and Theology of Religions*. London: SCM Press, 2010.

Hick, John, and Paul F. Knitter, eds. *The Myth of Christian Uniqueness: Toward a Pluralistic Theology of Religions*. Maryknoll, NY: Orbis, 1987.

Kim, Grace Ji-Sun. *The Grace of Sophia: A Korean North American Women's Christology*. Cleveland, OH: Pilgrim Press, 2002.

Pieris, Aloysius. "Christ Beyond Dogma: Doing Christology in the Context of the Religions and the Poor." *Louvain Studies* 25, no. 3 (2000): 187–231.

Yong, Amos. *Beyond the Impasse: Toward a Pneumatological Theology of Religions*. Grand Rapids, MI: Baker Academic, 2003.

Secondary

Adams, Graham. *Theology of Religions: Through the Lens of "Truth-as-Openness."* Leiden: Brill, 2019.

Cornille, Catherine. *The Im-possibility of Interreligious Dialogue.* New York: Crossroad, 2008.

Daggers, Jenny. *Postcolonial Theology of Religions: Particularity and Pluralism in World Christianity.* Abingdon: Routledge, 2013.

Ford, David F. "An Interfaith Wisdom: Scriptural Reasoning between Jews, Christians and Muslims." *Modern Theology* 22, no. 3 (2006): 345–66.

Harris, Elizabeth J., Paul Hedges, and Shanthikumar Hettiarachchi, eds. *Twenty-First Century Theologies of Religions: Retrospection and New Frontiers.* Leiden: Brill, 2016.

Phan, Peter. *Being Religious Interreligiously: Asian Perspectives on Interfaith Dialogue.* Maryknoll, NY: Orbis, 2004.

Theology Facing Contemporary Challenges

Theology and Capitalism

Devin Singh

Introduction

Theological reflection on capitalism has taken place for as long as something called "capitalism" has been in existence. To be sure, Christian theologizing on matters monetary and economic has existed since the rise of Christianity, incorporating long-standing Jewish and Greco-Roman concerns around wealth, poverty, and the ethics of exchange. Such reflection expanded and complexified during the Middle Ages, through influential scholastic casuistry around just prices, usury, and the legitimacy of wealth-seeking, for instance. Amid such theological and philosophical debates, social practices, technologies, and institutions were being transformed and would come to constitute the bedrock of a new economic system.

The story of the rise of capitalism and market society is tied together with the story of religious, political, and cultural transformations that occurred in Europe associated with the Renaissance and Reformation. The story of capitalism is also inextricably linked to the history of the colonial encounter, institutions of chattel slavery, and new definitions of the household and, with them, constructions of gender and reproduction. Many of the framing ideas of this new mode of production and exchange were heavily conditioned by theological and moral debate. Capitalism is a theologically freighted phenomenon, therefore, and invites theological analysis.

Given this volume's focus on *modern* theologians, particularly those of the twentieth and twenty-first centuries, this chapter will not rehearse the historical background or explore the theologians who lived and worked at the dawn of capitalism. Such considerations will come into view, however, as we review some of the questions pursued by contemporary thinkers engaging capitalism. Examining theological engagements with capitalism inevitably leads to debates about the "when" of capitalism as much as the "what," because efforts to define capitalism's essence and key characteristics are bound up with issues of periodization. The "when" of capitalism is also bound up with its "where," with spatial and geographic considerations, given the historical specificities of its emergence in the interchange between Western Europe and its colonies.

Mapping modern theological engagement with capitalism also includes examining methods, such as how one conceives the relationship between theology and economy and thereby justifies the points of contact,

Ford's The Modern Theologians: An Introduction to Christian Theology since 1918, Fourth Edition.
Edited by Rachel Muers and Ashley Cocksworth.

exchange, and influence between the two realms of thought and practice. Modeling the relation may lead to the inclusion of philosophy and critical theory as discourses concerned with epistemology and hermeneutics. Exploring theology and capitalism also involves ethical consideration, because much Christian thought about economic concerns involves moral judgments and prescriptions about what constitutes right economic relations. Calls toward mercy, compassion, and justice that figure centrally in Christian social and ethical traditions necessarily set their sights on economic matters under capitalism. Philosophy and ethics therefore remain intertwined and overlapping fields that inform theological engagement with capitalism.

Survey

This section explores some fundamental considerations around how we might define capitalism as an object of inquiry. It also attends to methodological issues and variations in framing engagements between theology and capitalism. It considers some of the conceptual and ethical challenges that emerge in the encounter.

Defining the object and scope

The question of what capitalism *is* is not as straightforward as it may seem. There are ongoing debates about periodization: the "when" of capitalism.[1] For instance, should the mercantilism that preceded full-fledged capitalism be considered a noncapitalist precursor or an early-stage form of capitalism? Is the "essence" of capitalism best captured in the agrarian transformations that shaped land access and use, particularly in England, in the seventeenth and eighteenth centuries, or in its industrial stage a century later? Or is capitalism's mid-twentieth-century financialized form more revelatory of its internal logic, driven as it clearly is by bank lending activity and the use of financialized instruments of credit and debt?

Diachronic differentiation is not the extent of the debate, however, as evidenced by the important contemporary field of comparative capitalisms. This synchronic approach shows that there is no one, fixed, master version of capitalism. Rather, capitalism is always marked by local variations with cultural and historical contingencies. One may be able to abstract from this diversity to some common denominator of characteristics, a contestable "ideal type" of capitalism. This can be important for analysis but must not be reified when it comes to recommendations for policy or praxis. The latter must always be correlated to actual manifestations of the economic system, lest it fight with phantoms.

If theologians seek to assess and possibly critique capitalism, it becomes necessary to define its key characteristics. While debate persists, such characteristics include the private ownership of the means of production and the alienation of labor, now priced through a wage system. Central as well is a banking system that drives the money supply through lending both to nation states and private actors, such that national fiat currencies are wedded to private credit money. This fuels business enterprise as the engine that seeks profit maximization and produces commodities, while extracting the highest possible value from labor at the minimum possible wage. The enforcement of private property rights and contracts also becomes essential. The capitalist era is marked by the intensity and extension of such practices. In other words, although historians may find instances of these practices in other periods, what marks capitalism is their pervasiveness and normative quality. They define the nature of production and exchange and contribute to the formation of an abstract entity – the market – that has become central to social, political, and, of course, economic life.

Theological engagement with capitalism is motivated not simply by concerns about the shortcomings of economic systems. Theorists also recognize how knowledge creation, symbolic power, cultural formation, and the forging of subjectivity itself are shaped by capitalism. Capitalism makes an existential purchase.

Specific claims about human nature justify capitalism, and the lifeworlds it generates both posit and limit what human being as such looks like. Capitalism conditions how we view ourselves, one another, and our world; it produces certain intimacies while eroding others.[2] Engaging capitalism theologically therefore includes responding to and potentially resisting the ways capitalism forms the self and influences relationships. Given Christianity's own existential claims and pretensions toward subject formation, it may find itself in competition with the worldviews generated by capitalism. This sense of competing claims about what constitutes "the good life" or what humans should value informs many critical accounts of the economy and influences how theology positions itself vis-à-vis capitalism.

Matters of existential influence lead to questions of the kinds of political and cultural regimes that travel with capitalism. Neoliberalism has thus emerged as a key object of inquiry in theological and ethical circles. Often confused with capitalism, neoliberalism defines a system and philosophy of governance that has developed alongside certain versions of capitalism. A defining characteristic is the use of government, paradoxically, to enforce ideologies of less governance and deregulation. Neoliberal ideology operates well beyond illusions of a free market, using state coercion to deregulate on behalf of private owners and corporate interests. State oversight extends with financialization, such that audit cultures, accounting practices, and the price mechanism are used as central methods for governmental administration. Neoliberalism propounds ideologies of bootstrap individualism, entrepreneurship, individual utility, self-interest and consumer preference, and the privatization of formerly public and common goods.[3]

Neoliberalism as a philosophy of governance raises the topic of economic theology and its links to political theology. Attention to the theological dimension here includes theology's impact on political and economic practice. Economic theology, like political theology, can be defined in varying ways, but central is its examination of the encounter between economic and theological ideas and practices. Stefan Schwarzkopf provides a succinct definition in his recent introduction to the field:

> [Economic theology] is the study of the forms of interaction between theological imaginaries on the one hand, and economic thought and economic-managerial practices on the other, both past and present. It identifies explicit and implicit theologies inherent in economic concepts, institutions and practices as well as the role of economic terminology within theological thought, both past and present.[4]

Schwarzkopf's definition highlights the reciprocal interaction between economic ideas/systems and theological claims, adding an additional layer of nuance: among the many theological critiques of capitalism and the handful of theological defenses of it, this approach moves beyond the binary to highlight mutual influence.

The proximity to political theology issues the reminder that theological engagement with capitalism requires assessment of political dynamics. Although temporary heuristic separation can be useful for assessments of certain economic aspects, one must not lose sight of the role that state institutions, policy, and law play in shaping market systems. Insight into the history of capitalism reveals that a series of deliberate legal and state administrative decisions enabled the rise of this economic system. To believe in the market's spontaneous self-emergence is to believe the myth that capitalism tells about itself.

Methodological considerations

Theological approaches to capitalism typically relate specific points of Christian doctrine to economic practices, themes, and concerns, and have emerged from various denominational traditions, theological movements, and geographical contexts.[5] Such tactics explore theological loci and then delineate their economic implications. Such engagements are typically ethically concerned. Nevertheless, other approaches give ethical theory center stage, striving to establish moral guidelines for the relationship between theology and capitalism.[6] Their aim is to construct a cohesive ethical system to guide economic actions rather than to delve deeply into theological imagery and doctrine. Theories such as narrative, virtue, and feminist ethics, deontology, and utilitarianism are dialogue partners. Still other ethicists draw on labor theory, work on global financial markets, womanism, intersectionality, and critical race theory to complexify Christian ethical evaluations of capitalism.[7] Theology and ethics use philosophical tools to articulate their claims. Nevertheless, other approaches take a more analytical approach to economic concerns by using philosophy and critical theory as sources of insight, while integrating theological perspectives and ethical concerns.[8] These approaches differ from traditional theological methods by relying on philosophical voices and being less bound to parameters such as tradition or scripture.

Regardless of disciplinary location, the engagement between theology and capitalism presumes some relation between Christian doctrine and practice, on one hand, and the ideas and institutions of capitalism, on the other. At the level of popular and pastoral practice, the presumption that Christians can and should just say and do things about capitalism is perfectly acceptable. Academic theology, however, calls for self-reflexivity about the justification for such engagement. The question of theology's relationship to capitalism can be located within a broader exploration of theology's relationship to the world, culture, and society. Although theology is certainly a product of the latter, its attempts to describe transcendent realities lead to epistemological and methodological challenges.

Various devices are invoked to bridge this gulf between transcendence and immanence, or God and creation: the analogy of being or the analogy of faith, or a model of Christ's incarnation as the basis for some union-in-distinction of these spheres, for instance. Debates about social Trinitarianism also hinge on the capacity or lack thereof for creaturely realities to mirror divine ones, and raise the question of how the inner world of Trinitarian life might "touch down" as it were in the human sphere to shape life accordingly. This example is relevant given the use of Trinitarian models by some theologians to advocate a particular economic ethic against capitalism.[9] The point here is that, when theologians seek to engage capitalism, included are the challenges of relating divine transcendence to the immanent human sphere.

The tension is heightened with economic matters, which have been highly vexatious for Christian thought and raise anxieties that have coursed within Christianity from the start. Many theologians have thus taken pains to imagine a theological space untainted by the world of exchange. If the love of money is the root of all kinds of evil, surely money itself is suspect, such that one must ensure that one's theology has not been influenced by it or by commodity exchange. If one cannot worship both God and Mammon, one's descriptions of God must have nothing to do with the realm of wealth and economy. The methodological ethos that emerges here is ethically freighted: to posit some kind of relationship between theology and capitalism is to risk idolatry or to confound what God has separated. Theologians who engage capitalism, and who want to make clear on what terms they do so, must face not only the conceptual challenges of relating transcendence to immanence but the ethical red flags of those concerned that said theologians are somehow up to no good by establishing a connection between the things of God and the "devilish" world of exchange.

An alternative mentality, which I advocate, accepts as a commonplace that language games and cultural forms influence one another, that cross-transmission is the norm and not the mark of ethical failure. In our case, it recognizes the ways theology has affected capitalism and capitalism has influenced theology. Studies about the role of theology in the formation of capitalism are one helpful entry point into understanding this linkage.[10] Such influence includes interpenetration of terms, tropes, metaphors, and other conceptual models. When theology engages capitalism, it may uncover theological ideas that were already embedded within economic reasoning and practice. Similarly, the influence that capitalism has upon theology may result from the already embedded economic concepts within theology.

I have elsewhere suggested homology to describe the connections between theology and economics. "Homology" as I use it indicates relations of filial connection, mutual dependence, and shared or related lines of conceptual descent.[11] Drawing from the use of biological metaphors to explore historical, textual, and conceptual relations, homology in this sense indicates that theological language and economic language have informed one another for centuries and that theologically engaging capitalism is best done with awareness of this long-standing connection. Beyond the linguistic realm, I claim that there is also a relationship between religious and economic institutions and practices. Homology emphasizes links and transfers and so moves beyond analogy as a way to grasp similarity across difference. Homology signals the endurance of material relations and the lingering traces glimpsed in metaphors and larger conceptual systems used within the two fields.

Viewing this normal influx and efflux of linguistic and cultural formations neutrally means to forestall ethical judgment about such influence until its impact can be assessed. It accepts as a necessary condition of human life that theological language will draw from and be shaped by the economic contexts of its production, internalizing certain economic concepts and assumptions. Such theological language will, in turn, shape economic context and be appropriated and used in the formation of new economic ideas and practices. The fact that, for example, theological models of divine providence were essential for framing the idea of market equilibrium is on its own neither an ethical failure nor triumph.[12] Closer examination of the uses toward which theologies of providence were put in actual deployments of market models would reveal such theologies at times facilitating arguments for deregulated markets and at times supporting views of market management and oversight to curb excesses.[13] One's ethical judgments about the impact of theology on capitalism would thus be conditioned presumably by one's position on the merits of these divergent visions of the market. Similarly, one can describe in neutral terms how language of financial calculation and purchase became essential to the logic of redemption theologies.[14] One may, however, choose to lament some unforeseen consequences of these mergers or the purposes toward which such doctrines are put, and at other times celebrate the immanent interventions theology can make precisely from its internalized economic language and logic.

Named Theologians

This section reviews some contemporary contributors to the conversation on theology and capitalism. By no means exhaustive or comprehensive, it aims to present some diversity of scope and method; thinkers discussed here are primarily theologians but also represent fields such as ethics, philosophy, and history. Each approaches the topic from their unique vantage point and with different aims in mind.

William Cavanaugh

Cavanaugh is an ethicist and moral theologian working within the Catholic tradition. His *Being Consumed* intervenes in several aspects of capitalist economies, taking on the ideal of the free market, consumption practices, dynamics of globalization, and the logic of scarcity that undergirds market competition.[15] He critiques capitalist anthropology that departs from a Christian vision of human fulfillment in God. In a market context, restless, unmet desires propel a continuous consumption that never satisfies, a consumption that supports and is in turn buttressed by an anemic view of freedom as the absence of constraints. Cavanaugh instead asserts freedom as the realization of the human *telos* in God. Such freedom is found in relationship with God and fellow Christians and is marked by the eucharist as the central practice that offers an alternative logic of consumption. As Christians consume the host they are in turn consumed by Christ and become his body, the church, which is a community of counter-consumption. This community is marked by relations of mutuality and abundance, which in turn mirror Trinitarian mutuality. In such contexts, Christians can achieve the true freedom of fulfillment in God, not freedom to compete within the scarcity of the market. Such communities of counter-consumption also challenge the injustice of globalization, and here Cavanaugh looks to fair trade and localized forms of production and exchange that embody a eucharistic ethic of mutuality and abundance.

Keri Day

Day is a constructive theologian and ethicist who draws on her experiences within Black Pentecostalism as well as on womanist and Black feminist traditions to evaluate and challenge elements of capitalism. Her work centers the experiences and practices of Black and Brown women and incorporates theological reflection from religious communities that have been marginalized by both mainstream economies and mainline Christianities. In *Religious Resistance to Neoliberalism* Day takes on neoliberalism, which, as we have seen, operates both as a philosophy of governance and cultural force shaping ways of life.[16] She decries competition and acquisitiveness as central values of a regime that encourages us to see self-formation through an entrepreneurial lens. Incorporating an important womanist suspicion of redemption narratives, she offers creativity as a better option for thinking through the limitations of neoliberal capitalism and fashioning more life-giving alternatives.

Day marshals a notion of the erotic that, she claims, figures centrally in marginalized communities of Black and Brown women. The erotic names the "shared deep feelings, sensations, and connection with and for each other that wake us up to love, freedom, and pleasure."[17] The erotic combats the closure, competition, and fear of difference in neoliberalism, inviting us to open, inclusive loves and new affective bonds with otherness. Building on this vision, Day's approach in *Azusa Reimagined* retrieves the experiences and communal forms of the Azusa Street revivals that marked one early manifestation of Pentecostalism.[18] Such communities also demonstrate the inclusive, erotic bonds that challenge the logic of scarcity in capitalism and provide a model for radical democracy as an alternative to the hegemonic application of neoliberal ideology, despite all its talk of personal agency. Day's work provides a view from the underside of capitalism and from minoritized Christianities, where horizons of alternative possibility are most visible.

Philip Goodchild

Philosopher Philip Goodchild's significant reflections on capitalism draw from biblical studies, theology, and forms of continental thought. Rather than construct, say, a systematic theology of money, he contends in *Theology of Money* that modern monetary systems themselves reveal an implicit theology seen in principles such as the faith that sustains the global credit system. Goodchild devotes primary attention to explicating and problematizing the thought systems, assumptions, and values undergirding modern money and the patterns of desire under capitalism.[19] He offers a normative ethical vision, resisting the corrosiveness of modern faith in an abstract credit system as opposed to faith and trust in communal relations. Central to his project is the claim that money has usurped the place of God as the ultimate measure of value and that to undo the power of global capitalism we must create (or restore) a valuation system beyond money that allows us to value things intrinsically and not according to price.

Goodchild's magnum opus, a trilogy titled *Credit and Faith*, moves this agenda forward through an extended reflection on the problem of value and related concerns of time and attention.[20] It also takes a step beyond a philosophical analysis of economy to probe the symbiotic relationship between philosophy and economy, asking how both might be transcended and reimagined. In this dense, challenging, complex, and wide-ranging philosophical work, Goodchild constructs his own philosophical system for valuation as a route for resistance to capitalism. He also indicts certain philosophical projects for their enmeshment in economic logic and centers other voices as more helpful resources for alternative valuation. These works offer many rich conceptual resources from which theologians and ethicists might construct visions and practices for change.

Mary Hirschfeld

Mary Hirschfeld brings an important interdisciplinary perspective as a trained economist who, following a conversion to Catholicism, added advanced training in theology to her expertise. Shaped by the thought of Thomas Aquinas, Hirschfeld examines what Thomistic thought has to offer the conversation between theology and economics. In *Aquinas and the Market*, she challenges aspects of orthodox economics while seeking a constructive dialogue between it and theology.[21] She critiques the governing role that efficiency plays as the determinative value in standard economic analysis and utility theory. Such thinking lends itself, she surmises, to the assumption that accumulation as such is a sufficient end in itself. Economics unmoored is unable to determine what the actual good is that economic actors should seek, and as such requires placement within a broader system of meaning and value. Thomas offers such a framework, one that includes significant attention to economic concerns. His assertion, and Hirschfeld's following him, is that human happiness comes from achieving our intended purpose, a purpose that is bound to creation's broader purpose of revealing divine goodness. Because economic thinking and action are legitimate pieces of purposeful human activity, it follows that happiness is a vital economic goal, one that is missed when efficiency is supremely prized. Theological economics recasts economic theory with such human ends in mind, ranking higher and lower order goods and centering virtue as a goal that supersedes economic satisfaction. Surplus wealth, i.e. that which exceeds what one needs in providing for oneself and one's family, is to be used to provide for others. Social discernment, including that of ecclesial communities, is essential in the process of determining whether wealth is fulfilling a legitimate need or an illegitimate desire and in deciding how best to redistribute resources. In drawing on Thomas, Hirschfeld contributes precapitalist theological and economic thinking in ways that may bring challenge to modern economies and the theories that support them.

Paul Oslington

Oslington is also a trained economist who, like Hirschfeld, sought further training in theology. Much of his work examines economic history, historical theology, the theologies operative in the thought of key economic thinkers. His research provides important context for constructive theologians making claims about capitalism and also gives historical insight into theology's influence at various points in economic history. *Adam Smith as Theologian* is an important edited collection of essays convened by Oslington that sheds light on Smith's religious milieu and on the theological themes present in Smith's work.[22] The essays explore the ways theology influenced foundational ethical and economic ideas in Smith and how theologians and ethicists might assess capitalism today in light of Smith's legacy.

Oslington's own later monograph, *Political Economy as Natural Theology*, takes up these themes and extends them in a wide-ranging examination of Smith and influential economic thinkers that preceded and followed him.[23] Oslington's aim is to demonstrate how central natural theology was for thinkers who established the field of political economy. Whereas extensive work exists on how natural theology was essential for the rise of the modern natural sciences, less attention has been devoted to its role in the social sciences and in economics, in particular. Oslington fills that gap and shows how the early modern British intelligentsia accepted such theology as foundational. Notions of an ordered creation reflecting God's power and goodness and a baseline faith in divine providence were the premises from which early moral philosophers extended their science of exchange. Not only were market dynamics conceptually modeled on a sense of divine management but the ameliorative potential of market society was offered as a kind of theodicy.

Oslington documents the rise and fall of this theological economic union in a way that reveals the mutual shaping and indeed dependence of these fields and opens fruitful new pathways for theological intervention in light of this shared history.

Kathryn Tanner

Theologian Kathryn Tanner approaches analyses of capitalism from traditional systematic theology, informed by Anglican, Reformed, and feminist perspectives. Her work relates core Christian doctrines, such as the Trinity and incarnation, to models of the economy and to economic concerns. Her *Economy of Grace* establishes a framework for thinking about the affinities, linking points, and contrasts between divine and earthly economies.[24] Tanner explicates the patterns of relationship in the economy of grace, God's theological economy, highlighting its contrasts with the capitalist sphere. She marshals reflections on God's noncompetitive relation to creation to establish principles for economic relations based in turn upon mutuality and noncompetition. The economy of grace is one where God bestows gifts upon creation that are not diminished even as they are shared. The Christian ideal involves in part serving as a channel of grace to others; both the giver and receiver are blessed. Tanner enjoins Christians to conceive of how a grace-oriented economy might improve the world market system. Claiming that post-World War II proposals by J. M. Keynes were never fully implemented, Tanner sets forth a series of Keynesian prescriptions for market intervention, including welfare and social safety net proposals and a revitalization of public and common goods.

Whereas *Economy of Grace* builds toward a more public theological set of policy proposals accessible to Christians and non-Christians alike, Tanner's *Christianity and the New Spirit of Capitalism* remains primarily confessional and is aimed to renew believers' faith.[25] The work sets theological principles of conversion, justification, and sanctification into contrast with countervailing principles of debt that lay claim upon and shape human lives in late finance capitalism. The theologically informed framework for conversion enables a conceptual break with the past to which many remain chained by the bonds of debt and the need to generate surplus through labor. Tanner further articulates a Protestant "anti-work ethic" that resists the links between productivity and self-worth so central to capitalism, links that foreclose openness to the future by forced attention to the present. She sets forth an alternative vision, indeed "an imaginative counter to the whole world of capitalism," of a life encompassed by divine grace.[26] Although lacking instructions for intervention, which, arguably, Tanner already provided in *Economy of Grace*, the upshot of this work is a contrasting vision of Christian values counterposed to those of finance capitalism that serves as a point of critique of the current regime.

Jonathan Tran

Theological ethicist Jonathan Tran's recent intervention into studies of capitalism marks an important inflection point. In *Asian Americans and the Spirit of Racial Capitalism* Tran relays crucial historical and theoretical work on the ways race, racism, and racialization function as elements of capitalism, claiming they are essential to capitalism's operations and successes.[27] Tran writes from the subject position of an Asian American facing the challenge of an American racial discourse that largely operates along a Black–White binary. Progressive politics that emerge from this nexus offer ambivalent horizons for Asian American praxis. Tran adds nuance to the conversation by showing that such binaries need disruption by a more textured picture of the racialized hierarchies that serve the interests of capitalism. In this way, economics alone is insufficient to understand how capitalism functions. More controversially, racial logic is itself a function of economy. As such, Tran intervenes in conversations about identity politics by resisting claims of independent social ontologies of race, arguing that we can make sense of race only by understanding the economics that undergird it and that we can dismantle racism only by undoing the capitalism that gives it life. Tran contributes a rich ethnography of an urban Asian American church attempting forms of racial and economic justice as one vision for a community guided by the "deep economy" of divine grace rather than the divisive, competitive, scarcity logic of capitalism.

Nimi Wariboko

Nimi Wariboko is a theological ethicist or self-described "theological theorist" who draws on African Pentecostalism and Indigenous African religions, while using his training in finance and accountancy to provide original engagements with aspects of capitalism. His *God and Money* models monetary relations in the global financial system after social Trinitarianism.[28] Wariboko establishes a mediation for this model by following Paul Tillich's work on the Trinitarian nature of the human condition. Money as a form of social relation expresses this structure of human nature. It follows that such relations might be patterned after relations among the persons of the Trinity. The risk is that humans continually elevate money to the place of God rather than pattern monetary relations after God. Drawing from Tillich's claim that human nature reflects tensions between a desire for particularity and diversity, on one hand, and universality and unity, on the other (which, for Tillich, are reflected in polytheism and monotheism, respectively), Wariboko suggests that the global financial system should retain a multiplicity of national currencies and also develop a single world currency that Wariboko terms the "earth dollar." Such unity-in-difference might be able to foster more just economic relations through the counterbalancing tensions between local and global currencies, much like the unity-in-difference in the Trinity can be understood nonhierarchically.

Wariboko has further developed his interventions by thinking through the nature of the economic subject and economy as such. In *Economics in Spirit and Truth*, he explores the care of the soul in light of the challenges of finance capital. He examines the links between theology and economics and articulates an antifragile ethic as a mode of reclaiming human freedom against the constraints of capitalism. He suggests that a split or fracture exists in finance that enables such interventions. In *The Split Economy*, Wariboko examines this split further, arguing that the roots to modern economy were established when early humans made the decision to begin saving surplus for the future, effectively splitting desire between present consumption and speculation about the future. The future was effectively created in this way and has come to govern increasingly more of economic decision making. Wariboko approaches the split nature of human subjectivity through Pauline analysis of grace and law, and argues that the ethical objective should be to abolish the future as generated by capitalism and construct a new, alternative future.[29]

Debate

A major point of ethical contention is the question of what stance Christian theology should take in its engagement with capitalism. Should it be critical, and if so, to what degree? Should it advocate reform or revolution? Should it be laudatory, offering endorsements and defenses of the market system? Should it be descriptive and exegetical, eschewing a normative position?

One recurrent site of historical contention concerns the role of theology in capitalist development. Given Max Weber's influential thesis about Calvinist communities fueling the rise of capitalist enterprise, debate persists about the accuracies of his assessment and the place of other theological traditions in supporting or resisting capitalism.[30] Contending against Weber's claims, some thinkers are concerned to exonerate Calvin from such associations or, at the least, heavily nuance interpretation by closer attention to Calvin's actual teaching. Although such interventions are at times motivated by the perceived scandal of association between Calvinism and worldly economy, the upshot of some of these studies is more historically nuanced examinations that contribute better pictures of the ideas and practices on the ground during a time of new economic emergences.

Some theologians willing to admit that theology shaped the rise of capitalism issue the caveat that such theology was heterodox or heretical. This is a confessional or dogmatic claim, one that may boost a sense of piety but not one that is social-scientifically persuasive. The claim attempts to maintain a boundary around orthodox (read: authentic and pure) theology as somehow disconnected from economy. Any theology that does give evidence of linkages to capitalism can therefore be designated a priori as heterodox. More careful exponents of this view may take the time to exegete the theological views of early market theorists to show how they fail the test of some standard of orthodoxy. What this move misses are examples of other economic thinkers whose theology could justifiably be construed as orthodox. It also misses the more interesting forms of indirect, cultural, and institutional influence by orthodox Christianity on market developments regardless of the self-conscious, espoused views of political economy's framing figures.

Methodological debates are concerned with how to approach and engage capitalism from the standpoint of theology and from within Christian communities. As noted, one overarching anxiety is to avoid impugning theology or reducing its capacity for virtuous judgment upon capitalism. Such undermining might take place, some worry, by suggesting that economic ideas and practices have influenced the shape of theology. It may also result from the inverse: if Christian doctrine helped give rise to capitalism, is such doctrine redeemable? D. Stephen Long, a theological ethicist who has contributed much rich work to the Christian conversation on capitalism, is concerned that "it will be difficult, if not impossible, to be a Christian theologian that affirms its central mysteries and rejects capitalism" if it can be shown that orthodox Christian thought contributed to the rise of market society.[31] For him, such a line of influence invalidates theological critique. Furthermore, if theology is a product of church communities, to suggest that theology and capitalism shape one another risks admitting to an ecclesial failure to maintain adequate distance from the world.

Although I grant that it is perfectly legitimate to attempt to order Christian communal life in ways that *appear* different from the world, to imagine that such communities can remain unchanged by it is illusory. No such hermetic seal exists. To foist it upon theology by doubling down on its distinctiveness from the economy ruptures the mirroring work that theology does of the communities who produce it. Furthermore, sequestering theology and church with such a boundary potentially undercuts theology's ability to speak to a world from which it is purportedly totally separate, and it thus interrupts the capacity for the sacred to transform the profane.

One way to allay such concerns is to emphasize that the homological relation between theology and economics need not lead to determinism. Economics need not take a particular shape despite its heritage in theologically laden worldviews, claims, and conceptual systems. Neither is theology somehow "warped" or "tainted" with a genetic disease due to its being influenced by the economy. Although the presence of economic logic has indeed influenced theology's trajectories in actual history, this does not fix theology's horizon of possibility. Theology's links with economic ideas and practices are impossible to extricate, but this is only a neutral observation and need not be taken on its own as a failure of theology. It simply sets the stage for more nuanced, social-scientifically responsible, and self-reflexive modes of theological engagement.

Agenda

A variety of directions for further research exist. Capitalism is a system in flux, despite the ideology espoused by some that we have reached the "end of history" or that "there is no alternative" to capitalism.[32] Two millennia of proclamation and intervention on economic matters notwithstanding, the need for Christian theological reflection and response continue. This section highlights just a few of the many possible routes for future engagement.

Money, credit, and debt

Money, credit, and debt continue to be central sites in need of analysis. So far, in-depth understanding of the complexities of these economic instruments has not permeated theological discussions of economics. Aside from important targeted studies by a handful of scholars, much theological critique takes place at a surface level or speaks in generalities. This is understandable given how complex these instruments are and how much debate persists among social scientists about how to understand them. Yet, theologians wishing to engage with capitalism meaningfully should make an effort to wade into the conversation because money, credit, and debt represent the lifeblood and sustaining features of capitalism.

Theological engagements with money, credit, and debt might attend to theological ideas that inform and shape these instruments or marshal ideas that resist and critique them. They might provide philosophical analysis of the assumptions that undergird such exchange systems. They might explore the relation of the economic dynamics in question to ways theology supports political concepts and regimes. The rise of digital and cryptocurrencies represents another key cutting-edge site for engagement.[33] There is much needed reflection on this merger of monetary dynamics with digital technologies, with all the complexities, promises, and pitfalls that such dimensions bring. Theologians versed in economics and technology should be in conversation about the implications of such developments.

Race, gender, and sexuality

Although it has long been recognized that class and the economy intersect with other identity categories, further theological reflection is called for. Work that centers these categories as necessary for analysis and constitutive of capitalism would offer fresh takes. Racial capitalism marks a variety of ways to think about the intersections of race, racism, and political economy.[34] It draws upon discussions of anti-Blackness, White supremacy, and the legacy of slavery in the West. Although definitions vary, the central point is that elements of race and racialization are endemic to capitalist dynamics such that analysis of one dimension requires the other. For some, the implication here is that capitalism cannot be adequately understood, let alone critiqued and transformed, without attending to the ways race enables the deployment of class dynamics. In such scenarios, race deserves more examination. For others, the implication is that racial issues operate almost superstructurally over economic ones and that the real target for analysis and challenge is the economy. In these approaches, racial challenges will be addressed as a byproduct of addressing capitalism. The opportunity here is for theologians addressing capitalism and those addressing race to converge and assess how to intervene in ways that show the interworkings of both sides.

Racialization of capital brings together race and class with attendant considerations of social reproduction that draw on gender and sexuality studies. Theologians have been addressing the role that religion has played in constructing and resisting this assemblage. It is important to consider the ways that theology has contributed to racial categories as well as upheld class and gender hierarchies. Some theological responses have sought to provide frameworks for understanding God and theology from the point of view of communities including people of color, the differently abled, and sexual minorities who have typically been othered and marginalized from religious communities. Considering the racialization of capital together with gender, sexuality, and social reproduction invites analyses of theology's role in maintaining or subverting the social, racial, and sexual contracts, and other matters related to so-called human capital and labor that are always raced and gendered.

Corporate form

A key area of inquiry is a theological analysis and genealogy of, and further critical engagement with, the corporation.[35] The history of the business corporation must be thought together with the history of the body politic, emerging notions of nationhood, and the vicissitudes of ecclesiastical structure in the West. The concept of *persona ficta* was created in the Middle Ages by papal decree and represents a watershed development in legal theory that has implications for law, business, and economy, as well as for religion, politics, and new forms of social organization. Fictitious corporate personhood raises ethical questions about the structures and activities of firms and raises broader metaphysical questions about personhood and subjectivity.

A variety of directions present themselves for Christian theological analysis. The most obvious are ethical concerns about the practices of corporations in terms of how they engage with society, how they treat their employees and the public, how they interact with and avoid legal regulations, and the kinds of direct impact they have through advertising and marketing. Concerns about consumption and commodification center on corporate practices as well, as the drivers and architects of such practices. In addition, the interaction between the business corporation and the church is a site of interest. This is seen within contemporary megachurch studies, where evangelical and other nondenominational churches emulate corporate practices of leadership, media communication, and even financial accountancy. The interchange of corporate and ecclesial practices invites further study to complement studies of the role of Christian businessmen's associations and other initiatives of Christian entrepreneurship that enthusiastically endorse capitalist work culture and practices.

Thinking exits and ends

Like all economic systems, capitalism will give way to something else – eventually. The question for many who resist capitalism is whether this transition can be hastened by further theological production, protest, and communal action. Either way, the critical edge for theological engagements with capitalism is to think about such transitions, whether they are exits created by historical actors (including theologians and church communities) or ends that come inevitably due to large-scale historical change. Even those who support capitalism will benefit by recognizing the inevitability of something beyond it. Rather than dogged resistance to such transitions, employing the theological imagination to anticipate other possible orders can facilitate better outcomes and improve communal response to such changes.

Such thinking is also practiced resistance to the totalization narrative offered by pundits of capitalism and the moves by capital firms to project the front of a unified, totalized system. Capitalism's historical contingency and systemic vulnerabilities induce its defenders to present it as a totality and inevitability. Theologians might highlight, instead, the rapid changes taking place that show forth the possibility for new arrangements. They might also enter debates about whether, say, accelerationism, inoperativity, or resistance are more useful interventions. Public theological contributions are especially needed around practical policy changes and new economic institutional arrangements.[36]

These are but a few of a vast set of possible directions needed in the engagement between theology and capitalism. Although much important and valuable work has been done, the need continues. As both theology and the economic system continue to change and evolve, new perspectives will emerge. As theologians seek better ways to assess capitalism, self-reflexivity will result in better ways to do theology as well.[37]

Notes

1 Giovanni Arrighi, *The Long Twentieth Century: Money, Power, and the Origins of Our Times* (London: Verso, 1994); Ellen Meiksins Wood, *The Origin of Capitalism: A Long View* (London: Verso, 2002); Jürgen Kocka, *Capitalism: A Short History*, trans. Jeremiah Riemer (Princeton, NJ: Princeton University Press, 2016).

2   See Devin Singh, "Speaking of Love in a Time of Capital," *Political Theology* 17, no. 5 (2016): 413–16.

3   Wendy Brown, *Undoing the Demos: Neoliberalism's Stealth Revolution* (New York: Zone Books, 2015); Melinda Cooper, *Family Values: Between Neoliberalism and the New Social Conservatism* (New York: Zone Books, 2017); Martijn Konings, *Capital and Time: For a New Critique of Neoliberal Reason* (Stanford, CA: Stanford University Press, 2018).

4   Stefan Schwarzkopf, "An Introduction to Economic Theology," in *The Routledge Handbook of Economic Theology*, ed. Stefan Schwarzkopf (London: Routledge, 2020), 4.

5   M. Douglas Meeks, *God the Economist: The Doctrine of God and Political Economy* (Minneapolis, MN: Fortress Press, 1989); Marion Grau, *Of Divine Economy: Refinancing Redemption* (New York: T&T Clark, 2004); Kathryn Tanner, *Economy of Grace* (Minneapolis, MN: Fortress Press, 2005); Kathryn Tanner, *Christianity and the New Spirit of Capitalism* (New Haven, CT: Yale University Press, 2019).

6   Max L. Stackhouse et al., *God and Gobalization*, 4 vols. (Harrisburg, PA: Trinity Press, 2000); D. Stephen Long and Nancy Ruth Fox, *Calculated Futures: Theology, Ethics, and Economics* (Waco, TX: Baylor University Press, 2007); William T. Cavanaugh, *Being Consumed: Economics and Christian Desire* (Grand Rapids, MI: Eerdmans, 2008); Mary L. Hirschfeld, *Aquinas and the Market: Toward a Humane Economy* (Cambridge, MA: Harvard University Press, 2018).

7   Joerg Rieger, *No Rising Tide: Theology, Economics, and the Future* (Minneapolis, MN: Fortress Press, 2009); Nimi Wariboko, *God and Money: A Theology of Money in a Globalizing World* (Lanham, MD: Lexington Books, 2008); Nimi Wariboko, *Economics in Spirit and Truth: A Moral Philosophy of Finance* (New York: Palgrave Macmillan, 2014); Keri Day, *Religious Resistance to Neoliberalism: Womanist and Black Feminist Perspectives* (New York: Palgrave Macmillan, 2016); Ilsup Ahn, *Just Debt: Theology, Ethics, and Neoliberalism* (Waco, TX: Baylor University Press, 2017).

8   Philip Goodchild, *Theology of Money* (Durham, NC: Duke University Press, 2009); Philip Goodchild, *Credit and Faith* (Lanham, MD: Rowman & Littlefield, 2020); Joshua Alan Ramey, *Politics of Divination: Neoliberal Endgame and the Religion of Contingency* (Lanham, MD: Rowman & Littlefield, 2016); Adam Kotsko, *Neoliberalism's Demons: On the Political Theology of Late Capital* (Stanford, CA: Stanford University Press, 2018); Hollis Phelps, *Jesus and the Politics of Mammon* (Eugene, OR: Cascade, 2019).

9   Meeks, *God the Economist*; Leonardo Boff, *Holy Trinity, Perfect Community* (Maryknoll, NY: Orbis, 2000); Wariboko, *God and Money*.

10 Robert H. Nelson, *Reaching for Heaven on Earth: The Theological Meaning of Economics* (Lanham, MD: Rowman & Littlefield, 1991); Paul Oslington, ed., *Adam Smith as Theologian* (New York: Routledge, 2011); Paul Oslington, *Political Economy as Natural Theology: Smith, Malthus and Their Followers* (London: Routledge, 2018); Eugene McCarraher, *The Enchantments of Mammon: How Capitalism Became the Religion of Modernity* (Cambridge, MA: The Belknap Press of Harvard University Press, 2019); Benjamin M. Friedman, *Religion and the Rise of Capitalism* (New York: Alfred A. Knopf, 2021).

11 Devin Singh, *Divine Currency: The Theological Power of Money in the West* (Stanford, CA: Stanford University Press, 2018), 17–22.

12 Lisa Hill, "The Hidden Theology of Adam Smith," *European Journal of History of Economic Thought* 8, no. 1 (2001): 1–29; Schwarzkopf, "Markets and Marketization."

13 Friedman, *Religion and the Rise of Capitalism*.

14 Singh, *Divine Currency*.

15 Cavanaugh, *Being Consumed*.

16 Day, *Religious Resistance to Neoliberalism*.

17 Day, *Religious Resistance to Neoliberalism*, 81.

18 Keri Day, *Azusa Reimagined: A Radical Vision of Religious and Democratic Belonging* (Stanford, CA: Stanford University Press, 2022).

19 Goodchild, *Theology of Money*. See also Philip Goodchild, *Capitalism and Religion: The Price of Piety* (London: Routledge, 2002).

20 Goodchild, *Credit and Faith*; Philip Goodchild, *Economic Theology: Credit and Faith II* (Lanham, MD: Rowman & Littlefield, 2020); Philip Goodchild, *The Metaphysics of Trust: Credit and Faith III* (Lanham, MD: Rowman & Littlefield, 2021).

21 Hirschfeld, *Aquinas and the Market*.

22 Oslington, *Adam Smith as Theologian*.

23 Oslington, *Political Economy*.

24 Tanner, *Economy of Grace*.

25 Tanner, *Christianity and the New Spirit of Capitalism*.

26 Tanner, *Christianity and the New Spirit of Capitalism*, 219.

27 Jonathan Tran, *Asian Americans and the Spirit of Racial Capitalism* (New York: Oxford University Press, 2022).

28 Wariboko, *God and Money*.

29 Wariboko, *Economics in Spirit and Truth*; Nimi Wariboko, *The Split Economy: Saint Paul Goes to Wall Street* (Albany, NY: State University of New York Press, 2020).

30 Max Weber, *The Protestant Ethic and the Spirit of Capitalism*, trans. Stephen Kalberg, rev. and updated ed. (New York: Oxford University Press, 2011).

31 D. Stephen Long, "Can Christians Be Capitalists?" *Marginalia: Los Angeles Review of Books* (15 February 2019). For my response to Long here, see Devin Singh, "The Anxiety of Influence," *Marginalia: Los Angeles*

Review of Books (15 March 2019). For Long's own important earlier intervention into theology and economics, see D. Stephen Long, *Divine Economy: Theology and the Market* (London: Routledge, 2000).

32   See, respectively, Francis Fukuyama, *The End of History and the Last Man* (New York: Free Press, 1992); Claire Berlinski, *"There Is No Alternative": Why Margaret Thatcher Matters* (New York: Basic Books, 2008).

33   See, for example, Devin Singh, "Crypto-Ethic? Presence, Relationality, and Care among Digital Currencies," in *Religious and Cultural Implications of Technology-Mediated Relationships in a Post-Pandemic World*, ed. Ilia Delio and Noreen Herzfeld (Lanham, MD: Lexington, 2023), 165–92.

34   See Eric Eustace Williams, *Capitalism and Slavery* (Chapel Hill, NC: University of North Carolina Press, 1944); Cedric Robinson, *Black Marxism: The Making of*

the Black Radical Tradition (Chapel Hill, NC: University of North Carolina Press, 2000); Nancy Leong, "Racial Capitalism," *Harvard Law Review* 126, no. 8 (2013): 2153–2226.

35   Perry Dane, "Corporations," in *The Routledge Handbook of Economic Theology*, ed. Stefan Schwarzkopf (London: Routledge, 2020), 144–53. One focused study is Amanda Porterfield, *Corporate Spirit: Religion and the Rise of the Modern Corporation* (Oxford: Oxford University Press, 2018).

36   Devin Singh, "Economics," in *T&T Clark Handbook of Public Theology*, ed. Christoph Hübenthal and Christiane Alpers (New York: Bloomsbury, 2022), 414–31.

37   Portions of this chapter reproduced with permission material contained in Devin Singh, *Economy and Modern Christian Thought* (Leiden: Brill, 2022).

Recommended Reading

Ahn, Ilsup. *Just Debt: Theology, Ethics, and Neoliberalism.* Waco, TX: Baylor University Press, 2017.

Cavanaugh, William T. *Being Consumed: Economics and Christian Desire.* Grand Rapids, MI: Eerdmans, 2008.

Day, Keri. *Religious Resistance to Neoliberalism: Womanist and Black Feminist Perspectives.* New York: Palgrave Macmillan, 2016.

Friedman, Benjamin M. *Religion and the Rise of Capitalism.* New York: Alfred A. Knopf, 2021.

Goodchild, Philip. *Capitalism and Religion: The Price of Piety.* London; New York: Routledge, 2002.

———. *Theology of Money.* Durham, NC: Duke University Press, 2009.

Grau, Marion. *Of Divine Economy: Refinancing Redemption.* New York: T&T Clark, 2004.

Hirschfeld, Mary L. *Aquinas and the Market: Toward a Humane Economy.* Cambridge, MA: Harvard University Press, 2018.

Long, D. Stephen. *Divine Economy: Theology and the Market.* London: Routledge, 2000.

McCarraher, Eugene. *The Enchantments of Mammon: How Capitalism Became the Religion of Modernity.* Cambridge, MA: The Belknap Press of Harvard University Press, 2019.

Oslington, Paul, ed. *The Oxford Handbook of Christianity and Economics.* New York: Oxford University Press, 2014.

———. *Political Economy as Natural Theology: Smith, Malthus and Their Followers.* London: Routledge, 2018.

Phelps, Hollis. *Jesus and the Politics of Mammon.* Critical Theory & Biblical Studies. Eugene, OR: Cascade, 2019.

Rieger, Joerg. *No Rising Tide: Theology, Economics, and the Future.* Minneapolis, MN: Fortress Press, 2009.

Schwarzkopf, Stefan, ed. *The Routledge Handbook of Economic Theology.* London: Routledge, 2020.

Singh, Devin. *Divine Currency: The Theological Power of Money in the West.* Stanford, CA: Stanford University Press, 2018.

———. *Economy and Modern Christian Thought.* Leiden: Brill, 2022.

Tanner, Kathryn. *Christianity and the New Spirit of Capitalism.* New Haven, CT: Yale University Press, 2019.

———. *Economy of Grace.* Minneapolis, MN: Fortress Press, 2005.

Tran, Jonathan. *Asian Americans and the Spirit of Racial Capitalism.* New York: Oxford University Press, 2022.

Wariboko, Nimi. *God and Money: A Theology of Money in a Globalizing World.* Lanham, MD: Lexington Books, 2008.

Theology and Race

Brian Bantum

Introduction

At the heart of Christianity is the problem and the possibility of difference. A God who is unseen becomes flesh. Who is God if we believe in the incarnation of the eternal Word? That God walked and talked and ate and suffered? And what does this mean for our bodies, our relations? People who were deemed defiled become brothers and sisters and mother and fathers. What are the marks of faithfulness in someone's life? In a community's life? Christian identity and the theological reflection that emerges from these communities are an ongoing negotiation of what our bodies mean in relationship to God and to one another. Who was in? What must inclusion look like?

Theology as a practice emerges from these questions and the answers that have been given over time. Although theology as a practice can be understood as reflection upon and expression of who God is, who we are, and what is the world we inhabit, theology should also be considered an act of identity. Theology emerges in the interplay of who people believe themselves to be in the midst of their descriptions of God and the world. Through confession and differentiation theology identifies its internal structures, its boundaries, and names the signs of belonging. From Justin Martyr's appeals to philosophy or Irenaeus's rebuttal of those described as Gnostics, to violent and enduring anti-Semitism, theological description emerges from an attempt to account for oneself in the world, or account for the differences among us.

The idea of race, the belief in the intrinsic meaning and value of who people are based on physical characteristics, is an iteration of this dynamic of identity. Part of the challenge of understanding the relationship between theology and race is identifying the relationship between these ideas. Does race have a fundamentally theological center? Does it arise from the very core of Christian theological convictions and structure? Or is race a cultural or economic phenomenon that found particularly fertile ground in European religious, economic, and cultural soil? The answer is likely all of the above. But it can be said that beginning at least as early as the fifteenth century, with Spanish, French, Portuguese, Dutch, and English colonial expansion into the rest of the world, the question of difference was refracted through the lens of racialized bodies. Encounter with the "new worlds" was accounted for in a theological language that circulated around an emerging description of Whiteness and a dark otherness of bodies they encountered in the rest of the world.[1]

Ford's The Modern Theologians: An Introduction to Christian Theology since 1918, Fourth Edition.
Edited by Rachel Muers and Ashley Cocksworth.
© 2024 John Wiley & Sons Ltd. Published 2024 by John Wiley & Sons Ltd.

The challenge of telling the story of theology and race is complicated by three realities. First, race is the product of the colonial imagination of England, France, Spain, Portugal, Italy, and the Netherlands. That is, race is not simply about the classification of differences among people. Race is a story about the creation of Whiteness through the creation of peoples deemed not-White. The story of race is not simply about physical attributes. Race is the erection of a scaffolding of normalcy and tradition and "humanness" from which everything else is measured. To speak of "racism" is not simply to speak of hatred or dislike for a particular people or person because of what they look like. Racism is the slow evolution of a social and economic system that implicitly or explicitly values bodies deemed White while submerging the very language of race in the process. How does one name a phenomenon that so often operates as a nameless, shapeless norm? One way of telling the story of theology and race would be to tell the story of Whiteness, or Christianity and Whiteness.[2]

Second, in the ubiquity and unrelenting creation of racialized spaces, those subjected to the violence of colonial terror and White supremacy also resisted, adapted, and created ways of surviving and sometimes flourishing despite the history and weight of racialized power. If race began as a story of Whiteness and White supremacy, it did not remain so. How do we tell the story of those who created culture, shaped a peoplehood in the face of the violence and attempts to subjugate them? For example, there was a time when Blackness was not, and yet in the wake of colonial expansion and chattel slavery, there is a Black diaspora.[3] It is varied and complicated but also has a center of its own, a mass, a gravity that can and should be understood apart from the forces that it may have emerged from. As Emilie Townes writes, "Defining Black people's otherness or subjectivity as victimization is a hollow and incomplete description of is-ness. We have narratives of resistance and rebellion as part of our story as well. Yet we must not rush too quickly to celebrate the victory of our diversity."[4]

Telling the story of theology and race is also navigating the manifold ways people resisted the violence of a racialized world without reducing those affected by it to perpetual victims. A story of theology and race must also account for the varied ways people articulated and rearticulated who they were and who God was in the face of racial terror and hegemony.

Third, descriptions of race can often become isolated to the context of the United States. Although race is undoubtedly a dominant force in American life, does this mean that these racialized patterns extend beyond US borders? Although the United States would become a particular lacuna of racialized life, the colonial projects that nurtured racialized life left profound marks wherever their ships landed. Although there are specific dynamics of race that are unique to the United States, how do we begin to understand the manifestation of racial imagination and how those patterns shape the theological reflection of Christians throughout the world? Understanding race as a dynamic of difference helps us to understand the permutations of racialized logics throughout the world. Violent differentiations work themselves out in national imaginations, imaginations that have seeds in a colonial theological claim that God and God's people *looked* a certain way.

Lastly, it is impossible to separate notions of race from the ways ideas of personhood were always braided with patterns of gender, sexuality, ability, and class. Race is never a singular issue but always amplifies or operates within or alongside or in contestation of patterns of subjugating description operative in the world.

Survey

What is race?

What is "race?" Before we consider the concept of race and its relationship to theology, we should first begin with a consideration of identity more broadly. When we consider any understanding of race we are working in the aftermath of *essentialist* understandings of identity. That is, the belief that fundamental characteristics of personhood are correlated to physical characteristics. The belief in an ontological relationship between the "unseen" and the "seen" is not peculiar to racial thinking. The attempt to understand and classify people based on physical differences has been an almost constant feature of human social life.[5] Along with notions of gender, racialized categories hardened these observations and organized them into categories of citizenship, civility, moral agency, beauty, and intelligence, to name a few. Essentialized understandings of identity presuppose aspects of a person's identity based on particular physical characteristics. Identity is fixed, stable, and unchanging.

When the histories of these seemingly immutable, unchanging identities are examined, it is quickly apparent that all identities have histories. "There was a time when they were not," so to speak. Opposed to an understanding of identity as fixed, or essential, race is understood to be *socially constructed*. For theorist Stuart Hall, identity is not the assertion of a certain, stable point of personhood. Rather,

> identity [refers] to the meeting point, the point of suture, between on the one hand the discourses and practices which attempt to "interpellate," speak to us or hail us into place as the social subjects of particular discourses, and on the other hand, the processes which produce subjectivities, which construct us as subjects which can be "spoken".[6]

He goes on to suggest identity is better understood as "identification," an ongoing, dynamic process where individuals and communities are negotiating who they are and who they are not through a complex circuit of representative signs, patterns of production and consumption (everything from food, to tools, to cars, to homes, to music, etc.), and means of disciplining those who transgress the boundaries of how identity is construed in a given moment. The particular configuration and movement of these forces create a web of shared meaning that constitutes a particular culture or subculture. For Hall, these dynamics of identity are what constitutes a culture. It is how social systems form and function. Within these systems there are competing forces of power, discipline, and resistance. Everyone is navigating the dynamics of power that function as the seemingly normal or natural way of being. These norms have a history, but they are obscured by the presumption of their eternal, natural, or divinely ordered origins. But even as there are norms and those whose identity is braided in the maintenance of those norms, there are those whose identities have been narrated as other, as the antithesis of the norm. For those whose marginality creates the center, they are either navigating their identities in approximation to power or articulating their personhood in opposition to the hegemony that attempts to determine the meaning of their bodies.

Understanding identity as an ongoing process is important because the notion of identity as social construction is often construed as race being a kind of myth. But the identities that are formed in these maelstroms of power and encounter and language also create material realities that then become forces in their own right. The dynamics of identity emerge in these social interactions, claims of peoplehood, and then become the formative lens that people live into or resist in often complicated, overlapping ways.

Identity as a process has two implications for any consideration of race and theology. First, Christian identity is not exempt from the dynamics of identification. In fact, its very beginnings exemplify the kind of "suturing" Hall speaks of. Christian identity is an ongoing process that is navigating belonging and exclusion in relationship to the first Jewish followers of Jesus and the broader varied Jewish community, the dynamics of class and power involved in navigating the Roman Empire, and the myriad peoples/movements/philosophies/religions that constituted the Roman Empire.

Although race as we understand it today was not an operative term in early Christian communities, there were nonetheless dynamics of power, differentiation, and negotiations of what being a follower of Jesus would look like. As Christianity distinguished itself from its Jewish beginnings, Jewishness no longer served as a mark of likeness or kinship but as a negation; some would believe they superseded the Jews as Christian belief came into the world.[7] Theologian Willie James Jennings points to this critical break in identification with Jesus's Jewishness and Jews as the people of God as the nascent moments of racial imagination.[8]

The relationship between modern conceptions of race and Christianity's understanding of itself in relationship to Jesus's Jewishness and the Jewish people cannot be overstated. Even prior to colonial expansion, anti-Semitism in Europe was the central axis of violent differentiation and what scholars such as Geraldine Heng and Matthew Vernon argue are the even earlier moments of European racial imagination.[9]

Throughout its existence Christian life has been a problem of identity. Who belongs? Who is outside and who is kin? In a way, Christian identity exemplifies the very suturing and ever-unfolding that Stuart Hall describes as identification. In our identification with the Word who becomes flesh, we are drawn into identification with one another, an identification that is not fixed, but fluid and constantly being renegotiated as we continue to meet others who are drawn into Christ's life.

But as we know, this was not the story of Christianity. In the biblical accounts of life with Jesus, the earliest followers of Jesus struggled to comprehend the transgressions of identity and the confusions of belonging Jesus's life called them to. Even while they walked with Jesus, the disciples bristled at the associations Jesus drew them into, and after Jesus's death we would see stark lines of exclusion and belonging emerge. These dynamics of identity are not exclusive to Christian life; they are intrinsic to all communities and the individuals who are a part of those communities. And at the same time, we must trace the formations of these claims and how they shape their society. A study of theology and race is an examination of how the negotiation of identity in Christian life both creates logics of race and finds new ways of understanding God and human existence.

The development of modern understandings of race

The idea of race as a "natural" category is a new concept in human history. Although difference between peoples and cultures has been prevalent throughout human history, the notion of race as a biological and theological category has its beginnings with European encounters with the world. In these encounters they sought first to account theologically for the physical differences that confronted them and the varying ways of life that seemed to accompany these physical differences. Jennings points to how all of these differences are then articulated within a grand theological concept, a racial scale that classified everything (including the differences among human beings) in relationship to a transcendent ideal of the *imago dei*, an ideal that looked curiously like the European Christian male.[10]

Encountering different people was certainly not new for Europeans. Trade with nations to the East and an awareness of the African continent brought with it stories of difference and of different religions. But in the fifteenth and sixteenth centuries European countries would begin more sustained contact with African countries looking for trade routes to Asia. As historian Winthrop Jordan describes some of these earliest encounters, there was not necessarily the frame of race or even inhumanity.[11] But there were observations of difference, of skin color in particular, and dress and customs that were inevitably compared to European customs, religious self-understanding, and the emerging judgments of what was "civilized" and what was "primitive."[12]

These encounters mingled with conceptions of difference that already associated evil with darkness and light with good and purity. Jordan writes:

> In England perhaps more than in Southern Europe, the concept of blackness was loaded with intense meaning. Long before they found that some men were black, Englishmen found in the idea of blackness a way of expressing some of their most ingrained values. No other color except white conveyed so much emotional impact . . . Black was an emotionally partisan color, the handmaid and symbol of baseness and evil, a sign of danger and repulsion.[13]

As Europeans moved westward to the newly discovered "Americas" two factors began to shift how physical and cultural differences were understood. The first was the slave trade and the second was the discovery of valuable resources in these lands. The questions began to shift from curiosity about how these differences between people emerged to whether these differences pointed to the African or the indigenous person's humanity. These were not only economic questions. They were also theological questions. Did the African have a soul? Could they be saved? If they had a soul could they be enslaved? (These questions became more critical as the profit of the slave trade grew.)

In the subsequent two hundred years and culminating in the scientific racism of the Enlightenment, the observed differences between people would become, as Jennings would describe it, a global racial scale where physical attributes signified fundamental characteristics of personhood. One's intelligence, capacity for self-governance, sexual appetites, moral agency, occupational prospects – to name a few – were understood to be intrinsically tied to their racial classification. And these categories were correlated to a normative standard cued to a particular implicit or explicit Christian self-understanding.

These theological interpretations of non-European bodies would become solidified through the emerging "scientific" and rational lens of Enlightenment Europe. Theological categories would be buttressed by scientific methods of classification. These scientific classifications would become the basis of understanding certain people's purposes, limitations, and possibilities. The study and comparison of skulls and body types were correlated to one's capacity to reason, to one's spirituality, to one's abilities and purposes in society. The American slave society was built upon these twin foundations of theological and scientific classification, attributing *essential* and *fundamental* meaning about their humanity (or inhumanity) to particular physical characteristics. And these classifications were not limited to non-Europeans. Immanuel Kant, in reading accounts of peoples, nations, and religions throughout the world, categorized all people according to their physical and intrinsic characteristics.[14]

Although a discussion about race often focuses on the objects of racialized thought and rhetoric, namely, people deemed non-White, what is often lost in these conversations is how the notion of race creates categories of non-Whiteness in order to shape and give coherence to notions of Whiteness. Here Whiteness has a certain corollary to skin color. But as with Kant's racial scale, there are, more critically, characteristics that are associated with Whiteness. These characteristics can be approximated by some people but are often out of reach for others. But the significance of these categories lies more in the creation of a central gravity of normativity that remains implicit, but nonetheless continually exerts force upon those whose orbit is close enough.

The notion of race is not simply about physical characteristics. The physical characteristics are signs of deeper ways of knowing and being in the world, sometimes cued by words like "civilization" or "tradition." The concept of race is not about description of bodies, it is fundamentally, about a way of knowing, an epistemology. Allen points to the development of Whiteness as a concept in England, drawing on distinctions between civilized Englishness and "savage" Irish identity and the subsequent logics of racial thought that would organize life in the Americas.[15]

Race becomes a way of understanding one's self and one's community in relation to others that legitimizes violence, marginalization, and the codification or particular differences. It becomes the assumed, enduring story of why the world or a community is the way it is and often obscures the histories of how those material realities came to be.

African American Responses: Howard Thurman, James Cone, Kelly Brown Douglas, Shawn Copeland

If race is a fallacy and a construct, an epistemological prison that seemingly circumscribes all bodies and land within its gaze, should the category have any meaning for us today? Here the framing of race as working within broader dynamics of identity as identification is helpful. Although notions of Whiteness seemed to categorize and sought to determine the totality of those deemed non-White, identity is not simply about the power to name. Identity is a dynamic negotiation where histories of policies or violent classification are not totalizing. That is, simply because a society describes my body as inhuman does not mean that I understand myself to be less than human. Because a society refuses baptism to me and my community because they do not believe we have a soul, it does not mean that we do not have a dynamic and rich faith that pulls from our own remembered traditions (texts on our Lady of Guadalupe, African religious sentiments in Black religion in the Americas, for example) or from the very book used to justify our subjugation.

The refusals of racialized frameworks of faith are most clearly seen in the ways communities articulated who God, and more specifically, Christ was for them. In these Christological descriptions we also see the embedded narratives of what it means to be human, what is the nature of sin and its social manifestations, and what salvation or wholeness might look like.

In 1969 James Cone published *Black Theology and Black Power.*[16] Cone's work sought to speak directly to the conditions and realities of Black people in the United States who had endured centuries of segregation and subjugation. He asked, "Who is Jesus for us?" His response was a rearticulation of the person of Christ drawing on the values of the Black Power movement that emphasized Black beauty and history, as well as a refusal of a theological system that did not account for the material conditions of the poor and oppressed.[17]

Cone's work, while the first formal academic treatment of Jesus as liberator, is drawing from a long tradition of Black theological reflection that identified God's repeated decision for the poor, the outcast, and the marginalized. Black Christian faith in the United States was a constant rereading of scripture and seeing elements of redemption and God's desire for people to be free. Prior to Cone's famous declaration, "Jesus is Black," Howard Thurman would point out the significance of Jesus's Jewishness. Reading the stories of Israel's oppression and God's liberation, in the early twentieth century Thurman suggested the significance of Jesus's identity as a Jew. He wrote:

> The economic predicament with which he was identified in birth placed him initially with the great mass of men on the earth. The masses of the people are poor. If we dare take the position that in Jesus there was at work some radical destiny, it would be safe to say that in his poverty he was more truly Son of man than he would have been if the incident of family or birth had made him a rich son of Israel. It is not a point to be labored, for again and again men have transcended circumstance of birth and training; but it is an observation not without merit. The third fact is that Jesus was a member of a minority group in the midst of a larger dominant and controlling group. In 63 BC Palestine fell into the hands of the Romans. After this date the gruesome details of loss of status were etched, line by line, in the sensitive soul of Israel, dramatized ever by an increasing desecration of the Holy Land.[18]

For Thurman, Jesus's Jewishness was not only a theological identity but a socioeconomic reality, one that could not be understood apart from his theological mission. For Thurman, the entirety of Jesus life and work was oriented toward freedom, for both those oppressed and those who oppress. But the locus, the center of this work, and who Jesus identified as and with, was central to who he was.

James Cone would pick up on Thurman's emphasis and speak of God's *identification* with the poor and oppressed, highlighting his identity as oppressed took on a fundamental likeness to all who were oppressed, marginalized, tortured, and subject to state-sanctioned violence. Building from Thurman's description of Jesus's socioeconomic situation, Cone frames Jesus's work within a wider systematic lens. He draws from a classic theological phrase, "God becomes like us so that we might become like God." This idea works as a systematic frame, suggesting both a claim about what went wrong and how the incarnation meets us.

In Cone's work, we see the significance of Jesus's humanity, but more critically, Jesus's oppressed Jewish humanity. Addressing the parallels between Jesus and Black American existence Cone writes:

What is this freedom for which black people have marched, boycotted, picketed, and rebelled in order to achieve? Simply stated, freedom is not doing what I will but becoming what I should. A man is free when he sees clearly the fulfillment of his being and is thus capable of making the envisioned self a reality. This is "Black power!" They want the grip of white power removed what black people have in mind when they cry "Freedom now!" Now and forever.

Is this not why God became man in Jesus Christ so that man might become what he is? Is not this at least part of what St. Paul had in mind when he said, "For freedom, Christ has set us free" (Gal. 5:1)? As long as man is a slave to another power, he is not free to serve God with mature responsibility. He is not free to become what he is—human.[19]

Although Cone builds from Thurman, Cone has put Jesus's work within a larger set of systemic claims. Notice the centrality of freedom in Cone's description both of what we are as human beings and as the center of the fallen condition. We were made to be free. But the problem, the fallenness in creation, is bondage and the determination of a people over others, limiting what they might become.

God's response is to become "like us." But this likeness is specific, particular. The Word becomes the oppressed, those in bondage, so that those who are in bondage might become free. Freedom here is self-determination, for Cone. As Cone reads Jesus's Jewishness he sees a solidarity, a sharing with the oppressed, dispossessed, and disinherited of the world, of whom he understands Black Americans to be the quintessential representation. This connection is what gives rise to Cone's eventual assertion that Jesus is Black. This claim is not one based on an ontological or even "biological" likeness but rather the sharing of an existential connection of oppression and marginalization. In the face of White supremacist ideologies and theologies, Black theologians speak to the centrality of freedom and the fullness of their humanity. God wants us all to be free.

Theologian Kelly Brown Douglas grounds these ideas of our freedom in a doctrine of creation, in particular, *creatio ex nihilo* where God is creator of all things, God is free, God nurtures and fosters life. From these theological starting points that arise from Black Christians' experience of a God who both met them while they were free and desired them to be free, Douglas writes, "What is clear now is the absolute relationship between the freedom of God and life."[20] Freedom is understood to be one of the fundamental characteristics of God and consequently, God's creation. Douglas continues, "The *imago dei*, therefore, is the Spirit of total liberation in all humanity."[21]

This underlying, constant belief in a God who creates and in a God who desires life animates Douglas' understanding of Black faith traditions. It is from these experiences of freedom and belief in a God of freedom that the community begins to imagine possibilities of life apart from the discourses and practices of death found in the Americas. "In other words, the black faith tradition itself generates a discourse of resistance that allows black people to affirm their innate and created worth, even when everything around them suggests their utter worthlessness."[22] The interrelationship between a God of freedom and life and the reality of violence becomes both a paradox and a testament. In the face of such utter violence, whether in the cross (and the state) or in the lynching tree or Manifest Destiny or police violence, the unrelenting desire for life points to the presence of the resurrection, to the reality of life overcoming death. These underlying frames of God's power and God's life are the articulation of justice, of what God desires for all of creation, and in particular Black lives in our contemporary moment. She writes, "The freedom/love/life of God that was expressed through the exodus of the Israelites from Egyptian bondage is expressed on the cross of Jesus as the triumph over all that denies life. It reveals that this love knows no bounds, as it reaches down into the vilest realities of human hate and evil."[23] In Douglas' work the cross is not so much a symbol of God's need for violence as, rather, a symbol of God's power to overcome violence. Jesus's life is lived into freedom and the creation of freedom for others. This enactment of freedom is resisted with violence, an attempt to reiterate the power of those in control through a symbolic death of one whose life displays the radical freedom of God and the freedom God desires for all of God's creation.

Douglas' work provides an example of how theologians respond to the hegemony of colonizing Christianity, with preconceptions of the very nature of God, creation, and what it means to be human having profound implications for our understanding of violence. For Douglas, this reconnection of the violence of the cross responds to the concept of Manifest Destiny that shaped the imperial growth of the United States in the nineteenth century, and critically, served as a justification of the violence necessary to subjugate people under the auspices of "law and order."

The last example of Black theological reimagination is the thought of theologian Shawn Copeland, who continues the womanist theological tradition we see in Douglas and the liberationist emphasis of James Cone but also points to the necessity of liberation as praxis. As Copeland builds her argument we begin to see the enactment of the body as a "discursive" presence, that is, a body that "speaks" in its negotiation of the social spaces it inhabits. The body is bound to discourses and languages and histories. The body, the person, is never simply an individual untethered from history or community or the narratives and descriptions of who a people are (or who they are not or can never be). Because of these connections and interconnections, the body speaks. The body does work as it walks in the world. People speak without uttering words and their lives are participating in these currents of history, language, and discourses about what their bodies are or are not. Theologically speaking, Copeland adds a layer of significance to the body as "sacramental."

Drawing on Catholic tradition about the "body as sacrament" Copeland suggests, "But, the body is a sacrament, it is the concrete medium through which persons realize themselves interdependently in the world and in freedom in Christ, and in Catholic sacramental economy to express is to effect."[24] The significance of the body is grounded in the person and work of Jesus where

> The only body capable of taking us all in as we are with all our different body marks – certainly including the mark of homosexuality – is the body of Christ. This taking us in, this incorporation, is akin to sublation, not erasure, not uniformity; the basileia praxis of Jesus draws us up to him. Our humble engagement in his praxis revalues our identities and differences, even as it preserves the integrity and significance of our body marks. At the same time, those very particular body marks are relativized, reoriented, and reappropriated under this sign, the sign of the cross. Thus in solidarity and in love of others and the Other, we are (re)made and (re)marked as the flesh of Christ, as the flesh of his church.[25]

This passage exemplifies Copeland's Christological approach. The problem of race and gender is a distortion of praxis and social space, one that distorts the significance of the body and creates a social system that subjects the body to a violent circumscription. It is reduced to parts to be consumed, used, and discarded. In the same way that our bodies point to a reality beyond ourselves, to histories and languages and discourses that we live within, Jesus's body participates in a social reality.

But this reality is not one that is constrained by the either/or discourses that require us to deny in order to be. Copeland's Christology points to a body that can hold these differences within God's own life without erasure. Put differently, God identifies with us and we become identified with God. The significance of Jesus's body as sacrament lies not only in what his praxis means in the lives of those he meets, but in his taking up of the human condition he also opens up a new "discursive" space in his life where we can be marked, where our identities become entwined with his. But for Copeland this markedness is not one in name alone but rather draws us into a praxis, a solidarity with the life, the body of Christ as we navigate a world that continues to be marked by patterns of empire. This life becomes a constant enactment of a life in Christ where "our daily living out, and out of, the dangerous memory of the torture and abuse, death and resurrection of Jesus Christ constitutes us as his own body raised up and made visible in the world . . . As his body, we pulse with new life, for Eucharist is the heart of Christian community."[26]

Black Christian theology in the United States is not reflective of the totality of responses to Christianity grounded in colonial and White racial imagination. These are only three examples of ways theologians have sought to address and refuse theologies of inhumanity. But in these three examples we see ways that theologians have sought to affirm the humanity and wholeness of Black life, and in the case of Douglas and Copeland, expand that understanding of wholeness and freedom beyond issues of race and toward the realities of gender, sexuality, and class. The methods of refusal of White supremacist logics and theologies were grounded in affirmations of their beauty and possibility, articulating who God was in light of the values and histories of the community and drawing upon a wide range of resources – from scripture to Christian teachings to secular movements to customs and practices that were folded into Christian practices – in order to express who God was and who they were.

Theologies that were grounded in the presupposition of superiority, classification, and racial hierarchy also presupposed the normativity of maleness, heterosexuality, intelligence, beauty, Tradition, economics, governance, education, to name a few. The question of race and theology is never a singular topic. Race is an idea that sought to circumscribe all people within certain conceptions of normalcy and theologize that normalcy as part of what it meant to be made in the image of God.

Agenda: Decolonial Approaches in a Globalized World

The previous section was devoted to thinking about several examples of Black Christian thought in the United States. The difficulty in considering a topic as unwieldy as race and theology is the danger of reducing many, disparate realities into a few singular narratives. One of these dangers comes in understanding the permutations of difference through the lens of permutations of racialized life in the United States. At the same time, how do we begin to account for the dynamics of identity wrought through the racialized project of colonization throughout the world, albeit in nuanced and differentiated ways?

Discussing her relationship to the work of womanist theologians, theologian Kwok Pui-lan wrote,

I realize my experience of Christianity is radically different from theirs. While black religious communities [in the United States] historically provided black people with support for their struggle and served as a base for them to see an alternative reality, I cannot say this for many of our Asian churches For many Asian folks, Christianity is the religion of the oppressors. My feminist critique, therefore, begins with the suspicion of such faith statements as "the Bible is the Word of God" or "Jesus is the savior of all people."[27]

Kwok points to a fundamental nuance in how both theology and race shape her understanding of God, herself, and her world. How do we begin to make sense of the relationship between race and theology in spaces where the language of race either has limited purchase or is wholly unintelligible in terms of physical characteristics? At the same time, how do we begin to account for the permutations of racialized thought, anti-Blackness in particular, that continue to work explicitly or implicitly in virtually all corners of the world?

First, we need to return to an understanding of race and racial oppression that extends beyond explicit views about physical characteristics. The racial logics of the European colonial project were braided with understandings of knowledge. Theorist Walter Mignolo describes this in terms of a global transformation where

Between 1500 and 2000 . . . the great transformation of the sixteenth century – in the Atlantic that connected European initiatives, enslaved Africans, dismantled civilizations . . . and encompassed the genocide in Ayiti – was the emergence of a structure of control and management of authority, economy, subjectivity, gender and sexual norms and relations that were driven by Western (Atlantic) Europeans (Iberian Peninsula, Holland, France, and England) both in their internal conflicts and in their exploitation of labor and expropriation of land.[28]

This reorganization of peoples and land and their interrelationships were indelibly marked by a racial logic. In spaces where the racial vernacular recedes, its structure remains.[29] This is not to say that every issue of violence or coloniality or marginalization is, at its heart, a racial reality. But given the fundamental reliance of the colonial project upon racialized difference, there must always be some attentiveness to how the assumptions of power, knowledge, land, beauty, etc., continue to work within historically racialized dynamics of identity and identification.

In response, decolonial movements have sought to decouple understandings of God and personhood from the European missionary presumptions. These varied movements may not explicitly point to race or racialized structures, but in their refusal of the equivalence of Christianity to "civilization" for example, these theologians are refusing the hegemonic imagination that accompanied European colonial endeavors.[30] The decolonial imperative looks to retrieve the stories, histories, and knowledges that were so often discarded or eradicated as missionaries gained ground.

Ghanaian theologian Mercy Oduyoye exemplifies this complicated refusal, reaching past, and yet incorporating all of it into a theological articulation of being human. Describing the theological task she writes, "In the eyes of Christian missionaries, African Religion was nothing but idolatry. Reflecting as it does in all of the culture, phenomena such as naming had to be abandoned to ensure the names of idols are not carried into the house of the 'jealous' God of Christianity. It is for this reason and the fact that the African Religion continues that we begin our 'God-talk' by rehearsing what we learn from African Religion."[31] Oduyoye goes on to draw upon creation narratives and practices of African tribal religions in relationship to Christian claims about the nature of God and humanity, weaving together a theological vision that speaks to the multiplicity of faith traditions and the realities of patriarchy in her Ghanaian context.

In decolonial approaches to Christian theology and identity, questions of race are sometimes more implicit. Histories of ethnicity and geographic difference, religious difference, a constant centering of Western European and US perspectives on identity and social/economic structures are challenges that are often addressed. At the same time, decolonial strategies share methods examined in the theological postures examined in the previous section. By centering communal practices and values, stories, and religious practices that preceded Christian encounter, decolonial theologies work against the ways racialized imperial and colonial encounters sought to structure their societies.

One challenge in thinking about how to understand the implications and presences of racialized thought on a more global scale are the complex ways marginalizations and exclusions can overlap. For instance, while theologians in East Asian countries such as South Korea express the theological implications of US military imperialism, there is also the reality of anti-Black racism prevalent in the social system.[32] If race is no longer the primary lens through which we understand identity or legacies of oppression, is race still a helpful framework? And what is lost or fills the gap if we do not understand the afterlives of racialized frameworks in our social systems?

A key decolonial hermeneutic for understanding the complexities of the world colonialism wrought is the language of hybridity. This is true of any colonial expansion, but it has been an especially important category for beginning to account for the world that was created in the Western European colonial project. In a global context where colonial conceptions of racial difference sought to delineate who people were (and who they were not), how do we begin to account for those who did not fall neatly within the categories created? How do we account for the violence that often conceived these children? And how do we begin to understand the significance of these blurring lines and shifting boundaries in an increasingly globalizing world? The question of hybridity is not simply one of race or ethnicity but also religion, practices, ways of being. If identity is better understood as a dynamic identification, how does the presence of people who disrupt or expand these boundaries shape our understandings of race? Of God? And are these hybrid people a kind of panacea? A hope for all people? Or a sign of what is inevitably lost when peoples encounter one another, and especially when power is involved?

Hybridity is a critical category of theological reflection on race in the contemporary world. Theorist Homi Bhabha suggests, "The borderline work of culture demands an encounter with 'newness' that is not part of the continuum of past and present. It creates a sense of the new as an insurgent act of cultural translation. Such art does not merely recall the past as social cause or aesthetic precedent; it renews the past, refiguring it as a contingent 'in-between' space, that innovates and interrupts the performance of the present. The past-present becomes part of the necessity, not the nostalgia, of living."[33] In a globalized world where there is no neat and clean before and after, theologies that wrestle with hybridities express race within this encounter. They explore both how race creates categories of difference and also how the "children" of those categories navigate the world, create new spaces of meaning. Whether the "mulattic" spaces of mixed race children offering new ways to understand Jesus and discipleship,[34] or the various ways Latino/a theologies consider the legacies of encounter that comprise language, customs, and ways of being in the world as mestizo or mestizaje or mujerista,[35] theologians are also wrestling with how the racial categories endure in problematic ways and how they continue to bend and shift as peoples continue to overlap more and more.

As an outworking of Christian identity, theology will always be an exercise of identity and identification. Grounded in the significance of our bodied lives, of our flesh as something God sees as good and becomes human in order to redeem, the question of the meaning of our bodies, their differences, and the ways our communities shape how we understand our bodies will be an enduring question. To address these questions faithfully and to account for life together, race is a category and a history that cannot be left unattended. Our understanding of God will always be filtered through the ways we see one another and ourselves.

Notes

1 Throughout this chapter I use the language of race in reference to the social and economic systems that revolve around the implicit or explicit relationship between physical characteristics and individual or communal qualities, capacities, or purposes. There is a critical issue regarding the distinction between race and ethnicity. We might understand racial characteristics as being developed and assigned in order to control, oppress, or emphasize negative characteristics or exclusion.

2 Nell Irvin Painter, *The History of White People* (New York: W. W. Norton & Company, 2010); Theodore W. Allen, *The Invention of the White Race*, 2 vols. (London: Verso, 2012); Jennifer Harvey, *Dear White Christians: For Those Still Longing for Racial Reconciliation* (Grand Rapids, MI: Eerdmans, 2014); George Yancy, *Christology and Whiteness: What Would Jesus Do?* (London: Routledge, 2012).

3 Christina Elizabeth Sharpe, *In the Wake: On Blackness and Being* (Durham, NC: Duke University Press, 2016).

4 Emilie M. Townes, *Womanist Ethics and the Cultural Production of Evil* (New York: Palgrave Macmillan, 2006).

5 See Painter, *A History of White People*.

6 Stuart Hall, "Introduction: Who Needs 'Identity'?," in *Questions of Cultural Identity*, ed. Stuart Hall and Paul du Gay (London: Sage, 1996), 5–6.

7 For critical examinations of racial constructs in the early church and biblical studies see Love L. Sechrest, *A Former Jew: Paul and the Dialectics of Race* (London: T&T Clark, 2009). For considerations of race in biblical studies and the use of scripture see Shawn Kelley, *Racializing Jesus: Race, Ideology, and the Formation of Modern Biblical Scholarship* (London: Routledge, 2002); Colin Kidd, *The Forging of Races: Race and Scripture in the Protestant Atlantic World, 1600–2000* (Cambridge: Cambridge University Press, 2006).

8 Willie James Jennings. *The Christian Imagination: Theology and the Origins of Race* (New Haven, CT: Yale University Press, 2010), 254. For further engagement with the relationship between Jewish and Christian identity see Daniel Boyarin, *Border Lines: The Partition of Judaeo-Christianity* (Philadelphia, PA: University of Pennsylvania Press, 2007).

9 Important studies on racial frameworks that precede the sixteenth century (the date typically given to the formal introduction of racialized frameworks) include Matthew X. Vernon, *The Black Middle Ages: Race and the Construction of the Middle Ages* (Cham, CH: Palgrave Macmillan, 2018) and Geraldine Heng, *The Invention of Race in the European Middle Ages* (New York: Cambridge University Press, 2018).

10 Jennings, *The Christian Imagination*, 29–30.

11 Winthrop D. Jordan, *The White Man's Burden; Historical Origins of Racism in the United States* (New York: Oxford University Press, 1974), 3.

12 Scholars are increasingly pointing to racialized structures of thought preceding encounters beyond Europe beginning as early as the Middle Ages. See Vernon, *The Black Middle Ages*, and Heng, *The Invention of Race in the European Middle Ages*.

13 Jordan, *The White Man's Burden*, 5–6.

14 See J. Kameron Carter, *Race: A Theological Account* (Oxford: Oxford University Press, 2008), 82–96 and Emmanuel Chukwudi Eze, ed., *Race and the Enlightenment: A Reader* (Cambridge, MA: Blackwell, 1997).

15 For more on understanding racism and English colonization of the Irish see Kimberly Anne Coles, *Bad Humor: Race and Religious Essentialism in Early Modern England* (Philadelphia, PA: University of Pennsylvania Press, 2022), and Maeve Callan, "'A Savage and Sacrilegious Race, Hostile to God and Humanity': Religion, Racism, and Ireland's Colonization," *Journal of Medieval Religious Cultures* 49, no. 1 (2023): 1–27.

16 James H. Cone, *Black Theology and Black Power*, 50th anniversary ed. (Maryknoll, NY: Orbis, 2018).

17 In the following example I will be exploring a constellation of African American theologians. This is not to suggest these are the only theologians who wrote against the world that colonialism created but is intended to offer an example of how theologians rearticulated who they were, who God was, and what it meant to be Christian in the face of White supremacy.

18 Howard Thurman, *Jesus and the Disinherited* (Boston, MA: Beacon Press, 1996), 17–18.

19 Cone, *Black Theology and Black Power*, 39.

20 Kelly Brown Douglas, *Stand Your Ground: Black Bodies and the Justice of God* (Maryknoll, NY: Orbis, 2015), 47.

21 Douglas, *Stand Your Ground*, 151.

22 Douglas, *Stand Your Ground*, 154.

23 Douglas, *Stand Your Ground*, 179.

24 M. Shawn Copeland, *Enfleshing Freedom: Body, Race, and Being* (Minneapolis, MN: Fortress Press, 2009), 74.

25 Copeland, *Enfleshing Freedom*, 83.

26 Copeland, *Enfleshing Freedom*, 127–8.

27 Kwok Pui-lan, "Speaking from the Margins," *Journal of Feminist Studies of Religion* 8, no. 2 (1992): 102.

28 Walter D. Mignolo, *The Darker Side of Modernity: Global Futures, Decolonial Options* (Durham, NC: Duke University Press, 2011), 7.

29 Paul Gilroy, *The Black Atlantic: Modernity and Double Consciousness* (Cambridge, MA: Harvard University Press, 1993); Sylvia Wynter, "1492: A New World View," in *Race, Discourse, and the Origin of the Americas: A New World View*, ed. Vera Lawrence Hyatt and Rex Nettleford (Washington, DC: Smithsonian Institution Press, 1995), 5–57.

30 For example, see Kwame Bediako, *Theology and Identity: The Impact of Culture upon Christian Thought in the Second Century and in Modern Africa* (Oxford: Regnum Books International, 1999). For engagements with postcolonial treatments of scripture see John S. Mbiti, *Bible and Theology in African Christianity* (Nairobi: Oxford University Press, 1986); Musa W. Dube Shomanah, *Postcolonial Feminist Interpretation of the Bible* (St. Louis, MO: Chalice Press, 2000); R. S. Sugirtharajah, ed., *Voices from the Margin: Interpreting the Bible in the Third World*, 25th anniversary ed. (Maryknoll, NY: Orbis, 2016).

31 Mercy Amba Oduyoye, *Introducing African Women's Theology* (Cleveland, OH: Pilgrim Press, 2001), 39.

32 For a helpful analysis of the complex pressure of accounting for marginality even while recognizing legacies of bias see Wonhee Anne Joh, *Heart of the Cross: A Postcolonial Christology* (Louisville, KY: Westminster John Knox Press, 2006).

33 Homi Bhabha, *The Location of Culture* (London: Routledge, 2004), 10.

34 Brian Bantum, *Redeeming Mulatto: A Theology of Race and Christian Hybridity* (Waco, TX: Baylor University Press, 2010).

35 See Ada María Isasi-Díaz, *En La Lucha/In the Struggle: A Hispanic Women's Liberation Theology* (Minneapolis, MN: Fortress Press, 1993); Néstor Medina, *Mestizaje: (Re)mapping Race, Culture, and Faith in Latina/o Catholicism* (Maryknoll, NY: Orbis, 2009); Michelle A Gonzalez, *Afro-Cuban Theology: Religion, Race, Culture, and Identity* (Gainesville, FL: University Press of Florida, 2006).

Recommended Reading

Theological Texts

Copeland, Shawn. *Enfleshing Freedom: Body, Race, Being.* Minneapolis, MN: Fortress Press, 2010.

Gonzalez, Michelle A. *Afro-Cuban Theology: Religion, Race, Culture, and Identity.* Gainesville, FL: University Press of Florida, 2006.

Jennings, Willie James. *The Christian Imagination: Theology and the Origins of Race.* New Haven, CT: Yale University Press, 2010.

Joh, Wonhee Anne. *Heart of the Cross: A Postcolonial Christology.* Louisville, KY: Westminster John Knox Press, 2006.

Kwok Pui-lan. *Postcolonial Politics and Theology: Unraveling Empire for a Global World.* Louisville, KY: Westminster John Knox Press, 2021.

Medina, Néstor. *Mestizaje: (Re)mapping Race, Culture, and Faith in Latina/o Catholicism.* Maryknoll, NY: Orbis, 2009.

Townes, Emilie M. *Womanist Ethics and the Cultural Production of Evil.* New York: Palgrave Macmillan, 2006.

Theory and History

Anzaldúa, Gloria. *Borderlands: The New Mestiza = La Frontera.* 3rd ed. San Francisco, CA: Aunt Lute Books, 2007.

Heng, Geraldine. *The Invention of Race in the European Middle Ages.* New York: Cambridge University Press, 2018.

Morrison, Toni. *The Origin of Others.* Cambridge, MA: Harvard University Press, 2017.

Ramos-Zayas, Ana Y., and Mérida M. Rúa, eds. *Critical Dialogues in Latinx Studies: A Reader.* New York: New York University Press, 2021.

Said, Edward W. *Orientalism.* 25th anniversary ed. New York: Vintage Books, 2003.

Theology and (Neo)Nationalism

Ulrich Schmiedel

Introduction

6 January 2021. A picture of Jesus of Nazareth stood out among the signs and symbols that were carried during the attack on the Capitol, the seat of the United States Congress, which was in a joint session to affirm the presidential election results:[1] a White Jesus, wearing a red cap with the caption "Make America Great Again."[2] "MAGA Jesus" – as the scholars who curated a stunning collection about the attack call the picture – symbolizes a surge of Christian nationalism that challenges democracies around the globe.[3]

The concept of nationalism has had a checkered career in the history of the humanities. "Nation" captures an idea. "Nationalism" captures an ideology. This ideology identifies people as a nation,[4] inscribing this nation at the center of their social and political imaginary.[5] Scholars used to understand nationalism as a nonreligious rather than a religious ideology. Coming out of the European Enlightenment, the age of nationalism in the nineteenth and twentieth century – or so the standard story goes – replaced community constructions rooted in religion with reason, ushering politics into modernity.[6] However, it is not only the Christian nationalism of the attack on the Capitol that casts doubt on the standard story. This story is itself a consequence and a component of the ideology of nationalism.[7] Both in the past and in the present, religions have distinguished between insiders and outsiders, demarcating those who do and those who do not belong to "the people" that define a nation.[8]

Today, nationalism is more and more connected to civilizational and cultural claims for which references to religion are crucial.[9] Such neonationalism is not interested in the establishment of a nation-state. On the contrary, it sees the nation-state as under attack from both internal and external enemies against whom it ought to be secured.[10] Neonationalism, then, is a contemporary nationalism championed by the political right rather than the political left. For the neonationalist attackers who carried his picture, "MAGA Jesus" stands up for both the security and the supremacy of the nation of the United States, provoking populist and polarizing politics.[11]

In what follows, I concentrate on Christian nationalism in European and American contexts in order to chart concepts, complications, and critiques of (neo)nationalism. To criticize Christian nationalism, I contend, theologians need to scrutinize how Christianity has been complacent or complicit with the racism and

Ford's The Modern Theologians: An Introduction to Christian Theology since 1918, Fourth Edition.
Edited by Rachel Muers and Ashley Cocksworth.
© 2024 John Wiley & Sons Ltd. Published 2024 by John Wiley & Sons Ltd.

the sexism that run through Christian nationalisms past and present. A compelling counter to "MAGA Jesus" requires that theologians take this Jesus seriously in order to offer reasons and rationales for practices that claim Christianity for new solidarities both within and without the nation-state.

Survey

Conceptualizing nationalism

Given the contested conceptualization of nationalism, there are conflicting arguments about the relationship between religion and nation so that it makes very little sense to ask for the relationship between religion and nation overall.[12] Instead, I chart the most important and the most instructive conceptualizations of nationalism in order to clarify how they conceive of the category of religion.

Benedict Anderson's *Imagined Communities* is a promising point of departure because it is a recurrent reference in studies of nationalism. For Anderson, the nation is imagined. It is defined and described as "an imagined political community."[13] Imagination is crucial because it allows people to identify themselves. Even if the members of a nation never meet each other in person, they can tell who is and who is not one of them because they imagine the nation. The connections between the people of a nation, then, are ideal rather than material – they are imagined. Yet the fact that they are imagined does not mean that they have no impact. Both nation and nationalism are real, but their reality differs from the tale that nationalists tell.

Anderson's concept of the nation is a critique of the nationalist tale that nations have always already been there, so that the age of nationalism in the nineteenth and the twentieth century can be seen as the awakening of a "sleeping beauty."[14] Interpreting the nationalist tale about nationalism itself, Anderson analyzes how the nation is invented. He contends that the imagination of the nation requires particular circumstances and precise conditions to arise. For Anderson, the Enlightenment is crucial.[15] Through the Enlightenment, the assumption that peoples and people ought to be ruled by dynasties of monarchs who derive their authority from God lost its appeal. According to Anderson, "nations dream of being free" – and if free "under God," then directly rather than indirectly, not mediated by a church that crowns the monarch.[16]

Of course, the critique of the hierarchy of the church can be traced back beyond the Enlightenment. David Little presents the Protestant Reformation as one of the origins of nationalism.[17] One of the consequences of the breakup of the *Corpus Christianum* caused by the Reformation was the conceptualization of sovereign nation-states. This conceptualization required a reimagination of "the people" at the core of the state.[18] Little contends that the current controversies in the conceptualization of nationalism – particularly the distinction between a more internationalist liberal nationalism based on equal access, on the one hand, and a more nationalist illiberal nationalism based on ethnic access, on the other – were anticipated by the Reformers.[19] Little compares what he calls the more reactionary theology of Martin Luther and the more revolutionary theology of Thomas Müntzer. Although Luther was a "complicated case," the difference between the reactionary and the revolutionary wing of the Reformation has consequences for the image of the people.[20] This image differs in a political-theological imagination that calls for the establishment of a church in cooperation with the government and in a political-theological imagination that calls for the disestablishment of a church in conflict with the government. For Little, the reactionary image of the people favors compromise over chosenness with a focus on the national, whereas the revolutionary image of the people favors chosenness over compromise with a focus on the international. Caught in the middle, according to Little, was the reformism of John Calvin. Although there was considerable change throughout Calvin's career – Little argues that he moved from a more optimistic to a more pessimistic anthropology – his political theology was capable of holding both images of the people in tension.[21]

Little's comparison stresses the significance of theology for both the idea of the nation and the ideology of nationalism, by showcasing how ecclesial and ecclesiological concepts have shaped the imagination of the nation.

For the history of nationalism, the confessionalization of Europe that followed from the Reformation is significant.[22] In 1555, representatives of both churches – Catholicism and Protestantism – came together in Augsburg to pacify the conflicts between them. In the Peace of Augsburg, they agreed on a connection between religion and realm: "one country one confession", with the ruler of the country deciding about it. According to Peter van der Veer, the Peace of Augsburg enabled what could be called the religionalization of the nation and the nationalization of religion,[23] leading to the assumption that the nation is one nation under God – directly rather than indirectly, as Anderson put it. In turn, this assumption had consequences for the conceptualization of sovereignty.

The Peace of Westphalia, signed in 1648, ended the Wars of Religion that had raged across Europe by establishing state sovereignty as the cornerstone of both the national and the international order. Each state exerts exclusive and exclusionary authority over its territory. Hugh McLeod has argued that Christianity was intertwined with the nationalism of the nineteenth and twentieth century that arose through the Westphalian order, even in countries with nonestablished rather than established national churches.[24] Often priests and pastors supported nationalism, leading to a conviction across almost all countries in Europe that their nation was fighting for a just cause during the so-called Great War, even if it meant that Christians were fighting Christians – "God with us."[25]

Although he underscores the consequences of the Enlightenment, Anderson is careful not to argue that nationalism assumes a simple or straightforward secularization of Europe. For Anderson, nationalism is not the outcome of secularization and secularization is not the outcome of nationalism.[26] The nation is not superseding religion either.[27] However, the social, cultural, and political processes coming out of the Enlightenment marked "a fundamental change … in modes of apprehending the world, which, more than anything else, made it possible to 'think' the nation."[28] Once it could be thought, "the 'nation' proved an invention on which it was impossible to secure a patent."[29]

Anderson's conceptualization of nation(alism), then, is paradigmatic for modernism. He presents nation-alism as a consequence of the European Enlightenment.[30] However, accounts such as Anderson's, which assume a radical rupture between the premodern and the modern, have a blind spot. Their assumption prevents them from analyzing modernity because any analysis that works with this assumption falls prey to the terms set by modernism itself.[31] Accordingly, alternatives to Anderson's concept of nation(alism) have pointed to connections that bridge the rupture between premodern and modern.

Religion is one connection. Among the scholars who counter the modernism of Anderson, Anthony Marx concentrates on the conflicts that he conceives of as constitutive of nation(alism), and Anthony Smith concentrates on the cohesion that he conceives of as constitutive of nation(alism), but for both of them religion is crucial – either as a factor for conflict or as a factor for cohesion.

Marx's *Faith in Nation* offers a critique of conceptualizations of the nation as community. He agrees with Anderson that scholars of nationalism have to go beyond the nationalist assumption that nations have always already been there.[32] There are invention and imagination in nationalism. However, for Marx, invention and imagination are not enough to bind people together amid conflicts in and between communities. On the contrary, he argues that conflicts are the key to the nation because they call for the differentiation between insiders and outsiders – a differentiation that is at the core of nationalism.[33]

Marx refers to the concept of enmity in Carl Schmitt's political theology – the notion that the differentiation between the friend and the foe is at the core of the political – to make the case for the construction of nationalism as "demarcating, demonizing, and depriving."[34] The cohesion of the community that is so crucial to the construction of the nation, then, follows a logic – yet it is not a logic of inclusionary cohesion, but a logic of exclusionary cohesion, which is to say: a logic of conflict. "And this logic has apparently often been put into practice."[35]

According to Marx, there are waves of nation-building, with the "imperative for intolerance" running through history,[36] connecting the premodern and the modern.[37] As the title *Faith in Nation* announces, religion is crucial for the logic of conflict. Pointing to the Wars of Religion, Marx argues that "faith was then the most pervasive form of identity among the populace whose loyalty was sought."[38] When political conflicts trigger religious passions and religious passions trigger political conflicts, "faith [is] emerging as a crutch for building or bounding community."[39]

Marx stresses that the logic of conflict that is so crucial to the construction of the nation has been forgotten because nationalism "is all about … purposeful manipulation of memory."[40] It is the Enlightenment with its ideas of liberal as opposed to illiberal nationalism that "eclipsed the memory of exclusion."[41] Modernist accounts of nation(alism) that draw a strict and stable distinction between the premodern and modern miss that religion has contributed to the conflictual construction of community.

Smith agrees with Marx that religion is crucial to connect premodern and modern nationalisms.[42] He argues that "it is not enough to see nationalism as a secular political ideology like liberalism and socialism."[43] Rather nationalism is itself a religion, a "belief system whose object is the nation conceived as a sacred communion."[44]

Conceptually, Smith returns to the category of ethnicity in order to trace unconscious and conscious nationalisms throughout history. However, he conceives of ethnicity not in terms of blood but in terms of belief – the "belief in … common descent," as Max Weber put it.[45] For Smith, nationalism presents ethnicity as sacred.[46] Nationalism constructs community through a shared story of origin, a common culture and a common cult.[47] Hence, it is a religion that is "heterodox" rather than "orthodox."[48] "Myths of ethnic descent, particularly myths of 'ethnic chosenness,' lie at its core."[49]

Smith's ethnosymbolism – the study of the symbols that make up the ethnic communities that are at the core of the sacred sources of nationalism[50] – is interested in the "power of ethnic traditions in the modern world," interpreting how ethnicity connects the present to the past, mixing with cultural or political modes of community construction.[51] He charts how "ethnic traditions … 'flow' into all kinds of communities."[52] According to Smith, religion lends itself to an exclusive rather than an inclusive "ethnicism."[53] However, when it is translated into celebrations of nationalism, it can change from more exclusivist to more inclusivist community cohesion, revolving around the "cult of self-sacrifice" that is on display during events such as Remembrance Sunday.[54] Modernist accounts of nation(alism) that draw a strict and stable distinction between the premodern and modern miss that religion has contributed to the cohesive construction of community.

Both critics of Anderson, then, point to the shortcomings of a modernism that assumes a radical rupture between the premodern and the modern. The Enlightenment is crucial for nation(alism), but there are connections between pre- and post-Enlightenment nationalisms. Religion is a case in point. Although they offer competing accounts of the construction of the nation that come with different and diverse understandings of the role of religion, both critics can be considered to complement each other.[55] Marx points to the role of religion in the conflict and Smith points to the role of religion in the cohesion that nationalism requires, but both insist that religion is crucial to nationalisms past and present.

Reflecting on the role of religion for the imagination of the nation, Steve Backhouse suggests that the "logic of nationalism follows contours recognizable to Christian theology."[56] For Backhouse, there is a mythology of creation that revolves around the nation's history, complemented by an "ecclesiology" that revolves around its present and an "eschatology" that revolves around its potential. Drawing on Smith, Backhouse even sees a soteriology for the nation, with nationalism "referred to as a 'salvation drama.'"[57]

Altogether, both nation and nationalism are complex and contested categories. The significance of religion for the construction of nations stresses that the distinction between liberal and illiberal nationalism is "a false dichotomy."[58] It makes the case for a modernist secularism that presents religious symbols and sentiments as problematic and nonreligious symbols and sentiments as promising for community building, as if religious communities would always come with exclusion and nonreligious communities would always come with inclusion.[59] Yet how the relation between "religion" and "nation" is described depends on the definition of the terms of the relation. Rogers Brubaker makes a convincing case in pointing to analogies between them. Both offer modes of identification and institutionalization for people,[60] including the "politicisation of culture and the culturalisation of politics."[61]

Building on these analogies, Backhouse proposes that "theology ... provides the best lens" to study nationalism.[62] Although his proposal might please theologians, it pits theology against scholarship in political, legal, and racism studies.[63] Yet these studies are crucial to uncover the complications in the conceptualization of the idea of the nation and the ideology of nationalism.

Complicating nationalism

In a clear and compelling overview of the scholarship on religion and nation(alism), Atalia Omer argues that a concentration on the intersections of the categories of race and religion, is crucial to analyze nationalism today.[64] The "MAGA Jesus" carried during the attacks on the Capitol clarified that Christian nationalism is White. In the United States, White Christian nationalism revolves around the claim that "America" was founded by White Christians who therefore deserve predominance – a predominance that is predicated on racialized and sexualized politics.[65] Building on Omer's argument, I chart the significance of religion for the racialized and the sexualized politics of Christian nationalism in order to clarify how neonationalism is itself transnational.

Racialized politics

As Randall Balmer suggests in *Bad Faith*, the roots of the Christian nationalism that "MAGA Jesus" symbolizes are to be found in the "defense of racial segregation."[66] This racism plays out today. In order to capture the intersection between the categories of race and religion, it is crucial to clarify the category of racism. Racism can be color-coded, referring to categories of biology, such as "race," or culture-coded, referring to categories of belonging, such as "religion."[67] Although both color-coded and culture-coded racism are prevalent on both sides of the Atlantic, the emphases and effects differ in European and American contexts.

Characterizing the history of Europe, Anya Topolski coined the concept of the "'race-religion constellation' to refer to the practice of classifying people into races according to categories we now associate with the term 'religion.'"[68] Historically, she contends, peoples in Europe were classified through religion, with the true Christian faith on the one hand, and the untrue non-Christian faiths on the other. With the Enlightenment, this theological classification was replaced by a philological classification. Topolski points out that philologists came up with the category of the "Semite."[69] In the nineteenth and the twentieth century, this categorization was then conceptualized through biology rather than philology, with catastrophic consequences in the Shoah. Historically, however, "European racism has its historical roots in a hierarchical binary between Christian and non-Christian religions."[70]

Crucially, these roots come to the fore in the shift from color-coded racism to culture-coded racism that is crucial to the neonationalism that draws on the construct of Christianity's civilizational clash with Islam. In *The Crisis of Multiculturalism in Europe*, Rita Chin pinpoints the shift in public debates about immigration across the continent. Considering how a variety of countries have coped with multiculturalism, Chin highlights a speech by the German politician Alfred Dregger.

In his speech, delivered in the Bundestag, the federal parliament of Germany, in the 1980s, Dregger suggests that Europeans and non-Europeans have been shaped by what he calls "high cultures," shaped in turn by religions. Christianity is crucial for the high culture of Europe. Turks, the immigrants he is interested in, have been shaped by Islam so that their high culture contrasts with the high culture of the Europeans.

"Even in its more secular form the cultural impulses of ... high culture have a lasting effect on our peoples. This contributes, in addition to a pronounced national pride of the Turks, to the fact that they are not assimilable. They want to remain what they are, namely Turks. And we should respect this."[71] Dregger's speech showcases the shift from color-coded to culture-coded racism.[72] Functionally, the reference to religion continues the reference to race, but without taking recourse to blood or biology. The other – in Dregger's case, the Turk – is essentialized through culture-coded, religious rather than color-coded, racial categories. The consequence is that a hierarchy between Europeans and non-Europeans is introduced to justify the withholding of social, cultural, and political equality for "the Turks" in Germany. According to Chin, Dregger's speech instigated the shift to culture and civilization that has shaped politics in Europe ever since.[73] Islamophobia, a racism that targets Muslimness or perceived Muslimness, is crucial to this politics.[74]

Christian nationalisms on both sides of the Atlantic draw on anti-Muslim racism. Ulf Hedetoft presents populism as intensified neonationalism that comes in three configurations.[75] There is what he interprets as a "substantial" connection between religion and neonationalist populism, more common in Eastern Europe, where the Christian church is seen to support Christian nationalism. There is what he interprets as a "secularized" connection between Christianity and neonationalist populism more common in Western Europe, where Christian culture is seen to support Christian nationalism. And there is the individual connection between the two in the United States, where the personal Christian faith maps onto Christian nationalism. Typologies of populist neonationalism, such as Hedetoft's, are contested. However, regardless of how the types are defined and differentiated, they clarify that, as Omer argues, "segregating religion and race as two distinct sides in the study of nationalism is myopic."[76]

Sexualized politics

Nationalism comes with positions and politics on gender. Nira Yuval-Davis stresses that studies of nationalism "have ignored gender relations as irrelevant."[77] By contrast, she concentrates on a "gendered understanding of nations and nationalisms, by examining systematically the crucial contribution of gender relations."[78]

Yuval-Davis' point of departure is that nationalism, particularly when it works with the concept of the nation-state, assumes that those who live in a state belong to the nation and that those who belong to the nation live in a state. The assumption of this "complete correspondence" is "virtually everywhere a fiction" because populations are mixed.[79] According to Yuval-Davis, this fiction naturalizes the "hegemony of one collectivity" in the state: in order to justify a differential distribution of power, some are marked as minority and some are marked as majority with access to political power.[80] Because the nation is conceptualized – fictionalized, in Yuval-Davis' account – as a consequence of kinship, the control of sexuality is crucial for the functioning of the differential distribution of power.[81]

According to Yuval-Davis, the "myth of common origin" comes with a concept of the nation that is rooted in birth, so that the procreation of the people has to be considered a central concern for nationalism.[82] Those who are marked as majority are called to procreate, whereas those who are marked as minority are not called to procreate, all in order to maintain the fiction of the nation. Where nationalism draws on "the notion of the common genetic pool," the category of race is vital for the control of sexuality.[83] It plays out in the rhetoric of politicians and pundits who are obsessed with the birth rates of whoever is othered – be it "the Mexican" in U.S.-American contexts, or "the Muslim" in European contexts, or indeed both.[84]

However, in addition to the myth of the common origin, Yuval-Davis stresses the significance of gender for dimensions of culture and citizenship. Although nationalisms that are based on shared culture or shared citizenship appear to be more open to otherness than a nationalism predicated on birth, Yuval-Davis argues that these nationalisms also require the control of reproduction.[85] Religion is crucial here.

Nationalism based on shared citizenship relies on resources to acquire membership that are differentially distributed in terms of gender.[86] Drawing on Yuval-Davis, Ludger Viefhus-Bailey argues that women exist in two bodies, their private and their public bodies. Privately, they are considered equal. "At the same time, the nation's reproductive needs require women's bodies to be controlled by the urgency to reproduce the sovereign people correctly. In this sense, every woman's reproductive body is public property."[87] As a consequence, procreation is regulated. According to Viefhues-Baily, the "theology of 'gender complementarity' ... serves to maintain this double-life of women."[88] It is a theology that is decisive for Christian nationalism.

Nationalism based on shared culture also relies on resources to acquire membership that are differentially distributed in terms of gender. According to Yuval-Davis, constructs of sexuality, manhood, and womanhood are crucial here.[89] These constructs can work either in the way that a particularly rigid understanding of sexuality, manhood, and womanhood is considered central to the cultural core of a nation or in the way that a particularly relaxed understanding of sexuality, manhood, and womanhood is considered central to the cultural core of a nation. Jasbir K. Puar coined the concept of homonationalism to capture a shift in the symbolization of the nation in the United States from heteronormativity to homonormativity after 9/11. Through homonationalism, the LGBTQ+ community is shifted from the outside to the inside of the nation, but only in order to draw a new distinction to control the nation.[90] Following the scripts of Islamophobia, it is presumed that Muslims are homophobic so that the presumed homophobia can be presented as argument for the closure of the community against them. According to Puar, "gay marriage ... is not simply a demand for equality with heterosexual norms, but more importantly a demand for reinstatement of white privileges," if these scripts are not criticized and challenged.[91] Again, it is a theology that is decisive for Christian nationalism.

Altogether, then, racialized and sexualized politics are crucial to understand the role of religion in nationalism. Arguably, these complications of the concept of nationalism are at the core of a paradox that characterizes current neonationalism across the globe – the transnationalization of nationalism.

The transnationalization of nationalism

Considering neonationalisms around the globe, Kristina Stoeckl points out that "while they seek the security of the nation-state in their desire for ... sovereignty, the very same actors actively connect ... across national borders."[92] Writing with Dimitry Uzlaner, Stoeckl draws on James D. Hunter's concept of the culture wars,[93] describing how "the globalization of the culture wars leads to the same realignment of the religious landscape that we have already seen in the national American context – but this time on a global scale": there are traditionalists, on the one hand, and nontraditionalists – Hunter called them "progressive"[94] – on the other.[95] Crucially, the new global scale allows for cooperations across religions, with traditionalist Jewish, Christian, and Muslim alliances and nontraditionalist Jewish, Christian, and Muslim alliances working against each other.[96] Concentrating on Russia, Stoeckl is interested in what she interprets as the "moralist international," the transnational traditionalism.

Analytically, one of Stoeckl's core concerns is to show that it is not simply religion shaping nationalism or nationalism shaping religion that scholars must be aware of here, but "the culture wars themselves that bring forth a specific kind of religious traditionalism."[97] Hence, in the transnationalization of neonationalism, religion is transformed.[98] "Religious traditions are substantially shaped by the culture-wars confrontation."[99] The identity of its traditions and its theologies – in the case of Christianity, that which makes Christianity Christian – are at stake. Neonationalisms, including Christian neonationalism, then, are a transnational challenge for theologians.[100]

Theologically, it is not enough to present analogies between religion and nation to argue that theology provides the best lens to study nationalism. The significance of religion for the racialized and the sexualized politics on which Christian nationalism is predicated requires theologians to draw on political, legal, and racism studies. Gender is a crucial category here. Omer has pointed out that the idea of the nation and the ideology of nationalism are so engrained in the self-understanding of modernity, that a "turn to the decolonial" is necessary.[101] She stresses that contemporary populist neonationalisms, with their reliance on Islamophobia on both sides of the Atlantic, are not a coincidental flaw but a feature of nationalism.[102] "In order to obtain a more robust analytic purchase on the relation between religion and nation," she suggests, "a discursive critique of the metamorphosis of Christianity in the production of modernity becomes a generative site of scholarship."[103] Such a critique would be a promising point of departure for theological responses to Christian nationalism.

Debate

Omer's turn to the decolonial stresses that strategies which separate religion and nation so that Christianity can be conceptualized as a critique of Christian nationalism are naïve. I chart scholarship that works with what could be called the metaphor of the hijacked faith as a persistent and pervasive formulation of these strategies.[104] Although the metaphor of the hijacked faith seems clear and compelling in its straightforwardness – there is no Jesus in "MAGA Jesus" – it comes with sociological and theological problems that prevent a more robust and a more radical theological response to Christian nationalism.

Sociologically, the metaphor of the hijacked faith has shaped scholarship on nationalist or neonationalist populism. In their introduction to *Saving the People: How Populists Hijack Religion*, Nadia Marzouki and Duncan McDonnell sketch how religion is interpreted to define "the people."[105] They suggest that these interpretations are instrumentalizations of religion because they reduce religion to belonging rather than believing. For them, nationalist populism is not about faith in God.[106] Concentrating on Christianity, Brubaker makes a very similar case. He suggests that the references to Christianity that prop up populist neonationalisms are nonsubstantial rather than substantial.[107] He captures them as "Christianism" rather than "Christianity," because according to him they offer nothing more than a "secularist posture."[108] They see Christianity not as a religion but as a civilization or culture – which is to say, a matter of belonging rather than believing. In his conclusion to *Saving the People*, Olivier Roy finally formulates the metaphor. He insists that the reductionist references to belonging rather than believing are a "'hijacking' of religion."[109] The metaphor of the hijacking indicates a distinction between the legitimate and the illegitimate owners of religion. This distinction comes to the fore when Roy wonders whether the nationalist or neonationalist populists will be able to "impose their vision of religion on the 'legitimate owners'" whom he identifies, seemingly with some hesitation, with "the Catholic Church."[110]

These sociological strategies show that the metaphor of the hijacked faith presupposes a normative distinction between honest religion, evaluated as positive, on the one hand, and hijacked religion, evaluated as negative, on the other. Hedetoft criticizes this presupposition as "normative essentialism."[111] He argues that it prevents the analysis of the object of study – in his case, populist neonationalism – because it presents what is at stake as an aberration rather than an actual object.[112] His criticism is not so much that the distinction between honest religion and hijacked religion is drawn normatively, although he is careful to present his own approach as descriptive rather than prescriptive.[113] Rather, his critique is that the distinction camouflages the connections between what is considered honest and what is considered hijacked. If the scholar approaches one type of religion as *by definition* authentic and the other type of religion as *by definition* inauthentic, then scholarship can only ever confirm its own presuppositions.

Theologically, the metaphor of the hijacked faith comes to the fore in one of the most popular and provocative critiques of Christian nationalism – the critique presented by Stanley Hauerwas. Concentrating on the United States, Hauerwas' critique of Christian nationalism is at its most comprehensive and clearest when he characterizes what he calls the "American god": "Americans continue to maintain a stubborn belief in a god, but the god they believe in turns out to be the American god. To … worship that god does not require a church to exist because that god is known through the providential establishment of a free people. Religious people on both the Right and the Left share the presumption that America is the church."[114] Hauerwas draws on studies that describe and define nationalism as religion-like.[115] Because both nation and religion are modes for the identification and institutionalization of a community, Hauerwas stresses that Christians have to choose: either they are loyal to the ecclesial community that is worshipping God or they are loyal to the nonecclesial community that is worshipping god. Christians cannot worship God and god at the same time, because the adoration of the American god is, in traditional theological terminology, idolatry. Nationalism confronts Christians with the *status confessionis*.

Hauerwas, then, offers one example of a theology that works with the metaphor of the hijacked faith by distinguishing honest faith, here identified with the ecclesial community, and the hijacked faith, here identified with the nonecclesial community, the nation-state. Although theologians might be more at ease with the normativity through which this distinction is drawn, the consequences of the metaphor of the hijacked faith are arguably even more problematic in theology than in sociology. The problem is that the metaphor lets theologians off the hook.[116] If theologians who are concerned with Christianity characterize the claims to Christianity communicated by Christian nationalism as "hijacked" rather than "honest" – which is to say, as something that comes from the outside rather than the inside of Christian traditions and theologies – they characterize themselves as *not* responsible for these claims. Once these characterizations are in place, theologians have no need to attend to the claims to Christianity stoked in competing and contradictory political causes. They always already know that there is no Jesus in "MAGA Jesus."

Agenda

In order to counter the naivety that comes with the normative essentialism captured by the metaphor of the hijacked faith, I suggest that theologians need to conceptualize Christianity as expansively and as elastically as possible.[117] Reflecting on how Christianity has come to be used for racism and sexism and antiracism and antisexism at the same time requires a conceptualization of Christianity that allows for both Christianities *as* Christianity in the first place. Instead of forcing a concept of Christianity onto the field, theologians need to ask how Christianity is formulated *in* the field: how Christianity is preached and how Christianity is practiced in its everyday social, cultural, and political entanglements. Lived Christianity is what is at stake here.

To be sure, I am not suggesting that each and every claim to Christianity has to be accepted as Christian. Normativity itself is not the issue here. Theologians have very good reasons to argue that theology ought to counter racism and sexism. However, in order to make these arguments, they need to analyze and assess both the positive and the negative politics propagated in the name of Christianity past and present. Dismissing Christian nationalism through normative accounts will not do the trick, because simplistic dismissals that allocate all positive features to "honest" Christianity and all negative features to "hijacked" Christianity prevent theologians from studying both racism and sexism on the inside and racism and sexism on the outside of what they consider Christianity. For theologians, then, the question is not *whether* there is normativity but *which* normativity there is in their studies of nationalism.

Gloria H. Albrecht has exposed a lack of criticism in Hauerwas's theology. According to Albrecht, Hauerwas insists that he takes the practice of the church as a point of departure for his critique of Christian nationalism, but ignores that women and men have experienced this practice in very different ways.[118] As a consequence, he cannot appreciate what impact these differences have on the identification of what is and what is not considered Christian. "Essentially, Hauerwas attempts to resist the rise of subjugated voices by creating a timeless story of what Christians ... always will be, regardless of specific conditions of history."[119] This timeless story comes close to the nationalist tale about nationalism. "Hauerwas imputes certainty and constancy to what is an interpreted and interpretive tradition."[120] According to Albrecht, the tale that Hauerwas tells is so successful because it secures the privileged position of those who tell it. "The social position of his Christian 'we' explains his successful communication. A gospel from a position of white male privilege and power is being heard by those who share that position."[121] Even consolation can be found in "a gospel that removes from us the ability ... to respond to structural injustice."[122] The consequence,

Albrecht concludes, is "the church's self-deception: the self-interest of a dominant group masked as God's will."[123] Albrecht's comments on Hauerwas clarify how a critique of Christian nationalism can confirm the racism and the sexism at the core of it, if the critique assumes that there is a hijacked and an honest Christianity, and that the honest is *by definition* beyond critique.

By contrast, theologians who analyze both racist and sexist practices of Christianity and antiracist and antisexist practices of Christianity – and everything in between – might be able to appreciate how churches in the past and in the present might have been complicit or complacent with regard to racism and sexism, even if they have criticized it. Such attentiveness allows these theologians to come close to what Omer calls "critical caretaking."[124] They critique theological traditions that side with the oppressors and confirm theological traditions that side with the oppressed, so as to reimagine the identity of Christianity in solidarity with the victims – those who have and those who have not survived the racism and the sexism of Christian nationalism. Normativity is crucial here, but it is constructed in a way that allows for both criticism and self-criticism. One example is Ulrike Auga's call for "a critical biotheology" that can offer a "a new understanding of kinship."[125] Auga points to the practices of a "Rainbow toddler group" because these practices carve out a "space where new … forms of action or agency can emerge from which a social imaginary of a more solidary society can develop."[126] Care is a central category in this new understanding.[127] Here, resistance to MAGA Jesus can begin – both within and without the nation-state.

Conclusion

To summarize, I have charted concepts, complications, and critiques of the idea of the nation and the ideology of nationalism. However "religion" and "nation" are conceptualized, these categories characterize modes for the identification and the institutionalization of people(s). Crucially, there is a racialized and a sexualized politics in Christian nationalism that regulates membership through birth, culture, or citizenship. The significance of religion for this politics highlights that the distinction between liberal and illiberal nationalism is too nice and too neat to convince. Religions have differentiated between insiders and outsiders throughout history, thus demarcating "the people" at the core of the nation. This demarcation continues.

Current neonationalisms, championed by the political right rather than the political left, see nations as under threat from internal and external enemies. As a consequence, these nationalisms draw more and more on civilizational and cultural claims for which references to religion are crucial. Islamophobia is one consequence. However, religions also connect neonationalist actors around the globe, giving rise to a transnationalization of nationalism that cuts across intra- and interreligious boundaries. Theologians, then, cannot conceptualize "religion" and "nation" as strong and stable categories so as to characterize Christian nationalism as a hijacking of Christianity. On the contrary, the Christian nationalism captured by "MAGA Jesus" needs to be taken seriously. For only if it is taken seriously, can it be criticized and countered.

Notes

1 For official reports about the attack, see "Capitol Breach Cases," https://www.justice.gov/usao-dc/capitol-breach-cases (accessed 6 January 2023).

2 See "MAGA Jesus," *Uncivil Religion: A Curated Resource of Media from the U.S. Capitol on January 6*, https://uncivilreligion.org/home/media/maga-jesus (accessed 20 October 2021).

3 See "Uncivil Religion," https://uncivilreligion.org (accessed 20 October 2021).

4 Atalia Omer and Jason A. Springs, *Religious Nationalism: A Reference Handbook* (Santa Barbara, CA: ABC-CLIO, 2013), 1.

5 Rogers Brubaker, "Religion and Nationalism: Four Approaches," *Nations and Nationalism* 18, no. 1 (2012): 16.

6 Omer and Springs, *Religious Nationalism*, 2–3.

7 Peter van der Veer and Hartmut Lehmann, "Introduction," in *Nation and Religion: Perspectives on Europe and Asia*,

ed. Peter van der Veer and Hartmut Lehmann (Princeton, NJ: Princeton University Press, 1999), 3.

8 See the cases and the chronologies in Omer and Springs, *Religious Nationalism*.

9 See Rogers Brubaker, "Between Nationalism and Civilizationism: The European Populist Moment in Comparative Perspective," *Ethnic and Racial Studies* 40, no. 8 (2017): 1191–226.

10 See Maureen Eger and Sarah Valdez, "Neo-Nationalism in Western Europe," *European Sociological Review* 31, no. 1 (2015): 115–30 as well as Maureen Eger and Sarah Valdez, "From Radical Right to Neo-Nationalist," *European Political Science* 18, no. 3 (2019): 379–99. The concept of neonationalism is problematic if it is meant to distinguish between present neonationalism and past nationalism. See Hans Joas, "Religion and Neo-Nationalism: A Commentary," in *Religion and Neo-Nationalism in Europe*, ed. Florian Höhne and Torsten Meireis (Baden-Baden: Nomos, 2020), 407–16. The case of Scotland demonstrates that there are contemporary nationalisms that call for the establishment of new nation-states. See the classic study by William Storrar, *Scottish Nationalism: A Christian Vision* (Haddington: Handsel Press, 1990). Following Maureen Eger and Sarah Valdez, I take the concept of neonationalism to characterize contemporary nationalisms of the political right rather than the political left.

11 Florian Höhne and Torsten Meireis, "Introduction: Religion, Populism, Neo-Nationalism," in *Religion and Neo-Nationalism in Europe*, 11. See also the contributions to *The Spirit of Populism: Political Theologies in Polarized Times*, ed. Ulrich Schmiedel and Joshua Ralston (Leiden: Brill, 2022).

12 Brubaker, "Religion and Nationalism," 2.

13 Benedict Anderson, *Imagined Communities: Reflections on the Origin and Spread of Nationalism*, rev. ed. (London: Verso, 2016), 6.

14 Omer and Springs, *Religious Nationalism*, 47. Ernest Gellner criticized the assumption that nations run through the history of Europe, with nationalism turning them from the unconscious to the conscious. He insisted that nations are invented. See Ernest Gellner, *Nations and Nationalism*, 2nd ed. (Oxford: Blackwell, 2006).

15 Anderson, *Imagined Communities*, 9–36, 64–5.

16 Anderson, *Imagined Communities*, 7.

17 David Little, "Religion, Peace, and the Origins of Nationalism," in *The Oxford Handbook of Religion, Conflict, and Peacebuilding*, ed. Atalia Omer, R. Scott Appleby, and David Little (Oxford: Oxford University Press, 2015), 61–99.

18 Little, "Religion, Peace, and the Origins of Nationalism," 66.

19 Little, "Religion, Peace, and the Origins of Nationalism," 66.

20 Little, "Religion, Peace, and the Origins of Nationalism," 67.

21 Little, "Religion, Peace, and the Origins of Nationalism," 73–7, drawing on John Witte, Jr., *Reformation of Rights: Law, Religion, and Human Rights in Early Modern Calvinism* (Cambridge: Cambridge University Press, 2007).

22 Brubaker, "Religion and Nationalism," 6–8.

23 Peter van der Veer, "Nationalism and Religion," in *The Oxford Handbook of the History of Nationalism*, ed. John Breuilly (Oxford: Oxford University Press, 2013), 657–9.

24 Hugh McLeod, "Christianity and Nationalism in Nineteenth-Century Europe," *International Journal for the Study of the Christian Church* 15, no. 1 (2015): 7–22.

25 Hugh McLeod, "Christianity and Nationalism in Nineteenth-Century Europe," 17–18.

26 Anderson, *Imagined Communities*, 12.

27 Anderson, *Imagined Communities*, 12.

28 Anderson, *Imagined Communities*, 22.

29 Anderson, *Imagined Communities*, 67.

30 Omer and Springs, *Religious Nationalism*, 47–9.

31 Atalia Omer, "Religion and Nationalism," in *Emerging Trends in the Social and Behavioral Sciences*, ed. Robert A. Scott, Marlis Buchmann, and Stephen Kosslyn (Hoboken: John Wiley & Sons, 2018), 5–6.

32 Anthony W. Marx, *Faith in Nation: Exclusionary Origins of Nationalism* (Oxford: Oxford University Press, 2003), 15.

33 Marx, *Faith in Nation*, 23.

34 Marx, *Faith in Nation*, 23, drawing on Carl Schmitt, *The Concept of the Political*, trans. George Schwab (Chicago, IL: University of Chicago Press, 2007).

35 Marx, *Faith in Nation*, 24.

36 Marx, *Faith in Nation*, 164.

37 Marx, *Faith in Nation*, 143–4. See also Anthony W. Marx, "The Nation-State and its Exclusions," *Political Science Quarterly* 117, no. 1 (2002): 103–26.

38 Marx, *Faith in Nation*, 25.

39 Marx, *Faith in Nation*, 26.

40 Marx, *Faith in Nation*, 29.

41 Marx, *Faith in Nation*, 31.

42 Anthony D. Smith, *Chosen Peoples: Sacred Sources of National Identity* (Oxford: Oxford University Press, 2003), 5.

43 Smith, *Chosen Peoples*, 18.

44 Smith, *Chosen Peoples*, 18.

45 Max Weber, *Economy and Society. An Outline of Interpretive Sociology*, ed. Guenther Roth and Claus Wittich (Berkeley, CA: University of California Press, 1978), 389.

46 Smith, *Chosen Peoples*, 32–3. See also Anthony D. Smith, *The Ethnic Origins of Nations* (Oxford: Blackwell, 1986).

47 Anthony D. Smith, "The Power of Ethnic Traditions in the Modern World," in *Nationalism and Ethnosymbolism: History, Culture and Ethnicity in the Formation of Nations,* ed. Athena Leoussi and Steven Grosby (Edinburgh: Edinburgh University Press, 2006), 327.

48 Smith, *Chosen Peoples,* 13.

49 Daniele Conversi, "Mapping the Field: Theories of Nationalism and the Ethnosymbolic Approach," in *Nationalism and Ethnosymbolism: History, Culture and Ethnicity in the Formation of Nations,* ed. Athena Leoussi and Steven Grosby (Edinburgh: Edinburgh University Press, 2006), 21.

50 Smith, *Chosen Peoples,* 5. See also Anthony D. Smith, *Ethno-Symbolism and Nationalism: A Cultural Approach* (London: Routledge, 2009).

51 Smith, "The Power of Ethnic Traditions," 325.

52 Smith, "The Power of Ethnic Traditions," 330.

53 Smith, "The Power of Ethnic Traditions," 334.

54 Smith, "The Power of Ethnic Traditions," 334.

55 Omer and Springs, *Religious Nationalism,* 39.

56 Stephen Backhouse, "Nationalism and Patriotism," in *The Oxford Handbook of Theology and Modern European Thought,* ed. Nicholas Adams, George Pattison, and Graham Ward (Oxford: Oxford University Press, 2013), 50.

57 Backhouse, "Nationalism and Patriotism," 52, citing Anthony D. Smith, *Nationalism and Modernism* (London: Routledge, 1998), 43.

58 Omer and Springs, *Religious Nationalism,* 60.

59 Omer and Springs, *Religious Nationalism,* 60.

60 Brubaker, "Religion and Nationalism," 4.

61 Brubaker, "Religion and Nationalism," 5.

62 Backhouse, "Nationalism and Patriotism," 41.

63 Backhouse, "Nationalism and Patriotism," 41.

64 Omer, "Religion and Nationalism," 1.

65 See Andrew L. Whitehead and Samuel L. Perry, *Taking America Back for God: Christian Nationalism in the United States* (Oxford: Oxford University Press, 2020) and Philip S. Gorski and Samuel L. Perry, *The Flag and The Cross: White Christian Nationalism and the Threat to American Democracy* (Oxford: Oxford University Press, 2022). For a succinct summary, see Philip S. Gorski, "Right-Wing Populism and Religious Conservatism: What's the Connection?" in *Religion and Neo-Nationalism in Europe,* ed. Florian Höhne and Torsten Meireis (Baden-Baden: Nomos, 2020), 333–46.

66 Randall Balmer, *Bad Faith: Race and the Rise of the Religious Right* (Grand Rapids, MI: Eerdmans, 2021), 44.

67 For a short summary, see Hannah Strømmen and Ulrich Schmiedel, *The Claim to Christianity: Responding to the Far Right* (London: SCM Press, 2020), 18–22. For the nexus of religion and race, see the contributions to *Racialization and Religion: Race, Culture and Difference in the Study of Antisemitism and Islamophobia,* ed. Nasar Meer (London: Routledge, 2014).

68 Anya Topolski, "The Race-Religion Constellation: A European Contribution to the Critical Philosophy of Race," *Critical Philosophy of Race* 6, no. 1 (2018): 59.

69 Topolski, "The Race-Religion Constellation," 66.

70 Topolski, "The Race-Religion Constellation," 75–6.

71 Alfred Dregger, cited in Rita Chin, *The Crisis of Multiculturalism in Europe: A History* (Princeton, NJ: Princeton University Press 2017), 159.

72 See again Strømmen and Schmiedel, *The Claim to Christianity,* 18–22.

73 Chin, *The Crisis of Multiculturalism in Europe,* 160.

74 For a helpful account of Islamophobia as anti-Muslim racism, see Farid Hafez, *Feindbild Islam: Über die Salonfähigkeit von Rassismus* (Vienna: Böhlau, 2019). For the construct of the clash of civilizations or cultures connected to Islamophobia, see the contributions to *Is There a Judeo-Christian Tradition? A European Perspective,* ed. Emmanuel Nathan and Anya Topolski (Berlin: De Gruyter, 2016).

75 Ulf Hedetoft, "Nationalism and the Political Theology of Populism: Affect and Rationality in Contemporary Identity Politics," in *Religion and Neo-Nationalism in Europe,* ed. Florian Höhne and Torsten Meireis (Baden-Baden: Nomos, 2020), 99–114.

76 Omer, "Religion and Nationalism," 3.

77 Nira Yuval-Davis, *Gender and Nation* (London: SAGE, 1997), 1.

78 Yuval-Davis, *Gender and Nation,* 3.

79 Yuval-Davis, *Gender and Nation,* 11.

80 Yuval-Davis, *Gender and Nation,* 11.

81 Yuval-Davis, *Gender and Nation,* 15.

82 Yuval-Davis, *Gender and Nation,* 22.

83 Yuval-Davis, *Gender and Nation,* 23.

84 Samuel Huntington, for example, is obsessed with differences in birth rates. With regard to the European context, he points to Muslims. See Samuel Huntington, *The Clash of Civilizations and the Remaking of World Order* (New York: Simon & Schuster, 1996). With regard to the U.S.-American context, he points to Mexicans. See Samuel P. Huntington, *Who Are We? The Challenges to America's National Identity* (New York: Simon & Schuster, 2004). On the connections between the two, see Luis N. Rivera-Pagán, "Toward a Theology of Migration," in *Christianity and the Law of Migration,* ed. Silas Allard, Kristin Heyer, and Raj Nadella (London: Routledge, 2021), 179–94.

85 Yuval-Davis, *Gender and Nation,* 21.

86 Yuval-Davis, *Gender and Nation,* 23–4.

87 Ludger Viefhues-Bailey, "Querying Populism by Queering Chantal Mouffe: Understanding Hetero-Patriarchal Populism," in *The Spirit of Populism: Political Theologies in Polarized Times,* ed. Ulrich Schmiedel and Joshua Ralston (Leiden: Brill, 2022), 173.

88 Viefhues-Bailey, "Querying Populism by Queering Chantal Mouffe," 173. See also Ludger Viefhues-Bailey,

Between a Man and a Woman? Why Conservatives Oppose Same-Sex Marriage (New York: Columbia University Press, 2010).

89 Yuval-Davis, *Gender and Nation*, 23.

90 Jasbir K. Puar, *Terrorist Assemblages: Homonationalism in Queer Times* (Durham, NC: Duke University Press, 2007).

91 Puar, *Terrorist Assemblages*, 29.

92 Kristina Stoeckl, "The Russian Orthodox Church and Neo-Nationalism," in *Religion and Neo-Nationalism in Europe*, ed. Florian Höhne and Torsten Meireis (Baden-Baden: Nomos 2020), 316.

93 James D. Hunter, *Culture Wars: The Struggle to Define America* (New York: Basic Books, 1991).

94 Hunter, *Culture Wars*, 43.

95 Kristina Stoeckl and Dimitry Uzlaner, *The Moralist International: Russia in the Global Culture Wars* (New York: Fordham University Press, 2022), 27.

96 Stoeckl and Uzlaner, *The Moralist International*, 28.

97 Stoeckl and Uzlaner, *The Moralist International*, 23.

98 Stoeckl and Uzlaner, *The Moralist International*, 3.

99 Stoeckl and Uzlaner, *The Moralist International*, 7.

100 Stoeckl, "The Russian Orthodox Church and Neo-Nationalism," 318.

101 Omer, "Religion and Nationalism," 6.

102 Omer, "Religion and Nationalism," 6.

103 Omer, "Religion and Nationalism," 8.

104 Here I draw on Ulrich Schmiedel, "Hijacked or Hooked? Religion in Populist Politics in Germany," in *Is God a Populist? Christianity, Populism, and the Future of Europe*, ed. Susan Kerr (Oslo: Frekk Forlag, 2019), 96–107 and Ulrich Schmiedel, "Introduction: Political Theology in the Spirit of Populism – Methods and Metaphors," in *The Spirit of Populism: Political Theologies in Polarized Times*, ed. Ulrich Schmiedel and Joshua Ralston (Leiden: Brill, 2022), 1–22.

105 Nadia Marzouki and Duncan McDonnel, "Populism and Religion," in *Saving the People: How Populists Hijack Religion*, ed. Nadia Marzouki, Duncan McDonnell, and Olivier Roy (London: Hurst, 2016), 1–12.

106 Marzouki and McDonnel, "Populism and Religion," 2.

107 Brubaker, "Between Nationalism and Civilizationism," 1199.

108 Brubaker, "Between Nationalism and Civilizationism," 1193.

109 Olivier Roy, "Beyond Populism: The Conservative Right, the Courts, the Churches, and the Concept of a Christian Europe," in *Saving the People: How Populists Hijack Religion*, ed. Nadia Marzouki, Duncan McDonnell, and Olivier Roy (London: Hurst, 2016), 190.

110 Roy, "Beyond Populism," 190.

111 Hedetoft, "Nationalism and the Political Theology of Populism," 109.

112 Hedetoft, "Nationalism and the Political Theology of Populism," 109.

113 Hedetoft, "Nationalism and the Political Theology of Populism," 109–110.

114 Stanley Hauerwas, *War and the American Difference: Theological Reflections on Violence and National Identity* (Grand Rapids, MI: Baker, 2011), 16. For a more comprehensive account of Hauerwas' critique of nationalism, see Ulrich Schmiedel, *Terror und Theologie: Der religionstheoretische Diskurs der 9/11-Dekade* (Tübingen: Mohr Siebeck, 2021), 171–206.

115 See Hauerwas' account of Carolyn Marvin and David Ingle, *Blood Sacrifice and the Nation: Totem Rituals and the American Flag* (Cambridge: Cambridge University Press, 1999), in *War and the American Difference*, 19–20, 28–9, 60, 67–8.

116 See Strømmen and Schmiedel, *The Claim to Christianity*, 1–10.

117 Here I draw on Ulrich Schmiedel, "The Cracks in the Category of Christianism: A Call for Ambiguity in the Conceptualization of Christianity," in *Contemporary Christian-Cultural Values: Migration Encounters in the Nordic Region*, ed. Cecilia Nahnfeldt and Kaia S. Rønsdal (London: Routledge, 2021), 164–82.

118 Gloria A. Albrecht, 'Myself and other Characters: A Feminist Liberationist Critique of Hauerwas's Ethics of Christian Character," *The Annual Society of Christian Ethics* 12 (1992): 107.

119 Albrecht, "Myself and Other Characters," 110.

120 Gloria A. Albrecht, review of *In Good Company: The Church as Polis* by Stanley Hauerwas, *Scottish Journal of Theology* 50, no. 2 (1997): 224.

121 Gloria A. Albrecht, *The Character of our Communities: Toward an Ethic of Liberation for the Church* (Nashville, TN: Abingdon Press, 1995), 112.

122 Albrecht, *The Character of our Communities*, 112.

123 Albrecht, review of *In Good Company*, 225. Stanley Hauerwas, "Failure of Communication or a Case of Uncomprehending Feminism," *Scottish Journal of Theology* 50, no. 2 (1997): 228–239, responds to Albrecht's critique but does not name any criteria through which the church could be critical with itself, because any problems are by definition allocated to the outside rather than the inside, the hijacked rather than the honest faith. "I have no reason to deny that the church … has oppressed women and men, but such claims only make sense by naming the practices that make the specific form of injustice intelligible. Albrecht comes close simply to equating any difference of treatment in the church as sufficient grounds for a claim of injustice …. In contrast, I believe good communities first discover the differences necessary for the whole community to work towards its telos." (235). Gloria A. Albrecht, "Response," *Scottish Journal of Theology* 50,

no. 2 (1997): 240–1, sharpens her challenge in response: "How has a tradition rooted in … Jesus become, in large part in the U.S., a tradition with … practices which not only separate us from the poor in our midst, but assure us that the distance is not theologically or ethically … significant?" (241).

124   Atalia Omer, *Days of Awe: Reimagining Jewishness in Solidarity with Palestinians* (Chicago, IL: University of Chicago Press, 2019), 10–11, 100–52.

125   Ulrike E. Auga, *An Epistemology of Religion and Gender: Biopolitics – Performativity – Agency* (London:

Routledge, 2020), 171. Auga points to Judith Butler, *Antigone's Claim: Kinship between Life and Death* (New York: Columbia University Press, 2000).

126   Auga, *An Epistemology of Religion and Gender*, 172.

127   For the significance of the ethics of care in response to neonationalism, see Ludger Viefhues-Bailey, *No Separation: Sexualities, Christianity, and the Making of Secular Democracies* (New York: Columbia University Press, 2023).

Recommended Reading

Anderson, Benedict. *Imagined Communities: Reflections on the Origin and Spread of Nationalism*. Revised Edition. London: Verso, 2016.

Hedetoft, Ulf. *Paradoxes of Populism: Troubles of the West and Nationalism's Second Coming*. London: Anthem Press, 2020.

Höhne, Florian, and Torsten Meireis, eds. *Religion and Neo-Nationalism in Europe*. Baden-Baden: Nomos, 2020.

Marvin, Carolyn, and David Ingle. *Blood Sacrifice and the Nation: Totem Rituals and the American Flag*. Cambridge: Cambridge University Press, 1999.

Marx, Anthony W. *Faith in Nation: Exclusionary Origins of Nationalism*. Oxford: Oxford University Press, 2003.

Omer, Atalia. "Religion and Nationalism." In *Emerging Trends in the Social and Behavioral Sciences*, ed. Robert A. Scott, Marlis Buchmann, and Stephen Kosslyn, 1–13. Hoboken: John Wiley & Sons, 2018.

Omer, Atalia, and Jason A. Springs. *Religious Nationalism: A Reference Handbook*. Santa Barbara, CA: ABC-CLIO, 2013.

Schmiedel, Ulrich, and Joshua Ralston, eds. *The Spirit of Populism: Political Theologies in Polarized Times*. Leiden: Brill, 2022.

Smith, Anthony D. *Chosen Peoples: Sacred Sources of National Identity*. Oxford: Oxford University Press, 2003.

Stoeckl, Kristina, and Dimitry Uzlaner. *The Moralist International: Russia in the Global Culture Wars*. New York: Fordham University Press, 2022.

Strømmen, Hannah, and Ulrich Schmiedel. *The Claim to Christianity: Responding to the Far Right*. London: SCM Press, 2020.

Viefhues-Bailey, Ludger. *No Separation: Sexualities, Christianity, and the Making of Secular Democracies*. New York: Columbia University Press, 2023.

Yuval-Davis, Nira. *Gender and Nation*. London: SAGE, 1997.

Theology and Ecological Destruction

Ernst M. Conradie

Introduction

Although the roots of "ecotheology" go much deeper, the English term as such gained currency only in the 1990s. This was signaled by an important World Council of Churches (WCC) volume titled *Ecotheology: Voices from South and North* (1994), edited by David Hallman, and by the name change of the journal *Theology in Green* (1992–6) to *Ecotheology* (1996–2006).[1]

The abbreviated term "ecotheology," instead of "ecological theology," must be understood against the background of the term "ecojustice," which is used in ecumenical discourse to capture the need for a comprehensive sense of justice that can respond to economic injustice, ecological degradation, *and* the interplay between them. It builds upon the recognition that the English words ecology, economy, and ecumenical share the same etymological root in the Greek *oikos* (household). Accordingly, ecology describes the underlying logic (*logos*) of the household, economy circumscribes the rules (*nomoi*) for the management of the household, and the "whole inhabited world" (*oikoumene*) refers to the (human) inhabitation of the household. In ecclesial terms one may also speak of "ecodomy" as the upbuilding of the household.

Ecotheology is therefore the English translation of the Greek oikos+theos+logos. Indeed, the "whole household of God" has become a dominant root metaphor in many strands of ecotheology, as far apart as the Pacific islands, South Africa, and South Korea.[2] However, if the earth is indeed our only "house," it does not provide a sense of "home" for all yet, while the habitat of many other forms of life is being destroyed.[3]

One may also find forms of ecotheology in other theistic traditions. It is therefore best to add the qualifier "Christian" to speak of Christian ecotheology. Christian ecotheology is arguably characterized by a dual critique, namely a Christian critique of ecological destruction *and* an ecological critique of Christian complicity in such destruction. The first critique tends to be dominant in prophetic forms of theology, discerning the signs of the time and a moment of truth (kairos). In multireligious and also multidisciplinary conversations it is the second critique that tends to dominate. One may say that the genius of ecotheology is to hold these two critiques together. Without a critique of Christianity, it can easily become an apologetic exercise that overlooks the need for a radical ecological reformation of Christianity and merely reiterates

Ford's The Modern Theologians: An Introduction to Christian Theology since 1918, Fourth Edition.
Edited by Rachel Muers and Ashley Cocksworth.
© 2024 John Wiley & Sons Ltd. Published 2024 by John Wiley & Sons Ltd.

human responsibility toward the environment through notions of stewardship or priesthood. Without a Christian critique of ecological destruction, ecotheology loses its ability to offer any distinct contribution to wider debates. Ecotheology then becomes nothing more than one branch of "religion and ecology" and cannot avoid the traps of self-secularization.

This dual critique is often complemented by a constructive contribution that is also of a dual nature, namely a constructive contribution to the common good and to Christian authenticity.[4] On the one hand Christians have to work with many others in addressing the full range of ecological challenges. This has to be a multidisciplinary effort in which civil society is only one role player, alongside government, business and industry, trade unions, science, and the media. Working with others implies having shared penultimate goals and agendas, even if the ultimate vision may remain distinct. At some point the question will emerge whether Christians have a specific contribution to offer. However, some would counter that the most significant contribution that Christianity could make is to get its own house in order.

The need for nothing short of an ongoing ecological reformation of the entire Christian tradition from within suggests a second constructive task for Christian ecotheology, namely, to contribute to Christian authenticity. It would not do merely to apply external criteria to Christianity without doing justice to the core of the Christian gospel. Arguably, the constructive task in society can come to fruition only if it is indeed based on the ongoing renewal of Christianity from within on the basis of a retrieval of its own core beliefs. This entails multiple tasks such as rereading the Bible, revisiting the history of the Christian tradition, reconsidering its worldviews and cosmological assumptions, and exploring its deepest convictions, symbols, moral visions, and forms of praxis (including spirituality, liturgy, preaching, pastoral care, ministry, and missions). A core aspect is to reflect on the identity and character of God in order to address the question what this (Triune) God may be doing in a time of unprecedented ecological destruction. Clearly, all the traditional subdisciplines of Christian theology are involved in these critical and constructive tasks.

Overview

Prompts for the emergence of Christian ecotheology

As an academic discourse ecotheology emerged in the 1970s. One may identify various secular *prompts*, theological *precursors*, and subsequent *developments* in the emergence of Christian ecotheology. Reconstructing the secular prompts may be facile, while the precursors are contested and the subsequent developments by now virtually impossible to survey.

One obvious prompt was the devastation wreaked by the nuclear bombs detonated over Hiroshima and Nagasaki on 6 and 8 August 1945, subsequent nuclear tests, the nuclear arms race, and the Cuban missile crisis of October 1962. The threat of a nuclear winter will remain as long as humans know how to make such bombs. A second prompt is the recognition of the impact of chemical pollution following Rachel Carson's *Silent Spring*, first published in September 1962. A perhaps less obvious prompt is associated with the messy process of decolonization after 1945 – in India and the East Indies, throughout Africa and around the world. The extraction and control over natural resources and the impact of such extraction remain contested ever since. In close proximity to 1970 one may mention the UN Conference on the Environment held in Stockholm in June 1972, the *Limits to Growth Report* to the Club of Rome (1972), the oil crisis of 1973, and the third World Population Conference in Bucharest (1974). In hindsight one may also mention the early work of climate scientists, symbolized by Charles Keeling's work at the Mauna Loa Observatory in Hawaii since 1958.

A more direct prompt for ecotheology was an (in)famous essay by the American historian (and Presbyterian layperson) Lynn White in which he related such roots to the medieval influence of the Jewish-Christian tradition. White maintains that "Christianity is the most anthropocentric religion the world has seen" and concludes that "Christianity bears a huge burden of guilt."[5] In a similar critique of Christianity, Carl Amery describes the "gnadenlose Folgen des Christentums" (merciless consequences of Christianity).[6] He highlights the impact of the history of interpretation of biblical motifs such as humanity being created in the image of God, the command to have dominion over the earth, the notion of original sin, and the history of human salvation. Similar critiques soon followed. One may observe that at least in the Western academy the early flourishing of ecotheology may be regarded as diverging responses to such critiques. Some offered an apology for Christianity, and others apologized on behalf of Christianity for the ecological destruction it has wreaked.

However, the prompts for the emergence of ecotheology go much deeper in Western history. White's thesis may be regarded as an ecological reformulation of Max Weber's even more famous and contested thesis on the influence of the spirit of Calvinism on the rise of capitalism. The critique of Christianity reveals an uneasy relationship between Christianity and modernity. Modernity may itself be understood as a critique of Christianity, but also emerged precisely within the context of Christendom. If Christianity did not always embrace the rise of modernity, at least Western Christianity found itself in collusion with four interrelated pillars of modernity.

The first pillar is the voyages of exploration and exploitation, partially based, as it was, on Eurocentrism, White supremacy, and the slave trade. Such voyages enabled successive waves of Portuguese, Spanish, Dutch, Danish, French, British, Belgian, and German colonialism, followed by neocolonial quests for American, Russian, Japanese, and Chinese supremacy. The second pillar is the intellectual movements associated with the Renaissance, the European reformations, the rise of empirical science from Galileo onwards, Cartesian rationalism, German idealism, and attempts to come to terms with positivism. The third pillar is the political movements associated especially with the French and American revolutions, the rise of democracy, the abolition of slavery, voting rights for women and other excluded groups, the emphasis on human dignity and subsequently on human rights and human responsibilities. The fourth pillar is the industrial revolution based on technological innovation, extended from Germany and Britain to Silicon Valley and sweatshops in Asia with at least four phases that are widely recognized. The industrial revolution itself became deeply intertwined with the rise of various forms of capitalism that spurred on the process of industrialization through the mantra of sustained economic growth. Indeed, ecological impact may be closely associated with the rise of industrialized capitalism (including the correctives of industrialized socialism). Despite shifts in the global economy from a focus on agriculture to mining and industry and then to services and the knowledge industry, there has been no actual decrease in such biophysical throughput (through dematerialization), while carbon emissions have not yet peaked either.

Globally, ecotheology may undoubtedly be understood as a response to modernity, more specifically to the long-term environmental impact of modernity and Christian complicity in that. Put differently, the root causes of ecological destruction are often located squarely in modernity itself, often in conjunction with critiques of capitalism, feminist critiques, and more recently postcolonial and decolonial critiques.

Ecotheology could therefore be said to be antimodern, in the sense of being a resistance movement against modernity, but that would underestimate the lasting legacy of modernity and the ways in which the intellectual and technological tools of modernity are employed in ecotheology. It would also not do to suggest that ecotheology is postmodern, at least insofar as the ecological impact of late modernity remains undeniable. Some forms of ecotheology may be premodern by retrieving the ecological wisdom from early Christian traditions or indigenous ecological wisdom, but none can escape the impact of globalized threats associated with climate change, ocean acidification, the rapid loss of biodiversity, the emergence of zoonotic diseases (of which COVID-19 is but one), or ozone depletion. One may also identify "submodern" forms of ecotheology, referring to the subdued and subjugated victims of modernity, including other forms of life, and the articulation of such concerns, for example in subaltern movements.[7] In one way or another, ecotheology therefore cannot be separated from the legacy of modernity. One may also argue that a focus on ecotheology under conditions of modernity may be regarded as an appropriate form of contextual theology in the global North, namely, to challenge such impacts of modernity from within – without assumptions around the universal validity of such theological reflections.

Precursors and early exponents of Christian ecotheology

One may identify some ecological sensitivities and wisdom in the biblical roots and subsequent history of the Christian tradition long before ecotheology emerged as a scholarly discipline. Although an ecological biblical hermeneutics is discussed in the literature only in the last four decades or so, the biblical texts are of course much older.[8] The ecological wisdom embedded in premodern examples such as the desert fathers and mothers, apophatic forms of spirituality, Benedictine monasteries, Celtic Christianity, Franciscan spirituality, medieval mystics including notable female mystics, the Protestant and Catholic reformations, the agrarian rootedness of Anabaptists, Puritans, and Amish – and many more – are retrieved and widely discussed in Christian literature.

The precursors and early exponents of ecotheology are more difficult to reconstruct, and may be readily contested given a Western stereotype that fails to recognize why ecotheology has become a global theological movement.[9] In a volume titled *Creation and Salvation: A Companion on Recent Theological Movements* (2012), a large group of scholars from six continents associated with the "Christian Faith and the Earth" project explored the roots of ecotheology, in chapters covering Eastern Christian thought, Roman Catholic theologies, North Atlantic Lutheran theologies, West-European Reformed theologies, Nordic theologies, science and theology discourse, process and relational theisms, Western ecofeminist theologies, North American perspectives from the margins, Latin American theologies, African theological perspectives, Asian theological perspectives, oceanic readings, and global ecumenical theology. In a recent essay George Zachariah observed that this does not provide a full picture yet. He notes that Indian theologians and lay economists such as M. M. Thomas, Paulos Mar Gregorios, S. L. Parmar, J. C. Kumarappa, and C. T. Kurien were instrumental in initiating an ecumenical engagement with economics, development, technology, and sustainability in the 1960s and 1970s.[10]

This does suggest the need to recognize four factors in reconstructing subsequent developments in ecotheology:

- The first is to recognize the role of theological developments from the margins of former colonial powers in order to gain a more global perspective. This requires attention to geographic context, and to the full spectrum of confessional traditions, cultures and languages.
- The second is to recognize the role of the laity, and forms of a Christian ethos, praxis, and spirituality from which any second-order theological reflection necessarily stems. Indeed, in theological reflection on ecological concerns the laity have often and appropriately taken the lead. This requires an emphasis on "doing theology," i.e. ongoing critical reflection on the Christian faith as embedded in Christian praxis. The production of scholarly research in the field of ecotheology is by now expansive, but this is only the proverbial tip of the iceberg.
- The third is to widen the lens of themes that are recognized as relevant for ecotheology. It simply cannot be reduced to the doctrine of creation, understanding the relationship between "man and nature," or an environmental ethics. It has to cover the full spectrum of Christian doctrine and the full range of theological subdisciplines.
- A fourth factor is the dominance of English in ecotheology. English is opted for as the preferred medium of communication not only in the United Kingdom, the United States, Canada, and Australia but also by many scholars from elsewhere in Europe, Africa, and India. Moreover, the other languages in which ecotheology is regularly published cannot be disassociated from the legacy of colonialism, including

Afrikaans, Dutch, French, German, Greek, Korean, Portuguese, Spanish, and Swedish. Either way, some vigilance is clearly required for any attempt to offer an overview of the emergence and flourishing of contemporary Christian ecotheology.

Mapping the global spread of ecotheology

In the Western academy, Christian ecotheology arguably emerged as an ecumenical scholarly discourse in 1970. This is marked by Frederick Elder's *Crisis in Eden*, Hugh Montefiore's *Can Man Survive?*, Paul Santmire's *Brother Earth*, and Joseph Sittler's *The Ecology of Faith*, all published in that year. This was soon followed by John Cobb's *Is It Too Late?*, Francis Schaeffer's *Pollution and the Death of Man*, and Sittler's *Essays on Nature and Grace*, all in 1972. Notably, each of these early books was written in English and mostly by American men. This would change significantly in decades to come.

Given the dominance of the Western academy, limitations of language, geographical context, and ecumenical contacts, it is far from easy to do justice to the flourishing of ecotheology since the early 1970s. Suffice it to say that it has touched all the traditional subdisciplines of Christian theology, has become embedded in all the major confessional traditions, is found in all bioregions and in most if not all schools of theology, and is a transversal in most of the theological discourses that are surveyed in this volume.

To illustrate this global spread, underplaying the role of confessional traditions, a few examples may be mentioned of early developments in a particular context:

First, in ecumenical theology, early milestones that prompted further reflection include a conference on "Science and Technology for Human Development" in Bucharest in 1974, the Nairobi Assembly (1975) of the WCC with its motto of "Towards a Just, Participatory and Sustainable Society," another conference on "Faith, Science and the Future" hosted by the WCC subunit on Church and Society at the Massachusetts Institute for Technology (1979), and the "Conciliar Process" toward "Justice, Peace and the Integrity of Creation," following the Vancouver Assembly (1983) and leading toward the World Convocation on Justice, Peace and the Integrity of Creation in Seoul (1990). Such work is sustained through ongoing ecumenical programs on climate change and on water networks, each with a huge corpus of publications.

Second, North Atlantic feminist theology developed an interest in ecological concerns already in the 1970s. Often this was related to a sense of embodiedness and to a critique of the interlocking dualisms of soul/body, heaven/earth, spirit/matter, human/animal, and God/world that are correlated with domination in the name of gendered differences. One may mention the early contributions by Rosemary Radford Ruether, e.g. in *New Woman/New Earth: Sexist Ideologies and Human Liberation* (1975), and by Mary Daly in *Gyn/Ecology: The Metaphysics of Radical Feminism* (1978). Other early contributions were by Mary Grey, Catharina Halkes, Grace Jantzen, Catherine Keller, Sallie McFague, Anne Primavesi, and Dorothee Sölle.

Third, Indigenous scholars from around the world made contributions to ecumenical reflection on the integrity of creation, and retrieved indigenous ecological wisdom in this regard. In the Native American context, Vine Deloria's *God Is Red* (1973) and influential essays by George Tinker are noteworthy. One may also mention the volume edited by Jace Weaver, *Defending Mother Earth: Native American Perspectives on Environmental Justice* (1996). Contributions from elsewhere in the world soon followed, including from Sami traditions in the Arctic, the Andean region, Aboriginal Australia, and the Pacific region.

Fourth, in the Indian context contributions to ecotheology placed an emphasis on linking environmental and economic concerns in the face of massive poverty. This ensured that ecotheology remained intersectional and justice oriented, as is illustrated in the work of K. C. Abraham, Geevarghese Mar Coorilose, Aruna Gnanadason, Paulos Mar Gregorios, Sebastian Kappen SJ, Samuel Rayan SJ, and George Zachariah. Another early contribution to ecotheology from South Asia is by Sri Lankan theologian Tissa Balasuriya in *Planetary Theology* (1984).

Fifth, in Orthodox theology the cosmic work of the Holy Spirit was easily extended to address ecological concerns, especially through the influence of the ecumenical patriarchs Dimitrios I (1972–1991) and

Bartholomew (1992–present) and scholars such as John Chryssavgis, Paulos Mar Gregorios, Elizabeth Theokritoff, Kallistos Ware, and John Zizioulas. Orthodox witnessing on ecological concerns culminated in the Orthodox conciliar document *The Witness of the Church in Today's World*, adopted by the Holy and Great Council of the Orthodox (2016).

Sixth, one may say that there is a sensitivity for ecological concerns as a transversal in most forms of Latin America liberation theology. This was made explicit by proponents such as Leonardo Boff in *Cry of the Earth, Cry of the Poor* (1997) and Ivone Gebara in *Longing for Running Water: Ecofeminism and Liberation* (1999). The "cry of the earth" was also picked up by the Argentinian Pope Francis in *Laudato Si'* (2015). More recently, responding to current challenges, *Voices*, the journal of the Ecumenical Association of Third World Theologians, published significant contributions to ecotheology. Guillermo Kerber from Uruguay became an important voice, also through his involvement in the climate change advocacy of the WCC.

Seventh, in the African context ecological concerns are prompted especially by deforestation, the impact on colonialism and of neocolonial extractive industries. Such concerns are evident in diverse schools of African theology, such as indigenization theology, theological reflection among African Instituted Churches, and theologies of liberation and reconstruction that focus on issues of international debt, the environmental impact of debt, structural adjustment programs, and climate justice. Following the pioneering work of Mercy Amba Oduyoye, ecotheology flourishes especially in the context of the Circle for Concerned African Women Theologians. It plays a more limited role in South African Black theology and in the critique of the prosperity gospel in Pentecostal churches.

Eighth, a significant contribution from the perspective of North American Black theology was made by James Cone through a paper titled "Whose Earth Is It Anyway?"[11] Ecowomanist theologies began appearing in the early 1990s, for example through contributions by Karen Baker-Fletcher, Shamara Shantu Riley, and Delores Williams. Numerous younger voices, led by Melanie Harris, soon followed.

Ninth, in *Minjung* theologies (in South Korea) the concept of "life" is sometimes used instead of "ecology," as illustrated in the early contributions of Kim Yong Bock, Heup Yong Kim, and Chung Hyun Kyung. Other recent Asian voices include contributions by Meehyun Chung, Grace Ji-Sun Kim, Lai Pan-Chiu, and Kwok Pui-lan. Such contributions are not necessarily translated into English and are easily marginalized in overviews from a Western perspective.

Finally, contributions to ecotheology from the Pacific region are becoming increasingly significant, not least given experiences of the impact of rising sea levels. Such voices are prominent in the lobbying of Small Island Developing States at the various Conferences of the Parties, at consultations of the WCC and through postgraduate studies by church leaders. By now there is a wealth of contributions, for example by Faafetai Aiava (Samoa), Cliff Bird (Solomon Islands), Ama'amalele Tofaeono (Samoa), and Upolu Lumā Vaai (Samoa/Fiji).

The academic field of religion and ecology, stimulated by the work of Thomas Berry and further developed through a series of conferences organized by Mary Evelyn Tucker and John Grim at the Harvard Center for the Study of World Religions, provided fertile soil for the growth of ecotheology. Such conversations between the various world religions, including Indigenous religions, have subsequently flourished in various other geographic regions. For some, discourse on "religion and ecology" cannot be clearly distinguished from Christian ecotheology, whereas others frame this as a debate on a "theology of religions." Because "religion and ecology" is indeed a distinct field, I refrain from subsuming that under Christian ecotheology.

Key figures in ecotheology

To identify a few key figures in the field of Christian ecotheology cannot do justice to its spread across confessional traditions, geographical regions, theological schools, and languages. It would also not reckon with the shift in the geographical center of global Christianity. Influential figures since 1970 could arguably include Joseph Sittler (1904–87), Thomas Berry (1914–2009), John B. Cobb (1925–), Jürgen Moltmann

(b. 1926), and Larry Rasmussen (b. 1939). This would clearly be to skew the picture given the role of prominent female scholars, for example, Dorothee Sölle (1929–2003), Sallie McFague (1933–2019), Anne Primavesi (1934–2019), and Rosemary Radford Ruether (1936–2022). There would then still be a North Atlantic bias so that others would want to include Kim Yong Bock (1938–2022), Leonardo Boff (b. 1938), and Ivone Gebara (b. 1944). What, then, about Australian pioneers such as Norman Habel (b. 1932) and Denis Edwards (1943–2019)? Clearly such a list is more indicative of those left out than those included. One may even say that the emphasis on key figures harks back to the era of theological "giants" that does not reflect current theological movements.

Instead, it may be more appropriate to single out some recent edited volumes that are indicative of an ecumenical and collaborative spirit and that deliberately bridge North-South divides. At the risk of grave omissions, seven such volumes are recommended for further reading in the final section.

Debate: Achievements and Contestations within Ecotheology

It may be helpful to discern and circumscribe some of the contestations within contemporary ecotheology. This is not to deny some overwhelming consensus that have emerged over the last five decades. Such consensus arguably includes the following: (1) prophetic resistance against ecological destruction; (2) a commitment to diagnose the economic, cultural, intellectual, and religious roots of the problem; (3) a willingness to engage in a response to the critique of Christianity in this regard; (4) concern over consumerist lifestyles in church and in society, not only in highly industrialized countries; (5) a critique of the prosperity gospel; (6) resistance against any escapist eschatology that relativizes the importance of this earthly life by longing for a heavenly hereafter; (7) an emphasis on the ecological significance of God's immanence, especially through the incarnation of Christ and the inhabitation of the Spirit; (8) a critique of understanding the place of humanity in God's creation in terms of domination; (9) an emphasis on the responsibility of the church to care for creation, to include ecological concerns in the churches' understanding of mission; and (10) a recognition that an ecological theology needs to be coupled with an ecological praxis, ethos, and spirituality.

Nevertheless, ecotheology is characterized by global divides – along confessional lines, between the North and the South, the West and the East, between academics and church practitioners, the clergy and the laity, on issues of gender and sexual orientation, and with reference to contemporary science (especially in the global North) and/or traditional, Indigenous wisdom (widespread in the global South). Worldviews clearly play an important role, although this category is itself contested and open to confusion.

Another crucial factor, prompting both a rich plurality of voices and considerable confusion, is the role of interlocutors and implied readers. These are found in the academy (with the full range of disciplines), the church, and various sectors of society (including activist movements in civil society). Often particular discourses in ecotheology remain isolated from others in "special interest" lobby groups characterized by the divides mentioned above.

In what follows a series of partially overlapping dualities are identified that typically lead to tensions. Sometimes fruitless binaries can be avoided but how to do that is not always clear.

On Western versus "restern" ecotheologies

The term "restern" was coined somewhat mischievously by the South African economist Sampie Terblanche to confront lasting inequalities in the global economy. Such tensions may well apply to contemporary ecotheology. In the North Atlantic region ecotheology needs to confront the massive ecological impact of Western economies. This may be symbolized by historical carbon emissions but the indirect impact is equally pertinent, namely through the forces of globalization in production, the rapid transfer of finance, the assumption that industrialized capitalism is the only viable alternative, the colonizing of markets, and the global spread of American-style consumerism.

The underlying problem is that the by now massive production of Christian ecotheology could tacitly follow the same assumptions as the economies where such publications originated from. At worst this means the production of ecotheology by scholars situated in the West (even if they come from elsewhere), aimed primarily at readers in the West but then exported for consumption elsewhere. Scholars situated in the restern world may follow suit by publishing their work in English (preferably!) through networks where globalized distribution seems assured. Often Eurocentric assumptions of Western superiority (and White supremacy) prevail on the basis of a focus on Western theological traditions without qualifying this as one limited perspective among others. As a result, promising developments in ecotheology in the restern world tend to remain marginalized. This suggests the need to decolonize ecotheology. This is possible only if what is "Western" is properly provincialized and not portrayed as "universal." This is also why an ecumenical orientation and a sense of "planetary solidarity" are so important.

On sustainable development versus "radical" critiques of capitalism

The term sustainability was coined at an ecumenical gathering in Bucharest in 1974. At first it had to be understood with reference to the report on *Limits to Growth* (1972) and the sustained use of nonrenewable sources. The question was how long such use can be stretched. In secular circles the focus shifted to the sustainable use of renewable resources and then with the Brundtland report on *Our Common Future* (1987) to discourse on sustainable development. The question was how socioeconomic development can be maintained without compromising the ability of future generations to sustain themselves. Following the World Summit on Sustainable Development in Johannesburg (2002), such a focus on sustainable development is nowadays framed in terms of the United Nations' seventeen interlinked Sustainable Development Goals (2015).

Such secular debates could not but influence theological reflection, often leading to Christians embracing the UN process. Soon questions were asked whether sustainable development assumes sustained economic growth and whether that is not a contradiction in terms. Others argued that the many failures of "development" cannot be addressed by coupling that with the term "sustainable." In short, does an emphasis on sustainable development not amount to an attempt at greening capitalism? In ecumenical discourse the emphasis thus shifted toward notions of sustainable community and sustainable livelihoods. This allowed for radical critiques of capitalism and of globalization, for example expressed in the Accra Confession (2004) and the WCC report on *Alternative Globalisation Addressing Peoples and Earth* (*AGAPE*, 2005). Such contestations remain unresolved in Christian ecotheology.

On the green versus the brown agenda

A closely related contestation, also mainly taking place in secular circles, is color coded to refer to the tension between nature conservation (the "green" agenda) and environmental justice (the "brown" agenda mixing "green" with "red"). Aligned with this tension is a focus on either population as the main driver of ecological destruction (pointing the finger at ruinous birth rates in the "Third World") or on consumption patterns (pointing the finger at an unequal distribution of wealth and the environmental impact of the "First World"). The green agenda is often accused of being misanthropic while the brown agenda is accused of remaining anthropocentric in its focus on human poverty, environmental racism, the plight of the poor, women, workers, slum dwellers and so forth. This all too real tension is necessarily fruitless – as is emphasized by virtually all Indigenous, Black, and womanist contributions to ecotheology.

The WCC clearly regards concerns over "justice, peace, and the integrity of creation" to be inseparable, but where the priority should be remains contested. From within the South African context Steve de Gruchy proposed "an olive agenda" to hold together the green and the brown agendas.[12] Whether this would allow for a "rainbow alliance," also involving the church ("purple"), labor unions ("red"), and the LGBQTIA+ movement ("pink"?) remains to be seen but is unlikely given the deep divisions in this regard.

On apologetic versus revisionist approaches

The accusation by Lynn White and others that Christianity is deeply implicated in the root causes of environmental destruction has prompted both apologetic and revisionist responses. Some defend Christianity, the Christian understanding of God, the Christian faith, the Bible, and so forth against such criticisms and hence seek to retrieve the ecological wisdom embedded in the larger Christian tradition. One may add that although the criticisms apply to Western Christianity and then only broadly speaking, it does not necessarily apply to other Christian traditions. By contrast there are others who recognize the legitimacy of the criticism and, short of abandoning Christianity, emphasize the need to revisit basically every aspect of it: reading the Bible with a hermeneutics of suspicion, radically reinterpreting the Christian faith, transforming Christian practices, and so forth. This tension could be a creative one, as calls for an ecological reformation amply illustrate.[13] The assumption is that Christianity is again in need of a reformation but also that it can indeed be reformed from within. However, maintaining such a creative tension is far from easy as diverging positions on (1) the appropriateness of the term stewardship, (2) the debate on the brown or the green agenda (see previous discussion), and (3) assumptions on human uniqueness and hence human supremacy quickly reveal.

On the role of doctrine versus other theological subdisciplines

"Ecology" operates as a transversal across various discourses. Likewise, ecotheology is typically interdisciplinary, multidisciplinary or transdisciplinary in orientation, not only within the family of disciplines comprising theological studies (e.g. biblical studies, the history of Christianity, systematic or constructive theology, Christian ethics, practical theology, missiology, and so on) but also in relationship to other academic disciplines. Nevertheless, the old, tired methodological disputes between the theological subdisciplines are readily revived in the context of ecotheology, often leading to misunderstanding if not conflict. Contributions from within such subdisciplines approach the subject matter in diverging ways. Consider the resistance to doctrine in biblical hermeneutics, or the difficulty of defining what is theological about the history of Christianity, the tensions between practical theology with its typical empirical orientation and systematic theology with its conceptual focus, or between the agenda of Christian mission and how this is related to all the other theological subdisciplines. As an aside one may note that it is exceptionally hard to introduce ecotheology into any theological curriculum because it is not clear where it should be made to fit in. It could fit everywhere but often fits nowhere.

On "ecclesiology" versus "ethics"

In addition, there is the long-standing ecumenical divide between discourse on "faith and order" and on "life and work." This is captured in old slogans such as "Doctrine divides but service unites" and the inverse "Service divides but doctrine unites." At times either the one or the other rings true. This stimulated a significant WCC project on "Ecclesiology and Ethics," i.e. to reflect on the conceptual links between what the church does *as church* and what the church actually *does* and should be doing in the world.[14] Theoretically, there should be no tension but in reality there is a deep divide here – likened to the failure to build a bridge over a wide river where the two sides don't come together. This divide cannot but influence ecotheology. Some are understandably keen for Christians (and for theological reflection on Christian praxis) to make a difference with regard to pressing ecological concerns at a local, regional, or global level. Others call for a radical ecological transformation of the church itself. Understandably, this divide also reflects the contrasting concerns of the clergy (on the church as an institution) and the laity (on the church as an organism in the world).

On a Christological focus versus a pneumatological width

A less obvious tension goes to the core of the Christian confession, namely the relationship between Jesus Christ and the Holy Spirit. This has long divided Christianity in the West and the East, symbolized by the Great Schism of 1054 and the *filioque* controversy. Does the Spirit "proceed" from the Father or also from the Son? Behind the terminological dispute lies a deeper concern: Does God's Spirit work in the world mainly through Christ and therefore through the witness to Christ (scripture), the body of Christ (the church), the offices of the church, the sacraments (communion with Christ) and the ministries and missions of the church? Or does the Spirit also (or even primarily) work independently of Christ's presence, far beyond the confines of the church? The latter position is affirmed by those who find the Spirit's presence in direct illuminations and interventions (as some Pentecostals assume), in diverse liberation movements, in women's movements, in indigenous (ecological) wisdom, and in non-Christian forms of spirituality. This divide is obviously also found in ecotheology. There are many who would find common ground and cooperation with secular climate activists much more congenial than with some of those who confess Christ, including fundamentalists and climate denialists. This divide cannot be tolerated given the Trinitarian heart of the Christian confession, but the simple "and" that links the first article of the creed with the second and the third cannot be taken for granted.[15]

On contemporary science versus indigenous worldviews

A quite different way of framing global tensions within Christian ecotheology is with reference to the question whether contemporary science or Indigenous worldviews are adopted as the dominant conversation partner. This may or may not coincide with the divide between the West and the Rest. Understandably, the focus on ecology in the narrower sense requires scientific expertise but the same applies to climate science and its multiple interactions with a wide array of natural sciences and, given anthropogenic climate change, also the social sciences. The use of science to address ethical concerns does not by itself shape worldviews. That is shaped by theological conversations with especially four disciplines, namely astrophysics (on the formation of the universe), geology (on the formation of the earth), evolutionary biology and palaeoanthropology (on the origin and evolution of species), and the cognitive sciences (on human origins and human distinctiveness). Together, insights emerging from such disciplines are often integrated in "the universe story," and a clear ecological moral is then discerned in that story.

In response, the victims of white supremacy, imperialism, and colonialism intuitively sense that modern science and technology as the products of modernity need to be regarded with a hermeneutics of suspicion. Instead, the ecological wisdom embedded in Indigenous traditions from around the world is retrieved, also in conversation with non-Western religious traditions such as Buddhism, Confucianism, Hinduism, and Taoism. Such insights are typically retrieved to reinterpret the place and vocation of humans and to resist capitalist exploitation of the earth. Most African contributions to ecotheology outside of South Africa seek to retrieve indigenous ecological African wisdom, often coupled with a decolonial critique. The same apply to Native American ecotheology.

It may be noted that Christianity is not necessarily tied to any one worldview. The cosmologies embedded in biblical narratives need not be normative. It is nevertheless striking that conversations either with contemporary science or with Indigenous wisdom tend to become one sided so that any specific Christian content becomes bracketed in order to embrace the one or the other. If the focus is on the themes of creation and anthropology, the Christian message of redemption is sidelined as implausible, either because science, education, and technology (or perhaps welfare, development, and aid) is regarded as salvific, or because of the allegiance between Christianity and colonialism so that the message of the gospel as "good news" for the whole earth is met with suspicion.

On religion and ecology versus ecotheology

A similar tension follows from the previous one. It is clearly necessary to address ecological concerns, most notably climate change, in a collaborative, multidisciplinary way. There is a need for common ground to collaborate with others in the global commons. Understandably, such collaboration leads to an emphasis on religious studies. In the public sphere Christianity is regarded as one religious tradition alongside others, whereas the role of religion in general is regarded, if not as something purely private, then as part of civil society. On this basis multifaith organizations have emerged all over the world to address common and indeed global concerns. Likewise, the field of "religion and ecology" has burgeoned through multiple conferences, forums, and publications. For some there is no clear border between ecotheology and discourse on religion and ecology. Others are more concerned with Christian particularity and authenticity and hence understand the "theos" in ecotheology in a more specifically Trinitarian way. Some evangelicals may regard "ecology" at best as another opportunity for Christian witness.

On the identity and character of the "theos" in ecotheology

All the disputes on the very existence, identity, and character of God (the *theos* in ecotheology) come into play when juxtaposed with the terms *oikos* and *logos*. There are not only diverging views on *theos* and *oikos* but also on the presumed *logos*/Logos given the long-standing disputes between the various subdisciplines of Christian theology and between theological studies, secular fields of ethics, religious studies, and philosophy. Not surprisingly, such disputes and interplay spill over into discourse on ecotheology. This does not need to inhibit multifaith cooperation on ecological concerns, but only if issues of identity and authenticity are not underplayed.

Achievements and Agenda: Current Paths and Emerging Horizons in Ecotheology

The phrases "current paths" and "emerging horizons" were used in the subtitle of a volume on *Christian Faith and the Earth* that concluded an international project in ecotheology.[16] A few personal impressions on such current paths and emerging horizons will have to suffice here.

A first impression is that ecotheology is becoming increasingly amorphous precisely due to its spread across confessional traditions, geographical contexts, and theological schools. As a result, it can easily become insular given the conflicting variety of scholars, topics, and approaches. Moreover, an ecological awareness is now found as a transversal in most forms of theological reflection so that it is hard to demarcate what counts as ecotheology and what does not. The same would apply to transversals around race, class, and gender and so forth. This tendency toward increasing diversity cannot be avoided and may even be a sign of its impact, but it does leave any attempt to offer an overview in danger of creating hegemony.

A second impression is that, precisely given this diversifying tendency, global ecumenical dialogue across the divides mentioned above remains vital but it is much harder than is often assumed. That applies especially to North–South and East-West dialogues where issues of language, worldviews (scientific / Indigenous), manifestations of religious plurality, and socioeconomic power inhibit respectful but also mutually critical conversation. This is my experience in working on multiple edited volumes in the field given the impact of the language of communication, publishers, countries of origin, current location, and dominant conversation partners. How a project is conceptualized, who is to be invited and within what institutional framework that is done is always tricky. Even where there is North–South dialogue it is often between like-minded scholars who agree to collaborate so that the harder conversations do not actually take place. Among those who profess to share the Christian faith deep divides remain, as is illustrated by creationists and proponents of the epic of evolution or climate activists and climate denialists. Likewise, there are diverging positions on how to interpret religious plurality theologically, but this theme is often avoided.

A third impression is that confessional divides are often underplayed or trivialized for the sake of ecumenical collaboration. That is hardly helpful as theological assumptions typically reemerge and are then harder to address than if they were acknowledged upfront. The classic theological debates on nature and grace, general and special revelation, natural theology or a theology of nature, creation and redemption, orthodox or liberal, Thomists or Scotists, a focus on Christ or on the Spirit, diverging views on the Lord's Supper, infant or adult baptism, episcopal versus presbyterian church structures, and so forth are never fully left behind, because the real differences do come to the fore through sustained conversations.

Such divides do not necessarily inhibit global ecotheology. In fact, an encounter of such differences may precisely energizes further reflection. The danger though is that when times get rough churches and individual theologians would give preference to purely local concerns, without addressing issues that are indeed of global concern. That would deflate the core intuition of ecotheology, namely that there are indeed concerns that have to be addressed by the whole household of God.

Notes

1 The journal *Ecotheology* was subsumed under the *Journal for the Study of Religion, Nature, and Culture* that started publishing in 2007, indicating another symbolic shift.

2 The metaphor of the whole household of God is widely explored in ecumenical theology since the early contributions by general secretaries such as Philip Potter and Konrad Raiser. Among countless publications, see Clive W. Ayre and Ernst M. Conradie, eds., *The Church in God's Household: Protestant Perspectives on Ecclesiology and Ecology* (Pietermaritzburg: Cluster, 2016).

3 For this distinction between a house and a home, a sense of belonging and an eschatological longing, between a house, a home, and a warm hearth, see Musimbi Kanyoro and Nyambura Njoroge, eds., *Groaning in Faith: African Women in the Household of God* (Nairobi: Acton, 1996).

4 See Ernst M. Conradie, "The Four Tasks of Christian Ecotheology: Revisiting the Current Debate," *Scriptura* 119 (2020): 1–13.

5 See Lynn White Jr., "The Historical Roots of our Ecological Crisis," *Science* 155 (1967): 1205, 1207.

6 Carl Amery, *Das Ende der Vorsehung. Die gnadenlosen Folgen des Christentums* (Hamburg: Verlag Reinbek, 1971).

7 See Jürgen Moltmann, *God for a Secular Society: The Public Relevance of Theology* (Minneapolis, MN: Fortress Press, 1999), 11.

8 On an ecological biblical hermeneutics, see especially the Earth Bible Series, the subsequent Earth Bible commentaries and the volume edited by David Horrell et al., *Ecological Hermeneutics: Biblical, Historical, and Theological Perspectives* (London: T&T Clark, 2010).

9 See, for example, Panu Pihkala, *Early Ecotheology and Joseph Sittler* (Berlin: LIT Verlag, 2017).

10 See George Zachariah, "Whose Oikos Is It Anyway? Towards a *Poromboke* Eco-theology of 'Commoning,'" in *Decolonizing Ecotheology: Indigenous and Subaltern Challenges*, ed. S. Lily Mendoza and George Zachariah (Eugene, OR: Pickwick, 2022), 201–18.

11 See James H. Cone, "Whose Earth Is It Anyway?" in *Earth Habitat: Eco-injustices and the Church's Response,*

ed. Dieter T. Hessel and Larry Rasmussen (Minneapolis, MN: Fortress Press, 2001), 23–32.

12 See Steve M. de Gruchy, "An Olive Agenda: First Thoughts on a Metaphorical Theology of Development," *Ecumenical Review* 59, nos. 2–3 (2007): 333–45.

13 For recent calls for an ecological reformation, see the Volos Call, the Wuppertal Declaration, and the volume edited by Lisa E. Dahill and James B. Martin-Schramm, *Eco-Reformation: Grace and Hope for a Planet in Peril* (Eugene, OR: Cascade, 2016).

14 See Thomas F. Best, and Martin Robra, eds., *Ecclesiology and Ethics: Ecumenical Ethical Engagement, Moral Formation and the Nature of the Church* (Geneva: WCC, 1997).

15 There is a significant corpus of literature on pneumatology and ecology but not equally on Christology and ecology. For an affirmation of the ecological significance of faith in a Triune God, see especially Denis Edwards, *Partaking of God: Trinity, Evolution and Ecology* (Collegeville, MN: Liturgical Press, 2014).

16 See Ernst M. Conradie, Sigurd Bergmann, Celia Deane-Drummond, and Denis Edwards, eds., *Christian Faith and the Earth: Current Paths and Emerging Horizons in Ecotheology* (London: Bloomsbury T&T Clark, 2014).

Recommended Reading

Andrianos, Louk, ed. *Kairos for Creation: Confessing Hope for the Earth.* Solingen: Foedus Verlag, 2019.

Beros, Daniel et al., eds. *International Handbook on Creation Care & Eco-Diakonia.* Oxford: Regnum Books, 2022.

Conradie Ernst M., and Hilda P. Koster, eds. *The T&T Clark Handbook of Christian Theology and Climate Change.* London: Bloomsbury T&T Clark, 2019.

Conradie Ernst M., and Pan-Chiu Lai, eds. *Taking a Deep Breath for the Story to Begin.* Durbanville: Aosis/Eugene, OR: Cascade, 2021.

Kim, Grace Ji-Sun, and Hilda P. Koster, eds. *Planetary Solidarity: Global Women's Voices on Christian Doctrine and Climate Justice.* Minneapolis, MN: Fortress Press, 2017.

Mendoza, Lily, and George Zachariah, eds. *Decolonizing Ecotheology: Indigenous and Subaltern Challenges.* Eugene. OR: Pickwick, 2022.

Yugar, Theresa, Sarah Robinson, Lilian Dube, and Teresia Hinga, eds. *Valuing Lives, Healing Earth: Religion, Gender, and Life on Earth.* Leuven: Peeters, 2021.

Index

Ford's The Modern Theologians: An Introduction to Christian Theology since 1918, Fourth Edition.
Edited by Rachel Muers and Ashley Cocksworth.
© 2024 John Wiley & Sons Ltd. Published 2024 by John Wiley & Sons Ltd.